A Dictionary of the Anglo-Saxon Language

or Egyptian / Cognate words — Preface 1866 –

In Hebrew & other oriental Langs written & read from right to left, & often without vowels or differently expressed, it is necessary to give the original characters, but for facility of comparison such oriental words, are also given printed in Roman letters which are printed in the usual manner from left to right.

see p 6 of Outline (MS) of Preface to Dict of 1838 –

Proof of 1st ½ sheet July 17th 1832 see p 2 MS top
2d July 30 " " "

Proof of last sheet of Dict Oct. 1834 Sig 3 T see p 505 top

Preface not begun to print Feby 10. 1835 see note Ref 1

Preface Finished writing — Jany 1st 1837 See Pref CLXXVI

A

DICTIONARY

OF THE

ANGLO-SAXON LANGUAGE,

CONTAINING

THE ACCENTUATION—THE GRAMMATICAL INFLECTIONS—THE IRREGULAR WORDS REFERRED TO THEIR THEMES—THE PARALLEL TERMS FROM THE OTHER GOTHIC LANGUAGES—THE MEANING OF THE ANGLO-SAXON IN ENGLISH AND LATIN —AND COPIOUS ENGLISH AND LATIN INDEXES, SERVING AS A DICTIONARY OF ENGLISH AND ANGLO-SAXON, AS WELL AS OF LATIN AND ANGLO-SAXON.

WITH

A PREFACE ON THE ORIGIN AND CONNEXION OF THE GERMANIC TONGUES—A MAP OF LANGUAGES—AND THE ESSENTIALS OF ANGLO-SAXON GRAMMAR.

BY

THE REV. J. BOSWORTH, LL.D.

DR. PHIL. OF LEYDEN;
B.D. OF TRINITY COLLEGE, CAMBRIDGE; F.R.S.; F.S.A.; CORRESPONDING MEMBER OF THE ROYAL INSTITUTE OF THE NETHERLANDS; M.R.S. OF LIT. LONDON; HONORARY F.R.S. OF SCIENCES, NORWAY; F.S.A. COPENHAGEN; F. OF THE LIT. S. LEYDEN, UTRETCHT, BRISTOL, ETC.; BRITISH CHAPLAIN AT ROTTERDAM.

LONDON:
LONGMAN, REES, ORME, BROWN, GREEN, AND LONGMAN;
TALBOYS, OXFORD; STEVENSON, CAMBRIDGE.

MDCCCXXXVIII.

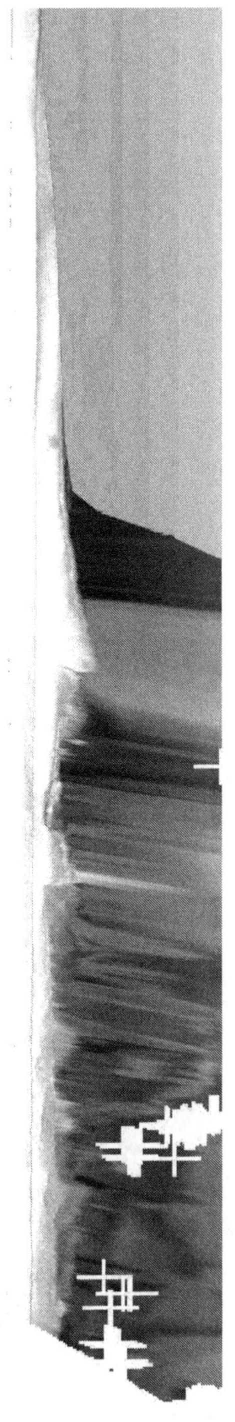

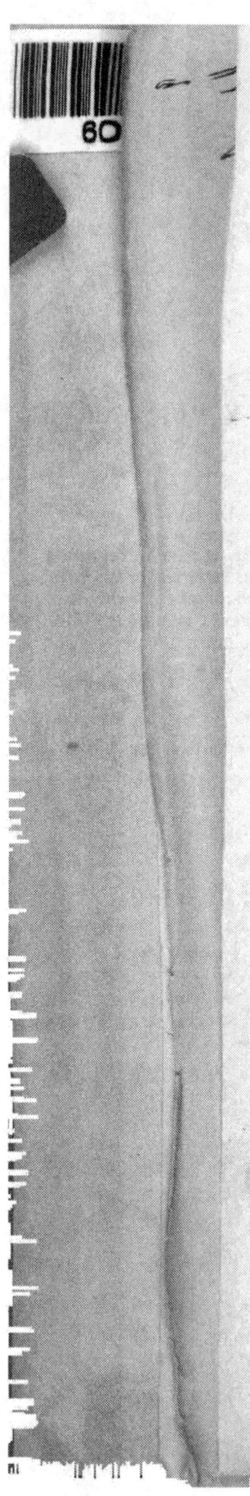

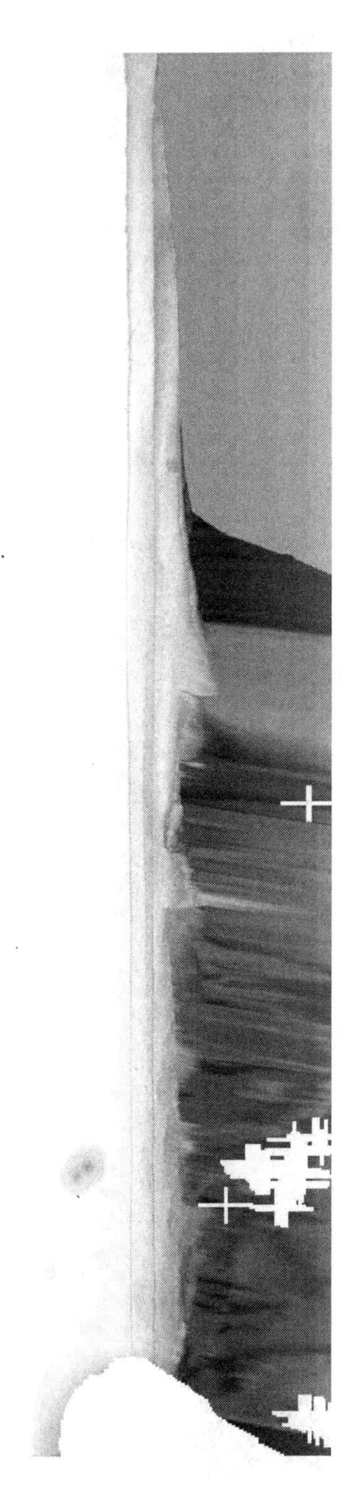

CONTENTS OF PREFACE.

CONTENTS.

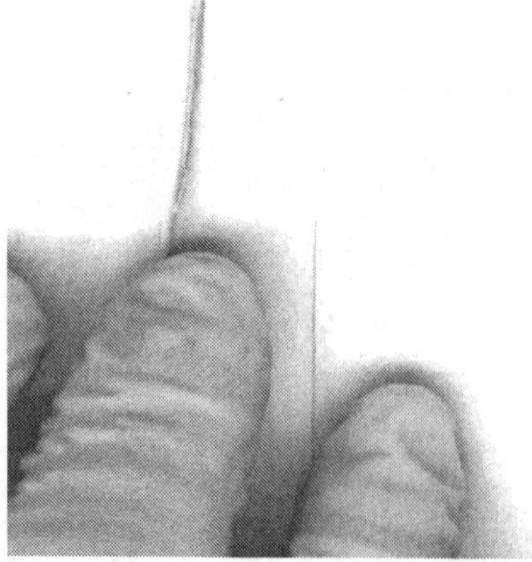

Preface ~~Index not~~ sent to the Printer after Feb 10. 1835. See p 2 of this note

Rotterdam Feby 10
1835

My dear Sir,

I am very much disappointed you do not proceed more rapidly with the Index. You really must arrange to get it out, Eng & Latin, this month. The Latin Index must be printed without spaces between the lines. I am anxious to see a specimen of it, & also a specimen of the Title. You may copy the Title given on the Circular but give my name thus

The Revd. J. Bosworth Dr. Phil. of Leyden
B.D. of Trinity Coll. Cambridge F.R.S.
&c. British Chaplain at Rotterdam

Pray let me have a specimen in a post or two. Send it directly thro' the Cambridge Post directed for the Revd. Dr. Bosworth Rotterdam.

As soon as I see you are coming nearer the close of the Index I will forward the Preface. You have not answered my last letter.

I am yours &c

Joseph Bosworth

Mr. Metcalfe
Printer
Cambridge

PREFACE.

I.—THE IMPORTANCE OF A CLOSE INVESTIGATION OF LANGUAGES IN CORROBORATING REVELATION, AND TRACING THE ORIGIN AND AFFINITY OF NATIONS.—ALL LANGUAGES HAVE A DISTANT VERBAL RESEMBLANCE, INDICATING A PRIMITIVE CONNEXION.—THERE IS ALSO A GREAT DIVERSITY IN THE FORM AND STRUCTURE OF LANGUAGES, WHICH IS MOST RATIONALLY ACCOUNTED FOR BY THE CONFUSION RECORDED BY MOSES.—LANGUAGES ARE DIVIDED INTO CLASSES, SUCH AS THOSE SPOKEN BY THE DESCENDANTS OF SHEM, HAM, AND JAPHETH.—THE PEOPLE AND LANGUAGES OF EUROPE WERE OF JAPHETIC ORIGIN.—THE FIRST TRIBES THAT ENTERED EUROPE WERE CELTS,—THE NEXT WERE THE TEUTONI OR GERMANS,—AND THE THIRD THE SCLAVONIANS.—AS WE ARE MOST CONCERNED WITH THE TEUTONIC, OR GERMAN TRIBES, THEY CLAIM A PARTICULAR NOTICE.

1. It is mind, understanding, or the power of reasoning, which is the distinguishing property of man. The mind is a man's self; by it we are allied to the highest intelligence. Can it then be unimportant for an intellectual being to examine the operations of the mind? But its operations or thoughts are so quick and fugitive, that no real apprehension of them can be obtained, except by their representatives, that is, by words. These, when spoken, quickly vanish from the mind. It is only when words are written, that they become tangible; they are then the lasting representatives or signs of ideas. Those, therefore, who philosophically and effectually examine the structure and the right meaning of words, the instruments of thought, are most likely to have the clearest apprehension of the mental powers and their operations.

2. Words, as the instruments for expressing thoughts,* are the constituent parts of language. It is by language that the feelings, experience, and indeed the whole mind of individuals, can be communicated and made the property of our whole species. The most sublime thoughts and extensive

* Whately's *Elements of Logic*, Ch. ii. p. 55.

knowledge of those who have been favoured with the highest order of intellect, are in their writings concentrated and perpetuated: thus the exalted endowment of reason is perfected by the gift of rational language.

3. The minute investigation of language is not only important in examining the mental powers, but in bearing its testimony to the truth of Revelation, and in tracing the origin and affinity of nations.

4. The physical history of man, the researches of the most eminent geologists, the investigations of the most able philosophers, and the close and patient examination of all the phenomena of nature, are so many distinct confirmations of the Mosaic record. At present we need only refer to the physical or natural history of man.* Here every candid inquirer is led to the conclusion, that all the diversities of the human race originally sprang from one father and mother; and hence we reasonably infer, that this primitive pair had one primitive language. We now find a great diversity of tongues. To account for this diversity, philosophers have started different theories:† but there is no theory which so satisfactorily accounts for the variety of languages, and yet the similarity observable in their fragments, as the plain statement of facts recorded by Moses.

5. "The whole earth was of one language and one speech," or of one *lip*,‡ and of like words.§ "And it came to pass, as they (the families of the sons of Noah) journeyed from the east, that they found a plain in the land of Shinar; and they dwelt there." Because the people said, "Let us build us a city and a tower, whose top may reach unto heaven; and let us make us a name, lest we be scattered abroad upon the face of the whole earth," when the Lord had determined that they should be dispersed, and thus "replenish the earth," God "confounded their *lip*, language, or pronunciation, that they could not understand one another's speech." "Therefore is the name of it called Babel; because the Lord did there confound the language of all the earth; and from thence did the Lord scatter them abroad upon the face of all the earth." (Gen. xi. 1, 2, 4, 7, 9.)

6. On a close examination and analysis of languages, even as we find them at the present day, nearly forty-two centuries after the confusion,

* *Researches into the Physical History of Mankind*, by C. J. Prichard, M.D., F.R.S., &c.

† Some French naturalists and physiologists, with a few writers on history and antiquities in Germany, speak of the Adamic race as of one among many distinct creations. Von Humboldt speaks of the Americans as a distinct stock. Malte Brun has taken it for granted that each part of the earth had its own race, of whose origin it was in vain to inquire. Niebuhr is of the same opinion as to the early inhabitants of Italy.—Dr. Prichard's *Eastern Origin of the Celtic Nations*, 8vo. Oxford, 1831.

‡ *Heb.* ויהי כל־הארץ שפה אחת: *Septuagint* Και ἦν πᾶσα ἡ γῆ χεῖλος ἐν: *Vulgate* Erat autem terra labii unius.—שפה *a lip, talk, margin;* labium, sermo, ora.

§ *Heb.* ודברים אחדים: *Septuagint* καὶ φωνη μια πᾶσι: *Vulgate* et sermonum eorundem.—אחדים *pl. ones, alike, the same,* from אחד *one; Arab.* أحدان *pl. ones,* from أحد *one.*—דברים *words, speech,* from דבר *a word, matter, thing;* verbum, res, aliquid.

there are, in almost every tongue, a few fragments and whole words so similar, as to indicate an original connexion. The great diversity in their vocabularies and grammatical structure is still more apparent. The facts recorded by the Hebrew legislator of one original language, the subsequent confusion of lip or pronunciation, and the consequent dispersion, alone account for this pervading identity or resemblance, and the striking diversity.* Both these claim a brief notice.

7. First, there are resemblances or identities still observable in the severed fragments of an original language. These occur most frequently in words of the commonest use. Such words, if not composed exactly of the same letters, are from letters of the same organ, or from those which are interchangeable.

8. A slight inspection of the ten numerals, even in a few languages, will prove that they had an original connexion.

* Those who wish to see this subject fully and satisfactorily discussed, are referred to the admirable papers of Sharon Turner, Esq., F.S.A. *On the Affinities and Diversities in the Languages of the World, and on their Primeval Cause*, in the *Transactions of the Royal Society of Literature of the United Kingdom*, Vol. I. Part I. 4to. 1827. p. 17—106, and Vol. II. Part II. 1834, p. 252—262. He has arranged the words used to denote *Father* in more than five hundred languages. He has also made a similar classification of the various terms to designate *Mother*, as well as the first two numerals. Mr. Turner observes: "In my letters on the first and second numerals, it was endeavoured to show, that the words which various nations have used to express them, were either simple sounds of one syllable, or compound terms resolvable frequently into these simpler elements, and most probably always made from them; but a more important object was to evince, that both the elementary and the composite sounds have resemblances and connected analogies, which, although used by nations that were strangers to each other, were too numerous to have been accidental.

I intimated that the languages or people, among whom such similarities prevailed, however disparted and divergent they had been, or now were, must have had some ancient and primeval consanguinity.—In meditating on this subject, it occurred to me, that if the mind were not pursuing an illusory idea, the same facts and the same intimation would appear as strikingly in some other words, as they were visible in the numerals. This impression, and the desire neither to mislead, nor to be misled, have induced me to observe, whether the words that are used in the different languages of the world to express the first, the dearest, the most universal, and the most lasting relations of life, *Father* and *Mother*, would be found to confirm, or overthrow the principles suggested. The words were arranged into classes, according to their primitive or more simple elements. These classes demonstrate that the common use of sounds to express the same ideas, must have had some common origin, and are evidences of a common and early affinity. While each class proves a similarity or an identity, the numerous classes indicate great diversity. Identity without diversity would have proved only a common derivation, and diversity without identities would disprove community of origin. But so much partial identity and resemblance remaining, at this advanced period of the world, visible amid so much striking and general disparity, exactly coincides with the Hebrew statement of an anterior unity, and of a subsequent confusion, abruption, and dispersion.

Amongst his deductions Mr. Turner observes, that the "primeval language has not been anywhere preserved, but that fragments of it must, from the common origin of all, everywhere exist; that these fragments will indicate the original derivation and kindredship of all; and that some direct causation of no common agency has operated to begin, and has so permanently affected mankind, as to produce a striking and universally experienced diversity." A gentleman, whose erudition is universally acknowledged, and whose opinions, from his extensive lingual knowledge, and especially from his critical acquaintance with the oriental tongues, deserve the greatest attention, has come to this conclusion; for he has stated ("De oorspronkelijke taal, wier oudste dochter het Sanskrit is, de vruchtbare moeder van zoovele dialekten, bestaat niet meer,") the original language, of which the oldest daughter is the Sanscrit, the fruitful mother of so many dialects, exists no longer.—Professor Hamaker's *Akademische voorlezingen*, &c. Leyden, 8vo. 1835, p. 7. These interesting lectures have just appeared; English and German translations of them are preparing for the press. Ere long we hope to see Professor Hamaker's two other learned works: *A Comparison of the Radical Words of the Sanscrit with those of other Dialects*; and, *Grammatical Remarks on the Indo-Germanic Languages*—on both of which he has for some time been diligently, and it may be added, very successfully engaged.

A TABLE OF NUMERALS.

Sanscrit.	Persian.	Welsh.	Erse.	Greek.	Latin.	Anglo-Saxon.	English.	Dutch.	Icelandic.	Danish.	Mœso-Gothic.	Old High German.	Russian.
एक aika	يكا yika	un	aen	εἱς, μια, ἑν	unus, a, um	an	one	een	einn	een	aina, aina, ain	ein	odin'
द्वि dwi द्वौ dwau	دو du	dau dwy	da do	δυω, δοιω	duo, duæ i. e. duai	twá twégen	two	twee	tvö	to	twai, twos, twa	tue	dva dvie
त्रि tri	سه seh	tri tair	tri	τρεῖς τρεες τρια	tres tria	þreo þry	three	drie	þrir	tre	thrins	thri	tri
चतुर् chatur	چهار chehaur	pedwar pedair	keathair	πισυρες, πεσσυρες τετορα	quatuor, petor *Oscan*	feower	four	vier	fiórir	fire	fidwor	fiuuar	chetyre
पंच pancha	پنج penj	pump	kuig	πεμπε πεντε	quinque	fif	five	vijf	fimm	fem	fimf	finfe	pyat
षष् shash	شش shesh	chwech	se	ἑξ	sex	six	six	zes	sex	sex	saihs	sehs	shest'
सप्तन् saptan	هفت heft	saith	secht	ἑπτα	septem	seofon	seven	zeven	siö	syv	sibun	sibun	sem
अष्ट ashta	هشت hesht	wyth	ocht	ὀκτω	octo	eahta	eight	acht	átta	aatte	ahtan	ohto	osm vosem
नवन् navan	نه nuh	naw	noi	’εννεα	novem	nigon	nine	negen	niu	ni	nihun	niguni	devyat'
दशन् dashan	ده deh	dêg	deich	δεκα	decem	tyn	ten	tien	tiu	ti	taihun	tehan	desyat'
विंशति vingshati	بيست bist	ugain	fichid	εἰκοσι Ϝεικοντι ?	viginti	twentig	twenty	twintig	tuttugu	tyve	twaimtigum	tuentig	dvatzat'
त्रिंशत् tringshat	سي si	deg ar ugain	deich ar hichid	τριακοντα	triginta	þrittig	thirty	dertig	þriatyu	trèdive	thrinstigum	thrittig	tritzat'
शतं shatum	صد sad	cant	kett	ἑκατον	centum	hund	hundred	honderd	hundrad	hundrede	hund	hunt	sto

9. By the common change of *t* into *d*, all the words in the different languages denoting *two* and *three*, are evidently cognate, or from one common source. The *Sans.* chatur; *Erse* keathair; *Pers.* chehaur; *Rus.* chetyre; *Grk.* τετταρες, πισυρες; *Wel.* pedwar; *Lat.* quatuor; *Oscan* petor; *Moes.* fidwor; *Old High Ger.* fiuuar; *A.-S.* feower; *Dut.* vier; *Dan.* fire; *Eng.* four, by the change of *ch, k, q,* τ, π, *p,* and *f,* have a distant connexion.* By a slight change of lip or pronunciation, the other numerals appear to be cognate.

10. The *Heb.* שׁשׁ sĕs *six,* seems to be allied to the *Sans.* shash; the *Chaldee* תליתי tliti *third,* to the *Sans.* tritaya. Other words have evidently a connexion: the *Heb.* בית bit *a house, dwelling; Chaldee* בות but *to tarry, dwell,* often used in the Targum for לון lun; in *Arab.* بات bat or بيت beit *to tarry, be situated;* the *Erse* beith; *Wel.* bŷdh, bôd; *Teutonic* be, beon *to be;* and the *Sans.* verbal root भू bhū, whence bhavami *I am,* are allied.—The *Heb.* יש *is; Wel.* oes *he is; Erse* is, as is me *I am,* seems connected with the *Sans.* verbal root अस् as, whence we have *Sans.* asmi, asi, asti *sum, es, est; Grk.* ἐιμι [ἐσμι] ἐσσι, ἐστι.†

11. Some Coptic words are very similar to Hebrew.

Coptic.	Hebrew.
ⲁⲗⲏⲓ alēi *to go up,*	עלה olē *to go up.*
ⲁⲗⲟⲩ alou *a boy,*	עול oul *an infant,* עולל oull *a boy.*
ⲁⲛ an *not,*	אין ain *not.*
ⲁⲛⲟⲕ anok *I,*	אנכי anki *I.*
ⲁⲛⲟⲛ anon *we,*	אנחנה anene, or אנן anĕn, הנן enĕn *Chl. we*
ⲁⲣⲉϫ areg *terminus,*	ארץ arĕj *terra, regio.*
ⲁⲣⲏⲃ arēb *a pledge,*	ערבה orbē *a pledge.*
ⲃⲉⲗ bel *to destroy,*	בלה blē *to wear, waste away.*
ⲃⲉⲣⲓ beri *new,* ⲉⲣ-ⲃⲉⲣⲓ *to renew,*	ברא bra *to create.*
ⲉⲓⲟⲩⲗ eioul *a stag,*	איל ail *a stag.*
ⲑⲁⲗ thal *a hill,*	תל tĕl *a heap.*
ⲑⲗⲱⲙ thlom *furrows,*	תלם tĕlm *furrows.*
ⲓⲁⲣⲟ iaro *a river,*	יאר iar *a river.*
ⲓⲟⲙ iom *the sea,*	ים Im *the sea.*
ⲕⲁϣ kash *a reed,*	קש qĕs *stubble, straw, &c.*

* See the change of letters admirably proved in the erudite and invaluable work of Dr. Prichard, *On the Eastern Origin of the Celtic Nations,* p. 27—91, 8vo. Oxford, 1831, to whose work the preceding table is much indebted. The regular interchange of consonants, and the laws that influence the vowel system, are also satisfactorily proved and fully treated by Dr. James Grimm in his *Deutsche Grammatik,* Gottingen, 1822, 8vo. Vol. I. p. 581, 584, 578; and in Professor Schmitthenner's valuable Introduction to his short German Dictionary. No one who has omitted to examine what these learned and laborious authors have written, ought to reject, and much less ridicule, the systematic and regular change of vowels and consonants.

† See more examples in Dr. Prichard's *Celtic Nations,* p. 192—194.

12. The table of numerals, with the preceding short collection of examples, may be sufficient to show that there are many words which are of cognate origin, even in languages often deemed the most dissimilar. It is not contended with the ancient fathers that the *Hebrew* is the primitive tongue, or with the modern philosophers that it is the *Sanscrit;* for it appears, on the evidence of Moses,* and from the conclusion of eminent philologists, that the original language of our first parents no longer exists. The similarity of the words previously cited, prove that these languages originally proceeded from one common source, and they thus verify that part of the Mosaic history which declares, that "the whole earth was of one language."

13. It is now necessary to advert to the vast diversity of languages, which is satisfactorily accounted for by the confusion of lip or pronunciation. Those who pronounced their words in the same manner, separating from those they could not understand, would naturally unite together, and form distinct tribes. In addition to the passages previously cited relative to the dispersion, Moses adds: "By these (the sons of *Japheth*) were the isles of the Gentiles (Europe) divided in their lands, every one *after his tongue,* after their families, in their nations.—These are the sons of *Ham,* after their families, *after their tongues,* in their countries, and in their nations.—These are the sons of *Shem,* after their families, *after their tongues,* in their lands, after their nations." (Gen. x. 5, 20, 31.)

14. Do they, who reject these and the preceding passages of the Sacred History, on account of their reference to a supernatural agency, suggest that various languages existed from the beginning, and that the faculty of expressing ideas by a different language was given to distinct creations of men in each particular region of the earth? This would imply, "that the world contained from the beginning, not three or four, as some writers are willing to believe, but some hundreds, and perhaps thousands of different human races."† These numerous creations must refer to a supernatural agency as many times more miraculous than the event recorded by Moses, as the miracle, according to their theory, was numerically repeated.

15. Whatever diversity of opinion there may have been, as to the origin of the great variety of tongues, the most eminent philologists have generally divided languages into classes, distinguished by remarkable differences in their grammatical structure and vocabularies.

16. One of these classes of languages is the *Shemitic,* or *Semetic,* so called from the supposition that the race of Shem alone spoke the language so denominated. Objections may be made to the term, as the

* Gen. xi. 1, 6, 7, 9; and Gen. x. 5, 20, 31. See § 6, note ‡.

† The languages of the African nations, according to Seetzen, who has made the most extensive and original researches into this subject, amount to 100 or 150. In America, there are said to be 1500 idioms, "notabilmente diversi." Such was the opinion of Lopez, a missionary of great knowledge in the languages both of South and North America. See Seetzen's *Letters in Von Zach's Monathliche Correspondenz,* 1810, p. 328; Hervas's *Catalogo delle Lingue,* p. 11; and Dr. Prichard's *Celtic Nations,* p. 11.

Phœnicians or Canaanites, who took their origin from Ham, spoke a Shemitic dialect; but as Shemitic is in general use and well understood, it is best to retain it. The race of Shem, who were much devoted to a pastoral life, spread over the finest part of Middle and Upper Asia, over Armenia, Mesopotamia, and Assyria. The following languages, distinguished by being written from right to left, and forming their grammatical connexions by prefixes and postfixes, are of the Shemitic race:—

Shemitic Languages.

Hebrew, { Chaldee,
Syriac,

Arabic,
Aramæan, &c.

17. The descendants of *Ham* were seafaring men, who founded the republics of Tyre, Sidon, Carthage, &c. Little appears to be known of the languages used by the race of *Ham*. Some name the following:—

The Dialect of Ancient Egypt.

Coptic, { Sahidic,
Bashmuric,

The numerous African dialects spoken by the *Kabyles* of Mauritania, the *Tuarik* of the Great Desert, the *Felatahs* of Nigritia, the *Foulahs* of the Senegal, &c.

18. Another class of idioms is the *Japhetic*, by some called Caucasian, from the supposition that the primitive seat of this race was near Mount Caucasus; by others denominated Indo-Germanic, indicating that all the Germanic tongues had an Indian origin. The compound Indo-Germanic, by not including the Celtic or Welsh, an important branch of these idioms, has been considered defective. A word of more extended signification has been adopted, namely, Indo-European,* to denote all those European languages which are clearly cognate with the Sanscrit, or ancient language of India. Other etymologists have proposed Arian or Persian, as it designates their origin amongst the Arians, Irenians, or Persians.† As some Asiatic as well as European dialects ought to be included in the name, it may be better to retain the old term Japhetic, comprising all the supposed descendants of Japheth, who diverged from Shinar throughout Asia and Europe; from the banks of the Ganges to the Atlantic ocean, and from the shores of Iceland to the Mediterranean Sea. They seem to have passed to the north of the great range of the Taurus, as far as the Eastern ocean, and probably passed over Behring's straits from Kamschatka to America.‡

19. A tabular arrangement will best show the extent of the languages of the Japhetic race.

* Dr. Prichard's *Eastern Origin of the Celtic Nations*, p. 19.

† Kurzes Deutsches Wörterbuch *fur Etymologie, Synonymik und Orthographie* von Friedrich Schmitthenner, 8vo. Darmstadt, 1834, p. 24.

‡ Dr. Hales's *Analysis of Chronology*, Vol. I. p. 352.

A singular congruity is said to exist in all the American languages, from the north to the southern extremity of the continent. They may be reduced to a few great divisions, several of which extend as radii from a common centre in the north western part near Behring's straits.—Dr. Prichard's *Eastern Origin of the Celtic Nations*, p. 6.

TABLE OF JAPHETIC LANGUAGES.

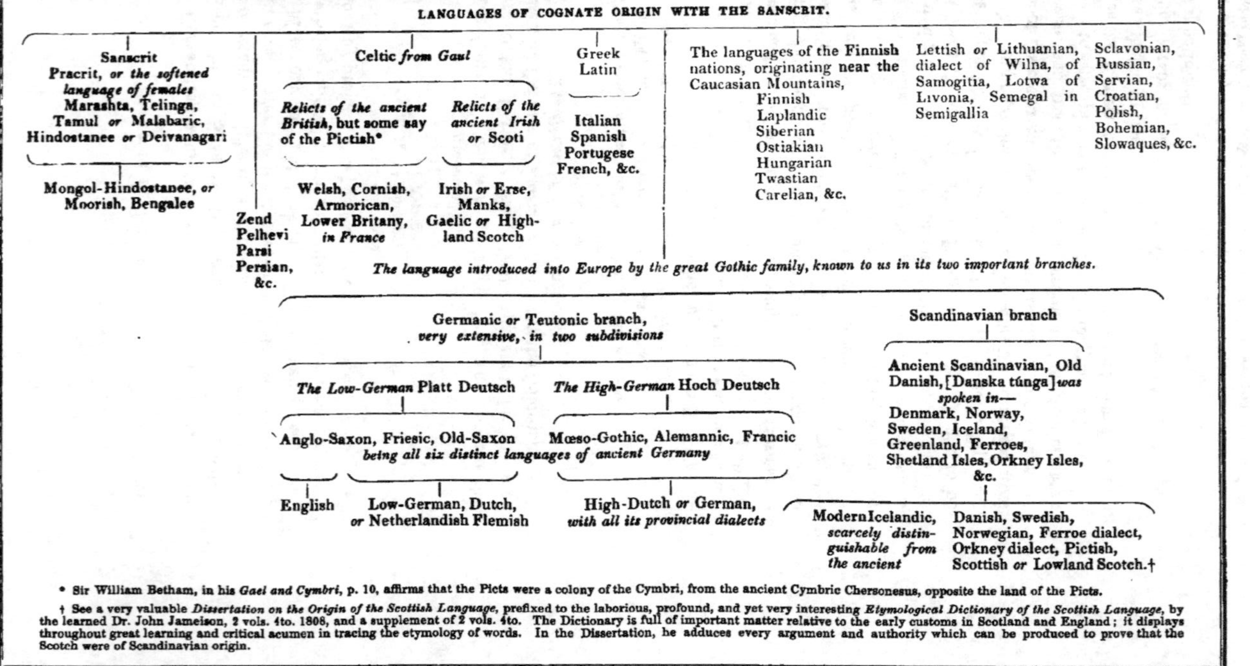

* Sir William Betham, in his *Gael and Cymbri*, p. 10, affirms that the Picts were a colony of the Cymbri, from the ancient Cymbric Chersonesus, opposite the land of the Picts.

† See a very valuable *Dissertation on the Origin of the Scottish Language*, prefixed to the laborious, profound, and yet very interesting *Etymological Dictionary of the Scottish Language*, by the learned Dr. John Jameison, 2 vols. 4to. 1808, and a supplement of 2 vols. 4to. The Dictionary is full of important matter relative to the early customs in Scotland and England; it displays throughout great learning and critical acumen in tracing the etymology of words. In the Dissertation, he adduces every argument and authority which can be produced to prove that the Scotch were of Scandinavian origin.

20. Little need be said here of the Asiatic nations proceeding from Japhet: a casual remark, however, may be admitted upon the language of the Hindoos. The Sanscrit* is that ancient tongue which once prevailed throughout all Hindoostan, from the Gulf of Bengal to the Arabian Sea, and from the southern extremity of the country to the Himalaya Mountains on the north. The Sanscrit is the most compositive, flexible, and complete language yet known. It admits of being perfectly analysed, by merely reducing its compound words to simple elements which exist in the language itself. It contains the roots of the various European dialects, of the Latin, Greek, Celtic, German, and Sclavonic. Having all its words composed of its own elements, and containing no exotic terms, proves it to be very near its primitive state.† The Sanscrit is, therefore, placed at the commencement of the languages here called Japhetic. That all these are closely connected with the Sanscrit, will clearly appear from a few examples.

EXAMPLES.

Sanscrit.	Greek.	Latin.	Persian.	German.	Anglo-Sax.	Dutch.	Danish.	English.
उपर upar	ὑπερ	super	عبور aboor	ober	ofer	over	over	over
जानु jānu	γονυ	genu	زانو zano	knie	cneow	knie	knæ	knee
नवं năwam	νεον	novum	نو nĕw	neu	niwe	nieuw	ny	new
नाम nāma	ονομα	nomen	نام nām	nahme	nama	naam	navn	name
नो no	νη	non	نه nĕh	nein	na	neen	nej	no
पितृ pitr	πατηρ	pater	پدر pădr	vater	fæder	vader	fader	father
मुष musha	μυς	mus	موش moosh	maus	mús	muis	muus	mouse
युगं yugam	ζευγος	jugum	یوغ yogh	joch	geóc	juk	—	yoke‡

Sans. क्रमिलं krimilam; *Grk.* καμελος; *Lat.* camelum; *Heb.* גמל gĕmĕl; *Ger.* kamel; *Eng. camel.* — *Sans.* युवन yuwănah, *young:* *Lat.* juvenis; *Pers.* جوان juwan; *Ger.* jung; *Heb.* יונק junq *a suckling, a twig, sucker;* *A.-S.* geong *young;* *Plat.* junk; *Dut.* jong; *Swed. Dan.* ung; *Wel.* jeuangc.—*Sans.* जनि jani *a woman; Celtic*

* Sanscrit, in derivation and sound, is very similar to συγκριτος *joined together, united.* Hence it is used for *a whole*, so completely possessing all *its parts*, as in its *union, parts*, or *decomposition*, to be *finished* or *perfect.*—Professor Hamaker's *Voorlezingen*, p. 6.

† Lieut. Col. Vans Kennedy's *Researches*, p. 196.

‡ See many more examples in Lieut. Col. Vans Kennedy's *Researches*, p. 278.

gean; *Rus.* jena; *Grk.* γυνη; *Pers.* زني zünné.—*Sans.* मातृ mātre; *Pers.* مادر mādr; *Rus.* mater; *Celtic, Erse* mathair; *Grk.* μητηρ; *Lat.* mater; *Ger.* mutter; *Dut.* moeder; *A.-S.* modor; *Dan. Swed.* moder.—*Sans.* भ्रातृ bhrātre; *Rus.* brātr; *Celtic, Wel.* brawd; *Erse* brathair; *Irish* brutha; *Grk.* φρατηρ; *Lat.* frater; *Fr.* frêtre, frère; *Pers.* برادر brādr; *Tar.* bruder; *Ger.* bruder; *Moes.* brothar; *A.-S.* broðor; *Dut.* broeder; *Dan. Swed.* broder; *Icel.* brodur; *Arm.* breur; *Eng. brother.**

21. The preceding remarks are by no means intended to serve as a complete classification of languages; they only afford a very superficial view, for the monosyllabic, or the Chinese, Indo-Chinese, &c. are entirely omitted. What is advanced relative to the inhabitants and languages of Europe must be more precise.

22. Europe appears to have been gradually occupied by successive waves of population from the east. Those now located most to the west, the Celts, were amongst the tribes who first left Asia, and were impelled westward by succeeding emigrations, and thus spread over a considerable part of Europe. The Celts, or Celtæ, were a people of Gaul, who, at a very early period, crossed the straits of Dover, and entered the British Isles. The ancient Britons were therefore Celts, who were subsequently conquered by the Romans, and then by the Saxons, and driven into Wales and Cornwal. Britain must have been inhabited even before the Trojan war, more than 1200 years before the Christian era, as tin was then brought from Britain by the Phœnicians.† It has been clearly proved that the Celtic dialects are of cognate origin with the Sanscrit, though differing so much in structure as to be distinct from the Teutonic or German.‡

23. The Teutonic, German, or Gothic tribes, were the second source of European population. Like their predecessors, the Celts, these tribes came out of Asia into Europe over the Kimmerian Bosphorus, between the Black Sea and the Sea of Azoph, but at a later period, perhaps about B.C. 680. In the time of Herodotus, about B.C. 450, the Teutonic tribes were on the Danube, and extended towards the south. Fifty years before the Christian era, in Cæsar's time, they were called Teutoni or Germans, and had established themselves so far to the westward as to have obliged the Celts to withdraw from the eastern banks of the Rhine. In later ages they became known by the name of Getæ or Goths.

24. The third and most recent stream of population which flowed into Europe, conveyed thither the Sclavonian or Sarmatian nations:

* See numerous instances in Dr. Prichard's *Celtic Nations*, p. 66—69.

† See the account of Herodotus on the Phœnician commerce.

‡ Dr. Prichard's *Eastern Origin of the Celtic Nations.*

they are mentioned by Herodotus as being on the borders of Europe in his time; they therefore probably entered Europe soon after 450. These coming last, occupied the most eastern parts, as Russia, Poland, Eastern Prussia, Moravia, Bohemia, and their vicinity. From these Sclavonic tribes a third genus of European languages arose, as the Russian, Polish, Bohemian, Livonian, Lusatian, Moravian, Dalmatian, &c.

25. As the tribes of Celtic origin, the first source of European population, are clearly distinguished from the Teutonic or German, and as the Sclavonic or Sarmatian tribes, the third wave of population, have never extended so far west as England, nor made any settlement among us, no further notice will be taken of them or of their languages. We are most concerned with the Teutonic, German, or Gothic, the second stream of European population, and the language spoken by these tribes. The language, brought into Europe by the great Gothic family, is chiefly known to us in its two important branches, the GERMANIC and SCANDINAVIAN. The Scandinavian branch includes the Icelandic, Danish, Swedish, Norwegian, &c. The Teutonic or Germanic branch is subdivided into Low-German and High-German. The Low-German comprises not only the older languages, such as the Anglo-Saxon, Friesic, and the Old-Saxon, but their immediate descendants, the modern English, with all its provincial dialects, the Dutch or Netherlandish, Flemish, and the present Low or Platt German dialects, spoken in the north or low and flat parts of Germany. The High-German includes an account of the Mœso-Gothic, Alemannic, and Francic, with the present High-German, and its modern dialects.

II.—GERMANIC AND SCANDINAVIAN LANGUAGES.

1. The Germanic or Teutonic languages, the Anglo-Saxon, Friesic, Old-Saxon, Mœso-Gothic, Alemannic, and Francic, are easily distinguished from the Scandinavian tongues, the Icelandic, Danish, Norwegian, and Swedish. The Germanic languages have no passive voice, and have only one definite article, which is always placed before the noun or adjective; but the Scandinavians have now, and have had from the earliest times, a passive form of the verb, and two definite articles—one placed before nouns, and the other affixed to them.

The Germans, Teutoni, Teutschen, Deutschen, speaking the German, Teutonic or Theotisc language.*

2. Each of the Teutonic tribes skirting the northern or north-eastern boundary of the Roman empire, had its own distinctive denomination. Their peculiar names were unknown or disregarded by the Romans; hence these hostile bands of the Teutoni, from their martial appearance, were classed together, and by the Gauls and Romans called Germani, or *war-men.*† We do not find in any remnant of their language, that the Germans ever applied this term to themselves.‡ When united as one people, under Charlemagne, the Germans styled themselves Teutschen or Deutschen, from the Teutoni§ mentioned by Cæsar and Livy.‖ These Teutoni were so powerful and influential, that (B. C. 102) they, united with the Cimbri, entered Italy, which was only preserved by the bravery and talent of Marius. While at the present day the Germans most frequently apply to themselves the name of Deutschen, they are generally called Germans by foreigners.

3. Wherever the Germanic or Gothic tribes appeared, liberty prevailed: they thought, they acted for themselves. They would not blindly follow any leader or any system: they were free. Hence Theodoric encouraged Gothic literature, and induced Cassiodorus to write a history of the Goths from their only records, their ancient songs. Another Teutonic or Theotisc monarch, Charlemagne, gave encouragement to genius. He saw and felt, that the only effectual mode of giving a full establishment to his authority over those whom he had conquered, was by enlightening their understandings, and influencing them by the solemn sanctions of religion. These he wisely attempted to convey in the vernacular idiom, convinced that his subjects loved even the language of

* See note (§) below.

† German, *pl.* Germanen—an appellation used by the Gauls and Romans to designate the inhabitants of Germany. The word *German* is Gallic, for the Gauls called the soldiers who received a stipend, Gaisaten [Plut. Marius, 6, 7]. If the French gais be the *Moes.* gais, *Franc.* ger *a spear*, then German would be *a spear-man, spear-bearer.*—*Schmitthenner's* Deutsches Wörterbuch sub voce, p. 102. Others say that German is the same as Wermann, from which the Romans derived their Germanus, and the Gauls their Guerra. Warr, were, is derived from the *Old Ger.* uuer *pl.* uueros, wer, war, waer, bar, baro *a man, brave man, warrior;* vir bellator.—*Radlof's* Die Sprachen der Germanen, p. 4, 28.

‡ Celebrant carminibus antiquis Tuistonem deum terra editum, et filium Mannum, originem gentis conditoresque. Deo ortos, Marsos, Gambrivios, Suevos, Vandalios, affirmant; eaque vera et antiqua nomina. Ceterum *Germaniæ vocabulum recens et nuper additum;* quoniam qui primi Rhenum transgressi Gallos expulerint, ac nunc Tungri, nunc Germani vocati sunt.—*Tacit. de Mor. Ger.* 2.—Cæsar, after enumerating the names of several nations, adds, "qui uno nomine Germani appellantur. *Cæsar. Bell. Gal.* ii. 4.—Γνησιοι γαρ ὁι Γερμανοι κατα την Ρωμαιαν διαλεκτον: for Gnesioi are the Germans in the *Roman language.*—*Strabo* 7.

§ The Teutoni of Cæsar, Livy, and Virgil; Tuisto of Tacitus, or Tuisco, which, as *Schmitthenner* and *Mone* observe, is a mutilation of Tiusco or Tiusto, signifying *the great, the powerful.* Deutsch, *Old Ger.* Diotisc, Diutisc, or Theotisc, signify *belonging to a people*, from diot *people.* The national name Theodisci, Theotisci, or Theudisci, was not used till the time of the Carlovingian dynasty. Then all the smaller nations were united into one great empire. This word, since that time, has assumed very different forms according to the provinces where it was used, as Dutsch, Dietsch, Teutsch, Deutsch.—*Schmitthenner's* kurzes Deutsches Wörterbuch, p. 301. *Mone's* geschichte des Heidenthumsa, vol. ii. p. 6—8.

‖ Cæsar 1, 33, 40: 7, 77.—Livi. Epit. 68.

freedom. He used his influence to preserve the songs of his native land, and to improve its language and fix its grammar. Thus stability was first given to the German tongue, from which period it has gradually advanced, till it has become one of the most cultivated and important languages in Europe. To trace its progress, it will be necessary to enter into detail, and to examine the German language in its two great divisions, the Low and High German.

Division into Low and High German.

4. The Germanic or Teutonic tribes may, according to the nature of their language, be separated into two divisions. The Low-German prevailed in the low or flat provinces of ancient Germany, lying to the north and west, and is used in modern Flanders, the Dutch provinces, Westphalia, Oldenburg, Hanover, Brunswick, Holstein, Sleswick, Mecklenburg, Prussia, Courland, and part of Livonia, where the Low-German, or Nieder or Platt-Deutsch is spoken. This dialect is more soft and flowing than the High-German. It changes the High-German *sch* into *s*; the harsh *sz* or *z* into *t*, and always delights in simple vowels.

5. The second division comprised the Upper or High German, which prevailed in the mountainous or southern parts of Germany, that is, in the north of Switzerland, in Alsace, Swabia, Baden, Wurtemberg, Bavaria, the Austrian States, Silesia, Upper Saxony, and Hesse. The High-German dialect is distinguished by its predilection for long vowels and diphthongs, and rough, hard, and aspirated consonants, especially by the harsh pronunciation of *sch, st, sz,* and *z*.

6. The Francic seems to occupy an intermediate state between the High and Low German; but as it appears most inclined to the High-German, it is placed in the second division. The earlier Francs inhabited the banks of the Rhine, from Mayence to Cleves, the present Rhine Provinces of Prussia, Wurzburg, Bamburg, and Franconia, now part of Bavaria, and they continually increased their territory till the immense empire of Charlemagne was founded.

Low-German.

7. The Low-German comprises—

1st. Anglo-Saxon, written by king Alfred, Ælfric, Cædmon, &c. sec. III. 9, note.

2nd. Friesic, the written remains of which are found in the Asega-buch, &c.

3rd. The Old-Saxon or Platt-Deutsch, which has employed the pens of many authors. Tatian's Harmony of the Gospels is translated into a sort of Old-Saxon.—The Heliand is in Old-Saxon.—Reineke Vos, &c.

High-German.

8. To the High-German belong—

1st. The Mœso-Gothic, written by Ulphilas.

2nd. The Alemannic or Suabian, written by Kero, Rhabanus Maurus, Otfrid, Notker, Chunrad von Kirchberg, Gotfrit von Nifen.

3rd. The Francic, or transition between High and Low, but approaching more to the High-German, the chief writers in which are Isidore, and Willeram.

9 The nature and peculiarity of these six dialects may be best shown by a short historical detail of each tribe, as an alteration in a language was generally produced by some influential political change. It seems impossible to say which of the Germanic tongues was first used in Europe, but probably that language which was spoken by the people located most to the west. If this be sufficient for priority, the Anglo-Saxons will claim the first notice.

III.—THE ANGLO-SAXONS.

1. The Anglo-Saxons derived their being and name from the Angles, a tribe of the Saxon confederacy, occupying Anglen in the south-east part of the Duchy of Sleswich in the south of Denmark. These Saxons, like all the Teutoni or Germans, were of oriental origin. They were as far westward as the Elbe in the days of Ptolemy, A.D. 90; and therefore in all probability they were amongst the first Germanic or Teutonic tribes that visited Europe. Their situation, between the Elbe and the Eyder in the south of Denmark, seems to indicate that they moved among the foremost columns of the vast Teutonic emigration. The Saxons, when first settled on the Elbe, were an inconsiderable people, but in succeeding ages they increased in power and renown. About A.D. 240, the Saxons united with the Francs (*the free people*) to oppose the progress of the Romans towards the north. By this league and other means the Saxon influence was increased, till they possessed the vast extent of country embraced by the Elbe, the Sala, and the Rhine, in addition to their ancient territory from the Elbe to the Eyder. In this tract of country were several confederate nations, leagued together for mutual defence. Although the Saxon name became, on the continent, the appellation of this confederacy of nations, yet at first it only denoted a single state.

2. It may be satisfactory to have a brief and clear account of the Germanic tribes, the Jutes, Saxons, and Angles, who successively obtained settlements in Britain.

3. The Jutes gained the first possessions. Hengist and Horsa, two brothers from Jutland or the Cimbric Chersonesus in Denmark, arrived in three ceols or small ships at Ebbs-fleet on the Isle of Thanet in A.D. 449. These Jutes, for assisting the Britons against the Picts and Scots, had the Isle of Thanet assigned to them. They subsequently obtained possession of Kent, the Isle of Wight, and part of Hampshire.

4. The Saxons had a very extended territory. After many of them had migrated to Britain, the parent stock on the continent had the name of *Old-Saxons.** The first Saxon kingdom† was established by Ella in A.D. 491, under the name of South-Saxons, or South-Sax, now Sussex. In 494, another powerful colony arrived under Cerdic, and being placed west of the other kingdoms, they were, on their full establishment in 519, called West-Saxons [West-Seaxe], in its fullest extent embracing the north part of Hampshire, Berks, Wilts, Dorset, Somerset, Devon, and part of Cornwall.—A third Saxon kingdom, in A.D. 527, was planted in Essex, Middlesex, and the south part of Hertfordshire, under the name of East-Saxons, East-Sax, or Essex.

* Hist. of Anglo-Saxons, by F. Palgrave, Esq. small 8vo. 1831, p. 83; The Rise and Progress of the English Commonwealth, by the same, 4to. 1832, p. 40.

† *The Saxon Chronicle gives the following account:* "An. CCCCXLIX. Her Martianus and Valentinianus onfengon rice, and ricsodon VII. winter. On heora dagum Hengest and Horsa, from Wyrtgeorne gelaðode Brytta cyninge to fultume, gesohton Brytene on þam stæðe, þe is genemned Ypwines-fleot, ærest Bryttum to fultume, ac hy eft on hy fuhton. Se cing het hi feohtan agien Pihtas, and hi swa dydan, and sige hæfdon swa hwar swa hi comon. Hi þa sende to Angle, and heton heom sendan mare fultum, and heom seggan Brytwalana nahtnesse, and þæs landes cysta. Hi þa sendon heom mare fultum, þa comon þa menn of þrim mægðum Germanie, of Eald-Seaxum, of Anglum, of Iotum.

"Of Iotum comon Cantware and Wihtware [þæt is seo mæið þe nu eardað on Wiht,] and þæt cynn on West-Sexum, þe man nu gyt het Iutna-cynn. Of Eald-Seaxum comon East-Seaxan, and Suð-Seaxan, and West-Seaxan. Of Angle comon, se á siððan stod westig betwix Iutum and Seaxum, East-Engle, and Middel-Angle, and Mearce and ealle Norðymbra. Heora here-togan wæron twegen gebroðra, Hengest and Horsa, þæt wæron Wihtgilses suna, Wihtgils wæs Witting, Witta Wecting, Wecta Wodning, fram þam Wodne awoc eall ure cyne-cynn and Suðan-hymbra eac."—*Ingram's Chr.* pp. 13—15.

Bede makes nearly the same statement. "Advenerant autem de tribus Germaniæ populis fortioribus, id est, Saxonibus, Anglis, Jutis. De Jutarum origine sunt Cantuarii et Victuarii, hoc est, ea gens quæ Vectam tenet insulam, et ea quæ usque hodie in provincia Occidentalium Saxonum Jutarum natio nominatur, posita contra ipsam insulam Vectam. De saxonibus, id est, ea regione quæ nunc antiquorum Saxonum cognominatur, venere Orientales Saxones, Meridiani Saxones, Occidui Saxones. Porro de Anglis, hoc est, de illa patria quæ Angulus dicitur et ab eo tempore usque hodie manere desertus inter provincias Jutarum et Saxonum perhibetur, Orientales Angli, Mediterranei Angli, Merci, tota Nordanhymbrorum progenies, id est, illarum gentium quæ ad Boream Humbri fluminis inhabitant cæterique Anglorum populi sunt orti. Duces fuisse perhibentur eorum primi duo fratres Hengist et Horsa; e quibus Horsa postea occisus in bello a Brittonibus, hactenus in Orientalibus Cantiæ partibus monumentum habet suo nomine insigne. Erant autem filii Victgilsi, cujus pater Vitta, cujus pater Vecta, cujus pater Voden, de cujus stirpe multarum provinciarum regium genus originem duxit."—*Bede*, lib. i. ch. 15, p. 52. *Alfred's Saxon translation of which is:* "Comon hi of þrim folcum þam strangestan Germanie, þæt of Seaxum, and of Angle, and of Geatum. Of geata fruman syndon Cantware, and Wihtsætan, þæt is seo þeod þe Wiht þæt Ealond oneardað. Of Seaxum þæt is of þam lande þe mon hateð Eald-Seaxan, coman East-Seaxan, and Suð-Seaxan, and West-Seaxan. And of Engle coman East-Engle and Middel-Engle, and Myrce, and eall Norðhembra cynn, is þæt land þe Angulus is nemned betwyh Geatum and Seaxum. Is sæd of þære tide þe hi þanon gewiton oð to dæge þæt hit weste wunige. Wæron þa ærest heora latteowas and heretogan twegen gebroðra, Hengest and Horsa. Hi wæron Wihtgylses suna, þæs Fæder wæs [Witta haten, þæs fæder wæs Wihta haten, þæs] fæder wæs Woden nemned, of þæs strynde monigra mægða cyning cynn fruman lædde."—*Smith's Bede*, p. 483.

5. The Angles (Engle), from Sleswich in the south of Denmark, about A.D. 527, settled themselves in East Anglia, containing Norfolk, Suffolk, Cambridge, and part of Bedfordshire.—Ida, in A.D. 547, began to establish himself in Bernicia, comprehending Northumberland, and the south of Scotland between the Tweed and the Firth of Forth.—About A.D. 559, Ella conquered Deira [Deoramægð] lying between the Humber and the Tweed, including the present counties of York, Durham, Northumberland, Cumberland, Westmoreland, and Lancashire.—Mercia was formed into an independent state by Crida, about A.D. 586, and comprehended the counties of Chester, Derby, Nottingham, Lincoln, Leicester, Northampton, Rutland, Huntingdon, the north of Beds, and Hertford, Warwick, Bucks, Oxon, Worcester, Hereford, Gloucester, Stafford, and Salop. Thus, one Jute, three Saxon, and four Angle, altogether eight kingdoms, were established in Britain, by the year 586.*

6. The Angles emigrated so numerously as to leave Angle, their original district, destitute of inhabitants. Though the Friesians are not named as uniting in the first conquest of Britain, it is clear, from their locality, that many of them accompanied the other Teutonic tribes.† Those now settled in Britain were denominated Anglo-Saxons to show their origin; Anglo-Saxon denoting that the people so called were the Angles, a nation coming from the Saxon confederacy. In subsequent times, when the Angles had been alienated from the Saxon confederacy by settling in Britain, they denominated that part of this kingdom which they inhabited Engla-land, the land of the Angles, Angle's land, which was afterwards contracted into England.

7. From the entrance of the Saxons into Britain in A.D. 449, they opposed the Britons, till, on the full establishment of the Saxon power in A.D. 586, the Britons were driven into Wales. As soon as the Britons ceased to oppose their invaders the Saxon kingdoms began to contend with each other. The West-Saxons, with varying success, gradually increased in influence and territory from Cerdic their first leader in A.D. 494, till 827, when Egbert, king of Wessex, defeated or made tributary all the other Saxon kingdoms. Egbert, his son Ethelwulph, and his grandsons Ethelbald, Ethelbert, Ethelred, and Alfred the Great, had to contend with new and fierce opponents in the Northmen, or Danes. The most energetic and renowned of the West-Saxon kings was Alfred the Great. He drove the Northmen from his kingdom, and found leisure

* Mr. Turner, in his Hist. of A.-S., b. iii. ch. 5, vol. i. p. 309, observes: "This state of Britain has been improperly denominated the Saxon heptarchy. When all the kingdoms were settled, they formed an octarchy. Ella, supporting his invasion in Sussex, like Hengist in Kent, made a Saxon duarchy before the year 500. When Cerdic erected the state of Wessex in 519, a triarchy appeared; East Anglia made it a tetrarchy; Essex a pentarchy. The success of Ida, after 547, having established a sovereignty of Angles in Bernicia, the island beheld an hexarchy. When the northern Ella penetrated, in 560, southward of the Tees, his kingdom of Deira produced an heptarchy. In 586, the Angles branching from Deira into the regions south of the Humber, the state of Mercia completed an Anglo-Saxon octarchy."

† See Friesians, iv. § 50—56.

not only to encourage literature in others, but, with great success, to devote himself to literary pursuits, as much as the proper discharge of the public affairs of his kingdom would allow. He translated into Anglo-Saxon, Boethius, Orosius, and Bede, and thus gave a preeminence to the West-Saxon language, as well as to the West-Saxon kingdom. The West-Saxons retained the government of this island till 1016, when Canute, a Dane, became king of England. Canute and his two sons, Harold and Hardicanute, reigned twenty-six years. The Saxon line was restored in 1042, and continued till 1066, when Harold the Second was slain by William duke of Normandy, commonly called William the Conqueror. Thus the Anglo-Saxon dynasty terminated, after it had existed in England about six hundred years. The Saxon power ceased when William the Conqueror ascended the throne, but not the language; for Anglo-Saxon, after rejecting or changing many of its inflections, continued to be spoken by the old inhabitants till the time of Henry the Third, A.D. 1258. What was written after this period has generally so great a resemblance to our present language, that it may evidently be called English.

8. From the preceding short detail, it appears that the Jutes had small possessions in Kent and the Isle of Wight: the Angles occupied the east and north of England, with the south of Scotland: and the Saxons had extensive possessions in the western and southern parts. The descendants of these Saxons were very numerous: their power and influence became most extensive under the dominion of West-Saxon kings, especially under Egbert and Alfred. It was the powerful mind of Alfred that drew into England the talent and literature of Europe, and induced him to benefit his country by writing so much in his native tongue, the Anglo-Saxon; thus giving the West-Saxon dialect so great a predominance as to constitute it the cultivated language of the Anglo-Saxons. This pure Anglo-Saxon may be found in the works of Alfred, Ælfric, the Anglo-Saxon Laws, Cædmon, &c.

9. Ethelbert, king of Kent, being converted to the Christian faith by the preaching of Augustine, in A.D. 597, was distinguished as the author of the first written Saxon laws which have descended to us, or are known to have been established. Some think that the laws of Ethelbert are the first Anglo-Saxon composition:* others give priority to Beowulf, the Traveller's Song, &c. Beowulf is said to have been nearly contemporary with Hengist;† but the poem contained in the Cotton MS. British Museum, Vitellius, A. xv. is not so old. There occur in it Christian allusions which fix this text at least at a period subsequent to A.D. 597. Some eminent scholars attribute this MS. to the early part of the 10th century.‡

* Turner's *Hist. of Anglo-Saxons*, b. iii. c. 6, vol. i. p. 332.

† See the very neat edition of *Beowulf*, by Mr. Kemble, *Pref.* p. xx. *London*, 1833.

‡ Conybeare's *Illustrations of Anglo-Saxon Poetry*, p. 32; Turner's *Hist. of Anglo-Saxons*, b. ix. c. 2, vol. iii. p. 281.

From this fine poem may be selected some early specimens of pure Anglo-Saxon. The Traveller's Song, in its original composition, is referred by Mr. Conybeare* to about A.D. 450. It was first printed by him with a literal Latin version, and a free poetical translation in English. An improved Saxon text is given in Mr. Kemble's Beowulf, p. 223—233. For an example of an early specimen of Anglo-Saxon poetry, compared with one of a subsequent date, see FRIESIC, § 58. As the works of Alfred, Ælfric, Cædmon, the poems of Beowulf, and many of the books specified in the note below,† afford ample specimens of pure

* Illustrations of A.-S. Poetry, p. 9—29; Exeter MS. p. 84.

† *A chronological list of the chief works printed in Anglo-Saxon, with a notice of Grammars and Dictionaries intended for junior students.*—[1567.] ÆLFRIC. 1. A Testimonie of antiqvitie showing the auncient fayth in the Church of England touching the Sacrament of the Body and Bloude of the Lord here publickely preached, and also receiued in the Saxons' tyme, above 600 yeares agoe, 16mo. Imprinted at London by John Daye, dwelling over Aldersgate beneath S. Martyns, 1567. *This little book contains* "A Sermon of the Paschall Lambe to be spoken unto the people at Easter." *Anglo-Saxon on the left-hand page, and an English translation on the right. It is paged only on the right to 75. Then follow 13 leaves, without being paged, containing the Lord's Prayer, the Creed, and the X Commandments in Saxon, with an interlinear English translation. The whole book, therefore, consists of 88 leaves, or 176 pages. It was published again in small 4to. with L'Isle's* "Treatise concerning the Old and New Testament," in 1623: *the Easter Homily was printed again in the 2nd vol. of Fox's* "Acts and Monuments," *and in the notes to Whelock's* "Bede," b. v. c. 22. *In the year of L'Isle's death, it appeared again with this title,* "Divers ancient Monuments in the Saxon Tongue," &c. 4to. 1638.—[1568.] LAWS. 2. Αρχαιονομια, sive de priscis Anglorum Legibus libri, Sermone Anglico, vetustate antiquissimo aliquot abhinc seculis conscripti, atque nunc demum magno Jurisperitorum et amantium antiquitatis omnium commodo, e tenebris in lucem vocati, Gulielmo Lambardo, 4to. ex officina Johan. Daye, *Lond.* 1568. *A greatly improved edition was published by* Whelock, in folio, Cambridge, 1644, pp. 226, 1*l. A still better edition, so much enlarged and improved as to be considered almost a new work, was published with the following title:* "Leges Anglo-Saxonicæ Ecclesiasticæ et Civiles, accedunt Leges Edvardi Latinæ, Gulielmi Conquestoris Gallo-Normannicæ, et Henrici I. Latinæ, subjungitur Domini Henr. Spelmanni Codex Legum Veterum Statutorum Regni Angliæ, quæ ab ingressu Gulielmi I. usque ad annum nonum Henr. III. edita sunt; toti Operi præmittitur Dissertatio Epistolaris admodum Reverendi Domini Gulielmi Nicolsoni Episcopi, Derrensis De Jure Feudali Veterum Saxonum, cum Codd. MSS. contulit, notas, versionem, et glossarium adjecit David Wilkins, S.T.P. fol. *Lond.* 1721, p. 434, 2*l.* 12*s.* 6*d. These are in Anglo-Saxon, with Latin translation and notes.*—Die Gesetze der Angelsachsen. In der Ursprache mit Uebersetzung und Erläuterungen herausgegeben von Dr. Reinhold Schmid, Professor der Rechte zu Jena, 8vo. Leipzig, 1832, pp. 304, about 8*s. There are two columns in a page; on the left is the Anglo-Saxon text, in Roman type except the* þ, ð, *and on the right a German translation. The second volume has long been expected. The Record Commission have undertaken an edition with an improved Anglo-Saxon text, carefully accented, and accompanied with an English translation and notes. It was prepared, and a considerable part printed, under the superintendence of the late Richard Price, Esq. whose critical acquaintance with the Anglo-Saxon has been manifested by his excellent edition of Warton's* "History of English Poetry." *This edition of the A.-S. Laws by Mr. Price, is not yet published.*—[1571.] GOSPELS. 3. The Gospels of the fower Euangelistes, translated in the olde Saxon, tyme out of Latin into the vulgare toung of the Saxons, newly collected out of auncient monumentes of the sayd Saxons, and now published for testimonie of the same, 4to. London, printed by John Daye, 1571. *It is accompanied with an English version out of the Bishop's Bible, so altered as to agree with the Saxon, and published by Fox, the Martyrologist, at the expense of Archbishop Parker. Price* 3*l.* 3*s.*—Quatuor D.N. Jesu Christi Evangeliorum Versiones per antiquæ duæ, Gothica scil. et Anglo-Saxonica: quarum illam ex celeberrimo Codice Argenteo nunc primum depromsit Franciscus Junius, hanc autem ex Codd. MSS. collatis emendatiùs recudi curavit Thomas Mareschallus Anglus; cujus etiam observationes in utramque versionem subnectuntur. Accessit et Glossarium Gothicum: cui præmittitur Alphabetum Gothicum, Runicum, &c. operâ ejusdem Francisci Junii, 4to. Dordrechti, 1665, et Amsterdam, 1684, pp. 383—431, 2*l.* 8*s. The Amsterdam edition appears, on collation, to be made up from the old copies with new title-pages, and a reprint of the first sheet in vol.* ii. *Moes. Glos.* The Anglo-Saxon Gospels from the text of Marshall, the Rushworth Gloss, MS. Bodl. together with all the A.-S. translations of the Gospels, are about to appear in a quarto volume from the Pitt Press, Cambridge.—[1623.] ÆLFRIC. 4. A Saxon Treatise concerning the Old and New Testament. Written abovt the time of King Edgar (700 yeares agoe) by Ælfricvs Abbas, thought to be the same that was afterward Archbishop of Canterbvrie. Whereby

Anglo-Saxon, it will not be necessary to occupy much space with quotations. One extract will be sufficient, and, for facility of comparison,

appeares what was the Canon of holy Scripture here then receiued, and that the Church of England had it so long agoe in her mother-tongue. Now first pvblished in print with English of our times by WILLIAM L'ISLE of Wilbvrgham, Esquier for the King's bodie: the originall remaining still to be seene in Sr Robert Cotton's Librarie, at the end of his lesser Copie of the Saxon Pentatevch. And herevnto is added ovt of the Homilies and Epistles of the fore-said Ælfricvs, a second edition of *A Testimonie of Antiquitie, &c. touching the Sacrament of the Body and Bloud of the* LORD, here publikely preached and receiued in the Saxons' time, &c. London, printed by John Haviland for Henrie Seile, dwelling in Paul's Church-yard, at the signe of the Tyger's head, 1623, small 4to. *The Dedication, Preface, &c. contain 30 leaves, the paragraphs numbered, but not the pages; then follow 43 leaves of the Treatise of the Old and New Testament, Saxon on the left, and English on the right-hand page. The first 12 leaves are without numbers, 13 is placed at the head of the Saxon on the left, and also at the head of the English on the right page, the same numeral serving for two pages.* The Testimony of Antiquity, &c. *has 9 leaves of Preface, &c., 14 leaves, with double numerals, of* "A Sermon of the Paschall Lambe, &c.;" *then follow 11 leaves unpaged, containing* the words of Elfrike Abbot, and the Lord's Prayer, Creed, and X Commandments, *in Saxon, with an interlinear English version*, 30 + 43 + 9 + 14 + 11 = 107 *leaves, or 214 pages.*—[1640.] PSALMS. 5. Psalterium Davidis Latino-Saxonicum Vetus, à Johanne Spelmanno, D. Hen. fil. editum, 4to. Londini, 1640, 1*l.* 1*s.*—Libri Psalmorum versio antiqua Latina; cum paraphrasi Anglo-Saxonica, partim soluta oratione, partim metrice composita, nunc primum e cod. MS. in Bibl. Regia Parisiensi adservato, descripsit et edidit Benjamin Thorpe, S.A.S. Soc. Lit. Isl. Hafn. Soc. Hon. 8vo. Oxonii, 1835.—[1644.] BEDE. 6. Bedæ Venerabilis Historia Ecclesiastica Anglorum, Anglo-Saxonicè ex versione Ælfredi Magni Gentis et Latinè, accessêre Chronologia Saxonica (*The Saxon Chronicle*, see 9.) et Leges Anglo-Saxonicè cum interpretatione Latinâ, curâ Abrahami Wheloci, fol. Cantabrigiæ, 1644. *A much improved and splendid edition was published with the following title:* "Bedæ Historia Ecclesiastica, Latinè et Saxonicè; una cum reliquis ejus operibus Historicis Latinè, curâ et studio Johannis Smith, S.T.P. fol. Cantabrigiæ, 1722, pp. 823, 2*l.* 16*s.*—[1655.] CÆDMON. 7. Cædmonis Monachi Paraphrasis Poetica Genesios ac præcipuarum sacræ paginæ historiarum, abhinc annos M.LXX. Anglo-Saxonicè conscripta, et nunc primùm edita à Francisco Junio, Amst. 1655, pp. 116. 1*l.*—Cædmon's Metrical Paraphrase of Parts of the Holy Scriptures, in Anglo-Saxon, with an English translation, notes, and a verbal index, by Benjamin Thorpe, F.S.A. 8vo. London, 1832, pp. 341, 1*l.* 1*s.*—[1659.] ÆLFRIC. 8. Ælfrici abbatis Grammatici vulgo dicti Grammatica Latino-Saxonica, &c. Guliel. Somnerus, fol. Oxon. 1659, pp. 52. *This is a Latin Grammar written in Anglo-Saxon for the use of those Saxon youths who were studying Latin. It is appended to Somner's A.-S. Dictionary, see* 22.—[1692.] CHRONICLE. 9. Chronologica Anglo-Saxonica, curâ Abrahami Wheloci, fol. Cantabrigiæ, 1644. *Appended to Whelock's edition of Bede, see Bede*, 6.—Chronicon Saxonicum; seu Annales Rerum in Angliâ præcipue gestarum ad annum MCLIV.; cum indice rerum chronologico. Accedunt regulæ ad investigandas nominum locorum origines; et nominum locorum et virorum in Chronico memoratorum explicatio; Latinè et Anglo-Saxonicè, cum notis Edmundi Gibson, 4to. Oxon. 1692, 2*l.* 8*s.*—The Saxon Chronicle, with an English translation, and notes, critical and explanatory, and chronological, topographical, and glossarial indexes; a short Grammar of the Anglo-Saxon Language, by the Rev. James Ingram B.D.; a new Map of England during the Heptarchy, plates of Coins, 4to. 1823, pp. 463, 3*l.* 13*s.* 6*d.* *The Saxon Chronicle has been translated into English, and printed with an improved A.-S. text, carefully accented from MSS. by the late Richard Price, Esq. for the Record Commission. It is not yet published. Miss Gurney printed and circulated privately among her friends a very useful work entitled* "A literal Translation of the Saxon Chronicle, 12mo. Norwich, 1819, pp. 324, *with 48 pages of Index.*—[1698.] ÆLFRIC'S *Bible.* 10. Heptateuchus, Liber Job, et Evangelium Nicodemi, Anglo-Saxonicè. Historiæ Judith Fragmentum; Dano-Saxonice, edidit nunc primùm ex MSS. Codicibus Edvardus Thwaites, 8vo. Oxon. 1698, pp. 168 + 30 = 198, 1*l.* 4*s.* *The first seven books of the Bible in Anglo-Saxon.*—[1698.] ALFRED'S *Boethius.* 11. Boethii (An. Manl. Sever.) Consolationis Philosophiæ libri V. Anglo-Saxonicè redditi ab Ælfredo; ad Apographum Junianum expressos edidit Christophorus Rawlinson, 8vo. Oxon. 1698, 1*l.* 8*s.*—King Alfred's Anglo-Saxon version of Boethius, de Consolatione Philosophiæ; with an English translation and notes, by J. S. Cardale, 8vo. London, 1829, pp. 425, 1*l.* 5*s.*—King Alfred's Anglo-Saxon version of the Metres of Boethius, with an English translation and notes, by the Rev. Samuel Fox, M.A. 8vo. London, 1835, pp. 144, 12*s.*—[1709.] ELSTOB'S *Hom.* 12. An English-Saxon Homily on the Birth-day of St. Gregory, anciently used in the English-Saxon Church, giving an account of the Conversion of the English from Paganism to Christianity; translated into modern English, with Notes, &c. by Elizabeth Elstob, 8vo. London, 1709, pp. Preface, lx. 44 + 10 + 49 = 103, 1*l.* 4*s.* *This work is in Anglo-Saxon and English. She also printed some sheets in folio of Anglo-Saxon Homilies, with an English translation. For reasons now unknown the press was stopped. A copy of what was printed is in the British Museum.*—[1773.] ALFRED'S *Oros.* 13. The Anglo-Saxon version from the historian Orosius, by Alfred the Great, together with an English translation from the Anglo-Saxon,

the parable of the Sower is selected from Marshall's Gospels, *Dordrecht*, 1665.

(by Daines Barrington), 8vo. London, 1773; Anglo-Saxon, pp. 242, English translation and notes, pp. 259, about 1*l.* 5*s.*—ALFRED'S *Will.* 14. Ælfred's Will, in Anglo-Saxon, with a literal and also a free English translation, a Latin version, and notes, (by the Rev. Owen Manning,) royal 4to. Oxford, at the Clarendon Press, 1788, pp. 51, about 7*s.* The same, reprinted from the Oxford edition of 1788, with a preface and additional notes, (by Mr. Cardale) London, Pickering, Combe, Leicester, 8vo. 1828, pp. 32, price 5*s.*—[1815.] BEOWULF. 15. De Danorum Rebus Gestis Secul. III. et IV. Poëma Danicum, Dialecto Anglo-Saxonica, ex Bibliotheca Cottoniana Musæi Britannici edidit versione Latinâ et indicibus, auxit, Grim Johnson Thorkelin, Dr. J. V. &c. 4to. Havniæ, 1815, pp. 299, 14*s.*—*An analysis of this fine poem, and an English translation of a considerable part of it, has been given by Mr. Turner in his History of the Anglo-Saxons*, b. ix. c. 2, vol. iii. p. 280-301.—*A still more complete analysis is given, with free translations in English verse, and a literal Latin version from a text formed from a careful collation with the MS. in Conybeare's* Illustrations of Anglo-Saxon Poetry, p. 30-167.—*A very neat edition of the Anglo-Saxon text has appeared, entitled* "The Anglo-Saxon Poems of Beowulf; the Traveller's Song, and the Battle of Finnes-burh, edited, together with a Glossary of the more difficult words, and an historical Preface, by John M. Kemble, Esq. M.A. of Trinity College, Cambridge," small 8vo. London, 1833, pp. 259, 13*s.* *A second edition, with an English translation and a complete Glossary, is on the eve of publication.*—[1826.] CONYBEARE'S *Poetry.* 16. Illustrations of Anglo-Saxon Poetry, by the Rev. John Josias Conybeare, M.A. late Anglo-Saxon Professor, &c. at Oxford, edited by his brother the Rev. W. D. Conybeare, M.A. &c. 8vo. London, 1826, pp. 286, 18*s.*—[1830.] Fox's *Menol.* 17. Menologium, seu Calendarium Poeticum, ex Hickesiano Thesauro: or, The Poetical Calendar of the Anglo-Saxons, with an English translation and notes, by the Rev. Samuel Fox, M.A. 8vo. London, 1830, pp. 64, 6*s.*—[1834.] THORPE'S *Analect.* 18. Analecta Anglo-Saxonica. A selection, in prose and verse, from Anglo-Saxon authors of various ages, with a Glossary; designed chiefly as a first book for students, by Benjamin Thorpe, F.S.A. 8vo. London, 1834, pp. 266, 20*s.* *This work gives specimens of Anglo-Saxon from its purest to its most corrupt state. As some of the specimens have been taken from MSS. and are here printed for the first time, this useful book has properly a place here.*—[1834.] THORPE'S *Apoll.* 19. The Anglo-Saxon version of the story of Apollonius of Tyre, upon which is founded the play of Pericles, attributed to Shakspeare; from a MS. in the Library of C.C.C. Cambridge, with a literal translation, &c. by Benjamin Thorpe, F.S.A. 12mo. London, 1834, pp. 92, 6*s.*—20. A MORE *minute account of works printed in Anglo-Saxon, especially of smaller detached pieces, may be found in* p. 134 *of* Hickes's Institutiones Grammaticæ Anglo-Saxonicæ, 4to. Oxoniæ, 1680; *and in Wanley's Catalogue of Anglo-Saxon MSS. forming the 3rd vol. of Hickes's Thesaurus*, p. 325. *A short notice of the principal A.-S. MSS. may be found in Hickes's Institutiones, from* p. 135 *to* 176, *but a minute account of all the A.-S. MSS. with many very interesting and valuable extracts, will be found in Wanley's Catalogue, which, as the 3rd vol. of Hickes's Thesaurus, has the following title:* "Antiquæ Literaturæ Septentrionalis Liber alter, seu Humphredi Wanleii Librorum Veterum Septentrionalium qui in Angliæ Bibliothecis extant, nec non multorum Veterum Codicum Septentrionalium alibi extantium *Catalogus* Historico-Criticus, cum totius Thesauri Linguarum Septentrionalium sex Indicibus, fol. Oxoniæ, 1705.—*An arranged Catalogue of all the extant relics of A.-S. poetry is given in Conybeare's* Illustrations of A.-S. Poetry, p. lxxvi—lxxxvi.

21. GRAMMARS. 1. Hickes's Institutiones Gram. A.-S. 4to. Oxon. 1689, 2*l.*—2. Hickes's Thesaurus, 3 vols. fol. Oxon. 1705, 12*s.*—3. (Thwaites's) Gram. A.-S. ex Hickesiano, 8vo. pp. 48, 2*l.*—4. Elstob's (Eliz.) Gram. of English-Saxon tongue, 4to. Lond. 1715, 1*l.*—5. Henley's Gram. of Anglo-Saxon, Lond. 1726, pp. 61, 4*s.*—6. Lye's Gram. Anglo-Saxon, prefixed to Junius's Etymologicum, fol. Oxon. 1743.—7. Manning's Gram. Anglo-Saxon et Mœso-Goth. prefixed to his edition of Lye's A.-S. Dict. 2 vols. fol. Lond. 1772.—8. Rask's Angelsaksisk Sproglære, 8vo. Stockholm, 1817, pp. 168; Mr. Thorpe's Translation of ditto, 8vo. Copenhagen, 1830, 15*s.* 6*d.*—9. Sisson's Elements of A.-S. Gram. 12mo. Leeds, 1819, pp. 84, 5*s.*—10. Dr. Jacob Grimm's Deutsche Grammatik, 3 vols. 8vo. Gottingen, 1822, 1826, 1831. *This is a Grammar of all the Germanic languages; it is the 2nd edit.*—11. Bosworth's Elements of A.-S. Gram. 8vo. 1823, pp. 330, 16*s.*—Bosworth's Compendious Gram. of Primitive Eng. or A.-S. 8vo. 1826, pp. 84, 5*s.*—12. Ingram's Short Gram. of A.-S. prefixed to his edition of the Saxon Chronicle, 4to. 1823, pp. 8.—13. Gwilt's Rudiments of A.-S. 8vo. Lond. 1829, pp. 56, 6*s.*

22. DICTIONARIES. Somner's Dict. Saxonico-Latino-Anglicum, folio, Oxon. 1659, 8*l.*—2. Benson's Vocabularium A.-S. 8vo. Oxon. 1701, 1*l.* 4*s.*—3. Lye's Dictionarium Saxonico et Gothico-Latinum, published by Manning, in 2 vols. fol. Lond. 1772, 7*l.* 17*s.* 6*d.*

Works relating to Anglo-Saxon.—[1650.] 23. CASAUBONI (Merici) de Linguâ Saxonicâ et de Linguâ Hebraicâ Commentarius; accesserunt Gulielmi Somneri ad verba vetera Germanica Lipsiana notæ, small 8vo. Londini, 1650, 8*s.* 6*d.*—[1678.] ALFRED'S *Life.* 24. Ælfredi Magni Vita, à Joanne Spelman, plates, folio, Oxon. 1678, about 16*s.*—[1709.] Ælfred's Life, by Sir John Spelman, Knt. from the original manuscript in the Bodleian Library, with considerable additions, and several historical remarks, by the publisher Thomas Hearne, M.A. small 8vo.

Mk. iv. 3—8.

3. Gehyrað, Ute eode se sædere hys sæd to sawenne. 4. And þa he sew, sum feoll wið þone weg, and fugelas comon and hyt fræton. 5. Sum feoll ofer stans-cyligean, þar hyt næfde mycel eorðan, and sona up-eode, forþam þe hyt næfde eorðan þiccnesse. 6. Þa hyt up-eode, seo sunne hyt forswælde, and hyt forscranc, forþam hyt wirtruman næfde. 7. And sum feoll on þornas, þa stigon þa þornas and forðrysmodon þæt, and hyt wæstm ne bær. 8. And sum feoll on god land, and hyt sealde, upstigende and wexende, wæstm, and an brohte þrittig-fealdne, sum syxtig-fealdne, sum hundfealdne.

The Anglo-Saxon Dialects.

10. The Jutes, Angles, and Saxons, had probably some little difference of dialect when they arrived in Britain. Distant tribes, from the disturbed state of the country, and the difficulties of travelling, could have very limited intercourse. The Jutes were few in number, and could not have much influence, especially as it regards the language. The descendants of the Angles were very numerous, and occupied the country north of the Thames: they settled in East-Anglia, Northumbria, south of Scotland, &c. Their language was more broad and harsh than the West-Saxon, and was formerly called the Dano-Saxon dialect. It may,

Oxford, 1709, about 9*s.*—Life of Alfred or Alured, by Robert Powell, 18mo. 1634, about 5*s.*—Ælfredi Regis præfatio ad Pastorale Sancti Gregorii, e Codd. MS. Jun. LIII. *Saxon and Latin. See Asserii Meneven. Ælfredi*, p. 81.—[1722.] Asserii Menevensis Annales Rerum Gestarum Ælfredi Magni, recensuit Franciscus Wise, M.A. small 8vo. Oxon. 1722, about 9*s.*—Mr. Turner's Hist. of Anglo-Saxons, b. iv. c. 6—11, and b. v. c. 1—6.—[1708.] Wotton's *View.* 25. Linguarum Veterum Septentrionalium Thesauri Grammatico-Critici et Archæologici, auctore Georgio Hickesio, Conspectus brevis, cum notis, Gulielmo Wotton, 12mo. 12*s.*—[1708.] Wotton's Short View of George Hickes's Grammatico-Critical and Archeological Treasury of the Ancient Northern Languages, translated, with notes, by Maurice Shelton, 4to. London, 1737.—[1715.] Elstob's *Saxon Devotion.* 26. Publick Office of daily and nightly devotion for the seven canonical hours of prayer, used in the Anglo-Saxon Church, with a translation and notes, together with the Rev. Dr. George Hickes's Controversial Discourses, by W. Elstob, 1 vol. 8vo. 1705, London, 5*s.*; the same, 2 vols. 8vo. 16*s.* 1715-27.—[1726.] Gavelkind. 27. Somner's (William) Treatise of Gavelkind, both name and thing, showing the True Etymologie and Derivation of the One, the Nature, Antiquity, and Original of the Other. To which is added the Life of the Author, by Bishop White Kennett, 4to. London, 1726. 17*s.*—[1798.] Henshall. 28. The Saxon and English Languages reciprocally illustrative of each other; the impracticability of acquiring an accurate knowledge of Saxon Literature through the medium of Latin Phraseology, exemplified in the errors of Hickes, Wilkins, Gibson, and other scholars; and a new mode suggested of radically studying the Saxon and English Languages, by Samuel Henshall, M.A. 4to. London, 1798, pp. 60. 5*s.*—[1807.] Ingram. 29. An Inaugural Lecture on the utility of Anglo-Saxon Literature; to which is added the Geography of Europe, by King Alfred, including his account of the Discovery of the North Cape in the 9th century, by the Rev. James Ingram, M.A. 4to. Oxford, 1807, pp. 112. 10*s.* 6*d.*—[1807.] Henshall. 30. The Etymological Organic Reasoner; with part of the Gothic Gospel of St. Matthew, from the Codex Argenteus (Cent. IV.) and from the Saxon Durham Book (Cent. VIII.), with an English Version, 8vo. 1807. 5*s.*—[1822.] Silver. 31. A Lecture on the Study of the Anglo-Saxon, (by the Rev. Thomas Silver, D.D.), 8vo. Oxford, 1822. 3*s.*—[1830.] 32. Mone's (Franz Joseph) Quellen und Forschungen zur Geschichte der Teutschen Lit. und Sprache, 8vo. Leipzig, 1830, 10*s.*—[1833.] 33. Collen's (George William) Britannia Saxonica, a Map of Britain during the Octarchy, 4to. London, 1833, 12*s.*—[1799-1834.] 34. Turner's (Sharon) History of the Anglo-Saxons; comprising the History of England from the earliest period to the Norman Conquest, 3 vols. 8vo. 5th edit. London, 1834, 2*l.* 5*s.*—Palgrave's (Sir Francis) Hist. of A.-S. 16mo. Lond. 1831, pp. 391, 5*s.*—Palgrave's Rise and Progress of the English Commonwealth, 4to. London, 1834, 3*l.* 3*s.* *Mr. Turner and Sir F. Palgrave's important works must be carefully read by every A.-S. student. These for History, and Rask and Grimm for Philology, are rich sources of information for those who are interested in the Anglo-Saxon language and literature.*

however, probably be rather denominated, from its locality,* the Northumbrian or East-Anglian dialect. As this is not the place to enter minutely into the subject of dialects, a few extracts are only given, that they may be compared with the specimen of pure Anglo-Saxon.

11. The parable of the Sower, from the Northumbrian Gloss or Durham Book, written about A. D. 900,† and now preserved in the British Museum, London, Cotton MSS. Nero, D. IV. fol. 100.

Mk. iv. 3—8.

3. heono eode ðe sawende l sedere to sawenne 4. and miððs geseuw,
3. Ecce exiit seminans ad seminandum. 4. et dum seminat,

oðer l sū feoll ymb ða stret, and cwomon flegendo and fretton l eton ðæt
aliud cecidit circa viā, et venerunt volucres et comederunt illud.

5 sum ec feoll of stæner, ðer ne hæfde eorðu michel l menig; and hræðe
5. aliud vero cecidit super petrosa, ubi non habuit terram multam; et statim

upp iornende wæs l arisæn wæs f̄ ðon niefde heanisse eorðes: 6. and ða
exortum est, quoniam non habebat altitudinem terræ: 6. et quando

arisen l ða upp eode wæs sunna; gedrugade l f̄bernde; f̄ ðon niefde
exortus est sol, exæstuavit, eo quod non haberet

wyrt-ruma, gedrugade. 7. and sum feoll in ðornum, and astigon l upp eodun ðornas,
radicem, exaruit. 7. et aliud cecidit in spinis, et ascenderunt spinæ,

* Mr. Cardale has well remarked:—"*Pure Anglo-Saxon* and *Dano-Saxon* were the two great dialects of the language. The pure A.-S. was used, as Hickes observes, in the southern and western parts of England; and the Dano-Saxon, in the north of England and south of Scotland. It is entirely a gratuitous supposition, to imagine that either of these dialects commenced at a much later period than the other. Each was probably as old as the time of Egbert.... The Saxons were predominant in the southern and western parts, and the Angles in the northern. As these nations were distinct in their original seats on the continent, so they arrived at different times, and brought with them different dialects. This variety of speech continued till the Norman conquest, and even afterwards.... These two great dialects of the A.-S. continued substantially distinct, as long as the language itself was in use .... that the Dano-Saxon, in short, never superseded the A.-S.... They were not consecutive, but contemporary."—*Notes prefixed to Mr. Cardale's elegant edition of Boethius.*

Another gentleman, to whom A.-S. literature is also much indebted, thus states his opinion: "Saxon MSS. ought to be locally classed, before any attempt be made at chronological arrangement; nor will this appear strange when we consider, that in early times the several divisions of the kingdom were, comparatively speaking, almost like foreign countries to each other; that in some parts the Saxon must have continued uninfluenced by foreign idioms much longer than in others; that the various provincial dialects must have been much more strongly marked than they are at present, and that they were all equally employed in literary composition."—*Mr. Thorpe's Preface to Cædmon*, pp. xii. xiii.

Mr. Thorpe mentions Mr. Joseph Stephenson, of the British Museum, as the gentleman from whom we may hope for a local classification of our Saxon MSS. Perhaps it would be difficult to find a gentleman more competent for so arduous a work, if we form a judgment of Mr. Stephenson's qualifications only from the valuable matter collected from old MSS. and judiciously inserted by him in the first two parts of Boucher's English Glossary of Archaic and Provincial Words, 4to. 1832-1833.

† This is one of the finest specimens of Saxon writing. The Vulgate Latin text of the Four Gospels was written by Eadfrid Bishop of Lindisfarne, about A. D. 680; the interlinear Anglo-Saxon gloss was added by Aldred, probably about 900. For a full account of this MS. see Mareschalli Observationes in Versionem Anglo-Saxonicam, Dordrechti, 4to. 1665, p. 492: Wanley's Catalogue, p. 252: Henshall's Etymological Organic Reasoner, p. 54: Ingram's Inaugural Lecture on Saxon Literature, p. 43: and Baber's Historical account of the Saxon and English Versions of the Scriptures, before the opening of the fifteenth century, prefixed to his edition of Wiclif's Gospels, 4to. 1810, p. lix. For facsimiles of the beautiful writing in this splendid Durham Book, see Astle's Origin and Progress of Writing, 4to, 1803, p. 96; and my Elements of Anglo-Saxon Grammar, 8vo. 1823, p. 18.

and under dulfon þæt, and wæstm ne salde. 8. and oðer feoll on eorðu
et suffocaverunt illud, et fructum non dedit. 8. et aliud cecidit in terram

godũ, and salde wæstm stigende, and wæxende, and to brohte enne ł an
bonam, et dabat fructum ascendentem, et crescentem, et adferebat unum

ðrittig and un sexdig, and an hundrað.
triginta et unum sexagenta, et unum centum.*

12. The parable of the Sower, from the Rushworth Gloss, which is an Anglo-Saxon gloss or version of the 10th century, written at Harewood or Harwood [æt Harawuda], over St. Jerome's Latin of the Four Gospels. The Latin text is about the age of the Latin of the Durham Book, as it was written towards the close of the 7th century. MS. Bibl. Bodl. D. 24. No. 3946, now (1835) D. 2. 19. Auct.†

MK. IV. 3—8.

3. Geherðe; heonu eode ðe sedere ł sawend to sawend. 4. and miððy giseow,
3. Audite; ecce exiit seminans ad seminandũ. 4. et dum seminat,

oðer ł sum gifeol ymb ða strete, and comun flegende, and fretan ł etan ðæt.
aliud decidit circa viam, et venerunt volucres, et comederunt illud.

5. oðer ł sum soðlice gifeol ofer stænere, ðer ne hæfde eorðo, and hræðe
5. aliud vero cecidit super petrosa, ubi non habuit terram, et statim

up iornende wæs, forðon ne hæfde heonisse eorðo. 6. and ða
exortum est, quoniam non habebat altitudinẽ terræ. 6. et quando

aras ł uparnende wæs sunne, and drygde ƥbernde; and for þon ne hæfde
exortus est sol, exæstuavit; et ex eo quod non haberet

wyrtruma, adrugade. 7. and oðer gifeol in þornas, and astigun ł upeadun ðornas
radicem, exaruit. 7. Et aliud cecidit in spinas, et ascenderunt spinae

and under dulfun ðæt, and wæstem ne salde. 8. and oðro gifeol on eorðo
et suffocaverunt illud, et fructum non dedit. 8. et aliud cecidit in terram

gode; and salde wæstem stigende, and wexende, and tobrohte an ł enne
bonã; et dabat fructum ascendentem, et crescentem, et adferebat unum

ðritig, and an sextig and an hundreð.
XXX., et unum LX. et unum C.‡

13. An extract from the Saxon Chronicle of the year 1135, will show how much the language was then corrupted in its idiom, inflections, and orthography.

AN. MCXXXV. On þis gere for se king Henri ofer sæ æt te Lammasse. and þæt oðer dei. þa he lai an slep in scip. þa þestrede þe dæi ouer all landes. and uuard þe sunne swilc als it uuare þre-niht-ald mone. an sterres abuten him at middæi. Wurðen men swiðe ofwundred and ofdred. and sæden þæt micel þing sculde cumme her efter. swa

* For the accurate collation of this extract with the MS. we are indebted to the polite attention of Sir Henry Ellis, of the British Museum.

† For a further account of this MS. see Mareschalli Observ. in Versionem A.-S. p. 492: Wanley's Catalogue, p. 81, 82: Henshall's Etym. Organic Reasoner, p. 63, 64: Astle's Origin and Progress of Writing, p. 99: Baber's Pref. to Wiclif's Test. p. lx.

‡ The transcript of this extract was obligingly compared with the MS. by a well-known Saxon scholar, Dr. Ingram, President of Trinity College, Oxford, and editor of the Saxon Chronicle, with an English translation, notes, &c. see note to § 9, No. 9.

dide. for þæt ilc gær warð þe king ded. þæt oðer dæi efter s. Andreas massedæi. on Normandi. Þa wes tre sona þas landes. for æuric man sone ræuede oðer þe mihte. Þa namen his sune and his frend and brohten his lic to Engle-land. and bebiriend in Reding. God man he wes. and micel æie wes of him. Durste nan man misdon wið oðer on his time. Pais he makede men and dær. Wua sua bare his byrðen gold and silure. durste nan man sei to him naht bute god.—*Ingram's Saxon Chronicle*, p. 364.

LITERAL ENGLISH.

An. 1135. In this year went the king Henry over sea at the Lammas; and the next day, as he lay asleep on ship, darkened the day over all lands, and was the sun so as it were a three-night-old moon, and the stars about him at mid-day. Men were very much astonished and terrified, and said that a great event should come hereafter. So it did; for that same year was the king dead, the next day after St. Andrew's mass-day, in Normandy. Then was tribulation soon in the land; for every man that might, soon robbed another. Then his sons and his friends took his body, and brought it to England, and buried it at Reading. A good man he was; and there was great dread of him. No man durst do wrong with another in his time. Peace he made for man and beast. Whoso bare his burthen of gold and silver, durst no man say ought to him but good.

14. The Grave, a fragment. It is found in the margin of Semi-Saxon Homilies in the Bodleian Library,* and is supposed by Wanley to be written about the year 1150.

SEMI-SAXON.	LITERAL ENGLISH.
Ðe wes bold gebyld	For thee was a house built
er þu iboren were;	Ere thou wert born;
ðe wes molde imynt	For thee was a mould appointed
er ðu of moder come;	Ere thou of mother camest;
ac hit nes no idiht,	But it is not prepared,
ne þeo deopnes imeten;	Nor the deepness meted;
nes gyt iloced,	Nor is yet seen,
hu long hit þe were:	How long for thee it were:
Nu me þe bringæð	Now I bring thee
þer ðu beon scealt,	Where thou shalt be,
nu me sceal þe meten,	Now I shall thee measure,
and ða mold seoððа, &c.	And then earth afterwards.

15. The Ormulum is a metrical paraphrase of the Gospels and Acts, in lines of fifteen syllables, written in Semi-Saxon by an ecclesiastic named Orm, probably in the north of England, about the year 1180.† The author gives the following reason for the name of the work:

This book is named Ormulum, for that Orm made it.
Ðiff boc iff nemmnedd Orrmulum, forrþi þæt Orrm itt wrohhte.—*Preface.*

Mr. Thorpe observes, that the author seems to have been a critic in his mother-tongue; and from his idea of doubling the consonant after a short

* Bibl. Bodl. Codex NE. F. 4. 12, Wanley, p. 15.—Mr. Conybeare's *Illustrations of A.-S. Poetry*, p. 270, for the first printed text with a verbal Latin and English translation. Mr. Thorpe's *Analecta*, p. 142, for an improved text.

† Wanley's *Catalogue*, p. 59—63: Conybeare's *Illustrations of A.-S. Poetry*, Introd. p. lxvii: Turner's *Hist. of Eng. Middle Ages*, b. ix. 1, vol. v. p. 435, 436: Mr. Thorpe's *Analecta*, Pref. p. ix: Baber's *Wiclif*, Pref. p. lxiv.

owel, as in German, we are enabled to form some tolerably accurate otions as to the pronunciation of our forefathers. Thus he writes *min* and *in* with a single *n* only, and *lif* with a single *f*, because the *i* is long, as *mine, wine,* and *life.* On the other hand, wherever the consonant is oubled, the vowel preceding is short and sharp, as *winn*, pronounced *win*, ot *wine*. Orm's dialect merits, if any, to be called Dano-Saxon: his ame also betrays a Scandinavian descent.*

Uppo þe þridde dagg bilammp, swa summ þe Goddspell kiþeþþ,
þatt i þe land off Galile waff an bridale garrkedd;
And itt waff garrkedd inn an tun þatt waff Cana gehatenn,
and Cristeff moderr Marge waff att tatt bridaless sæte.
And Crist wass clepedd till þatt hus wiþþ hise lerninng cnihhtess.
And teggre win waff drunnkenn swa þætt tær nass þa na mare.

Wanley, p. 62.†

VERBAL ENGLISH.

Upon the third day (it) happened, as some of the Gospels say,
that in the land of Galilee was a bridal prepared;
And it was prepared in a town that was Cana called,
and Christ's mother, Mary, was at that bridal's seat.
And Christ was invited to that house with his disciples.
And their wine was drunk, so that there was not then any more.

16. Robert of Gloucester‡ was a monk belonging to the abbey at loucester, who wrote a history of England in rhyming verse about .D. 1280. He declares that he saw the eclipse which happened in 1264, the day of the battle at Evesham, and thus describes it:

As in þe Norþ West a derk weder þer aros,
Sodeinliche suart inou, þat mani man agros,
And ouer caste it þoȝte al þut lond, þat me miȝte vnneðe ise,
Grisloker weder þan it was ne miȝte an erþe be.
An vewe dropes of reine þer velle grete inou.
Þis tokninge vel in þis lond, þo me þis men slou
Wor þretti mile þanne. þis isei Roberd,
þat verst þis boc made, and was wel sore aferd.

17. John de Wiclif was born about 1324, at Wiclif, a village on the anks of the river Tees, near Richmond, Yorkshire. He translated the ible and Testament, and even the Apocryphal books, from Latin into nglish, in the year 1380. Though Wiclif's writing may be called Old nglish, yet a specimen from the parable of the Sower is given that it ay be compared with the preceding translations.

* Analecta, Pref. p. ix.

† Bodleian Library, Cod. Junii, i. p. 330.

‡ Turner's *Hist. of Eng. Middle Ages*, b. viii. 1, vol. v. p. 217; ix. 2, vol. v. p. 442.—arton's *Hist. of Eng. Poetry*, 8vo. 1824, vol. i. p. 52.

Mk. iv. 3—8.

Here ye, lo a man sowinge goith out to sowe, and the while he sowith sum seed fel aboute the weye, and briddis of hevene camen and eeten it. other felde doun on stony places where it hadde not myche erthe, and anoon it sprong up; for it hadde not depnesse of erthe, and whanne the sunne roos up it welewide for hete, and it driede up, for it hadde no roote. And other fel doun into thornes: and thornes sprungen up and strangliden it, and it gaf not fruyt: And othere felde doun into good lond: and it gaf fruyt spryngyng up and wexinge, and oon broughte thritty fold, and oon sixty fold, and oon an hundrid fold.

18. Semi-Saxon, in the dialect of Kent, written in A.D. 1340.

Nou ich wille þet ye ywyte hou hit iſ ywent
Þet þiſ bociſ ywrite mid engliſſ of Kent.
Þiſ boc iſ ymad uor lewede men |
Vor uader | and uor moder | and uor oþer ken |
Ham uor to berȝe uram alle manyere zen |
Þet ine hare inwytte ne bleue no uoul wen.
Huo aſe god iſ hiſ name yzed |
Þet þiſ boc made God him yeue þet bread |
Of angleſ of heuene and þerto his red |
And onderuonge hiſ zaule huanne þet he iſ dyad.
Amen.

Ymende. Þet þiſ boc iſ uolueld ine þe eue of þe holy apoſtleſ Symon an Judaſ | of ane broþer of þe choyſtre of ſaynt Austin of Canterberi | Ine þe yeare of oure lhordes beringe. 1340.—*Arundel MSS. No.* 57, *British Museum.**

19. It is evident, from the preceding extracts, that the pure West-Saxon did not ever prevail over the whole of England, and that in process of time the language approached more or less to the present English, according to its relative position to the West-Saxons. In early times there was, clearly, considerable dialectic variety in the writings of men residing in different provinces. This will be evident by comparing the short specimens from the Northumbrian and Rushworth glosses,† and the extract from the Saxon Chronicle,‡ with the quotation from Marshall's Anglo-Saxon Gospels,|| and other works in pure Anglo-Saxon. The difference observable in the language of the most cultivated classes would be still more marked and apparent in the mass of population, or the less educated community. These, from their agricultural pursuits, had little communication with the inhabitants of other provinces; and having few opportunities and little inducement to leave their own neighbourhood, they intermarried among each other, and, from their limited acquaintance and circumscribed views, they would naturally be much attached to their old manners, customs, and language. The same cause operating from age to age would keep united the greater part of the population, or the

* Mr. Thorpe's *Pref. to Cædmon*, p. xii.

† § 11 and 12. ‡ § 13. || § 9.

amilies of the middle stations of life, it may, therefore, be well expected that uch of the peculiarity of dialect prevalent in Anglo-Saxon times, is preerved even to the present day in the provincial dialects of the same districts. n these local dialects, then, remnants of the Anglo-Saxon tongue may be ound in its least altered, most uncorrupt, and therefore its purest state. Iaving a strong and expressive language of their own, they had little esire and few opportunities to adopt foreign idioms or pronunciation, nd thus to corrupt the purity of their ancient language. Our present olished phrase and fashionable pronunciation are often new, and, as eviating from primitive usage, faulty and corrupt. We are, therefore, uch indebted to those zealous and patriotic individuals who have referred s to the archaisms of our nervous language, by publishing provincial lossaries, and giving specimens of their dialects.*

20. So much has been advanced with the view of showing, that what is enerally termed "vulgar language," deserves some notice, and claims ur respect from its direct descent from our high-spirited Anglo-Saxon ncestors, and from its power of expression. It is not asserted that any rovincial dialect has issued in a full and uncontaminated stream from the ure Anglo-Saxon fountain; but in every province some streamlets flow own from the fountain-head, retaining their original purity and flavour, hough not now relished perhaps by fastidious palates. None can boast hat they retain the language of their early forefathers unimpaired, but all nay prove that they possess strong traces of it.†

* The following is a list of the principal provincial Glossaries:—1. A Collection of English Words not generally used, &c. by John Ray, F.R.S. 3rd edit. 8vo. *London*, 1737, pp. 150, rice about 4*s*.—2. An Exmoor Scolding, and also an Exmoor Courtship, with a Glossary, 7th dit. 8vo. *Exon*. 1771, pp. 60, price 9*d*.—3. The Lancashire Dialect, with a Glossary, Poems, &c. by Tim Bobbin, Esq. (Mr. John Collier, Schoolmaster at Milnrow, near Rochdale,) 2mo. *Manchester*, 1775; *London*, 1818, pp. 212, price 3*s*.—4. A Provincial Glossary, with Collection of Local Proverbs, &c. by Francis Grose, Esq. F.A.S. 2nd edit. 12mo. *London*, 790, price 5*s*.—5. Anecdotes of the English Language, chiefly regarding the Local Dialect of ondon and its environs, which have not corrupted the language of their ancestors, *London*, 803, 8vo. 2nd edit. 1814.—6. An Etymological Dictionary of the Scottish Language, &c. by ohn Jamieson, D.D. F.R.S.E. &c. 2 vols. 4to. 1808, *Edinburgh*; 2 vols. 4to. Supplement, 1825. —7. A List of ancient Words at present used in the mountainous Districts of the West Riding f Yorkshire, by Robert Willan, M.D. F.R.S. and S.A. 1811; Archæologia, vol. xvii. 1814, p. 29.—8. An Attempt at a Glossary of some Words used in Cheshire, by Roger Wilbraham, Esq. F.R.S. and S.A. 1817; Archæologia, vol. xix. 2nd edit. *Rod, London*, 12mo. 1826, price 5*s*. p. 117; The Hallamshire Glossary, by the Rev. Joseph Hunter.—9. Suffolk Words and Phrases, by Edward Moor, F.R.S. F.A.S. &c. 12mo. *Woodbridge*, 1823.—10. Horæ Momenta Cravenæ, or, the Craven Dialect: to which is annexed a copious Glossary by a native of Craven, 12mo. *London*, 1824, pp. 125, price 4*s*. *This is a very valuable little book, the work of scholar.*—11. A Glossary of North Country Words in use, by John Trotter Brockett, F.S.A. ondon and Newcastle, 8vo. *Newcastle-upon-Tyne*, 1825, pp. 243, price 10*s*. 6*d*.—12. Obserations on some of the Dialects in the West of England, particularly Somersetshire, with Glossary of Words now in use there, and poems and other pieces exemplifying the Dialect, y James Jennings, Honorary Secretary of the Metropolitan Literary Institution, London, 2mo. *London*, 1825, pp. 191, price 7*s*.—13. The Vocabulary of East-Anglia; an attempt to ecord the vulgar tongue of the twin-sister counties, Norfolk and Suffolk, as it existed in the ast twenty years of the 18th century, and still exists; with proofs of its antiquity from etymoogy and authority, by the late Rev. Robert Forby, Rector of Fincham, Norfolk, 2 vols. 12mo. *London*, 1830, price 1*l*. 1*s*.—14. A Glossary of Archaic and Provincial Words, by the late Rev. Jonathan Boucher, F.S.A. Vicar of Epsom, edited jointly by the Rev. Joseph Hunter, F.S.A. and Joseph Stevenson, Esq. part I. 1832, part II. 1833, 4to.

† Forby's *East-Anglia*, vol. i. p. 18.

21. A few specimens of provincial dialects are given, beginning with extracts from Mr. Jennings's neat and valuable little work, being the present dialect of that part where the West-Saxon or pure Anglo-Saxon was once spoken, and then proceeding to East-Anglia, and terminating with the broad dialect of Craven in Yorkshire. In attempting to give the exact pronunciation of each district, some words are so disguised as, at the first view, to be scarcely recognised, and occasionally two or more words are pronounced, and therefore written, as one word. This is an ambiguity which could not be entirely avoided; but an ample compensation is made for it by giving the words, as far as possible, in the pronunciation of the several provincial districts.

22. *Dialects of the West of England, particularly Somersetshire.*

The following are some of the peculiarities observable in the West of England.

The people of Somersetshire, east of the river Parret, make the third person singular of the indicative mood, present tense, to end in *th* or *eth;* thus for he loves, he reads, they uniformly say, *he lov'th, he read'th.* They use *Ise* for I, *er* for he, and *her* for she.—They sound â as *a* in *father;* and *e* as the French *e*, or as the English *a* in *cane, fane,* &c.—*Th* is sounded as *d:* for thread they say *dread* or *dird;* for through *dro,* thrash *drash:* *s* as *z, Zummerzet* for Somerset, &c.—They invert the order of some consonants: for thrush, brush, rush, they say *dirsh, birsh, hirsh;* for clasp, hasp, asp, they use *claps, haps, aps.*—They annex *y* to the infinitive mood, and some other parts of many of the common verbs, *I can't sewy, he can't reapy, to sewy, to nursy:* they also prefix letters; for lost, gone, bought, they say *alost, agone, abought.* —They often make dissyllables of monosyllables: for air, both, fair, fire, sure, &c. they say, *ayer, booäth, fayer, shower,* &c.—*I be, thou beest* or *bist, thee beest, we be, they* or *thâ be,* are commonly heard; but rarely or never *he be,* but *he is.*—*War* is always used for was and were; as *I war, thee* or *thou wart, he war, we war, they* or *thâ war.*—We often hear *we'm, you'm, they'm,* for we are, you are, they are.—They use *thic* for that; as *thic house, thic man,* for that house, that man.—The diphthong *oi* is often pronounced *wi:* for spoil, boil, point, soil, we have *spwile, bwile, pwint, swile,* &c.—In and, *d* is often omitted, as *you an I.*—In the present participle and other words in ing, *g* is omitted; for loving, hearing, singing, lightning, they say *lovin, hearin* or *hirin, zingin, lightnin.*

As specimens of the Somerset dialect, a dedication in verse, and a short dialogue in prose, will be sufficient.

TO THA DWELLERS O' THE WEST.

Tha fruit o' longvul labour, years,
In theäze veo leaves at last appears.
Ta you, tha Dwellers o' tha West,
I'm pleas'd that thâ shood be addresst:
Vor thaw I now in Lunnun dwell,
I mine ye still—I love ye well;
An niver, niver sholl vorget
I vust drâw'd breath in Zummerzet;
Amangst ye liv'd, an left ye zorry,
As you'll knaw when you hire my storry.
Theäze little book than take o' me;
'Tis âll I hâ jist now ta gee.

FARMER BENNET AN JAN LIDE.

A Dialogue.

Farmer Bennet. Jan! why dwon't ye right my shoes?

Jan Lide. Bin, maester 'tis zaw cawld, I can't work wi' tha tacker at âll; I've)rawk it ten times I'm shower ta dâ—da vreaze za hord. Why, Hester hanged out ɪittle-smock ta drowy, an in dree minits a war a vraur as stiff as a pawker; an can't avoord ta keep a good vier—I wish I cood—I'd zoon right your shoes an thers too—I'd zoon yarn zum money, I warnt ye. Can't ye vine zum work vor ɜ, maester, theäze hord times—I'll do any theng ta sar a penny. I can drash— ɔan cleave brans—I can make spars—I can thatchy—I can shear ditch, an I can ɨpy too, bit da vreaze za hord. I can wimmy—I can messy or milky nif ther be ed o't. I ood'n mine dreavin plough or any theng.

Farmer Bennet. I've a got nothin vor ye ta do, Jan; bit Mister Boord banehond I jist now that thâ war gwain ta wimmy, an that thâ wanted zumbody ta help 'em.

Jan Lide. Aw, I'm glad o't. I'll hirn auver an zee where I can't help 'em; bit ıan't a bin athin tha drashel o' Maester Boord's door vor a longful time, bin I thawt ɪt missis did'n use Hester well; but I dwon't bear malice, an zaw I'll goo.

Farmer Bennet. What did Missis Boord zâ or do ta Hester, than?

Jan Lide. Why, Hester, a-mâ-be, war zummet ta blame too; vor she war one n, d'ye zee, that rawd Skimmerton—thic mâ-game that frunted zum o' tha gennel-wk. Thâ zed 'twar time to a done wi' jitch litter, or jitch stuff, or I dwon knaw ıat thâ call'd it; bit thâ war a frunted wi' Hester about it; an I zed nif thâ war a unted wi' Hester, thâ mid be a frunted wi' I. This zet missis's back up, an Hester n't a bin a choorin there zunz. Bit 'tis niver-the-near ta bear malice; and zaw I'll o auver an zee which wâ tha wine da blaw.

The Exmoor Dialect.

23. Exmoor is in the north of Somersetshire and Devonshire; it is so lled, being the forest or moor in which the river Exe rises.

AN EXMOOR COURTSHIP.

Andrew. Well, cozen Magery, cham glad you're come agen.

Margery. Wull ye eat a croust o' brid and chezee, cozen Andra?

Andrew. No, es thankee, cozen Magery; vor es eat a crub as es come along; zides es went to dinner jest avore.—Well, bet, cozen Magery, whot onser dest ' ma to tha quesson es put vore now-reert.

Margery. What quesson was et?

Andrew. Why, zure, ya bant zo vorgetvul. Why, tha quesson es put a little ther.

Margery. Es dont know what quesson ye meean; es begit whot quesson twos.

Andrew. Why, to tell tha vlat and plane agen, twos thes: Wut ha' ma, ay or no?

Margery. Whot! marry to Earteen?—Es gee tha zame onser es geed avore, es udent marry the best man in oll Ingland. Es cud amorst zwear chud ne'er marry at ɪ. And more and zo, cozen Andra, cham a told ya keep company wey Tamzen osegood. And nif ya keep hare company, es'll ha no more to zey to tha.

Andrew. Ay, thes es Jo Hosegood's flim-flam.—Oh! tha very vengance out o'en.

Margery. No, no; tes none of Jo Hosegood's flim-flam.

Andrew. Well, well, cozen Magery, be't how twull, whot caree I?—And zo, od-buy, good-buy t' e, cozen Magery.—Nif voaken be jealous avore they be arried, zo they mey arter. Zo good-buy, cozen Magery. Chell net trouble ye en vor wone while, chell warndy.

Margery. [*Calling after him.*] Bet hearky, hearky a bit, cozen Andra! Es wudent ha ye go away angry nether zure; and zure you wont deny to see me drenk? Why ya hant a tasted our cyder yet. [*Andrew returns.*] Come, cozen Andra, here's t'ye.

Andrew. Na, vor that matter, es owe no ill-will to enny kesson, net I.—Bet es wont drenk, nether, except ya vurst kiss and vriends.

The Dialect of East-Anglia, or Norfolk and Suffolk.

24. "The most general and pervading characteristic of East-Anglian pronunciation," says Mr. Forby, "is a narrowness and tenuity, precisely the reverse of the round, sonorous, 'mouth-filling' tones of the north of England. The broad and open sounds of vowels, the rich and full tones of diphthongs, are generally thus reduced. Generally—not universally. Some few words become broader, but they become also harsher and coarser. This narrowness of utterance is, in some parts, rendered still more offensive by being delivered in a sort of shrill whining recitative. This prevails chiefly in Suffolk, so as to be called in Norfolk the 'Suffolk whine.' The voice of the speaker (or singer) is perpetually running up and down through half or a whole octave of sharp notes, with now and then a most querulous cadence.*

The following are a few of the common contractions and changes: *Duffus* for dove or pigeon-house; *wuddus* wood-house; *shant* shall not; *cant* cannot; *ont, wont* will not; *dint* did not; *shunt* should not; *wunt* would not; *mant* may not; *warnt* were not; *eent* is not; *aint* is not; *heent* has not; *hănt* had not.—*Tut* is used for to it; *dut* do it; *wut* with it; *het* have it; *tebbin* it has been.—We hear *cup* for come up; *gup* go up; *gout* go out; *gin* go in; *giz* give us.—The following are very peculiar: *k'ye here*, or *k'ere; k'ye there; k'ye hinder*, or *k'inder; k'ye thinder*, for look ye here, there, and yonder.—Words are often jumbled together, as in this sentence. *M'aunt bod me g'into th'archard, and call m'uncle into house.*

Derbyshire Dialect.

25. This dialect is remarkable for its broad pronunciation. In *me* the *e* is pronounced long and broad, as *mee.* The *l* is often omitted after *a* or *o*, as *aw* for all, *caw* call, *bowd* bold, *coud* cold.—Words in *ing* generally omit the *g*, but sometimes it is changed into *k*; as *think* for thing, *lovin* for loving. They use *con* for can; *conner* for cannot; *shanner* for shall not; *wool, wooner* for will, and will not; *yo* for you, &c.

A Dialogue between Farmer Bennet and Tummus Lide.

Farmer Bennet. Tummus, why dunner yo mend meh shoon?

Tummus Lide. Becoz, mester 'tis zo cood, I conner work wee the tachin at aw; I've brockn it ten times I'm shur to de—it freezes zo hard. Why, Hester hung out a smock-frock to dry, an in three minits it wor frozzen as stiff as a proker, an I conner afford to keep a good fire—I wish I cud—I'd soon mend yore shoon, an uthers tow.—I'd soon yarn sum munney, I warrant ye. Conner yo find sum work for m', mester, these hard times?—I'll doo onny think to addle a penny. I con thresh

* Vocabulary of East-Anglia, Introduction, p. 82.

—I con split wood—I con mak spars—I con thack. I con skower a dike, an I con trench tow, bur it freezes zo hard. I con winner—I con fother, or milk, if there be need on't. I woodner mind drivin plow, or onny think.

Farm. B. I hanner got nothin for ye to doo, Tummus; bur Mester Boord towd me jist now that they wor gooin to winner, an that they shud want sumbody to help 'em.

Tummus L. O, I'm glad on't. I'll run oor an zee whether I con help 'em; bur I hanner bin weein the threshold ov Mester Boord's doer for a nation time, becoz I thoot misses didner use Hester well, bur I dunner bear malice, an zo I'll goo.

Farm. B. What did Misses Boord za or doo to Hester then?

Tummus L. Why, Hester may-be wor summet to blame too; for her wor one on 'em, de ye zee, that jawd Skimmerton,—the mak-gam that frunted zum o' the gente-fook. They said 'twor time to dun wee sich litter, or sich stuff, or I dunner know what they cawd it; bur they wor frunted wee Hester bout it; an I said, If they wor frunted wee Hester, they mid bee frunted wee mee. This set misses's back up, an Hester hanner bin a charrin there sin. But 'tis no use to bear malice; an zo I'll goo oor, and zee which we the winde blows.

Cheshire Dialect.

26. One peculiarity in the province is to change, or soften, the pronunciation of many words in the middle of which the letter *l* is preceded by *a* or *o*.

Thus in common discourse we pronounce *bawk* for balk, *cauf* for calf, *hauf* for half, *wawk* for walk, *foke* for folk, and *St. Awbuns* for St. Albans; but in the Cheshire dialect, as in all the north, the custom of substituting the *o* for the *a*, and the double *ee* for the *igh*, prevails in a still greater degree: thus we call all *aw;* always *awways;* bold *bowd;* calf *cauf;* call *caw;* can *con;* cold *cowd;* colt *cowt;* fold *fowd;* gold *gowd;* false *fause;* foul *fow;* fool *foo;* full *foo;* fine *foin;* hold *howd;* holt *howt;* half *hauf;* halfpenny *hawpenny;* hall *haw;* long *lung;* man *mon;* many *mony;* manner *monner;* might *meet;* mold *mowd;* pull *poo;* soft *saft;* bright *breet;* scald *scawd;* stool *stoo;* right *reet;* twine *twoin;* flight *fleet;* lane *loan* or *lone;* mol *mal;* sight *see;* sit *seet;* such *sich.*

The Lancashire Dialect.

27. Observations on the Lancashire dialect. All and al are generally sounded broad, as *aw* or *o:* thus, awl *haw* or *ho*, *awlus* for all, hall, always. —In words ending in *ing*, *k* is used for *g*, as *think, wooink,* for thing, wooing, &c.—At the end of words *d* and *ed* are often changed into *t;* thus *behint, wynt, awtert,* for behind, wind, awkward.—The *d* is sometimes omitted in and, for which they say *an.*—It is common, in some places, to sound *ou* and *ow* as *a*; thus *tha, ka* or *ca,* for thou, cow. In other places, *ou* and *ow* have the sound *eaw;* thus, for thou, cow, house, mouse, they say *theaw, keaw, heawse, meawse.*—In some parts *o* is used for *a*, and *a* for *o*; thus, for part, hand, they say *port, hont;* and instead of for, short, they say *far, shart.*—The syllable *en* or *'n* is generally used in the plural of verbs, &c. as *hat'n, lov'n, think'n.*—In Lancashire they generally speak quick and short, and omit many letters, and often pronounce two or three words together; as, *I'll got'* or *I'll gut'* for I'll go to; *runt'* for run

to; *hoost* for she shall; *intle* or *int'll* for if thou will; *I wou'didd'n* for I wish you would.

Tummus and Meary.

Tummus. Odds me! Meary, whooa the dickons wou'd o thowt o' leeting o thee here so soyne this morning? Where has to bin? Theaw'rt aw on a swat, I think; for theaw looks primely.

Meary. Beleemy, Tummus, I welly lost my wynt; for I've had sitch o'traunce this morning as eh neer had e' meh live: for I went to Jone's o'Harry's o'lung Jone's, for't borrow their thible, to stur th' furmetry weh, an his wife had lent it to Bet o' my gronny's; so I skeawrt eend-wey, an' when eh coom there, hoo'd lent it Kester o' Dick's, an the dule steawnd 'im for a brindl't cur, he'd mede it int' shoon pegs! Neaw wou'd naw sitch o moon-shine traunce potter any body's plucks?

Tummus. Mark whot e tell the, Meary; for I think lunger ot fok liv'n an' th' moor mischoances they han.

Meary. Not awlus.—But whot meys o't' sowgh, on seem so dane-kest? For I con tell o' I'd fene see o' whick an hearty.

Tummus. Whick an hearty too! oddzo, but I con tell the whot, its moor in bargin ot I'm oather whick or hearty, for 'twur seign peawnd t'a tuppunny jannock, I'd bin os deeod os o dur nele be this awer; for th' last oandurth boh one me measter had lik't o killt meh: on just neaw, os shure os thee and me ar stonning here, I'm actilly running meh country.

The Dialect of Craven.

28. The Deanery of Craven is in the West Riding of Yorkshire. A short specimen will be sufficient.

Dialogue between Farmer Giles and his neighbour Bridget.

Giles. Good mornin to the, Bridget, how isto?

Bridget. Deftly as out, and as cobby as a lop, thanksto.

Giles. Wha, marry, thou looks i gay good fettle.

Bridget. What thinksto o't' weather? Awr house is vara unrid and grimy, t'chimla smudges an reeks seea, an mackst' reckon, at used to shimmer and glissen, nowght bud soote an muck.

Giles. It's now a vara lithe day, bud there war a girt roak, an a rag o't' fells at delleet, an it looked feaful heavisome.

Bridget. I oft think a donky, mislin, deggy mornin is a sign o't' pride o't' weather, for it oft worsels up, an is maar to be liked ner t' element full o' thunner packs er a breet, scaumy sky.

Giles. Wha, when't bent's snod, hask, cranchin an slaap, it's a strang sign of a pash.

Bridget. I've oft obsarved there hes been a downfaw soon efter; bud for sure, I cannot gaum mich be ouer chimla at prisent, it's seea smoored up wi mull an brash. Yusterday about noon, t' summer-goose flackered at naya lile rate, an t' element, at edge o' dark, wor feaful full of filly tails an hen scrattins.—Thou knaws that's a sartain sign ov a change, sometimes I've knaan it sile and teem efter.

An Alphabetical Glossary of most of the peculiar Words used in the preceding specimens of Provincial Dialects.

29. A-mâ-be *as may be, perhaps: s.* Arter *after: e.* Auver *over: s.* Aw *all: d.* Awlus *always: l.*—Banehond *to intimate: s.* Becoz

ecause: d. Begit *to forget*: e. Brans *brands, fire-wood*: s. Brash ash, *impetuous*: c. Bur *but*: d.—Cawd *called*: d. Cham *I am*: e. Charrin *jobbing*: d. Chel *I shall*; e. Chorrin *jobbing*: s. Cobby ively: c. Conner *can not*: d. Cood *cold*: d. Cranchin *scranching*, rinding, *crackling*: c. Crub *a crumb*: e.—Deggy *foggy*: c. De ay: d. Deftly *decently, well*: c. Dickons, Deuce *the devil*: d. Donky *wet, dark, gloomy*: c. Drash *to thrash*: s. Dunner *do not*: d. Dwon't *don't, do not*: s.—Es, ise *I, is*: e.—Fettle *condition*: c. Fok olk: l. Fother *to fodder*: d.—Gaum *to know, distinguish*: c. Gee o *give*: e. Girt *great, friendly*: c. Gripy *to cut in gripes, to cut* trench: s.—Hâ *have*: s. Han *have*: l. Hanner *has* or *have not*: d. Hask *dry, parched*: c. Hirn *to run*: s. Hoo'd *her had, she had*: l.— annock *oat cake, bread made of oatmeal*: l. Jawd *scolded*: d. Jitch uch: s.—Kesson *Christian*: e. Kittle-smock *a smock-frock*: s.—Lile ittle: c. Lithe *blithe, mild*: c. Lop *a flea*: c.—Marry *truly*: c. Mess, messy *to serve cattle*: s. Mine *to mind, regard*: s. Mislin *misty*, mall *rain*: c. Mul *dust or refuse of turf or peat*: c.—Nation *great*, ery: d. Never-the-near *useless*: s. Now-reert *now right, just now*: e. —o' *of*: s. Oandurth *afternoon*: l. Odds me *bless me*: l. Ood'n *would* ot: s.—Pash *a fall of rain*: c. Pride *fineness*: c. Proker *a poker*: d. —Rag *mist*: c. Rather *soon, early*: e. Reckon, reek on *what is smoked* n, *an iron bar over the fire to support a boiling pot*: c. Reek *to* moke: c. Roak *a reek, smoke*: c.—Sar *to earn*: s. Seign *seven*: l. Shimmer *to shine*: c. Shoon *shoes*: d. Sile *to pour with rain*: c. Sin ince: d. Skeawr *to make haste*: l. Slaap *slippery*: c. Smoored mothered: c. Snod *smooth*: c. Sowgh *to sigh*: l. Spars *pointed* ticks, *doubled and twisted in the middle to fasten thatch upon a roof*: s. Summet *somewhat*: d.—Tacker: s. tachin: d. *a waxed thread*. Teem o *pour out*: c. Thâ *they*: s. Thack *to thatch*: d. Thaw *though*: s. Theaw *thou*: l. Theaze *these, this*: s. Thibble *a thin piece of wood* o *stir meat in a pot*: l. Think *thing*: d. Towd *told*: d. Traunce troublesome *journey*: l. 'Twar *it was*: s. Twull *as it will*: e.—Vine o *find*: s.—Warnt *to warrant, assure*: s. Whick *quick, alive*: l. Wimmy *to winnow*: s. Wine *wind*: s. Withers *others*: s. Wood-er *would not*: d. Worsel *to wrestle*: c. Wynt *wind*: l.—Ya *you*: e. Yarn *to earn*: s. Yo *you*: d. Yore *your*: d.—Zaw *so*: s. Zo *so*: d. Zunz *since*: s.

Contractions. c. *Craven*. d. *Derbyshire*. e. *Exmoor*. l. *Lancashire*. s. *Somerset*.

30. Many expressive Anglo-Saxon words, which are no longer in use among the refined, have been retained in the provincial dialects. These then ought not to be neglected. The facility and simplicity of combining several short indigenous words to express any complex idea, practised by the Anglo-Saxons and other Gothic nations, is now too seldom used. Instead of adopting technical terms from other languages, or forming

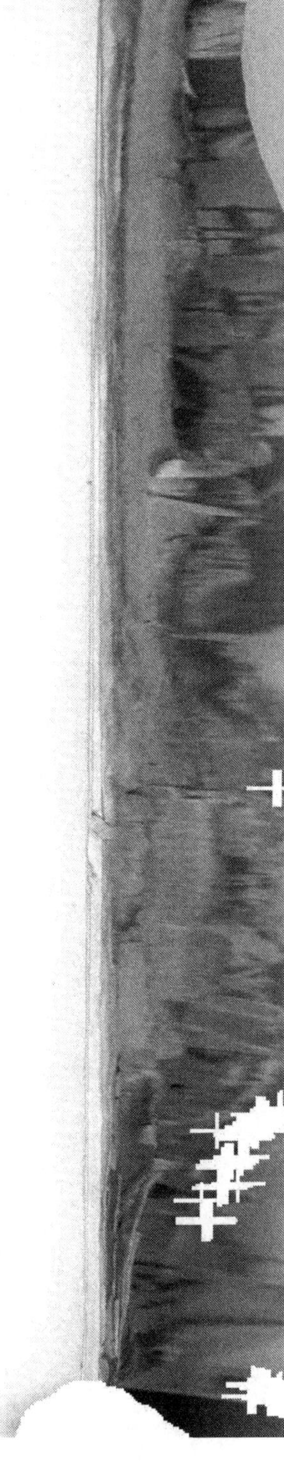

them from the Greek or Latin, as is the present English custom, our Anglo-Saxon forefathers formed words equally expressive by composing them from their own radical terms. For our *literature* they used boccræft *book-craft*, from boc *a book*, cræft *art, science;* for *arithmetic* rimcræft, from rim *a number*, cræft *art;* for *astronomy* tungelcræft, from tungel *a star*, &c. If, however, we have lost in simplicity, we have gained in copiousness and euphony. In collecting from other languages, the English have appropriated what was best adapted to their purpose, and thus greatly enriched their language. Like bees they have diligently gathered honey from every flower.* They have now a language which, for copiousness, power, and extensive use, can scarcely be surpassed. It is not only used in England, Scotland, and Ireland, but in the whole of North America and Australia: it prevails in the West Indies, and is more or less spoken in our vast possessions in the east. Indeed, wherever civilization, science, and literature prevail, there the English language is understood and spoken.

* Camden observes: "Whereas our tongue is mixed, it is no disgrace. The Italian is pleasant, but without sinewes, as a still fleeting water. The French delicate, but even nice as a woman, scarce daring to open her lippes, for fear of marring her countenance. The Spanish majesticall, but fulsome, running too much on the *o*, and terrible like the Divell in a play. The Dutch manlike, but withall very harsh, as one ready at every word to picke a quarrell. Now we, in borrowing from them, give the strength of consonants to the Italian; the full sound of words to the French; the variety of terminations to the Spanish; and the mollifying of more vowels to the Dutch; and so, like bees, we gather the honey of their good properties, and leave the dregs to themselves. And thus, when substantialnesse combineth with delightfulnesse, fullnesse with finenesse, seemlinesse with portlinesse, and currentnesse with staydnesse, how can the language which consisteth of all these, sound other than full of all sweetnesse?"—*Camden's Remains*, p. 38, *edit. of* 1623.

In the following comparison of the Anglo-Saxon with the ancient and modern Friesic, though there may be, in some minor points, a little diversity of opinion between the author and his friend the Rev. J. H. Halbertsma, yet it would be unjust to make alterations. Mr. Halbertsma has, therefore, been always permitted to speak for himself, and to give his reasons in his own way. Where opinions vary, the author has generally referred to both statements, leaving it to the reader to form his own conclusions from the evidence adduced. Considering this the most equitable mode of statement, he has adopted it, not only in regard to the valuable Essay of Mr. Halbertsma, but towards the works of those from whom he may differ far more widely. He is too conscious of his own liability to err, to be overconfident in his own views. He has given his reasons or authorities, and all that he can confidently assert is, that it has been his constant and earnest wish and endeavour to avoid the natural bias towards the idol self, or that of any party, and to discover and follow truth, whether it favour his own previous opinions, or those of others. Perhaps he may have failed even here. If he have, he will, as soon as it is pointed out, gladly make every acknowledgement and reparation in his power.

IV.—FRIESIC.*

Ancient and Modern Friesic† *compared with Anglo-Saxon.*

1. Anglo-Saxon being one of those languages called dead, no information about its pronunciation can be obtained from the people themselves. Of course, all knowledge in these matters depends upon the written letters, and upon determining the sound of those letters.

2. This, however, is a very difficult task. There is no connexion at all between visible marks and audible sounds: the letters serve more to indicate the genus, than the species of the sounds, and use alone can teach us the shades (*nuances*) of pronunciation.

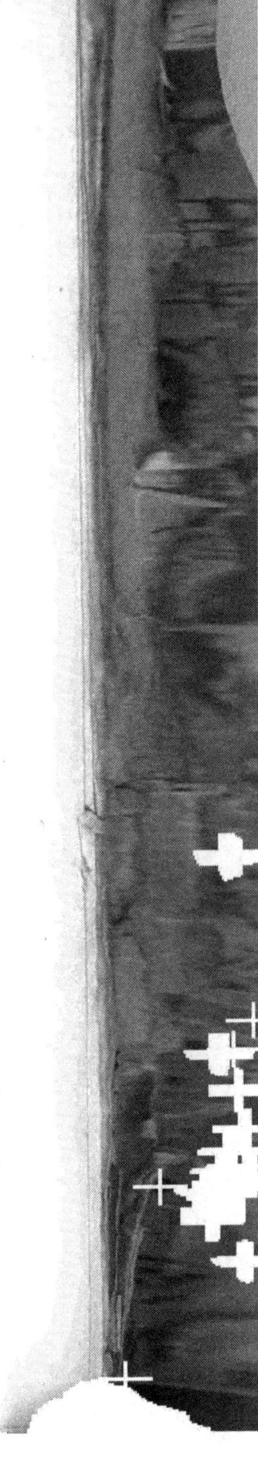

* "In comparing kindred languages with each other, the scholar will generally start from the point where he was born. Rask usually refers the A.-S. to the Scandinavian tongues, especially to the Icelandic. Germans have chiefly recourse to the Theotisc, and what is called by them Saxon. Others will bring it back to the dialects of their country; all with the same aim of elucidating the grammar, or discovering the sounds in A.-S. The reason of this is evidently the intimate acquaintance each of them has with the old and modern dialects of his own country, and most likely the scholar would compare the A.-S. with another class of dialects, if all the tongues of the Germanic branch were as thoroughly known to him as those of his native country. Being a native Friesian, and comparing the A.-S. chiefly with the Friesic, I could scarcely escape the suspicion of having yielded to the same influence as others, if I did not explain my reasons. This, I hope, will be a sufficient excuse for my entering into some details about the primitive relationship between the Anglo-Saxons and the Friesians.

"As every scholar has his own *point de vue* in matters of language, I beg leave to have mine. If my principles were unknown to my readers, my rules, depending on these principles, would, as void of foundation, be unintelligible. It is for this reason that I have here inserted some of my opinions about the pedigree and comparison of languages, appearing properly to belong more to general grammar than to my present subject.

"As history often fails in showing the full truth of my opinion about the relationship between the Angles and the Friesians, I had recourse to the languages. Hence a view of the remnants of the Friesic both dead and still flourishing is here presented, and compared with the English and A.-S. It pleases not the muse of history to speak but late, and then in a very confused manner. Yes, she often deceives, and before she is come to maturity, she seldom distinctly tells the truth. Language never deceives, but speaks more distinctly, though removed to a far higher antiquity.

"It is at the request of my dear friend Bosworth that I write in English, a language in which I have not been favoured with any instruction. I possess only some dim feeling of analogy between its manner of speaking and my native tongue. I, therefore, grant to my English readers the full freedom of smiling at my thousand and one Friesianisms, while I shall have reached my aim if I am only understood.

"J. H. HALBERTSMA."

DEVENTER, *August* 10*th*, 1834.

† Mr. Halbertsma, to promote Friesian literature, amongst other works, has published Hulde aan Gysbert Japiks, 2 vols. 8vo. Bolsward, 1824-1827.—De Lapekoer fen Gabe Scroar, 12mo. Dimter, 1834.—Friesche Spelling, 18mo. 1835.—The following are by other hands: Dr. Epkemate published Gysbert Japicx Friesche Rijmlerye, 4to. Ljeauwert, 1821.—Woordenboek op de gedichten van Japicx, 4to. *id.* 1824.—Mr. Postumus translated into Friesic two of Shakspeare's plays, entitled, De Keapman fen Venetien in Julius Cesar, 8vo. Grintz, 1829.—Jonkh. Mr. Montanus Hettema has shown his patriotism by giving to the public the following valuable works:—Emsiger Landrecht Beknopte handleiding om de oude Friesche taal, 8vo. Leeuwarden, 1829.—Proeve van een Friesch en Nederlandsch Woordenboek, 8vo. Leeuwarden, 1832.—Friesche Spraakleer van R. Rask, 8vo. *id.* 1832.—Jurisprudentia Frisica, of Friesche Regtkennis, een handschrift uit de vijftiende eeuw, 8vo. *id.* 1834-35, 2 parts, &c. &c. Many more Friesians ought to be named as great promoters of their literature.—Professors Wassenberg, Hoekstra, Mr. Hoeufft, Wielinga Huber, Scheltema, Beuker Andreae, van Halmael, and others. See paragraphs 86—102, for an account of ancient Friesic works.

3. The simple sounds we assign to letters, bears no proportion to the diphthongal nature of almost every sound in A.-S.

The inhabitants of Hindelopen still retain some A.-S. sounds undefiled. When I first heard some old people speak in this little town, I was quite astonished how sounds so compounded and diphthongal as those could be pronounced with so much ease and fluency. What is more simple in writing than the words lêod, A.-S. leód *people;* neugen, A.-S. nigen *nine?* When you hear these words at Hindelopen, you will find that the pronunciation baffles every effort of the grammarian to invent signs giving an adequate idea of its nature. In the *eu* you hear first the *y*, then the *eu* blended with the French *ou*, ending in *oi*. Such words as lêod *people*, and neugen-end-neugentig *nine-and-ninety*, are, for this reason, Hindelopean shibboleths above all imitation of their own countrymen, the other Friesians.

4. Besides this, the sounds of letters are in restless fluctuation. If we could trace the changes in the sound of letters, our success would exceed our hopes; but even this discovery could not give an adequate idea of the sound of letters in use at any period, for sounds are altered when the letters remain still unchanged. The English and French languages give full proof of this truth.

When they enter into the class of dead languages, there will still be greater difficulties in ascertaining the pronunciation of *chateau*, and *eschew*. When, after long investigation, you discover that *chateau* ought to be pronounced *ka-te-au*, as the Picardians pronounce it at this very day, you find that by the tyranny of custom it is enervated to *sya-to;* when also you discover that the English first pronounced *e-schew*, and afterwards *es*-tshow (*ou* French), how few readers will believe your assertions, seeing that these words remain expressed by the same letters.

5. The sounds of a language, like other things, are, by time, subject to mutations, and these changes are homogeneous or heterogeneous, according as the cause of change is internal or external. In this way, diphthongs become vowels, and vowels again diphthongs. An elaborate treatise would point out the changes in a language, if an uninterrupted succession of MSS. of different ages could be procured.

6. Independent of these succeeding general changes of the whole language, there are diversities existing at the same time, called dialects. The A.-S. is subject to these diversities in the highest degree, and with a free people it could not be otherwise. When a nation easily submits to an absolute sway, individuals have little attachment to what is their own in character and opinions, and easily suffer themselves to be modelled in one general mould of the court or priesthood. On the other hand, when a nation, as the Angles and Friesians, is jealous of its liberty, and will only submit to the law enacted for the public good, while every individual regulates his private affairs for himself, the slightest peculiarity of character, unrestrained by the assumed power of any mortal, developes itself freely in the proper expressions, and every individuality is preserved. This I believe is the reason why in the province of Friesia are more peculiarities than in the other six provinces of the present kingdom of the Netherlands, and more in England alone than in the whole of Europe.

Applying this principle in language, the very mirror of the soul, we find the same variety; so that among a people so fond of liberty as the Angles and Friesians, not only every district, but every village, nay, every hamlet, must have a dialect of its own. The diversity of dialects since the French Revolution of 1795, is much decreasing by the centralisation of power taking daily more effect in the Netherlands: the former republic, by leaving to every village the management of its domestic affairs, preserved every dialect unimpaired. Nevertheless, at this very time, those living on the coast of *Eastmahorn*, in Friesia, do not understand the people of *Schiermonikoog*, a little island with one village of the same name, almost in sight of the coast. The *Hindelopians* speak a dialect unintelligible to those living at the distance of four miles from them. Nay, the Friesians have still dialects within a dialect.

In the village where I was born, we said indiscriminately, after, efter, and æfter, *A.-S.* æfter; tar, and tær, *A.-S.* tare; par, and pær, *A.-S.* pera; tarre, and tære *consumere*, *A.-S.* teran; kar, and kær, *A.-S.* cyre; hi lei, and hi lái, *A.-S.* læg; perfect tense of ik lizz', hi leit, *A.-S.* licge, liȝ; smarre, and smære, *A.-S.* smerian; warre and wære, warge and wærge, *A.-S.* weran, werian *tueri, resistere*. On this matter I can produce a very striking example in the centre of Friesian nationality. It is now, I believe, sixteen years since I spoke to an old woman at *Molquerum*, a village now almost lying in ruins, but still divided into seven little islands, called *Pollen*, joined to each other by (breggen *A.-S.* bricgas) *little bridges*. Now the good woman told me in her homely style, that when she was a child, every island had its peculiar way of pronouncing, and that when an inhabitant of any of the villages entered her mother's house, she could easily ascertain to which *Pol* the person belonged, merely by some peculiarity of speech. Dependence may be placed on this fact, as I have ascertained its truth by strict inquiry. I have no doubt the same peculiarity was observable in almost every village of the Anglo-Saxons. Every Englishman who notices the diversity of dialects to be found in Yorkshire, Durham, Northumberland, Cumberland, or Lancashire, and by these judges of the rest, and considers what they have formerly been, will perhaps enter, in some measure, into my views.

7. This fact fully accounts for the discrepancies in the forms of words, occurring nearly in every page of a genuine A.-S. author. Not writing by established, often arbitrary rules of grammar, he wrote just as he spoke; his writing was, therefore, the true representation of his dialect.

8. There still exists another cause, which, though not less productive of variety in writing, ought to be carefully distinguished from variety of dialect. The diphthongal nature of the whole system of A.-S. vowels made it difficult for every writer to know by what letters to indicate the proper sounds of his words. Unable to satisfy himself, he often interchanged kindred vowels in the same words, at one time putting *a* or *éo*, and afterwards *æ* and *y*. Diversities arising from this cause are of the most frequent occurrence even in the oldest Anglo-Saxon MSS.

9. This diversity in the spelling of a word is of the greatest importance to one who would ascertain the true pronunciation of the Anglo-Saxon. While the writer is groping about him for proper letters, we guess the

sound he wished to express by assuming some middle sound between the letters he employs. This advantage would have been totally lost to us if the orthography of the Anglo-Saxon could boast of the same uniformity as that of the English recorded in Walker's Pronouncing Dictionary.

10. In this respect we owe a thousand thanks to *Lye,* who gives us the Anglo-Saxon words as he found them, and never alters the orthography to suit his own views.

At the head of his articles he occasionally attributes to the word a vowel which it has not. For instance, he puts the *a* in staf and lat, which these words have only when a second syllable is added, as in late, stafa: when monosyllables, they are written stæf *a staff,* læt *late.* Whether he considered the vowel he inserts as the primitive one, or did not know the laws of permutation in Anglo-Saxon vowels, matters not, as it is impossible to be misled by them, standing alone and without any authority. He moreover rectifies his faults by his citations, in which neither staf nor lat occur. Such trifling mistakes should not obscure his immense merits in faithfully giving us the vowels of the Anglo-Saxon authors, with all their odd and lawless exertions to express the sounds they heard.

11. I fear that those who credit what I have stated about the diversity of Anglo-Saxon and Friesian dialects, will consider these infinite variations as the curse of Babel. They will, however, permit me to say, that human speech in general has its mechanical rules fixed by the frame of the organs of speech, to which all tongues submit. This frame admits modifications to which every nation yields. These modifications admit of farther modifications, to which not only districts, but even villages are liable. Therefore, every language is of necessity what it is, and it is not in the power of fancy or choice to obey or disobey these laws. From this cause proceeds much of the diversity in language.

12. From the sounds which can be pronounced, every nation selects those which are best adapted to the frame of his organs, and the feelings he endeavours to express.

Now this choice, in which we are free, opens an immense field for diversities in tongues; but, whatever the choice may be, the first grasp decides all the rest: every consonant brings its corresponding consonant, and the vowel its corresponding vowel. In a word, every language is a compact, well-framed whole, in which all the parts sympathize with each other. Insult one of its essential properties, and the disgrace will be felt through the whole system. Remove one series of its original place, and all the others will follow the motion. What is true of any language may be asserted of any of its branches or dialects. Reason and never-failing experience vindicate the justice of these conclusions. The dialect corresponds to itself in its dialects, and the principle on which the form of a word is framed, is always followed in similar cases. If this analogy be unobserved, it is not the fault of the dialect, but of the dim sight of the observer. The majority of grammarians deem dialects lawless deviations in the speech of the dull mob, to which they attach all that is coarse, vulgar, confused, and ridiculous. Indeed, the chaos of tongues then begins, when grammarians, ignorant of the operations of the mind, and its exertions to express its thoughts, obtrude their arbitrary rules,* and, by heterogeneous mixtures, ever fertile in producing others, set

* This assertion may be verified by many examples in English. On this point, the 467th paragraph of the Principles prefixed to Walker's Pronouncing Dictionary, is very striking.

e well-framed system of sounds in inextricable confusion. Regardless of the interior ucture, wholly unknown to eyes gliding over the surface of things, they use language the rich but ignorant man his library, who, deeming it to be a matter of chief imporıce that his books should be of the same size, ordered them all to be cut to 8vo. and mo. The public is not generally expert in forming a judgment on these matters: ighing no argument, it regards only the tone of the proposer, and places its conence in him who is the boldest in his assertions, though he is generally the most ıorant—for the greatest ignorance is ever accompanied with the greatest assurance. owever men may suffer themselves to be imposed upon, nature still defends her hts. As our bodies have hidden resources and expedients, to remove the obstacles ich the very art of the physician often puts in its way, so language, ruled by an lomitable inward principle, triumphs in some degree over the folly of grammarians. ok at the English, polluted by Danish and Norman conquests, distorted in its nuine and noble features by old and recent endeavours to mould it after the ench fashion, invaded by a hostile entrance of Greek and Latin words, threatening increasing hosts to overwhelm the indigenous terms; in these long contests ainst the combined might of so many forcible enemies, the language, it is true, has t some of its power of inversion in the structure of sentences, the means of noting the differences of gender, and the nice distinctions by inflexion and terminan—almost every word is attacked by the spasm of the accent and the drawing of nsonants to wrong positions; yet the old English principle is not overpowered. ampled down by the ignoble feet of strangers, its spring still retains force enough restore itself; it lives and plays through all the veins of the language, it impregtes the innumerable strangers entering its dominions with its temper, and stains em with its colour, not unlike the Greek, which in taking up oriental words ipped them of their foreign costume, and bid them appear as native Greeks.

13. But to return.—In human language, as in the whole creation, the eat law of beauty and happiness is this—*variety in unity*. Though there e great difficulties in discovering the true pronunciation of Anglo-Saxon, e have still left to us two means of investigation. First, the comparison its vowels and consonants with those of a kindred dialect existing at more remote period; and secondly, the same comparison with a kindred alect of posterior age, both as it is written and still spoken—for, however ered in some of its features, it must still retain genuine traits of its iginal countenance. The Gothic or Mœso-Gothic* will answer for the st, and the Friesic the second; two languages combining the advantage at the nations who spoke them bordered on the Anglo-Saxons, the œso-Goths on the north, and the Friesians on the south, and by closing the Anglo-Saxons, limit their influence, both as it respects their ography and language.

14. It is evident that all the tongues spoken by the great people which e Romans called Germani, considered on a large scale, appear as alects all issuing from one common source. There was a time when all ese languages were one. If we could mount sufficiently high in the ale of time, we should arrive at the period when the progenitors of all e tribes were gathered within the compass of a little camp under a few

* See VII. §. 1, and note 2.

tents, and spoke one language, containing the germs of all the diversities by which the dialects of their posterity were distinguished. The nearer we approach this time and place, the more will all the Germanic tongues become similar to each other, and their boundaries vanish by which at present they are enclosed. For this reason, the oldest and best poet of the Greeks, retaining symptoms of a particular dialect, blends in his poems all the dialects of Greece. In regard to antiquity, the Gothic of Ulphilas, being written about A.D. 360, has the precedence of any Anglo-Saxon MSS. by four or five hundred years. In comparing the Anglo-Saxon with the Gothic, we shall have the double advantage of measuring by a standard approaching nearest the genuine dimensions, and of approaching to a nearer contact with those kindred tongues which subsequently developed themselves into more striking differences.

15. The nearer we approach the source, the more pure will be the water. If the development of language were left to its natural course, without any disturbing shock or foreign influence, all things would change according to the established rules of nature, and every word bear in its changes some resemblance to its primitive state. But every age brings on some disturbance of the system, and the intermixture of foreign ingredients, originating in wars, migrations, revolutions, and other causes, introduces so many changes, that in some respects the rule is overthrown by the exceptions, and the language rendered quite unfit for comparison. A sufficient reason can be given for the present state of disorder only by ascending to the period of order, and not by a comparison of the dialects lying in their present confusion. Now the higher the step on which we can observe the language, the less it is disturbed in its original structure, and the better adapted for the standard of comparison. It is the high age of the Gothic, and its real character, known by what is remaining of it, which in these respects stamps its value. Spoken by one unmixed tribe of warriors, it appears on the stage fresh and unpolluted, quite original and sui generis, with members of due proportion, and dressed in its own native costume, without a shred of foreign ornament.

16. The advantages derived from a comparison with a language of this sort, may be exemplified by some names of the numbers.

The English having composed *eleven* and *twelve* from én, twé, and lifen, you would conclude that they would express *unus*, *duo*, by én, twé; but no, they say *one*, *two*. The Dutchman says twaalf, veertien, from twa and veer; but his simple numbers are twé, víer. The German has his zwanzig *twenty*, and zwei *two*. The country Friesian uses olwe, tóalf, tretjen, with manifest indication of Runic admixture, from ellefu *eleven*, tólf *twelve*, þrettán *thirteen*, from the Icelandic tveir and þrír. Their twenty has the sound of tweintich—ought they not to say also to *two*, træ *three*, one *one*, as the Hindelopians do? Rather incongruously they use ien, twá, trye; and having fjouwer *four*, they compose tsjien with víer into fjirtjen *fourteen*. Hence, when the numbers were composed, the English had the Dutch én and twé; the Dutch had the Gothic, Anglo-Saxon, and modern Friesic twa, with the Germans; the country Friesians had the *one*, *two*, of the English. Would not these ngues, when taken as a basis for analogical research, lead into a thousand mistakes? in English the number *eleven* were unknown to you, would you not say, from alogy, that it was formed from one, on-leven contracted into olven? It is not own in Gothic, but we may be sure that *ai* in ains *one*, will not be disowned in lif, as twa is not in twalif, nor twaim *duobus* in twaimtigum (*d. pl.*) *twenty*. In e same analogical manner the Anglo-Saxons compose words, þreo *three*, þreotyne rteen, twegen *two*, originally twen, twenluf contracted to twelf; án by pushing the ent æn-d-lufan. Does not *Kero* make, from zuene *two*, zuelifin *twelve?* In frid, from zuei *two*, zueinzig? Finally, does not the old Friesian, from twia *twice*, twi, *Ab.* 1, 93; thrē *three*, *Ab.* 177, træ Hindelopian; fiuwer *four*, fiower, *Ab.* 5, 87, form analogically twilif *twelve*, *Ab.* 14; thredtine *thirteen*, *Ab.* 19, 93; wertine *fourteen*, *Ab.* 19, 94?

17. There still exists another anomaly in the numerals.

The Greeks and Romans, counting only by tens, composed their numbers from ten twenty with δεκα, decem *ten;* ἑνδεκα, undecim *eleven;* δωδεκα, duodecim *twelve.* ne German tribes form the same numerals in a similar manner, except *eleven* and elve, which were composed with *Ger.* lif; *A.-S.* læfan, lif, lef, l'f, in other dialects. ut as this anomaly entered our numeral system in a period anterior to the history of r tongues, and is common to all the Germanic languages, the analogy between the ndred dialects is not disturbed by these irregularities, but rather advanced.

18. The cause of this disturbance lies in the old practice of using both n and *twelve* as fundamental numbers.

The advance was by ten, thus þrittig, *Country Friesic* tritich; feowertig, *Ab.* 2, &c. ut on arriving at sixty the series was finished, and another begun, denoted by efixing hund. This second series proceeded to one hundred and twenty, thus: undnigontig *ninety;* hundteontig *a hundred;* hundenlufontig *a hundred and ten;* undtwelftig *a hundred and twenty:* here the second series concluded. It thus pears, that the Anglo-Saxons did not know our *hundred* = 100, as the chief vision of numbers; and, though they counted from ten to ten, they, at the same ne, chose the number *twelve* as the basis of the chief divisions. As we say × 10 = 50, 10 × 10 = 100, they multiplied 5 and 10 by 12, and produced 60 and 0. When the Scandinavians adopted a hundred as a chief division [100 = 10 × 10], ey still retained one hundred and twenty; and calling both these numbers *hundred*, ey distinguished them by the epithets *little* or ten hundred, lill-hundrad or hundrad æd, and *great* or the twelve number hundred, stor-hundrade or hundrad tólfræd. he Danes count to forty by tens, thus, tredive *thirty*, fyrretyve *forty;* and then mmence by twenties, thus, halvtrediesindstyve, literally in *A.-S.* þridda héalf siðon entig* [*two twenties*], and *the third twenty half*, i. e. *fifty*. The Icelanders call 00 half þridie þusand, [*Dut.* derdehalfduizend,] i. e. *two thousand*, and *the third ousand half;* firesindotyve [*four-times twenty*] *eighty*, and so on to a hundred. he Francs, being a mixture of kindred nations from the middle of Germany, when ey entered Gallia, partly adopted the Anglo-Saxon mode of numeration, and partly at of the Danes, and they afterwards translated verbally their vernacular names of

* The ellipsis of the *two twenties* is supplied in the expression twa geare and þridde healf o *years and half the third year*, literally in *Frs. c.* twa jier in 't tredde heal, but custom conacts it to tredde heal jier. Hickes compares this ellipsis with the Scotch expression *half n*, which is also the *Dut.* half tien, but in this he is not accurate. The Country Friesians ot having this ellipsis, prove that it must be supplied in another way. They say, healwei jienen *half way of the present hour to ten o'clock*. Dr. Dorow has also fallen into the same istake, p. 127, *Denkmäler*, I. 2 and 3.

the numerals by Latin words. From twenty to fifty it proceeds in the usual manner, vingt, trente, quarante, cinquante, soixants; but having arrived at seventy, the same place where the Anglo-Saxons commenced with hund, hundseofontig, it uses soixantedix, quatrevingt, just as the Danes express eighty by firesindstyve *four-times twenty*. As it appears that the old Germans had two fundamental numbers, *ten* and *twelve*, it follows that *eleven* and *twelve* are the *last two* numerals of the twelve series, and the *first two* in the ten series; hence perhaps came the use of the termination lif or luf, in *eleven* and *twelve*.

19. Let us still add another example.

The conjugation of the Anglo-Saxon verb stigan *ascendere*, and the Gothic steigan, is thus inflected: ic stige, steiga; he stihð, steigith *he ascends*; he stáh, staig *he ascended*; we stígon, stígum *we ascended*. Here it appears, that the Gothic *ei* corresponds with the A.-S. *i*; *ai* with *á*; *í* with *í*. Now I conclude, if the evolution of both languages was regulated by the same principle, there must be an analogy between the vowels in similar instances. Indeed we do observe the same analogy preserved in verbs of the same class. Let us take, for instance, gripan, arisan, and spiwan:

A.-S. gripan *to gripe*;	gripe, gripð;	gráp, grípon.
Moes. greipan *to gripe*;	greipa, greipith;	graip, gripum.
A.-S. arisan *to arise*,	arise, arist;	arás, arison.
Moes. reisan *to arise*;	reisa, reisith;	rais, risum.
A.-S. spiwan *to vomit*;	spiwe, spiwð;	spáw, spíwun.
Moes. speiwan *to spit*;	speiwa, speiwith;	spaiw, spiwum.

20. These instances are all regular, but as soon as ever the accustomed evolution is disturbed in its course, the analogy is gone.

Thus, the verb scinan *to shine*, ic scine *I shine*, he scinð *he shines*, we scínon *we shone*, corresponds to skeinan, skeina, skeinith, skinum. The long *á*, however, in scán, Gothic skain, by some error being changed into short *a*, this short *a* is converted into éat and forms scéan *shone*. It has already been observed, that every dialect corresponds in its several parts, and that a certain form in the *present tense* brings on a certain form in the *perfect tense*. Of course the practice of some grammarians, in forming the conjugation of a verb out of the present tense of one dialect, and the perfect tense of another dialect, is contrary to the first rule of sound analogy. If any dialect had scunan or scéonan, the perfect tense scéan would not be an exception, as it is when appertaining to scinan.

21. It is a most happy circumstance, that the Gothic, and not the Theotisc, had the advantage of being recorded in the oldest monument of Germanic literature. Though much of the coincidence of this language with all its kindred dialects may be owing to its age, it owes still more in this respect to its locality in the genealogy of language.

22. It is hardly necessary to observe, that there is scarcely a single word in the *A.-S.* which we do not also find in all the kindred German dialects. We do not ask whether an *A.-S.* word can be found in the language of the Scandinavians, the Goths, or Theotiscans, but, to which of these it has the nearest relationship? In an etymological point of view, the great point is to ascertain the species, and not merely the genus; to discover to which particular dialect a word is most closely allied, and not to be satisfied with pointing out to what sort of language it belongs.

23. There are three chief species, of which the Anglo-Saxon and the 'riesic take the left side, the Theotisc or Alemannic the right side, and e Icelandic, Mœso-Gothic, Westphalian or Saxon, and Netherlandish, e middle: that is, so far as the vowels and consonants are concerned.

The Anglo-Saxon agrees in the consonants with the middle series, represented by e Mœso-Gothic, but in some important points it differs from the Mœso-Gothic and e Theotisc in its vowels, and has a system of its own. On the other hand, the 'heotisc agrees with the Gothic in its vowels, having regard to the lapse of time and alectic variations. In the consonants, the Theotisc is as different from Gothic and nglo-Saxon, as the Anglo-Saxon is in its vowels from the Gothic and Theotisc, and venture to say still more original; for, the consonants have not only quitted their d ranks, but those into which they have entered are also disorbed. The Gothic, en, being allied to the consonants of the Anglo-Saxon and the vowels of the heotisc, is thus the proper standard of comparison for all the Gothic tongues, ving been, from its locality, connected with them all. Thus the Gothic diups *deep* allied by the vowels *iu* to the Theotisc tiuf, and by the consonants *d* and *p* to the nglo-Saxon deop.

24. The Gothic has some peculiarities, which, whether they arise from s place in the pedigree of tongues, or its seniority, exemplify similar pecuarities in other languages.

For instance, the Icelandic is noted for the termination *r* or *ur*, which, in kindred ngues, changes into one of the vowels, and these vowels again into the lean sheva *e*; us, diupr *deep*, *A.-S.* deop, or deope. For the *r* the Gothic uses *s*, as the Latin *bos, honos*, for *arbor, honor;* thus *Goth.* diups *deep; A.-S.* wæg, geard; *Theotisc* c, karto; *Gothic* wigs, gards, are in *Icelandic* vegr and gardr.

25. These observations may account for the different opinions of ilologers in determining the just relations of the Germanic tongues. he reducing them all to Gothic origin was an exuberant spring of error. he Gothic is not of such antiquity as to boast in being the mother of all ermanic tongues with which we became acquainted in a latter period. the age of Ulphilas, it was a dialect of Germanic lineage, having other alects by its side, as the Anglo-Saxon, which in the 4th century ffered less from the Gothic than in the 9th century. It will be enough my purpose to observe, that all critics do not agree in arranging the digree of the Gothic. The reason is evident.

26. The Gothic or Mœso-Gothic is a language of transition or ssage. If you consider the vowels of a word, you make it of Gothic igin: another, only looking at the consonants, will assert it has nothing do with the Gothic. Some, only keeping in view grammatical forms, scover similarity of structure in the language of the Heliand; while hers, neglecting vowels, consonants, and grammatical forms, will only fix eir attention on the etymological meaning of the word, and will find other filiation.

It is evident that the *A.-S.* mot *a coin*,* as to the vowel, is nearer the *Gothic* mota

* q. *Tribute money*, numisma census, vectigal.—J. B.

*custom-house,** than *Ger.* maut *custom-house;* but, as to etymological sense, maut is nearer to the *Gothic* mota; and though the word mota may be older and more complete than the *A.-S.* mot, the signification of *coin* was anterior to that of *custom-house.* In this case, the *Icelandic* and *Friesic* still mount a step higher than the Gothic, Anglo-Saxon, or German, *e.g.* the *Icel.* móta *insculpo, typico,* and mót *typus; Frs. c.* moet *an impression,* gives origin to the idea of a *coin,* as coin does of the house where the tax-money was gathered.—The *Theotisc* mahal *concio, curia,* agrees with the *Moes.* mathls *forum,* as to the vowel and signification, but the *A.-S.* meðel *sermo* as to the consonant ð: we find also *Moes.* mathlei *sermo,* which agrees with *A.-S.* meðel, both in the consonants and the signification.—Feawa *few,* pauci, has the *w* of *Moes.* fawai *pauci,* but the *Theotisc* fahe *few,* the vowel. If we consider the *a* in *Icel.* vargr *furiosus,* it is nearer the *Moes.* wargjan *damnare,* than the *A.-S.* wergean *to curse,* maledicere, but in the signification the *A.-S.* draws nearer. Let us take an English example: the word abb *the yarn on a weaver's warp.* The *w* (pronounced nearly as Eng. *v*) being the aspiration of the lips, is often changed into *h,* the aspiration of the throat, as fahe, for fawai. The *Moes.* biwaibjan *to surround, encompass,* from waips *a garland,* sertum, *A.-S.* wefan *to weave, Theotisc* uueban, *Grk.* ὑφαειν, from ὑφειν. The Scandinavians cast away both these aspirations in the *perf.* of eg vef *I weave,* saying vóf, vaf, and of, hence of *tela* in use by the Scandinavians. In abb, then, the *a* is Icelandic, from vaf, and without the *w* in of *texebam;* but the *b* changes into *f,* or remains a *b,* as in the *Moes.* and in the *A.-S.* web; *Frs. c.* wob; both *e* and *o* originating from *a.*

27. From these few examples, it is evident that a word may have as many affinities as the points of view from which it may be observed. The Gothic was a tongue of transmigration, and all Germanic languages coming in contact with it in some point or other, it was very easily imagined to be the mother of the whole race. I may lastly add, on the ground of my own experience, that, having regard only to vowels and consonants, I cannot arrive at the common source of the Germanic tongues, as we trace back human kind to one common father in paradise. History begins too late to permit us to trace, with any satisfaction, even the first half of the period. Let us, therefore, not attempt what is impracticable; but, keeping in mind the seniority of the class at the head of each column, let us range them all in one line, as dialects of the same language. Finding, 1st. the *Anglo-Saxon* older than the *English,* the *Old Friesic* than the *Country Friesic,*—2ndly, the *Mœso-Gothic* older than the *Swedish,*—3rdly, the *Theotisc* or *Alemannic* older than the present German; and considering how much of grammatical forms, in the present languages, time may have destroyed, as to the vowels and consonants, the languages must be classified in the following order:—

* Telonium.

ANGLO-SAXON,	MŒSO-GOTHIC,	THEOTISC.
by the intermixing of Old Danish, Norman French, Latin, Greek, &c. is formed into *English*, *Scottish*, &c.* *Friesic*, at present divided into *Hindelopian*, *Country Friesic*, *Schiermonnikogian*, *Saterlandic*, *North Friesic*, [A small part of the Dutchy of *Sleswick*] All these dialects are more or less tainted by the languages of the respective surrounding people.	*Old and Modern, Icelandic*, mixed with German, Saxon, &c. forms the present *Swedish*, *Danish*, *&c*. *Saxon* or *Westphalian* language of the poem *Heliand*,† *Low-Saxon*.‡ [*Reineke de Vos*,‖ *of Henry van Alkmar, Lubek*, 1498.] From the Province of Overyssel, along the whole coast of the North-Sea to Sleswick, the Baltic, &c. *Netherlandish* [*Coren van stat der van Bruessele*, 1229.§] Statutes of the town of Brussels. *Dutch*, now daily becoming more defiled by Gallicisms and Germanisms.	[Language of *Kero* of the *xxvi Hymns*,¶ &c.] *High German*, *Bavarian*, *Austrian*, and other dialects. *German*, a mixture of High-German and some Saxon, [Low-German] as established by the version of the Bible by Martin Luther, and since adopted as the general language through the whole of Germany, A.D. 1555.**

* See Jameson's opinion of the origin of the Scottish in Table I. § 19, p. viii.

† Heliand oder die altsächsische Evangelien-Harmonie. Herausgegeben von J. Andreas Schmeller, Monachii, nptibus J. G. Cottæ, 1830. The Cottonian MS. of the Heliand is of the 9th century. The MS. of Bamberg century later. With the Heliand compare *Denkmäler*, alter sprache und kunst von Dr. Dorow, I. 2nd and l part, Berlin, 1824, where are explained some admirable specimens of the dialect spoken between Munster d Paderborn in the 10th century. It is a list of the rents of the convent Freckahorst near Waxendorf.

‡ *Niedersächsisch*, *Platt-deutch* [Low-deutch] in German as opposed to *High-deutch*. See the history of these lects in *Geschichte der Nieder-sächsischen sprache* von J. F. A. Kinderling, Magdeburg, 1800.

‖ See VI. 13—18.

§ First published in a treatise entitled *Verhandeling over de Nederduytsche tael en Letterkunde opzigtelyk de ydelyke provintien der Nederlanden door J. F. Willems, Antwerpen*, 1819, tom i. p. 133. This piece being the lest specimen of Netherlandish now extant, fully proves that the present Dutch is mere Brabandish, and that strongly marked dialectic diversities of these two sisters were formed when the Netherlandish was cultivated the seven United Provinces. The Netherlandish was called the *Vlaemsche tael*; the Flemish tongue, *la langue amande*, as long as the southern part of the Netherlands was the most flourishing, and Flanders the chief ovince. It was called Hollandish [Dutch] after the Spanish revolution, when the northern part was become owerful republic, and the province of Holland a ruling province. To be a language or dialect, is often merely uestion of predominant influence. See VI. 11, 20.

¶ Hymnorum veteris ecclesiæ XXVI. interpretatio Theotisca, ed. Jacobus Grimm, Gottingæ, 1830.

** See X. 51.

28. Considering the frame of the whole, I take no notice of the little terchanges between the columns—for instance, that the Friesic is nearer the Icelandic than the Anglo-Saxon. All the three columns are onsidered as proceeding together, and developing themselves in succeedg ages with more or less facility.* An attempt shall subsequently be ade to show the locality of the Germanic languages in a higher period, nd how they developed themselves in advancing to the station of the Iœso-Gothic.

* This hypothesis must be regulated by a due attention to the fact, that the first appearnce of the Anglo-Saxon in the orbit of languages, is some centuries later than the Mœsoothic, which has, therefore, its phases more advanced than the Anglo-Saxon. This conderation is of common application.

29. It must be observed, that the monuments of Friesian literature are of a far more recent date than the Anglo-Saxon; but the development of language does not always depend upon its age. The Friesians, encompassed on the one side by the sea, and on the other by the Saxons, owe it to their greographical position that they have experienced no mutations but those of a Saxon origin, and in many respects homogeneous with their own language. I do not recollect any intermixture of a foreign language with the Friesian, except what was caused by the frequent inroads of Normans, and by the settlement of some bands of the same race among the Friesians.

30. Add to this, that the language of the Friesians never felt the shock caused by migrations. From the time of Cæsar to this very day, amongst the endless revolutions of nations, they have never changed their name or the place of their residence, and they are noted as an exception to the locomotive temper of the Germanic race.*

31. These causes would render the language so stationary, that it would be less altered in the 12th century, than others in the 10th. In the following comparison, many instances will occur of true Anglo-Saxon sounds still flourishing in Friesland. What I consider still more important, the development of some vowels has produced now the same result as it did eight centuries ago—a convincing proof that the germ of both languages must be homogeneous.

32. Discovering such striking features of likeness, after a separation of almost fourteen centuries, a complete separation by the ocean, by the adventures and the diversity of their means of subsistence, and of the land they occupied, I conclude, that at the time of their union, about the middle of the 5th century, the Anglo-Saxon was distinguished from the Friesic only by slight differences of dialect. We do not become acquainted with the A.-S. before the 8th or 9th century, and with the Friesian not before the 12th or 13th century, about four and eight hundred years after their separation. The series of evolutions each tongue has sustained, affords a full account of the chief discrepancies then existing.†

33. As this whole matter can be proved by a strict comparision, we need not seek for authorities.

If authority were wanted, that of Francis Junius would be amply sufficient. After a long scrutiny of the whole Germanic antiquity in regard to languages; after the compilation of glossaries of almost every dialect of the race, unparalleled in labour and accuracy; after a stay of two years [1652-1654] in those parts of Friesia noted as tenacious of their old manners and language, this scholar has always declared it as his opinion, that, of all the Germanic tongues, none approached so closely to the Anglo-Saxon as the Friesian. This decision will, I trust, outweigh all contrary opinions. As there are few in this century even deserving to march by the side of Junius, so I do not think any one can be vain enough to imagine he is superior.

* *Précis de la Geographie Universelle, par M. Malte-Brun, Paris,* 1810, vol. i. p. 344.

† See § 14, 58, &c.

34. The geographical position of this people in question coincides with eir philological pedigree. Let us begin with the Goths, taking care at the epithet Mœsian, coupled with their name, does not deceive the mmon reader.

Some fragments of the Periplus of Pytheas, the renowned navigator from Marseilles, orm us, that he, being in search of the amber coasts in the Baltic, doubled the cape Jutland, and sailed about 6,000 stadia along the coasts of the Guttones and utones, through the gulf Mentonomon [Kattegat, Belt, &c.] This was about 5 years before the Christian era. The Guttones or Goths, seated in Jutland, scended afterwards to their brethren at the southern coast of the Baltic,* for the ief seat of the race was on the banks of the Vistula [Weichsel]. After a part s gone into Scandinavia, the great bulk moved thence to the banks of the Danube)onau] in Dacia [Moldavia and Wallachia, about A.D. 180]. A part of the Goths, lled West-Goths, pushed on by the Huns, retired, about A.D. 377, into Mœsia ervia and Bulgaria], and hence these Western-Goths obtained the name of Mœso-oths. It was to this people that Ulphilas, the renowned translator of the Scriptures, as bishop.

35. On the southern borders of the ancient Goths were seated the ngles, spreading southward perhaps to the banks of the Eider. The iief town of these people at a later date was Haddeby or Haithaby, .-S. Hæðe in Schleswig, or Sleswick.

36. While the Angles filled nearly the whole of the Chersonesus Cimricus, they were bordered on the west by another people of their kindred. 'hese were the Friesians, whose posterity still live in the district of Brededt near the coast of the sea, and whose dialect will afford some words ›r comparison.

Hence the Friesians spread themselves in one uninterrupted line along the coast of e German sea to the mouth of the Scheld;† though the extremities of this line were ery distant from each other, and the people subdivided into sections denominated rocmans, Segelterlanders, Rustrunger, Hunsingoër, and Emlander, each people ruling s own section by its own private statutes; still they were one people, and spoke the me language, and ruled by the same common law, as a close examination of its *'etus jus Frisionum* will prove. We remark that the Friesians lived close to the oast, as if allured by some magic attraction of the water; and, though when exigences equired it, they sometimes extended into the interior parts, they never spread far in readth, and even in their partial extension they soon relinquished their internal

* See VII. § 1, &c.

† The learned S. Turner cites six lines of Melis Stoke, in which the chronicler asserts that *ower Saxony* has been confined by the Scheld. This accurate historian would not place any onfidence in these words, if he had been acquainted with the following edition of the Rhymer: *Rijmkronijk van Melis Stoke, met aanmerkingen door Balthazar Huydecoper*, tom. iii. 8vo. Leyen, 1772; i. p. 9. See *Lex Frisionum edita et notis illustrata à Sibrando Siccama; Franekeræ*, 617.—*Van Wijn, bijvoegzels en aanmerkingen op de Faderl-Geschiedenis van Wagenaar*, om. i.—iv. p. 83—90. The same remark is of still more forcible application on a passage of 'olijn, also cited by Mr. Turner. Colijnus is a supposititious child. *History of the Anglo-'axons*, i. p. 328 and 150, London, 8vo. 1828. In the history of Friesia after the time of 'harlemagne, those Friesians who governed by their own laws, and spoke Friesic, must be arefully distinguished from the surrounding people, who are also called Friesians because the *olitical* division of countries refers them to Friesia. The blending of these two races has een the source of endless errors in history.

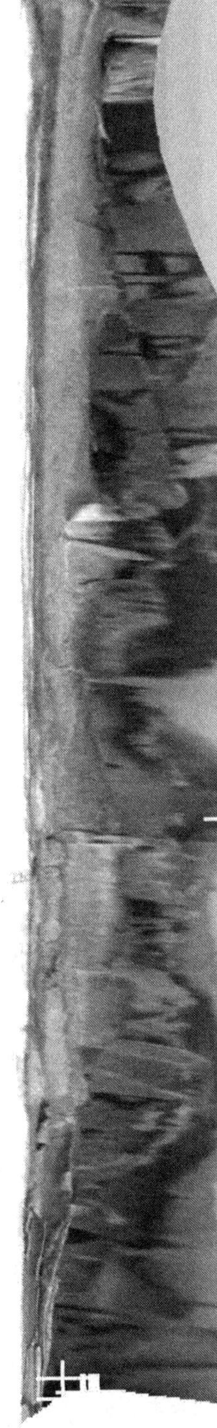

possessions. The historian, recollecting these facts, will not overlook the importance of the Friesians, though they only inhabited the borders of the continent, and the little islands by which the coast of the German ocean is covered.

37. This Friesian line was early broken in two places by two mighty nations—one making its appearance from the continent, the other from the ocean.

Between the Ems and the Weser were settled the *Chauci Minores*, and between the Weser and the Elbe the *Chauci Majores*. It is reported by Tacitus, that this immense extension of land, even from the borders of Hessia, was not only under the dominion, but was inhabited by the *Chauci*, but, he adds, they only kept some part of the strand, leaving the Friesians for the most part in their old possessions. The Chauci, entering into alliance with other people against the declining power of Rome, and assuming the name of Francs, left this country, and their name, being absorbed in that of the Francs, disappears from historic record. The Friesians availed themselves of this opportunity to occupy the vacated possessions of the Chauci, it not being unusual for a steady people like the Friesians to make use of the changes produced by the roving disposition of their neighbours to increase their own territory.

38. Two descriptions of the Chauci are given by Tacitus. He first records some facts, and then, in the thirty-fifth chapter *De Moribus Germanorum*, he draws their portrait.

In the record of the facts,* the Chauci appear cruel oppressors of the feeble, vindictive pirates, and to be prone to foreign military expedition, and also to make inroads on their neighbours. In delineating their character,† it is said that they wish to support their grandeur by justice, being free from covetousness, masters of themselves, calm, modest, and retired. They never excite wars, nor harass their neighbours by predatory excursions or highway robbery. It is deemed the strongest proof of their bravery and might, that they act as superiors, and never pursue anything by injustice. Nevertheless, every one is ready to take up arms, and, in case of exigency, to unite in forming an army. They have plenty of men and horses, and their placitude detracts nothing from their valour. Had Tacitus first given this description, and afterwards recorded the facts, one might have supposed that he was misled through ignorance of the facts; but how he could contradict known facts related by himself, is hardly to be conceived. It must be clear to all who know the Friesians and their disposition, that the character ascribed to the Chauci agrees even in the least particulars with that of the Friesians. Is it then impossible that Tacitus at a distant period, and mislead by later reports, should blend two neighbouring people together, and attribute to the Chauci what was alone applicable to the Friesians?

39. The line of the Friesian tribes was broken again in a second place, to the north of the Elbe.

The Saxons, occupying only some islands, such as Nordstrand, and some points on the continent to the westward and south of the Angles, and their western neighbours the strand Friesians, were in time so increased that they descended from their narrow

* *Taciti Annales* xi. 18, 19. *Dion. Cass.* ix. 30. *Tac. Ann.* xiii. 55. Didius Julianus restitit iis Belgicam aggredientibus, *Spartianus in Did. Jul.* I.

† *Taciti Germania*, cap. 36. It is said that he wrote his *Germania* later than his *Annales* or *History*. Whether this be true or not, the facts and the description must apply to different people.

abodes, and spread along the northern banks of the Elbe, and filled up the whole extent of country between this river and the land of the Angles.* This second breach, being near and enlarging that of the Chauci, was never entirely filled up again; and where it was afterwards, either by the departure of the Chauci, or the expeditions of the Saxons, the bishops of Bremen and Hamburg determined, by their power and spiritual influence, to destroy the Friesic spirit of freedom, by subjugating the Friesians to their sway in government, religion, and language.

40. Hence two divisions of Friesia originated at an early date: the southern part began at the mouth of the Weser, and terminated at the mouth of the Scheld; the northern part from the west strand of Schleswig [Sleswick], towards the mouth of the Elbe, much less than the southern part, and for this reason called *Friesia Minor*. In the 13th century, this small territory had power to raise for the king of Denmark an army of sixty thousand men.†

41. The Mœso-Goths are traced to their first position in the northern parts of Chersonesus Cimbricus [Jutland, Denmark]; the Angles in the narrower part and to the banks of the Eider; the Friesians extended on the sea-coasts by the side of the Angles to the mouth of the Elbe. We intend to place our philological comparison in the same order; first the *Gothic*, then the *Anglo-Saxon*, and finally the *Friesic*.

42. It must not be overlooked, that the geographical position of the whole Germanic race coincides with the arrangement of the preceding table of their languages. Going from the Baltic to the Netherlands, you pass through the original seats of the *Icelandic*, *Mœso-Gothic*, *Westphalian*, *Netherlandish;* on the left you find the *Angles* and *Friesians;* and on the right you have the *Alemannic* or *Theotisc* race.‡

43. This position may, perhaps, afford some idea of the order in which the respective tribes marched from the orient to the west of Europe.

The foremost were the Anglo-Friesic race, who, being pushed forward by following tribes, did not halt till they arrived on the shore of the German ocean. The Goths with their attendants followed, and the train of the Germani was closed by the Theotisc race. The coast of the German ocean, along which the Anglo-Friesic race was forced to spread itself, was the basis of the direction in which the two following races took their position, and were placed nearly in three parallels from north-east to south-west. These parallels are crossed and disturbed in a thousand ways by migrations and wars, but their general direction manifests itself to this very day in the remnants of the respective old languages.

44. The adventurers who subdued Britain are called Anglo-Saxons; but here an important question arises—what is implied in this name? First, it is to be observed, that this people never called themselves Anglo-

* As the Saxons were unknown to Tacitus, the irruption of the Chauci was, of course, anterior to that of the Saxons.

† "Imperator Otto, Holsatiam sibi subigere volebat, contra quem venit rex Waldemarus cum exercitu copioso, habens secum de solis Frisionibus sexaginta millia hominum."—*Ericus Rex, ad ann.* 1215.

‡ § 27.

Saxons; but this name is given them by historians. *Paulus Diaconus* called them *Angli-Saxones;** *Codoaldus, rex Anglonum-Saxonum;*† and, inverting the construction of the words, he says, *Hermelinda ex Saxonum-Anglorum genere.*‡ They did not call themselves by these compound names, but indiscriminately, *Angles* or *Saxons. Anglorum, sive Saxonum gens.*|| The case seems to me as follows.

45. After the Goths had evacuated the Chersonesus Cimbricus, and left only their name to the country, colonies of the neighbouring Angles succeeded in their place, and assumed the name of the Country Geatas, Eotas, Ytas.

The *Scandinavians,* and more particularly the *Danes,* were quite distinct from these *Juths,*§ being their mortal enemies, and being distinguished from them by some strong features in the respective languages. Neither did the Danes originally possess any part of the Chersonesus Cimbricus, unless it was the very northern point. In later ages they succeeded in gradually subduing the population of the Chersonesus, and mingling their language with that of the innates; but this very mixture proves by its ingredients, now visible, that nearly the whole peninsula was before populated by a race different to the Danes, and similar to the Angles. The definite article *the,* both in *Danish* and *Icelandic,* is placed after the noun and made to coalesce with it, while in the Anglo-Saxon and the kindred tongues it is always set before the noun: thus *A.-S.* seo stræt *the street; Icel.* strætit; *A.-S.* se strand *the strand; Icel.* ströndin; *A.-S.* se man *the man; Dan.* manden, *gen.* mandens *of the man.*¶ This peculiarity of the Danish idiom is not to be found in the dialect of the Jutes, however Danish it may be. If you draw a line from Skanderburg to Wiburg, and to the gulph of Liim, what lies south and west of this line, Thysted not excepted, retains still the remains of its Anglo-Saxon, or rather its antiscandinavian origin.**

46. The combined power of the Angles and Jutes was easily overcome by that of their southern neighbours; for such was the number, the power, and the extent of the Saxons along and above the northern banks of the Elbe, that all the surrounding people, whether Friesians, Angles, or Jutes, were considered by foreigners as subdivisions of the Saxons; even what was effected by a union of all these tribes, was often ascribed to the Saxons alone.

It is likely that the Saxons were the most prominent, and therefore attracted the greatest attention from southern scholars, while the Friesians, Angles, and Jutes were less observed on the strand or the inner part of the peninsula. It is known, from their geographical position, that the Angles constituted a part, and being the chief actors, probably a great part of the migrating allies; so that, on their departure, their native soil was left nearly destitute of inhabitants.†† The Angles, however, were considered a subdivision of the more powerful Saxons, and took a share in their

* De gestis Longobard. iv. 23. † *Id.* vi. 15. ‡ *Id.* v. 37. || Bede, i. 15.

§ "Guti cum veniunt suscipi debent, et protegi in regno isto sicut conjurati fratres, sicut propinqui et proprii cives regni hujus. Exierunt enim quondam de nobili sanguine Anglorum, scilicet de Engra civitate, et Anglici de sanguine illorum, et semper efficiuntur populus unus et gens una."—*Leges Edwardi, Wilkins,* p. 206.

¶ See II. § 1.

** See this position defended by a Danish gentleman, Dr. C. Paulsen, in the Nordisk Review, No. I. p. 261, Copenhagen, 1833.

†† See III. § 5, 6.

edition: this union is correctly expressed in the denomination *Anglo-Saxons.* r, whether this word be considered as German or Latin, the first part denotes the cies, and the second the genus, and the whole implies the tribe of the Angles onging to the Saxon confederacy. The Angles bore the chief and leading part in expedition to Britain, though considered as only a part of the Saxon confederacy, therefore denominated Anglo-Saxon.* Time has done justice to the Angles; while the name of Saxons has either completely disappeared, or has only a faint tige in such words as *Essex,* (*East-Saxons,*) *Middlesex,* &c., the name of the gles is still embodied in England and Englishmen, and is in full vigour and known m pole to pole; nor will it ever die, unless the declining empires of Germanic e should be washed away by a flood of barbarians, as the Roman empire was by Germanic.

47. It has already been shown that *Anglo-Saxon* is a word formed by l Latin authors, and not by the Saxons themselves. Independently of torical proof, the foreign descent of the word is proved by its for- tion.

Thus we say, in the Latin form, Anglo-Saxones, Hiberno-Anglus, Polono-Russus, ether we take *Anglo, Hiberno, Polono,* for substantives or adverbs; but in expres- g these words in the Germanic tongues, we should say *English Saxon, Polish ssian;* in German, *Englischer Sachse, Russischer Pole.* Thus the Dutch poet erlant, Dus werden heren dingelsche sassen, *Thus the English Saxons turned ers.* (iii. 29.) This Germanic form is verbally translated by Paulus Diaconus, (iv.15,) *gli-Saxones.*

48. It is often stated that the word Seaxan *Saxons* is derived from x *a sword;* in East Friesia, saeghs *a little sabre.*

If this be true, there is some reason for the supposition that the kindred nations ived their names from the weapon which they chiefly used. Thus, *Franc,* from nca *a javelin; German,* from gár *jaculum; Dut. Kil.* gheer *fuscina;* and man an, that is, *a dart man.* Angle *the Angles,* from angel *aculeus hamatus.* The word x is nothing else but *Moes.* ahs *spica; Sans.* असि asc *a sword,* ensis; *A.-S.* air, ear *an ear;* æx, eax *an axe, an instrument consisting of a metal head with harp edge,* preceded by the sibilant *s;* and perhaps gar is the same word as (ar) ; *Dut.* aar, air, aer *arista,* preceded by the guttural *g; Dut. Kil.* anghel *an ear spike of corn*—all proving the idea of something pointed. The word franca is seen *Ger.* fram, properly *the sharp end of an instrument, the beginning of any thing, and ce the preposition* from, agreeing in signification with the *Moes.* fram. Fram ma, (*Moes. Jn.* 15, 27,) is on that account properly *the edge, commencement of the inning,* that is, *from the beginning.* Is it not also possible that the Brondingas, eo. K.* p. 37, 11,) are so called from *Icel.* brandr *lamina ensis.*

49. In the comparison of languages, care should be taken not to be slead by mere names. The Saxons increased so much in power, as to re to oppose the hosts of Charlemagne, and at last they occupied an mense territory about the Elbe and the Weser, which, after their name, s called Saxony. This Saxony was subsequently occupied by other

* It is remarkable that king *Ine,* who commenced his reign in A.D. 700, calls himself, at the inning of his laws, a *West-Saxon.* Ic Ine, mid Godes gyfe West-Seaxana cyning, *I Ine, by 's grace king of the West-Saxons.* But the people of his kingdom he denominates *English-* . Gif wite-þeow Englisc mon hine forstalige, *if an Englishman condemned to slavery steal,* 24. Gif Englisc mon stealð, *if an Englishman steal, In.* 46: 54: 74. An Englishman, in the paragraphs, is opposed to Wealh *a Welshman.*

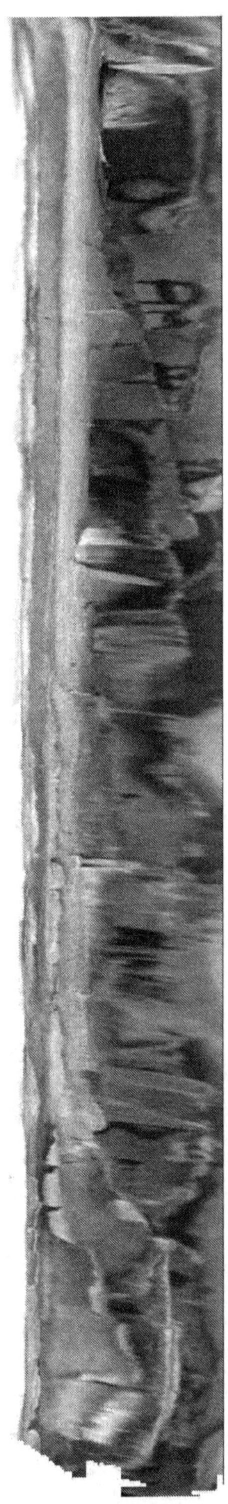

tribes, whose system of vowels approached to that of the Theotisc race, and therefore differed very much from the Anglo-Saxon sounds. These tribes, taking the name of *Saxons* from the country they inhabited, their language is also called Saxon. I need not remark, that we can neither compare Anglo-Saxon nor the English to this Saxon as their nearest relative, if the mistakes of the most celebrated philologists did not render it necessary.*

Dr. Johnson did not regard this rule, and therefore he often compares English words with the most remote German. "After cat you first find *Teuton* katz (*read* katze), then *French* chat, and afterwards *A.-S.* cat; while *A.-S.* cat, *Frs.* and *Dut.* kat, being the proper form of the word, ought to have stood first." Some hundred examples of this sort, and worse, may be quoted from this celebrated lexicographer: his errors, instead of being removed by his editor, Mr. Todd, are in this respect, and some others, increased: added to this, that many words are not to be found in the languages referred to. In the article *hay*, the *Icel.* hey is also said to be *Dut.*, while the *Dut.* word is hooi; and thus in almost every page. An impartial judge, considering the medley of materials, the blunders, the negligence or typographical errors occurring in deducing words from their originals, will conclude, that the etymological part of Johnson's Dictionary, even in the edition of 1827, is not deserving of the expense and the labour bestowed upon it, and is quite unworthy of the nation of whose language it is the chief interpreter, if not the uncontrolled lawgiver. The English etymologist will only meet with the proper forms of its words by consulting the nearest relatives of the English language. We may illustrate this by the preceding example of *hay*. Here we find the same change of *g* to *y* in the Country Friesian as in the English—a change which is not to be found so often in any other Germanic tongue. *A.-S.* heg, in *Frs. c.* is hêa; but hâye (*Italian a*) *to make hay*, agrees with *hay*, having both *a*, as *Moes.* hawi. So also *A.-S.* mæg *potest*, dæg *dies*, weg *via*, cæg *clavis*, were changed into *may*, *day*, *way*, *key*, of which the Englishman will scarcely discover instances, unless he goes to his nearest kinsmen the Friesians, *Frs. c.* mei, dei, wei, kâi, (*Italian a*).†

50. It may be asked whether, when the Anglo-Saxons left their native soil, any of the neighbouring Friesians accompanied them, and whether any intercourse was subsequently maintained between the separated brethren? ‡

* It has already been observed, (§ 22,) that the question is not whether a word exists in *one* of the Germanic languages, which is generally the case, but whether the proper form of the word is to be found in the *nearest* kindred dialect. When we cannot discover it in this dialect, then only we may apply to languages of more remote relationship. The question, for instance, is not whether the word *cat* exists in other Germanic tongues, but whether it is found in *A.-S.*, *Frs.* or *Dut.*

† There is another class of Germanic words introduced in this century, or the two preceding, and making no part of the original frame of the language. The correct derivation of these words depends more upon an extensive knowledge of many thousand terms in modern tongues, than upon analogical acuteness: I should wish to bestow more praise upon this part of Johnson's Dictionary, but it is not better than the other. One example will be sufficient. What can be more simple than the derivation of the word TATTOE, *the beat of a drum warning soldiers to their quarters*, from the *Dut.* taptoo, *id.* properly signifying *tapping shut*, *the taps or ginshops shut* from the soldiers? Even in the last edition of Johnson, by Todd, it is derived from *Fr.* tapotez tous.

‡ The old Chroniclers are at a loss whether to make Hengist a Friesian or a Saxon. Maerlant speaks of him thus.

Een hiet Engistus een vriese, een sas,
Die vten lande verdreuen was;
One was named [*A.-S.* het] Engist, a Friesian or a Saxon,
Who was driven away out of his land.—*Spiegel Historial*, c. xv. p. 16.

Upon which I would remark, that the faces of the Anglo-Saxon and the Friesic nguages would have the more marked and decided likeness to each other, when the paration was the most complete. If a continued intercourse between the Friesians 1 the continent, and the Anglo-Saxons in Britain, had been maintained, the Anglo-axon would have been supplied with Friesian ingredients of a later date, in such way as languages not otherwise homogeneous may form a distant similitude; but hen there are innumerable resemblances between Anglo-Saxon and the Friesian f this very day, originating in the latter part of the 5th century, without being creased by a subsequent intercourse, it is a proof that this striking similitude must ave been laid in the basis of the languages. I feel much inclined to think that this the truth, while I allow that many of the neighbouring Friesians accompanied the nglo-Saxons in their expedition.

51. It is true that the Friesian is noted for his tenacity to his native oil. His residence about the mouths of the Ems and the Rhine for enturies before our era, in the midst of a wandering people, is a sufficient roof of this character.

The Friesians on the confines of the Angles were not of such quiet and sedentary abits as those on the Ems and the Rhine. They acquired the restless habits of their eighbours. Suppose then a portion of the *Saxons*, many thousand *Jutes*, and nearly l the *Angles*, leaving their country for glory and riches; would it not be a miracle, if e Friesians in the neighbourhood of the moving tribes were alone insensible of the eneral impulse? This is on the supposition that the movement was voluntary; but, nsidering the subsequent emigration of the *Cimbrians*, the *Goths*, and *Angles*, from e same peninsula, I cannot help retaining the supposition, that some cause, now iknown, might operate to produce these migrations. This cause, whether famine,* inroads from the Scandinavians, being general, would have the same influence upon e Friesians as upon their neighbours.

52. I am aware that inquiry will be made, why Bede, in enumerating e tribes who peopled Britain, omitted the Friesians.†

As well may we inquire why Procopius omits the Saxons, and names the riesians. Bede was born about A.D. 673, and died in 735. Though he was well

Thus again:

Engistus wart dus outeert
Ende is in Vrieseland gekeert.

Engist was thus disgraced,
And is into Friesia returned.—tom. iii. p. 29.

The Chronicle of Maerlant is founded upon the *Speculum Historiale* of Monk Vincentius, ho wrote about A. D. 1245.

* Nennius says, that the first settlers arrived in three vessels, and that Hengist and Horsa ere exiles: this intimates some internal combustion in Gothland. In those nations averse to e sedentary occupation of agriculture, famine was always the most efficient and general use of emigration. This was at least the case with the Scandinavians, who, pressed by earth, determined by lot who should emigrate. It is likely that the Scandinavians fell upon e Jutes, who, being settled in the corner of the peninsula, were the first prey of the hungry vaders. The Jutes fell upon Britain, and were the first Saxon settlers in Kent and Wight. The andinavians then descended further to the south on the Angles and Saxons, and induced e tribes to comply with the request of Hengist and other leaders to come to Britain. The rthern pirates, still descending further, ravaged the whole coast of the German sea: the iesians were, therefore, the never-ceasing objects of their piratical incursions. In still ter times they settled in France, and ultimately reached the descendants of the same tribes the Anglo-Saxons, who, in the two preceding centuries, were exiled from their native soil. e on this subject, *Normannernes sötoge og deres nedsættelse i Frankerig Historik Fremstillet af B. Depping med adskillige forandringer oversat af N. M. Petersen Köbenhavn*, 1830, p. 57, *et seq.*

† Bede i. 15.

acquainted with the affairs of England in his time, he never left his native land. Procopius was a Greek of Cæsarea, and after the year 535 the secretary of Belisarius, the companion of his general in his expeditions against the Vandals and Goths, and of course well acquainted with the general circumstances and relations of the Germanic tribes. He was also two hundred years nearer the Saxon expedition to Britain than Bede. This Procopius states in his fourth book on the Gothic war, that Britain was peopled by three nations, the *Britons*, the *Angles*, and the *Friesians*, Αγγιλοι και Φρισσονες. Could Procopius be mistaken or mislead in an historical fact of such notoriety as the overthrow of an important island by swarms from the continent, an event in which the political interests of his master Justinian, as to the influence of its example, were highly concerned? It was to Procopius a comparatively recent event, happening about 449, and therefore only about a hundred years before he wrote his history. If he were mislead, how is it that he does not mention some nation of wider fame, and is satisfied to select the Angles and the remote tribe of the Friesians to be the inhabitants of Britain?

53. I cannot omit to mention, that the leaders of the Anglo-Saxons bear names which are now in use by the Friesians, though by time a little altered or abbreviated.

They have *Hortse, Hengst,* Witte, Wiggele, Eske, Tsjisse, Tsjerk, Ealse, Hessel;* for *A.-S.* Horsa, Hengest, Witta, Wihtgil, *Chr. Ing.* p. 15; Æsc. Cissa, *Chr. Ing.* p. 16; Cerdic, Elesa, *Chr. Ing.* p. 17. Also *Lense, Timen, Elle,* for *A.-S.* Wlencing, Cymen, Ælle, [*Icel.* at ellda *ignem facere; A.-S.* ellen *virtus, robur,*] *Chr. Ing.* 16; *Ine, Ide, Offe,* for *A.-S.* Ine, Ide, Offa. There are indeed but few A.-S. names which may not be found in use with the present Friesians.

54. The story of Geoffrey of Monmouth about *Vortigern* and *Rouin,* or *Rowen,* daughter of Hengist, is known. She welcomed him with, "Lauerd king, wacht heil," *Lord king, wait for my hailing draught.* He, by the help of an interpreter, answered, "Drinc heil," *Drink hail to me.*†

I intend not to discuss the verity of the history, but only to allude to the ceremony which was observed. The Friesian Chronicles represent *Rowen* as drinking the whole, in compliance with the royal command, "Drink hail!" and then taking the right hand of the king in hers and kissing him, while she offered him the cup with her left hand. This is quite a Friesian custom.‡ The female is not named Rouin by the Friesian Chronicle, as the text of Geoffrey badly states, but Ronixa, a name still in use with us, though, by an analogical permutation of consonants, it is written Reonts.

* See § 50, note ‡.

† Galfredi Monumetensis Historia Regum Britanniæ, iv. 12.

‡ Est præterea et alia quam pro lege vel quasi observant (Frisii) ut videlicet quoties alicui patheram vel poculum vino, vel cerevisia plenum propinant, tum dicunt sua materna lingua, Het gilt, ele frye Frieze! [*It concerns thy hail, O free Friesian!*] et non tradunt patheram sive poculum, nisi datis dexteris, cujuscumque etiam conditionis, aut sexus fuerunt, quique tum accipientes prædictum poculum respondent eadem lingua, "Fare wâl, ele frye Frieze! [*Farewell, O free Friesians!*] Etsi personæ dissimiles fuerint, aut utræque feminei sexus nihilominus *addito osculo* idem perficiunt; quem etiam morem in hunc usque diem Frisii pertinaciter retentum observant.—*De orig. situ, qualit. et quant. Frisiæ, M. Corn. Kempio authore, Coloniæ Agr.* 1588.

"Respondens deinde Vortegirnus, Drinc heil jussit puellam potare, cepitque de manu ipsius scyphum et osculatus est eam et potavit."—*Galfredus Monum,* vi. 12. The maiden's taking hold of the king's hand and kissing him, is reported by Winsemius Frieschi Historien, p. 43, and others, who may be compared with Geoffrey of Monmouth. See *Junii Etymol. Anglic. in voce* WAIT.

55. Whatever may be the truth of the story, it is most certain that "Wacht hail" is changed into *Wassail;* that *wassail-cup* is sometimes ısed at feasts and on New-year's day in England; and that its origin is raced back to the supposed meeting of Vortigern and Ronixa.

What has particularly struck me is, that the figure of the old English wassail-bowl s exactly the same as the silver cups in which, at weddings, the Friesians offer to the uests brandy with raisins, [*spicy wassel-bowl*]. This cup passes from the married ouple to their guests on their left-hand, and from them to their left-hand neighbour, s in the corporation festivals in England. The liquor is called in the Friesian ongue, "breid's trienen" *bride's tears,* alluding to her reluctant willingness to enter nto wedlock.

56. I will only add that the Danes were the common enemies of the riesians and Angles, and as much opposed by national hatred, as the riesians and Angles were united by the ties of national sympathy.

The Saxon Chronicle records, in the year A. D. 897, that the Friesians and Angles ought under the command of king Alfred against the Danes, who were defeated near xmouth, Devonshire. The Friesians were of some repute, or the names of three of hem would not have been preserved from oblivion in this record: Æbbe, *Frs. c.* bbe; Æðelere, *Frs. c.* Eldert; Wulfheard, *Frs. c.* Olfert. Were these Friesians e allies of Alfred, recently come to his assistance from the banks of the Elbe or hine, or his subjects settled in England?

Before entering upon the comparison of the Friesic with the Anglo-axon, it will be necessary to form accurate ideas about the state in which he Anglo-Saxon language has reached our time.

57. One common fate accompanied all the MSS. of the middle ages, hat the text was modernised, and therefore spoiled when copied by person who spoke the same language, and nothing but the ignorance of e scribe could give security from this perversion. Not understanding e MS. he was compelled to copy literally, and his errors, whether rising from inadvertence or the indistinctness of the old letters, are easily ectified by the critic. The fact is, that the copyist, considering the words nly as a vehicle of the sense, did not care about the language. Every ribe, therefore, changed the language of his MS. into the dialect of his wn time and dwelling-place.

In this way *the Roman du Renard,** which can be traced to the time between the st and second crusade, is come down to us in the language of the 13th century, D. 1288, 1290, 1292. It is on this account that Mr. Roberts observes—"Avant invention de l' imprimevie le style ne conduit qu' imparfaitement a reconnoitre la

* *Le Roman du Renart public,* par M. D. M. Méon, Paris, 1826. This poem was the basis of poem in the language of Flanders, van den Vos Reynaerde, A. D. 1404. This was followed the *Dutch Renard in prose, Gouda,* 1479, and this again by the renowned *Reincke de Vos* of *enri van Alkmar, Lubek,* 1498, the parent of all later European versions. *Caxton's folio ition* of 1481, was a translation of the work published at Gouda. To the researches of cent scholars, we owe *Reinardus Vulpes, carmen epicum seculis* IX. *et* XII. *conscriptum: ad em codd. MSS. ed. et annotationibus illustravit, Fr. Jas. Mone, editio princeps,* 8vo. pp. 336. is proved by comparison, that this Latin poem has given rise to the very *Roman du Renart,* blished by Mr. Méon, and also that the author was an inhabitant of the Belgic Netherlands, the localities of which, allusion is often made. See VI. § 13—17.

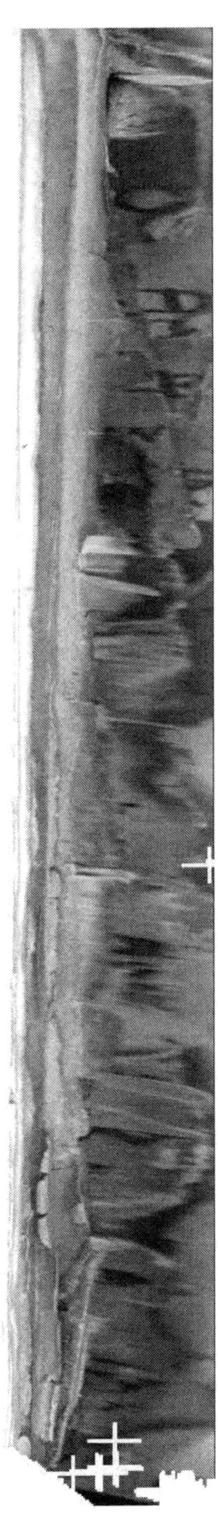

différence des temps. Les copistes ne se bornoient pas a transcrire ; ils corrigeoient l' ortographe substituoient des vers nouveaux à ceux qu' ils avoient sous les yeux, et des expressions nouvelles a celles qui tomboient si rapidement en désuétude. La langue, qui changeoit d' un joura l' autre devoit les engager à multiplier ces altérations que le peu de sévérité de l' art poetique rendoit alors si faciles."* The scribe, however, found some restraint in the alliteration, which was observed by Cædmon and other poets. In those MSS. where there was little except the rhyme to indicate the mechanism of the verses, or where the MS. was in prose, the scribe had more liberty to change. This was the fate of the oldest Dutch poet, *Maerlant.* Some leaves of parchment containing fragments of his *Spiegel Historial,* much older than the MS. from which the edition of 1785 was printed, afford conclusive evidence, that neither the construction of the words, nor the manner of spelling in the MS. used in printing this edition, was that of Maerlant himself. Therefore, the question about language during the middle ages, is reduced to the question of the time and place of the MS.

58. The same fate attended the most ancient pieces of Anglo-Saxon poetry, not to speak of prose. Let me exemplify my assertions by the poems of Cædmon. The MS. of the Cædmon on which Mr. Thorpe† founds his text, is apparently of the 10th century, and it strictly expresses the language of that period. Cædmon, the author of the poem, died about A.D. 680. He was first a cowherd at Whitby, and afterwards became a monk. Would it not be a little strange to assert, that a man brought up in his station of life, especially in the uncivilized northern parts of England, and in the 7th century, has spoken the same dialect as the far more civilized inhabitants of southern England two centuries later? This too in an age, when some parts of England had as little communication with each other, as with foreign countries. In this case, Anglo-Saxon would be an exception in the history of languages; it would be without dialect, time, and place, having produced no change in its forms. How far an assertion of this sort is distant from truth, is proved by the oldest remnant of Anglo-Saxon poetry now extant, compared with its appearance two and three centuries later. In a codex referred by Wanley to A.D. 737,‡ we read a few lines of Cædmon which are translated into Latin by Bede,§ and we have the same lines as they are modernized by Alfred in his Anglo-Saxon version of Bede, about two hundred years after Cædmon. Let us compare these two specimens with each other:—

* *Fables inédites des* XII., XIII., *et* XIV. *siècles, par A. C. M. Robert, Paris,* 1825, p. cxxii.

† *Cædmon's Metrical Paraphrase in Anglo-Saxon, with an English translation, notes, and a verbal index, by Benjamin Thorpe, London,* 1832.

‡ "Hisce pene omnibus in A.D. 737, concurrentibus, verisimile mihi videtur hunc ipsum codicem eodem anno, Ceolwlfo adhuc regnante, seu saltem ante Eadberhti inaugurationem, duobus quoque annis post Bedæ obitum, in Wiremuthensi monasterio fuisse scriptum."—*Wanley,* p. 288.

§ Bede, lib. iv. cap. 24.

edmon died A.D. 680: *this MS. is of* A.D. 737. *d. MSS. Epis. Norwicensis* Wanley*, p. 287.	*About* A.D. 885, *by King Alfred. MS. C.C.C. Oxon. Thorpe Pref. Cædm.* xxii.	*Literal English Version.*
Nu scylun hergan	Nu we sceolan herian.[f]	Now must we praise
hefaen ricaes uard	heofon-ríces weard.	the guardian of heaven's kingdom,
metudæs mæcti[a]	metodes mihte.	the creator's might,
end his mod gidanc	and his mod-geþonc.[g]	and his mind's thought,
uerc uuldur fadur	wera[h] wuldor-fæder.	glorious Father of men!
sue he uundra gihuaes	swa he wundra[i] gehwæs.	as of every wonder he,
eci drictin[b]	ece dryhten.[j]	Lord eternal,
or astelidæ.	oord[k] onstealde[l].	formed the beginning.
He ærist[c] scop	he ærest gescéop.[m]	He first framed
elda barnum	eorðan bearnum.	for the children of earth
heben til hrofe	heofon to hrófe.[n]	the heavens as a roof;
haleg scepen	halig scyppend.	holy Creator!
tha[d] middun geard	þa middan geard.	then mid-earth,
mon cynnæs uard	mon cynnes weard.	the guardian of mankind,
eci dryctin	ece dryhten.[o]	the eternal Lord,
æfter tiadæ	æfter teode.	afterwards produced;
firum foldu[e]	firum foldan.	the earth for men,
frea allmectig.	frea ælmihtig.	Lord Almighty!

Primo cantavit Cædmon istud carmen.

[a] maecti. [b] dryctin. [c] aerist. [d] þa. [e] fold:. [f] herigean. [g] geþanc. [h] *abest.* [i] wuldres. [j] drihten. [k] ord. [l] astealde B. [m] gescop. [n] rofe. [o] drihtne. *Various readings in Smith's edition of Bede*, 597, 20.

Whether the reference of the *MS. Episc. Norwicensis* to the precise year, A.D. 737, correct or not, every one will agree with Wanley, that it is far before the age of fred,† and is by no means a re-translation of the Latin words of Bede. *King Alfred* ictly follows the lines and the words of the *MS. Episc. Norwicensis*. The obser- ion of Bede,‡ that he followed the sense of *Cædmon*, and not the construction of words, applies particularly to the latter part of the *MS. Episc. Norwicensis*, l is an additional proof that Bede found his original almost in the same form as it is sented to us in *MS. Episc. Norwicensis*. Alfred seems convinced that he had the e song of Cædmon before him, as in his Anglo-Saxon translation, he not only its Bede's remark about giving merely the sense, and not the same collocation of rds, but immediately before the insertion of this Anglo-Saxon song, he asserts, ara endebyrdnes þis is" *the order of which is this.*§

* Codex MS. omnium vetustissimus non ita pridem erat penes egregium illum literarum torem *Joannem Morum* Episcopum nuper Eliensem, hodieque in Bibliotheca Regia, *Cantagiæ* asservatur, *Smith's Bede, Cantabrigiæ*, folio, 1722, *Pref.* p. 3. The MS. named by nley in note [‡ p. lvi.] described in his Catalogue as *Cod. MSS. Episcopi Norwicensis*, p. 288, is same as that mentioned by Smith in this note. *Dr. John Moore* was bishop of Norwich when nley made his Catalogue; he was afterwards bishop of Ely; after his death, king George First purchased this MS. with the Doctor's library, which he presented to the University Cambridge, where the MS. is now preserved in the Public Library.—J. B.

† Ego iterum publicandum censeo, tanquam *omnium* quæ in nostra Lingua etiamnum ent monumentorum pene vetustissimum.—*Wanley*, p. 287.

‡ Hic est sensus, non autem ordo ipse verborum quæ dormiens ille canebat; neque enim sunt carmina, quamvis optime composita, ex alia in aliam linguam, ad verbum, sine detrinto sui decoris ac dignitatis transferri.—*Bede* 4, 24; *Sm.* p. 171, 10.

§ *Bede Sm.* p. 597, 19, and just afterwards, l. 26, adds, "And þam wordum sona monig word æt ylce gemet, Gode wyrðes songes togeþeodde," *and to those words soon joined many words ong worthy of God*, IN THE SAME MEASURE.—J. B.

59. Having here the same words written in different ages, it is my intention to notice the discrepancies, that the changes the language underwent in the interval may be clearly seen.

60. In the *MS. Episc. Norwicensis*, we find no characters for þ and ƿ, the one being designated by *u*, the other by *d*, as in gidanc, or by th, as in tha for þa. In the same MS. *casula* is translated hearth for hearð. Hence may it not be inferred, that the þ and ƿ were introduced later than the date of the MS.? Or was the þ a letter of the heathen Runic alphabet, and for that reason was not admitted amongst the letters of the holy Roman church?

61. The *æ* is divided into its compounds *a* and *e*, as in hefaen, ricaes, in which a long *a* seems to be implied. Mr. Thorpe, in his second edition, p. 22, follows neither Wanley nor Smith, having hefæn, metudaes, for hefaen, metudæs; but in this, Smith also differs from Wanley, who puts mæcti for Smith's maecti.

62. The *c*, when it had the sound of *ch* was not yet changed into *h*, as in mæcti, drictin; but in later times became mihte, dryhten.

63. We find here two forms of *heaven*, the one written with *b*, and the other with *f*, hefaen ricaes and heben;* and in the *Vetus Jus Frisicum*, which is about four centuries older than the oldest laws written in Friesic, we have (Tit. iii.) thivbda for thiaftha, when the inscription is not from the hand of any Francic-Theotisc lawyer under Charlemagne.

64. The resolving of *a* into *æ* was not yet accomplished, we have fadur for fæder; *Frs. feder*, *Asg. bk*, 2, *Ch.* I. 389, 475, 612, contracted, *Frs. h.* feer.

65. The *g* in the termination of the infinitive had not yet undergone any change; hergan *celebrare* was changed by Alfred into herian, and to supply the hiatus, replaced the *g*, and changed *a* into *ea*, making herigean.

66. The *a* was already changed into *e*, where the more modern A.-S. still retains the *a*, as in end, sue, scepen, for and, swa, scapen. This was, perhaps, something peculiar to the Northumbrian dialect, agreeing with the Friesic in scepene clather *made clothes*, (*Asg. bk.* 84), but not in and *and*, (*Asg. bk.* 1); nor in *Old Frs.* and *Frs. v.* sa *thus*. Later in the *Frs. l.* we find ende like the above. They probably pronounced the words thus, éand, suéa, scéapen.

67. The *a* changed into *e* was not yet gone into *i*, as mectig, but at a later period mihtig; with *æ*, as in mæcti later mihte. Heliand has hêlag *holy*, *MS. Episc. Norwicensis* haleg, not yet halig; on the contrary, Heliand mahtig, and of course *MS. Episc. Norwicensis* mectig. It further appears, from the exchange of *e* for *æ*, that *æ* had nearly the sound of *e*, and of course like the *Fr. ai*. In terminations we find also *æ* used for *e*.

68. The vowel has undergone a different change in the enclytic *gi*. *Moes. ga* produces the usual A.-S. *ge*, when pronounced broad and like a diphthong, *ge* becomes *gi*; as, gidanc, gihuaes, for geþonc, gehwæs.

69. The vowel in the terminations of words and in all syllables unaccented, is sounded as indistinctly as the short *ĕ* or *Heb.* sheva [:]. It is a proof that a dialect has some antiquity, when these unaccented syllables have not entirely lost a distinguishing feature. The *MS. Episc. Norwicensis* has ricaes, metudæs, astelidæ, moncynnæs, tiadæ, for rices, metudes, astelide, moncynnes, tiade; and mæcti, dricti, for mæcte, dricten.

70. It is a principle in English pronunciation, that the vowel before *r* in terminations takes the sound of *u*, [Walker's *Pron. Dict.* § 98, 418]. In *MS. Episc. Nor-*

* Like *b* in *A.-S.* lybban *vivere*, *Asg. bk.* libba; in *Frs. v.* libben *vita*; *Frs. v.* libje *vivere*, and *A.-S.* lyfan *vivere*; *Asg. bk.* 189, lif *life*.

icensis we have, uuldur, fadur, for uuldor, fader. Before *n* the *a* is also changed to *u*, as fold." or foldun, middun, for foldan, middan.

71. The *a* was not yet resolved into *ea*, as ward, barnum, for wéard, béarnum; or the *o* into *eo*, as scôp [*Old. Dut.* schóep; *Ger.* gaskop *creabat*] for gescéop reeing with the present *Dut.* schíep.

72. The *e*, which has its origin in *i*, and was afterwards changed into *eo*, remained ıaltered in heben, hefaen for heofon. It seems that *eo* has produced *o* in -fon, in e same manner as *æ* proceeded from *e*, and affords an instance of some assimilation vowels in two succeeding syllables. I must add, however, that it is questionable hether the vowel of the latter syllable operates upon that of the former, or the rmer upon that of the latter. If the vowel of the former syllable depend upon that the latter, then -fæn and -fon were changed before he- and héo-; but if the latter ›on that of the former, then he- and heo- before -fæn and -fon. I do not lay much ress upon this observation, as languages in their most ancient state have not this nd of assimilation; it seems, however, to rest in the mind on the same foundation alliteration, both being a feeling for rhythm. For whatever may be the assimilation of ıe syllable to another in the same word, the same relation one word has to another two successive lines of poetry. This assimilation of vowels is called by German ammarians *umlaut*.

73. The *ia* being proper to the old Westphalian and Zelandic, undergo no change tiadæ; the *i* being changed into *e*, the *a* ought to follow the impulse and pass to *o*, ıd make teode from teon *producere*; to hape tiath *in unum conveniunt, Asg. bk.* 335; a *ducere, Em. l.* 88; tíoda *ducebat*; *Icel.* tiadi, *id.* The *Moes.* tiuhan *ducere*; uch *ducebat*; hence the *Frs. v.* teach, taech, *Frs. l.* 79, 81: but there was once an *ld Frs.* imperfect tíade, as the *Dut.* tijde.

74. So *i* had not yet passed to *e*, nor *u* to *o*, in metudæs, later metodes.

75. The imperfect astelidæ was not yet contracted to astealde.

76. It is clear that the earliest languages consisted of single words, and ıat two separate ideas were expressed by two separate words; but, by eing constantly used together, at last united in one idea and one word. he adjective, in this process, passing from adjectives, separately existing, the first and specifying component of the word, loses the adjective rmination, by doubling its accent on the principal vowel, and looks like ı adverb or preposition compounded with a word.

Thus, on ealddagum *olim*, originally on ealdum dagum *olim*; *Dut.* eertyds, iginally eeres tijds *in former times*. *Dut.* oudvader; *Ger.* altvater *a patriarch*, rmerly oude vader, and alte vater. In the *MS. Episc. Norwic.* we meet with an stance in which the meaning of such a compound appears, but the grammatical form not yet developed. The compound aelda barnum appears as two words, yet aelda not in the *dat.* as it ought to be when separate, and it only requires the process time to become one word aeldbarnum, the same as *Ger.* altvater. Aelda barnum es not signify *antiquis liberis*, but *children of old*; and thus it has the whole eaning of the compound, but only half its grammatical form. Alfred, finding the rase a little antiquated, used eorðan bearnum *filiis terræ*. There could be no jection to the form, because, in Alfred's time, ealda-fæder, ealde-moder, and ealde-ta, were sometimes used for ealdfæder *avus*, ealdmoder *avia*, ealdwita *senior clesiæ*.

77. The pronoun þe was omitted before scylun *we must*, precisely as the *Moes.* ulum *debemus, Lk.* xviii. 1.

78. In this word the *u* had not yet been changed into *eo*. From *Moes.* skulum was rived *A.-S.* scylun, the more modern scéolon.

79. As *a* had not yet gone over into *éa*, or *o* into *éo*, or *e* into *éo*, so also *e* had not yet been changed into *ea*: thus we find astelidæ for astéalde.

80. This comparison affords a few important deductions. As there appears to be no mixture of the dialect of the Northmen, the MS. must be of a date anterior to their conquest of Northumberland, which agrees with the statements of Wanley.

81. In it we find also many analogies with cognate languages not apparent in the writings of Alfred, and this affords a further proof of the antiquity of the MS.; for we have already observed, that the resemblance of languages is greater in proportion to their age, and, on the other hand, that dialect differs most which has most diverged from the parent stock.*

82. The development of the diphthongs *ea* and *eo* from simple vowels, was the result of nearly two centuries between the date of the *MS. Episc. Norwic.* and the time of Alfred; for no one, I believe, will pretend that the simple vowel in these instances was a dialectic variation peculiar to Northumberland, as these diphthongs are still distinctly pronounced there, like *death* in Yorkshire. The diphthong was of course developed in the north, as well as in the south of England. If we now go back still further, from the time of the *MS. Episc. Norwic.* to the descent of the Anglo-Saxons on Britain, [from 737 to 449,] and if we suppose that during this period the cognate languages approached nearer to the *A.-S.* in the same proportion as they did from Alfred to Cædmon, then indeed we have a clear conception how all these tribes of Jutes, Angles, Saxons, and Friesians, whose languages some centuries later were quite unintelligible to one another, could, at their departure from their native shores to Britain, as men of one speech, unite in council and action.

83. This comparison implies further, that the peculiarities by which the A.-S. is distinguished, relate to the state in which this tongue has come down to us.

84. I have nothing more to add about the Mœso-Gothic, to what I stated in the fourteenth and fifteenth paragraphs. The peculiar character of the A.-S., as distinguished from the Mœso-Gothic, would for the most part be removed, if we could trace the A.-S. to the time of the Mœso-Gothic, about the middle of the 4th century. The means of comparison are greatly increased by the exertions of Angelo Mai, Count Castiglione and Massmann.† The stores within the reach of Junius were exhausted by him, for comparison with the A.-S. in almost every word of his Glossarium Gothicum, in many articles of his Etymologicon Anglicanum, and in his other Dictionaries, still sleeping, to the common shame of the English and Friesians, in the Bodleian Library, Oxford. The first that made a classification and comparison of the Gothic languages was Lambert ten Kate, a Dutchman. The foundation laid by him has more

* § 14. † See VII. 7—11.

ently been greatly extended by the unwearied toil of Rask and Grimm. eed not boast that I have done the same, for it requires no genius—the our is purely mechanical. Some will present you with the oldest form of vord, but this is not right, when it has to be compared with a subse- ent and more advanced development. For my part, I shall not hesitate avail myself of the labours of my predecessors, and to cite parallel rds in different cases and times, when I think it does not affect the vel or consonant to be compared.

85. I do not know any A.-S. scholar, who has instituted a comparison tween the Anglo-Saxon and Friesic so minute as their near relationship ims. Some did not see the force of the comparison, and all wanted terials. A brief account of the materials I have used may not be interesting.

86. The *Asega-bôk,** the book of the judge, contains the laws of the istringian Friesians located around the gulf of the Jade, as far as the ithern banks of the Weser. Its date may be about A.D. 1212-1250.

87. *Littera Brocmannorum,*† the letter, *i.e.* the written law of the ôcmen, Friesians bordering on the sea in the western part of East- iesia, [*Dut.* Oostvriesland]. Its date is reckoned between A.D. 1276 d 1340.

88. The *Amesga-riucht,*‡ the code of the country of the Ems, con- ning registers of the mulcts for the Friesians situated about the eastern nks of the Ems, A.D. 1276-1312.

89. The *Keran fon Hunesgena londe,*§ [*Dut.* Het Hunsingoër land- cht,] the statutes of the country of Hunsingo, A.D. 1252, revised and rrected, but as to their origin of a far earlier date. This most remark- le monument of Friesian antiquity is published in the *Verhandelingen n het genootschap pro excolendo jure patrio,* tom. ii. Groningen, '78, but in a manner so negligent, that I deem it matter of great danger r a critic to cite words from this edition. I, however, entertain the easing hope, that this defect will soon be redressed by one of my friends, ho intends to publish a second edition, founded on an excellent codex ithin our reach, as soon as the literary public feel inclined to defray the sts of the press.

90. *Jeld and botha,*‖ the value of the money and the mulcts, to be

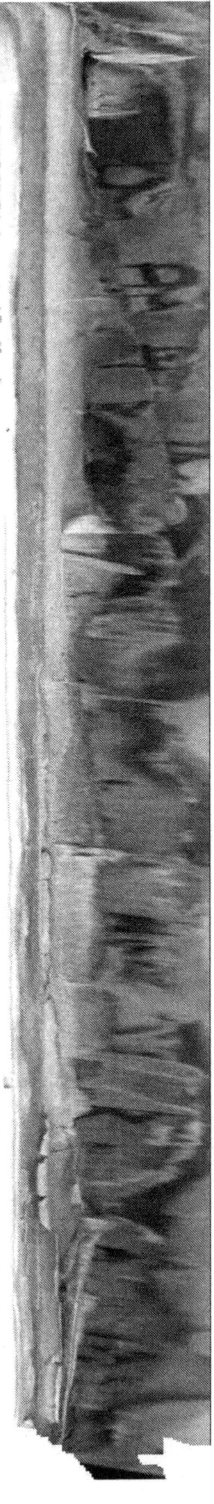

* Asega-buch ein Alt-friesisches gesetzbuch der Rustringer, herausgegeben, übersetzt und läutert von *F. D. Wiarda,* Berlin, 1805.

† Willküren der Brockmänner eines freyen Friesischen volkes, herausgegeben von *F. D. iarda,* Berlin, 1820.

‡ Het Emsiger landregt van het jaar, 1812. Leeuwarden, 1830, published by *Mr. Hettema.*

§ Verhandelingen ter nasporinge van de wetten en gesteldheid onzes vaderlands door een nootschap te Groningen, pro excolendo jure patrio, tom. v. Groningen, 1773-1828.

‖ Groot placaat en Charterboek van Vriesland, verzamelt door *G. F. Baron* thoe Schwart- nberg en Hohenlansberg, 5 vols. folio; Leeuwarden, 1768-1793. The pages 59—461, ntaining a catalogue of the ecclesiastical estates in Friesia, made up by order of Charles V. ough already printed, are suppressed in the 3rd volume, and replaced by other materials. great number of the estates, after the Spanish revolution, having fallen into unjust hands, it as feared that the publication would be an inducement to endless curses and persecutions ainst the aristocracy. The 6th tome is also printed, but not yet published, for the reatest number of the copies was burnt during the disorders of the French Revolution.

observed in several parts of the country of Friesia, forming a part of the present kingdom of the Netherlands. This piece is of A.D. 1276, and published in the Groot placaat en Charterboek van Vriesland, tom. i. p. 97, together with a great many little records of latter times in the Friesian tongue.

91. The most complete system of Friesian laws,* though of a more recent date than the foregoing, is contained in the *Old Friesian Laws*, published by two eminent Friesian lawyers, *P. Wierdsma* and *Brantsma*, whose commentary bears witness to the depth and extent of their erudition. The laws in this collection, as well as those found in the Charterboek, had force chiefly within the limits of the country of Friesia in the Netherlands.

92. To the same country belongs also the collection of charters dispersed in the history of its capital Leeuwarden, by Gabbema.† They are all of a recent date, when the Friesic was about to be disused in public charters. In the enumeration of these laws and records, I have descended from the north to the south, beginning at the Wezer and ending at Old Friesia, situate at the mouth of the Rhine. But let us now ascend still higher, beginning with the Friesians conterminous with the Angles.

93. Friesic is still spoken in a tract of country bordering the coast of the German sea, in the district of Bredsted, dutchy of Schleswig. It is strongly tainted with Danish; but a corn-merchant of my native village, [Friesia, part of the Netherlands,] on going there to buy rapeseed, was not a little surprised that he and the peasants could understand each other in their respective mother-tongues. The late Reverend N. Outzen has left a glossary of the Friesic dialect, which for some years has been in the press, at the expense of the Royal Society of Copenhagen. The first eighty-eight pages, which were intended for me by my friend the late Professor Rask, and sent to me through the courteous attention of Professor Rafn, have fully convinced me of the identity of this dialect with the other branches of the Friesic.

94. Of the language of the Ditmarsian Friesians, and those living between the Elbe and Wezer, nothing remains. Their long and obstinate struggle against the aggressions of the Danish kings, Bremish bishops, or dukes of Oldenburg,‡ terminating with the extinction of their liberty and language, has long since effaced the last trace of the Friesian tongue and nationality, and destroyed the MSS. of their ancient laws.

95. A more lucky fate was allotted to the land between the Wezer and

* Oude Friesche wetten met eene Nederduitsche vertaling en ophelderende aantekeningen voorzien. Part I. Campen en Leeuwarden, 1782. The Preface and Part II., though prepared by the publishers, were lost after the death of Wierdsma.

† Verhaal van de stad Leeuwaarden-beschreeven van *Simon Abbes Gabbema*, Franeker, 1701.

‡ U. Emmius, Hist. Fries. 145, 588, &c. Wiarda, Ostfrisische geschichte, I. 202.

e Ems. The latter subjugation of this country has caused the eserving of a single codex of the Asega-bôk in the archives of .denburg. I here give a specimen of its language.

Thit is thet twintegoste londriucht. hwersa northmann an thet lond hla- ;h. and hia enne mon fath. and bindath. ut of lande ledath. and eft withir to ıde brangath and hini ther to twingath et hi husbarne. and wif nedgie. and ın sle and gadis hus barne. and hwed hi to lethe dwa mi. alsa hi thenne dfliuch ieftha lesed werth. and withir londe kumth. and to liodon sinon. willath him tha liode thing to seka. d sinne opa werpa[a] truch thet ginte[c] ɔrth ther hi er mith tha witsingon[d] enuth[e] heth. Sa mire thenne afara ene warf gunga. and iechta mire tala. ne eth hach[f] hi thenne opa tha heligon swerande. thet hit al dede bi there de. alsa him sin hera bad. ther hi was es. and lethana[g] en unweldich mon. ne thuruon[h] him tha liode ne frana. halda seka ni sinna truch thet thi frana muchte him thes fretha[i] waria[j] thi alk[k] skolde dwa alsa him sin hera bad uch thes liues willa.—*Asega-bôk*, p. 97.

This is the twentieth landright (law). When any Northman leaps on the land (*shore*), and he takes a man, and binds and leads (*him*) out of the land, and brings (*him*) after (*wards*) to the land (*ashore*) and forces him to this, that he burns houses and violates wives, and slays men and burns God's houses, and what he may do to harm, (A.-S. laðe.) When he then flees away or is loosed, and again comes to land, and his lede[b] (*is restored to his land and kindred*). If then the court of justice of the people will seek him (*prosecute him*), and his relations intend to charge him with the horrible murder which he has ere (*formerly*) framed (*committed*) with the pirates; he may then go (*appear*) before the court, and he may tell (*confess*) known and proved facts; he ought then to swear an oath by the saints, that he did it all by need (*force*), as his lord bade him, because he was a man not wielding his life (*body*) and members. In this case, neither the lede (*people*), nor the king's attorney, nor his relations, e allowed to seek him (*harass him*) with fetters, through (*because*) that the torney might not (*was unable*) to secure him his safety. The servant should as his lord bade him through will of the life (*for the sake of his life*).

[a] A.-S. weorpan, werpan, *jacere*. [b] Lede *people*, *Jun. Et. Angl.*

[c] ginte Wiarda translates *yonder*. I deem it to be *horrible, tremendous murder*, which agrees th the Low-Saxon version of the Asega-bôk, which has *great, enormous murder*. This word connected with A.-S. ginian, of course *yawning, enormously vast, horrible*. In this way the nglish adj. huge *vast, great even to deformity*, explains the meaning of *Icel.* ugr *terror*, whence ly; of A.-S. oge, whence *Frs. v.* [ouw-lik] onjouwlik *horrible*, all derived from the idea of ide vastness, still apparent in *Moes.* auhn, *Swed.* ogn, ugn.

[d] *A.-S.* wicing *pirata*. The *c* by the Friesic and English being changed into *tsh*, wicing ecomes witsing. Thus *A.-S.* cerene, *Frs. v.* tsher'ne or tsjerne, *Eng. churn*. Sometimes the rs. v. retains both forms with some shade of the signification: *Frs. v.* kâtje *to talk*, but jatterje *to chat, chatter*. From *A.-S.* cidan, properly *to make a noise as an inharmonious bird*, ıd hence *to quarrel*, the *Frs. v.* has only tsjitte *to make a noise as quarrelling sparrows and omen*. The original signification, now lost in English, was very well known in the old nglish. "The swalowes *chyterid* and songe."—Golden Legend, I. 493. *Frs. v.* De swéalen jittene in songen.—It is dubious whether wicing is to be derived from wic-cing *sinus vel pæ unde insidiabantur pirata, rex*, or from wig-cing *the king of slaughter*.

[e] *A.-S.* fremad. Wiarda not knowing this Anglo-Saxon word, deems *efrenuth* to be ɔurious; for this word does not occur elsewhere. This instance may teach us how easily the ost difficult words are explained in Anglo-Saxon and Friesic, when aided by each other.

[f] Ah *possidet*, proprie, *vinctus est*, of the verb agan. [g] *A.-S.* liðа.

[h] The Anglo-Saxon has the Friesian form in this verb thurfon.

[i] *A.-S.* friðian *protegere*, frið *pax*. [j] *A.-S.* warian *cavere*. [k] *A.-S.* scéalc *servus*.

96. Let it be remarked, that the *u* having the power of *ou* in *Fr.* doux, or *Eng. cube*, is changed by the *Frs. v.* into *o*; undfliuch, unweldich, mucht, truch, gunga, are now pronounced *ontflyucht, onweldich, mocht, troch, gonge.*

97. Brocmen kiasath thet to enre kere[a] thet ther nene burga and mura[b] and nannen hach sten hus ne mota wesa bi achta mercum. and hoc redieua thit naud ne kerth and efter naud ne dele leith. sa geie[c] hi mith achta mercum and mitha huse wit [h]liude. hine skiriene[d] fon. and werther aeng mon [h]agera sa tuelef ier[d]foda hac [h]andre[e] tiuke, and wasa welle makia enne szelnre sa mot hi ne makia vr tua feke.[f] ief hi welle. andre thiuke. and makath aeng otheres sa geie hi mith achta mercum,[g] thi ther otheres wercth. and tha nya redieua skelin hit onfa,[h] efter tham ther tha erra[i] thene frethe vt kethet[j] bi alsa denre geie. Stenslek[k] hwile efter al tha londe buta munekum and godes husen bi alsa denre geie.—*Statutes of the Brocmen*, p. 130.

Brocmen choose (*made*) this to a statute, that there no borough (*castle*) and wall, and no high house of stone must be by (*the mulct*) of eight marks: and whatsoever rede-giver (*counsel, judge*) hinders not this, and after (*being built*) lays not (*pulls*) down, he may atone for it with eight marks, and with the house with (*the*) lede (*people*), unless he clears himself. And turns (*builds*) any man higher than twelve earth-feet (*a measure*) high to the roof, and who will (*intends to*) make a cellar, he must not make over (*above*) two stories. If he will (*intends*) to the roof and makes any (*thing*), otherwise let him atone for it with eight marks, who works otherwise. And the new judges shall accept it after the former (*judges*) have proclaimed the peace (*this statute for the public security*) by the mulct mentioned. Let stone-cutting cease through all the land, but (*except in building*) monks' and God's houses by the mulct mentioned.

98. From this example it may be seen that the text is corrupt, and cannot be cited without employing some criticism. It suffices, however, to show the extreme jealousy of a free people for their liberty, so as even not to allow the building of a house of stone, or of more than two stories above a cellar, that the possessor might not thence annoy his countrymen, and use his house as an instrument of tyranny. Building their churches alone of stone, they fortified them at the same time, together with the surrounding parishes; and this forming a single connected stronghold, they retired there after the loss of a battle, and defended at the same moment the two dearest possessions of mankind, their liberty and their altars, against the insults of oppression. It is for this reason that Friesland does not offer any ruins of castles of the middle age to the eye of the antiquary, which are of so frequent occurrence on the borders of the Rhine and almost in every part of Europe. They still retain their ground, name,

[a] *A.-S.* curan *eligere.* [b] *A.-S.* mur *murus.*
[c] *Icel.* geigr *offensa, clades.* [d] *A.-S.* scir *purus.*
[e] An *there.* [f] *A.-S.* fæc *spatium.* [g] *A.-S.* mearc *moneta quædam.*
[h] *A.-S.* andfoa *accipere.* [i] *A.-S.* ærra, æra *prior.* [j] *A.-S.* cyðan *notum facere.*
[k] *A.-S.* stæn *lapis,* slæge *ictus,* slecge *malleus major. Frs. v.* slei *malleus major ligneus.*

nguage and national character, the only remnant of Friesian antiquity nknown to the travelling antiquary, whose eyes are attracted by the ore glaring objects of old walls, palaces, tombs, and castles. It is most kely that we are indebted to these statutes for the absence of any vaulted llar in Friesia. What castles there are, owe their origin to the fatal ternal wars of the Schieringers and Vetkopers in the 14th and 15th nturies. The Friesians, however, stood not in want of cellars as they not like any salted vegetables, or vegetables at all; flour, peas and beans, lted meat in the winter, and some fresh in summer, being their ordinary od, they do not lay up any provisions. I speak from the experience of my n childhood, when every one, in winter as well as summer, daily bought at he wanted, and a single cellar was amongst the curiosities of the llage and its neighbourhood.

99. § VI. Ther ne mot nen mon er wiwe god wrkapie[a] er thet hie der[b] to hape[c] tein[d] hebbath.—*nasga-riucht*, p. 59.

There must no man sell the goods (bona *possessions*) of his wife before they have reared children.

§ LXV. Hvasa[e] annen vnseheldigen n feth sunder ther rediewe willa sa ckt hi en grat merc anda alsa ful to e.[f]—p. 84.

Whoso arrests an unguilty (*innocent*) man without the will (*authority*) of the judge, he so breaks (*forfeits*) a great mark (*to the judge*) and as much to the injured person.

§ LXXI. Ther ne mey nen munik e erfnisse ieftha lawa fagie alsa hi wen is fon feider noch fon moder, fon ter noch fon broder noch fon sine ndem nen god wither eruie[g] ther hi ath[h] claster brocht heth ieftha inna ster wunnen heth.—p. 89.

There may no monk, as he is withdrawn (*from the world*), fetch (*accept*) an inheritance or leavings (*bequests*) from father or from mother, from sister or from brother, or from his friends; (on the contrary) let nobody inherit any possession he has brought into the cloister, or has won in the cloister.

100. Let us now pass over the Ems in the northern part of the gdom of the Netherlands, called the province of Groningen [en de nmelanden], containing close to the sea the district of Hunsingo.

Prima Petitio.

Thet is thiu forme kest end' thes enges Kerles jeft end' riucht alra[i]

This is the first statute and the gift of king Charles, and the right of all

A.-S. ceapian *emere et vendere; Frs. v.* kéapje *emere*, forkéapje *vendere*, here wrkapie.

A.-S. cenned *natus, productus*, contracted to cen'd, kind *child*, like bearn *filius*, from n *ferre utero*, hio kenneð *or* bereð sunu *pariet filium, R. Mt.* 1, 21.

A.-S. héapum *by troops;* to hape *in a single heap*, i. e. *together.*

Tia *producere*, part. tegen, contr. tein *productus; A.-S.* téon *ducere*, part. tegen *vel* togen.

A.-S. swa hwylcman swa *quicumque homo.*

Bote, *A.-S.* bote *reparation* [*of the harm*] *to the injured person.* But *A.-S.* brecan *to k*, relates to the breaking of the law, and indicates the mulct to be paid to the representer e law, the judge.

A.-S. yrf, erf *pecus, bona, hæreditas.*

[h] Inna ith.

Hwelic, contr. *A.-S.* hwelc, *omnium hominum quisque*, alra monna hwelic.

Fresena thet alra monna hwelic and sine gode bisitte [a] alsa longe saret [b] unforwerkat [c] hebbe.—p. 2.

Friesians, that every one occupies his possessions as long as he has not forfeited them.

Decima Petitio.

Thet is thiu tiande kest thet Fresan ni thuren nene hereferd [d] firra fara sa aster tore [e] Wisere and wester to tha Fli be thiu thet hia hira lond bihelde [f] wither thet hef [g] and wither there hethena here. Thia bed thi kenenk Kerl thet hia firra tha hereferd fore aster til Hiddes [h] eckere ande wester til cincfallum. [i] tha bihelden hit tha liude wither thene keneng thet hia nene hereferd firra fara ne thorste sa aster til there wisere and wester to tha Fli. truch thet as scelen alle Fresa fon tha North fri [j] wesa.—*Keran fon Hunesgena londe*, p. 6.

This is the tenth statute, that the Friesians need not follow a campaign further eastward than to the Weser, and westward to the Flie; that they may hold their land against the sea, and against the host of the heathens (*Northmen*). Then king Charles bade that they should fare (*follow*) the campaign further eastward to Hitsakker, and westward to Sinkfal. Then the people maintained their right against the king, that they needed not fare (*follow*) the campaign further eastward than to the Weser, and westward to the Flie. Through this all Friesians shall be free (*protected, secured*) from the north.

101. Over the river Lauwers, now but a brook, we pass into Old-Friesia, properly so called.

Old-Friesian Laws.	*Country-Friesian.*	*English.*
Dat oder landriucht is. hweerso dyo moder her kyndes eerwe foerkapet, jefta foerwixled [k] mit her fryonda reed eer dat kind [l] jerich is; als hit jerich se likje him di kaep so halde	Dat óare lóan-riúcht is: hwersa dy móar [m] hjar berns erfscip forkéapet of forwixelt mei hjar fréonen ríed foár 't it bern jirrich is; as it jirrich is, liket [n] hìm dy kéap, sa halde hy	The other land right is: whenever the mother sells the inheritance of her child, or exchanges (*it*) with rede (*counsel*) of her friends (*kindred*), before the child is of age; when

[a] *A.-S.* besittan *possidere.* [b] Sa er het.

[c] *A.-S.* wyrcan *facere.* *A.-S.* forwyrcan *faciendo perdere, amittere, mulctari.*

[d] *A.-S.* here *exercitus*, fere *iter*. Thus the *A.-S.* heregang *irruptio*, faran *ire*.

[e] To there. [f] *A.-S.* behéaldan *custodire.*

[g] *A.-S.* ofer héafo *super mare*, Beow. Ed. Kemble, 1833, p. 171.

[h] A little town or village near Danneberg, close to the Elbe—at present, Hitzacker.

[i] Sinkfal close to the mouth of the Schelde. See Van Wijn and Siccama, cited § 36. It is now called *het Zwin* and *het Hazegat.*

[j] Friðian *protegere.*

[k] The word wixelje, whose theme wix or wex, is obvious nearly in all kindred dialects; it sounds in *A.-S.* wrix. *A.-S.* wrixian *permutare.* The Scots, however, use to *whissle.*

[l] Kynd is unknown in the Country-Friesic, as in the *A.-S.* and Eng.

[m] Móar is now used in contempt, or to indicate the mother of a beast. The term equal to mother is *mem.*

[n] Lykje and *A.-S.* lician are neuter verbs with the regimen of a dative, like the Lat. in placet mihi, mannum lycað *hominibus placet.* In English, the neuter signification has nearly degenerated into the active; for *to like* signifies more to approve with preference, than to please.

ten[a] ende liker[b] him et so fare hit[c] oen syn ı eerwe sonder stryd le sonder schulde.

't him, in lykke er him net sa farre hy it óan syn ein erfscip sonder striid in sonder scild.

he is of age, likes he the bargain, let him hold it (*to the purchaser*), and does he not like it, let him fare (*enter*) on his own inheritance without strife and without debts.

So hwaso dat kind bicht jefta birawet op syn n eerwe so breckt hy en lyoedmerck ende to as dine frana[d] dat sint ı schillingen: ende alle lyoed agen him to lpen ende di frana, dat comme op syn ayn rwe, deer hy eer bi chta aechte: hit ne se t hioet[e] seld habbe jef th, jef wixled truch dera a haudneda een, deer o dis kyndes des lives ede hulp. Dyo forme ed is: hweerso een nd jong is finsen ende ered noerd oer hef, jefta ther wr birgh,[f] soe moet o moder her kyndes rwe setta ende sella de her kynd lesa ende s lives bihelpa. Dive der need is jef da jere ore wirdet ende di heta nger wr dat land faert de dat kynd honger era wil, so moet dio oder her kyndes eerwe tta ende sella ende capia er bern ku[g] ende ey[h]

Hwasa it bern befiúcht of bestelt op syn eigen erf sa brekt hy tsjíen ljomerk in tsjin de frana binne dat iénintweintich sceljen, in al de ljo hawwe de frana in him to helpjen, dat hy op syn ein erf komt der 't him eren nei riúchten takaém, as it net is dat hja it forkoft het, of forset, of wixle troch íén fen de tryë haédneden, der hja it berns libben mei holp. Dy eerste need is: hwersa ien bern jong is finsen in fitere nóard oer sé of suwdlik oer berch, sa mat de móar hjar berns erfscip forsette in forkéapje, in hjar bern losse in it libben beholpje (bewarje). De óare need is: as de jirren djoer wirde in de hjitte honger oer it lóan fart in it bern fen honger stjerre wol, sa mat de móar hjar berns erfscip forsette in forkéapje, in kéapje hjar bern ky[i] in eikes (sciep) in kóarn der me

Whoever fights or bereaves the child on his own ground, he forfeits ten ledemarks (marks to be paid to the people as wronged), and to the king's attorney[d] the mulct is XXI shillings; and all the lede (*people*) ought to help him and the king's attorney, that he may come to his own inheritance, which he owned before by right; unless she has sold, or set (*pawned*), or exchanged it through one of the three head needs (*necessities*) by which she helped the life of the child. The first need is: whenever a child is made prisoner and fettered[j] northward over the sea, or southward over the mountains, the mother must set (*pawn*) and sell her child's inheritance, and release her child and save its life. The other need is: if the years become dear, and sharp hunger goes over the land, and the child will starve[k] of hunger, then the mother

[a] Hi *or* hjam it him. [b] Like er. [c] Hi it.

[d] From *fra*, properly the first, fréa *dominus*, and frana *the lord*, *i. e.* the king's attorney in e court of justice; summus, princeps, *i. e.* judex populi, § 48.

[e] Hioe it, effer hjoe it. [f] *A.-S.* béorh, byrg *collis, arx, civitas; borough.*

[g] Ku *cow*. Of ku pl. Lf. 91, 93, 152. *A.-S.* cu *cow*, pl. cu, gen. cuna.

[h] *A.-S.* Eowu *ovis matrix; ewe.*

[i] Kou *cow*, pl. ky; *y* sounds like *e* in *me*, or like the Dut. *ij* in *mij*.

[j] *A.-S.* feter *pedica*.

[k] Starve is not to be derived from *Dut.* sterven *to die*, but from *Ic.* at starfa *laborare, ærumis premi*. For to starve, is to suffer all sorts of misery, in use chiefly that of hunger; for this eason *starveling*, properly *ærumnosus*, is used in the sense of *hungry, lean, pining*. Lye has téarfian without authority; but steorfa *pestis* is in Lup. I., where Lye properly cites the English phrase, A starfe take you, *te pestis perdat*. *Dut.* sterven *to die*, is not the first, but he second meaning.

ende coern, deerma da kinde des liues mede helpe. Dyo tredde need is: als dat kynd is al stocknaken[a] jefta huuslaes, ende dan di tiuestera[b] nevil[c] ende calda winter oencomt, so faert aller manick oen syn hof[d] ende oen syn huis ende an waranne[e] gaten, ende da wylda dier seket dyn holla baem ende der birgha hly, aldeer hit syn lyf oen bihalda mey; sa weinet[f] ende scryt[g] dat onjeriga kind ende wyst[h] dan syn nakena lyae ende syn huuslaes ende syn fader deer him reda schuld to jenst dyn honger ende winter nevil cald dat hi so diepe ende dimme mitta fiower neylen is onder eke ende onder

it bern mei yn 't libben helpt (halt). De tredde need is: as it bern alleheel stóaknéaken of huwsléas is, in den de tsiústere nevel in de kalde winter óankomt, sa fart (tsjocht) alle man yn syn hóaf in yn syn huws in yn warjende gatten, in de wylde djier siikje de holle beam in de lyte fen de bergen, der it syn liif yn behalde mei; sa weint in scriemt it onjirrige bern in wiist den syn néakene léa in syn huwsléazens, in syn faer, der him rede scoe tsjin de honger in de winter-nevel-kalde, that hy sa djip in dimster (tsiúster) mei de fjouwer neilen onder de iik in onder de ierde is besletten in be-

must set (*pawn*) and sell her child's inheritance, and buy her child cows and ewes and corn, wherewith the life of the child is helped (*preserved*). The third need is: when the child is stark-naked, or houseless, and then the dark fog and the cold winter come on, when every man fares (*enters*) his house and its appurtenances, and lurking holes, and the wild deer (*beasts*) seek the hollow beam (*tree*) and the lee[1] of the mountains, where it may save its life; then moans and weeps the minor child, and shows his naked limbs and his being houseless, and [points at] his father, who should provide for him against hunger and the

[a] *A.-S.* stoc *stipes, truncus; stock.*

[b] *A.-S.* þéoster *dark.*

[c] *A.-S.* newelnysse *nubes.*

[d] *A.-S.* hôf *domus, spelunca.*

[e] *A.-S.* warian *to defend*, wariande, by assimilation, waranne, part. pres. act. *defending* Wara, inf. Sch. 103, a. *to defend.* The first stronghold was an enclosure, and the root of the signification of the verb is in *A.-S.* wær *septum.* Wera or wer *hedge, fence*, Lf. 204.

[f] *A.-S.* Wanian *plorare.* Weine is in *Frs. v. to moan like a sick man*, sc. *to croon.*

[g] Likewise scria *to weep*, from *Icel.* kria *quæri; Icel.* at krita *minurire*, or rather from *to cry*, also *to scream: Frs. v.* scrieme *to weep*, from *A.-S.* hreman.

[h] *A.-S.* wisian *to show*, obvious in *weather-wiser.*

[1] The root *hle* and *le* exists in *A.-S.* hligan: þe þec men hligað *which incline thee to man;* where the reading of hnigað for hligað is to no purpose at all, *Cd.* 235, 25, *Ed. Thorpe.* The Icelanders have the same root in their hlickr *obliquitas, curvamen.* To this is perhaps also related *A.-S.* ligan, (*inclinare*) *cubare, jacere,* (*tegere*) *mentiri.* *Moes.* hliga *tabernaculum*, shows that the aspiration originally belonged to *Moes.* ligan *jacere.* The other form, *Moes.* laugnjan, nearly equivalent to *Goth.* liugan (*tegere*) *mentiri et uxorem ducere*, whence *A.-S.* leogan *to lie*, signifies to hide and to deny, in which the same transition of the sense is observable. In the same manner, *A.-S.* þacian *tegere*, and *Moes. Gott.* thahan *tacere.*

The second form is furnished with a *d* in *Icel.* at hlída *inclinare, cedere, obedire*, from *Icel.* hlíd *devexitas vel latus montis*, whence also *Dan.* en fjeldlie. Lida, besides the *h*, takes also *s* and *g* in to slide and to glide, *per devexa labi.* To cover by inclining, hence *A.-S.* hlid *covering, potlid; Ems. Land.* 8, 82, hlid *eyelid; Frs. v.* éachlid, lid *potlid; Icel.* hlid *ostium, porta* (*the cover of the entrance*). The Goths had likewise this form in their hleithva *a tent.*

I return to *le* without a final consonant, *A.-S.* hleo *covering, shelter, refuge; Ab.* 86, *place sheltered from the wind. The lee side, Dut.* de lij (a sea term) *the side of the ship not exposed to the wind.* As the sailor must determine the situation of surrounding objects from the relative position of his vessel, the coast opposite to his lee-side is called by him the lee-shore, though it is the shore towards which the wind blows, and necessarily must blow. The sailor does not regard the position of the shore as to the wind, but as to the sides of his vessel, and lee in this phrase denotes too, *calm, quiet.* I was induced to make these remarks to silence an objection of Dr. Jamieson, who concludes, from the signification of lee-shore, that lee, *Scot.* le, cannot be *sheltered from the wind*, and derives the word from *Icel.* lá, lea. See Todd's Johnson in loco, Jamieson in loco.

eerda bisloten[a] ende acht;[b] so moet dio der her kindes eerwe ta ende sella, om dat da bihield[c] habbe le biwaer also lang so onjerick is, dat hit forste ner oen hoen- naet forfare.[d]

ditsen; sa mat de mŏar hjar berns erfscip forsette in forkéapje, om dat hja it opsicht het in de be- wæring sa lang as it on- jirrich is, dat it ŏan frŏast of ŏan honger net for- farre (forreisgje, stjerre).

wintry fog-cold, that he so deep and dim (*dark*) is locked up and covered under the oak and under the earth with four nails (*spikes to fasten the coffin*): so the mother must set (*pawn*) and sell her child's inheritance, since she has the keeping and guarding as long as [the child] is under age, that it dies not from frost or from hunger.

102. Let us now pass over the Zuiderzee, formerly the northern tlet of the Rhine, and by the irruptions of the German ocean enlarged a mediterranean sea. The Friesians living on that side were ever the ject of the tyranny of the Dutch counts, [Hollandsche Graven,] and ter a furious struggle of three hundred years, in which their love of edom and undaunted bravery recalled the days of Greece, they were at st subdued by the united forces of the Count and Emperor. Political wer, assisted by the influence of the priests, soon triumphed in spoiling eir national language and character. The country is, however, in some aps still marked Westfriesland, now called Noordholland; and when at msterdam you pass the Y, a narrow water separating this town from estfriesland, you perceive distinctly that you are amongst another ople. The peculiarities of Zaandam, Broek, and other villages by hich the inhabitants of North Holland are distinguished from other utchmen, are too well known to be recorded here. I will only mention e particular, that the peasants of Waterland still spoke Friesic in the iddle of the 17th century.

103. We pass from North to South Holland. As we proceed and proach nearer to Sincfalla, (now the *Swin* or *Hazegat*, on the left side the mouth of the Scheld,) the ancient southern border of Friesia, we nd the Friesians, who were thinly scattered along the coasts, were the rlier blended with their more powerful neighbours. Nor are any aces of their tongue and character to be found, except in a few names of llages. It, however, deserves our attention, that the Flemish tongue

[a] Read bisletten, part. præt. pass. of the verb bisluta *to enclose*. Hence the *Scot.* to slott *to lt.* The root is *Moes.* and *A.-S.* lukan *to close*, preceded by the sibilation.

[b] Bitekka *to cover*, bitacht *covered*. *A.-S.* þeccan *to cover*, þéaht *covered*. Hence takere *e case which covers and holds the feathers of a bed.* Takeres-jefta *the sum paid by the bride to r brother-in-law for ceding her his half in the bed of her man*, *Frs. l.* 29. The Dutch in full *ddetijk*, and by ellipsis *tijk*, like the Eng. *tick*; *Frs. v.* teek, from *A.-S.* þecan. It is singu- r, that the *Eng.* thatch, and the *Frs. v.* tek, have passed both in the special signification of *raw laid upon the top of a house to keep out the weather.*

[c] *A.-S.* behéoldan *custodire, despicere; to behold.* The *Frs. v.* have behald *to keep, to have;* it not in the signification of *to view.*

[d] *A.-S.* forfaran *perire*, compounded of for and faran *to go*, as perire of per and ire.

now in use in that part of Belgium, bordering the southern frontier of Friesia, has retained a great many Friesian forms of words.

104. It is for the third time that I return to Jutland, to investigate the relics of the Friesian tongue, still existing in some dialects.

105. The remains of the Friesic on the western coast, conterminous to that of the Angles, have been mentioned, § 93.

106. East-Friesia, lying between the Ems and the Jade, has forfeited all its claims to Friesian nationality. About the end of the 17th century, the people still spoke Friesic, though greatly corrupted by broad Low-Saxon. I am in possession of the celebrated *Memoriale Linguæ Friesicæ*, exhibiting the state of this language in 1691, composed by Johannes Cadovius Muller, the clergyman of Stedesdorf.

107. On the east side of East-Friesia, lies a small tract of country enclosed by the Ems and the Lee, which from its marshy ground is inaccessible during several months of the year; it is called Sagelterland, or Saterland, where Friesic is still spoken. In this retired spot, which has no way of access, and offers no allurements to strangers in hopes of gain, many thousand words represent the true sounds of Friesian speech.

Amongst these many bear a striking resemblance to English words, not apparent in the present Country-Friesic. For instance, *Sagel.* ji; *Frs. v.* ja; *Eng.* yes; *A.-S.* gise. *Sagel.* jier; *Frs. v.* jíer; *Eng.* year; *A.-S.* géar. *Sagel.* liddel; *Frs. v.* lyts; *Frs. h.* lyk; *Eng.* little. *Sagel.* noase; *Frs. v.* noas; *Eng.* nose; *A.-S.* nose. *Sagel.* queden; *Eng. imperf.* quoth; *A.-S.* cweðan. *Sagel.* slepen; *Frs. v.* sliepe; *Eng.* to sleep. *Sagel.* two; *Frs. v.* twa; *Eng.* two; *A.-S.* twa. *Sagel.* fiaurtin; *Frs. v.* fjirtjin; *Eng.* fourteen: and as to the shades of signification in such words as *Sagel.* miede *meadow; Frs. v.* miede *hayland.* Saterland, forming part of the kingdom of Hanover, has the same king as England.

108. We lastly enter Friesia, properly so called, which is surrounded on the north, west, and south, by the Zuiderzee, forming almost a peninsula, and frequented little by strangers, unless it be for the sake of commerce. Here the Friesians have manifested their national feelings; here Tacitus and his contemporaries fixed their residence; here the Friesians dwelt in past ages, and, through all the vicissitudes of time, here they remain to the present day. It is for this reason that the French geographer observes: "Dixhuit siécles ont vu le Rhin changer son cours et l'ocean engloutir ses rivages; la nation Frisonne est restée debout comme un monument historique, digne d'interesser egalement les descendans des Francs, des Anglo-Saxons, et des Scandinaves."* This country bears the simple name of Friesia [Friesland], which has continued unaltered through all ages, and was respected even by Napoleon himself, who altered all other names. The surrounding parts are named according to their relative position with regard to this centre; hence the name of East-Friesia between the Ems and the Jade, and West-Friesia on the opposite coast of the Zuiderzee.

* Précis de la Geographie Universelle, par M. Malte-Brun, tom. i. p. 344, Paris, 1810.

109. It is, however, not merely the name which distinguishes Old-riesia in the present day, it is also the language of its inhabitants, hich, from the circumstance of its being unintelligible to the Dutch, still roves itself to be Friesian. At least a hundred thousand people speak e language commonly called Country-Friesic, which on comparison ill be found to possess more true Anglo-Saxon sounds than any other ialect. In § 101, I have already given a specimen of the Old-Friesic of e 13th century, with a Country-Friesic version. I shall now add other specimen, being a literal version of some stanzas by the Countess Blessington, occurring in the Book of Beauty of the year 1834.

110. This and the other specimen (§ 101) exhibit the Country-Friesic its present state.

Country-Friesic.

Hwat bist dou, libben?[a]
Ien wirch[b] stribjen[c]
Fen pine, noed[d] in soárch;
Lange oeren fen smerte,
In nochten[g]—ho koárt!
Det fordwine de moárns.

Déad, hwat bist dou,
Ta hwaem allen buwgje,
Fen de scepterde kening ta de slawe?
De lætste, bæste fréon,[h]
Om uws soárgen to eingjen,
Dyn gebiet is yn 't græf.

Wenneer se allen binne fled
Jouwst dou ien bæd,
Wær wy kalm yn sliepe:
De wounen alle hele,
De digerige éagen segele,
Dy lang díene[k] wekje in gepje.[l]

Stanzas by the Countess of Blessington.

What art thou, Life?
A weary strife
Of pain, care,[e] and sorrow;
Long hours of grief,[f]
And joys—how brief!
That vanish the morrow.

Death, what art thou,
To whom all bow,
From sceptred king to slave?
The last, best friend,
Our cares to end,
Thy empire is in the grave.

When all have fled
Thou giv'st a bed,
Wherein we calmly[i] sleep:
The wounds all heal'd,
The dim[j] eyes seal'd,
That long did wake and weep.

a & c As *strife* is to stribjen, so is *life* to libben, § 63.

b From wirich, *A.-S.* werig *fatigatus*, by contraction wirch.

d Noed *solicitude, risk.*

e *Moes. A.-S.* car, and *Eng.* care, all signifying cura, find their original signification in the s. v. kar *choice.* For as the *Dut.* proverb says, Keus baart angst *in optione cura.*

f The word grief is *Eng.* and *Dut.*, whence the *Fr.* grief. It is not from gravis, but from t. grieven *to stab;* the same with greva *to dig*, *Frs. l.* 303; *Dut.* graven, whence *Eng.* grave; -S. græft *sculptura;* *A.-S.* græf; *Frs. v.* græf *grave.*

g Nocht *pleasure*, properly *plenty*, from nôach, *A.-S.* nôh *enough*, or nóachje *to satisfy.*

h The Old-Friesic has fríond, *Asg. bk.* 20, 91; *Frs. l.* 162, and fríund, being part. act. of e verb fría *to love, court.* The *Frs. v.* agrees with the *A.-S.* fréond in fréon, pronounced also eun. Friend is the *Dut.* form vriend.

i Calm. The analogy of the consonants points out γαληνη as the same word, but the deriva-n cannot be pursued further, unless in the Greek itself.

j Dimme *obscure*, *Asg. bk.* 87, b.

k Diene. A literal version, contrary to the genius of the Friesic, which forms its imp. like e *A.-S.* without the auxiliary verb *to do.* Low-Saxon characters, however, offer often the words, er doet men het niwasschen, mangelen, &c., literally *Here men (people) do calendering*, &c. calender, calenders.

l Gepje. This word is not *Frs. v.*, it is *Hindelopian*, putting *g* for *w*.

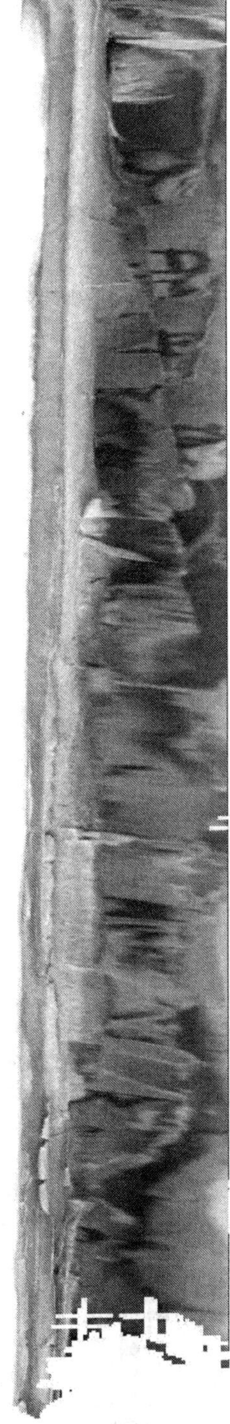

111. The following specimen shows what the same dialect was about 1650, nearly two centuries earlier. It is a rustic song composed by Gysbert Japicx, supposed to be sung by a peasant on his return from a wedding-feast.

I	I
Swíet,[a] ja swíet is 't, oer 'e míete[b]	Sweet, yes sweet is over (*beyond*) measure
'T Boáskien fóar[c] 'e jonge lie;[a]	The marrying for the young lede (*people*);
Kreftich swíet is 't, sizz' ik jíette,[d]	Most sweet is it, I say yet (*once more*),
As it gíet[a] mei âlders ríe.[a]	When it goes with the rede (*counsel*) of the elders.
Mar óars tiget 'et to 'n pléach	But otherwise it tends to a plague (*curse*),
As ik óan myn géafeint séach.[e]	As I saw on (*by the example of*) my village fellow.
2	**2**
Goune swobke, lit uws péarje,	Golden Swobke, let us pair,
Béa hy her mei mylde stemm,	He bade her with a mild voice,
Ofke, sei se, ho scoe 'k it kléarje![f]	Ofke, she said, how should (*would*) I clear it! (*free from obstacles*)
Wist du[g] rie to heite in mem?	Knowest thou rede, father and mother?
Ljéaf,[h] dat nim ik to myn læst.	(*My*) love! I nim (*take*) this to my last (*charge*);
Dear mey wier dy knôte[i] fæst.	Therewith the knot was fast.
3	**3**
Da dit pear to géar[j] 'scoe ite	When this pair should (*would*) eat together,
In hjæ híene nin gewin,	And they had no gain (*livelihood*),
Heite[k] séach, as woe hy bite,	Father (*the husband*) saw as if he would bite (*looked angry*);
Mem wier stjoersch in lef fen sin.	Mother (*the wife*) was stern and cross of humour.

[a] It is the genius of the Anglo-Friesic, 1st, to change the *u* after *s*, obvious in all other dialects, into the consonant *w*; thus súet becomes swêt: 2nd, to change the *e* into *i*; swet, *A.-S.* swete, whether written or not with *i*, is pronounced like *i*. In the same way, lede *people*, rede *counsel*, were pronounced lide, ride, by contraction *Frs. v.* lie, rie.

[b] Miete, at present *Frs. v.* mjitte.

[c] Fóar, at present *Frs. v.* foár.

[d] Yet present *Frs. v.* just as it is pronounced in English. It is the Anglo-Friesic fashion to change *g* into *y* in many instances where all other dialects retain the *g*. Thus *Old Eng.* yern *readily; Frs. v.* jern; jerne, *Asg. bk.* 2, b; *A.-S.* géorn. *Yesterday*, *Frs. v.* jister; *A.-S.* gistra. *Old Eng.* to yet *to pour*; *Frs. v.* jitte; *A.-S.* géotan. Yet *adhuc*, *Frs. v.* yet; *A.-S.* gyt. Yond *ibi*, *Frs. v.* jinder; *A.-S.* geond. The German-Saxon dialect uses jot for gott.

[e] Séach *saw*, séa-gen *videbant*; *A.-S.* séah *videbat*; *A.-S.* séagon *videbant*.

[f] Kléarje, at present kljerge.

[g] This du is now become dou, as the *A.-S.* þu sounds in the present *Eng.* thou. Tongues of the same original frame show the same development in their consonants as in their vowels.

[h] Ljéaf, *A.-S.* léof *charus*.

[i] Knô-te, present *Frs. v.* knotte, an ellipsis for *love-knot*. It was a knotted handkerchief in which was a coin; when presented by the woer and accepted by the maiden, the knot was fastened.

[j] To géare, now to gjerre, contr. for *A.-S.* geader *to gather*; compounded of ge and eader *septum, septo includi*, i. e. *conjunctim*; *together*, *to encompass*.

[k] This word heite *father* is *Frs. v.* and *Moes.* atta *pater*, aithei *mater*. I wonder that the word is neither in the Old-Friesic nor in the A.-S.

ɛe, sei se, elk jíer ien bern	Ofke, she said, each (*every*) year a child . . .
er ik fáem![a] Ik woe 't so jern.[b]	Were I maiden! I would (*wish*) it so yern (*so willingly*).
4	4
ite in Hóatske[c] sneins[d] to kéamer	Hoite and Hoatske every Sunday in the inn
kken 't mei elkóarme kléar.	Made it clear (*settled it*) with each other.
ɛke krigge Sjolle-kréamer[e]	Tetke got Sjolle the pedlar
sint Eal by wyn in bjéar.	To St. Alof's fair unto wine and bear.
rint elk om as ien slet,[f]	Now each runs about as a slut,
bekleye 't: mar to let.	And complains (*of*) it, but too late.
5	5
ds die better nei ik achtje	Oeds did better in my opinion
[g] hy sæts syn trou[h] tosei;	When he said (*gave*) his troth to Sæts;
liet de alders even plachtje[i]	He let the elders even plight (*contract*)
ret se óan elke ich[j] joene mei.	What they on each edge (*side*) gave with (*the married couple*).
besit hy huws in schuwr',	Now he possesses house and barn,
syn bern fleane alle man uwr.	And his children outdo all men.
6	6
k, myn sóan, wolt du bedye,[k]	Ork, my son, wouldst thou prosper,
ı náet óan allyk ien moll'![l]	Run not on all like a mole;
d in rie lit mei dy frye,	Let age and rede (*good counsel*) woo thee,
rn, so géan' dyn saken wol;	Child, then thy affairs go well;
n scil de himel uwr dyn dwáen	Then the heaven shall (*will*) give over thy doings
k in mylde seining' jáen.[m]	Luck (*fortune*) and mild (*liberal*) blessings.

[a] Faem, in the dialect of Hindelope, faen *maiden; A.-S.* fœmna *virgo*. The common eek γυνη is a corruption of the Doric βανα, corresponding with the *Lat.* fœmina, and the *glo-Friesic* fana; for the Greek β corresponds with the *Ger. p*, sometimes going over to *f*. vonder this word, obvious in *A.-S.* and *Friesic*, is totally lost in *Eng*.

[b] See note ([d]) at p. lxxii. on jíette.

[c] Hóatse, the proper name of a man, becomes that of a female by adding ke, Hóatske, at esent Hoátse and Hoátske. A great many of these proper names of the Friesians are come familiar names in Eng. by adding *son*. Thus, Watse, Ritse, Hodse, Gibbe, Friesian oper names, become Watse-son, Ritse-son, Hodse-son, Gibbe-son; in the Friesian syntax, e son of Watse, &c., by contraction, Watson, Ritson, Hodson, Gibbson (Gibbon).

[d] Snein *Sunday*, Senen-dei, by contraction Sneen-dei, and casting away dei, Sneen, whence ien and Snein. The Hindelopians still say Senne-dei or Sendei. Galbema, p. 30, has nendei; and the Charter-boek, I. p. 534, 536, Snayndé *dies solis*. *dei* is also cast away in e, and *Frs. v.* freed *Fri-day*. Correct, Junius, *Gloss. Goth.* p. 310.

[e] From *Frs. v.* kream, *Scot.* craim *a merchant's stall*, is derived kreamer *a merchant in a stall.*

[f] The etymology of *slut* is not apprehended either by Johnson, Jamieson, or Tooke. From *-S.* slidan *to slide; Dut.* sleden *labi, trahere*, comes sledde *traha*, now sled. The other form sletan or slutan, producing *Frs. v.* slet *a clout, towel, a dirty woman*, and *Eng.* slut *a dirty man*. The Friesians in the same way form sleep *a slut*, from *Frs. v.* sleepje *trahere*.

[g] *A.-S.* þa, the same as *Frs. v.* da *then*, is not in *Eng*.

[h] Trou *fidelity; A.-S.* treowa, treowð; *Scot.* trouth *truth; Scot.* to trow *to believe*.

[i] Plachtje *to plead, bargain*. It is the same word as *A.-S.* plihtan *spondere, oppignorare*.

[j] *A.-S.* ecge forms by assimilation egge, *Asg. bk.* 273, *edge* (*of a sword*); igge, *Asg. bk.* 365. ge or ich means here *side, part*, as in *Scot. the edge of a hill, the side and the top of a hill.*

[k] For be the A.-S. used ge, as ge-þeän *to thrive;* the *e* pronounced like *i*, this in Friesic, ence di-ja, *i.e.* dye.

[l] Mole is an ellipsis for mouldwarp, *i.e. A.-S.* moldweorp, as molle is for the common *s. v.* mol-wrot, from molde *terra*, and *A.-S.* wrotan, *Frs. v.* wrotte *rostro versare*. The Scots e by inversion of letters mawdiwart and moudiewort. The *Eng.* mouldwarp has warp from e *A.-S.* wand-wyrp, properly the *turn-cast*, i.e. *who casts up mould by turning it.*

[m] *Frs. v.* jaen *to give, Frs. l.* 26, 28, and ja *to give, Frs. l.* 53, 101, for *Scot.* ga' *to give.*

112. To give some idea of the Hindelopian dialect, I shall add a few lines which I found written above the months of January, February, and May, in a Hindelopian calendar for seamen. The Hindelopians were formerly all seamen, even in the beginning of the present century.

Januarius het xxxi deggen.	January has xxxi days.
Nyje deggen,[a] nyje winscen,	New days, new wishes,
Nyje ré[b] fan nyje minschen!	New rede (*counsel*) of new men.
Weer ûs livven ek[c] su ny	Were our life (*conduct*) eke so (*also as*) new
Sunden wârdven lichst[d] fan fry.	We grew lightly free from sins.
Februarius het xxviii deggen.	February has xxviii days.
Silers[e] meye winters reste,[f]	Sailors may rest in winter,
Thûs tu blieuwen mut jerm leste;	To stay at home (*to house*) must please them.
Lot[g] men iertske surg mêr stân	(*If*) one let earthly sorrow more stand (*be*)
Mengwar[h] scoe men better dwân.	Many times we should (*would*) do better.
Majus het xxxi deggen.	May has xxxi days.
As we tommelje oeuwer 't wetter[i]	As we tumble (*are tossed*) over the water
Heuwe[j] 't slim[k] en soms hwet better.	(*Then*) we have it slim (*bad*[m]) and sometimes (*then*) what (*a little*) better.
Su 's de wrâld ek as de sê,	So the world is eke (*also*) as the sea,
Soms fol kurje,[l] soms fol nê.	Sometimes full of delight, sometimes full of need.

[a] As we have had in the preceding læst for last *a burden*, fæst for fast, let for late, so here deggen for daggen. The *A.-S.* used also fæst, dæg: but what may be the reason why the Eng. in a thousand such words write *a*, although they have ever retained the old pronunciation of *e*? Does this oddity date from the time when *a*, losing entirely its genuine meaning, was called *e*?

[b] Ré, contraction of the *Old Eng.* rede *counsel.*

[c] *Frs. v.* eak; *A.-S.* éac; *Hindl.* ek, contr. of *Old Eng.* eke *also.*

[d] It is a very remarkable property of the Hindl. dialect to insert *s* between *ch* and *t*; lichst for licht *light*; ânsichst *visage*; suchst *sickliness*; for ânsicht (*A.-S.* onsien *vultus, sight*) sucht.

[e] I have not found this word in the particular signification of *a seaman* (matelst) anywhere but in *Eng.* and *Hindl.* In *Dut.* een zeiler is *a sailing vessel*; and in *Frs. v.* siler is *a swimmer.*

[f] We have *u* in the *Ger.* ruhe and the *Dut.* rust, but *e*, originating from *u*, in the Anglo-Friesic rest.

[g] Lot *let*; *Frs. v.* lit.

[h] Meng-war is a compound of menig (men-ig) *many*; and *A.-S.* hweorf (*itus et reditus*) *vices, many times.*

[i] Wetter: in this word the Eng. is inconsequent by retaining the broad *a* in the pronunciation.

[j] Heuwe *we have*; *Frs. v.* wy hawwe.

[k] Slim *bad, wrong*; properly *curved, crooked*; *Dut. Kil.* slimvoet *loripes*; slim *distortus.* In the same way, *wrong* (derived from *A.-S.* wringan, *Frs. v.* wringe *to wring*) is properly *tortus.* This primary signification of *wringing* is likewise in *A.-S.* slincan, slingan *to sling*; whence the frequentative form *Frs. v.* slingerje, and in slang *a snake.* In *Dut.* as in the north of England, slim *tortuous* has the analogical signification of *sly.* But slim denotes also *weak and thin of shape* in Eng. In *Icel.* lam is *a fracture*, lama *fractus viribus*, whence at slæma (as *Eng.* slîm from lîm *limus*) *debilitare*; *Eng.* slim *weak, slight.* It is not impossible that *A.-S.* lim *limb*, as *a fracture, division*, or *member*, belongs to this class. Further we find *A.-S.* hlæne *lean*, and with the sibilant instead of the aspirate: *Dut. Frs. v.* slank *thin of shape, opposed to the swelling of an inflamed wound.* *Frs. v.* linkje *to grow less in bulk.* Slink *furrow between banks in sea.* *Eng.* slim *slender, thin of shape.*

[l] Kurje *security and peace.* From *A.-S.* cyse or cyre *electio*; kar in the Swed. laws is *full freedom in his actions, and security against all violence in his house.* In the same way, *Frs. v.* wâld, and *A.-S.* wela *felicity*, is from *Dut.* walen and welen *eligere.*

[m] The form of this word is one of the most ancient extant in the Eng. language not to be found in A.-S. nor any Germanic tongue, but only in the *Persian* بد bad *malignus*; in the Mogul language badd. The European form is wâd, from *A.-S.* wedan; *Dut.* woeden *insanire, furere*—whence *Dut.* k-waad, kwaad *bad.*

113. The never-ceasing floods of Germans at last overwhelmed the riesians and their nationality. Had the Friesians sought for some fuge in the heart of the ocean, like their English brethren, they would ave braved the combined force of all the continental tyrants, whether owned, or representing the hydra of democracy. Only the North-Friesic, aterlandic, Sciermonnikoogian, Country-Friesic, and Hindelopian remain fragments that have resisted the influence of invaders to the present ay.

114. Low-Saxon has prevailed in all the country between Schleswic d the Dutch Zuiderzee, once possessed by the Friesians: it varies deed in its dialects being always affected by the tongue of the bordering ople; in one part smooth and fluent, in another broad and coarse, as in e province of Groningen. All, however, are of an homogeneous nature, that a person acquainted with one of them easily understands all the hers.

115. Glossaries of all these dialects have been formed.

Of the dialect of Holstein by J. F. Schutze in his *Holsteinisches Idiotikon,* 4 tom. amburg, 1800;—of the dialect of Hamburg by Michael Richey, in his *Idioticon amburgense,* Hamburg, 1754;—of that of Bremen and Werden by Kelp, on which tes are to be found in the *Collectanea Etymologica* of Leibnitz I. p. 33, Hanover, 17; and not only of the dialect of Bremen, but also of the Low-Saxon in general, by ociety of Bremish philologists in their *Versuch eines Bremisch-Niedersächsischen 'örterbuchs,* Bremen, 1767, 5 vols; it will be unnecessary to cite more. I must, wever, add, that a specimen of the present East-Friesic is to be found in the *Sangh-a,* a collection of songs and poetry, printed at Emden, 1828, Woortman.

116. While these dialects prevail in those parts of Old-Friesia extend-g from Schleswic nearly to the northern coasts of the Zuiderzee, Dutch spoken in North Holland, South Holland, and Zealand, and Flemish in e country surrounding Antwerp, and in Flanders.

117. I beg leave to draw the attention of the Anglo-Saxon scholar to e Low-Saxon glossaries above mentioned. Many hundred Anglo-Saxon rds will be elucidated, as to their form and meaning, by closely comparing em with the Low-Saxon. Low-Saxon has all the appearance of German afted on an Anglo-Friesic tree. The words are Anglo-Friesic with erman vowels, as if the Friesians, in adopting the German, retained the nsonants of the old language. This observation may with still greater opriety be applied to the syntax and phraseology, that is, to the mental rt or soul of the language. They continued to think in Anglo-Friesic rms, whilst their organs adopted the vowels and some other mechanical rts of the German. Hence there is scarcely a single expression or rase extant in Anglo-Saxon, Friesic, or Dutch, of which the parallel is t to be found in the Low-Saxon glossaries. In short, it is the Anglo-iesic idiom, with words of Germanic form. This observation also plains another phenomenon, which is, that scarcely a single scholar, native of any place on the coast of the German sea, where Low-Saxon is

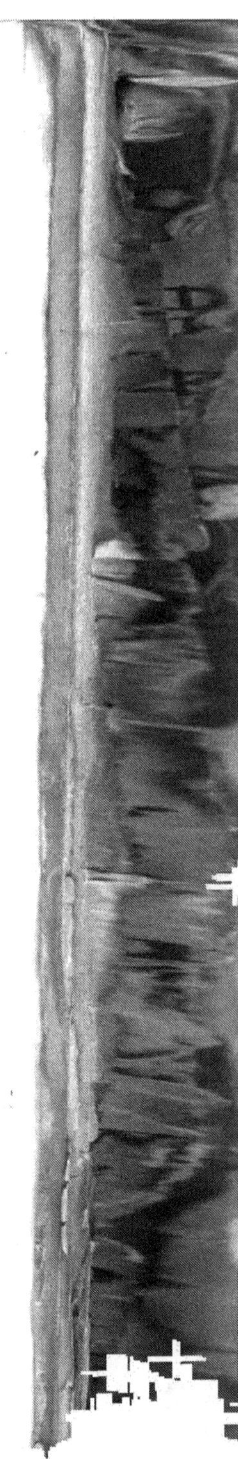

the mother-tongue, possesses the true genius of the German language. Though Klopstock was born at Hamburg, yet I venture to affirm that no scholar of the stamp of T. D. Wiarda is acquainted with the true spirit of the German tongue.

118. It is for this reason, that any one who intends to compose a syntax of the Anglo-Saxon, after having thoroughly investigated the Friesic and Dutch, must not omit to compare almost every part with the Low-Saxon glossaries. This is an important and almost a new task. To this day the syntax of the Anglo-Saxon, requiring a deep insight into the hidden springs of speech, has been but rudely developed, only hinted at even by Rask, while the different forms of conjugation and declension have been analyzed with the most minute attention.

119. Moreover, if the syntax of the Anglo-Saxon be the basis of the English syntax, as I think it is, notwithstanding a partial degeneration since the Norman conquest by a mixture with French,* the absurdity is felt of modelling the construction of the English according to that of corrupt Latin, known by the name of French. The construction of the French language is as regularly arranged as the pipes of an organ, while the most diversified inversion, exceeded only by that of the Latin and Greek, characterizes the Anglo-Saxon and Friesic; and the more the English is made to differ from this standard of propriety, the more it deviates from its original form and its very nature. The diction and idiom, forming the mirror of the soul of nations, are in English and French as widely different as the character of the respective people. Hence the phenomenon, that when a foreigner well acquainted with the French easily understands an English author, it is certain that this writer is not possessed of the true genius of the English language. Addison may be deemed neat, pure, elegant, and fluent—but he is not English. Shakspeare wrote English; in him the English tongue and genius are represented.

120. Great clamours have arisen about the total corruption of the English language by the mixture of French and other foreign words, and I readily grant that a rich language, possessed of the power of forming compound words from simples, wants no foreign words to express even new objects and ideas. But permit me to observe, that the deficiency has not hitherto been supplied with due consideration and taste. For when an author (the translator of the Lord's Prayer for instance) uses a certain number of foreign words, it is no proof that the English language had not words of its own to express the same ideas. The fact is, that many thousand foreign words have been introduced when native terms already existed, and the English has, in this way, been endowed with the power of expressing the same idea by two different

* "Children in scole against the usage and manir of all othir nations beeth compelled for to leve hire owne langage, and for to construe hir lessons and hir thynges in Frenche."—*Trevisa's Translation of [illegible].* See "The causes of the corruption of the English language," *Boucher's Glossary*, London, 18[illegible], Introd. p. 39, 40.

words—or, what is of still greater value, of appropriating this new word to mark some modification in the meaning of the indigenous word. In the phrases "Forgive us our debts, lead us not into temptation, but deliver us from evil," could there not be found amongst all the stores of the English language some words to express the ideas of *debt*, *temptation*, and *deliver?* If these words now bear significations somewhat different from those of the foreign ones, if foreign words have usurped the office of native ones, this is no argument that at all affects the richness and proper essence of the language.

121. For a proof of what I have advanced, I beg to refer the English reader to the Friesic pieces I have translated into English: this, however imperfect, will not I hope be entirely disregarded.

My object was to show the analogy between the two languages, by translating them as literally as possible; and the cognate words in English which do not perfectly agree with the Friesic in sense, I have explained by others in parentheses. In 1200 words I have only had recourse to 50 which are not of Saxon origin—a number which might be greatly diminished by a scholar thoroughly acquainted with the original stores of the English language. At this rate, about every twenty-fourth word of the original fund of the language is lost. In 125 words in parentheses, I used 50 foreign words: here one word is lost out of every $2\frac{1}{2}$. The number of words was 1200; add the words in parentheses 125, it makes a total of 1325. The foreign words in 1200 were 50, and in parentheses, 50, making the sum of 100. Then $\frac{1325}{100} = 13\frac{1}{4}$; shows that there is one foreign word for every thirteen English.

122. The stanzas of the Countess of Blessington contain seventy-seven words, of which eight are of foreign origin, namely, *pain*, *hours*, *joy*, *scald*, *vanish*, *sceptred*, *empire*, *brief*. Thus in nine and a half English terms, one word is exotic.

123. The foreign words in the English language are, for the most part, used to express scientific or abstract ideas, and were introduced from the French. These terms, however, do not suit the feelings of the poet; he involuntarily has recourse to the original stores of his native tongue—to the varied construction, and the energetic and picturesque diction of the Anglo-Saxon—a language formed by his valiant forefathers in their savage, that is, poetical state. This remark fully accounts for the phenomenon, that a reader who is a little acquainted with French and Latin, easily understands the writings of an English lawyer, divine, or philosopher, while he boggles at every sentence of the poets, whose Anglo-Saxon words and construction are equally unknown to him.

124. The Anglo-Saxon appears greatly disfigured as it is at present represented in the English. But as the granting of citizenship to foreign words, and the moulding of them to an English form, have led to fundamental laws in the English language, every one will allow the great advantage that results from such a change. While all the stores of the numberless tongues on the globe became perfectly English when introduced into England, the Dutch, on the contrary, which may boast of

exquisite purity, cannot adopt a single word without its bearing the mark of its foreign origin.

125. Finally, it scarcely needs be mentioned, that as genuine English words are for the most part Anglo-Saxon, an agreement of Friesic with English naturally implies an agreement of Friesic with Anglo-Saxon. It is for this reason, that the parallel Anglo-Saxon words are not always cited in the specimens in §§ 95, 97, &c. This comparison would also have taken too much time to pay due attention to the different degrees of development by which words of the same age are often distinguished from one another.

126. All that has been said about the analogy between the Anglo-Saxon and Friesic, tends to prove that the Friesic tongue is absolutely indispensable in determining, as far as it is now possible, the genuine pronunciation of the Anglo-Saxon; and that preceding writers, in passing over the Friesic, overlooked an important source of knowledge.

127. What is less pardonable in modern Anglo-Saxon scholars, is their complete neglect of English in this respect. Their ignorance of the English, as of the Friesic, will not, I hope, be alleged as an excuse. Is not the English tongue, as to its descent and substance, still a genuine daughter of the Anglo-Saxon? Does she not bear to this very day some features of her fair mother, notwithstanding her foreign ornaments? Do not many Anglo-Saxon vowels still exist in Yorkshire, in Scotland, and in other provincial dialects of England? May not the English alone boast of having preserved the true sound of the old *etch* (þ *th*), which has disappeared from the whole continent of Europe, so as not even to leave the means of forming a faint idea of the sound of this consonant, without the aid of the English? Why should we consult only the Gothic, or the Icelandic, which is still more remote from the Anglo-Saxon? Why should that which is unknown be sought amongst the unknown, rather than in that which is known in the remains of the old sounds of the language? With a competent knowledge of the subject, and fair induction, I presume that no source can afford so much light in the pronunciation and other peculiarities of the Anglo-Saxon as the English.

128. Of late, the accent by which some Anglo-Saxon MSS. are marked, is held as one of the most efficient means of ascertaining the true pronunciation of the Anglo-Saxon, and Wilkins and other publishers are to be blamed for omitting them. It is here necessary to state my opinion on this subject. A mark of accent, in modern tongues, may have three applications:—1st. It may denote the stress of the voice on a certain syllable, and this is perhaps the only purpose for which the accent (′) may be lawfully used. 2nd. But, improperly and contrary to its original design, it may denote the very nature of the sound of the vowel. And 3rd. it may be used to designate the lengthening of a short vowel, without altering the nature of its sound.

In *above* and *comfort*, you hear the short sound of *o*, and in *ghost*, *potent*, *low*, we have the long sound; but in *loose*, the very nature of the sound is changed and varies from *o* to the French *ou*, and in *for* to *au*. Suppose *pôtent* to be noted by the accent, and the sound of the *o* to be unknown to you: what will this accent then mean? Will it signify simply the lengthening of the short *o*? or one of the four or five modifications of the sound of *o*? and which of the modifications? Or does it mean that *po* in potent has the stress? If no one can ascertain to which of these six or seven purposes this single mark is applied, of what use can it be in settling the pronunciation of Anglo-Saxon?

129. Let us endeavour to illustrate the subject by some instances from Cædmon, published by Mr. Thorpe.

Is the *a* long in þá *then*, (*Cd. Th.* p. 20, 11,) [þa, 20, 6,] contrary to the short *a* in *Frs. v.* da: *Moes.* than; *Dut.* dan *then*, and agree with the Icelandic þá *tunc*, pronounced *thau* or *tau*? Or does it denote *a* inclining to *o*? Or does it mean *a* modified a little by *i*? Is *a* long in náman, (*Cd. Th.* p. 9, 11,) contrary to *Moes.* namo; *Frs. v.* namme; *Icel.* namn and nafn, which have all short *a*? Or does it mean an inclination of the *a* to the sound of the old *o* in ὀνομα and nomen? The same question may be applied to hám, (*Cd. Th.* p. 108, 33,) *Eng.* home; and we further ask if the accent, in this instance, can also signify the verging of *a* to *i* (âi) apparent in *Moes.* haim *abode*; *Icel.* heimr *domus*; Hesychius ειμαδες ποιμενων οικιαι; *Frs. v.* hiem *homestead* or *the land just around a farm-house, enclosed by a ditch*. What is the pronunciation of éngel, (*Cd. Th.* p. 137, 1,) written engel, p. 137, 23? If the *e* is long, then it is pronounced eengel, contrary to the pronunciation of the continental descendants of the Anglo-Saxons, but agreeing with that of their direct posterity the English in their angel? What is the sound of ý in þýsne *this*, (*Cd. Th.* p. 52, 6)? Is it long, and opposed to the present *Eng.* this, and *Frs. v.* disse, *Asg. bk.* 2, 3, 271, 278, thesse: *Frs. l.* 2, 5, disse? Tell me also the meaning of the accent in lífe, (*Cd. Th.* p. 103, 4). Is the vowel only lengthened, and life pronounced liife? Or has it the diphthongal nature of the *Eng. i* in life? Or is it perhaps like ij in *Dut.* lyf *body*? If the *i* in wítan *to reproach*, (*Cd. Th.* p. 51, 9,) in wíte-hús *torture-house*, (p. 3, 21,) differ in its sound from *i* in witan *to know*, *Frs. v.* wite, like *Icel.* víta *reprehendere*, from *Icel.* vit *ratio*, has the *í* then a long sound as wiitan, or like the *Dut. ij* in wijten *imputare*, or *ei* in weitan?—What do you say of ó in nóm *cepit*? Must the ó only be made long, as noom, or is the *o* modified as if united with *a*, as in *Frs. v.* nóam? Is the ó long in bórd *shield*, (*Cd. Th.* p. 193, 28,) contrary to *Icel.* bord, *Dut.* bord, both being short like *Moes.* baurd? Or is it something similar to the *Frs. v.* ou, or *Frs. v.* oe in boerd? What is the sound of ó in wordum *with words*? Is the *o* long as in *Dut* woord, opposed to *Moes.* waurd; *Frs. v.* wird; *Icel.* ord? Or is it pronounced like woárden, as the inhabitants of the Friesian towns speak? Or does it denote the stress of the voice falling upon wor? Is ón, (*Cd. Th.* p. 64, 1,) pronounced oon, contrary to *Moes.* ana [short *a*] and *Eng.* on? Or does it agree with *Dut.* aan, *Frs. v.* óan? Finally, what does the accent mean above rǽd *narration*, derived from short *a* in *Moes.* rathan *numerare*, *A.-S.* rædan *to read*? Is the vowel long? Or is some sound like *Fr.* ai in mais designated? As soon as Anglo-Saxon scholars will answer these questions, and show me the rule which regulates the application of this single mark, in every particular instance, I will gladly observe every accent found in the MSS., and in the mean time I beg to be allowed my own opinion.

130. Far* from depreciating the use of marks of accents, I am fully

* As the sounds were more numerous than the letters, especially in the earliest state of the language, when the system of the vowels was more developed, and the letters fewer, being only sixteen Runes, it is evident that many letters must have had a double and even a triple

convinced of their being indispensable in the dead languages; but if two marks are used to denote the spiritus, and three the accent, in Greek, [ʽ ʼ ´ ` ˜]—and these are far from conveying a just idea of the pronunciation of this language—how could a single mark effect this in Anglo-Saxon? And how is this single mark used? It is sometimes inserted, and sometimes omitted, even in MSS. boasting of some accuracy in this respect, as the MSS. of Cædmon. I will not mention other MSS., as Beowulf in the British Museum, Vitellius A. xv., in which three marks [´ ` ˉ] are employed with so much confusion, that the grammarian, in using them, has not only confounded the ideas of emphasis, the nature of sound, and the simple lengthening of sound, as perhaps all who have used the accents in Anglo-Saxon MSS. have done, but he has often misapplied the marks. Several attempts have been made in our day to invent proper signs, and to define the true force of each; but, as if it were to increase the confusion, the two principal advocates of accents, Rask and Grimm, differ in the import they ascribe to the same sign.

131. It may be here asked, whether the authors themselves made use of accents, or their copiers, or if a later hand added them? Finally, whether it was the hand of a genuine Anglo-Saxon, or whether, after the Danish conquest, it was some writer who had a strong tincture of Danish pronunciation that accented the MSS. Should I live to make my intended inquiries on the changes of the vowels, I may perhaps throw some light on the subject.

132. Since the pronunciation of the old languages depends on the sound of the letters, it is important to inquire what these letters were.

I answer, that the old Saxon letters were Runic. Rhabanus Maurus has left a Runic alphabet of the Marcomanni, called by some Nordmanni and Northalbingii,* located on the northern banks of the Elbe, and thus on the same spot that the allies of the Angles, the Saxons, inhabited. On comparing the form of these letters with the Runic alphabet of the Anglo-Saxons,† we shall perceive, on the whole, a striking resemblance, which is to me a convincing proof that the Anglo-Saxons brought with them the Runic alphabet into Britain. That these letters were once in common use among them, has been lately proved by the discovery of two sepulchral stones at Hartlepool,‡ bearing Runic inscriptions.§

sound. When, in process of time, the sounds which were sensibly distinct approached each other, the evil became still worse. Thus the *e* in red became in time the representative of *éo* in réod *arundo;* of *éa* in réad *ruber*, and of *æ* in ræd, *Old Eng.* rede *consilium*. This fully proves the necessity of marks to guide the pronunciation.

* Consult Ueber Deutsche Runen von W. C. Grimm, Göttingen, 1821, in general, and p. 149 in particular.

† Hickes's Gram. Goth. et Anglo-Saxonica, in the Thes. L. L. Sept. tom. i. p. 135, 136.

‡ An accurate delineation of these stones is to be found in the Gentleman's Magazine, Sept. 1833, p. 219.

§ Annuente Deo, Mr. Halbertsma intends to add in another publication, a second and third part to what is here given: the second on the sound of each Anglo-Saxon Letter—and the third part on the practical application of the preceding rules relative to the vowels, diphthongs, and consonants.

V.—THE SAXONS, OR OLD-SAXONS.

1. The Saxons* spoke the Old-Saxon, now called Low-German, or Platt-Deutsch.

2. The German confederacy, known under the name of Saxons, occupied the greater part of Low, Platt, or Northern Germany. They were divided into—1. *Eastphalians*, on the eastern borders of the Weser; 2. *Westphalians*, on the Western borders of the Weser down to the Rhine and the North Sea; 3. *Angrivarians*, situated between the Eastphalians and Westphalians, and the borders of the North Sea; 4. *North-Albingians*, from the north of the river Elbe to Denmark; 5. *Trans-Albingians*, comprising the whole country from the Elbe to the river Oder, with the exception of those districts occupied by the Wends or Sorbians, near the Baltic, and in the neighbourhood of the Oder. These Saxons, or Old-Saxons, chiefly remaining in their ancient localities, retained their low, soft, or Old-Saxon dialect in great purity. The Anglo-Saxons, a branch of the Old-Saxons, wrote and matured their language in England; hence it differs from the tongue of their continental progenitors. The Old-Saxon, now called Low or Platt-German, seems to be conveyed down to the present day with few alterations, and those only such as time always produces; but as we have no specimen of it earlier than the Heliand in the 9th century, we do not know the exact form of the Old-Saxon from which the Anglo-Saxon was derived. This Low-German, so called from being the vernacular language of Platt, or Low-Germany, or of the common people, is, even in the present day, very extensive, being spoken by the lower classes in the greater part of Westphalia, in Hanover, Holstein, Sleswick, a part of Jutland, in Mecklenburg, Magdeburg, Brandenburg, Pomerania, the kingdom of Prussia, and as far north as Livonia and Estonia.†

3. The origin and ancient history of the Saxons are enveloped in much darkness. The Fosi mentioned by Tacitus‡ were most likely Saxons,

* Those who wish for a full view of Low-German literature, may consult—Geschichte der Nieder-Sächsischen oder Plattdeutschen Sprache von M. Joh. Fried. August Kinderling, Magdeburg, 1800.—Bücherkunde der Sassisch-Niederdeutschen Sprache, von Dr. Karl, F. A. Scheller, Braunschweig, 1826.

† Melis Stoke says,

	Verbal English.
Oude Boeken horic ghewaghen,	Old books hear I mentioning,
Dat al tlant, beneden Nimaghen,	That all the land below Nimeguen,
Wilen Neder Zassen hiet;	Formerly (*was*) called Low-Saxony.
Also alst de stroem versciet	So as the stream flows
Vander Mazen eñ vanden Rine.	Of the Maas, and of the Rhine.
Die Scelt was dat Westende sine,	The Scheld that was its western end (*boundary*).
Also als si valt in de zee,	So as it falls into the sea,
Oest streckende min no mee,	Eastward stretching less or more
Dan toter Laveeen of ter Elven.	(*Than*) to the Laveeen or the Elbe.

Huydecoper's edition, lib. i. v. 41, p. 9.

‡ De Moribus Ger. cap. xxxvi.

for Ptolemy,* who wrote in the beginning of the 2nd century, mentions the Saxons, and assigns to them nearly the same situation as Tacitus.

4. The Anglo-Saxons, as has just been stated, were a branch of the Saxons, who, for distinction, are denominated Old-Saxons.† In the short account of the Anglo-Saxons ‡ will be found most of what is known of the origin and progress of this people. It is there ascertained that the Saxons were a confederacy of different tribes united for mutual defence against the Romans. Two of these were the *Angles* and *Jutes*, who, in A.D. 449, were among the first and chief settlers in Britain.

5. Subsequent to this emigration, the Saxons, remaining on the continent, were in a constant conflict with the Francs. These Old-Saxons preserved their freedom till about A.D. 785, when, after a gallant opposition of thirty-three years, they were subdued by Charlemagne, who, by much cruelty, forced them to embrace Christianity. Charlemagne would scarcely have succeeded in inducing the Saxons to submit, if their celebrated duke *Wittekind*, who was never entirely subdued, had not terminated the cruelties of Charlemagne by consenting to be baptized. Wittekind, by treaty, remained in possession of the greater part of Saxony till his death in 807.

6. From Wittekind, not only the German emperors of the Saxon line, Henry I., Otto I. and II., and Henry II., from A.D. 918 to 1024, and the house of Hanover, the royal family of Great Britain, but also the present king of Saxony, and the other princes of the house of Saxony, take their origin.

7. The most flourishing period of the Platt-Deutsch was just before the Reformation. Luther was accustomed to speak and write in High-German, in which he wrote his version of the Scriptures. As Luther's translation soon came into general use throughout Germany, the high dialect of his translation was not long before it prevailed over all the Low-German dialects. The influence of the Reformation in preventing the further cultivation of the Platt or Low-German, and in confining its use only to the lower orders, is regretted by all who are acquainted with its beauties. The most learned agree, that while the Low-German or Platt-Deutsch is equal to the High in strength and compositive power, the Platt is much softer and richer. The true old German freedom, sincerity, and honesty, can have no better medium to express its full mental and political independence, its genuine and confidential feelings of the heart, than its old, unsophisticated, open, Low-German dialect.

8. Where the High-German is obliged to employ most of the organs of speech to pronounce words, such as ochse *ox*, flachs *flax*, wachs *wax*, the Platt-German with the greatest ease says oss, flass, wass. The High-

* Cellarius, lib. II. cap. v. p. 303.

† Anglo-Saxon, Eald-Seaxan *Old-Saxons*, *Chr.* 449, *Ing.* p. 14, 22. See also the ANGLO-SAXON DICTIONARY, under the word *Seaxan*.

‡ III. § 1–8.

German *pfeifer pfeif auf*, is in Platt, like the English, piper pip up *piper pipe up*. The Low-German and Dutch proverbs are nearly all the same, both equally expressive, and in phraseology like English.

As dat beer is in den man
Is de wyshet in de kan.

As (*when*) the beer is in the man
The wisdom is in the kan.

9. From the great extent of the territory where the Low-German is spoken, it may be easily conceived that it does not always assume the same shape. Mr. Kinderling,* in his history of the Low-German or Platt-Deutsch language, names all the minute peculiarities; here the most essential need only be noticed.

10. It is generally acknowledged that the purest Low-German, or Platt-Deutsch dialect, is spoken in Holstein and Sleswick, particularly in the neighbourhood of Kiel. The Brunswick and Hanoverian dialect is broad and coarse. In the south-east of Westphalia, it mixes with the High-German, while on the borders of the Netherlands it melts into Dutch. The dialect of Gelderland and Overyssel preserves many Platt forms, as the Dutch gout, zout, hout, *gold, salt, wood*, is golt, zolt, holt; the *u*, written *w*, is pronounced like the Platt and High-Ger. *u*, Eng. *oo*.

11. The *Platt* changes the *High-Ger. au* into *oo* and *u;* as, auge *eye*, oog (*o* in no); auch *also*, ook (*o* in no); auf *up*, *Platt* up; bauch *belly, stomach*, in *Platt* makes buuk (the *uu* pronounced like the *Eng. oo* in wood). The *High-Ger. a* is changed into *oo;* as, alt *old*, *Platt* oold. The *High-Ger. ei* into *y* and *ee;* as, mein, dein, sein *mine, thine, his*, *Platt* myn; geist *spirit*, *Platt* geest. The *High-Ger. i* very often changes into *e;* as, wissen *to know* into weten;—*ie* into *ee* or *ä;* as, lieb *dear*, *Platt* leev; viel *much*, *Platt* väl;—*i* into *jü;* as, immer *always*, *Platt* jümmer. The *High-Ger. o* often changes into *a* long and broad *a;* as, oben *above*, bawen. *High-Ger.* alt, *Platt* old, like the *Eng.* in signification and pronunciation. The *High-Ger. ü* or *ue* changes into *ö;* as, vergnügt *content*, vergnögt;—the *u* into *o;* as, zu *at*, *Platt* to; rufen *to call*, roopen (pronounced *ropen*); gut *good*.

12. Change of the consonants.—*b* often changes into *f* and *v, w;* as, dieb *thief*, deef; lieb *dear*, leev;—*ch* changes into *k;* as, ich *I*, ik or ick;—*ch* into *y;* as, mich *me*, my (pronounced like the *Eng.* me);—*r* into *y;* as, mir *to me*, my (pronounced mee); dir *to thee*, dy (pronounced dee);—*ss* into *t;* as, wasser *water*, water;—*chs* into *ss;* as, flachs *flax*, flass. The *ch* with the *s* preceding is often omitted; as, schlagen *to beat*, slagen; schweigen *to be silent*, swigen; schwimmen *to swim*, swimmen. The *Low-Ger.* in this respect has great correspondence with the old *High-Ger.* which avoids this unpleasant hissing sound in all those words where it is omitted in the *Low-Ger.* as, *High-Ger.* schwester *sister; Old High-Ger.* suester; *Platt-Ger.* suster; *Sanscrit* suasr; *A.-S.* suster, sweoster; *High-Ger.* schweiss *sweat; Platt* swêt. In some parts of Holstein and Sleswick, particularly near the borders of Jutland, the *sch* is changed into *sk;* as, schuld *debitum; Platt* skuld; *Old High-Ger.* sculd; *Dan.* skyld; *A.-S.* scyld. The auxiliary verb *shall* is in *High-Ger.* sollen; *Moes.* skulan, skallan; *Dut.* zullen, in *Platt* commonly schüllen, süllen, or like the *Icel.* skal,

* See note (*), § 1.

High-Ger. suche changes into *Platt* syke; sicher *sure* into seker;—*t* very often changes into *d*; as, teufel *devil*, düvel; tief *deep*, deep; Gott *God*; gut *good*; tod *death*, dod; tochter *daughter*, dochter;—*v*, with a few exceptions, is used instead of the *High-Ger. f*;—*w* is used and pronounced like the *High-Ger. w*;—*z* occurs only in a few instances, and is pronounced softer than the *High-Ger. z*, which in *Platt* is mostly changed into *t*; as, zu *to, at*, to; zichen *to pull*, tên; zwey *two*, twe; zeichen *token*, têken; zeit *time*, tyd; zoll *toll*, toll. The *High-Ger. pf* always changes into a single *p*; as, pflug *plough*, ploog; pfanne *pan*, pann; pflanze *plant*, plant; pfund *pound*, pund; pflaume *plum*, plum; pfeife *pipe*, pipe; pflücken *to pluck*, plükken.

13. HELIAND. An unknown author, in the early part of the 9th century, wrote, in alliterative lines, a Harmony of the Gospels in the Old-Saxon dialect. The MSS. are preserved at Munich, and in the British Museum, London. Some extracts were published under the name of Franco-Theotisc in *Hickes's Thes.* vol. ii. p. 101, and also by *Nyerup* at Copenhagen, 1787; but the whole was well edited, and splendidly published, with the following title:—

Heliand; Poema Saxonicum seculi noni. Accurate expressum ad exemplar Monacense insertis e Cottoniano Londinensi supplementis nec non adjecta lectionum varietate, nunc primum edidit J. Andreas Schmeller, Bibliothecæ Regiæ Monacensis Custos, &c., Monachii, 1830.

PARABLE OF THE SOWER, *Mt.* xiii. 3—6; *Mk.* iv. 1—4; *Lk.* viii. 4—6.

Huat ik iu seggean mag quad he· gesidos mine. huo imu en erl bi-
gan· an erdu sehan· hren corni mid is handun. Sum it an hardan
sten· obanuuardan fel· erdon ni habda. that it thar mahti uuahsan·
eftha uurteo gifahan. kinan eftha bicliben. ac uuard that corn
farloren. that thar an theru leian gilag.—*Heliand*, p. 73, l. 6—10.

LITERAL GERMAN.

Was ich euch sagen möchte, sprach er, Genossen meine, wie sich ein Landmann be-
gann in die Erde zu säen rein Korn mit sein' Händen; Etliches aber auf harten
Stein oberwärts fiel, Erde nicht hatte, dass es da konnte wachsen,
oder Wurzel erfassen, keimen oder bekleiben, auch ward (ging) das Korn
verloren, das da auf der strasse lag.

LITERAL ENGLISH.

What (*now*) I may say (*tell*) you, quoth he, my companions, how a farmer be-
gan on earth to sow clean corn with his hands. Some of it on hard
stone fell, had not earth that it there might wax (*grow*),
or roots take, germinate, or stick, and that corn was
lost, that there on the road lay.

14. TATIAN'S HARMONY. An unknown author, about A.D. 890, translated Tatian's Harmony of the Gospels into a softer dialect than the Alemannic and Bavarian: this translation contains words peculiar to the Old-Saxon dialect, and may be considered a sort of transition between Low and High-German. MSS. are preserved at Oxford and St. Gallen. This Harmony was first printed with this title: Tatiani Harmonia Evangelica e Latina Victoris Capuani versione translata in linguam Theotiscam antiquissimam per Jo. Phil. Palthenius, 4to. 1706; and again in Schilter's Thes. vol. ii. towards the end.

THE PARABLE OF THE SOWER.

Matt. xiii. 3.—Senu gieng tho uz thie thar sauuit, zi sauuenne samon sinan. 4. Mitthiu her tho sata, sumiu fielun nah themo uuege, inti uurdun furtretanu, inti quamun fugala himiles, inti frazun thiu. 5. Andaru fielun in steinaht lant, thar nih habeta mihhila erda, inti sliumo giengun uf, uuanta sie ni habetun erda tiufi. 6. Ufganteru sunnon furbrantiu uuirdun, inti bithiu sie ni habetun uurzala, furthorretun.—*Schilter's Thes.* vol. ii. p. 54, *towards the end.*

LITERAL GERMAN.

Matt. xiii. 3.—Sieh, es gieng da aus, der da säet, zu säen Samen seinen. 4. Indem er da säete, etliche (Samen) fielen nach dem Wege, und wurden vertreten; und (es) kamen die Vögel des Himmels, und frassen diese. 5. Andere fielen in steinig Land, wo (es) nicht hatte (gab) viele Erde; und schleunig giengen sie auf, weil sie nicht hatten Erde tiefe. 6. (Bey) aufgehender Sonne, wurden sie verbrannt; und da sie nicht hatten Wurzeln, verdorrten sie.

LITERAL ENGLISH.

Matt. xiii. 3.—See now, there went out (he) who there soweth, to sow his seed. 4. While he there sowed some fell on the way, and was trodden down, and came the fowls of heaven and devoured it. 5. Others fell on stony land, there had not much earth, and quickly went (grew) up, for they (it) had not deep earth; 6. (By) risen sun were burnt, and, because they had not roots, withered.

15. An Old-Saxon Chronicle in Rhyme of the year 1216, published in J. G. Leuçkfeld's Antiquitates Gandersh. in Leibnitii Scriptores Rerum Brunsv., and in Harenberg Historia Gandersh. with the following title, "Battle of Henry I. the Saxon, against the Huns."

Na by der Oveker lag koning Hinrik:
Up hôv he sek an der naten nagt alse ein dägen;
He en shuwede dûsternisse nog den rägen,
Dog folgeden öme kume halv de dâr waren.—*Scheller*, p. 9.

LITERAL ENGLISH VERSION.

Near by the shore lay King Henry,
Exposed to the wet night as a hero;
He did not shun darkness nor the rain,
But scarcely half those who were there followed him.

16. An allegorical Old-Saxon Poem, on love and fidelity, of the year 1231. Published in Eschenburg's Denkmale altdeut: Dichtkunst, Berlin, 1792.

FIDELITY.

Mine truwe folget or alleine.
Fôr allen frouwen is se here,
Ik wil nemandes syn wän ere.
Gôd geve or sulven sinen sägen,
Unde dusend ängele, de or plägen.—*Scheller*, p. 13.

LITERAL ENGLISH.

My fidelity follows her alone.
Above all ladies she is noble,
I will be nobody's but hers.
May God give her his blessing,
And a thousand angels attend her.

17. THE PRIVILEGE conferred upon the citizens of Itzehoe in Holstein, in the year 1260, by Count John and Gerhard of Holstein, about the Staple-right, from Westphalen's Monumenta Inedita, &c. vol. iv., and Halthaus's Glossarium, under the word *Stapel*, p. 1730.

Dat alle de Schiphern—ere kopenschop schullen affleggen vnde beden den Borgeren vnde Gesten to Itseho de to verkopende.

LITERAL ENGLISH.

That all the shippers shall deposit and offer their merchandise to the burghers and guests of Itzehoe to sale.

18. THE CATELNBURG SONG, made in 1350, on the rebuilding of the convent of that name, published in Letzner's Chronica of Dassel and Eimbeck, vol. ii.

THE CATELNBURG SONG.

Dat kloster ward gebuwet fyn
Edt gifft nu einen nien scyn,
Help Godt van Himelricke,
Dat wol geraden ore swyn
Vnnd werden wedder ricke.—*Scheller*, p. 36.

LITERAL ENGLISH.

The cloister was built fine,
It gives now a new shine;
God help from heaven on high,
That prosper well their swine,
And so grow rich thereby.

19. A LOW-GERMAN translation of the Speculum Humanæ Salvationis of the 14th century, published in E. Nyerup's Specim. Literat. Teuton. p. 446—454.

Dit buk is den vnghelerden bereyt,
Vnde het en spegel der mynsliken salicheit,
Dar in mag man prouen, dor wat sake
Got den mynschen wolde maken,
Unde wo de mynsche vordomet wart,
Unde wo dat god wedder vmme heft ghekart.
Lucifer houarde tegen gode synen heylant,
Dar vmme warp he ene in dat afgrunde altohant.
Kinderling, p. 296.

LITERAL ENGLISH.

This book is for the unlearned prepared,
And is called a mirror of human happiness,
Therein may one learn, by what means
God would make man,
And how man was condemned,
And how God again that has changed.
Lucifer boasted against God his Saviour,
Therefore threw he him into the gulph instantly.

20. A JOURNEY to the Holy Land made in the year 1356, written in Low-Saxon probably by Ludolfs, and copied from a MS. in 1471, by Nicholas Culenborch. The MS. in possession of Kinderling.

In allen (guden) Dingen de eyn mynsche deyt edder wil vullen bringhen, schal dar tho bidden bevoren god, de den mynschen heft vterkoren, so blift dat warck un verloren.—*Kinderling*, p. 341.

LITERAL ENGLISH VERSION.

In all good things which a man does or will perform, he shall before pray to God, who has chosen man, then this work will not be lost.

21. A LOW-SAXON epitaph on the Duke Adolph of Sleswick and Holstein, in the year 1459. In Arnkiel's Cimbrischen Heidenthum (Cimbric Paganism), vol. iii. p. 400.

Da man schref ein Ring von der Taschen (CIↃ),
Und veer Hängen van einer Flaschen, (cccc)
Vief Duven Föt vnd negen I (xxxxxIIIIIIIII)
Dar denk man Hartoch Adolf by,
Twischen Barber vnde Niclas Dagen,
O weh der jammerliken Klagen!
Do ward manch Og gewenet roth
Wol um des edlen Försten Dod.—*Kinderling*, p. 158.

LITERAL ENGLISH.

As men wrote a ring of a pocket (CIↃ)
And four hangers (handles) of a flask, (cccc)
Five doves feet and nine I (xxxxxIIIIIIIII)
Thereby think men on Duke Adolf,
Between Barbara and St. Nicholas days (Dec. 4.)
Alas for the grievous sorrows!
When many an eye was red with weeping
For the noble Prince's death.

22. THE LIFE of the holy Virgin Mary, from a MS. of the year 1474, in the Low-Saxon dialect, in possession of Kinderling, partly published in Adelung's Magazine for the German Language, vol. ii. No. I. p. 63, and in the Deutsches Museum, Oct. 1788, p. 340.

THE VIRGIN MARY.

Se was de schoneste aller wyue
Se was schone wyt vnde blanck,
Se was nicht kort, to mate lanck,
Ore Hende weren wyt gevar
Ane aller hande wandels gar,
Gel vnde goltvar was er har.—*Kinderling*, p. 343.

LITERAL ENGLISH.

She was the most beautiful of all wives.
She was fine white and blank.
She was not short, (but) moderately lank.
Her hands were of a white appearance,
Entirely without any kind of defect,
Yellow and of a gold colour was her hair.

23. A Bible printed at Cologne, 1480, folio.

Mk. iv. 3—4. Hort, de dar seyet, de is uitgegaen to seyen. Eñ do he seyede, dat eyn vyl by den wech. eñ de vogel des hemels quemen eñ eten dat.

24. A Bible printed at Lubeck, 1494, folio.

Mk. iv. 3—4. Horet. seet de dar seyet is vtghegan to seyende. vñ do he seyede. dath ene vyl by dē wech. vñ de voghele des hemmels quemen vñ eten dat.

25. Mirror for the Laymen (Speygel der Leyen), printed at Lubeck, 1496. This work is quoted in Brun's Old Platt-Ger. Poems, Berlin, 1798.

Der leyen speygel heft hyr eyn ende,
Den les gherne in desseme elende
Uppe dat god dy syne gnade sende,
Vn eynt leste dyme sele entfange in syne hende.
De dyt boek leeth maken. vnde ok de dar inne lesen,
Leue here god wyl den io gnedig wesen. Amen.
Anno dm. mccccxcvi, Lubeck.—*Scheller*, p. 107.

LITERAL ENGLISH.

The laick mirror has here an end,
Read it willingly in this distress
That God to thee his blessing send,
And at last thy soul receive into his hand.
(He) who this book made and also those who read in it,
Dear Lord God, be merciful to them. Amen.
Anno Domini 1496, Lubeck.

26. Reineke Vos,* an allegorical and satirical Poem in the Low-Saxon dialect, by Hinreck van Alkmar, founded and for the greater part literally translated from the Flemish original of Willem van Utenhoven. The first edition of this Low-Saxon poem was printed at Lubeck, 1498. In the years 1517 and 1522, two other editions accompanied with remarks were published by Nicholas Baumann, and printed by Lewis Dietz at Rostock. All the numerous subsequent editions are founded on these three.

Dat êrste bôk.
Dat êrste kapittel.

Wo de louwe, konnink aller deren, lêt ûtkrejêren unde vasten vrede ûtropen unde lêt beden allen deren to synem hove to komen.

It geschach up enen pinkstedach,
dat men de wolde uñ velde sach
grone stân mit lôf uñ gras,
uñ mannich vogel vrolik was
mit sange in hagen uñ up bomen;
de krûde sproten uñ de blomen,
de wol rôken hier uñ dâr:

* See Netherland, or Holland, VI. § 17, and High-German, X. § 56, 57.

de dach was schone, dat weder klâr.
Nobel de konnink van allen deren
hêlt hof un̄ lêt den ûtkrejêren
syn lant dorch over al.
dâr quemen vele heren mit grotem schal,
ôk quemen to hove vele stolter gesellen,
de men nicht alle konde tellen:
Lütke de krôn un̄ Marquart de hegger,
ja, desse weren dâr alle degger;
wente de konnink mit synen heren
mênde to holden hof mit eren,
mit vrouden un̄ mit grotem love,
un̄ hadde vorbodet dâr to hove
alle de dere grôt un̄ klene
sunder Reinken den vos allêne.
he hadde in dem hof so vele misdân,
dat he dâr nicht en dorste komen noch gân.
de quât deit, de schuwet gêrn dat licht,
also dede ôk Reinke de bosewicht,
he schuwede sere des konninges hof,
darin he hadde sêr kranken lof.

Reineke Vos, p. 1.*

LITERAL ENGLISH.

The First Book.
The First Chapter.

How the lion, king of all animals, ordered to be proclaimed and published a fast peace, and commanded all animals to come to his court.

It happened on a Whitsunday,
That men saw the woods and fields
Green, standing with leaves and grass,
And many a fowl joyful was,
With song in hedges and on trees;
The herbs and the blooms sprouted,
Which well perfumed here and there:
The day was fine, the weather clear.
Nobel the king of all beasts
Held a court, and had it proclaimed
Throughout his land every where.
There came many lords with great noise
Also came to the court many stately fellows
Whom men could not all tell.
Lutke the crane, and Marquart the magpie,
Yes, these were there altogether;
For the king, with his lords,
Meant to hold court with splendour,
With rejoicing and with great honour,
And had summoned there to the court,

* Reineke Vos. Nach der Lübecker ausgabe vom jahre, 1498. Mit einleitung, glossar und anmerkungen von Hoffmann von Fallersleben. Breslau, 1834.

All the beasts great and small
Except Renard the fox alone.
He had at court so much misdone
That he there durst not go or come.
Who does a wrong shuns much the light,
So did Renard, the wicked wight,
He shunned much the king's court
Wherein he had a sad report.

27. THE BOOK of the holy Gospels, Lessons, Prophets, and Epistles, &c. Brunswick, 1506, fol.

Mk. iv. 3—4. He ghink vth de dar seyede sin saet vn̄ do he seyede do vil des sades ein deel bi dē wech vn̄ wart ghetreden van den luden vnd de voghele des hēmels ethen yd vp.

28. A BIBLE printed at Halberstadt, 1522, fol.

Mk. iv. 3—4. Horet, seet, de dar seyet, ys uthgegan tho seyende. Und do he seyede, dat eyn veyl by den wech, und de voghele des hymels quemen, und eten dat.

29. THE NEW TESTAMENT, printed at Cologne, 1525.

Mk. iv. 3—4. Hoort toe, siet, het ginck een Saeyman wt om te saeyen. Ende het gescyede als hi saeyde dat Saet, dat somige viel by den Wech, doen quamen die Vogelen onder den Hemel, ende aten dat op.

30. A BIBLE—Lübeck, 1533, fol.

Mk. iv. 3—4. Höret tho. sêth, Ein sädtseyer ginck vth tho seyende. Vnde ydt begaff syck, jn dem alse he seyede, vell etlick an den wech: do quemen de vögel vnder den hemmel, vnde fretent vp.

31. BUGENHAGEN'S Bible, Magdeburgh, 1578.

Mk. iv. 3—4. Höret tho. Seet, Eyn Saedtseyer gynck vth tho seyende, Vnde ydt begaff sick, yn deme alse he seyede, vell etlyck an den Wech, Do quemen de Vögele vnder dem Hemmel, vnde fretent vp.

Low-German Dialects.

32. The following are specimens of the provincial dialects, spoken in Low or North-Germany, as collected and written down in 1827.

33. The provincial dialect spoken about *Nienburg*, 1827.

Mk. iv. 3—4. Hört to: Seeth En Seyer günk ut to seyen. Un et begaff sick, unner't Seyen vull etlick an de Wech, do kemen de Vägels unner'n Himmel un fretent up.

34. PLATT-GER. dialect spoken about *Hanover*, 1827.

Mk. iv. 3—4. Härt tau, et gunk ein Sägemann ut, tau sägen. Und et begaf seck, weil hei sögte, fellen edliche Kören en den Weg; da keimen dei Vögeln under dem Himmel und fratten sei up.

35. PLATT-GER. dialect of the Old Mark of *Brandenburg*, 1827.

Mk. iv. 3—4. Horch tau, et gink en Buer up't Feld tum Seén. Un (et begap sick) indem hê seété, föhl wat an der Side (oder: ob de Halve); da kamen de Vögel von Himmel (oder: von boben) un fratent up.

36. PLATT-GER. dialect of *Hamburgh*, 1827.

Mk. iv. 3—4. Hör't to: Een Buhr güng ut, sien Saat to say'n: As he nu say't, full een Deel von de Saat by den Wegg, un wurr von de Vägel unnern Himmel oppfrêten.

37. BRUNSWICK dialect, 1827.

Mk. iv. 3—4. Höret tau! Süh et gung en Saiemann ut to saien, Un et begaf sik, bi den Saien, fell wat an den Weg; do kaimen de Vöggel under den Himmel un freiten et up.

38. MECKLENBURG-SCHWERIN dialect, 1827.

Mk. iv. 3—4. Hüret to: Sü, dâr gink een Sajer uut, to sajen. Un et begav sik, as he sajete, feel weck (wat) an de Straat, dâr kemen de Vägel unner den Hewen, un freten't upp.

VI.—THE NETHERLANDS, OR HOLLAND.*

1. Holland† is as remarkable for its origin, as for the intellectual energy of its inhabitants. About fifty years before the christian era, Cæsar speaks

* The author has been very anxious to be correct. He has generally cited his authorities, and to secure as much accuracy as possible, he has consulted his friends, amongst whom he ought to mention Professor Siegenbeek, with gratitude, for his kindness in correcting the manuscript. Those who wish for more minute information on the Dutch language and literature, will find ample information in the following works:—Beknopte Geschiedenis der Nederlandsche Letterkunde, door *Professor M. Siegenbeek*, 8vo. Haarlem, 1826.—J. de 'S Gravenweert, Essai sur l' Histoire de la Littérature Neerlandaise, 8vo. Amsterdam, 1830.—Beknopte Geschiedenis der Nederlandsche tale, door *Professor A. Ypey*, 2 vols. 8vo. Utrecht, 1812-1832.—*Collot d'Escury* Hollands roem in kunsten en wetenschappen, 6 vols. Hague, 1824-1833.—Proeve eener Geschiedenis der Nederduitsche Dichtkunst, door *J. de Vries*, 2 vols. 8vo. Amsterdam, 1809.—Beknopte Geschiedenis der Letteren en Wetenschappen in de Nederlanden, door *N. G. van Kampen*, 3 vols. 8vo. Hague, 1821-1826.—Biographisch, Anthologisch en Critisch Woordenboek der Nederduitsche Dichters, door *P. G. Witsen Geysbeek*, 6 vols. 8vo. Amsterdam, 1821-1827.—Verhandeling over de Nederduytsche Tael en Letterkunde, opzigtelyk de zuydelyke Provintien der Nederlanden, door *J. F. Willems*, 8vo. Antwerpen, 1819.—Over de Hollandsche en Vlaemsche Schryfwyzen van het Nederduitsch, door *J. F. Willems*, 8vo. Antwerpen, 1824.—Batavian Anthology, by *John Bowring* and *Harry S. van Dyk*, 12mo. London, 1824.—Sketch of the Language and Literature of Holland, by *John Bowring*, 12mo. Amsterdam, 1829.—*Van Wijn's* Huiszittend Leven; also *van Wijn's* Historische en Letterkundige Avondstonden, 8vo. Amsterdam, 1800.—Aenleiding tot de Kennisse van het Verhevene Deel der Nederduitsche Sprake, door *Lambert ten Kate*, 2 vols. 4to. Amsterdam, 1723.

† The name of Holland, as Mr. Halbertsma observes, is not heard of before the eleventh century [1064]. The meaning of Holland exactly suits the *fenny* and *boggy* soil which it designates. The oldest Dutch authors write it *ollant*. Thus *Maerlant* says—

> "Doe wart coninc Loduwike
> Karel die caluwe, die wel geraecte,
> Die eerst graue jn *ollant* maecte."
> Vol. iii. p. 13, v. 8.

And again, "Comes de Ollandia," *a Count of Holland*. See Huydecoper on Melis Stoke, vol. i. p. 524. Look for this word in the Teuthonista of van der Schueren, and you will find "Beven daveren als eyn ollant, *Scatere*," *tremble under the feet as a marshy ground.*

The word *ol*, in the sense of *dirty* or *glutinous matter, mud*, does not appear in Anglo-Saxon, but it is found in a derived signification. *Ol*, occasionally changed to *hol*, signifies *calumnia*. Wachtendonk, in his Rhyme Chronicle, observes:

> "Hollant, een nieuwe naem, die schijnt 't lant te passen,
> Alsoo het meest bestaet in veenen en moerassen."
> *Matthæus de Nobilitate*, p. 50.

of the *Batavi*,* the first inhabitants on record, as being located towards the mouths of the Rhine, between the Whaal,† the most southerly stream of the Rhine, and the other branches to the north: thus the dominions of the Batavi appear to have extended from Dordrecht to about Haarlem. The country is generally low and marshy, and seems formed or enriched by the alluvial deposits brought down by the various streams into which the Rhine was divided as it approached the sea. Pliny, the naturalist, about a century after Cæsar, gives a minute description of it as a land, where "the ocean pours in its flood twice every day, and produces a perpetual uncertainty whether the country may be considered as a part of the continent or the sea."‡ The genius and industry of men have prevailed. The Hollanders or Dutch have originally taken their possessions from the dominion of the deep; and the exercise of the perpetual thought, care, and industry, necessary first to raise, and then keep up such mighty embankments as defend them from their constant assailant the raging sea, has educated a people, adventurous, brave, and cautious. The Dutch, applying these habits to the cultivation of their intellectual powers, have thus taken the first rank in polite literature, and have also been successful cultivators of the arts and sciences. We are indebted to the Dutch not only for the discovery of oil painting,§ but for the finest specimens of the art: they were also the inventors of printing,‖ painting on glass, and, as some say, of the pendulum, the microscope, &c.

* Bataver is thought by many to be contracted from Bat-auwers, that is, *inhabitants of good or fruitful land*, from bat, bet *good* (still found in beter), and auwe *ground* or *country*. It is supposed that the name is preserved in a part of Gelderland, the Betuwe *fruitful country*, in opposition to Veluwe *bad land*, from vale *falling*, *defective*, and ouwe *land*, *country*.—*Hist. of Dut. Language, by Ypey*.

† Cæsar's Comment. lib. iv. 10.

‡ Plin. Hist. Nat. lib. xvi.

§ By John van Eyck, better known by the name of John of Bruges, in 1410. Korte leevensschets der Graaven van Holland, door *Ludolf Smids*, 4to. Haarlem, 1744.

‖ At Haarlem, by *Laurence Koster*, about 1423. His real name was *Lourens Janszoon Koster*, a celebrated citizen of Haarlem, born about 1370. He was treasurer of the city, and held other important offices. I once thought that Gutenburg of Mayence was the inventor of printing in 1440, (Elements of Anglo-Saxon Gr. p. 16); but every impartial person, upon a close investigation of the evidence produced in recent works, must ascribe the honour of the invention to Koster. Ample proof will be found in Verhandeling van Koning over den oorsprong, de uitvinding, verbetering en volmaking der Boekdrukkunst te Haarlem, 1816, bij Loosjes. Gedenkschriften wegens het vierde eeuwgetijde van de uitvinding der Boekdrukkunst door Lourens Janszoon Koster van stadswege gevierd te Haarlem den 10 en 11 Julij 1823, bijeenverzameld door Vincent Loosjes, te Haarlem 1824. Mr. Jacobus Scheltema's geschied en Letterkundig Mengelwerk, vol. v. vi. One authority, among many others, is so strong in favour of Holland, that it cannot be omitted. A German chronicle of the year 1499, acknowledges that though Mayence improved the art, it was first known in Holland. "Item wie wail die kunst is vonden tzo Mentz, als vursz up die wyse, als dan nu gemeynlich gebruicht wirt, so is doch die eyrste vurbyldung vonden in Hollant uyss den Donaten, die daeselffst vur der tzyt gedruckt syn. Ind van ind uyss den is genommen dat begynne der vursz kunst. Ind is vill meysterlicher ind subtilicher vonden, dan die selve manier was, und ye langer ye mere kunstlicher wurden." Item, though this art was found (out) as aforesaid at Mayence, in that manner in which it is now commonly practised, yet the first idea was taken in Holland from the Donates which were there published before that time. And from and out of them is taken the beginning of the aforesaid art. And is much more masterly and neatly performed than the former manner was, and the longer (it has continued) the more perfect it has become.—*Cronica van der hilliger stat v̄ Coellē*. Gedrukt te Keulen, by Johannes Koelhoff, in den jare 1499. Gedenkschriften van de uitvinding der Boekdrukkunst, p. 437.

2. This small country has had more than its share of eminent men. It has produced an *Erasmus*, a *Vossius, Lipsius, Junius, Grotius, Heinsius, Rubens, van Dyk, Rembrandt, Boerhave, van Lennep,* and *Bilderdijk*. *Ten Kate* developed the grammatical principles which have been so fully and ably illustrated by Dr. J. Grimm in his Deutsche Grammatik. Let it also be ever remembered that this land of freedom has not only fostered native talent, but supported and encouraged it wherever it was found. Here *Linnæus* formed and matured his *Systema Naturæ:* here *Haller* studied, *Descartes* first received encouraging support, and at Gouda *Locke* finished his immortal work on *Human Understanding*. From Holland also has flowed a stream of classical erudition, conveyed in pure Latinity, and benefited the whole of Europe by the accurate and beautiful specimens of typography which issued fróm the press of the *Elzevirs, Wetsteins,* and other eminent printers. While, for their skill in the learned languages, their classical scholars have acquired European fame, the native tongue, which informed the mind and warmed the heart of the Hollander, has been either entirely unknown or disregarded by other nations, though it is a language of Teutonic origin, and well deserves the attention of the philologer, being one of the purest, most nervous, and expressive of the Gothic root.

3. We have no evidence of the language which was spoken by the Batavi in Cæsar's time, but, as they were a German race, it must have had a Teutonic origin. That this language has undergone some mutations, will be evident from a very short view of the political changes which have taken place. Such changes as affected the language arose from tribes of Teutonic origin; their language, therefore, was only altered by some small dialectic variations, and still remained Teutonic.

4. The *Batavi* were allies of the Romans, who constantly eulogize Batavian bravery and fidelity; but about the end of the 3rd century the Batavi were much oppressed by other Gothic nations, as the Saxons, Salian Francs, and other hordes, which forcibly obtained the settlements of the Batavi. Thus the country became inhabited by a mixture of Germanic tribes,* which were subject to the Francic power till the time of Charlemagne and his sons.

Vincent Loosjes, Haarlem, 1824. A learned Italian, Tommaso Tonelli of Florence, after visiting Holland, and making minute and personal inquiries concerning the discovery of printing, unhesitatingly declares that the invention must be ascribed to Lawrence Koster.—*Antologia di Firenze, Vol.* 41, *Jan.—April*, 1831.

* That the present Dutch are descended from the Batavi, is the opinion of some learned Dutch authors, such as Erasmus, Junius, Dousa, Grotius, and Scriverius. Grotius asserts boldly, [*De Antiquitate Reipublicæ Batavicæ*, c. iii. ad finem,] that the ever-succeeding invaders of the *Insula Batavorum* were swallowed up in the bulk of the Batavian population, and that of course the present Dutch are the genuine offspring of the Batavians. Such was the importance of the Batavian support, that even the insurrection of the Batavi under Civilis could not prevent their restoration to the friendship of the proud conquerors of the world. As long as their name appears in history, the Batavi were the allies of the Romans. But that the present Dutch are the direct offspring of the Batavi, is still a controverted point; for the Batavians were exhausted by the never-ceasing levies of troops, and by the bloody battles of the Romans, often decided by Batavian valour, and being the last supports of the tottering

5. These pagan inhabitants and the Friesians did not listen to the preaching of the Francic monks. The Anglo-Saxons being more allied to the old Dutch, their missionaries had greater success. ***Willibrord,**** with eleven Anglo-Saxon associates, in A.D. 692, left England, as missionaries to Heligoland, Friesland, Holland, Zealand, &c. They were countenanced by Pepin, Duke of the Franks.† Willibrord exerted himself so much, and was so successful, that he became the first bishop of Utrecht in A.D. 697.‡

6. In the 10th century this country had its own particular sovereigns, known by the name of Counts. ***Diederik***§ was the first raised to the dignity of Count of Holland, in A.D. 903. There was a succession of thirty-six Counts, till ***Philip*** II. king of Spain in 1581, who was the last Count.|| Philip, being a bigoted catholic, and infringing the rights of Holland and the neighbouring states, ***Holland,*** united with four other provinces, at Utrecht in 1579, to resist the Spanish oppression. Soon after, in 1581, two other states joined, and constituted ***The Seven United Provinces,*** which solemnly renounced the authority of Philip. William, Prince of Orange and Nassau, first held the dignity as Stadtholder under the authority of Philip. After the rejection of Philip, William was to be made Count of Holland: all preliminary steps were taken, and there was nothing wanted but the solemn inauguration, when he was assassinated at Delft in 1584. His sons, Maurice and Frederic Henry, held the dignity

empire, they were crushed and almost annihilated by its downfal. The Germanic crowds of Saxons, Francs, and Cauchi, rushing on the borders of the Roman empire, could not suffer these *socii*, these *amici et sodales populi Romani*, to dwell with them on the same spot. Afterwards the Insula Batavorum is reported to be inhabited by the Francs, and the name of Batavi is never mentioned again in all the changes their country underwent. In succeeding periods the Insula Batavorum was occupied by the Chamari; [A.D. 287], by the Salii [A.D. 358], shortly after by the Guadi (read perhaps Cauchi) and in the reports of the battles of the Romans against these invaders, or of the invaders against each other, the name of Batavi is never mentioned. Eumenius states, that towards the end of the third century, the Insula Batavorum was possessed by Francic tribes. At last, about A.D. 470, the name of Batavi disappears for ever from history, and on this period it is justly observed by the Dutch historian Wagenaar, "This nation (the Batavi) seems to have been partly slain in the Roman armies, partly transplanted by the Romans, partly killed by foreign adventurers, or drawn away from their native soil, and partly blended amongst the Francs, the Saxons, and the Friesians, so as soon to obliterate even their name in this country." Now if the Batavi were extinguished in the fifth century, it will be difficult to discover much of Batavian blood in those who occupy their territories in the nineteenth century. See *Wagenaar Vaderlandsche historie*, tom. i. p. 243, 244, 251, 295, 296. *Nalezingen op de Nederlandsche Geschiedenis*, tom. i. p. 93, 97. Inleiding tot de geschiedenis van Gelderland door W. A. van Spaan, tom. iii. p. 2. *Eumenius Panegyricus Constant.* August. c. v. *Leibnitz* rerum Brunswicensium Scriptores, I. 26.—The substance of this note is taken from a communication of the Rev. J. H. Halbertsma; it rests on his authority and the authors he has quoted.

* Alcuin. Vita Willibr. Die sprachen der Germanen von Dr. T. G. Radlof, p. 4.

† Advenissent ad Pippinum Ducem Francorum, *Bd.* v. 10, 11; *Sm.* p. 192, 9.

‡ Historia Episcopatuum Fœderati Belgii, utpote Metropolitani Ultrajectini, &c. folio, Antverpiæ, 1755, p. 1.

§ Some refer the origin of the Counts of Holland to the time of Charlemagne, Holland being one of the feudal grants of this emperor. "Noverint universi, quod serenissimus Dominus Rex Albertus Romanorum semper invictus, vacantem *Hollandiæ Principatum, quem Carolus Imperator olim magnus Theodorico* (Diederik) *Comiti concessit in beneficium feudale*, tam jure, quam gladio ad Sacrum Romanum intendit revocare imperium. *Trithemius Chr. Hirsaug. ad a.* 1300. *Struvii Corpus Hist. Germaniæ, Periodus nona*, § 8, note 33, vol. i. p. 574.

|| Smids's *Graven van Holland*, 4to. Haarlem, 1744.

of Stadtholder in succession till 1647, when William II. son of Frederic Henry, was invested with this authority.

7. The Stadtholder fled in 1795, and Holland became a more democratic republic. In 1806, Lewis Buonaparte, by the powerful influence of his brother Napoleon, was proclaimed King of Holland. This prince abdicated in 1810, and Holland was united to the French empire. In 1815, Belgium was joined to Holland, and the Prince of Orange Nassau was inaugurated King of the Netherlands under the name of William I. Belgium revolted in 1830.

From these political changes the language, especially in early times, must have been affected. A few specimens will best show the mutations and the progress of the Dutch tongue; but, before these are introduced, a few remarks upon its nature and character may not be useless.

8. The distinguishing characteristic of the Dutch language,* is descriptive energy. If it be not soft and musical, it is dignified, sonorous, and emphatic. It has great compositive power; all technical terms, which the English borrow from exotic sources, from the Latin and Greek, are composed by the Dutch from their own indigenous roots. Almost every polysyllabic word is descriptive of the object which it designates. In this respect the Dutch is much superior to the present English.† There is, however, a striking affinity between our language and the Dutch. Take as instances a Dutch proverb, and a short extract from Spieghel.

A DUTCH PROVERB.

"Als de wyn is in de man,
Is de wysheid in de kan."

TUINMAN's *Sprkw. Nalz*. p. 19.

LITERAL ENGLISH.

As (*when*) the wine is in the man,
Is the wisdom in the can.—*Bowring*.

"Parnassus is te wijd; hier is geen Helicon,
Maar duinen, bosch en beek, een lucht, een zelfde zon,
Dit water, dit land, beek, veld, stroom en boomgodinnen,
Met maghteloose liefd wij hartelijk beminnen."

Hartspiegel, I. 127—130.

LITERAL ENGLISH.

Parnassus is too wide; here is no Helicon,
But downs, wood, and beck, one air, one selfsame sun,
This water, this land, beck, field, stream, and wood-goddesses,
With mightless love we heartily admire.‡

* I cannot omit a remark on the importance of language, in designating the mental powers of a nation, written by a learned and truly patriotic Dutchman. "Elk volk hecht prijs aan het eigendommelijke van zijn karakter, aan hetgeen, waarin het zijne zedelijke waarde, het uitmuntende van zijne verstandsvermogens acht te bestaan; het moet dus, bij wettig gevolg, belang in die Taal stellen, welke het van alle volken onderscheidt."—*Collot d'Escury Hollands roem in kunsten en wetensch.* iii. bl. 9.

† Astronomy is in Dutch sterrekunde, from ster *a star*, kunde *knowledge, science*; or hemelloopkunde, from hemel *heaven*, loop *a course*, kunde *science*.—Taalkunde *grammar*, from taal *language*, kunde *science*.—Telkunst *arithmetic*, from tel *a number*, kunst *science, art*.—Aardrijkskunde *geography*, from aarde *earth*, rijk *realm*, kunde *science*, &c.

‡ Bowring's Batavian Anthology, 12mo. London, 1834, from which interesting little work these translations and some other poetic versions are taken.

9. The correct and emphatic version of the Scriptures, which owes its origin to the Synod of Dordrecht 1618—1619, affords a fine specimen of the expressive powers of the Dutch language. It is one of the best established versions, and the language of this translation is well calculated to express the devout and dignified emotions of the Christian.

10. The earlier the specimens of the Teutonic languages, the more striking are their affinity and analogy, which prove that they originally sprung from one source. The oldest compositions in Dutch are very similar to Low-German (*Platt-Deutsch.*)

THE FIRST SPECIMEN OF THE DUTCH LANGUAGE is taken from a translation of the Psalms made about A.D. 800. These Low-German Psalms, written in the time of the dynasty of Charlemagne, were published for the first time by F. H. von der Hagen Breslaw, 1816.* The manuscript of this translation is first mentioned in a letter of Lipsius to his friend Schottius, at Antwerp, dated Louvain, January 14th, 1599.† Professor A. Ypey of Groningen claims this fragment as a specimen of the old Low-German or Dutch. (*Nederduitsch.*)‡

PSALM lvi. 2—5.

2. Ginathi mi got ginathi mi. uuanda an thi gitruot sila min. In an scado ftheraco thinro sal ic gitruon untis farliet unreht.

3. Ruopen sal ik te gode hoista. got thia uuala dida mi.

4. Sanda fan himele in ginereda mi. gaf'an bismere te tradon mi.

5. Santa got ginatha sina in uuarheit sina. in generida sela mina fan mitton uuelpo leono. slip ik gidruouit. Kint manno tende iro geuuepene in sceifte. in tunga iro suert scarp.

THE SAME IN MODERN DUTCH.

2. Begenadig mij, God! Begenadig mij; want op U vertrouwt mijne ziel. En in de schaduw uwer vederen zal ik vertrouwen tot dat het onregt moge voorbijgaan.

3. Roepen zal ik tot den hoogsten God, God die mij wel deed.

4. Hij zond van den hemel en verloste mij; Hij gaf aan den smaad over, die mij vertraden.

5. God zond zijne genade en waarheid; en Hij verloste mijne ziel van het midden der leeuwen welpen. Ik sliep ongerust. Kinderen der menschen; hunne tanden (waren) wapenen en schichten en hunne tong een scherp zwaard.

11. The Flemish is so closely allied to the Dutch, that it may, especially in its earliest form, be considered the same language. In the thirteenth century, because of the flourishing state of the Flemings, and the care of their writers to observe great purity in their diction, and to express correctly the gender and inflection of words, this improved form of the Dutch language was denominated Flemish. Even at the present day Flemish appears to be nothing more than the Dutch of the preceding century.

* Niederdeutsche Psalmen aus der Karolinger Zeit, zum ersten mahl herausgegeben von Friedrich Heinrich von der Hagen, 8vo. Breslau, 1816.

† Opera omnia Justi Lipsii, vol. ii. p. 986, Vesaliæ, 1675.

‡ A. de Jager, Taalkundig Magazijn, No. I. p. 65, Rotterdam, 1833.

12. A LITERAL COPY OF THE CHARTER OF BRUSSELS in A.D. 1229, from the Book of Privileges, called the Book with the Hairs (*Boek met den Hairen*) from *Verhandeling over de Nederduytsche tael en Letterkunde, opzigtelyk de zuydelyke Provintien der Nederlanden*, door J. F. Willems, Antwerpen, 2 vols. 8vo. 1819—1824.

"Ic heinric bi der gratien goeds hertoghe van Brabant, Ende ic heinric sijn oudste sone wi doen u cont dit ghescrifte allen dengenen die nu syn ende die nacomende sijn. dat wi overmids vroeden rade onser mannen en der scepenen en der gesworne van bruesele desen coren hebben geset binnen Bruesele bi trouwen en de bi eede onser manne ende gemeinleec den poerteren van Bruesele Desen core te houden om gemeine orbore ende vordane meer in deser manieren."—WILLEMS' *Verhandeling*, p. 133.

MODERN DUTCH.

"Ik Hendrik, bij de gratie Gods, hertog van Braband, en ik Hendrik, zijn oudste zoon, wij doen u weten dit geschrift aan al degenen, die nu zijn, en die nakomende zijn, dat wij, ten gevolgen van wijzen raad onzer mannen en der schepenen en der gezworencn van Brussel, deze keuren hebben gezet binnen Brussel door trouw en door ede onzer mannen, en gemeenlijk de Poorteren (*Burgers*) van Brussel deze keuren te houden tot algemeen gemak en voortaan meer op deze wijze."

LITERAL ENGLISH.

"I Henry, by the grace of God, Duke of Brabant, and I Henry, his eldest son, we make (to) you known this writing to all those who now are, and who are to come, that we, in consequence of the wise counsel of our men, and of the sheriffs, and of the sworn of Brussels, these statutes have established in Brussels through the fidelity and oath of our men, and commonly the citizens (Burghers) of Brussels these statutes to keep, for general convenience, and for the future more in this wise."

13. Reinaert de Vos, an allegorical and satirical poem, is one of the most popular works ever published. The story soon spread over the whole of Europe, by translations into almost every language. The poem was first written in the old *Flemish* dialect, affording a fine and very early specimen of the language. The Flemish manuscript is undoubtedly the original of which the famous *Low-Saxon Reineke Vos*, published at Lubeck, 1498, is a free translation. The old prose editions of Reineke Vos, printed at *Gouda*, 1479, and *Delft*, 1485, appear to be only a negligent translation of the Flemish poem, even preserving, in many instances, the metre and rhyme of the original. The English version, by *William Caxton*, 1481, was made from the Delft edition. By the indefatigable researches of Mr. J. F. Willems, it appears that the first part of the Flemish Reinaert was written about 1150, and by recent inquiries, as well as by the preface to his modernized Flemish Reinaert de Vos naer de oudste beryming, Eecloo, 1834, it is concluded that *Willem van Utenhoven*, a priest of Aerdenburg, was the real author* of the second

* *Madok* was not the author, for the name of such a writer cannot be found. In the passage where Madok occurs, it cannot be the name of a man; for, as *Maerlant* observes, it merely designates a poem, (Hoffmann's *Horæ Belg* i. 21, by the fertile and learned writer

part which was composed about the year 1250. Jacob van Maerlant, the father of the Flemish chroniclers and poets, so early as 1270, complains of the alterations and additions made by copyists of Reinaert's boerden, *merry jests and tricks.*

14. That some of the materials of this fine poem are taken from French works, is confessed by Willem van Utenhoven himself:

> Daerom dedi de vite soeken,
> Ende heeftse uten walschen boeken
> In dietsche aldus begonnen.— *Willems' Pref.* p. xiv. l. 7.
>
> Therefore did he the tricks (*of the fox*) seek,
> And has them out of Welsh (*foreign*) books
> In Dutch thus begun.

15. There have been many editions of this work. We have the erudite volume of Reinardus Vulpes, *Carmen epicum seculis* IX *et* XII *conscriptum,* ad fidem Codd. MSS. edidit et adnotationibus illustravit *Franciscus Josephus Mone, Stuttgardiæ et Tubingæ,* 1832; also *Mr. O. M. Meon's* highly interesting edition of nearly all the parts of the fables and tales of the Fox, treated by *Piere de St. Cloud, Richard de Lison, Marie de France,* &c. which appeared under the title *Le Roman du Renard,* publié d'après les MSS. de la Bibliothèque du Roi des XIII. XIV. et XV. siécles, *Paris,* 1826, chez Treuttel et Würz, 4 vols. 8vo. avec figures. The indefatigable researches of the learned *Professor J. Grimm* are published under the title *Reinhart Fuchs,* Berlin, 1834, These and other numerous editions, as well as the complaint of Waltherus de Coinsi, Prior of Vic sur Aisne in his Louanges de nostre Dame, and Miracles de la Vierge, that Renard was preferred to the reading of legends, sufficiently show how many pens it has occupied, and at what an early period this celebrated poem served for entertainment and instruction. A slight comparison of all these productions with the Flemish *Reinaert de Vos* must lead to the conviction, that whatever use its author may have made of the works of his predecessors, he has far surpassed them all, and has composed a work fully deserving the praises which the most competent judges have bestowed upon it. It is important both for matter and composition; and if it were the only interesting and valuable work existing in the old Dutch, it alone would fully repay the trouble of learning that language. This poem gives a true picture of the world, with all its orders, states, conditions, passions, and characters, in an easy

Hoffmann von Fallersleben, to whom we are indebted for a very correct edition of Reineke Vos, from the Lubeck edition of 1498, with a valuable glossary). Besides, the article *de* is never used before Dutch proper names. That all may judge for themselves, the passage is here cited:—

"Willem die Madok maecte Daer hi dicken omme waecte Hem vernoide so haerde Dat die geeste van Reinaerde Niet te recht en es geschreven." *Willems' Reinaert de Vos,* p. XIII.	"Willem, who wrote (made) Madok, About which he was much awake, Annoyed himself so much That the actions of Reinaerde Were not correctly written."

and flowing versification, in a rich, powerful, and sonorous language, hitherto, for want of knowing its powers, not so valued as it deserves.

16. Professor Grimm's invaluable Reinhart Fuchs is a rich mine of philology, history, and general information, that cannot fail to revive a love for the old Dutch or Flemish, which, notwithstanding all endeavours to suppress it, has still preserved its pristine vigour and strength. In the present age, the Flemish owes much to the patriotic feeling and well-directed energy of a native Fleming, *J. F. Willems, Esq.* whose exertions are above all praise.*

17. The first example is taken from *Grimm's Reinhart Fuchs*, Berlin, 1834, printed from the Codex Comburgensis, an old Flemish manuscript preserved at Stuttgardt. There is still a manuscript of it at Antwerp; there was also one at Amsterdam, which a few years ago was sold to an Englishman.† The other example is taken from the *modernised Flemish edition by J. F. Willems*, 12mo. Eecloo, 1834. These may serve to show the great affinity of the Flemish dialect with the English:

OLD FLEMISH.

Het was in enen pinxen daghe,
dat bede bosch ende haghe
met groenen loveren waren bevaen.
Nobel die coninc hadde ghedaen
sîn hof craieren over al,
dat hi waende, hadde hîs gheval,
houden ten wel groten love.
Doe quamen tes coninx hove
alle die diere, grôt ende clene,
sonder vos Reinaert allene.
hi hadde te hove so vele mesdaen,
dat hire niet dorste gaen:
die hem besculdich kent, onsiet.
also was Reinaerde ghesciet:
ende hier omme scuwedi sconinx hof,
daer hi in hadde cranken lof.

Grimm's Reinhart Fuchs, p. 116.

MODERNISED FLEMISH VERSION.

'T was omtrent de Sinxendagen.
Over bosschen over hagen
Hing het groene lenteloof.
Koning Nobel riep ten hoov'

* Verhandeling over de Nederduitsche tael en letterkunde opzigtelyk de zuydelyke Provintien der Nederlanden, *J. F. Willems, Antwerpen*, 1819.—*Willems'* over de hollandsche en vlaemsche schryfwyzen van het Nederduitsch, *Antwerpen*, 1824, 8vo.

† Mr. Heber at whose sale, as I am informed by the friendly communication of Mr. Willems, it was purchased by the Belgian government, and it is now printing under the learned and judicious superintendence of Mr. Willems. A warm interest for the early literature of the Belgians has recently been revived, not only by the publications of Mr. Willems, but by Theophilus, a Flemish poem of the 14th century, and other pieces, just published by Mr. Blommaert of Ghent.

Al wie hy, om hof te houden,
Roepen kon uit veld en wouden.
Vele dieren kwamen daer,
Groot en klein, een bonte schaer.
Reinaert Vos, vol slimme treken,
Bleef alleen het hof ontweken;
Want hy had te veel misdaen
Om er heen te durven gaen.
Die zich schuldig kent wil vluchten.
Reinaert had er veel te duchten;
Daerom schuwde hy het hof,
En dit bracht hem kranken lof.—*Willems*, p. 1.

LITERAL ENGLISH.

It was upon a Whitsunday,
When over hedge and bush so gay
Waved the greeny leaves of spring.
At the command of Nobel, king,
To his court they did convene
All whom he did faithful ween,
Bowing with submission true.
Then to the royal court there drew
All the beasts, both great and small,
But one was missing of them all,
Renard whose misdeeds were so great
He durst no more approach the gate:
A guilty conscience shuns the light,
And such was Renard's evil plight,
That to the court no more he came,
Where he did bear so ill a name.*—*Morrell.*

18. JACOB VAN MAERLANT is the father of the Dutch Poets. He was born at Damme in Flanders, A.D. 1235, and died in 1300. Maerlant was a layman, and distinguished as a philosopher and orator. He translated several works into Dutch rhyme, such as *The Beauties of Aristotle*, of which

MAERLANT SAYS:

Dese bloemen hebben wi besocht
En uten Latine in Dietsche brocht
Ute Aristotiles boeken.

IMITATED IN THE ENGLISH OF CHAUCER.

All these beauties haue we soughte,
And out of Latin to Dutche broughte,
From the bookes of Aristotle.

19. His famous work is, "Spiegel Historiael," or "*Historic Mirror.*" In his *Leven van Franciscus*, he makes the following apology for using Flemish words.

* For the German of this passage, see *High-German*, § 56, 57; and *Low-German*, § 26.

MAERLANT'S FRANCISCUS.

Ende, omdat ic Vlaminc ben,
Met goeder herte biddic hen,
Die dit Dietsche sullen lesen,
Dat si myns genadich wesen;
Ende lesen sire in somich woort,
Dat in her land es ongehoort,
Men moet om de rime souken,
Misselike tonghe in bouken.

IMITATED IN THE STYLE OF CHAUCER.

For I am Flemysh, I you beseche
Of youre courtesye, al and eche,
That shal thys Doche chaunce peruse,
Unto me nat youre grace refuse;
And yf ye fynden any worde
In youre countrey that ys unherde,
Thynketh that clerkys for her ryme
Taken an estrange worde somtyme.

Bowring's Batav. Anthol. p. 25.

20. In power, extent, and population, Holland soon became the predominant province; and after the Union, the States-General was held at the Hague in this district: hence, the language of Holland became the language of the government, the learned, and the press—in short, the arbiter of what was to be considered true Dutch, and it is therefore often denominated *Hollandsche taal* or *Hollandsch.*

21. Melis Stoke began his "Rijmkronijk," or "*Poetical Chronicle,*" before the year 1296, perhaps about 1283, as it was dedicated to Count Floris the Fifth, who died in 1296.* This Chronicle was published in 1591, and again in 3 vols. 4to. 1772, by *Huydecoper*, with valuable notes. This last is by far the best edition.†

MELIS STOKE'S DEDICATION.

Dese pine ende dit ghepens
Sendic u, Heer Grave Florens,
Dat ghi moghet sien ende horen
Wanen dat ghi sijt gheboren,
Ende bi wat redenen ghi in hant
Hebbet Zeelant ende Hollant;
Ende bi wat redenen dat ghi soect
Vrieslant, dat u so sere vloect.

Huydecoper's Melis Stoke, b. i. v. 27.

LITERAL ENGLISH.

The fruit of my pains, and thoughts also,
Sir Count Florens, send I to you;

* Ypey's Beknopte geschiedenis der Nederlandsche Taal, Utrecht, O. S. van Paddenburg, 1812, vol. i. p. 334.

† B. Huydecoper Rijmkronijk van Melis Stoke, met Historie-Oudheid-en Taalkundige aanmerkingen, Leyden, Johannes Le Mair, 1772, vol. i. p. 7, 8.

That you might see, and also hear,
From whence they came that did you bear,
And by what right, within your hand,
You hold both Zealand and eke Holland,
And by what right you seek yet more
Friesland, that curses you so sore.

Morrell.

22. Charter of Leyden, A.D. 1294.

In het Jaar, 1294.

Wy Florens, Grave van Hollant, van Zelant, ende Here van Vrieslant, maken cont alle den ghenen, die desen brief sullen sien, of horen lesen, dat wi hebben ghegheven Rutghere den Scomakere, ende Kerstanse sinen broder, derdalf morghens Lants in eghindoem, die ligghen alrenast der Burch van Leiden, ende dat vorseide Lant hevet Daniel van den Warde quite gheschouden, als dat hy't held van ons te lene.

Ghegheven alsmen scrivet vire ende neghentie.

Handvesten der Stad Leyden, folio, *Leyden*, 1759, p. 478.

LITERAL ENGLISH.

In the year 1294.

We Florens, Count of Holland, of Zealand, and Lord of Friesland, make known to all those who this letter shall see, or hear read, that we have given to Rutghere the Shoemaker, and Kerstanse his brother, two and a half acres of land, in property, which lie nearest the castle of Leyden, and this aforesaid land has Daniel van den Warde quite paid, so as he held it from us in fief.

Given, as men date, four and ninety.

Jan van Heelu.

23. Jan van Heelu, or van Leeuwe, so called from the name of the place in Braband where he dwelt. About 1291 he wrote the chronicle of the feats of Jan I. Duke of Braband,* which has just appeared in a splendid edition with this title " Rijmkronijk van Jan van Heelu, &c. van J. F. Willems Lid der Koninglijke Academie van Brussel. 4to. 1836.

JAN VAN HEELU.

Want, gelyc dat die Euerzwyn,
Daer si moede gejaget zyn,
Verbeiden spieten ende sweert,
Alsoe drongen si, onuerueert,
Jeghen die Brabantre weder,
Dat si doen den Hertoghe neder
Twee orsen onder hem staken.

A VERSION IN THE LANGUAGE OF CHAUCER.

As the furious boare, pursued
By the daring hunter rude,
Teares the earth, and, raging loudlie,
Rushes on the hunter proudlie,
So the fierce Brabanter then
Driues the Hertoch back agen,
Under him two horses stagger.

* Professor Siegenbeek's Beknopte Geschiedenis der Nederlandsche Letterkunde, 8vo. 1826, p. 27.

24. The Life of Jesus, an interesting and a very useful harmony of the Gospels, most probably formed from the Vulgate, as the parables and other parts are in Dutch prose, and almost a literal Dutch translation from the Latin of this celebrated version. This early Harmony of the Gospels must be interesting to divines, while the philologist will rejoice at the discovery of this pure specimen of ancient Teutonic. The MS., written on one hundred and two leaves of coarse parchment, was preserved in the Abbey of St. Trond, and presented to Dr. Meijer, in 1828, while he was Professor in the University of Louvain. It is the opinion of his friend, Professor F. J. Mone, and of Mr. Willems of Ghent, as well as his own, that this MS. is a composition of the latter part of the 13th century. It was published with the following title:

Het Leven van Jesus.—Een Nederlandsch Handschrift uit de dertiende eeuw, met taalkundige aanteekeningen, voor het eerst, uitgegeven door G. J. Meijer, Hoogleeraar te Groningen.—*Te Groningen bij J. Oomkens*, 8vo. 1835, pp. 431.

A very short specimen from the parable of the sower will be sufficient.

Een sayere ghinc ut sayen syn saet. en alse hi sayde so uil som dat saet neuen den weghe. Aldar wardt vertorden. eñ de voghele quamen eñ atent op. (Chap. 89, p. 77, l. 9.)

25. Spiegel onser behoudenisse. This is one of the first books printed at Haarlem by Laurens Janszoon Koster; it is in the old German character, and in a quarto form, consisting of sixty-two pages. The printing is only on one side of the leaf, the blank sides being pasted together, and the pages are without numbers. Many of the letters stand out of their connexion, and irregularly in the lines. The book has not any title, but its object is to illustrate Scripture history by means of woodcuts. It is without date, but supposed to have been printed about the year 1424. The introductory sentence will be an interesting specimen of the Dutch language about the time when it was printed:

SPIEGEL ONSER BEHOUDENISSE.

Dit is die prologhe vãder spieghel onser behoudenisse so wie ter rechtuaerdichet vele mẽschẽ lerẽ sellẽ blenckẽ alse sterrẽ in die ewighe ewichhede. Hier om ist dat ic tott' lerĩge vele mẽschẽ dit boek heb aẽgedacht te vgaderen (vergaderen).

LITERAL ENGLISH.

This is the prologue of the mirror of our redemption, such as for justification, many men shall teach to shine as stars in the everlasting eternity. Therefore it is that I, to the instruction of many men, this book have meditated to compose.

26. Evangelium, is a translation from the Latin Vulgate, a monument of the Dutch language, and a fine specimen of typography: it was printed at *Gouda*, 1477, in 4to. The Evangelium was just preceded by *Nederduitsche Bybel*, Delft, Jacob Jacobsz (van der Meer) en Mauritius Yemantsz van Middelborch, 10 Jan. 1477, small fol.

Lk. viii. 4, 5.

4. In dien tiden doe ene grote scare vergaderde, ende uten steden quamē to thē seide hi bi ghelikenisse. 5. Hi ghinc wt saeyen die syn saet saeyet Ende als hyt saeyet. sommic hviel biden weghe. ende het wort vertreden ende die voghelen des hemels atent.

27. Dat niewe Testament, *Delft*, 1524, 8vo.

Mk. iv. 3, 4.

3, 4. Hoert toe Siet, een sayer ginc wt om te sayen, ende het geboerde onder tsayē, dattet soommich saet viel bij den wech, ende die vogelē des hemels syn gecomen, ende hebbē dat opgegetē.

28. Dat gheheel Nyeuwe Testament, *Thantwerpe*, 1527, 8vo.

Mk. iv. 3, 4.

3, 4. Hoor toe, siet, een sayer ghinc wt om te sayen. En tgebuerde onder tsayen, datt et sommich saeyt viel bey den wech, ende die vogelen des Hemels zijn gecomen ende hebben dat opgegeten.

29. Biblia, *tot Leyden*, 1581.

Mk. iv. 3, 4.

3, 4. Hoort, siet een Zaeyer ginck wt om te zaeyen. Ende het gheschiede dat als hy zaeyde, een deel (des zaets) viel by den weech, ende de voghelen des hemels quamen ende aten dat op.

30. Jacob Cats, generally styled Father Cats, was born at Brouwershaven, a small town in Zealand, 1577, and died 1660. He is the poet of the people: everywhere practical and useful, everywhere original, and often sublime. Bilderdijk says—

> Goede, dierbre Vader Cats,
> Wat behelst ge niet al schats!
>
> Good, beloved Father Cats,
> How much treasure dost thou contain!
>
> Gij, daerom, geeft uw liefde niet
> Aen ieder die u liefde biet;
> Maer eerst op alle saecken let
> Eer dat gij sucht of gunste set;
> Want die te licht een vrient verkiest,
> Wel licht sijn vrient en al verliest.
>
> *Minne en Sinnebeelden*, I. D. p. 133. 1828.
>
> Then love not each who offers thee
> In seeming truth his amity;
> But first take heed, and weigh with care,
> Ere he thy love and favour share;
> For those who friends too lightly choose,
> Soon friends and all besides may lose.
>
> Geluckigh is de mensch die gelt en hooge staten
> Kan hebben buijten sucht, en willigh achterlaten;
> Kan seggen tot de pracht, tot eer, en tot de lust,
> Al ben ick sonder u, soo ben ick toch gerust.
>
> *Spiegel van den ouden en nieuwen tijt*, I. D. p. 539. 1828.

Oh! happy, happy he, whose generous soul can rise
Above the dross of wealth, or pomp, or vanities—
Scorn splendour, pleasure, fame; and say with honest pride,
I have ye not indeed, but yet am satisfied.—*Bowring.*

31. PIETER CORNELIUS HOOFT, born at Amsterdam, March 16th, 1581, and died 1647. Vondel said of him—

Dat Doorluchtig Hooft der Hollandsche Poeten.
Of Holland's poets most illustrious head.

He was also so eminent a prose writer as to obtain the appellation of the Tacitus of Holland.

32. HUIG DE GROOT, better known by his Latinised name Hugo Grotius, was born at Delft in 1583. He had extraordinary and precocious talents, and was a zealous Arminian. Grotius was one of those whose influence excited some of that universal attention to religion so prevalent in Holland. When imprisoned at Loevesteyn, he wrote his most celebrated poem in Dutch, "*Bewijs van de ware Godsdienst,*" Evidences of the true Religion.* Though he was one of the most learned men Holland ever produced, and is deservedly eulogised for his critical as well as for his historical writings, his reputation as a poet is not very great. One short specimen is given from the conclusion of his Evidences.

Neemt niet onwaerdig aen dit werkstuk mijner handen,
O des aerdbodems markt, o bloem der Nederlanden,
Schoon Holland: laet dit sijn in plaets van mij bij u
Mijn koningin: ik toon soo als ik kan noch nu
De liefde die ik heb altijd tot u gedragen
En draeg en dragen sal voorts alle mijne dagen.—p. 136. 1728.

ENGLISH VERSION.

Receive not with disdain this product from my hand,
O mart of all the world! O flower of Netherland!
Fair Holland! Let this live, tho' I may not, with thee,
My bosom's queen! I show e'en now how fervently
I've loved thee thro' all change—thy good and evil days—
And love, and still will love, till life itself decays.

33. DIRK RAFAEL CAMPHUYSEN, a disciple of the famous Arminius, was a native of Gorkum, born in 1586, and died in 1626. He wrote a paraphrase on the Psalms, and much religious poetry. One of the most popular pieces of the Dutch poets is *Camphuysen's "May Morning.*"

Wat is de Meester wijs en goed,
Die alles heeft gebouwt,
En noch in wezen blijven doet:
Wat's menschen oog aanschouwt.

* Better known in England by its Latin title, *De Veritate Religionis Christianæ.* He wrote this work in Dutch verse for fishermen, and sailors on long voyages. The Rev. J. Halbertsma says, "I have often heard old Friesian sailors reciting whole pages from this book. Grotius was afterwards induced by the learned to translate it into Latin, and it has been since translated into almost all the languages of Europe, and I believe into Arabic."

Ach! waren alle Menschen wijs,
En wilden daar bij wel!
De Aard' waar haar een Paradijs,
Nu is ze meest een Hel.

Stichtelyke Rymen, 1727, p. 639.

What love, what wisdom, God displays
On earth, and sea, and sky,
Where all that fades and all that stays
Proclaim his Majesty!

Ah! were the human race but wise,
And would they reason well,
That earth would be a paradise,
Which folly makes a hell.

A line is often quoted from his Lawful Amusement, [*Spels Mate*]:

'T is wel, goedheyts fonteyn, 't is wel al wat gy doet.
Fountain of goodness Thou—and all thou dost is well.

34. Joost van den Vondel was born in 1587, and lived to the age of ninety-one. He is the Dutch Shakspeare in his Tragedies: his "Lucifer" is one of the finest poems in the language, and is compared to Milton's "Paradise Lost."

VONDEL'S LUCIFER.

——— O noit volprezen
Van al wat leeft, of niet en leeft,
Noit uitgesproken, noch te spreecken;
Vergeef het ons, en schelt ons quijt
Dat geen verbeelding, tong, noch teken
U melden kan. Ghij waert, ghij zijt,
Ghij blijft de zelve.

A FREE TRANSLATION.

Forgive the praise—too mean and low—
Or from the living or the dead.
No tongue thy peerless name hath spoken,
No space can hold that awful name;
The aspiring spirit's wing is broken;—
Thou wilt be, wert, and art the same!

35. The Established Dutch Version, according to the Synod of Dordrecht, 1618-1619.

Mk. iv. 3—8.

3. Hoort toe, Ziet, een zaeijer gingh uyt om te zaeijen. 4. Ende het geschiedde
in het zaeijen, dat het een [*deel zaets*] viel by den wegh, ende de vogelen des hemels
quamen, ende aten het op. 5. Ende het ander viel op het steenachtige, daer het niet
veel aerde en hadde: ende het gingh terstont op, om dat het geen diepte van aerde
en hadde. 6. Maer als de sonne opgegaen was, soo is het verbrant geworden, ende
om dat het geen wortel en hadde soo is het verdorret. 7. Ende het ander viel in de

doornen, ende de doornen wiessen op, ende verstickten het selve, ende het en gaf geen vrucht. 8. Ende het ander viel in de goede aerde, ende gaf vrucht: die opgingh ende wies, ende het een droegh dertigh, ende het ander sestigh, ende het ander hondert [*vout*].

36. As the chief object of this short account of the Dutch language and literature is philological, to show the close analogy between all the Teutonic languages, especially in their earliest form, very little of more recent literature can with propriety be introduced; but the 17th century is so splendid an era, that a few remarks and extracts must be excused in this period, and even one or two in the 18th and 19th centuries. In the 17th century, Holland had its heroes in *De Ruiter* and *Tromp:* its statesmen in *Barneveldt* and the *De Wits.* Its learned writers are *Huig de Groot* [Grotius], *Daniel* and *Nicolaas Heins* [Heinsius], *P. Schryver* [Schriverius], *John Frederick Groenhof* [Gronovius], *Casper van Baerle* [Barlæus], *Gerard Vos* [Vossius],* and many other eminent classics. For science, *Huygens, Leeuwenhoek, Ruysch, Tulp, Swammerdam.* For its painters, it had *Rubens, Van Dyk, Rembrandt, Mierevelt,* the *Teniers,* the *Van de Veldes, Jordaans, Kuyp,* the *Ostades, Gerard Douw, Mieris, John* and *Philip Wouwerman, Metsu, Berchem, Paul Potter, Pynaker,* the *Ruysdaels, Van Huysem, Wynants, Steen;* and during this period the Universities at *Groningen* in 1614, *Utrecht* in 1636, and *Gelderland,* 1648, and the celebrated school at *Amsterdam* in 1629,† were established. "The age of which we speak," says the learned *Professor Siegenbeek,* "and more especially the earlier part of it, was, in every point of view, so glorious to the Dutch nation, that it would be difficult to discover, in the history of any other people, a period of such resplendent fame and greatness."‡

37. "JACOBUS BELLAMY, born at Flushing in 1757, after gaining much applause, died at Utrecht at the early age of twenty-nine.§ A ballad of his [*Roosje*] is perhaps the most touchingly told story which the Dutch possess. It is of a maid—a beloved maid—born at her mother's death—bred up amidst the tears and kisses of her father—prattling thoughtlessly about her mother—every one's admiration for beauty, cleverness, and virtue—gentle as the moon shining on the downs. Her name was to be seen written again and again on the sands by the Zealand youths—and scarcely a beautiful flower bloomed but was gathered for her. Now in Zealand,

* Of whom Vondel said—

"Al wat in boeken steekt is in zyn brein gevaren."
Whatever is anchored in books, floated about in his brain.

† The University of Leyden was founded in 1574.

‡ Bowring's *Batavian Anthology,* p. 15.

§ Some of the beautiful little poems of *van Alphen* ought to be given, but want of room will only admit of a short eulogy from the pen of Dr. Bowring. "Van Alphen's *Poems for Children* (Gedichtjes voor de Jeugd) are among the best that were ever written. They are a precious inheritance for the youth of the *Netherlands.* They teach virtue in simple eloquence, and are better known in Holland, than are the hymns of Dr. Watts or Mrs. Barbauld here."—*Sketch of the Lang. and Lit. of Holland,* p. 79.

when the south winds of summer come, there comes too a delicate fish, which hides itself in the sand, and which is dug out as a luxury by the young people. It is the time of sport and gaiety—and they venture far, far over the flat coast into the sea. The boys drag the girls among the waves—and Roosje was so dragged, notwithstanding many appeals. "A kiss, a kiss, or you go further," cried her conductor—she fled—he followed, both laughing:—"Into the sea—into the sea," said all their companions; he pushes her on—it is deeper, and deeper—she shrieks—she sinks—they sink together—the sands were faithless—there was no succour—the waves rolled over them—there was stillness and death. The terrified playmates looked—

BELLAMY'S ROOSJE.

De jeugd ging, zwijgend, van het strand,
En zag gedurig om:
Een ieders hart was vol gevoel,—
Maar ieders tong was stom!

De maan klom stil en statig op,
En scheen op 't aaklig graf
Waarin het lieve, jonge paar
Het laatste zuchtje gaf.

De wind stak hevig op uit zee
De golven beukten 't strand;
En schielijk was de droeve maar
Verspreid door 't gansche land.

FREE TRANSLATION.

All silently—they look'd again—
And silently sped home;
And every heart was bursting then,
But every tongue was dumb.

And still and stately o'er the wave,
The mournful moon arose,
Flinging pale beams upon the grave,
Where they in peace repose.

The wind glanced o'er the voiceless sea,
The billows kissed the strand;
And one sad dirge of misery
Filled all the mourning land.

Bowring's Batavian Anthol. p. 75—77.

38. WILLEM BILDERDIJK, born at Amsterdam, 1756, and died at Haarlem, December 18th, 1831, was educated for the law. He was a giant in literature and intellectual strength, the most fertile of the Dutch writers. Willem Bilderdijk is the Samuel Johnson of the Dutch.

Bilderdijk wrote on almost every subject, but poetry was his fort, and he stands in the foremost rank of the Dutch poets.*

PRAISE OF SPEECH.

O vloeibre klanken, waar, met d' adem uitgegoten,
De ziel (als Godlijk licht, in stralen afgeschoten,)
Zich-zelve in meêdeelt! Meer dan licht of melody;
Maar schepsel van 't gevoel in de engste harmony
Die 't stofloos met het stof vereenigt en vermengelt!
Door wie zich 't hart ontlast, verademt, en verengelt!
Gij, band der wezens; en geen ijdel kunstgewrocht,
Door arbeidzaam verstand met moeite en vlijt gezocht,
Maar goddelijke gift, met d' ademtocht van 't leven,
Aan 't schepsel ingestort zoo verr' er geesten zweven.
Bilderdijk's De Dieren, p. 19.

LITERAL ENGLISH.

Ye flowing sounds, in which, with breath pour'd forth,
(Like Godlike light in rays) the soul imparts
Itself! surpassing light or melody;
Deep feeling's offspring, in close harmony,
Spirit and matter blending and uniting!
Thro' which the soul, unburden'd, breathes and lives
The life of angels! Thou tie of beings;
No vain attempt of human skill art thou,
By toilsome minds with pains and care sought out,
But heaven's own gift, breathed with breath of life,
Shed thro' creation, far as mind pervades.—*Morrell.*

39. The services of Professor Siegenbeek, in restoring and remodelling the Dutch language, have been so highly estimated by his country, that his system of Orthography obtained the sanction of the Dutch government in 1806. Since this time, for the sake of uniformity in expressing words, it is required that every public document should be written in strict accordance with the Professor's orthographical system.

40. A free translation of the whole Scriptures, in the modern Dutch style and orthography, was made by the learned and eloquent Professor van der Palm, of Leyden. It was published in 4to. in 1825; and, though it has not the sanction of the States-General, nor is it adopted in the churches, it is greatly esteemed, and in general use. The following extract may serve as a specimen.

Mk. iv. 3—8.

3. Hoort toe! ziet, een zaaijer ging uit om te zaaijen. 4. En het geschiedde, terwijl hij zaaide, viel een deel (*van het zaad*) op den weg; en de vogelen des hemels

* Though living authors scarcely come within the scope of this work, *Tollens* cannot be omitted. He is styled, "the most agreeable, the most popular living poet of Holland." An edition of ten thousand copies of three volumes of his poetry was promptly sold among a population of no more than three millions of people. This itself is no small praise, and implies no small merit, to have so happily touched the feelings of an entire nation. His power is descriptive, his characteristic is originality.—See more in Dr. Bowring's *Sketch*, p. 98.

kwamen, en aten het op. 5. En een ander deel viel in steenachtigen grond, waar het niet veel aarde had; en het schoot terstond op, omdat het geen diepte van aarde had. 6. Doch toen de zon opging, verbrandde het, en omdat het geen' wortel had, verdorde het. 7. En een ander deel viel onder de doornen; en de doornen wiessen op en verstikten het; en het bragt geen vrucht voort. 8. En een ander deel viel in de goede aarde, en bragt vrucht voort, die uitbottede en opwies; en het een droeg dertig, en het andere zestig, en het andere honderd.

41. The established version of the Scriptures, made according to the regulations of the Synod of Dort, 1618-1619, and first published at Leyden in 1637, had its orthography modernised, according to the system of Professor Siegenbeek, by the Rev. Henry Cats, minister of the Dutch Reformed Church at Leyden. Mr. Cats dying before the work was completed, it was finished by Professor van Hengel, and published in 4to. by Thieme of Arnhem, in 1834. The same passage is selected as in the last paragraph, for facility of comparison with Professor van der Palm's translation, and with the old orthography in the 34th paragraph.

Mk. iv. 3—8.

3. Hoort toe! ziet, een zaaijer ging uit om te zaaijen. 4. En het geschiedde in het zaaijen, dat het ééne [*deel zaads*] viel bij den weg; en de vogelen des hemels kwamen, en aten het op. 5. En het andere viel op het steenachtige, waar het niet veel aarde had; en het ging terstond op, omdat het geene diepte van arde had. 6. Maar als de zon opgegaan was, zoo is het verbrand geworden, en omdat het geen' wortel had, zoo is het verdord. 7. En het andere viel in de doornen, en de doornen wiessen op, en verstikten hetzelve, en het gaf geene vrucht. 8. En het andere deel viel in de goede aarde, en het éène droeg dertig, en het andere zestig, en het andere honderd [*voudig*].

42. It is difficult to pass over many of the fine passages to be found in Feith's Old Age, [*Ouderdom*]; The Grave, [*Het Graf*], &c.; Helmers's Dutch Nation, [*Hollandsche Natie*], &c.; and also in the works of many of the old as well as the modern Dutch poets. It would be gratifying to name their divines, philosophers, and those numerous individuals excelling in science and literature; but even a list of their names would far exceed the limits of this brief sketch. A reference can therefore, only be made to those, who have professedly treated the subject more fully.* Enough has been probably advanced to prove that Holland has cast more than her share into the intellectual treasury of the world, and this must suffice for the present.

Dutch Dialects.

43. There are several dialects of the Dutch language, such as the Flemish, the Gelderic, &c. The Friesic need not be here named, as the peculiarities of the country and town Friesic are both pointed out and compared with Anglo-Saxon in IV. page xxxv.

* See note to § 1, page xci.

44. The modern Flemish dialect, according to *Mr. J. F. Willems,** is distinguished from the Dutch,—First, by a too far-fetched inclination to express the distinctions and shades of all varying sounds and significations of words, united with a careful endeavour to preserve in the pronunciation the radical syllable. For this reason the Flemings not only double the long *e* and *o*, but when doubled they also accentuate them, as *eé*, *eê*, and *oó*. They endeavour, in all inflections of words, constantly to write *ae* or *ee*, as plaegen *to plague;* verdraegen, beklaegen, neémen, geéven, graeven; from plaeg *plague*, verdraegt *he agrees*, klaegt *he complains*. They also try to distinguish, by orthography, all words of the same sound, but different in signification; as, wagen *to hazard*, waegen *to weigh*, leven *life*, leeven *to live*. They distinguish compound words by always uniting them with a hyphen, as spraek-konst, grond-word, haeg-appel-boom, aen-nemen, aen-te-nemen.

Secondly.—The long sound of the vowels *a*, *e*, *i*, and *u*, is expressed by immediately adding an *e* in syllables where the vowel is followed by a consonant. Some words are exceptions; as, vader *father;* nader *nearer;* vergaderen *to gather;* kamer *chamber;* averechts *preposterous;* where the single vowel is considered as sufficient. The *y* is considered a real vowel, and thus the Flemings have a vowel more than the Dutch. The *o* is not lengthened by the additional *e*. These two letters are pronounced short, like the French *ou*, or the German *u*.

Thirdly.—By the particular pronunciation of the *ei* or *eê* in beêr, *Dut.* bier *beer;* peêrd, *Dut.* paard *a horse;* peêrel, *Dut.* paarel or parel *a pearl;* geêrne, *Dut.* gaarne, gaarn *willingly*, *readily;* rechtveêrdig, *Dut.* regtvaardig *righteous*, *just;* weêrd, *Dut.* waard *dear*. To this pronunciation the Dutch object, and call it the blaetende, *bleating sound*, though in reality it appears to be the true pronunciation of the Low-Saxon.

The *modernised Flemish version* of the extract from Reinaert de Vos will serve as a specimen.†

45. The dialect of Gelderland will be sufficiently illustrated by the following extract, which will serve both as a specimen and an explanation of its peculiarities. Slichtenhorst, the writer, lived in the 16th century.

GELDERSCHE TAAL.

Geene spraek van Nederland, en koemt de Duitsse moeder-tael naerder dan de Geldersse, als de welke 't eenemael mannelijk is, en de woorden volkomen wtbrengt: wtgezonderd daar de ingezeetenen aen 't Sticht van Utrecht of Holland belenden, die een botter tael hebben dan de binnen-landers. Want daar men hier golt, holt, zolt, zeght, gebruijken de anderen *gout*, *hout*, *zout*, breekende de woorden op zijn Frans, die de letter *l*, vooral in woorden van 't Latijn herkomstigh, ofte smelten ofte 't eenemael verzwijghen, gelijk in hault, altus, *hoogh*, assault en andere meer is te speuren.—*Slichtenhorst, over de Geldersche Taal. Geldersche Volks-Almanak*, 1835, p. 69.

* Over de Hollandsche en Vlaemsche Schryfwyzen van het Nederduitsch, Antwerpen, 1824, pp. 66.

† See § 17, page xcix.

LITERAL ENGLISH.
(Dialect of Gelderland.)

No dialect of the Netherlands comes nearer to the German mother-tongue than that of Gelderland, which is singularly strong, and pronounces the words fully, except where the inhabitants border the provinces of Utrecht or Holland, who have a blunter dialect than those of the interior. For where we here (in Gelderland) say, golt *gold*, holt *wood*, zolt *salt*, the others use gout, hout, zout, pronouncing the words according to the French, who, particularly in words derived from the Latin, either melt (soften) or entirely omit the letter *l*, as in hault altus *high*, assault, and more that may be found.

Non vox, sed votum;
Non musica chordula, sed cor;
Non clamor, sed amor,
Clangit in aure Dei.

Niet de stemmen klaer en soet,
Maar de suchten van 't gemoet;
Niet muzijk van 't snaeren-spel,
Maar het hart oprecht en wel;
Niet 't geroep, maar liefde en min
Klinkt tot Godes ooren in.

Sluijter, 1660, *Geldersche Volks-Almanak*, 1835, p. 124.

46. The peculiarities of the Overijssel Dialect, with many useful documents, and a Dictionary of the chief words, are given by the Rev. J. H. Halbertsma in *Overijsselche Almanak voor Oudheid en Letteren*, 1836, published by J. de Lange, at Deventer. Want of room prevents quotations from this very interesting work.

VII.—THE GOTHS.*

1. The Goths were of Asiatic origin, and it is supposed that they formed a part of the second wave of European population. Many centuries before our era the Goths must have been in Europe, though Pytheas,† the famous navigator born at Marseilles, is the first who

* That great pains have been taken to give an accurate and succinct account of the Goths and their literature, will be evident, when it is known that, besides many alterations, this short and still imperfect abstract has been transcribed four times. A large volume might easily have been written; the difficulty has been in attempting to give a clear epitome. Those who wish for further information may consult "Historia Gothorum, Vandalorum, et Langobardorum ab *Hug. Grotio*, partim versa, partim in ordinem digesta. Præmissa sunt ejusdem prolegomena, ubi Regum Gothorum ordo et chronologia cum elogiis. Accedunt nomina appellativa, et verba Gothica, Vandalica, Longobardica, cum explicatione. Amstelodami, 1655, in gr. 8vo." This is an invaluable work. See also the works cited in the following abstract. There is an article which deserves attention in Schilter's Thesaurus, vol. iii. p. 395, sub voce *Gothe*.

† Strabo I. 23.

mentions them by name. Strabo* assures us, that Pytheas, about 325 before Christ, undertook a voyage to explore the amber coasts in the Baltic. He sailed to Thule, probably Tellemark on the west borders of Norway, then turned southward and passed the cape of Jutland, and proceeded eastward along the coasts of the Guttones and Teutones. If credit be given to this account of Pytheas, the Goths, at this early period, had extended far over Europe, and had arrived on the coast of the Baltic. We know, upon the better authority of Tacitus,† who wrote with great precision towards the end of the first century in the christian era, that in his time the Goths were near the mouth of the Vistula.

2. According to the opinion of many Scandinavian antiquaries, the Goths who overran the Roman empire, came from Scandinavia or Sweden;‡ but Tacitus§ speaks of no Goths in Scandinavia, and only of Suiones, which is the same name that the Swen-skar (*Swedes*) apply to themselves at the present day. It is therefore more probable, as some learned Swedes‖ acknowledge, that when the Goths wandered towards the west and south, some of them, in early times, crossed the Baltic and established themselves in the south of Sweden and the island of Goth-land.¶ We know from Tacitus, just cited, that the Goths were in

* Strabo, the Greek geographer, who died about A.D. 25, is the chief writer recording particulars and giving quotations from the lost works of Pytheas. Strabo I. 63; II. 114.—Pliny also mentions Pytheas, Nat. Hist. xxxvii. 2; iv. 13.

† Annal. II. 62; De Mor. Ger. 43.

‡ They support their assertion by the traditions of Jornandes. Cassiodorus, the learned minister of Theodoric, the Gothic king of Italy in the 6th century, was the first who attempted to write a history of the Goths. This history consisted of twelve books, compiled from old chronicles and songs. The work of Cassiodorus is lost, and all that remains is an imperfect abridgment by Jornandes, (*Jornandes* de Getarum sive Gothorum Origine, et rebus gestis, ad Castalium, cap. 3, 4, 13, &c., Leyden, 1595, 8vo.; *Gibbon's* Decline and Fall of the Roman Empire, chap. 10) bishop of Ravenna, who states that the Goths were from Scandinavia, or the present Sweden, Norway, and Denmark. They traced the genealogies of their hereditary princes up to the race of Odin, called Æsir, [æsir *pl.* of the *Icel.* ás *an Asiatic; vir Asiaticus,*—*Jornandes*, 3, &c.; *Ynglinga Saga. Wheaton Hist.* p. 110,]or Asiatic Odin, and his followers are supposed to have come from the banks of the Tanais or Don. At the present day we find in Sweden, East, West, and South Gothland, and the island near the east coast of Sweden is still called Gothland. From the south of Sweden the Goths crossed the Baltic, and settled on the coast of Prussia, about the mouth of the Vistula. We are informed by some fragments of Pytheas, that he, being in search of the amber coasts, sailed about 6,000 stadia along the coasts of the Guttones and Teutones, through the gulph of Mentonomon [Kattegat, Belt, &c.] to Baltia, the Baltic. (*Plin. Hist. Nat.* xxxvii. 2; iv. 13; *Wachter's Gloss. Ger. Pref.* § XLV.) About the time of the Antonines, A.D. 180, [Ptolemy II.] from some unknown cause or other, the Goths, in vast hordes, leaving the mouth of the Vistula, and other parts, followed the course of this river, and migrated to the northern coast of the Black Sea: hence they made inroads into the Roman empire. In this way Gibbon, following Jornandes, brings the Goths in contact with the Romans.—See *Decline and Fall of the Roman Empire*, chap. 10.

§ Tacitus de Mor. Ger. 44, 45. See the judicious dissertation of *Mr. Gräberg de Hemso*, written in Italian and entitled "Su la Falsità dell' Origine Scandinava data di Popoli detti Barbari chi distrussero l'Impero di Roma," Pisa, 1815.

‖ A. W. de Schlegel sur l'Origine des Hindous.—*Transactions of the Royal Society of Literature*, vol. II. part ii. p. 408.

¶ In the preface to "*Historisch Antiquarische Mitheilungen*," published by the Copenhagen Royal Society of Northern Antiquities, it is said, that "The Goths were found not only in Scandinavia, but Germany; they are, therefore, properly designated by Gotho-Germans (Gotho-Germanen). The old northern Sagas acknowledge that Odin and his Asas first occupied and peopled Saxony, Westphalia, and different other German provinces, before they founded their government in Denmark and Sweden."—*Pref.* p. iii. 1835.

Pomeralia and Prussia, near the Vistula, about A.D. 80, and in the time of the Antonines, A.D. 180. The Vandals and Burgundians are considered as belonging to this race. After conquering different smaller nations in the east of Germany and the present Poland, the Goths, sword in hand, opened themselves a way to the Lower Danube. They took possession of all the northern coasts of the Black Sea, and made inroads into the neighbouring countries, particularly into Dacia, where they settled, and divided themselves into the East and West Goths.* The Visi-Gothi, Visigoths, or, as Jornandes calls them, Vesegothæ, and others Wisigothi or West-Goths, had their name from their western situation. For the same reason the East-Goths were denominated Ostro, or Austro-Gothi.

3. The Goths having conquered and occupied the country on the north of the Black Sea, where, according to Herodotus, the Scythians had dwelt, were often called Scythians by Greek and Roman writers, to the great confusion of history.

4. The West-Goths must have been numerous on the west of the Black Sea, and have made inroads into the Roman empire, as we find them so powerful in Thracia in the time of Decius, A.D. 250, that they took and sacked Philippolis.† Even before this period, about A.D. 180, these Goths had so far increased as to occupy Dacia, the present Transilvania, Moldavia, Wallachia, and Bessarabia.

5. The Getæ, a Thracian race, who had previously inhabited Dacia, were, with the Romans still remaining in the country, amalgamised with their conquerors, the West-Goths. As the East-Goths had been confounded with the Scythians, their predecessors, so there are some who suppose that the West-Goths and the Getæ were the same nation, because they found these Goths occupying the same territory, formerly inhabited by the Getæ. Jornandes, by birth a Goth, probably with the view of exalting his nation by attributing to them all that was done by the Getæ, makes the Goths and the Getæ to be the same people. Had he only been guided by the languages of these nations, he would have seen that the Getæ must have a different origin to the Goths.‡

6. When the West-Goths settled in Dacia, they not only found remnants of Roman civilisation, but Christianity established.§ The mild but powerful influence of the christian religion soon prevailed over their cruel heathen rites; for as early as the Council of Nice, in A.D. 325, the

* Zahn's Ulphilas, p. 2; Adelung's Ælteste Geschichete der Deutschen, p. 202.

† Ammianus, 31, 5; Aurelius Victor, 29.

‡ Herodotus, Strabo, and Menander who was a Getian by birth, and many others, declare that the Getæ were of Thracian origin. Stephanus of Byzantium says expressly "Γετια, ἡ χωρα τῶν Γετῶν. Εστι δε Θρακικον εθνος *Getia, the country of the Getæ. It is a Thracian nation.* — Sub voce ΓΕΤΙΑ, p. 207; *Virg. Æn.* iii. 35; *Ovid. Trist.* v. 7; *Epist. Pont.* lib. iv. *Ep.* xiii. 17. Strabo declares that the Getæ and Thracians spoke the same language, and that the Thracian and the Gothic or Old-German are *quite distinct languages.* See Zahn, p. 4, note *a.* In Adelung's Geschichte der Deutschen there is a long list of Thracian words, not one of which has the least resemblance to German, p. 284—290.

§ Sozomen's Eccl. Hist. lib. ii. 6.

christian Goths had their bishop, Theophilus, whose signature appears in the records of this celebrated council. The Ostro or Eastern Goths, having no such advantages, remained for a long time heathens. In the latter part of the 4th century, the whole of the Goths were governed by Ermanneric, one of their greatest conquerors, who subdued the western nations, and extended his empire from the river Don, through Sarmatia to the Vistula, and even to the Baltic.

7. The Visigoths or West-Goths being greatly oppressed by the Huns from the north of China or Tartary, induced Ulphilas,* their bishop, to implore the protection of the Roman emperor, Valens, in A.D. 376. He pleaded their cause successfully, and the province of Moesia was assigned to them; their innumerable tribes were then permitted to pass over the Danube.† It was from the residence which Valens gave them in Moesia, now Servia and Bulgaria, south of the Danube, that the Visigoths obtained the name of Moeso-Goths. Considering themselves oppressed in Moesia, the Goths revolted, gained several victories over the Romans, and at last under Alaric desolated the Illyrian provinces, and in A.D. 409 took and pillaged Rome. In 412 they established themselves in the south of France, and crossing the Pyrenees, fixed the seat of their empire in Spain, where they reigned nearly three hundred years. They were first weakened by the Francs, and finally subdued by the Saracens.

8. The Ostro or East-Goths, though they applied to Valens, were not permitted to enter Moesia, and were therefore subjugated by the Huns; but after liberating themselves, they embraced Christianity, and were received into Pannonia in A.D. 456, following the Visi or West-Goths into Moesia. The emperor Theodoric the Great, the hero of this nation, conquered Italy, and in A.D. 493 became the founder of a new monarchy at Ravenna. The Gothic government continued in Italy till the year 554, when it was terminated by Belisarius and Narsus under Justinian, emperor of the east. Cassiodorus,‡ the minister of Theodoric, wrote a history of the Goths, which was abridged by his secretary Jornandes.

* This name has great variety in its orthography: we find Ulphilas, Urphilus, Gilfulas, Gudillas, Galfilas, Gulfilas, Ulphias, Ulpias, Gulfias, Hulfias, Wulfila, &c. It is written אולפילאס Aulpilas by R. Abraham in his work entitled שלטי הגבורים. It is inflected *nom.* Ulphilas; *g.* Ulphilæ, exactly as Æneas, Æneæ, &c. after the Greek form Ουλφιλας (*Socrates' Hist. Eccles.* II. 41; IV. 33; *Theodoret.* IV. 33; *Epist.* 104; *Philost.* II. 5; *Sozomen Hist. Eccles.* VI. 37.) Some of the most eminent German scholars have recently adopted a new orthography, or as they affirm, reverted to the old Teutonic spelling, and write it Ulfila from Wulfila *a little wolf*, formed from *Moes.* wulfs *a wolf*, (*Mt.* vii. 15,) in the same manner as magula *puerulus*, (*Jn.* vi. 9,) from magus *puer*, and the diminutive fiskila *pisciculus*, from the root fisk *piscis*. (*Grimm's Deut. Gramm.* vol. iii. p. 666). This, according to the Moeso-Gothic idiom, appears quite correct as it regards the termination; but if a close adherence to the Moeso-Gothic word be followed, it ought to be as precise in the commencement as in the termination, and to be written Wulfila, not Ulfila. Rather than adopt the new mode, which appears incorrect in this particular, the old spelling is here retained, and the word is written Ulphilas Οὐλφιλας, as received from the Greek ecclesiastical historians. *Canzler*, in his *Deutsche Vor und Zunnamen*, thinks that Ulfila, Hulfias, &c. has some affinity with *A.-S.* ulph: *Plat.* hülp: *Dut.* hulp: *Ger.* hülfe: *Old-Ger.* hilfa: *Dan.* hjælp: *Swed.* hjelp: *Icel.* hiálp—all denoting *help, aid, assistance*. Then, with the addition of the diminutive ila, we have Hulpila, or Ulfila *a little help, infantine aid*.

† Jornandes, 25, 26.

‡ See § 2, note (‡).

9. Ulphilas,* born of Cappadocian parents,† was made bishop of the West or Moeso-Goths about A.D. 360. He was so eminent in his talents, learning, and prudence, that he had the greatest influence amongst the Goths, and thence originated the proverb "Whatever is done by Ulphilas is well done." They received with implicit confidence the doctrines of the gospel which he enforced by a blameless life. That he might lead them to the fountain of his doctrine, he translated the Bible from the Greek into the language of the Moeso-Goths, between A.D. 360 and 380. Those who are best acquainted with the subject‡ declare that the language of this ancient translation ought not to be called Moeso-Gothic, as this name leads to the erroneous supposition that this dialect was formed in Moesia. The language of Ulphilas's version is, in fact, the pure German of the period in which it was written, and which the West-Goths brought with them into Moesia. The term Moeso-Gothic is still retained in this work, as it at once shows that the words to which *Moes.* or Moeso-Gothic is applied are taken from the version of Ulphilas, while however the Moeso-Gothic is considered as the earliest German dialect now in existence.

10. Several fragments of Ulphilas's celebrated translation have been discovered. The most famous is *The Codex Argenteus*, or *Silver Book*, so called from being transmitted to us in letters of a silver hue. The words appear to be formed on vellum by metallic characters heated, and then impressed on silver foil, which is attached to the vellum by some glutinous substance, somewhat in the manner that bookbinders now letter and ornament the backs of books.§ This document, containing fragments of the four gospels, is supposed to be of the 5th century, and made in Italy.|| It was preserved for many centuries, in the monastery of Werden on the river Rhur, in Westphalia. In the 17th century it was transmitted for safety to Prague; but Count Konigsmark, taking this city, the Codex Argenteus came into the possession of the Swedes, who deposited it in the library at Stockholm. Vossius, in 1655, when visiting Sweden, became possessed of it, and brought it to Holland; but Puffendorf, as he travelled through Holland in 1662, found it in the custody of Vossius, and purchased it for Count de la Gardie, who, after having it bound in silver, presented it to the Royal Library at Upsal, where it is still preserved.

11. This mutilated copy of the Four Gospels was first published with a Glossary by Junius and Marshall, in 2 vols. 4to. at Dort, 1665, from a beautiful facsimile manuscript made by Derrer, but now lost. There are two columns in each page, Gothic on the left column, and Anglo-Saxon on the right, both in their original characters, the types for which were cast at Dort. The same book, apparently

* See § 7, note (*).

† Theodoret, iv. 37; Sozomen, vi. 37; Socrates, iv. 33.

‡ See Grimm's Deutsche Grammatik, 1st edit. 1819, pref. xlv. xlvi.

§ Ihre's Ulphilas Illustratus, edited by Büsching, Berlin, 1773; Meerman's Origines Typographicæ, Hag. Comit. 2 vols. 4to. 1765, vol. i. p. 2, cap. 2.

|| In Italia scriptus fuit—Ulphilæ partium ineditarum in Ambrosianis Palimpsestis ab Angelo Maio repertarum Specimen, 4to. pp. 1—36. Mediolani, 1819, Pref. p. iv. 12.

published with new titles, and a reprint of the first sheet in Vol. II. or Glossary, appeared again at Amsterdam in 1684. Stiernhelm sent forth an edition in Gothic, Icelandic, Swedish, German, and Latin, 4to. Stockholm, 1671. A new one was prepared by Dr. Eric Benzelius, and published by Lye, 4to. Oxford, 1750, with a Latin translation, and notes below the Gothic: a short Gothic Grammar is prefixed by Lye. A learned Swede, Ihre, a native of Upsal, and afterward Professor, in 1753 favoured the literati with his remarks upon the editions of Junius, Stiernhelm, and Lye. He had constant access to the Codex, and his criticisms and remarks upon the editors' deviations from it are very valuable. All Professor Ihre's treatises on the Gothic version, and other tracts connected with the subject, were published under the following title: — J. ab Ihre scripta versionem Ulphilanam et linguam Moeso-Gothicam illustrantia, edita ab Anton. Frid. Büsching, Berolini, 4to. 1773. The Codex was again prepared and printed in Roman characters, after the corrected text of Ihre, with a literal interlineal Latin translation, and a more free Latin version in the margin, with a Grammar and Glossary by F. K. Fulda. The Glossary revised and the text corrected by W. F. H. Reinwald, published by J. C. Zahn, Weissenfels and Leipzig, 4to. 1805. One short specimen will be sufficient.

THE PARABLE OF THE SOWER.

Mk. iv. 3, 4.—Hauseith. sai. urrann sa saiands du saian fraiwa seinamma. 4. Jah warth miththanei saiso. sum raihtis gadraus faur wig. jah quemun fuglos, jah fretun thata.—*Zahn's Edition*, p. 45.

Title-deed at Naples.

12. This document was discovered in modern times, and is now preserved in the archives of the church of St. Annunciata at Naples. It is defective, and written in very corrupt Latin, bearing no date, but appearing to have been written in the beginning of the 6th century, soon after the arrival of the Goths in Italy. According to this title-deed, the clergymen of the church St. Anastasia, sell some land, and ratify the sale in several Latin attestations, with four in Gothic. These four subscriptions are, as regards the language, of no importance, for they contain no new Gothic words; but they are highly valuable as affording an incontestible proof that the language and writing of the Codex Argenteus are genuine Gothic. Some have questioned whether this Codex be Gothic, but it is in the same language and the same character as these attestations, and they are written, at the period of Gothic influence in Italy, in the Gothic language and character by Gothic priests, having Gothic names; therefore the Codex Argenteus must also be Gothic.

The title-deed preserved at Naples was minutely copied by Professor Massmann. As all the published copies are very defective, he has promised shortly to give to the world a faithful facsimile.*

One attestation will be a sufficient specimen of the language.

Ik winjaifrithas diakon handu meinai ufmelida jah (andnemum) skilliggans. I.
Ego Winefridus Diaconus manu mea subscripsi et accepimus solidos 60

* See Zahn's Gothic Gospels, p. 77; Massmann's St. John, pref. p. ix.: a facsimile is given by Sierakowsky, 1810, also in Marini's tab. 118.

jah faurthis thairh kawtsjon mith diakon(a) (ala) myda unsaramma jah mith-
et antea per cautionem cum Diacono . . . . . . nostro et con-
gahlaibaim unsaraim andnemum skilliggans. RK. wairth thize saiwe.
ministris nostris accepimus solidos 120 *pretium horum paludum.*

Title-deed at Arezzo.

13. This is a contract written on Egyptian papyrus. A deacon, Gottlieb sells to another deacon, Alamud, an estate with some buildings. This document is written in barbarous Latin, and only contains one Gothic attestation. It is contemporary with the Neapolitan document, and of equal importance: the original MS. is unfortunately lost, but the following is copied from Zahn.*

Ik guthilub• dkn• tho frabauhta boka fram mis gawaurhta thus dkn•
Ego Gottlieb Diaconus hæc vendidi librum a me feci tibi Diacone
alamoda fidwor unkjana hugsis kaballarja jah killiggans• RLG• andnahm jah
Alamod quatuor uncias fundi Caballaria et solidos 133 *accepi et*
ufmelida.
subscripsi.

14. Knittel, Archdeacon of Wolfenbuttel, in the Dutchy of Brunswick, found a palimpsest † manuscript of the 8th century, containing part of the 11th and following chapters, as far as the 13th verse of the xvth chapter of St. Paul's Epistle to the Romans, in Gothic and Latin.

This document is denominated Codex Carolinus, from Charles, Duke of Brunswick, who enabled Knittel to give his work to the world. He published it in twelve plates, 4to. 1761.‡ Republished by Ihre in Roman characters, with Latin version, notes, index, &c. pp. 90, Upsal, 1763. Again, by Manning, in the Appendix to his edition of Lye's Anglo-Saxon Dictionary, 2 vols. folio, 1772. And by Büsching, Berlin, 4to. 1773.

15. Angelo Mai, while keeper of the Ambrosian Library at Milan, discovered some fragments of Gothic in palimpsest manuscripts, and, with Count Castiglione, published the following extracts:—

Esdras ii. 28—42: Nehem. v. 13—18; vi. 14—19; vii. 1—3: Mt. xxv. 38—46; xxvi. 1—3; 65—75; xxvii. 1: Philip. ii. 22—30; iii. 1—16: Titus i. 1—16; ii. 1:

* A more circumstantial description of both these documents is given in Zahn's preface, p. 77, 78, and in the following works:—Versuch einer Erläuterung der Gothischen Sprachüberreste in Neapel und Arezo als eine Einladungsschrift und Beilage zum Ulphilas, von *J. C. Zahn*, Braunschweig, 1804. Antonius Franciscus Gorius was the first who, in the year 1731, published the document of Arezzo in the following work: *J. B. Doni* Inscriptiones antiquæ nunc primum editæ notisque illustratæ, &c. ab *A. F. Gorio*, Florent. 1731, folio. Professor H. F. Massman observes, that, notwithstanding the most minute investigation, he has not been able to discover the Gothic document of Arezo. (Preface to the Gothic Commentary on St. John, p. x.) It is, however, copied in No. 117 of *Gaetano Marini's* Papiri Diplomatici, &c. Romæ, 1805, folio, from the original attributed to A. D. 551, and again published in Codice diplomatico Toscano dal antiquario *Brunetti*, 11, p. 209—213, Firenze, 1833, 4to.

† *Rescript*, from παλιν *again*, and ψαω *to wipe* or *cleanse*. For an interesting account of the discoveries made in palimpsest MSS. see a paper by *the venerable Archdeacon Nares* in the Transactions of the Royal Society of Literature, Vol. I. part i. p. 122.

‡ Friedrich Adolph Ebert, late librarian of the King of Saxony, has declared, after having collated it in the most minute manner, that this edition is the most correct copy of the MS. For want of sale many copies were used as waste paper, and the copper-plates were sold for old copper: it is therefore become very scarce. See Allgemeines bibliographisches Lexicon von F. A. Ebert, vol. ii. p. 992, Leipzig, F. A. Brockhaus, 1830, 4to.

Philem. i. 11—23;—A page from a Homily—A fragment of a Gothic Calendar. He concludes his small volume with a Glossary and two plates. The Gothic fragments are accompanied with a Latin version, and in the parts taken from the Scriptures the Greek text is given. This work was published with the following title:—Ulphilæ partium ineditarum in Ambrosianis Palimpsestis ab Angelo Maio repertarum specimen conjunctis curis ejusdem Maii et Caroli Octavii Castillionæi editum. Mediolani, 4to. 1819, pp. 1—36, Pref. xxiv.*

16. Count Castiglione again proved his zeal for Gothic literature by publishing—

Ulphilæ Gothica versio, epistolæ Divi Pauli ad Corinthios secundæ quam ex Ambrosianæ Bibliothecæ palimpsestis depromptam cum interpretatione adnotationibus, glossario edidit Carolus Octavius Castillionæus, Mediolani, 4to. 1829.

17. Count Castiglione, rather than increase suspense by delay, most generously determined to satisfy at once the anxious wishes of the learned world, by publishing the text of the following work without preface or glossary:—

Gothicæ versionis epistolarum Divi Pauli ad Romanos, ad Corinthios primæ, ad Ephesios, quæ supersunt ex Ambrosianæ Bibliothecæ palimpsestis deprompta cum adnotationibus edidit Carolus Octavius Castillionæus, Mediolani, Regiis typis, 1834, 4to. p. 64.

18. A commentary on parts of the Gospel according to St. John, written in Moeso-Gothic, has been published in Germany by Dr. H. Massmann, from a MS. in the Vatican.

It is a 4to. vol. of 182 pages, to which is prefixed a dedication and an account of the manuscript, in 17 pages. Then follow 34 pages of two columns in a page of the Commentary in Moeso-Gothic, printed in facsimile types. Immediately afterwards is given in 15 pages the same Moeso-Gothic, text in Roman type, in one column, and a literal Latin version in the other, with notes at the foot of the page. Then succeed an account of the proposed emendations of the MS., a short notice of the life of Ulphilas, and a complete Glossary of all the *Moes.* words not only in the text of the Commentary, but those found in Castiglione's extracts from St. Paul's Epistle to the Romans, first of Corinthians, and the Ephesians mentioned in the last paragraph. At the end is a copper-plate containing several facsimiles of MSS.† The full title of the work is, Skeirein's Aiwaggeljons thairh Johannen: Auslegung des Evangelii Johannis in gothischer Sprache. Aus römischen und mayländischen Handschriften nebst lateinischer Uebersetzung, belegenden Anmerkungen, geschichtlicher Untersuchung, gothisch-lateinischem Wörterbuche und Schriftproben. Im Auftrage seiner Königlichen Hoheit des Kronprinzen Maximilian von Bayern erlesen, erläutert und zum ersten Male herausgegeben von H. F. Massmann, Doctor der Philosophie, Professor der älteren deutschen Sprache, etc. 4to. München, 1834.

* Transactions of the Royal Society of Literature, Vol. I. part i. p. 129.

† A new edition of all that is discovered of Ulphilas's translation of the Scriptures is advertised to appear in the course of this year, with this title: *Ulfilas*, vet. et novi test. versionis Goth. fragmenta quæ supersunt—cum glossario et grammatica, edid. *H. C. de Gabelentz et Dr. J. Loebe*, 2 tom. 4to. maj. Altenburgi, Schnuphase. See Allgemeines Verzeichniss der Bücher der Frankfurter und Leipziger Oster-messe, 1836, p. 251. In a critique inserted in the Göttinger gelehrte Anzeigen, it is mentioned that the celebrated philologist, Prof. Jacob Grimm, has been long preparing a complete edition of all the fragments of Ulphilas's version of the Bible. The original text is to be printed in the Latin character.

The Gothic begins thus:	*Latin version.*
saei frathjai áiththáu	si est intelligens aut
sôkjái Guth.	requirens Deum.
Allái usvandidêdum.	Omnes declinaverunt.
samana unbrûkjái vaúrthun,	simul inutiles facti sunt,
jah ju uf dáutháus	ac jam sub mortis
atdrusun stáuái.	inciderunt judicium.—p. 37.

19. With the extinction of the Gothic dynasties, this pure and rich German tongue, though vestiges still remain, ceased to be a prevailing dialect. Like the Scandinavian branches, the Gothic retained a distinct form for the passive voice. The Scandinavians, having little interruption from other nations, would most likely retain their grammatical forms much longer than the southern German tribes, who (from the 4th century, when the Moeso-Gothic Gospels were written, to the 8th, when we find the next earliest specimen of German) must have lost many of the old forms, and with them probably the passive voice.

VIII.—THE ALEMANNI OR SUABIANS.

1. There are various opinions about the derivation of the word *Alemanni*. It was a name given to the Suabians,* who appear to have come from the shores of the Baltic to the southern part of Germany. This locality of the Suabians is, in some measure, confirmed by the ancient name of the Baltic, Mare Suevicum, Suavian, or Suabian Sea. In the beginning of the 3rd century, the Suabians assembled in great numbers on the borders of the Roman empire, between the Danube, Rhine, and Main,† and united with other tribes. To denote this coalition or union of various nations, they were called Alemanni *various men, all men.*‡

* Schwaben (Suavi) according to Schmitthenner, Schwabe, *m. pl.* Schwaben, in *Old High-Ger.* Suab, *pl.* Suaba, and signifies *the wise, the intelligent, a person full of understanding and discernment*, from the *Old High-Ger.* sueban *to perceive, understand, know, discern, comprehend.*

† Walafridus Strabo de Vita B. Galli apud Goldastum, tom. I. rer Alemann. p. 143: Igitur quia mixti Alemannis Suevi partem Germaniæ ultra Danubium, partem Retiæ inter Alpes et Histriam, partemque Galliæ circa Ararim obsederunt.—Jornandes de rebus Geticis, cap. lv.: Theodemir Gothorum rex emenso Danubio, Suevis improvisus a tergo apparuit. Nam regio illa Suevorum ab oriente Baiobaros habet, ab occidente Francos, a meridie Burgundiones, a septentrione Thuringos. Quibus Suevis tunc juncti Alemanni etiam aderant, ipsique alpes erectas omnino regentes.

‡ *Ger.* allerley *various, different:* mann *man.* Schmitthenner says from the *Old-Ger.* alloman *each*, in the plural alamanna *many, a nation, community.*—Von Schmid in his Suavian Dictionary, sub *Alb, alp*, informs us that alm, almand, or almang, denoted not only *a common, a pasture*, but *a mountain;* hence the people dwelling on the mountains in Austria, Tyrol, &c.

Thus increased in power, they soon ventured to make formidable inroads into the Roman territory, and not only entered the plains of Lombardy, but advanced almost in sight of Rome. They were repelled, and, in a new attack, vanquished by Aurelian.* The term Alemanni was used by foreigners as synonymous with Germans,† and, while in English they are called Germans, in French and Spanish they are to this day denominated Alemanns. This great confederacy terminated in A.D. 496, by a bloody victory of the Francic king, Clovis (Chlodovæus), at Tolbiac, near Cologne on the Rhine, the present Zullich or Zulpich.

2. The peculiarities of the Suabian or Alemannic dialect are these:

The first vowel *a* very much prevails, and the final *n* of verbs is omitted: thus they say, saga for sagen *to say;* fraga for fragen *to ask.* They change the *Ger. o* into *au*, and use braut for brot *bread;* grauss for gross *great.* For the *Ger. st*, they put *scht* (sht); they use du bischt, kannscht, for du bist *thou art;* kannst *canst.* They form diminutives in *li*, *le*, as herzli for *Ger.* herzchen *a little heart.* In the inflections of sollen *shall*, wollen *will*, the *l* is generally omitted; as, du sottascht di doch schema, for du solltest dich doch schämen *thou shouldst be ashamed.* The oldest Suabian and Upper German dialect contained very few rough hissing sounds. In old documents, and till the time of Emperor Maximilian I. the *sch* is rarely found. The hissing sounds begin on the borders of Italy and France, diminish in the middle of Germany, and nearly disappear in North or Low-Germany.

3. The Suabians of the present day speak in a lively and quick manner.

4. The Alemannic or Suabian dialect prevails in the north of Switzerland, in Alsace, Baden, Wurtemberg, Bavaria, and the western part of the Austrian States.

5. Some of the authors who are generally said to have written in Alemannic, and some of the early compositions in this dialect, are—

An exhortation to Christians, A.D. 720 (x. 2).—Kero, A.D. 800 (x. 7).—Rhabanus Maurus, A.D. 850 (x. 11).—Otfrid, A.D. 860 (x. 12).—Notker, A.D. 1020 (x. 16).—Nibelungen Lied, A.D. 1150 (x. 24).—Walter von der Vogelweide, A.D. 1190 (x. 25).—Chunrad von Kirchberg, A.D. 1195 (x. 26).—Gotfrit von Nifen, A.D. 1235 (x. 29).—Schwaben-Spiegel, A.D. 1250 (x. 31), &c.

were called Alemanni. *Οι δε Αλαμανοι ειγε χρη Ασινιῳ Κουαδρατῳ ἑπεσθαι, ανδρι Ιταλιωτῃ, και τα Γερμανικα ἐς το ακριβες αναγραψαμενῳ ξυνηλιδες ἐισιν ἀνθρωποι και μιγαδες· και τουτο δυναται ἀυτοις ἡ ἐπωνυμια.* Alemanni, si Asinio Quadrato fides, viro Italo et Germanicarum rerum exacto Scriptori, communes sunt variis e nationibus collecti, id ipsum apud eos consignificante vocabulo.—*Agathias*, lib. i. *Hist.* p. 7.

* Gibbon, ch. xi.

† Nota, quod partes viciniores Italicis, sicut sunt Bavaria, Suevia, dictæ fuerint, ab Italis primo Alemannia, et homines dicebantur Alemanni, nota secundum Orosium et Solinum, quod tunc temporis Germania et Alemania habebantur pro uno et eodem. Nam Ungaria dicebatur Pannonia, et ab Ungaria usque ad Rhenum dicebatur Germania, vel Alemania, et ultra Rhenum Gallia.—*Auctor Hist. Landgrav. Thur.* c. vi.; *Struvii Corpus Hist. Ger.* § 1; *de Ger. orig. &c.* p. 10, n. 22.—See II. § 2, and note (†).

IX.—THE FRANCS.

1. The Francs,* or Freemen, were a confederacy of high-spirited and independent German tribes, dwelling between the Rhine and Elbe. They were composed of the Tencteri, Catti, Sali, Bructeri, Chamavi, Chauci, &c. who occupied the modern Prussian provinces on the Rhine, Zwey-Brücken or Deux-Ponts, part of Hesse, the south of Saxony, and the northern part of Bavaria. The Francs lying to the north-east were called Salian Francs from the river Sala, and those on the Rhine were, from their situation, denominated Ripuarian Francs.

2. This confederation was known, under the denomination of Francs, about A.D. 240.† According to Schilter,‡ the Francs were first mentioned by Eumenius, a Latin orator, born at Autun in France, at the beginning of the 4th century. They had been harassed by the Romans; and having felt the importance of union for self-defence, they, when united, soon discovered not only an ability to resist their enemies, but in turn to invade some of the Roman territories. In the beginning of the 5th century they took possession of the west bank of the Rhine, and began to make incursions into Gaul.

3. About A.D. 420, their power extended from the Rhine nearly over the whole of Gaul, and they founded the Merovingian dynasty, under Pharamond their king, who, according to their custom, was elected by the chiefs of the nation, constituting the Francic confederacy. The Merovingian line continued for 323 years through a succession of twenty-two kings, from A.D. 428 to 751. One of the Merovingian kings, Clodwig, Chlothovecus, Clovis, Ludewig, or Lewis, subdued the Alemanni in A.D. 496; and, immediately after this conquest, he and many of his subjects made a public profession of the Christian faith by being baptized at Rheims.

4. After the Merovingian succeeded the Carlovingian family, which supplied eleven kings, who held the reins of the Francic government for 236 years; then succeeded in France the Capetian line, which needs not be further noticed, as it would lead to a history of France beyond the object of this notice.

5. Pepin, the first king of the Carlovingian race, seized the Francic crown in A.D. 751, and divided the kingdom between his two sons, Charlemagne and Carloman. After the death of his brother, Charlemagne became sole possessor of the kingdom in 768. As some short historical

* Frank, according to Schmitthenner, signifies originally, *preceding, bold, upright, free;* hence, der Franke *the Franc.; Old Ger.* franho; *Icel.* frackr *m. francus, liber, generosus, elatus, tumidus.* Frackar *m. pl. Francones, Franci;* fracki *m. virtuosus, potens.*

† Gibbon, ch x. Turner's Hist. of Anglo-Saxons, bk. 2, ch. iii.

‡ Schilter's, Gloss. to Thes. vol. iii. p. 316.

remarks* will be made when specimens of the language are introduced, it will only be necessary to observe here, that Charlemagne, after showing himself one of the greatest men that ever reigned over a most extensive empire, died in A.D. 814.

6. It is difficult to name with minuteness and precision all the writers and the compositions in the Francic dialect; but the following are generally considered as written in this idiom :—

A translation of Isidore, A.D. 800 (x. 8).—Hildibraht and Hadubrant, A.D. 730 (x. 3).—Ludwigslied, A.D. 883 (x. 14).—A Translation of Boethius, A.D. 950 (x. 18).—Willeram's Paraphrase, A.D. 1070 (x. 20).—The Praise of St. Anno, A.D. 1075 (x. 21), &c.

X.—HIGH-GERMAN, OR THE ALEMANNIC, SUABIAN, AND FRANCIC DIALECTS.

1. The translation of the Scriptures by Bishop Ulphilas, about A.D. 360, affords the earliest specimen of German. Almost four centuries elapsed between the writings of Ulphilas, and the composition of the following exhortation. When the Francs and Alemanni were converted to Christianity, their instructors not only wrote prayers, exhortations, sermons, hymns, and commentaries on the Scriptures, but also composed glossaries; thus preserving specimens of the German language in the 7th and 8th centuries.

2. An exhortation to Christians (exhortatio ad plebem Christianam) is taken from a MS. of the early part of the 8th century, originally preserved in the bishoprick of Freisingen in Bavaria, and Fulde in Hesse, but now in Munich and Kassel. It was published in *Hottinger's* Historia Ecclesiastica, vol. viii. p. 1220; in *B. J. Docen's* Miscellaneen, vol. i. p. 4—8; and in *Wackernagel's* Altdeutsches Lesebuch, 8vo. Basel, 1835.

EXHORTATIO.

Hlosêt ir, chindô liupôstun, rihtida therâ galaupâ the ir in herzin kahucclicho hapên sculut, ir deu christânun namun intfangan eigut, thaz ist chundida iuuererâ christânheiti, fona demo truhtine in man gaplâsan, fona sin selpes jungirôn kasezzit.—*Wackernagel's Altdeut. Les.* p. 6.

LITERAL GERMAN.

Lauschet ihr, Kinder liebsten, der zucht des Glaubens, den ihr im Herzen behütlich haben sollet, (wenn) ihr den Christennamen empfangen habt, das ist Kunde eurer Christenheit, von dem Herrn eingeblasen, von seinen eigenen Jüngern gesetzt.

* See X. § 9, 10.

LITERAL ENGLISH.

Listen ye, children dear, to the instruction of the belief, which you shall preserve in your hearts, (when) you have received the Christian name, that is, the knowledge of your Christianity, inspired by the Lord, (and) established by his own disciples.

3. THE HEROIC *Song, relating the combat between Hildibraht and Hadubrant.* The language of this song is Francic, with a great intermixture of the Low-German dialect. Bouterweck considers it just what one would expect from the attempt of a Low-Saxon to write Francic. Like the Wessobrunn Prayer, it is alliterative,* and ascribed to the 8th century. It was first published by *Eckard*, in *Commentariis de rebus Francorum*, vol. i. p. 864, from the Fulda manuscript, now kept at Kassel, by *Grimm, at Kassel*, 1812, and in his *Altdeutsche Wälder*, vol. ii. p. 97. A lithographic specimen of the fragment preserved at Göttingen was given by Professor Grimm in 1830. An edition appeared in 1833, by Lachmann. An explanation of the difficult passages by W. Mohr, in 12mo. pp. 16, Marburg, 1836.

Old German.	*Literal Modern German.*	*Literal English.*
Ik gihôrta dhat seggen,	Ich hörte das sagen,	I heard it said
. . . .	. . . .	. . . .
dhat sih *u*rhêttun	dass sich herausforderten	that Hiltibraht and Hadubrant
*ê*nôn muotin	einstimmig	with one voice
*H*iltibraht joh *H*adubrant	Hildebrand und Hadubrand	challenged
untar *h*erjun tvêm.	unter einander.	one another.
*s*unufatarungôs	Sohn und Vater, wie	Son and father, when
iro *s*aro rihtun,	sie ihren Kampfplatz bestimmt	the (combat) place they fixed,
*g*arutun se iro *g*ûdhamun,	thaten sie ihre Kriegshemden an	their coat of war they put on,
*g*urtun sih svert ana,	gürteten sich ihr Schwert um	girded their sword on,
*h*elidôs, ubar *h*ringâ,	die Helden zum Ringen (Kampf)	the heroes for the fight,
dô sie ti derô *h*iltju ritun.	da sie zum Kampf ritten.	when they to combat rode.
*H*iltibraht gimahalta:	sprach Hildebrand:	Hiltibraht spoke:
er was *h*êrôro man,	er war ein hehrer Mann	he was a stately man,
*f*erahes *f*rôtôro:	Geistes weise:	of a prudent (*wise*) mind:
er *f*râgen gistuont	er fragen that	he did ask
*f*ôhêm wortum	mit wenigen Worten	with few words
hver sîn *f*ater wâri	wer sein Vater wäre	who his father was
*f*ireô in *f*olche,	im Männer Volke,	among the race of men,
. . . .	. . . .	. . . .
. . . .	. . . .	. . . .
eddo hvelihhes cnuosles du sîs.	oder welches Stammes du seyst.	or of what family (*he was*) thou art.

Wackernagel, p. 14.

* The alliteration in the example is denoted by *italic* letters.

4. The following Latin hymns are ascribed to St. Ambrose, who was Bishop of Milan from A.D. 374 to 397. The German translations, made by an unknown hand, are thought to be of the 8th century. They are found in *Wackernagel's* Altdeutches Lesebuch, 8vo. Basel, 1835.

The Original Latin.	*Old German Translation.*
Deus qui cœli lumen es	cot dû der himiles leoht pist
satorque lucis, qui polum	sâio joh leohtes dû der himil
paterno fultum brachio	faterlîchemu arspriuztan arme
præclara pandis dextera.	duruheitareru spreitis zesauûn
Aurora stellas jam tegit	tagarod sternâ giu dechit
rubrum sustollens gurgitem,	rôtan ûfpurrenti uuâk
humectis namque flatibus	fuhtêm kauuisso plâstim
terram baptizans roribus.	erda taufantêr tauum.
Wackernagel, p. 7.	

TE DEUM.*

The Original Latin.	*Old German Translation.*
Te Deum laudamus.	thih cot lopêmês
te dominum confitemur.	thih truhtnan gehemês
te æternum patrem	thih êuuîgan fater
omnis terra veneratur.	êokiuuelih erda uuirdit (êrêt).
Tibi omnes angeli, tibi cœli	thir allê engilâ thir himilâ
et universæ potestates,	inti allô kiuualtidô
tibi cherubim et seraphim	thir cherubim inti seraphim
incessabili voce proclamant.	unbilibanlîcheru stimmô forharênt.
Sanctus sanctus sanctus	uuîhêr uuîhêr uuîhêr
dominus deus sabaoth.	truhtin cot herrô
pleni sunt cœli et terra	folliu sint himilâ inti erda
majestate gloriæ tuæ.	therâ meginchreftî tiuridâ thinerâ.
Wackernagel, p. 11.	

5. A HYMN to the honour of St. Peter, by an anonymous author of the 8th century, published from a MS. of Freisingen, in Docen's Miscellaneen, 2 vols. Munich, 1809: Hoffmann's Fundgruben, 8vo. 1 vol. Breslau, 1830.

Vnsar trohtin hat farsalt sancte petre ginualt,
daz er mac ginerian ze imo dingenten man.
Kyrie eleyson. Christe eleyson.
Er hapet ouh mit vuortun himilriches portun,
dar in mach er skerian, den er uuili nerian.
Kirie eleison. Christe (eleison).
Fundgruben, p. 1.

LITERAL GERMAN.

Unser Herr hat verliehen St. Peter gewalt,
das er kann erhalten (den) zu ihm bittenden mann.
Κυριε ἐλεησον, Χριστε ἐλεησον.
Er hat auch mit worten (des) himmelreiches pforten,
dahin kann er bringen den er will erhalten
Κυριε ἐλεησον, Χριστε ἐλεησον.

* For a specimen of the *Te Deum*, in German of the 12th century, see § 22.

LITERAL ENGLISH.

Our Lord has given St. Peter power,
that he may preserve, the man that prays to him.
Lord have mercy, Christ have mercy.
He also keeps, with words, the portals of heaven's kingdom
wherein he may take, whom he will preserve.
Lord have mercy. Christ have mercy.

6. THE WESSOBRUNN PRAYER, so called from the MS. being first discovered in the monastery of Wessobrunn, in Bavaria. The MS. is of the latter part of the 8th century; it was published by *Professor J. Grimm* at Kassel, 1812, by *Massmann* at Berlin, 1824, and in *Wackernagel's* Altdeutsches Lesebuch, 8vo. Basel, 1835. The alliteration is denoted by italic letters.

Old German.	*Literal Modern German.*	*Literal English.*
Dat ga*f*regin ih mit *f*irahim	Das hörte ich bey Menschen	This I heard from men
*f*iriwizzô meista,	mit Fürwitz meistem,	of most curiosity,
dat *e*ro ni was	dass Erde nicht war	that (*the*) earth was not
noh *û*fhimil,	noch Aufhimmel,	nor heaven,
noh *p*aum nohheinig	noch Baum einiger	nor any tree
noh *p*ereg ni was;	noch Berg nicht war;	nor mountain was;
ni	nicht	not . . . .
noh *s*unna ni *s*cein	noch Sonne nicht schien	nor sun did shine
noh *m*âno ni liuhta	noch Mond nicht leuchtete	nor moon gave light
noh der *m*areosêo.	noch der Meersee.	nor the main (*sea*).
dô dâr ni*w*iht ni *w*as	Als da Nichts nicht war	when there was no wight
enteô ni *w*enteô,	Ende noch Wende,	end nor wend (*turn*),
enti dô was der *e*ino	und da war der eine	and then was the one
*a*lmahtico cot, &c.	allmächtige Gott, &c.	Almighty God, &c.

Wackernagel, p. 17.

7. KERO, a monk in the abbey of St. Gallen in Switzerland, made a German translation of the Rules of St. Benedict, about A.D. 800, under the title, Interpretatio Regulæ Sancti Benedicti Thetisca, *Schilter's* Thes. at the end of vol i. p. 25, and a part of it in *Graff's* Althochdeutscher Sprachschatz.

De Taciturnitate, chap. VI.

Tuamees. daz qhuad vvizzago qhuad ih kehalte vveka mine daz nalles
Faciamus quod ait Propheta: Dixi, custodiam vias meas, ut non
missitue in zungun mineru sazta munde minemu kehaltida ertumbeta indi
delinqam in lingua mea: Posui ori meo custodiam: Obmutui et
kedeomuatit pim indi suuiketa fona cuateem hiar keaugit uuizzago ibu fona
humiliatus sum, et silui â bonis; hic ostendit propheta, si â
cuateem sprahhom ofto duruh suuigalii sculi suuigeen huueo meer
bonis eloquiis interdum propter taciturnitatem debet taceri. Quanto magis
fona vbileem vvortum duruh vvizzi dera sunta sculi pilinnan.
á malis verbis propter poenam peccati debet cessari?

Graff, p. xlviii.

LITERAL GERMAN.

Thuen wir das, was der Weissager sagt: ich habe gesagt, ich werde bewachen, die Wege mein, dass ich nichts missethue mit meiner Zunge; ich setzte dem Munde mein eine Wache, ich bin verstummt, und gedemüthiget und schweige von den Guten. Heir zeigt der Weissager, wenn von guten Reden oft wegen der Verschwiegenheit soll geschwiegen werden, wie viel mehr von übeln Worten wegen der Strafe der Sünde soll geschwiegen werden.

LITERAL ENGLISH.

Let us do what the sayer (*Prophet*) saith: I have said I will keep my ways, that I nothing misdo with my tongue: I have set a watch over my mouth, I was dumb, and humbled, and silent (even) from good; here the wise-sayer shows, if from good speeches often for taciturnity we should be silent, how much more from evil words should we cease for punishment of the sin.

8. Isidore, born at Carthage, was archbishop of Seville, from 600 to 636. Amongst other works, he wrote a treatise, *De Nativitate Domini*, of which a Franc is supposed to have made a translation. The MS. is preserved at Paris. It was published by *Jo. Phil. Palthen*, at Greifswald, 1706, and again in *Schilter's Thes.* at the end of vol. i. Ulm, 1728: it was also inserted by *Rostgaard* in the Danish Bibliotheca, No. 2, Copenhagen, 1738.

The following specimen of Isidore is from *Graff's Althochdeutschen Sprachschatz*, vol. i. p. xlv. Berlin, 1834,* most carefully collated by this indefatigable scholar with the original MS. at Paris. It is to be found also in *Schilter's Thes.* p. 4 of vol. i., *Isidore*, ch. iv. 1.

Hear quhidit umbi dhea Bauhnunga. dhero dhrio heideo gotes.

Araugit ist in dhes aldin uuizssodes boohhum. dhazs fater endi sunu endi heilac geist got sii. Oh dhes sindun unchilaubun iudeo liudi. dhazs sunu endi heilac gheist got sii. bi dhiu huuanda sie chihordon gotes stimna hluda in sina berge quhedhenda. Chihori dhu israhel druhtin got dhin. ist eino got.

LITERAL GERMAN.

Hier wird gesprochen von der bedeutung der Dreieinigkeit Gottes.

Sichtbar ist in den alten bundes büchern, dass Vater und Sohn und heiliger Geist Gott seyn. O der sündigen (thörichten) Juden leute, unglaubig dass Sohn und heiliger Geist Gott seyn, darum weil sie hörten Gottes stimme laut auf dem berge Sinai sprechend: Höre du Israel der Herr dein Gott ist einge Gott.

LITERAL ENGLISH.

Here is spoken about the signification of the Trinity of God.

It is visible, in the books of the Old Testament, that the Father and Son and Holy Ghost is God. O the sinful Jewish people, disbelieving that the Son and the Holy Ghost is God, because they heard God's voice loud on mount Sinai, saying, Hear thou, Israel, the Lord thy God is one God.

* In the preface to this laborious and learned work, from p. xxxiii. to lxxiii. there is a very valuable account of old Ger. MSS. Some specimens are given of unpublished glossaries and fragments of a translation of *Boetius* de consolatione philosophiæ, supposed to be Notker's work (in cod. 5, gall. 825) of Mart. Capella de Nuptiis Mercurii et Philologiæ, (in cod. 5, gall. 872,) and of Aristotle's Organon (in cod. 5, gall. 818). The glossaries are from the 7th to the 9th century. To give a *true idea* of the quality and state of the MSS. Graff has very properly given them with all their faults, &c. exactly as he found them.

9. CHARLEMAGNE,* who reigned from 768—814, united the German tribes, the *Francs, Alemanni, Bavarians, Thuringians, Saxons, Longobards, Burgundians,* &c. into one mighty empire, and governed all the nations from the *Eider* in the north of Germany, to the *Ebro* in Spain—from the *Baltic* sea to the *Tiber* in Italy. Arts and sciences declined more and more after the time of Gregory the Great, in 604, who himself discouraged scientific pursuits so much, that at the time of Charlemagne there was scarcely a trace of science or literature on the continent. Charlemagne arose, and obtained the aid of the most learned men of his time for the improvement of his mighty empire. A few of these eminent men may be named. *Alkuin,* an Anglo-Saxon monk, born about 732, educated at York, was well versed in Latin, Greek, Hebrew, theology, rhetoric, poetry, and mathematics, and was also distinguished for his piety. He died, abbot of Tours, in 804. *Theodulph* died 821, bishop of Orleans. *Eginhard,* born in Odenwalde, South Germany, wrote the History of Charlemagne, and died in 839. Schools were also established in different parts of the empire. By these means science and literature were supported in the 9th and following centuries. Charlemagne enjoined the clergy to preach in German, and to translate homilies into that language. He himself attempted to form a German Grammar, and ordered a collection of the national songs to be made, which unfortunately are lost, but we may form some judgment of them from the Hildibraht, a remarkable fragment of early German.

10. The successors of Charlemagne inherited his empire, but not his talents. The second son of Charlemagne, *Ludwig* or *Lewis* the pious, in the year 843, divided the empire among his three sons:—1. *Lewis* had Germany, which comprised Suabia, East Franconia, Bavaria, Thuringia, Saxony. Germany, from this early period to the present day, has preserved its language, its customs, and independence. 2. To *Charles,* Gallia was assigned. 3. *Lothar* received for his portion, Dauphine, Alsace, and Burgundy.

At first the Francs, in Gallia under Charles, spoke German, but they soon mixed it with the language of the subdued Gauls. The oaths which Charles and Lewis and their subjects took near Strasburg in 842, to protect their empire against Lothar, their eldest brother, are preserved. The grandson of Charlemagne, *Abbot Nidhart,* who died 853, in his history of the disputes of the sons, has preserved the form of the oath in German and French. It is a curious specimen of both languages at this early period.†

Charles's Oath in Francic, or Old German.

In godes minna ind in thes christiânes folches ind unser bêdherô gehaltnissi, fon thesemo dage frammordes, sô fram sô mir got geuuizci indi mahd furgibit, sô haldih

* Eginharti de Vita Carolimagni commentariis, cum annotationibus Ger. Nicolai Heerkens, Groningiæ, 12mo. 1755. Histoire de Charlemagne par Gaillard, 2 vols. 8vo. Paris, 1819.

† Roquefort gloss. de la langue romane, tom. i. disc. prel. p. xx. Wackernagel's Altdeutsches Lesebuch, 8vo. Basel, 1835, p. 26.

tesan mînan bruodher sôsô man mit rehtû sinan bruodher scal, in thiû thaz er mig sô soma duo, indi mit Ludherem in nohheiniu thing ne gegangu, thê mînan uuillon imo ce scadhen werdhên.

LITERAL GERMAN.

In Gottes Minne und in (wegen) des christlichen Volkes und unser beider Erhaltung von diesem Tage fortan, so fern so mir Gott Weisheit und Macht giebt, so halte ich diesen meinen Bruder, so wie man mit Recht seinen Bruder soll, und dass er mir auch so thun und mit Ludherem (will ich) in keine Sache nicht gehen, mit meinem Willen ihm zu Schaden werden.

LITERAL ENGLISH.

In God's love and for the christian folk and our common preservation, from this day henceforth, so far as God gives me wisdom and power, so hold I (*shall I preserve*) this my brother, so as one (*man*) by right his brother should (*preserve*) and that he to me also so may do, and with Lothar I (*will*) not enter into any thing, with my will, to be an injury to him.

The Oath of Lewis, in the Romanic, or French.

Pro deo amur et pro christian poblo et nostro commun salvament, dist di in avant, in quant deus savir et podir me dunat, si salvarai eo cist meon fradre Karlo et in adjudha et in cadhuna cosa, si cum om per dreit son fradra salvar dist, in o quid il mi altresi fazet, et ab Ludher nul plaid nunquam prindrai, qui meon vol cist meon fradre Karle in damno sit.

LITERAL ENGLISH.

For God's love and for the christian people and our common preservation from this day and henceforth, in so far as God gives me wisdom and power, so shall I assist this my brother Charles, and in assistance and in any cause so as one (*man*) by right his brother ought to assist in such a manner as he may do to me; and with Lothar I will not enter into any treaty (*placitum*) which to me, or to this my brother Charles, can be an injury.

Oath of Charles's army, in Romanic or Old French.

Si Lodhuvigs sagrament quæ son fradre Karlo jurat conservat, et Karlus meos sendra de suo part non lo stanit, si io returnar non lint pois, ne io ne neuls cui eo returnar int pois, in nulla ajudha contra Lodhuwig nun li iver.

LITERAL ENGLISH.

If Lewis keeps the oath which to his brother Charles he swore, and Charles my Seignior (*Lord*) on his part does not keep it, if I cannot prevent him, neither I, nor any one whom I can prevent, shall give him any assistance against Lewis.

Oath of Lewis's army, in Francic or Old German.

Oba Karl then eid, then er sinemo bruodher Ludhuuuîge gesuor geleistit, indi Ludhuuuîg min hêrro then er imo gesuor forbrihchit, ob ih inan es iruuenden ne mag, noh ih noh therô nohhein, then ih es iruuenden mag, uuidhar Karle imo ce follustî ne uuirdhu.

LITERAL GERMAN.

Wenn Karl den Eid, den er seinem Bruder Ludwig schwur, leistet (hält) und Ludwig, mein Herr (den Eid), den er ihm schwur, bricht, wenn ich ihn davon abwenden (abhalten), nicht kann, (so) werden weder ich, noch deren einer, den ich davon abwenden (abhalten) kann ihm wider Karl zu Hülfe nicht seyn (beistehn).

LITERAL ENGLISH.

If Charles keeps the oath, which he swore (to) his brother Lewis, and Lewis my Lord breaks the (oath) which he swore (to) him, in case I cannot prevent him, (then) neither I, nor any one whom I can prevent, shall give him any assistance against Charles.

11. Rhabanus Maurus, born at Mayence in 776, became a celebrated teacher at Fulda. His attention was attracted to the German language, and, in a council at Mayence, A.D. 848, he succeeded in passing a canon that in future the clergy should preach in Romanic (*French*) or Theotisc (*German*). He died, Archbishop of Mayence, Feb. 4th, 856. Rhabanus Maurus compiled *Glossæ Latino barbaricæ de partibus humani corporis Goldast script. rerum Alemannic*, vol. i. p. 66—69.—*Glossarium Latino Theodiscum in tota Biblia V. et N. Test. Goldast. id.*

12. Otfrid belonged to the Alemanni or Suabians, and was educated at Fulda under Rhabanus Maurus. He was a Benedictine monk at Weissenburg in Alsace, a learned theologian, philosopher, orator, and poet, who flourished between 840 and 870. Otfrid wrote in rhyme a poetical paraphrase of the Gospels in Alemannic, his native language, to banish the profane songs of the common people. In this work there is a disregard of chronological order, for the poet seems to have written down the circumstances as they came into his mind. The MS. was first discovered by Beatus Rhenanus in the monastery at Freisingen, near Munich; there are two other MSS., one at Heidelburg, and the other at Vienna. It was first published by *Flaccius* (*Illericus*), *at Basle*, 1571, in *Schilter's Thes.* vol. i. *with Scherz's annotations;* also at Bonn in 4to. *Bonner Bruchstüche vom Otfried, durch H. Hoffmann von Fallersleben*, 1821. Again in 4to. by *E. G. Graff, Königsberg*, 1831, under the title of *Krist.*

Otfrid's Krist.

Séhet these fógala. thie hiar flíagent óbana.
  zi ákare sie ni gángent. ioh ouh uuíht ni spinnent
Thoh ni brístit in thes. zi uuáru thoh ginúages.
  ní sie sih ginérien. ioh scóno giuuerien.
Biginnet ána scouuon. thie frónisgon blúomon.
  thar líuti after uuége gent. thie in themo ákare stent.
Sálomon ther ríchо. ni uuátta sih gilícho.
  thaz ságen ih íú in ala uuár. so ein thero blúomono thar.

Krist by Graff, ii. 22, 9: p. 165, 9.

LITERAL GERMAN.

Sehet diese vögel, die hier fliegen oben.
Zum acker sie nicht gehen, und auch nichts nicht spinnen,
Doch nicht fehlt ihnen etwas, fürwahr zum genügen,
Nicht sie sich ernähren, und schön gewähren.
Beginnet anzuschauen, die herrlichen blumen
(Wo leute nach wege gehen) di in dem acker stehen:
Salomon der reiche, nicht kleidete (wattete) sich gleich mässig
Das sage ich euch in aller wahrheit, so wie eine der blumen dar.

LITERAL ENGLISH.

See these fowls, which here fly above.
To the field they go not (i. e. *they till not*), and also nothing spin,
Yet want not any thing, they truly have enough,
They do not nourish themselves, nor make fine.
Begin to look on the splendid flowers
(After which people go) standing in the field:
Solomon, the rich, did not dress (wodded) himself like
(That say I to you, in all truth) one of the flowers there.

13. MUSPILLI, a fragment of an old High-German alliterative Poem on the end of the world, from a MS. of the middle of the 9th century, in the Royal Library at Munich, published by *J. A. Schmeller, Munich*, 1832.

. . . Dar ni mac denne mak andremo
helfan· uora demo muspille· denne· daz
preita uuasal allaz uar prinnit· enti uugir
enti luft iz allaz arfurpit; uuar ist denne
diu marha dar man dar heo· mit sinen ma
gon piehc;

Thus arranged and corrected by Schmeller.

Dar ni mac denne mâk andremo helfan vora demo Muspille.
Denne daz preita wasal allaz varprinnit,
enti viur enti luft iz allaz arfurpit,
war ist denne diu marha, dar man dar eo mit sinen mâgon piehc?

LITERAL GERMAN.

. . . . Da mag Kein Mage dem anderen
helfen vor dem Muspille wenn die
breite Erdfläche ganz verbrennet, und Feuer
und Luft ist ganz verworfen; wo ist dann
die marke, darum man hier mit seinen magen strit?

LITERAL ENGLISH VERSION.

. . . . Then may no kindred assist the other
for the Muspille. When the
broad surface of the earth all is burning, and fire
and air are all cast away; where is then
the mark about which one has been quarrelling here with his relatives?

14. LUDWIGSLIED, a German heroic song by an unknown author, in praise of the East Francic King Lewis III. in the year A.D. 883. The MS. was originally at St. Amand, near Tournay, but it is now lost. It was published first in *Schilter's Thes.*, then by *Docen*, Munich, 1813, and in 1835 in *Wackernagel's* Altdeutsches Lesebuch, 8vo. Basel, p. 46.

HEROIC SONG.

Sang uuas gesungen. Thâr vaht thegenô gelih,
Uuig uuas bigunnen: Nichein sô sô Hluduuig:
Bluot skein in uuangôn, Snel indi kuoni,
Spilôd under vrankon. Thaz uuas imo gekunni.

LITERAL GERMAN.

Sang war gesungen,
Kampf war begonnen,
Blut schien in Wangen
Kämpfender Franken.

Da focht Degen (heroes) gleich
Keiner so wie Ludwig,
Schnell und kühn,
Das war ihm angeboren.
Schilter, Thes. vol. ii. p. 17.

LITERAL ENGLISH.

Song was sung,
Fight was begun:
Blood shone in the cheeks
Of fighting Francs.

There fought like a hero
Not one so as Lewis,
Quick and bold,
Which was in him inborn.

15. Saxon Emperors. During the reign of the Saxon emperors, from 919 till 1024, literature and science made some progress. The *Ottoes* valued and loved the sciences, and patronised *Gerbert* the most learned man of their time. Gerbert became pope under the name Silvester II. and died 1003.

16. Notker wrote in the period of the Saxon emperors. The only important monument in High-German literature of this age is a translation and commentary on the Psalms by this learned monk, *Notker of St. Gallen.* He was called Labeo, from his broad lips. His Alemannic translation is free and natural; and, as it respects power and strength of expression, it equals the best modern translation. Notker died in 1022. His work was published in *Schilter's Thes.* vol. i.

Psalm i.

1. *Beatus vir qui non abiit in consilio impiorum,*
Der man ist salig, der in dero argon rat ne gegieng.
So Adam teta, do er dero chenun rates folgeta uuider Gote, *Sicut adam fecit, cum mulieris consilium sequeretur adversus Deum.*

Et in via peccatorum non stetit.
Noh an dero sundigon uuege ne stuont.
So er teta. Er cham dar ana, er cham an den breiten uueg ter ze hello gat, unde stuont dar ana, uuanda er hangta sinero geluste. Hengendo stuont er. *Sicut idem fecit. Processit eò, processit ad viam latam qui ad Infernum ducit, et stetit ibi, namque pendebat à concupiscentia sua. Pendulus stetit.*

Et in cathedra pestilentiæ non stetit.
Noh an demo suhtstuole ne saz.
Ih meino daz er richeson ne uuolta, uuanda diu suht sturet sie nah alle. So sie adamen teta, do er Got uuolta uuerden. Pestis chit latine pecora sternens (fieo niderslahinde) so pestis sih kebreitet, so ist iz pestilentia, *i.e.* late peruagata pestis (uuito uuallonde sterbo). *Intelligo, quod gubernare,* (pro tribunali) *nollet. Namque hæc pestis corripuit fere omnes, sicut Adamo fecit, quum vellet Deus fieri. Pestis dicitur Latinè, quasi* pecora sternens. *Quando pestis se dilatat, dicitur Pestilentia,* i.e. *latè pervagata pestis.*

17. After the extinction of the Saxon emperors, the line of *Salian Francs* governed in Germany from A.D. 1024 to 1125. The authors of this period generally wrote in Latin. *Adam,* called *Bremensis,* born

at Meissen, Canon at Bremen, wrote in Latin a History of the Church which gives an account of Hamburg and Bremen, from the time of Charlemagne to Henry IV. It is of great value for the history of North Germany.

18. German literature had very few monuments in the time of the Salian Francs: the language is very stiff and mixed with Latin. The few specimens of German, in this period, are translations, such as the version of *Boethius* and *Aristotle*, by an unknown monk of St. Gallen, and the paraphrase of Canticum Canticorum by *Willeram*. *E. G. Graff*, in his Althochdeutschen Sprachschatz, vol. i. No. I. pref. p. xxxvi. 4to. Berlin, 1834, mentions a St. Gallen MS. of the 10th and 11th century, containing an old High-German translation of Boethius Cons. philos., and gives a specimen of this translation. The following extract is interesting, from the additions which the monk makes to the Latin text of Boethius,* showing the astronomical knowledge of his time.

Boethius.

Uuír uuízen. dáz tia érda daz uuázer úmbe gât. únde der fíerdo téil nàhôr óbenân erbárôt íst. án démo sízzent tie ménnisken. Ter hímel lêret únsíh. táz iz ter fíerdo téil íst. Alle díe astronomiam chúnnen. díe bechénnent táz æquinoctialis zona den hímel réhto in zuéi téilet. únde fóne íro ze dien ûzerôsten polis íouuéder hálb ében fílo íst íh méino ze demo septentrionali. únde ze demo australi. Sô ist tiu érda sínuuelbíu. únde íst úns únchúnt. úbe si. úndenân erbárôt sí. óbenân dâr sî erbárôt íst. târ sízzent tie líute ab æthiopico oceano. usque ad scithicum oceanum. Tíe férrôst sízzent ad austrum. díe sízzent in æthiopicis insulis. tíen íst tiu súnna óbe hóubete. sô si gât ûzer ariete in uerno tempore. únde sô si begínnet kân in libram in autumno.—*Graff's Sprachschatz, pref.* p. xxxvi.

LITERAL ENGLISH.

We know that the water goes round the earth, and the fourth part above is bare; on it sit the men. The heaven learns (*teaches*) us that it is the fourth part. All, who know astronomy, confess that the equinoctial zone divides the heaven right in two, and that from it to the uttermost pole of each half is an equal distance, I mean to the north, and to the south. So is the earth round, and it is to us unknown, if it be bare underneath; above, where it is bare, there sit the people from the Ethiopian ocean to the Scythian ocean. The farthest sitting to the south, they sit in Ethiopian islands; to those is the sun over head, when he goes out of Aries in the spring, and when he begins to go into Libra in autumn.

19. Parable *of the Sower*, in old High-German, taken from MS. fragments of Homilies in the Imperial Library at Vienna, written at the beginning of the 11th century, and printed in *Lambecsii Commentariis*, &c. 2nd edit. l. 11, p. 550: *Schilter*, vol. i. p. 76, at the end.

Lk. 8.—Unser Herro der almahtige Got der sprichet in desmi Euangelio, suenne der acchirman sait sinen samen, so fellit sumelichis pi demo uuege, unde uuirdit firtretin, oder is essant die uogile.

* Boethius de consolatione philosophiæ, 12mo. Lugd. Batavorum, 1656, p. 42, Prosa 7.—King Alfred's Anglo-Saxon Translation, with an excellent English Version by Cardale, ch. xviii. 1, p. 95.

20. Willeram was educated at Fulda. He died 1085, abbot of the monastery Ebersberg in Bavaria, and probably composed his Paraphrase between 1070 and 1084. MSS. are preserved at Vienna, Breslaw, Stuttgard, Einsiedeln, published with this title, *Willerami Abbatis* in Canticum Canticorum paraphrasis, Latina et veteri lingua Francica, ed. P. Merula, Leyden, 1598, and by *F. Vögelin, Worms*, 1631, and in *Schilter's Thes.* Also by *Hoffman, Breslaw*, 1827.

Sage mir uuine min. uua du dine scaf uueidenes. uua du ruouues umbe mitten dag. Umbe uuaz biten ih des? Daz ih niet irre ne beginne gen. unter den corteron dinero gesellon. Kunde mir o sponse. den ih mit allen chreften minno. uuer die ueræ fidei doctores sin. die dine scaf uuisen ad pascua uitæ. unte die solich sin. daz du in iro herzen dir hereberga machest. unte sie beskirmes ab omni feruore temptationis.—*Schilter's Thes.* vol. i. p. 6, *in fine*.

LITERAL GERMAN.

Sage mir, mein Geliebter, wo du deine Schafe weidest, wo du ruhest um Mittag. Warum warte ich dessen? dass ich nicht irre noch fehl gehe unter den Hürden deiner Gesellen. Verkünde mir, o Gespons, den ich aus allen Kräften liebe, wer die veræ fidei doctores sind, die deine Schafe weisen ad pascua vitæ, und die solche sind, dass du in ihren Herzen Herberge machest und sie beschirmst ab omni fervore temptationis.

VERBAL ENGLISH VERSION.

Say to me, my beloved, where thou pasturest thy sheep, where thou restest at midday. For what ask I this? That I may not err, nor begin to go among the number of thy companions. Inform me, O bridegroom, whom I love with all might, who are the teachers of true faith, who show thy sheep to the pastures of life, and who are such that you make dwellings in their hearts, and shelter them from all heat of temptation.

21. St. Anno. The praises of the archbishop of Cologne, *St. Anno*, who died 1075, concludes this period. The writer is unknown, but this poem was probably composed, soon after St. Anno's death, before the end of the 11th century. It is in rhyme, and consists of forty-nine stanzas, written, as Herzog says, in the *Low-Rhinish* or *Francic* dialect (Nieder Rhinisch). Meusel calls it *Alemannic*. Fragments of this poem were first published by *Martin Opitz*, 1639, who discovered them at Breslaw. The MS. is lost. It was printed by *Schilter* and others, and in 1816 by Goldmann. All the latter editions depend on the first incorrect publication.

MAN'S INGRATITUDE.	LITERAL GERMAN.
Mit bluomin cierint sich diu lant,	Mit Blumen zieren sich die Lande,
mit loube dekkit sich der walt;	Mit Laube decket sich der Wald,
daz wilt habit den sînin ganc,	Das Wild hat seinen Gang
scône ist der vôgil sanc:	Schön ist der Vogelsang;
ein iwelich ding die ê noch havit,	Ein jeglich Ding das Gesetz noch hat,
diemi got van êrist virgab:	Das ihm Gott zuerst gab.
newære die zuei gescephte,	Nur die zwei Geschöpfe,
di her gescuoph die bezziste,	Die er schuf die besten,
die virkêrten sich in die dobeheit:	Die verkehrten sich in die Tollheit,
dannin huobin sich diu leith.	Davon erhub sich das Leid.
Wackernagel, p. 117.	

POETICAL VERSION.

The flow'rs adorn the fields,
Green leaves bedeck the groves,
The beasts their courses run,
Soft rings the sweet bird's song:
All things obey the laws
That God creating gave,
Save the two latest born,
Whom noblest, best, he framed;
They spurn his high command,
And turn to folly's course,
From hence began the pain.*

22. *Te Deum of the* 12*th century.*†

Prof. Graff observes that the MS. is of the 12th century. It was originally the property of the monastery of St. Maria at Windberg, and contains many very rare words and expressions. The following extract is from the MS. in the Royal Library at Munich. It is inserted in the *Diutiska* of *Prof. C. G. Graff*, vol. iii. No. III. p. 459.

Daz lobesanch dere saligen bischoue den si sungen
Ymnus beatorum episcoporum Ambrosii et Augustini quem cantaverunt
deme herren wehsellichen unter in fure die becherde des uileheiteren lerares
domino vicissim inter se pro conversione preclari doctoris
unde uateres. Dih got wir loben Dih herren wir ueriehen dih ewigen
et patris Augustini. Te deum laudamus te dominum confitemur. Te æternum
uater elliu diu erde erwirdit. Dir alle engile dir die himile unde alle
patrem omnis terra veneratur. Tibi omnes angeli tibi cœli et universæ
gualte Dir die guizzeneuolle. unde die minnefiurige mit untuallicher stimme
potestates. Tibi cherubim et seraphim incessabili voce
furruoffent. Heiliger heiliger heiliger herro got dere here. Volle sint himile
proclamant. Sanctus, sanctus, sanctus dominus deus sabaoth. Pleni sunt cœli
unde erde dere magenchrefte eren diner.
et terra maiestatis gloriæ tuæ.

MINNESINGERS.‡

23. *German national poetry and prose compositions, from the* 12*th to the* 14*th century.* The Hohenstauffen or Suabian race of German emperors were great admirers and promoters of literature. Frederic I., Henry VI., Frederic II. and Conrad IV. were themselves poets, as well as the patrons of Minnesingers. A few of the chief Minnesingers and other authors will now be mentioned.

24. The *Nibelungen Lied*, or Song of the Nibelungen, is one of the most ancient and perfect Suabian epic poems. Pelegrin, bishop of Passau, who died in 991, is supposed to have collected the story of the *Nibelungen*, and to have written it in Latin by the aid of his scribe Conrad. The present poem is probably founded upon the Latin, and apparently written by Henry of Ofterdingen, about the middle of the 12th century. The following specimen and the English version are from the interesting

* This flowing and spirited translation, with some others that follow, is taken from *Lays of the Minnesingers*, 8vo. Longman, London, 1825, a valuable little work, which is full of interesting information respecting the Minnesingers, and contains many beautiful specimens of their poetry.

† See § 4, for a specimen of the *Te Deum* in German of the 8th century.

‡ Minne *love*, sänger *singer*.

work, "*Lays of the Minnesingers*," p. 114: the substance of the extract will be found in the edition of *van der Hagen*, 8vo. Berlin, 1807, p. 47, verse 1145.

SONG OF THE NIBELUNGEN.	FREE ENGLISH VERSION.
Sam der liehte mane	And as the beaming moon
Vor der sternen stat,	Rides high the stars among,
Der schin so lûterliche	And moves with lustre mild
Ab' den wolchen gat,	The mirky clouds along;
Dem stûnt si nu geliche	So, midst her maiden throng,
Vor maneger vrowen gût.	Up rose that matchless fair;
Des wart da wol gehôhet	And higher swell'd the soul
Den zieren helden der mût.	Of many a hero there.

25. WALTER *von der Vogelweide*, of Thurgau in Switzerland, flourished from 1190 to 1227.

SUMMER.	FREE ENGLISH VERSION.
Do der sumer komen was,	'Twas summer—through the opening grass
Und die bluomen dur das gras	The joyous flowers up sprang,
Wunneklich entsprungen,	The birds in all their diff'rent tribes
Und die vogel.sungen, &c.	Loud in the woodlands sang.

Minnesingers, p. 206.

26. GRAVE CHUNRAD *von Kilchberg* or *Kirchberg*, of Suabia, wrote in the latter part of the 12th century.

ON MAY.	FREE ENGLISH VERSION.
Meige ist komen in dú lant,	May, sweet May, again is come,
Der uns ie von sorgen bant:	May that frees the land from gloom;
Kinder, kinder, sint gemant!	Children, children, up and see
Wir sun schouwen wunne manigvalde;	All her stores of jollity!
Uf der liehten heide breit	On the laughing hedgerow's side
Da hat er uns fúr gespreit	She hath spread her treasures wide;
Manig bluemelin gemeit,	She is in the greenwood shade,
Erst bezeiget in dem gruenen walde;	Where the nightingale hath made
Da hört man die nahtegal,	Every branch and every tree
Uf dem bluenden rise,	Ring with her sweet melody.
Singen lobelichen schal, &c.	*Minnesingers*, p. 141.

27. HENRY RISPACH, commonly styled Der tugendhafte Schreiber *the virtuous Clerk*, lived about 1207.

THE LOVER'S LAMENT.	FREE ENGLISH TRANSLATION.
Es ist in den walt gesungen	The woodlands with my songs resound,
Das ich ir genaden klage	As still I seek to gain
Dú min herze hat betwungen	The favours of that lady fair
Und noh twinget alle tage.	Who causeth all my pain.
Mir ist sam der nahtegal,	My fate is like the nightingale's
Dú so vil vergebne singet,	That singeth all night long,
Und ir doh ze leste bringet	While still the woodlands mournfully
Niht wan schaden ir suezer schal.	But echo back her song.

Minnesingers, p. 144.

28. Wirnt von Grafenberg wrote a poem styled, *Wigalois*, about 1212. MSS. are preserved at Cologne, Leyden, Bremen, and Hamburg. A very valuable edition was published in 8vo. by *Benecke*, *Berlin*, 1819.

Artus Hofhaltung.	*Court of King Arthur.*
Ez was hie vor, so man seit,	Heretofore there was, as men say,
Ein Kunech der ie nach Eren streit;	A king who always for honour fought,
Des Name witen was erkant.	Whose name was widely known.
Britanie hiez sin Lant;	Britain was called his land,
Selbe hiez er Artus.	He himself was called Arthur.
Ze Karidol da het er Hus.	At Karidol there had he a house,
Mit solhen Freuden stunt ez do,	With such delights it stood there
Daz uns daz nu machet fro.	That it now gives us pleasure.
	Herzog, p. 79.

29. Gotfrit von Nifen, a Suabian nobleman, wrote about the year 1235. The following specimen is taken from *Benecke's Additions to Bodmer's Versuche über die alte schwäbische Poesie*, *Zürich*, 1748.

SPRING.	FREE ENGLISH VERSION.
Nu woluf! grüssen	Up, up, let us greet
Wir den süssen,	The season so sweet,
Der uns büssen	For winter is gone;
Wil des winters pin;	And the flowers are springing,
Der uns wil bringen	And little birds singing,
Vogelin singen,	Their soft notes ringing,
Blümen springen,	And bright is the sun!
Und der sunnen schin.	Where all was drest
Da man sach e	In a snowy vest,
Den kalten sne,	There grass is growing,
Da siht man gras,	With dew-drops glowing,
Von touwe nas,	And flowers are seen
Bruevent das	On beds so green.
Blumen unde der kle.	*Minnesingers*, p. 155.

30. A notice of the following didactic poems in the old High-German dialect cannot be omitted. 1. Der König Tyrol von Schotten und sein sohn Fridebrant, *King Tyrol of Scotland and his son Fridebrant.* 2. Der Winsbeke an sinen sun, *Winsbeke to his son.* 3. Du(i) Winsbekin an ir Tohter, *Winsbekin to her daughter.* These three are by unknown authors, but they most likely belong to the beginning of the 13th century. They are printed in *Schilter*, vol. ii.; and in *Manesse's Collection.* 4. Frigedanks Bescheidenheit, *Sentiments and Sentences.* Whether Frigedank be the real or fictitious name of the author, is very doubtful. The poem was written before 1230. Published by *Sebastian Brand*, *Strasburg*, 1508, 4to., and lately by *W. Grimm.* These didactic poems, particularly the latter, are distinguished by elevated and philosophical views of life.

DER WINSBEKE.	LITERAL ENGLISH VERSION.
Sun ellú wisheit ist ein wiht,	Son all wisdom is nothing,
Dú herze sin ertrahten kan,	(Thy heart can do without it)
Hat er ze Gote minne niht,	If to God it has no love,
Vnd siht in niht mit vorhten an.	And do not look to him in fear.

Schilter's Thes. vol. ii. p. 20, *in fine.*

FRIGEDANKS BESCHEIDENHEIT.	LITERAL ENGLISH VERSION.
Gote dienen ane Wank	God serving without irresolution
Deist aller Wisheit Anvank.	That is of all wisdom the beginning.
Der hat sich sëlben betrogen	He has deceived himself
Und zimbert uf den Regenbogen.	Who builds upon the rainbow.

31. SCHWABEN-SPIEGEL, or *Suabian Mirror*, the Alemannic provincial law, probably compiled in the 13th century. Published in *Schilter's* Thes. vol. ii.

Introduction to the Laws.

Herre Got himelischer Vater, durch din milte gute geschufte du den menschen mit drivaltiger wirdikeit.

2. Diu erst ist daz er nach dir gebildet ist.

3. Daz ist auch ain alz groz uuirdikeit, der dir allez menschen kunne ymmer sunderlichen danken sol, uuan dez haben uuir groz reht, Vil lieber herre himelischer Vater sit du unz zu diner hohen gothait also uuirdiclich geedelt hast.

4. Diu ander uuirdikeit ist da du Herr almächtiger Schöpfer den menschen zu geschaffen hast, daz du alle die uuelt die sunnen und den maun die sterne und diu vier elemente, fiur, uuazzer, luft, erde, die vogel in den luften, die vische in dem uuage, diu tier in dem uualde, die uuurme in der erde, golt, silber, edelgestain und der edeln uuurtze suzzer smak, der plumen liehtiu varuue, der baume frucht korn und alle creatur, daz haust du herre allez dem menschen ze nutze und ze dienst geschaffen durch die triuuue und durch die minne die du zu dem menschen hetest.

5. Diu dritt uuirdikait ist da du Herr den menschen mit geedelt hast, daz ist diu daz der mensche die uuirde und ere und freude und uuunn die du selb bist ymmer mit dir euuiclich niezzen sol.

LITERAL ENGLISH.

Lord God, heavenly father, by thy kind goodness, createst thou man with threefold dignity.

2. The first is, that he after thee is formed.

3. That is such a great dignity, for which all mankind always particularly shall thank thee, for which we have great right (obligation), much beloved Lord, heavenly father, since thou to thy high Godhead hast so honourably ennobled us.

4. The second dignity to which thou, Lord, almighty Creator, hast formed man, is that thou, all the world, the sun and moon, the stars, and the four elements, fire, water, air, earth, the fowls in the air, the fish in the waves, the animals in the wood, the worms on the earth, gold, silver, and precious stones, and the sweet flavour of costly spices, the shining colour of flowers, the fruit of the trees, corn, and all creatures, hast, the Lord, created for the use and service of man, by the favour and love which thou hadst to man.

5. The third dignity with which thou, Lord, hast ennobled man is this, that man shall enjoy the dignity and honour and pleasure and delight which thou thyself art (hast) always and eternally with thee.

32. THE EDELSTEIN, or *the Gem*, a collection of fables by Boner, Dominican monk whose name is often mentioned in documents from 324—1349. An excellent edition of the Edelstein, with a glossary, is iven by *Prof. G. F. Beneke,* of Gottingen, published at Berlin, 1816, vo.

Von einem Hund und einem Esel. (*Von unbedachter Narreheit.*)	*Of a Dog and an Ass.* (*Unthinking folly.*)
Wel rechter Tore des begert,	He (is) a complete fool, who asks
Des sin Nature in nicht gewert,	What his nature does not grant,
Der mag des wol entgelten.	He may for it well suffer.
Dar zu sol man in schelten,	Besides that we shall blame him,
Der sich des Dinges nimet an,	Who undertakes a thing,
Das sin Geslechte nie gewan.	Which his species never acquired.
Was du Nature hat gegeben,	What nature has given
Dem mag der Mensch kum wider streben.	Man may hardly oppose.
	Herzog, p. 144.

33. The following specimens show, from the year 1400, the gradual formation of the modern German. As best indicating the change in the language, the extracts are chiefly given from the same passage of the Scriptures.

34. THE GOSPELS (*Evangelien uber al daz Jar*) from a MS. at Munich of the 13th century.

LK. viii. 3.—(Do ein michel Menig chom zu Jesu, und von den Steten eilten zu im, do sprach er ei Bispel :) Der Ackerman gi aus seen sinen Samen.—4. Und do er ge seet, do viel ein Sam pi dem Weg und ward vertreten und gazzen in di Vogel.

35. THE EPISTLES and Gospels in High-German (Hoch-Teutsch), "*Lectiones, Epistolæ et Evangelia per annum,*" A.D. 1431, from a MS. at Munich.

LK. viii. 3.—(Do ain michel menig cham zue iesu vnd von den stetten eilten zv im do sprach er ain peichspill) der Akcherman gie aus säen seinen samen.—4. Vnd do er gesäett, do viell ain sam peij dem weg vnd ward vertreten und azzn in auch die vogel.

36. GOSPELS for every day of the year (*Evangelien auf alle Tage des Jahres*), from a MS. at Munich, about 1450. *Domin. Sexagesima.*

LK. viii. 3.—Do ein michl menig chom zu jhm vnd võ dē stetn eylten zu jm do sprach er ein peyspill d' ackerman gye aus sänd seiñ samē,—4. vnd do er gesät do viel ein samē pey dē weg vnd wart vertretten vnd gassn jn auch die vogl.

37. AIN POSTIL *uber dij Evangelij*, from a MS. at Munich, about 1460.

LK. viii. 3.—(Vnd da das volck nū chom zu im da hueb er auf und sagt in ain peyspil vnd sprach) Es gie ain man aus zu ainen zeitn vnd sät, 4. vnd da er nu ward seen da viel ain sam zu dem weg vnd der ward vertreten vnd dartzu komen die vogel und assn den samen.

38. BIBLE in High-German (*teutsche Bibel*). One of the earliest Bibles, but without date; some say it was printed at Mayence, 1462, others at Strasburg, 1466.

MK. iv. 3.—Hört secht der Seer gieng aus ze seen. 4. Vnd do er seet: der ein viel bey dem Weg, vnd die Vogel des Himels kamen vnd assen jn.

39. A Plenarium (*Sammlung der Episteln und Evangelien*), Augsburg, 1473.

Mk. iv. 3.—Er get auss der da säen will seinen samen vn̄ sät, 4. Vnd als er säet, das ein felt in den weg. vnd wirt verträtten, vnd die Vögel des hymels die essent es auff.

40. Plenarium, *Augsburg*, 1474.

Mk. iv. 3.—Der ist aussgangen der da seet zu seen seinen somen,—4. Vn̄ als er seet da ist einer gefallen an den weg vnnd ist getretten worden, vnnd auch die vogel des himels habendt den gegessen.

41. Bible (*teutsch*), *Augsburg*, 1476.

Mk. iv.—Hört secht d' da seet der ist aussgegangē ze seen. Vnd da er seet. der ein viel bey dem weg vn̄ die vogel des hymels kamen vnd assen in.

42. Bible (*teutsch*), *Augsburg*, 1487.

Mk. iv.—Hört. secht. der do seet, der ist aussgegangen ze seen. Vnd do er seet. der ein viel bey dem weg. vnd die vögel des hÿmmels kamen vnd assen jn.

43. Bible, printed by H. Schonsperger, *Augsburg*, 1490.

Mk. iv.—Hört. sehet. der da säet. d' ist aussgegangen ze säen. Vnnd da er säet. der ein viel bey dem weg. vnd die vögel des hymmels kamen vnnd assen jn.

44. Gospels, *Strasburg*, 1517.

Lk. viii.—Do zuomal als vil volcks gesammē kam zu Jesu, vn̄ vō dē stettē zu im yltē. Jn der zeit da sagt er inē ein gleichniss Der da seiet d' ist vssgangen zu seen seinen somē. Vn̄ als der seet da ist etlichs gefallē in dē weg, vn̄ ist zertrettē worden vn̄ die vögel des himels haben es gessen.

45. Dr. Keiserssberg's Postil, *Strasburg*, 1522.

Am Sonnentag Sexagesimæ. Horēt (sprach der her) nement war, der d' do seyet ist vssgangē zu seyen seinē somē. Vn̄ so er seyt, ist d' ander som gefallē vff dē weg. (secus via, uit neben den weg. er wer sust ī dē acker gefallē) vn̄ ist zertrettē wordē vō den wādleren, vn̄ die fögel des hīmels seind kūmen vn̄ habend den vffgessen.

46. New Testament, *Zurich*, 1524.

Mk. iv. 3, 4.—Hörend zu, sich es gieng ein säyer vss zu säyen, vn̄ es begab sich in dem er säyet, fiel etlichs an den weg, do komend die vögel vnder dem himel vnd frassends vff.

47. Bible, by Dr. I. Eck, *Ingolstadt*, 1537.

Mk. iv. 3.—Höret zu, Sihe, Ainer der da säiet, giēg auss: zu säien:—4. Vnd in dem er säiet. fiel etlichs an den weg, da kamen die vögel des lufts vnd frassens auf.

48. New Testament (*Deutssch*), *Wittenberg*, 1522.

Mk. iv. 3.—Horet zu, Sihe, Es, gieng eyn seeman aus zu seen,—4. vnd es begab sich, ynn dem er seet, fiel ettlichs an den weg, da kamen die vogel vnter dem hymel vnd frassens auf.

49. HISTORY of the Gospels (*Evangelisch Hijstori*), by Othmaren Nachtgall, Augsburg, 1525.

MK. iv. 3.—Es was ainer ausgegangen zu seen seynen Somen,—4. Vnnder dem ainer gefallen was auff den Weg, vñ zertretten worden, auch hetten in die Vogel des Hymels auffgessen.

50. BIBLE, *Zurich*, 1530.

MK. iv. 3.—Hörend zu, sihe, es gieng ein Säyer auss ze säyen,—4. vnd es begab sich in dem er säyet, fiel etliches an den wäg, do kamend die vögel vnder dem himel, vnd frassends auf.

51. The present German language* (Hoch-Deutsch) has a greater affinity to the Alemannic and Francic than to the Platt-Deutsch. This inclination towards the High-German, or southerly branch of the German dialects, arose from the influence of Luther at the Reformation. Luther was Professor of Divinity at Wittenberg, where the high dialect prevailed, and in which he wrote his translation of the Bible. The New Testament first published in 1523, and the Old Testament from 1523 to 1534, was revised and the whole Bible published from 1541 to 1545. This revised translation soon became generally known, and the numerous students that crowded Wittenberg to benefit by the lectures of Luther, and subsequently dispersed into the different provinces, carried with them this High-German version, and a predilection for this dialect. Thus High-German became generally known, and was adopted as the language of the church, the learned, and the press. This tongue spread with the Reformation, and as it advanced in extent it increased in perfection, till it has become one of the most cultivated and extensive of all the Gothic or Teutonic dialects. It not only prevails in the German confederacy, but in the north of Switzerland, Alsace, in a great part of Hungary, Transylvania, Bohemia, the kingdom of Prussia, in Schleswick, part of Jutland, and in Russia as far north as Courland. Amongst the Germans are writers of the first order in every branch of literature and science: they are most prolific in the production of new works, nor can any easily exceed them in freedom of inquiry, in labour, or erudition.

52. BIBLE, by Dr. M. Luther, *Wittenberg*, 1545.

MK. iv. 3.—Höret zu! Sihe, es gieng ein Seeman aus zu seen.—4. Vnd es begab sich, in dem er seet, fiel etlichs an den Weg, da kamen die Vogel unter dem Himel vnd frassens auff.

53. DER LÄYEN Biblia, by J. Freydang, *Frankfort*, 1569.

LK. viii.—Es gieng ein Säemann auss seim Hauss,
Zu säen seinen Samen auss,
Vnd etlichs fiel an weges gstetn,
Das wurd gentzlich in staub vertretn,

Vnd die Vögel vnder dem Himml
Frassen das auff mit eim gewimbl:
Auff den Felsen fiel etliches,
Da es auffgieng verdorret es.

* For the origin of the Germans and their name, see § II. 1, 2, 3, note (†).

54. The Froschmäuseler, oder der Frösch und Mäuse wunderbare Hofhaltung, *The court of the frogs and mice*, Magdeburg, 1595, 8vo. is one of the most remarkable epic poems. It was written by George Rollenhagen, who was born 1542, at Bernau in Brandenburg, and died 1609, when rector of the Latin school of Magdeburg. He attempts to describe eternity in the following striking allegory.

ETERNITY.	ENGLISH VERSION.
* * * *	* * * *
Ewig, Ewig, ist lange Zeit.	For ever and ever is a long time.
Wēr ein Sandberg uns vorgestelt,	Were a heap of sand before our eyes,
Viel grösser denn die gantze Welt,	Exceeding the whole world in size,
Und ein Vogel all tausend Iahr kēm,	And a bird ev'ry thousand years should come,
Auff einmahl nur ein Kornlein nem,	To take but a single grain therefrom,
Und Gott uns denn erlösen wolt,	And God would grant deliverance
Wenn er das letzte Körnlein holt,	When the last grain were taken thence,
So wēr Hoffnung das uns elende,	We might have hope that our wretched state,
Zwar langsam, aber doch het ein ende.	Tho' long, might yet still terminate.
Nun bleiben wir in Gottes Zorn	But now beneath God's wrath we lie
Ohn all Hoffnung ewig verlorn.	Lost, without hope, eternally.
Chap. xiii.	*Morrell.*

55. Bible, *Nuremberg*, 1703, 1708, &c.

Mk. iv. 3.—Höret zu, Sihe, es gieng ein Sāe-Mann aus zu säen.—4. Und es begab sich, in dem er säete, fiel etliches an den Weg, da kamen die Vögel unter dem Himmel, und frassens auf.

56. New Testament, translated by J. Maria, *Passau*, in Bavaria, 1752.

Mk. iv. 3. Höret: siehe, es gieng ein Sämann aus zu säen.—4. Und es begab sich, indem er säete, fiel ein Theil an den Weg, da kamen die Vögel, und frassen es auf.

57. A High-German translation of Reineke de Vos in the same metre as the Low-German of Henry van Alkmar, by *Dietrich Wilhelm Soltau*, Lüneburg, 1830. This extract will not only serve as a specimen of modern High-German, but as an example of the difference in the dialects.*

REINEKE DE VOS.

Es war an einem Mayentag,	Und Marks der Häher kamen sogar;
Wie Blum' und Laub die Knospen brach;	Denn Nobel wollte Herr'n und Sassen
Die Kräuter sprossten; froh erklang	Ein frohes Gastmahl feyern lassen;
Im Hain der Vögel Lobgesang;	Darum er alles her berief,
Der Tag war schön, und Balsamduft	Was ging, was kroch, was flog, was lief,
Erfüllte weit umher die Luft;	Thier' und Gevögel, gross und klein,
Als König Nobel, der mächtige Leu,	Bis auf Reinhard den Fuchs allein,
Ein Fest gab, und liess mit Geschrey	Der sich so frevelhaft benommen,
Hoftag verkünden überall.	Dass er nicht durft' nach Hofe kommen.
Da kamen hin mit grossem Schall	Wer Böses thut, der scheu't das Licht;
Viel edle Herr'n und stolze Gesellen;	So ging's auch diesem falschen Wicht;
Es war kaum möglich sie zu zählen.	Er hatt' am Hofe schlimmen Geruch,
Der Kranich Lütke, Matz der Staar	Drum er zu kommen Bedenken trug.

* See Dutch, VI. 17; and Low-German, V. 26.

58. A free High-German translation of Henry van Alkmar's Reineke de Vos by *Göethe.*

Pfingsten, das liebliche Fest, war gekommen; Es grünten und blüthen
Feld und Wald; auf Hügeln und Höhn, in Büschen und Hecken
Uebten ein fröhliches Lied die neuermunterten Vögel;
Jede Wiese sprosste von Blumen in duftenden Gründen,
Festlich heiter glänzte der Himmel und farbig die Erd.
Nobel, der König, versammelt den Hof; und seine Vasallen
Eilen gerufen herbey mit grossem Gepränge; da kommen
Viele stolze Gesellen von allen Seiten und Enden,
Lütke, der Kranich, und Markart der Häher und alle die Besten.
Denn der König gedenkt mit allen seinen Baronen
Hof zu halten in Feyer und Pracht; er lässt sie berufen
Alle mit einander, so gut die grossen als kleinen.
Niemand sollte fehlen! und dennoch fehlte der eine,
Reinecke Fuchs, der Schelm! der viel begangenen Frevels
Halben des Hofs sich enthielt. So scheuet das böse Gewissen
Licht und Tag, es scheute der Fuchs die versammleten Herren.

59. The MODERN GERMAN of 1835 only differs in orthography from the first edition of Luther's Bible of 1545.*

High-German Provincial Dialects.

60. The following are a few specimens of the various provincial dialects spoken in Upper Germany in 1827.

61. SWISS provincial dialect in the canton *Zurich,* 1827.

MK. iv. 3.—Losät uf, äs ischt en Ackhersmā uffs Fäld gangä ge säen.—4. Und da er gsät hät, ischt öbbis ā d' Strass gfallä, da sind d' Vögel cho und händs ufgrässä.

62. SWISS provincial dialect in the canton *Uri,* 1827.

MK. iv. 3.—Hört zuŏ, ksöscht, a Mā ischt üssgangă go saïa; 4. und wie 'ne sait, falt'n öpis an die Strass, da sind die Vögel chŏ, und hand's aweg gefrässă.

63. SUABIAN provincial dialect near the *Alps,* 1827.

MK. iv. 3.—Lōsät und lûogăd, as īscht a Sayer ussi gangă z' saiid;—4. Und wie êar g'sait hêat, īscht a Dôal uf a Wêag, g'falla, dên hĕnn-da d' Vögel g'uoh', und ufg'frêassa.

64. SUABIAN provincial dialect about *Stuttgard,* 1827.

MK. iv. 3.—Höhret me an̄: A Bauer ischt zum sää̆ naus gangă ufs Feld.—4. Äbbes vom rumg' streutā Sohmā ischt uf da Weeg g'fallă, do sind d' Vögel kommā, und hends g'fressă.

65. SUABIAN provincial dialect about *Ulm,* 1827.

MK. iv. 3.—Hairet zûe, séand, es ischt a Sæmâ ausganga z' sæ̂a.—4. Und wïa æ̂r g'sæ̂t haut, do ischt a Thoil an Wêag g'fallâ, dā̆ sénd d' Vegel kommâ und hann̄ds aufg' fressâ.

66. ALSACIAN dialect about *Strasburg,* 1827.

MK. iv. 3.—Hèrt, sîet der Ackersmann esch üssgange zu'm Säije.—4. Un wie er g'saijit hätt, èsch eins (ebbs) ouf de Waij g'falle; dā̆ sind d' Vögel komme ounterm Himmel, un häns ouffg'frässe.

* See § 51, 52.

67. SALTZBURG dialect, 1827.

MK. iv. 3.—Höscht's: Schau, ös gàng à Sàmōn aus zum Sàn̄.—4. Und ös gàb si, indem à sát, völd à Doal an dem Wög, da kàmàn d' Vögl und fràss'ns auf.

68. TIROLESE dialect, 1827.

MK. iv. 3.—Då hëärts à Mål zuê; às ischt à Mål a Paur zê sàn aussi gàngn.—4. und às ischt g'schöch'n, wie ëar g' sànt hât, ischt ôàn Thail àffn Wög g' fäll'n, und då hànn d' Fögl kemmen, und håb'ns àffg'frössen.

69. BAVARIAN dialect about *Eichstadt*, 1827.

MK. 4. 3.—Iză schau! a Baur is zum sàn gangă.—4. Und do, wi-a gsàt hăt, iss epàs an Wég hing'falln; dēs håbn d' Vögl wek g'fressn.

70. BAVARIAN dialect about *Munich*, 1827.

MK. iv. 3.—Lossts enk sogn̄g! à Moĭ is ă Baur aufs Sàhn' naus gangă.—4. Und wia r-a denn do g'saht hot, is e'am à Thoâi Sammă-r-ånn Weg nō gfôin; do sànn d' Vögl vonn Himmi rō kemma, und hammatn aufg'frössn.

71. BAVARIAN dialect about *Nuremberg*, 1827.

MK. iv. 3.—Höirt zôu, segt, es iss a Bauer (a Säemoh) ausgangă z'sææ̆.—4. Und dâu hâuts es si zoutrågn̄, wöi er g'sät hâut, iss etli's an Weeg g'falln; da senn die Vügel unterm Himmel kummă und hâbens âfg'fressn.

72. DIALECT about *Frankfort* on the Maine, (Sachsenhausen), 1827.

MK. iv. 3.—Hihrt zôu, Sich, es gung ĕ Mōl a Sihmann ĕnausser z' sihn̄.—4. Unn dò hőt sech's begäwwe, wäi ĕr gesiht hőt, fäil Epäs d'rvun̄ ån'n̄ Wäg; do sénn (sain̄) di Vigel unnerm Hémmel kumme, unn håwwe's uffgĕfresse.

73. DIALECT of *Wetteravia*, or the district enclosed by the Sahn, Rhine, and Maine, 1827.

MK. iv. 3.—Hirt zôu! Sich, es geng ĕ mohl ĕ Sehmann naus, der wullt sihĕ,—4. Önn wêi ĕ sēt', do fêil a Dàl uf de Wèk; då kohme de Vigel onnerm Himmel onn frossens uf.

74. HESSIAN dialect about *Kassel*, 1827.

MK. iv. 3.—Hehrt zu, sich, es gink en Sehmann us ze sehen. 4. Un es begab sich, wie hä (he) sehte, fiel etliches uf den Wäk; do kamen de Väggel unner dem Himmel und frassens uf.

75. HIGH-SAXON dialect about *Leipsic*, 1827.

MK. iv. 3.—Hürt zu säht! 's gung ä mal a Siämann aus zu siän.—4. Un da hä siäte, da feel eeniges an'n Wäg; da kamen de Vegel (Veggel) unggern Himmel, un frassens uf.

76. HIGH-SAXON dialect about *Ansbach*, 1827.

MK. iv. 3.—Härt zu! sich, es gieng à Sôamå auf's Soâ aus.—4. und es iss g' seheg'n, indemm ehr säte, fiel Etlichs ån den Weeg. Dôa kamm die Viegel unt'rn Himmel und frassens auf.

XI.—SCANDINAVIAN LITERATURE,* INCLUDING A SKETCH OF THE LANGUAGES OF ICELAND, DENMARK, NORWAY, AND SWEDEN.

1. ICELAND has been supposed to be the remote *Thule* † of Virgil, Pliny, and other classical authors; but it is more probable, that when they mention Thule, they refer to part of South Norway, probably the province of Tellemark. It is denominated *Thyle* ‡ by king Alfred in his translation of Boethius, and *Thila* § in his Orosius. The cluster of islands called *Ferroes* were discovered by Scandinavian navigators at an early period, and in A. D. 861, *Naddod*, a Norwegian, was driven by storms on the coast of Iceland, which, from the snow, he named *Snoeland*. Soon after, *Gardar Svarfarson*, a Swede, by circumnavigation, ascertained it to be an island, and named it *Gardarsholm*, or the island of *Gardar*;|| it has, however, become generally known by the descriptive name Iceland.¶

2. *Harald Hárfager*, or the Fairhaired, subduing all the petty kings of Norway, obtained the supreme power about A. D. 863, and continued king of Norway till his death in 934. Some of the independent and high-spirited nobles spurned the usurped authority of Harald, and when, in their deadly feuds, they had slain an adversary, or in some other way broken the laws, rather than submit to Harald, they fled to Iceland, a land of prodigies, where subterraneous fires burst through the frozen soil, and boiling springs shoot up amidst eternal snows; where the powerful genius of liberty, and the no less powerful genius of poetry, have given most brilliant proofs of the energies of the human mind at the remotest confines of animated nature.** Among those who first fled to this land of freedom, we have, in 874, a record of Ingolf, the son of a Norwegian Jarl, Comes, or Earl, and his brother-in-law *Hjörleif*, who settled on the promontory on the south-east coast, still called Ingolf-shöfdi. In the next century, *Thornvald* with his son Erik, surnamed Raudi, or the red,†† escaped to Iceland. In the space of 50 or 60 years

* This short sketch is much indebted to the important works published by THE ROYAL SOCIETY OF NORTHERN ANTIQUARIES, COPENHAGEN, a Society which claims the especial regard of Englishmen. While too much praise cannot be given to the Professors Finn Magnusen and Rafn, as well as to the late Professor Rask, and the other active members of this Institution, for their erudite publications, feelings of the highest respect and the warmest gratitude must ever be excited, when the author recollects the constant literary communications and the very friendly assistance of Dr. Rafn and Dr. Rask. An account of part of Professor Rafn's valuable works will be found in § 17, 18, and 19.

† The ultima Thule of Virgil, *Georg*. i. 30, and Pliny, iv. 16.

‡ Bo. 29, 3; Card. p. 166, 1. § Ors. 1, 1; Bar. p. 31, 1.

|| Islands Landnámabók, sive Liber originum Islandiæ, I. 1. I'slendinga Sögur, I. p. 25, 26. Schöning, Norges Riges, Historie, vol. ii. p. 101. Wheaton's Hist. of Northmen, p. 17.

¶ Is ice, land *land*. Dr. Ingram thinks, in Orosius, Bar. 25, 4, Ira-land ought to be Isa-land. *Inaugural Lect*. p. 79, note *q*.—Isa-land is the reading adopted by Professor Rask.

** Malte *Brun's Geog*. vol. v. p. 98.

†† Landnámabók, i. 6—8. *Schoening*, vol. i. p. 107. *Malte Brun's Geog*. vol. v. p. 98.

u

the inhabitable parts of Iceland were occupied by refugees from Norway, who brought with them their families and a numerous retinue of dependants. Here they were amply repaid for their hardships and toil, in this severe clime, by the full enjoyment of liberty and independence; here they imported their language, the old Danish, their rites of heathen worship, and their civil institutions. They established a great national assembly, held annually, where all freeholders had a right to be present. This assembly bore a great resemblance to the Anglo-Saxon Witenagemot, and was called *Alþing*.* The president of this meeting was elected for life, and was denominated *Lögsögumaðr*† or Promulgator of the law. Iceland continued this species of government, or republic, for about three centuries, that is, till A.D. 1275, when it became subject to the kings of Norway. Christianity was introduced into Iceland about the end of the 10th century, and was established in 1016.

3. Iceland, in its pagan state, had a literature, a poetry, and mythology, peculiarly its own. The Icelanders preserved their learning and history in oral tradition, by means of their *Skalds*,‡ who were at once poets and historians. These Skalds were a sort of travelling minstrels, who composed and recited the praises of kings and heroes in verse, and continually migrated from one northern country to another. They were the chroniclers, and often the companions of kings, attended them in their conflicts, and thus, from their presence at the scenes they had to record, they were able to give a lively and faithful description. In the Icelandic language a list is kept of the 230 chief Skalds or poetical historians from *Ragnar Lodbrok* to *Valdemar* II. amongst whom are several crowned heads, and celebrated warriors.‖

4. *A Saga-man* § recalled the memory of past events in prose narratives as the Skalds did in verse. The memory of past transactions was thus transmitted from age to age by the poets or Skalds, and the Saga-men or story-tellers, till the introduction of writing, gave them a fixed and durable record.

5. The literature, mythology, and history of the Icelanders, and the old Scandinavians in general, in their pagan and early christian state, are chiefly preserved in the poetic or elder Edda,¶ the prose or younger Edda, and the Sagas, the *Njála*, the *Heimskríngla*, the *Konúngsskuggsjá*, and the *Landnámabók*. A short account of these works, and their various editions, may be useful.**

* Þing in Icelandic signifies *forum, conventus, a court of justice, an assize;* and alþing *a general meeting, or assize.*

† *Icl.* Lögsaga *f.* (*gen.* lögsögu) *recitatio legum*, from lög *law;* saga *a telling, speaking;* maðr *a man, the man propounding the law.*

‡ Skald from *Icl.* skálld *a poet.*

‖ Wheaton's History of Northmen, p. 51.

§ Saga *historia, narratio;* maðr *gen.* manns, *acc.* mann *man*, that is, *a story-teller.*

¶ Edda *a grandmother*, quasi prima mater ethnicæ religionis.

** A minute account of the Icelandic works which are published may be found in "*Lexicon Islandico Latino-Danicum Biörnonis Haldersonii, curâ R. K. Raskii, editum Havniæ,*" 4to. 1814.

6. SÆMUND SIGFUSSEN, a clergyman, born in Iceland in 1056, was the first compiler of the *Poetic Edda.* He appears to have written some of these poetic effusions from the recital of contemporary Skalds, and to have collected others from manuscripts.

The Icelandic text of the poetic Edda was published in 4to. at Copenhagen in 1787, with a Latin translation, notes, and glossary. A second volume was not printed till 1818, and a third in 1828, by *Professor Finn Magnusen.* *Professor Rask* and the *Rev. Mr. Afzelius*, in 1818, published, at Stockholm, the original of this Edda, carefully accented, and distinguishing *i* from *j*, *u* from *v*, and *ö* from *o*.

7. THE POETIC EDDA contains the *Völu-spá,** which gives an account of the creation f the universe, and the gods and men who inhabited it. The *Gróu-galdr* or Groa's ſagic Song. The *Sólarljóð* or Song of the Sun which is almost entirely Sæmund's wn composition, containing ideas of a future life, evidently derived from a christian ›urce. The *Vafþrúðnis-mál,* which is a sort of poetic dialogue between Odin and famous giant.

8. THE GRÍMNIS-MÁ'L, or the Song of Grimner, describing the habitations of the ities. The *Alvis-mál, Hyndlu-ljóð*, &c., *Hýmnisquiða*, or the Song of Hymer, &c. any of these poems can be traced back to the 10th, or even the 9th century.

9. THE PROSE OR YOUNGER EDDA was written by the famous *Snorre* *'urleson,* who was born of a noble family in 1178, at Hvamm on the ›st coast of Iceland, and was murdered in 1241. The Prose Edda was, ›refore, more than a century later than the Poetic.

Γhe first edition of the Prose Edda was published in an abridged form at Copen- ;en in 1665, by *Resenius*, in Icelandic, Danish, and Latin. He appended to this tion the Völu-spá and Háva-mál, two poems from the Poetic Edda. A complete tion of the original text of the Prose Edda was published at Stockholm in 1818, Professor Rask. The Prose Edda is a course of poetical lectures, drawn up for ›e young Icelanders who intended to become Skalds or poets. It consists of two s. The first part, properly called the Edda, explains the mythology of the Poetic la, and forms a complete northern Pantheon in the form of fables. The second is the Skalda or Poetics, which is the art of poetry adopted by the Skalds. It ains a dictionary of poetic synonymes, and the whole art of versification, allitera- species of verse, &c. In explaining the mythology, and illustrating the different ies of versification, Snorre extracted the most interesting parts of the Poetic ı, and thus contrived in the form of dialogues to give the substance of it in a more ligible form.

. NJA'LA, or Life of the celebrated Icelander, Njáll Þorgeirsson, and his sons. It ıutiful in style, and correct in its statements. The Icelandic text was published ›penhagen, 1772, in 4to. and a Latin version in 1809.

. *Snorre* may be justly called the Herodotus of the north, if we consider his great historical work, *Heimskringla,*† or Annals of the vegian kings from Odin.‡

* ölu-spá *the oracle or prophecy* of vala, *gen.* völu.

† eims-kringla *orbis terrarum;* heimr *mundus*, kringla *orbis.*

‡ ı this account of the Edda and other Icelandic works, much use has been made of on's Hist. of Northmen, where more satisfactory information will be found. In Mallet's rn Antiquities there is an English translation of the Prose Edda, and many useful with the Icelandic text, and an English translation of five pieces of Runic poetry, ıt which is Ragnar Lodbrok.

It was published by Peringskjöld, with a Latin and Swedish translation, in 2 vols. fol. Stockholm, 1697, and with a Latin and Danish translation by *Schöning* and *Thorlacius*, in 3 vols. fol. Copenhagen, 1777—1783, and continued by the younger *Thorlacius* and *Werlauff*, in 3 vols. 1813—1826.*

12. Kónungsskuggsja',† or Royal Mirror. This is supposed to be the work of *Sverre*, king of Norway. It is in the form of dialogue, and gives a view of human life, with practical rules for different stations. It was published in Icelandic, Danish, and Latin, by *Halfdan Einarsen*, in 4to. 1768, Sorö.

13. The Landna'mabók is an account of the most remarkable events connected with the first settlement of Iceland, its revolutions, and the introduction of Christianity. This history commences in the 9th, and extends to the 12th century. It was begun by *Are Frodi*, and continued by other hands. Are Frodi was born in Iceland in 1067; he was the friend and fellow-student of Sæmund. His work is remarkable as being the earliest historical composition written in the Old Danish or northern tongue, which still remains the living language of Iceland. Only a few fragments of his works are remaining, which have been published under the title of *Schedæ*‡ and *Landnámabók*.§

14. The Sagas are very numerous. These were popular narratives, recording the lives of kings, chieftains, and noble families. To aid the memory of the *Saga-man* or *Story-teller*, he contrived to introduce the most striking metrical passages from the poems of the Skalds.

15. Under the well-directed patronage of *The Royal Society of Northern Antiquaries at Copenhagen*, the following works have appeared.‖

Fornmanna *Sögur*, vol. i.—xi.; *Oldnordiske Sagaer*, vol. i.—xi.; *Scripta Historica Islandorum*, vol. i.—vii. containing—of the historical Sagas, recording events out of Iceland—the history of the Norwegian kings from *Olaf Tryggvason* to *Magnus Lagabœtir*, and of the Danish kings (*Knytlinga*) from Harald Blue-tooth to Canute VI., or the period between the middle of the 10th century, and the year 1274; in Icelandic, Danish, and Latin.

16. I'slendínga Sögur, vol. i. ii. containing—*of the historical Sagas, recording events in Iceland itself*—Are Frodi's *Schedæ*, *Landnámabók*,¶ and *Heiðarviga-*, *Ljósvetnínga*, *Svarfdæla-*, *Vallnaljóts-*, *Vemundar ok Víga-Skútu*, and *Víga-Glúms Sagas*, in Icelandic.

17. The following works are edited by the learned Secretary of the Society, Professor Rafn:—*Færeyinga Saga*, or the history of the inhabitants of the Farroes; in Icelandic, the Farroe dialect, and Danish, and with a map of the islands.

18. Fornaldar *Sögur Norðrlanda*, vol. i.—iii.; *Nordiske Fortids Sagaer*, vol. i.—iii., being a complete edition of the mytho-historical Sagas, recording events in

* Rask's A.-S. Gr. by Thorpe, pref. p. iv. note 1.

† Rask's A.-S. Gr. by Thorpe, pref. p. iv. note 2. Kóngr *a king;* skuggsia *a mirror, speculum.*

‡ Are Frodi's Schedæ were published by C. Wormius, Oxford, 1716; by A. Bussæus, Copenhagen, 1733; but most correctly by the Royal Society of Northern Antiquaries at Copenhagen in *Islendinga Sögur*, vol. i.

§ Wheaton's Northmen, p. 59, 99. Müller, Saga bibliothek, i. p. 34. *Schedæ Ara Prestz Fróda um I'sland*, was published in 4to. pp. 26, Skálholt, 1688; *Sagan Landnáma*, in 4to. pp. 182, Skálholt, 1688. Again with a Latin version, index, &c. under the title *Islands Landnámabók*, 4to. pp. 510, Copenhagen, 1774; and in *Islendinga Sögur*, vol. i. See § 16.

‖ See Annual Report for 1834.

¶ See § 13 for the particulars of this work.

ıe north, assignable to the period anterior to the colonization of Iceland, or the era 'authentic history; in Icelandic and Danish.

19. Kra'kuma'l, *sive Epicedium Ragnaris Lodbroci,** or Ode on the heroic deeds d death of the Danish king, Ragnar Lodbrok, in England; in Icelandic, Danish, ıtin, and French. This *Krákumál* is by some called *Loðbrókarkviðu*, or *the Death-ıg of Ragnar Lodbrok*, who is said to have reigned in Denmark and Sweden in the ter part of the 8th century.† Ragnar invaded Northumbria, and was opposed by la, king of Deira. This fact ascertains the date of the event, as Ella usurped the ırthumbrian crown in 862, and perished in 867. Ragnar was taken prisoner, and a ordered him to be cast into a dungeon, where he might perish by venomous kes.‡ This *song* is sometimes quoted as the composition of Ragnar.§ It is bable that the first twenty-three verses constituted the war-song of Ragnar and followers. The remaining six strophes may have been composed after the king's th by his queen Aslaga, or Kráka, or by some of the contemporary or later ds.‖ This song celebrates the fifty-one depredations of Ragnar in various coun-ı. The death of Ragnar is not only important in an historical point of view, ıing his sons Halfden, Ingwar, and Ubbo to undertake an invasion which destroyed Octarchy of England, and, for a time, dethroned Alfred; but if the song were posed by him or in his time, it will serve as a very early specimen of the Scan-vian language.¶

). From the Old Danish (*Danska túnga*) or Scandinavian (*Norræna*), ıg those languages and dialects which are spoken from the coasts of ınland to those of Finland, from the Frozen Ocean to the Eider.** Old Danish was, in its purest state, carried into Iceland by the first vegian refugees in the 9th century. Hence the Icelandic is the same ıage as the Old Danish, and the Icelanders, from their insular and northern locality, have retained the *Old Danish* in such purity and such slight variations, that it may still be considered the living age of Iceland. There is so little difference between the present ıg and the most ancient records, that modern Icelandic scholars can he oldest documents with the greatest facility.

vas first printed in 4to. at Copenhagen, 1636, in the work of *Olaus Wormius*, in his *Runir ica literatura antiquissima*, vulgo Gothica dicta. It was afterwards printed six times different persons in various forms before it appeared in the original, with an English on, entitled "*Five pieces of Runic Poetry translated from the Icelandic language*," London, 33. These pieces were translated by Dr. Thomas Percy, bishop of Dromore, and at the end of the 2nd vol. of his translation of Mallet's Northern Antiquities. The time of its appearance was in 12mo. with the title of *Lodbrokar-Quida; or, the Death-odbroc, with a free English translation, an Islando-Latino glossary, and explanatory notes, Johnstone, printed* [*at Copenhagen by Aug. Ferd. Steen*] 1782. The twenty-seventh vhich this celebrated song has appeared is the most splendid and complete. This is e best edition; followed by a Latin and French translation, and a complete critical ı, with a minute account of every edition, and a facsimile of the first page of a manu-nd in the Royal Museum, Copenhagen, 1821. The title of this work is "*Krákumál, dium Regnaris Lodbroci Regis Daniæ.*"—Vide Fornaldar Sögur Norðrlandi, i. p. 305; Fortids Sagaer, i. p. 282.

ıton's Hist. of Northmen, p. 150.

er's Hist. of A.-S. bk. iv. ch. iii. Langb. 277.

Wormius, Bartholin, Stephanius, &c.; Turner, bk. iv. ch. iii. note 37.

ton's Hist. of Northmen, p. 153.

ıe specimen, § 25.

:'s Gr. of the Anglo-Saxon tongue, translated into English by Thorpe, p. 42.

Specimens of Old Danish and its dialects, from the earliest age to the present time.

21. A specimen of Old Danish composed by *Starkad the Old*, whose verses are supposed to be the most ancient of all the specimens of the *Danska Túnga* that are still extant, but the precise age of which is not ascertained,* though it was long before A.D. 645.

OLD DANISH.	MODERN DANISH.
Þann hefi ek manna	Ham har jeg blandt Mænd
mennskra fundit	af Menneske-Herkomst,
hríng heyjanda	blandt Stridsmænd fundet
hrammastan at afli.	stærkest af Kræfter.

LITERAL ENGLISH.

Him have I among men	among warriors, found
of the human race,†	the strongest of body.

22. A specimen of Old Danish, composed at so remote a period in heathen times, that it is impossible now to ascertain its age. It is from the Poetic Edda.

The first verse of the Völu-spá.‡

OLD DANISH.	MODERN DANISH.
Hljóþs biþ ek allar	Lytter til min Tale,
helgar kindir,	alle hellige Væsener,
meiri ok minni	större og mindre
mögu Heimþallar;	af Heimdals Slægt;
vildo'at ek Valföþur	jeg vil fortælle
vèl framteljak,	Valfaders Bedrifter
fornspjöll fíra,	Mænds gamle Sagn,
þau ek fremst of-nam.	de förste jeg lærte.
	Finn Magnusen, p. 31.

LATIN.

Silentium rogo omnia	Velim cœlestis patris
Sacra entia;	Facinora enarrare,
Majores et minores	Antiquos hominum sermones,
Posteros Heimdalli.	Quos primos recordor.

23. A specimen of Old Danish, composed probably during the former part of the 7th century, being the beginning of the *Bjarka-mál hin fornu*, so called after *Bödvar Bjarke*, one of king Rolf Krake's warriors, a song sung before a battle.§

* Halfdani Einari Hist. lit. Islandiæ, p. 49. This specimen is from the *Snorra Edda ásamt Skáldu*, edited by Rask, p. 311, 312.

† *i.e.* not of the Aser race.

‡ From the *Edda Sæmundar hins Fróða* ex recensione E. C. Rask, Holmiæ, 1818, p. 1. See the edition of the same, at the expense of the Arna-Magnæan Commissioners by Prof. Finn Magnusen, as also his modern Danish version of it, under the title of *Den ældre Edda*, vol. i. p. 31.

§ Published by Professor Rafn in the *Fornaldar Sögur Norðrlanda*, vol. i. p. 110. See his modern Danish version in the *Nordiske Fortids Sagaer*, vol. i. p. 103. This ancient song was sung at dawn of the day of the great battle of Stiklestad, A.D. 1030, in which king St. Olaf fell; vide *Fornmanna Sögur*, vol. v. p. 59, 60, and the Latin version by S. Egilsson in the *Scripta historica Islandorum*, vol. v. p. 64.

OLD DANISH.	MODERN DANISH.
Dagr er uppkominn,	Solen er oprunden,
dynja hana fjaðrar,	ryste Hanens Fjædre,
mál er vilmögum	Tid er nu for Drenge
at vinna erfiði;	til Daad at gange;
vaki ok æ vaki	vaager, stedse vaager,
vina-höfuð,	Venner kjære,
allir hinir æztu	alle I ypperste
Adels ofsinnar.	Adils Hofsinder.
Hár hinn harðgreipi,	Har hin haardföre,
Hrólfr skjótandi,	Rolf den Skytte,
ættgóðir menn,	ætgode Mænd, som
þeir er ekki flýja!	Flugt ei kjende!
vekjat yðr at víni	eder jeg vækker ei til Viin,
nè at vífs rúnum,	ikke til Kvinders Tale,
heldr vek ek yðr at hörðum	men jeg eder til Hildes
Hildar leiki.	haarde Leg nu vækker.

LATIN.

Dies exortus est,	Har, manu fortis,
pennæ galli strepunt,	Rolvus jaculator,
tempus est, ut servi	genere præstantes viri,
opus incipiant;	qui non fugiunt!
vigilent, semper vigilent	Ad vina vos non excito,
amicorum capita,	neque ad puellarum colloquia,
præstantissimi quique	sed excito vos ad durum
Adilsis comites.	Bellonæ ludum.

24. A specimen of Old Danish of about the year 770, cut in Runic characters in a flat rock at Runamo, in the parish of Hoby in Bleking, now a province of Sweden, but formerly of Denmark, as interpreted by Professor Finn Magnusen.*

OLD DANISH.	MODERN ICELANDIC.
Hültekinn ríki nam,	Hildikinn ríki nam,
Garþr in hió,	Garðr inn hjó,
U'li eit gaf	O'li eið gaf . . . .
vígi O'þin rúnar!	vígi O'ðinn rúnar!
Hríngr fái	Hríngr fái

* The Danish king Valdemar the First, sent, probably at the suggestion of the historian Saxo Grammaticus, some individuals skilled in Runes to Bleking, between the years 1157 and 1182, with the view of having this inscription deciphered. His emissaries, however, failed to accomplish the object of their mission. Subsequently, and especially during the last century or two, the attempt from time to time was renewed under the auspices of some of the most learned men of the day, but their endeavours led to no more satisfactory results. It was reserved for the great Archæologist and Runologist *Finn Magnusen*, after a personal inspection of the inscription on the spot, to interpret it in its entire state in May 1834, and to determine the form of verse (the ancient *Fornyrðalag*) in which it was written. Professor Magnusen's remarks upon this subject are inserted in the Transactions of the Royal Society of Northern Antiquaries, *Nordisk Tidsskrift for Oldkyndighed*, vol. ii. p. 276—304; and in *Historisch-Antiquarische Mittheilungen*, herausgegeben von der Königlichen Gesellschaft für Nordische Alterthumskunde, Kopenhagen, 1835, pp. 109—117. In p. 111 of the latter work, it is recorded that Professor Finn Magnusen for more than ten months tried in vain to decipher the inscription. On the 22nd of May, 1834, by attempting to read from right to left, he immediately succeeded in deciphering the first three words, and in less than two hours he explained the whole inscription.

fall á mold! . . . .
A'lfar, ástagoð
O'la (fjái);
O'þin ok Frei
ok A'sakun
fari (fari)
fiandum varum,
unni Haraldi
ærin sigr!

fall á mold!
A'lfar, A'stagoð
O'la fjái (hati)
O'ðinn, og Frey
og A'sakyn
fari, fari
fjandum vorum,
unni Haraldi
ærinn sigr!

MODERN DANISH.

Hildekind modtog Riget,
Gard indhug (Runerne),
Ole aflagde Ed . . . .
Odin vie Runerne!
Gid Ring faae
Fald paa Muld!
Alfer Elskovsguder
Ole (forlade)!
Odin og Freij
og Asers Slægt
ödelægge (ödelægge)
vore Fjender,
unde Harald
fuldstændig Seier!

ENGLISH.

Hildekinn received the kingdom,
Gard hewed out (these characters),
Ole took the oath . . . .
Odin consecrate these Runes!
May Ring get
a fall on the mould;
Elves, gods of love,
Ole hate!
Odin and Frey
and the Aser-race
destroy (destroy)
our enemies,
grant to Harald
a great victory!

25. A specimen of Old Danish from Krákumál, or the Death-song of Ragnar Lodbrok,* probably composed between A.D. 862 and 867.

OLD DANISH.

Hjuggu vèr með hjörvi!
hörð kom hríð á skjöldu,
nár fèll niðr til jarðar
á Norðimbralandi;
varat um eina óttu
öldum þörf at frýja
Hildar leik, þar er hvassir
hjálmstofn bitu skjómar;
böðmána sá ek bresta,
brá því fira lífi.
Krákumál Str. 14.

MODERN DANISH.

Svunge vi med Sværdet!
stormede Regn mod Skjolde,
Lig i Nordhumberland da
laae paa Jorden strõede;
man ei nödtes den Morgen
Mænd til Strid at egge,
der hvor skarpe Kaarder
skare Hjelmens Flade;
Kampmaaner saae jeg klöves,
Kæmperne misted Livet.
Rafn, p. 13.

LITERAL LATIN.

Percussimus nos cum gladio
Dura venit procella in scuta,
cadaver cecidit deorsum ad terram
in Northumbriâ terrâ.
Non erat, tempore matutino,
viris opus, ciere.
Ad Bellonæ ludum ibi anhelant,
galeæ fulcrum mordebant fulgores,
peltas lunatas vidi ego confractas,
invertit ideo virorum vita.

LITERAL ENGLISH.

We hewed with swords!
Hard came the storm on our shields,
dead they fell down on the earth,
in Northumberland.
None, on that morning,
needed men to incite.
For Bellona's sharp sport,
the glittering sword split the steel-capt skull,
the moon-round shield saw I broken,
and thus men's lives were lost.

* See § 19.

26. A specimen of Old Danish of the 10th century, being the Runic inscriptions at Jellinge in Jutland, on the tumulus of king Gorm the Old, and his consort Thyre, as interpreted by Professor Finn Magnusen.

OLD DANISH.

Gurmr kunugr gerþi kubl þusi eft Þurvi kunu sína Danmarkar-but.

Haraldr kunugr baþ giorva kubl þösi eft gurm faþur sin ök eft Þiurvi muþur sina; sa Haraldr ies van Danmörk ala ök Nurvieg ök tók kristno.

MODERN ICELANDIC.

Gormr konúngr gerði kumbl þessi eftir Þýri konu sína Danmarkarbót.

Haraldr konúngr bað gjörva kumbl þessi eftir Gorm feður sinn og eftir Þýri, móður sína; sá Haraldr, er (es) vann Danmörk alla og Norveg ok tók kristni.

MODERN DANISH.

Kong Gorm gjorde denne Höi efter sin Kone Thyre Danmarks-Bod.

Kong Harald bad (bod) gjöre denne Höi efter Gorm, sin Fader og efter Thyre sin Moder; den Harald som vandt al Danmark og Norge, og antog Christendommen.

LITERAL ENGLISH.

King Gorm raised this barrow after (in memory of) his queen Thyre Danmarks-bod (the improver of Denmark).

King Harald bade make this barrow for his father Gorm and his mother Thyre, the same Harald who conquered all Denmark and Norway, and embraced Christianity.

Antiquariske Annaler, vol. iv. p 110—112.

27. A specimen of Old Danish or Icelandic of the former part of the 11th century, from Ottar Svarte's ode on king St. Olaf.

OLD DANISH OR ICELANDIC.

Komtu i land ok lendir,
ládvörðr! Aðalráði,
þín naut rekka reynir
ríki efldr at slíku;
harðr var fundr, sá er færuð
friðland á vit niðja
rèð ættstudill áðan
Eátmundar þar grundu.

MODERN DANISH.

Landbeskytter! du atter
Adelraad til sit Rige
förte, sligt dig Folkets
mægtige Fyrste skijlder;
haardt var Slaget, da Edmunds
Arving du indsatte
i det fredede Rige,
för behersket af Slægten.

LATIN.

Terræ custos, valens potentia!
Venisti in terram, et Adalradum
in regnum restituisti; tua ope
est usus hac in re virorum amicus.

Durus erat conflictus, quo
nepotem Jatmundi pacato
reddidisti regno; huic terræ
avita proles imperaverat antea.*

28. A specimen of Old Danish or Icelandic, written before 1150, according to the opinion of Professor Rafn.†

OLD DANISH OR ICELANDIC.

Maðr er nefndr Grímr kamban, hann bygði fyrstr Færeyjar á dögum Haralds hins hárfagra; þá flýðu fyrir hans ofríki fjöldi manna, settust sumir í Færeyjum, ok bygðu þar, en sumir leituðu til annarra eyðilanda.

MODERN FERROE DIALECT.

Ajn Mävur èr nevndur Grujmur Kamban, han fowr fistur at biggja Förjar, meni Häraldur hin hårfagri vär å Dövun; tå flujddi firi Owdömi hansara mengur Mävur; summir settu se uj Förjun og bigdu här, men summir lajtavu til annur Ojulond.

* Fornmanna Sögur, vol. iv. p. 50, and vol. xi. p. 185; Oldnordiske Sagaer, vol. iv. p. 47, and vol. xi. p. 164; Scripta historica Islandorum, vol. iv. p. 49.

† See Færeyínga Saga, p. 1. Improperly, by a pleonasm, called Ferroe Islands,—Islands being unnecessary, as Ferroe is derived from fær or faar, c. *a sheep*, ovis; ö, c. *an island*, insula, *pl.* öer *islands*, insulæ; Færoerne or Faar-öer *ovium insulæ*, in Danish commonly called the Færöer.

LITERAL ENGLISH.

A man named Grim Kamban cultivated first the Fær islands in the time of Harald the fair-haired; then (*when*) many fled from his tyranny, some settled on the Fær islands, and built houses, and some sought for other uncultivated lands.

MODERN DANISH.

Grim Kamban hed en Mand; han bebyggede först Færöerne i Harald Haarfagers Dage. Der vare den Gang mange, som flyede for Kongens Her-skesyge, af hvilke nogle nedsatte sig paa Færöerne, og toge sig der Bopæl, men nogle sögte til andre öde Lande.

29. A specimen of Icelandic, written about A.D. 1200, from Snorre's Edda.

ICELANDIC.

Almáttigr guð skapaði í upphafi himin ok jörd ok alla þá luti er þeim fylgja, ok síðarst menn tvâ, er ættir eru frá komnar, Adam ok Evo, ok fjölgaðist þeirra kynslóð, ok dreifðist um heim allan. En er fram liðu stundir, þá újafnaðist mannfólkið, voru sumir góðir ok rètt-trúaðir, en miklu fleiri snerust þá eptir girndum heimsins, ok úrækti guðs boðorð.—*Snorra-Edda, Rask, Stockholm*, 1818, p. 1.

MODERN DANISH.

Den almægtige Gud skabte i Begyndelsen Himlen og Jorden og alle de Ting som dertil höre, og tilsidst to Mennesker, fra hvem Slægter nedstamme, Adam og Eva, og deres Stamme formerede sig, og udbredtes over hele Verden. Men da Tiderne lede frem, blev Menneskeslægten ulig, nogle vare gode og rettroende, men langt flere vendte sig efter Verdens Begjerligheder, og forsömte Guds Bud.

LITERAL ENGLISH.

The Almighty God created, in the beginning, heaven and earth, and all the things which thereto belong, and at last, men from whom families sprung forth, Adam and Eve, and their race increased themselves and spread over all the world. But as time passed (*led*) on, the race of men became different (*unlike*), some were good and right believing, but far more turned themselves to (*after*) the desires (*lusts*) of the world, and neglected God's commandment.

30. A specimen of Old Danish or Icelandic, as written towards the close of the 13th century, but dating from an earlier period, the year A D. 1117, being an extract from the ancient Icelandic Law-book, entitled the Grágás (*The Gray-goose*).*

OLD DANISH OR ICELANDIC.

Ef utlendir menn verþa vegnir á landi hèr, danskir eþr sönskir eþr norrönir, or þeirra konga veldi III. er vâr túnga er, þar eigo frændr þeirra þær sakir, ef þeir eru út hèr, en af öllum túngum öþrum enn af danskri túngo, þá á engi maþr hèr vígsök at sökja af frændsemis sökum, nema faþir eþr sonr eþr bróþir, oc því at eino þeir, ef þeir höfþo hèr áþr viþkennzt.

LATIN.

Si exteri, Dani, Sveii, vel Norvegi e tribus illorum regum imperiis, quæ lingva nostra utuntur, oriundi his in terris interfecti fuerint, cæsi propinqui si adfuerint actionem cædis suscipere liceat. Sedalia quam Danica lingva utentium nemo propinquitatis nomine, cædis causam hic agendi jure gaudeat, nisi pater, filius vel frater, iique tantummodo, si hic antea noti fuerint.

* See *Hin forna lögbók Islendinga sem nefnist Grágás.* Codex juris Islandorum antiquissimus qui nominatur Grágás, Hafniæ, 1829, at the expense of the Arna-Magnæan Commissioners, Part II. p. 71, 72.

31. Old Danish before the Calmar Union in A.D. 1397.

OLD DANISH.

Sattær war ræt thænne . . . . tvém win-trum oc fæm ukum, sidæn Rō war wnnin til Cristendóms af Waldemar kunungi, oc laght til Sjálanzs biscopsdóm(s) af Waldemare kunungi oc Alexandær paue.

ICELANDIC.

Settr var rèttr þessi tveim vetrum oc fimm vikum, siðan Rö var unnin til Cristindóms af Valdimar konúngi, oc logð til Sjálanz biskupsdóms af Valdimari konúngi oc Alexandri páua.

Rask's Anglo-Saxon Gr. Pref. p. xxii.

ENGLISH.

Set was this law, two winters and five weeks; since peace was bestowed on Christianity by Waldemar the king, and a law made for Sjálans bishoprick by Waldemar the king, and Alexander the pope.

32. *Danish in* 1433.

DANISH.

Wii Erick meth guths nathe Danmarks, Swerghes, Norghes-koning göre witerlikt alle the, thette breff see eller höre, at wi vor serdelis Nadhe for Hr Erick Niëlsons wor elschelike tro mans oc radhs bön huld sva oc for troscap oc willich tieniste hanne oc giue hanum . . . friihet oc frelsse med suadane wapen . . . som her vnder nidhen vtmaledh sta . . .

Datum 1433.

ENGLISH.

We Erick, by God's grace, king of Denmark, Sweden, Norway, make known to all, who see or hear this letter, that we by our peculiar grace for Mr. Erick Nielsöns, our beloved faithful man and counsellor, praying, and for fidelity and willing services, have conferred and given him . . . liberty and franchisement with such coat of arms as here under beneath painted stand.

Given 1433.

Rask's Anglo-Saxon Gr. Pref. p. xxi.

33. Old Danish, from a MS. of Homilies, or meditations, belonging to the Royal Swedish Historiographer of Hallenberg. It is without date, but appears to be about A.D. 1450.

DANISH.

Ther æffther drogh Nichodemus then annen spiger pa vinstræ handh, oc fæk han sammeledes Iohannes. Sidhen foor Nichodemus nether, oc foor op at ien liden stie, och togh spigene af födærnæ, mædæn Joseph hiolt pa ligommæt.

ENGLISH.

Hereafter drew Nichodemus the other nail from the left hand, and gave it in the same manner to John. Afterwards Nichodemus went nearer, and went upon the small steps, and drew the nails from the feet, while Joseph held the corpse.

Rask's Anglo-Saxon Gr. Pref. p. xviii.

34. A few examples of Danish are given from the Scriptures, to facilitate the comparison, and thus shew the connexion of this tongue with those of Teutonic origin. The first example is from the Danish Epistles and Gospels, *Leipsic*, 1518, fol.

Mark. iv. 3, 6.—En mand gick wd ath saa sin Sæd. Som hā saade da falt somt aff hannd hoss vegn. Oc det bleff traad bort oc sompt der aff ode fuglene i væred.

35. Bible, *Copenhagen*, 1589, fol.

Mark. iv. 3, 4.—Hörer til! See, der gick en Sæmand ud ad saa. Oc det skede, weil hand saade, at noget falt hoss Veyen: Da komme Fulene under Himmelen oc aad det.

36. Bible, 1647, 8vo.

Mk. iv. 3, 4.—Hörer til; See, der gik en Sædemand ud at saae. Og det skede i det hand saaede, at noget faldt hos Vejen; og der komme Himmelens Fugle og saede det op.

37. New Testament, *Copenhagen*, 1717, 8vo.

Mk. iv. 3, 4.—Hörer (til): see, en Sædemand gik ut at saae. Og det skede, i det hand saade, at noget faldt hos Veyen, og Himmelens Fugle kom og aad det op.

38. New Testament, *London*, 1827, 8vo.

Mk. iv. 3, 4.—Hörer til; see, en Sædemand gik ud at saae. Og det skede, i det han saaede, at noget faldt ved Veien, og Himmelens Fugle kom, og aad det op.

39. As a specimen of the present Danish, a better cannot be selected than the following National Song, which is to the Danes what "God save the King" is to the English. It was written by Johannes Evald, a poet who flourished in the latter part of the last century. (Born 1743, died 1781).*

Kong Christian stod ved höien Mast	King Christian stood by the lofty mast
I Rög og Damp.	In mist and smoke.
Hans Værge hamrede saa fast,	His sword was hammering so fast,
At Gothens Hielm og Hierne brast.	Through Gothic helm and brain it passed.
Da sank hver fiendtligt Speil og Mast	Then sank each hostile hulk and mast
I Rög og Damp.	In mist and smoke.
Flye, skreg de, flye, hvad flygte kan!	Fly, shouted they, fly, he who can!
Hvo staaer for Danmarks Christian	Who braves of Denmark's Christian
I Kamp?	The stroke?
Niels Juel gav Agt paa Stormens Brag:	Niels Juel gave heed to the tempest's roar;
Nu er det Tid!	Now is the hour!
Han heisede det röde Flag,	He hoisted his blood-red flag once more,
Og slog paa Fienden Slag i Slag.	And smote the foe of the Dane full sore.†
Da skreg de höit blant Stormens Brag:	And shouted loud through the tempest's roar:
Nu er det Tid!	Now is the hour!
Flye, skreg de, hver, som veed et Skiul!	Fly, shouted they, for shelter fly!
Hvo kan bestaae for Danmarks Juel	Of Denmark's Juel who can defy
I strid?	The power?
O Nordhav, Glimt, af Vessel bröd	North Sea! a glimpse of Wessel rent
Din mörke Skye:	Thy murky sky!
Da tyede Kæmper til dit Skiöd;	Then champions to thine arms were sent;
Thi med ham lynte Skræk og Död;	Terror and death glared where he went;
Fra Vallen hortes Vraal, som bröd	From the waves was heard a wail, that rent
Din Skye:	Thy murky sky!
Fra Danmark lyner Tordenskiold;	From Denmark thunders Tordenskiol';
Hver give sig i Himlens Vold,	Let each to heaven commend his soul,
Og flye!	And fly!

* For this piece and the translation, I am indebted to my friend, H. W. Longfellow, Esq. M.A. Professor of Belles Lettres in Harvard University, Cambridge, America, Nov. 1835.

† "And smote upon the foe full sore."

Du Danskes Vei til Roes og Magt,	Path of the Dane to fame and might,
Sortladne Hav!	Dark-rolling wave!
Modtag din Ven, som uforsagt	Receive thy friend, who scorning flight
Tör möde Faren med Foragt,	Goes to meet danger with despite,
Saa stolt, som du, mod Stormens Magt,	Proudly as thou meetest the tempest's might,
Sortladne Hav!	Dark-rolling wave!
Og rask igiennem Larm og Spil,	And amid pleasures and alarms
Og Kamp og Seier föer mig til	And war and victory, be thine arms
Min Grav!	My grave!

40. *The Icelandic, here called Norræni.* For facility of comparison, few extracts are given from the Icelandic Scriptures. Nach: Thetta hid nye Testament Jesu Christi, &c. utlogd a Norræni, &c. or *The ew Testament in the Norrænn, northern, Old Danish, or Icelandic ngue,* 8vo. 1539.

Mk. iv. 3, 4.—Og i sine predikan, tha sagdi han til thra. Heyre thier, siaet! ein lsædare gieck vt at saa. Thad vard tha han sadi, at sumt fiell vtan hia veginum, og komu fuglar loptzins og atu thad vpp.

41. Biblia thad er, öll Heilög Rituing vtlógd a Norrænu, med forlum Mart. Lutheri, Prentad a Holum, af Ione Ionas Syne, fol. 1584, *The Bible, in Norse or Icelandic, after the version of Luther.* Bible, ckholm, 1584, fol.

Ik. iv. 3, 4.—Og i sine Predikan, tha sagde han til thra, Heyre thier. Sia: Eirn sædare gieck ut at sa. Og thad vard tha han sade, at sumt fiell utan hia veigenum, ıar komu fuglar Lopisins og aatu thad vpp.

2. Stiernhelm's Gospels of Ulphilas, in *Moes., Icel., Swed., Ger.,* and *in,* 4to. Stockholm, 1671.*

k. iv. 3, 4.—Heyred til. Sia, eirn Sadmadur gieck ut ad saa. Og thad vard i han saade, ad sumt fiell utann hia Veigenum; og tha komu Fuglar under Himm, og aatu thad upp.

. Old Swedish can scarcely be distinguished from Danish; and Noran has been, from the earliest times on record, and is now, identical Danish; but as more modern Swedish differs a little from the Danish, specimens may be desirable.

A specimen of Swedish from a document issued by king Magnus in 1354.

SWEDISH.	ENGLISH.
magnus, med guds nadh Sverikis ;, norghis oc skane, wiliom at thet om mannom witerlikt wara, at wi a serdelis nadh hafwm vnt bergxnen a noreberge thænnæ ræt oc , som hær æpter fölger: fförst wi stat oc skipat, at tolff skulu som fore bergheno sculu standa ræœt wæria oc fulfölghia i allom tc.	We Magnus, by the grace of God, king of Sweden, Norway, and Scania, will that it shall be known to all men that we by our peculiar grace have conceded to Bergxman (miner) of Noreberge the right and power as hereafter follows: first have we constituted and ordained, that twelve shall be the sum, &c.

* See Gothic, § 11.

45. Swedish Bible, *Upsal*, 1541, fol.

Mk. iv. 3, 4.—Hörer til. Sij, en Sädhesman gick vth til at sââ. Och hende sigh widh han sâdde, föll somt widh wâghen, och foghlanar vnder himmelen komo, och âto thet vp.

46. *The Swedish*, from the Gospels of Ulphilas, *Stockholm*,* 1671.

Mk. iv. 3, 4.—Hörer til; sÿ en Sädesman gik uth, til at sââ. Och hende sigh wid han sâdde, föll somt wid Wägen, og Foglarna under Himmelen komo, och âto thet up.

47. Bible, 8vo. *London*, 1828.

Mk. iv. 3, 4.—Hörer til: Si, en Sädesman gick ut, til at sâ. Och hände sig, wid han sâdde, föll somt wid wägen, och foglarne under himmelen kommo, och âto thet up.

48. One of the most eminent of modern Swedish poets is Bishop Tegnér. He took the story of Frithiof from one of the old Sagas, and under the title of Frithiof's Saga, he has written in flowing verse a most interesting story of royal affection. The following extract is from the *Exile of Frithiof*, in the original Swedish, in the Norwegian or Danish translation, and with a poetical version of the Rev. W. Strong.

SWEDISH.	DANISH.	ENGLISH.
Nu sol går opp	Nu Sol gaaer op	The orb of day,
bak fjällens topp,	Bag Fjeldets Top;	Now tints the spray;
och vinden ljuder	Landvinden lyder,	From piping heights,
från land och bjuder	Hver Vove byder	The breeze invites
hvar våg till dans	Den op til Dands	Each beam and wave,
i morgonglans.	I Morgenglands.	To dance and lave.
På böljans toppar	Paa Bölgetoppe	O'er the gay group,
Ellida hoppar	Assted de hoppe	Ellida's poop
i fröjd åstad,	Saa fro og glad,	Bounds light along;
men Frithiof qvad.	Men Frithjof qvad.	To Frithiof's wilder song.
Tegnér, cant. xiv. p. 113.	*Foss*, p. 135.	*Strong*, p. 187.

49. A fine passage from *The Reconciliation*, cannot be omitted: it is a description of Balder the good.

SWEDISH.

Frid var hans härski, härlek var hans blanka svärd,
och oskuld satt som dufva på hans silfverhjelm.
From lefde han och lärde, dog han och förlät,
och under fjerran palmer står hans graf i ljus.
Hans lära, sägs det, vandrar ifrån dal till dal,
försmälter hårda hjertan, lägger hand i hand,
och bygger fridens rike på försonad jord.—*Tegnér*, p. 164.

DANISH.

Fred var hans Hærraab, Kjerlighed hans blanke Sværd,
Og Uskyld sad som Due paa hans Sölverhjelm.
Fromt leved han og lærte, döde og tilgav,
Og under fjerne Palmer staaer hans Grav i Lys.
Hans Lære, siges der, gaaer vidt fra Dal til Dal,
Samsmelter haarde Hjerter, lægger Haand i Haand,
Og bygger Fredens Rige paa forsonet Jord.—*Foss*, p. 194.

* See § 42, and Gothic, § 11.

ENGLISH.

His war-cry, peace, good-will: love was his two-edged sword;
Crest of his silver helm, sat dove-like innocence;
Grace mark'd his life, his word: his death-sigh breath'd 'Forgive.'
In light 'neath distant palms, far pilgrims seek his tomb.
'Tis said his tidings walk, peace-shod from dale to dale,
Melting the flinty heart, cementing man to man,
Building of living stones, a temple to this God.—*Strong*, p. 303.

*Dialect of Dalecarlia.**

50. The principal dialect† of Sweden is the Dalecarlian. The Dalcarls re spoken of as the Swedish Highlanders. Inhabiting that secluded region hich stretches westward from the Silian Lake to the Alps of Norway, they ave preserved comparatively unchanged the manners, customs, and lanuage of their Gothic forefathers.

"Here," says Serenius,‡ "are the only remains in Sweden of the ancient Gothic ock, whereof the aspiration of the letters *l* and *w* bears witness upon their tongues, infallible characteristic of the Moeso-Gothic, Anglo-Saxon, and Icelandic." In other place, speaking of the guttural or aspirated *l*, he says: "Germans and Danes nnot pronounce it, no more than the aspirated *w*; for which reason this was a fatal ter three hundred years ago in these nations, when Engelbrect, a born Dalcarl, set p for a shibboleth, and whoever could not say *Hivid hest i Korngulff*, was taken a foreigner, because he could not aspirate the *w*, nor utter the guttural *l*."§ It is n asserted, that with their ancient customs and language the Dalcarls have preserved use of the old Runic alphabet, although from feelings of religious superstition it prohibited by Olaf Shätkonung at the beginning of the 11th century, and distinued in all other parts of Sweden. This is mentioned on the authority of man, who wrote in the first half of the last century.‖

1. The Dalecarlian dialect is spoken in its greatest purity in Elfdalen, ra, and Orsa, parishes of East Dalecarlia.

West Dalecarlia it is mingled with the dialects of the Norwegian mountains, and the name of *Mahlungs Skinnarmål*. The peculiarities of this jargon are these: Prefixing the letter *v* to all monosyllables which begin with a vowel, as vom for *f;* vord for ord *a word*, &c. 2. The transposition of syllables, as jasel for selja *l;* lata for tala *to speak*, &c. Thus they say—

Kan du lâta tæ korba, so kimi du lâvi?
Kan du tala tæ baka, so miki du vilâ?
Canst thou speak backwards, as much as thou wilt?

rofessor Longfellow, of Harvard University, Cambridge, America, who has recently ed from Sweden, was so obliging as to draw up this notice of the Dalecarlian dialect, r, 1835.

lbi and Malte Brun make two great divisions in the Swedish. I. *Swedish proper*, spoken north and east; and II. *Modern Gothic*, used in Gothland to the south.—I. SWEDISH R, subdivided into 1. The dialect of Upland, 2. Norland, 3. Eastern Dalecarlian, and ialect of Finland. II. MODERN GOTHIC, divided into 1. West Gothic, 2. East Gothic, neland, 4. Smoland, and 5. Runæ in Livonia.—*Balbi's Atlas*, Table xiii.; *Malte Brun*, i. vol. vi. p. 109.

Serenius' English and Swedish Dictionary, 4to. Nyköping, 1757, Pref. p. iii.

d. p. ii.

sman (R. E.) Historiola Linguæ Dalekarlicæ, 4to. Upsaliæ, 1733, p. 30.

52. The inhabitants of the town of Särna, on the borders of the Norwegian Alps in East Dalecarlia, speak a mixed dialect of Dalecarlian and Norwegian; and it is said, that they understood the language spoken by certain Dutchmen, who were in the habit of visiting those mountains for the purpose of taking falcons, then used in hunting.* We are also told of a Dalecarlian boy who was taken by a Swedish ambassador to England, and who easily understood the language of the peasants of the northern counties.†

53. The three branches of the Dalecarlian dialect, as spoken in *Elfdalen, Mora*, and *Orsa*, differ from each other not only in the change of letters and the inflexion of words, but also in accent and pronunciation. Between those of Elfdalen and Mora the difference is not, however, very great. That of Orsa stands more apart, as may be seen by the following versions of the Lord's Prayer.

54. *Dialect of Elfdalen.*

Fad uoer, so ir i himbluma.
Hielit ir dætt nam. Tilkum dætt riki.
Ski dænn uilja, so i himblum så å jordi.
Uott dagli brod giæf oss i dag.
Og firilat oss uoræer skulldær.
Soss uir firilatum diöm so i oss nod skilldug.
Læd int uoss i nân jælok fræstilsæ
Autå los oss frå uondu. Amen.

55. *Dialect of Mora.*

Fad uær so ir i himmelim.
Hællit æ dætt nam. Tilkum dett rikiæ.
Ske dænn uilli so i himmelim so å jordi.
Uott dagli brod giæf huåss i dag.
Firilat huåss huåræer skulldur.
Sos huir firilatum diöm så æ huåss nå skilldå.
Led int huåss i nân uondan fræstilsæ.
Int' åt fræls huåss frå illu. Amen.

56. *Dialect of Orsa.*

Falla orn, sa ir i himblim.
Hælgat uæri dætt nam. Tilkæmi dætt rikia.
Ski dæina uilju, så i himblum sa å jordi.
Ort dagliga brod gia huåss i dag.
Å farlåt huass oræer skulldær,
Skai sa ui færlatum dæm huåss skilldugær irå.
Å inled huoss int i fræstilse.
Mæld fræls huåss frå uåndu. Amen.

Norwegian.

57. For several centuries, and especially since the Danish became a fixed and regular tongue, Norwegian has been identical with Danish.

* Näsman, p. 12.

† Ibid. p. 17.

'his common dialect has perhaps been as much settled and polished by 'orwegians as by natives of Denmark.* As there is this identity in the 'anish and Norwegian, the copious examples of the *Danska túnga* pre- ously given, will serve also for the Norwegian, and will render further marks unnecessary.

Ferroe Dialect.

58. A specimen of early Ferroe taken from Professor Rafn's Færeyínga ıga, Pref. p. iv. Thrand was one of the first inhabitants of Ferroe. any religious verses are ascribed to him, and are still preserved by oral ıdition among the inhabitants of the Ferroes. The following Creed, itten down by a native Ferroe clergyman, Pastor Schröter, now neritus, who translated the Gospel of St. Matthew,† will serve as an ımple of this dialect.

FERROE DIALECT.	LITERAL ENGLISH.
Gjivnir eru Ajnglar gowir [af Gudi]	Good angels are given by God,
Aj gengji e ajna udi,	I go not alone,
Ferun mujnun filgja	My steps follow
Fim Guds Ajnglar;	Five angels of God;
Bije e firi mär Bön,	Pray I for me a prayer,
Bera tajr tä [Bön] firi Kriste.	They bear it to Christ.
Singje e Sålmana sjej,	Sing I seven Psalms,
Sär Gud til Såluna mujna!	Sees God for my soul!

MODERN FERROE DIALECT.	OLD ICELANDIC.
Gengji e aj ajna út,	Gángat ek einn út,
fujra mär filgja,	fjórir mèr fylgja,
fim Guds Ajnglar,	fimm guðs einglar;
beri e Bön firi mär,	ber ek bæn fyrir mèr,
Bön firi Krist,	bæn fyrir Kristi,
singji e Sålma sjej,	sýng ek sálma sjö,
sjåji Gud til Luta mujn!	sjái guð hluta minn!
	Written about A.D. 1150.

LITERAL ENGLISH.	MODERN DANISH.
Go I not alone out,	Ene jeg ei gaaer ud,
Four me follow,	fire mig fölge,
Five God's angels,	fem Guds Engle,
I pray a prayer for me,	Bön for mig jeg frembærer
A prayer for Christ,	Bön for Christus,
I sing seven Psalms,	syv Salmer jeg synger,
God will see for my lot!	Sörge Gud for mit Bedste!

* ee § 42, and Rask's A.-S. Gr. by Mr. Thorpe, p. xvi.
† vangelium St. Matthæussa å Færöisk o Dansk, Randers, 1823—8.

XII.—THE AFFINITY OF THE GERMANIC LANGUAGES.

1. THE Germanic languages, comprehending not only the Low and High-German, but also the Scandinavian, have a striking similarity, and are evidently of cognate origin. The short history of each language, accompanied with extracts, and a detail of their most evident peculiarities, have occupied so much space, and engaged the attention so long, that it may be desirable to advert again to their similarity. They appear as dialects of one extensive language, branches of one vigorous stock, or streams from the same copious fountain. A recollection of this will, in some degree, restore to order the confusion of Babel, and therefore very much facilitate the acquisition of languages.* An appeal to the Germanic languages will be a sufficient proof, not only of their similarity, but of their identity. This likeness and close relationship will be clearly manifest by a few examples from their vocabularies and grammatical inflections.

2. In the following examples, the *v* in the Dutch visch has exactly the same sound as the English *f*; hence fish has the same name in all the Germanic languages.

Eng.	*A.-S.*	*Dut.*	*Frs.*	*Ger.*	*Moes.*	*Dan.*	*Swed.*	*Icel.*
a fish	fisc	visch	fisk	fisch	fisk-s	fisk	fisk	fisk-r
a fish's	fisc-es	visch-es†	fisk-es	fisch-es	fisk-is	fisk-s	fisk-s	fisk-s
to a fish	fisc-e	visch-e	fisk-e	fisch-e	fisk-a	fisk	fisk	fisk-i
a fish	fisc	visch	fisk	fisch	fisk	fisk	fisk	fisk
fishes	fisc-as	visch-en	fisk-ar	fisch-e	fisk-os	fisk-e	fisk-ar	fisk-ar
fishes'	fisc-a	visch-en	fisk-a	fisch-e	fisk-e	fisk-es	fisk-ars	fisk-a
to fishes	fisc-um	visch-en	fisk-um	fisch-en	fisk-en	fisk-e	fisk-ar	fisk-um
fishes	fisc-as	visch-en	fisk-ar	fisch-e	fisk-ans	fisk-e	fisk-ar	fisk-a.

3. The identity of the Germanic languages will be still more evident if a few examples be taken from what has been generally called the irregular parts of these languages. It may be useful to remark, that the *Moes. A.-S.* and *Eng.* þ or *th*, in *Dut. Dan.* and *Swed.* is changed into *d*. The *Dan.* jeg and mig are pronounced yih and mih: the *Swed.* jag and mig are sounded yih and mih.

* Classification and association are of the utmost importance in learning languages. The greater part of European tongues in the south and west are those of Germanic, and those of Roman origin. The Germanic class embraces the modern English, German, Dutch, Danish, Swedish, Norwegian, Icelandic, &c.; the Roman or Latin comprises the Spanish, Italian, Portuguese, French, &c. To this subject has been drawn the attention of an old friend, the Rev. W. Pulling, M.A., A.S.L. Rector of Dymchurch, Kent. He was induced to deliver in the University of Cambridge "A course of Lectures on the French, Italian, Spanish, and Portuguese languages, and their chief dialects, Cambridge, 1834." These interesting and valuable Lectures deserve attention, and it is greatly to be wished that Mr. Pulling may receive sufficient encouragement to carry into effect his intention of publishing a volume containing short grammars of the languages of Roman origin, to be followed by another volume comprising grammars of the Germanic tongues.

† The Dutch, &c. now generally use prepositions instead of the old terminations: thus, *Dut.* van een visch *of a fish*, instead of visches.

Eng. I am, be: *A.-S.* ic eom, beo: *Frs.* ik ben: *Plat.* ick bin, em: *Dut.* ik bin, ım: *Moes.* ik im: *Ger.* ich bin: *Icel.* ek er, em: *Dan.* jeg er: *Swed.* jag är.—*Eng.* . was: *A.-S.* ic wæs: *Frs.* ik was: *Plat.* ick was: *Dut.* ik was: *Moes.* ik was: *Ger.* ich war: *Icel.* er var: *Dan.* jeg var: *Swed.* jag vas.—*Eng.* come, *p.* came, *pp.* ome: *A.-S.* cume, *p.* com, *pp.* cumen: *Frs.* kem, *p.* kom, *pp.* kemen: *Plat.* kom, ·. kwam, *pp.* gekomen. *Dut.* kome, *p.* kwam, *pp.* gekomen: *Moes.* quima, *p.* quam, *p.* quuman(s): *Ger.* komme, *p.* kam, *pp.* (ge)kommen: *Icel.* kem, *p.* kom, *pp.* koıinn: *Dan.* kommer, *p.* kam, *pp.* kummen: *Swed.* kommer, *p.* kom, *pp.* kommen. -*Eng.* thou: *A.-S.* þu: *Frs.* thu: *Plat.* thû: *Flem.* du: *Moes.* thu: *Ger.* du: *cel.* þu: *Dan.* du: *Swed.* du.—*Eng.* who: *A.-S.* hwa: *Frs.* hwa: *Plat.* huie: *Dut.* wie: *Moes.* hwa(s): *Ger.* wer: *Icel.* hwa(r): *Dan.* hwô: *Swed.* hô.—*Eng.* ood, better, best. *A.-S.* gód (bet), betra, betst: *Frs.* gód, bettre, (betere), beste: *Dut.* goed, beter, best: *Moes.* goths (god(s) *or* bats), batiza, batist(s): *Ger.* gut, esser, beste: *Icel.* gód(r) bettri, bestr: *Dan.* god, bedre, beste: *Swed.* god, bättre, ist.

4. If these examples do not convince the reader that these languages e mere dialectic variations of one ancient tongue, perhaps the following eclension of the pronoun of the first person may produce full conviction.

Eng.	*A.-S.*	*Dut.*	*Frs.*	*Ger.*	*Moes.*	*Dan.*	*Swed.*	*Icel.*
I	ic	ik	ik	ich	ik	jeg	jag	ek
mine	min	mins	min	mein	meina	min	min	min
to me	me	mij	mi	mir	mis	mig	mig	mér
me	me	mij	mi	mich	mik	mig	mig	mik
we	we	wij	wi	wir	weis	wi	wi	wër
our	úre	onzer	use	unser	unsara	vor	wår	wår
to us	us	ons	us	uns	uns	os	oss	oss
us	us	ons	us	uns	uns	os	oss	oss.

5. In the most irregular parts of the Germanic languages, even at the esent day, there is a complete correspondence, which shows that there st have been a time when the nations of Germanic origin were all ted in one tribe. Some branches of this great Gothic family have not l any close intercourse or alliance for many centuries; the present simity of their languages must then have arisen from a close anterior nexion. The period of this connexion it is not easy to specify; but it ıt have been very early and intimate, as the similarity is most evident he words which designate what was most necessary, in the rudest state ociety, and in those verbs generally called irregular,* and which are ı now most in use. This early connexion it is very important to observe, it is the part of scientific etymology to show it in the clearest light.

Ten Kate's Anleiding tot de Kenisse van de Nederduitsche Sprake, vol. ii. p. 12, § XI.

XIII.—THE IMPORTANCE OF ETYMOLOGY,* THE MANNER OF FORMING WORDS, AND AN OUTLINE OF THE GERMAN SYSTEM.

1. Words are the creation of mind. As the true philosopher looks with humble adoration, from the variety and perfection of God's visible creation to the power and goodness of the Creator, so the philosophic etymologist is constantly led, from the various forms and applications of words, to contemplate the intellectual powers in which man most resembles his Creator. The true and judicious etymologist is anxious to obtain the right meaning and application of words, and thus a good etymologist is most likely to become the best metaphysician. He is not satisfied with the common and external signification of words received from popular use, but he examines their structure, their radical, that is, their real and internal meaning, and thus endeavours to discover the reason of the application of the term. When the understanding is thus called into exercise in the formation of words, precision is not only given to expression, but the higher faculty of reason lends its powerful aid to the memory, and greatly facilitates the acquisition of a language. The etymology of a word being understood, and thus the sanction of reason obtained, neither that word nor any of its family can scarcely ever escape from the memory. The use of etymology will, however, be best proved by a few plain examples, showing the real meaning of some common words.

Acorn, *A.-S.* æceren, æcern, from æc, ác *an oak;* cern or corn *corn, the corn or fruit of the oak.*—Childhood, *A.-S.* cildhád, from cild *a child,* hád *a condition, state, a child's condition.*—Kingdom, *A.-S.* cyngdóm, cyningdóm, from cyning, cyng *a king;* dóm *power, jurisdiction, a king's jurisdiction, or dominion.*—Island, *A.-S.* ealand, from ea *water,* land *land; water-land, land surrounded with water.*—Sheriff, or shirereeve, *A.-S.* scir-gerefa, from scir *a share, division, shire, county;* gerefa *a reeve, governor, a governor of a shire.*—Neighbour, *A.-S.* neah-bur, from neah *near;* bur *a bower, dwelling, one who has a dwelling near.*—Righteous, *A.-S.* rihtwís, from riht *right, just;* wís *wise, right wise, honest, virtuous.*—Fosterchild, *A.-S.* foster-cild, from foster *food, nourishment;* cild *a child, a child that receives food from a person who is not its parent, &c.*

2. In looking at the first formation of words in the origin of language, it may be observed, that a knowledge of things appears to be conveyed to the mind through the medium of the five senses, especially by the sight. An idea or image of a visible object is formed in the mind by means of the eye; and the word which, when written or spoken, conveys this image

* Etymology is thus defined:—Optime Cicero ἐτυμολογιαν. Latine vertit *veriloquium.* Eumque merito defendit Martinius: certe verbotim non potuit melius Cicero. Nam certum est, quod ἐτυμον sit *verum;* et ἐτυμολογος, qui το ἐτυμον λεγει. Scaliger tamen Etymologiam sic definit, tanquam esset a λογος *ratio.* Etymologia, inquit, est vocis ratio, id est vis, qua vox a voce generatur.—*Wachter's Glos. Germ. Prolegom. VII.*

o the mind, is called a *noun*. If it be most probable that the general ppearance of a material thing would be impressed on the mind before ny particular part or action of the thing, then nouns* must be the primi- ve words in language. Every noun or thing which has an existence, ust have either an action or state of being, and the word which expresses ıat action or state of being is denominated a *verb*. If, after the general ıtline of an object was formed in the mind, the attention were fixed upon ; action or state of being, then verbs were formed subsequently to nouns. ıus all things material were first designated by the *noun*, while the bsequent motions of these objects were indicated by the *verb* in its ıplest form.†

3. This reasoning is corroborated by the structure not only of the Ger- nic languages but of the Shemitic.

ı few examples may be first cited from the Hebrew. where the roots of words have ı generally said to exist only in the verb, from which nouns were always said to ɔrmed. The following verbs, however, evidently spring from nouns. From אט *ı stooping*, נטה něthe *to incline, bow down*;—אל al *power, strength*, אלה ale *to :ise power in injuring, to curse*;—אן an *labour*, אנן aněn *to be faint with labour, mplain*;—אף ap *heat, anger*, אפה ape *to operate as heat, to bake*;—אר ar *a river, flows*, ארה are *to be flowing off, to crop*, ארר arěr *to flow or take from, to curse*; א as *fire*, אשש asěs *to be fired, angry, or grieved*;—את at *a sign, thou, the sub- e of a thing*, אתה ate *to come, come near, to approach*;—בד běd *what is separate, nch, desert*, בדד běděd *to be alone*;—בן běn *a son*, בנה běne *to build, to build ı continue, as a son builds up or continues the family or line of his father*;—יד *and*, ידה ide *to put forth, to extend*;—עץ oj *a tree*, עצה oje *to be as a tree, to firm or steady*.

In Greek some verbs appear also to be formed from nouns.

ıs *agitation of the sea, the sea*, σαλευω *I sea, I act as the sea, I shake, or agitate*: λος *a messenger, angel*, αγγελλω *I act as a messenger, I bring information*,

mkhi expressly declares הפעל יצא מהשם *the verb proceeds from the noun*. See *r Lee's Heb. Gram.* 8vo. London, 2nd edit. 1832, Lect. VI. Art. 144, 146; and Lect. X. ', § 2, note, for some interesting facts on this subject. "In Burman, verbs are nothing an nouns conjugated with the pronouns."—*Id.* Lect. VI. Art. 144, § 1, note (*). See *Compendious Gram. of the Anglo-Saxon Language*, 8vo. London, 1826, ch. VII. p. 57.

› says, "I doubt not, if we could trace words to their sources, we should find, in all :s, the names that stand for *things that fall not under our senses*, to have had their first ı sensible objects.—*On Human Understanding*, bk. 3, ch. I.

ıes verborum propriæ *omnes* sunt corporeæ, sive ad res pertinentes, quæ sensus nos- unt.—*Van Lennep*, p. 7. Nec alias esse (verborum significationes) nisi *corporeas*, quibus *res, sensibus*, exterius *expositæ*, designantur.—*Id. Anal.* p. 41. *Mr. Richardson Mag. April*, 1836, p. 373.

ermanic literati differ in opinion on this subject. Many eminent etymologists declare roots of all words were originally verbs. Professor J. Grimm, though of the same uses a more cautious expression, and says verbs *appear* to be the foundation of all *Deutsche Gram.* II. 5.) It is true that many words originate from verbs; but it is ; to attempt to trace all words to verbs as their root. Professor Grimm, on the ›n that all roots were verbs, has quoted a great number of verbs as lost which ıever existed: this great investigator, adds Schmitthenner, *is certainly led astray by position.* (*Schmitthenner's Etymol. Darmstadt*, 8vo. 1833, p. 20—23.) In § 17 he says, is neither a noun nor a verb, but what precedes both," &c.

raves C. Haughton's "Inquiry into the nature of Language," prefixed to his elaborate earned *Dictionary of Bengali and Sanskrit*, 4to. London, 1833, p. 4.

I tell:—αγων, -ωνος *a combat, battle,* αγωνια *a conflict of mind, distress, agony,* αγωνιαω *I am in agony, am distressed:*—αεθλος, ἄθλος *a combat,* αεθλευω, αθλεω *I fight, combat:*—αἱμα, -ἄτος *the effusion of blood,* αἱμας, -ἄδος *blood streaming from a wound,* αἱμασσω *I stain with blood:*—αιχμη *a spear,* αιχμαζω *I fight with a spear, brandish:*—ακμη *the point, top, maturity,* ακμαζω *I grow up to maturity, ripen, &c.*

5. The root or origin of a verb in Welsh is, as the learned Dr. Davies remarked, for the most part, a noun, as dysc *doctrina;* dyscais *docui;* câr *amicus,* carav *amo,* vel *amabo.* This substantive, adds the same writer, is generally identical with the third person singular of the future indicative, (as in Hebrew the third of the preterite is the root,) or with the second of the imperative, which forms are generally the same.*

6. The Germanic languages afford many examples of verbs evidently derived from nouns.

From *A.-S.* dæl: *Plat. Dut.* deel: *Frs.* del: *Moes.* dails: *Ger.* theil: *Old Ger.* deil: *Icel.* deil: *Dan.* deel: *Swed.* del *a part,* pars; we have the following verbs in *A.-S.* dæl-an: *Plat.* del-en: *Dut.* deel-en: *Frs.* del-a: *Moes.* dail-jan: *Old Ger.* deil-an: *Icel.* deil-a: *Dan.* deel-e: and *Swed.* del-a *to give a part, to separate, divide.*—From *A.-S.* meolc, milc: *Plat. Dut.* melk: *Ger.* milch: *Old Ger.* miluh, milich: *Icel.* miólk: *Dan.* malk: and *Swed.* mjölk MILK, lac, we have the following verbs in *A.-S.* meolc-ean: *Plat. Dut.* melk-en: *Ger.* melk-en: *Old Ger.* melk-an: *Icel.* miolk-a: *Dan.* malk-e: and *Swed.* mjolk-a *to afford or give milk, to milk,* to draw *milk;* mulgere.—From *A.-S.* rec: *Plat. Dut.* rook: *Frs.* rec, rek: *Ger.* rauch: *Icel.* reykr: *Dan.* rög: and *Swed.* rök *smoke,* exhalatio; we have the following verbs in *A.-S.* rec-an: *Plat. Dut.* rook-en: *Frs.* rek-a *to smoke, dwell in, inhabit: Ger.* rauch-en: *Icel.* reyk-ia: *Dan.* rög-e: and *Swed.* rok-a *to give a smoke, to smoke, to* REEK; fumare, exhalare.

7. Both nouns and verbs are formed into adjectives.

Some nouns are used as adjectives without any alteration; but adjectives in A.-S. are generally formed by annexing to the noun or verb, -en, -ig, -isc, from an, unnan, ican or ecan *to give, add, eke;* also, -bær *bearing, producing;*—cund *born, a kind, sort;* -ece *eternal;* -ende; -fæst *fast, firm;* -full *full, plenty;* -lic *like;* -sum *some, part,* &c.—As lað *n. evil, mischief;* lað *adj. evil, pernicious;* gold *gold,* -en *add, add or join something,* as golden þræd *golden thread;* blod *blood,* blodig *bloody;* wit *mind, wit,* witig *witty;* folc *folk,* folcisc *like the people, plebeian;* æppelbær *apple-bearing;* leohtbær *light-bearing;* eorðcund *earthly;* godcund *divine;* efenece *coeternal;* cennan *to bear,* cennende *bearing;* drincan *to drink,* drincende *drinking;* faran, feran *to go,* ferende *going;* æ *law,* æfæst *fast in the law, firm, religious;* tungful *full of tongue, talkative;* eorð *earth,* eorðlic *earthlike, earthly;* lufu *love,* luflic *lovelike, lovely;* lang *long,* langsum *longsome, lasting;* wyn *pleasure,* wynsum *some pleasure, pleasant.*

8. Adverbs are often formed by frequently using nouns in certain cases.

Thus hwilum *awhile, now, d. of* hwil *time, space;* þonces *of gratitude,* þonce *with gratitude, gratefully, thankfully, g.* and *d. of* þanc *favour,* &c.

9. The remarks in paragraphs 3 and 4 can only refer to words in their first formation. In a subsequent stage of language, many nouns have evidently had their origin from verbs, adjectives, &c.

* See Dr. Davies' Antiquæ Linguæ Britannicæ Rudimenta, and Dr. Prichard's Celtic Nations, p. 178.

Thus huntað *a hunting, chase,* from huntian *to hunt;* fiscoð *a fishing,* from fiscian)*fish;* gelicnes *likeness,* from gelic *like;* hrædnes *readiness,* from hræd *ready;* hrædcnys *readiness,* from hrædlic *ready, quick;* blawung *a blowing,* from blawan *to blow;* ıl *healthy, sound;* halig *holy,* haligan *to consecrate;* haligdom *a sanctuary;* halignes)*liness;* halgung, gehalgung *a hallowing, consecration, &c.*

10. All that is here stated, as well as what is advanced in the preceding ıragraphs, is the mere threshold of etymology, that which is the most ident and palpable; but perhaps it may have appeared that even this :ipient knowledge is not destitute of utility. Should there be a desire enter into the arcana of etymology, or to fathom its deep abyss, much ıe and attention must be devoted to the works of German philologists,* the etymology of the Teutonic languages has been carried to great ent by some of the most able men in Germany. They have adopted · principle, and introduced much of the refinement discovered and)lied by Sanscrit grammarians. Every one who investigates the subject ɜt acknowledge there is much metaphysical nicety in their mode of .ting it, and much laborious exertion to make it intelligible. Though ı talents and industry certainly deserve attention, yet the great question vhether in the western tongues these metaphysical subtleties can be e available to practical utility. The learned and indefatigable Dr. ker, in his German Grammar for Englishmen, with many of his counıen, asserts that their system is found most efficient in practice. It is, ɜfore, only common justice to let these erudite Germans speak for ɪselves, or rather to allow one to explain for the whole. A recent ·r, and one of the least diffuse and most able after Professor Bopp† Grimm, is Professor Schmitthenner, from whose Introduction to the *t German Dictionary*‡ the following abstract of the German language en. The substance is only given, but where it is translated the version close as possible.

Of VOWELS. The modern German has five simple vowels, *a, e, i, o, u.* ee of these are radical vowels, *a, i, u.* The two others, *e* and *o,* are only shades *u.* The *y* of the A.-S. and the old northern dialects has something analogous ft *u,* but it is unknown to the other German dialects. It is borrowed from the

ɜ Von der Wortbildung, in vol. ii. p. 1—923 of Professor J. Grimm's Deutsche Gram- 8vo. Göttingen, 1826.—Die Deutsche Wortbildung von Dr. Becker, 8vo. Frankfurt n, 1824, and all the other valuable publications of Der frankfurtischen Gelehrten- ;ung für deutsche Sprache, Herman, Frankfurt, &c.

ɔugh Professor Bopp, whose general erudition, and critical knowledge of Sanscrit cular, are universally admitted, was so obliging as to send the author a copy of his *ɪus* immediately on publication; it is impossible to give a clear abstract of so learned found a work in the short space which can be here devoted to the subject. Those, ɜ, who read German, must peruse and reperuse *Vocalismus, oder Sprachvergleichende über J. Grimm's deutsche Grammatik, und Graff's althochdeutchen Sprachschatz, mit ɪng einer neuen Theorie des ablauts von Franz Bopp,* 8vo. *Berlin,* 1836. An English ɔn of this work would be a most acceptable boon to the public. Professor Bopp goes :o the oriental source, and with a new theory of the ablaut, opposed to Dr. Grimm,) he shows how much the vocalism of the Germanic languages may be philosophically i by the system of Indian grammarians, and proves that the *ablaut,* or change of the owel, is influenced by the vowel of the termination.

ɪes Deutsches Wörterbuch für Etymologie, Synonymik, und Orthographie von Friedɪitthenner, Darmstadt, 8vo. 1834.

Greek; but in earlier times it was also used in some original German words to express *i*. It must be ascribed to the form of the epiglottis, that there can only be three original vowels, though in a variety of shades and colouring. This is a natural fact in language and grammar. All other vowels are only considered as shades and approximations. Of these three,* the vowel *a* is the easiest, most simple, and universal sound.—The radical vowels undergo various changes in the declension and formation of words.—1. By a shade changing the *i* into *e*, and the *u* into *o*; as *Moes.* niman, *Ger.* nehmen *to take*: *Moes.* giban, *Ger.* geben *to give*: *Moes.* uftô, *Ger.* oft *often*: *Moes.* fugls, *Ger.* vogel *a bird*.—2. By upsound (auflaut) or thinning of the vowel or sound, by earlier etymologists called (umlaut). If, for instance, in the inflection or formation of a radical syllable which has *a*, *o*, or *u*, and consequently a strong full vowel, an *i* is added, but which in the new German is changed into *e*, or entirely omitted; then these three vowels change into a higher but weaker sound, the *a* into ä or *e*, the *o* into ö, and the *u* into ü; as adel, edel: *Old Ger.* adal, edili: ast *a branch*, æste *branches*: Gott *God*, götter *gods*: *Old Ger.* kot, kotier: blut, blütig, and blutig: *Old Ger.* pluot, pluotic, or pluotac.—3. By change of vowels (umlaut), or change of one vowel into another, by some etymologists improperly called offsound (ablaut). In the formation of a word it thus happens that some roots of *a* go over into *i* and *u*, as binde, band, gebunden, properly band, binde, gebunden. —4. By insound (inlaut), in the Sanscrit called Guna, that is, in the formation of a word another vowel is placed before the radical vowel, like an internal augment, to denote the change which an idea undergoes. From the nature of the vowels the following law is deduced,—that the insound or guna can only proceed in the following order, *a*, *i*, *u*. *A* can be placed before *a* (*a* + *a*), before *i* (*a* + *i*), and *u* (*a* + *u*); *i* only before *i* (*i* + *i*), and before *u* (*i* + *u*), and *u* only before *u* (*u* + *u*).—According to the radical vowels, or what we call organic sounds, there can, in reality, only exist the following six diphthongs, *aa*, *ai*, *au*, *ii*, *iu*, *uu*.—In the reverse series, the vowels may be also compounded, but they form, as the pronunciation directly shows, no simple diphthongs. The diphthongs in the new High-German are formed partly by shades which the radical vowels or sounds suffer, and partly according to the peculiarity of the dialect which is become the written language, as *û*, (*ô*), *ai*, *au*, (*ô*), *ei*, *eu*, and *ie*.—In pronunciation and writing, the *û* as a diphthong is put aside; but it ought to have the power of *a* + *a* in the explanation of words. The three simple vowels *a*, *i*, *u*, with the guna † *aa*, *ai*, *au*, *ii*, *iu*, *uu*, are partly the natural and partly the historical normal sounds, and the original type of vocalism.

12. In the different dialects, the vowels, by upsound, shading, disorganization, &c. are softened and tinged different ways, but all in a certain order and according to determined rules. Thus, as the comparative zoologist is able to recognise the type of the genus in all deviations of the form of the single animal, so the comparative etymologist must be able to reduce the vocalism of the dialect to its original type, and thus comprehend it, for otherwise his perception is dark, and his whole proceeding uncertain, and vain error. Some complain that the doctrine of the guna is difficult, but nothing is more simple. In the diphthong we have only to consider the first letter as a prefix, denoting the formation, an inserted vowel equal to the insound

* A table of the changes of the radical vowels in the Germanic tongues will be found in Dr. Grimm's Deutsche Grammatik, vol. i. 573, 575; a table of the long vowels in p. 578.

† A table of the vowel forms, by the application of guna, in the Germanic languages may be seen in p. 59 of Schmitthenner's Deutsche Etymologie, 12mo. Darmstadt, 1833.

inlaut), and the last letter as the radical vowel. In some cases, only *ie* nakes an exception.

13. The modern German has the following sounds: *A*, ä = *ae*; *ai* = *a* + *i*; *au* = + *u*: *E* = *a*, *ë*, *ei*, *ê*: *Ei* = *ai*, *î* (*i* + *i*): *Eu* = *iu*: *I* = *old iu, io, ai, ei* : = *u*; *ô* = *au*, *old uo*, *â*; ö = *the increased sound of o*: *U*, *û* = *gunited a*; ü the sound of *u* and *û*.—*A*. By the preceding, it is clear there are only three radical wels from which the others take their origin; thus from *A* originates *o*, ä, *e*, *i* (*e*), (*o*), *ü*, *ô*; *I* goes over into *e*, *ei*, (*ai*), *ie*: *U* changes into *o*, *ie*, *eu*, *au*.—Hence it very easy, in a great number of cases, to recognize the radical vowel in a word, pecially by comparing it with other words of the same family. We often find the t in verbs, as soon as the vowel of the perfect tense is divested of all its changes guna and upsound. From binde, band, bund *bind, bound, bound*, we find *band* he root. From ritt *rode*, reiten *to ride*, is the root rit *a riding*. From fliege, flog *flew* is the root flug *a flight*.

4. OF CONSONANTS. The natural articulation of the consonants acding to the organs, is represented in the following table.

		a. *labial.*	*b.* *lingual.*	*c.* *palatine.*
A.	*Half mute sounds.*	w	h (*Breathing sound*, Spirans.)	j
B.	The sibilant (sibilans) ſ, s.			
C.	The liquids	m	l	nr
D.	The mutes (mutæ).			
aa. *Simple.*	*soft*	b	d	g
	hard	p	t	k
bb. *Aspirate.*		v	(dh)	—
		f	(th)	ch
cc. *Sibilant.*		—	sz	—
		ψ	z	x,

evident, by this table, that in the modern *Ger.* the aspirated palatine and the t labial sounds are wanting, while it has a double aspirated labial and a double ; lingual sound. The *q* is a double letter. The *s* possesses a double sound, e is expressed by *s*, and the other by *sh*.

No root or radical word has originally a double consonant of the same kind. ginal *i* in the derivation has given rise to gemination or hardening of the sound, s found nearly in all words of the same family. In this manner originated

nm	*from* mj	*as* schemmen	*from* suamjan
l	— lj	— hölle	— helja
nn	— nj	— rennen	— ranjan
r	— rj	— sperren	— sparjan
f (*Old Ger.* pph)	— phj	— hüpfen	— huphjan
z (zz)	— zj (tj)	— setzen	— satjan
k (*Old Ger.* cch)	— kj or hj	— zicke	— zikja.

aw is of great importance in etymology, showing how to reduce words with final letter to their roots. Instead of the double letter, we ought to put the le letter; and, instead of the upsound, originated by the derivative *i*, there a full original vowel. Thus, for example, from kennen *to know*, comes the root kan; *Old Ger.* chan; from fallen *to fall*, the root fal, *Old Ger.* val; from bücken *to bow*, the root bug—by guna biegen *to bend* (*Old Ger.* puk—piokan); from ricke *a doe*, reh (instead of rih), &c. In the old as well as in the modern *Ger.* language, a double consonant is used in writing only to express the sharpening of the consonant.

16. Of the root. The root is the simple syllable which designates the first appearance of a thing. According to its signification it has a simple vowel *a, i, u,* and a single consonant. It is often very easy to discover the root, for we need only take from the word the vowel forming the umlaut, and the guna (inlaut); the gemination, and the terminating syllables.

For example, let us take from the verb leuchten *to light*, the guna *e*, and the postfixed syllable *ten;* then will remain luch, *Old Ger.* luh, *Lat.* luc-ere.—From fuhr (*Old Ger.* vuor) take the guna, then remains fahr (*Old Ger.* var), &c. In general, a comparison with the old form is quite necessary.

17. According to its signification the root is neither a noun nor a verb, but it is what precedes both. It is the expression of the simplest intuition by a sound, without determining any associate idea of the gender, the time, &c.

Let us take the appearance of blau,—then the root is blu, *f. Lat.* fulvus (which, however, signifies something else,) and by guna blau the expression of the sound instead of it without any further determination, whether it be a thing, a quality, or only a relation. But being in reality a quality, it is afterwards used as an adjective, and the principal word or noun bläue *blueness*, and the verb bläuen *to blue* or *to make blue*, are only derived from it by additional letters. In the same manner let us take the impression which the cry of chickens or crows produces on the ear; the simplest expression of the sound will be kra, *Old Ger.* chra. As this impression quickly vanishes, there is directly formed the verb krähen *to crow, Old Ger.* chrâhan; present tense ich krähe *I crow, Old Ger.* chrâ-hu, and krähte, *Old Ger.* chrâ-ta *I crew*, and also in the same manner the noun das krähen *the crowing, Old Ger.* chrâ-t; die krâhe *the crow, Old Ger.* chrâ-ja, &c. In this manner language springs up everywhere full of fine signification and inexhaustible life.

Of the formation of words by umlaut and inlaut, or by change of vowels and by guna.

18. This takes place when, for the designation of the gender, case, or time, vowels or sounds are added. The transition of the root into different words is in all cases easily understood. Let us take the root luh, *New Ger.* hell *clear, light*, then by guna (inlaut) and an added *t*, is formed lioht, *New Ger.* licht (instead of liecht) *the clearness, light;* and also the *adj.* licht *light*, &c.

The determination of the signification of words and roots.

19. Language generally originates from the most simple perception of our senses. The appearances which offer themselves to the sight, not yet dimmed by any reflection, are the qualities and the relation of things

in time and space, such as, *light, dark:—black, white:—great, small:—standing, running—to rise, to fall*, &c.

20. These appearances are immediately determined or marked by the language, whether they are resting qualities, as; *blue, yellow, great, small*, &c., or a temporal relation, as, *flows, stands, burns, smokes*, &c., or only relations of space and number, as; *by, at, for—one, two*, &c. Things, of which the appearance only shows the special situation, the number and their relation, can only be designated by language in such a manner that it either points to their situation in space, by which pronouns originate, as, *I, he, his, that*, &c., or it describes them by nominating their qualities and their temporal relation, as, *the bird, the floating in air*. Thus originate the names of things, and each name is originally a short description.

21. It is the task of etymology to pursue the signification now in use, hrough all changes, till we come to the radical signification. So we are ed to a proper knowledge of the language, as a clear conception of the ommon signification can, in general, be only discovered in the light of the adical meaning.

22. Easy as it may be, in most cases, to find the form of the root by ecomposing the words, yet it is often difficult to ascertain the original gnification. Where it remains perceptible to the senses, it is immeately discovered: thus, fliessen *to flow*, from the moving on of the fluid; hen *to blow*, from the soft movement of the air; blau *blue*, from a colour, c. In other cases there are difficulties which can only be overcome by ose investigation.

23. The doctrine of the interchange of consonants,* and that of umlaut† d guna‡ are the two gates which lead into the sanctuary of etymology. e former opens the insight into the true nature of the consonants, the ter into that of the vowels. He, then, who has a clear view of these o doctrines, has received the consecration, and can look into the interior the sanctuary.§

§ 14. † § 11, iii. ‡ § 11, iv.; § 12, 13.

It ought to be acknowledged again, that this is a very imperfect view, but the shortest best that could be found. Those who would enter fully into the subject, must consult original authorities quoted throughout this abstract, and especially Professor J. Grimm's luable Deutsche Grammatik, 3 vols. 8vo. Göttingen; Bopp's Vocalismus, with the works chmeller, Becker, Wüllner, Graff, &c. See xiii. § 10.

XIV.—AN ACCOUNT OF THE WORK.

1. After much consideration, the Roman character has been adopted in printing the A.-S. words, with the exception of the two peculiar letters þ and ð, an account of which will be found under þ in the Dictionary. With all the prejudices of an antiquarian taste, and an eye long familiar with the form in which the words had been accustomed to be read, in what has been called the Anglo-Saxon character, and with the difficulty of recognizing the same words when presented in a different dress, it required a strong reason to justify the rejection of the old letters. Nothing but a thorough conviction that the Roman character would be the most legible, and would best show the identity of the present English with the Anglo-Saxon, as well as the clear analogy existing in the words of all the other Germanic languages, would have led to the adoption of this type. As a table is given for the sound of the letters in the chief languages used in the Dictionary, this opportunity is taken to introduce the peculiar characters of each language.* Words from the oriental tongues being written from right to left, and difficult to express in European letters alone, are given in their original characters; but for facility of comparison they are also represented in Roman letters.

2. It was originally intended to exclude all impure Anglo-Saxon words, and to introduce none of a later date than A.D. 1100. Subsequently it was found desirable to take a wider range, and to include some terms of a more recent formation.† These are mostly from the Anglo-Saxon Chronicle, with their date affixed. As the authors are always quoted, the age and purity of a word can at once be seen. The radical and some other chief words are generally printed in capitals. Accents are now adopted, as they were evidently employed by the Anglo-Saxons to distinguish long from short vowels: thus, ác *an oak*, ac *but;* ís *ice*, is *is;* þé *thee*, þe *the;* fór *went*, for *for*, &c. They are only used in this Dictionary on the word and its variations standing at the head of each article, this being sufficient for all practical purposes.—That orthography is, for the most part, strictly followed which is found most frequently in the best authors: still the principal variations in the literal expression of a word are added in the order in which they vary from what is deemed the correct spelling. No fancy or presumption has been permitted in the orthography; but all authors have been allowed to answer for themselves and to appear in their own dress, without a wish to dictate the mode in which it is now presumed they ought to have written.

* See the table at the end of the Dictionary.

† As many words were omitted in the early part of the alphabet, the supplement is rendered much more extensive than would otherwise have been necessary.

ı reference is constantly made to the place where the word is found, and ıe reader left to form his own judgment. Even verbs in -gian are ıserted when they are discovered so written. Verbs with the prefixes e-, ge-, on-, &c., are frequently placed under the radical word; but if ıund in the infinitive mood, or in any form directly derived from the finitive, such verbs are given, with a brief explanation, in the alphaetical order of the prefixes be-, ge-, &c., with a reference to the dical word for a full explanation. The majority of words have exactly e same sense with or without the prefixed ge-, as nyðerian, and genyðern *to humble*, (*Lk.* xiv, 11: *Ps.* xvii, 29.)—No pains have been spared ascertain and express the precise grammatical inflections. Every ıown irregularity in a word is placed in its alphabetical order, with meaning: thus, eóde *went, delivered*, the perfect tense, is referred to e infinitive gan *to go*. If the meaning be all that is required, it is us ascertained at once; but should the derivation and other particulars desired, they may be found under the word to which a reference is ıde.

3. With the view of illustrating the Anglo-Saxon, nearly all the radical rds, and a few important compounds, are followed by the parallel ms* from the cognate dialects. Synonymes without a meaning attached re the same signification as the A.-S. word under which they are ought. When it was difficult to ascertain whether the noun or verb s the radical, parallels are occasionally inserted under both. To show re clearly the analogy of cognate languages, an attempt has been made arrange the parallel terms in the most natural order. The Low (Platt) rman is generally placed first, because it is now spoken by the people o inhabit the territory formerly occupied by the Old-Saxons, the genitors of our Anglo-Saxon ancestors. The Dutch and Friesic rds follow, because they are of the same Low-German branch, and st similar to the A.-S. and Platt. The German then succeeds with the mannic from Kero, Otfrid, &c. Francic, from a translation of Isidore Nativitate, &c. and from Willeram's Canticum Canticorum: these are owed by the Mœso-Gothic. With this Teutonic or German branch onnected the Scandinavian, including the Danish, Swedish, Norwe-ı, Icelandic, Old Danish or Norse. The Sclavonic, Latin, Greek, Celtic synonymes are not given unless they bear some striking ıity to the word under consideration. The following arrangement, inning with the Low-German, and, as frequently as practicable, tracing word through the cognate dialects, up to some oriental source,

* The author has here the pleasure of recording the exertions of a very learned and zealous d, a native of Holstein, well acquainted with all the Teutonic and Scandinavian dialects. erudite friend, who will not allow his name to appear, has used his utmost efforts to every word introduced amongst the parallels, and to give the orthography and gender ctly. The laborious work of Meidinger, entitled Etymologische Wörterbuch Frankfurt, Iain, 8vo. 1833, has been occasionally used. The Rev. G. Phillips, M.A. Fellow of ns' Coll., Cambridge, has enriched the latter part of this Dictionary by his knowledge of riental languages, in selecting some parallel words from the Shemitic family.

will make the matter clear. This tracing of the languages upwards is nearly the reverse of the table of Japhetic languages in page viii.

I. 1. Low-German, Platt-Deutsch, or Old-Saxon being the dialects spoken in the northern or flat and low provinces of Germany, from which the A.-S. originally came into Britain. Written in
Heliand, A.D. 840.
Tatian's Harmony, A.D. 890.

2. Friesic, from the Asega-bôk, Hettema's Friesch en Nederlandsch Woordenboek, &c.

3. Dutch, from Kilian, and Holtrop's Dictionaries, &c.

II. 1. High-German, modern High-German, or Hoch-Deutsch; which, since the time of Luther, has become the cultivated language of Germany.

2. Francic, which was spoken by the independent tribes dwelling between the Rhine and Elbe, is an intermediate dialect between the German and Alemannic. Written in
Hildibraht and Hadubrant, A.D. 730.
Isidore's De Nativitate, A.D. 800.
Willeram's Canticum, A.D. 1070.

3. Alemannic or Suabian, which prevailed in the southern or hilly part of Germany. Written in
Exhortation to Christians, A.D. 720.
Kero, A.D. 800.
Rhabanus Maurus, A.D. 850.
Otfrid, A.D. 860.
Notker, A.D. 1020.

III. Mœso-Gothic. Written in
The Gospels, A.D, 370.

IV. Scandinavian:
1. Danish
2. Swedish } from Dictionaries.
3. Norwegian
4. Icelandic from Halderson's Lexicon Islandico-Latino-Danicum, by Rask, 4to. 1814.

V. The Latin Dialects are less useful in illustrating A.-S., and therefore not so frequently introduced.
1. Italian.
2. Spanish.
3. Portuguese.
4. French.
5. Latin.
6. Greek.

VI. The Celtic Dialects.
1. Welsh.
2. Cornish.
3. Irish.
4. Gaelic.
5. Armorican.

VII. 1. Arabic.
2. Hebrew.

VIII. 1. Persian,
2. Sanscrit.

4. The derivation immediately follows the synonymes. If the word be uncompounded in A.-S. it is occasionally traced to an oriental origin. From the danger of giving way to fancy, on the debateable ground of etymology, it has been an anxious wish and constant care rather to do too little than too much, and to avoid a dictatorial and dogmatical spirit on every point, but especially in the derivation of words. Immediately after compound terms will be found their constituent parts with their separate meanings: but such compounds as at once indicate their composition, are ... words
een no

nation,
tained,
æ *law*,
The
n iden-
c Latin
hat this
sanction
are also
al from
ie exact
onsisted
ius, and
rom the
lation is
rom the
e Saxon
English
al order
adopted
s various
ppeared
ien prac-
thors by
rked(¶).
ave been
lanations
t in view.
pace as is
ctical in-
of Lye.
r part of

g attentions
Cambridge,

July 11th 1866

The Dean of Ch. Ch. Oxford Dr. Liddell, recommends Arrangement of each article in Dr. Bosworth's Ang.-Sax. Dicty.

1 Cognate forms within brackets [ ] after the inflection

2 Capitals not to be used except in proper names, at the beging. of each article when there are not Roman Numerals & at the beging. of each body (or set) of quotations

3 Give the authorities & quotations after each set of meanings

4 — —

5 Yes —

Latin

Old Italic Version of the Scriptures, The Homilies of Alfric &c

will make the matter clear. This tracing of the languages upwards is nearly the reverse of the table of Japhetic languages in page viii.

I. 1. Low-German, Platt-Deutsch, or Old-Saxon being the dialects spoken in the northern or flat and low provinces of Germany, from which the A.-S. originally came into Britain. Written in
Heliand, A.D. 840.
Tatian's Harmony, A.D. 890.

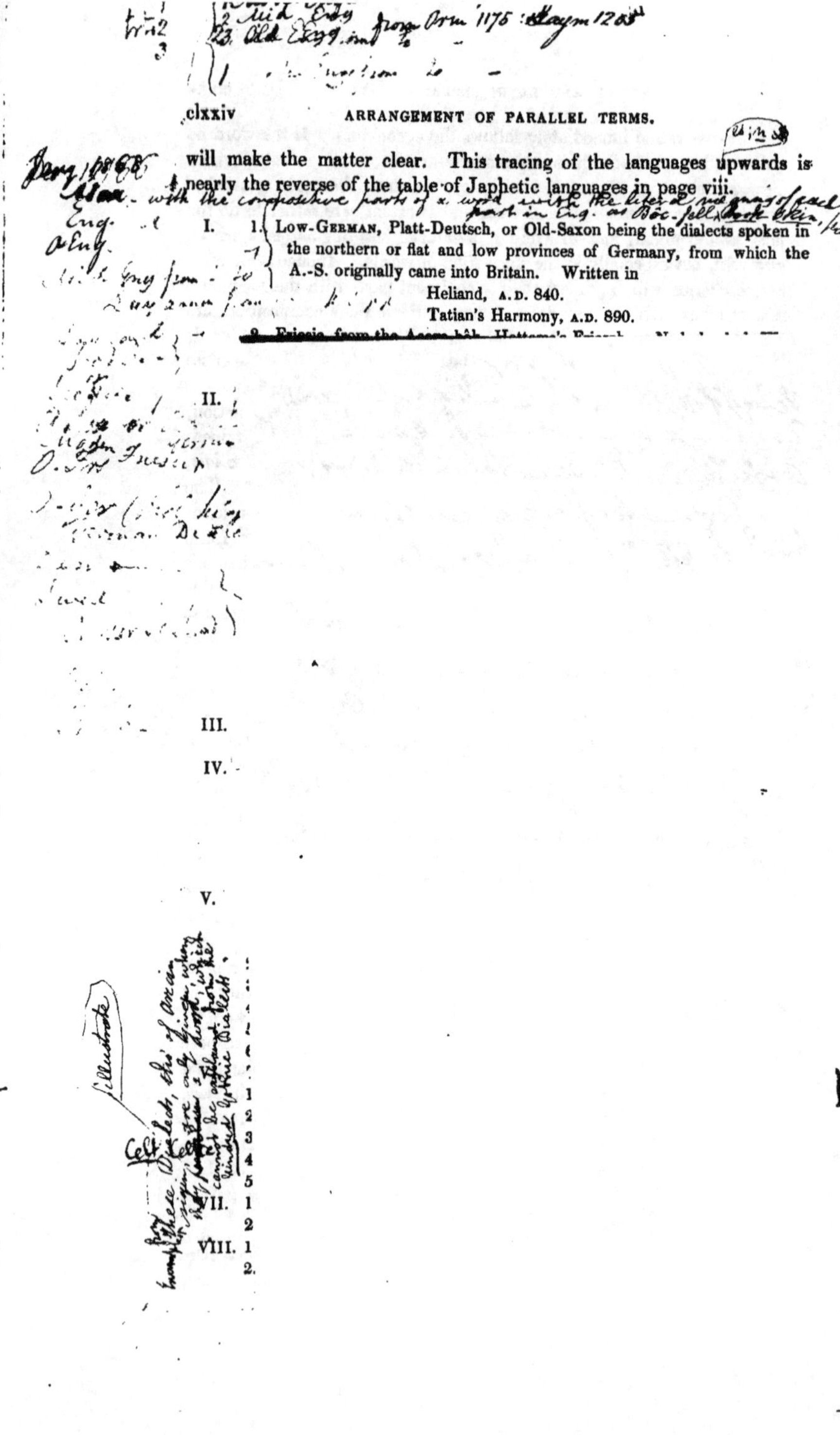

II.

III.

IV.

V.

VII. 1
2

VIII. 1
2.

4. The derivation immediately follows the synonymes. If the word be ncompounded in A.-S. it is occasionally traced to an oriental origin. rom the danger of giving way to fancy, on the debateable ground of ymology, it has been an anxious wish and constant care rather to do too :tle than too much, and to avoid a dictatorial and dogmatical spirit on ery point, but especially in the derivation of words. Immediately after mpound terms will be found their constituent parts with their separate eanings: but such compounds as at once indicate their composition, are t analyzed; the literal sense of each part is then only given, in words iich most resemble the A.-S., and for this purpose there has been no 'uple in using some obsolete and modern provincial terms.

5. The synonymes and derivation were placed before the explanation, the radical meaning of the separate parts of a word being ascertained, uld naturally lead to the first sense of the compound; thus æfest [æ *law*, t *fast, fixed*] *fixed in the law, religious, devout;* religiosus. The planation of the A.-S. is in English, one word of which is often iden- l with the Saxon; hence the necessity of a long paraphrastic Latin dering is superseded, and the definition much shortened: but that this :tionary may have the authority of Somner and Lye, and the sanction he most important A.-S. authors, the principal significations are also ed in Latin. The Latin explanation is generally the original from ch the A.-S. translation was first made, and thus confirms the exact ning on the authority of the translators, whose chief literature consisted nglo-Saxon versions from the Latin of Bede, Boethius, Orosius, and Vulgate, or Latin Scriptures. In the quotations, except from the e, which is too well known to require it, an English translation is 1, as literal as possible; but in those from Bede, and often from the e, the Latin is retained, as it is the original from which the Saxon on was made, and therefore the best explanation. To the English lation the Latin is appended, when it indicates the grammatical order e inflections of the Saxon. The following is the general plan adopted e explanation:—The radical meaning is placed first, then its various ications are numbered, and arranged in that order which appeared accordant with the association of ideas;—each meaning, when prac- e, is confirmed by quotations, with a reference to the authors by the word is used. Next follow the idiomatical expressions marked(¶). ecting examples to confirm the different meanings, those have been red which illustrate the grammatical inflections. In the explanations lustrations, brevity and perspicuity have always been kept in view. ese means, and a proper attention to as much economy of space as is tible with neatness in typographical execution, more practical in- ion is comprised in this volume than in the two folios of Lye. e English and Latin Indexes,* the Saxon to the greater part of

Latin

Old Italic Version of the Scriptures, The Homilies of Alfric &c

preparing the Indexes and carrying them through the press, the obliging attentions ev. J. Williamson, and Mr. O. H. Flowers, both of St. John's College, Cambridge, e forgotten.

English and Latin terms may be found, the derivation and original meaning of most English words may be ascertained, and a comparison instituted with their radical cognates in the other Gothic languages.

6. Some words have been collected from old Glossaries, with a mere Latin meaning. In such cases, the only mode of discovering the real sense was by the derivation and analogy of cognate words of Teutonic origin. When this failed, there was no alternative but to translate the Latin signification into English: thus, geman *the hollow of the hand, sole of the foot*, could only be known by translating, vola, *Cot.* 198. Some words are from Somner, Benson, and Lye, for which no other authority could be found. The orthography, inflection, and meaning of these words are given, without alteration, on the responsibility of these authors.

7. As there has been a careful citation of authorities, and at the same time particular obligations expressed, very little more can be now required. A free use, without continued reference, has been made of preceding Dictionaries and Vocabularies, and of the A.-S. Grammar of an erudite friend, the late Professor Rask. Mr. Thorpe's Glossaries, appended to his Analecta Anglo-Saxonica, and Apollonius, and his index to Cædmon, have been useful auxiliaries. Citations from Cædmon have always been made from Mr. Thorpe's improved text, through whom, and the kindness of Sir Nicholas Carlisle, the learned secretary of the Society of Antiquaries, the perusal of some sheets was allowed before the work was published. Amongst those to whom the greatest debt of gratitude is due, is an old and faithful friend, C. S. Cardale, Esq., known to A.-S. students by the benefit he has rendered them in publishing his elegant and correct edition of Boethius. This gentleman allowed the full and free use of his extensive and very valuable Anglo-Saxon and English Dictionary in MS. It would be ingratitude not to mention the friendly communications of the Rev. S. Fox, or to leave unnoticed the advantages derived from his published works.* A well known collector of choice books, Mr. Bohn, was so obliging as spontaneously to lend an interleaved copy of Lye's Dictionary, with MS. notes by the late Rev. S. Henshall. The Rev. M. White, B.D. Professor of A.-S. in the University of Oxford, had given notice of his intention to prepare an A.-S. Dictionary, but being informed that this work was far advanced, Mr. White, in the most gentlemanly manner, gave up his intended publication. He has, however, taken the most lively interest in the progress of this Dictionary.

8. This work was begun with a sanguine hope of soon bringing it to a satisfactory conclusion; but it has employed every leisure hour of the compiler for more than seven years, four of which it has been in the

* The following neat and valuable publications of Mr. Fox deserve the especial notice of Anglo-Saxon students:—Menologium, or the Poetical Calendar of the Anglo-Saxons, 8vo. 1830. See p. xx. note No. 17.—King Alfred's A.-S. version of Boethius, with an English translation and notes, 8vo. 1835. See p. xix. note No. 11.

press. It is at last brought to a close; and, though he has used all the diligence, and availed himself of every means in his power, having the patriotism, amidst many disadvantages, to print in his own country at his own expense and risk, it is far, very far from answering even his own expectations. He can, however, honestly declare that his utmost exertions have been continually made to lay before the public, in this Dictionary, a brief but comprehensive summary of the Anglo-Saxon language. The sources of information are constantly pointed out; hence, where there are errors, there also are the means of discovering truth. Though he has always endeavoured to guard against prejudice and predilection, he is conscious that opinions have sometimes been advanced which may appear to want support. In such, and indeed in all cases, as he has stated in another place, he invites liberal criticism, being assured that, by the collision of opposite opinions, new light, if not truth, is often elicited; and should this be the case, he will have cause to rejoice, whether it be produced by himself or by a more successful investigator.

ROTTERDAM, *January* 1*st*, 1837.

THE ESSENTIALS

OF

ANGLO-SAXON GRAMMAR,

WITH AN OUTLINE OF

PROFESSOR RASK AND GRIMM'S SYSTEMS.

PREFACE.

Thirteen years have elapsed since a zealous, but very imperfect attempt was made to divest Anglo-Saxon Grammar of its Latin incumbrances, and to offer one formed on the true genius and structure of the language in the publication of *The Elements of the Anglo-Saxon Grammar with copious Notes*, 8vo. 1823, pp. 330. Before committing this work to the press every accessible source of information was explored, and a complete English Translation made of *Angelsaksisk Sproglære ved R. K. Rask*, 8vo. Stockholm, 1817. In 1826, the most practical part of The Elements with such corrections and additions as naturally arose from a farther consideration of the subject, appeared with the title of *A Compendious Grammar of the primitive English or Anglo-Saxon Language*, 8vo. pp. 84.* The following Essentials are given as the result of a still longer and closer investigation of the language in the preparation of the Anglo-Saxon Dictionary, and a continued appeal to the grammar of a lamented friend, the late Professor Rask, and to the learned Deutsche Grammatik of Professor Grimm. It will be seen that, as information has increased, there has been a gradual approximation, in grammatical forms and accents, to the views of Professor Rask and Grimm. While there is a hope that these Essentials, referring only to Etymology, may be found the most simple and practical, a very short abstract is given of Professor Rask and Grimm's Grammars for the use of those who prefer, what may be considered the more complete systems of these celebrated men.

* See Preface to Dictionary of the Anglo-Saxon Language, p. xx. note (§) 21.

THE ESSENTIALS,

&c.

---

1. The Anglo-Saxon letters are *a, b, c, d, e, f, g, h, i, (k), l, m, n, o, p, (q), r, s, t, u, w, x, y, þ, ð.**

2. The letters *j, k, q, v,* and *z,* are not found in genuine Anglo-Saxon; for *k* and *q* the Anglo-Saxons used *c* and *cw.* Þ, þ had the hard sound of *th* in *th*in, *th*ing; and Ð, ð soft, as *th* in *th*ine, smoo*th*.

3. All nouns, having the *nom. s.* ending in -a, -scipe, -dóm, -end, and -ere, are masculine: those having the *nom. s.* in -nes, -um, -uð, -ð, and -estre, are feminine: and those in -ærn, -ed, are neuter. All nouns having the *nom.* and *ac. pl.* in -u are of the first declension, neuter gender. Every noun, having the *nom.* and *ac. pl.* in as, is masculine—All nouns making *g. s.* in -e are feminine.

4. If a noun be masculine and have the *nom. s.* in -e, it always makes the *g.* in -an; it is therefore of the second declension. All other masculine nouns make the *g. s.* in -es, and are hence of the first declension.—All neuter nouns make the *g. s.* in -es, and are of the first declension, except a very few in -e, which are of the second declension, and have the *g.* in -an.—All feminine nouns having the *nom. s.* in -e are of the second declension, and make the *g.* in -an; all other feminine nouns make the *g.* in -e, and are of the third declension.

5. *Synopsis of the declensions of nouns.*

	1st declension.			*2nd declension.*			*3rd declension.*	
	m.	*n.*	*n.*	*m.*	*f.*	*n.*	*f*	*f.*
s. nom.	[e]	—	[e]	-a	-e	-e	—	-u
g.	-es	-es	-es	-an	-an	-an	-e	-e
d.	-e	-e	-e	-an	-an	-an	-e	-e
ac.	[e]	—	[e]	-an	-an	-e	-e	-e
pl. nom. ac.	-as	—	u	-an	-an	-an	-a	-a
g.	-a	-a	-a [ena]	-ena	-ena	-ena	-a	-ena
d.	-um	-um	-um	-um	-um	-um	-um	-um.

6. *The first declension,* (except those in -u, see § 13) only comprehending *m.* and *n.* nouns, is known by the genitive case singular ending in -es. It includes almost

* The following characters have been generally called Anglo-Saxon:—

A a, B b, C c, D ꝺ, E e, F ꝼ, G ᵹ, H h, I ı, K k, L l, M m, N n, O o, P p, R ꞃ, S ꞅ, T ꞇ, U u, X x, Y ẏ, Z z, Þ þ, Ð ð.

all masculine nouns, not ending in -a or -u, such as those in -dóm, wisdóm, es; *m. wisdom;* -end (derived from participles) as Hælend, es; *m. the healer, Saviour:* -ere, fiscere, es; *m. a fisher:* -els, récels, es; *m. incense:* -ing, cyning, es; *m. a king:* -erd, -ord, -est, as hlaford, es; *m. a lord:* -að, -eð, -oð, as monað, es; *m. a month:* -scype, or -scipe, as freondscipe, es; *m. friendship:* and generally, nouns ending in -l, -m, -n, -r, as eorl, es; *m. a nobleman:* æðm, es; *m. breath:* also neuter nouns ending in a consonant, or in two or more consonants; as word, es; *n. a word:* neuters in -e and -incle; as ríce, es; *n. a kingdom:* dissyllables in -el, -ol, -en, -er; as tungel, es; *n. a star:* nouns in -ed, -et, -od, heafod, es; *n. a head.*

	m.	*m.*	*m.*	*n.*	*n.*	*n.*
s. nom. ac.	smið	end-e	stæf	word	ríc-e	fæt
g.	smið-es	end-es	stæf-es	word-es	ríc-es	fæt-es
d.	smið-e	end-e	stæf-e	word-e	ríc-e	fæt-e
pl. nom. ac.	smið-as	end-as	staf-as	word	ríc-u	fat-u
g.	smið-a	end-a	staf-a	word-a	ríc-a	fat-a
d.	smið-um	end-um	staf-um	word-um	ríc-um	fat-um.

7. In this declension the *nom.* and *ac.* cases are always the same. Masculines ending in a consonant, like smið *a smith;* and those in e like ende *an end,* are the most regular: nouns in -e are declined as if they had no e, like smið, except in the *nom.* and *ac. s.* where it is preserved.—Monosyllables with æ before a single consonant, and before st, sc, assuming another syllable with *a, o,* or *u,* in declining, change æ into a, as in stæf *a letter,* stafas *letters;* fæt *a vat,* fatu *vats;* gæst *a guest,* gastas *guests;* but the æ is unchanged in stæfes *of a letter,* in fæte *to a vat,* or in cræft *craft,* cræftas *crafts;* because the syllables es, e, assumed in declining, do not contain *a, o,* or *u,* or because æ comes before other double consonants, than st, sc.—Dissyllables in -l, -n, -r, -d, are often contracted when a vowel follows, as tungel *a star, g.* tungles *of a star,* instead of tungeles; heáfod *a head, g.* heáfdes *of a head.*—Neuters ending in a single or double consonant as word *a word,* make the *nom.* and *ac.* in the *s.* and *pl.* all alike; but dissyllable nouns of the neuter gender ending in -el, -ol, -en, -er, diminutives in -incle and neuters ending in -e, make the *nom.* and *ac. pl.* in -u, as tungel *a star,* tunglu *stars,* ricu *kingdoms;* neuter monosyllables having the diphthong æ make the *pl.* in -u, and also change the vowel, as fæt *a vat, pl. nom. ac.* fatu *vats.**

8. *The second declension* has the genitive case singular ending in -an, as wítega, an; *m. a prophet:* wuce, an; *f. a week:* eáre, an; *n. an ear.* All nouns having the *nom.* ending in -a are masculine, and of this declension; so also are all feminine nouns in -e, -estre, -istre, as sangistre, an; *f. a songstress;* and names of men and women in -a, as Attila, Anna, &c.

	m.	*f.*
s. nom.	wíteg-a	wuc-e
g.	wíteg-an	wuc-an
d.	wíteg-an	wuc-an
ac.	wíteg-an	wuc-an
pl. nom. ac.	wíteg-an	wuc-an
g.	wíteg-ena	wuc-ena
d.	wíteg-um	wuc-um.

9. Very few neuters have been found of this declension, eáre *an ear,* and eáge *an eye,* stace *a stake,* like all neuters, make the *ac. s.* like the *nom.,* thus, *nom. ac.* eáre, eáge; in the other cases they are declined exactly like wuce.

* See example in § 6.

10. Names of countries and places in -a, are sometimes indeclinable, and sometimes they take the Latin form. Európa has Európam, Európe, Európe (*i. e.* Europæ) in Orosius.*

11. *The third Declension*, which only includes feminine nouns, is known by the genitive case singular ending in e. All feminine nouns ending in a consonant, or in -u, or -o; as wylen or wyln *a female slave*, gifu *a gift*, syn *sin*, are of this declension. Nouns in -ung, styrung, e; *f. a motion*, and a few in -ing; those in -nis, -nes, -nys, as gelícnes, se; *f. a likeness*, -uð, geoguð, e; *f. youth* are all feminine, and of this declension.

	f.	*f.*	*f.*	*f.*
s. nom.	wyln	gif-u	syn	gelícnes
g.	wyln-e	gif-e	syn-ne	gelícnes-se
d.	wyln-e	gif-e	syn-ne	gelícnes-se
ac.	wyln-e	gif-e	syn-ne	gelícnes-se
pl. nom. ac.	wyln-a	gif-a	syn-na	gelícnes-sa
g.	wyln-a	gif-ena	syn-na	gelícnes-sa
d.	wyln-um	gif-um	syn-num	gelícnes-sum.

12. Nouns ending in a consonant make the *g. pl.* in -a, as wylna *of female slaves*, synna *of sins*; those in -u or -o have the *g. pl.* in -ena, as gif-ena *of gifts*, and sometimes the *ac.* in u. Those which end in a single consonant, after a short vowel, double the final letter in the *g.* and all the other cases formed from it, as sin *sin*, synne *of sin*, gelícnes *a likeness*, gelícnesse *of a likeness*. Nouns in -ung sometimes make the *d. s.* in -a. A few words have the *ac.* like the *nom.* as tíd *time*, hand *a hand*, miht *might*.

Irregular Nouns.

13. The few masculine nouns which end in -u, such as, lagu *water*, medu *mead*, sidu *custom*, sunu *a son*, are thus declined: *s. nom. ac.* sunu *a son*; *g. d.* suna; *pl. nom. ac.* suna, *g.* suna, or sunena; *d.* sunum. In the *pl.* they are declined like nouns of the second declension.—A few names of nations are only used in the plural, and end in -e, as Romane *the Romans*, Angle *the Angles*, Dene *the Danes*. They are declined, *nom ac.* Romane, *g.* Romana, *d.* Romanum.

14. A few words ending in -or, and -er denoting relationship, such as bróðor *a brother*, dóhter *a daughter*, whether masculine or feminine, are thus declined *s. nom. g.* Bróðor; *d.* bréðer: *pl. nom. g. ac.* bróðra, *d.* bróðrum.

15. Some nouns chiefly monosyllables, containing the vowels a, u, ú, and ó, change those vowels in *d. s.* and *nom. ac, pl.* as man *a man*, in *d. s.* is men *to* or *with a man*, and *pl. nom. ac.* men *men*: also fót *a foot*, tóð *a tooth*, bóc *a book*, bróc *breeches*, gós *a goose*, turf *a turf*, burh *a castle*, cu *a cow*, lus *a louse*, mús *a mouse*, módor *a mother*, dóhtor *a daughter*, make in the *d.* singular, and in the *nom.* and *ac. pl.* fét, téð, béc, bréc, gés, tyrf, byrh, and byrig, cy, lys, mys, méder, déhter. They are mostly regular without change of vowel in the *g. s.* as mannes, fótes, tóðes, bóce, bróce, góse, múse, turfe; and also in the *g.* and *d. pl.* as manna, mannum; fóta, fótum; tóða, tóðum, bóca, bócum; bróca, brócum; gósa, gósum; músa, músum; turfa, turfum; dóhtra, dóhtrum.†

Adjectives.

16. Anglo-Saxon adjectives have variable terminations to correspond with their nouns.

* Mr. Thorpe's translation of Rask, § 65.

† See Dr. Grimm's Deutsche Grammatik, vol. i. p. 646, 647.

17. There is an indefinite and a definite form of declension.

18. *Synopsis of Adjective terminations.*

	Indefinite Adjectives.				*Definite Adjectives.*				
	m.	*f.*	*n.*	*m. f. n.*		*m.*	*f.*	*n.*	*m. f. n.*
s. nom.	—	—	—	*pl.* -e	*s.*	-a	-e	-e	*pl.* -an
g.	-es	-re	-es	-ra		-an	-an	-an	-ena
d.	-um	-re	-um	-um		-an	-an	-an	-um
ac.	-ne	-e	—	-e		-an	-an	-e	-an.

Indefinite Adjectives.

19. Gód *good,* læt *late,* will serve as examples of declining indefinite adjectives. All adjectives of one syllable, except when the vowel is æ before a single consonant; also those ending in -e, participles in -ende, -od, -ed; dissyllables in -el, &c., as sóð *true,* hál *sound,* leoht *light,* niwe *new,* willende *wishing,* gehered *praised,* mycel *great,* are declined like gód *good.*

	m.	*f.*	*n.*		*m. f. n.*
s. nom.	gód	gód	gód	*pl. nom.*	gód-e
g.	gód-es	gód-re	gód-es	*g.*	gód-ra
*d.**	gód-um	gód-re	gód-um	*d.*	gód-um
ac.	gód-ne	gód-e	gód	*ac.*	gód-e.

20. Those that end in -e, drop the e in declining; as niwe *new, g.* niw-es, niw-re, niw-es. Adjectives, ending in a single consonant, after a short vowel, double the consonant in declining; but one consonant is omitted before -ne, -re, -ra; as, grim *severe, g. m.* grim-mes, *f.* grim-re.

21. Polysyllabic adjectives formed by the derivative terminations, -ful, -ig, -isc, -leás, -lic, -sum, &c., make the *nom. s. f.* and the *nom. pl. n.* in -u; and monosyllables, ending in a single consonant preceded by æ, have the same cases in -u. The latter, when æ is followed by a single consonant, and *a, e, o,* or *u,* change æ into a; but before double consonants æ is unchanged. An example will make the matter plain: læt *late.*

	m.	*f.*	*n.*		*m. f.*	*n.*
s. nom.	læt	lat-u	læt	*pl.*	lat-e	lat-u
g.	lat-es	læt-re	lat-es		læt-ra	læt-ra
*d.**	lat-um	læt-re	lat-um		lat-um	lat-um
ac.	læt-ne	lat-e	læt		lat-e	lat-u.

22. Dissyllables, when the inflection begins with a vowel, are often contracted; as, hálig *holy; g. s. m.* hálg-es, but not when the inflection begins with a consonant; as, *g. s. f.* hálig-re.

Definite Adjectives.

23. The definite declension is used when the adjective has before it a definite article, or a demonstrative or possessive pronoun. The inflections are exactly the same as nouns of the second declension.

* Professor Rask gives a distinct form for the ablative singular.

	m.	*f.*	*n.*
ab.	gód-e,	gód-re,	gód-e.
ab.	lat-e,	læt-re,	lat-e.

	m.	f.	n.		m. f. n.
s. nom.	se gód-a	seo gód-e	þæt gód-e	*pl.*	þá gód-an
g.	þæs gód-an	þære gód-an	þæs gód-an		þára gód-ena
*d.**	þám gód-an	þære gód-an	þám gód-an		þám gód-um
ac.	þone gód-an	þá gód-an	þæt gód-e		þá gód-an.

24. Adjectives of one syllable with *æ* before a single consonant, in all cases reject the *e* from *æ*, hence the simple vowel *a* remains, or, in accordance with the rule in § 21, when a single consonant is followed by *a, e, o, u, æ* is changed into *a*. Læt *late* is declined definitely, thus:

	m.	f.	n.		m. f. n.
s. nom.	se lat-a	seo lat-e	þæt lat-e	*pl.*	þá lat-an
g.	þæs lat-an	þære lat-an	þæs lat-an		þára lat-ena
*d.**	þám lat-an	þære lat-an	þám lat-an		þám lat-um
ac.	þone lat-an	þá lat-an	þæt lat-e		þá lat-an.

Comparison.

25. The comparative degree is formed both definitely and indefinitely by annexing -ra, *m.* -re, *f.* -re, *n.* to the positive; the superlative indefinite by annexing -ost or -est, and the definite by -esta or -osta, *m.* -este, *f.* -este, *n.*, and sometimes by -mest, -mæst.

	Positive.	*Comparative.*	*Superlative.*
Indefinite.	Smæl	smæl-ra *m.* smæl-re *f. n.*	smal-ost
	small	*smaller*	*smallest*
Definite.	se smal-a	se smæl-ra seo, þæt smæl-re	se smal-esta, seo, þæt smal-este
	the small	*the smaller*	*the smallest*
Indefinite.	swið	swið-ra *m.* swið-re *f. n.*	swið-ost
	strong	*stronger*	*strongest*
Definite.	se swið-a	se swið-ra seo, þæt swið-re	se swið-esta, seo, þæt swið-este
	the strong	*the stronger*	*the strongest*
	læt	læt-ra	lat-ost *or* lat-emest
	late	*later*	*latest, most late*
	úteweard	útre	ytemest
	outward	*outer*	*outermost.*

26. The irregular comparisons, as gód *good*, betera *better*, betst *best*, &c. will be found in the Dictionary.

27. All *adj.* in the comparative degree, and all definite superlatives, are declined like se gód-a; all indefinite superlatives like gód *good.*

Pronouns.

28. Personal pronouns.

	I	*thou*	*he*	*she*	*it*		*we*†	*ye*‡	*they*
s. nom.	ic	þú	he	heo	hit[f]	*pl.*	we	ge	hí[k]
g.	mín	þín	his	hire[e]	his		úre[g]	eower	hira[l]
d.	me	þe	him[c]	hire[e]	him		us	eow	him[m]
ac.	me[a]	þe[b]	hine[d]	hí	hit[f]		us[h]	eow[i]	hí[k].

[a] meh, mec—[b] þeh, þec—[c] hym—[d] hyne—[e] hyre—[f] hyt—[g] user—[h] usih, usic—[i] eowih, eowic—[k] híg, heo, hie—[l] heora—[m] heom.

* Professor Rask gives an express form for the ablative case.

	m.	f.	n.
ab.	þy gód-an,	þære gód-an,	þy gód-an,
ab.	þy lat-an,	þære lat-an,	þy lat-an.

† 1. *Dual of* ic.
nom. wit, wyt *we two.*
g. uncer *of us two.*
d. unc *to us two.*
ac. unc *us two.*

‡ 2. *Dual of* þu.
git, gyt *ye two.*
incer *of you two.*
inc *to you two.*
inc[a] *you two.*

[a] incit.

29. Sylf *self* is declined like gód indefinitely and definitely, and is added to personal pronouns in the same gender and case, as ic sylf *I myself,* mín sylfes *of myself,* me sylfum *to myself;* but the *d.* of the personal *pron.* is sometimes as in *Eng.* prefixed to the *nom.* of sylf, me-sylf *myself,* þe-sylf *thyself,* him-sylf *himself.* Definitely it signifies *the same,* as, se sylfa man *the same man.* Sometimes agen *own,* declined like the indefinite of gód *good,* is added. To his agenum *to his own, Jn.* i. 11. The reciprocal sense of *his,* as *his own* is also expressed by sín.

Adjective Pronouns.

30. Adjective pronouns are only the genitive cases of the personal pronouns taken and declined as the indefinite adjective gód. They are mín *my,* þín *thine,* uncer *our two,* ure, or user *our,* incer *your two,* eower *your.*

	m. f. n.		*m.*		*f.*		*n.*
s. nom.	mín	*g.*	mín-es	*g.*	mín-re	*g.*	mín-es[a], &c.
	þín		þín-es		þín-re		þín-es, &c.
	uncer		unc-res		unc-re		unc-res, &c.
	úre[b]		úr-es		úre		úr-es, &c.
	incer		inc-res		inc-re		inc-res, &c.
	eower		eow-res		eow-re		eow-res, &c.

[a] *ac.* míne *or* mínne; [b] *nom. s. m. f. n.* user; *g. m. n.* usses, *f.* usse; *d. m. n.* ussum, *f.* usse; *ac. m.* userne, *f.* usse, *n.* user; *pl. nom. ac. m. f. n.* usse, user; *g. m. f. n.* ussa; *d. m. f. n.* ussum.

Definite or Demonstrative Pronouns.

31. The article or definite se *the,* and the definite þes *this,* are thus declined.

	m.	*f.*	*n.*		*m.f.n.*		*m.*	*f.*	*n.*		*m.f.n.*
s. nom.	se	seó	þæt	*pl.*	þá	*s.*	þes	þeós	þis	*pl.*	þás[h]
g.	þæs	þære	þæs		þára[d]		þises[e]	þisse[g]	þises[e]		þissa[i]
*d.**	þám[a]	þære	þám[c]		þám[a]	†	þisum[f]	þisse[g]	þisum		þisum[f]
ac.	þone[b]	þá	þæt		þá		þisne	þás	þis		þás.[h]

[a] þæm—[b] þæne—[c] þan, þon—[d] þæra—[e] þisses, þesses—[f] þissum, þis—[g] þissere—[h] þæs—[i] þissera.

32. The indeclinable article þe is used instead of the various cases of se, seo, þæt. Se, seo, þæt are used relatively like the English *that* for the relative hwá *who,* hwæt *what.*

Relative Pronouns.

33. The article or definitive se, seo, þæt, þe are generally used for the relative *who, which.* The interrogatives hwá *who?* hwæt *what?* are thus declined.

	m. f.		*n.*
s. and pl. nom.	hwá	*s.*	hwæt
g.	hwæs		hwæs
d.[c]	hwám[a]		hwám[a]
ac.	hwone[b].		hwæt.

[a] hwæm—[b] hwæne—[c] *ablative* hwi.

* Professor Rask makes a distinct ablative case, and says: "þy seems justly to be received as a proper *ablativus instrumenti,* as it occurs so often in this character, even in the masculine gender, as mid þy aþe *with that oath, L. In.* 53; and in the same place, in the dative, on þæm aþe *in that oath.*"—*Mr. Thorpe's Trans.* § 147.

	m.	*f.*	*n.*
ab.	þy	þære	þy.
† *ab.*	þise	þisse	þise.

34. Hwylc, hwilc, hwelc *which?* hwæðer *which of the two?* are declined indefinitely like gód *good.*

Numerals.

35. The numerals will be found in the Dictionary. A'n *one* is declined like gód *good.* Twegen *m.* twa *f. n. two,* begen *m.* bá *f. n. both,* and þry *three,* are declined thus:

	m.	*f. n.*	*m.*	*f. n.*
nom.	twegen	twá[c]	þry	þreó
g.	twegra[a]	twegra[a]	þreóra	þreóra
d.	twám[b]	twám[b]	þrym	þrym
ac.	twégen	twá	þry	þreó.

[a] twega—[b] twæm—[c] tú.

36. Feower *four* makes the *g.* feowera; fif *five,* six *six,* seofon *seven,* are also found in the *g.* fifa, sixa, and seofona. When used absolutely, tyn *ten* makes in *nom. ac.* tyne, and *d.* tynum; also twelf, *nom.* twelfe; *g.* twelfa; *d.* twelfum, but they are often undeclined. Twentig, and other words in -tig, are thus inflected in all genders, *nom. ac.* -tig; *g.* -tigra; *d.* -tigum. The ordinal numbers are all declined definitely like se góda, as se forma; seo, þæt forme *the first,* except oðer *second,* which has only the indefinite declension like gód *good.*

Verbs.

37. *The conjugation of Anglo-Saxon verbs,* like the English, is very simple.* According to the inflection, all Anglo-Saxon verbs may be divided into two classes, the one more simple and regular, the other more complex and irregular; hence, formerly called regular and irregular.

38. The most simple, regular, and prevailing mode of forming the perfect tense and perfect participle is by the addition of a syllable. Hence in Anglo-Saxon, as in the modern English, this plan universally prevails when new verbs are formed, or when verbs from a foreign language are adopted; when verbs are formed from adjectives, nouns, or from the perfect tense of complex verbs with a modified meaning. This prevalence in forming the principal parts of such verbs requires that they should be placed in the first class, especially since it is the permanent and unalterable inflection of verbs; for, though there is an increased and continued verging of complex verbs to the simple mode of formation, yet the simple or more regular class of verbs are always stable, and never assume the complex form.

39. *The simple and more regular class of verbs* is distinguished by having the perfect tense of two or more syllables, and the termination in -ode, -ede, -de, or -te, while the perfect participle ends in -od, -ed, -d, or -t; as, luf-ian *to love; p.* luf-ode; *pp.* luf-od; segel-ian *to sail; p.* segel-ede, or segel-ode; *pp.* gesegel-ed, gesegel-od: bærn-an *to burn; p.* bærn-de; *pp.* bærn-ed; met-an *to meet; p.* met-te; *pp.* met, or gemet.

40. *The more complex* and irregular verbs are known by having the perfect tense a monosyllable, ending in the last consonant coming before the infinitive -an, with a change of the vowel, and the perfect participle ending in -en, or -n; as, far-an *to go; p.* fór; *pp.* far-en; sing-an *to sing; p.* sang; *pp.* gesung-en.

* What is generally termed the passive voice has no existence in A.-S. any more than in modern English. The Anglo-Saxons wrote, he is lufod *he is loved.* Here he is, is the *ind. indef. of the neut. verb* wesan, and lufod *loved,* is the *pp.* of the verb lufian *to love.* In parsing, every word should be considered a distinct part of speech: "*to a king,*" is not called a dative case in English, as *regi* in Latin, because the English phrase is not formed by inflection, but by the auxiliary words "*to a.*" If auxiliaries do not form cases in English nouns, why should they be allowed to form various tenses, and a passive voice either in the English, or in its parent the Saxon? Thus, Ic mæg beon lufod *I may be loved,* instead of being called the *potential mood, pass.* mæg is more rationally considered a verb in the *indic. mood, indef. tense,* 1st sing. beon, the neut. verb in the *infin. mood,* after the verb mæg: lufod is the *perf. part.* of the verb lufian.

41. There are four moods—the indicative, imperative, subjunctive, and infinitive, with a sort of second infinitive, and two participles. The infinitive does not admit of a preposition before it, but the second infinitive is always preceded by tó, as tó etanne *to eat;* it seems to be the dative case of the *infin.* etan *to eat,* which is a sort of a noun. With the neuter verb it has a passive signification, or seems to denote a duty. Hit is tó witanne *it is to be known, it must or ought to be known, Elf. Pref. Gen.*

42. There are two tenses—the indefinite and perfect. The indefinite* tense may refer either to the present period or to a future, and thus comprehend what are generally termed the present and future tenses. Ic write *I write now,* or *I write to-morrow.*

43. *The conjugation of a regular verb, or a verb of the simple class,* § 39.

THE PRINCIPAL PARTS.

infinitive.	*perfect.*	*perfect participle.*
bærn-an *to burn,*	bærn-de *burned,*	bærn-ed *burned.*
luf-ian *to love,*	luf-ode *loved,*	luf-od *loved.*

They are thus conjugated :

INDICATIVE.			SUBJUNCTIVE.	
	indefinite.	*perfect.*	*indefinite.*	*perfect.*
	do or shall burn.	*burned or have burned.*	*if I, etc. burn.*	*if I, etc. have burned.*
s.	ic bærn-e	bærn-de	bærn-e	bærn-de
	þu bærn-st	bærn-dest	bærn-e	bærn-de
	he[a] bærn-ð	bærn-de	bærn-e	bærn-de
pl.	we bærn-að[b]	bærn-don	bærn-on[d]	bærn-don
	ge bærn-að[b]	bærn-don	bærn-on[d]	bærn-don
	hi bærn-að[b]	bærn-don	bærn-on[d]	bærn-don.

IMPERATIVE.	INFINITIVE.	PARTICIPLES.	
		indef.	*perf.*
s. bærn þu *burn thou,*	bærn-an *to burn,*		
pl. bærn-að[b]ge *burn ye,*	tó bærn-enne *to burn,*	bærn-ende *burning,*	bærn-ed *burned.*

INDICATIVE.			SUBJUNCTIVE.	
	indefinite.	*perfect.*	*indefinite.*	*perfect.*
	do or shall love.	*loved or have loved.*	*if I, etc. love.*	*if I, etc. have loved.*
s.	ic luf-ige	luf-ode	luf-ige	luf-ode
	þu luf-ast	luf-odest	luf-ige	luf-ode
	he[a] luf-að	luf-ode	luf-ige	luf-ode
pl.	we luf-iað[b]	luf-odon[c]	luf-ion[d]	luf-odon[c]
	ge luf-iað[b]	luf-odon[c]	luf-ion[d]	luf-odon[c]
	hi luf-iað[b]	luf-odon[c]	luf-ion[d]	luf-odon[c].

IMPERATIVE.	INFINITIVE.	PARTICIPLES.	
		indef.	*perf.*
lufa þu *love thou,*	luf-ian *or* -igean *to love,*		
luf-iað[b] ge *love ye,*	tó luf-ienne *or* -igenne *to love,*	luf-iende *loving,*	luf-od *loved.*

[a] Also heo *she,* hit *it*: [b] bærn-e and lufige are used when the pronoun follows the verb, as in asking a question, or commanding: but when the pronoun is omitted, or it precedes the verb -að is used: [c] also, -edon : [d] also, -an.

* The future form is the same as the present, for example: "Hi doð eow of gesomnungum, ac seo tid cymð þæt ælc þe eow ofslyhð, wenð þæt he þenige Gode *they shall put you from the synagogue: and the time shall come that every one who slayeth you, will think that he serveth God.*" St. John xvi. 2.

The words Ic wille, sceal, &c. generally signify *volition, obligation,* and *injunction,* rather than the *property of time.* Sometimes, however, they have some appearance of denoting time.

Remarks on the formation of Moods, Tenses, and Persons.

44. The imperative mood is formed from the infinitive by rejecting the infinitive termination -an, as, bærn-an *to burn,* bærn *burn.* If the consonant be double, after the rejection of the *infin.* an, one consonant is rejected, and *e* added; as, syll-an *to give, sell; imper.* syle *give, sell.* Verbs in -ian, make the *imper.* in -a, as luf-ian *to love,* luf-a *love.*

45. The *p.* tense is formed by changing the infinitive -an, or -ian, into -ode, -ede, or -de; and the *pp.* by changing -an, or -ian, into -od, or -ed: as luf-ian *to love; p.* luf-ode; *pp.* luf-od: segl-ian *to sail; p.* segl-ede; *pp.* segl-ed.

46. Verbs having the consonants *d, f, g, l, m, n, r, s, w,* and ð, before the infinitive termination, often contract the *p.* tense, and have only -de added instead of -ede or -ode; as, betyn-an *to shut,* betyn-de *I shut* or *have shut;* alys-an *to redeem,* alys-de *I redeemed.*

47. Verbs which end in -dan or -tan with a consonant preceding, do not take an additional *d* or *t* in the past tense; as, send-an *to send,* send-e *I sent;* ahred-dan *to liberate,* ahred-de *I liberated;* pliht-an *to plight* or *pledge;* pliht-e *I plighted* or *pledged;* set-tan *to set,* set-te *I set.* Those with *c* or *cc* change the *c* or *cc* into *h* before *t;* as, rec-can *to regard; p.* reh-te *regarded.*

48. When verbs have the letters *t, p, c, h, x,* and *s,* after another consonant before the infinitive -an, they often not only reject the vowel before *d* in the *p.* and *pp.*, but change *d* into *t;* as from dypp-an *to dip,* would be regularly formed dypp-ede, dypp-ed *dipped,* but they are contracted into dypde, dypte, dyppd, dyppt, and dypt *dipped.*

49. *Formation of persons.* The first person singular is formed from the infinitive by changing -an, &c. into -e, and the second into -st, -ast, or -est, and the third into -ð, -að, -eð.

50. In the third person singular, the aspirate ð is changed into the soft *t,* when the infinitive ends in -dan, or -san; as, fed-an *to feed,* fet *he feedeth* or *will feed;* ræs-an *to rush,* ræst *he rusheth:* verbs in -þan or -tan receive no additional ð; as, cyð-an *to tell,* he cyð *he makes known;* hat-an *to name, to call,* hæt *he calls.* Verbs in -dan have the *2nd s.* in -tst; as, send-an *to send,* þu sentst *thou sendest,*—yet sendest is sometimes found.

51. When the infinitive ends in -an with a vowel before it, the plural persons end in -iað; as, hingr-ian *to hunger,* hingr-iað *we, ye, they hunger;* wyr-ian *to curse,* wyr-iað *we, ye, they curse;* but if a consonant go before -an, then they end in -að; as, þyrst-an *to thirst,* þyrstað *we, ye, they thirst.*

52. The plural persons often end in the same manner as the first person singular, especially when the Saxon pronoun is placed after the verb: as, hwæt ete we *what shall we eat?* (See note b to § 43.)

53. If there be a double consonant in the verb, one is always rejected in forming the persons when another follows: as, spillan *to spill,* spilst *spillest,* spilð *spilleth,* spilde *spilled.* Where it would be too harsh to add *st* and ð to the bare root, an *e* is inserted, but only in the indefinite tense; as, nemn-an *to name,* nemn-est *namest,* nemn-eð *nameth:* the perfect is regularly formed, nem-de *named;* and so is the perfect participle, nemn-ed *named.*

54. On all occasions when *e* follows *i,* a *g* is inserted between them; hence, lufie *I love,* becomes lufige *I love;* and lufiende *loving,* becomes lufigende *loving; g* is also often found before an *a* or *ea;* as, sceawigan *or* sceawigean *to shew,* which are the same as sceawian *to shew.*

55. *Complex verbs.* Those verbs which become monosyllables after casting away the infinitive termination, are called complex, because the *perf.* tense is formed by various

or complex modifications or changes of the radical vowel. Though there are only about 188 complex radical verbs, they are divided into many classes, and can hardly be known without giving a complete list. It is not deemed necessary to give them here, as they are all inserted in the Dictionary. For Englishmen, such a list is not absolutely required, as almost all the A.-S. verbs which have been usually called irregular form their *p.* and *pp.* as in English, thus ete, æt, eten *eat, ate, eaten;* gifan, geaf, gifen *give, gave, given;* writan, wrát, writen *write, wrote, written.* The following rules will, however, be useful in forming the *p.* and *pp.* of these verbs.

56. Verbs which become monosyllables after casting away the infinitive termination when the remaining vowel is *a,* often change it into *o,* and occasionally into *eo;* and *ea* generally into *eo,* in the past tense, while the vowel in the *pp.* remains unchanged; as *infin.* stand-an *to stand, p.* stód *stood; pp.* gestanden *stood; infin.* beát-an *to beat; p.* beot *beat; pp.* beáten *beaten.*

57. Verbs which have *e* or *eo* before the letters *ll, lf, lg, lt, rp, rf, rg,* and the like, have *ea*—and in a few cases *æ*—in the past tense, and *o* in the *pp.*, as delft-an *to dig; p.* dealf *dug; pp.* dolfen *dug.*

58. Verbs which have *i* before the double consonants *rn, nn, ng, nc, nd, mb, mp,* &c. often change the *i* into *a* in the past tense, and into *u* in the *pp.*; as, sing-an *to sing; p.* sang *sang; pp.* sungen *sung.* Those which have *i* before a single consonant also changed the *i* into *a* in the perfect tense; the *pp.* is like the infinitive, or in *u;* as, bít-an *to bite; p* bát *bit; pp.* biten *bitten;* nim-an *to take; p.* nam *took; pp* numen *taken.*

59. Verbs, with *ú* or *eó* in the infinitive, have the *p.* in *eá* and the *pp.* in *o;* as, clúf-an *to cleave; p.* cleáf *clove; pp.* clofen; creóp-an *to creep; p.* creáp *crept; pp.* cropen *crept.*

60. *Formation of persons in complex verbs.* The personal terminations are most commonly like those in the simple or more regular verbs; the first vowel in the verb, however, is often changed in the second and third persons of the singular in the indefinite tense; but the plural persons retain the vowel of the first person singular: thus *a* is generally changed to *æ,* and sometimes to *e* or *y;*—*c, ea,* and *u* often become *y,* and sometimes *i:*—*ó* is converted into *é:*—*ú* or *eó* becomes *y.* The other vowels *i* and *y* are not changed. From bac-an *to bake,* we have Ic bace *I bake,* þu bæcst *thou bakest,* he bæcð *he baketh: pl.* we, ge, hi bacað *we, ye, they bake.* From stand-an *to stand,* we also sometimes find Ic stande *I stand,* þu stenst *thou standest,* he stent *he standeth; pl.* we, ge, hi standað *we, ye, they stand.* From et-an *to eat,* we have Ic ete *I eat,* þu ytst *thou eatest,* he yt *he eateth:* we, ge, hi etað *we, ye, they eat.* From sceót-an *to shoot,* are formed Ic sceóte *I shoot,* þu scytst *thou shootest,* he scyt *he shooteth; pl.* we, ge, hi sceotað *we, ye, they shoot.*

61. The same observations which were made on the formation of the third person of simple verbs ending in -dan, -san, -tan, &c. (see § 50), will be applicable here: as, Ic ríde *I ride,* he rít *or* rídeð *he rides;* Ic cweðe *I say,* þu cwyst *thou sayest,* he cwyð *he saith;* Ic ceóse *I choose,* þu cyst *thou choosest,* he cyst *he chooses;* and in et-an *to eat,* as in § 60.

62. The persons in the perfect tense are often formed like regular verbs; but the second person singular more frequently ends in *e:* as, from bacan *to bake,* we have the past tense boc, boce; thus *p. s.* Ic boc *I baked,* þu boce *thou bakedst.* he, &c. boc *he, &c. baked; pl.* we, ge, hi bocon *we, ye, they baked.*

63. Verbs which have *u* or *o* for the first vowel in the *perfect participle,* mostly have *u* in the second person singular, and all the plural persons of the *p.* tense; as in simple verbs, the third person singular is like the first: thus *p. s.* Ic sang *I sang,* þu sunge *thou sangest,* he *or* heo sang *he* or *she sung; pl.* we, ge, hi sungon *we, ye, they sang.*

64. Verbs, having *a* for the first vowel of the *p.* and *i* for the *pp.* make the second person *s.* and all the persons in the *pl.* of the *p.* in *i*; as, arisan *to arise; p.* ic, he, aras *I, he arose,* þu arise *thou arosest;* we, ge, hi arison *we, ye, they arose.*—wrítan *to write; p.* ic, he wrát *I, he wrote;* þu write *thou wrotest;* we, ge, hi writon *we, ye, they wrote.*

65. Verbs of one syllable, terminating in a vowel, have an *h* annexed to them; and those in *g.* generally change the *g* into *h* in all parts of the verb, as well as in the imperative mood; as þwean *to wash; imp.* þweah *wash; p.* þwoh *washed.* Stigan *to rise; p.* stah *rose.*

The conjugation of complex, or more irregular verbs.

wrítan *to write; p.* wrát *wrote; pp.* writen *written.*
standan *to stand; p.* stód *stood; pp.* gestanden *stood.*

INDICATIVE.		SUBJUNCTIVE.	
indefinite.	*perfect.*	*indefinite.*	*perfect.*
I, etc. do or shall write.	*I, etc. wrote.*	*if I, etc. write.*	*if I, etc. wrote.*
s. ic wrít-e	wrát	wrít-e	writ-e
þu wrít-st	writ-e	wrít-e	writ-e
he[c] wrít	wrát	wrít-e	writ-e
pl. we wrít-að[a]	writ-on	wrít-on[d]	writ-on[d]
ge wrít-að[a]	writ-on	wrít-on[d]	writ-on[d]
hi wrít-að[a]	writ-on	wrít-on[d]	writ-on[d].

IMPERATIVE.	INFINITIVE.	PARTICIPLES.
wrít þu *write thou.*	wrít-an *to write.*	*indef.* wrít-ende *writing.*
wrít-e[e] ge *write ye.*	tó writ-anne	*pp.* writ-en *written.*

INDICATIVE.		SUBJUNCTIVE.	
indefinite.	*perfect.*	*indefinite.*	*perfect.*
I, etc. do or shall stand.	*I, etc. stood.*	*if I, etc. stand.*	*if I, etc. stood.*
s. ic stand-e	stód	stand-e	stód-e
þu stenst[b]	stód-e	stand-e	stód-e
he[c] stent[b]	stód	stand-e	stód-e
pl. we stand-að[a]	stód-on	stand-on[d]	stód-on[d]
ge stand-að[a]	stód-on	stand-on[d]	stód-on[d]
hi stand-að[a]	stód-on	stand-on[d]	stód-on[d].

IMPERATIVE.	INFINITIVE.	PARTICIPLES.
stand þu *stand thou.*	stand-an *to stand.*	*indef.* stand-ende *standing.*
stand-e[e] ge *stand ye.*	tó stand-anne.	*pp.* ge-stand-en *stood.*

[a] wrít-e and stand-e are used when a pronoun follows the verb, see § 43, note b.—[b] Also þu stand-est *or* þu stand-st; he stand-eð.—[c] Also heo *she,* hit *it,* as, he, heo, hit stent *he, she, or it stands.*—[d] Also, -en.—[e] When the pronoun is omitted, the termination is -að, as wrít-að *write,* stand-að *stand.* See § 43, note b.

66. The auxiliary verbs wesan *or* beón *to be,* habban *to have,** magan *to be able,* sceal *shall,*† wyllan *to will, wish, &c.* need not be conjugated here, as all these will be found in the Dictionary.

* Habban is used with a *pp.* to express what is called in Latin the preterperfect tense; as, ic hæbbe geset *I have set* or *placed,* posui, for ic sette *I placed* or *have placed.*

† Ic sceal fæstan *I shall fast;* jejunabo: here ic sceal is a verb of the first person *s. indef.* and fæstan is in the *inf.* governed by sceal. See § 37, note (*), and § 42, note (*).

AN ABSTRACT

OF

PROFESSOR RASK'S ANGLO-SAXON GRAMMAR.

1. **Nouns** are divided into two orders. I. The Simple order. II. The Complex order.

2. I. *The Simple order* of nouns contains only words ending in an essential vowel; viz. -a in the *m.* as steorra *a star;* and -e in the *f.* and *n.* as tunge *a tongue,* and eáge *an eye.*

	SINGULAR.			PLURAL.		
	n.	*m.*	*f.*	*n.*	*m.*	*f.*
nom.	eág-e	steorr-a	tung-e	eág-an	steorr-an	tung-an
ac.	eág-e	steorr-an	tung-an	eág-an	steorr-an	tung-an
ab. d.	eág-an	stèorr-an	tung-an	eág-um	steorr-um	tung-um
g.	eág-an	steorr-an	tung-an	eág-ena	steorr-ena	tung-ena.

3. II. *The Complex order* comprehends all words ending in a consonant, and some also in an unessential, -e, (for *i*) or u.

4. *2nd Declension,* 1*st class,* most neuters ending in a consonant; as, leáf *a leaf,* and word *a word.*

s. nom. ac.	leáf	word	*pl.*	leáf	word
ab. d.	leáf-e	word-e		leáf-um	word-um
g.	leáf-es	word-es		leáf-a	word-a.

5. *2nd Declension, 2nd class,* nearly all masculines not ending in -a or u; as, smið *a smith,* ende *an end,* and dæg *a day.*

s. nom. ac.	smið	end-e	dæg	*pl.*	smið-as	end-as	dag-as
ab. d.	smið-e	end-e	dæg-e		smið-um	end-um	dag-um
g.	smið-es	end-es	dæg-es		smið-a	end-a	dag-a.

6. *2nd Declension. 3rd class,* all feminines ending in a consonant; as, wylen *a female slave,* and spræ'c *a speech.*

s. nom.	wylen	spræ'c	*pl.*	wyln-a	spræ'c-a
ac.	wyln-e	spræ'c-e		wyln-a	spræ'c-a
ab. d.	wyln-e	spræ'c-e		wyln-um	spræ'c-um
g.	wyln-e	spræ'c-e		wyln-a	spræ'c-a.

7. *3rd Declension, 1st class,* all neuters in -e (for *i*); as, treow *a tree,* ríce *a kingdom,* and fæt *a vessel.*

s. nom. ac.	treow	ríc-e	fæt	*pl.* treow-u	ríc-u	fat-u
ab. d.	treow-e	ríc-e	fæt-e	treow-um	ríc-um	fat-um
g.	treow-es	ríc-es	fæt-es	treow-a	ríc-a	fat-a.

8. *3rd Declension, 2nd class,* all masculines in -u, which form their *pl.* in -a; also words for kindred in -or; as, sunu *a son,* bróðor *a brother,* man *a man.*

s. nom. ac.	sun-u	bróð-or(er)	man	*pl.* sun-a	bróðr-a(u)	menn
ab. d.	sun-a	bréð-er	men	sun-um	bróðr-um	man-num
g.	sun-a	bróð-or(er)	man-nes	sun-ena	bróðr-a	man-na.

9. *3rd Declension, 3rd class,* all feminines in -u or -o; as, gifu *a gift,* and denu *a den.*

s. nom.	gif-u	den-u	*pl.* gif-a	den-a
ac.	gif-e(u)	den-e(u)	gif-a	den-a
ab. d.	gif-e	den-e	gif-um	den-um
g.	gif-e	den-e	gif-ena	den-ena.

10. For the declension of adjectives, see § 18—27; pronouns, § 28—34; and numerals, § 35 and 36.

11. Verbs are divided into I. the Simple, and II. the Complex order.

12. I. *The Simple order of verbs* contains one conjugation and three classes. In this order the *p.* is more than one syllable, and ends in -de or -te; and the *pp.* in -d or -t.

1st conjugation.

class.	*inf.*	*indf.*	*p.*	*pp.*
1.	luf-ian *to love*	luf-ige	luf-ode	geluf-od
2.	bærn-an *to burn*	bærn-e	bærn-de	bærn-ed
3.	syll-an *to give*	syll-e	seald-de	seald.

1st conjugation, indicative mood.

pres. s.	ic lufige	bærne	sylle
	þu lufast	bærnst	sylst
	he lufað	bærnð	sylð
pl.	we, ge, hi lufiað	bærnað	syllað
	lufige	bærne	sylle
p. s.	ic lufode	bærnde	sealde
	þu lufodest	bærndest	sealdest
	he lufode	bærnde	sealde
pl.	we, ge, hi lufodon(edon)	bærndon	sealdon

subjunctive mood.

pres. s.	ic, þu, he lufige	bærne	sylle
	we, ge, hi lufion(an)	bærnon(an)	syllon
p. s.	ic, þu, he lufode	bærnde	sealde
pl.	we, ge, hi lufodon(edon)	bærndon	sealdon

imperative mood.

s.	lufa þu	bærn	syle
pl.	lufiað ge	bærnað	syllað
	lufige ge	bærne	sylle

INFINITIVE MOOD.

pres. lufian	bærnan	syllan
gerund. (tó)lufigenne	bærnenne	syllanne (enne)

PARTICIPLES.

act. lufigende	bærnende	syllende
pp. (ge)lufod	bærned	seald.

13. *1st Class.** As lufian are also conjugated all verbs in -ian; as, þeowian, *pres.* þeowige, *p.* þeowode, *pp.* geþeowod *to serve*, clypian *to call*, hálgian *to consecrate, hallow*, macian *to make*, eardian *to dwell*, laðian *to invite*, fúlian *to rot*, fullian *to baptize*, wunian *to dwell*, getimbrian *to build*, neósian *to spy*, bletsian *to bless*, ŕicsian *to govern*, gitsian *to desire*, syngian *to sin*, myngian *to admonish*, gehýrsumian *to obey*.

14. *2nd Class.* As bærnan are inflected all verbs derived from nouns, adjectives, and other verbs; as, belæ'wan, *pres.* belæ'we, *p.* belæ'wde, *pp.* belæ'wed *to betray*, adræ'fan *to expel*, wrégan *to accuse*, læ'ran *to instruct*, todæ'lan *to divide*, déman *to deem*, wénan *to imagine, ween*, fyllan *to fell*, drencan, drencean *to give to drink, to drench*, bæ'tan *to bridle*, weccan *to awaken*, alýsan *to redeem*, amyrran *to waste*, métan *to meet*, dyppan *to dip*, nemnan *to name*, grétan *to greet*, scrýdan *to clothe*, ræsan *to rush*, gán *or* gangan *to go*.

15. *3rd Class*, includes those verbs not belonging to the other two classes, and yet having the *p.* of more than one syllable; as, tellan, *pres.* ic telle, *imp.* tele þu, *p.* tealde, *pp.* geteald, stellan *to leap*, cwellan *to kill*, gedwellan *to mislead*, þeccan *to thatch*, reccan *to care about*, secgan *to say*, lecgan *to lay*, bycgan *to buy*, sécan *to seek*, ŕecan *to care for*, wyrcan *to work*, bringan *to bring*, þencan *to think*, þincan *to seem*, habban *to have*, willan *to will*.

16. Anomolous verbs—Ic, he can (þu cunne, canst) *pl.* cunnon, *inf.* cunnan, cuðe, cuðon, *pp.* cuð *know*.—An, ic an *I grant* (þu unne) *pl.* unnon, *inf.* unnan, uðe, uðon *give, bestow*. Also ic gean, we geunnon, geunnan, geuðe, *pp.* geunnen.—Geman, *Jn.* 16, 21, (þu gemanst, *Bt.* p. 118), *pl.* gemunon, gemunan, gemunde, gemundon *remember*.—Sceal (þu scealt), sculon, (sceolon), *pres. sub.* scyle, *imp.* sceolde, sceoldon *shall, should*.—Dear (þu dearst, *Beo.* 42), durron, *sub.* durre, dorste, dorston *dare*.—Þearf (þearft, *Bt.* p. 8, *or* þurfe, *Elf.,gr.* p. 5), þurfon, *subj.* þurfe, þorfte, þorfton *need*. Also beþearf, beþurfon, &c.—Deáh, dugon, *inf.* dugan, dohte, *Bt.* p. 158, *Beo.* 42, þu dohtest, *Deut.* 15, 11, dohton, *Bt.* p. 40, (not dûhte) *help, be good for* (*Icel.* dugi).—Mæg (þu miht, *Jn.* 13, 36), magon (not mâgon), *sub.* mæge (mage), mihte, mihton *or* meahte, meahton *may, might*.—Ah (þu áge), ágon, *sub.* áge, ágan, áhte, áhton *possess, own*. Also the negative náh, *Elf. gr.* 2, he náh, *Jn.* 10, 12, *pl.* nágon, and *sub.* náge, *Wilk. L.* p. 160, náhte, náhtest, náhton *I do not possess*.—Wát, (þu wást), witon, wite, witan, wiste, wiston *supine*, witod *know*. Likewise the negative nát (þu nást), nyton, nyte, nytan, nyste, nystest *or* nestest, *Bt.* 5, 3, nyston.—Mót (þu móst) móton, móte, móste, móston *must*.

17. II. *Complex order* makes the *p.* a monosyllable with a change of vowel, and the *pp.* in -en, or -n; as,

2ND CONJUGATION.				3RD CONJUGATION.			
class. inf.	*pres.*	*p.*	*pp.*	*class. inf.*	*pres.*	*p.*	*pp.*
1. et-an	ete	æt	eten *to eat.*	1. byrn-an	byrne	barn	burnen *to burn.*
2. læt-an	læte	let	læten *to let.*	2. wrít-an	wríte	wrát	writen *to write.*
3. far-an	fare	fór	faren *to go.*	3. sceót-an	sceóte	sceát	scoten *to shoot.*

* This abstract is taken from the English Translation of Mr. Thorpe, 8vo. *Copenhagen*, 1830.

2ND CONJUGATION, INDICATIVE MOOD.

pres.s.	ic ete	læ'te	fare
	þu ytst	læ'tst	færst
	he yt	læ't	færð
pl.	we, ge, hi etað	læ't-að	farað
	or ete	*or* læ'te	*or* fare
p. s.	ic æ't	let	fór
	þu æ'te	lete	fóre
	he æ't	let	fór
pl.	we, ge, hi æton	leton	fóron

SUBJUNCTIVE MOOD.

pres.s.	ic, þu, he ete	læ'te	fare
pl.	we, ge, hi eton	læ'ton	faron

SUBJUNCTIVE MOOD.

p. s.	ic, þu, he æ'te	lete	fóre
pl.	we, ge, hi æ'ton	leton	fóron

IMPERATIVE MOOD.

s.	et þu	læ't	far
pl.	etað ge	læ'tað	farað
	or ete ge	*or* læ'te	*or* fare

INFINITIVE MOOD.

pres.	etan	læ'tan	faran
gerund.	etanne	læ'tanne	faranne

PARTICIPLES.

act.	etende	læ'tende	farende
pp.	eten	læ'ten	faren.

18. *1st Class,* conjugated like etan, contains those verbs which have a long -e or -i before a single characteristic; as, *inf.* sprecan, *pres.* ic sprece, he spricð, *p.* ic spræc, we spræ'con, *pp.* gesprecen *to speak,* wrecan *to revenge,* tredan *to tread,* fretan *to fret,* metan *to measure,* genesan *to recover,* lesan *to gather,* biddan *to bid, beg,* sittan *to sit,* licgan *to lie,* ongitan *to understand,* gifan *to give,* swefan *to sleep,* beran *to bear,* teran *to tear,* sceran *to shear,* acwelan *to perish,* forhelan *to conceal,* stelan *to steal,* niman *to take.*—Irregulars, geseón *to see,* cweðan *to say,* wesan *to be,* beón *to be;* for their formation, see the Dictionary.

19. *2nd Class,* includes verbs which have short *e* and short *eo* in *p.* conjugated like lætan; as, *inf.* hátan, *pres.* he hæ't, *p.* ic het, we heton, *pp.* háten *to command,* healdan, *pres.* he hylt, healt, *p.* ic heold, we heoldon, *pp.* healden, ondræ'dan *to dread,* slápan *to sleep;* hón, *p.* heng, *pp.* hangen *to hang;* onfon *to receive,* fealdan *to fold,* wealdan *to govern,* feallan *to fall,* weallan *to boil,* weaxan *to grow,* sceádan *to divide,* gesceátan, *to fall to,* beátan *to beat,* blótan *to sacrifice,* hleápan *to leap,* swápan *to sweep,* wépan *to weep,* bláwan *to blow,* cnáwan *to know,* cráwan *to crow,* sáwan *to sow,* heawan *to hew,* flówan *to flow,* spówan *to succeed,* grówan *to grow,* rówan *to row.*

20. *3rd Class,* includes verbs which form the perfect in *ó;* as, wacan, *pres.* he wæcð; *p.* ic wóc, we wócon; *pp.* wacen *to arise, awaken,* bacan *to bake,* wiðsacan *to deny,* scacan *to shake,* dragan *to draw,* gnagan *to gnaw,* hlihhan *to laugh,* slean *to slay,* þweân *to wash,* leán *to blame,* wadan *to wade,* hladan *to load,* grafan *to dig,* scafan *to shave,* hebban *to lift,* steppan *to step,* scyppan *to create,* wacsan *to wash,* standan *to stand,* galan *to enchant,* spanan *to allure,* cuman *to come.*

3RD CONJUGATION, INDICATIVE MOOD.

pr.s.	ic byrne	wríte	sceóte
	þu byrnst	wrítst	scýtst
	he byrnð	wrít	scýt
pl.	we, ge, hi byrnað	wrítað	sceótað
	or byrne	*or* wríte	*or* sceóte
p. s.	ic barn	wrát	sceát
	þu burne	write	scute
	he barn	wrát	sceát
pl.	we, ge, hi burnon	writon	scuton

SUBJUNCTIVE MOOD.

pr.s.	ic, þu, he byrne	wríte	sceóte
pl.	we, ge, hi byrnon	wríton	sceóton

SUBJUNCTIVE MOOD.

p. s.	ic, þu, he burne	write	scute
pl.	we, ge, hi burnon	writon	scuton

IMPERATIVE MOOD.

s.	byrn þu	wrít þu	sceót þu
pl.	byrnað ge	wrítað ge	sceótað ge
	or byrne ge	*or* wríte ge	*or* sceóte ge

INFINITIVE MOOD.

pres.	byrnan	wrítan	sceótan
gerund.	byrnanne	wrítanne	sceótanne

PARTICIPLES.

act.	byrnende	wrítende	sceótende
pp.	burnen	writen	scoten.

21. *1st Class,* comprises those verbs which have a short *i* (*y*) before *rn, nn, ng, nc, nd, mb, mp;* a short *a* (*o*) in the *p.* and *u* in the *pp.;* also those with a short *e* or *eo*

before *ll*, *lg*, *lt*, *rp*, *rf*, *rg;* in the *p. ea* (*æ*) short, and *o* in the *pp.*; as, spinnan, *pres.* he spinð; *p.* ic span, we spunnon; *pp.* spunnen; yrnan *to run*, blinnan *to cease*, onginnan *to begin*, winnan *to war*, frinan *or* fregnan *to ask*, singan *to sing*, swingan *to scourge, beat*, springan *to spring*, ofstingan *to sting, stab*, wringan *to wring*, þringan *to throng*, drincan *to drink*, besincan *to sink*, forscrincan *to shrink, wither*, stincan *to stink*, swincan *to toil*, bindan *to bind*, findan *to find*, grindan *to grind*, swindan *to vanish*, windan *to wind*, swimman *to swim*, climban *to climb*, gelimpan *to happen*, swellan *to swell*, belgan *to be wroth*, swelgan *to swallow*, meltan *to melt*, sweltan *to die*, geldan *to pay*, helpan *to help*, gelpan *to boast*, delfan *to delve*, murnan *to mourn*, spurnan *to spurn*, gesweorcan *deficire*, beorgan *to save*, weorpan *to throw*, ceorfan *to cut*, gedeorfan *to suffer*, steorfan *to die*, hweorfan *to return*, berstan *to burst*, þerscan *to thresh*, bredan *to braid*, bregdan *to braid*, feohtan *to fight*.

22. 2*nd Class*, includes all verbs with a hard *i* in the *pres.* and *a* in the *p.*; as, dwinan, *pres.* he dwinð; *p.* ic dwân, we dwinon; *pp.* dwinen *to pine, fade*, hrínan *to touch*, scinan *to shine*, arísan *to arise*, blícan *to shine*, beswícan *to seduce*, hnígan *to sink, bow*, mígan *mingere*, sígan *to fall*, stígan *to ascend*, wrígan *to cover*. bítan *to bite*, flítan *to contend*, slítan *to tear, slit*, smítan *to smite*, gewitan *to depart*, wlitan *to look*, bídan *to stay, bide*, glídan *to glide*, gnídan *to rub*, aslídan *to slide*, grípan *to seize*, toslipan *to dissolve*, belífan *to remain*, slífan *to split*, spiwan *to spit, vomit*.

23. 3*rd Class*, bears a near resemblance to the preceding; as, brúcan, *pres.* he brycð; *p.* ic breác, we brucon; *pp.* brocen *to use*, belúcan *to shut up*, súcan *to suck*, reócan *to reek*, smeócan *to smoke*, gebúgan *to bow*, dreógan *to do*, leógan *to lie*, fleógan, fleon *to fly, flee*, teógan, teon *to draw*, wreón *to cover*, geþeon *to thrive*, lútan *to bow, incline*, geótan *to pour*, fleótan *to float*, hleótan *to obtain; sortiri*, neótan *to enjoy*, þeótan *to howl*, toslúpan *to dissolve*, creópan *to creep*, clúfan *to cleave*, gedúfan *to dive*, scúfan *to shove*, ceówan *to chew*, hreówan *to rue*.

AN ABSTRACT

OF

PROF. GRIMM'S* DECLENSIONS AND CONJUGATIONS.

Strong Masculine Nouns.

1. *1st Decl.* fisc *a fish*; *2nd Decl.* hirde *a shepherd*; *3rd Decl.* sunu *a son*; *4th Decl.* lëóde *people*.

1st.	fisc	*pl.*	fisc-as	*2nd.*	hird-e	*pl.*	hird-as
	fisc-es		fisc-a		hird-es		hird-a
	fisc-e		fisc-um		hird-e		hird-um
	fisc		fisc-as		hird-e		hird-as
3rd.	sun-u		sun-a	*4th.*	——		lëód-e
	sun-a		sun-a		——		lëód-a
	sun-a		sun-um		——		lëód-um
	sun-u		sun-a		——		lëód-e.

Strong Feminine Nouns.

2. *1st Decl.* gifu *a gift*; *2nd Decl.* æðelo *nobility*; *4th Decl.* dæd *a deed.*

1st.	gif-u	*pl.*	gif-a	*2nd.*	æðel-o	*4th.*	dæd	*pl.*	dæd-a
	gif-e		gif-ena		æðel-o		dæd-e		dæd-a
	gif-e		gif-um		æðel-o		dæd-e		dæd-um
	gif-e		gif-a		æðel-o		dæd-e		dæd-a.

Strong Neuter Nouns.

3. *1st Decl.* word *a word*, fæt *a vat*; *2nd Decl.* rìce *a kingdom*.

1st.	word	*pl.*	word	fæt	*pl.*	fat-u	*2nd.*	rìc-e	*pl.*	rìc-u
	word-es		word-a	fæt-es		fat-a		rìc-es		rìc-a
	word-e		word-um	fæt-e		fat-um		rìc-e		rìc-um
	word		word	fæt		fat-u		rìc-e		rìc-u.

* This abstract is taken from the Göttingen edition of 1822, vol. I. p. 638—647 : 732—735 : 895—910.

Weak Nouns.

4. A weak masculine, hana *a cock;* a weak feminine, tunge *a tongue;* a weak neuter, eáre *an ear.*

m. han-a	*pl.* han-an	*f.* tung-e	*pl.* tung-an	*n.* eár-e	*pl.* eár-an
han-an	han-ena	tung-an	tung-ena	eár-an	eár-ena
han-an	han-um	tung-an	tung-um	eár-an	eár-um
han-an	han-an	tung-an	tung-an	eár-e	eár-an.

Adjectives.

5. Declension of strong adjectives.

	m.	*f.*	*n.*		*m.*	*f.*	*n.*
s.	blind	blind(u)	blind	*s.*	hwæt	hwat-u	hwæt
	blind-es	blind-re	blind-es		hwat-es	hwæt-re	hwat-es
	blind-um	blind-re	blind-um		hwat-um	hwæt-re	hwat-um
	blind-ne	blind-e	blind		hwæt-ne	hwat-e	hwæt
pl.	blind-e	blind-e	blind-u	*pl.*	hwat-e	hwat-e	hwat-u
	blind-ra	blind-ra	blind-ra		hwæt-ra	hwæt-ra	hwæt-ra
	blind-um	blind-um	blind-um		hwat-um	hwat-um	hwat-um
	blind-e	blind-e	blind-u		hwat-e	hwat-e	hwat-u.

6. Weak adjectives are declined exactly like the weak nouns, see § 4 in this page, and Definite Adjectives in § 23 and 24 of the Essentials.

7. The pronouns and articles, see Essentials, § 28—31.

Verbs.

8. In strong verbs, there are twelve conjugations;* viz.

		p.	*p. pl.*	*pp.*
1.	Fëalle *cado*	fëol	fëollon	fëallen
2.	Swâpe *verro*	swëop	swëopon	swâpen
3.	Hleápe *salio*	hlëôp	hlëôpon	hleápen
4.	Slæpe *dormio*	slêp	slèpon	slæpen
5.	Blâwe *spiro*	blëôw	blëôwon	blâwen
6.	——	——	——	——
7.	Gale *cano*	gôl	gôlon	galen
8.	Dwine *tabesco*	dwân	dwinon	dwinen
	Gripe *arripio*	grâp	gripon	gripen
9.	Crëópe *repo*	creáp	crupon	cropen
10.	Drëpe *ferio*	dräp	dræpon	drëpen
11.	Cwële *necor*	cwäl	cwælon	cwëlen
12.	Swëlle *tumeo*	swëall	swullon	swollen
	Binde *necto*	band	bundon	bunden.

* In the first edition, Professor Grimm made fourteen conjugations.

9. *Terminations of strong verbs.*

ind. pres. s.	-e	-est	-eð	*sub.* -e	-e	-e
pl.	-að	-að	-að	-en	-en	-en
p. s.	—	-e	—	-e	-e	-e
pl.	-on	-on	-on	-en	-en	-en

imp. s. — *pl.* -að; *inf.* -an; *part. pres.* -ende; *pp.* -en.

10. Bindan *to bind*, and gripan *to gripe.**

ind. pres. s.	bind-e	bind-est	bind-eð	grip-e	grip-est	grip-eð
pl.	bind-að	bind-að	bind-að	grip-að	grip-að	grip-að
p. s.	band	bunde	band	grap	gripe	grap
pl.	bund-on	bund-on	bund-on	grip-on	grip-on	grip-on
sub. pres. s.	bind-e	bind-e	bind-e	grip-e	grip-e	grip-e
pl.	bind-en	bind-en	bind-en	grip-en	grip-en	grip-en
p. s.	bund-e	bund-e	bund-e	grip-e	grip-e	grip-e
	bund-en	bund-en	bund-en	grip-en	grip-en	grip-en.

imp. s. bind, grip; *pl.* bind-að, grip-að; *inf.* bind-an, grip-an; *past. pres.* bind-ende, grip-ende; *pp.* bunden, gripen.

Weak Verbs.

11. There are two conjugations of weak verbs.
Terminations of weak verbs.

ind. pres. s.	-e	-st	-ð	*sub. pres.* -e	-e	-e
pl.	-að	-að	-að	-en	-en	-en
p. s.	-de	-dest	-de	-de	-de	-de
pl.	-don	-don	-don	-den	-den	-den.

imp. s. — *pl.* -ð; *inf.* -an; *part. pres.* -ende; *pp.* -d.

12. First conjugation, nerian *to keep*. 13. Second conjugation, sealfian *to anoint.*

ind. pres. s.	ner-je	ner-ëst	ner-ëð	sëalf-ige	sëalf-ast	sëalf-að
pl.	ner-jað	ner-jað	ner-jað	sëalf-jað	sëalf-jað	sëalf-jað
p. s.	ner-ëde	ner-ëdest	ner-ëde	sëalf-ode	sëalf-odest	sëalf-ode
pl.	ner-ëdon	ner-ëdon	ner-ëdon	sëalf-edon	sëalf-edon	sëalf-edon
sub. pres. s.	ner-je	ner-je	ner-je	sëalf-ige	sëalf-ige	sëalf-ige
pl.	ner-jen	ner-jen	ner-jen	sëalf-jon	sëalf-jon	sëalf-jon
p. s.	ner-ëde	ner-ëde	ner-ëde	sëalf-ode	sëalf-ode	sëalf-ode
pl.	ner-ëden	ner-ëden	ner-ëden	sëalf-eden	sëalf-eden	sëalf-eden.

imp. s. ner-ë; *pl.* ner-jað; *inf.* ner-jan; *part. pres.* ner-jende; *pp.* ner-ëd.

imp. s. sëalfa; *pl.* sëalf-jað; *inf.* sealf-jan; *part. pres.* sëalf-igende; *pp.* gesëalf-od.

The Anomolous Verbs.

14. *Pres. ind. s.* ëom, ëart, is; *pl.* sind, sindon; *sub.* sî, sî, sî, *or* sig, *or* sëó; *pl.* sîn, sîn, sîn; *p.* wäs, wære, wäs; *pl.* wæron; *inf.* wësan; *imp.* wës; *pl.* wësað;

* These examples are from the first edition, 1819.

pres. part. wësende; *pp.* gewësen.—*Future* or *pres.* bëo *or* bëom, bist, bið; *pl.* bëoð; *sub.* bëo; *pl.* bëon; *inf.* bëon; *imp.* bëo; *pl.* bëoð.—Môt, môst, môt; *pl.* môton; *p.* môste.—Wât, wâst, wât; *pl.* witon; *p.* wiste.—Nât *nescio*, nâst, nât; *pl.* nyton; *p.* nyste.—Ah *possideo*, âge? âh; *pl.* âgon; *p.* âhte.—Deáh *prosum*, duge, deáh; *pl.* dugon; *p.* dûhte.—Mäg, mëaht, mäg; *pl.* mâgon; *p.* mëahte.—Scëal, scëalt, scëal; *pl.* sculon; *p.* scëolde.—Gemon memini, *Beo.* 90, *pl.* gemunon; *p.* gemunde. Dëar, dëarst *or* durre, dëar; *pl.* durron; *p.* dorste.—Þëarf, þurfe *or* þëarft? þëarf; *pl.* þurfon; *p.* þorfte.—Can, canst, *or* const, *or* cunne,can; *pl.* cunnon; *p.* cuðe.—An, unne, an; *pl.* unnon; *p.* uðe.—Wille, wilt, wille; *pl.* willað; *p.* wolde.—Nylle *nolo*, nylt, nylle; *pl.* nyllað; *p.* nolde.—Dô, dêst, dêð; *pl.* dôð; *p.* dide, didest, dide; *pl.* didon; *inf.* dôn; *pp.* gedôn.—See Dictionary for gangan *ire*, bûan *habitare, &c.*

ot,
con;
rylon;
cleáh;
scéalt,
inde.
éarl;
e.—
ylle
ide;
&c.

used by

used by

1400

1865

96

Alfc. gl. in Somner p 53–80

a Alfc. Alfric

Alfc. gr. Alfric Gram in Somner Quote

Brun v. A. Brun.

London

Andr Kmb. The Legend of St Andrew edited with an Eng translation by J. M. Kemble M.A. for the Ælfric Society

8vo

l Andr. Grim Andreas und Elene von Jacob Grimm Cassel 1840

z Celt. Celtic

z Chauc. Chaucer

m A Sax or A S Anglo Saxon see O. Sax

Met

(m) Bos. ... Bosworth Gothic v Mt. Bos.

Anglo Saxon Gospels in parallel columns with the version of Wycliffe & Tyndale 4to. & 8vo Smith London 1865

Bt. Fox. Fox's Boethius John ... 1864 ... Bt

Bt. ... Fox King Alfred's Metres of Boethius by Fox

Bt. ... Tupper v Bt. Fox p 263–352

y Camb. Mt. The manuscript of the A Saxon Gospels in the Univ Lib Cambridge marked Ii, 2.11 ...

Bos. Gothic & Anglo Sax Pref. p xlii § II. C

Cod. Dipl. v. Kmbl. Cod Dipl & Th Dipl

EXPLANATION

OF THE

PRINCIPAL CONTRACTIONS.

a. or *act.* stands for active verb.
ab. ablative case.
ac. or *acc.* accusative case.
adj. adjective.
ad calc. ad calcem *at the end.*
Adl. Adelung.
adv. adverb.
Ælf. Ælfredus, v. *Alf.*
Ælf. Ælfricus, v. *Elf.*
Al. Alemannic from which the High Dutch or South German is derived.
Alb. Resp. Albini responsa ad Sigewlfi interrogationes. Bibl. Bodl. Cod. Jun. xxiii. fol.122; xxiv. p. 300: Cod. civ. Bibl. C.C.C. Cant. S. 5, p. 139: S. 17, p. 317, Bibl. Cott. Julius, E. 7, fol. 228.
Alf. or *Ælf.* Alfred, Ælfredus, king of England, A.D. 890.
an. anno *in the year.*
Apol. Apollonius, v. *Th. Apol.*
Arb. or *Arab.* Arabic.
Arm. Armenian.
A.-S. Anglo-Saxon, or Anglo-Saxons.
A.-S.-L. Anglo-Saxon laws.
Asg. bk. The Friesic Asega book.
Asser. Asserius Menevensis, A.D. 900.
Athan. Athanasian Creed.
—— Symb. Athanas. v. Symb.

b. book.
B. v. *Brom.*
Bar. Barrington's Orosius, 8vo. London, 1773, v. *pref.* p. xix. note, number 13.
Bd. Venerable Bede, A.D. 730.
Bd. S. or *Sm.* Bede, by Smith, Camb. fol. 1722, v. *pref.* p. xix. note, number 6.
Bd. W. or *Wh.* Bede, by Wheelock, Cambridge, fol. 1644, v. *pref.* p. xix. note, number 6.
Bel. v. *Fl.* Flemish.
Ben. Benson's vocabularium Anglo-Saxonicum, Oxford, 8vo. 1701, v. *pref.* p. xx. note, number 22.
Beng. Bengalee language.
Beo. Beowulf, by Thorkelin, 4to. Copenhagen, 1815.
Beo. K. —— Kemble, London, 1833, *2nd vol.* 1837, v. *pref.* p. xx. note, number 15.
Bl. Bilderdijk's Geslachtlijst.
Boh. Bohemian.
Box. or *Boxh.* Boxhornii Glos.
Brem. Bremish Dictionary of the Low-German dialect about Bremen, 5 vols. 1767.
Bret. Celto Breton.
Brit. British.
Brock. Brockett's Glossary of North-country words, Newcastle-upon-Tyne, 1825.
Brom. Bromtonus, A.D. 1330.
Bt. Boethius, v. *pref.* p. xix. note, number 11.
Bt. Card. Boethius, Saxon and English, by Cardale, Pickering, 8vo. London, 1829, v. *Bt.*
Bt. F. Fox's Boethius, 8vo. London, 1835, v. *Bt.*
Bt. Rawl. Boethius, by Rawlinson, 8vo. Oxon. 1698, v. *Bt.*

c. chapter.
C. vel. *Cot.* Glossarii Ælfrici exemplar Cottonianum Bibl. Cott. Jul. A. 2.
calc. ad calcem *at the end.*
Cant. Moys. or *Cant. M.* Canticum Moysis, at the end of Thwaites' Heptateuch, v. *pref.* p. xix. note, number 10.
C. v. *Cot.*
Cd. or *Cædm.* Cædmon. The references are to the figures, within brackets, in the body of the page of Junius's edit. and to the figures, within brackets, between the columns of Mr. Thorpe's, v. *pref.* p. xix. note, number 7.
Cd. Jun. Junius's Cædmon, small 4to. Amsterdam, 1655, v. *Cd.*
Cd. Th. Cædmon, by Thorpe, Black & Co. London, 1832, v. *Cd.*
Celt. Celtic.
Charl. Charlemagne.
Chauc. Chaucer.
Chl. Chaldee.
Chr. Anglo-Saxon Chronicle, v. *pref.* p. xix. note, number 9.
Chr. Gib. Gibson's Chronicle, 4to. Oxford, 1692, v. *Chr.*
Chr. Ing. Ingram's Chronicle, 4to. London, 1823, v. *Chr.*
C. Mt. Mk. &c. the Gospels of Matthew, Mark, &c. in the Pub. Lib. Cambridge, Wanley's Catalogue, p. 152.
Cod. Ex. Exeter MS. v. Wanley's Catalogue, p. 279, but especially Conybeare's illustration of A.-S. poetry, p. 9 and 189.
Coll. Mon. or *Coll. Monast.* Colloquium Monachicum; Mr. Thorpe's Analecta, p. 101, Wanley, p. 95 and 193.
comp. comparative degree.

Conyb. Conybeare's Illustrations of A.-S. Poetry, 8vo. London, 1826, v. *pref.* p. xx. note, number 16.
conj. conjunction.
Corn. Cornish.
Cop. Coptic.
Cot. Glossarii Ælfrici exemplar Cottonianum Bibl. Cott. Jul. A. 2. British Museum.
C. Ps. Cantabrigiense Psalterium: the Saxon psalms in the Public Library at Cambridge, Wanley's Cat. p. 152.
C. R. Ben. Cantabrigiensis Regula Benedicti, Bibl. C.C.C. Cant. S. 6, p. 263.

D. Vocabularium Dewesianum, scilicet a Joh. Jocelino digestum, a Sim. D'Ewes autem Barto. descriptum, Bibl. Cott. Tit. A. 15, 16.
d. or *dat.* dative case.
Dan. Danish.
def. the definite declension.
Deut. Deuteronomy, v. *Gen.*
Dial. Gregory's Dialogues, translated into A.-S. by King Alfred, v. *Wanl.* p. 71, 92, 99, 130, 212.
Doug. or *Doug. Virg.* The translation of Virgil into Scottish metre, by Gawin Douglas, Bp. of Dunkeld, born 1474, died 1521.
Dun. the historian Sim. Dunelmensis, A.D. 1164.
Dut. Dutch.

E. v. Ethel.
Elf. Elfric, an *Abbot*, and afterwards Archbishop of Canterbury, died A.D. 1005. The great luminary of his age. He translated the Scriptures into A.-S., also Sermons, Grammar, &c., v. *pref.* p. xviii. note, numbers 1, 4, 8, and 10.
Elf. Can. Elfric's Canons, *Wilk.* p. 153, v. *L. Can. Eccl.*
Elf. ep. Elfric's Epistles, v. *Wilk.* p. 161.
Elf. gr. or *gl.* or *Elf. gr. Som.* Elfric's Grammar or Glossary at the end of Somner's Dictionary, *Elf. gr.* 9, 26, is chapter 9, and xxvi. in the body of the page, v. *pref.* p. xix. note, number 8.
Elf. T. Elfric concerning the Old and New Testament, v. *pref.* p. xviii. note, number 1.
Els. Elstob (Miss) Homily of St. Gregory. The portraits of Miss E. and the Pope are beautifully engraved in the initial letters of the Homily, v. *pref.* p. xix. note, number 12.
Em. l. The Friesic Emsiger Landregt, or code of the country of Ems, A.D. 1276.
ep. Epist. Epistle.
etc. et cætera.
Ethel. the Latin writer Ethelredus, Abbas Rievallis, A.D. 1166.
Ethelw. the Latin writer Ethelwerdus, A.D. 977.
Ex. Exodus, v. *Gen.*

f. Feminine, or, of the feminine gender.
F. v. *Flor.*
Fin. Finlandish.
Fl. Flemish, or Belgic.
fl. fluvius.
Flor. Florentius, a Latin Historian, A.D. 1117.
Fr. French.
Franc. Francic.
Fr. Jud. Fragmentum libri Judithæ, at the end of Thwaites' Heptateuch, v. *Jdth.*
Frs. Friesic from Hettema,—with *H.* from Halbertsma.
Frs. c. Friesic of the cities.
Frs. h. Friesic of Hindelopen.
Frs. l. Old Friesic laws, by Wierdsma.
Frs. v. Friesic of the villages, or Country Friesic.

g. or *gen.* genitive case.
Gael. Gaelic, the language of the highlands of Scotland.
Gen. Genesis, from Thwaite's Heptateuch, 8vo. Oxon. 1698, v. *Thw.*
Ger. German.
Gerv. the Latin writer Gervasius, A.D. 1200.
Gib. Gibson's Saxon Chronicle, v. *Chr.*
gl. or *glos.* glossary.
Gm. I. II. or III. Deutsche Grammatik von Dr. Jacob Grimm, 3 vols. 8vo. Göttingen, 1822, 1826, 1831: references are to vol., page, and line.
Gm. Myth. Deutsche Mythologie, von Jacob Grimm, 8vo. Göttingen, 1835.
Gm. Recht. Deutsche Rechtsalterhümer, von Jacob Grimm, Göttingen, 8vo. 1828.
Gr. Dial. or *Greg.* Gregorii Papæ Dialogi, Saxonicè redditi à Werfertho episcopo Wigorniensi. Bibl. Bodl. Hatt. 100: 1, Coll. C. C. Cant. S. 10: Cott. Otho, C. 1, fol. 136, v. Wanley, p. 70, 92, 114, 153, 168, 217, &c. v. *Dial.*
Greg. v. *Gr. Dial.*
Grk. Greek.
Gr. Proœm. Gregorii Papæ Proœmium, Preface to Gregory's Pastoral Care in A.-S. v. Wanley, p. 153.
Guth. Guthlaci monachi vita et miracula. Bibl. Cott. Vesp. D. 21.

H. Halbertsma, a writer on the Friesic language.
Hag. the Latin writer Hagustaldensis Prior, Joannes, A.D. 1180.
Heb. Hebrew.
Hem. or *Heming.* Heming's Chartulary; Hemingi Chartularium Eccl. Wigorniensis, edidit T. Hearn, 8vo. Oxon. 1723, tom. ii.
Herb. Herbarium, scilicet L. Apuleii Madaurensis, Saxonicè redditum. Bibl. Bodl. Hatt. 100: Jun. 58: Bibl. Cott. Vitellius, C. 3, fol. 19. In Wan. p. 73—75; 176—180, are the A.-S. names of plants, and A.-S. extracts, v. *L. M.*
Het. Hettema's Friesic Dictionary, with explanations in Dutch, 8vo. Leeuwarden, 1832.
Hexaëm. Hexaëmeron: *i. e.* Homilia Saxonica de Dei opere sex diebus exacto, Bibl. Bodl. Jun. 23: Wanley, p. 36; Wanley, p. 40, item 47: C. C. C. Cant. S. 6, p. 16: S. 17, p. 1: Cott. Otho, B. 10, fol. 8.
Hic. or *Hick.* Hickes' Thesaurus, London, 3 vols. fol. 1705, v. *pref.* p. xx. note, number 21.
Hind. Hindoo, Hindostanne.
H. Mt. Mk. &c. Evangeliorum secundum Matth. Marc. &c. exemplar Hattonianum. Bibl. Bodl. Hatt. 65: Wanley, p. 76.
Hom. homily.
Hom. Greg. the Homily of St. Gregory, v. *Els.*
Hovd. the Latin writer Hovdenus, A.D. 1204.
Hun. Hungarian.
Hun. the Latin writer, Henr. Huntingdoniensis, A.D. 1148.
Hymn. Hymnarium, Bibl. Cott. Jul. A. 6.

ib. ibidem, the same.
Icl. or *Icel.* Icelandic.
id. idem, the same.
i. e. id est, that is.
imp. imperative.
imprs. impersonal.
ind. indicative mood.
indecl. indeclinable.

CCIV a

18 Grm.

Ex. Exodus Exod Grein
E Exon. Codex Exoniensis
Copy Thorpe

Grm, Grin
James Grimm
v. Grm.

Grm. Grein's Bible: Angelsach. of
Copy Title

h Cri. Cynewulfs Crist v. Grm.

v Al. Fox

n Der. Derivatives, or words derived from the subject of the article

Al. Fox's Boethius, small 8vo Bohn 1864.
F.Al. Met. The Metres of Alfred's Boethius in Mr Fox's edn. with a free metrical translation by Martin F. Tupper Esqr D.C.L. p 263–352

Fr. French

Frs Japa the Fragment of the Book Japick AD 1650

n v. OFrs.

n Elen Grm. Andreas und Elene von Jacob Grimm, Cassel 1840

Aelfc v. Alfc.

Ger. New High German. v. Nhg.

Grm, Grin

Heyn Gr. Kurze Grammatik der Altgermanischen Sprachstämme Goth: OHGer: OSax ASax. OFrs: ONrs. von Moritz Heyne Paderborn 1862

Gr. Grammar v. Heyn Gr.

Goth. Gothic often called Moeso Gothic, from their residing in Moesia south west of the Black Sea

Hrn Thomas Hearne born 1678 d 1735 ... Esq. A ... Glossary & Peter Langtoft's Chronicle 1724

Grg, Greg. Dial. Gregorii Dialogues
Grg. Past. Gregorii Pastoral Care
Copy from Bosh. ccvi

Lind the Lindisfarne or Northumbrian Gospel ~~Edited by~~ St. Matthew Edited by the Rev Joseph Stevenson for the Surtees Society 8vo 1854. St Mk. Lk & Jn by Geo Waring Esqr in 1861, 1863, & 1866

Ex E

g Itl. It Italian

n ~~Jpn~~ Jap. or ~~Jpn~~ Japa
d v Frs. Japa.

π Lith. Lithuanian the
~~Language of~~

of origin

Dict. D

n Jn Bos. v Mt Bos.
Jn Boutr. v Mt. Boutr.

p Jul. Grn Bibliothek Angelsachsischen Poesie, Göttingen 8vo. 1858

Kmbl. Cod. Dipl.
Copy Title

q Kmbl Kemble v
Andr. Kmb: Mt. Kmble
Kmbl Sax. Eng. ~~Hosl~~ The Saxons in England. A History of the English Commonwealth till the Norman conquest by Jn. Mitchell Kemble M.A. 2 vols 8vo Longman & Co. London 1849.

For Met. & Dutr.

x M Dut. Middle Dutch or
x Met. The Metrum or Metres of Boethius
Mhger. Middle High German
w Mhg. Middle High German

Mlhger or Mlg. Middle Low German, the Plat or Low German of the Low or northern part of Germany

w Laym. = Layamons Brut by Madden Copy Title

y Lat. Latin

indf. or *indef.* indefinite tense, present and future tenses.
inf. infinitive.
Ing. Ingram, v. *Chr. Ing.*
Ing. Lect. Ingram's A.-S. Lecture, 4to. Oxford, 1807.
Ing. or *Ingul.* the Latin writer Ingulphus, A. D. 1109.
Ingul. Contin. Ingulphi Continuatores, A. D. 1486.
interjec. interjection.
Ir. Irish.
irr. irregular.
Isd. Isidore de Nativitate, translated into Francic, about A. D. 800.
It. Italian.

Jap. Gysbert Japicx, a Friesian poet who wrote about A. D. 1650.
Jdth. or *Fr. Jud.* Judith, a fragment of an A.-S. poem, printed as prose at the end of Thwaites's Heptateuch, but very properly as poetry in Mr. Thorpe's Analecta, p. 131, v. *Thw.*
Jn. 1, 3: 7, 6, 8. St. John's Gospel, by Junius and Marshall, 4to. Dordrecht, 1665, v. *pref.* p. xviii. note, number 3, 1st chap. 3rd verse: 7th chap. the 6th and 8th verse.
Job. v. *Gen.*
Jos. Joshua, v. *Gen.*
Jud. Judges, v. *Gen.*
Jun. Junius.

Ker. Kero an Alemannic or High-German writer about A. D. 800.
Kil. Kilian, the compiler of a Dutch Dictionary, with Latin explanations. 4to. Antwerp, 1599: Utrecht, 1777.
Kni. the Latin writer Knighton, A. D. 1395.

l. line.
L. Anglo-Saxon Laws, by Wilkins, fol. Lond. 1721, v. *pref.* p. xviii. note, number 2.
L. Ænh. the Concilium Ænhamense in Wilkins's Anglo-Saxon Laws, p. 119.
L. Alf. Leges Ælfredi, *W.* p. 28.
L. Alf. Guth. Leges Ælfredi et Guthruni, *W.* p. 47.
L. Alf. pol. The second division of King Alfred's Laws, *W.* p. 34.
L. Athel. Leges Æthelstani, *W.* p. 54.
L. Can. Eccl. and *L. Elf. Can.* Liber Canonum Ecclesiasticorum, *W.* p. 153.
L. Can. Edg. Canones editi sub Eadgaro rege, *W.* p. 82.
L. Can. Edg. conf. Canones editi sub Eadgaro rege de confessione, *W.* p. 87.
L. Can. Edg. pen. or *pœn.* —— modus imponendi pœnitentiam, *W.* p. 89.
L. Can. Edg. pen. or *pœn. magn.* —— de magnatibus, *W.* p. 96.
L. Can. Edg. pol. or *Pol.* the first division of King Edgar's laws, *W.* p. 76.
L. Cnut. or *L. Cnut. Eccl.* Leges Cnuti regis, *W.* p. 126.
L. Cnut. pol. the second division of Canute's laws, *W.* p. 133.
L. Const. Liber Constitutionum, *W.* p. 147.
L. Const. Ethel. Liber Constitutionum tempore regis Æthelredi, *W.* p. 106.
L. Eccl. Liber legum Ecclesiasticarum, *W.* p. 173.
L. Edg. Leges Eadgari, p. 76.
L. Edg. pol. the first division of King Edgar's laws, *W.* p. 76.
L. Edg. sup. Legum Eadgari supplementum, *W.* p. 79.
L. Edm. Leges Edmundi regis, *W.* p. 72.
L. Edw. Leges Eadweardi, *W.* p. 48.
L. Edw. Guth. Fœdus Eadweardi et Guthruni regum, *W.* p. 51.
L. Elf. Can. Liber Ælfrici Canonum, *W.* p. 153, v. *L. Can. Eccl.*
L. Elf. ep. Ælfrici Epistolæ, *W.* p. 161.
L. Ethel. Leges Æthelredi, *W.* p. 102.
L. Ethel. Anlaf. or *Anl.* Leges Æthelredi cum Anlavo, *W.* p. 104.
L. Ethelb. Leges Æthelbirhti, *W.* p. 1: *Th.*
L. Hloth. Leges Hlotharii et Eadrici, *W.* p. 7.
L. In. Leges Inæ, *W.* p. 14.
L. Lond. or *Lund.* Judicia Civitatis Lundoniæ, *W.* p. 65.
L. North. pres. Northumbrensium presbyterorum leges, *W.* p. 98.
L. Wal. Senatus Consultum de Monticolis Walliæ, *W.* p. 125.
L. Wiht. Leges Wihtrædi, *W.* p. 10.
Lamb. Lambard's Anglo-Saxon laws, v. *L.*
Lanc. Lancashire.
Lap. Laplandish.
Lat. mid. Latin of the middle and later age.
Lett. Lettish.
Lev. Leviticus, v. *Gen.*
Lin. Linnæus.
Lip. Lipsius's Glossary, Opera Omnia Versal. 4 vols. 8vo. vol. ii. p. 988.
Lk. St. Luke's Gospel, v. *Jn.*
L.M. Liber Medicinalis, v. *Herb.* a Baldo quodam, ex scriptis Marcelli, Scribonii Largi, C. Plinii, aliorumque Medicorum Latinorum, uti censet Wanleius, compilatus, Bibl. D. Jac. Westm. v. the Titles of Chapters in A.-S. and quotations in Wanley's Cat. 176—180, 72.
L. Lambeth Psalter. v. *Lps.* and *M. Ps.*
Lps. or *L. Ps.* Lambeth Psalter, Bibl. Lambeth, 4to. 188, Art. 5.
Lup. Lupus's Sermons, in Hickes's Thes. vol. ii. p. 99. Reference to sections and lines of sections.

m. mas. masculine, or, of the masculine gender.
M.A. Monasticon Anglicanum.
Malm. Will. Malmesburiensis, A. D. 1140.
Mann. Manning's edition of Lye's A.-S. Dict. particularly the Supplement: 2 vols. fol. v. *pref.* p. xx. note, number 22.
Mart. Martinii Lexicon philologicum, 2 vols. fol. 1711.
Martyr. Mart. or *Menol.* Martyrologium, sive potius Menologium seu Calendarium poeticum, or The poetical calendar of the Anglo-Saxons, Hickes's Thes. I. p. 203, Fox, 8vo. London, 1830, v. *pref* p. xx. note, number 17.
Med. ex Quadr. Medicina ex quadrupedibus, Bibl. Bodl. Hatt. 100, Art. 4, Jun. 58, Art. 2, Bibl. Cott. Vitell. C. 3, fol. 75: Wanley, p. 75.
Menol. the Menology, v. *Martyr.*
Menol. F. Fox, v. *Martyr.*
Mk. Mark, v. *Jn.*
Moes. Moeso-Gothic, the earliest High-German dialect yet known, preserved in the Gospels, &c. A. D. 370, v. *Jn.*
Mone. Mone's Quellen und Forschungen zur Geschichte der teutschen Literatur und Sprache, 8vo. Leipzig, 1830.
Mone. A. —— the Glossary (in p. 314) of natural history. The MS. is of the 10th century, and is in the Jesuits' Library at Brussels, in 4to. No. 539.

Conyb. Conybeare's Illustrations of A.-S. Poetry, 8vo. London, 1826, v. *pref.* p. xx. note, number 16.
conj. conjunction.
Corn. Cornish.
Cop. Coptic.
Cot. Glossarii Ælfrici exemplar Cottonianum Bibl. Cott. Jul. A. 2. British Museum.
C. Ps. Cantabrigiense Psalterium: the Saxon psalms in the Public Library at Cambridge, Wanley's Cat. p. 152.
C. R. Ben. Cantabrigiensis Regula Benedicti, Bibl. C.C.C. Cant. S. 6, p. 263.

D. Vocabularium Dewesianum, scilicet a Joh. Jocelino digestum, a Sim. D'Ewes autem Barto. descriptum, Bibl. Cott. Tit. A. 15, 16.
d. or *dat.* dative case.
Dan. Danish.
def. the definite declension.
Deut. Deuteronomy, v. *Gen.*
Dial. Gregory's Dialogues, translated into A.-S. by King Alfred, v. *Wanl.* p. 71, 92, 99, 130, 212.
Doug. or *Doug. Virg.* The translation of Virgil into Scottish metre, by Gawin Douglas, Bp. of Dunkeld, born 1474, died 1521.
Dun. the historian Sim. Dunelmensis, A.D. 1164.
Dut. Dutch.

E. v. Ethel.
Elf. Elfric, an *Abbot*, and afterwards Archbishop of Canterbury, died A.D. 1005. The great luminary of his age. He translated the Scriptures into A.-S., also Sermons, Grammar, &c., v. *pref.* p. xviii. note, numbers 1, 4, 8, and 10.
Elf. Can. Elfric's Canons, *Wilk.* p. 153, v. *L. Can. Eccl.*
Elf. ep. Elfric's Epistles, v. *Wilk.* p. 161.
Elf. gr. or *gl.* or *Elf. gr. Som.* Elfric's Grammar or Glossary at the end of Somner's Dictionary, *Elf. gr.* 9, 26, is chapter 9, and xxvi. in the body of the page, v. *pref.* p. xix. note, number 8.
Elf. T. Elfric concerning the Old and New Testament, v. *pref.* p. xviii. note, number 1.
Els. Elstob (Miss) Homily of St. Gregory. The portraits of Miss E. and the Pope are beautifully engraved in the initial letters of the Homily, v. *pref.* p. xix. note, number 12.
Em. l. The Friesic Emsiger Landregt, or code of the country of Ems, A.D. 1276.
ep. Epist. Epistle.
etc. et cætera.
Ethel. the Latin writer Ethelredus, Abbas Rievallis, A.D. 1166.
Ethelw. the Latin writer Ethelwerdus, A.D. 977.
Ex. Exodus, v. *Gen.*

f. Feminine, or, of the feminine gender.
F. v. *Flor.*
Fin. Finlandish.
Fl. Flemish, or Belgic.
fl. fluvius.
Flor. Florentius, a Latin Historian, A.D. 1117.
Fr. French.
Franc. Francic.
Fr. Jud. Fragmentum libri Judithæ, at the end of Thwaites' Heptateuch, v. *Jdth.*
Frs. Friesic from Hettema,—with *H.* from Halbertsma.
Frs. c. Friesic of the cities.
Frs. h. Friesic of Hindelopen.
Frs. l. Old Friesic laws, by Wierdsma.
Frs. v. Friesic of the villages, or Country Friesic.

g. or *gen.* genitive case.
Gael. Gaelic, the language of the highlands of Scotland.
Gen. Genesis, from Thwaite's Heptateuch, 8vo. Oxon. 1698, v. *Thw.*
Ger. German.
Gerv. the Latin writer Gervasius, A.D. 1200.
Gib. Gibson's Saxon Chronicle, v. *Chr.*
gl. or *glos.* glossary.
Gm. I. II. or III. Deutsche Grammatik von Dr. Jacob Grimm, 3 vols. 8vo. Göttingen, 1822, 1826, 1831: references are to vol., page, and line.
Gm. Myth. Deutsche Mythologie, von Jacob Grimm, 8vo. Göttingen, 1835.
Gm. Recht. Deutsche Rechtsalterhümer, von Jacob Grimm, Göttingen, 8vo. 1828.
Gr. Dial. or *Greg.* Gregorii Papæ Dialogi, Saxonicè redditi à Werfertho episcopo Wigorniensi. Bibl. Bodl. Hatt. 100; 1, Coll. C. C. Cant. S. 10: Cott. Otho, C. 1, fol. 136, v. Wanley, p. 70, 92, 114, 153, 168, 217, &c. v. *Dial.*
Greg. v. *Gr. Dial.*
Grk. Greek.
Gr. Proœm. Gregorii Papæ Proœmium, Preface to Gregory's Pastoral Care in A.-S. v. Wanley, p. 153.
Guth. Guthlaci monachi vita et miracula. Bibl. Cott. Vesp. D. 21.

H. Halbertsma, a writer on the Friesic language.
Hag. the Latin writer Hagustaldensis Prior, Joannes, A.D. 1180.
Heb. Hebrew.
Hem. or *Heming.* Heming's Chartulary; Hemingi Chartularium Eccl. Wigorniensis, edidit T. Hearn, 8vo. Oxon. 1723, tom. ii.
Herb. Herbarium, scilicet L. Apuleii Madaurensis, Saxonicè redditum. Bibl. Bodl. Hatt. 100: Jun. 58: Bibl. Cott. Vitellius, C. 3, fol. 19. In Wan. p. 73—75; 176—180, are the A.-S. names of plants, and A.-S. extracts, v. *L. M.*
Het. Hettema's Friesic Dictionary, with explanations in Dutch, 8vo. Leeuwarden, 1832.
Hexaëm. Hexaëmeron: *i.e.* Homilia Saxonica de Dei opere sex diebus exacto, Bibl. Bodl. Jun. 23: Wanley, p. 36; Wanley, p. 40, item 47: C. C. C. Cant. S. 6, p. 16: S. 17, p. 1: Cott. Otho, B. 10, fol. 8.
Hic. or *Hick.* Hickes' Thesaurus, London, 3 vols. fol. 1705, v. *pref.* p. xx. note, number 21.
Hind. Hindoo, Hindostanne.
H. Mt. Mk. &c. Evangeliorum secundum Matth. Marc. &c. exemplar Hattonianum. Bibl. Bodl. Hatt. 65: Wanley, p. 76.
Hom. homily.
Hom. Greg. the Homily of St. Gregory, v. *Els.*
Hovd. the Latin writer Hovdenus, A.D. 1204.
Hun. Hungarian.
Hun. the Latin writer, Henr. Huntingdoniensis, A.D. 1148.
Hymn. Hymnarium, Bibl. Cott. Jul. A. 6.

ib. ibidem, the same.
Icl. or *Icel.* Icelandic.
id. idem, the same.
i. e. id est, that is.
imp. imperative.
imprs. impersonal.
ind. indicative mood.
indecl. indeclinable.

Grm.

Ex. Exodus. Exod. Grein. Exon. Codex Exoniensis. Copy Thorpe

Grm, Grim. James Grimm &c. v Grm.

Grn. Grein's Bibl. Angelsach. [illegible] Copy Title

Cri. Cynewulf's Crist v. Grn.

v Bt. Fox

Bt. Fox's Boethius, small 8vo. Bohn. London 1864.

Fox. Met. The Metres of Alfred's Boethius in Mr Fox's ed: with a free metrical translation by Martin F. Tupper Esqr D.C.L. p. 263–352

Der. Derivatives, or words derived from [illegible]

Fr. French

Frs. Japx. The Friesian [illegible] of Gysbert Japick AD 1650

v. O.Frs.

Elen. Grm. Andreas und Elene von Jacob Grimm, Cassel 1840, 8vo.

Ger. New High German. v. Adler

Elfc. v Alfc.

v Grm, Grim

Heyn. Gr. Kurze Grammatik der altgermanischen Sprachstämme. Goth: O.H.Ger: O.Sax. A.Sax. O.Frs: O.Nrs. von Moritz Heyne Paderborn 1862

Gr. Grammar v Heyn. Gr.

Goth. Gothic often called Moeso Gothic from their residence in Moesia south west of the Black Sea

Hrn. Thomas Hearne born 1678 [illegible] 1735 [illegible] Esqr B [illegible]

Grg. Greg. Dial. Gregorij Dialogus [illegible]

Grg. Past. Gregorij Pastoral Care Copy from Past. ccvi

Ex

Dict. 2

[illegible]

[illegible]

r.

ndr

War.

War

[illegible]

und War

Ex:

g Itl. = Italian

u ~~Jpn~~ Jap. or ~~Jpn~~ Japa

d v Frs. Japa.

† Dict.: u Ju Bos. v Mt Bos.

Ju Boutr. v Mt. Boutr.

ρ Jul. Grein Bibliothek Angelsachsischen Poesie, Göttingen 8vo. 1858

Kmbl. Cod. Dipl. Copy Title

q Kmbl Kemble — v Andr. Kmb: Mt, Kmble

Kmbl Sax. Eng. ~~Hand~~ The Saxons in England a History of the English commonwealth till the Norman conquest by Jn. Mitchell Kemble M.A. 2 vols 8vo Longman & Co London 1849.

w Laym = Layamons y Lat. Latin

Brut by Madden

Copy Title

s Lind The Lindisfarne or Northumbrian Gospel ~~Edited by~~ St. Matthew Edited by the Revd Joseph Stevenson for the Surtees Society 8vo 1854: St Mk. Lk & Jn by Geo Waring Esqr in 1861, 1863, & 1866

π Lith. Lithuanian the ~~language of~~

of origin

(For Mat. & Dictr)

x { M Dutch ~~Middle~~ Middle Dutch or Hollandish

{ Mat. The ~~Metrum~~ Archives & Metre of

} Mger. Middle High German

w { Mhg. Middle high German

Mdlger or Mdlg. Middle Low German, the Plat or Low German of the Low or northern part of Germany

indf. or *indef.* indefinite tense, present and future tenses.
inf. infinitive.
Ing. Ingram, v. *Chr. Ing.*
Ing. Lect. Ingram's A.-S. Lecture, 4to. Oxford, 1807.
Ing. or *Ingul.* the Latin writer Ingulphus, A. D. 1109.
Ingul. Contin. Ingulphi Continuatores, A. D. 1486.
interjec. interjection.
Ir. Irish.
irr. irregular.
Isd. Isidore de Nativitate, translated into Francic, about A. D. 800.
It. Italian.

Jap. Gysbert Japicx, a Friesian poet who wrote about A. D. 1650.
Jdth. or *Fr. Jud.* Judith, a fragment of an A.-S. poem, printed as prose at the end of Thwaites's Heptateuch, but very properly as poetry in Mr. Thorpe's Analecta, p. 131, v. *Thw.*
Jn. 1, 3: 7, 6, 8. St. John's Gospel, by Junius and Marshall, 4to. Dordrecht, 1665, v. *pref.* p. xviii. note, number 3, 1st chap. 3rd verse: 7th chap. the 6th and 8th verse.
Job. v. *Gen.*
Jos. Joshua, v. *Gen.*
Jud. Judges, v. *Gen.*
Jun. Junius.

Ker. Kero an Alemannic or High-German writer about A. D. 800.
Kil. Kilian, the compiler of a Dutch Dictionary, with Latin explanations. 4to. Antwerp, 1599: Utrecht, 1777.
Kni. the Latin writer Knighton, A. D. 1395.

l. line.
L. Anglo-Saxon Laws, by Wilkins, fol. Lond. 1721, v. *pref.* p. xviii. note, number 2.
L. Ænh. the Concilium Ænhamense in Wilkins's Anglo-Saxon Laws, p. 119.
L. Alf. Leges Ælfredi, *W.* p. 28.
L. Alf. Guth. Leges Ælfredi et Guthruni, *W.* p. 47.
L. Alf. pol. The second division of King Alfred's Laws, *W.* p. 34.
L. Athel. Leges Æthelstani, *W.* p. 54.
L. Can. Ecc. and *L. Elf. Can.* Liber Canonum Ecclesiasticorum, *W.* p. 153.
L. Can. Edg. Canones editi sub Eadgaro rege, *W.* p. 82.
L. Can. Edg. conf. Canones editi sub Eadgaro rege de confessione, *W.* p. 87.
L. Can. Edg. pen. or *pœn.* —— modus imponendi pœnitentiam, *W.* p. 89.
L. Can. Edg. pen. or *pœn. magn.* —— de magnatibus, *W.* p. 96.
L. Can. Edg. pol. or *Pol.* the first division of King Edgar's laws, *W.* p. 76.
L. Cnut. or *L. Cnut. Eccl.* Leges Cnuti regis, *W.* p. 126.
L. Cnut. pol. the second division of Canute's laws, *W.* p. 133.
L. Const. Liber Constitutionum, *W.* p 147.
L. Const. Ethel. Liber Constitutionum tempore regis Æthelredi, *W.* p. 106.
L. Eccl. Liber legum Ecclesiasticarum, *W.* p. 173.
L. Edg. Leges Eadgari, p. 76.
L. Edg. pol. the first division of King Edgar's laws, *W.* p. 76.
L. Edg. sup. Legum Eadgari supplementum, *W.* p. 79.
L. Edm. Leges Edmundi regis, *W.* p. 72.
L. Edw. Leges Eadweardi, *W.* p. 48.
L. Edw. Guth. Fœdus Eadweardi et Guthruni regum, *W.* p. 51.
L. Elf. Can. Liber Ælfrici Canonum, *W.* p. 153, v. *L. Can. Eccl.*
L. Elf. ep. Ælfrici Epistolæ, *W.* p. 161.
L. Ethel. Leges Æthelredi, *W.* p. 102.
L. Ethel. Anlaf. or *Anl.* Leges Æthelredi cum Anlavo, *W.* p. 104.
L. Ethelb. Leges Æthelbirhti, *W.* p. 1.
L. Hloth. Leges Hlotharii et Eadrici, *W.* p. 7.
L. In. Leges Inæ, *W.* p. 14.
L. Lond. or *Lund.* Judicia Civitatis Lundoniæ, *W.* p. 65.
L. North. pres. Northumbrensium presbyterorum leges, *W.* p. 98.
L. Wal. Senatus Consultum de Monticolis Walliæ, *W.* p. 125.
L. Wiht. Leges Wihtrædi, *W.* p. 10.
Lamb. Lambard's Anglo-Saxon laws, v. *L.*
Lanc. Lancashire.
Lap. Laplandish.
Lat. mid. Latin of the middle and later age.
Lett. Lettish.
Lev. Leviticus, v. *Gen.*
Lin. Linnæus.
Lip. Lipsius's Glossary, Opera Omnia Versal. 4 vols. 8vo. vol. ii. p. 988.
Lk. St. Luke's Gospel, v. *Jn.*
L.M. Liber Medicinalis, v. *Herb.* a Baldo quodam, ex scriptis Marcelli, Scribonii Largi, C. Plinii, aliorumque Medicorum Latinorum, uti censet Wanleius, compilatus, Bibl. D. Jac. Westm. v. the Titles of Chapters in A.-S. and quotations in Wanley's Cat. 176—180, 72.
L. Lambeth Psalter. v. *Lps.* and *M. Ps.*
Lps. or *L. Ps.* Lambeth Psalter, Bibl. Lambeth, 4to. 188, Art. 5.
Lup. Lupus's Sermons, in Hickes's Thes. vol. ii. p. 99. Reference to sections and lines of sections.

m. mas. masculine, or, of the masculine gender.
M.A. Monasticon Anglicanum.
Malm. Will. Malmesburiensis, A. D. 1140.
Mann. Manning's edition of Lye's A.-S. Dict. particularly the Supplement: 2 vols. fol. v. *pref.* p. xx. note, number 22.
Mart. Martinii Lexicon philologicum, 2 vols. fol. 1711.
Martyr. Mart. or *Menol.* Martyrologium, sive potius Menologium seu Calendarium poeticum, or The poetical calendar of the Anglo-Saxons, Hickes's Thes. I. p. 203, Fox, 8vo. London, 1830, v. *pref* p. xx. note, number 17.
Med. ex Quadr. Medicina ex quadrupedibus, Bibl. Bodl. Hatt. 100, Art. 4, Jun. 58, Art. 2, Bibl. Cott. Vitell. C. 3, fol. 75: Wanley, p. 75.
Menol. the Menology, v. *Martyr.*
Menol. F. Fox, v. *Martyr.*
Mk. Mark, v. *Jn.*
Moes. Moeso-Gothic, the earliest High-German dialect yet known, preserved in the Gospels, &c. A. D. 370, v. *Jn.*
Mone. Mone's Quellen und Forschungen zur Geschichte der teutschen Literatur und Sprache, 8vo. Leipzig, 1830.
Mone. A. —— the Glossary (in p. 314) of natural history. The MS. is of the 10th century, and is in the Jesuits' Library at Brussels, in 4to. No. 539.

Mone. B. Mone's Quellen und Forschungen zur Geschichte der teutschen Literatur und Sprache, 8vo. Leipzig, 1830; the A.-S. Gloss. (in p. 329), on Aldhelm's Latin treatise *De laude virginitatis*, taken from the Burgundian Library at Brussels, No. 471.

Mone C. —— the Gloss. (in p. 442) from the Brussels MS. No. 539.

Mons. or *Mons. Glos.* Monsee Glossary, so called from a Codex of the Convent Monsee, published under the title Glossæ Monseenses, by B. Pez, in Thes. Anecdotorum, nov. I. col. 319—414.

M. Ps. Mareschalli Psalterium; *i. e.* Versio Psalmorum in Bibl. Tho. Comitis Arundeliæ, nec non Comitis Mareschalli Angliæ, quam Regiæ Societati dedit Hen. Dux. Norf. Ao. 1679.

M.S. Manuscript.

M.SS. Manuscripts.

M.S. C. Manuscriptus codex Cantabrigiensis.

M.S. T. Manuscriptus codex in bibliotheca Coll. S. Trinitatis Cantabrigiæ.

Mt. Matthew, v. *Jn.*

n. neut. neuter, or, of the neuter gender.

N. Noeli (Laur.) Vocabularium; in Bibl. Bodl.

Nat. S. Greg. a Homily on the Birth-day of St. Gregory, v. *Els.*

Nath. Nathanis Judæi legatio fabulosa ad Tib. Cæsarem; in Bibl. Publ. Cantabr. unde descripsit Junius id quod extat apographum in Bodl. Jun. 74. Art. 2.

Nic. or *Nicod.* Nicodemi pseudo-evangelium, at the end of Thwaites's Heptateuch, v. *Thw.*

nn. a noun.

nom. the nominative case.

Norse. Norse, or Old Danish, spoken throughout Scandinavia, the nearest approach to which is the Icelandic.

Norw. Norwegian.

Not. Notker's translation of the Psalms into Alemannic or High-German, about A. D. 1020.

Num. or *Numb.* Numbers, v. *Gen.*

Ol Ger. Old High-German.

Ors. Orosius, by Barrington, Saxon and English, 8vo. London, 1773, v. *Bar.*

Ot. Ott. or *Otlf.* Otfrid's poetical paraphrase of the Gospels in Alemannic or High-German, published by Graff, 4to. Königsberg, 1831.

p. or P. with figures following denotes page.

p. or *per.* perfect tense.

par. paragraph.

part. participle.

Past. Gregorii P. Liber de cura Pastorali, Saxonicè redditus ab Ælfredo Rege. Bibl. Bodl. Hatt. 88, Jun. 53, 2: Bibl. Publ. Cant. C.C.C. Cant: S. 1, Coll. Trin. Cant: Cott, Otho, B. 2, v. *Dial.* and *Gr. Dial.*

Pecc. Med. Peccatorum Medicina; in Bibl. Cott. Tib. A. 3, fol. 93, unde suum desumpsit Junius, in Bodl. Jun. 59.

Pers. Persian.

pl. plu. plural.

Plat. Plat-Dutch, or Low-German spoken in the flat or north part of Germany.

pœn. pen. or *pn.* pœnitentia, pœnitens in the Laws, v. *L. Can. Edg. pen.*

Port. Portuguese.

pp. perfect participle.

pr. or *pref.* preface.

prep. preposition.

pres. present tense.

Pri. Price's edition of Warton's History of English Poetry, 4 vols. 8vo. 1824.

pron. pronoun.

Prœm. R. Conc. Prœmium Regularis Concordiæ Anglicæ nationis Monachorum Sanctimonialiumque. Edidit in notis suis ad Eadmeri historiam Novorum, p. 145, Cl. Joh. Seldenus, e Bibl. Cott. Tib. A. 3, fol. 1.

Prov. Glossæ in Proverbia Salomonis; in Bibl. Bodl. Jun. 71, Art. 2, desumptæ vero a Junio e Cott. Vesp. D. 6.

Ps. Psalms, by Spelman, 4to. London, 1640, v. *pref.* p. xix. note, number 5. The division of the Vulgate is used, which varies a little from the English division of the Psalms and verses.

P.S. Paraphrasis Saxonica, Cædmon's Paraphrase of Genesis, v. *Cd.*

Ps. Th. Psalms, by Thorpe, 8vo. Oxford, 1835.

q. quære, doubt.

q.d. quasi dicat.

Q. v. or *q. v.* Quod vide.

R. Reubenii Glossarium; *i. e.* Ælfrici Glossarii exemplar inter membranas Cl. Pet. Paul. Reubenii repertum, et a Francisco Junio integre descriptum, Bibl. Bodl. Jun. 71, 1.

Rab. Rhabanus Maurus, who wrote in Alemannic or High German, about A. D. 850.

Rawl. Rawlinson, v. *Bt. R.*

R. Ben. Regulæ Benedictinæ exemplar aliud.

R. Conc. Regularis Concordia Angliæ nationis Monachorum Sanctimonialiumque, Bibl. Bodl. Tib. A. 3: Claud, D. 3.

resp. responsum, answer.

Ric. Ricardus, Prior Hagustald, who wrote in Latin, about A. D. 1184.

R. Mt. Mk. &c. Evangeliorum secundum Matth. Marc. &c. exemplar Rushworthianum, in Bibl. Bodl. v. autem Wanl. Cat. p. 82. Written about the 10th century, v. *pref.* § 21, p. x xiii.

R. T. or *R. Th.* or *Th. R.* Mr. Thorpe's Translation of Rask's Anglo-Saxon Grammar, 8vo. Copenhagen, 1830.

Rubr. Rubric.

Rus. Russian.

S. or *sing.* singular.

Sal. Salic laws, the laws of the Francs, published by Charlemagne, A. D. 798, v. Schilter's Thes. vol. ii. p. 49.

Sans. Sanscrit, the ancient Hindoo language, v. *pref.* p. ix. § 20.

sc. scilicet, namely.

S. C. de Mont. Wall. Senatus Consultum de Monticolis Walliæ, v. *W.* p. 125, v. *L. Wal.*

Schw. Schwabenspiegel.

Scint. Scintillarius, sive Liber Scintillarum; *i. e.* Sententiarum ex S. Scriptura et Patrum libris a Beda Venerabili collectarum. Bibl. D. Jac. Westm. Excerpsit autem quædam ex his Cl. Junius, quæ extant in Bibl. Bodl. Jun. 40.

Scot. Scottish.

Ser. or *Serm.* Ælfric's Sermon on Creation, v. Elements of A.-S. Grammar, p. 272, note (*).

Shaks. Shakespeare.

Slav. Slavonic.

Sol. vel *Solil.* Soliloquia Augustini selecta et Saxonicè reddita ab Ælfredo Rege.

R. Brun. Peter Langtoft's Ch by Hearne – v Rob of Glouc

l Ox. MS. The Oxford Manuscript of the Anglo Gospels in the Bodleian No. 441 The basis of the text of Foxe in 1571 & Junius & Marshall in 1665

c Gregory's ~~Lessons~~ Pastoral Care translated into Anglo-Saxon by King Alfred Hanley v Greg.

The Gospel according to St. Matthew

† Piers. Piers Ploughman

K P. Langt. ~~Peter~~ v R. Brun. ~~Langtoft's Ch~~ ~~[illegible]~~

R. Glouc – Robert of Gloucester's Chronicles by T. Hearne M.A. 2 vols 8vo. Oxford 1724 reprinted by J Bagster 1810

Rob. gr. the or Rob. Th. Rasks ~~Gram~~ translated by ~~Thorpe~~ 8vo 1830 – 1c

m Pref. Preface

Copy Bos.

n Mt. Bos. v. Jn. & Bos.
~~Mt. Kmbl.~~ Copy Title & pp
Mt. Lind. Stev. } St. Matthew. Lindisfarne & Rushworth by Rev Jos. Stevenson M.A. for the Surtees Society 8vo. 1854
Mt. Rush. Stev. }
~~Mt Lind. War.~~
~~Mt Rush. War.~~
Mt Lind.
Mt. Rush

3 Rush. ~~Rune~~ The Runic ~~Inscriptions of~~ Gospel Book from Hicks Thes. fol 1705 I p. 135 Kemble. ~~Archae~~ ~~Archaeol~~ Archaeolog. vol XXVIII. 1840 p. 344.

3 Salm. Kmbl. The Dialogue

S Provn – Provence?

† Skrt. Sanskrit

t ~~[illegible]~~ Ps. Spl. { Psalms by Spelman v. Text v Pref. p XIX note, number 5.

Ps Spl. Copy 4to 1640

W Ps. Th. Libri Psalmorum versio antiqua Latina; cum paraphrasi Anglo-Saxonica, edidit Benjamin Thorpe F.S.A. 8vo Oxonii 1835

† N Dut. New Dutch or Hollandish

6. NGer. New High Ger See Ger.
NLGer. New Low Germ

(v) Nrs. Norse
† va Norw. or ~~[illegible]~~ Norw Norwegian
† ODut. Old Dutch or Hollandish
† w OEng. Old English
† x OFri. Old Frisic of the Laws
† OHGer. Old High Ger.
† ONrs. Old Norse, old Danish or Icelandic?
OSax. or OS. Old Saxon see Plat
OSlav. Old Slavonic.
OLGer. Old Low Ger

Shks = Shakespeare.

OSlav. Old Slavonic or Russian

Sm. v Bd.

† Orm Ormulum
† Ors. Bos. Orosius by Bosworth with Eng. Tran 8vo. 1859 Copy
† Ors. Th. Orosius by Thorpe 12mo 18– – Copy
† Owl. Nightingale Owl & Nightingale

The Dialogue of Salomon & Saturnus [illegible]

Mone. B. Mone's Quellen und Forschungen zur Geschichte der teutschen Literatur und Sprache, 8vo. Leipzig, 1830; the A.-S. Gloss. (in p. 329), on Aldhelm's Latin treatise *De laude virginitatis*, taken from the Burgundian Library at Brussels, No. 471.
Mone C. —— the Gloss. (in p. 442) from the Brussels MS. No. 539.
Mons. or *Mons. Glos.* Monsee Glossary, so called from a Codex of the Convent Monsee, published under the title Glossæ Monseenses, by B. Pez, in Thes. Anecdotorum, nov. I. col. 319—414.
M. Ps. Mareschalli Psalterium; *i.e.* Versio Psalmorum in Bibl. Tho. Comitis Arundeliæ, nec non Comitis Mareschalli Angliæ, quam Regiæ Societati dedit Hen. Dux. Norf. Ao. 1679.
M.S. Manuscript.
M.SS. Manuscripts.
M.S. C. Manuscriptus codex Cantabrigiensis.
M.S. T. Manuscriptus codex in bibliotheca Coll. S. Trinitatis Cantabrigiæ.
Mt. Matthew, v. *Jn.*

n. neut. neuter, or, of the neuter gender.
N. Neeli (Laur.) Vocabularium; in Bibl. Bodl.
Nat. S. Greg. a Homily on the Birth-day of St. Gregory, v. *Els.*
Nath. Nathanis Judæi legatio fabulosa ad Tib. Cæsarem; in Bibl. Publ. Cantabr. unde descripsit Junius id quod extat apographum in Bodl. Jun. 74. Art. 2.
Nic. or *Nicod.* Nicodemi pseudo-evangelium, at the end of Thwaites's Heptateuch, v. *Thw.*
nn. a noun.
nom. the nominative case.
Norse. Norse, or Old Danish, spoken throughout Scandinavia, the nearest approach to which is the Icelandic.
Norw. Norwegian.
Not. Notker's translation of the Psalms into Alemannic or High-German, about A.D. 1020.
Num. or *Numb.* Numbers, v. *Gen.*

Ol. Ger. Old High-German.
Ors. Orosius, by Barrington, Saxon and English, 8vo. London, 1773, v. *Bar.*

Ot. Ott. or *Ottf.* Otfrid's poetical paraphrase of the Gospels in Alemannic or High-German, published by Graff, 4to. Königsberg, 1831.

p. or P. with figures following denotes page.
p. or *per.* perfect tense.
par. paragraph.
part. participle.
Past. Gregorii P. Liber de cura Pastorali, Saxonicè redditus ab Ælfredo Rege. Bibl. Bodl. Hatt. 88, Jun. 53, 2: Bibl. Publ. Cant. C.C.C. Cant: S. 1, Coll. Trin. Cant: Cott. Otho, B. 2, v. *Dial.* and *Gr. Dial.*
Pecc. Med. Peccatorum Medicina; in Bibl. Cott. Tib. A. 3, fol. 93, unde suum desumpsit Junius, in Bodl. Jun. 59.
Pers. Persian.
pl. plu. plural.
Plat. Plat-Dutch, or Low-German spoken in the flat or north part of Germany.
pœn. pen. or *pn.* pœnitentia, pœnitens in the Laws, v. *L. Can. Edg. pen.*
Port. Portuguese.
pp. perfect participle.
pr. or *pref.* preface.
prep. preposition.
pres. present tense.
Pri. Price's edition of Warton's History of English Poetry, 4 vols. 8vo. 1824.
pron. pronoun.
Prœm. R. Conc. Prœmium Regularis Concordiæ Anglicæ nationis Monachorum Sanctimonialiumque. Edidit in notis suis ad Eadmeri historiam Novorum, p. 145, Cl. Joh. Seldenus, e Bibl. Cott. Tib. A. 3, fol. 1.
Prov. Glossæ in Proverbia Salomonis; in Bibl. Bodl. Jun. 71, Art. 2, desumptæ vero a Junio e Cott. Vesp. D. 6.
Ps. Psalms, by Spelman, 4to. London, 1640, v. *pref.* p. xix. note, number 5. The division of the Vulgate is used, which varies a little from the English division of the Psalms and verses.
P.S. Paraphrasis Saxonica, Cædmon's Paraphrase of Genesis, v. *Cd.*
Ps. Th. Psalms, by Thorpe, 8vo. Oxford, 1835.

q. quære, doubt.
q.d. quasi dicat.
Q.v. or *q.v.* Quod vide.

R. Reubenii Glossarium; *i.e.* Ælfrici Glossarii exemplar inter membranas Cl. Pet. Paul. Reubenii repertum, et a Francisco Junio integre descriptum, Bibl. Bodl. Jun. 71, 1.
Rab. Rhabanus Maurus, who wrote in Alemannic or High German, about A.D. 850.
Rawl. Rawlinson, v. *Bt. R.*
R. Ben. Regulæ Benedictinæ exemplar aliud.
R. Conc. Regularis Concordia Angliæ nationis Monachorum Sanctimonialiumque, Bibl. Bodl. Tib. A. 3: Claud, D. 3.
resp. responsum, answer.
Ric. Ricardus, Prior Hagustald, who wrote in Latin, about A.D. 1184.
R. Mt. Mk. &c. Evangeliorum secundum Matth. Marc. &c. exemplar Rushworthianum, in Bibl. Bodl. v. autem Wanl. Cat. p. 82. Written about the 10th century, v. *pref.* § 21, p. xxiii.
R. T. or *R. Th.* or *Th. R.* Mr. Thorpe's Translation of Rask's Anglo-Saxon Grammar, 8vo. Copenhagen, 1830.
Rubr. Rubric.
Rus. Russian.
s. or *sing.* singular.
Sal. Salic laws, the laws of the Francs, published by Charlemagne, A.D. 798, v. Schilter's Thes. vol. ii. p. 49.
Sans. Sanscrit, the ancient Hindoo language, v. *pref.* p. ix. § 20.
sc. scilicet, namely.
S. C. de Mont. Wall. Senatus Consultum de Monticolis Walliæ, v. *W.* p. 125, v. *L. Wal.*
Schw. Schwabenspiegel.
Scint. Scintillarius, sive Liber Scintillarum; *i.e.* Sententiarum ex S. Scriptura et Patrum libris a Beda Venerabili collectarum. Bibl. D. Jac. Westm. Excerpsit autem quædam ex his Cl. Junius, quæ extant in Bibl. Bodl. Jun. 40.
Scot. Scottish.
Ser. or *Serm.* Ælfric's Sermon on Creation, v. Elements of A.-S. Grammar, p. 272, note (*).
Shaks. Shakespeare.
Slav. Slavonic.
Sol. vel *Solil.* Soliloquia Augustini selecta et Saxonicè reddita ab Ælfredo Rege.

C Ox. MS. The Oxford manuscript of the Anglo Gospels in the Bodleian No. 441 The basis of the text of Foxe in 1571; & Junius & Marshall in 1665

R. Anna. Peter Langtoft's Ch by Hearne. v Robt of Glouc

Gregory's Pastoral Care translated into Saxon by King Alfred. v Greg.

R. Glouc. Robert of Gloucester's Chronicle by T. Hearne M.A. 2 vols 8vo. Oxford 1724 reprinted by S. Bagster 1810

Rsk. gr. Th. or Rsk. Th. Rask's Gram translated by Thorpe 8vo 1830

The Gospel according to St. Matthew

Piers. Piers Plowman

P. Langt. v R. Br.

Copy Bos.

m Prof. Rosen

n Mt. Bos. v. Jn. & Bos.

Mt. Kmbl. Copy title

Mt. Lind. Stev.

Mt. Rush. Stev.

St. Matthew Lindisfarne & Rushworth by Rev. Jos. Stevenson M.A. for the Surtees Society 8vo. 1854

~~Mt Lind. War.~~

~~Mt Rush. War.~~

Mt. Lind.

Mt. Rush

Rush

Anna. Bon. Annis Beowulf ... Boe. fol. 1705 I p 136

Kemble. Archaeolog. Vol XXVIII. 1840 p 34?

Salm. Kmbl. The Dialogue of Solomon & Saturn ... Kemble ... 8vo. 1848

S Brown. Provence?

Skrt. Sanskrit

N Dut. New Dutch or Hollandish

N Ger. New High Ger See Ger.

N Lat. New Lat.

Ps. Spl. Psalms by Spelman v Text

v Pref.

p XIX note, number 5.

Ps Spl. Copy 4to 1640

v Nrs. Norse

Norw. or Norwegian

O Dut. Old Dutch or Hollandish

O Eng. Old English

O Frs. Old Frisic of the Laws

O Ger. Old High Ger.

O Nrs. Old Norse, old Danish or Icelandic?

O Sax. or O S. Old Saxon see Hel.

O Slav. Old Slavonic.

OS Ger. Old Sax Ger

Shks = Shakespeare

O Rsv. Old Slavonic or Russian

Sm. v Bd.

Orm Ormulum

Ors. Bos. Orosius by Bosworth with Eng. Tran 8vo. 1859 copy

Ors. Th. Orosius by Thorpe 12mo 18 - - Copy

Owl Nt Owl & Nightingale

[illegible]

Promises [illegible] [illegible] Copy

[illegible]

Bar [illegible]

[illegible]

[illegible]

c Th. Dipl Copy

Vulg. The Latin version of the Scrip by St. Jerome ?

h Th. B. ~~Thorpe's ed.~~ ~~Vocabulary Title~~ v Vo. Th

War. Waring, v Mr. Smith War.

h Spn. Spanish

i Spl; Spel Spelmanis Balins v Vo. Spl.

Tupp, Martin F. Tupper Esq. v. F. Bt. Met. v. Bt. Tupp

Wilk. Wilkins v S.

m better Rek. Th.

Voc. vocab.

Wr. Wright Thos. A Volume of Vocabularies from the ~~Appdx~~ 10th ~~to the 15th~~ century

Wycl = Wycliffe

Zend The Zend or old Persian ?

to the 15th. by Thomas Wright Esqr. M.A: F.S.A. &c

From A Library of National Antiquities in a series of Volumes illustrating the General Archaeology & History of our Country. published at the expense of Joseph Mayer Esqr F.S.A &c Privately Printed large 8vo 1857. D. Marples, Printer, Liverpool

Bibl. Cott. Vitell. A. 15, fol. 1, unde descripsit Junius quod in Bodl. Jun. 70.

Som. Somner's A.-S. Dictionary, v. *pref.* p. xx. note, number 22.

Somn. Somniorum diversitas, Bibl. Cott. Tib. A. 3, fol. 36 and 40, unde descripsit Junius quæ extant in Bodl. Jun. 43, Art. 1, 2, 3, and 44, Art. 12.

Sp. Spanish.

Spen. Spencer, the poet.

Spl. or *Supl.* Supplement.

Stub. the Latin writer Stubbes, A. D. 1360

sub. subjunctive mood.

sup. superlative degree.

Supl. The Supplement.

Swd. or *Swed.* Swedish.

Symb. Athanas. Athanasian Creed.

Syr. Syriac.

Th. R. Thorpe's translation of Rask's A.-S. Grammar, 8vo. 1830.

Th. An. Thorpe's Analecta Anglo-Saxonica, 8vo. London, 1834.

Th. Apol. Apollonius, of Tyre, by B. Thorpe, 12mo. London, 1834.

Tart. Tartaric.

Tat. Tatian's Harmony of the Gospels in Low-German, about A. D. 890.

Thork. Thorkelin's edition of Beowulf, v. *pref.* p. xx. note, number 15.

Thorn, a Latin writer, about A. D. 1390.

Thw. Thwaites, editor of the Heptateuch, v. *pref.* p. xix. note, number 10: 21, 3.

T. Ps. Psalterii exemplar in Bibl. Coll. S. Trin. Cant.

T. T. Taylor's edition of Tooke's Diversions of Purley, 2 vols. 8vo. 1829.

Turner. Hist. of A.-S.; the references are to the 4th edit. 3 vols. 8vo. 1823.

v. vide, see.

v. a verb.

v. a. or *act.* verb active.

v. irr. verb irregular.

v. l. vide locum.

v. n. verb neuter.

V. Ps. or *Vps.* Vossianum Psalterium. Exemplar scil. quod ab Is. Vossio accepit Fr. Junius. Extat autem in Bibl. Bodl. Jun. 27.

W. or *Wilk.* Wilkins' A.-S. laws, v. *L.*

W. v. *Wan.*

Wac. or *Wach.* Wachter's Glossarium Germanicum, Lips. fol. 1737.

W. B. or *Wh.* or *Whel.* Wheelock's Bede, v. *pref.* p. xix. note, number 6.

Wan. or *Wanl. Cat.* Wanley's Catalogue of A.-S. M.SS. forming the 3rd vol. of Hickes's Thesaurus, v. *pref.* p. xx. note, number 21.

Wel. Welsh.

West. the Latin writer Mattheus Westmonasteriensis, A. D. 1377.

Wil. Willeram's paraphrase of the Canticle in Francic, about A. D. 1070.

Weston. B.D. F.R.S. (Stephen). A specimen of the Conformity of the European languages, particularly the English, with the Oriental languages, especially the Persian, London, 8vo. 1802, price 7*s.*

In the English and Latin Indexes the references are to the numbers and letters at the head of the page: as, Mulberries 47a, is found under number 47a, at the head of the page in the Dictionary, and the first column after a in the margin.

Mone. B. Mone's Quellen und Forschungen zur Geschichte der teutschen Literatur und Sprache, 8vo. Leipzig, 1830; the A.-S. Gloss. (in p. 329), on Aldhelm's Latin treatise *De laude virginitatis*, taken from the Burgundian Library at Brussels, No. 471.

Mone C. —— the Gloss. (in p. 442) from the Brussels MS. No. 539.

Mons. or *Mons. Glos.* Monsee Glossary, so called from a Codex of the Convent Monsee, published under the title Glossæ Monseenses, by B. Pez, in Thes. Anecdotorum, nov. I. col. 319—414.

M. Ps. Mareschalli Psalterium; *i. e.* Versio Psalmorum in Bibl. Tho. Comitis Arundeliæ, nec non Comitis Mareschalli Angliæ, quam Regiæ Societati dedit Hen. Dux. Norf. Ao. 1679.

M.S. Manuscript.

M.SS. Manuscripts.

M.S. C. Manuscriptus codex Cantabrigiensis.

M.S. T. Manuscriptus codex in bibliotheca Coll. S. Trinitatis Cantabrigiæ.

Mt. Matthew, v. *Jn.*

n. neut. neuter, or, of the neuter gender.

N. Noeli (Laur.) Vocabularium; in Bibl. Bodl.

Nat. S. Greg. a Homily on the Birth-day of St. Gregory, v. *Els.*

Nath. Nathanis Judæi legatio fabulosa ad Tib. Cæsarem; in Bibl. Publ. Cantabr. unde descripsit Junius id quod extat apographum in Bodl. Jun. 74. Art. 2.

Nic. or *Nicod.* Nicodemi pseudo-evangelium, at the end of Thwaites's Heptateuch, v. *Thw.*

nn. a noun.

nom. the nominative case.

Norse. Norse, or Old Danish, spoken throughout Scandinavia, the nearest approach to which is the Icelandic.

Norw. Norwegian.

Not. Notker's translation of the Psalms into Alemannic or High-German, about A. D. 1020.

Num. or *Numb.* Numbers, v. *Gen.*

Ot. Ger. Old High-German.

Ors. Orosius, by Barrington, Saxon and English, 8vo. London, 1773, v. *Bar.*

Ot. Ott. or *Ottf.* Otfrid's poetical paraphrase of the Gospels in Alemannic or High-German, published by Graff, 4to. Königsberg, 1831.

p. or P. with figures following denotes page.

p. or *per.* perfect tense.

par. paragraph.

part. participle.

Past. Gregorii P. Liber de cura Pastorali, Saxonicè redditus ab Ælfredo Rege. Bibl. Bodl. Hatt. 88, Jun. 53, 2: Bibl. Publ. Cant. C.C.C. Cant: S. 1, Coll. Trin. Cant: Cott, Otho, B. 2, v. *Dial.* and *Gr. Dial.*

Pecc. Med. Peccatorum Medicina; in Bibl. Cott. Tib. A. 3, fol. 93, unde suum desumpsit Junius, in Bodl. Jun. 59.

Pers. Persian.

pl. plu. plural.

Plat. Plat-Dutch, or Low-German spoken in the flat or north part of Germany.

pœn. pen. or *pn.* pœnitentia, pœnitens in the Laws, v. *L. Can. Edg. pen.*

Port. Portuguese.

pp. perfect participle.

pr. or *pref.* preface.

prep. preposition.

pres. present tense.

Pri. Price's edition of Warton's History of English Poetry, 4 vols. 8vo. 1824.

pron. pronoun.

Prœm. R. Conc. Prœmium Regularis Concordiæ Anglicæ nationis Monachorum Sanctimonialiumque. Edidit in notis suis ad Eadmeri historiam Novorum, p. 145, Cl. Joh. Seldenus, e Bibl. Cott. Tib. A. 3, fol. 1.

Prov. Glossæ in Proverbia Salomonis; in Bibl. Bodl. Jun. 71, Art. 2, desumptæ vero a Junio e Cott. Vesp. D. 6.

Ps. Psalms, by Spelman, 4to. London, 1640, v. *pref.* p. xix. note, number 5. The division of the Vulgate is used, which varies a little from the English division of the Psalms and verses.

P.S. Paraphrasis Saxonica, Cædmon's Paraphrase of Genesis, v. *Cd.*

Ps. Th. Psalms, by Thorpe, 8vo. Oxford, 1835.

q. quere, doubt.

q.d. quasi dicat.

Q. v. or *q. v.* Quod vide.

R. Reubenii Glossarium; *i. e.* Ælfrici Glossarii exemplar inter membranas Cl. Pet. Paul. Reubenii repertum, et a Francisco Junio integre descriptum, Bibl. Bodl. Jun. 71, 1.

Rab. Rhabanus Maurus, who wrote in Alemannic or High German, about A. D. 850.

Rawl. Rawlinson, v. *Bt. R.*

R. Ben. Regulæ Benedictinæ exemplar aliud.

R. Conc. Regularis Concordia Angliæ nationis Monachorum Sanctimonialiumque, Bibl. Bodl. Tib. A. 3: Claud, D. 3.

resp. responsum, answer.

Ric. Ricardus, Prior Hagustald, who wrote in Latin, about A. D. 1184.

R. Mt. Mk. &c. Evangeliorum secundum Matth. Marc. &c. exemplar Rushworthianum, in Bibl. Bodl. v. autem Wanl. Cat. p. 82. Written about the 10th century, v. *pref.* § 21, p. x xiii.

R. T. or *R. Th.* or *Th. R.* Mr. Thorpe's Translation of Rask's Anglo-Saxon Grammar, 8vo. Copenhagen, 1830.

Rubr. Rubric.

Rus. Russian.

S. or *sing.* singular.

Sal. Salic laws, the laws of the Francs, published by Charlemagne, A. D. 798, v. Schilter's Thes. vol. ii. p. 49.

Sans. Sanscrit, the ancient Hindoo language, v. *pref.* p. ix. § 20.

sc. scilicet, namely.

S. C. de Mont. Wall. Senatus Consultum de Monticolis Walliæ, v. *W.* p. 125, v. *L. Wal.*

Schw. Schwabenspiegel.

Scint. Scintillarius, sive Liber Scintillarum; *i. e.* Sententiarum ex S. Scriptura et Patrum libris a Beda Venerabili collectarum. Bibl. D. Jac. Westm. Excerpsit autem quædam ex his Cl. Junius, quæ extant in Bibl. Bodl. Jun. 40.

Scot. Scottish.

Ser. or *Serm.* Ælfric's Sermon on Creation, v. Elements of A.-S. Grammar, p. 272, note (*).

Shaks. Shakespeare.

Slav. Slavonic.

Sol. vel *Solil.* Soliloquia Augustini selecta et Saxonicè reddita ab Ælfredo Rege.

The Gospel according to St. Matthew

Copy Bos.

Ox. MS. The Oxford Manuscript of the Anglo-Saxon Gospels in the Bodleian No. 441 The basis of the text of Foxe in 1571; & Junius & Marshall in 1665

Gregory's ~~[illegible]~~ Pastoral Care translated into Saxon by King Alfred ... v. Greg.

R. Brun. Peter Langtoft's Ch. by Hearne. v Rob. of Glouc

R. Glouc. Robert of Gloucester's Chronicle by T. Hearne M.A. 2 vols 8vo Oxford 1724 reprinted by ...

Piers. Piers Ploughman

P. Langl. ~~[illegible]~~ v. R. Brun.

~~Langtoft's Ch. Copy Title~~

Prof. Rosen

Rsk. gr. Rask's Grammar ... translated by Thorpe 8vo 1830 ...

Mt. Bos. v. Jn. & Bos.

~~Mt. Kmbl.~~ Copy Title page

Mt. Lind. Stev.

Mt. Rush. Stev.

St. Matthew Lindisfarne & Rushworth by Rev Jos. Stevenson M.A. for the Surtees Society 8vo 1854

~~Mt. Lind. War.~~

~~Mt. Rush. War.~~

Mt. Lind.

Mt. Rush.

Rush. ~~Runic~~ Runic ... Hickes Thes. fol 1705 p. I p. 135

Kemble. ~~[illegible]~~ Archaeolog. vol XXVIII, 1840 p. 344?

Salm. Kmbl. The Dialogue of Salomon & Saturnus ... edited by ... 1848

Provn. Provence?

Skrt. Sanskrit

N. Dut. New Dutch or Hollandish

N. H. Ger. New High Ger See Ger.

N. L. Ger. New Low Germ

~~[illegible]~~ Ps. Spl. Psalms by Spelman v. Text v Pref. p. XIX note, number 5.

Ps. Spl. Copy 4to 1640

Ps. Th. Libri Psalmorum versio antiqua Latina; cum paraphrasi Anglo-Saxonica, edidit Benjamin Thorpe S.A.S. 8vo Oxonii 1835

Nrs. Norse

Norw. or Nrw. Norwegian

O. Dut. Old Dutch or Hollandish

O. Eng. Old English

O. Frs. Old Frisic of the Laws

O. H. Ger. Old High Ger.

O. Nrs. Old Norse, old Danish or Icelandic?

O. Sax. or O. S. Old Saxon See Plat

O. Slav. Old Slavonic.

O. L. Ger. Old Low Ger

Shks = Shakespeare.

O. Slav. Old Slavonic or Russian

Sm. v Rd.

Orm. Ormulum

Ors. Bos. Orosius by Bosworth with Eng. Tran 8vo. 1859 Copy

Ors. Th. Orosius by Thorpe 12mo 18 - Copy

Owl & Ng. Owl & Nightingale

c Th. Bibl. Copy

x Vulg. The Latin version of the Script by St. Jerome ?

h Th. B. ~~Thapsi at~~ ~~Rudimentary Title~~ v Ps. Th

ʒ War. Waring v Mk. Lint. War.

h Spn. Spanish

i Spl; Spel Spelman's Balms v Ps. Spl.

n Tupp. Tupper Esqr. Martin F. v. Bt. Tupr

v. F Bt. Met

w Wilk. Wilkins v L.

in better Rsk. Th.

w ~~Wr~~ Wr. Wright Thos. A Volume of Vocabularies from the ~~Appx~~ 10th ~~to the 15th~~ century

Wycl = Wycliffe

x Zend The Zend or old Persian ?

to the 15th. by Thomas Wright Esqr. M.A: F.S.A. &c

From A Library of National Antiquities in a series of Volumes illustrating the General Archaeology & History of our Country. published at the expense of Joseph Mayer Esqr F.S.A. &c Privately Printed large 8vo 1857 - D. Marples, Printer, Liverpool

Bibl. Cott. Vitell. A. 15, fol. 1, unde descripsit Junius quod in Bodl. Jun. 70.

Som. Somner's A.-S. Dictionary, v. *pref.* p. xx. note, number 22.

Somn. Somniorum diversitas, Bibl. Cott. Tib. A. 3, fol. 36 and 40, unde descripsit Junius quæ extant in Bodl. Jun. 43, Art. 1, 2, 3, and 44, Art. 12.

Sp. Spanish.

Spen. Spencer, the poet.

Spl. or *Supl.* Supplement.

Stub. the Latin writer Stubbes, A. D. 1360

sub. subjunctive mood.

sup. superlative degree.

Supl. The Supplement.

Swd. or *Swed.* Swedish.

Symb. Athanas. Athanasian Creed.

Syr. Syriac.

Th. R. Thorpe's translation of Rask's A.-S. Grammar, 8vo. 1830.

Th. An. Thorpe's Analecta Anglo-Saxonica, 8vo. London, 1834.

Th. Apol. Apollonius, of Tyre, by B. Thorpe, 12mo. London, 1834.

Tart. Tartaric.

Tat. Tatian's Harmony of the Gospels in Low-German, about A. D. 890.

Thork. Thorkelin's edition of Beowulf, v. *pref.* p. xx. note, number 15.

Thorn, a Latin writer, about A. D. 1390.

Thw. Thwaites, editor of the Heptateuch, v. *pref.* p. xix. note, number 10: 21, 3.

T. Ps. Psalterii exemplar in Bibl. Coll. S. Trin. Cant.

T. T. Taylor's edition of Tooke's Diversions of Purley, 2 vols. 8vo. 1829.

Turner. Hist. of A.-S.; the references are to the 4th edit. 3 vols. 8vo. 1823.

v. vide, see.

v. a verb.

v. a. or *act.* verb active.

v. irr. verb irregular.

v. l. vide locum.

v. n. verb neuter.

V. Ps. or *Vps.* Vossianum Psalterium. Exemplar scil. quod ab Is. Vossio accepit Fr. Junius. Extat autem in Bibl. Bodl. Jun. 27.

W. or *Wilk.* Wilkins' A.-S. laws, v. *L.*

W. v. *Wan.*

Wac. or *Wach.* Wachter's Glossarium Germanicum, Lips. fol. 1737.

W. B. or *Wh.* or *Whel.* Wheelock's Bede, v. *pref.* p. xix. note, number 6.

Wan. or *Wanl. Cat.* Wanley's Catalogue of A.-S. M.SS. forming the 3rd vol. of Hickes's Thesaurus, v. *pref.* p. xx. note, number 21.

Wel. Welsh.

West. the Latin writer Mattheus Westmonasteriensis, A. D. 1377.

Wil. Willeram's paraphrase of the Canticle in Francic, about A. D. 1070.

Weston. B.D. F.R.S. (Stephen). A specimen of the Conformity of the European languages, particularly the English, with the Oriental languages, especially the Persian, London, 8vo. 1802, price 7*s.*

In the English and Latin Indexes the references are to the numbers and letters at the head of the page: as, Mulberries 47a, is found under number 47a, at the head of the page in the Dictionary, and the first column after a in the margin.

General Remarks upon the Gender and Declension of Anglo-Saxon Nouns.

EVERY noun, which has the *nom. s.* in -a is *m.* and makes the *g. s.* in -an. All *m.* nouns ending in a consonant, or -e, make the *g. s.* in -es: those nouns which terminate in -dóm, -els, -end, -ere, -ing, -erd, -ord, -scipe; -feld *a field, plain;* -ford *a ford;* -hám *a home;* -hlæw *rising ground;* -stede *a place*; -tun *an inclosure, a town,* &c.; likewise all nouns, making the *nom.* and *ac. pl.* in -as, are all *m.* and, therefore, make the *g. s.* in -es.

All *f.* nouns, which have the *nom. s.* in -e, make the *g. s.* in -an. Every *f.* noun, ending in a consonant, such as words in -ceaster *a city;* -dun *a hill;* -scir, -scyr, *a shire;* -stow *a place,* &c. has the *g. s.* in -e: indeed, every noun having the *g. s.* in -e is *f.*

All nouns, having the *nom.* and *ac. pl.* in -u, are *n.*, and, like all *n.* nouns, ending in a consonant, make the *g. s.* in -es.

Observations upon inflections, useful for finding words in the Dictionary.

In nouns, when *a* comes before a single consonant, or *st. sc* followed by *a, o,* or *u,* and, in adjectives, when *a* comes before a single consonant followed by *a, e, o,* or *u,* the *nom. s.* is found by rejecting all the letters after the second consonant, or *st. sc.* and by changing *a* into *æ*: as in the nouns fatum *with vats,* stafas *letters,* gastas *guests,* by casting away um, as, as, and changing *a* into *æ,* we have fæt *a vat,* stæf *a letter;* gæst *a guest,* and in the adjectives, lates, latena *of late,* latum *to late,* se smala *the small,* smalost *smallest,* se smalesta *the smallest,* by taking away es, ena, um, a, ost, esta, and changing *a* into *æ,* we have læt *late,* and smæl *small.*

Synopsis of the terminations of verbs.

Simple verbs, or verbs which have the *p.* of two or more syllables.				Complex verbs, or verbs which have the *p.* a monosyllable.
		INDICATIVE, *indf.*		INDICATIVE, *indf.*
		1.*	2.*	3.*
s.	*I,*	-e	-ige	-e[d]
	thou,	-st[a]	-ast	-st, -est[d]
	he,	-ð[b]	-að	—, -ð, -eð
pl.	*we, ye, they,*	-að, -e	-iað, -ige	-að, -e.
		perfect.		*perfect.*
s.	*I,*	-de[c]	-ode	—[e]
	thou,	-dest	-odest	-e[e]
	he,	-de	-ode	—[e]
pl.	*we, ye, they,*	-don	-odon, -edon	-on
		SUBJUNCTIVE, *indf.*		SUBJUNCTIVE, *indf.*
s.	*if I, thou, he,*	-e	-ige	-e
pl.	*if we, ye, they,*	-on, -an	-ion, -ian	-on, en
		perfect.		*perfect.*
s.	*if I, thou, he,*	-de	-ode	-e[e]
pl.	*if we, ye, they,*	-don, -den	-odon, -eden	-on, en
		IMPERATIVE, &c.		IMPERATIVE, &c.
	s.	—	-a	—
	pl.	-að, -e	-iað, -ige	-e, -að
	inf. to,	-enne	-igenne	-anne
	part. -ing,	-ende	-igende	-ende
	pp.	-ed	-od	-en.

1.* By substituting the *inf.* -an, for -e, -st, -de, &c., and prefixing the radical part of the verb, as bærn-e, bærn-st, bærn-de, we have the *inf.* bærn-an *to burn.* [a] -tst is changed into -dan in the *inf.* as þu lætst *thou leadest,* becomes lædan *to lead.* [b] -t is changed into -tan, as he gret *he greets,* becomes gretan *to greet:* -ð, after a vowel, is -ðan, as he cyð *he tells,* cyðan *to tell.* [c] -hte is the *inf.* -htan, or -ccan, as *p.* he plihte *he plighted, inf.* plihtan; he rehte *he cared for, inf.* reccan. In the *p.* and *pp.* -eal-, before -de, or -d, is the *inf.* -ellan; as tealde, geteald *told, inf.* tellan *to tell:* -eah- before -te, -t is *inf.* -eccan, as þeahte *thatched, inf.* þeccan *to thatch.*

2.* By substituting -ian for -ige, -ast, -ode, &c. as luf-ige, luf-ode, we have luf-ian *to love.*

3.* By substituting -an for -e, -st, -est, &c., and changing the vowels of the first syllable as in the following directions, the *inf.* is found. [d] In the 1st and 2nd persons *indf. æ, e* are generally from *a* of the *inf.* as þu bæcst *thou bakest,* he bæcð *he bakes, inf.* bacan *to bake:* þu stenst *thou standest,* he stent *he stands, inf.* standan *to stand: y* is from *e, eo,* or *u,* as þu ytst *thou eatest,* he yt *he eats, inf.* etan *to eat:*—þu cyst *thou choosest,* he cyst *he chooses, inf.* ceosan *to choose:*—he sycð *he sucks, inf.* súcan *to suck.* [e] The 1st and 3rd persons end in the last consonant of the verb, and change the preceding vowel: thus, *o* and sometimes *eo* in the *p.* are from the *inf. a;* but *eo* in the *p.* is generally from *ea;* as *p.* he stód *he stood, from inf.* standan *to stand; p.* he bleow *he blew, inf.* blawan *to blow;* he beot *he beat, inf.* beatan *to beat.* The *p. ea, æ,* and the *pp. o* before *ll, lf, lg, lt, rp, rf, rg,* &c. are from the *inf. e, eo,* or *u;* as, *p.* he mealt *he melted, pp.* molten *melted,* from *inf.* meltan *to melt;* he stærf *he died, pp.* storfen *died, inf.* steorfan *to die; p.* cleáf *clove, pp.* clofen *cloven, inf.* clúfan *to cleave.* The *a* of the *p.* and *u* or *i* of the *pp.* are from *i* of the *inf. p.* he sang *he sang; pp.* sungen *sung; inf.* singan *to sing:*—he bat *he bit, pp.* biten *bitten, inf.* bitan *to bite.*

First steps to A. S.
or

First steps to Anglo-Saxon
shewing the composition & descriptive
power of some English
words

First steps to A. S.
or
the use of a slight
knowledge of A.S. in
ascertaining the composition
power & radical
meaning of many
Eng. words.

First steps to A. S.
or
the composition power &
radical meaning of many
Eng. words by ascending
to their parental form
in the A. S.

Words for Sir Walter — explaining customs &c. — Manors

Ea-land an island.

Engle the Angles
Eorl, es; m an earl
Gicel an icicle
Hreopandun Repton

Wer a fine
Wild-deor a wild b
Wic a dwelling
Ham a home & — ham
For
Þegen
Wite the wite &

Gligman
Mor a moor
Morgan-gifu
Mund, e f protection
Neah-bur a neighbour
Pening, es; m a p
Pund, es; m a pound
Rihtwis-
Rice, &c — ric
Scillin a shilling

Ric — as Ricard
Fred-ric —
See Dict.

were
× Gemot
Gerefa —
Sceatt —

Shows the origin of the word Wednesday

Q Would it not be better to have words in -nes, thus — ness, e; f as licness, gelicness, e; f

-scipe ship et dom &c

Sibb, e f peace
Synn, e; f sin
See Gen III 446. a Pall, es m a pall

V. A. copy in Emerenges

not in K's index

Sib-æþeling

Sawl the soul
Scir a shire
Scyld a shield
Scearu es m or scearu
Seaxan the Saxons
Secan to seek
Smiþ a smith
Steallere
Swefel es m brimstone
Templ es; n a temple
Tor, es; m to hill
Tyn ten
Usa the Ouse
Wer: were a fine
Winter winter
Wisdom wisdom
× Abbandune, e; f Abingdon
Wildernes in Supp

Q 1, 2 All nouns which have the nom in x ne m

Scill, scilling or a shilling —
Pencg a penny
Wic a dwelling place — &
-wic as a termination
Wild-deor a wild beast.
Wild-deor-nes in the supplement p 719.

Wendan to go

2 Abacan to bake Ben. 4
v 1 bacan

1 Abelgan to be angry
the Index to Cdt.
Cd 217 th p 276, 27
v belgan

Witan to know
Wita a fine
Woden woden
Wuduwe an[illegible] widow
Þegen es a servant
Þeof a thief
Þeow a servant
Þor es m Thor

A DICTIONARY

OF THE

ANGLO-SAXON LANGUAGE.

[a] A often interchanges with other vowels; thus, æ and a, as æc and ac *an oak;* æcer and acer *a field;* habban *to have;* ic hæbbe *I have;* stan *a stone,* stænen *stony;* lar *doctrine,* læran *to teach;* an *one,* ænig *any one.*

A and O interchange, particularly before *n*, in a short syllable, as mon, man *a man;* long, lang *long;* sond, sand *sand;* an, on *on;* etc.

[b] A prefixed to words, sometimes denotes a negative, deteriorating, or opposite signification, as *from, out, away;* thus, awendan *to turn from, to subvert, from* wendan *to turn;* atynan *to open, expose,* from tynan *to enclose, hedge;* agylde, *or* ægilde *without payment, without amends;* amod *or* æmod *out of,* or *without mind, mad;* adon *to do away, to banish, composed of* a *from,* don *to do:* for æ v. 2 *i.*

[c] A, prefixed, does not always appear to alter the signification; *in this case,* it is generally omitted in modern English words derived immediately from Saxon; *thus,* arisan *to rise;* aberan *to bear;* abrecan *to break;* abitan *to bite.* The prefixed a, however, generally adds some little force, or intensity, to the original signification of the word to which it is joined.

[d] A, be, for, ge, and to, are often indifferently and interchangeably prefixed to verbs, especially to perfect tenses and to perfect participles, as well as to verbal nouns. If a word, therefore, cannot be found under a, it may be sought for under be, for, ge, *or* to, or rather under the first letter that remains, after rejecting these prefixes.

[e] A, added to words, denotes *a person, an agent,* or *actor,* and occasionally it denotes *inanimate things;* as cum *come thou,* cuma *a person who comes,* or *a guest;* swic *deceive thou,* se swica *the traitor;* worht *wrought,* wyrhta *a workman, a wright;* foregeng *foregoing,* foregenga *a foregoer;* bead *or* gebed *a supplication, a praying,* beada *a person who supplicates* or *prays;* bytl *a beetle,* or *hammer,* bytla *a hammerer, a builder;* cræft *art,* cræfta *an artist, artificer;* geman *to assemble,* gemana *an assembly, a congregation;* gewuna *a custom, habit.*

[f] A', aa; *adv.* [*Frs.* æ: *Moes.* aiw: *Grk.* ἀεί. The original signification seems to be *a flowing,* referring *to time,* which every moment flows on, *to water,* etc. v. ea *a river*] *Always, ever, for ever; hence the Old English* AYE, *ever;* semper:—Ac a sceal þæt wiðerwearde gemetgian *but ever must the contrary moderate, Bt.* 21. Aa, oð weorulde ende *always, until the end of the world, Bd.* 4, 19. ¶ A world *forever, Ex.* 21, 6. A forð *ever forth, from thence, Bt. R.* p. 168.

Aac *an oak,* v. ac.

Aad *a heap,* v. ad.

Aar *honour,* v. ar.

[g] Aar *morning,* v. ær.

Ab[illegible], v. ob.

Abacen *baked,* v. bacan.

Abad *expected,* v. abidan.

Abæd, abædon *asked,* v. abiddan.

Abælige *may be angry,* v. belgan.

Abær *bore,* sustulit, v. aberan.

A'bal *Ability, power of body, strength;* robur corporis:—*Cd.* 25.

Abannan; *pp.* ed, en; *v. a.* [bannan *from Al.* ban *a prince, command.*]—1. *To command, order;* mandare.—2. *To publish, proclaim; with* ut *to order out, call forth, call together, congregate, assemble;* edicere:—1. Aban þu þa beornas *command thou the children, Cd.* 193. 2. Þa het se cyng abannan ut ealne þeodscipe *then the king commanded to order out* [*to assemble*] *all the population, Chr.* 1006.

[h] Abárian; *pp.* ěd; *v. a.* [bar *bare, naked*] *To make bare, to manifest, detect, discover, disclose;* denudare:—Þu abarast ure spræce, *Jos.* 2, 20.

ABBAD, abbod, abbud, es *or* an; *pl.* as *or* an; *m.* [*Plat. Dut. Ger.* abd, abt: *Grk.* ἀββα: *Syr.* ܐܒܐ aba: *Heb.* אָב ab, *a father.*] *An abbot;* abbas:—Se arwurþa abbad Albinus *the reverend abbot Albinus, Bd. pref.* Swa gebireð abbodan *as becometh abbots, L. Const. W. p.* 150, 27.

Abbadisse, abbatisse, abbúdisse, an; *f. An abbess;* abbatissa:—Abbodas and huru abbatissan on mynstrum wunigean *abbots, and at least abbesses, should remain in monasteries, L. Const. W. p.* 150, 21: *Bd.* 3, 11.

Abbandun, es [abban *abbot's;* dun *a down, hill*] *Abingdon, in Berkshire:*—*Chr.* 985.

Abbod *an abbot,* v. abbad.

Abbotrice, abbuddóm, es; *m.* [abbad *an abbot;* rice, dóm *a province*] *The dominion or dignity of an abbot, an abbacy;* abbatis dignitas:—Guðfrið

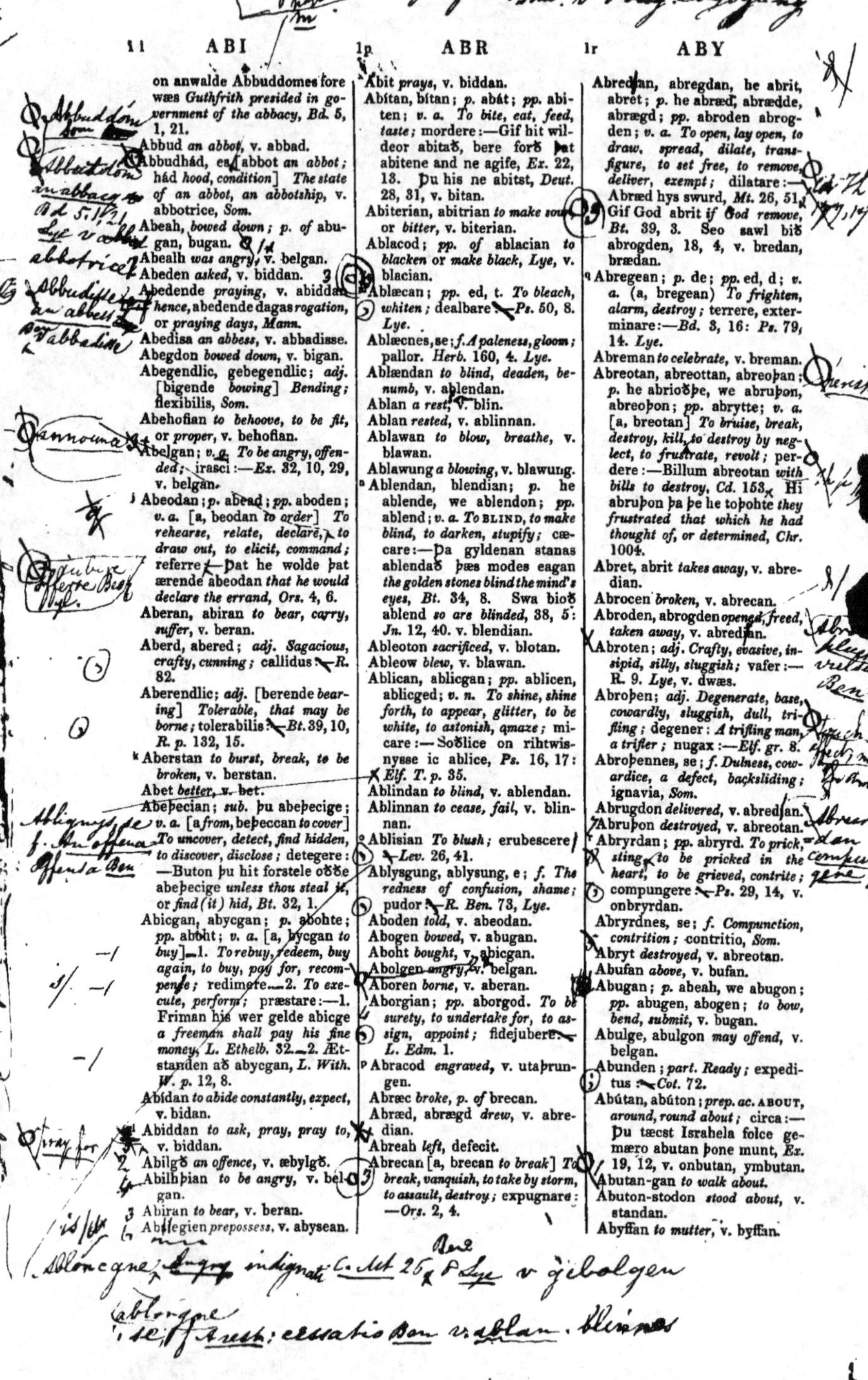

on anwalde Abbuddomes fore wæs *Guthfrith presided in government of the abbacy, Bd.* 5, 1, 21.

Abbud *an abbot*, v. abbad.

Abbudhád, es [abbot *an abbot;* hád *hood, condition*] *The state of an abbot, an abbotship*, v. abbotrice, *Som.*

Abeah, *bowed down; p. of* abugan, bugan.

Abealh *was angry*, v. belgan.

Abeden *asked*, v. biddan.

Abedende *praying*, v. abiddan; *hence*, abedende dagas *rogation, or praying days, Mann.*

Abedisa *an abbess*, v. abbadisse.

Abegdon *bowed down*, v. bigan.

Abegendlic, gebegendlic; *adj.* [bigende *bowing*] *Bending;* flexibilis, *Som.*

Abehofian *to behoove, to be fit, or proper*, v. behofian.

Abelgan; *v. a. To be angry, offended;* irasci:—*Ex.* 32, 10, 29, v. belgan.

Abeodan; *p.* abead; *pp.* aboden; *v. a.* [a, beodan *to order*] *To rehearse, relate, declare, to draw out, to elicit, command;* referre:—Þat he wolde þat ærende abeodan *that he would declare the errand, Ors.* 4, 6.

Aberan, abiran *to bear, carry, suffer*, v. beran.

Aberd, abered; *adj. Sagacious, crafty, cunning;* callidus:—*R.* 82.

Aberendlic; *adj.* [berende *bearing*] *Tolerable, that may be borne;* tolerabilis:—*Bt.* 39, 10, *R. p.* 132, 15.

Aberstan *to burst, break, to be broken*, v. berstan.

Abet *better*, v. bet.

Abeþecian; *sub.* þu abeþecige; *v. a.* [a *from*, beþeccan *to cover*] *To uncover, detect, find hidden, to discover, disclose;* detegere:—Buton þu hit forstele oððe abeþecige *unless thou steal it, or find (it) hid, Bt.* 32, 1.

Abicgan, abycgan; *p.* abohte; *pp.* aboht; *v. a.* [a, bycgan *to buy*] 1. *To rebuy, redeem, buy again, to buy, pay for, recompense;* redimere.—2. *To execute, perform;* præstare:—1. Friman his wer gelde abicge *a freeman shall pay his fine money, L. Ethelb.* 32.—2. Ætstanden að abycgan, *L. With. W. p.* 12, 8.

Abidan *to abide constantly, expect*, v. bidan.

Abiddan *to ask, pray, pray to*, v. biddan.

Abilgð *an offence*, v. æbylgð.

Abilhþian *to be angry*, v. belgan.

Abiran *to bear*, v. beran.

Abisegien *prepossess*, v. abysean.

Abit *prays*, v. biddan.

Abítan, bítan; *p.* abát; *pp.* abiten; *v. a. To bite, eat, feed, taste;* mordere:—Gif hit wildeor abitað, bere forð þat abitene and ne agife, *Ex.* 22, 13. Þu his ne abitst, *Deut.* 28, 31, v. bitan.

Abiterian, abitrian *to make sour or bitter*, v. biterian.

Ablacod; *pp. of* ablacian *to blacken or make black, Lye*, v. blacian.

Ablæcan; *pp.* ed, t. *To bleach, whiten;* dealbare:—*Ps.* 50, 8. *Lye.*

Ablæcnes, se; *f. A paleness, gloom;* pallor. *Herb.* 160, 4. *Lye.*

Ablændan *to blind, deaden, benumb*, v. ablendan.

Ablan *a rest*, v. blin.

Ablan *rested*, v. ablinnan.

Ablawan *to blow, breathe*, v. blawan.

Ablawung *a blowing*, v. blawung.

Ablendan, blendian; *p.* he ablende, we ablendon; *pp.* ablend; *v. a. To* BLIND, *to make blind, to darken, stupify;* cæcare:—Þa gyldenan stanas ablendað þæs modes eagan *the golden stones blind the mind's eyes, Bt.* 34, 8. Swa bioð ablend *so are blinded*, 38, 5: *Jn.* 12, 40. v. blendian.

Ableoton *sacrificed*, v. blotan.

Ableow *blew*, v. blawan.

Ablican, ablicgan; *pp.* ablicen, ablicged; *v. n. To shine, shine forth, to appear, glitter, to be white, to astonish, amaze;* micare:—Soðlice on rihtwisnysse ic ablice, *Ps.* 16, 17: *Elf. T. p.* 35.

Ablindan *to blind*, v. ablendan.

Ablinnan *to cease, fail*, v. blinnan.

Ablisian *To blush;* erubescere:—*Lev.* 26, 41.

Ablysgung, ablysung, e; *f. The redness of confusion, shame;* pudor:—*R. Ben.* 73, *Lye.*

Aboden *told*, v. abeodan.

Abogen *bowed*, v. abugan.

Aboht *bought*, v. abicgan.

Abolgen *angry*, v. belgan.

Aboren *borne*, v. aberan.

Aborgian; *pp.* aborgod. *To be surety, to undertake for, to assign, appoint;* fidejubere:—*L. Edm.* 1.

Abracod *engraved*, v. utaþrungen.

Abræc *broke, p. of* brecan.

Abræd, abrægd *drew*, v. abredian.

Abreah *left*, defecit.

Abrecan [a, brecan *to break*] *To break, vanquish, to take by storm, to assault, destroy;* expugnare:—*Ors.* 2, 4.

Abredian, abregdan, he abrit, abret; *p.* he abræd, abrædde, abrægd; *pp.* abroden abrogden; *v. a. To open, lay open, to draw, spread, dilate, transfigure, to set free, to remove, deliver, exempt;* dilatare:—Abræd hys swurd, *Mt.* 26, 51. Gif God abrit *if God remove, Bt.* 39, 3. Seo sawl bið abrogden, 18, 4, v. bredan, brædan.

Abregean; *p.* de; *pp.* ed, d; *v. a.* (a, bregean) *To frighten, alarm, destroy;* terrere, exterminare:—*Bd.* 3, 16: *Ps.* 79, 14. *Lye.*

Abreman *to celebrate*, v. breman.

Abreotan, abreottan, abreoþan; *p.* he abrioðþe, we abruþon, abreoþon; *pp.* abrytte; *v. a.* [a, breotan] *To bruise, break, destroy, kill, to destroy by neglect, to frustrate, revolt;* perdere:—Billum abreotan *with bills to destroy, Cd.* 153. Hi abruþon þa þe he toþohte *they frustrated that which he had thought of, or determined, Chr.* 1004.

Abret, abrit *takes away*, v. abredian.

Abrocen *broken*, v. abrecan.

Abroden, abrogden *opened, freed, taken away*, v. abredian.

Abroten; *adj. Crafty, evasive, insipid, silly, sluggish;* vafer:—R. 9. *Lye*, v. dwæs.

Abroþen; *adj. Degenerate, base, cowardly, sluggish, dull, trifling;* degener: *A trifling man, a trifler;* nugax:—*Elf. gr.* 8.

Abroþennes, se; *f. Dulness, cowardice, a defect, backsliding;* ignavia, *Som.*

Abrugdon *delivered*, v. abredian.

Abruþon *destroyed*, v. abreotan.

Abryrdan; *pp.* abryrd. *To prick, sting, to be pricked in the heart, to be grieved, contrite;* compungere:—*Ps.* 29, 14, v. onbryrdan.

Abryrdnes, se; *f. Compunction, contrition;* contritio, *Som.*

Abryt *destroyed*, v. abreotan.

Abufan *above*, v. bufan.

Abugan; *p.* abeah, we abugon; *pp.* abugen, abogen; *to bow, bend, submit*, v. bugan.

Abulge, abulgon *may offend*, v. belgan.

Abunden; *part. Ready;* expeditus:—*Cot.* 72.

Abútan, abúton; *prep. ac.* ABOUT, *around, round about;* circa:—Þu tæcst Israhela folce gemæro abutan þone munt, *Ex.* 19, 12, v. onbutan, ymbutan.

Abutan-gan *to walk about.*

Abuton-stodon *stood about*, v. standan.

Abyffan *to mutter*, v. byffan.

First ½ sheet proof July 17. 1832
2nd July 30 "
See p 505 dated Oct. 2. 1834 See page 19

Abredwian? to send abroad, to banish; exulare, pellare Bosk 5235

Q 1x Cd 222 Th p. 290, 4

(Q) 3 [8a, 1]

Q 3 Te abegdan seal from thee shall draw Cd 125 Th p 159, 22: 176, 19

2 Abeced abecedarius Wan. p 88 Lye

Q abedan exigere: Ben.

3 Abelgan v. a.* to anger

6 Abegan to bow depart inclinare Ben Bos p 1544 v abugan

Abrosdan plucked; vulsum Ben

Q Abryran pungere Ben

Abrytan extermi-nari Ben

(8) Abegan q p. of begnan

Abededse an abbess Th. An v abbedesse

5 Abilgian to offend? words; exacerbare Ben

Q 2d Th p 28, 4

4 Abotrice an abbess Th. An v abbotrice

Gif he abelgþe ahwam

Abreda [illegible] coarse, [illegible] stupa Lye Ben.

Abifian to tremble Th. Apol

3 Abisgian to busy engage oneself occupare Th. Apol

(Q) Abrecan to break (into) Th. Apol

Q Abutan-faran to go about Lye

6 Abisgung employment v abysgung

pr. 16 Wil p. 95, 63

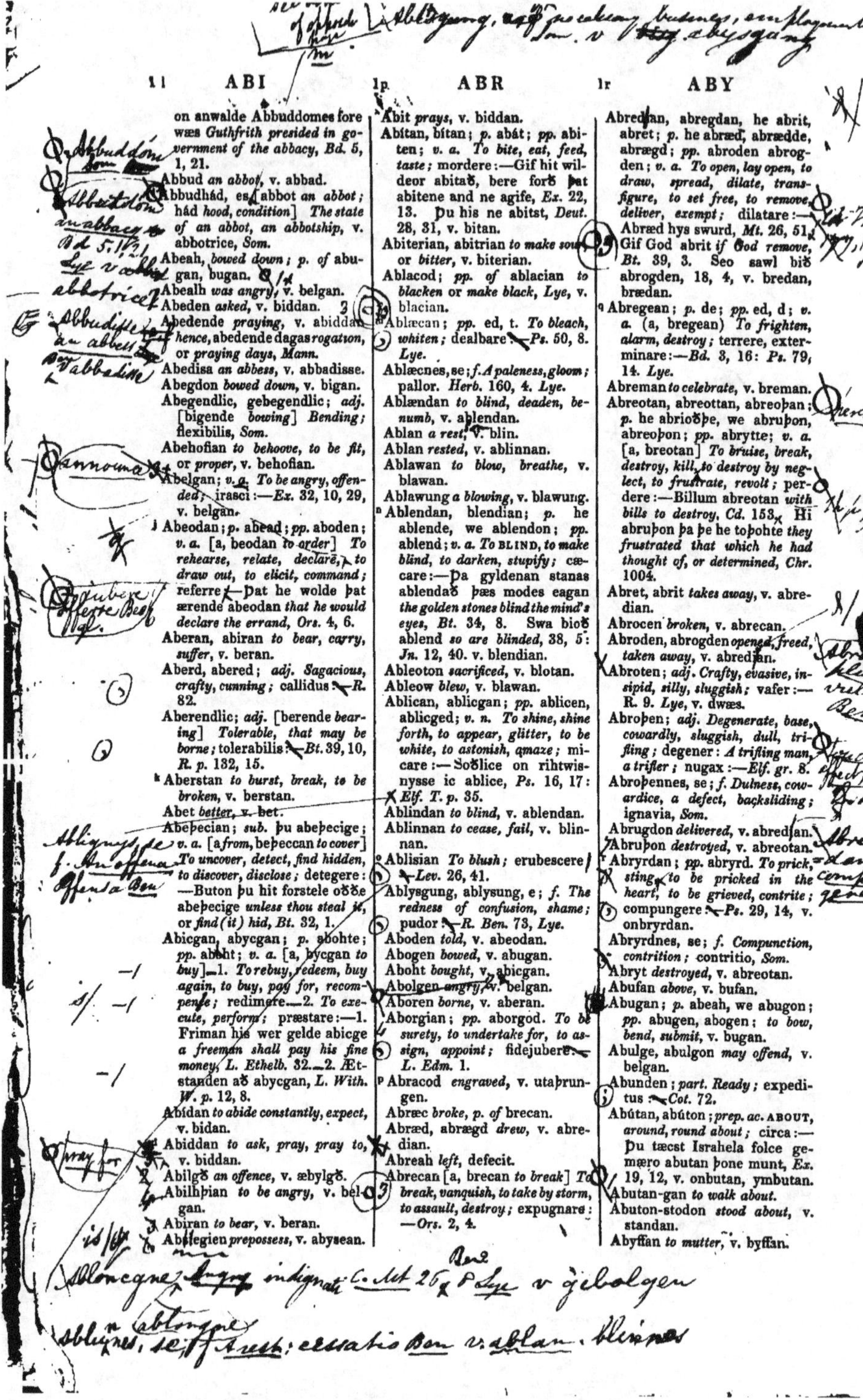

on anwalde Abbuddomes fore wæs *Guthfrith presided in government of the abbacy, Bd.* 5, 1, 21.

Abbud *an abbot*, v. abbad.

Abbudhád, es [abbot *an abbot*; hád *hood, condition*] *The state of an abbot, an abbotship*, v. abbotrice, *Som.*

Abeah, *bowed down*; *p. of* abugan, bugan.

Abealh *was angry*, v. belgan.

Abeden *asked*, v. biddan.

Abedende *praying*, v. abiddan *hence*, abedende dagas *rogation, or praying days, Mann.*

Abedisa *an abbess*, v. abbadisse.

Abegdon *bowed down*, v. bigan.

Abegendlic, gebegendlic; *adj.* [bigende *bowing*] *Bending*; flexibilis, *Som.*

Abehofian *to behoove, to be fit, or proper*, v. behofian.

Abelgan; *v. a. To be angry, offended*; irasci:—*Ex.* 32, 10, 29, v. belgan.

Abeodan; *p.* abead; *pp.* aboden; *v. a.* [a, beodan *to order*] *To rehearse, relate, declare, to draw out, to elicit, command*; referre:—Þæt he wolde þæt ærende abeodan *that he would declare the errand, Ors.* 4, 6.

Aberan, abiran *to bear, carry, suffer*, v. beran.

Aberd, abered; *adj. Sagacious, crafty, cunning*; callidus:—*R.* 82.

Aberendlic; *adj.* [berende *bearing*] *Tolerable, that may be borne*; tolerabilis:—*Bt.* 39, 10, *R. p.* 132, 15.

Aberstan *to burst, break, to be broken*, v. berstan.

Abet *better*, v. bet.

Abeþecian; *sub.* þu abeþecige; *v. a.* [a *from*, beþeccan *to cover*] *To uncover, detect, find hidden, to discover, disclose*; detegere:—Buton þu hit forstele oððe abeþecige *unless thou steal it, or find (it) hid, Bt.* 32, 1.

Abicgan, abycgan; *p.* abohte; *pp.* aboht; *v. a.* [a, bycgan *to buy*] 1. *To rebuy, redeem, buy again, to buy, pay for, recompense*; redimere. 2. *To execute, perform*; præstare:—1. Friman his wer gelde abicge *a freeman shall pay his fine money, L. Ethelb.* 32. 2. Ætstanden að abycgan, *L. With. W. p.* 12, 8.

Abídan *to abide constantly, expect*, v. bidan.

Abiddan *to ask, pray, pray to*, v. biddan.

Abilgð *an offence*, v. æbylgð.

Abilhþian *to be angry*, v. belgan.

Abiran *to bear*, v. beran.

Abiegien *prepossess*, v. abysean.

Abit *prays*, v. biddan.

Abitan, bítan; *p.* abát; *pp.* abiten; *v. a. To bite, eat, feed, taste*; mordere:—Gif hit wildeor abitað, bere forð þat abitene and ne agife, *Ex.* 22, 13. Þu his ne abitst, *Deut.* 28, 31, v. bitan.

Abiterian, abitrian *to make sour or bitter*, v. biterian.

Ablacod; *pp. of* ablacian *to blacken or make black, Lye*, v. blacian.

Ablæcan; *pp.* ed, t. *To bleach, whiten*; dealbare:—*Ps.* 50, 8. *Lye.*

Ablæcnes, se; *f. A paleness, gloom*; pallor. *Herb.* 160, 4. *Lye.*

Ablændan *to blind, deaden, benumb*, v. ablendan.

Ablan *a rest*, v. blin.

Ablan *rested*, v. ablinnan.

Ablawan *to blow, breathe*, v. blawan.

Ablawung *a blowing*, v. blawung.

Ablendan, blendian; *p.* he ablende, we ablendon; *pp.* ablend; *v. a. To* BLIND, *to make blind, to darken, stupify*; cæcare:—Þa gyldenan stanas ablendað þæs modes eagan *the golden stones blind the mind's eyes, Bt.* 34, 8. Swa bioð ablend *so are blinded*, 38, 5: *Jn.* 12, 40. v. blendian.

Ableoton *sacrificed*, v. blotan.

Ableow *blew*, v. blawan.

Ablican, ablicgan; *pp.* ablicen, ablicged; *v. n. To shine, shine forth, to appear, glitter, to be white, to astonish, amaze*; micare:—Soðlice on rihtwisnysse ic ablice, *Ps.* 16, 17: *Elf. T. p.* 35.

Ablindan *to blind*, v. ablendan.

Ablinnan *to cease, fail*, v. blinnan.

Ablisian *To blush*; erubescere:—*Lev.* 26, 41.

Ablysgung, ablysung, e; *f. The redness of confusion, shame*; pudor:—*R. Ben.* 73, *Lye.*

Aboden *told*, v. abeodan.

Abogen *bowed*, v. abugan.

Aboht *bought*, v. abicgan.

Abolgen *angry*, v. belgan.

Aboren *borne*, v. aberan.

Aborgian; *pp.* aborgod. *To be surety, to undertake for, to assign, appoint*; fidejubere:—*L. Edm.* 1.

Abracod *engraved*, v. utaþrungen.

Abræc *broke*, *p. of* brecan.

Abræd, abrægd *drew*, v. abredian.

Abreah *left*, defecit.

Abrecan [a, brecan *to break*] *To break, vanquish, to take by storm, to assault, destroy*; expugnare:—*Ors.* 2, 4.

Abredan, abregdan, he abrit, abret; *p.* he abræd, abrædde, abrægd; *pp.* abroden abrogden; *v. a. To open, lay open, to draw, spread, dilate, transfigure, to set free, to remove, deliver, exempt*; dilatare:—Abræd hys swurd, *Mt.* 26, 51: Gif God abrit *if God remove, Bt.* 39, 3. Seo sawl bið abrogden, 18, 4, v. bredan, brædan.

Abregean; *p.* de; *pp.* ed, d; *v. a.* (a, bregean) *To frighten, alarm, destroy*; terrere, exterminare:—*Bd.* 3, 16: *Ps.* 79, 14. *Lye.*

Abreman *to celebrate*, v. breman.

Abreotan, abreottan, abreoþan; *p.* he abrioðþe, we abruþon, abreoþon; *pp.* abrytte; *v. a.* [a, breotan] *To bruise, break, destroy, kill, to destroy by neglect, to frustrate, revolt*; perdere:—Billum abreotan *with bills to destroy, Cd.* 153. Hi abruþon þa þe he toþohte *they frustrated that which he had thought of, or determined, Chr.* 1004.

Abret, abrit *takes away*, v. abredian.

Abrocen *broken*, v. abrecan.

Abroden, abrogden *opened, freed, taken away*, v. abredian.

Abroten; *adj. Crafty, evasive, insipid, silly, sluggish*; vafer:—R. 9. *Lye*, v. dwæs.

Abroþen; *adj. Degenerate, base, cowardly, sluggish, dull, trifling*; degener: *A trifling man, a trifler*; nugax:—*Elf. gr.* 8.

Abroþennes, se; *f. Dulness, cowardice, a defect, backsliding*; ignavia, *Som.*

Abrugdon *delivered*, v. abredian.

Abruþon *destroyed*, v. abreotan.

Abryrdan; *pp.* abryrd. *To prick, sting, to be pricked in the heart, to be grieved, contrite*; compungere:—*Ps.* 29, 14, v. onbryrdan.

Abryrdnes, se; *f. Compunction, contrition*; contritio, *Som.*

Abryt *destroyed*, v. abreotan.

Abufan *above*, v. bufan.

Abugan; *p.* abeah, we abugon; *pp.* abugen, abogen; *to bow, bend, submit*, v. bugan.

Abulge, abulgon *may offend*, v. belgan.

Abunden; *part. Ready*; expeditus:—*Cot.* 72.

Abútan, abúton; *prep. ac.* ABOUT, *around, round about*; circa:—Þu tæcst Israhela folce gemæro abutan þone munt, *Ex.* 19, 12, v. onbutan, ymbutan.

Abutan-gan *to walk about.*

Abuton-stodon *stood about*, v. standan.

Abyffan *to mutter*, v. byffan.

First ½ sheet proof July 17. 1832
2nd July 30 "
See p 505 dated Oct. 2-1834 See page 19

Abredwian? to send abroad, to banish; exulare, pellere Bosk 5235

1 x Cd 222 3 [8ai]

Vi p 290. 4

2 Abecedabecedarius Wan. p 28 Lye

Abedan exigere: Ben.

3 Abelgan v. a* to anger

Þe abregdan scеal from thee shall draw Cd. 125 th p 159, 22: 176, 19

6 Abégan to bow depart inclinare Ben Bosk 1544 v abegan

Abrosdan plucked; vulsum Ben

Abryran pungere Ben

Abryttan exterminari Ben

Abuddise an abbess th an v abbodisse

Belgian to exasperate provoke; exacerbare Ben

2d th p 28, 4

Abbotrice an abbacy th an v abbotrice

Gif he welhye ahwam ... aliquem exacerbet ... Can Edg

Abræda ~~a~~ cease tow; hands stupa ~~Lye~~ Ben.

Abifian to tremble th. Apol

Abisgian to busy (into) engage oneself th. Apol occupare

Abrecan to break th. apol

Abutan-faran to go about Lye

6 Abisgung, es employment th an v abysgung

pn. 16 Wid p. 95, 63

X Abylgean ~~to trouble~~ to offend anger, or vex; offended, vexed Som v
~~Hindr~~ ~~Fr~~ Som v K abelgan abelgan

X 2 — X

O 1× for id 72 Tl.
86, 3

X

O [Derivation]

O to bear, sustain ih. apol.

X. Ac, aac, e; f.
an oak te Elf. Som p 7. 42

Acleac
X. ~~Ac leac~~ porrum R 45
~~Som~~ Lye

X. Acnisum i.e rankere
Ben, acnised
percussus Lye

O

O Acold

3 —— X 3

4

4

5

X× Acemannes, burh, -
-burge, d. byrig. byrih; Ibyri, beirg, also
~~Acemannes~~ ceaster, e; f. ete;
~~ceastre; f.~~ Bath O tr/

X —— X 4

O 5

O 3 Acsan to ask Ben
v acsian

X V Ascian to ask xi.
to be transferred
V Leo 107 Dereloc

Abylgð *offends*, v. belgan.

Abyrgean, abyrigean *To taste;* gustare, v. brygan.

Abysean, abysgan abysgean; *sub.* hi abisegien, on; *p.* gode; *pp.* god; *v. a.* [a, bysgian *to busy*] *To occupy, preoccupy, prepossess;* occupare:—Ðeah unþeawas oft abisegien þat mod *though imperfections oft prepossess the mind, Bt.* 35, 1.

Abysgung, e; *f. Necessary business, employment;* occupatio:—*Past.* 18, 1, *Som.*

Ac; *conj.* [æc *or* eac. *imp. of* eacan *to eke, add,*] *But, whether;* sed:—Ne com ic na to wurpan, ac gefyllan, *Mt.* 5, 17, *Som.*

A'c, aac [*Plat.* eke *f: Dut.* eik *f: Frs.* eek, iek: *Swed.* ek: *Ger.* eiche.] *An* OAK; quercus:—*Elf. gr.* 8.

Acægan *to name*, v. cegan.

Acænned *brought forth*, v. acennan.

Acænnednys, acænnys *nativity*, v. acennednes.

Acærran *to avert;* acærred *averted*, v. cerran.

Acalian *to cool*, v. acolian.

ACAN, we acað; *pp.* acen; *v. n.* [*Plat.* aeken] *To* AKE, *pain;* dolere:—Acað mine eagas *my eyes ake, I am dark, Elf. gr.* 36, *Mann.*

Acas, acase *an ax*, v. æx.

Accærn, accorn *an acorn*, v. æceren.

Accutan *to prove*, v. cunnian.

Accyn [ac *oak*, cyn *kind*] *A species of oak*, ilex, *Mann.*

Acdrenc, acdrinc *oak-drink, a kind of drink made of acorns, Som.*

Ace *ake, pain*, v. æce.

Acealdian *to cool*, v. acolian.

Aceapian *to buy;* aceaped *bought*, v. ceapian.

Acearfan *to cut off*, v. ceorfan.

Acelan *to cool;* aceled *cooled*, v. acolian.

Acemannes-beri,-ceastre, [æce *ake*, mannes *man's*, ceaster *or* burh *a city*] *Bath, Somersetshire:*—Æt Acemannes-beri, þat is at Baþine *at Akemansbery, that is, at Bath, Chr.* 973, *Ing. p.* 158, *note, l.* 10, v. Bað.

Acen *oaken*, v. æcen.

Acen *pained*, v. acan.

Acennan, þu acents, he acenð; *p.* acende; *pp.* accenned; *v. a. To bring forth, produce, beget;* parere:—*Bt.* 31, 1: *Gen.* 3, 16: *Mt.* 2, 1, v. cennan.

Acennedlic; *adj. Native;* nativus:—*Cot.* 138, *Som.*

Acennednes, acennes, acennys, acænnednys, acænnys, se; *f. Nativity, birth, generation;* ortus:—Manega on hys acennednesse gefagniað, *Lk.* 1, 14: *Ps.* 106, 37.

Aceocan; *pp.* aceocod *to suffocate, choke, Som.*

Aceocung, e; *f. A consideration;* ruminatio, *R.* 99, v. ceosung.

Aceorfan *to cut off*, v. ceorfan.

Acer, acera *a field*, v. æcer.

Acerran *to return*, v. cerran.

Acerrednes *an aversion*, v. acyrrednes.

Achsian *to ask*, v. acsian.

Aciende *Troubling, shivering, rough;* horrens:—*Hymn, Lye.*

Acigan *to call:*—*Bd.* 2, 12, v. cygan.

Acl; *adj. Clear, sonorous;* clarus:—Aclum stefnum *with clear voices, Cd.* 171, *Mann.*

Aclænsian *to cleanse, purify*, v. clænsian.

Aclea [ac *an oak*, lea, *or* lega *a lay, meadow*] *The name of a place, as Oakley:*—Sinoð wæs gegaderod æt Aclea *a synod was assembled at Acley or Oakley, Chr.* 789.

Acliopian *to call, to call out*, v. clypian.

Acmistel *mistletoe of the oak:*—*L. M.* 1, 36.

Acnised, *expelled, driven out, chased away*, v. chysan.

Acofran *to recover;* convalescere:—*Observ. Lun.* 2, *Lye.*

Acol, acul; *adj. Acold, chilled with fear, terrified;* perterritus, *Mann.*

Acolian, æcelan, acelan; *p.* de; *pp.* ed, od. *To become cold, to wax* or *grow cold;* frigescere:—*Mt.* 24, 12.

Acolmod *of a fearful mind, timid.*

Acordan; *p.* we acordedan. *To* ACCORD, *agree, reconcile;* reconciliare:—*Chr.* 1119.

Acoren *chosen*, v. coren.

Acorenlic; *adj. Likely to be chosen;* eligibilis:—*Past.* 52, 8.

Acorfen *carved*, v. ceorfan.

Acostnod *tried*, v. costian.

Acræftan *To devise, plan, contrive as a craftsman;* excogitare:—*Ors.* 2, 5.

Acreowed *q.* acreoped *crept over:*—*Ex.* 16, 20. v. creopan.

Acrummen *crammed*, v. crammian.

Acruman, acrymman; *pp.* men. *To crum, crumble;* friare, *Som.*

Acs *an ax*, v. æx.

Acsan-mynster, Axanminster *Axminster in Devonshire:*—*Chr.* 755.

Acse, v. axe *ashes*, v. æx *an ax*, v. *also* æsc, *an ash-tree.*

ACSIAN, acsigan, ahsian, ascian, axian, axigean; *p.* de, ede, ode; *pp.* od. [*Plat.* ésken: *Dut.* eischen] *To* ASK, *inquire, explore;* rogare:—Mot ic acsian, *Bd.* 4, 3. Hu mæg ænig man acsigan, *Bt.* 35, 1. Ne nan ne dorste axigean, *Mt.* 22, 46.

Acsung, ascung, e; *f. An* ASKING, *a question, an inquiry, inquisition, interrogation, that which is enquired about, information;* interrogatio:—Uneaþe ic mæg forstandan þine acsunga *I can scarcely understand thy questions, Bt.* 5, 3. Mid ascunga *by enquiries, Id.* 35, 1.

Acucian *to revive*, v. cucian.

Acul *cold*, v. acol.

Acuman; *pp.* acumen. *To come to, to pursue, bear, suffer, perform, to overcome;* attingere, ferre:—*Gen.* 36, 7.

Acumba, acumbe, æcemba, æcumbe *Oakum, the coarse part of flax, hards, a kind of marley,* or *chalky clay, shales* or *parings;* stupa:—*R.* 64, *Som.*

Acumendlic; *adj. Tolerable, bearable;* tolerabilis:—Acumendlicre byð, *Mt.* 10, 15.

Acumendlicnes, se; *f. The possibility to bring any thing to pass;* possibilitas, *Som.*

Acunnian *to prove*, v. cunnian.

Acuron *chose*, v. ceosan.

Acwæden *said*, v. cwæþan.

Acwælan *died*, v. acwelan.

Acwæþan *to say*, acwæð *said*, v. cwæþan.

Acwalde *killed*, v. cwellan.

Acwan, acwanc *quenched*, v. acwencan.

Acweald, acwealde *killed*, v. cwellan.

Acwelan, acwylan, cwelan, he acwilð, hi acwelað; *p.* acwæl; *pp.* acwolen; *v.n. To die, perish;* mori:—Ða fixas acwelað, *Ex.* 7, 18.

Acwellan *to kill*, v. cwellan.

Acwellednes, se; *f. A quelling, killing, slaying;* occisio, Som.

Acwencan, acwinan, cwencan; *p.* acwanc; *pp.* acwenced, acwenct, acwent, acwan, acwinen. *To* QUENCH, *extinguish, to put out;* extinguere:—Ure leohtfatu synt acwencte, *Mt.* 25, 8. Fyr ne byð acwenced, *Mk.* 9, 44. Ðæt fyr acwan wæs *the fire was put out, Bd.* 2, 7.

Acwern, wern [ac *an oak*, wern] *The name of an animal, a squirrel*, etc.; scirra:—*Elf. gl. Som.*

Acwerran, acworren *drunk, Ps.* 77, 71.

Acweþan *to answer*, v. cwæþan.

Acwician acwucian, gecwican; *pp.* acwicod, gecwicod. *To quicken, revive, to come to life, to create;* reviviscere:—*Bd.* 5, 6, 12, *Lye.*

Acwillan *to kill*, v. cwellan.

Acwinen *quenched*, v. acwencan.

Acwoellan *to kill*, v. cwellan.

Acwolen *dead*, v. acwelan.

Acworren *drunk*, v. acwerran.

Acwucian *to quicken*, v. acwician.

Acwylan *to die*, v. acwelan.

Acxan *ashes*, v. axe.

Acyd *said, confirmed*, v. acyþan.

Acyr *a field*, v. æcer.

Acyrran; *p.* acyrde; *pp.* acyrred, acyrd *to avert*, v. cyrran.

c Acyrrednes, acerrednes, se; *f.* *A turning, aversion, a turning from, apostacy, backsliding, revolting*; aversio, *Som.*

ÁD, aad, ade; *m.* [*Al.* od *substance, goods, Icel.* aud: *Heb.* עדה ode, *an assembly.*] *A heap, a pile*; congeries:—*Bd.* 3, 16.

Adæled *divided*, v. dælan.

Adastrigan *To discourage, dismay, to frighten away*; deterrere: Hence DASTARD, *a coward, Som.*

Adeadan, deadian; *p.* ode; *pp.* od, gedead. *To fail, decay* or *die, to mortify, to lay waste, to destroy*; fatiscere:—*Heb.* 35, *Som.*

Adeaf *deaf*, v. deaf.

Adeafian; *p.* ede. *To become* or *wax deaf*; surdescere, *Som.*

Adeafung earena *a deafening of the ears, a deafening, Lye.*

Adel *a disease*, v. adl.

Adelfan *to dig*, v delfan.

Adeliht; *adj. Dirty, filthy*; coenosus:—*Cot.* 48.

Adelseað, adulseað *A sewer, gutter, sink*; cloaca, *Som.*

Adelyng *a prince*, v. æþeling.

Ademan *To judge, doom, deem, try*; examinare:—*Bd.* 4, 23.

e Adeorcian; *p.* ade; *pp.* ad. *To obscure, dim, darken, hide*; obscurare, *Som.*

Adesa, adese *An addice* or *adz, a cooper's instrument*; ascia:—*Bd.* 4, 3.

Adihtod *made, composed*, v. dihtan.

Adilegian, adilgian, adylegian; *p.* ode; *pp.* adilegod, adilgod, adylegod; *v. a. To abolish, to blot out, to destroy, to do away*; delere:—His sawul bið adilegod, *Gen.* 17, 14: *Ex.* 32, 32, v. dilgian.

Adimmian; *p.* de; *pp.* od, ad. *To dim, darken, obscure, to make dull*; obscurare:—Ðeah heora mod sie adimmad *though their mind be obscured, Bt.* 24, 4.

ADL, e; *pl.* a, u; *f.* [*Heb.* חדל hedel, *to fail*] *A disease, grief, pain, a languishing sickness, consumption*; morbus:—Hu manega adla *how many diseases, Bt.* 31, 1: *Bd.* 3, 12. ¶ Seo mycle adl *the leprosy.* Laman legeres adl *the palsy*, v. leger.

Adl, adlic, adlig; *adj. Sick, ill, diseased, corrupted, putrid*; morbidus: Hence ADDLE egg:—*Bd.* 3, 2, *Mann.*

Adlian *To ail, to be sick, to languish*; ægrotare:—*Elf. gr.* 26.

g Adlic, adlig *sick*, v. adl.

Adol *a disease*, v. adl.

Adolfen, *dug*, v. delfan.

Adon; *p.* we adydon; *imp.* ado; *v. a.* [a *from* don *to do*] *To take away, remove, banish*; tollere:—Ado þas wylne, *Gen.* 21, 10: *Bt.* 16, 1.

Adrædan *to dread*, v. ondredan.

Adræfan *to drive away*, v. adrifan.

Adrænct *sunk*, v. adrencan.

Adreag, adreah *bore*, v. adreogan.

Adred *feared*, v. ondredan.

Adrefed *driven*, v. adrifan.

Adreið *dries*, v. adrigan.

Adremnt *the herb feverfew* or *mugwort, Som.*

Adrencan; *p.* adrænct, adrencte; *pp.* adrenced, adroncen, adruncen, adronct; *v.a. To plunge under, to immerge, drown*; immergere:—Wolde hine adrencan on þære ea *would drown him in the river, Bt.* 16, 2.

Adreogan, gedreogan, adreohan, adriogan, adriohan; *p.* adreag, adreah, we adrugon; *pp.* adrogen; *v. a. To bear, suffer, lead, endure*; pati:—Hi adreogan magan *they may bear, Bt.* 40, 3. Ic ne mæg adreohan þine seofunga *I cannot tolerate thy lamentations, Bt.* 11, 1. ¶ Adreogan lif *to lead a life, to live*, v. dreogan.

Adreogendlic; *adj. Bearable, endurable*; tolerabilis, *Lye.*

Adrifan, ædrifan, adræfan; *p.* adraf, adrof, adræfde, we adrifon; *pp.* adræfed, adrifed, adrefed, adrifen.—1. *To drive away, to expel, repel*; expellere.—2. *To drive, impel*; agere:—1. He adræfed wæs, *Gen.* 3, 24.—2. Ða Walas adrifon sumre ea ford ealne mid scearpum pilum greatum innan þam wætere *the Welsh drove all the ford of a certain river with great sharp piles within the water, Chr. Introd.* ¶ Adrifene fatu *graven* or *embossed vessels, R.* 67, v. drifan.

Adrigan, -ygan, -igean, -yggean, -iggan, -ugian, -uwian; *p.* ic adrigde, -ugode, þu adrigdest, we adrugodon, -uwedon; *pp.* adruged, -uwod, -uwud. *To dry, dry up, rub dry, to wither*; siccare:—*Ps.* 73, 16: *Gen.* 8, 11, 13, v. drigan.

Adriogan, adriohan *to bear*, v. adreogan.

Adrogen *done*, v. adreogan.

Adronc, adroncen, adronct *drowned*, v. adrencan.

Adrugian *to dry*, v. adrigan.

Adruncen *drowned*, v. adrencan.

Adruwian; *p.* adruwedon *to dry up*, v. adrigan.

Adrygan, -yggean *to dry*, v. adrigan.

Adrysnian *to extinguish*, v. drysnian.

Adulseað *a sewer, sink*, v. adelseað.

h Adumbian; *p.* ede; *pp.* ed; *v. n. To hold one's peace, to keep silence, to become mute* or *dumb*; obmutescere:—Adumba and ga of þisum men, *Mk.* 1, 25.

Adún, adúne, ofdúne *adv.* [a, dun *a hill*] *Down*, ADOWN, *downward*; deorsum:—Adun of þam wealle *down from the wall, Bd.* 1, 12. Ða dura bræcon adune *broke the doors down, Chr.* 1083. Adune asetton *(they) put down, deposed, Bd.* 4, 6. He adune astah, *Ps.* 71, 6.

Adunweard; *adv. Downward*; deorsum:—*Chr.* 1083.

i Adwæscan, dwæscan; *p.* -cede; *pp.* -ced adwæsct; *v. a. To quench, to put out, to staunch, appease*; extinguere:—Smeocende flex he ne adwæsceð, *Mt.* 12, 20: *Bd.* 2, 7, 12.

Adwelian *To seduce, to lead into error*; seducere:—*Elf. ep.* 29, *Lye.*

Adwinan *to put out*, v. dwinan.

Adydan, adyddan; *p.* yde; *pp.* yd; *v. a.* [dydan *to die*] *To put to death, to destroy, kill, mortify*; perdere:—Wolde hig adydan *would destroy them, Elf. T.* p. 22, 19: *Gen.* 9, 11.

Adylegian, adylgian *to destroy*, v. adilegian.

Æ, prefixed to words, like *a*, often denotes, *a negative, deteriorating* or *opposite* signification, as *from, away, out, without*, etc.; thus æhiwness *paleness*, æ *without*, hiwnes *hue*; æmen *depopulated*, æ *without*, men *men*; æmod *mad*, æ *without*, mod *mind*; æscær *unshorn*, æ *not*, scær *cut*; ætynan *to open*, æ *not*, tynan *to shut*; æwena *doubtful*, æ *from*, wena *hope*. Sometimes æ *prefixed* to words does not appear to alter the signification, as æbere, abare, *or* bare *bare, naked*; æbilgð, abylgð, belgð *is angry*; æblece *or*

1× Þu scealt ád ge=
=gærwan bæl-fyr, &
blotan sylf. thou shalt
a pile prepare, a balefire
& sacrifice thyself Cd. 138
Th p 173, 3: 175, 25:
176, 20: 177, 14.
Oe 8

× Adrincan, p
we adruncon
a drang × to drown
to quench th. a.
adrencan, drincan, E.

For [illegible] see [illegible]
[illegible]

2

× Adranc quenched
Cd 146 Th 182, 18
p of adrincan v. Dpl
4 Adremint
5 parthenium.

× ——— 1

3 Adestrigan detes-
tari C. Mt 26, 74
Ben, Lye.

——— 5 × Cd
220 Th. 283, 17

× 2 × Ad-fyr a pile
fire, fire of the funeral
pile - Ad-fyr on=
bran a pile fire
kindled Cd. 162 Th
p 203, 4

× 2c × Adilgian to abolish. dl. adilgean

12 × Ádel, ádl, e. f
a disease Gm II, 100, 6

Ælma, chafing of horses with saddles; fadum intertrigo Som

Ædwines-clif, es. n Edwinscliff, Edwinstow Notts. Ch. 761

Æfen-gram evening rage, Beo K 4143

Æcin Tibetum, wd. forte tabes. Som Lye Bone

Æ-cræft, es; m Law craft, adeq[?] Institute Cd 173 Th p 217, 7

Æddre, ædre, æ; f a vein, drain, water course Gmth. 134, 8 III 407, 26; Alone A. 196: Beo[?] ædre

also Ædre, an; f see opposite

Æder, æ; f Th p 83, 3

Æcræftigo pharisees C. Mt 12, 24

Æbilgnes, se; f Anger Th. Apol

Æbreda a kind of marl or clay; naphtha Cot 138 Lye, Som

Æfen-leóht, es; n evening light Beo K 821

Æfen-ræst, e; f evening rest Beo K 2504

Æfen-spræc, e; f an evening speech Beo K 1511

abræda

He sende graman æbylignysse (æbylgðe) mid[?] iram indignationis Ps 77.54. On æbylignysse Ps 94, 8

Æddre nædle[?] Cd 140, Th p 175, 32

Ædre a vein v. also ædre

blæce *pale;* æaldorman, ealdorman, aldorman *an alderman.* Like a, ge, etc., æ is sometimes prefixed to perfect tenses and perfect participles without any perceptible alteration in the sense, æceled, acoled, coled *cooled.*

Æ; *f. indecl.* [*Al. Franc.* e, ee, ehe *a law*, from a,e, ἀεὶ *always, flowing on for a long time, till it has become a custom, a law*] *A law, right, testament;* lex:—God him sette æ þat ys open lagu *God set them law, that is plain direction, Elf. T.* p. 10, 20. Æ Drihtnes *God's law, Ps.* 18, 8: *Mt.* 26, 28. Wircað his bebodu and his æ, *Deut.* 11, 1. ¶ Cristes æ *the Gospel.* Butan æ *or* utlaga *an outlaw, Elf. gr.* 47. Seo æftere æ *Deuteronomy, Bd.* 1, 27.

Æ, æa *water*, v. ea.

Æaht *property*, v. æht.

Æall *all*, v. eal.

Æala *alas!* v. eala.

Æaldian *to grow old*, v. ealdian.

Æaldermen, æaldormen *noblemen*, v. ealdorman.

Æargian; *p.* hi æargadon *they were slothful*, v. eargian.

Æbbad *ebbed*, v. ebban.

Æbbung *an ebbing.* ¶ Sæ æbbung *a bay;* sinus:—*R.* 67.

Æbec *law books, books of the law.*

Æbed, æbod *an affair of law, business.*

Æber; *adj. Clear and evident by proof, manifest, apparent, notorious;* manifestus:—Se æbera þeof, *L. Edg.* 7.

Æbesne *pasturage*, v. æfesne.

Æbilgað, æbiliað *vex*, v. belgan.

Æblec; *adj. Pale, wan, whitish, bleak;* pallidus, *Som.*

Æblecing, æblecnys *paleness*, v. blacung.

Æbod *a business*, v. æbed.

Æbrec [ea *water*, bræc] *A catarrh, rheum;* rheuma, *Som.*

Æbs *a fir tree, Elf. gr.* 5.

Æbyld *An injury;* injuria:—*L. Cnut. pol.* 37.

Æbyligan *to be angry*, v. abelgan.

Æbylgð, æbylhð, abilgð, æbylignis, se; *f.* [bylgð, v. belgan] *An offence, a fault, scandal, anger, wrath, indignation;* offensa:—*Ors.* 4, 1.

Æc *also*, v. eac.

Æ'c *an oak*, v. ac.

Æcan *to eke*, v. eacan.

Æcced *acid*, v. eced.

Æccer *a field*, v. æcer.

Æce *eternal*, v. ece.

Æce, ece, ace; *m.* [*Plat.* aak *a disease in the finger; Ger.* ach: *Grk.* ἄχος: *Heb.* אח ah, *a place for fire, heat*] *An* AKE, *pain;* dolor:—Eal þat sar and se æce onwæg alæded wæs *all the sore and ake were (led) taken away, Bd.* 5, 3, 4.

Æced *vinegar*, v. eced: Æcedfæt *a vessel for vinegar*, v. eced-fæt.

Æceled *cooled*, v. acolian.

Æcemba *oakum*, v. acumba.

Æcen, acen; *adj. Oaken, made of oak;* quernus:—*Cot.* 165.

ÆCER, æcyr, es; *pl.* æceras, æcras; *m.* (*Plat. Dut. Ger.* akker *m.*: *Moes.* akrs: *Heb.* אכר akr, *a farmer*) *A field, land, any thing sown, sown corn, corn, an* ACRE; ager, seges:—Forþam is se æcer gehaten Acheldemah, *Mt.* 27, 8.

Æcer-ceorl, æcer-mon *a fieldman, a farmer, ploughman, clown.*

Æceren, æcern, æcirn [ac *an oak*, corn *corn*] *The corn or fruit of an oak, an* ACORN, *a nut;* glans:—*Gen.* 43, 11.

Æcer-spranca, æcer-spranga *Young shoots springing up from acorns, saplings, the holm oak, scarlet oak;* ilex:—*Elf. gr.*: *Som.* p. 13, 48.

Æchir *an ear of corn*, v. ear.

Æciorfan *to cut to pieces*, v. ceorfan.

Æcirnu *nuts*, v. æceren.

Æcne; *adj. Fruitful;* fœcundus, *Som.*

Æcrum *with fields*, v. æcer.

Æ-cræftig *law-crafty, one skilful in law, a lawyer, pharisee.*

Æcse *an ax*, v. æx.

Æcumbe *oakum*, v. acumba.

Æcyr *a field*, v. æcer.

Æcyrf *that which is cut off, a fragment, piece*, v. cyrf, ceorfan.

Æddre, æddra, ædra, ædre [æ *water*, dri *dry*, or *drain*]—1. *A passage for liquid, a drain, hence an artery, a vein, pore, kidney, a fissure or rent;* vena.—2. *A vessel, nerve, sinew;* nervus:—1. Æddran *kidneys, Ps.* 7, 10.—2. *Ors.* 3, 9.

Ædre-seax, ædre-seax *a vein knife, a lancet.*

Ædfæst [ead *substance*, fæst *fast, fixed*] *Goods, property;* bona:—Ædfæst tæht to healdenne *property taken to hold, a pledge, Elf. gl.*: *Som.* p. 58.

Ædlean *a reward*, v. edlean.

Ædra, ædre *a drain for liquid*, v. æddra.

Ædre; *adv. Directly, quickly, forthwith, by and by;* confestim:—*Menol.* 259.

Ædre-seax *a lancet*, v. æderseax.

Ædre wegga *a drain way, a vein, an artery.*

Ædrifan *to expel*, v. adrifan.

Ædwist *substance*, v. edwist.

Ædwit *a reproach*, v. edwit.

Ædwitan *to reproach;* ædwitod *derided*, v. edwitan.

Æene *once*, v. æne.

Æfæst *envy*, v. æfista.

Æfdæl *a descent*, v. ofdæl.

Æfelle, afelle (æ, fell *a skin*) *Barked, peeled, skinned;* decorticatum:—*R.* 115.

Æfen *even*, v. efen.

ÆFEN, æfnung, æfyn, efen, [*Plat.* avend; *m.*: *Dut.* avond: *Ger.* abend] *The* EVEN, *evening, eventide;* vesper, vespera:—On æfen, on æfnunge *or* to æfen *at even, in the evening, Ps.* 29, 6. Heo com þa on æfnunge eft to Noe. *Gen.* 8, 11. ¶ Æfen-dream *an evening song.*—Æfen-gebed *a prayer or evening duty, R.* 34.—Æfengereord *an evening meal, a supper, Bd.* 3. 7, v. æfenmete.—Æfen-gereordian (gereordian *to feed*) *to sup, or take supper.*—Æfen-gloma, glommung, glomung *the evening twilight, Bd.* 1, 1.

Æfen-gyfl *a supper, Past.* 1, 2, v. æfenmete.

Æfen-hlytta *A fellow, consort, companion* or *mate;* consors, *Som.*

Æfen hrepsung [æfen, hrepsung *evening*] *The evening, even, Som.*

Æfenlæcan *to match*, v. efenlæcan.

Æfenlæcend *an imitator*, v. efenlæcend.

Æfenlæcð *it draweth nigh the evening;* advesperascit:—*Lk.* 24, 29.

Æfenleoð *an evening song, Cd.* 151. v. æfendream.

Æfenlic; *adj. Vespertine, of the evening;* vespertinus:—*Ps.* 140, 2.

Æfen-mete *evening meat, supper:*—*Cot.* 42.

Æfenn *the evening*, v. æfen.

Æfen-rima *twilight;* crepusculum, *Lye.*

Æfen-sang *an evening song.*

Æfen-scima *evening splendour, Cd.* 112.

Æfen-steorra, an; *m. The twilight star, evening star, morning star;* hesperus:—Se steorra þe we hatað æfen-steorra *the star which we call evening star, Bt.* 39, 13. Se morgen-steorra, we hatað oþre naman, æfensteorra, *Bt.* 4, v. æfentungel.

Æfen-þenung *an even repast, a supper.*

Æfen-þeowdóm *an evening duty, attendance:*—*R.* 34.

Æfen-tid, æfen-tima, *The*

eventide, evening; hora vespertina:—Da æfentima wæs, *Mk.* 11, 11. Seo æfen-tide þæs dæges *the eventide of the day, Dial.* 1, 10.

Æfen-tungel *the evening star, Som.*

t ÆFER, æfre; *adv. Always,* EVER; semper:—Æfer ge fliton ongen God, *Deut.* 31, 27.

Æfesne, æbesne *Pasturage, the hire of pigs going into the wood to fatten on acorns;* pasnagium:—Gif mon nime æfesne on swinum *if [a man] any one take pasturage on swine, L. In.* 49.

Æfest, æfst, æfestig, æwfest [æ *law,* fæst *fast, fixed*]—1. *Fixed in the law, religious, devout;* religiosus.—2. *Fastened by the law, married;* matrimonio conjunctus.—3. *Fixed in mind, zealous, envious, spiteful, malicious;* invidus:—1. Wæs he æfest and arfæst *was he devout and good, Bd.* 3, 14.—2. *L. Cnut. pol.* 47, v. æwfestman.—3. *Bd.* 5, 22.

Æfestian *to envy, Cot.* 119.

Æfestig *a contender,* v. æfista, æfest.

Æfestig *religious,* v. æfest.

u Æfestlice; *adv. Religiously;* religiose:—*Bd.* 5, 13: *Chr.* 656.

Æfestnes, æfæstnes, se; *f.*—1. *Religion, devotion;* religio.—2. *Envy, spite, emulation;* invidia:—1. He wæs mycelre æfæstnesse wer *he was a man of much religion, Bd.* 4, 31.—2. *Som.*

Æffrica, African, Africa *Africa, an African;* Africa, Afer, Africanus.—Æffrica cynnes, Africa-cynnes *of African race;* genere Afer, *Bd.* 1, 5.

Æfgræf, æfgræfa *A tax-gatherer, a collector;* exactor, *Som.*

Æfista, æfæst, æfest, æfst, æfestig, æfstig *Envy, zeal, spite, a striver, an opposer, a rival;* invidia, æmulator:—*Past.* 13, 2, v. æfestnes.

Æfnan *to perform,* v. efnan.

Æfne *behold,* v. efne.

v Æfnian *To grow towards evening, Dial.* 1, 10, v. æfenlæcð.

Æfre *ever,* v. æfer.

Æfst *envy,* v. æfista.

Æfstian *to hasten,* v. efstan.

Æfstig *a contender,* v. æfista.

Æf-sweorce *Fruit;* fructus:—*Cot.* 92, *Lye.*

Æft, eft, æfter, æftan; *adv.* AFTER, *again, behind, afterwards;* postea:—Moises cwæð æft to Israel, *Deut.* 28, 15. Cwæð heo eft *said she again, Bd.* 4, 8. Swilce ær nas ne æfter ne cymð, *Ex.* 11, 6. He cymð him sylf æfter, *Gen.* 32, 19. Earn æftan hwit *an eagle white behind, Chr.* 938. ¶ Ær oþðe eft *ere or aft, before or after, Athan.*

Æftan; *prep. After, behind;* post:—*Lup.* 8, v. bæftan.

Æftbeteht *reassigned,* v. eftbetæht.

Æftemest,-myst *last,* v. æfter, *adj.*

ÆFTER, efter; *prep. dat.* [*Frs. Dan. Swed.* efter: *Al.* after: *Moes.* afar: *Norse* aptir] AFTER, *for, on account of, according to, through, over;* post:—Se þe æfter me towerd ys, *Mt.* 3, 11. Ne swincð he nauht æfter þam *he labours not for this, Bt.* 33, 2. Æfter Moyses æ, *Lk.* 2, 22. Æfter burgum *through the cities, Bt. R.* p. 155:—¶ Æfter rihte *justly.* Æfter þam þe, *Mk.* 14, 28, Æfter þon þe, *Bd.* 3, 20, *after that, after, afterwards.*

Æfter *after,* v. æft.

Æfter, *comp.* re, ra; *sup.* mest. myst; *adj.* AFTER, *next, second, new, last;* posterus, novus:—Se æftera dæl þæs heafdes *the after, or hinder part of the head,* v. æfteweard. Æftera dæg *the next day, Lk.* 13, 33. Þeos boc ys æftemyst *this book is the last, Elf. T.* p. 31, 23.

w Æftera Geola *January,* v. geol.

Æftera Liþa *July,* v. liþa.

Æfterboren; *part. Born after the father's death;* posthumus:—*Elf. gr.* 47, *Som.*

Æftercwæþan *To speak after, to answer, revoke, renounce, abjure;* revocare:—*Bd.* 5, 2.

Æftereala *after-ale, small beer, or ale, Elf. gl.* p. 62.

Æfter-fæce; *adv.* [æfter *after, and the dat. of* fæc *a space*] *Afterward, after that;* postmodum, *Som.*

x Æfterfolger, es; *m. A follower, a successor:*—*Ors.* 3, 2.

Æfterfolgiende *following after.*

Æfter-fylian, -filian; *To follow or come after, to succeed;* subsequi:—Þæs æfter-filiendan tacnes, *Ex.* 4, 8.

Æfterfylging; *f. A following after, a sequence;* sectatio, v. æfterfylignes.

Æfterfyligend; *m. One who follows, or succeeds, a follower;* successor, *Bd.* 2, 20, v. æfterfylian.

y Æfterfylignes, se; *f. A following after, a succession, succeeding;* successio, *Som.*

Æftergan [gan *to go*] *To follow after;* subsequi:—*Past.* 15, 2.

Æftergencnys, se; *f.* [gengnys *a going*] *Extremity;* extremitas:—*R. Ben. Interl.* 7, *Lye.*

Æftergenga [genga *goer; from* geng *or* gang *a walk*] *One who goes, or follows after, a follower;* successor:—Þu me ne derige, ne minum æftergengum, *Gen.* 21, 23.

Æfter-gengle [q æftergenga] *Successors, they who succeed, posterity, offspring;* posteri, *Som.*

z Æftergengnys, se; *f. Posterity, succession;* posteritas, *Som.*

Æfterhæþe, -hæþa [æfter *after,* hætu *heat*] *Afterheat;* insequens calor:—*Ors.* 3, 3.

Æfterhyrigean *To follow another's example, to imitate, resemble;* imitari:—*Bd.* 3, 18.

Æfterleán *An after-loan, a reward, a recompence;* præmium:—*Cd.* 4.

Æftermest *aftermost,* v. æfter, *adj.*

Æfterra *second,* v. æfter, *adj.*

Æfterran acennes *regeneration, Som,* v. acennednes.

Æfterran siþe *secondly,* v. siþe.

a Æfterrap, es; *m. An* AFTER-ROPE, *a crupper;* postilena:—*Elf. gl. p.* 59, *Som.*

Æfterridan *To ride after;* equo insequi:—*Jos.* 2, 7.

Æfter-rihte *according to right, justly, Som,* v. rihte.

Æfter-ryne *An encountering, a meeting, running against one;* occursus:—*Ps.* 18, 7, *Som.*

Æftersang *The after-song;* posterior cantus:—*Elf. ep.* 1, 31, *Mann.*

Æftersingend *an after-singer,* v. singan.

Æfterspræc *after-speech,* v. spræc.

Æfter-spræcan *To seek after, sue for, to require;* petere:—*Cd.* 162.

Æfterspyrian, -spyrgean *to enquire after,* v. spirian.

b Æfterweardnes, se; *f. Posterity;* posteritas:—*Cot.* 149, *Som.*

Æfter-wearð *Being away, absent, Bd.* 3, 15, *Som,* v. æfweard.

Æfter yldo *an after age,* v. yld.

Æfteweard; *adj. After, back, late, latter, full;* posterior:—Æfteweard lencten *full spring, R.* 95. Æfteweard heafod *the back of the head, R.* 69.

Æftewearde; *adv. Afterward, after, behind;* post, pone:—Þu gesihst me æftewearde, *Ex.* 33, 23: ¶ On æfteweard *on after, behind, Deut.* 28, 13.

c Æfþanc, es; *m. Offence, displeasure, zeal;* offensa:—*Ps.* 118, 139: æfþonca, *Fr. Jud.* 12.

Æftmest *last,* v. æfter *adj.*

Æftra dæl *the last part.*

X

Ø 2

Ø 1 ×

Ø 1

Ø 2 hátu, e. f

O 9 ——— 9 per 155
after burgum
through cities, abroad, op. Cd 169 Th p 210, 4 OH F p 19.5

2 Æfterlic after second; secundus Cot 191 Lye

O 2 Secund - Pas æfteran sealmes capitul secundi psalmi caput OE Ps Th. title to 2.

• 2× Ø

Æfter-singende, es m an after singer, succentor Æ 33 Lye

Ø 4 Æflast Cd 166, Th p 207, 27

Ø 3 Æfter-eala sapa (eala, e. f. Ziusas; n) Elf gl Som p 62, 22

Ø 4 - folgere, es, m

×

Ø 5

O Æfestig Matt 13, 2 Lye

Ø 6

Æfteward afterward Gen 33, 2 v æfteweard

6 Æf-punga, an m Wolves, nes, dis like, disgust; taedium, aversio Bes K 999 v Æso...

Æg-lac v. ?

Æg-lác, es; n Misery, trouble; misery Cd p 230 Beo sl in lác v. aglac

a-hiwnes deficientia coloris Mann Lex.

(aglæca)

Æglaca, an; m A wretch, miscreant; miser Cd 216 Th p 274, 28: 214, Th p 269, 14: Beo of in lác

[a sea guard or keeper] æg-weard, e; f [in Beo gl. in warian] for

Æg, e; f an island v. ieg Beo K 480

v. æg-weard

Æg-flotan, sailors, nautæ Cod verc Beo Th apx 480

Ægles-burh, Egles-burh, g. -burge; d. -byrig Aylesbury, Bucks Cuþwulf genam Æglesburh Cuthulf took Aylesbury Chr 571 Ing p 26, 14 — Betwux Burnewuda ⁊ Æglesbyrig between Burnham wood & Aylesbury 921 Ing p 135, 10

Æhte-geweald, æhta-geweald pr. perty power; property possessions Cd 212 Th 263, 5: 139, Th p 235, 15

Æggewritere, es. m law writer

Æg-gemang, gemenced æg ocastrum, ogastrum Cot 145: 168 Lye

Æg-[illegible]

Æh-þyrl, es; n [eage an eye hole, or window Th An Ex]

v eagh-þyrl

either Th An [illegible]

Aine any Th An v ænig

Æfweard, æfward *adj. Absent, distant;* absens:—*Bd.* 3, 15, v. æfterwearð, *Lye.*

Æfweardnes, se; *f. Absence, removal, posterity;* absentia:—For þinre æfweardnesse *because of thy absence, Bt.* 10.

Æfwyrdla, æwyrdla, awyrdla, an. *Damage, injury, loss, the amercement for it;* detrimentum:—*L. In.* 40, 42.

Æfyn *the evening,* v. æfen.

Æfyrmþa [æ, fyrmþa *washing*] *Ablutions, the sweepings of a house, the refuse of things, or things of no value;* ablutiones, quisquiliæ:—*Elf. gr.* 13.

d ÆG, es *plu.* ægru, ægeru; *n.* [*Plat. Dut.* ei *n.*: *Ger.* ey *n.*: *Dan.* eg, æg] *An* EGG; ovum:—Gif he bit æg, *Lk.* 11, 12. ¶ Ægru lecgan *to lay eggs, Som.* 121. Æges hwite *white of an egg.*

Æg *or* ge [æg is contracted from ælc *all,* as Hickes says, or it may be from a, aa, æ *ever, always* strongly enunciated] The *Swed.* prefix *e,* the *Dan. i,* to some pronouns and adverbs, which signify the same as the A. S. æg, or ge; that is, *ever, always;* as, æghwa *every one;* quisque: æghwær *every where;* ubique: æghwilc *every one;* quisque.

Ægan *to own,* v. agan.

Æge *fear,* v. ege.

Æge *An island;* insula:-Eþeling æge *the island of nobles; Sim. Dunelm an.* 888. *Lye,* v. ealand.

Ægelesford *Ailsford,* v. Æglesford.

Ægewriter, es; *m.* [æ *law,* gewriter *a writer*] *A writer or composer of laws;* legum conditor:—*Prov.* 8.

Ægeru *eggs,* v. æg.

Ægh *an eye,* v. eage.

e Æghwa *neut.* æghwæt *or* æghwæs; *pron.* [æg *or* ælc *all* hwa *who*] *Whoever, whosoever, every one;* quicunque:—God æghwæs wealt *God governs every thing, Bt.* 35, 4.

Æghwær, æghwar, ahwær; *adv. Every where;* ubique:—Hi þa farende æghwar bodedon, *Mk.* 16, 20.

Æghwæt *whatever;* quodcunque, v. æghwa.

Æghwæþer; *pron. Both, each, both one and the other;* uterque. ¶ Æghwæþer ge—ge *both—and;* et—et, *Bd.* 3, 13, v. ægþer.

Æghwanon, -hwonon, -hwonene, -hwanun, -hwanum; *adv. Every where, every way, on all sides;* undique:—Hi æghwanon to hym comon, *Mk.* 1, 45. Æghwanone, *Elf. gr.* 45. Æghwanan, *Bd.* 4, 19.

Æghwar, æghwer *every where,* v. æghwær.

Æghwider, -hwyder; *adv. On every side, every way;* quoquoversum:—*Bd.* 2, 16.

f Æghwilc, æghwylc, alhwylc *adj. Every, all, all manner of, whosoever, whatsoever, every one;* unusquisque, omnis:—Æghwylc dæg *every day, Mt.* 6, 34. Æghwilce wisan *all manner of ways.* Æghwilc þinga *of all manners, or fashions, Som.*

Æghwonene *on all sides,* v. æghwanon.

Æghwyder *every way,* v. æghwider.

Ægift *A legal gift, restitution;* legalis dos, restitutio:—*Cart. Eadgif R.*

Ægiptisc *Egyptian,* v. Egiptisc

Æglæc *miserable,* v. aglæc.

Ægleaw, ægleawa, æ-gleawman, [æ *law,* gleaw *skilful*] *One skilful in the law, a lawyer, counsellor;* legis peritus:—Þa andswarude hym sum ægleaw, *Lk.* 11, 45.

Æglesburh, Ægelesbyrig, Ægelesburh, Æglesbyrig. AYLESBURY, *in Buckinghamshire;*—*Chr.* 571, *Ing. p.* 26, 13. Manning says, "Potius Ellesborough prope Wendover."

Æglesford, Ægelesford, AYLESFORD *on the Medway near Maidstone, Kent:*—*Chr.* 455.

g Æglesþrep AYLESTHORPE, *a village near Aylesford, Kent:*—*Chr.* 455, *p.* 15, *note h.*

Ægleswurð *The village of Eylesworth, Northamptonshire:*—*Chr.* 963.

Æglim, [æg *an egg,* lime *lime, glew*] EGG-LIME, *the sticky part, or white of an egg;* ovi viscum, glarea:—*R.* 81.

Ægn *own,* v. agen.

Ægnes þonces *of his own accord,* v. agen.

Ægnian *to own,* v. agnian

Ægru *eggs,* v. æg.

Ægsa *fear,* v. egsa.

Ægþer; *pron. Either, each, both,* uterque:—Ægþer byð gehealden, *Mt.* 9, 17. ¶ Heora ægþer *either,* or *both of them, each,* Gen. 21, 31. On ægþer hand, on ægþere healfe *on either hand or half, on both sides, Ors.* 1, 11, 14. On ægþre healfe weard *towards both sides, Elf. gr.* Ægþer ge—ge, *both—and; as well—as; so—as.* Ægþer ge heonan ge þanan *both here and there, on this side and that,* v. æghwæþer.

h Ægweard *a warden, keeper, guard, Beo.*

Ægylde, agilde; *adv.* [æ *without,* gild *payment*] *Without amends;* sine compensatione:—Licge he ægylde *he shall lie,* or *remain without amends, L. Edw. Guth.* 6, *W. p.* 52, 33, *note, n.*: *L. Cnut.* 2, 45.

Ægylt, es; *m.* [æ *a law,* gylt *gilt, fault*] *A breach* or *violation of the law, a trespass, a fault;* delictum:—*Ps.* 24, 7.

Ægypte *Egypt,* v. Egypte.

Æher *an ear of corn,* v. ear.

Æhiwnes, se; *f. Paleness, gloom;* pallor, deficientia coloris:—Æhiwnes þæs lichoman *paleness of the body, Herb.* 160, 4, v. ablæcnis.

Æhlyp, æt-hlyp, es; *m.* [æ *law,* hleap *or* hlyp *a leap*] *A transgression, breach of the law;* legis transgressio:—To wite forþon æhlype *to wit for the transgression, L. Athel,* 1, 6, *W. p.* 57, 40.

Æhsc *an ax,* v. æx.

i ÆHT, eht, eaht, e; *f.* [*Plat. Dut. Ger.* echt: *Frs.* aet, eat: *Franc.* eht, æht *or* aht *owned,* v. agan *to own*] *Property, substance, cattle, possessions, lands, goods, riches, value, estimation;* substancia, opes:—He hæfde mycele æhta, *Mk.* 10, 22. Esau nam ealle his æhta, and eall þat he æhte *Esau took all his goods, and all that he had, or possessed, Gen.* 36, 6.

ÆHTA eahta; *adj.* [*Plat. Dut. Ger. Al. Franc.* acht: *Moes.* ahtau] EIGHT: octo:—Æhta siðe *eight times.* Æhte siðe twenti *eight times twenty,* or *one hundred and sixty, Chr.* 1071.

Æhte *had, p. of* agan.

Æhteland, es; *n.* [æht *property*] *Landed property;* terra possessionis:—*Bd.* 4, 26, v. land.

Æhteman, nes *plu.* men; *m. A husbandman, a farmer, ploughman, drudge;* colonus:—Laboratores sind yrðlingas and æhte men *labourers are ploughmen and husbandmen, Elf. T. p.* 40, 20.

Æhtere; *m. An estimator, a valuer;* æstimator, *Lye.*

l Æhteswan [swan *a swain*] *A preserver of property, a cowherd, a swineherd;* fundi bubulcus, villicus, *Mann.*

Æhtige *the rich, Cot.* 211.

Æhtung; *f. Estimation, valuing;* æstimatio:—*R.* 114.

Æhwyrfan *to turn from, avert;* avertere:—*Ps.* 53, 5.

Æker *a field,* v. æcer.

Æl *all,* v. eall.

Æl *oil,* v. ele.

ÆL, es; *m.* [*Plat. Dut. Ger. Dan.* aal *m*: *Frs.* iel: *Al,* al, ahl] An EEL; anguilla:—Hwilce fixas gefehst þu? ælas and hacodas *What fishes catchest thou? Eels and haddocks*:—*Cot. M. S. Tib. A. III. p.* 19: *Bd.* 4, 13. Smæl æl *a small eel, Cot.* 161.

ÆL, eal, al, awul, awel [*Plat.* aal: *Dut.* else, els: *Ger.* ahl: *Al.* ahl, al: *Norse.* alur] *An* AWL, *a fork, a flesh-hook*; subula:—Þirlige his eare mid ale, *Lev.* 25, 10.

Ælædend, es; *m.* [lædend *part.* from læden *to lead*] *A lawgiver*; legislator:—*Ps.* 9, 21.

Ælan; *p.* de; *pp.* ed. *To oil, kindle, light, to set on fire, to bake*; accendere, coquere:—Ne hi ne ælað hyra leohtfæt, *Mt.* 5, 15. Uton ælan us hig on fyre, *Gen.* 11, 3, v. onælan.

Ælareow, es; *m.* [æ *law*, lareow *a master*] *A master of the law, one learned in the law, a lawyer, a pharisee*; legis doctor:—*Mt.* 22, 35.

Ælarwas *pharisees or* ælareowas.

Ælbeorht; *adj. All bright, all shining*; fulgentissimus:—*Cd.* 190.

ÆLC; *adj.* [*Plat. Dut.* elk:] *Each, every, every one, all*; unusquisque, omnis:—Ælc god tryw byrð gode wæstmas, *Mt.* 7, 17. ¶ On ælcere tide *at all times, Lk.* 21, 36. Elces cynnes *of each sort* or *all sorts.* Ælce healfe, *or* ælce wise *in all ways.*

Ælceald *all cold, most cold.*

Ælcera *of each*, v. ælc.

Ælcian *to delay*, v. elcian.

Ælcor, ælcra; *adv. Elsewhere, besides, otherwise*; aliter:—*Elf. gr.* 38: *Bd.* 2, 13.

Ælcræftig; *adj. All-skilful, ingenious, all-virtuous, perfect*; omnis habens virtutes:—*Bt. R. p.* 174.

Ælcumende; *part. Doubtful*; dubitans, *Som.*

Æld *fire*, v. æled.

Æld, ældo, ældu *old*, v. eald.

Ældian *to put off, to delay*, v. yldan.

Ælding *delay*, v. ylding.

Ældomen *pharisees*, v. aldu.

Ældro *parents*, v. ealdor.

Ælecung *An allurement, a blandishment*; blandimentum:—*C. R. Ben.* 2, *Lye.*

Æled, [*Dan.* ild: *Swed.* eld: *Norse.* elldr] *Fire*; ignis.

Æled weccan *to excite*, or *light a fire, Cd.* 140, v. fyr.

Ælednys, se; *f. A burning*; incendium, *Lye.*

Æleng; *adj. Long, protracted, lasting, troublesome*; longus, molestus:—To ælenge *too long, Bt.* 39, 4.

Æleputa, an, [*Plat.* aalput, *or* putte: *Dut.* aalpuit, aelputi: æl *an eel*, pytt *a pit*] *An* EELPOUT. Hwilce fixas gefehst þu? Mynas and æleputan *What fishes catchest thou? Minnows and eelpouts, Cot. M.S. Tib. A. III. p.* 19, v. myne.

Ælete, æleten, alæten; *part.* [*from* alætan *to let go*] *One let go, divorced*; repudiata uxor:—*L. Cnut. ecl.* 7.

Ælf *an elf, fairy*, v. elf.

Ælfcyn, es. *A kind of elves, or fairies*; ephialtum genus, *Som.*

Ælfe *the night mare*, v. ælfsidenne.

Ælfere [*Swed.* elf *a river*, erian *to dig*] *A ditch*; fossa:—*Cd.* 146, *Lye.*

Ælfremd, ælfremed; *adj. Strange, foreign*; alienus:—Bearn ælfremde, *Ps.* 17, 47.

Ælfremda, ælfremeda, an; *m.* [æl, eall *all*, fremd *estranged*] *A stranger, foreigner*; alienigena:—Þes ælfremeda, *Lk.* 17, 18.

Ælfsidenne, ælfe *the night mare*; incubus:—*Herb.* 3, 6.

Ælfsogoþa [sogeþa *juice*] *Fairy influence, inspiration of the Muses*; castalidum impetus:—*L. M.* 3, 62.

Ælgrén *adj. Full green, entirely green*; perviridis:—*Cd.* 10.

Ælgylden; *part. Gilded, golden, gilded over*; deauratus:—*Som.* v. gildan.

Ælic; *adj. Belonging to law, lawful*; legalis:—*Bd.* 1, 27. ¶ Tyn ælican word *the ten commandments, Som.*

Ælincge, *a conflagration*, or *burning*; conflagratio, *Som.*

Ælinge *Weariness*; tædium:—*Bt. pref. Cot.*

Ællmihtig *Almighty*, v. ælmiht.

Ællreord *barbarous*, v. ælreord.

Ællþeodignes *a wandering*, v. ælþeodignes.

Ællyfta *the eleventh*, v. endlefta.

Ælmas, ælmæsa, an; ælmæsse, ælmysse, ælmesse, plu. [*Plat.* allmisse *f*: *Frs.* ealmis: *Dut.* aelmoesse, aalmoes *f*: *Ger.* almosen: æl, eall *all*, mese, myse *a table*; *all that was given from the table.*] ALMS, *almsgiving*; eleemosyna, agape:—Soðlice þonne þu þine ælmessan do, *Mt.* 6, 4. ¶ Ælmessan dælan *or* syllan *to give*, or *distribute alms.* Ælmes lac *the gift of alms.* Almes bæð *an alms' bath, a bath free of cost.* Ælmes dæd ALMS' DEED. Ælmes feoh *alms' money.* Ælmes gedal, *or* sylene *alms' dole, the dealing, doling, or giving of alms.*

Ælmes georn *an alms' giver, Elf. T. p.* 21, 24.

Ælmæst *almost*, v. ealmæst.

Ælmiht Ælmihti, Ælmihtig, Ællmihtig *The Almighty*; Omnipotens:—*Bd.* 3, 15.

Ælnet *an eel net.*

Ælpig; *adj. Each, single*; unicus:—*Chr.* 1085, v. ænlipig.

Ælr, ælre, *an elder tree*, v. alr.

Ælreord, ælreordig, eallreord, elreord, elreordig *adj. Barbarous, of a strange country* or *speech*; barbarus:—*Bd.* 1, 13, *Som.*

Ælsewalda *the universal ruler, Ben.* v. ælwalda.

Ælswa *also*, v. eallswa.

Ælsymle *always*, v. simle.

Æltæw, *comp.* re, ra; *adj. Good, excellent, entire, sound, healthful, perfect, honest*; bonus, sanus:—Næfð no æltæwne ende *has no good end, Bt.* 5, 2. Ful æltæwe geboren *born quite* [*full*] *sound or healthy, Bt.* 38, 5.

Æltæwestan *Nobles*; primates:—*Ors.* 4, 4.

Æltæwlice; *adv. Well, soundly, piously, perfectly*; bené, *Som.*

Æltæwre *better*, v. æltæw.

Ælþeod *a stranger*, v. ælþeodig.

Ælþeodelice, ælþeodiglice; *adv. From a strange country, abroad, out of a man's native soil, from far*; peregrinè:—*Elf. gr.* 38. *The following phrases have the same signification as these adverbs*:—On ælþeodignesse, *Gen.* 12, 10. On ælþeode, *Bt.* 27, 3.

Ælþeodige, elþeodige, ælþeod; *f. A stranger, foreigner, pilgrim, proselyte*; advena:—Bið þam ælþeodegan *is to the foreigners, Bt.* 27, 3.

Ælþeodig, ælþiodig, elþeodin, elþeodisc; *adj. Strange, foreign*; exterus:—On ælþeodig folc *to a foreign people, Bt.* 27, 3. ¶ Ælþeodigra manna gisthus *foreign men's guest house, an inn, R.* 109.

Ælþeodiglice *from abroad*, v. ælþeodelice.

Ælþeodignes, elþeodignis, se; *f. A going abroad, peregrination, pilgrimage*; peregrinatio:—*Mt.* 25, 14. On ælþeodignesse *from abroad*, v. ælþeodelice.

Ælþiodig *foreign*, v. ælþeodig.

Ælwalda, ealwalda, [eall *all*, wald *power, rule*] *Universal ruler*, or *governor*; imperium in omnia tenens:—Se ealwalda *the Almighty, the Omnipotent, Cd.* 14.

Ælwiht *every creature.*

Æmelle; *adj. Unsavoury, without taste*; insipidus:—*Cot.* 116.

O ϕ1

O ϕ2 a jolthead; capito Th. An

O 6 Alet q

O 7 Alfcynne ~~Grim II 44, 713~~

Alfet-ée (æl an eel fæt a vat, receptacle, ea water) Adlingfleet Yorkshire Cd 763

~~Al-fyfe all people folk~~ foreign folk Beo K 4737

Alfscine elfin-bright Th. An. elfin beauty Ælf-sciene Cd 86 1302 Ap 109, 23; 165, 11

Q 12 Alfþone herba genus Som.

Almes-man an almsman Th. An.

Almysse, an f. alms plu

Altewe see opposite margin

Alfscien, ne f. ly

O 2 q

Ælda-cyn, nes; n. the human race Cd Ex 19 Beo gl.

Bdl Almas ~~alt~~ ele

~~dupl~~ Almesse, ælmysse, ælmysse, an; f. Alms etc.

ale oil Th. An, ele

Æled-leóma, an m fire light, a blaze, flamma Beo ~~2311~~ K 6244 ~~Grim II 448, 23~~

ϕ 14

Elþeodung, e; f a going abroad Som v. elþeodignes

Al-timbred strangely built, peregrine structus Beo K 2612

3 Æg-lac q.v.
~~Æg~~-lác, es; m. Misery, trouble; miseria Cd p 230 Beo ed in lac v. æglac

1 [a-hiwness deficientia coloris Mann Sup.]

(ægleca)
Æglaca, an; m. A wretch, miscreant, miser Cd 216 Th p 274, 28: 214, Th p 269, 14: Beo ed in lác

(a law warden or keeper; æg-weard, e; f. in Beo. ed. in wararn) for

Æg, e; f. an island v ig. v æg-weard Beo Th 480

Æg-flotan, dm. m. A sailors, nauta Cod verc Beo Th apx 480

Æglesburh, Egles-burh, g.-burge; d. -byrig Aylesbury, Bucks
Cuthwulf genam Ægles-burh Cuthulf took Aylesbury Chr 571 Ing p 26, 14 — Betwebx Burnewuda ⁊ Æglesbyrig betwixt Burnham wood & Aylesbury 921 Ing p 135, 10

Æhte-geweald, æhta-geweald property power; property possessions Cd 212 Th 263, 5: 139, Th p 235, 15

Æ-gewritere, es. m law writer

Æg-gemang, gemenced æg ocastrum, ogastrum Cot 145: 168 Lye

4 either Th An

3 Æine ang Th An v ænig

Æh-pyrl, es; m. [eage an eye hole, a window Th. An Gr.]
v eagh-pyrl

Æfweard, æfward *adj. Absent, distant;* absens:—*Bd.* 3, 15, v. æfterweard, *Lye.*

Æfweardnes, se; *f. Absence, removal, posterity;* absentia:—For þinre æfweardnesse *because of thy absence, Bt.* 10.

Æfwyrdla, æwyrdla, awyrdla, an. *Damage, injury, loss, the amercement for it;* detrimentum:—*L. In.* 40, 42.

Æfyn *the evening,* v. æfen.

Æfyrmþa [æ, fyrmþa *washing*] *Ablutions, the sweepings of a house, the refuse of things, or things of no value;* ablutiones, quisquiliæ:—*Elf. gr.* 13.

d **ÆG**, es *plu.* ægru, ægeru; *n.* [*Plat. Dut.* ei *n.*: *Ger.* ey *n.*: *Dan.* eg, æg] *An* EGG; ovum:—Gif he bit æg, *Lk.* 11, 12. ¶ Ægru lecgan *to lay eggs, Som.* 121. Æges hwite *white of an egg.*

Æg *or* ge [æg is contracted from ælc *all,* as Hickes says, or it may be from a, aa, æ *ever, always* strongly enunciated] The *Swed.* prefix *e,* the *Dan. i,* to some pronouns and adverbs, which signify the same as the A. S. æg, or ge; that is, *ever, always;* as, æghwa *every one;* quisque: æghwær *every where;* ubique: æghwilc *every one;* quisque.

Ægan *to own,* v. agan.

Æge *fear,* v. ege.

Æge *An island;* insula:—Eþeling æge *the island of nobles; Sim. Dunelm an.* 888. *Lye,* v. ealand.

Ægelesford *Ailsford,* v. Æglesford.

Ægewriter, es; *m.* [æ *law,* gewriter *a writer*] *A writer or composer of laws;* legum conditor:—*Prov.* 8.

Ægeru *eggs,* v. æg.

Ægh *an eye,* v. eage.

e **Æghwa** *neut.* æghwæt *or* æghwæs; *pron.* [æg *or* ælc *all* hwa *who*] *Whoever, whosoever, every one;* quicunque:—God æghwæs wealt *God governs every thing, Bt.* 35, 4.

Æghwær, æghwar, ahwær; *adv. Every where;* ubique:—Hi þa farende æghwar bodedon, *Mk.* 16, 20.

Æghwæt *whatever;* quodcunque, v. æghwa.

Æghwæþer; *pron. Both, each, both one and the other;* uterque. ¶ Æghwæþer ge—ge *both—and;* et—et, *Bd.* 3, 13, v. ægþer.

Æghwanon, -hwonon, -hwonene, -hwanun, -hwanum; *adv. Every where, every way, on all sides;* undique:—Hi æghwanon to hym comon, *Mk.* 1, 45. Æghwanone, *Elf. gr.* 45. Æghwanan, *Bd.* 4, 19.

Æghwar, æghwer *every where,* v. æghwær.

Æghwider, -hwyder; *adv. On every side, every way;* quoquoversum:—*Bd.* 2, 16.

f **Æghwilc**, æghwylc, ahwylc *adj. Every, all, all manner of, whosoever, whatsoever, every one;* unusquisque, omnis:—Æghwylc dæg *every day, Mt.* 6, 34. Æghwilce wisan *all manner of ways.* Æghwilc þinga *of all manners,* or *fashions, Som.*

Æghwonene *on all sides,* v. æghwanon.

Æghwyder *every way,* v. æghwider.

Ægift *A legal gift, restitution;* legalis dos, restitutio:—*Cart. Eadgif R.*

Ægiptisc *Egyptian,* v. Egiptisc

Æglæc *miserable,* v. aglæc.

Ægleaw, ægleawa, æ-gleawman, [æ *law,* gleaw *skilful*] *One skilful in the law, a lawyer, counsellor;* legis peritus:—Þa andswarude hym sum ægleaw, *Lk.* 11, 45.

Æglesburh, Ægelesbyrig, Ægelesburh, Æglesbyrig. AYLESBURY, *in Buckinghamshire;*—*Chr.* 571, *Ing. p.* 26, 13. Manning says, "Potius Ellesborough prope Wendover."

Æglesford, Ægelesford, AYLESFORD *on the Medway near Maidstone, Kent:*—*Chr.* 455.

g **Æglesþrep** AYLESTHORPE, *a village near Aylesford, Kent:*—*Chr.* 455, *p.* 15, *note h.*

Ægleswurð *The village of Eylesworth, Northamptonshire:*—*Chr.* 963.

Æglim, [æg *an egg,* lime *lime, glew*] EGG-LIME, *the sticky part, or white of an egg;* ovi viscum, glarea:—*R.* 81.

Ægn *own,* v. agen.

Ægnes þonces *of his own accord,* v. agen.

Ægnian *to own,* v. agnian

Ægru *eggs,* v. æg.

Ægsa *fear,* v. egsa.

Ægþer; *pron. Either, each, both,* uterque:—Ægþer byð gehealden, *Mt.* 9, 17. ¶ Heora ægþer *either,* or *both of them, each,* Gen. 21, 31. On ægþer hand, on ægþere healfe *on either hand or half, on both sides, Ors.* 1, 11, 14. On ægþre healfe weard *towards both sides, Elf. gr.* Ægþer ge—ge, *both—and; as well—as; so—as.* Ægþer ge heonan ge þanan *both here and there, on this side and that,* v. æghwæþer.

h **Ægweard** *a warden, keeper, guard, Beo.*

Ægylde, agilde; *adv.* [æ *without,* gild *payment*] *Without amends;* sine compensatione:—Licge he ægylde *he shall lie,* or *remain without amends, L. Edw. Guth.* 6, *W. p.* 52, 33, *note, n.*: *L. Cnut.* 2, 45.

Ægylt, es; *m.* [æ *a law,* gylt *gilt, fault*] *A breach* or *violation of the law, a trespass, a fault;* delictum:—*Ps.* 24, 7.

Ægypte *Egypt,* v. Egypte.

Æher *an ear of corn,* v. ear.

Æhiwnes, se; *f. Paleness, gloom;* pallor, deficientia coloris:—Æhiwnes þæs lichoman *paleness of the body, Herb.* 160, 4, v. ablæcnis.

Æhlyp, æt-hlyp, es; *m.* [æ *law,* hleap *or* hlyp *a leap*] *A transgression, breach of the law;* legis transgressio:—To wite forþon æhlype *to wit for the transgression, L. Athel,* 1, 6, *W. p.* 57, 40.

Æhse *an ax,* v. æx.

i **ÆHT**, eht, eaht, e; *f.* [*Plat. Dut. Ger.* echt: *Frs.* aet, eat: *Franc.* eht, æht *or* aht *owned,* v. agan *to own*] *Property, substance, cattle, possessions, lands, goods, riches, value, estimation;* substancia, opes:—He hæfde mycele æhta, *Mk.* 10, 22. Esau nam ealle his æhta, and eall þat he æhte *Esau took all his goods, and all that he had, or possessed, Gen.* 36, 6.

ÆHTA eahta; *adj.* [*Plat. Dut. Ger. Al. Franc.* acht: *Moes.* ahtau] EIGHT: octo:—Æhta siðe *eight times.* Æhte siðe twenti *eight times twenty,* or *one hundred and sixty, Chr.* 1071.

Æhte *had, p. of* agan.

Æhteland, es; *n.* [æht *property*] *Landed property;* terra possessionis:—*Bd.* 4, 26, v. land.

Æhteman, nes *plu.* men; *m. A husbandman, a farmer, ploughman, drudge;* colonus:—Laboratores sind yrðlingas and æhte men *labourers are ploughmen and husbandmen, Elf. T. p.* 40, 20.

Æhtere; *m. An estimator, a valuer;* æstimator, *Lye.*

j **Æhteswan** [swan *a swain*] *A preserver of property, a cowherd, a swineherd;* fundi bubulcus, villicus, *Mann.*

Æhtige *the rich, Cot.* 211.

Æhtung; *f. Estimation, valuing;* æstimatio:—*R.* 114.

Æhwyrfan *to turn from, avert;* avertere:—*Ps.* 53, 5.

Æker *a field,* v. æcer.

Æl *all,* v. eall.

Æl *oil,* v. ele.

ÆL, es; *m.* [*Plat. Dut. Ger. Dan.* aal *m*: *Frs.* iel: *Al,* al, ahl] *An* eel; anguilla:—Hwilce fixas gefehst þu? ælas and hacodas *What fishes catchest thou? Eels and haddocks*:—*Cot. M. S. Tib. A. III. p.* 19: *Bd.* 4, 13. Smæl æl *a small eel*, *Cot.* 161.

k **ÆL**, eal, al, awul, awel [*Plat.* aal: *Dut.* else, els: *Ger.* ahl: *Al.* ahl, al: *Norse.* alur] *An* awl, *a fork, a flesh-hook*; subula:—Þirlige his eare mid ale, *Lev.* 25, 10.

Ælædend, es; *m.* [lædend *part.* from læden *to lead*] *A law-giver*; legislator:—*Ps.* 9, 21.

Ælan; *p.* de; *pp.* ed. *To oil, kindle, light, to set on fire, to bake*; accendere, coquere:—Ne hi ne ælað hyra leohtfæt, *Mt.* 5, 15. Uton ælan us hig on fyre, *Gen.* 11, 3, v. onælan.

Ælareow, es; *m.* [æ *law*, lareow *a master*] *A master of the law, one learned in the law, a lawyer, a pharisee*; legis doctor:—*Mt.* 22, 35.

Ælarwas *pharisees or* ælareowas.

Ælbeorht; *adj. All bright, all shining*; fulgentissimus:—*Cd.* 190.

l **ÆLC**; *adj.* [*Plat. Dut.* elk:] *Each, every, every one, all*; unusquisque, omnis:—Ælc god tryw byrð gode wæstmas, *Mt.* 7, 17. ¶ On ælcere tide *at all times*, *Lk.* 21, 36. Ælces cynnes *of each sort* or *all sorts*. Ælce healfe, *or* ælce wise *in all ways*.

Ælceald *all cold, most cold.*

Ælcera *of each*, v. ælc.

Ælcian *to delay*, v. elcian.

Ælcor, ælcra; *adv. Elsewhere, besides, otherwise*; aliter:—*Elf. gr.* 38: *Bd.* 2, 13.

Ælcræftig; *adj. All-skilful, ingenious, all-virtuous, perfect*; omnis habens virtutes:—*Bt. R. p.* 174.

Ælcumende; *part. Doubtful*; dubitans, *Som.*

Æld *fire*, v. æled.

Æld, ældo, ældu *old*, v. eald.

Ældian *to put off, to delay*, v. yldan.

Ælding *delay*, v. ylding.

Ældomen *pharisees*, v. aldu.

Ældro *parents*, v. ealdor.

m Ælecung *An allurement, a blandishment*; blandimentum:—*C. R. Ben.* 2, *Lye.*

Æled, [*Dan.* ild: *Swed.* eld: *Norse.* elldr] *Fire*; ignis. ¶ Æled weccan *to excite*, or *light a fire*, *Cd.* 140, v. fyr.

Ælednys, se; *f. A burning*; incendium, *Lye.*

Æleng; *adj. Long, protracted, lasting, troublesome*; longus, molestus:—To ælenge *too long*, *Bt.* 39, 4.

Æleputa, an, [*Plat.* aalput, *or* putte: *Dut.* aalpuit, aelputi: æl *an eel*, pytt *a pit*] *An* eel-pout. Hwilce fixas gefehst þu? Mynas and æleputan *What fishes catchest thou? Minnows and eelpouts*, *Cot. M.S. Tib. A. III. p.* 19, v. myne.

n Ælete, æleten, alæten; *part.* [*from* alætan *to let go*] *One let go, divorced*; repudiata uxor:—*L. Cnut. ecl.* 7.

Ælf *an elf, fairy*, v. elf.

Ælfcyn, es. *A kind of elves, or fairies*; ephialtum genus, *Som.*

Ælfe *the night mare*, v. ælfsidenne.

Ælfere [*Swed.* elf *a river*, erian *to dig*] *A ditch*; fossa:—*Cd.* 146, *Lye.*

Ælfremd, ælfremed; *adj. Strange, foreign*; alienus:—Bearn ælfremde, *Ps.* 17, 47.

Ælfremda, ælfremeda, an; *m.* [æl, eall *all*, fremd *estranged*] *A stranger, foreigner*; alienigena:—Þes ælfremeda, *Lk.* 17, 18.

o Ælfsidenne, ælfe *the night mare*; incubus:—*Herb.* 3, 6.

Ælfsogoþa [sogeþa *juice*] *Fairy influence, inspiration of the Muses*; castalidum impetus:—*L. M.* 3, 62.

Ælgrén, *adj. Full green, entirely green*; perviridis:—*Cd.* 10.

Ælgylden; *part. Gilded, golden, gilded over*; deauratus:—*Som.* v. gildan.

p Ælic; *adj. Belonging to law, lawful*; legalis:—*Bd.* 1, 27. ¶ Tyn ælican word *the ten commandments*, *Som.*

Ælincge, *a conflagration*, or *burning*; conflagratio, *Som.*

Ælinge *Weariness*; tædium:—*Bt. pref. Cot.*

Ællmihtig *Almighty*, v. ælmiht

Ællreord *barbarous*, v. ælreord.

Ællþeodignes *a wandering*, v. ælþeodignes.

Ællyfta *the eleventh*, v. endlefta.

Ælmas, ælmæsa, an; ælmæsse, ælmysse, ælmesse, plu. [*Plat.* allmisse *f*: *Frs.* ealmis: *Dut.* aelmoesse, aalmoes *f*: *Ger.* almosen: æl, eall *all*, mese, myse *a table*; *all that was given from the table.*] Alms, *almsgiving*; eleemosyna, agape:—Soðlice þonne þu þine ælmessan do, *Mt.* 6, 4. ¶ Ælmessan dælan *or* syllan *to give*, or *distribute alms*. Ælmes lac *the gift of alms*. Almes bæð *an alms' bath, a bath free of cost*. Ælmes dæd alms' deed. Ælmes feoh *alms' money*. Ælmes gedal, *or* sylene *alms' dole, the dealing, doling*, or *giving of alms*.

Ælmes georn *an alms' giver*, *Elf. T. p.* 21, 24.

Ælmæst *almost*, v. ealmæst.

Ælmiht Ælmihti, Ælmihtig, Ællmihtig *The Almighty*; Omnipotens:—*Bd.* 3, 15.

Ælnet *an eel net.*

q Ælpig; *adj. Each, single*; unicus:—*Chr.* 1085, v. ænlipig.

Ælr, ælre, *an elder tree*, v. alr.

Ælreord, ælreordig, eallreord, elreord, elreordig *adj. Barbarous, of a strange country* or *speech*; barbarus:—*Bd.* 1, 13, *Som.*

Ælsewalda *the universal ruler*, *Ben.* v. ælwalda.

Ælswa *also*, v. eallswa.

Ælsymle *always*, v. simle.

Æltæw, *comp.* re, ra; *adj. Good, excellent, entire, sound, healthful, perfect, honest*; bonus, sanus:—Næfð no æltæwne ende *has no good end*, *Bt.* 5, 2. Ful æltæwe geboren *born quite* [*full*] *sound or healthy*, *Bt.* 38, 5.

Æltæwestan *Nobles*; primates:—*Ors.* 4, 4.

r Æltæwlice; *adv. Well, soundly, piously, perfectly*; bené, *Som.*

Æltæwre *better*, v. æltæw.

Ælþeod *a stranger*, v. ælþeodig.

Ælþeodelice, ælþeodiglice; *adv. From a strange country, abroad, out of a man's native soil, from far*; peregrinè:—*Elf. gr.* 38. *The following phrases have the same signification as these adverbs*:—On ælþeodignesse, *Gen.* 12, 10. On ælþeode, *Bt.* 27, 3.

Ælþeodige, elþeodige, ælþeod; *f. A stranger, foreigner, pilgrim, proselyte*; advena:—Bið þam ælþeodegan *is to the foreigners*, *Bt.* 27, 3.

Ælþeodig, ælþiodig, elþeodin, elþeodisc; *adj. Strange, foreign*; exterus:—On ælþeodig folc *to a foreign people*, *Bt.* 27, 3. ¶ Ælþeodigra manna gisthus *foreign men's guest house, an inn*, *R.* 109.

Ælþeodiglice *from abroad*, v. ælþeodelice.

Ælþeodignes, elþeodignis, se; *f. A going abroad, peregrination, pilgrimage*; peregrinatio:—*Mt.* 25, 14. On ælþeodignesse *from abroad*, v. ælþeodelice.

Ælþiodig *foreign*, v. ælþeodig.

s Ælwalda, ealwalda, [eall *all*, wald *power, rule*] *Universal ruler*, or *governor*; imperium in omnia tenens:—Se ealwalda *the Almighty, the Omnipotent*, *Cd.* 14.

Ælwiht *every creature.*

Æmelle; *adj. Unsavoury, without taste*; insipidus:—*Cot.* 116.

O ϕ1

O ϕ 2x a jolthead; capito Th. An

O 6 Ælet... q

O ~~ælfcynne~~ ...

X Ælfet-ée [æl an æl fæt, a vat, receptacle, ea water] Sdlingfleet Yorkshire Cd 763

X Æl-fyle ~~all~~ ... ~~folk~~ foreign folk Beo K 4737

X Ælfscine elfin bright Th. An.

Ælf-sciene elfin beauty Cd 86 Thp 109, 23; 130 22 165, 11

O 12 Ælfþone herba genus Som.

4x Ælmes-man an almsman Th. An.

Ælmysse, an f. alms, dole

X Æltæwe see opposite margin

X Ælfsiden, ne f. q

O

O 2 q.

X Ældan cyn, nes; n. the human race Cod Ex 19 Beo q.

X 3 dl. Ælmas ate ~~...~~ ~~Al~~

~~Ælmesdæl~~ ...

Xx ǣle oil; ele Th. An

X Ælmesse, ælmæsse, ælmysse, an; f. Alms etc

ϕ 14

X 8x Æled-leóma, an m fire light, a blaze; flamma Beo ~~...~~ K 6244 ~~Grm II 448, 23~~

X Ælfædung, e; f a going abroad Som v. ælfædignes

Æl-timbred strongly built; peregrine structus Beo K ~~...~~ 2612

See note in red ink p 11

Ana narrow, Cd 18 Th p 23, 9

1 Amenne desolate
Th. An of ablatin of
a-man
Amete[?]an an ant
Ametgian to beat
[illegible] vanitian

Anigweata in any way, any how Th An

2 Æppyl an apple
in æpl
Æpse, æspe an asp tree Gm I 251, 11, 12

4

Amtegian to be at leisure vacare
Grimm II 58, 23 v amtian
Past 18, 4 Lye

3 — 03

Anotes ... a without note use [?] useless

5 A' always eode went

8

Amgrian 2a

Æpeningas fructus, vel fructus quædam stomachico præscripta ... L.M. 2.2 Som

æpl, æpl, æppel, ge. æppels m an apple

On æple in an apple Cd 43 Th 57, 33. Se æppel hoc malum Elf gr. 6 Som p 5, 31

Æppel-fealuwe apple-fallow apple gray Beo K 4325 Beogl in fealo

1 Ær pisson, ær pissum hereto fore, ere or before this time; antehac Som.

5

Æmelnys, æmylnys, se; *f. Loathsomeness, weariness, disdain, falsehood, unfaithfulness, false dealing, treason;* fastidium, *Som.*

Æmen; *adj.* [æ *without*, man *man*] *Unmanned, depopulated, desolate;* hominibus nudus:—*Ors.* 2, 4.

t ÆMET, æmette *An* EMMET, *an ant;* formica:—*Elf. gl.* 14.

Æmet-hwile [æmta *leisure, spare-time*, hwil *while, time*] *Leisure, spare-time, respite;* otium:—*Elf. gr.* 8.

Æmethyll *An* EMMET HILL, *an ant-hill;* formicetum:—*Past.* 28, 1.

Æmetta *rest*, v. æmta.

Æmettig *idle*, v. æmti.

Æmnitta *a balance;* statera, *Som.*

a Æmod; *adj.* [æ *without*, mod *mind*] *Out of mind, mad, dismayed, discouraged;* amens:—*Ors.* 3, 4.

Æmta, emta, æmetta, an *Quiet, leisure, rest;* quies:—Ic ne æmtan nabbe *I have no leisure, Bt.* 39, 4. Be his æmettan *by his leisure, Bt. pref.*

Æmtege *free*, v. æmti.

Æmtegiõ *is at leisure*, v. æmtian.

Æmtian, æmtigean *To be at leisure, to be vacant;* otiosum esse:—*Ps.* 45, 10.

ÆMTI, æmtig, æmteg, emtig, æmetig, emetig, æmettig; *adj. Vacant,* EMPTY, *free, idle;* vacuus:—Seo eorþe wæs æmtig, *Gen.* 1, 2. Hig synd emtige *they are idle, Ex.* 5, 8. ¶ Æmtege wifemen *unmarried women, Past.* 21, 8.

Æmtigean *to be at leisure*, v. æmtian.

Æmuða [æ *without*, muða *a mouth*]; cæcum intestinum:—*R.* 75.

v Æmyce, æmyrce; *adj. Excellent, singular;* egregius:—*Cot.* 74.

Æmylnys, se; *f. Weariness;* tædium:—*Pref. R. Conc.*

Æmyrian *ashes;* cineres, *Ben.*

Æmytta *an emmet*, v. æmet.

Æn *one*, v. an.

Ænd *an end*, v. end.

Ænde *and*, v. and.

Ændemes, ændemest *likewise*, v. endemes.

Ændian [*Plat.* endigen: *Dut.* einden *or* eindigen] *To* END; finire:—*Solil.* 12.

Ændlefene *eleven*, v. endlufon.

Ændlyfta *eleventh*, v. endlefta.

Æne, æene; *adv. Once;* semel:—Nu ic æne begann, *Gen.* 18, 31.

Æneg, ænegu *any*, v. ænig.

w Ænette *solitude;* solitudo:—*Dial.* 2, 3.

Ænfilt *an anvil*, v. anfilt.

Ænforleten; *part. Clothed;* amictus:—*Ps.* 103, 2.

Æng *any*, v. ænig.

Ænga *a narrowness*, v. enga.

Ængel *an angel*, v. engel.

Ængellic *angelic*, v. engelic.

Ænglisc *English*, v. englisc.

Ænig, æneg, ani; *adj.* [*Dut.* eenig: *Frs.* ienich] ANY, *any one;* ullus:—Þæt ænig man ænig fæt þurh þat templ bære, *Mk.* 11, 16.

Ænige, ænigge *one-eyed*, v. aneage.

Æniht *any*, v. ænig.

Æninga *entirely*, v. aninga.

Ænlep *each*, v. ænlipig.

x Ænlepnes, anlepnes, se; *f. Solitude, privacy;* solitudo:—*Bd.* 2, 12.

Ænlic, anlic; *adj.* [an *one*, lic *like*] ONLY, *solitary, singular, incomparable, excellent, golden, precious, beautiful, elegant;* unicus, excellens:—He is min anlica sunu, *Lk.* 9, 38. He hæfde an swiþe ænlic wif *he had a very excellent wife, Bt.* 35, 6. Ænlices hiwes *of an excellent shape, Elf. T.* p. 33, 16.

Ænlice, anlice; *comp.* or; *sup.* ost; *adv.* ONLY, *singularly, elegantly;* eleganter:—*Ors.* 2, 4.

Ænlipig, ænlipug, anlipig, ænlep, anlepig, anlip, anlypi; *adj. Each, every, singular, solitary, private;* singuli, solus:—Be ænlipugum mannum, *Jos.* 7, 14.

Ænlypie *each*, v. ænlipig.

Ænne *one, ac. of* an.

Ænot; *adj.* [æ *without*, not *use*] *Useless, of no use, unprofitable;* inutilis, *Lye.*

A'eode *afterwards happened*, v. gan.

y Æpel-sceal *an apple-shale, or film about the kernels or pips.*

Æpel-tre, apple-treow, apulder, *an apple-tree*, v. æpl-treow.

Æpel-treowu *pomegranates;* granata:—*Cot.* 99, *Lye.*

ÆPL, apl, æppel, e; *pl.* a [*Plat. Dut.* appel *m: Frs.* apel: *Ger.* apfel *m: Dan.* æble *n: Swed.* äple *n.*]—1. *An* APPLE, *fruit;* malum.—2. *The apple, or pupil of the eye;* pupilla:—1. *Cd.* 43. Æppla *apples.* Liþe æppla *ripe apples, or fruit.*—2. Swa swa man deð þone æpl on his eagan, *Bt.* 39, 10.

z Æppelbær; *adj. Apple bearing, fruit bearing;* pomifer:—Æppelbære treow, *Gen.* 1, 11.

Æppel-cyrnla, appel-cyrnlu *A pomegranate;* malogranatum:—*Cot.* 128, v. æpel-treowu.

Æppel-hus *an apple-house, a place for fruit.*

Æppel-leaf *an apple-leaf*, v. appelleaf.

Æppel-screada, *or* corn-æsceda *apple-parings, the chaff, or refuse of corn.*

Æppel-treow, *an apple-tree*, v. æpl.

a Æppel-tun, apple-tun, apuldertun *an apple-garden, orchard.*

Æppel-win *apple-wine, cider, Som.*

Æppuldre, æpuldre *an apple-tree*, v. æpl.

Æppuldre-tun *an orchard, for* æppeltun.

ÆPS, æspe [*Dut.* espe *f: Ger.* aspe *f: Dan.* espetræe: *Swed.* asp *f.*] *An asp-tree, a species of poplar, a fir-tree;* populus tremula:—*Elf. gl.* 17.

Æpsenys, se; *f. Disgrace, dishonour, shame;* dedecus:—*Scint.* 56, *Som.*

Ær *brass*, v. ar.

Æ'R, æror; *sup.* ærost, ærst; *adv.* [*Plat. Dut.* eer: *Frs.* eren: *Ger.* ehe, eher: *Al.* er: Icel. ár: *Moes.* air *early in the morning, before day,* diluculum, as the *Heb.* אור *aur*, and the *Grk.* ἦρ *the morning, the time* BEFORE *day;* and then it might denote what was *antecedent*, or *before* any other time, or *before* any thing] ERE, *before, sooner, earlier, first, heretofore, formerly, already, some time ago, lately, just now, till, until;* prius, dudum:—Gang ær, *Mt.* 5, 24. He wæs ær þonne ic, *Jn.* 1, 15, 30. Æron morgen, *Ex.* 12, 22. Ic æron nyste *I before knew not, Nic.* 12. p. 6. 21. Ærost *first*, Gen. 19, 33. Þat is ærost *that is first, in the first place, Cod. Ex.* 10. ¶ Ær þe, ærþam þe *before that, Bt.* 41, 3. Noht micle ær *not much before, Bd.* 4, 23. Hwene ær *scarcely before, just before, Bt.* 23. Swyþe ær *very early, very soon, Mk.* 16, 2.

b Æ'R; *prep.* ERE, *before;* ante, præ:—Ær þam hode, *Mt.* 24, 38. Ær þe *before thee, Bt.* 41, 3.

Æ'ra, (se æra; *def.*) ære, ærre, ærer, æror, ærur; *sup.* ærest; *adj.* [*Plat. Dut.* eer, eerst] *Former, early, superior, ancient;* prior:—He wæs gyrstan dæg and þis æran dæg, *Gen.* 31, 5. Forlyst he his ærran god *he loses his former good, Bt.* 35, 6. Wurþe ærest stan, *Jn.* 8, 7. ¶ Æt ærestan, ærest þinga *or* ærest sona *at first, first of all.* To þam ær dæge, *or* mid ær dæge *at the early day, first dawn, Cd.* 153. On æran, on æron, *or* on ær dagum *formerly, Ors.* 1, 12. Ærn micel *very much, Beo.* 1, 32.

Æra-geblond, ær-geblond, ear-gebland *the sea, the ocean, the briny deep;* mare:—*Chr.* 938: *Bt. R. p.* 158.

Æ'r-boren *first-born, Cd.* 47.

Ærcebiscop, ærcebisceop *an archbishop.*—Ærcebisceophad *the dignity of an archbishop,* v. arcebisceop, etc.

Ærcediacn *an archdeacon,* v. arcediacn.

Æ'r-dæd, e; f. *Former conduct, offence, demerit, vice;* anteactus:—Wyt witodlice bi uncer ær-dædum onfoð, *Lk.* 23, 41.

Æ'rdæg, æ'rdæg *a former day,* v. æra.

Ærdian *to inhabit,* v. eardian.

Ærdung, ærdung-stow *a tabernacle,* v. eardung.

Ærefnan *to bear,* v. aræfnan.

ÆREN, æryn; *adj. Made of brass, brazen;* æreus:—Wirc ane ærenan næddran, *Num.* 21, 8.

Ærenbyt [byt *a butt, vessel*] *Brass pan,* or *vessel;* lenticula:—*R.* 26, *Ben.*

Ærend, ærynd [*Dan.* ærende *f*: *Swed.* arende *n*: *Icel.* erende: *Norse,* eirendi] *An* ERRAND, *a message, an embassy, business, news, tiding, an answer, business, care;* nuntium:—He sent on his ærenda *he sends on his errands, Bt.* 39, 13. Hig lægdon ærende *they imposed an errand, Chr.* 1065.

Æ'rendæg [*contracted for* on ærran dæg *on a former day*] *The day before, yesterday;* pridie:—*R.* 96, v. dæg.

Ærend-boc *a letter,* v. ærendgewrit.

Ærend-gast *a spiritual messenger, an angel.*

Æren-geat [æren *brazen,* geat *gate*] *Arpa, R.* 17, *Lye.*

Ærend-gewrit, ærendwrit, ærendboc, *A message,* or *report in writing, a letter, an epistle, letters mandatory, a brief writing, short notes, a summary;* epistola:—Þurh his ærend gewritu *by his letters, Bd. pref. S. p.* 472, 22.

Ærendian; p. de; pp. od; *v. a. To go on an errand, to carry news, tidings,* or *a message, to intercede, to plead the cause;* annuntiare:—*Bd.* 2, 12.

Ærend-raca, ærend-wraca, ærendwreca; *m. A messenger, ambassador, an apostle;* nuntius:—Se ærendraca nys mæra, *Jn.* 13, 16. Ærendracan *apostles, R.* 68. ¶ Ærendracan unnytnes *a tale-bearer.* Gesibbe ærendracan *messengers of peace.*

Ærendran *messengers.*

Ærend-secga *an errand-deliverer, a messenger.*

Ærendsecgian *to deliver a message.*

Ærendung; *f. A command;* mandatum:—*C. R. Ben.* 38.

Ærendwraca *a messenger,* v. ærendraca.

Ærendwrit *a letter,* v. ærendgewrit.

Æ'rer *former,* v. æra.

Æ'rest *first,* v. æra.

Ærest *the resurrection,* v. æryst.

Ærfe-land, *heritable land,* v. yrfeland.

Ærfesten; *adj. Full of words;* linguosus:—*Ps.* 139, 12.

Ærfestnys *piety,* v. arfæstnys.

Ær-geblond *the sea,* v. ærageblond.

Æ'r-gedon; *adj. Done before;* anteactus:—*Bd.* 1, 6, 12. v. ær-dæd.

Æ'r-genemned *before-named.*

Æ'rgód *very* or *exceeding good.*

Æ'r-gystrandæg *ere yesterday, before yesterday.*

Æriesned *scattered;* distulit:—*Ps.* 77, 25.

Æriht [æ *law,* riht *right*] *Right, justice, lawful;* jus, legum jus:—*Cot.* 113.

Æring; *f. The dawning, day break, C. R. Mk.* 1, 35.

Ærisc *a bulrush,* v. rics.

Æ'rist *a resurrection,* v. æryst.

Æ'r-leoht, ær-tid *early light, day-break.*

Ærleat *iniquity,* v. arleasnes.

Ærlice *early in the morning,* arlice.

Ærm *poor,* v. earm.

Æ'r-mæl *before dinner,* v. mæl.

Ærmergen, ærnemorgen, ærmorgen, armorgen, ærnemergen; *m. The morning, the early part of the morning, the early dawn, day-break;* diluculum:—Se ærnemorgen þat ys betwux þam dægræde and þære sunnan upgange *the morning, that is, betwixt the dawn and the sun's rising, Æqu. vern.* 5. ¶ On ærnemergen *in the morning, Mt.* 20, 1.

ÆRN, *es; n.* [*Frs.* earne: *Dan.* arne *m*: *Icel.* ar, arn *m.*] *A place, secret place, closet, an habitation, a house, cottage;* locus, domus:—Bereð into his ærne *beareth into his house, L. In.* 57. Heal ærna mæst, *Beo.* 1, 50.

-ærn, -ern [from ærn *a place*] is used as a termination to some words, and denotes *a place.* Nouns ending in -ærn, *or* -ern are *neuter;* thus, Domern *a judgment-place, a judgment-hall, a court of justice.* Heddern *a hiding place, a storehouse, a cellar.* It denotes towards a place; as, -*ern* in English; thus, Suðern *southern;* australis: Norðern *northern;* septentrionalis: Western *western;* occidentalis, etc.

Ærn *brazen,* v. æren.

Ærnamæst *most honourable,* v. æra *superior.*

Ærnan; *v. a. To let run,* v. yrnan.

Ærnddedon; *p. of* ærendian *to go on an errand.*

Ærnemergen *the morning,* v. ærmergen.

Ærne-weg, es; *m. A course, way, broad road,* or *great street;* platea:—Æt sumes ærneweges ende *at the end of some course, Bt.* 37, 2.

Ærnian *to earn,* v. earnian.

Ærning, e; *f. A running, a course;* cursus:—Þa þe hiora ærninge trewað *those who are confident in their course, Bt.* 37, 2.

Ærnung, e; *f. An* EARNING, *stipend, hire, wages;* merces, *Som.*

Æron *before,* v. ær; *adv.*

Æ'r-onfangian *To take up before, to anticipate;* antecapere, *Som.*

Æror *before,* v. æra.

Ærost *first,* v. ær.

Ærra *the former,* v. æra.

Ærra geola *December,* v. geol.

Ærra liþa *June,* v. liþa ærra.

ÆRS, [*Plat. Dan.* ars: *Frs.* ears] *The buttocks, the hind part;* anus, podex:—*R.* 46.

Ærschen *a quail,* v. erschen.

Ærst *first, for* ærost, v. ær.

Æ'r-tid *early time,* v. ær-leoht.

Æ'r-toweard; *adv. Before, a little before;* paulo antea, *Som.*

Ærur *before,* v. æra.

Ærwe *an arrow,* v. arewa.

Ærwyrð *honourable,* v. arwurð.

Æryn *brazen,* v. æren.

Ærynd *an errand,* v. ærend.

Æryndwrit *a letter,* v. ærendgewrit.

Æryr *former,* v. ær.

Æryst, ærist, ærest, arist; *m. The rising, resurrection;* resurrectio:—Þe god farað on lifes æryste, *Jn.* 5, 29.

ÆS [*Dut.* aas *n*: *Ger.* az *f*: *Frs.* *Al.* as, az] *Meat, food,* esca:—*Scint.* 28, *Som.*

Æsc, es; *m.* [*Frs.* esk: *Plat. Dut. Ger.* esche *f*: *Dan.* ask, esk, esktræ: *Icel.* aas: *Al.* asche, esche: "*Ind.* askr baculus de fraxino," *Wach.*] 1. *An* ASH *tree, a shield* or *lance, a small ship, a vessel to sail* or *row in,* (so named from the wood of which *it was made*); fraxinus. 2. *A man,* (because the *Norreni,* or *Cimbri,* supposed that the first man was made of *Ash,* as the first woman was of *Elm,* v. *Mall. North. Antiq. by Percy,* vol. 2. p. 28—30); vir, homo. 3. *The chief of men, a leader,* (hence

O

X 2 Orbenuma, an m an heir, Th. gpe yrfenuma

X Or-fæder, es; m fore father, Beo K 5241

O [Pa 4]

X

2 Orfæst pious, religious Th. an v æfest

3 × Or-dæg early day early morn Beo K 252

5 Orfe, erfe, es; n succession; hærede; Th. an tras Th. an yrfe

Cd 25 Cd 32, 7

X Orian to plough Th. an v erian

4 × Orend, e; f. It Orende, es; n An errand, message Th. An Cd 139, Th p 174, Cd 160 Th p 210, 20 Beo yl.

Or- gescód shod with brass Beo K 5551

Or- gestreon brass treasure, wealth treasure Cd 98 Th

Beo K 3511

Beo K 1102

Or- geweorc, es; n ancient work

1356

9 × Oernum bearum with brazen trumpets Cd. 156 Th 191. 18; 200, Th p 248, 28

O 9 a message Cd 212. Th p 261, 32

Orran dæge on the day before; pridie Som.

6 × Or- morien, es; m early morn, dawn Th. an

8 X Orþam ere that, antequam v ær

O Oar person, or pissem before this here to fr. antehac Som.

O 10

Th an Orþes, es m

X Oran, es; m der oppose

Orpon before Bd 5, 2 antea

X Or- wela; an m old wealth Beo K 5491

Oes [56]

8 × bait; esca

X Os, es; n [But, plat, few is m] Old Ger äsz, as, ase Used as m [Oesc 56] Dead carcass, carrion; cadaver Th. An

O 10 ×
Cd 32, Th p 41, 31

X Orendra, an, m A messenger; Cd 111 Th p 147, 3

X Orend-secg, es; m an envoy a message deliverer Cd 30, Th p 41, 17

X

None

After the D & P insert C p. 7 3a 16 ...
~~P in this, the next col. & in page 12~~
Æl-spring, es; m a fountain
... 7, 1

O

2 Æswic, es; m
Pork æswicas Lup 16, 12.

Æswicnis reverentia Ben

Æswidiste juris-periti Ben

Ætefing-stoc Tavistock Chr 997 v Tæfingstoc

4 Æsc-bora, an m A spear or lance bearer hastifer Grim II 448, 9

Æsce, an; f. ashes; cinis Ic æt æscean Ps. Th 101, 7

See margin

At farode at the shore Beo K 3828 v farod

Æt-fealh approached Beo K 1930 p. of æt-filhan

Æsc-here, es; m a naval band Th. An

2 Æsc-róf spear-famed Th. An

Æta, an m An eater v man-æta

3 Æsc-stede, es m a battle place Cod. Ex 838

Ætad eat, for etad pl. indef. of etan

Æt-filhan to ~~approach~~ to approach see æfingern ~~Beo K 1930~~

4 Æsc-wiga, an m A fighter with a lance champion; pugil Beo ~~153~~ K 4079

7 Æsmogu the skin or slough of senectus: Nædran æsmogu a snake's slough Lye

Æsmælo morbus quidam oculorum æsmælum 7 wið eallum eagna wærce L. M. 1, 2 Som

the proper name Æsc, the name of Hengist's son, *Chr.* 455, 457.); dux.—1. Ongen þa æscas *against the vessels, Chr.* 897. 2. *Mann.* 3, v. æsc-tir.

Æsca, æsce *Search, inquisition, examination, enquiry, trial of,* or *asking after any matter,* or *thing;* disquisitio:—*R. Ben. pref. Som.*

Æscær; *adj. Without shearing, untrimmed, uncut, without tonsure;* incultus:—*L. Can. Edg.*

j Æscapo; *part. Spared, borrowed,* or *separated from other affairs;* subsecivus:—*Cot.* 167, *Som.*

Æsc-berend, es; *m.* [æsc *a shield,* or *spear,* berend *a bearing*] *A lance-bearer, shield-bearer, soldier;* hastifer:—*Cd.* 94.

Æsceda *A farrago, mixture, perfume;* migma:—*R.* 59, *Lye.*

Æsceman, æscman *A pirate;* pirata:—*Cot.* 155.

Æscen [*Plat.* aesch, aesk *f. Ger.* asch *m*: *Dan.* aeske *c.*] *A vessel made of wood, such as a bottle, bucket, pail,* etc.; lagena:—Æscen þe is oðre namon hrygilebuc gecleopad *an ascen, its other name is called Rigelbuc,* q. *back-bucket, Heming,* p. 393.

k Æscen, æscenne; *adj. Ashen, ash, made of ash;* fraxineus, *Som.*

Æscesdun, assandun [æsc *ash,* dun *a down,* or *hill*] ASHDOWN, *Aston in Berkshire,* ASHENDON *in Bucks,* etc., *Chr. Ing.* p. 38, 47, 100, 180.

Æscholt *an haft,* or *handle of ash, Beo.* 5, 22: *Thork.* p. 27.

Æscian *to ask,* v. acsian.

Æscman *a pirate,* v. æsceman.

Æscplega [plega *play*] *the sport* or *play of lances,* or *spears, war;* bellum:—*Fr. Jdth.* p. 24, 31.

Æscrof [æsc *a man,* rof *roof, high*] *An eminent man, a nobleman;* homo clarus:—*Fr. Jdth.* p. 26, 20.—Æscþræc; *m.* (þræc *strength*) *strength of spear, power, a battle.*

l Æscþrote, ascþrotu *an herb, the big-fennel,* or *fennel-giant;*—*Herb.* 4, 1, *Som.*

Æsc-tir, æsc-tyr *spear-glory, Cd.* 95.

Æscwig [wig *warlike*] *A general, an hero, a proper name:—Chr.* 992: *Gib.* p. 127, 3:—Æscwin [win *a friend*] *a man's friend, a proper name:—Chr.* 495: *Gib.* p. 16, 11.

Æsellend *a law-giver,* v. æsyllend.

Æsne, æsne-mon *a man,* v. esne.

Æsp *the asp-tree,* v. æpse.

m Æspen; *adj.* ASPEN, *belonging to the asp-tree;* populeus, *Som.*

Æspring; [æ *water,* spring] *A water-spring, a fountain;* fons.

Æst *estimation,* v. est.

Æstel, es; *m.* [stel *a column, division*] *An index,* or *table of contents ranged in columns, a label, guide, a stile,* or *division in wainscotting, a handle;* index:—*Elf. gr.* 8, *Som.*

Æswapa, aswapa *sweepings, dust;* pergamentum, *Som.*

Æswic, æswicung [æ *law,* swic *an offence*] *An offence, a scandal, stumbling-block, sedition, deceit;* scandalum:—*Ps.* 48, 13.

n Æswica, æswicend, es; *An offender of the law, a deceiver, an hypocrite, apostate;* legis violator, *Som.*

Æswician, æswican *to depart from the law, to dissemble,* v. swican.

Æswicung *an offence,* v. æswic.

Æswind *idle,* v. aswind.

Æswutol *A lawyer;* legisperitus, *Som.*

Æsyllend, es; *m.* [æ *law,* syllende *giving*] *A lawgiver;* legislator:—*Ps.* 83, 7.

ÆT; *prep. dat.* [*Moes.* at: *Heb.* את at, *denoting nearness, approach,* v. ארח at *to come to*]. 1. AT, *to, next, with, against, in;* apud. 2. *Of, from,* because you approach a person or thing when you wish to take something away, as they say in and about Nottingham, "*Take this at me,*" i.e. *from me;* a, ab, de:—1. Sittende æt toll-sceamule, *Mt.* 9, 9. Ge ne comun æt me, *Mt.* 25, 43. Æt feawum wordum *in few words, briefly, Bd.* 3, 17. 2. Animað þat pund æt hym, *Mt.* 25, 28. Leorniað æt me *learn by coming near me, learn at, of,* or *from me, Mt.* 11, 29. Æt his sylfes muþe *at,* or *from his own mouth, Bd.* 3, 27. ¶ Æt handa *at hand, Bd.* 2, 9.

Æt, es; *m. Meat, food;* cibus:—*R. Ben.* 43, 49.

Æt *ate, devoured,* v. etan.

Ætarn *ran,* v. yrnan.

Ætbær *shewed,* v. ætberan.

Ætbeon *to be at, to be present.*

Ætberan; *p.* ætbær [æt *out,* beran *to bear*] *To* BEAR OUT, *to shew;* præferre:—*Cd.* 202.

Ætberstan; *p.* ætbærst, hi ætburston; *pp.* ætborsten *To break out,* or *loose, to escape, to get away;* erumpere:—Þa fif cyningas ætburston, *Jos.* 10, 16. Þat he þanon ætberste, *L. Cnut.* 2.

Ætbredan, he ætbryt; *p.* ætbræde, we ætbrudon; *pp.* ætbrodon, ætbreden; *v. a. To take away, withdraw, set at liberty, to enlarge, release, rescue;* tollere, eripere:—Se deofol ætbryt þat word, *Lk.* 8, 12.

Ætbredendlic gebigednys *the ablative case:—Elf. gr.* 7.

Ætbrodon, ætbrudon *taken away,* v. ætbredan.

Ætbyrstan *to break out,* v. ætberstan.

Ætclifian *to cleave to, adhere.*

Ætdon *To take away, to take;* eripere:—*L. Can. Edg. W.* p. 83, 17.

Æte *food,* v. æt.

p Ætearnnis *an argument.*

Æt-ecan [æt *at,* eacan *to eke*] *To add, to increase;* adjicere:—*Bd.* 3, 27, *Lye.*

Æt-eom, þu æt-eart, he æt-ys; *v. n.* [æt *at,* eom *I am*] *To be present;* adesse:—Þat rip æt ys, *Mk.* 4. 29.

Æteorian *to be wanting,* v. ateorian.

Æteowednis *a revelation.*

Æteowian, ic æteowige; *imp.* æteow, ædeau; *p.* æteowde, atiwede; *pp.* æteowd *To shew, appear, tell, declare;* ostendere:—Þa æteowde se coccel hine, *Mt.* 13, 26.

q Æteowigendlice; *adv. Evidently, demonstratively;* demonstrative, *Lye.*

Æteren, ætern *poisonous,* v. ættrene.

Æternes, se; *f. Venomousness, full of poison;* venenositas, *Som.*

Ætewung, e; *f. A shewing, manifesting, epiphany;* manifestatio:—*Elf. gl.* p. 55.

Ætfaroð *An approach, entrance, return;* aditus, *Beo.*

Ætfæstan *to dash against,* v. æt-bræppan.

Ætfeohtan *to fight for,* or *at.*

Ætfeolan; *p.* ætfealh, ætfalh, ætfelh, ætfeolh; *pp.* ætfeallen [æt, feallan *to fall*] *To stay, fall, lean,* or *insist upon, to stick to, to trust in, labour in, to happen;* insistere:—Me soðlice ætfeolan Gode gód is, *Ps.* 72, 27. Ætfeolan wæccum and gebedum *to continue in watchings and prayers, Bd.* 4, 25.

Ætferian *to carry out, to take away.*

Ætfiolan *to persist,* v. ætfeolan.

r Ætflean, ætfleon; *p.* ætfleah, we ætflugon; *pp.* ætflogen [æt, fleogan *to flee*] *To flee away, to escape by flight, to eschew;* aufugere:—Ætfleon ne mihte, *Jos.* 10, 35.

Ætflowan *To flow to,* or *together, to increase;* affluere:—Gyf welan ætflowon, *Ps.* 61, 10.

Ætfó, ætfon [æt *from,* fon *to take*] *To take away, to seize, claim;*

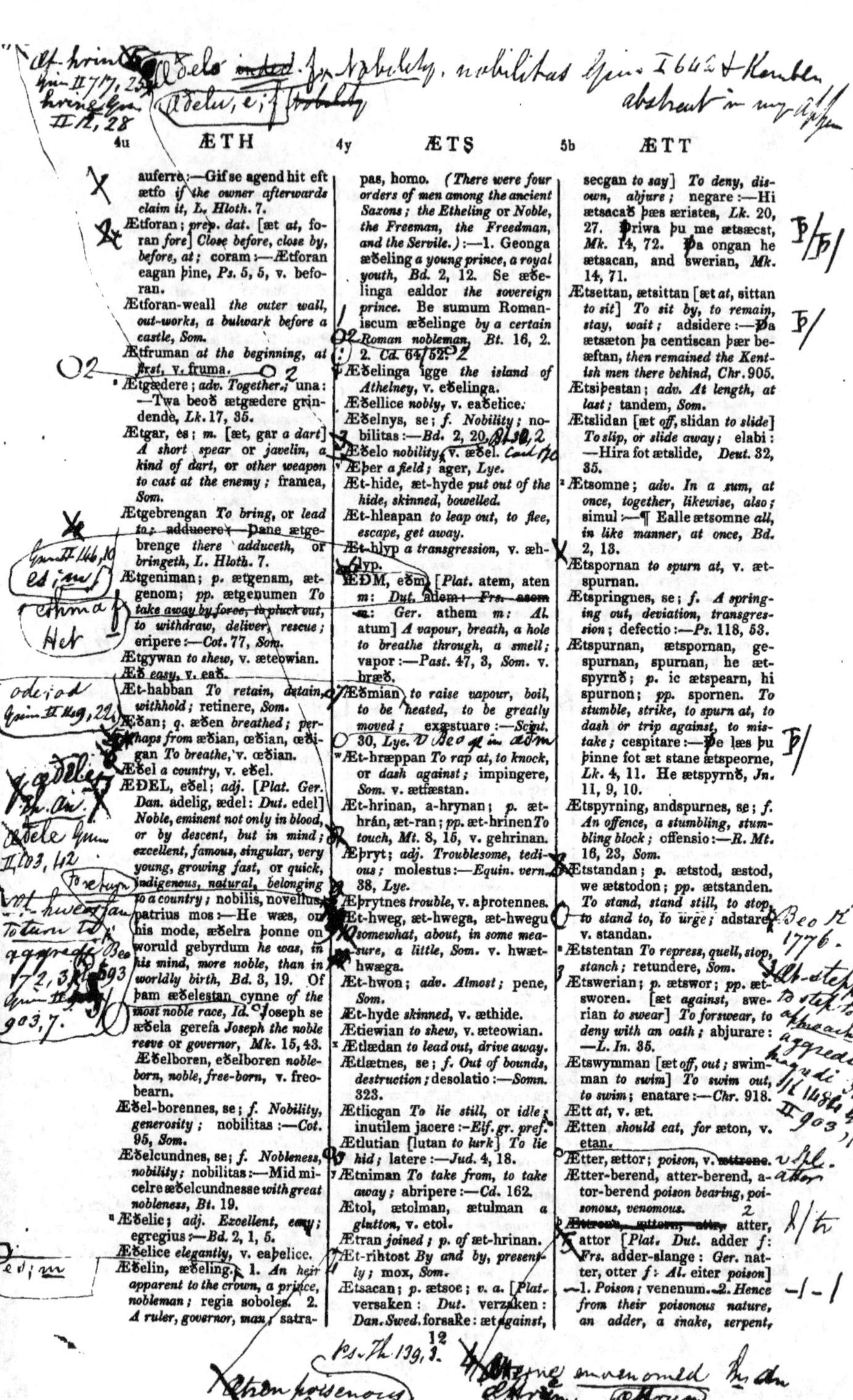

auferre:—Gif se agend hit eft ætfo *if the owner afterwards claim it*, *L. Hloth.* 7.

Ætforan; *prep. dat.* [æt *at*, foran *fore*] *Close before, close by, before, at*; coram:—Ætforan eagan þine, *Ps.* 5, 5, v. beforan.

Ætforan-weall *the outer wall, out-works, a bulwark before a castle, Som.*

Ætfruman *at the beginning, at first*, v. fruma.

Ætgædere; *adv. Together*; una:—Twa beoð ætgædere grindende, *Lk.* 17, 35.

Ætgar, es; *m.* [æt, gar *a dart*] *A short spear* or *javelin, a kind of dart*, or *other weapon to cast at the enemy*; framea, *Som.*

Ætgebrengan *To bring*, or *lead to*; adducere:—Þane ætgebrenge *there adduceth*, or *bringeth*, *L. Hloth.* 7.

Ætgeniman; *p.* ætgenam, ætgenom; *pp.* ætgenumen *To take away by force, to pluck out, to withdraw, deliver, rescue*; eripere:—*Cot.* 77, *Som.*

Ætgywan *to shew*, v. æteowian.

Æð *easy*, v. eað.

Æt-habban *To retain, detain, withhold*; retinere, *Som.*

Æðan; *q.* æðen *breathed*; *perhaps from* æðian, œðian, œðigan *To breathe*, v. œðian.

Æðel *a country*, v. eðel.

ÆÐEL, eðel; *adj.* [*Plat. Ger. Dan.* adelig, ædel: *Dut.* edel] *Noble, eminent not only in blood, or by descent, but in mind; excellent, famous, singular, very young, growing fast*, or *quick, indigenous, natural, belonging to a country*; nobilis, novellus, patrius mos:—He wæs, on his mode, æðelra þonne on woruld gebyrdum *he was, in his mind, more noble, than in worldly birth*, *Bd.* 3, 19. Of þam æðelestan cynne *of the most noble race*, *Id.* Joseph se æðela gerefa *Joseph the noble reeve* or *governor*, *Mk.* 15, 43. Æðelboren, eðelboren *noble-born, noble, free-born*, v. freobearn.

Æðel-borennes, se; *f. Nobility, generosity*; nobilitas:—*Cot.* 95, *Som.*

Æðelcundnes, se; *f. Nobleness, nobility*; nobilitas:—Mid micelre æðelcundnesse *with great nobleness*, *Bt.* 19.

Æðelic; *adj. Excellent, easy*; egregius:—*Bd.* 2, 1, 5.

Æðelice *elegantly*, v. eaþelice.

Æðelin, æðeling. 1. *An heir apparent to the crown, a prince, nobleman*; regia soboles. 2. *A ruler, governor, man*; satrapas, homo. (*There were four orders of men among the ancient Saxons; the Etheling* or *Noble, the Freeman, the Freedman, and the Servile.*):—1. Geonga æðeling *a young prince, a royal youth*, *Bd.* 2, 12. Se æðelinga ealdor *the sovereign prince.* Be sumum Romaniscum æðelinge *by a certain Roman nobleman*, *Bt.* 16, 2. 2. *Cd.* 64.

Æðelinga igge *the island of Athelney*, v. eðelinga.

Æðellice *nobly*, v. eaðelice.

Æðelnys, se; *f. Nobility*; nobilitas:—*Bd.* 2, 20.

Æðelo *nobility*, v. æðel.

Æþer *a field*; ager, *Lye.*

Æt-hide, æt-hyde *put out of the hide, skinned, bowelled.*

Æt-hleapan *to leap out, to flee, escape, get away.*

Æt-hlyp *a transgression*, v. æhlyp.

ÆÐM, eðm [*Plat.* atem, aten *m*: *Dut.* adem: *Frs.* azem *m*: *Ger.* athem *m*: *Al.* atum] *A vapour, breath, a hole to breathe through, a smell*; vapor:—*Past.* 47, 3, *Som.* v. bræð.

Æðmian *to raise vapour, boil, to be heated, to be greatly moved*; exæstuare:—*Scint.* 30, *Lye.*

Æt-hræppan *To rap at, to knock*, or *dash against*; impingere, *Som.* v. ætfæstan.

Æt-hrinan, a-hrynan; *p.* æthrán, æt-ran; *pp.* æt-hrinen *To touch*, *Mt.* 8, 15, v. gehrinan.

Æþryt; *adj. Troublesome, tedious*; molestus:—*Equin. vern.* 38, *Lye.*

Æþrytnes *trouble*, v. aþrotennes.

Æt-hweg, æt-hwega, æt-hwegu *somewhat, about, in some measure, a little, Som.* v. hwæthwæga.

Æt-hwon; *adv. Almost*; pene, *Som.*

Æt-hyde *skinned*, v. æthide.

Ætiewian *to shew*, v. æteowian.

Ætlædan *to lead out, drive away.*

Ætlætnes, se; *f. Out of bounds, destruction*; desolatio:—*Somn.* 323.

Ætliegan *To lie still*, or *idle*; inutilem jacere:—*Elf. gr. pref.*

Ætlutian [lutan *to lurk*] *To lie hid*; latere:—*Jud.* 4, 18.

Ætniman *To take from, to take away*; abripere:—*Cd.* 162.

Ætol, ætolman, ætulman *a glutton*, v. etol.

Ætran *joined*; *p. of* æt-hrinan.

Æt-rihtost *By and by, presently*; mox, *Som.*

Ætsacan; *p.* ætsoc; *v. a.* [*Plat.* versaken: *Dut.* verzaken: *Dan. Swed.* forsake: æt *against*, secgan *to say*] *To deny, disown, abjure*; negare:—Hi ætsacað þæs æristes, *Lk.* 20, 27. Þriwa þu me ætsæcst, *Mk.* 14, 72. Þa ongan he ætsacan, and swerian, *Mk.* 14, 71.

Ætsettan, ætsittan [æt *at*, sittan *to sit*] *To sit by, to remain, stay, wait*; adsidere:—Þa ætsæton þa centiscan þær beæftan, *then remained the Kentish men there behind*, *Chr.* 905.

Ætsiþestan; *adv. At length, at last*; tandem, *Som.*

Ætslidan [æt *off*, slidan *to slide*] *To slip, or slide away*; elabi:—Hira fot ætslide, *Deut.* 32, 35.

Ætsomne; *adv. In a sum, at once, together, likewise, also*; simul:—¶ Ealle ætsomne *all, in like manner, at once*, *Bd.* 2, 13.

Ætspornan *to spurn at*, v. ætspurnan.

Ætspringnes, se; *f. A springing out, deviation, transgression*; defectio:—*Ps.* 118, 53.

Ætspurnan, ætspornan, gespurnan, spurnan, he ætspyrnð; *p.* ic ætspearn, hi spurnon; *pp.* spornen. *To stumble, strike, to spurn at, to dash or trip against, to mistake*; cespitare:—Þe læs þu þinne fot æt stane ætspeorne, *Lk.* 4, 11. He ætspyrnð, *Jn.* 11, 9, 10.

Ætspyrning, andspurnes, se; *f. An offence, a stumbling, stumbling block*; offensio:—*R. Mt.* 16, 23, *Som.*

Ætstandan; *p.* ætstod, æstod, we ætstodon; *pp.* ætstanden. *To stand, stand still, to stop, to stand to, to urge*; adstare, v. standan.

Ætstentan *To repress, quell, stop, stanch*; retundere, *Som.*

Ætswerian; *p.* ætswor; *pp.* ætsworen. [æt *against*, swerian *to swear*] *To forswear, to deny with an oath*; abjurare:—*L. In.* 35.

Ætswymman [æt *off, out*; swimman *to swim*] *To swim out, to swim*; enatare:—*Chr.* 918.

Ætt *at*, v. æt.

Ætten *should eat, for* æton, v. etan.

Ætter, ættor; *poison*, v. ættrene.

Ætter-berend, atter-berend, ator-berend *poison bearing, poisonous, venomous.*

[illegible] atter, attor [*Plat. Dut.* adder *f*: *Frs.* adder-slange: *Ger.* natter, otter *f*: *Al.* eiter *poison*]—1. *Poison*; venenum. 2. *Hence from their poisonous nature, an adder, a snake, serpent,*

X Ætforan tëawian to provide Th. An

2 X Ætfore before v ætforan

○ 3 at the same time Th. An.

X Æt-gifan to restore reddere Beo K 5751

X Æþelinga-denu f. (the nobles' valley) Alton Hants. To Æþelinga-dene To Alton Chr 1001 Ing 173, 30

○ 2 Æþelinga ord men's origin Cd. 64 Th p 77, 20

X Ædele, alu ale boiled to the third part; carenum Som. Ben v ealu

X Æt-sprang spring out Beo K 2236 f. of. at-springan, v springan

X Ædelo see top of p

X Æþelferþing-wyrt herba genus plagam sanans et carbunculos Herb. 1. c 39 & 38 Som Ben

X Æþele adj noble nobilis Th. An

X Ædan to deluge overwhelm Cd 64. Th p 77. 24

X Æþelcundnes nobilitas Ben

○ 6 8 70

X Æþung, eþung breath Th. An

æþung

○

2 X Æt-standan p æt-stód to stand out, cease Beo K 1776 Beo Th in standan

3 See back margin

○

○ 3 Æt nextan, at nyhstan at length, at last; tandem Som.

○ Æt-samon cyrre sometimes, quandoque Som

X

Ættrene, ætern ætter, dl.

5 X Ættor, ætter, ater es; n; poison

5 ~~ater~~

~~Beo Attor~~

X

○ 8

— Beo K 3233 Beo Th in ættor

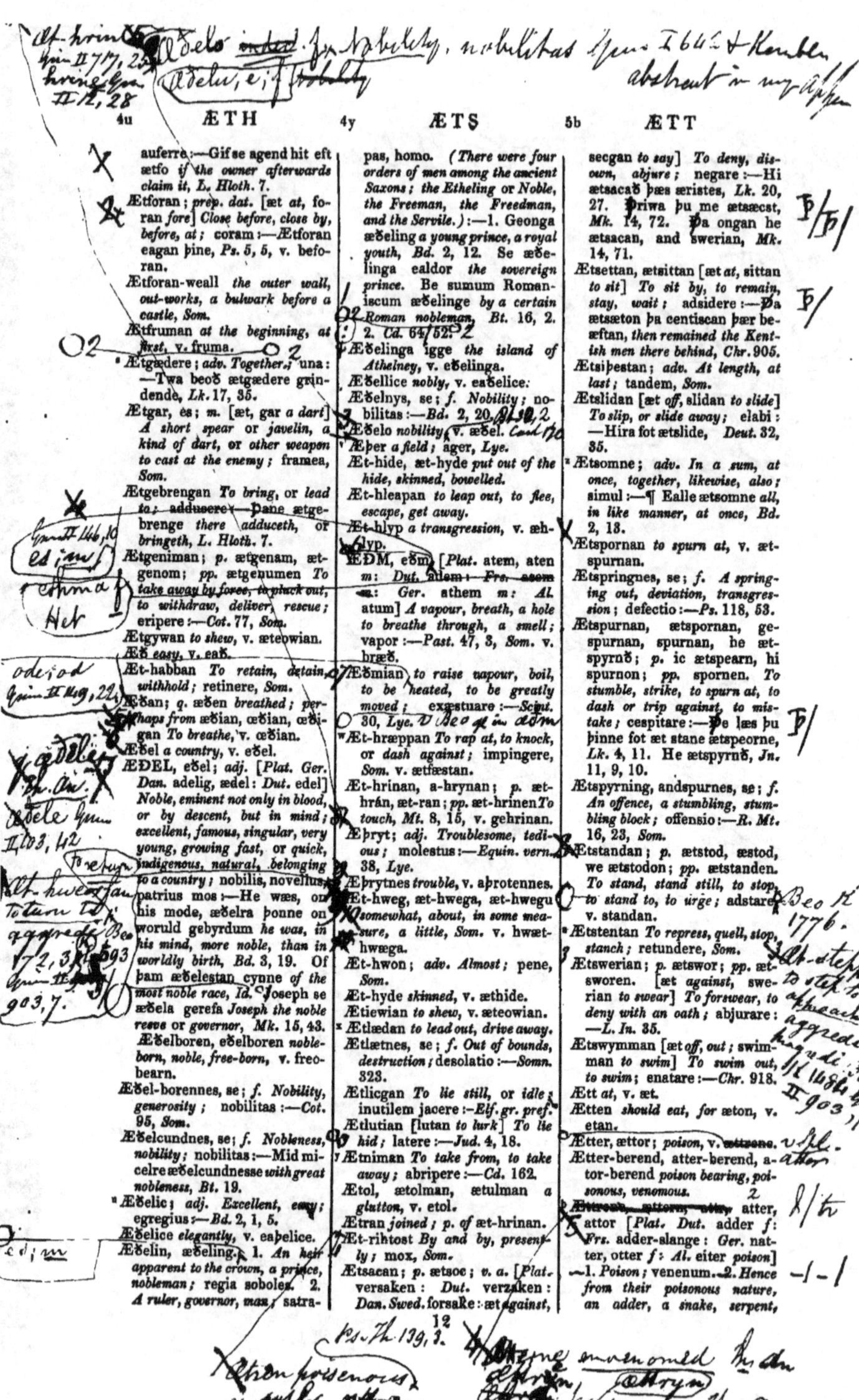

auferre:—Gif se agend hit eft ætfo *if the owner afterwards claim it, L. Hloth.* 7.

Ætforan; *prep. dat.* [æt *at,* foran *fore*] *Close before, close by, before, at;* coram:—Ætforan eagan þine, *Ps.* 5, 5, v. beforan.

Ætforan-weall *the outer wall, out-works, a bulwark before a castle, Som.*

Ætfruman *at the beginning, at first,* v. fruma.

Ætgædere; *adv. Together;* una:—Twa beoð ætgædere grindende, *Lk.* 17, 35.

Ætgar, es; *m.* [æt, gar *a dart*] *A short spear* or *javelin, a kind of dart,* or *other weapon to cast at the enemy;* framea, *Som.*

Ætgebrengan *To bring,* or *lead to;* adducere:—Þane ætgebrenge *there adduceth,* or *bringeth, L. Hloth.* 7.

Ætgeniman; *p.* ætgenam, ætgenom; *pp.* ætgenumen *To take away by force, to pluck out, to withdraw, deliver, rescue;* eripere:—*Cot.* 77, *Som.*

Ætgywan *to shew,* v. æteowian.

Æð *easy,* v. eað.

Æt-habban *To retain, detain, withhold;* retinere, *Som.*

Æðan; *q.* æðen *breathed; perhaps from* æðian, œðian, œðigan *To breathe,* v. œðian.

Æðel *a country,* v. eðel.

ÆÐEL, eðel; *adj.* [*Plat. Ger. Dan.* adelig, ædel: *Dut.* edel] *Noble, eminent not only in blood, or by descent, but in mind; excellent, famous, singular, very young, growing fast,* or *quick, indigenous, natural, belonging to a country;* nobilis, novellus, patrius mos:—He wæs, on his mode, æðelra þonne on woruld gebyrdum *he was, in his mind, more noble, than in worldly birth, Bd.* 3, 19. Of þam æðelestan cynne *of the most noble race, Id.* Joseph se æðela gerefa *Joseph the noble reeve* or *governor, Mk.* 15, 43.

Æðelboren, eðelboren *noble-born, noble, free-born,* v. freobearn.

Æðel-borennes, se; *f. Nobility, generosity;* nobilitas:—*Cot.* 95, *Som.*

Æðelcundnes, se; *f. Nobleness, nobility;* nobilitas:—Mid micelre æðelcundnesse *with great nobleness, Bt.* 19.

Æðelic; *adj. Excellent, easy;* egregius:—*Bd.* 2, 1, 5.

Æðelice *elegantly,* v. eaþelice.

Æðelin, æðeling. 1. *An heir apparent to the crown, a prince, nobleman;* regia soboles. 2. *A ruler, governor, man;* satrapas, homo. (*There were four orders of men among the ancient Saxons; the Etheling* or *Noble, the Freeman, the Freedman, and the Servile.*):—1. Geonga æðeling *a young prince, a royal youth, Bd.* 2, 12. Se æðelinga ealdor *the sovereign prince.* Be sumum Romaniscum æðelinge *by a certain Roman nobleman, Bt.* 16, 2. 2. *Cd.* 64.

Æðelinga igge *the island of Atheiney,* v. eðelinga.

Æðellice *nobly,* v. eaðelice.

Æðelnys, se; *f. Nobility;* nobilitas:—*Bd.* 2, 20.

Æðelo *nobility,* v. æðel.

Æþer *a field;* ager, *Lye.*

Æt-hide, æt-hyde *put out of the hide, skinned, bowelled.*

Æt-hleapan *to leap out, to flee, escape, get away.*

Æt-hlyp *a transgression,* v. æhlyp.

ÆÐM, eðm [*Plat.* atem, aten *m: Dut.* adem: *Frs.* asem *m: Ger.* athem *m: Al.* atum] *A vapour, breath, a hole to breathe through, a smell;* vapor:—*Past.* 47, 3, *Som.* v. bræð.

Æðmian *to raise vapour, boil, to be heated, to be greatly moved;* exæstuare:—*Scint.* 30, *Lye.*

Æt-hræppan *To rap at, to knock,* or *dash against;* impingere, *Som.* v. ætfæstan.

Æt-hrinan, a-hrynan; *p.* æthrán, æt-ran; *pp.* æt-hrinen *To touch, Mt.* 8, 15, v. gehrinan.

Æþryt; *adj. Troublesome, tedious;* molestus:—*Equin. vern.* 38, *Lye.*

Æþrytnes *trouble,* v. aþrotennes.

Æt-hweg, æt-hwega, æt-hwegu *somewhat, about, in some measure, a little, Som.* v. hwæthwæga.

Æt-hwon; *adv. Almost;* pene, *Som.*

Æt-hyde *skinned,* v. æthide.

Ætiewian *to shew,* v. æteowian.

Ætlædan *to lead out, drive away.*

Ætlætnes, se; *f. Out of bounds, destruction;* desolatio:—*Somn.* 323.

Ætlicgan *To lie still,* or *idle;* inutilem jacere:—*Elf. gr. pref.*

Ætlutian [lutan *to lurk*] *To lie hid;* latere:—*Jud.* 4, 18.

Ætniman *To take from, to take away;* abripere:—*Cd.* 162.

Ætol, ætolman, ætulman *a glutton,* v. etol.

Ætran *joined; p. of* æt-hrinan.

Æt-rihtost *By and by, presently;* mox, *Som.*

Ætsacan; *p.* ætsoc; *v. a.* [*Plat.* versaken: *Dut.* verzaken: *Dan. Swed.* forsake: æt *against,* secgan *to say*] *To deny, disown, abjure;* negare:—Hi ætsacað þæs æristes, *Lk.* 20, 27. Þriwa þu me ætsæcst, *Mk.* 14, 72. Þa ongan he ætsacan, and swerian, *Mk.* 14, 71.

Ætsettan, ætsittan [æt *at,* sittan *to sit*] *To sit by, to remain, stay, wait;* adsidere:—Þa ætsæton þa centiscan þær beæftan, *then remained the Kentish men there behind, Chr.* 905.

Ætsiþestan; *adv. At length, at last;* tandem, *Som.*

Ætslidan [æt *off,* slidan *to slide*] *To slip, or slide away;* elabi:—Hira fot ætslide, *Deut.* 32, 35.

Ætsomne; *adv. In a sum, at once, together, likewise, also;* simul:—¶ Ealle ætsomne *all, in like manner, at once, Bd.* 2, 13.

Ætspornan *to spurn at,* v. ætspurnan.

Ætspringnes, se; *f. A springing out, deviation, transgression;* defectio:—*Ps.* 118, 53.

Ætspurnan, ætspornan, gespurnan, spurnan, he ætspyrnð; *p.* ic ætspearn, hi spurnon; *pp.* spornen. *To stumble, strike, to spurn at, to dash* or *trip against, to mistake;* cespitare:—Þe læs þu þinne fot æt stane ætspeorne, *Lk.* 4, 11. He ætspyrnð, *Jn.* 11, 9, 10.

Ætspyrning, andspurnes, se; *f. An offence, a stumbling, stumbling block;* offensio:—*R. Mt.* 16, 23, *Som.*

Ætstandan; *p.* ætstod, æstod, we ætstodon; *pp.* ætstanden. *To stand, stand still, to stop, to stand to, to urge;* adstare, v. standan.

Ætstentan *To repress, quell, stop, stanch;* retundere, *Som.*

Ætswerian; *p.* ætswor; *pp.* ætsworen. [æt *against,* swerian *to swear*] *To forswear, to deny with an oath;* abjurare:—*L. In.* 35.

Ætswymman [æt *off, out;* swimman *to swim*] *To swim out, to swim;* enatare:—*Chr.* 918.

Ætt *at,* v. æt.

Ætten *should eat, for* æton, v. etan.

Ætter, ættor; *poison,* v. ættrene.

Ætter-berend, atter-berend, ator-berend *poison bearing, poisonous, venomous.*

Ættrene, ættern, ættre atter, attor [*Plat. Dut.* adder *f: Frs.* adder-slange: *Ger.* natter, otter *f: Al.* eiter *poison*] 1. *Poison;* venenum. 2. *Hence from their poisonous nature, an adder, a snake, serpent,*

X Ætforan tēawian to provide Th. An

2 Ætfore before v ætforan

○ 3 at the same time Th. An.

4 Æt-gifan to restore reddere Beo K 5751

Æþelinga-ig, -ige f.

X Æþelinga-dene f. (the nobles valley) Alton Hants. To Æþelinga-dene to Alton Chr 1001 Ing 173, 30

○ 2 Æþelinga ord men's origin Cd 64 Th. 77, 20

X Æðele, alu ale boiled to the third part; carenum Som. Ben v ealu

Æþelo; fe ge top of k 7

X Æþelferþing-wyrt herba genus plagam sanans et carbunculos Herb. 1. c 33 & 13 8 Som. Ben. Lye

X Æt-sprang sprungon ... Beo K 2236 ... Æt-springan, v ætspringan

X Æþele adj noble, nobilis Th. An Beo gl

X Ældan to deluge, overwhelm Cd 64. Th p 77, 24

X 6 Æðeundnes nobilitas Ben

X Æþung breath Th. An ... æþung

○

2 Æt standan p æt-stód to stand out; exstare Beo K 1776 gl Beo gl in standan

3- See text marcii

○

○ 3 Æt nextan, æt nyhstan at length, at last; tandem Som.

○ Æt sumon cyrre sometimes, quandoque Som

Ættrene, ætterne ætter. dl.

5 X Ættor, ætter, ater es; n; poison

~~5 X ater~~

~~Beo gl Ættor~~

○ 8

— Beo K 3233 Beo gl in ættor

ϕ 1 Awinbre cynnigas
relevs for new year
condalo consules
dan

ϕ

O

Hæ nagu

3 Æt-wegan p æt-wæg-
to take or bear away Beo
K 2397

ϕ

ϕ Æwisc-mód
a disgraced mind
Cd 42 Th p 55, 18

ϕ 1 es; m
ælbrycas Sup 16, 14

2 Ætwitan to twit
reproach Th. An

O

3 food Hickes Thes. I 135, 14
Cd. 60 Th p 73, 21

ϕ 4 Awelm, es; m
Th. An

4 Ax, eax, e; f

ϕ 2 an own brother
eldwere gebroðre

O

3 Æxian, pode, to ask
V acsian
Ps 136, 3

Æw, e f. ~~tan~~ wife

viper; anguis, vipera:—1. Ættrene or attor nædrena, Ps. 139, 3. 2. Cyn ætterna seed of vipers, Cot. Mt. 3. 7. Cynn aterne is found in Rush Codex, Lk. 3, 7, v. attr poison, næddra a serpent.

Ættrian; pp. ættrod, geættrod To poison, envenom; venenare:—Pref. R. Conc.

Ætul-man a glutton, v. ætol.

Æt-unlage; adv. Unjustly, wrongfully, wickedly; injuste, Som.

Ætwæsend, ætwesend, ætweosend, [æt at, wesende being; p. of wesan to be] At hand, approaching, hard by; imminens:—Cot. 107, Som.

Ætwenan, aðwænan [æt from, wenan to wean] To deliver from, to wean, to pluck out, to deprive of, to diminish, lessen, abate; segregare:—L. Cnut. in Epil.

c Ætwesan [æt at, wesan to be] To be present; adesse:—Bd. 4, 5.

Ætwindan; p. ætwand; pp. ætwunden. To wind off, escape, flee away; aufugere:—Job. Thw. p. 165.

Ætwist substance, v. edwist.

Ætwitan to reproach, v. edwitan.

Ætwunden fled, v. ætwindan.

Ætycean; p. ætecte, ætycte; v [æt, ycan, ecan to eke] To add to, to augment, increase; adjicere:—Bd. 4, 30.

Ætycenys, ætycnys, se; f. An increase, an addition; augmentum:—Bd. 1, 27.

Ætynan; p. de; pp. ed; v. a. [æ not, tynan to shut] To open; aperire:—Dura heofonas he ætynde, Ps. 77, 27.

Æt-ys is present, adest; v. æt-eom.

Ætywan, ætywian to shew, v. ywan.

d Ætywednes, ætywnys, se; f. A shewing, manifestation, laying open, a declaration; ostensio:—Oð þone dæg hys ætywednessum, Lk. 1, 80.

Æven evening, v. æfen.

Ævesa fruit; fructus, Mann.

Ævestlice, ævostlice religiously, v. æfestlice.

Æufest religious, v. æfest.

Æure always, v. æfer.

ÆW, æwe [æ law]. 1. Law, what is established by law, hence wedlock, marriage, a marriage vow; matrimonium. 2. A female bound by the law of marriage, a wife, spouse; conjux:—1. Æwe bryeð breaketh the marriage vow; adulteriam committit, L. Edg. 17: W. p. 90, 44. 2. Se þe hæfð æwe he who has a wife, Id. 19.

Æw; adj. Lawful, legitimate, related by the law of marriage, married, german; legitimus, nuptus, germanus:—Mid his æwum wife with his lawful wife, L. Alf. 38, W. p. 44, 21. Mid his dohtor æwum borenre with his daughter-in-law; cum filia sua germana, Id. l. 23. Æwe gebroðru brothers german; germani fratres, Bd. 1, 27. Æwen-broðor brother-in-law, Cot. 97.

Æwbrecca, æwbrica [æw marriage, breca a breaker] A breaker of the marriage vow, an adulterer, adulteress; adulter:—Se þe his æwe forlet and nymð oþer wif he bið æwbrica he who his wife leaves, and taketh another woman, he is an adulterer, L. Edg. 18, W. p. 91, 3.

Æwbrece, æwbryce [æw marriage, bryce a breaking] Adultery, fornication; adulterium:—Wið æghwylcne æwbryce from all adultery, L. Cnut. 24.

Æwd, an; æwdman A juror, one who serves on a jury, a juryman; fidejussor:—Hæbbe him in aþe oþerne æwdan godne let him have on oath another good juror, L. With. W. p. 12, 21. Mid godum æwdum by good jurors, L. Hloth. 2.

Æwe law, v. æw.

Æwelm, æwellm, æwylm, eawylm [æ or ea water, wælm boiling] A boiling up of water, a spring, fountain, head of a river; fons:—Swa sum mical æwelm and diop as some great and deep fountain, Bt. 34, 1. Þe mæg geseon þone hluttran æwellm, Id. 35, 6.

Æwenbroðor a brother german, v. æw; adj.

Æwende, membrum virile, Som.

Æwen; adj. [æ without, wen hope] Doubtful, uncertain; dubius:—And eow bið eowre lif æwene, Deut. 28, 66.

f Æwerd; adj. [æ law, werd from, werdan to corrupt] Perverse, froward, averse; perversus, Som.

Æwfest religious, v. æfest.

Æwfest-man A man restricted by law, a husband; maritus:—Yfel æwbryce þat æwfest man wið æmtige ænige forlicge, malum adulterium [est] quod uxoratus homo cum vacua ulla coeat, L. pol. Cnut. 47., v. æfest.

Æwfesten [æ, æw law, fæsten a fast] A fixed fast, a fast-day before Christmas-day; jejunium recurrens in adventu.

Æwfestnys religion, piety, v. æfestnes.

Æwfull religious, v. æfest.

Æwintre one winter, or year, v. anwintre.

Æwisc, æwist A dishonour, disgrace; dedecus:—Cwæð þat him to micel æwiste wære þat etc. Ors. 4. 6.

Æwisc; adj. Ashamed, disgraced, debased; dedecoratus:—Chr. 938.

Æwiscberend; adj. Bearing disgrace, unchaste, lewd, unclean, shameless, impudent; impudicus, Som.

Æwiscnys, ewiscnes, se; f. A disgrace, obscenity, filthiness, a blushing for shame, reverence; dedecus:—Ps. 34, 30. ¶ On æwiscnesse openly, as not being ashamed to be seen; in propatulo, Cot. 110, 202.

Æwist a disgrace, v. æwisc.

Æwlic lawful, v. ælic.

Æwritere, es; m. A writer, composer or framer of laws; legum conditor:—Prov. 8, Lye.

Æwul A twig-basket for catching fish; nassa:—Ælf. gl. 77, Lye.

Æwum-borenre to one lawfully born, v. æw; adj.

h Æwung, on æwunge openly, abroad, in the sight of all; in propatulo, Som.

Æwylm a fountain, v. æwelm.

Æwyrdla, æwyrdlea damage, v. æfwyrdla.

Æwyrp [æ from, wyrp cast, from wyrpan or weorpan to cast] A castaway, an abject, one lost; abjectus:—R. Ben. 7.

ÆX eax, acas; f. [Plat. Ger. axt f: Dut. aks f: Ottf. akus: Dan. öxe: Swed. Icel. yxa: Lat. ascia: Grk. ἀξίνη] Any thing that is brought to a sharp edge, an AXE, a hatchet, knife; securis:—Eallunga ys seo æx to þæra trywa wurtrumum asett, Mt. 3, 10. Seo eax ys the ax is, L. In. 43.

Æx an axis, v. eax.

Æxe ashes, v. axe.

Æxodon asked, v. acsian.

Af of, v. of.

Afæded; part. [feded fed, from fedan to feed] Fed, nourished, brought up, educated; nutritus:—Bd. 1, 27.

Afægd, afæged, adorned, v. afægrod.

Afægniend rejoicing, as fægniende; part. of. fægnian.

Afægrod, afægd, afæged; part. Coloured, adorned, embroidered; depictus, ornatus:—Bd. 1, 25.

i Afælan, gefælan To overthrow, overturn; evertere:—Ps. 105, 25.

Afællan To cast out, to oppose, offend; ejicere:—R. Mt. 18, 6, Lye.

Afæran, færan; p. æfærde, we æferdon; pp. æfæred, afered,

æfæryd *To frighten, to make afraid, to astonish, terrify;* terrere :—*Gen.* 42, 35.

Afærð *he goes, or shall go out,* v. afaran.

Afæstan *to fast,* v. fæstan.

Afæstla; *interjec.* [*Dut.* vastelyk: *Ger.* festiglych: *Dan.* visselig: a *intensive,* fæst *fast,* la *O!*] *O certainly! O assuredly;* O certè :—Afæstla, and hi la hi, and wella wel, and þyllice oðre syndon Englisc interjectiones *O certainly, and alas, and well well, and such other are English interjections, Elf. gr. interj., Som. p.* 49, 28.

Afæstnian, gefæstnian, FÆSTNIAN; *p.* de; *pp.* od. [*Plat.* vesten: *Dut.* vestigen: *Ger.* festigen, festen: *Dan.* faeste] *To fix, fasten,* or *make firm, to strengthen, fortify, confirm, betroth, espouse, inscribe;* figere :—Ðat we hi þonne moton afæstnian on þe *that we may fix them* [*our eyes*] *on thee, Bt.* 33, 4. Afæstnod ic eom, *Ps.* 68, 2. Mid gewritum gefæstnod *confirmed by writings, Ors.* 5, 13.

Afandelic *probable,* v. afandigendlic.

j Afandian, afandigean; *p.* -dode; *pp.* -dod, -dud, -dad, gefandod; *v. a. To prove, try, to make a trial, to discover by trying, to experience;* probare :—Ðu afandodest heorte mine, *Ps.* 16, 4. La liceteras, cunne ge afandigean heofones ansyne and eorðan, humeta na afandige ge þas tide? *Lk.* 12, 56. Ðu hit hæfst afandad be þe selfum, *Bt.* 31, 1.

Afandigendlic, afandelic, afandodlic; *adj. What may be tried, proved, probable;* probabilis :—*Scint. de prædest.*

Afandung *a trying,* v. fandung.

Afangen *taken, received,* v. fon.

Afaran, afearrian, fearran, he færð; *p.* afor; *pp.* afaren; *v. n. To depart, to go out of, or from a place;* exire :—*Ps.* 51, 5.

Afaran *children,* v. eafora.

Afdæl *a descent,* v. ofdæl.

Afeallan *to fall down,* v. feallan.

Afearrian *to depart,* v. afaran.

Afecan *To receive;* accipere :—He afecð me, *Ps.* 48, 16.

Afed, afeded *fed; part. of* afedan.

Afedan *to feed,* v. fedan.

Afehð *receives,* v. fon.

Afelle *barked, peeled,* v. æfelle.

Afene, Afon, an; AVON, *the name of a river in Somersetshire* :—East oð Afene muðan *east at the Avon's mouth, Chr.* 918. Also of other rivers in different parts of England. Into Afenan muðan *into Avon's mouth, Chr.* 1067.

k Afeohtan; *p.* we afuhton. [a *intensive,* feohtan *to fight*] *To win by assault,* or *force, to vanquish* or *conquer by fighting;* expugnare :—*Bd.* 5, 23.

Afeoll *fell; p. of* afeallan, v. feallan.

Afeormian; *p.* ode; *pp.* od; *v. a.* [a *intensive,* feormian *to cleanse*] *To cleanse, to clean thoroughly, to purge, to wash away;* emundare :—Mid besmum afeormod, *Lk.* 11, 25. He afeormað his þyrscel-flore, *Mt.* 3, 12.

Afeormung *A cleansing, purging;* purgatio, *Scint.* 2.

Afeorrian *to remove, Bt.* 32, 2, v. afyrran.

Afeorsian *to depart,* v. afyrsian.

Afera *a child,* v. eafora.

Afered *frightened,* v. afæran.

Aferran *to remove,* v. afyrran.

l Aferscean [a, fersc *fresh*] *To freshen, to become fresh;* salsuginem deponere :—Ðær aferesceað *there fresheneth, Bt.* 34, 6.

Afersian *to take away,* v. afyrsian.

Afesian *to shear,* v. efesian.

Afestnian *to fix,* v. afæstnian.

Afetian; *indef.* ic afetige *To beat with the feet, to praise;* plaudere :—*Elf. gr.* 31.

Affrican, es; *m. An African;* Africanus :— Regulus feaht wið Affricanas *Regulus fought against Africans, Bt.* 16, 2, Æffrica.

Afgod [*Plat. Dut.* afgod *m.*: *Ger.* abgott *m.*: *Dan.* afgud *m.*] *An idol, an image;* idolum, *Som.*

Afgodnes, se; *f. Idolatry, the worshipping of images;* idololatria, *Som.*

Afindan *to find,* v. findan.

Afirran *to depart,* v. afyrran.

Afirsian *to take away,* v. afyrsian.

m Afleotan *To float off, to scum, clarify, purify liquor by scumming;* despumare, *Som.*

Afleow *overflowed; p. of* aflowan.

Afligan; *p.* de; *pp.* ed, aflogen; *v. a.* [a, flion *to flee*] *To drive away, put to flight;* fugare :—Afliged beon *to be driven away, R. Ben.* cap. 48. Affliged mon *an apostate, Prov.* 6.

Afligengce *A putting to flight, a driving away;* fugatio, *Som.*

Afliung *A fleeing;* rejectio :—Metes afliung *a rejecting of meat;* atrophia :—*R.* 10.

Aflogen *driven away,* v. afligan.

n Aflowan; *p.* afleow *To flow from, to flow over;* effluere :—Atna fyr afleow up *Etna threw up fire, Ors.* 5, 4.

Aflyg *Flight;* fuga, *Som.*

Aflyman, geflyman, gefleman; *p.* de; *pp.* ed, d; *v. a. To drive away, to disperse, eject, banish, scatter;* fugare :—Ðu me aflymst, *Gen.* 4, 14. *Banished, a banished man;* fugatus, exul :—Sy he aflymed *let him be banished;* sit exul, *L. Alf.* 1, *W.* p. 34, 48.

Afoed *brought up together,* v. fedan.

Afole *The soul, mind;* anima, mens :—Eallum his afole *with all his soul, L. Const. W.* p. 147, 6, v. sawl.

Afon *the river Avon,* v. Afene.

Afon *to receive,* v. fon.

Afongen *delivered, cast into prison; pp. of* afon, v. fon.

Afor *departed; p. of* afaran.

Afor, afre; *adj. Bitter, sour, sharp, hateful;* amarus, odiosus :—*Fr. Jdth.* 12, *Lye.*

Afora *a child,* v. eafora.

Aforfeorsod; *pp. Lengthened out, prolonged;* prolongatus, *Ps.* 119, 5, *Lye.*

o Aforhtian; *p.* aforhtode, afyrht; *pp.* aforhtod, afyrhted, afyrht. [a *intensive,* forhtian *to fear*] *To be very much afraid, to tremble with fear, to be affrighted, amazed;* expavescere :—Ða aforhtode Isaac micelre forhtnisse, *Gen.* 27, 33.

Aforð; *adv.* [a *always,* forð *forth*] *Always, continually, daily, still;* indies :—*Cot.* 115.

Aforud *higher,* v. yfer.

Afre *bitter,* v. afor.

Afrefrian *to comfort,* v. frefrian.

Afrian *to liberate, free,* v. freon.

Africa *Africa, an African.* v. Æffrica.

Africanisc, Afrisc; *adj. Belonging to Africa, African;* Africanus :— Africanisca æpple *a pomegranate;* malum punicum, *Som.*

Afrisc *African,* v. Africanisc.

Afroefred *comforted,* v. frefrian.

After *after,* v. æfter.

p After-fylgean *to follow after, to prosecute.*

Afterfylgend, es; *A follower of another, a successor;* successor, *Som.*

Aftergenga *a follower,* v. æftergenga.

Afterra geola *January,* v. æftera geola.

Aful *A fault;* culpa, *Lye.*

Afulað, afuloð *putrified,* v. afylan.

Afulan *to putrify,* v. afylan.

Afunden *found,* v. findan.

Afundennis, se; *f. An experi-*

~~a~~ afeng received
p. of afon

Øq

O1 past ~~afon~~ afonde receiving
susceptus 1214 b v afon,
fon to receive
Oq

Ø2 sons Cd 208
Th p. 258,7

Ø2 African-cyn ~~~~ African
race, an African; Afer,
Africanus Sone
Afrigen frixum Cot 86

aferran pafrde
to banish, expellere
Cd. 219 Th; 282
9: 214, ... p 269,
3

Øx afeded brought
forth, nourished
Cd 79 Th p 99, 5:
82 Th p 102, 29
~~...~~ OBe afene inv 652. O, afene mutan to avoni
ej afon mon the Chr 918

Afysan To hurry, hasten, rush, Th. An

7 Agend, es m. A lord, owner possessor Beow m agan

Agende Having, habens part. of agan Beow in agan

Afyldum effeta Cot 75 Lye

A-galan to p ágol to sound, sing; intonare Bed K 304 2

5 Agen-lædan to lead back Th An

6 Agen-hwyrfan To return, redire Som. v hwerfan

Cd. 223. th p 2951

Afyrd, afyrred An eunuch Eunuched, spado Cot. 189 Som Lye v afyrran

Agann began Th. An Forangan

Afyrhtan, to affright Th An v aforhtian

Afyrred disbarred Cd 19 th p 24, 17 v afyrran

96 Ageat understood Cd. 169, th 210, 12

Agelan to hinder Th. An

Aged strewed pt of agotan arum agoted by darts strewed Chr 938 Ing 142, 21 pieces walk L. XCII, 11

ment, an invention, a discovery; experimentum:—R. Ben. interl. 59.

Afundian to find, v. findan.

Afylan, afulan; p. ede; pp. ed, ad, od. To foul, defile, pollute, to make filthy, to corrupt, putrify, disgrace, condemn; inquinare:—L. Cnut. 43, W. p. 141, 18.

q Afyllan; p. de; pp. ed; v. a. [a, fyllan to fill] To fill up, or full, replenish, satisfy; replere:—Afyllað þa eorþan, Gen. 9, 1. He ne mæg þa gitsunga afyllan he cannot satisfy the desires, Bt. 16, 3.

Afyllan; indef. he afylð, afylð; p. de; pp. ed; v. a. [a, feol, fell; p. of feallan to fall] To fell, to strike, or beat down, to overturn, subvert, condemn, destroy; prosternere:—Drihten afylð þine fynd, Deut. 28, 7. To eorðan afyllað þe, Lk. 19, 44. Hu man mæg afyllan how one may overturn, L. Cnut. 11.

Afyran; p. de; pp. ed, yd; v. a. [a, fyran castrare] To take away, castrate; castrare:—Twegen afyryde men, Gen. 40, 1. Afyred olfend a dromedary, a kind of swift camel; dromeda, v. afyrran.

Afyrht, afyrhted affrighted, v. aforhtian.

Afyrhto fear, v. fyrhto.

Afyrida, afyryda, afyrd, an; m. An eunuch, a castrated animal, a servant, a courtier; eunuchus, servus:—Se afyrida the servant, courtier [eunuch], Gen. 39, 1. Sealdon Josep þam afyrydan, Gen. 37, 36.

Afyrran, afeorran, afirran; p. ede; pp. ed; v. a. [a, feor, fyrr far] To remove to a distance, to take away, to take away time, to tarry, delay; amovere, elongare:—Nædran hi afyrrað, Mk. 16, 18. Beoð afyrrede are taken away, Ps. 57, 8. Afirreð takes away, 75, 12. Magon beon afeorred may be taken away, Bt. 32, 2. Mæg bion afyrred, Rawl. p. 71, note c. Þu afeorrodyst [afirdest] fram me freond, Ps. 87, 19. Deað hit afirreð death shall take it away, Bt. 8. ¶ Aferede awæg carried away, Cot. 14.

Afyrsian, afeorsian; p. ede; pp. ed; v. a. [a, fyrsian to remove] To remove farthest away, to depart, drive away, dispel; pellere, propellere:—He feorsode fram us unrihtwisnysse ure, Ps. 102, 12. Afeorsiað, Ps. 72, 25. Afyrseð, Ps. 75, 12. Deofla afyrseð, L. ecl. Cnut. 4, v. afyrran, fyrsian.

Afyryd an eunuch, v. afyrida.

Ag Wickedness; nequitia, Ps. 72, 8.

Agæf returned; p. of agefan, from agyfan.

Agælan to hinder, P. 88, 34, v. gælan.

Agæled, agælwed astonished, v. gælan.

Agælend enchanting, v. galan.

Agæn gone, past, v. gan.

Agæð happens, v. agan.

Agalod loosed, dissolved, Som.

r Agan, ægan; indef. ic age, þu age, he ah, we agan, agon, agun; p. he aht, ahte, æhte, we ahton; pp. agen; v. a. [Plat. egen: Frs. eigenje: Dut. eigenen: Al. eigan: Dan. eje: Icel. Norse, eiga].—1. To OWN, possess, have, obtain; possidere.—2. To make another to own, or possess: Hence to give, deliver, restore; dare in possessionem, reddere:—1. Þat ic ece lif age, Mk. 10, 17. Þe micel agan willað who desire [will] to possess much, Bt. 14, 2.—2. On hand agan to deliver in hand, Ors. 3, 11. ¶ Agan ut to have, or find it out. Lett agan ut hu fela permit to find out how many, Chr. 1085.

Agan gone, past, v. gan.

Agan began; p. of aginnan.

Agan own; proprius, v. agen.

Agangan; p. ic, he aeode; pp. agangen, agongen. To go from, to go, or pass by, or over; præterire:—Cd. 224.

Ageaf gave up; p. of agyfan.

Agald rewarded; p. of agyldan.

Agean again, v. ongean.

Agean-feran to go again, to return

Agean-hwyrfan to turn again, to return.

Ageara, agearwa prepared, v. gearw.

Agearwian to prepare, v. gearwian.

Ageat understood; p. of agytan.

Ageat poured out, v. ageotan.

Agefan to give back, v. agyfan.

Agelde may pay, v. agyldan.

Agelwed astonished, v. gælan.

A'gen, agan; adj. [Plat. Dan. egen: Dut. Ger. eigen; pp. of agan to possess] OWN, proper, peculiar; proprius:—Secð hys agen wuldor, Jn. 7, 18. Ic sylle min agan lif, Jn. 10, 15. ¶ Agenes þances of his own accord, freely. Agen broþer own brother, Bd. 3, 22.

Agen; prep. ac. [a, gan to go] Against; contra:—Se þe nis agen eow, Mk. 9, 40.

Agen again; iterum, v. ongean.

Agen gone, past, v. gan.

Agen-arn met; p. from agenyrnan.

Agen-bewendan; p. de. To turn again, return.

Agen-cuman; p. -com; pp. -cumen to come again.

Agen-cyrran to return again, to return; agen again, cyran to turn.

Agend, agendfrea; m. An owner, a possessor, a lord of a thing; proprietarius, L. In. 53.

t Agendlice; adv. Properly, as his own; proprie, Bd. 1, 1.

Agene-cyre, -cyrre own turn, one's own choice, will, or pleasure.

Agen-frige a possessor, v. agend.

Agen-gecyrran to turn again, recur.

Agen-gehwyrfan to change again, to return.

Agenlice; adv. Powerfully; potenter, Som.

Agen-namæ an own name, a proper name.

u Agennys, se; f. An owning, a possession, property; possessio, Lye.

Agensendan to send again, to send back.

Agenslaga a self-slayer, self-murderer.

Agenspræc; f. [agen own, spræc speech] One's own tongue, an idiom, the peculiarity of a language; idioma, Lye.

Agenstandan To STAND AGAINST to withstand, resist, oppose, hinder; obsistere:—Lk. 11, 53.

v Agenung, agnung, ahnung, e; f. An OWNING, a possessing, possession, claiming as one's own, power, or dominion over any thing; possessio, dominium:—L. Ethelb. 10.

Agen-yrnan; p. arn; v. a. [agan against, yrnan to run] To run against, to meet with, to meet; occurrere:—Hym agenarn an man, Mk. 5, 2. Inc agenyrnð sum man, Mk. 14, 13.

Ageofan to give, v. agyfan.

Ageolwian [a, geolewe yellow] To make yellow, or red, to make to glitter as gold; flavescere, Som.

Ageomrod lamented, v geomerian.

Ageotan, agitan; p. ageat, agute, aguette, þu agute, we aguton; pp. ageoted, ageted, ageoten, ageaten, agiten, agoten; v. a. [a from, geotan to pour] To pour out, to strew, spread, spill, draw out, disperse; effundere:—Hi aguton blod, Ps. 78, 3. Ageot cocor, Ps. 34, 3.

Aghwær every where, v. æghwær.

Agien own, v. agen.

Agieta, agita A shedder, a pourer out, a spendthrift; effusor:—Past. 20.

Agifan *to restore*, agifen *restored*, v. agyfan.
ʷ Agift; *m. A giving back, restoration;* restitutio.
Agild *without amends*, v. ægylde.
Agildan *to repay*, v. agyldan.
Agiltan *to offend*, v. agyltan.
Agiltst *thou repayest*, v. agyldan.
Agimmed, agymmed; *part. Gemmed, set with gems;* gemmatus:—Agimmed and gesmiðed bend *a gemmed and worked crown, a diadem.* Agimmed gerdel, *or* gyrdel, *or* angseta, *or* hringc *a gemmed girdle or ring*, *R.* 64, v. atæned.
Aginnan, he agynð; *p.* agan; *v.a. To begin, to set upon, undertake, take in hand;* incipere:—And agynð beatan hys efenþeowas, *Mt.* 24, 49.
Agita *a spendthrift*, v. agieta.
Agitan *to pour out*, v. ageotan.
Agiten *dispersed*, v. ageotan.
Agiten *known*, v. agytan.
Aglac [*Plat.* lak *a fault*] *Misery, grief, trouble, vexation, sorrow, torment;* miseria:—*Cd.* 184, *Som.*
Aglad *failed; p. from* eglian.
AGLÆC, æglæc; *def.* se aglæca; *adj. Miserable, tormented, wicked, mischievous;* miser, cruciatus:—Wið þam aglæcan *among the wicked*, *Beo.* 6, *Thork.* p. 34, 21.
Agn *own*, v. agen.
Agnegan *to possess*, v. agnian.
ˣ Agnette *Usury;* usura:—*C. Lk.* 19, 23.
Agnian, geagnian; *p.* hi ahnodon; *part.* agnigende, ahniende; *v. a. To own, to possess, to appropriate to himself;* possidere:—Hu miht þu þonne þe agnian heora god *how canst thou, then, appropriate to thyself their good? Bt.* 14, 1. Hi ahnodon eorðan, *Ps.* 43, 4.
Agniend, ahniend *An owner, a possessor;* possessor:—*Gen.* 14, 22.
Agniendlic, geagnigendlic; *adj. Possessive, pertaining to possession, or owning;* possessivus, *Som.*
Agnu *own*, v. agen.
Agnung *an owning*, v. agenung.
ʸ Agnys *Sorrow, affliction;* ærumna, *Ben.*
Agolden *repaid*, v. agyldan.
Agon, agun *they own*, v. agan.
Agongen *passed*, v. agangan.
Agoten, agotten *poured out*, v. ageotan.
Agotenes, agotennys, se; *f. An effusion, a pouring,* or *shedding forth, out* or *abroad;* effusio:—Agotennys teara *a shedding of tears, Med. pec.* 16.
Agræfen, agraf, agrafen *engraved, carved*, v. grafan.
Agrafenlice; *s.* [agrafen *carved*, lice *body*] *That which is carved, a carved image;* sculptile:—Hi gebædon þat agrafenlice, *Ps.* 105, 19.
Agrisan *To dread, to fear greatly;* horrere:—For helle agrise *shall have dread of hell, L. eccl. Cnut.* 25.
Agrisenlic *horrible*, v. grislic.
ᶻ Agrof *engraved*, v. grafan.
Agrowan [a, growan *to grow*] *To grow under, to cover;* succrescere:—Seo eorðe stod mid holtum agrowen *the earth was* [*stood*] *covered* [*overgrown*] *with groves* [*holts*], *Hexaem.* 6, v. growan.
Agryndan, gryndan; *p.* [*Plat. Ger.* grunden: *Dut.* gronden: a, grund *the ground*] *To ground, to descend to the earth;* ad solum descendere:—*Menol.* 212: *Hickes's Thes.* vol. 1, p. 205.
Agu *A pie, a magpie;* pica, *Ben.*
Aguette, agute *poured out*, v. ageotan.
Agyfan, agifan; *p.* ageaf, agæf; *pp.* agyfen, agifen; *v. a. To restore, give back, give up, return, repay;* reddere:—Agyf þat þu me scealt, *Mt.* 18, 28. Ða het Pilatus agyfan, *Mt.* 27, 58. He ageaf hys gast, *Jn.* 19, 30, v. gifan.
ᵃ Agyldan, agildan, ageldan; *p.* ageald, we aguldon; *pp.* agolden; *v. a. To pay, fulfil, repay, restore, reward, offer sacrifice;* solvere:—*Mt.* 5, 33, v. gildan.
Agyltan, agiltan; *p.* te; *pp.* t; *v.* [a, gyltan *to make guilty*] *To fail in duty, to commit, to become guilty, to offend, to sin against;* delinquere:—Ðæt he agylte on him sylfum, *Ps.* 35, 1. Agyltan wið *to offend*, or *sin against.* Twegen men agylton wið heora hlaford, *Gen.* 40, 1. Ic agilte wið eow, *Ex.* 10, 16.
Agymmed *set with gems*, v. agimmed.
Agynð *beginneth*, v. aginnan.
Agytan; *p.* ageat; *pp.* agyten, agiten; *v. a.* [a *from*, gytan *to get*] *To discover, know, understand, consider;* deprehendere. Gif æni man agiten wurðe *if any man should be known, L. North. pres.* 48. Gecyðnyssa þine ic ageat, *Ps.* 118, 95.
ᵇ AH; *adv. Whether, but;* nunquid, sed:—*Ps.* 7, 12. Ah ne *whether or not;* nonne, *C. Mk.* 6, 3. Ah nuu *now.*
A'h *has, owns;* habet, v. agan.
Ahabban, ahæbban; *v.* [habban *to have*] *To abstain, restrain;* abstinere:—*Bd.* 3, 22: 5, 6, v. habban.
Ahældon; *declined; p. of* ahildan.
Ahafen *lifted up, puffed up*, v. ahebban.
Ahafennes, ahafennys, se; *f. An elevation, a lifting up, a loftiness, pride, arrogance;* elevatio:—Ahafennys handa minra, *Ps.* 140, 2: 92, 6.
Ahangen, ahangan *hung; pp. of* ahon, v. hon.
ᶜ Aheardian; *p.* ahyrde, ahyrte; *pp.* aheardod, ahyrd; *v. a.* [*Plat. Dut.* verharden: *Ger.* verharten: *Dan.* forhearte: a *intensive*, heardian *to harden*]. 1. *To harden, make hard;* durare. 2. *To endure, continue, secure:* perdurare:—1. Ic ahyrde Pharaones heortan, *Ex.* 4, 21. 2. Aheardað his gebod *secureth his power, R. Ben.* 6, 8.
Aheardung *A hardening;* induratio, *Som.*
Aheawian; *p.* aheow: *pp.* aheawen. [a *from*, heawan *to hew*] *To hew, or cut out, to carve, make even, smooth;* resecare:—He aheow on stane, *Mt.* 27, 60. Of aheawenum bordum *of hewed or planed boards, Gen.* 6, 14. Aheawen treow *timber, Elf. gl.* 17.
Ahebban, þu ahefst, he ahefð; *imp.* ahefe; *p.* ic ahefde, ahof, we ahefdon; *pp.* ahafen, ahefen; *v. a. To lift up, to raise, elevate, exalt;* elevare, v. hebban.
Ahefednes *pride*, v. ahafennes.
Ahefegod, ahefgad *weighed down*, v. ahefigan.
Ahefen *elevated; pp. of* ahebban.
ᵈ Ahefigad, ahefgad, ahefegod; *part. Weighed down, burdened, grieved;* gravatus:—Ðonne hit bið ahefigad *when it is weighed down, Bt.* 24, 4, v. hefigan.
Ahefst, ahefð, v. ahebban *to raise.*
Aheð *shall crucify;* suspendet:—*Deut.* 21, 22, v. hon.
Aheld *inclined*, v. ahildan.
Ahencg *hung*, v. hon.
Ahened *despised, trod upon*, v. hynan.
Aheng *hung;* hi ahengon; *p. of* ahon, v. hon.
Aheolorod; *part. Weighed, balanced;* libratus, *Som.*
Aherian *to hire*, v. hyrian.
Aherian; *v. To benefit, profit;* prodesse:—*Prec. ad calc.* 3, *Cd. l.* 5.
Ahicgan, ahycgan *to seize, pursue earnestly;* assequi, v. hicgan.
Ahildan, aheldan *to incline*, ahild, ahældon *inclined*, v. hyldan.
ᵉ Ahildenlice; *adv. Incliningly;* inclinative, *Som.*
Ahioloran *to balance*, v. heoloran.

1

Agroette iesit
C R Lk 9,42

4 of litle agryt
from (cls) statin
descending accend
F. 220

Aglad
1. Aad aited v eglian
Mann Sup

Agneras, keah hyrne
ygrgie: volvos dicimus
angulos oculorum
R 70 Lye

ahefd ahefteid up B Mk 3,2
ahefd heaves
31. indef of ahebban

Agniden sie defricabitur Co L63
Lye

Agyt pours out
31. indef of agea-
tan, geotan

Aheran to hear
audire Som. v
hyran

1 aticgan to search
Cd 178 Th 224,3

A-gol sang Beo K 3062
p of agalan. Ispl

ϕ

p ahlog
A-hleahhan to laugh
~~Beo K 1454~~
ahlæca a wretch &c. Beo K 1286 v aglæc
A-hlóg laughed
Beo K 1454 p of
~~Ahlog~~ hliehan

ϕ

ϕ, Cd 109 Th. p ~~14~~ 143, 16

X. Ahydan to hide v hydan
Cd. 148 Th p 184, 30
Som
Ahyrded hardened
Beo K 2919 ~~1154~~ v aheardian

X Aidlian to render vain Th.

X. Ahnian; ~~past~~ ahniende to own
Gen. 14, 22 v agnian
~~X Ahniend, es; m an owner Gen 14, 22 v agnian~~

X Ahwa any one
aleges [illegible] v hwa

X. Ahwanne any one [illegible] ahwa
v. hwa Saxon

Alag
X A-læg ceased, failed ~~[illegible]~~ v licgan

X. Ahweorfan
p ahwearf
pl. we ahwurfon
[v, ~~see~~ hweorfan to turn]
To turn away
to bend - ahwearf Cd 206 Th p 255, 26
ahwurfon Cd
O Th. p 2, 26

X Ahræcan p ahræhte
to reach Th-An

ϕ to ~~[illegible]~~, save, rescue
redeem Th-An in ah.
reddan

ahredde
O 3 ahred rescued Cd 94
Th p 122, 26; Ps Th 17, 3

Ahiscean *to hiss at, to mock;* irridere, *Lye,* v. hiscan.
Ahiþan *to rob,* v. hyþian.
Ahiþend, *A robber, an extortioner;* grassator:—*Cot.* 95, *Som.*
Ahladan [a *from,* ladan *to lade*] *To draw out;* exhaurire, *Elf. gr.*
Ahlænsud; *part. Soaked, steeped, watered, made lean;* maceratus:—*Scint.* 10, *Som.*
Ahlas *levers, bars;* vectes:—*Past.* 22, 1, *Lye.*
Ahleapan; *p.* ahleop, hi ahleopon [a *from,* hleapan *to leap*] *To leap up, out* or *upon;* exilire, insilire:—*Ors.* 3, 9.
Ahlinode *loosed, delivered;* solvit; *p. from,* a *not,* hlænan *for* lænan *to lend.*
Ahlocan *to pull out,* v. alocan.
Ahlóh *laughed at,* v. hlihan.
Ahlowan [a *intensive,* hlowan *to low*] *To low,* or *bellow again;* reboare, *Som.*
Ahlytred, ahlutred; *part. Purified, scummed, refined, cleansed;* purgatus:—Ahlutred win *refined wine, Cot.* 68, v. hlyttrian.
Ahne *whether* or *not,* v. ah.
Ahnescian *to mollify,* v. anescian.
Ahnipan; *p.* ahneop; *v. a. To pluck, gather;* carpere:—Ahneop wæstem *gathered the fruit, Cod. Ex.* 45. *a.,* v. hnipan.
Ahnodon *owned,* v. agnian.
Ahniend *an owner,* v. agniend.
Ahnung *an owning,* v. agenung.
Ahnyscton *they mocked, Ps.* 79, 7, v. ahiscean.
Aho *crucify;* suspendo:—*Elf. gr.* 26, 119, v. hon.
Ahof *raised; p. of* ahebban.
Ahofyn *elated; pp. of* ahebban.
Ahoh *crucify,* v. hon.
Aholan; *p.* ede; *pp.* od; *v. a.* [a, holian *to hollow*] *To dig;* fodere:—Aholað ut *to pluck out.* Ahola hit ut, *Mt.* 5, 29.
Ahold *faithful,* v. hold.
Aholede [*p. of* aholan *to dig*] *An engraved,* or *embossed work;* opera lacunata, *Mann.*
Ahon *to hang, Gen.* 40, 19, v. hon.
Ahongen *hung, Fr. Jud.* 10; *pp. of* ahon, v. hon.
Ahorn [*Plat. Dut. Ger.* ahorn; *m.*] *A plane tree;* acer platanoides, *Ben.*
Ahræddan, ahreddan, ariddan, berædan; *p.* de; *pp.* ahreded, ahred, arydid [a *from,* hreddan *to rid*] *To rid, liberate, set free, deliver, draw out, cast out, to rob;* liberare, eruere:—Forhwy þu ariddest, *Ps.* 42, 2.
Ahreht *erect, upright; pp. of* recan.
Ahreofod; *adj. Leprous;* leprosus:—*Martyr.* 21, *Sep.*
Ahreosian *to rush,* v. hreosan.

Ahrepod *touched,* v. hrepan.
Ahrered *reared,* or *lifted up,* v. hreran.
Ahrinað *will touch,* v. æt-hrinan.
Ahruron *rushed,* v. hreosan.
Ahrydred *robbed,* v. ahryd.
Ahrynan *To touch;* tangere, v. æt-hrinan.
Ahryre *should rush,* v. hreosan.
Ahrysod *shaken, disturbed,* v. hreosan.
Ahsa *ashes,* v. axe.
Ahsian *to ask; part.* ahsiende; *p.* ahsode, v. acsian.
A'HT, uht, auht, wiht, wuht, awiht, awuht; *pron.* [*Plat.* icht, ichts, ichtens, echt, iht: *Frs.* hwat, wat, watte, hwet, het, hette: *Dut.* iets: *Ger.* etwas, v. æht] AUGHT, *any thing, something;* aliquid, quidquam:—Afandian hwæþer he aht sy, oððe naht, *Mt.* 16, 18. Þe ahtes wæron *who were of aught, of any account,* or *value, Chr.* 992. Þat an man, þe himsylf aht wære, mihte faran *that a man, who himself was aught, might go, Id.* 1087.
Ahta *eight,* v. æhta.
Ahte *owned; p. of* agan.
Ahtihting *An intention, a purpose, an aim;* intentio, *Som.*
Ahtlice; *adv. Courageously, manfully, triumphantly;* viriliter, *Chr.* 1071; *Gib.* p. 172, 27.
Ahtswan *a cow-herd,* v. æhteswan.
Ahudan [a *from,* huð *prey*] *To spoil, rob;* spoliare, *Mann.*
Ahwænan *To oppress, vex, trouble;* opprimere, *Som.*
Ahwæned *Weaned;* ablactatus:—*Herb.* 20, 7.
Ahwænne *when, some time,* v. hwænne.
Ahwær *every where,* v. æghwær.
Ahwær-gen *every where again, continually.*
Ahwar, ahwer, awer; *adv. Some where, any where, any wise;* alicubi:—*Jos.* 1, 18. Ahwar on lande *wheresoever, L. Edw. Guth.* 11. Habbe ic awer *have I in any wise, Bt.* 7, 3.
Ahwerfed *turned,* v. hweorfed.
Ahwettan *to whet,* v. hwettan.
Ahwider *every where,* v. æghwær.
Ahwilc; *adj. Terrible;* terribilis:—*R.* 116, *Lye.*
Ahwonan, ahwonon; *adv.* [a *from,* hwonan *whence*] *From what place, whence, some where, any where;* alicubi:—*Bd.* 5, 12. ¶ Ahwonan utan *from without, outwardly, extrinsically, Bt.* 34, 3.
Ahworfen *moved,* v. hweorfan.
Ahwylc *whatsoever,* v. æghwilc.
Ahwylfan, behwylfan [a *intensive,* hwealfian *to cover*] *To cover over, overwhelm;* obruere:—*Ex.* 14, 27.
Ahwyrfð *turns,* v. hweorfan.
Ahycgan *to seize,* v. ahicgan.
Ahyddon, ahyded *hidden,* v. hydan.
Ahyldan *to incline,* v. hyldan.
Ahyldendlice *incliningly,* v. ahildenlice.
Ahyrd, ahyrde *hardened,* v. aheardian.
Ahyrdincg *a hardening,* v. aheardung.
Ahyrian, ahyrod, v. hyrian *to hire.*
Ahyrst *fried,* v. hyrstan.
Ahyrte *hardened; p. of* aheardian.
Aide AID; adjumentum, *Lye.*
Aidlian, he aydlige; *p.* ede; *pp.* ed, ad [adlian *to fail,* v. adl *a disease,* adilegian *to abolish*] *To* AIL, *to be sick, to languish, profane, frustrate, empty, deface, destroy;* ægrotare, profanare:—*Bd.* 5, 3.
Aieþende *demolishing,* v. aiþan.
Ain, aina *one,* v. an.
Aiþan; *part.* aiþende [a *from,* uþian or utian *to put out*] *To cast out, to put out of doors;* eliminare:—*Cot.* 71, 76.
Aisil *vinegar,* v. eced.
Aizon, aizoon [ἀειζωον *from* ἀει *always,* ζωη *life, always alive,* or *green*] *The herb aygreen, sengreen,* or *houseleek;* sempervivum, herba:—*Herb.* 146, *Som.*
Akauertune *the courts;* atria:—*Ps.* 83, 1, v. cafertun.
Al *an eel,* v. æl.
Al *an awl,* v. æl.
Al *all,* v. eall.
Aladian [a *from,* ladian *to clear*] *To excuse, to make excuse for;* excusare:—Hu magon hi hi aladigen *how can they excuse themselves, Bt.* 41, 3.
Alæcgan *to lay away,* v. alecgan.
Alædan; *p.* de; *pp.* ed, æd [a *from,* lædan *to lead*] *To lead, to lead out, withdraw, take away;* educere:—Ic alædde þe of lande, *Ps.* 80, 9. Alæd, ælæd or aledd ic eom *I am taken away, Ps.* 108, 22.
Alæned *lent,* v. lænan.
Alætan, alétan; *p.* alét, alæt; *pp.* alæten; *v. a.* [a *from,* lætan *to let*] *To let go, to lay down, cease, leave off, lose;* dimittere, deponere:—Ic hæbbe anweald mine sawle to alætanne, *Jn.* 10, 18. Ic þat aletan ne sceal *I will not let that go, Solil.* 8. Þu hine alætst *thou lettest it go, Bt.* 25.
Alætnes, se; *f. A loss, a losing;* amissio:—*Somn.* 326.

Alættan [lætan *to let*] *To let, hinder*; impedire, *Som.*

Alan; v. *To appear*; apparere:—*C. R. Lk.* 11, 44.

Alað *ale*, v. aloð.

Albe, *f.* [*Lat.* alba *from,* albus *white*] *An* ALB, *a surplice*; alba, vestis sacerdotalis:—*Elf. gl.* 19.

Ald, alda *old*, v. eald.

Ald *An age, old age*; senectus, *Mann.*

Aldagian; *v. To grow, or wax old*; *Som.* v. ealdian.

Aldaht *a basket,* or *maund*; alveolum, *Som.*

n Aldefæder *a grandfather*, v. ealdfæder.

Alder, es; *m. An author, originator*; auctor:—Þe alderas forlorene wæron *the authors were destroyed*, *Bd.* 2, 5, v. ealdor.

Alderdóm *authority*, v. ealdordom.

Aldhád [eald *old,* had *hood*] *Old age*; senectus, *Som.*

Aldhelm [eald *old,* helm *an helmet*] ALDHELM, *a name of a man*; Aldhelmus, vetus galea, *Lye.*

Aldian *to grow old*, v. ealdian.

Aldlic *old*, v. ealdlic.

Aldor *life*, v. aldr.

Aldor *an elder*, v. ealdor.

Aldor *elder, former*, v. eald.

Aldor-apostol *the chief of the apostles*; apostolorum princeps:—*Bd.* 3, 17.

Aldor-bana [aldr *life,* bana *a killer*] *A murderer, manslayer, fratricide*; homicida:—*Cain was so called*, *Cd.* 49.

Aldor-birig [ealdor *chief,* burg *a city*] *A chief city, metropolis*; urbs primaria:—*Bd.* 1, 26.

Aldor-déma [ealdor *chief,* dema *a judge*] *A supreme judge, a prince*; supremus judex:—*Cd.* 57.

Aldordóm *a principality*, v. ealdordom.

Aldor-duguðe *A chief nobility*; principalis nobilitas, v. ealdorduguðe.

o Aldor-frea *A chief lord*; princeps dominus:—*Cd.* 174.

Aldor-gedál [aldr *life,* gedal *a separation*] *A divorce, separation from life*; vitæ divortium:—*Cd.* 52, *Lye.*

Aldorleas; *adj.* [ealdor *a father,* leas *less*] *Fatherless, deprived of parents*; orphanus:—*C. Jn.* 14, 18.

Aldorlege [eald *old,* orleg *fate*] *Fate, fortune*; fatum:—*Cd.* 179.

Aldorlic *principal*, v. ealdorlic.

Aldorman *a prince*, v. ealdorman.

Aldor-nere, ealdor-nere [ealdor *life,* ner *refuge*] *A life's safety, a refuge, sanctuary, an asylum*; refugium:—*Cd.* 117.

Aldornes *authority*, v. ealdordom.

Aldorþægn *a principal servant, a minister*, v. ealdorþægn.

Aldor-wisa [ealdor *chief,* wisa *a ruler*] *A chief director,* or *disposer*; principalis director:—*Cd.* 63.

p Aldr, aldor, ealdor, ealdr [*Plat.* older: *Ger.* alter *n*: *Dan.* alder *n*: *Swed.* älder *n*: ældian, or yldan *to put off, the imp. is* æld *lengthen,* and *comp.* er *more*] *That which is deferred* or *lengthened, an age, the term of a man's remaining on the earth, the life*; ævum, vita:—Aldre scyldig *the forfeit of life*; vitæ, vel capitis reus, *Cd.* 196. Þonne þu of lice aldor asendest *when thou sendest life from the body*, *Cd.* 133. ¶ A to aldre, æfre to aldre *or,* in aldre *for ever*, *Cd.* 227. Ne on aldre *never*, *Cd.* 21.

Aldr *a parent,* aldro *parents*, v. ealdor.

Aldu, ældo-men; *pl. Pharisees*; pharisæi:—*R. Mk.* 2, 24.

Aldur *chief,* as aldur-sacerdas, *the chief priests*, v. ealdor.

Ald-wif *an old woman*, v. ealdwif.

Aleah, aleag *falsified*; mentitus, *p. of* aleogan.

Aleat *bent down, flat*; pronus:—*Num.* 22, 31, v. alutan.

q Alecgan, *imp.* alege; *p.* alede, hi aledon; *pp.* aled, alegd, alegen; *v.a.* [a *from,* lecgan *to lay*] 1. *To place, lay down, lay along*; ponere, deponere. 2. *To lay aside, confine, diminish, take away, put down, depress, confute*; imminuere, deprimere:—1. Hig ne mihton hine alecgan, *Lk.* 5, 19. 2. Godes lof alecgan *to diminish God's glory*, *Elf. T. p.* 22, 20. Godes monnes lof alegen bið *good men's praise is confined*, *Bt.* 18, 3. ¶ Alecgende *part.* or alecgendlice word *a verb deponent, because it has deposed* or *left out some of its inflections.*

Alede, aledon *put down*, v. alecgan.

Alefan *to permit*, v. alyfan.

Alefed, alefed *permitted*, v. alyfan.

Al efne [*from* al *all,* efne *behold*] *Behold all!* omnis ecce.

Alegd *deposed, frightened*, v. alecgan.

Alege *lay down*, v. alecgan.

Alegen *confined*, v. alecgan.

Aleh *placed*; posuit:—*Beo.* 1: *Thork.* p. 8, 54, v. alecgan.

Alend; q. alenð *or* alænð *lendeth*; commodat:—*Ps.* 36, 22, v. lænan.

r Alenian [a, lænian *to be lean*] *To make lean, to soak*; macerare:—*Elf. pref. Hom. p.* 4.

Aleógan; *p.* aleág, aleáh; *pp.* alogen. *To lie, to tell lies, to deceive*, v. leogan.

Aler *the alder*; alnus, v. alr.

Alerholt *an alder wood*; alnetum, v. alr.

Alesan *to redeem*, v. alysan.

Alesen *chosen*, v. lesan.

Alesenis *redemption*, v. alysednes.

Alet *fire, combustibles*; ignis, pabulum ignis:—*Cd.* 186, *Lye.*

Aletan *to cease*, v. alætan.

Aletlic; *adj. Pardonable*; remissibilis, *Mann.*

Alewa, an [*Lat.* aloë: *Heb.* אהלי ahli or אהלים ahlim *the aloe trees*] *The aloe, bitter spices,* in the plural *aloes*; aloe:—Brohte alewan, *Jn.* 19, 39.

Alewed; *adj. Weak*; debilis:—*R. Ben.* 27.

s Alfæt; *pl.* alfati *A pot* or *kettle to boil in*; coculum:—*Cot.* 210, *Som.*

Algeats; *adv.* [eal *all,* geatas *gates,* ALL GATES, Chau. and Spenc.] *Always, altogether*; omnifariam, omninò, *Som.*

Algeweorc *Tinder, touchwood, a fire-steel*; igniarium:—*Cot.* 107, 164, v. tyndre.

Alh, ealh *A temple, church, a hall*; templum, basilica:—*Cd.* 162, v. heal.

Alh-sted, ealh-sted [heal *a hall,* sted *a place*] *A palace, a royal residence*; palatia:—*Cd.* 209.

Alibban *to live*, v. lybban.

Alibbe, alibbend *A survivor, one who lives after*; superstes, *Som.*

Aliefan, alifan *to permit, p.* ed, v. alyfan.

Aliesan *to redeem*; *part.* aliesend, v. alysan.

Alifian *to live*, v. alybban.

t Alihtan; *v. a.* [a *intensive,* lihtan *to light*] 1. *To enlighten*; illuminare. 2. *To* ALIGHT, *come down*; desilire:—1. Hig alihton þa eorðan, *Gen.* 1, 15. 2. *Elf. gr.* 30.

Alinnan; *v. To* LIN, *cease, stop*; cessare, *Som.*

Alis *loose*, v. alysan.

Alisendnes *redemption*, v. alysednes.

Alisian *to try*, v. halsian.

All *all*, v. eall.

Allic; *adj.* [eall *all,* lic *like*] *Universal, general, catholic*; universus:—Allic geleafa *the catholic,* or *general belief*, *Bd.* 4, 17.

Allinga, allunga *altogether*, v. eallunga.

X 7

X A-lamp happened; occurred Beo K 1238 v shl limpan

Φ 1 an; f Som: 9

O 2

X Aldor, e; f life Cd 124 Th p 158, 29 f. ealdor ~~...~~

X Aleodian, p ode [a, leod a limb] To dismember Cd 9. Th 11, 18

O 3

X Alf-walda, an, m ruler of ~~elfs~~ elves, God; alforum dominus, Deus Beo ~~...~~ K 2628 Beo gl in waldan

O

O

X Aldor-bealo es m life bale Beo K 3350 v balew

X Ale with an awl v æl

X Aldor-burh, (ealdor chief, burh a city) a chief city giburge; d, byrig

X Aldor-ceare, e f fatal care Beo K 1806

X Aldor-dæg, dies vitæ Beo 56 K ~~...~~ 1429 [life or life-day, day of life, life]

Φ 5 X Alh-stede, es m [stede a place] a palace, a hall, high

Φ 8

X Alecgan to lay down, ikach Cd 127 Th p 162, 21 Φ 6 v alecgan

Φ 9

O

Φ

Φ 2 Alefed permitted v alefan, alyfan

X A-leh belied p of aleogan Beo K 1594 Beo gl in leogan

O

for Almihtigan

1. Almihtega, the Almighty, the Almighty God; Al-miht

2 Alwalda, among allestway ing; Goth. An. Abes (?) Sn. K 630 yl in waldan 3

4

3. Almes-land, land given or granted in frankalmoigne; fundus in eleemosynam datus Som.

3. Alotyn, falling down, prostrate; provolutus Som. vt. alutan

4 Alot, ealu; ... K Alysniane to prefle out, deliver; vellere Som. Ben

5

2

3 v spl ombihte

4 a certain measure Th. An.

Alse as; sicut v Syn Spl form

3, as; m Bo Ch. 17, 2

5 Ambiht

5 Ambiht, seleg or sem

... Ch. 17, 2

... ambiht seleg

... mentere ...

Allwalda *the Omnipotent*, v. ælwalda.

Almerige [*hence the old English* almery, almonry, almry, amry, ambry, *and the Norman-French* ambrey, the *Irish* amri, *the Welsh* almeri *a cupboard*] *A cupboard, a chest, an* AMBRY; repositorium, scrinium, *Som.*

Almes *alms*, v. ælmes.

Alne *an ell*, v. elne.

Alocan, alucan; p. ede; pp. alocced, alocen; *v.a.* [a *from*, loc *an enclosure, or* læcan *to approach*] *To put out of an enclosure, to expose, cast out, separate, pull out, take away, root up*; ejicere, avellere:—He wæs fram hym alocen, *Lk.* 22, 41. Aluc þu hine *take him away, L. Alf.* 13: *W.* p. 29, 33.

Alogen *false, feigned*, v. aleogan.

Alor *an alder-tree*; alnus, v. alr.

Aloten *prone, submissive*, v. alutan.

ALOD, eale, eala, ealu [*Dan. Swed. Icel.* öl *n*: *Norse*, aul] ALE; cerevisia:—Ale and mead were the favourite drinks of the Anglo-Saxons. They had three sorts of ale. *In the Chr.* 852, *Ing.* p. 93, 16, *we find*, Wulfred scolde gife twa tunnan fulle hlutres aloð, and ten mittan Wælsces aloð *Wulfred should give two tuns full of clear ale, and ten mittan or measures of Welsh ale.* Hwæt drincst þu! Ealu, gif ic hæbbe, oððe wæter gif ic ne hæbbe ealu *ale if I have* [*it*], *or water if I have not ale. M. S. Cott. Tib. A.* iii. p. 63, v. brydeala.

ALR [*Plat.* eller *f*: *Dut.* els *f*: *Ger.* erle *f*: *Dan.* alletrae *n*: *Swed.* al *f*. IHRE *supposes this word to be derived from the Swedish word* al *water, because the* alnus *grows best in wet ground.*] *An* ALDER-*tree, a sort of birch* in the north of England, called ELLER and ALLER; alnus, betula alnus. *It is quite distinct from* ellen *the elder-tree*; sambucus:—*Elf. gl.* 17. ¶ Alrholt *an alder-holt*, or *grove*.

Alsian *to intreat*, v. halsian.

Alsuic; *conj. for* eall swilc *all such*.

Alswa *also*, v. eallswa.

Altar [*Plat. Dut.* altaar *m.* and *n*: *Ger.* altar *m*: *Dan.* alter *n*: *Swed.* altare *m*: *Lat.* altare, *from* alta *high*, and ara *a place for sacrifice*] *An altar*; altare:—Beforan þam altare, *Mt.* 5, 24.

Alucan, aluccan *to pull out*, v. alocan.

Alutan, anlutan; *p.* aleat; *pp.* aluten, aloten [a, lutan *to bend*] *To bend, incline, bend*, or *bow down*; procumbere:—Alutende he geseah, *Lk.* 24, 12. He aleat to eorðan *he bowed to the earth, Elf. T.* p. 37, 8.

Alwalda, alwaldend, alwealda *the Omnipotent*, v. ælwalda.

Alwan *aloes*, v. alewa.

Alwiht *every creature, Cd.* 10.

Alybban, alibban, þu alyfast; *p.* aleofode, hi alyfden; *pp.* aleofod; *v.* [a, lybban *to live*] *To survive, live after, live*; vivere:—Heo alyfað, *Ex.* 21, 22. Ic alybban ne mæg *I cannot live, Nicod.* 26: *Thw.* p. 13, 36. Heo wolde libban, *Ors.* 3, 6.

Alyfan, hit alyfð; *imp.* alyfe; *p.* alyfde, hi alyfdon; *pp.* alyfed; *v. a. To give leave, permit, suffer*, v. lyfan.

Alyfedlic; *adj. Allowable, quick*; expeditus:—Alyfedlice þing *an allowable thing, Elf. gr.* 9, 25.

Alyfedlice; *adv. Lawfully, allowably*; licite, *Lye.*

Alyfednes, se; *f. Permission, sufferance, leave, grant*; permissio, *Som.*

Alyhtnys, se; *f. An enlightening, illumination, a lightness*; illuminatio:—*Ps.* 89, 8.

Alynian, alynnan *To pull down, liberate, deliver, free from*; evellere:—Alinian of rode Cristes lichaman *to unfasten Christ's body from the cross.* De offic diurn, et noct, *Lye.*

Alysan, lysan; *p.* alysde; *pp.* alysed; *v. a.* [*Plat.* verlösen: *Dut.* verlossen: *Ger.* erlösen: *Dan.* forlöse: *Swed.* förlossa: a *from*, lysan *to loose*] 1. *To let loose, free, deliver, liberate*; liberare. 2. *To pay for loosing, to pay, redeem, ransom*; redimere:—1. Hwæþer Helias wylle hine alysan, *Mt.* 27, 49. Þat þu beo fram hym alysed, *Lk.* 12, 58. 2. Ic alysde *I paid, Ps.* 68, 6. His fæsten alysan, *Bd.* 5, 4. Broþor ne alyseð, *Ps.* 48, 7. God alyseð sawle mine of handa helle, *Ps.* 48, 16.

Alysednys, alysnes, se; *f. Redemption, a ransom*; redemptio:—Weorð alysednysse sawle his, *Ps.* 48, 8.

Alysend, alesend *A liberator, deliverer, redeemer*; liberator:—Ic lufige þe Driht alysend min, *Ps.* 17, 1, 48.

Alysendlic; *adj. Free, loose*; solutorius:—*Bd.* 4, 22.

Alystan *to list, to wish*, v. lystan.

Am *am*; sum, v. eom.

Amæran ute *to exterminate*, v. utamæran.

Amæstan, gemæstan; *p.* ede; *pp.* ed [*Plat. Dut.* mesten: *Ger.* mästen: a *from*, mæst *mast*, the fruit of trees on which some animals are fattened, as nuts, acorns, berries: *Moes.* mats: *Ger.* mast *food*] *To fatten*; saginare:—*Cod. Ex.* p. 111. b. ¶ Amæst, *or* amæsted beon *to be fattened*; impinguari. Amæste fuglas, *or* gemæsted fugelas *fattened fowls, fatlings, Cot.* 16.

Amætan *to find*, v. metan.

Amang *among*, v. gemang.

Amanian; *p.* ade, ode. 1. *To admonish strongly, to fine*; admonere. 2. *To direct, govern, send*; dirigere:—1. Se bisceop amanige, *L. Athel.* 26. Be gerefan þe mid riht ne amanige *concerning a governor who fines not with justice, L. Edw.* 5. 2. And amanige þære scyrbisceop þa bote *and shall send the offering to the bishop of the shire, Edg.* 3: *W.* p. 78, 5.

Amánsumian; *p.* de; *pp.* ed od [a, mænsumian *to marry*] *To disjoin, excommunicate*; excommunicare:—*Bd.* 3, 22. Amansumod, -ed *excommunicated, Chr.* 675. *This word is opposed to* mænsumian, *or* gemænsumian *to join*, or *marry*.

Amansumnung, amansumung, amænsumung; *f. Exclusion, excommunication, a curse*; excommunicatio:—Mid þære amansumunge, *Jos.* 7, 12.

Ambeht, embeht, ymbeaht, ombiht [ymb *about*, æht *property*] *A joining, collection, an office, a ministry, message, a servant*; collatio, officium:—*Bt. Rawl.* p. 163. Þa Abraham spræc to his ombihtum *then Abraham spoke to his servants, Cd.* 139.

Amber, omber, es; *m.* [*Plat.* ammer *m*: *Dut.* emmer *m*: *Ger.* eimer *m*: *Swed.* ämbar *m.*] *A vessel to carry about liquids, having two ears, a tub; tankard*; amphora:—*Ors.* 1, 1.

Ambiht-hus [ambeht *an office*, hus *house*] *A shop*; officina:—*R. Concord.* 11.

Ambiht-men, embeht-men [*Dut.* ambachtman *m*: ambeht *office*, men *men*] *Persons who go about on being ordered, servants, ministers, pages*; servientes, satellites:—Habbað oðre ambihtmen *have other servants, L. Lib. eccl.* 12.

Ambiht-scealcas, ombihtscealcas [ambeht *office*, scealc *a servant*] *The same meaning as* ambihtmen *above, Fr. Jud.* 10.

Ambiht-smið; *m.* [ambeht, smið *a workman*] *An overlooker of workmen, an ambassador, L. Ethelb.* 7.

a Ambyht *a message*, v. ambeht.

Ambyht-secg [ambyht *a message*, secga *a sayer*] *A messenger, an ambassador*; nuntius :—*Cd.* 27.

Ambyrne wind *a prosperous wind, Ors.* 1, 1.

Ameallud; *part. Emptied, brought to nought*; exinanitus :—*C. M. Ps.* 74, 8.

Amearcan *to mark*, v. mearcian.

Amel, es; *m. A vessel for holy water*; amula, vas lustrale :—*Cot.* 2.

Ameldian *to betray*, ic ameldige ameldod, v. meldian.

b Amerian, amyrian; *p.* ede; *pp.* ed. *To examine, try, prove*; examinare :—Oþer dæl sceal beon amered on þam fyre *the other part shall be proved in the fire, Bt.* 38, 4. Amered, amyred beon *to be examined.*

Amerran *to hinder*, v. amyrran.

Amersod; *part.* [q. amansod, *or* amansumod, v. amansumian *to disjoin*] *Excommunicated*; excommunicatus :—Gif hwa amersodne oððe utlahne healde, plihte him sylfum, *L. Cnut.* 64.

Amet, amett; *part. Decked, adorned, clothed, furnished*; ornatus, *Som.*

Ametan; *p.* amæt; *pp.* ameten *To measure*, v. metan.

Amethwile [amet, hwile *while*] *Leisure*; otium :—*Elf. gr. Lye.*

Amett *painted*; pictum, v. amet.

Amiddan *To weigh, poise, ponder, esteem*; appendere, *Som.*

c Amiddan *in the middle.*

Amolsnian *to putrify*, v. formolsnian.

Amorreas, Amorreiscas; *pl. The Amorites*; Amoritæi :—*Gen.* 15, 16.

Ampella, ampolla, ampulla *A vial, bottle, flagon*; ampulla :—Ampellan, *or* elefæt *an oil-vat*; legithum, *Cot.* 119. Ampellan, *or* crogen *small vessels, Chrismatories*; lenticulæ :—*Cot.* 124.

Ampre, ompre *A crooked swelling vein, an herb, sweet marjoram, feverfew*; varix, herba quædam, ut amaracus, origanum majorana, *Lin.* :—*L. M.* p. 1. c. 39.

Amundbræg [a *from*, mund *a mound, protection, peace*, bræga *a breaker*] *A peace-breaker, a disturber*; pacis violator :—*Chr.* 1087, v. mundbrece.

Amundian *to preserve*, v. mundian.

Amyrdran; *p.* ede; *pp.* ed [*Plat. Dut.* vermoorden: *Ger.* ermorden: *Dan.* myrde: *Swed.* mörda: a, myrðra *murder*] *To murder, kill*; trucidare :—Þat man sy amyrdrede *that one be murdered, L. Cnut.* 53.

Amyrian *to examine*, v. amerian.

d Amyrran, amerran; *p.* de; *pp.* ed; *v. a.* 1. *To dissipate, spend, distract, defile, mar, lose, spoil*; dissipare, perdere. 2. *To hinder, mislead*; impedire :—1. Þa he hæfde ealle amyrrede, *Lk.* 15, 14, 30. Ne amyrð he hys mede, *Mt.* 10, 42. And eorðe wæs amyrred, *Ex.* 8, 24. 2. Wela amerð and læt *wealth obstructs and hinders, Bt.* 32, 1.

An, æn, ain; *gen.* es; *def.* se ana; seo, þæt áne; *pron.* [*Plat. Dut.* een: *Frs.* ien: *Ger. Al. Franc.* ein: *Moes.* ains, aina, ain: *Dan. Swed.* en, et: *Icel.* einn: *Norse*, einr. These various forms seem to denote *the beginning, the origin. Wachter* says *an*, as a noun, significat principium, seu nascendi originem :—Hence the *Al.* æne *a grandfather*, ane *a grandmother*]—1. One; unus. 2. *Alone, only, sole, another*; solus—with these meanings it is used *definitely*, and *generally written* ana *m, and sometimes* aina, anne, anga; *f. and n*: ane. 3. *A certain one, some one*; quidam, v. sum. Sometimes, though rarely, *an* may be used as the English article *a, an.* It does not, however, appear to be generally used as an indefinite article, but more like the *Moes.* ain, or the *Lat.* unus.—When a noun was used indefinitely by the Saxons, it was without an article prefixed, as Þeodric wæs Cristen *Theodoricus fuit Christianus, Theodric was a Christian, Bt.* 1. 4. *Any, every one, all*; quisque :—1. An of þam, *Mt.* 10, 29. Ain wæs on Ispania *one was in Spain, Ors.* 4, 9. He is an God, *Mk.* 12, 29. 2. An God ys god *only God is good, Mt.* 19, 17: 8, 8. Ge forlæton me anne, and ic ne eom ana, *Jn.* 16, 32. Angum, *Bt.* 29, 1: *Card.* p. 158, 12. Þat ge aina gebroðra hæfdon, *Gen.* 43, 6. 5. An man hæfde twegen suna, *Mt.* 21, 28. *In this sense it is used as* sum, *as in the parallel passage*, Sum man hæfde twegen suna, *Lk.* 15, 11. Cynric ofslogon ænne Bryttiscne cyning *Cynric slew a British king, Chr.* 508. Wirc þe nu ænne arc, *Gen.* 6, 14. Ane lytle hwyle *a little while, Bt.* 7, 1. 6. *In this sense it admits of a plural form, as* anra gehwa, anra gehwylc *every one*, or literally *every one of all.* Swelte anra gehwilc for his agenum gilte, *Deut.* 24, 16. Anes hwæt, *Bt.* 18, 3, denotes *any thing*, literally *any thing of all*, and is used adverbially for *at all*, in *any degree.* ¶ *One, other.* An æfter anum *one after another, Jn.* 8, 9. To anum to anum *from one to the other, only*; duntaxat. Þat an, *or* for an, *Mk.* 5, 36. Anne finger, and anne *one finger, and then another, Ors.* 2, 3. Ænne and ænne *one and the other, one after another, Herb.* 1, 20. Ymb an beon *to agree*; consentire, *C. Mt.* 18, 19. On an, *in one, continually, Gen.* 7, 12.

e An *in*, v. on.

An *give*, v. unnan.

An the termination of most Anglo-Saxon verbs. Mr. Turner says, "if we go through the alphabet, we shall find that most of the verbs are composed of a noun, and the syllables -an, -ian, *or* -gan. Of these additional syllables," he adds, "-gan is the verb of motion *to go*, or the verb agan *to possess*, and -an seems sometimes to be the abbreviation of unnan, or, according to *Lye*, anan *to give*, which is probably a double infinitive like gangan *to go*, and that an is the original infinitive of the verb *to give.*" Thus deagan *to tinge* appears to be from deag *a colour*, and an *to give*, dælan *to divide*: dæl-an *to give apart*: cyssan *to kiss*: cos-an *to give a kiss*: blostmian *to blossom* is blostmagan *to have a flower*: byan *to inhabit* is by-agan *to have an habitation*:—*Hist. of A.-S.* vol. ii. p. 424.

f An is sometimes used in composition for and-, *or* un-, *or* in-, as, anweorc *for* andweorc: anbindan *for* unbindan *to unbind, loosen.*

Ana *alone*, v. an.

Anælan; *pp.* anæled [an, ælan *to light*] *To kindle, inflame, light*, anneal; accendere, inflammare :—*Chr.* 694.

Anæþelan [un *not*, æþel *noble*] *To dishonour, degrade*; ignobilem reddere :—And þonan wyrð anæþelad oð þat he wyrð unæþele *and thence becomes degraded till he is unnoble, Bt.* 30, 2.

Anan, *or* anum *by this alone, only*; *d. of* an.

Anawyrm [ana, wyrm *a worm*]

[Birm Ambresbury]

Φ 1 Ambres-buri, g burge; d. byrig, byri [Also Ambresbury-burh the city of] Amesbury, Wilts. On Ames-byri Chr 994 Ing 170, 3.

~~Ambihtsecga~~ v ombiht

Ɣ ambyht, a message; officium Cd 25 ?33, 10 v ambeht

Ɣ to inform, announce Th. An.

Φ 2 Ameos the herb ameos, bishopweed, bullwort, or bishops weed; ammi vel ammium Som

~~Ɣ And only alone~~ ~~Th. An~~

Φ

Φ

Ɣ Amore A kind of bird; avis genus, Scorellus Cot 160 Som. Lye. O[7 b]

Ɣ Ampull a bottle Th. An v ampella

Φ 1 Amm-beam Arboris genus, cujus cortex in aquâ decoctus in balneo utilis est adversus scabiem L. M. 1, 32 Som

Ambiht-smið; *m.* [ambeht, smið *a workman*] *An overlooker of workmen, an ambassador, L. Ethelb.* 7.

a Ambyht *a message*, v. ambeht.

Ambyht-secg [ambyht *a message*, secga *a sayer*] *A messenger, an ambassador;* nuntius:—*Cd.* 27.

Ambyrne wind *a prosperous wind, Ors.* 1, 1.

Ameallud; *part. Emptied, brought to nought;* exinanitus:—*C. M. Ps.* 74, 8.

Amearcan *to mark*, v. mearcian.

Amel, es; *m. A vessel for holy water;* amula, vas lustrale:—*Cot.* 2.

Ameldian *to betray*, ic ameldige ameldod, v. meldian.

b Amerian, amyrian; *p.* ede; *pp.* ed. *To examine, try, prove;* examinare:—Oþer dæl sceal beon amered on þam fyre *the other part shall be proved in the fire, Bt.* 38, 4. Amered, amyred beon *to be examined.*

Amerran *to hinder*, v. amyrran.

Amersod; *part.* [q. amansod, *or* amansumod, v. amansumian *to disjoin*] *Excommunicated;* excommunicatus:—Gif hwa amersodne oððe utlahne healde, plihte him sylfum, *L. Cnut.* 64.

Amet, amett; *part. Decked, adorned, clothed, furnished;* ornatus, *Som.*

Ametan; *p.* amæt; *pp.* ameten *To measure*, v. metan.

Amethwile [amet, hwile *while*] *Leisure;* otium:—*Elf. gr. Lye.*

Amett *painted;* pictum, v. amet.

Amiddan *To weigh, poise, ponder, esteem;* appendere, *Som.*

c Amiddan *in the middle.*

Amolsnian *to putrify*, v. formolsnian.

Amorreas, Amorreiscas; *pl. The Amorites;* Amoritæi:—*Gen.* 15, 16.

Ampella, ampolla, ampulla *A vial, bottle, flagon;* ampulla:—Ampellan, *or* elefæt *an oil-vat;* legithum, *Cot.* 119. Ampellan, *or* crogen *small vessels, Chrismatories;* lenticulæ:—*Cot.* 124.

Ampre, ompre *A crooked swelling vein, an herb, sweet marjoram, feverfew;* varix, herba quædam, ut amaracus, origanum majorana, *Lin.*:—*L. M.* p. 1. c. 39.

Amundbræg [a *from*, mund *a mound, protection, peace*, bræga *a breaker*] *A peace-breaker, a disturber;* pacis violator:—*Chr.* 1087, v. mundbrece.

Amundian *to preserve*, v. mundian.

Amyrdran; *p.* ede; *pp.* ed [*Plat. Dut.* vermoorden: *Ger.* ermorden: *Dan.* myrde: *Swed.* mörda: a, myrðra *murder*] *To murder, kill;* trucidare:—Þat man sy amyrdrede *that one be murdered, L. Cnut.* 53.

Amyrian *to examine*, v. amerian.

d Amyrran, amerran; *p.* de; *pp.* ed; *v. a.* 1. *To dissipate, spend, distract, defile, mar, lose, spoil;* dissipare, perdere. 2. *To hinder, mislead;* impedire:—1. Þa he hæfde ealle amyrrede, *Lk.* 15, 14, 30. Ne amyrð he hys mede, *Mt.* 10, 42. And eorðe wæs amyrred, *Ex.* 8, 24. 2. Wela amerð and læt *wealth obstructs and hinders, Bt.* 32, 1.

An, æn, ain; *gen.* es; *def.* se ana; seo, þæt áne; *pron.* [*Plat. Dut.* een: *Frs.* ien: *Ger. Al. Franc.* ein: *Moes.* ains, aina, ain: *Dan. Swed.* en, et: *Icel.* einn: *Norse*, einr. These various forms seem to denote *the beginning, the origin. Wachter* says *an*, as a noun, significat principium, seu nascendi originem:—Hence the *Al.* æne *a grandfather*, ane *a grandmother*]—1. One; unus. II. *Alone, only, sole, another;* solus—with these meanings it is used *definitely*, and *generally written* ana *m, and sometimes* aina, anne, anga; *f. and n:* ane. III. *A certain one, some one;* quidam, v. sum. Sometimes, though rarely, *an* may be used as the English article *a, an.* It does not, however, appear to be generally used as an indefinite article, but more like the *Moes.* ain, or the *Lat.* unus.—When a noun was used indefinitely by the Saxons, it was without an article prefixed, as Þeodric wæs Cristen *Theodoricus fuit Christianus, Theodoric was a Christian, Bt.* 1. IV. *Any, every one, all;* quisque:—I. An of þam, *Mt.* 10, 29. Ain wæs on Ispania *one was in Spain, Ors.* 4, 9. He is an God, *Mk.* 12, 29. 2. An God ys god *only God is good, Mt.* 19, 17: 8, 8. Ge forlæton me anne, and ic ne eom ana, *Jn.* 16, 32. Angum, *Bt.* 29, 1: *Card.* p. 158, 12. Þat ge aina gebroðra hæfdon, *Gen.* 43, 6. III. An man hæfde twegen suna, *Mt.* 21, 28. *In this sense it is used as* sum, *as in the parallel passage*, Sum man hæfde twegen suna, *Lk.* 15, 11. Cynric ofslogon ænne Bryttiscne cyning *Cynric slew a British king, Chr.* 508. Wirc þe nu ænne arc, *Gen.* 6, 14. Ane lytle hwyle *a little while, Bt.* 7, 1. IV. *In this sense it admits of a plural form, as* anra gehwa, anra gehwylc *every one*, or literally *every one of all.* Swelte anra gehwilc for his agenum gilte, *Deut.* 24, 16. Anes hwæt, *Bt.* 18, 3, denotes *any thing*, literally *any thing of all*, and is used adverbially for *at all*, in *any degree.* ¶ *One, other.* An æfter anum *one after another, Jn.* 8, 9. To anum to anum *from one to the other, only;* duntaxat. Þat an, *or* for an, *Mk.* 5, 36. Anne finger, and anne *one finger, and then another, Ors.* 2, 3. Ænne and ænne *one and the other, one after another, Herb.* 1, 20. Ymb an beon *to agree;* consentire, *C. Mt.* 18, 19. On an, *in one, continually, Gen.* 7, 12.

e An *in*, v. on.

An *give*, v. unnan.

-an the termination of most Anglo-Saxon verbs. Mr. Turner says, "if we go through the alphabet, we shall find that most of the verbs are composed of a noun, and the syllables -an, -ian, *or* -gan. Of these additional syllables," he adds, "-gan is the verb of motion *to go*, or the verb agan *to possess*, and -an seems sometimes to be the abbreviation of unan, or, according to *Lye*, anan *to give*, which is probably a double infinitive like gangan *to go*, and that an is the original infinitive of the verb *to give*." Thus deagan *to tinge* appears to be from deag *a colour*, and an *to give*, dælan *to divide:* dæl-an *to give apart:* cyssan *to kiss:* cos-an *to give a kiss:* blostmian *to blossom* is blostmagan *to have a flower:* byan *to inhabit* is by-agan *to have an habitation:*—*Hist. of A. S.* vol. ii. p. 424.

f An is sometimes used in composition for and-, *or* un-, *or* in-, as, anweorc *for* andweorc: anbindan *for* unbindan *to unbind, loosen.*

Ana *alone*, v. an.

Anælan; *pp.* anæled [an, ælan *to light*] *To kindle, inflame, light*, ANNEAL; accendere, inflammare:—*Chr.* 694.

Anæþelan [un *not*, æþel *noble*] *To dishonour, degrade;* ignobilem reddere:—And þonan wyrð anæþelad oð þat he wyrð unæþele *and thence becomes degraded till he is unnoble, Bt.* 30, 2.

Anan, *or* anum *by this alone, only; d. of* an.

Anawyrm [ana, wyrm *a worm*]

[Brom Ambresbury]

Φ 1 Ambres-burh, g. burge; d. byrig, byri [Mod. Ambrasbury-burh the city of] Amesbury, Wilts. On Ambres-byri Chr 994 Ing 170, 3.

~~[illegible]~~ v ombiht

X Ambyhto, f. a message; officium Cd 25 Th 33, 10 v ambeht

X to inform, announce Th. An.

Φ 2 Ameos The herb ameos, William, bullwort, or bishop's weed; ammi vel ammium Som ~~[illegible] only alone Th. An.~~

Φ

Φ

X Amore A kind of bird; avis genus, scorellus Cot 160 Som, Lye. O[7 p]

X Ampull, a bottle Th. An v ampella

Φ 1 Ampre, ampore [?] Anam-beam Arboris genus, cujus cortex in aqua decoctus in balneo utilis est adversus scabiem L. M. 1, 32 Som.

ϕ1

Ambidan to abide Th. An

Anegmod sad

ϕ4

An-cnawan to know, C. R. Bosw Lye, on-cnawan

Ancra an; m An anchorite, hermit Solitarius: Th An

ϕ2

ϕ7

Anbyrme scip trabaria navis R. 103, Lye

[8b]

Anbyht sceale, es; m A servant, attendant Th. An v Ambiht-scealcas

ϕ7

ϕ9 [old Ger ante: Ger ande: Norse anti]

Ancenned onlybegotten Th. An.

Ancer, es m An ancher; anchora Beo K 603: 3763 Beo gl

Andættan to confess Th. An v andettan

Andfenga an, m A receiver Th. An an undertaker ps 45.7 susceptor

ϕ5

ϕ5 Anfengend, es; m an undertaker Ps. Th 45.7

ϕ6 Andget, andgit and-gyt, es; m, n

An earth-worm, an intestinal worm; lumbricus:—*L. M.* p. 1, c. 46.

Anbærnys, onbærning, onbærnes, se; *f. Incense, frankincense;* thus:—*Ps.* 140, 2.

Anbelæd *introduced,* v. inbelædan.

Anbestungnan *introduced, Past.* 21, 1.

Anbid *expectation,* v. anbiding.

Anbidian; *p.* anbad; *pp.* anbiden *To abide, await,* v. bidan.

Anbiding, anbidung, anbid *An* ABIDING, *expectation, awaiting, tarrying;* expectatio:—Hwylc is abidung min, *Ps.* 38, 11. Þa wæron ærendracan on anbide *then ambassadors were in waiting, Ors.* 3, 9.

Anbidude *waited,* v. bidan.

Anbigan, anbugan [an, bigan *to bow*] *To bow to, obey, submit;* submittere:—*Ors.* 1, 12, v. bigan.

Anbindan [*Dut.* ontbinden: *Ger.* entbinden: un *un,* bindan *to bind*] *To* UNBIND, *untie;* absolvere:—Seo wiðerwearde anbint and gefreoð *the adverse unbinds and liberates, Bt.* 20.

Anbiscopod; *part. Unconfirmed;* non confirmatus:—To lange anbiscopod ne wurðe *should not be too long* [*unbishoped*] *unconfirmed, L. Can. Edg.* 15.

Anbryrd *vexed, grieved,* v. onbryrdan.

Anbryrdnes *sorrow,* v. onbryrdnys.

Anbugan *to obey,* v. bigan.

Anbyrdnys, se; *f.* [un *un,* byrdnys *bearableness,* v. geanbyrdan, geanbæran] *Unbearableness, resistance;* resistentia:—*L. Edg. p.* 81.

Anbyrignes *a taste, R.* 70, v. byrignes.

Ancenneda; *adj. Only-begotten;* unigenitus:—*Jn.* 1, 18.

ANCER, ancor, ~~ancr, ancra~~ [*Ger.* anker *m*: *Swed.* ankar: *Plat. Dan. Dut.* anker.] 1. *An anchor;* anchora. 2. *One held from the world, an anchorite, a hermit;* solitarius:—1. Þin ancor is git fæst *thine anchor is yet fast, Bt.* 10. On ancre fæst *fast at anchor, Beo.* 4, 92. 2. Slefleas ancra scrud *a hermit's sleeveless vest, Elf. gl.* 3. p. 86.

Ancerlic; *adj. Like a hermit, anchoretic;* anachoreticus, *Som.*

Ancer-lif *a hermit's life, a solitary life;* vita anachoretica:—*Bd.* 4, 28.

Ancer-man *the ruler, or guider of a ship;* proreta:—*Elf. gl.* 6.

Ancer-setl, es; *n.* [ancer, setel *a seat*] *A hermit's cell, a hermitage, the dwelling of an anchorite;* anachoresis:—*R.* 104. Twegen halige menn on ancersettle wuniende, wæron forbærnde, *Chr.* 1087.

Ancer-streng *An anchor-string, a cable;* anchorarius funis:—*Solil.* 4.

Ancgel *a hook,* v. angel.

Ancmod; *adj.* [ange *sorrowful,* mod *mind*] *Sad, sorrowful;* anxius:—*R. Ben.* 64.

Ancleow [*Plat. Dut. Ger.* enkel *m*: *Swed.* ankel *n.*] *The* ANCLE; talus:—*Elf. gl.* 3. Lytel ancleow *a little bone, die, R.* 75.

Ancor *an anchor.* Ancorlic *like a hermit, etc.,* v. ancer, ancerlic, etc.

Ancr, ancra *an anchor,* v. ancer.

Ancsum, ancsumlic *troublesome,* v. angsum.

Ancsumnes *troublesomeness,* v. angsumnes.

Ancummum; *adv.* [an *one,* cummum *the dat. of* cum *a coming*] *One by one, singly;* singulatim:—*C. Jn.* 21, 25.

Ancynne sunu *an only son.*

AND; *conj.* [*Plat.* un: *Frs.* en, in, ende: *Dut.* en, ende: *Ger.* und: *Otf.* unde: *Icl.* end] AND; et, atque, ac:—Gesceop God heofenan and eorðan, *Gen.* 1, 1. Cum and geseoh, *Jn.* 1, 46. ¶ And swa feorð *and so forth, or* and gehu elles *and the like;* et cætera.

And *against, through;* contra. An inseparable preposition denotes opposition, like the *Icl.* and, önd: *Moes.* and: *Norse,* and: *Ger.* und: and the *Grk.* ἀντι: thus, andwyrd *an answer:* andsacian *to deny.*

Anda, onda, handa, an; *m. Malice, envy, hatred, anger, zeal;* rancor, invidia:—Næfst þu nanne andan to nanum þinge *thou hast not any envy to any thing, Bt.* 33, 4. Hig hyne for andan sealdon, *Mt.* 27, 18. On minum handan *in my anger, envy, Gen.* 4, 23. Nyste nænne andan *know not any hatred, Bt.* 35, 6. ¶ For hwilcum liðrum andan *for any jealousy, L. Edg. poen.* 14.

Andæg fyrst *one day first, in a day's time.*

Andaga, an; *m. A fixed day, a time appointed, a term;* dies dictus:—Gesette me anne andagan, *Ex.* 8, 9.

Andatre *A shrub bearing capers;* capparis, *Som.*

Andbidian *to expect,* v. anbidian.

Andbidung *an expectation,* v. anbiding.

Andbita *the feast of unleavened bread;* azyma:—*Cot.* 17, v. beorma.

Andbyfene *A quantity;* quantitas, *Som.*

Andeaw; *adj.* [un *un,* þeaw *custom*] *Undutiful, disobedient, arrogant, presumptuous, proud;* arrogans:—*Scint.* 46, *Som.*

Andefer, an. ANDOVER, *Hants:*—Hi læddon Anlaf to Andeferan, *Chr.* 994.

Andefn [and, efen *even*] *An equality, a proportion, a measure, an amount;* proportio:—Be hire andefne *by its proportion, Bt.* 32, 2.

Andel-bæfetide *overhastily.*

Andetnys, se; *f. A confession, professing, an acknowledgment;* confessio:—Andetnys don *to make confession.* Seo andetnes þe we deð *the confession that we make, L. Lib. eccl.* 30.

Andetla *an acknowledgment.*

Andetta, an; andetter, es; *m. One who confesses, a confessor, an acknowledger;* confessor:—Se þæs slæges andetta sy *who is an acknowledger of the murder, L. Alf.* 26: *Bd.* 1, 7.

Andettan, ondettan; *v.a. To confess, to acknowledge, to thank;* fateri:—Gif he wille and cunne his dæda andettan *if he will and can confess his deeds, L. Edg.* 2. Ic andette Ælmihtigum Gode *I confess to Almighty God, Id.* 5: *Wilk.* p. 88, 11. Seo andetnes þe we Gode anum andettað, deð to gode *the confession that we confess to God alone tendeth to good, L. Lib. eccl.* 30. Ic andette þe, *Mt.* 11, 25.

Andetter *a confessor,* v. andetta.

Andetting *a confession,* v. andetnys.

Andfang *an undertaker,* v. anfeng.

Andfege *made bald,* v. andfexe, *Som.*

Andfegnessa *places for receiving, receptacles;* receptacula:—*Cot.* 190.

Andfenege *accepted,* v. anfeng.

Andfeng *an assumption,* v. anfeng.

Andfengend, andfenga *an undertaker,* v. anfeng.

Andfexe [and *without,* feax *hair*] *Baldness;* calvities, *Som.*

Andfindende; *part. Finding, getting;* nanciscens:—*Cot.* 138.

Andfon, anfon *to perceive, follow, receive,* v. fon.

Andgeloman, andloman; *pl. Implements, tools, utensils;* instrumenta:—*Cot.* 104, v. geloma.

ANDGET, es; *m.* 1. *The understanding, the intellect;* intellectus. 2. *Knowledge, cognizance;* cognitio. 3. *Sense, meaning, one of the senses;*

sensus:——1. Þas andgites mæð *the measure of the understanding, Bt.*41, 4. 2. Andget þe syle, *Ps.* 31, 10, v. ongitenes. 3. Hwilum andgit of andgita *sometimes meaning for meaning, Bt. pref.* Þa fif andgita þæs lichoman synd, gesiht, hlyst, spræc, stæng, or stenc and hrepung *the five senses of the body are sight, hearing, speech, smell, and touch, L. Modus, confit.*

Andgetfull, andgitlic; *adj. Sensible, discerning, knowing;* intelligibilis:—Þæt æenig mon sie swa andgetfull *that any man is so discerning, Bt.* 39, 9.

Andgitan *to understand,* v. angytan.

Andgitfullice, *comp.* or; *sup.* ost; *adv. Sensibly, wisely, clearly, plainly, distinctly;* intelligenter:—Swa swa he hit andgitfullicost gereccan mihte *as he most clearly might explain it, Bt. pref.*

Andgitleas; *adj. Foolish, senseless, doltish;* stolidus:—Andgitlease man sceal swingan *a foolish man shall be beaten, L. Edg. poen.* 16.

Andgitleaste, andgytlest, *Foolishness, senselessness;* stoliditas, *Som.*

Andgitlic *sensible,* v. andgetfull.

Andgitlice *clearly,* v. andgitfullice.

Andgyt *the understanding,* v. andget.

Andgytan *to understand,* v. angytan.

Andgytfull *intelligible,* v. andgetfull.

Andgytfullice *clearly,* v. andgitfullice.

Andgytlest, *foolishness,* v. andgitleaste.

Andgyttol, andgytol *sensible,* v. andgetfull.

Andhwæðer [*Ger.* entweder *whether*] *Notwithstanding, but yet;* attamen, *Som.*

Andian, ic andige, he andgað; *part.* andigende *To envy, hate;* invidere:—Ic andige on þe *I envy you, Elf. gr.* 41.

Andig; *adj. Envious;* invidus —*Scint.* 15.

Andigende *envying,* v. andian.

Andlang; *prep. g. d. ac.* [*Plat. Dan. Swed.* langs, enlangs: *Dut.* onlang: *Ger.* entlang: and *through,* lang *long*] 1. *On length,* ALONG, *by the side of;* in longum. 2. *Through, during;* per:—1. Þat wæter wyrð to ea, þonne andlang ea to sæ *the water runs to the river, then along the river to the sea, Bt.* 34, 6. 2. Andlang þas westenes, *Jos.* 8, 16. Onlongne dæg, or andlangne dæg *during the day,* or *through the day, Chr.* 938: *Ing.* p. 142, 22.

Andleofen, andlyfen. 1. *Food, sustenance, nourishment, pottage;* victus, alimenta. 2. *That by which food is procured, money, substance, wages;* stipendia:—1. He sealde him andlyfene wið horsum, *Gen.* 47, 17. 2. Ealle hyre andlyfene, *Mk.* 12, 44. On eowrum andlyfenum, *Lk.* 3, 14.

Andlicnis *likeness,* v. anlicnes.

Andlomon, andluman, *utensils,* v. andgeloman.

Andmitta [mitta *weight*] *A weight, a standard weight;* exagium, v. mitta.

Andrædan, andredan; *part.* andrædende *to fear,* v. ondredan.

Andræccan *To relate, report, bring back;* referre:— Andræccan spræce, *Bt. Lye.*

Andrece; *adj. Twisted, squeezed;* tortus:—Andrece fæt *a pressing vat, Elf. gl. Som.* p. 60.

Andred, Andredes leage, Andredes wald *Andred, Andredsley, Andred's weald, the name of a large wood in Kent, Chr.* 893: *Id. an.* 477: *Ing. Id. an.* 755. Andredes ceaster *Andredescester, a city in the same wood, Pevensey,* or *Pemsey Castle, Sussex, Chr.* 490: *Ing.* p. 17, 13.

Andres ea *a British island called Andersey Isle, Som.*

ANDRYSN, ondrysn, ondryslic, ondrysenlic; *adj.* 1. *Terrible, fearful, dreadful;* terribilis. 2. *Causing fear, venerable, respectable;* reverendus: — 1. Ondryslic on to seonne *terrible to be seen, Bd.* 2, 16. Ondrysnlico gesihð *a dreadful sight, Bd.* 5, 19. 2. He mæg hine gedon andrysn *he may make him respectable, Bt.* 27, 1.

Andrysn, ondrysn *Terror, force, power;* terror:— Ondryson halwendes eges *by the power of salutary fear, Past.* 49, 5, v. drysn.

Andrysnlice; *adv. Fearfully, dreadfully;* terribiliter:—*Past.* 15, 2.

Andsaca, an. *A denier, a forswearer, an opposer, an enemy;* negator:—Ofer eorðan andsaca ne wæs *there was not an opposer on the earth, Cd.* 208. Godes andsaca *an opposer,* or *a forsaker of God, Id.* 23. Godes andsacan, *God's enemies, Id.* 219.

Andsacian, andsacigan; *v. To deny, refuse, gainsay, forsake, abjure;* negare:—Ne mæg ic ne andsacigan *I cannot deny, Bt.* 10.

Andsæc, ansæce [and, sac *a contention*] *A denying, refusing, an abjuring, a forswearing, resistance;* negatio:—Be borges andsæce *concerning a refusing of a pledge, L. In.* 41. Butan ansæce *without resistance, Chr.* 796: *Ing.* p. 83, 5.

Andsæt; *adj.* [and *against,* sæt *set, from* sætan] *Set against, odious, hateful, abominable;* exosus, odiosus:—*Elf. gr.* 33.

Andspurnan *to stumble,* v. ætspurnan.

Andspurnes *an offence,* v. ætspyrning.

Andstandan [and, standan *to stand*] *To sustain, abide, stand by, bear;* sustinere, *Som.* Andstandond ongean *contending against, R. Ben.* 1.

Andswar, andswaru; *f.* [and *against,* swar *from* swaran *to swear, anciently, to speak,* or *Norse,* swar *a speech*] *An* ANSWER; responsum:—Hi afengon andsware, *Mt.* 2, 12. Andswaru liðe *a soft answer, Scint.* 77, v. andwyrd.

Andswarian, answarian, geandswarian, onswærian, ic answarige; *p.* -sworede, swarode; *pp.* ed; *To give an answer, to* ANSWER, *respond;* respondere:—Þa ne myhton hig him andswarian, *Mt.* 22, 46. Andswarode ic *answered I, Bt.* 26, 2.

Andsyn *a face,* v. ansyn.

Andþracian *to tremble,* v. anþracian.

Andþwære; *adj.* [and *against,* þwær *quiet*] *Perverse, froward, athwart, cross;* perversus, *Som.*

Andtimber *wood,* v. antimber.

Andustrian; *To hate, detest;* detestari:—*R. Mt.* 26, 74.

Andustrung *Abomination;* abominatio:—*R. Mt.* 24, 15.

Andward *present,* v. andweard.

Andwardnys *presence,* v. andweardnys.

Andweald *right, power,* v. anweald.

Andweard, andward, andwerd, andwyrd, anweard; *adj. Present;* præsens: — Oð þisne andweardan dæg, *Mt.* 28, 15. On þis andweardan life *in this present life, Bt.* 10.

Andweardian *To be present, to present, to make ready;* præsentare, *Som.*

Andweardlice; *adv. In the presence of, present;* præsentialiter;—Þe hine andweardlice gesawon *who saw him present, Bd.* 4, 17.

Andweardnes, andwardnys, se; *f. Presence, presentness;* præsentia:—*Bd.* 4, 25.

Andwended; *part. Changed, exchanged;* mutatus, *Som.*

andsæc

And-sæc ~~an~~ an-sæcc e; f ~~enmity, contention~~ ~~denial~~ ~~renunciation~~

5 And-sacu ~~Beo 1140 Grn 715, 15~~ Beo K 3711

[Sacu, e; f, contention; sæc, e f. war] enmity contention, ~~denying~~ resistance denying

Ø 1

And-leofen, andlifen Cd 43, Th 157, 28

And-lifen, food and-lyfen victus, alimentum Grn II 715, 13 Lk 3, 14

1 x Andræd constant v anræd

x Andgiet-tacen a sensible token Cd 75 Th 93, 3

And-lyfen food Lk 12, 44 v and-lifen leofne

x 3 Andswaru, e; f Th. An: Beo 91 ~~and sware Beo 113~~ swerian

Ø

Ø

Ø [ge]

x Andswerian to answer Th Apol v swerian lye andswarian

3 x Andryslic terrible v. adrysne

Ø 5

ondrysne

Ø 2 Andrysne terrible formidable Th. An lye

Ø

x

x Andrysn; Ondrysn fear

Ø

Ø

x Andwealcan to rolle Th. An v wealcan

Ø

Ø 1 And-saca, an m O 3 [10a] renunciator, apostata Beo K 1566: 3363

[Ic a]

[Ic b]

Anduzit ...

Andweltaz face coun-
tenance

andwyrd ...
andwyrde ... n ...
andswor ...

... andswyrde ...

... stone ...

... on ... Ande ...

... Anne ... gynod ... ne korned
... hyrned ... ale ...
an ... ... yrn

... Angeat found ...
... Beo K 2573 ...
... angeotan ...
... eotan

2 5 In-getwyle ...
... An

3 ... angim ...

4 ... angie ...
... an bloak, gengi-
gear ... solitary ...
... 325 ... 792

5 ... a rocks
... angel
... solitary
... Beo K 2 ...

... geotan, ...
... geat to pour
... ... taken, tilfundin
Beo K 1553 ...
geotan
... ongitan

an Angan kegan ... - 15 ... ongetan ...
... ongimman ... Beo K 2583
... ongeman
difficult ... 11
... ... angin ...

872 Ingnes - ...
... Angnes
modi ...

Andwendednys, se; *f. A changing, change*; mutatio:—*Ps.* 76, 10, v. onwendidnes.

Andweorc, anweorc *Matter, material, metal, cement, cause*; materia:—Andweorc to weall *mortar, or other stuff of which a wall is made.* To wepenne buton andweorce *in weeping without a cause, Bt.* 10. Buton anweorc *without cause, Id.* 32, 2.

Andwerd *present,* v. andweard.

Andwerdan, andwyrdan, aðwyrdan; *p.* de; *pp.* ed; *v. a.* [and word *a word,* an] *To answer*; respondere:—Abram hire andwerde, *Gen.* 16, 6: 3, 2.

Andwis; *adj. Expert, skilful, Som.*

Andwisnes, se; *f. Experience, skilfulness*; experientia, *Som.*

Andwlit, andwlita, andwlite, anwlita, an [*Plat.* antlaat *n*: *Dut.* gelaat *n*: *Ger.* antlitz *n*: *Swed.* anlete: *Icl.* andlite: and *intensive,* wlite *beauty, countenance*] *Personal appearance, a countenance, face, form*; vultus:—Leoht andwlitan þines, *Ps.* 4, 7. Geseah andwlite his, *Ps.* 10, 8. Hi onfoð andwlitan *they received form, Bt.* 39, 5.

Andwyrd *present,* v. andweard.

Andwyrd [*Plat. Dut.* antwoord *f. n*: *Ger.* antwort: *Moes.* andawaurd: *Dan. Frs.* antwort *a delivering, tradition: and* word *a word*] *An answer*; responsum:—Andwyrd secgan *to say, or give an answer, Ors.* 1, 10, v. andswar.

Andwyrdan *to answer,* v. andwerdan.

Andwyrding *A consent, an agreement, a conspiring, a conspiracy*; conspiratio:—*Cot.* 46.

Andyttan *to thank,* v. andettan.

Ane *one,* v. an.

x An-eage, anege, aneged, æn-ige, an-ige, æ-nigge; *adj.* [*Swed.* enogd: an *one,* eage *eye*] *One-eyed, blind of one eye*; luscus:—*Ex.* 21, 26.

Anecge; *adj. One-edged, having one edge*; unam habens aciem:—An-ecge sword *a sword, Elf. gl.* p. 66.

Anege, aneged *one-eyed,* v. an-eage.

Aneglod *nailed, fastened with nails, crucified, Som.,* v. næglian.

Anehyrned *one-horned,* v. anhyrne.

Anes *an agreement,* v. annes.

Anes bleos *of one colour*; unicolor:—Anes geares *of one year.* Anes hiwes *of the same hue or shape.* Ane siðe *one time, once.* Anes wana *wanting of one,* as anes wana twentig *wanting one of twenty, nineteen.*

Anescian, ahnescian *to make nesh,* v. hnescian.

Anfæreld *A journey*; iter:—*Nathan.* 2.

An-fah; *adj. Of one colour*; unicolor, *Som.,* v. fah.

Anfangen beon *to be received,* v. fon.

y Anfangennes *a receiving,* v. onfangenes.

A'nfeald; *adj.* [*Plat.* eenfold: *Dan.* eenfoldig: *Swed.* enfaldig: an *one,* feald *fold,* or *plait*] ONE FOLD, *simple, single, one alone, singular, peculiar, matchless*; simplex:—Gif þin eage bið anfeald, *Mt.* 6, 22, v. clæn, *and* hluttor *simple, pure.* Anfeald getel *the singular number, Elf. gr.* 13, 23. Anfeald gewin *single combat, R. Ben. interl.* 1. ¶ Anfealdan stræcan *those who are uniformly strict, Past.* 42, 1, *v. l.*

Anfealdlice; *adv. Singly, simply, without intermission*; simpliciter:—*R. Ben.* 52, *Som.*

Anfealdnes, se; *f. Oneness, unity, simplicity, singleness, agreement*; simplicitas:—Ymbe þa anfealdnesse *concerning the simplicity, Bt.* 35, 5.

Anfeng, andfeng; *m.* [an, feng *taken, from* fon] 1. *An undertaker, a defender*; susceptor. 2. *An assumption, a reception, taking, an undertaking*; assumptio:—1. Anfeng min, *Ps.* 61, 2. Andfeng min eart þu, *Ps.* 90, 2: 45, 7. 2. Anfeng ure, *Ps.* 88, 18: *Lk.* 9, 51.

z Anfeng, andfeng; *adj. Fit, acceptable, approved*; aptus:—Nys andfenge Godes rices, *Lk.* 9, 62. Nan witega nys andfenge, *Lk.* 4, 24, 19.

Anfeng *received*; *pp. of* fon.

Anfengednes *a receiving,* v. onfangenes.

An feþe *in walking, Bt.* 36, 5, v. feþe.

Anfilt *An* ANVIL; incus:—*Elf. gr.* 28.

Anfindan *to discover, find,* v. findan.

Anfon *to follow,* v. andfon.

Anforlætan *To lose, relinquish, forsake*; amittere:—Þu nu anforlete *thou hast now lost, Bt.* 7, 3.

Anfunden *found, taken,* v. findan.

Anga *any one, only,* v. an.

a Ang-breost [ange *contracted, troubled,* breost *a breast*] *An asthma, a difficulty of breathing*; asthma, *Som.*

ANGE [*Plat. Dut. Ger.* enge *f*: *Frs.* eang: *Heb.* אנח anh *oppression,* or אנק anq *to groan*] *Vexation, trouble, sorrow, affliction,* ANGUISH; vexatio:—Þa weas þam cynge swiðe ange on his mode *then was there great sorrow to the king's mind, Ors.* 2, 5.

Ange; *adj. Vexed, troubled, sorrowful, troublesome, vexatious*; vexatus, *Som.*

Angean *again,* v. ongean.

ANGEL, [*Plat. Dut. Ger. Dan.* angel *f. m.*] *A hook, a fishing-hook*; hamus:—Wurp þinne angel ut, *Mt.* 17, 27. Swa swa mid angle fisc gefangen bið *as a fish is caught by a hook, Bt.* 20.

Angel *an angel,* v. engel.

Angel-cyning *an English king,* v. Engel.

Angel-cynn, angel-þeod *the English nation,* v. Engel, cynn *a race, tribe,* þeod *a people.*

Angelic *like, similar,* v. gelic.

b Angeltwecca, angeltwicca *A red worm used for a bait in angling or fishing*; lumbricus:—*Elf. gl.* 13.

Angemitte, *for* gemette *found, from* gemetan *to find.*

Angeng; *adj. Going,* or *wandering alone*; solivagus, *Som.*

Angenga *A traveller,* or *passer-by*; viator:—*Beo.* 6: *Thork.* p. 36, 15.

Angeræd *foolish,* v. ungerad.

Angestliðnes *hospitality,* v. gæstliðnes.

Angeweald *power,* v. geweald.

Angin; *pl.* anginnu *A beginning, commencing, an attempt, an essay, opportunity*; initium:—Ælc angin *every beginning, Bt.* 5, 3. Synt þæra sara anginnu, *Mt.* 24, 8. Sara angin, *Mk.* 1, 1: 13, 8.

Anginnan *to begin, enter upon,* v. beginnan.

Angl *a hook,* v. angel.

Angle *the Angles,* v. engle.

c Angles-ege [æge *the island,* Angles *of the Angles*] ANGLESEY, so called after it was conquered by the English; it was anciently called Mona:—Hugo eorl wearð ofslagen innan Angles-ege, *Chr.* 1098.

Angletwicce *a red worm,* v. angeltwecca.

Angmod; *adj.* [ange *vexed,* mod *mind*] *Vexed in mind, sad, sorrowful, anxious*; tristis, *Som.*

Angmodnes, se; *f. Sadness, sorrowfulness*; tristitia, *Som.*

Angnægl [ange *troublesome,* nægel *a nail*] *An* AGNAIL, *a whitlow, a sore under the nail*; dolor ad ungulum, *Mann.*

Angnes, se; *f. Sorrowfulness, sorrow, anxiety, anguish*; ærumna:—On agnysse min, *Ps.* 31, 4. Geswinc and angnys gemetton me, *Ps.* 118, 143. Ag-

9 10 , 10 a - 13,
13.

1

4. Angeat poured out fell Beo K 2583 p of angeotan v. geotan

an, m; andwlite, n

[10a]

5. An-gehwylc every Th. An

Andwlit. dl.

3 Angel, g angles m a

[10b]

An-wlita face, countenance

4 Angengia, an genga an, m (an alone, genga a goer) a solitary Beo K 328 : 892

Andwyrd dl.

2 Andwyrde es; n an answer also Lye. — l. 6 Andwyrde secgan

5 7. Angil a hook one who goes alone Th. An v. angel

3 Ane alone, only Th An v. and

6 8. Angin in beginning solitarius

Angles-ea, an island Anglesey

an-geotan, p an-geat to pour out; diffundere Beo K 2583 v geotan Angitan

4. Angan began p. v. onginnan

10 Angitan to get Beo K 2583

2 4 Ane hyrned one horned v. an-hyrned, also Spl. an-hyrn

5. Angesum difficult narrow R Ben v angsum

11

8 12 Angnes — L. 5 Angnes modes

Andwendednys, se; *f. A changing, change*; mutatio:—*Ps.* 76, 10, v. onwendidnes.

Andweorc, anweorc *Matter, material, metal, cement, cause*; materia:—Andweorc to weall *mortar, or other stuff of which a wall is made.* To wepenne buton andweorce *in weeping without a cause, Bt.* 10. Buton anweorc *without cause, Id.* 32, 2.

Andwerd *present*, v. andweard.

Andwerdan, andwyrdan, aðwyrdan; *p.* de; *pp.* ed; *v. a.* [and word *a word*, an] *To answer*; respondere:—Abram hire andwerde, *Gen.* 16, 6: 3, 2.

w Andwis; *adj. Expert, skilful, Som.*

Andwisnes, se; *f. Experience, skilfulness*; experientia, *Som.*

Andwlit, andwlita, andwlite, anwlita, an [*Plat.* antlaat *n*: *Dut.* gelaat *n*: *Ger.* antlitz *n*: *Swed.* anlete: *Icl.* andlite: and *intensive*, wlite *beauty, countenance*] *Personal appearance, a countenance, face, form*; vultus:—Leoht andwlitan þines, *Ps.* 4, 7. Geseah andwlite his, *Ps.* 10, 8. Hi onfoð andwlitan *they received form, Bt.* 39, 5.

Andwyrd *present*, v. andweard.

Andwyrd [*Plat. Dut.* antwoord *f. n*: *Ger.* antwort: *Moes.* andawaurd: *Dan. Frs.* antwort *a delivering, tradition: and* word *a word*] *An answer*; responsum:—Andwyrd secgan *to say, or give an answer, Ors.* 1, 10, v. andswar.

Andwyrdan *to answer*, v. andwerdan.

Andwyrding *A consent, an agreement, a conspiring, a conspiracy*; conspiratio:—*Cot.* 46.

Andyttan *to thank*, v. andettan.

Ane *one*, v. an.

x An-eage, anege, aneged, æn-ige, an-ige, æ-nigge; *adj.* [*Swed.* enogd: an *one*, eage *eye*] *One-eyed, blind of one eye*; luscus:—*Ex.* 21, 26.

Anecge; *adj. One-edged, having one edge*; unam habens aciem:—An-ecge sword *a sword, Elf. gl.* p. 66.

Anege, aneged *one-eyed*, v. aneage.

Aneglod *nailed, fastened with nails, crucified, Som.*, v. næglian.

Anehyrned *one-horned*, v. anhyrne.

Anes *an agreement*, v. annes.

Anes bleos *of one colour*; unicolor:—Anes geares *of one year.* Anes hiwes *of the same hue or shape.* Ane siðe *one time, once.* Anes wana *wanting of one*, as anes wana twentig *wanting one of twenty, nineteen.*

Anescian, ahnescian *to make nesh*, v. hnescian.

Anfæreld *A journey*; iter:—*Nathan.* 2.

An-fah; *adj. Of one colour*; unicolor, *Som.*, v. fah.

Anfangen beon *to be received*, v. fon.

y Anfangennes *a receiving*, v. onfangenes.

A'nfeald; *adj.* [*Plat.* eenfold: *Dan.* eenfoldig: *Swed.* enfaldig: an *one*, feald *fold*, or *plait*] ONE FOLD, *simple, single, one alone, singular, peculiar, matchless*; simplex:—Gif þin eage bið anfeald, *Mt.* 6, 22, v. clæn, *and* hluttor *simple, pure.* Anfeald getel *the singular number, Elf. gr.* 13, 23. Anfeald gewin *single combat, R. Ben. interl.* 1. ¶ Anfealdan stræcan *those who are uniformly strict, Past.* 42, 1, *v. l.*

Anfealdlice; *adv. Singly, simply, without intermission*; simpliciter:—*R. Ben.* 52, *Som.*

Anfealdnes, se; *f. Oneness, unity, simplicity, singleness, agreement*; simplicitas:—Ymbe þa anfealdnesse *concerning the simplicity, Bt.* 35, 5.

Anfeng, andfeng; *m.* [an, feng *taken, from* fon] 1. *An undertaker, a defender*; susceptor. 2. *An assumption, a reception, taking, an undertaking*; assumptio:—1. Anfeng min, *Ps.* 61, 2. Andfeng min eart þu, *Ps.* 90, 2: 45, 7. 2. Anfeng ure, *Ps.* 88, 18: *Lk.* 9, 51.

z Anfeng, andfeng; *adj. Fit, acceptable, approved*; aptus:—Nys andfenge Godes rices, *Lk.* 9, 62. Nan witega nys andfenge, *Lk.* 4, 24, 19.

Anfeng *received*; *pp. of* fon.

Anfengednes *a receiving*, v. onfangenes.

An feþe *in walking, Bt.* 36, 5, v. feþe.

Anfilt *An* ANVIL; incus:—*Elf. gr.* 28.

Anfindan *to discover, find*, v. findan.

Anfon *to follow*, v. andfon.

Anforlætan *To lose, relinquish, forsake*; amittere:—Þu nu anforlete *thou hast now lost, Bt.* 7, 3.

Anfunden *found, taken*, v. findan.

Anga *any one, only*, v. an.

a Ang-breost [ange *contracted, troubled*, breost *a breast*] *An asthma, a difficulty of breathing*; asthma, *Som.*

ANGE [*Plat. Dut. Ger.* enge *f*: *Frs.* eang: *Heb.* אנחה anh *oppression*, or אנק anq *to groan*] *Vexation, trouble, sorrow, affliction*, ANGUISH; vexatio:—Þa weas þam cynge swiðe ange on his mode *then was there great sorrow to the king's mind, Ors.* 2, 5.

Ange; *adj. Vexed, troubled, sorrowful, troublesome, vexatious*; vexatus, *Som.*

Angean *again*, v. ongean.

ANGEL, angl [*Plat. Dut. Ger. Dan.* angel *f. m.*] *A hook, a fishing-hook*; hamus:—Wurp þinne angel ut, *Mt.* 17, 27. Swa swa mid angle fisc gefangen bið *as a fish is caught by a hook, Bt.* 20.

Angel *an angel*, v. engel.

Angel-cyning *an English king*, v. Engel.

Angel-cynn, angel-þeod *the English nation*, v. Engel, cynn *a race, tribe*, þeod *a people.*

Angelic *like, similar*, v. gelic.

b Angeltwecca, angeltwicca *A red worm used for a bait in angling or fishing*; lumbricus:—*Elf. gl.* 13.

Angemitte, *for* gemette *found, from* gemetan *to find.*

Angeng; *adj. Going*, or *wandering alone*; solivagus, *Som.*

Angenga *A traveller*, or *passer-by*; viator:—*Beo.* 6: *Thork.* p. 36, 15.

Angeræd *foolish*, v. ungerad.

Angestliðnes *hospitality*, v. gæstliðnes.

Angeweald *power*, v. gewald.

Angin; *pl.* anginnu *A beginning, commencing, an attempt, an essay, opportunity*; initium:—Ælc angin *every beginning, Bt.* 5, 3. Synt þæra sara anginnu, *Mt.* 24, 8. Sara angin, *Mk.* 1, 1: 13, 8.

Anginnan *to begin, enter upon*, v. beginnan.

Angl *a hook*, v. angel.

Angle *the Angles*, v. engle.

c Angles-ege [æge *the island*, Angles *of the Angles*] ANGLESEY, so called after it was conquered by the English; it was anciently called Mona:—Hugo eorl wearð ofslagen innan Angles-ege, *Chr.* 1098.

Angletwicce *a red worm*, v. angeltwecca.

Angmod; *adj.* [ange *vexed*, mod *mind*] *Vexed in mind, sad, sorrowful, anxious*; tristis, *Som.*

Angmodnes, se; *f. Sadness, sorrowfulness*; tristitia, *Som.*

Angnægl [ange *troublesome*, nægel *a nail*] *An* AGNAIL, *a whitlow, a sore under the nail*; dolor ad ungulum, *Mann.*

Angnes, se; *f. Sorrowfulness, sorrow, anxiety, anguish*; ærumna:—On agnysse min, *Ps.* 31, 4. Geswinc and angnys gemetton me, *Ps.* 118, 143. Ag-

§. B.

Φ1

7 4 Angeat poured out fell Beo K 2583 p of angeotan v. geotan

an. m; andwlite, n.

[10 a]

Andwlit dl.

Andwlita face, countenance

[10 b]

Andwyrd dl.

Andwyrde es; n. answer, also Gen 715, 19 — l. 6 Andwyrde secgan

Φ-3 Ane alone, only Th An v. and

2 5 An-gehwylc every Th. An

3 Angel, angles m a hook

4 Angenga, an genga an m an alone, genga a goer a solitary Beo K 328 : 892

5 7 Angil a hook Th. An v. angel

6 8 Anginnga solitarius in a beginning

Φ an-geotan, p an-geat to pour out; diffundere Beo K 2583 v geotan

Angles-ea, le; f [of an island] Anglesey

4 Angan began p. v. onginnan

7 10 Angitan to get Beo K 2583

Anehyrned one horned v. an-hyrned, also Spl. an-hyrn

2 5 Angesum difficult narrow R Ben 4 ye v angsum

Φ 11

8 12 Angnes — L. 5 Angnes modes

Andwendednys, se; *f. A changing, change;* mutatio:—*Ps.* 76, 10, v. onwendidnes.

Andweorc, anweorc *Matter, material, metal, cement, cause;* materia:—Andweorc to weall *mortar, or other stuff of which a wall is made.* To wepenne buton andweorce *in weeping without a cause, Bt.* 10. Buton anweorc *without cause, Id.* 32, 2.

Andwerd *present,* v. andweard.

Andwerdan, andwyrdan, aðwyrdan; *p.* de; *pp.* ed; *v. a.* [and word *a word,* an] *To answer;* respondere:—Abram hire andwerde, *Gen.* 16, 6: 3, 2.

w Andwis; *adj. Expert, skilful, Som.*

Andwisnes, se; *f. Experience, skilfulness;* experientia, *Som.*

Andwlit, andwlita, andwlite, anwlita, an [*Plat.* antlaat *n*: *Dut.* gelaat *n*: *Ger.* antlitz *n*: *Swed.* anlete: *Icl.* andlite: and *intensive,* wlite *beauty, countenance*] *Personal appearance, a countenance, face, form;* vultus:—Leoht andwlitan þines, *Ps.* 4, 7. Geseah andwlite his, *Ps.* 10, 8. Hi onfoð andwlitan *they received form, Bt.* 39, 5.

Andwyrd *present,* v. andweard.

Andwyrd [*Plat. Dut.* antwoord *f. n*: *Ger.* antwort: *Moes.* andawaurd: *Dan. Frs.* antwort *a delivering, tradition: and* word *a word*] *An answer;* responsum:—Andwyrd secgan *to say, or give an answer, Ors.* 1, 10, v. andswar.

Andwyrdan *to answer,* v. andwerdan.

Andwyrding *A consent, an agreement, a conspiring, a conspiracy;* conspiratio:—*Cot.* 46.

Andyttan *to thank,* v. andettan.

Ane *one,* v. an.

x An-eage, anege, aneged, æn-ige, an-ige, æ-nigge; *adj.* [*Swed.* enogd: an *one,* eage *eye*] *One-eyed, blind of one eye;* luscus:—*Ex.* 21, 26.

Anecge; *adj. One-edged, having one edge;* unam habens aciem:—An-ecge sword *a sword, Elf. gl.* p. 66.

Anege, aneged *one-eyed,* v. aneage.

Aneglod *nailed, fastened with nails, crucified, Som.,* v. nægglian.

Anehyrned *one-horned,* v. anhyrne.

Anes *an agreement,* v. annes.

Anes bleos *of one colour;* unicolor:—Anes geares *of one year.* Anes hiwes *of the same hue or shape.* Ane siðe *one time, once.* Anes wana *wanting of one,* as anes wana twentig *wanting one of twenty, nineteen.*

Anescian, ahnescian *to make nesh,* v. hnescian.

Anfæreld *A journey;* iter:—*Nathan.* 2.

An-fah; *adj. Of one colour;* unicolor, *Som.,* v. fah.

Anfangen beon *to be received,* v. fon.

y Anfangennes *a receiving,* v. onfangenes.

A'nfeald; *adj.* [*Plat.* eenfold: *Dan.* eenfoldig: *Swed.* enfaldig: an *one,* feald *fold,* or *plait*] ONE FOLD, *simple, single, one alone, singular, peculiar, matchless;* simplex:—Gif þin eage bið anfeald, *Mt.* 6, 22, v. clæn, *and* hluttor *simple, pure.* Anfeald getel *the singular number, Elf. gr.* 13, 23. Anfeald gewin *single combat, R. Ben. interl.* 1. ¶ Anfealdan stræcan *those who are uniformly strict, Past.* 42, 1, *v. l.*

Anfealdlice; *adv. Singly, simply, without intermission;* simpliciter:—*R. Ben.* 52, *Som.*

Anfealdnes, se; *f. Oneness, unity, simplicity, singleness, agreement;* simplicitas:—Ymbe þa anfealdnesse *concerning the simplicity, Bt.* 35, 5.

Anfeng, andfeng; *m.* [an, feng *taken, from* fon] 1. *An undertaker, a defender;* susceptor. 2. *An assumption, a reception, taking, an undertaking;* assumptio:—1. Anfeng min, *Ps.* 61, 2. Andfeng min eart þu, *Ps.* 90, 2: 45, 7. 2. Anfeng ure, *Ps.* 88, 18: *Lk.* 9, 51.

z Anfeng, andfeng; *adj. Fit, acceptable, approved;* aptus:—Nys andfenge Godes rices, *Lk.* 9, 62. Nan witega nys andfenge, *Lk.* 4, 24, 19.

Anfeng *received; pp. of* fon.

Anfengednes *a receiving,* v. ofangenes.

An feþe *in walking, Bt.* 36, 5, v. feþe.

Anfilt *An* ANVIL; incus:—*Elf. gr.* 28.

Anfindan *to discover, find,* v. findan.

Anfon *to follow,* v. andfon.

Anforlætan *To lose, relinquish, forsake;* amittere:—Þu nu anforlete *thou hast now lost, Bt.* 7, 3.

Anfunden *found, taken,* v. findan.

Anga *any one, only,* v. an.

a Ang-breost [ange *contracted, troubled,* breost *a breast*] *An asthma, a difficulty of breathing;* asthma, *Som.*

ANGE [*Plat. Dut. Ger.* enge *f*: *Frs.* eang: *Heb.* אנח anh *oppression,* or אנק anq *to groan*] *Vexation, trouble, sorrow, affliction,* ANGUISH; vexatio:—Þa weas þam cynge swiðe ange on his mode *then was there great sorrow to the king's mind, Ors.* 2, 5.

Ange; *adj. Vexed, troubled, sorrowful, troublesome, vexatious;* vexatus, *Som.*

Angean *again,* v. ongean.

ANGEL, angl [*Plat. Dut. Ger. Dan.* angel *f. m.*] *A hook, a fishing-hook;* hamus:—Wurp þinne angel ut, *Mt.* 17, 27. Swa swa mid angle fisc gefangen bið *as a fish is caught by a hook, Bt.* 20.

Angel *an angel,* v. engel.

Angel-cyning *an English king,* v. Engel.

Angel-cynn, angel-þeod *the English nation,* v. Engel, cynn *a race, tribe,* þeod *a people.*

Angelic *like, similar,* v. gelic.

b Angeltwecca, angeltwicca *A red worm used for a bait in angling or fishing;* lumbricus:—*Elf. gl.* 13.

Angemitte, *for* gemette *found, from* gemetan *to find.*

Angeng; *adj. Going,* or *wandering alone;* solivagus, *Som.*

Angenga *A traveller,* or *passer-by;* viator:—*Beo.* 6: *Thork.* p. 36, 15.

Angeræd *foolish,* v. ungerad.

Angestliðnes *hospitality,* v. gæstliðnes.

Angeweald *power,* v. geweald.

Angin; *pl.* anginnu *A beginning, commencing, an attempt, an essay, opportunity;* initium:—Ælc angin *every beginning, Bt.* 5, 3. Synt þæra sara anginnu, *Mt.* 24, 8. Sara angin, *Mk.* 1, 1: 13, 8.

Anginnan *to begin, enter upon,* v. beginnan.

Angl *a hook,* v. angel.

Angle *the Angles,* v. engle.

c Angles-ege [ege *the island,* Angles *of the Angles*] ANGLESEY, so called after it was conquered by the English; it was anciently called Mona:—Hugo eorl wearð ofslagen innan Angles-ege, *Chr.* 1098.

Angletwicce *a red worm,* v. angeltwecca.

Angmod; *adj.* [ange *vexed,* mod *mind*] *Vexed in mind, sad, sorrowful, anxious;* tristis, *Som.*

Angmodnes, se; *f. Sadness, sorrowfulness;* tristitia, *Som.*

Angnægl [ange *troublesome,* nægel *a nail*] *An* AGNAIL, *a whitlow, a sore under the nail;* dolor ad ungulum, *Mann.*

Angnes, se; *f. Sorrowfulness, sorrow, anxiety, anguish;* ærumna:—On agnysse min, *Ps.* 31, 4. Geswinc and angnys gemetton me, *Ps.* 118, 143. Ag-nes modes *anxiety of mind, Somn.* 854, v. angsumnes.

Angolden *paid, suffered; p. of* angildan, v. gildan.

Angol-þeod *the English nation*, v. Engel-cyn.

Angrislic *horrid*, v. grislic.

Angrysendlice; *adv. Terribly;* terribiliter:—*Nicod.* 26.

d Angset, angseta *A disease with eruptions, a carbuncle, a pimple, a pustule, an eruption, St. Anthony's fire;* carbunculus:—*Cot.* 157.

Angsum, angsumlic; *adj. Narrow, straight, troublesome, hard, difficult;* angustus:—Eala hu neara and hu angsum is þat geat, and se weg þe to life gelædt, and swyðe feawa synd þe þone weg finden, *Mt.* 7, 14.

Angsumian *To vex, afflict, to be solicitous;* vexare, solicitum esse, *Som.*

Angsumlic *troublesome*, v. angsum.

Angsumlice; *adv. Sorrowfully;* triste, *Som.*

Angsumnes, se; *f. Troublesomeness, sorrow, anxiety, anguish;* ærumna:—*Ps.* 118, 143. We gesawon hys angsumnisse, *Gen.* 42, 21, v. angnes.

e Angyld, es; *n.* [an *one*, gild *a payment*] *A single,* or *simple recompence, payment, amends, satisfaction;* simplex compensatio:—Mana þone þæs angyldes *admonish that* [*man*] *of the recompence, L. In.* 22: *Wilk.* p. 18, 27. Gyld þu þat angylde *pay thou the recompence*, p. 18, 28.

Angyn *a beginning*, v. angin.

Angytan [an, gytan *to get*] *To find, discover, understand, know;* invenire, intelligere:—*Ors.* 2, 1.

Anhafen *elevated; pp. of* anhebban.

Anhaga *Alone, vacant, solitary;* solitarius:—Þær se anhaga eard bihealdeð, *Cod. Ex.* 57, a. 10.

Anhagian *to be at leisure*, v. onhagian.

Anhebban; *p.* anhof; *pp.* anhafen *To lift up*, v. onhebban.

Anhefednes, se; *f. Exaltation;* exaltatio:—*C. R. Ben.* 7.

Anhend; *adj.* [*Plat. Dut.* eenhandig: *Ger.* einhandig: an *one*, hand *hand*] *One-handed, lame, imperfect, weak;* unimanus:—*Elf. gl.* 9.

Anhon *to hang*, v. hon.

Anhrædlice *unanimously*, v. anrædlice.

Anhreosian *to rush upon*, v. onhreosian.

f Anhydig; *adj.* [un, hydeg *cautious, heeding*] UNHEEDING, *immoveable, stubborn, rash;* pervicax:—*Cd.* 199.

Anhyldan *to incline*, v. onhyldan.

Anhynd *one-handed*, v. anhend.

Anhyran *To be anxious, emulous;* æmulari:—Ne anhyre þu, *Ps.* 36, 8, v. onhyrgan, onhyrgan.

Anhyrned; *adj.* [an *one*, hyrn *a horn*, as the *Dut.* eenhorn] *One-horned, having one horn;* unicornis:—Anhyrned deor, or anehyrned deor *a one-horned deer, an unicorn;* monoceros:—*Elf. gl.* 12.

Anhyrnend, es *A unicorn;* unicornis:—Swa anhyrnende horn, *Ps.* 91, 10. Fram hornum anhyrnendra, *Ps.* 21, 20.

Anidde *restrained; pp. of* anydan.

Anig *any*, v. ænig.

Anige, anigge *one-eyed*, v. aneage.

Animan; *p.* anam; *pp.* anumen [a *from*, niman *to take*] *To take away, remove;* tollere:—Animað þat pund at hym, *Mt.* 25, 28.

Aninga, æninga, anunga; *adv.* [an *one*, inga] *One by one, singly, at once, clearly, plainly, entirely, altogether, necessarily;* singulatim, omninò:—Hogedon aninga *they at once endeavoured, Jdth.* p. 25, 9.

g Aniðerian [a *intensive*, niðerian *to thrust down*] *To put down, condemn, damn;* deorsum trudere:—Þa wurðe he aniðrod mid Judas, *Chr.* 675: *Ing.* p. 52, 11.

Aniwan *to restore*, v. niwian.

Ankor *an anchor, a hermit*, v. ancer.

Anlæc *A respect, regard, consideration;* respectus:—*Elf. gr.* 28.

An læste, an laste, an luste *at the instant, at the moment;* e vestigio:—*Cot.* 72.

Anlætan [an *alone*, lætan *to let*] *To let alone, forbear, relinquish;* relinquere:—*Cd.* 30.

Anlaga; *adj. Alone, solitary, without company;* solitarius: —*Cot.* 198.

Anlang cempa *arranged soldiers*, v. andlang.

Anlapum; *adv.* [an *one*, læppan *with part*] *With one part, at once, one by one;* singulatim: —*C. Jn.* 21, 25, v. ænlipig.

h An laste *at the instant*, v. an læste.

Anlec *a respect*, v. anlæc.

Anleger; *adj.* [an *one*, leger *a layer*] *Lying with one person;* unicubus:—Anlegere wifman *a woman with one husband, R.* 8.

Anleofa *wages*, v. andleofene.

Anlepig *each*, v. ænlipig.

Anlepnes *solitude*, v. ænlepnes.

Anlic *only*, v. ænlic.

Anlic, onlic; *adj.* [*Dut.* gelyk: *Ger.* ähnlich: an *alone*, lic *like*] *Like, similar;* similis:—Forþam ys heofona rice anlic þam cyninge, *Mt.* 18, 23. Þat he bioð swiðe anlic *that he is very like, Bt.* 37, 1.

Anlice *only*, v. ænlice.

i Anlicnes, andlicnis, onlicnis, se; *f.* [*Dut.* gelyknes *f*: *Ger.* gleichniss *n.*] 1. *A likeness, a similitude, resemblance, an idea, an image;* similitudo. 2. *A statue, an idol, a stature, a height;* statua, simulacrum: —1. Hwæs anlicnys ys þis? *Mt.* 22, 20. God gesceop þa man to his andlicnisse, *Gen.* 1, 26, 27. 2. Tobrec hira anlicnyssa, *Ex.* 23, 24. Ic an ane elne to hys anlicnesse, *Lk.* 12, 25.

Anlifene *food*, v. andleofene.

Anlip, anlypi, anlipig *single, solitary*, v. ænlipig.

An luste *at the instant*, v. an læste.

Anlutan *to incline*, v. alutan.

Anmedla *Pride, arrogance, presumption;* superbia:—*Cd.* 212.

An mitta *a measure*, v. mitta.

Anmod, anmodlic; *adj.* [*Plat.* eenmödig: *Dut.* eenmoedig: an *one*, mod *the mind*] *All of one mind, unanimous, stubborn, obstinate;* unanimus: — Þu soðlice man anmod, *Ps.* 54, 14. Hi ealle anmodlic, *Jos.* 9. 2.

j Anmodlice; *adv. Unanimously, with one accord;* unanimiter: —Hi anmodlice comon, *Jos.* 11, 4.

Anmodnes, se; *f. Unity, unanimity;* unitas, unanimitas, *Som.*

Anne *only*, v. an.

Annes, annys, anes, se; *f.* 1. *Oneness, unity;* unitas. 2. *A covenant, an agreement;* conventio. 3. *Solitude;* solitudo:—1. On þa annysse þære halgan cyrican *in the unity of the holy church, Bd.* 2, 4. 2. Gewearð him and þam folce on Lindesige anes þat *there was with him and the people in Lindsey an agreement that—, Chr.* 1014: *Ing.* p. 193, 12. 3. Annys þæs widgillan westenes *the solitude of the wide desert, Guthl. vit.* c. 3.

Anoða *fear, amazement;* formido, *Som.*

k Anræd; *adj.* [an *one*, ræd *council*] *One-minded, unanimous, agreed, constant, persevering, prompt, diligent, vehement;* unanimus, diligens:—And þonne beon hig anræde *and when they be unanimous, L. In.* 77: *Wilk.* p. 27, 29. Þis swefen ys anræde, *Gen.* 41, 25. Ealle anræde *already, L. Can. Edg.*

××Angol, es, m English an Englishman Th. an v Engle

1 × ~~An hyrn~~ An-hyrn, An-hyrne deor a unicorn 2.18 Sm.

2 Anlifen food v and leofen

1 Anmedla an; m Cd. Th. Index presence 262, 22 arrogance 269, 16 Gm. El p 170 l 266 v also on-medla

) 2

2 Anlædan ~~to~~ to lead on Cd 151 Th 190, 5. v lædan

3. * Anhaga, an; m a hermit Beo K. 4731

) 4

1 2. Anon singly Cd 158 Th. 197, 26

2 3 Anpad, es; m A pass Cd 145 Th 181, 8

a narrow path Beo K 2819

) 5 Anhend Som An-hende Lye q. wh.

Anhorna, an m a unicorn Ps Th ~~[illegible]~~ 91, 9

2 6 * An-hydig one-minded, single-minded, sincerus Beo K ~~[illegible]~~ 5330

1 Án-tíd, e.i.f. one hour Beo K 436

Ø 2

Ø 1

2 3. Antymber matter wood
Ben. v ~~wood~~ antimber

3 4 Ánum adv. with one, only; solum, ~~unice~~ unice Beo ~~K~~ K 2156

4 [5] Án-walda, an. m ~~the only~~ one ruler, the Almighty Beo K 2544

Answeop adflavat Cot 14 [illegible]

Ø 2 Ánsyn, e.i.f. [illegible] gl in seon [illegible] ~~[illegible]~~ an-syne for this sight Beo K 1849; 5663

[10e]

Ø 2 aspect Cd 64 Th 76, 22

Ø 3-

Ø 4 Ánstandan [illegible] to resist [illegible] [illegible] som has-ian

5 Ánstapa an; m one going or stepping alone, a hermit; solitarius Cod Ex 95 b Bea gl in stapen

Ø

Anrædlice, anhrædlice; *adv. Unanimously, instantly, constantly, vehemently;* unanimiter:—Hi þohton anhrædlice, *Ps.* 82, 5. Þe anrædlice wile his sinna geswican, *L. Can. Edg. pn.* 17: *W. p.* 96, 15.

Anrædnys, se; *f. Unanimity, concord, agreement, constancy, steadfastness, diligence, earnestness, vehemency;* concordia:—Broðerlice anrædnys *brotherly unanimity, Scint.* 11. Anrædnys godes weorces *constancy of good works; Oct. vit. cap. Scint.* 7. *Opposed to* twyrædnes *dissention, quod v.*

Anra-gehwa, anra-gehwylc *every one,* v. an, 4.

l Anreces *continually,* v. anstreces.

Anrin [an *in,* ryne *a course*] *An inroad, incursion, assault;* incursio:—Fram anrine, *Ps.* 90, 6.

Ansaca *a denier,* v. onsace, andsaca.

Ansæce *a denying,* v. andsæc.

Ansæt *hated,* v. andsæt.

Ansceat, ansceot *the bowels, the intestines;* exentera:—*Cot.* 73.

Anscod *unshod,* v. unsceoda.

Anscunian *to shun,* v. onscunian.

Anscuniendlic, anscunigendlic *abominable,* v. onscuniendlic.

Ansecgan [*Plat.* anseggen: *Dut.* aanzeggen: *Ger.* ansagen: an, secgan *to declare*] *To affirm, avouch;* affirmare:—Mon ansecgan wolde *one would affirm, L. Edg. pol.* 4, v. secgan.

Ansegednes, ansegdnes, se; *f.* [ansecged *affirmed*] *A thing which is vowed,* or *devoted, an oblation, a sacrifice;* victima:—*Bd.* 1, 7.

Ansendan *to send,* v. onsendan.

Ansettan *to impose,* v. onsettan.

Ansien *a figure,* v. ansyn.

Ansin *a view, sight,* v. ansyn.

m Anspeca, onspæca [an *against,* spæc *a speech*] *A speaker against, an accuser, a persecutor;* persecutor, *Som.*

Anspel [an, spel *a speech, fable*] *A conjecture;* conjectura:—*Cot.* 56.

Anstandende, anstonde *or* munuc *one standing alone, a monk; part. of* anstandian.

Anstandian; *p.* anstod; *pp.* anstanden *To stand against, resist, withstand, to be firm,* or *steadfast, inhabit, dwell;* adversari, constare, habitare, *Som.*

Ansteled; *adj.* [*Dut.* eenstelig: *Ger.* einstielig: an *one,* stele *a stale,* or *handle*] *One staled, having one handle* or *stalk;* unicaulis, *Som.*

Anstonde *a monk,* v. anstandende.

Anstræcan *the determinate;* pertinaces:—*Past.* 42, 2.

Anstreces, ansreces, anreces; *adv.* [an *one, the gen. of* strec *a stretch*] *Of one stretch, with one effort, continually;* sine intermissione:—And foron on anstreces dæges and nihtes *and went in one stretch day and night, Chr.* 894: *Ing.* p. 119, 9. And eodon ansreces *and went continually, Chr.* 1010: *Ing.* p. 184, 25.

Ansund; *adj.* [an *one,* sund *sound, whole*] *One whole, entire;* integer:—Seo heofen is sinewealt and ansund *heaven is circular and continued, Æqu. vern.* 3.

n Ansundnes, se; *f. Wholeness, soundness, integrity;* integritas:—Ansundnesse lufigend *a lover of integrity, Wan. cat.* p. 292, 36.

Answarian *to answer,* v. andswarian.

Answeg; *adj.* [an *one,* sweg *a sound*] *Of the same sound* or *tune, consonant, agreeable;* consonus:—Answege sang, *Elf. gl. Som.* p. 62.

Ansyn, ansin, ansien, andsyn, onsyn [*Plat.* anseen *n*: *Dut.* aanzien *n*: *Ger.* ansehen *n*: *Dan.* seen *n*: an *one,* siene *a sight*] 1. *A face, countenance;* vultus. 2. *A view, an appearance, a sight, form, figure;* aspectus, figura. 3. *A thing to be looked upon, a spectacle;* spectaculum:—1. Ansyne þin ic sece, *Ps.* 26, 13. Fægere onsyne *with a fair countenance, Bd.* 5, 2. 2. Mid þære ansine *with the view, Bt.* 22, 2. Astah lichamlicre ansyne on hine, *Lk.* 3, 22. Ansien þyses middan-geardes *the figure of this world, Past.* 51, 2. 3. *Ors.* 6, 7.

Ant *and,* v. and.

o Antalic; *adj.* [an *not,* tællic *wicked*] *Not wicked, clean, pure;* immaculatus:—Æ drihtnes antalic, *Ps.* 18, 8.

Antecrist, anticrist *antichrist, Elf. T.* p. 6, 22.

Antefen; *f.* [an *against,* stæfen *a voice, contracted into* antefen, *written by Chaucer* antem] *An* ANTEM *or* ANTHEM, *a hymn sung in alternate parts;* antiphona:—Þat hi antefn gehleoðre stæfne sungan *that they sang the anthem with an harmonious voice, Bd.* 1, 25: *Sm.* p. 487, 24.

Antfeng *acceptable,* v. anfeng.

Anþracian, aþracian [an *intensive,* þracian *or* þræcian *to fear*] *To fear, to be afraid, to dread;* revereri, horrere:—*Ps.* 6, 19. Ic onginne to anþraeigenne *I begin to dread, Elf. gr.* 35.

Anþræc, anþræclic; *adj. Fearful, terrible, horrible;* terribilis, *Som.*

p Antibre *a condition,* or *state of things;* status, *Som.*

Anticrist *antichrist,* v. antecrist.

Antimber *Matter, materials, substance, a theme;* materies, materia:—Ungehiwod antimber *rude matter, Alb. resp.* 15, 22, v. timber.

Antrumnys *an infirmity,* v. untrumnes.

Antute *on the contrary;* e contrario, *Som.*

Antynan *to open,* v. untynan.

Anumen *taken away; pp. of* animan.

Anunga *one by one,* v. aninga.

Anunga *Zeal, an earnest desire, envy;* zelus:—*R. Jn.* 2, 17.

Anwadan; *p.* anwod *To invade, intrude;* invadere:—Hie anwod *invaded them, Cd.* 173, *Lye.*

Anwald *power,* v. anweald.

Anwalda *a magistrate,* v. anwealda.

Anwaldan *to rule,* v. waldan.

q Anwaldeg; *adj.* [*Plat.* weldig: *Dut.* geweldig: *Ger.* gewaltig: *Swed.* waldig] *Powerful;* potens:—Se sie anwaldegost *who is most powerful, Bt.* 36, 5.

Anwalg, anwealg; *adj. Entire, whole, sound;* integer:—*Past.* 52, 2.

Anwann *fought against; p. of* anwinnan.

Anweald, anwald, wald, es; *m.* [*Plat.* waldt *f*: *Dut.* geweld *n*: *Ger.* gewalt *f*: *Swed.* wälde *n.*] *Power, empire, dominion, jurisdiction, rule, government;* potestas:—Anweald or mihte Godes is, *Ps.* 61, 11. Ælc anweald on eorðan, *Mt.* 28, 18. He wæs of Herodes anwealde, *Lk.* 23, 7. On abbades anwalde, *Bd.* 4, 32. On his anwealde, *Gen.* 42, 6.

Anwealda, *A governor,* or *magistrate,* or *ruler,* or *prince,* or *monarch;* gubernator:—Se anwealda hæfð befangene *the governor hath restrained, Bt.* 21.

Anwealg *whole,* v. anwalg.

r Anwealglice; *adv. Wholly, soundly;* integrè:—*Past.* 33, 5.

Anwealgnes, se; *f. Wholeness, soundness, entireness;* integritas, *Som.*

Anweard *present,* v. andweard.

Anweardnes *presence,* v. andweardnes.

Anweg *away,* v. aweg.

Anweorc *a cause,* v. andweorc.

Anwig, es [an *one,* wig *a contest*] *A single combat, a duel;*

certamen singulare:—Hi gefuhton anwig *they fought a duel*, *Ors.* 3, 9: 3, 4, 6.

Anwiglice; *adv. By single combat.* Anwiglice feohtende *fighting in single combat*, *Cot.* 186.

Anwil, anwill; *adj.* [an *one*, will *a will*] *Following one's wish, self-willed, obstinate, stubborn;* pertinax:—*Elf. gl.* 28.

Anwillice; *adv. Obstinately, stubbornly, pertinaciously;* pertinaciter:—Ic to anwillice winne *I too pertinaciously attack*, *Bt.* 20.

Anwilnes, se; *f. Obstinacy, self-will, contumacy;* pertinacia:—*Past.* 32, 1.

Anwinnan; *p.* anwann *To fight against, to attack;* impugnare:—*Ors.* 3, 7.

An-wintre, æ-wintre; *adj.* [an *one, every,* winter *a winter*] *Of one year, one year old, continuing for a year;* hornus, anniculus:—Þat lamb sceal beon an-wintre, *Ex.* 12, 5.

Anwite, es; *n.* [an *one*, wite *a fine*] *A simple* or *single fine, a mulct* or *amercement;* simplex mulcta:—*L. Alf.* 26: *W.* p. 41, 5.

Anwlæta *Envy;* livor:—*Med. ex. quadr.* 7, 3.

Anwlita *a personal appearance*, v. andwlit.

Anwlitegan *to change the form of*, v. unwlitegan.

Anwlow, anwloh: *adj.* [an *without*, wloh *a fringe, ornament*] *Untrimmed, neglected, without a good grace, deformed, ill-favoured;* inornatus, deformis:—Þin rice restende bið anwloh *thy kingdom is remaining neglected*, *Cd.* 203.

Anwod *invaded*, *p.* of anwadan.

Anwreon; *p.* anwroh; *pp.* anwrogen [an *un*, wreon *to cover*] *To uncover, reveal;* revelare:—*R. Ben.* 3.

Anwrigenys, se; *f. A revealing, disclosing, an opening, a sermon, a homily;* explicatio, expositio, *Som.*

Anwunigende *inhabiting*, v. onwunian.

Anxsumnes *anxiety*, v. angsumnes.

Anydan; *p.* de; *pp.* ded, de, anidde [a *from*, nydian *to need, to compel*] 1. *To repel, thrust* or *beat back, keep from, restrain, constrain, force;* repellere. 2. *With* ut *to expel, to drive out;* expellere:—1. Mid unryhte anydde wærum *with injustice had been kept from*, *Chr.* 823. 2. Ic anyde hig ut, *Deut.* 32, 21.

Anywan *to shew, demonstrate*, v. niwian.

A of tide *on a sudden, forthwith;* ex tempore, *Som.*

Apa [*Plat. Dut.* aap *m*: *Frs.* ap: *Swed.* apa *f*: *Icel.* ape: *Wel.* eppa] *An* APE; simia:—*Elf. gl.* 3.

Apæcan *To seduce, mislead;* seducere:—Gif hwa fram him apæce, *L. Edg pæn.* 25.

Apæran *to pervert*, v. forpæran.

Aparod; *part. Apprehended, found, taken;* deprehensus:—Seo wæs aparod, *Jn.* 8, 3.

Apelder-tun *an apple-tree-garden*, v. æpel-treow.

Apel-treo *an apple-tree*, v. æpel-treow.

Apflod; *m.* [ap *up*, flod *a flood*] *An overflowing of the sea;* ledo, *Martyr.* 20, *Mart.*

Apinsian; *p.* de; *pp.* ed, od, ud *To ponder, weigh;* ponderare:—*Past.* 53, 3.

Apl *an apple*, v. æpl.

Aplantode, ed *planted*, v. plantian.

Apostata *Apostacy, revolt;* apostata:—*Lup. Serm.* 1, 19.

Apostol *One sent, an apostle;* apostolus:—Þæra twelf apostola naman, *Mt.* 10, 2.

Apostolic, apostollic; *adj. Apostolical;* apostolicus:—*Bd.* 1, 26.

Appel *an apple*, v. æpl.

Appel-leaf, æppel-leaf *an apple-leaf, violets;* pomi folium, violæ, *Som.*

Appelscreada *apple-parings*, v. æppel-screada.

Appl *an apple*, v. æpl.

Apple-treow *an apple-tree*, v. æpel-treow.

Apple-tun *an orchard*, v. æppeltun.

Aprotaman, aprotane *The herb southernwood, wormwood;* abrotonum [artemisia, *Lin.*], *Som.*

Apulder *An apple-tree*, v. æpeltreow:—Surmelst apulder; *q. souring apple-tree;* pyrus malus, *Lin.*:—Swite apulder *a sweeting apple-tree;* malomellus, *R.* 45.

Apuldre *an apple-tree*, v. æpeltreow.

Apuldre APPLEDORE, *a village, in Kent, near Tenterden, a harbour on the coast of Devon:*—Apuldre comb APPLEDORE COMB *Isle of Wight*, *Mann.*

Apuldur *an apple-tree.*

Apullod *pulled*, v. pullian.

Aquald *killed*, v. cwellan.

Aqueorna *a kind of ointment;* scirra, *Som.*, v. acwern.

Aquilegia *the herb columbine;* aquilegia, aquileia:—*Ors.* 6, 36.

Ar [*Frs.* eren *brazen, made of brass*] ORE, *brass, copper;* æs, v. bræs. Grene ar *green copper, brass;* aurichalcum.

A'r, aar; *pl. g.* ára, árna [*Plat. Frs.* ere *f*: *Dut.* eer *f*: *Ger.* ehre *f*: *Dan.* aere: *Swed.* ära *f*: *Icel.* æra: *Al.* ar, or, ur *beginning*: *Heb.* אור aur *light, splendour*] 1. *Glory, honour, respect, reverence;* gloria. 2. *Kindness, goodness, favour, use, care, benefit, power, wealth, money, riches, property, substance, support, wages;* benignitas, opes, substantia:—1. Ne wolde he ænige are witan *nor would he ascribe any honour*, *Bd.* 2, 20. He sundor lif wæs foreberende eallum þam arum *he a private life was preferring to all honours*, *Bd.* 4, 11: *Sm.* p. 579, 8. Nyton nane are *they know no respect*, *Bt.* 35, 6. 2. Him wæs ara þearf *to him was need of wealth*, *Cd.* 97. Arra biddan *to ask for power*, *Cd.* 131. To godre are *to good use*, *Herb.* 2, 9. Eallum to are ylda bearnum *for the benefit of all the sons of men*, *Jul. A.* 2. (Vid. *Price's Walton*, ci. *note* 34). Be ealre are *by all* [*his*] *wealth*, *Cnut.* 46. Hyra ar is mæst *their property is most*, *Ors.* 1, 1. Hi are forgeafen *they gave wages*, *Bd.* 1, 15.

A'r, es; *m.* [ær *before*, *as Moes.* airu *messenger from*, air *before*] *One going before, a legate, a messenger, an angel;* nuntius:—Lædan ut halige aras *lead out holy messengers*, *Cd.* 112. Þes ar sægeð *this messenger sayeth*, *Cd.* 32, v. ærend.

A'r, [*Dan.* aare: *Swed.* ara *c*: *Icel.* ar] *An* OAR; remus:—Sume hæfdon LX ara *some have 60 oars*, *Chr.* 897.

Ar *before*, v. ær.

Ar in marne, *or* ærist *early in the morning*, v. ær.

Arad *rode*, v. ridan.

Arade; *part. Relieved;* relevatus, *Som.*

Aræcan; *p.* aræcte *To reach out, extend, reach, lay hold of, hold up;* attingere:—Þat man aræcan mihte *that one could reach*, *Chr.* 1014: *Ing.* p. 193, 19. Arecð *or* aræcð *shall hold up*, *Ps.* 145, 6.

Aræd [a *intensive*, ræd *counsel*] *Counsel, welfare, safety;* consilium, salus:—Se aræda *one who consults for safety, a patriot.* Smeagende ymbe heora sawla aræd *considering about their souls' welfare*, *L. Edm. pref.* Se aræda, Romwara heretoga, se wæs hatan Brutus *the patriot, the consul of the Romans, who was called Brutus*, *Bt.* 19, v. ræd.

Arædan, aredan, aredian; *p.* aræd, arod, arædde hi aræd-

are
g. d. ac. ; pl
nom ac ara
g ára, or árna
d. arum
aar f

*Ár, ~~ár f. Honour~~

~~Ælfc Deuts~~

O 1. Apa [12 d]

O [13 a]

O a benefice

g— séo ár is

the benefice is

Eth. [illegible] p. 316, 1

Dolige þære áre

forfeit the benefice

Id. p. 316, 3

O 1

O 2 es; m. Th an

O 1 [wrætt nausea f.]

O 2 airus m [12 e]

O Are, an; f an oar

O 3 [13 b]

O [13 c]

O 2

[3 Apulder-tun ary apple garden, an orchard Som. Ben v. Æppel-tun

2/4 Apuldre tree malus An ~~Apuldre~~

~~[illegible]~~

þeos apuldre

O hæc malus Elfgr Som 6, 31. ~~apel tun~~

'3 * Anwyngenys, se f a revealthy

2 Aracan to relate Th An

O [12 f]

4/5 [* Ar, ær, es; m brass

106. 22

5 Aræd, se arede adj. Full of counsel benefit, patriotic; consilii plenus. Se forem ære 7 se areda Romwara heretogas the illustrious patriotic consul of the Romans [illegible]

dl.

Arædan *

to read, guess

6 Arædan the Ap

6

arædan

91 + ?

Φ 2 -es; m Th. An

Φ 4 Aretan to gladden Th. An

[14d & 8a 3]

Φ [1d] 2 *Arewe, an, ? *? Spl arewe, arwe arwe

Φ 3 es; m Th. An

[4] 5 Arfæst *holy, pious Th. An q æfest

○ 2 Aræfnan is ?
Bd 4, 31 In Ps 610, 27
Φ 3 Aræfnan to endure Th. Apol.

[4] * Ard, that which gives honour

[2] 6 Arfæstlice ~~honestly~~, *piously mercifully Th. An q æfestlice

[3] 7 Arfæstnes *piety Th. An. q ~~æfestlice~~ æfestnes

[2] 4 Aræsan to rush Th. An.

[3] 5 Aran parcere Ben.

Φ

○ Arc
Φ

& carc f
v in alph. order

[2] 5 Arefnan to bear ? 3, 7
Bar ? 104, 20 v arefnan
[3] 6 Areodian to become red Th. Apol

don; *pp.* aræded, aredad [*Plat. Dut.* raden: *Dan.* raade: *Swed.* rada.—a, rædan] 1. *To read, read through, peruse, tell, utter, speak;* perlegere. 2. *To conjecture, guess, divine, prophesy, discover, find out, examine, take counsel, care for, pursue, effect;* conjectare, decernere:—1. Þa se wisdom aræd hæfde *when wisdom had spoken, Bt.* 23. Orationem arædde *delivered an oration, Bd.* 4, 4. 2. And him to cwædon; aræd, *Mk.* 14, 65. Weg aredian *to discover the way, Bt.* 22, 2. Aredian þearfum *to regard, or take care for the poor, Bd.* 3, 9. Ic þæne ræd arædige *I will take that counsel, Mod. Confit.* 6. Ceap aredian *to make a bargain, L. Edg. Wilk.* p. 81, 8. Aredan his willan *to effect,* or *do his will, H. in. verba. Hieremiæ,* v. rædan.

f Arædnis *a condition,* v. arednes.

Aræfnan; *p.* de; *pp.* ed [a, ræfnan *to sustain*] *To bear, take away, suffer, sustain, undergo, bear in mind, to think;* tolerare:—Þe ic ærefne, *Ps.* 24, 5.

Aræfniende, aræfnigende; *part. Bearing in mind, considering;* expendens:— *Hom. in Nat. Dom.*

Aræfniendlic; *adj. Possible, tolerable;* possibilis, *Som.*

Aræman; *p.* de *To raise, lift up, erect, elevate;* excitare, erigere:—Þa ge mihton rædan and eow aræman on þam *which ye may read, and elevate yourselves in them, Elf. T.* p. 31, 15.

Aræran *to rear up,* arærende *lifting up,* aræred *lifted up,* v. ræran.

Arærnes, se; *f. A raising, an exaltation, a restitution;* exaltatio:—*Ors.* 3, 1.

Arafan [a *from,* reaf *clothing*] *To unclothe, let loose, unwind;* dissolvere:—Arafan þat cliwen *to unrove the clew, unwind the ball, Past.* 35, 5.

Arás *arose,* v. arisan.

A'ras *messengers,* v. ar.

Arasian; *p.* ade; *pp.* ad, od; *v. a. To raise, to be laid open, discover, try, raise the hand, take hold of, raise the mind, to suspect;* elevare, explorare:—God hæfð arasod ure unrihtwisnissa, *Gen.* 44, 16.

Arasod beon *to be held,* v. arasian.

Arblæd *the oar-blade;* palmula remi:—*Elf. gl. Som.* p. 77.

Arc, erc, earc, es; *m.* [*Plat. Dut. Al.* ark *f: Swed.* ark *m: Moes.* arka: *Ger.* arche *f: Basq.* arc: *Wel.* arch: *Dan.* ark: *Lat.* arca *a chest*] *A vessel to swim on water, an* ARK, *a coffer, chest, hutch, bag;* arca:—Þa ætstod se arc, *Gen.* 8, 4. Wirc þe nu ænne arc, *Gen.* 6, 14.

b Arcebisceop, arcebiscop, ærcebisceop, ærcebiscop *a bishop of the first class, an archbishop;* archiepiscopus, *Bd.* 1, 27.

Arcebisceop-hád, ærcebisceop-hád *an archbishop-hood, the degree* or *dignity of an archbishop;* archiepiscopi gradus, *vel* dignitas, *Bd.* 4, 6.

Arcediacon, archidiacon, ærcediacon. *An archdeacon, a bishop's vicegerent;* archidiaconus, *R.* 69.

Arcestol [arce *chief,* stol *a stool*] *An archiepiscopal see,* or *seat;* sedes archiepiscopalis, *Som.*

c Arcræftig; *adj.* [ar *respect,* cræftig *crafty*] *Skilful* or *quick in shewing respect, respectful, polite;* morigerus, obsequens:—Arcræftig ar *a respectful messenger, a prophet, Cd.* 202.

Arde [arde *honoured; p. of* arian *to honour*] *That which gives honour, an ensign of office, such as a pall,* or *staff;* honoris signum:—Ælfric arceb ferde to Rome æfter his arde *Archbishop Ælfric went to Rome for his ensign of office, Chr.* 997.

Ardlice, arudlice; *adv.* [arod *quick,* lice] *Quickly, immediately;* prompte:—Efstað nu ardlice, *Jos.* 2, 5.

Are *honour,* v. ar.

Are; *m. A court-yard;* area, *Alb. resp.* 48.

Areafian; *p.* areafode; *pp.* areafod [a *from,* reafian *to tear*] *To tear from, lacerate, divide;* discerpere:—Bring is areafod *the sacrifice is divided, Cd.* 158.

Areaht *explained; part. of* arecan, v. recan.

Arecan, areccan *to explain,* v. recan.

Areccean *to reckon, translate,* v. areccende, recan.

d Areccende *explaining,* v. recan.

Arecð *holdeth up,* v. aræcan.

Ared *counsel,* v. aræd.

Aredad *discovered; pp. of* arædan.

Aredan *to effect, to do,* v. arædan.

Areddan *to liberate,* v. ahreddan.

Aredian *to search out,* v. arædan.

Arednes, arædnes, se; *f. A degree, condition, covenant;* consultum, conditio:—Þære arednesse *on that condition, Bd.* 1, 1.

Aredod *furnished, Som.*

Arefian *to bear,* v. aræfnan.

Areht *erected; part. of* reccan.

Areosian *to fall down, perish;* decidere:—Ic areose *I shall fall down, Ps.* 7, 4.

Aretan, geretan; *p.* aret, geret; *pp.* aret, areted, gereted, aretten, aretne; *v. a.* [a *or* ge, retan *to delight*] *To restore, invigorate, refresh, renew, inspirit, repair, correct, set right;* reficere:—Hi hæfdon þat mod aret *they have restored* or *refreshed the mind, Bt. Tit.* 22, *Card.* p. 8. Þu me hæfst geretne, 22, 1, *Card.* p. 118, 5, and aretne, 41, 2, *Card.* p. 374, 28, *thou hast corrected me.*

e Arewa *An* ARROW; sagitta:—Sume scotedon adunweard mid arewan *some shot downward with arrows, Chr.* 1083.

Arewe [arewa *arrow*] ARROW, the name of a river in several counties, called so either from its *swiftness* or *straightness;* fluvii nomen.

Areweorð *honourable,* v. arwurð.

Arfæst; *adj.* [ar *honour,* fæst *fast*] *Honest, good, virtuous, gracious, merciful;* honestus, clemens:—Wæs he se mon æfæst and ærfæst *he was the religious and honest man, Bd.* 3, 14: *Sm.* p. 539, 33. Þat Drihten him arfæst and milde wære *that the Lord might be to him merciful and mild, Bd.* 4, 31.

Arfæstlice; *adv. Honestly;* honeste, *Som.*

Arfæstnes, arfestnys, se; *f. Honesty, goodness, virtue, clemency;* honestas, pietas:—Þat he wæs mycelre arfæstnesse and æfæstnesse wer *that he was a man of great virtue and piety, Bd.* 4, 31. Heo arfæstnisse cydde, *Jos.* 6, 17.

f Arfæt, arfat, es; *n. A brazen vessel;* æramentum:—Halgode þat arfæt, *Lev.* 8, 11.

Arfest *merciful,* v. arfæst.

Arful; *adj. Respectful, favourable, merciful, mild;* honorabilis:—Sy arfull, *Ps.* 102, 3. Beo arful fæder and meder, *Wulfst. Par.* 7.

Arfullice; *adv. Mildly, gently;* clementer:—Josep hig onceneow arfullice, *Gen.* 43, 27.

Arg; *adj.* [*Plat. Dut. Ger. Franc. Dan. Swed.* arg: *Grk.* ἀργος *idle:* *Norse,* argur *bad*] *Wicked, depraved, bad;* pravus:—Cneorisse yflo and arg *an evil and wicked generation,* v. forliger, earg.

Argentilla, argentille *Camomile;* anthemis chamomilla, *Lin.*:—*Elf. gr.* 15.

Ar-geotere [ar *brass,* geoter *a pourer*] *A caster* or *pourer of brass, a melter of brass;* æramentarius:—*Ors.* 1, 20.

g Ar-geweorc *Brass-work, copper-work;* æramentum:—*Cot.* 79.

Arhlice *disgracefully*, v. earhlice.

Arhwate; *adj.* [ær *before, most*, hwata *keen*] *Most bold, most valiant;* fortissimus:—Oforcomon eorlas arhwate *overcame most valiant earls, Chr.* 938: *Ing.* p. 145, 26.

Arian, gearian; *part.* ende, gende; *p.* ede; *pp.* ed, od; *v. a.* [*Plat. Dut.* eeren: *Ger.* ehren: *Dan.* aere: *Swed.* ara: ar *honour*, ian] 1. *To give honour, to honour, reverence, have in admiration;* honorare, venerari. 2. *To regard, care for, spare, pardon, forgive;* parcere:—1. Is to arianne *is to be honoured, Bt.* 32, 2. Onsægednys lofes areð me, *Ps.* 49, 24. 2. He þearfum arede *he cares for the poor, Bd.* 3, 9. Ac arodon heora life, *Jos.* 9, 21. He arað þa godan *he pardons the good, Bt.* 41, 2. Se Cyning arian wille *the king will pardon, L. In.* 36: *Wilk.* p. 20, 38.

Arianisc; *adj. def.* se Arrianisca ARIAN, *belonging to Arius, an Alexandrian, who lived in the fourth century:*—Se Arrianisca gedweolda aras *the Arian heresy arose, Bd.* 1, 8.

Ariddan *to rid, deliver*, v. ahræddan.

Ariende, arigende *sparing*, v. arian.

h Ariht; *adv.* [*Plat. Ger.* recht: *Dut.* regt: *Dan.* ret: *Swed.* rätt: a, riht *right*] ARIGHT, *right, well, correctly;* probe, recte:—Gif man hit ariht asmeað *if one considereth right, L. Can. Edg.* 13, v. riht.

Ariman *to number*, arimed *numbered*, arimende *numbering*, v. riman.

Aring *Honour, respect;* honoratio:—Buton aringe *without honour, Ors.* 5, 10.

ARISAN; *part.* arisende, he arist; *p.* arás, hi arison; *pp.* arisen; *v. n.* [*Plat.* risen: *Frs.* rieze: *Dut.* ryzen, opryzen: *Ger.* reisen: *Al.* reison: *Moes.* urreisan *or* riesan: *Dan.* reise: *Swed.* resa: *Norse*, risa] *To* ARISE, *rise, rise up, rise again;* surgere:—Ydel is eow arisan, *Ps.* 126, 3. He aras sona, *Gen.* 19, 1. Đa arison þa þri weras, *Gen.* 18, 16. Arisen wæs sunne, *C. Mk.* 4, 6. Đy þriddan dæge arisan, *Mt.* 16, 21.

Ariseð *it behoveth;* oportet, v. gerist.

Arist *a resurrection*, v. æryst.

Ariwe *an arrow*, v. arewa.

i A'rleás; *def.* se árleása; *adj.* [*Plat. Dut.* eerloos: *Ger.* ehrlos: *Dan. Swed.* aerelös: ar *honour*, leas] *Void of good, vile, impious, wicked;* impius:—Wið þam arleassestan eretice *against the most wicked heretic, Bd.* 4, 17. Forweorðað se arleasa *the wicked perisheth, Ps.* 9, 5.

j A'rleáslice; *adv. Wickedly, impiously;* impie:—Ne arleaslice ic dyde fram Gode, *Ps.* 17, 23.

A'rleásnes, se; *f.* [arleas *wicked*] *Wickedness, acts of wickedness, impiety;* iniquitas:—Æfter manigo arleasnyssa heora, *Ps.* 5, 12.

A'rlic; *adj.* [*Plat. Dut.* eerlyk: *Ger.* ehrlich: *Dan.* aerlig: *Swed.* ärlig: ar *honour*, lic] *Honourable, noble, venerable;* honorabilis:—*Bd.* 3, 7: *Ors.* 2, 7.

A'rlice; *adv. Honourably;* honorifice:—He wolde swiðe arlice underfon *he would very honourably receive, Bt.* 16, 2.

Arlice, ærlice; *adv.* [ær *early*, lice] EARLY, *betimes;* mane:—Swiðe arlice *very early, C. R. Mk.* 16, 2.

Arm *an arm*, v. earm.

Arm *miserable*, v. earm.

k Armelu [ær *early*, melu *moly* or *garlic*] *The early garlic, the moly, hermel, the wild rue*, or *garlic;* allium moly, *Lin.*:—*L. M.* 1, 64.

Armorgen *early dawn*, v. ærmergen.

Arna *honour*, v. ar.

Arnaleas *void of honour*, v. arleas.

Arn *ran;* p. *of* yrnan.

Arod *a species of herb;* herbæ genus, arum:—Nim lybcornes leaf, oððe arod *take a leaf of saffron*, or *arod, L. M.* 1, 2, p. 102.

Arod *ready, conjectured, pardoned*, v. arædan, arian.

Aroda *counsel, wisdom*, v. aræd.

Arodlice *quickly*, v. ardlice.

Arodscipe *Dexterity, readiness, aptness, dignity, honour;* dexteritas:—*Past.* 20.

Arra *of favours;* facultatum, *gen. plu. of* ar.

Arrianisc *Arian*, v. Arianisc.

Arsgang [ærs *anus*, gang *a passage*] *Anus;* arsganga, *Latrinæ, Lye.*

l Ar-smið, es; *m.* [ar *brass*, smið *a smith*] *A copper smith, a brazier, a worker in brass;* faber ærarius:—*Col. Mon.*

Arð *thou art*, es, v. eom.

Arþegn, arþeng, es; *m.* [ar *honour*, þegen *a servant*] *A servant* or *minister by his place* or *employment;* servus, minister honorabilis:—Cumena arþegn *the servant of guests, Bd.* 4, 31.

Arudlice *quickly*, v. ardlice.

Arung, e; *f.* 1. *An honouring, a reverence;* honoratio. 2. *A regarding, sparing, pardoning;* remissio, *Som.*

Arweorðe *honourably*, v. arwurðlice.

Arweorðian *to honour*, v. arwurðian.

Arweorðlice *solemnly*, v. arwurðlice.

Arweorðnes, arwyrðnes, se; *f.* arweorðung, arwurðung, e; *f.* [ær *before*, weorðnes *honour*] *Reverence, great honour, dignity, worship;* reverentia:—Bryngað Drihtne arwurðunge *bring to the Lord reverence, Ps.* 28, 2. Gif þu nu gemunan wilt eallra þara arwyrðnessa *if thou now wilt be mindful of all the honours, Bt.* 8: *Card.* p. 36, 18. ¶ Mid arweorðnesse *with honour, honourably.*

Arwiðþe [ar *an oar*, wiðþe *withe*] *An oar-withe, a willow-band to tie oars with;* struppus:—*Ælf. gl. Som.* p. 77.

m Arwunga, arwunge; *adv. Acting favourably, honourably, gratuitously;* gratis:—*R. Mt.* 10, 8.

Arwurð, arwyrð, arwurðlic; *def.* se arwurða, seo het arwurðe [ær *before, highly*, weorð *worthy*, or ar *honour*, wearð *worth, honour-worth, honourable*] *Highly honourable, venerable, worshipful, reverend;* honorabilis, venerandus:—Se arwurða wer *the very venerable man, Bd.* 4, 18: 5, 1. Se goda bið simle arwyrðe *the good is always highly honourable, Bt.* 39, 2. ¶ Arwurðe wuduwe *or* nunne *a nun, R.* 69.

Arwurðian, arweorðian, arwyrðian; *pp.* gearwurðod; *v.* [ar *honour*, weorðan *to be, to be made*] *To give honour, to reverence, celebrate, extol, worship;* honorare:—Onsægednys lofes arwurðað me, *Ps.* 49, 23. Đæt ealle arwurðigeon þone Sunu, swa swa hig arwurðigeað þone Fæder, se þe ne arwurðað þone Sunu, ne arwurðað he þone Fæder, *Jn.* 5, 23. Arwurða þinum Fæder, *Deut.* 5, 16.

Arwurðig *reverend*, v. arwurð.

Arwurðlic *venerable*, v. arwurð.

n Arwurðlice, arweorðe, arwyrðlice; *adv. Honourably, reverently, solemnly, mildly;* honorifice:—Swiðe arwurðlice onfangene wæron *were very honourably received, Bd.* 2, 20. Đa grete hig arwurðlice, *Gen.* 45, 4.

Arwurðung *honour*, v. arweorðnes.

~~X~~ Ar-hwat ~~fortes~~ ar-hwate
fostes Athelst Grein II
550, 78

1 Arewe arrow
~~1 Arewe an arrow~~
~~arrow~~ Th. An

2

O [Pa 3]

2 Arewe Ar arrow,
sagitta Som v ~~arewe~~
arewe, Spl arewe

3 Arwurde venerable, reverend; venerabilis
Th. An.

~~2~~ Arna ~~honoris~~ (for ara) of.
p of ar

O 4

3 Arra power, ~~favour~~
honours Cd. 131. Th p 166;
20. v. ár

4 Ar-staef ~~An~~ honor esm hf ar-stafas
staff, honor Beo ~~31-27~~ K 631 (usually used in the pl. for honour, protection)
Grein II 525, 19

5 Arwurdnys honour
Som v arwurdnes

9 + 6

ϕ 4 aretan to gladden Th. An

ϕ 2 -es; m Th. An

([14d & 8a 3]

ϕ 12 2 * arewe, an; f. q * 3pl arewe, arewe

arewe

ϕ 3 es; m Th. An

15 Arfæst * holy, pious Th. An q æfest

)2 Arefnian is iemd Bd 4, 31 In Lk 610, 27

ϕ3 Areefnian to endure Th. Apol

4 * Ard, that which gives honour

26 Arfæstlice ~~honestly~~, * piously mercifully Th. An q æfestlice

37 Arfæstnes * piety Th. An. q æfestnes

24 Aresan to rush Th. An.

35 Aran parcere Ben

ϕ

O Arc Dearcf v in alph. order

ϕ

25 Arefnan to bear Lrs 3, 7 Bar h 104, 20 v arefnan

36 Areodian to become red Th. Apol

don; *pp.* aræded, aredad [*Plat. Dut.* raden: *Dan.* raade: *Swed.* rada.—a, rædan] 1. *To read, read through, peruse, tell, utter, speak;* perlegere. 2. *To conjecture, guess, divine, prophesy, discover, find out, examine, take counsel, care for, pursue, effect;* conjectare, decernere:—1. Þa se wisdom aræd hæfde *when wisdom had spoken, Bt.* 23. Orationem arædde *delivered an oration, Bd.* 4, 4. 2. And him to cwædon; aræd, *Mk.* 14, 65. Weg aredian *to discover the way, Bt.* 22, 2. Aredian þearfum *to regard,* or *take care for the poor, Bd.* 3, 9. Ic þæne ræd arædige *I will take that counsel, Mod. Confit.* 6. Ceap aredian *to make a bargain, L. Edg. Wilk.* p. 81, 8. Aredan his willan *to effect,* or *do his will, H. in. verba. Hieremiæ,* v. rædan.

a Arædnis *a condition,* v. arednes.

Aræfnan; *p.* de; *pp.* ed [a, ræfnan *to sustain*] *To bear, take away, suffer, sustain, undergo, bear in mind, to think;* tolerare:—Þe ic ærefne, *Ps.* 24, 5.

Aræfniende, aræfnigende; *part. Bearing in mind, considering;* expendens:— *Hom. in Nat. Dom.*

Aræfniendlic; *adj. Possible, tolerable;* possibilis, *Som.*

Aræman; *p.* de *To raise, lift up, erect, elevate;* excitare, erigere:—Þa ge mihton ræddan and eow aræman on þam *which ye may read, and elevate yourselves in them, Elf. T.* p. 31, 15.

Aræran *to rear up,* arærende *lifting up,* arærde *lifted up,* v. ræran.

Arærnes, se; *f. A raising, an exaltation, a restitution;* exaltatio:—*Ors.* 3, 1.

Arafan [a *from,* reaf *clothing*] *To unclothe, let loose, unwind;* dissolvere:—Arafan þat cliwen *to unrove the clew, unwind the ball, Past.* 35, 5.

Arás *arose,* v. arisan.

A'ras *messengers,* v. ar.

Arasian; *p.* ade; *pp.* ad, od; *v. a. To raise, to be laid open, discover, try, raise the hand, take hold of, raise the mind, to suspect;* elevare, explorare:—God hæfð arasod ure unrihtwisnissa, *Gen.* 44, 16.

Arasod beon *to be held,* v. arasian.

Arblæd *the oar-blade;* palmula remi:—*Elf. gl. Som.* p. 77.

Arc, erc, earc, es; *m.* [*Plat. Dut. Al.* ark *f*: *Swed.* ark *m*: *Moes.* arka: *Ger.* arche *f*: *Basq.* arc: *Wel.* arch: *Dan.* ark: *Lat.* arca *a chest*] *A vessel to swim on water, an* ARK, *a coffer, chest, hutch, bag;* arca:—Þa ætstod se arc, *Gen.* 8, 4. Wirc þe nu ænne arc, *Gen.* 6, 14.

b Arcebisceop, arcebiscop, ærcebisceop, ærcebiscop *a bishop of the first class, an archbishop;* archiepiscopus, *Bd.* 1, 27.

Arcebisceop-hád, ærcebisceophád *an archbishop-hood, the degree* or *dignity of an archbishop;* archiepiscopi gradus, *vel* dignitas, *Bd.* 4, 6.

Arcediacon, archidiacon, ærcediacon. *An archdeacon, a bishop's vicegerent;* archidiaconus, *R.* 69.

Arcestol [arce *chief,* stol *a stool*] *An archiepiscopal see,* or *seat;* sedes archiepiscopalis, *Som.*

c Arcræftig; *adj.* [ar *respect,* cræftig *crafty*] *Skilful* or *quick in shewing respect, respectful, polite;* morigerus, obsequens:—Arcræftig ar *a respectful messenger, a prophet, Cd.* 202.

Arde [arde *honoured; p. of* arian *to honour*] *That which gives honour, an ensign of office, such as a pall,* or *staff;* honoris signum:—Ælfric arceb ferde to Rome æfter his arde *Archbishop Ælfric went to Rome for his ensign of office, Chr.* 997.

Ardlice, arudlice; *adv.* [arod *quick,* lice] *Quickly, immediately;* prompte:— Efstað nu ardlice, *Jos.* 2, 5.

Are *honour,* v. ar.

Are; *m. A court-yard;* area, *Alb. resp.* 48.

Areafian; *p.* areafode; *pp.* areafod [a *from,* reafian *to tear*] *To tear from, lacerate, divide;* discerpere:—Bring is areafod *the sacrifice is divided, Cd.* 158.

Areaht *explained; part. of* arecan, v. recan.

Arecan, areccan *to explain,* v. recan.

Areccean *to reckon, translate,* v. areccende, recan.

d Areccende *explaining,* v. recan.

Areð *holdeth up,* v. aræcan.

Ared *counsel,* v. aræd.

Aredad *discovered; pp. of* arædan.

Aredan *to effect, to do,* v. arædan.

Areddan *to liberate,* v. ahreddan.

Aredian *to search out,* v. arædan.

Arednes, arædnes, se; *f. A degree, condition, covenant;* consultum, conditio:—Þære arednesse *on that condition, Bd.* 1, 1.

Aredod *furnished, Som.*

Arefian *to bear,* v. aræfnan.

Areht *erected; part. of* recan.

Areosian *to fall down, perish;* decidere:—Ic areose *I shall fall down, Ps.* 7, 4.

Aretan, geretan; *p.* aret, geret; *pp.* aret, areted, gereted, aretten, aretne; *v. a.* [a *or* ge, retan *to delight*] *To restore, invigorate, refresh, renew, inspirit, repair, correct, set right;* reficere:—Hi hæfdon þat mod aret *they have restored* or *refreshed the mind, Bt. Tit.* 22, *Card.* p. 8. Þu me hæfst geretne, 22, 1, *Card.* p. 118, 5, and aretne, 41, 2, *Card.* p. 374, 28, *thou hast corrected me.*

e Arewa *An* ARROW; sagitta:—Sume scotedon adunweard mid arewan *some shot downward with arrows, Chr.* 1083.

Arewe [arewa *arrow*] ARROW, the name of a river in several counties, called so either from its *swiftness* or *straightness;* fluvii nomen.

Areweorð *honourable,* v. arwurð.

Arfæst; *adj.* [ar *honour,* fæst *fast*] *Honest, good, virtuous, gracious, merciful;* honestus, clemens:—Wæs he se mon æfæst and ærfæst *he was the religious and honest man, Bd.* 3, 14: *Sm.* p. 539, 33. Þat Drihten him arfæst and milde wære *that the Lord might be to him merciful and mild, Bd.* 4, 31.

Arfæstlice; *adv. Honestly;* honeste, *Som.*

Arfæstnes, arfestnys, se; *f. Honesty, goodness, virtue, clemency;* honestas, pietas:—Þat he wæs mycelre arfæstnesse and æfæstnesse wer *that he was a man of great virtue and piety, Bd.* 4, 31. Heo arfæstnisse cydde, *Jos.* 6, 17.

f Arfæt, arfat, es; *n. A brazen vessel;* æramentum:—Halgode þat arfæt, *Lev.* 8, 11.

Arfest *merciful,* v. arfæst.

Arful; *adj. Respectful, favourable, merciful, mild;* honorabilis:—Sy arfull, *Ps.* 102, 3. Beo arful fæder and meder, *Wulfst. Par.* 7.

Arfullice; *adv. Mildly, gently;* clementer:—Josep hig oncneow arfullice, *Gen.* 43, 27.

Arg; *adj.* [*Plat. Dut. Ger. Franc. Dan. Swed.* arg: *Grk.* ἄργος *idle*: *Norse,* argur *bad*] *Wicked, depraved, bad;* pravus:—Cneorisse yflo and arg *an evil and wicked generation,* v. forliger, earg.

Argentilla, argentille *Camomile;* anthemis chamomilla, *Lin.*:—*Elf. gr.* 15.

Ar-geotere [ar *brass,* geoter *a pourer*] *A caster* or *pourer of brass, a melter of brass;* æramentarius:—*Ors.* 1, 20.

g Ar-geweorc *Brass-work, copper-work;* æramentum:—*Cot.* 79.

Arhlice *disgracefully*, v. earhlice.

Arhwate; *adj.* [ær *before, most*, hwata *keen*] *Most bold, most valiant;* fortissimus:—Oforcomon eorlas arhwate *overcame most valiant earls, Chr.* 938: *Ing.* p. 145, 26.

Arian, gearian; *part.* ende, gende; *p.* ede; *pp.* ed, od; *v. a.* [*Plat. Dut.* eeren: *Ger.* ehren: *Dan.* aere: *Swed.* ara: ar *honour*, ian] 1. *To give honour, to honour, reverence, have in admiration;* honorare, venerari. 2. *To regard, care for, spare, pardon, forgive;* parcere:—1. Is to arianne *is to be honoured, Bt.* 32, 2. Onsægednys lofes areð me, *Ps.* 49, 24. 2. He þearfum arede *he cares for the poor, Bd.* 3, 9. Ac arodon heora life, *Jos.* 9, 21. He arað þa godan *he pardons the good, Bt.* 41, 2. Se Cyning arian wille *the king will pardon, L. In.* 36: *Wilk.* p. 20, 38.

Arianisc; *adj. def.* se Arrianisca Arian, *belonging to Arius, an Alexandrian, who lived in the fourth century*:—Se Arrianisca gedweolda aras *the Arian heresy arose, Bd.* 1, 8.

Ariddan *to rid, deliver*, v. ahrædden.

Ariende, arigende *sparing*, v. arian.

Ariht; *adv.* [*Plat. Ger.* recht: *Dut.* regt: *Dan.* ret: *Swed.* rätt: a, riht *right*] Aright, *right, well, correctly;* probe, recte:—Gif man hit ariht asmeað *if one considereth right, L. Can. Edg.* 13, v. riht.

Ariman *to number*, arimed *numbered*, arimende *numbering*, v. riman.

Aring *Honour, respect;* honoratio:—Buton aringe *without honour, Ors.* 5, 10.

Arisan; *part.* arisende, he arist; *p.* arás, hi arison; *pp.* arisen; *v. n.* [*Plat.* risen: *Frs.* rieze: *Dut.* ryzen, opryzen: *Ger.* reisen: *Al.* reison: *Moes.* urreisan *or* riesan: *Dan.* reise: *Swed.* resa: *Norse*, risa] *To* arise, *rise, rise up, rise again;* surgere:—Ydel is eow arisan, *Ps.* 126, 3. He aras sona, *Gen.* 19, 1. Þa arison þa þri weras, *Gen.* 18, 16. Arisen wæs sunne, *C. Mk.* 4, 6. Þy þriddan dæge arisan, *Mt.* 16, 21.

Triseð *it behoveth;* oportet, v. gerist.

Arist *a resurrection*, v. æryst.

Ariwe *an arrow*, v. arewa.

A'rleás; *def.* se árleása; *adj.* [*Plat. Dut.* eerloos: *Ger.* ehrlos: *Dan. Swed.* aerelös: ar honour, leas] *Void of good, vile, impious, wicked;* impius:—Wið þam arleassestan eretice *against the most wicked heretic, Bd.* 4, 17. Forweorðað se arleasa *the wicked perisheth, Ps.* 9, 5.

A'rleáslice; *adv. Wickedly, impiously;* impie:—Ne arleaslice ic dyde fram Gode, *Ps.* 17, 23.

A'rleásnes, se; *f.* [arleas *wicked*] *Wickedness, acts of wickedness, impiety;* iniquitas:—Æfter manigo arleasnyssa heora, *Ps.* 5, 12.

A'rlic; *adj.* [*Plat. Dut.* eerlyk: *Ger.* ehrlich: *Dan.* aerlig: *Swed.* ärlig: ar *honour*, lic] *Honourable, noble, venerable;* honorabilis:—*Bd.* 3, 7: *Ors.* 2, 7.

A'rlice; *adv. Honourably;* honorifice:—He wolde swiðe arlice underfon *he would very honourably receive, Bt.* 16, 2.

Arlice, ærlice; *adv.* [ær *early*, lice] Early, *betimes;* mane:—Swiðe arlice *very early, C. R. Mk.* 16, 2.

Arm *an arm*, v. earm.

Arm *miserable*, v. earm.

Armelu [ær *early*, melu *moly* or *garlic*] *The early garlic, the moly, hermel, the wild rue*, or *garlic;* allium moly, *Lin.*:—*L. M.* 1, 64.

Armorgen *early dawn*, v. ærmergen.

Arna *honour*, v. ar.

Arnaleas *void of honour*, v. arleas.

Arn *ran;* p. *of* yrnan.

Arod *a species of herb;* herbæ genus, arum:—Nim lybcornes leaf, oððe arod *take a leaf of saffron, or arod, L. M.* 1, 2, p. 102.

Arod *ready, conjectured, pardoned*, v. arædan, arian.

Aroda *counsel, wisdom*, v. aræd.

Arodlice *quickly*, v. ardlice.

Arodscipe *Dexterity, readiness, aptness, dignity, honour;* dexteritas:—*Past.* 20.

Arra *of favours;* facultatum, *gen. plu. of* ar.

Arrianisc *Arian*, v. Arianisc.

Arsgang [ærs *anus*, gang *a passage*] *Anus;* arsganga, *Latrinæ, Lye.*

Ar-smið, es; *m.* [ar *brass*, smið *a smith*] *A copper smith, a brazier, a worker in brass;* faber ærarius:—*Col. Mon.*

Arð *thou art*, es, v. eom.

Arþegn, arþeng, es; *m.* [ar *honour*, þegen *a servant*] *A servant* or *minister by his place* or *employment;* servus, minister honorabilis:—Cumena arþegn *the servant of guests, Bd.* 4, 31.

Arudlice *quickly*, v. ardlice.

Arung, e; *f.* 1. *An honouring, a reverence;* honoratio. 2. *A regarding, sparing, pardoning;* remissio, *Som.*

Arweorðe *honourably*, v. arwurðlice.

Arweorðian *to honour*, v. arwurðian.

Arweorðlice *solemnly*, v. arwurðlice.

Arweorðnes, arwyrðnes, se; *f.* arweorðung, arwurðung, e; *f.* [ær *before*, weorðnes *honour*] *Reverence, great honour, dignity, worship;* reverentia:—Bryngað Drihtne arwurðunge *bring to the Lord reverence, Ps.* 28, 2. Gif þu nu gemunan wilt eallra þara arwyrðnessa *if thou now wilt be mindful of all the honours, Bt.* 8: *Card.* p. 36, 18. ¶ Mid arweorðnesse *with honour, honourably.*

Arwiðþe [ar *an oar*, wiðþe *withe*] *An oar-withe, a willow-band to tie oars with;* struppus:—*Elf. gl. Som.* p. 77.

Arwunga, arwunge; *adv. Acting favourably, honourably, gratuitously;* gratis:—*R. Mt.* 10, 8.

Arwurð, arwyrð, arwurðlic; *def.* se arwurða, seo het arwurðe [ær *before, highly*, weorð *worthy*, or ar *honour*, wearð *worth, honour-worth, honourable*] *Highly honourable, venerable, worshipful, reverend;* honorabilis, venerandus:—Se arwurða wer *the very venerable man, Bd.* 4, 18: 5, 1. Se goda bið simle arwyrðe *the good is always highly honourable, Bt.* 39, 2. ¶ Arwurðe wuduwe *or* nunne *a nun, R.* 69.

Arwurðian, arweorðian, arwyrðian; *pp.* gearwurðod; *v.* [ar *honour*, weorðan *to be, to be made*] *To give honour, to reverence, celebrate, extol, worship;* honorare:—Onsægednys lofes arwurðað me, *Ps.* 49, 23. Þæt ealle arwurðigeon þone Sunu, swa swa hig arwurðigeað þone Fæder, se þe ne arwurðað þone Sunu, ne arwurðað he þone Fæder, *Jn.* 5, 23. Arwurða þinum Fæder, *Deut.* 5, 16.

Arwurðig *reverend*, v. arwurð.

Arwurðlic *venerable*, v. arwurð.

Arwurðlice, arweorðe, arwyrðlice; *adv. Honourably, reverently, solemnly, mildly;* honorifice:—Swiðe arwurðlice onfangene wæron *were very honourably received, Bd.* 2, 20. Þa grete hig arwurðlice, *Gen.* 45, 4.

Arwurðung *honour*, v. arweorðnes.

ar. hwæte
~~fold~~
✗*Ar. hwæt ~~fortis~~
fortis Æthelst. Grein II
550, 18

1 Arewe arrow
~~1 Arewe an arrow~~
~~arrow~~ th. Au

Φ 2

O [8a 3]

2 Arwe An arrow, sagitta Som v ~~arewe~~ arwe, Skl arewe

Φ 3 Arwurde venerable, reverend; venerably th. Au.

~~Arna~~ (for ara) of honours 7. pl. of ar

O 4

Φ 3 Arra power, ~~favour~~ honours Cd 131. Th p 166; 20. v. ár

4* Ar-stæf An honor staff, honor Beo ~~31, 27~~ K 631 (generally used in the pl. for honours, protection) es m pl. ar-stafas Grein II 525, 19

5 Arwurdnes honour Som v arweordnes

Φ 1

2 ~~Ascrafan~~ Ascrēpan; p ascræp To scrape Th. An

2 Asændan to send th apol v sendan

2 3. Asara The herb foalsfoot asarum Som

3 4 * Ascæfen shaven

5 Ascan to ask Ben ~~acsian~~ v ascian

1 * Asciregendlic dis-junctively Lye II 689, 22 v ascyrigendlic

2 * Ascreadian to prune to lop Th. An

3 Asc v alse in MS. p19

Arwyrð *venerable*, v. arwurð.
Arwyrðian *to reverence*, v. arwurðian.
Arwyrðlice *reverently*, v. arwurðlice.
Arwyrðnes *dignity*, v. arweorðnes.
Arydid *robbed; pp. of* ahræddan.
Arynd-raca *an ambassador*, v. ærend-raca.
Aryst *resurrection*, v. æryst.
Arytrid *robbed*, v. arydid.
As *brass*, v. ar.
Asæd *said out, finished*, v. asægan.
Asæcga *to offer sacrifice*; immolare:—*C. Mk.* 14, 12, *Lye.*
Asægan; *p.* asæde, asægde; *pp.* asæd, asægd [a *out*, sægan *or* secgan *to say*] *To speak out, relate, tell, finish speaking, conclude, end;* perloqui, eloqui:—Gif heo asæd bið *if it [she] be told, related, Bd.* 4, 22. Se wisdom þa þis spell asæd hæfde *when wisdom had ended this discourse, Bt.* 34, 8: 35, 1.
o Asægdnis, se; *f. A mystery, sacrifice;* mysterium:—*C. Lk.* 8, 10: *C. R. Lk.* 11, 24, v. ansegednes.
Asæled; *part.* [a, sæled *from*, sælan *to bind*] *Bound;* astrictus:—*Cd.* 100: 166.
Asah *set; p. of* sigan.
Asal, asald *an ass*, v. assa.
Asawan *to sow*, asawen *sowed*, v. sawan.
Asca *dust*, v. axe.
Ascacan *to brandish*, ascaden *separated*, v. asceacan.
Ascadian *to separate*, v. asceadan.
Ascæfen *shaven*, v. sceafan.
Ascære; *adj.* [a, scear *shears*] *Without tonsure, untrimmed;* incultus:—*Peccat. Med.* 8, *Lye.*
Ascamian *to be ashamed*, v. scamian.
Asce *ashes*, v. axe.
Asceacan, ascacan; *p.* asceoc; *pp.* asceacen, asceacyn; *v. a.* 1. *To shake off, remove;* excutere. 2. *To forsake, desert, revolt, flee;* deserere. 3. *To shake, brandish;* vibrare:—1. Asceacað þat dust of eowrum fotum, *Mr.* 6, 11. 2. He asceacen wæs fram Æþelrede *he had deserted from Æthelred, Chr.* 1001: *Ing.* p. 174, 16. 3. Ascæcð sweord his, *Ps.* 7, 13.
p Asceadan, ascadian; *p.* asceod; *pp.* asceaden, ascaden, asced; *v. a.* [a *from*, sceadan *to divide*] *To separate, disjoin, exclude;* separare:—And hine from nytenum asced *and separated him from beasts, L. Eccles. Wilk.* p. 184, 52. Hi of ciricean gemanan ascadene sien *they from the church communion shall be excluded, L. With. Wilk.* p. 10, 36.
Asceaf *expelled; p. of* ascufan.
Ascealian, ascilian; *p.* de; *pp.* ed, od, ascyled; *v.* [a *from*, sceal· *a scale*] *To pull off the scales or shells, to scale, shell, expound, declare;* decorticare:—*Cot.* 79, *Lye.*
Ascearpan *to sharpen*, v. ascyrpan.
Asced, ascede *separated*, v. asceadan.
Ascendan *to send;* v. asendan.
Asceofen *expelled*, v. ascufan.
Asceonendlic *detestable*, v. ascuniendlic.
q Asceonia *to detest, avoid;* detestari:—*R. Ben.* 2, *Lye.*
Asceonung *detestation*, v. ascunung.
Asceop *gave*, v. sceapian.
Asceortian, ascortian; *p.* de; *pp.* ed. *To be short, to grow short, shorten, elapse, diminish, fail;* breviare, effluere:—Ten þusend geara ascortað *ten thousand years will elapse, Bt.* 18, 3. Þat wæter asceortode, *Gen.* 21, 15.
Asceotan; *p.* asceat, hi ascuton; *pp.* ascoten [a, sceotan *to shoot*] *To shoot, shoot through, break through, fall;* cum impetu erumpere:—*Ors.* 6, 36.
Ascerpan, ascirpan; *p.* de; *pp.* ed. *To sharpen, clear from, save from;* exacuere:—Wracu ascirped *cleared* or *saved from destruction, Bt.* 20.
Ascian *to ask*, v. acsian.
Ascilian *to shell*, v. ascealian.
Ascimod *shining, Herb.* 2, 31, v. sciman *to glisten, Som.*
Ascinan *To shine forth, to be clear, evident;* clarescere:—Cuðlicor ascineð *will be more truly evident; Bd.* 5, 1.
Asciran, ascyrian; *p.* ede; *pp.* ed, ud; *v. a.* [*Plat. Dut.* afscheuren: a *from*, sciran *to sheer*] *To cut from, to separate, divide, part, sever, excommunicate;* resecare, separare:—He ascirede Adames bearn *he separated Adam's sons, Deut.* 32, 8. Ascyrud beon fram mannum, *Somn.* 280.
r Ascirped *cleared*, v. ascerpan.
Ascofen *banished*, v. ascufan.
Ascop *gave*, v. sceapian.
Ascortian *to shorten*, v. asceortian.
Ascræp *scraped*, v. ascreopan.
Ascrencan; *pp.* ascrenct, ascruncen [a, screncan *to supplant*] *To supplant, press, stamp, squeeze, pull, shrink;* supplantare:—*Past.* 48, 9: 53, 5: *Cot.* 71.
Ascreopan; *p.* ascræp; *pp.* ed [a *from*, screopan *to scrape*] *To scrape off, scrape;* scalpere:—Job ascræp þone wyrms of his lice, *Job.* p. 166, 33.
Ascrepan, ascrypan; *p.* de; *pp.* en. *To bear, carry, cast or vomit out;* egerere:—*Cot.* 71.
Ascruncen *pressed*, v. ascrencan.
Ascrutnian [a, scrudnian *to scrutiny*] *To search out, scrutinize, trace out;* scrutari, *Som.*
Ascrypan *to cast out*, v. ascrepan.
Ascþrotu *fennel-giant*, v. æscþrote.
s Ascufan; *p.* asceaf; *pp.* ascufen, -ofen, -eofen, -eafen [a *from*, scufan *to shove*] *To drive away, expel, banish, repel, shove away;* expellere:—*V. Ps.* 77, 66.
Ascunan; *v. a. To convict, accuse;* arguere:—Hwylc eower ascunað me for sinne, *Jn.* 8, 46.
Ascung *a question*, v. acsung.
Ascunian; *p.* de; *pp.* ed, od; *v. a.* [a *away*, scunian *to shun*] 1. *To avoid, shun, fly from;* evitare. 2. *To hate, detest;* detestari:—1. Mot he ascunian *must he avoid, L. Cnut.* 7. 2. Esau ascunode Jacob, *Gen.* 27, 41. Þa ascunodon hig hine, *Gen.* 37, 4.
Ascuniendlic, asceonendlic; *adj. Detestable, abominable;* detestabilis:—Beforan Gode ys ascuniendlic, *Lk.* 16, 15.
Ascunung, asceonung *An execration, abomination, a detestation;* execratio:—Ge geseoð þære toworpennysse ascunungge, *Mk.* 13, 14.
Ascuton *fell down*, v. asceotan.
Ascyled, od *taken out of the shell, shelled, declared*, v. ascealian.
t Ascyndan [a *from*, scyndan *to meet*] *To separate, remove, take away, lengthen;* tollere:—Þu ascyndest fram me freond, *Ps.* 87, 19.
Ascypan *to sharpen*, v. ascyrpan.
Ascyrian *to separate*, v. asciran.
Ascyrigendlic; *adj.* [ascirigende *disjoining, from* asciran] *Disjoining, disjunctive;* disjunctivus:—*Elf. gr.* 44.
Ascyrigendlice; *adv. Disjunctively, severally;* disjunctive:—*Elf. gr.* 44.
Ascyrpan; *p.* hi ascyrpton; *pp.* gescyrped *To sharpen;* exacuere:—Hi ascyrpton swa swa sweord tungan heora, *Ps.* 63, 3. Hi ascirpan *they sharpen, Bt.* 34, 8.
Ase *as.*
Asealcan; *pp.* asolcen *To depress, languish, to be weak;* languescere:—*Cd.* 99, v. asolcen, solcen.

x Asearian *To become dry, to sear, dry up;* arescere, *Som.*

Asecan; *p.* asohte; *pp.* asoht [a *from,* secan *to seek*] *To search, seek out, enquire;* requirere:—*Bd.* 1, 27.

Asecgan; *v.* [a *out,* secgan *to say*] *To speak out, declare, express, tell, publish, explain;* edicere:—Heofonas asecgað wuldor Godes, *Ps.* 18, 1.

Asecgendlic; *adj. That which may be spoken, expressible;* effabilis, *Som.*

Asend, asende *sent, emitted, thrown out,* v. sendan.

Aseowe *sowed,* aseowen *sowed,* v. sawan.

Aset *placed,* v. settan.

y Asetan *To appoint, design;* destinare:—*R. Conc. pref.*

Aseted, asett, asette, *set, placed, stored, built,* v. settan.

Aseðan *to boil,* v. seoðan.

Aseþian *to affirm,* v. seþan.

Asian *To put out, eject, sile;* expuere:—*R. Mt.* 23, 24.

Asicyd, gesiced; *part.* [a *from,* sucian *to suck*] *Taken from suck, weaned;* ablactatus:—Swa asicyd ofer moder, *Ps.* 130, 4.

Asigen *fallen; pp. of* sigan.

z Asindrod *sundered, separated, severed,* v. gesundrian.

Aslacian; *p.* aslacude, aslæcte; *pp.* aslacad, aslæcud *To slacken, loosen, untie, remit, dissolve, enervate;* laxare:—*Cot.* 103, v. slacian.

Aslacigendlic; *adj. Slack, remiss;* remissivus:—*Ælf. gr.* 38, *Lye.*

Aslacigendlice; *adv. Slackly, remissly;* remissè:—*Ælf. gr.* 38, *Som.*

Aslad *slipped away,* v. aslidan.

Aslæcte *loosed,* v. aslacian.

Aslæcud *sent off,* v. aslacian.

Aslægen, aslagen *struck, fixed,* v. slean.

a Aslapen; *adj. Sleepy, drowsy;* somnolentus, *Som.*

Aslawian *To be heavy, dull, sluggish;* torpescere:—*Ors.* 4, 13.

Aslean *to strike,* v. slean.

Aslegen *slain,* v. slean.

Aslídan, slidan; *p.* aslád; *pp.* asliden *To slide,* or *slip away, dash against;* labi, elidere:—Asliden beon, *Scint.* 13, 24, 78. Aslad, gefioll, wagað *slid, moved, waggle, Cot.* 120, *Lye.*

Aslitan, aslytan; *p.* aslat; *pp.* aslyten, asliten; *v. a.* [a *from,* slitan *to slit*] *To cleave, rive, destroy, fail, cut off;* discindere, diruere:—Aslat þa tunas ealle *destroyed all the villages, Bd.* 3, 16. Mildheortnysse his aslyteð of cneorysse on cynrine, *Ps.* 76, 8.

Aslogen, asloh *struck, fixed,* v. slean.

b Aslupan *To slip away;* labi:—*Cd.* 134.

Aslyteð *shall fail,* v. aslitan.

Asmeagende *enquiring; part. of* asmean.

Asmean; *p.* asmeade; *pp.* asmead; *v. a.* 1. *To search, enquire, elicit;* investigare. 2. *To contemplate, consider, ruminate, ponder, bethink, think;* ruminare, sentire:—1. Stige mine þu asmeadest, *Ps.* 138, 2. 2. Gif man hit ariht asmeað *if one rightly considers it, L. Can. Edg.* 13, v. smean.

Asmiðod *worked,* v. gesmiðed.

Asmoran, smoran; *p.* de; *pp.* ed, od; *v. a.* [*Plat. Dut.* smooren: *Ger.* schmoren: a *intensive,* smoran *to suffocate*] *To strangle, stifle, smother;* suffocare:—Þat ge forberen þicgan asmorod *that ye forbear to eat what is strangled, L. Alf.* 49: *W.* 33, 25. Hi hine on his bed asmoredon *they smothered him on his bed, Som.*

c Asnasan, asnæsan; *p.* he asnæst; *v. a. To hit,* or *strike against, to rush, pull out;* impingere:—Gif hine mon on asnæseð *if any one strike against him, L. Alf.* 32: *Wilk.* p. 42, 15. Gif foran eagum asnæse, *Id.* p. 42, 16.

Asnydan *to cut off,* v. snidan.

Asoden *sodden, boiled, melted,* v. seoðan.

Asoht *sought out, searched,* v. asecan.

Asolcen, aswolcen; *part. Idle, lazy, dissolute, slow, slothful;* remissus, ignavus:—*Scint.* 16.

Asolcennys, se; *f. Idleness, slothfulness, laziness;* ignavia:—*Scint.* 24.

Aspætan, þu aspeast, aspeost; *v. To spit out;* expuere:—*R. C. Jn.* 9, 6.

d Aspanan; *p.* aspón, aspeón; *pp.* aspanen *To allure, entice, Lye,* v. spanan.

Aspaw *vomited out; p. of* aspiwan.

Aspelian; *part.* aspeliende *To supply another's room, to be deputy* or *proxy;* vicario munere fungi:—*Jud. civ. Lund.* p. 71.

Aspendan, spendan; *p.* de; *pp.* ed [*Plat.* spenden: *Dan.* spendere: *Swed.* spendera] *To spend, lay out, bestow, employ;* expendere:—Aspendan þearfum *to spend on the poor, R. Ben. interl.* 58. Ic aspende yfele, *Ælf. gr.* 47.

Aspeon *invited, secretly enticed,* v. aspanan.

Aspirian *to enquire,* v. aspyrian.

Aspiwan; *p.* aspaw, aspau *To spew, vomit, eject;* evomere:—*Cot.* 78, *Lye,* v. spiwan.

Aspon *allured,* v. aspanan.

Asprettan *to sprout out,* v. asprytan.

Asprian, sprian; *v. a.* [*Dut.* spreyen: *Ger.* spreiten: *Swed.* sprida] *To display, lay before, shew;* prætendere:—Aspriað mildheortnysse þine, *Ps.* 35, 11.

Asprincan *to arise,* v. aspringan.

Asprindlad; *part. Extended,* or *stretched out with little rods* or *twigs;* virgulis extensus:—*L. M.* 2, 24.

Aspring *a fountain,* v. spring.

Aspringan; *p.* he, asprang, asprong, hi asprungon; *pp.* aspruncen; asprungen. 1. *To spring up, to arise, originate, break forth;* surgere, prorumpere. 2. *To spring out, escape, lack, fail;* deficere, imminuere:—1. Aspruncen is leoht, *Ps.* 111, 4. Apryngð rihtwisnys, *Ps.* 71, 7. Þa asprungon ealle wylspringas, *Gen.* 7, 11. 2. Þon aspringað miht min, *Ps.* 70, 10. Asprang gast min, *Ps.* 76, 3.

Aspruncen *arisen,* v. aspringan.

e Asprungennes, se; *f. An eclipse, a deficiency, want, misery;* eclipsis, defectio:—Sunnan *or* monan asprungennes *an eclipse of the sun or moon, Som.* Asprungynes nam me, *Ps.* 118, 53.

Asprytan; *pp.* yted, ytten *To sprout out,* v. sprytan.

Aspyligan; *v.* [*Plat.* afspölen: *Dut.* afspoelen: *Ger.* abspülen] *To cleanse, wash, purify;* abluere:—Swin nyllað aspyligan on hluttrum wæterum *swine will not wash in pure waters, Bt.* 37, 4.

d Aspyrgeng *A curious invention;* inventio:—*Cot.* 186.

Aspyrian; *v. To seek, search, explore, trace, discover, explain;* investigare:— *L. Ethel.* 2: *Wilk.* p. 63, 3, *Lye.*

Assa; *gen.* an; eosol, es [*Plat. Ger.* esel: *Al.* esel, esil: *Dut.* ezel: *Moes.* asil: *Dan.* aesel: *Swed.* äsna. *Icel.* esne: *Wel.* asen: *Lat.* asinus] *An* Ass; asinus:—Wilde assa *a wild ass.* Anbidiað eow her mid þam assum, *Gen.* 22, 5. Gif þu gemete þines feondes assan, *Ex.* 22, 4. Uppan assan folan sittende, *Jn.* 12, 15. And xx ass myrena *and* 20 *of mare asses or she asses, Gen.* 32, 15.

Assald *an ass,* v. assa.

Assandun *Ashdown,* v. Æscesdun.

e Assedun; *adj.* [axe, *or* asce *ashes,* dun *dun or grey colour*] Ashdun *of a dun* or *dark colour;* dosinus, cinereus:—*R.* 79, *Lye.*

1 Asead boiled, p of aseodan, seodan

6 Aslydan to slide slip, err Th. An

27 Asmeagan, to contemplate, investigate, imagine. Th An

2 Asendan to send Th. An

38 Asmeagung, e;f Meditation investigation Th. Apol v smeagung

3 Aseodan p. asead; pp asoden to boil, scorch, perh vex Th. An v seodan

9 Asmoran - l.9 his bedde

Asettan to set, place propose Ors 6, 15 pt. settan

1 Asprungen escaped dispaired Cd 5. Th p 6, 4 pp of aspringan

5 Asingan to sing Bt 39,4 Card p 334, 9 singan

10 Asogen sucked Cot 193 asucyd pp. v sugan, sucdn

2

Aslawian dl. *

6 Aslapian; p ede to be asleep; torpere Ors 4, 13 Bart 176, 16

Aspanan; p. aspeon (aspon) pp aspannen to entice Rask 229 Th. An

3 Assa, an asinus Ass v Spl Bidad assan Ps Th. 103, 11

7 Aslepen may slip Bt. F. 154, 18 v aslupan

5 Aspendan [15e]

4 Assa, an f. A she ass Th. An asina

12

[15d]

Ø 1. to go, proceed, step, mount Th. An

2 Astigie go, for astige v astigan

2 3 Astigend, es; m Ainder m ascendor; ascensor Ex. 15, ~~at end of Hepta p 29~~ Thw. ~~Hep~~ p 29

O 1 Astellan [16a]

O 1

Ø 2* Aswærnung; e f. modesty v scamu

Aswanian dl. *

3 Aswamad abateth Cd. 19 Th p 24. 12

Ø 4

O 5 [16e]

O 3 Aswefd for aswefed to appeased v aswefian

2 Aswican* to decrease, cease Th. An v swican

Cd 137 Th. 173. 20

Assirige *Assyria, Ors.* 2, 5.
Ass-myra *a she-ass,* v. assa.
Ast *A kiln;* siccatorium :—*R.* 109, v. cyln.
Astælan [a *out,* stælan *to steal*] *To steal out, to creep on, to seduce;* obrepere :—Ϸat me næfre deofol on astælan ne mæge *that the devil may never secretly creep on me* [*seduce me*], *L. Can. Edg. Confes.* 9: *Wilk.* p. 88, 49.
Astæned; *part. Set with precious stones;* gemmatus :—Astæned gyrdel *a girdle set with stones, Cot.* 201, *Lye,* v. agimmed.
Astærfed; *part. Starved out, dried up, withered,* or *killed as a plant or shrub;* exsiccatus :—*R. Mt.* 15, 13.
Astah, astahg *ascended,* v. astigan.
f Astandan; *p.* he astod, we astodon *To stand out, remain long, endure, last, continue, rise up;* durare: — Hig astodon *they urged, Lk.* 23, 23.
Astellan, asteallan; *p.* astealde; *pp.* asteald; *v. a.* [*Plat. Dut. Ger.* stellen: *Dan.* stille: *Swed.* stalla] 1. *To appoint, undertake, establish, ordain, decree, confirm, resolve upon;* statuere. 2. *To give, afford, yield, give away, to go out;* præbere, v. stellan :—1. Crist hit astealde and tæhte *Christ established and taught it, Hom. in dedic. Eccles.* Astealde gewin [*he*] *undertook the war, Ors.* 2, 5. Ϸone fleam ærest astealde Ϸurcytel *Thurkytel first undertook the flight, Chr.* 1010: *Ing.* p. 185, 8. Asteald to bysne *established for an example, Ors.* 2, 4. 2. Astellan bysene *to give an example, Past.* 3, 1.
Astemnian; *p.* nde; *pp.* ned [a *from,* stemn *a foundation*] *To proceed from a foundation, to found, build, erect;* condere :—Ϸe hi sylf astemnedon *which they themselves built, Bd. Pref. Sm.* p. 472, 17.
Astenct; *part. Scattered, dispersed, dissipated, routed;* dissipatus, *Som.*
Asteped *left childless,* v. stepan.
g Astepnes, se; *f. A privation;* orbatio :—*Cot.* 187.
Astepte *orphans, V. Ps.* 108, 8.
Astereð *moves,* v. astyrian.
Astered *disturbed,* v. astyrian.
Asterion *The herb pellitory, so called from its star-like form;* astericum :—*Herb.* 61.
Astifian; *p.* ede, ode; *pp.* ed *To stiffen, grow, or wax stiff;* obrigere :—*Cot.* 146. His sine astifode *his sinew stiffened, Gen.* 32, 32.
Astifician, astifecian; *v. a. To eradicate, extirpate, destroy, exterminate;* eradicare. Ϸat he astificige unþeawas *that he exterminate vices, Bt.* 27, 1.
h Astigan, astigð, astihð; *imp.* astih; *p.* astáh, astág, astáhg; *pp.* astiht *To go* or *come from,* v. stigan.
Astignes, se; *f. An ascent, ascending;* ascensus :—*Ps.* 103, 4.
Astihcest; *q.* astagest, astahest *thou removedst,* v. astigan.
Astiht *separated,* v. astigan.
Astintan; *p.* de; *pp.* ed, astynt *To blunt, to make dull, to stint, assuage;* obtundere :—*Scint.* 12: *Cot.* 101.
Astirian *to move,* v. astyrian.
Astiðian; *p.* ðude; *pp.* ðed [a *intensive,* stið *hard,* ian] *To become hard, dry, dry up, wither;* indurare arescere :—Astiðude swa swa tigle miht min *my strength dried up as a tile, Ps.* 21, 14.
Astod *urged; p. of* astandan.
i Astondnes, se; *f. An existence, a subsistence;* subsistentia :—An God on þrym astondnessum *one God in three subsistences, Bd.* 4, 17: *Sm.* p. 585, 38.
Astorfen; *part. Starved, like a dead body;* cadaverosus :—*Wanl.* p. 43, 17.
Astreccan, astrecan, astræcan; *p.* astrehte; *pp.* astreht; *v. a.* [*Plat.* uutstrekken: *Dut.* uitstrekken: *Ger.* aussrekken: *Dan.* udstraeke: *Swed.* utsträcka: a *out,* streccan *to stretch*] *To stretch out, to extend, prostrate,* or *lay low, to prostrate one's self, bow down;* prostrare extendere :—Ϸe les he astrecce his hand, *Gen.* 3, 22. Ϸa feoll Abram astreht to eorðan, *Gen.* 17, 3. Astrehte hine to eorðan, *Gen.* 18, 2.
j Astregdan; *q.* astregan; *p.* astregde; *pp.* astregd [a *out,* stregan *to sprinkle*] *To sprinkle, scatter, strew;* aspergere: —*Ps.* 50, 8, *Lye.*
Astreht *prostrated,* v. astreccan.
Astrengd *malleable, R.* 15; *perhaps* astreht, *Lye.*
Astrican; *v. To strike, smite;* percutere, *Som.*
Astrienan, astrynan; *p.* astrynde; *v. a. To engender, procreate,* v. strynan.
Astrihilthet [astre *a house,* hold *a master,* þeowet *a fine*] *A fine levied on a house-holder;* compensatio facta a domino mansionis, *L. Edw. Con.* 30, *Mann.*
Astundian *To* ASTOUND, *grieve, suffer grief, to bear;* dolere; *R. Ben.* 36.
Astyfecige; *q.* astificige *to terminate,* v. astifecian.
Astyltan; *v. To astonish;* stupescere, *Lye.*
Astyndende *blunting, Lye.*
k Astyrian *to stir,* v. stirian.
Astyrred *starred, Scint.* 58.
Astyrung *a motion,* v. stirung.
Asuab *erred,* v. aswifan.
Asuand *weakened,* v. aswindan.
Asuanian *to languish,* v. aswindan.
l Asundran, asundron; *adv.* ASUNDER, *apart, alone, privately;* seorsim :—He hys leorning cnihtum asundron rehte, *Mk.* 4, 34, v. sunder.
Asungen *sung,* v. singan.
Asuond *weakened,* v. aswindan.
Asurian; *p.* de; *pp.* ed, od. *To be,* or *become sour, tart, bitter;* acescere :—*Cot.* 10, 177.
Aswæfan, aswæft; *q.* aswapan, he aswapeð, aswæpð; *p.* asweop; *pp.* aswapen; *v. To sweep away, to cleanse;* abstergere :—*Past.* 36, 8. v. swapan.
Aswærnunga *Modesty, bashfulness, confusion;* modestia :—*Ps.* 43, 17, v. scama.
Aswanian *to languish,* v. aswindan.
Aswapa *sweepings,* v. æswapa.
Aswarcod; *part. Confounded, dismayed, abashed;* confusus :—*Ps.* 70, 26.
Aswarnian. Ϸat hi aswarnian *that they be confounded, Ps.* 85, 16, v. awarnian.
Aswearc *languished, failed,* v. geswearcan.
m Asweartian; *p.* ede; *pp.* ed, od *To blacken, darken, to be made* SWARTHY or *black, obscured, darkened;* denigrari :—Asweorted seo heofen *the heaven darkened, Æqu. vern.* 11, 39.
Aswefian; *p.* fede; *pp.* fed [a *intensive,* swefian *to sleep*] 1. *To sooth, appease, set at rest;* sopire. 2. *To strike with astonishment, to be stunned, made insensible;* percutere :—1. *Bd.* 3, 15. 2. Swyrdum aswefede, *Fr. Jud. Thw.* p. 26, 11.
Aswefecad *driven out,* v. aswyfecian.
Aswellan *to swell,* v. swellan.
Asweltan *to die, depart,* v. sweltan.
Aswengde *shaken,* v. swengan.
Asweotole *clearly,* v. sweotole.
n Aswican *to deceive,* v. swican.
Aswifan; *p.* asuab *To wander out of the way, to stray;* exorbitare, v. swifan.
Aswind, æswind; *adj. Slothful, sluggish, idle;* iners :—*Cot.* 108.
Aswindan; *p.* aswand; *pp.* aswunden; *v.* 1. *To languish through dulness, to enervate, pine, consume away;* tabescere. 2. *To decay, perish, dis-*

Asearian *To become dry, to sear, dry up;* arescere, *Som.*

Asecan; *p.* asohte; *pp.* asoht [a *from,* secan *to seek*] *To search, seek out, enquire;* requirere:—*Bd.* 1, 27.

Asecgan; *v.* [a *out,* secgan *to say*] *To speak out, declare, express, tell, publish, explain;* edicere:—Heofonas asecgað wuldor Godes, *Ps.* 18, 1.

Asecgendlic; *adj. That which may be spoken, expressible;* effabilis, *Som.*

Asend, asende *sent, emitted, thrown out,* v. sendan.

Aseowe *sowed,* aseowen *sowed,* v. sawan.

Aset *placed,* v. settan.

Asetan *To appoint, design;* destinare:—*R. Conc. pref.*

Aseted, asett, asette, *set, placed, stored, built,* v. settan.

Aseðan *to boil,* v. seoðan.

Aseþian *to affirm,* v. seþan.

Asian *To put out, eject, sile;* expuere:—*R. Mt.* 23, 24.

Asicyd, gesiced; *part.* [a *from,* sucian *to suck*] *Taken from suck, weaned;* ablactatus:—Swa asicyd ofer moder, *Ps.* 130, 4.

Asigen *fallen; pp. of* sigan.

Asindrod *sundered, separated, severed,* v. gesundrian.

Aslacian; *p.* aslacude, aslæcte; *pp.* aslacad, aslæcud *To slacken, loosen, untie, remit, dissolve, enervate;* laxare:—*Cot.* 103, v. slacian.

Aslacigendlic; *adj. Slack, remiss;* remissivus:—*Elf. gr.* 38, *Lye.*

Aslacigendlice; *adv. Slackly, remissly;* remissè:—*Elf. gr.* 38, *Som.*

Aslad *slipped away,* v. aslidan.

Aslæcte *loosed,* v. aslacian.

Aslæcud *sent off,* v. aslacian.

Aslægen, aslagen *struck, fixed,* v. slean.

Aslapen; *adj. Sleepy, drowsy;* somnolentus, *Som.*

Aslawian *To be heavy, dull, sluggish;* torpescere:—*Ors.* 4, 13.

Aslean *to strike,* v. slean.

Aslegen *slain,* v. slean.

Aslidan, slidan; *p.* aslád; *pp.* asliden *To slide,* or *slip away, dash against;* labi, elidere:—Asliden beon, *Scint.* 13, 24, 78. Aslad, gefioll, wagað *slid, moved, waggle, Cot.* 120, *Lye.*

Aslitan, aslytan; *p.* aslat; *pp.* aslyten, asliten; *v. a.* [a *from,* slitan *to slit*] *To cleave, rive, destroy, fail, cut off;* discindere, diruere:—Aslat þa tunas ealle *destroyed all the villages, Bd.* 3, 16. Mildheortnysse his aslyteð of cneorysse on cynrine, *Ps.* 76, 8.

Aslogen, asloh *struck, fixed,* v. slean.

Aslupan *To slip away;* labi:—*Cd.* 134.

Aslyteð *shall fail,* v. aslitan.

Asmeagende *enquiring; part. of* asmean.

Asmean; *p.* asmeade; *pp.* asmead; *v. a.* 1. *To search, enquire, elicit;* investigare. 2. *To contemplate, consider, ruminate, ponder, bethink, think;* ruminare, sentire:—1. Stige mine þu asmeadest, *Ps.* 138, 2. 2. Gif man hit ariht asmeað *if one rightly considers it, L. Can. Edg.* 18, v. smean.

Asmiðod *worked,* v. gesmiðed.

Asmoran, smoran; *p.* de; *pp.* ed, od; *v. a.* [*Plat. Dut.* smooren: *Ger.* schmoren: a *intensive,* smoran *to suffocate*] *To strangle, stifle, smother;* suffocare:—Þat ge forberen þicgan asmorod *that ye forbear to eat what is strangled, L. Alf.* 49: *W.* 33, 25. Hi hine on his bed asmoredon *they smothered him on his bed, Som.*

Asnasan, asnæsan; *p.* he asnæst; *v. a. To hit,* or *strike against, to rush, pull out;* impingere:—Gif hine mon on asnæseð *if any one strike against him, L. Alf.* 32: *Wilk.* p. 42, 15. Gif foran eagum asnæse, *Id.* p. 42, 16.

Asnydan *to cut off,* v. snidan.

Asoden *sodden, boiled, melted,* v. seoðan.

Asoht *sought out, searched,* v. asecan.

Asolcen, aswolcen; *part. Idle, lazy, dissolute, slow, slothful;* remissus, ignavus:—*Scint.* 16.

Asolcennys, se; *f. Idleness, slothfulness, laziness;* ignavia:—*Scint.* 24.

Aspætan, þu aspeast, aspeost; *v. To spit out;* expuere:—*R. C. Jn.* 9, 6.

Aspanan; *p.* aspón, aspeón; *pp.* aspanen *To allure, entice, Lye,* v. spanan.

Aspaw *vomited out; p. of* aspiwan.

Aspelian; *part.* aspeliende *To supply another's room, to be deputy* or *proxy;* vicario munere fungi:—*Jud. civ. Lund.* p. 71.

Aspendan, spendan; *p.* de; *pp.* ed [*Plat.* spenden: *Dan.* spendere: *Swed.* spendera] *To spend, lay out, bestow, employ;* expendere:—Aspendan þearfum *to spend on the poor, R. Ben. interl.* 58. Ic aspende yfele, *Elf. gr.* 47.

Aspeon *invited, secretly enticed,* v. aspanan.

Aspirian *to enquire,* v. aspyrian.

Aspiwan; *p.* aspaw, aspau *To spew, vomit, eject;* evomere:—*Cot.* 78, *Lye,* v. spiwan.

Aspon *allured,* v. aspanan.

Asprettan *to sprout out,* v. asprytan.

Asprian, sprian; *v. a.* [*Dut.* spreyen: *Ger.* spreiten: *Swed.* sprida] *To display, lay before, shew;* prætendere:—Aspriað mildheortnysse þine, *Ps.* 35, 11.

Asprincan *to arise,* v. aspringan.

Asprindlad; *part. Extended,* or *stretched out with little rods* or *twigs;* virgulis extensus:—*L. M.* 2, 24.

Aspring *a fountain,* v. spring.

Aspringan; *p.* he, asprang, asprong, hi asprungon; *pp.* asprunen; asprungen. 1. *To spring up, to arise, originate, break forth;* surgere, prorumpere. 2. *To spring out, escape, lack, fail;* deficere, imminuere:—1. Aspruncen is leoht, *Ps.* 111, 4. Apryngð rihtwisnys, *Ps.* 71, 7. Þa asprungon ealle wylspringas, *Gen.* 7, 11. 2. Þon aspringað miht min, *Ps.* 70, 10. Asprang gast min, *Ps.* 76, 3.

Aspruncen *arisen,* v. aspringan.

Asprungennes, se; *f. An eclipse, a deficiency, want, misery;* eclipsis, defectio:—Sunnan *or* monan asprungennes *an eclipse of the sun or moon, Som.* Asprungynes nam me, *Ps.* 118, 53.

Asprytan; *pp.* yted, ytten *To sprout out,* v. sprytan.

Aspyligan; *v.* [*Plat.* afspölen: *Dut.* afspoelen: *Ger.* abspülen] *To cleanse, wash, purify;* abluere:—Swin nyllað aspyligan on hluttrum wæterum *swine will not wash in pure waters, Bt.* 37, 4.

Aspyrgeng *A curious invention;* inventio:—*Cot.* 186.

Aspyrian; *v. To seek, search, explore, trace, discover, explain;* investigare:—*L. Ethel.* 2: *Wilk.* p. 63, 3, *Lye.*

Assa; *gen.* an; eosol, es [*Plat. Ger.* esel: *Al.* esel, esil: *Dut.* ezel: *Moes.* asil: *Dan.* aesel: *Swed.* äsna. *Icel.* esne: *Wel.* asen: *Lat.* asinus] *An* ASS; asinus:—Wilde assa *a wild ass.* Anbidiað eow her mid þam assum, *Gen.* 22, 5. Gif þu gemete þines feondes assan, *Ex.* 22, 4. Uppan assan folan sittende, *Jn.* 12, 15. And XX ass myrena *and* 20 *of mare asses or she asses, Gen.* 32, 15.

Assald *an ass,* v. assa.

Assandun *Ashdown,* v. Æscesdun.

Assedun; *adj.* [axe, *or* asce *ashes,* dun *dun or grey colour*] ASHDUN *of a dun* or *dark colour;* dosinus, cinereus:—*R.* 79, *Lye.*

1 Asead boiled, p of aseoðan, seoðan

6 Aslydan to slide slip, err Th. An

7 Asmeagan, to contemplate, investigate, imagine. Th An

2 Asendan to send Th. An

8 Asmeagung, e; f Meditation & investigation Th a Pol v smeagung

3 Aseoðan to boil p. asead; pp asoden to boil, scorch, prove Th. An v seoðan

9 Asmoran — l. 9 his bedde

4 Asettan to set, place propose Ors 6, 15 pt. settan

5 Asingan to sing Bt 39, 4 Card p 334, 9 singan

1 Aspringen escaped dispelled Cd 5. Th p 6,4 pp of aspringan

10 Asogen sucked asicyd [cf. 19] pp. v sugan, sucan

2

Aslawian dl. *

6 Aslapian; p ode to be asleep, torpere Ors 4,13 Bar p 176, 16

~~7 ... is there such a word as aslawan~~

Aspanan; p aspeon (aspon) pp asponnen to entice Rask Gr 23

3 Assa, an m asinus Ass v spl assa Bidað assan Ps Th 103, 11

7 Aslepen may slip Bt F. 154.18 v aslupan

8 Aspendan [15c]

4 Asse, an f A she ass Th. An asina

[15d]

12

O 1 Astellan [16a]

Φ 1 to go, proceed, step, mount Th. An

2 Astigie go, for astige v astigan

2 3 Astigend, es; m A nder; an ascendor; ascensor Ex 15, [illegible] ~~at 2nd of Hept. p 24~~ Thw. ~~Hept~~ p 29.

Φ 4

O 5 [16e]

O 1

Φ 2 Aswœrnung; e f, modesty, v scamu

Aswanian dl.

3 Aswamad abeteth Cd. 19 Th p 24, 12

O 3 Aswefd for aswefed appeased v aswefian

2 Aswican to decrease, cease Th An v swican

Cd 138 Th [illegible]

Assirige *Assyria*, Ors. 2, 5.
Ass-myra *a she-ass*, v. assa.
Ast *A kiln*; siccatorium :—R. 109, v. cyln.
Astælan [a *out*, stælan *to steal*] *To steal out, to creep on, to seduce*; obrepere :—Þat me næfre deofol on astælan ne mæge *that the devil may never secretly creep on me* [*seduce me*], L. Can. Edg. Confs. 9: Wilk. p. 88, 49.
Astæned; *part. Set with precious stones*; gemmatus :—Astæned gyrdel *a girdle set with stones*, Cot. 201, Lye, v. agimmed.
Astærfed; *part. Starved out, dried up, withered*, or *killed as a plant or shrub*; exsiccatus :—R. Mt. 15, 13.
Astah, astahg *ascended*, v. astigan.
f Astandan; p. he astod, we astodon *To stand out, remain long, endure, last, continue, rise up*; durare: — Hig astodon *they urged*, Lk. 23, 23.
Astellan, asteallan; p. astealde; pp. asteald; v. a. [Plat. Dut. Ger. stellen: Dan. stille: Swed. ställa] 1. *To appoint, undertake, establish, ordain, decree, confirm, resolve upon*; statuere. 2. *To give, afford, yield, give away, to go out*; præbere, v. stellan :—1. Crist hit astealde and tæhte *Christ established and taught it*, Hom. in dedic. Eccles. Astealde gewin [*he*] *undertook the war*, Ors. 2, 5. Þone fleam ærest astealde Þurcytel *Thurkytel first undertook the flight*, Chr. 1010: Ing. p. 185, 8. Asteald to bysne *established for an example*, Ors. 2, 4. 2. Astellan bysene *to give an example*, Past. 3, 1.
Astemnian; p. nde; pp. ned [a *from*, stemn *a foundation*] *To proceed from a foundation, to found, build, erect*; condere :—Þe hi sylf astemnedon *which they themselves built*, Bd. Pref. Sm. p. 472, 17.
Astenct; *part. Scattered, dispersed, dissipated, routed*; dissipatus, Som.
Asteped *left childless*, v. stepan.
g Astepnes, se; f. *A privation*; orbatio :—Cot. 187.
Astepte *orphans*, V. Ps. 108, 8.
Astereð *moves*, v. astyrian.
Astered *disturbed*, v. astyrian.
Asterion *The herb pellitory, so called from its star-like form*; astericum :—Herb. 61.
Astifian; p. ede, ode; pp. ed *To stiffen, grow, or wax stiff*; obrigere :—Cot. 146. His sine astifode *his sinew stiffened*, Gen. 32, 32.
Astificiah, astifecian; v. a. *To eradicate, extirpate, destroy, exterminate*; eradicare. Þat he astificige unþeawas *that he exterminate vices*, Bt. 27, 1.
h Astígan, astígð, astíhð; imp. astih; p. astáh, astág, astáhg; pp. astiht *To go* or *come from*, v. stigan.
Astignes, se; f. *An ascent, ascending*; ascensus :—Ps. 103, 4.
Astihcest; q. astagest, astahest *thou removedst*, v. astigan.
Astiht *separated*, v. astigan.
Astintan; p. de; pp. ed, astynt *To blunt, to make dull, to stint, assuage*; obtundere :—Scint. 12: Cot. 101.
Astirian *to move*, v. astyrian.
Astiðian; p. ðude; pp. ðed [a *intensive*, stið *hard*, ian] *To become hard, dry, dry up, wither*; indurare arescere :—Astiðude swa swa tigle miht min *my strength dried up as a tile*, Ps. 21, 14.
Astod *urged*; p. *of* astandan.
i Astondnes, se; f. *An existence, a subsistence*; subsistentia :—An God on þrym astondnessum *one God in three subsistences*, Bd. 4, 17: Sm. p. 585, 38.
Astorfen; *part. Starved, like a dead body*; cadaverosus :—Wanl. p. 43, 17.
Astreccan, astrecan, astræcan; p. astrehte; pp. astreht; v. a. [Plat. uutstrekken: Dut. uitstrekken: Ger. ausstrekken: Dan. udstraeke: Swed. utsträcka: a *out*, streccan *to stretch*] *To stretch out, to extend, prostrate*, or *lay low, to prostrate one's self, bow down*; prostrare extendere :—Þe leas he astrecce his hand, Gen. 3, 22. Þa feoll Abram astreht to eorðan, Gen. 17, 3. Astrehte hine to eorðan, Gen. 18, 2.
j Astregdan; q. astregan; p. astregde; pp. astregd [a *out*, stregan *to sprinkle*] *To sprinkle, scatter, strew*; aspergere: —Ps. 50, 8, Lye.
Astreht *prostrated*, v. astreccan.
Astrengd *malleable*, R. 15; *perhaps* astreht, Lye.
Astrican; v. *To strike, smite*; percutere, Som.
Astrienan, astrynan; p. astrynde; v. a. *To engender, procreate*, v. strynan.
Astrihilthet [astre *a house*, hold *a master*, þeowet *a fine*] *A fine levied on a house-holder*; compensatio facta a domino mansionis, L. Edw. Con. 30, Mann.
Astundian *To* ASTOUND, *grieve, suffer grief, to bear*; dolere; R. Ben. 36.
Astyfecige; q. astificige *to terminate*, v. astifecian.
Astyltan; v. *To astonish*; stupescere, Lye.
Astyndende *blunting*, Lye.
k Astyrian *to stir*, v. stirian.
Astyrred *starred*, Scint. 58.
Astyrung *a motion*, v. stirung.
Asuab *erred*, v. aswifan.
Asuand *weakened*, v. aswindan.
Asuanian *to languish*, v. aswindan.
l Asundran, asundron; adv. ASUNDER, *apart, alone, privately*; seorsim :—He hys leorning cnihtum asundron rehte, Mk. 4, 34, v. sunder.
Asungen *sung*, v. singan.
Asuond *weakened*, v. aswindan.
Asurian; p. de; pp. ed, od. *To be*, or *become sour, tart, bitter*; acescere :—Cot. 10, 177.
Aswæfan, aswæft; q. aswapan, he aswapeð, aswæpð; p. asweop; pp. aswapen; v. *To sweep away, to cleanse*; abstergere :—Past. 36, 8. v. swapan.
Aswærnunga *Modesty, bashfulness, confusion*; modestia :—Ps. 43, 17, v. scama.
Aswanian *to languish*, v. aswindan.
Aswapa *sweepings*, v. æswapa.
Aswarcod; *part. Confounded, dismayed, abashed*; confusus :—Ps. 70, 26.
Aswarnian. Þat hi aswarnian *that they be confounded*, Ps. 85, 16, v. awarnian.
Aswearc *languished, failed*, v. geswearcan.
m Asweartian; p. ede; pp. ed, od *To blacken, darken, to be made* SWARTHY or *black, obscured, darkened*; denigrari :—Asweorted seo heofen *the heaven darkened*, Æqu. vern. 11, 39.
Aswefian; p. fede; pp. fed [a *intensive*, swefian *to sleep*] 1. *To sooth, appease, set at rest*; sopire. 2. *To strike with astonishment, to be stunned, made insensible*; percutere :—1. Bd. 3, 15. 2. Swyrdum aswefede, Fr. Jud. Thw. p. 26, 11.
Aswefecad *driven out*, v. aswyfecian.
Aswellan *to swell*, v. swellan.
Asweltan *to die, depart*, v. sweltan.
Aswengde *shaken*, v. swengan.
Asweotole *clearly*, v. sweotole.
n Aswican *to deceive*, v. swican.
Aswifan; p. asuab *To wander out of the way, to stray*; exorbitare, v. swifan.
Aswind, æswind; adj. *Slothful, sluggish, idle*; iners :—Cot. 108.
Aswindan; p. aswand; pp. aswunden; v. 1. *To languish through dulness, to enervate, pine, consume away*; tabescere. 2. *To decay, perish, dis-*

9

Ø 1* to go, proceed, step, mount Th. An

~~2 Astige~~ go, for astige v astigan

2 3 ~~A~~ Astigend, es; m A rider, an ascendor; ascensor ~~Ex 15, 1~~ ~~at end of Hepte p 24~~ Thw. ~~Hept~~ p 29

Ø 4

O 5 [16e]

O 1 Astellan [16a]

9

O 1

Ø 2* Aswærnung; e f. modesty v scamu

Aswanian dl. *

3 Aswamad abateth Cd. 19 Th p 24. 12

O 3 Aswefd for aswefed appeased v aswefian

2 Aswican* to decrease, cease Th An v swican

Cd 137 Th p 173, 3

Assirige *Assyria*, *Ors.* 2, 5.
Ass-myra *a she-ass*, v. assa.
Ast *A kiln*; siccatorium :—*R.* 109, v. cyln.
Astælan [a *out*, stælan *to steal*] *To steal out, to creep on, to seduce*; obrepere :—Ðat me næfre deofol on astælan ne mæge *that the devil may never secretly creep on me* [*seduce me*], *L. Can. Edg. Confes.* 9: *Wilk.* p. 88, 49.
Astæned; *part. Set with precious stones*; gemmatus :—Astæned gyrdel *a girdle set with stones*, *Cot.* 201, *Lye*, v. agimmed.
Astærfed; *part. Starved out, dried up, withered*, or *killed as a plant or shrub*; exsiccatus :—*R. Mt.* 15, 13.
Astah, astahg *ascended*, v. astigan.
f Astandan; *p.* he astod, we astodon *To stand out, remain long, endure, last, continue, rise up*; durare: —Hig astodon *they urged*, *Lk.* 23, 23.
Astellan, asteallan; *p.* astealde; *pp.* asteald; *v. a.* [*Plat. Dut. Ger.* stellen: *Dan.* stille: *Swed.* ställa] 1. *To appoint, undertake, establish, ordain, decree, confirm, resolve upon*; statuere. 2. *To give, afford, yield, give away, to go out*; præbere, v. stellan :—1. Crist hit astealde and tæhte *Christ established and taught it*, *Hom. in dedic. Eccles.* Astealde gewin [*he*] *undertook the war*, *Ors.* 2, 5. Ðone fleam ærest astealde Ðurcytel *Thurkytel first undertook the flight*, *Chr.* 1010: *Ing.* p. 185, 8. Asteald to bysne *established for an example*, *Ors.* 2, 4. 2. Astellan bysene *to give an example*, *Past.* 3, 1.
Astemnian; *p.* ode; *pp.* ned [a *from*, stemn *a foundation*] *To proceed from a foundation, to found, build, erect*; condere :—Ðe hi sylf astemnedon *which they themselves built*, *Bd. Pref. Sm.* p. 472, 17.
Astenct; *part. Scattered, dispersed, dissipated, routed*; dissipatus, *Som.*
Asteped *left childless*, v. stepan.
g Astepnes, se; *f. A privation*; orbatio :—*Cot.* 187.
Astepte *orphans*, *V. Ps.* 108, 8.
Astereð *moves*, v. astyrian.
Astered *disturbed*, v. astyrian.
Asterion *The herb pellitory, so called from its star-like form*; astericum :—*Herb.* 61.
Astifian; *p.* ede, ode; *pp.* ed *To stiffen, grow, or wax stiff*; obrigere :—*Cot.* 146. His sine astifode *his sinew stiffened*, *Gen.* 32, 32.
Astificiah, astifecian; *v. a.* *To eradicate, extirpate, destroy, exterminate*; eradicare. Ðat he astificige unþeawas *that he exterminate vices*, *Bt.* 27, 1.
h Astigan, astigð, astihð; *imp.* astih; *p.* astáh, astág, astáhg; *pp.* astiht *To go* or *come from*, v. stigan.
Astignes, se; *f. An ascent, ascending*; ascensus :—*Ps.* 103, 4.
Astihcest; *q.* astagest, astahest *thou removedst*, v. astigan.
Astiht *separated*, v. astigan.
Astintan; *p.* de; *pp.* ed, astynt *To blunt, to make dull, to stint, assuage*; obtundere :—*Scint.* 12: *Cot.* 101.
Astirian *to move*, v. astyrian.
Astiðian; *p.* ðude; *pp.* ðed [a *intensive*, stið *hard*, ian] *To become hard, dry, dry up, wither*; indurare arescere :—Astiðude swa swa tigle miht min *my strength dried up as a tile*, *Ps.* 21, 14.
Astod *urged*; *p. of* astandan.
i Astondnes, se; *f. An existence, a subsistence*; subsistentia :—An God on þrym astondnessum *one God in three subsistences*, *Bd.* 4, 17: *Sm.* p. 585, 38.
Astorfen; *part. Starved, like a dead body*; cadaverosus :—*Wanl.* p. 43, 17.
Astreccan, astrecan, astræcan; *p.* astrehte; *pp.* astreht; *v. a.* [*Plat.* uutstrekken: *Dut.* uitstrekken: *Ger.* ausstrekken: *Dan.* udstraeke: *Swed.* utsträcka: a *out*, streccan *to stretch*] *To stretch out, to extend, prostrate*, or *lay low, to prostrate one's self, bow down*; prosternere, extendere :—Ðe leas he astrecce his hand, *Gen.* 3, 22. Ða feoll Abram astreht to eorðan, *Gen.* 17, 3. Astrehte hine to eorðan, *Gen.* 18, 2.
j Astregdan; *q.* astregan; *p.* astregde; *pp.* astregd [a *out*, stregan *to sprinkle*] *To sprinkle, scatter, strew*; aspergere: —*Ps.* 50, 8, *Lye.*
Astreht *prostrated*, v. astreccan.
Astrengd *malleable*, *R.* 15; *perhaps* astreht, *Lye.*
Astrican; *v. To strike, smite*; percutere, *Som.*
Astrienan, astrynan; *p.* astrynde; *v. a. To engender, procreate*, v. strynan.
Astrihilthet [astre *a house*, hold *a master*, þeowet *a fine*] *A fine levied on a house-holder*; compensatio facta a domino mansionis, *L. Edw. Con.* 30, *Mann.*
Astundian *To* ASTOUND, *grieve, suffer grief, to bear*; dolere; *R. Ben.* 36.
Astyfecige; *q.* astificige *to terminate*, v. astifecian.
Astyltan; *v. To astonish*; stupescere, *Lye.*
Astyndende *blunting*, *Lye.*
k Astyrian *to stir*, v. stirian.
Astyrred *starred*, *Scint.* 58.
Astyrung *a motion*, v. stirung.
Asuab *erred*, v. aswifan.
Asuand *weakened*, v. aswindan.
Asuanian *to languish*, v. aswindan.
l Asundran, asundron; *adv.* ASUNDER, *apart, alone, privately*; seorsim :—He hys leorning cnihtum asundron rehte, *Mk.* 4, 34, v. sunder.
Asungen *sung*, v. singan.
Asuond *weakened*, v. aswindan.
Asurian; *p.* de; *pp.* ed, od. *To be, or become sour, tart, bitter*; acescere :—*Cot.* 10, 177.
Aswæfan, aswæft; *q.* aswapan, he aswapeð, aswæpð; *p.* asweop; *pp.* aswapen; *v. To sweep away, to cleanse*; abstergere :—*Past.* 36, 8. v. swapan.
Aswærnunga *Modesty, bashfulness, confusion*; modestia :—*Ps.* 43, 17, v. scama.
Aswanian *to languish*, v. aswindan.
Aswapa *sweepings*, v. æswapa.
Aswarcod; *part. Confounded, dismayed, abashed*; confusus :—*Ps.* 70, 26.
Aswarnian. Ðat hi aswarnian *that they be confounded*, *Ps.* 85, 16, v. awarnian.
Aswearc *languished, failed*, v. geswearcan.
m Asweartian; *p.* ede; *pp.* ed, od *To blacken, darken, to be made* SWARTHY or *black, obscured, darkened*; denigrari :—Asweorted seo heofen *the heaven darkened*, *Æqu. vern.* 11, 39.
Aswefian; *p.* fede; *pp.* fed [a *intensive*, swefian *to sleep*] 1. *To sooth, appease, set at rest*; sopire. 2. *To strike with astonishment, to be stunned, made insensible*; percutere :—1. *Bd.* 3, 15. 2. Swyrdum aswefede, *Fr. Jud. Thw.* p. 26, 11.
Aswefecad *driven out*, v. aswyfecian.
Aswellan *to swell*, v. swellan.
Asweltan *to die, depart*, v. sweltan.
Aswengde *shaken*, v. swengan.
Asweotole *clearly*, v. sweotole.
n Aswican *to deceive*, v. swican.
Aswifan; *p.* asuab *To wander out of the way, to stray*; exorbitare, v. swifan.
Aswind, æswind; *adj. Slothful, sluggish, idle*; iners :—*Cot.* 108.
Aswindan; *p.* aswand; *pp.* aswunden; *v.* 1. *To languish through dulness, to enervate, pine, consume away*; tabescere. 2. *To decay, perish, dis-*

solve; consumere:—1. Hwy ge swa aswundene sion *why are ye so enervated, Bt.* 40, 4. 2. Þylæs ealle gesceafta aswindað *lest all creatures perish, Bt.* 33, 4. Aswindan me dyde anda min, *Ps.* 118, 139, v. swindan.

Aswindung *Idleness, sloth*; desidia, *Som.*

Aswipan; *pp.* aswopen *To sweep, scour, clean,* or *brush away*; verrere, *Som.*

Aswogen; *part. Overgrown, covered over, choked*; obductus:—*Past.* 52, 9.

Aswolcen *idle*, v. asolcen.

Aswollen *swollen*, v. aswellen.

Aswond, aswonden *weakened*, v. aswindan.

Aswondennes *sloth*, v. aswundennes.

Aswopen *swept*, v. aswipan, aswæfan.

Asworettan; *v. To breathe, sigh,* v. sworetan.

Aswunan *To swoon*; deficere animo, *Som.*

Aswunden *weakened, slothful*, v. aswindan.

Aswundenlice; *adv. Slothfully*, segniter, *Som.*

Aswundennes, se; *f. Slothfulness, idleness*; inertia:—Fram ussa tida aswundennysse, *Bd.* 3, 5.

Aswyfecian; *pp.* aswefecad *To pull up by the roots, to eradicate*; eradicare, v. astifecian.

Aswylegan; *v. To soil, sully, deface, disgrace*; devenustare, *Som.*

Aswyðerad *burdened, aggravated*, v. swyðran.

Asyndrian; *part.* asyndrigende, ic asyndrige; *p.* ede; *pp.* ed, od [a *from*, syndrian *to sunder, part*] *To put* ASUNDER, *to separate, disjoin, sever*; separare:—Ic com asyndrian, *Mt.* 10, 35, v. syndrian.

Asyndrung *A division, separation, divorce*; divortium:—*Cot.* 68.

Ata, ate, atih [*Frs.* ôat] OATS, *tares, darnel, cockle*; avena fatua, *Lin.*:—Wilde ata *wild oats, C. Mt.* 13, 30, 38. Atan *or* lasor *tares*; zizania, *Cot.* 204. Þat acer-sæd aten *the acre-seed of oats, Chr.* 1124, v. coccel.

Atæfran, atifran; *pp.* atefred, atifred, atiefned *To depict, paint*; depingere:—*Past.* 21, 3.

Atbærst *escaped*, v. ætberstan.

Ate *oats*; avena, v. ata. Urinæ, lotium, *Som.*

Ateah *took off*, v. ateon.

Atefred *painted*, v. atæfran.

Ategar *a javelin*, v. ætgar.

Atelan *to reckon*, v. tellan.

Atelic; *adj. Deformed, foul, ill-favoured, corrupt, shameful*; deformis:—*Bd.* 4, 32, v. atol.

Atellan *to tell out, number*, v. tellan.

Atelucost *or* atelicost; *sup. of* atelic *foul.*

Atemian; *p.* ede; *pp.* ed [a *intensive*, tamian *to tame*] *To make very tame* or *gentle, to tame*; domare:—*Past.* 46.

Aten *oats*; avenæ, v. ata.

Atendan; *p.* de; *pp.* ed; *v.* [a *intensive*, tendan *to tind*] *To set on fire, kindle, enrage, inflame*; incendere:—Hi atendon heora here-beacna *they lighted their camp-beacons, Chr.* 1006. Hi mid fyre atendan wolden *they would set it on fire, Chr.* 994.

Atendend *An incendiary, inflamer, exciter*; accensor:—*Scint.* 78, *Lye.*

Atendincge *A fire-brand, an incentive, a provoking*; incentivum:—*Scint.* 81, *Lye.*

Ateon, ation; ic ateo, he atihð, ateohð, we ateoð; *p.* þu ateodest, atuge, he ateh ateah, we atugon; *pp.* atiht, atogen [a *from*, teon *to tow, or draw*] 1. *To draw, move, draw* or *pluck out, attract*; trahere. 2. *To employ, dispose of, treat*; disponere:—Hi ne mihton hyt ateon, *Jn.* 21, 6. Mid atogenum swurde, *Numb.* 22, 22. 2. Hu hig sceoldon þæs Halendes wurð ateon *how they should dispose of the Saviour's price, Mt.* 27, 7. Ateoh hyne swylce broðer *treat him as a brother, Scint.* 60: *Nicod.* 14. ¶ *Used with prepositions thus:* Ateon fram *or* of *to draw from, Deut.* 13, 10. Ateon to *to draw to, attract.* Men beoð atihte to gesælþum *men are attracted to happiness, Bt.* 32: 1. *Tit.* 32: *Ps.* 118, 131. Ateon ut *to draw out, Ors.* 5, 13, v. teon.

Ateorian, æteorian, aterian, atiarian; *p.* ode; *pp.* ed. *To fail, tire, corrupt*; desistere:—Him æteorode se mete, *Jos.* 5, 12, v. geteorian.

Ateorigendlic; *adj. Defective, lacking, frail, brittle, ruinous*; defectivus:—*H. in die Pasch.* p. 3, *Som.*

Ateorung *a failing, a tiring*, v. geteorung, *Som.*

Ateowad, ateowed; *part. Shown, made known*; ostensus, *Som.*

Ater *poison*, v. attrene.

Ateran; *pp.* ed [a *from*, teran *to tear*] *To tear from, seize, fatigue*; diripere:—*R.* 87.

Ater-drinca, ator-drinc, attordrinca *A poisonous potion* or *drink, bile*; potio venenata:—*Cot.* 24.

Aterian *to fail*, v. ateorian.

Aterlaðe, atorlaðe, atterlaðe; *m. The herb betony, penny grass*; venenifuga, gallicrista, betonica:—*Cot.* 24.

Aterlic; *adj.* [ater *a serpent*, v. attrene, lic] *Snakelike, horrible, terrible, gorgonian*; gorgoneus:—*Cot.* 98, v. biter.

AÐ, -es; *m.* [*Frs. Dut.* eed, eet] *An oath, a swearing*; juramentum:—Þu agyltst þine aðas, *Mt.* 5, 33. Þa behet he mid aðe, *Mt.* 14, 7, 9. ¶ Að syllan *to take an oath, to swear.*

Aþanon *from thence*; inde, *Som.*

Aðbrice; *m. A breaking of an oath, perjury*; perjurium:—*Wulf.* 8.

Aðburstan [að *an oath*, berstan *to burst*] *To break an oath, to perjure*; perjerare:—Gif him aðburste wære, *L. Edw.* 3.

A þe, a þy; *conj. Therefore, so far that, so much*; idcirco:—It more properly means *ever the*, as a þy *or* a þe deorwyrðran *ever the more precious, Bt.* 14, 2. A þy ma *ever the more, Bt.* 40, 2. A þy betera *ever the better, Bt.* 13, v. þy.

Aþed *skinned*, v. æthide.

Aðe-gehat *an oath*, v. að-gehat.

Aþegen; *part. Full, stuffed out*; distentus:—*Cot.* 63.

Aþencan *to recollect, devise, invent, Ors.* 1, 10, v. þencean.

Aþenian; *p.* ede, ode; *pp.* ed, od; *v.a.* [a *out*, þenian *to stretch*] 1. *To stretch out, extend*; extendere. 2. *To prostrate*; prosternere. 3. *To expand, apply, stretch*; expandere:—1. Aþene þine hand, and he hi aþenede, *Mt.* 12, 13. 2. Hi aþenedon hi, *Mt.* 2, 11. 3. Bogan his he aþenede, *Ps.* 7, 13. Aþenian mod *to apply the mind, Bd.* 4, 3, *Lye*, v. þenian.

Aþenung *An extending, extension*; extensio, *Som.*

Aþeodan; *p.* de; *pp.* aþeodd, aþied [a *from*, þeodan *to join*] *To disjoin, separate*; disjungere:—Aþeodde from Gode, *Gr. Dial.* 2, 16.

Aþeostriað *darken*; aþeostrod *darkened*, v. aþystrian.

A'ðer, oððe *either*, v. aðor, oððe.

Aþexe *a lizard, newt*; lacerta, *Som.*

Aðfultum [að *an oath*, fultum *a helper*] *One who supports by an oath, who will swear for another, a witness*; sacramentales:—Þe aðfultum næbbe, *L. Cnut.* 5.

Að-gehat, aðe-gehat, es; *n.* [að *an oath*, gehat *a promise*] *A sacred pledge, an oath, sacrament*; sacramentum:—*R.* 13.

-ad, -od a torment; a month; v. -od. m. es monad, es. Cf. Rask 205, 206

1

2

3 × Ater-tán, es; m. a poisoned rod. Beo K. Grein II 529, 26. Beo K 2918

1

4 × Adburste from að an oath; berstan to burst.

5 Æþelo nobility Beo. Pl. Æþelu v. Spl

1 Aswyndan, to melt, to fail. Ben v swindan

2

3 syndrige separately, asunder. Som v asundrian

4 Ata, an m; oats

5 All. Unie lotium

1 × Ateowan, ateowian to appear, show Th. an. v æteowian

2 × Ater, atter, es; n poison Th. An. v Spl áttor

2 Aperigende extending. Lueb of aperian

3 Apeodian; p de, pied

4 [17]

solve; consumere:—1. Hwy ge swa aswundene sion *why are ye so enervated, Bt.* 40, 4. 2. Þylæs ealle gesceafta aswindað *lest all creatures perish, Bt.* 33, 4. Aswindan me dyde anda min, *Ps.* 118, 139, v. swindan.

Aswindung *Idleness, sloth;* desidia, *Som.*

Aswipan; *pp.* aswopen *To sweep, scour, clean,* or *brush away;* verrere, *Som.*

Aswogen; *part. Overgrown, covered over, choked;* obductus:—*Past.* 52, 9.

Aswolcen *idle,* v. asolcen.

Aswollen *swollen,* v. aswellen.

Aswond, aswonden *weakened,* v. aswindan.

Aswondennes *sloth,* v. aswundennes.

Aswopen *swept,* v. aswipan, aswæfan.

Asworettan; *v. To breathe, sigh,* v. sworetan.

Aswunan *To swoon;* deficere animo, *Som.*

Aswunden *weakened, slothful,* v. aswindan.

Aswundenlice; *adv. Slothfully,* segniter, *Som.*

Aswundennes, se; *f. Slothfulness, idleness;* inertia:—Fram ussa tida aswundennysse, *Bd.* 3, 5.

Aswyfecian; *pp.* aswefecad *To pull up by the roots, to eradicate;* eradicare, v. astifecian.

Aswylegan; *v. To soil, sully, deface, disgrace;* devenustare, *Som.*

Aswyðerad *burdened, aggravated,* v. swyðran.

Asyndrian; *part.* asyndrigende, ic asyndrige; *p.* ede; *pp.* ed, od [a *from,* syndrian *to sunder, part*] *To put* ASUNDER, *to separate, disjoin, sever;* separare:—Ic com asyndrian, *Mt.* 10, 35, v. syndrian.

Asyndrung *A division, separation, divorce;* divortium:—*Cot.* 68.

ATA, ate, atih [*Frs.* ðat] OATS, *tares, darnel, cockle;* avena fatua, *Lin.*:—Wilde ata *wild oats, C. Mt.* 13, 30, 38. Atan or lasor *tares;* zizania, *Cot.* 204. Þat acer-sæd aten *the acre-seed of oats, Chr.* 1124, v. coccel.

Atæfran, atifran; *pp.* atefred, atifred, atiefned *To depict, paint;* depingere:—*Past.* 21, 3.

Atbærst *escaped,* v. ætberstan.

Ate *oats;* avena, v. ata. Urinæ, lolium, *Som.*

Ateah *took off,* v. ateon.

Atefred *painted,* v. atæfran.

Ategar *a javelin,* v. ætgar.

Atelan *to reckon,* v. tellan.

Atelic; *adj. Deformed, foul, ill-favoured, corrupt, shameful;* deformis:—*Bd.* 4, 32, v. atol.

Atellan *to tell out, number,* v. tellan.

Atelucost or atelicost; *sup. of* atelic *foul.*

Atemian; *p.* ede; *pp.* ed [a *intensive,* tamian *to tame*] *To make very tame* or *gentle, to tame;* domare:—*Past.* 46.

Aten *oats;* avenæ, v. ata.

Atendan; *p.* de; *pp.* ed; *v.* [a *intensive,* tendan *to tind*] *To set on fire, kindle, enrage, inflame;* incendere:—Hi atendon heora here-beacna *they lighted their camp-beacons, Chr.* 1006. Hi mid fyre atendan wolden *they would set it on fire, Chr.* 994.

Atendend *An incendiary, inflamer, exciter;* accensor:—*Scint.* 78, *Lye.*

Atendincge *A fire-brand, an incentive, a provoking;* incentivum:—*Scint.* 81, *Lye.*

Ateon, ation; ic ateo, he atihð, ateohð, we ateoð; *p.* þu ateodest, atuge, he ateh ateah, we atugon; *pp.* atiht, atogen [a *from,* teon *to tow, or draw*] 1. *To draw, move, draw* or *pluck out, attract;* trahere. 2. *To employ, dispose of, treat;* disponere:—Hi ne mihton hyt ateon, *Jn.* 21, 6. Mid atogenum swurde, *Numb.* 22, 22. 2. Hu hig sceoldon þæs Halendes wurð ateon *how they should dispose of the Saviour's price, Mt.* 27, 7. Ateoh hyne swylce broðer *treat him as a brother, Scint.* 60: *Nicod.* 14. ¶ *Used with prepositions thus:* Ateon fram or of *to draw from, Deut.* 13, 10. Ateon to *to draw to, attract.* Men beoð atihte to gesælþum *men are attracted to happiness, Bt.* 32: 1. *Tit.* 32: *Ps.* 118, 131. Ateon ut *to draw out, Ors.* 5, 13, v. teon.

Ateorian, æteorian, aterian, atiarian; *p.* ode; *pp.* ed. *To fail, tire, corrupt;* desistere:—Him æteorode se mete, *Jos.* 5, 12, v. geteorian.

Ateorigendlic; *adj. Defective, lacking, frail, brittle, ruinous;* defectivus:—*H. in die Pasch.* p. 3, *Som.*

Ateorung *a failing, a tiring,* v. geteorung, *Som.*

Ateowad, ateowed; *part. Shown, made known;* ostensus, *Som.*

Ater *poison,* v. attor.

Ateran; *pp.* ed [a *from,* teran *to tear*] *To tear from, seize, fatigue;* diripere:—*R.* 87.

Ater-drinca, ator-drinc, attordrinca *A poisonous potion* or *drink, bile;* potio venenata:—*Cot.* 24.

Aterian *to fail,* v. ateorian.

Aterlaðe, atorlaðe, atterlaðe; *m. The herb betony, penny grass;* venenifuga, gallicrista, betonica:—*Cot.* 24.

Aterlic; *adj.* [ater *a serpent,* v. atterne, lic] *Snakelike, horrible, terrible, gorgonian;* gorgoneus:—*Cot.* 98, v. biter.

AÐ, -es; *m.* [*Frs. Dut.* eed, eet] *An oath, a swearing;* juramentum:—Þu agyltst þine aðas, *Mt.* 5, 33. Þa behet he mid aðe, *Mt.* 14, 7, 9. ¶ Að syllan *to take an oath, to swear.*

Aþanon *from thence;* inde, *Som.*

Aðbrice; *m. A breaking of an oath, perjury;* perjurium:—*Wulf.* 8.

Aðburstan [að *an oath,* berstan *to burst*] *To break an oath, to perjure;* perjerare:—Gif him aðburste wære, *L. Edw.* 3.

A þe, a þy; *conj. Therefore, so far that, so much;* idcirco:—It more properly means *ever the,* as a þy or a þe deorwyrðran *ever the more precious, Bt.* 14, 2. A þy ma *ever the more, Bt.* 40, 2. A þy betera *ever the better, Bt.* 13, v. þy.

Aþed *skinned,* v. æthide.

Aðe-gehat *an oath,* v. að-gehat.

Aþegen; *part. Full, stuffed out;* distentus:—*Cot.* 63.

Aþencan *to recollect, devise, invent, Ors.* 1, 10, v. þencean.

Aþenian; *p.* ede, ode; *pp.* ed, od; *v.a.* [a *out,* þenian *to stretch*] 1. *To stretch out, extend;* extendere. 2. *To prostrate;* prosternere. 3. *To expand, apply, stretch;* expandere:—1. Aþene þine hand, and he hi aþenede, *Mt.* 12, 13. 2. Hi aþenedon hi, *Mt.* 2, 11. 3. Bogan his he aþenede, *Ps.* 7, 13. Aþenian mod *to apply the mind, Bd.* 4, 3, *Lye,* v. þenian.

Aþenung *An extending, extension;* extensio, *Som.*

Aþeodan; *p.* de; *pp.* aþeodd, abied [a *from,* þeodan *to join*] *To disjoin, separate;* disjungere:—Aþeodde from Gode, *Gr. Dial.* 2, 16.

Aþeostriað *darken;* aþeostrod *darkened,* v. aþystrian.

A'ðer, oððe *either,* v. aðor, oððe.

Aþexe *a lizard, newt;* lacerta, *Som.*

Aðfultum [að *an oath,* fultum *a helper*] *One who supports by an oath, who will swear for another, a witness;* sacramentales:—Þe aðfultum næbbe, *L. Cnut.* 5.

Að-gehat, aðe-gehat, es; *n.* [að *an oath,* gehat *a promise*] *A sacred pledge, an oath, sacrament;* sacramentum:—*R.* 13.

-ad, -od, *a torment* nocuus *a* m *an* monad, es ...

ϕ1

2

3 Ater-tán, es; m a poisoned rod, ~~virga venenata~~ Beo ...

Gü II 529, 26

Beo K 2918

4 Adburste from ad ...oath; berstan to burst

5 Apelo nobility Beo ... æþelu

(v. Spl)

ϕ1

1 Aswyndan, to melt, decay tabesc... Ben v ~~...~~ swindan

-2 ...

3 ...syndrige ~~separately~~ asunder ... som v asund~~...~~ ran

4 Ata, an m; oats

5 ~~Ate~~ dl Unic ...

2 Apenigende extending Lat. ... extension

3 Apeodian; ...

4 [176]

1 Ateowan, ateowian to appear, show Th. an ... ateowian

2 Ater, ætter, es; n poison Th. An v Spl ... ættor

4 Ápswian to suf-
fer ²½. An

5 Hi hine on his bedde
aþryseno dan Ors 5,4 Bar
p. 185. 25

7 [See MS. M 4a .3]

3 Áþ-sware with
oath swearing Cd. 170. Th.
213, 26 - For heora áþ-
6 - swara Jos. 19, 18.

2 4 Áþ-sweord, es; n.
[Old Higher. suart, suert,
jusjurandum eid-suart]

5 An oath, jusjurandum ~~Bes. 29, p. 155.~~
~~K. 4123. See Kl. Aes.~~
~~p. 239~~ Grein II. 529, 16
Beo K 4123

3. Átiwan to ap-
pear v. ateowan
5 ~~Átor-lán~~ ...
Átor-sceaða an
a poisonous plague
~~venefica~~ Beo. K. 5673
10

3 6 Áþung, es; breath ½. An

7

2 Áttr. attre dl.
ator
atter, ater, gattres
dattre m.

3 8 *Áttor, n.
Poison venenum
Beo K 5426: Deut
32, 33.

9

1 2 Apríd robbed; ex-
pilatus Ben. N
aþryd

4 7 *Áþ-wyrde oath
worthy

8

18

Aþied *separated*, v. aþeodan.
Aþierran *To wash off* or *away, rinse, make clean, purge, clear;* diluere:—*Past.* 13, 1.
Aþiestrode *obscured*, v. aþystrian.
w Aþindan; *pp.* aþinden, aþunden *To puff up, swell, inflate;* intumescere:—He þa þone aþundenan sæ gesmylte *he then calmed the enraged sea, Bd.* 5, 1, v. þindan.
Aþindung *A swelling* or *puffing up;* tumor, *Som.*
Aþinnod, aþynned *thinned, made thin*, v. þinnian.
Aþistrod *obscured*, v. aþystrian.
Aþlans þat beorg *Mount Atlas;* Atlas mons:—*Ors.* 1, 1.
Aþnyid *pilled;* expilatus, v. aþryd.
Aþoht [a *out*, þoht *a thought*] *A thinking out, an excogitation, a device, an invention;* commentum:—*Cot.* 35, *Som.*
Aþolian *to sustain, endure*, v. þolian.
x Aðolode *Whole, not cut, or parted;* integer, *Som.*
Aðor, auðer, awðer; *pron. Either, the one or the other, other, both;* alteruter, uterque:—And seþe aðor fulbrece *and he who violates another, L. Cnut.* 2. On aðrum *on both, Cot.* 214. On aðre hand *on either hand, Ors.* 1, 14. Þissa twega yfela auðer ricsað *of these two evils, either reigns, Bt.* 6.—Naðor *neither.*
~~Aðor; *adj. Higher, former; sublimior:—Cd.* 228.~~
Aðor, auðer, aðor, oððe *either, or;* sive, v. oððe.
Aþracian *to fear*, v. anþracian.
Aþræste *wrested, Cot.* 73, v. þræstan.
Aþræt *Irksomeness;* tædium, *Som.*
Aþrawen, geþrawen; *part. Thrown out, twisted, wreathed, twined, wound;* projectus, contortus:—Aþrawenan gold þræddas *twisted gold thread.* Aþrawenum þrædum *with thrown thread, Cot.* 50, v. þrawan.
y Aþreotan; *indef.* hit aþryt; *p.* aþriet; *pp.* aþroten, aþriet *To loathe, disdain, be weary of;* tædio afficere; *also actively, to tire, weary, warn;* monere:—Me aþryt *it wearies me, I am weary, Elf. gr.* 33. Hwi ne læte ge eow þonne aþreotan *why then suffer ye [it] not to warn you, Bt.* 32, 2. Þat ic þe hæbbe aþriet *that I have wearied thee, Bt.* 39, 12.
Aþroten *loathed*, v. aþreotan.
Aþrotennes, aþrotenes, se; *f. Tediousness, loathsomeness, wearisomeness;* tædium:—*Cot.* 91, *Som.*

Aþrotsum; *adj. Troublesome, irksome, wearisome;* tædiosus:—Aþrotsum is *is weary, Cot.* 188.
Aþroxen; *part. Spoiled, robbed, disarmed;* spoliatus, *Som.*
Aþrungen; *part. Concealed;* celatum:—*Cot.* 33, *Lye.*
Aþrunten, aþruten; *part. Molested, infested, annoyed;* infestatus:—*Cod. Ex.* 109, *b. l.* 10.
Aþryd, ahrydred; *part. Wrested, wrung, driven out, robbed, pilled;* expressus:—*Cot.* 73, *Som.*, v. atredan.
z Aþrysemian; *v. To choke, suffocate, stifle;* suffocare:—*Ors.* 5, 4.
Aþryt *wearies*, v. aþreotan.
Að-stæf *an oath;* juramentum:—*Ps.* 104, 8.
Að-swar, aðswara *A solemn oath, an oath;* juramentum:—*Jos.* 9, 18. ¶ Aðsware pytt *the well of the oath, Beersheba, Gen.* 46, 1.
Að-swaring, að-swerung *An oath;* juramentum:—*Ps.* 104, 8: *Chr.* 1070.
Aðswefrian; *v. To devote, dedicate;* devotare:—*Cot.* 64.
Aðswerung *an oath*, v. aðswaring.
Aðswird *an oath;* juramentum:—*Ps.* 104, 8.
Aðsyllan; *v. To take an oath;* jurare, *Som.*
a AÞUM *A son in law, a daughter's husband, a brother in law, a sister's husband;* gener; sororis, ut et patris, sororis maritus:—Hæfst þusun a oððe þe aþum, *Gen.* 19, 12. To his twam aþumum, *Gen.* 19, 14. For to þam cynge his aþume *went to the king his sister's husband, Chr.* 1091.
Aþunden *swollen*, v. aþindan.
Aþundennes, se; *f. A tumour, a swelling;* tumor:—Geswel þat is aþundennesse *a swelling, that is a tumour, Herb.* 2, 17.
Aþwægen *washed*, v. aþwean.
Aþwænan *to take away*, v. ætwenan.
Aþwat *as*, na aþwat him *shall not disappoint him, Ps.* 131, 11.
b Aþwean *To wash from, cleanse, baptize, anoint;* lavare:—Aþweah me, *Ps.* 50, 3, v. þwean.
Að-wed *A solemn oath, sacrament;* sacramentum:—*R.* 13.
Aþwegen *washed*, v. þwean.
Aþweran; *v. To beat, move,* or *shake together;* agitare, *Som.*
Aþwog, aþwogen, aþwoh *washed*, v. þwean.
Aþwyrdan *to answer;* aþword *answered*, v. andwerdan.
Að-wyrð; *adj. Worthy of an oath, worthy of credit;* dignus qui juret:—Gif he að wyrðe bið *if he be oath-worthy, L. In.* 46.
Aþy, *therefore*, v. aþe.
Aþyd *skinned*, v. æthide.

Aþylgian; *p.* ode *To support, sustain;* sustinere:—*Ps.* 129, 4, 5.
c Aþystrian, aþeostrian; *p.* ode, ade; *pp.* aþystrod *To obscure, darken, to become dark, eclipse;* obscurare:—Syn aþystrode eagan heora, *Ps.* 68, 28. Þonne aþeostriað ealle steorran *then the stars become dark, Bt.* 9. Byð sunne aþistrod, *Mk.* 13, 24. Her sunne aþystrode *here the sun was eclipsed, Chr.* 538.
Aþywan; *p.* de; *pp.* ed *To lead* or *drive from, to discard;* ejicere:—*Ors.* 6, 36, v. aweg.
Aþywian, atywian; *v. To appear, shew;* apparere:—*Ps.* 77, 14, v. þywan.
Atiarian *to want*, v. ateorian.
Atifran *to paint;* atiefred *or* atifred *painted*, v. atæfran.
Atih *tares, C. Mt.* 13, 27, v. ata.
Atiht, atihta *attracted, intent upon*, v. ateon.
Atihting *Intention, an aim;* intentio, *Scint.* 6, 7.
Atillan *to touch*, v. getillan.
d Atimbrian, atymbran *To erect, build;* ædificare:—Het atymbran þa burgh *ordered the town to be built, Chr.* 643, v. timbrian.
Ation of *to draw out*, v. ateon.
Atiwede *appeared*, v. æteowian.
Atogen *drawn*, v. ateon.
Atol, atola, atoll, atollic, atelic *deformed, foul*, v. atelic.
Ator *poison;* ator-bærend *poisonous;* ator-cræft *the art of poisoning;* ator-drinc *a poisonous drink*, v. ættrene, ater, atterberend, &c.
Atorfian *to boast*, v. torfian.
Atorlað *Betony;* betonica, v. aterlaðe.
Atredan; *pp.* aþryd *To tread, twist* or *extort from* or *out;* extorquere:—*L. Can. Edg.*
Atrendlod; *part. Trundled, rolled;* volutatus:—*Bt. Rawl.* p. 155, v. trændel.
Atter *poison;* atter-berend *poisonous*, v. attr, ætter-berend.
e Atter-coppa, an [attr *poison*, copp *a cup, a head*] *A spider;* aranea:—*Ps.* 38, 15. ¶ Attercoppan-bite *a spider-bite, spider-wort, a sort of herb.*
Atter-laðe *avoiding poison*, v. aterlaðe.
Attor *poison;* attor-drinca *poisonous drink*, v. ættrene, aterdrinca.
Attor-laðe *penny grass*, v. aterlaðe.
Attr, attre [v. ættrene] *Poison, the herb snakeweed, or dragon wort;* venenum:—¶ Drenc wið attre *a drink or potion against poison;* theriaca, *R.* 12. Attre gemæled *spoken with poi-*

son, quarrels, Cot. 124. Fleogend attre *flying poison, a disease, L. M.* p. 1, cap. 25.

f Attred, od; *part. Poisoned*; venenatus:—*Ors.* 3, 9.

Atuge *drawn out*, v. ateon.

Atymbran *to build*, v. timbrian.

Atynan; *p.* de; *pp.* ed; *v. a.* [a *not*, tynan *to hedge*] *To open, lay open, leave out, shut out, exclude*; aperire:—Atyn us, *Lk.* 13, 25. Ic atynde muð minne, *Ps.* 38, 13.

Atyrian *to fail*, v. ateorian.

Atywde *shewed*, v. aþywian.

Auht *any thing*, v. aht.

Aurnen *run out, passed*, v. ayrnan.

Auðer *other*, v. aðor.

Auðer *either*, v. oððe.

AWA; *adv. Always*; semper:—Awa to aldre *for ever, Cd.* 220, v. aldr.

g Awacian, gewacan, on-wacan; *indef.* ic awacige; *p.* awacode; *pp.* cod. *To weaken, to grow weak*, or *effeminate, to languish, decline, fail, relax, to be indolent*; infirmari, deficere:—Awacode mid langre ealdunge *weakened with old age, Gr. Dial.* 2, 15. Awaciað on þære costnunge timan, *Lk.* 8, 13, Gif hy þær ne gewacodan *if they relaxed not there, Ors.* 3, 4.

Awacod, *softened, awaked*, v. awacan, awæcnian.

Awæcan *to awake, arise, take origin, to be born*, v. wæcan.

Awæcnian, onwæcnian, awacian; *p.* code, cnede, cenede; *pp.* cod, cned, cened. 1. *To* AWAKE, *arouse, revive*; expergefacere. 2. *To stir up, originate, arise, vegetate*; excitare, ortum ducere:—1. Swilce of hefegum slæpe awacode, *Gen.* 45, 26. He eft awacenede *he again revived, Bd.* 5, 12. 2. Of þam frumgarum folc awæcniað *from these patriarchs shall spring people, Cd.* 104. Eall heora gewinn awæcnedon ærest fram Alexandres epistole *all their contests first arose from Alexander's letter, Ors.* 3, 11.

Awægan, awregan; *p.* gde; *pp.* ged, gen; *v. To deceive, delude, frustrate, disappoint*; eludere:—Awæged nedo þu wedd *make not thou a vain* [*deluded*] *treaty, Hymn.* Awægune yrfebec *a useless will, Cot.* 116, *v. l.*

h Awæged *void, useless*, v. awægan.

Awægen, awægun *vain*, v. awægan.

Awæh *vegetated*, v. awæcan, wæh.

Awæh *weighed out*, v. wægan.

Awæht *aroused*, v. aweccan.

Awæht *Wearied*; defessus:—*Hymn. Cot.* 157, *Lye.*

Awælian *To revolve, suffer, vex*; revolvere:—*R. Mt.* 28, 2. Awæled *vexed*, v. wæled.

Awændan *to turn from*, v. awendan.

Awærde *A stupid, foolish man*; fatuus:—*R.* 9, v. awerdan.

Awærgda *reviled*, v. awyrian.

Awæscen *washed*, v. wæscan.

Awæstan *to destroy, eat up*, v. awestan.

Awanian *to diminish*, v. wanian.

i Awannan; *p.* ede; *pp.* od. *To make wan* or *pale*; pallescere:—*Dial.* 1, 2.

Awar; *adv. Somewhere*; alicubi, *Som.*

Awariged; *part. Accursed*; execrandus, *Som.*

Awarnian; *v. To confound*; confundere:—*Ps.* 85, 16, v. aswarnian.

Awarpen *cast out*, v. aworpan.

Aweaht *awakened*, v. aweccan.

Aweallan, he awylð; *p.* aweol; *pp.* aweallen *To boil* or *bubble up, to break forth, issue, flow, stream* or *gush forth*; ebullire, erumpere:—Þa fruman aweallað Deorwentan streames *the sources of the Derwent's stream flow forth, Bd.* 4, 29. Wylle aweolle *a spring issued forth, Bd.* 5, 10.

Aweardian; *v. To defend, ward, protect*; tueri:—Hi hi sylf aweardedon *they defended themselves, Ors.* 5, 3.

Awearpan *to cast away*, v. aweorpan.

j Aweb *The cross threads in weaving, called the woof*, or *weft*; subtegmen:—*Cot.* 161.

Aweccan, he aweccð; *imp.* awecc, awecce; *p.* awehte, awæhte, aweahte; hi awehton; *pp.* aweht, awæht; *v. a.* 1. *To awake from sleep, arouse, stir up, excite, consider*; expergefacere. 2. *To awake from death, to revive, raise up*; resuscitare. 3. *To produce, beget, raise up children*; gignere:—1. Hig awehton hyne, *Mk.* 4, 38. Hatung aweccð saca *hatred awaketh strife, Scint.* Heo awehte hine, *Judg.* 16, 19. Þa awæhte heo þa sweostera *then awoke she the sisters, Bd.* 4, 23. 2. Ic hine awecce, *Jn.* 6, 40. Swa se Fæder aweccð þa deadan, *Jn.* 5, 21. Awecceað deade *raise up* [*awake*] *the dead, Mt.* 10, 8. 3. He mæg bearn aweccan, *Lk.* 3, 8, (aweccean, *Mt.* 3, 9.) *he can raise up children.* Þæt he hys broðor sæd awecce, *Lk.* 20, 28, v. weccan.

Awece *arouse*, v. aweccan.

k Awecgan *to shake, Job. Thw.* p. 167, 33, v. wecgan.

Aweccð *rouses*, v. aweccan.

Awed *mad*, v. awedan.

Awedan, awoedan; *p.* awedde; *pp.* awed, aweden, *v. n. To be mad, to rage, to be angry, to go* or *wax mad, to revolt, apostatize*; in furorem agi:—Aweddan þa nytena *the cattle became mad, Ors.* 5, 10, *Som.*, v. wedan.

Awefen, aweuen; *part. Woven*; textus:—*Jn.* 19, 23, v. wefan.

Aweg, anweg; *adv.* [a *from*, wæg *a way*] AWAY, *out*; (this is its meaning both in and out of composition); auferendi vim habet:—Þa eode he aweg, *Mt.* 19, 22. Ge drehnigeað þone gnæt aweg, *Mt.* 23, 24. He hi raðe aweg aþywde *he quickly drove them away, Ors.* 6, 36.

l Awegadrifan *To drive* or *chase away*; expellere:—*Ps.* 35, 13, v. drifan.

Awegaferian *To leave entirely*; evehere:—*Cot.* 205.

Awegalucan [aweg *away*, alocan *to expose*] *To shut* or *lock out, to separate*; discludere:—*Cot.* 67, *Som.*

Awegan; *p.* de; *pp.* ed, yd, en. *To turn aside* or *away, move from, dissuade, lift up, balance, weigh, to weigh as an anchor, to agitate, shake*; avertere, agitare:—Mod bið aweged of his stede *the mind is moved from his place, Bt.* 12. Winde aweged hreod *a reed shaken* [*wagged*] *by the wind, Mt.* 11, 7, v. awecgan.

Aweganumen; *part. Taken away*; sublatus:—*Jn.* 20, 1.

Awegawylt; *part.* [awylt *rolled, from* awylian] *Rolled away*; revolutus:—*Mk.* 16, 4.

Awegbæran; *v. To bear, carry* or *convey away*; asportare:—*Elf. gr.* 47.

Awegcuman; *p.* com; hi awegcomon; *pp.* cumen *To go away, to leave, escape*; dimittere:—Sume awegcomon *some went away, Ors.* 3, 3: 4, 1.

Awegde *weighed*, v. awegan.

Aweged *shaken*, v. awegan.

m Awegen *weighed as in a balance*, v. awegan.

Aweggan *To go away*; abire:—Ongan aweggan *began to go away, Bd.* 4, 22.

Aweggeniman; *v. To take away*; auferre, *Som.*

Aweggewitan; *p.* gewat; *pp.* gewiten *To go away, to depart*; discedere:—Ic eom aweg-gewiten *I am passed away, Ors.* 2, 4.

Awegewitenes, se; *f. A going away, a departure*; abscessio:—*Bd.* 4, 12.

Aweglætan *To let go away, send*

Attor-sceaþa, an; m a poison, a plague Beo K 5673

Awendednes a translation Th a pol v awendednys

ϕ 1

ϕ 2 Awærgda, an; m one accursed Cd 222 Th p 290, 16

2 Atywian to appear reveal, disclose show, manifest ostendere Ps 14 Lye ~~Th An~~ v ætewian

3 Awarian to curse Th An

3

4 Awacened awaked revived Bd 5, 12 v awæcnian

O 4 None

O 5

2 Awegaþywde expulit ~~[illegible]~~ Ors 6, 36 v þywan

(intexere)

he awint
1 Awindan, to wind
of, to fly off
or to take off; evolare, detrahere Past. 21, 7: Bt 37, Card p 288, 13 v windan
winds

2 Awirt-walian to root up Som v awyrt-walian

2 Awendendlic changeable Som. Ben. v awendedlic
3 awenduncg a changing v awendincg

1 *awildian to grow wild Th. an.

away; dimittere :—*L. Pol. Cnut.* 26.
Awegonwendan; *v. To move away, to remove, to wend* or *wind away*; divertere : — *Ps.* 65, 19.
n Awegweorpan *To cast* or *throw away*; abjicere, *Som.*
Awegyd *shaken*, v. awegan.
Aweht *aroused*, v. aweccan.
Awehte *revived*; *p. of* aweccan.
Awehtnes, se; *f. An awaking, a stirring up, excitation, quickening, encouraging*; excitatio: *Bd.* 5, 12.
Awel *an awl*, v. æl.
Awenan; *p.* ede; *pp.* ed *To wean*; ablactare :—Awened beon *to be weaned*, *Bd.* 1, 27.
Awendan, awændan; *p.* awende, awent; *pp.* awend, awended, awoend; *v. a. To turn, change, translate, depart, pervert*; avertere :—*Gen.* 19, 26, v. wendan.
Awendedlic, awendelic, awendendlic; *adj. Moveable, changeable, alterable, mutable*; mobilis :—*Albin. resp.* 42, *Som.*
o Awendednys, se; *f. A change, alteration*; commutatio :—*Ps.* 54, 22: 88, 50.
Awendelicnes, se; *f. Mutableness, mutability, changeableness, inconstancy*; mutabilitas, *Som.*
Awend-gewrixl *on the other side*; versâ vice, *Som.*
Awendung *An overthrowing, a change, ruin*; subversio :—*Scint.* 61.
Awend-spræce to oðrum hiwe, *a word changed to another* [*hue*] *meaning, Metaplasm. Som.*
Awened *weaned*, v. awenan.
Aweodian; *v. a. To weed, root* or *rake up, to destroy*; sarculare :—Þat man aweodige unriht *that one should root up injustice*, *L. Pol. Cnut.* 1.
Aweol *flowed forth*, v. aweallan.
Aweorpan, awyrpan, awurpan; *p.* awearp, þu awurpe, hi awurpon; *pp.* aworpen; *v. a.* [a *from*, weorpan *to throw*] *To throw* or *cast down, to degrade, to cast away* or *off, cast out, reject, divorce*; abjicere :—Þu awurpe hi, *Ps.* 72, 18. Þa woldan senatus hine aweorpan *then would the senate degrade him*, *Ors.* 3, 10. Ne aweorp þu me, *Ps.* 70, 10. Ic awurpe deoflu, *Mt.* 12, 28. Þat mannes sunu gebyreð beon aworpen, *Mk.* 8, 31. Aworpen wif *a divorced wife*. Aworpen mon *an apostate man*, *Past.* 47, 1. Used also with the prepositions on *into*, as awurpan on *to cast into*, *Mt.* 13, 50. Fram *from*, *Mt.* 5, 29, 30. Ut *out*, *Mt.* 13, 48. Under *below*, *Bt.* 37, 4.

p Aweorpnis, se; *f. A divorce, a bill of divorce*; repudium :—*R. Mt.* 19, 7.
Aweorðan, he awyrð; *p.* awearð; *v. n.* [a *not*, weorðan *to be*] *Not to be, to vanish, spoil*; evanescere :—Gif þat sealt awyrð *if the salt be not, exist not*, or *be vanished*, *Mt.* 5, 13.
Aweosung, e; *f. The being, essence*, or *subsistence of a thing*; subsistentia :—*Cot.* 170.
Aweox *waxed, increased*, v. weaxan.
Awepan *To wipe out, cleanse*; abstergere, *Lye*, v. wipian.
Awer *any where*, v. ahwar.
Aweran *to wear*, v. weran.
Awerdan, awyrdan; *p.* de; *pp.* ded, awerde, awærde, awyrd; *v. To injure, deprive, vanish, hurt, spoil, forbid*; vapidus fieri, vitiari :—Gif spræc awyrd weorð *if speech be injured*, *L.* [illegible] 52, v. awærde.
Awerdnys, awyrdnys, se; *f. Downfal, injury, loss, ruin*; labes :—*Elf. gr.* 13.
Awered *worn*, v. weran.
Awered *protected*, v. awerian.
Awerged *cursed*, v. awyrian.
q Awerian *To protect, defend, guard, despise*; defendere :—*Ors.* 3, 9, v. werian.
Awerpan *to cast away*, v. aweorpan.
Awersian *To make worse*; deterius facere :—*Cart. Edwardi R. Lye*, v. wyrsian.
Awest; *adj.* or *part. Waste, void, deserted*; desertus :—Þæt eall seo þeod awest awearð *that all the country was* [*waste*] *deserted*, *Ors.* 3, 9.
Awestan; *p.* he aweste, hi aweston; *pp.* ed; *v. a.* [a *intensive*, westan *to waste*] *To waste, to lay waste, eat up, destroy, reduce, demolish, depopulate*; vastare :—And hi aweste, *Jos.* 10, 39. Swa swa oxa gewunað to awæstenne gærs, *Numb.* 22, 4. Hi ealle Egypta aweston, *Ors.* 1, 10. Þe burh awested wæs, *Ors.* 2, 2.
r Awestendnes, se; *f. A wasting, a laying waste*; vastatio, *Som.*
Awestnis, awoestenis, se; *f. Destruction, desolation*; desolatio :—*R. Mt.* 21, 20.
Aweuen *woven*, v. awefen.
Awht *aught*, v. aht.
Awidlan *To defile, profane*; violare :—*C. Mt.* 12, 5.
Awierdan *To corrupt, spoil*; corrumpere : — He awiert þæt mod *he corrupts the mind*, *Past.* 53, 5, *Lye*, v. awyrian.
Awiergda, awierged *cursed*, v. awyrian.
Awiht *any thing*, v. aht.
Awildan; *pp.* dod *To become wild* or *fierce*; sylvescere :—*Off. Epis.* 7, *Som.*
Awilled; *part. Well boiled*, or *sodden*; decoctus :—Awilled meolc *boiled milk, pottage*, *Cot.* 168. Awilled hunig *pure honey*, *Herb.* 1, 20. Awilled wine, awylled win, awyrd win or cyren *new wine, just pressed from the grape*, or *new wine boiled till half evaporated*, *Cot.* 62, 168, v. awylian, cæren.
s Awinnan *To labour, contend, fight, overcome, conquer*; laborare :—*Cot.* 211, v. winnan.
Awint *wound, wove, stript*; *p. of* windan.
Awirged *execrable, cursed*, v. awyrian.
Awirgean *to destroy*, v. awyrian.
Awirgnis *slander*, v. awyrgednys.
Awise-ferinend *Publicans*; publicani :—*Cot.* 204, v. æwisc.
Awisnian *To be dry, to become dry*, WIZZEN; arescere :—*C. Lk.* 8, 6.
Awlættan; *p.* te. *To defile*; fœdare :—*Hymn. Mod. Confit.* 1.
Awo *always*, v. awa.
Awoc *awoke, arose*, v. wæcan.
Awodian *to root up*, v. aweodian.
Awœdan *to be mad*, v. awedan.
Awœnd *returned*; reversus, *Lye*, v. awendan.
Awœrdan *to forbid*, *C. Lk.* 18, 16.
Awœstednis *destruction*, v. awestendnes.
Awœstenis *destruction*, v. awestnis.
Awogod *Wooed*; petitus, *Som.*, v. wogan.
t Awoh; *adv.* [a *out*, wo, woh *a turning, an error*] AWRY, *unjustly, wrongfully, badly*; *the same as* mid woh *or* woge, *with injustice*, or *unjustly*; tortè, obliquè, malè :—Gif mon þat trod awoh drife *if one wrongfully pursue the* [*tread*] *footstep*, *L. Wal.* 1. Ær awoh to somne gedydon *before unjustly joined* [*done*] *together*, *L. Edm.* 9.
Awolde *would*, *for* wolde, *from* wyllan.
Aworden *done*, v. weorðan.
Aworden; *part.* [awyrden, *from* awyrian *to curse*] *Execrated, cursed*; reprobatus :—Þu awordena *thou, the cursed*; racha, *Mt.* 5, 22.
Aworold *for ever*, v. weorold.
Aworpan *to reject*, aworpen *cast away*, v. aweorpan.
Aworpenlic; *adj. Damnable*; damnabilis :—*Past.* 52, 8.
Aworpenes, aworpennys, aworpnes, se; *f. A rejection, casting away, reprobation, reproving*; abjectio :—*Ps.* 21, 5.
v Aworðane *The cast away, the heathen*; ethnici, *Lye*.

Awoxe *Should sift*; cribraret:—*C. R. Lk.* 22, 31, *Lye*.
Awræste *extorted*, v. awrestan.
Awrat *wrote*, v. awritan.
Awrað *bound up*, v. awriðan.
Awrecan; *v. To revenge, avenge, vindicate, defend, free*; ulcisci:—Gif hine hwa awrecan wille, *L. Athel.* 20, v. wrecan.
Awreccan; *p.* awrehte; *pp.* awreht; *v. a. To arouse, awake, revive*; resuscitare:—Ic wyllegan and awreccan hyne of slæpe, *Jn.* 11, 11, v. aweccan.
Awrecen; *adj. One banished, driven away*; extorris:—*Cot.* 212, 5, *Lye*, v. wrec.
Awregan *to deceive*, v. awægan.
Awregennes *a discovery*, v. awrigenes.
Awreon, awrion, awrihð; *p.* ic, he, awreah, þu awruge, we awrugon; *pp.* awrogen, awrigen; *v. a.* [a *not*, wreon *to cover*] *To uncover, discover, disclose, open, reveal*; revelare:—Se Sunu hit awreon wyle, *Lk.* 10, 22. Syn awrigene *be revealed, Lk.* 2, 35, v. wreon.
Awrestan; *p.* awræste *To wrest from, to extort*; extorquere:—*Cot.* 78.
Awreþian; *p.* ode; *pp.* ed; *v. a. To support, underprop, sustain, lean upon*; sustentare:—Augustinus fram Gode awreþed wæs *Augustin was sustained by God, Bd.* 2, 3. He mid his crycce hine awreþiende ham becom *he, with his crutch supporting him, came home, Bd.* 4, 31.
Awridan; *v. To originate, generate*; pullulare, *Lye*, v. wridan.
Awrigde *cursed*, v. awyrian.
Awrigen *revealed*, v. awreon.
Awrigenes, awregennes, se; *f. A discovery, revelation*; revelatio:—*Lk.* 2, 32.
Awringan; *p.* awrang; *pp.* awrungen *To wring out, to squeeze out, express*; exprimere:—*Cot.* 196.
Awrion *to uncover*, v. awreon.
Awritan; *p.* awrat; *pp.* awriten; *v. a.* [a *from*, writan *to write*] *To write out, transcribe, draw out, describe, dispose, write, publish*; transcribere, describere:—Eall ic awrat *I transcribed all, Bd.* 5, 23. Geræde worde ic awrat *in simple speech*, [*prose*] *I transcribed, Id.* Nu hæbbe we awriten þære suð *now have we described the south, Ors.* 1, 1. Hi bæron alicnysse Hælendes on brede afægde and awritene *they bore the Savi[illegible]s likeness ornamented* [*figure[illegible]*] *and drawn on a tablet*, [illegible]. 1, 25.
Awri[illegible]n; *p.* awrað; *pp.* awri[illegible]; *v. a. To loose*; solvere; *to deliver from an injury, as a wound*; hence *to bind up*; alligare:—His wunda awrað *bound up his wounds, Bd.* 4, 22, v. wriðan.
Awriðþe *A strap*; struppus:—*R.* 103, v. strop.
Awruge *revealedst*, v. awreon.
Awrungen *wrung*, v. awringan.
Awuht *aught*, v. aht.
Awðre, awðer *another*, v. aðor.
Awul *an awl*, v. æl.
Awunden *woven*, v. windan.
Awunian *to abide, remain, inhabit, to be wont*, v. wunian.
Awunnen *fought*, v. winnan.
Awurpan *to cast away*, v. aweorpan.
Awurtwarude *rooted up*; exterminavit:—*Ps.* 79, 14.
Awyht *something*, v. aht.
Awylian; *p.* hi awylton; *pp.* awylten, awyltn, *v. a. To roll, roll away, revolve*; volutare:—Þat hig awylton þone stan, *Gen.* 29, 3. Awylt *rolled away, Lk.* 24, 2.
Awylð *shall spring forth*, v. aweallan.
Awyndwian *To blow away*; ventilare:—*Ps.* 43, 7.
Awyrcan *To do, effect*; facere:—*L. Hloth.*, v. wyrcan.
Awyrdan *to hurt*; awyrd *hurt*, v. awerdan.
Awyrdla *damage*, v. æfwyrdla.
Awyrgd *cursed*, v. awyrian.
Awyrgedlic; *adj. Wicked, evil*; malignus:—Awyrgedlic geþanc *a wicked thought, Nicod.* 20: *Thw.* p 10, 11.
Awyrgednys, awirgednys, awirgnis, se; *f. A cursedness, wickedness, a curse, reviling*; malignitas:—*Deut.* 11, 29, v. wyrgednes.
Awyrgendlic; *adj. Detestable, abominable*; detestabilis:—*Nathan.* 7.
Awyrian, awirian, awirgean; *p.* awirgede, awrigde; *pp.* awyrged, awyrgd, awirged, awierged, awiergd, awerged, awærgd; *v. a.* [a, wirian, wirgian *to curse*] *To curse, execrate, revile, corrupt, destroy*; execrari, maledicere:—Nelle ic awirgean þa eorðan, *Gen.* 8, 21. Gewitað ge awyrgede fram me, *Mt.* 25, 41. He hine sylfne hæfde awirged *he had destroyed himself, Ors.* 6, 36. Awrigde hine, *C. Mt.* 27, 5. The perfect participle signifies *execrable, wicked, detestable*, execrabilis:—Gewitað nu awirgede woruld sorga *depart now execrable worldly* [illegible] *Ps.* 3.
[illegible]wyrn; [illegible] [*perhaps for* ahwær] *Any where, in any place*; alicubi:—*Menol.* 193: *Hickes' Thes.* vol. i. p. 205.
Awyrpan *to cast away*, v. aweorpan.
Awyrð *exist not*, v. aweorðan.
Awyrðian *To give honour, glorify*; glorificare;—*Cant. Moys. Lye.*
Awyrtwalian; *p.* ode; *pp.* od, ud; *v. a.* [a *out*, wyrtwalian *to root, to fix roots*] *To root up, eradicate, extirpate, exterminate*; eradicare:—Ælc plantung byð awyrtwalod, *Mt.* 15, 13. Þelæs ge þone hwæte awyrtwalion, *Mt.* 13, 29.
Awystelian [a, wistlian *to whistle*] *To hiss, to lisp, whistle*; sibilare, *Som.*
Axan *for* oxan *oxen*, v. oxa.
Axan *ashes*, v. axe.
Axanminster *Axminster, Devon*, v. acsanmynster.
Axbaken; *part. Baked in ashes*; subcinericius:—*Gr. Dial.* 1, 11.
Axe, æxe, ahsa, axsa, an [*Frs.* yeske: *Dut.* asch] Ash, *ashes*; cinis, cineres:—Swa swa dust and axe *as dust and ashes, Bt.* 33, 4. On þære stowe þe man þa axan git, *Lev.* 1, 16. Ahsan [axan] swa swa hlaf ic æt, *Ps.* 101, 10.
Axian *to ask*, v. acsian.
Axiendlic, axigendlic; *adj. Enquiring, inquisitive*; interrogativus, *Som.*
Axigean *to ask*, v. acsian.
Axode *asked*, v. acsian.
Axsa *ashes*, v. axe.
Axung *inquiry*, v. acsung.
Aydlian *to fail*, v. aidlian.
Aydlige *fails*, v. aidlian.
Ayrnan, he ayrnð; *p.* aarn, hi aurnon; *pp.* aurnen [a *out*, yrnan *to run*] *To run over, to pass* or *go over, passed, gone*; præterire. Swa neah wæs þusend aurnen *so near was a thousand gone, Chr.* 971. Aurnenre tide *in* or *at a declining time, the time being far spent* or *gone*. Aurnen bið *is run out, passed, Som.*
Aytan [a *from*, ytan, ytian *for* utian *to out*] *To expel, drive out*; expellere:—He þa aytte þa Swegen ut *he then drove Sweyne out, Chr.* 1047.

1 Awrœc ~~sfm~~ told, related Bo.K ~~4212~~ 4212 v. ~~wrecan~~ wrecan

2 Awreat ~~[illegible]~~ avenged Son pp. of awrecan

3

4 Awrigan; pp. awrah wé awrigon to reveal, disclose Th. An v awreon

1 Awrygan discovered Son v awreon ~~[illegible]~~

4 Awrygenes a reveal ing Som v awrigene

7 Awurfwælan turned up Ben v. awyrtwalian

3 Awylled-win boiled wine; defrutum Som v. awilled

5

1 Awyrdnys a blemish injury Elf. gr. 9.27 v awerdnys

2 Awyrgian to curse Th. An v awyrian

1 Awyrigednes wicked ness Som v awyr gednys

2 Awyrtwalian to root up

1 Axan cinis Elf. gr. Som 9.28 line 236

3 Axigian to ask Ben v acsian

4

2 ~~Aidlad~~ pp. aidlud Ben

O [19a]

Baca of backs, bacu backs pl. of bæc

Bacan [18a]

[18b]

Bád, g. bæde f. a pledge

Baddan-burh, g. -burge; d. -byrig; f. Badbury

Æt Baddan-byrig at Badbury Chr. 901 Ing. p. 125, 3

Ø2

Ø3

Ø3 es; m; an m v before

Ø2. Bæftan, sittende sitting behind, or still idle, slothful; Som.

d The sound of B is produced by the lips; hence it is called a labial consonant. In all languages, and especially in the dialects of cognate languages, the letters employing the same organs of utterance are continually interchanged. In Anglo-Saxon, therefore, we find that B interchanges with the other labials F, P, and V, and with U: Ic hæbbe *I have*, he hæfð *he hath*. When words are transferred into modern English, B is sometimes represented by V; as Beber, *or* befor *a beaver;* Ifig, *or* iuig *ivy;* Ober, ofer, ouer *over;* Ebolstan, efolstan *to blaspheme*; Fot, uot *a foot;*
e Ebul *evil;* b *or* bb is sometimes omitted or superseded by f, p, u *or* v; as Ic lybbe *I live*, lif *life;* Diobul *for* deofl *a devil.*

Bá, bu; *gen.* begra; *dat.* bam; *acc.* bá; *adj. Both*, v. begen.

Bac *a back, found in composition*, v. bæc.

Bacan, ic bace, þu bæcst, he bæcð; *p.* ic bóc, we bócon; *pp.* bacen; *v. a.* [*Plat. Dut.* bakken: *Frs.* backe: *Ger.* backen] *To* BAKE; pinsere:—. Fif bacað on anum ofene, *Lev.* 26, 26. Hi bocon þat melu, *Ex.* 12, 39.

Bacberend *Taking on the back, taking secretly as a thief;* in furto deprehendens, *Mann.*

Bacen *baked*, v. bacan.

Bachilers; *m.* BACHELORS; baccalaurei, *Lye.*

Bacslitol; *m.* [bac *a back*, slitol *or* slite *a slit, cut*, or *bite*] *A slanderer, backbiter;* detractor:—*Off. reg.* 15. Opposed to wærsagol.

f Bá'd, báde; *f. A pledge, stake, a thing distrained;* pignus:—Gif bad genumen sy-þonne begyte þa bade ham *if a pledge be taken—then shall he obtain the pledge home again*, or *back*, *L. Wal.* 3, v. wædd.

Bad *expected; p. of* bidan.

Baddan-byrig [Baddan *for* Bieda, Biedda, *or* Bedd *a Saxon chief, Chr.* 501, byrig *a burg, town, place of defence*] BADBURY, *Dorsetshire, formerly Baddanburgum, Chr.* 901.

Badian; *v. a.* 1. *To pledge, to lay in*, or *to pawn;* pignerare. 2. *To seize on*, or *take for a distress*, or *by way of a pledge;* pignus auferre:—1. *Som.* 2. Of ægþran staþe on oþer man mot badian, *L. Wal.* 2.

Bæc [*Plat. Norse*, bak: *Al.* back: *Frs.* to bek *backwards*] A BACK; tergum:—Þa wendon hi me heora bæc to *then turned they their back to me*, *Bt.* 2. ¶ On bæc, *Jn.* 6, 66: *and* under bæc, *Ps.* 43, 12: *at his back, behind, backward*, v. under-bæc. Clæn bæc hæbban *to have a clean back, to be free from deceit, L. Alf. Guth.* Gang on bæc, *Mt.* 4, 10. Ga on bæc, *Mk.* 8, 33. GANG, or *go behind*, or *away.*

g Bæcbord [*Plat. Dut.* bakboord] *The larboard*, or *left-hand side of a ship when looking towards the prow*, or *head;* navigii sinistra pars:—Burgenda land wæs us on bæcbord *the land of the Burgundians was on our larboard*, or *left*, *Ors.* 1, 1.

Bæce *a beech tree*, v. boc.

Bæcere; *m.* [*Plat. Dut.* bakker *m.*: *Ger.* bäcker *m.*] A BAKER; pistor:—*R.* 50, *Lye.*

Bæc-ering [bæc *a back*, iren, eren *iron*] *A gridiron;* craticula, *Som.*

Bæc-ern [bæc *from*, bacan *to bake*, ern, *or* æren *a place*] *A baking place, a bakehouse;* pistrinum:—*Elf. gl.* 22.

Bæcestre, bæcistr, *or* bæcistre, an; *m. f.* 1. *A woman who bakes;* pistrix. 2. Because men performed that work which was originally done by females; this occupation is sometimes denoted by a feminine termination; hence, *a baker;* pistor:—1. *Som.* 2. Egypta cynges byrle and his bæcistre, *Gen.* 40, 1, 2, 16, 20.

h Bæchus A BAKEHOUSE; pistrinum:—*Elf. gl.* 22, v. bæcern.

Bæcling *used adverbially; thus*, On bæcling *backward*, *Ps.* 113, 3, v. bæc, under-bæc.

Bæcslitol *a backbiter*, v. bacslitol.

Bæcst *bakest*, v. bacan.

Bæcð *bakes*, v. bacan.

Bæcþearm, es; *m.* [bæc *a back*, þearm *a gut*] *The entrails;* anus longanum:—*Cot.* 15, 163. Bæcþearmas *the bowels;* extales, *Elf. gr.* 13. Bæcþearmes utgang *morbus*, fortasse, *ani procidentia, Som.*

Bæd *prayed*, v. biddan.

Bædd *a bed*, v. bed.

Bædde *A thing required, tribute;* exactum:—*Cot.* 73.

Bæddel *An animal uniting two sexes, a wether;* hermaphroditus, vervex:—*R.* 76, *Lye.*

Bæddryda *bedridden*, v. beddredda.

Bædel *a beadle*, v. bydel.

Bædend; *m. A vehement*, or *earnest persuader, a solicitor, stirrer;* impulsor:—*Cot.* 115, *Som.*

Bædeweg, bædewig *a contest*, v. beado.

i Bædling, es; *m.* [bæd *or* bedd *a bed*, ling *from*, linigan *to lie*] 1. *A delicate fellow, tenderling, one who lies much in bed;* homo delicatus. Bædlingas *effeminate, Cot.* 71. 2. *A carrier of letters*, as if derived from bæd *a prayer*, or *command*, ling *from* linigan *or* lingan *to lie, lie under, tend, bring;* tabellarius.

Bædt *commanded*, v. biddan.

Bædþearm; *mentera, pars hominis:*—*R.* 76, *f.*

Bædzere, bæzere, bæzera; *m. A baptist, baptizer;* baptista:—*R. Mt.* 3, 1: 16, 14. *An impure word for* fulluht. *quod*, v.

Bæfta; *m. The after part, the back;* tergum:—Ic geseah þone bæftan *I saw thy back, Gen.* 16, 13.

Bæftan, be-æftan, beftan; *prep. dat.* [be *by*, æftan *after*] 1. *After, behind;* post, pone. 2. *Without;* sine:—1. Gang bæftan me, *Mt.* 16, 23. 2. Bæftan þam hlaforde *without the master, Ex.* 22, 14: *Mt.* 16, 27.

i Bæftan, bæfta; *adv. After, hereafter, afterwards;* postea:—Git synd fif hungor ger bæftan, *Gen.* 45, 11. He ana belaf þær bæfta, *Gen.* 32, 24.

Bægeras, bægðware; *plu. The Bavarians;* Bavarii, *or* the Boiari, *or* Bajuvarii, [viri e Bojis oriundi, *Wachter.*] whose country was called Boiaria, its German name is Bayern, now called the kingdom of Bavaria. Mid Bægerum *with the Bavarians, Chr.* 891. Syndon Bægðware *are the Bavarians, Ors.* 1, 1.

Bæh *a crown*, v. beag.

BÆ'L, bæl *A funeral pile, or fire in which dead bodies were burned;* rogus:—*Cd.* 140. Bælfyr *the fire of the funeral pile, Cd.* 138. Bæl-blyse *a blaze of the funeral pile, Cd.* 162.

BÆLC, bealceten. 1. A BELCH; eructatio. 2. *The stomach, pride, arrogance;* superbia. 3. *A covering;* tegmen, v. balc:—1. *Mann.* 2. Bælc forbigde *pride, bowed, diminished, Cd.* 4. Swete to bealcetenne *sweet* or *pleasant to the stomach, Bt.* 21, 1. 3. Bælce ofer-brædde *with a covering overspread, Cd.* 146.

k Bælded; *part. Animated, encouraged, emboldened;* animatus, *Som.*

Bældu *Confidence;* fiducia:—*R. Mt.* 14, 27, *Lye.*

Bælfyr *a funeral fire,* v. bæl.

BÆLG, bælig, es; *m.* [*Plat. Dut. Ger. Dan.* balg *m*: *Frs. v.* bealg: *Moes.* balgs] A BULGE, *budget, bag, purse,* BELLY; bulga:—*Cot.* 27. ¶ Beanbelgas *beanshells.* Blast-belg [*Dut.* blaasbalg] *blast-bag, bellows.* Metbælg *a wallet for meat.*

Bælignis; *f. An injury;* injuria:—*C. Mt.* 20, 13, *Lye.*

Bæm *for* bam; *dat. of* ba *both,* v. ba, begen.

BÆNCE, benc, banc [*Plat. Dut. Ger.* bank *f*: *Dan. Swed.* baenk] 1. A BENCH, *form;* scamnum. 2. *A bed, bedstead, the side of a bed;* lectus, *Som.*

BÆND, bend, es; *m.* [*Plat. Dut. Ger. Icel.* band *m.* and *n*: *Frs.* bôan: *Frs. h.* biend: *Dan.* baand *n*: *Moes.* bandi, band, binde, bint *from,* bindan *to bind*] 1. A BAND, *any thing that tieth, bindeth* or *bendeth;* vinculum. 2. *A crown, chaplet, ornament for females;* diadema:—1. On bendum *in bonds,* or *prison, Mt.* 11, 22. 2. Bend mid golde gescrud *a crown* or *diadem decked with gold, R.* 64.

Bændan *to bind,* v. bindan.

l BÆR, bære, beer, bere. [*Plat.* baar, böre *f*: *Frs. v.* bier: *Dut.* baar *f*: *Ger.* bahre *f*: *Dan.* baare *c*: *Al.* para: *Per.* بير bir] 1. A BIER; feretrum. 2. *A portable bed;* grabatus:—1. *Elf. gl.* 26. 2. *Bd.* 5, 19.

Bær *bore;* portavit; *p. of* beran.

Bær *bear;* nudus, v. bar.

-bær, -bære, -bor *an adjective termination from the perfect tense of* beran *to bear, produce;* or *from the Teutonic* bar, *fruit, a production, producing, bearing: Ger. Dan.* -bar: *Per.* بر -ber: as wæstmbær *fruitbearing, fruitful.* Æppelbær *applebearing;* pomifer:—and hornbær *horn-bearing;* corniger, *Elf. gr.* 8. Leoht-bær *bearing light,* v. bora.

Bæræden; *part.* [be, hreddan *to rid*] *Rid of,* BERIDDEN, *deprived, driven away;* privatus, *Som.*

Bærcþearm, *or* snædel *the bowels, R.* 74, v. bæcþearm, snædel.

Bærdisc, es; *m.* [bær *bier,* disc *a dish, table*] *A frame on which several dishes were brought in at once and set upon the table, a course, service;* ferculum:—*Elf. gl.*

Bærefot, bærfot; *adj.* BAREFOOT, or *that goeth barefooted;* nudipes:—*Peccat. Med.* 8.

m Bærlice; *adv. Openly, nakedly,* BARELY; palam, *Som.*

Bærm *a bosom,* v. bearm.

Bærman, nes; *nom. plu.* bærmenn; *d.* bærmannum; *m. A man who bears, a bearer, carrier, porter;* bajulus:—Ða bærmenn gesetton heora fotlæst *the porters set their footstep, Jos.* 3, 3, 14.

Bærn *a barn,* v. bern.

Bærnan, forbærnan, onbærnan; *p.* bærnde, hi berenedon; *pp.* bærned; *v. a.* [barn *burned; p. of* byrnan] *To kindle, light, set on fire,* TO BURN, *burn up;* accendere, exurere:—Bærnað nu eower blacern *light now your lamp, Bd.* 4, 8. Ða ceafu he forbærnð, *Mt.* 3, 12. Hy onbærdon hit *they set it on fire, Ors.* 4, 1, v. byrnan.

Bærnes, bærnis, se; *f. A burning;* incendium:—*Bd.* 1, 6.

Bærnet, bærnytt, bernet *A combustion, burning up;* combustio:—*Gen.* 22, 9, v. bærnes.

Bærning, berning; *f.* A BURNING; adustio:—Bærninge wið bærninge *burning for burning, Ex.* 21, 25.

Bærs, bears [*Plat. Dut.* baars: *Ger.* bars: *Al.* baers, bars, barsch] *A perch;* perca, lupus:—*R.* 101, *Som.*

Bærst *burst; pp. of* berstan.

n Bærstlað *broke, burst;* crepuerit:—*Cot.* 39.

Bærsuinig,-suinih,-sunnig,-syndig, -synnig, -suining, beorswinig [bær *bare, open* from bar *naked, open;* synnig, or *Norse,* syndugr *a sinner*] *An offender, a sinner, a public sinner, a publican;* peccator:—*C. Mt.* 18, 17.

Bærw *a grove,* v. bearw.

BÆST [*Plat. Dut. Ger. Dan. Swed.* bast *m. n.*] *The inner bark of a tree, of which ropes were made;* tilia. In *Plat.* and *Dut.* bast *signifies a rope; because the inner part of the lime tree was most used for making ropes,* bæst *came to denote not only the bark, but probably the linden,* or *teil tree,* v. lind.

Bæsten rap *A linden,* or *bast rope, a rope made of the fibres of the linden tree;* tiliaceus funis:—Hig þa hine gebundon mid twam bæstenum rapum, *Jud.* 15, 13.

Bæstere *a baptizer,* v. bædzere.

Bæswi [basu *purple*] 1. *A scarlet robe;* coccinum, *Cot.* 208. 2. *A scarlet,* or *crimson colour;* coccineus, *Cd.* 210, *Som.*

Bæt *a bat,* v. bat.

o Bætan; *p.* bæted *or* bætte; *v. a. To bridle, rein in, restrain, curb, bit;* frænare:—Esolas bætan, *Cd.* 138.

BÆTE, gebæte, bitol, gebætel; *n.* [*Icel.* bitill: *Dut.* byt *or* bit: *Norse,* bit] A BIT *of a bridle, a bridle, trappings, harness;* lupatum, frænum:—Þæt gebetel of ateah *took the bridle off, Bd.* 3, 9. Mid þam gebætum *with the trappings, Bd.* 3, 14, v. bridel.

BÆÐ, bað, es; *pl.* baþo; *n.* [*Icel. Al. Ger. Dut.* bad] A BATH; balneum:—*Bd.* 1, 1: 2, 5. On hatum baðum *in hot baths, Bd.* 4, 19.

Bæðhus, es A BATH-HOUSE, *a bath enclosed;* thermarum domus:—*R.* 55.

Bæðian *to bathe,* v. baðian.

Bæð-stede, or -stow *A place of baths;* thermarum locus:—*R.* 55, and 109.

Bæðweg, es; *m.* [bæð *a bath, water;* wæg *a way, wave*] *A wave of the sea, the sea;* oceani fluctus, mare:—Bæðweges blæst *a blast,* or *wind of the sea, a sea breeze, the south wind.* Suðwind *is so called, Cd.* 158.

Bæting, beting, e; *f. A cable, a rope, any thing that holds,* or *restrains;* funis, retinaculum:—Lætan þa bætinge *to slip the cable, Bt.* 41, 3.

Bættan *beaten down;* straverunt:—*Cot.* 208, *Lye,* v. beatan.

Bætte *restrained,* v. bætan.

Bæzera, bæzere *a baptizer,* v. bædzere.

p Balc, an [*Dut.* balk: *Ger.* balken: *Swed.* bielka: *Icel.* bialki] 1. A BALK, *a heap, a ridge;* porca, terra inter duos sulcos congesta. 2. *A beam, roof, covering,* BALCONY; trabs, v. bælc:—1. On balcan legan *to lay in heaps, Bt.* 16, 2. 2. *Wachter* and *Mann.*

Balcettan *to belch,* v. bealcan.

O [19b & 32c] vs 91 – soe –

2 Bæl, ~~bæl~~ es; n a funeral pile, a burning Beo K 2226 : 4638 –

2 Bæl-stede, es; m a funeral pile place Beo K 6188 –

4 Bæl-wudu wood of the funeral pile; lig, num rogi Beo ~~xxx~~ 230 K 6219

O 3 Bælg [19c]

Φ 1 Bærefót

O 1 [21a]

g bædes; pl nom ac. bad-u, g bad-a, d bad-um Th. R.

3 Bæd, ~~xxx~~ n a bath Th apol.

O [19 d]

3 Bænc, e; f a bench Th Ex. spl benc

O ~~of bad~~ [21b]

2 Bærnan – l 10

2 bathing place Th. apol.

O 8 Bænd [20a]

2 Hy onbærndon

Φ 3 Bæd-stow a bath place Mann Sup & bæt-stede

3 Bærnete, es; n a combustion

5 Bær, e; f, a bier

O 4 [20c]

O [20b]

6 Bær, g; bæres; d. bærum; ac bærne : se bara; seo. pæt bære & adj bære, naked

O Bærsuiing – sinfuly Norse syndugor sinful [20d]

O 5 [21c]

O 4 [20e]

– bære adj terminatn denoting bearing &c as wæstm-bære fruit bearing

○[21d]

1 Bald – C2 Mors
barths

○2[22a]

~~Bān c12. Banes of the bones~~ ~~B.~~ Mannes ~~bāna~~ syndon mans bones are th an
p100,15

○3[23c]

○2[23a]

2 Balde adv Boldly audenter Cd. 182
Th p 228,11

○[22b]

[24b]

○7[23b]

2 Baldor, bealdor, es m a prince or Beogl

2 Ban-cofa, an m the bone dwelling, the body Beo K 2789

○4.

4 Balew ~~&~~ ~~the whole~~ article ~~and~~ ~~bealu~~ spl.

6 Balewa, an; m the baleful ~~or~~ wicked one, scelestus, satanas; Cd 224 Th p 295,11 v spl bealu

3 Bancorena burh, Bancorna burh, burge d byrg. Bangor

3 Barm-clāð a barm cloth v bearm ~~rægl~~ rægl

4 Ban-fat es n the bone ~~vessel~~ vat, the body Beo K 2225

4 Baroc scyre, f. Chr. 1103 Ing p 326,4

○ 8[24a]

○9

○ Mid Bearruc scyre with Berkshire Chr. 860 Ing p 97,1

5 Balew adj, l4 Bealu
+ sit..

5 Ban-hring es m bone ring neck bone Beo K 3133

○7

5 9 Basing [24c]

6 Ban-loca, an m A bone inclosure, the skin, body, cutis, corpus Beo 56 Grin II 506,16

67

[Plat. Dutch Ban been n: Frs Swed. ben n: Ger. Icel. bein n: Old Ger. pein n: Grm says from veinen to bind, unite; Schmitthenner from pi to stand forth, to be]

d p 27

○a 7 Bān, es, n a bone
9013 m

Bald, beald; *adj.* [*Al.* bald: *Ital.* baldo: *Moes.* balths: *Norse,* balda] BOLD, *audacious, adventurous;* audax: — *Bd.* 1. 12.

Bald, bold; as the incipient, or terminating syllable of proper names denotes *bold, courageous, honourable;* audax, virtuosus:—Baldewin, Balduin *from* bald, *and* win *a contest, battle.* Cuthbold, Cuðbald *from* cuð *or* cuða *known, well known,* and *bold.* Eadbold *or* Eadbald *happily bold, from* ead *or* eadig *and* bald.

Baldlice *boldly,* v. bealdlice.

Baldor [the *comp. of* bald *is* baldor *more bold, courageous, honourable, hence*] *A prince, ruler;* princeps, dominus:—*thus,* Gumena baldor *a ruler of men, Cd.* 128: *Fr. Jud.* p. 8, 24. Rinca baldor, *Idem,* p. 26, 21. Wigena baldor *a prince of warriors, Id.* p. 22, 5.

Baldra *bolder,* v. bald.

q Baldsam, es [*Dut.* balsem: *Moes.* balsan: *Ital.* balsamo: *Heb.* בעל שמין bol smin *the chief of oils, Amos.* 6, 6.] *Balsam, balm;* balsamum:—*Bd.* 3, 8.

Balew, beal, balo, balewa, bealo, bealu, bealew, bealw, es [*Moes.* balwei: *Icel.* bola: *Norse,* baul, bol: *Heb.* בלי bli *wasting, destruction*] 1. BALE, *evil, misery, torment, mischief, danger, a mark of injury, lividness, destruction;* malum, exitium: 2. *Depravity, wickedness, the devil;* pravitas:—1. Beornende bealo *burning, torment, Cd.* 214. Mannum to beala *destruction to men, Chr.* 1075. 2. Bealowes gast *the spirit of wickedness, the devil, Cd.* 228.

Balew, bealu, &c.; *adj.* 1. *Miserable, severe, deadly;* miser: 2. *Depraved, wicked;* scelestus:—1. Bealu sið *a miserable lot, Cd.* 143. 2. Bealowe gast *a wicked ghost* or *spirit, Cd.* 229. Mid balo cræftum *with wicked crafts* or *arts, Bt. Rawl.* p. 190. Balewe geþohtas *wicked thoughts, Cd.* 224.

Ballice *boldly,* v. bealdlice.

Balo *misery,* v. balew.

r Balsames blæd *The balsam's fruit;* carpobalsamum:—Balsames tær *the tear* or *juice of the balsam tree;* opobalsamum, *R.* 48.

Balsminte BALSAM-MINT, *spearmint, water-mint;* sisymbrium: *q.* mentha aquatica, *Lin. R.* 43.

Balzame *balsam,* v. baldsam.

Bám *with both; dat. of* ba, begen.

BA'N, es; *pl.* bán; *n.* [*Al. Icel.* bein: *Franc.* bein, bain, pein: *Frs. v.* ban, bien: *Dut. Swed.* been] A BONE; os:—Þis ys nu ban of minum banum, *Gen.* 2, 23. Moises nam Josepes ban mid him, *Ex.* 13, 19. Hi synt innan fulle deadra bana, *Mt.* 23, 27. Ban mine *my bone, Ps.* 6, 2. Banes bite *a bit* or *fragment of bone, L. Ethel.* 36. Bane *the hip or huckle bones, Cot.* 42.

Bána, an [*Icel.* bani *slaughter; Al.* ban: *Dan.* bane] 1. *A killer, murderer, manslayer;* interfector. 2. *Destruction, the undoing,* BANE; pernicies:—1. Hy næfre his banan folgian noldan *they never would follow his murderer, Chr.* 755. 2. *Som.* and *Lye,* v. aldorbana, broðrbana, feorhbana, ordbana.

s Bánbeorg, es; *m.* [ban *a bone,* beorg *a defence: old Dut.* beenberghe *boots: hence* banbeorgas] *Boots, buskins, greaves;* ocreæ:—*Cot.* 17, 145, v. banrift.

Bánbrice [ban *a bone,* bric *or* brice *a breaking*] A BONE-BREACH, *a breaking,* or *fracture of a bone;* ossis fractura:—*q. the plant* anthericum ossifragum, *Lin. Herb.* 15, 13.

BANC [*Fr. Armor,* banc: *Frs. v.* bank: *Al. Dut.* bank: *Dan.* bank: *Swed.* bænk: *Ital.* banco] *A bench, bank, hillock:* tumulus, *Som.*

Bancorena burh, bancorna byrig [banc *a bank, an elevation,* chor *a choir,* burh *or* byrig *burg* or *city*] *Bangor, in Wales;* civitas Bangor, *Som.*

Bancoþe [ban *bone;* coþe *disease*] *An erysipelas, a burning ulcer, St. Anthony's fire;* ignis sacer:—Bancoþe, þat is oman, *Liber. Medicus,* p. 1, c. 39, v. oman.

Band *bound,* v. bindan.

Banda *a band,* v. bonda.

t Bánfag; *adj.* [ban *bone,* fag *changeable*] *Mortal, deadly;* lethifer:—*Beo.* c. 11, 145.

Bánhús, es *The bone-house, the breast, the body;* ossea domus, pectus:—He þa banhus gebrocen hæfde *he the bone-house, the breast,* or *body, hath broken, Beo.* c. 43, 21. *Hence* banhuses weard *the body's guard, the mind, Cd.* 169.

Bannan *to command,* v. abannan.

Bannuccamb [camb *a comb*] *A wool-comb;* pecten textorium:—*R.* 3.

Bánrift, banryft [ban *bone,* rift *a cover*] *Boots, greaves;* ocreæ:—*Cot.* 174, v. ban-beorg.

Bansegn [*Al.* bann *an edict,* segn *a sign*] *A banner, an ensign;* vexillum:—*Cot.* 23, v. treuteru.

Bánwærc, es; *n.* [ban *a bone,* wærc *or* weorc *work, pain*] *Grief, pain,* or *ache in the bones;* dolor ossium, *Som.*

Bánwyrt [ban *bone,* wyrt *an herb*] *Bone-wort, a violet, perhaps the small knapweed;* viola, centauria minor:—*R.* 24: *Herb.* 141. *There is also* Seo greate banwyrt, *R.* p. 3, c. 8.

Baorm *bosom,* v. bearm.

BAR, es; *m.* [*Frs. Dut.* beer: *Ger. Not.* eber: *Al.* bær: *Heb.* בעיר boir *a brute or gluttonous animal, from* בער *to consume*] A BOAR; aper:—*Elf. gl.* 13, v. wild-bar, tam-bar.

u BAR bær; *adj.* [*Plat. Dut. Ger. Al. Dan.* bar: *Frs. v.* bear: *Norse,* ber: *Heb.* באר bar *to open, make evident*] BARE, *naked;* nudus:—On barum sondum *on bare sands, Bt.* 34, 10.

Barbacan, barbycan *An outwork, a promontory;* antemurale, *Lye.*

Barenian; *p.* hi barenodon, barendon *To make bare;* denudare se:—Sand barenodon, *Cd.* 166.

Barm *a bosom,* v. bearm.

Barn *burned,* v. byrnan.

Barocscire *the bare oak shire* or BERKSHIRE, so called from a polled oak in Windsor forest, where public meetings were held, *Brompt.* p. 801. It was written most commonly by the Anglo-Saxons—Barruc, Bearruc, and Bearwucscire, *Chr.* 860.

Baron *A man;* homo, *Lye.*

Barspere, barspreote [bar *boar,* spere *spear*] A BOAR SPEAR; venabulum:—*Elf. gr.* 6.

Barð [*q.* bærs] *A kind of fish;* dromo:—*R.* 103, *Lye.*

Basing *A short cloak, a cloak;* chlamys, pallium:—Ic geseah wurm readne basing *I saw a purple* [*worm* or *shell-fish reddened*] *cloak, Jos.* 7, 21. The name of a place, BASING, old Basing, near Basingstoke, Hampshire. Wið þone here æt Basingum *with the army at Basing, Chr.* 871.

Basnian; *v. To expect;* expectare:—*C. R. Lk.* 23, 35.

Basnung *Expectation;* expectatio:—*C. R. Lk.* 21, 26.

Baso, basu. 1. *Purple;* purpura:—*Cot.* 85. 2. *A kind of colour mixed with blue and purple;* indicum, *Som.,* v. brun baso, wealh-baso.

w Basterne *The people of Sarmatia in Europe* or *upper Hungary;* Bastarnæ, *Lye.*

Basu; *adj. Purple;* purpureus:—Basu hæwen *of purple co-*

lour or *hue, of scarlet* or *crimson colour, Cot.* 117, *Som.*

Basuian *To be clad in purple*; purpurâ vestiri, *Som.*

Baswe *a scarlet robe*, v. bæswi.

Baswon stan [basu *purple*, stan *stone*] *A topaz, a precious stone varying from a yellow to a violet colour*; topazium:—*Ps.* 118, 127.

Bat, batt A BAT, *club, staff* or *stick*; fustis, *Lye.*

Bat, bæt, bate [*Al.* bot: *Frs. v.* bôat: *Dut.* boot: *Swed.* bææt] A BOAT, *ship, vessel*; linter:—*Elf. gr.*

Bát *bit*; momordit, v. bitan.

Batan *To* BAIT *or lay a bait for a fish, to bait a hook*; inescare, *Som.*, v. bitan.

Bate *Contention*; contentio:—*R. Ben.* 21.

Bað *a bath*, v. bæð.

Bað *or* Baðan ceaster *The city of Bath, Somersetshire*, so called from its baths, *Chr.* 577, v. Ace-mannes ceaster.

Baðian, beðian, ic beðige *or* beðyge; *p.* ode, ede; *pp.* od, ed. *To* BATHE, *wash, foment, cherish*; lavare:—Seldon heo baðian wolde *she would seldom bathe* or *wash, Bd.* 4, 19. Hi baðedon þone lichoman *they washed the body, Bd.* 4, 19. Baðiendra manna hus *the house of bathing men, R.* 55.

Baðo *baths*, v. bæð.

Batswan A BOATSWAIN; scaphiarius, proreta, *Lye.*

Bátwá, buta, butu, butwu; *adj.* [bá *both*, twá *two*] BOTH THE TWO, *both.* Batwa Adam and Eue, *Cd.* 37: *Gen.* 26, 35, v. begen.

Batweard [bat *boat*, weard *keeper*] *Keeper or commander of a ship*; navis custos, *Beo.*

Be, bi, big; *prep. dat.* [*Moes.* bi: *Swed.* bi, be: *Al.* bei: *Frs. Dut. Icel.* by: *Ger.* bey. *The prepositions* be, bi, big *are perhaps the imperative mood of* big-an, bi-an, by-an *to inhabit, occupy, possess*, or *from* by or bye, *a place occupied*, or *an habitation*, all which denote nearness to one; in this case the primary signification would be *proximity, nearness*] 1. BY, *near to, to, at, in, upon, about, with*; juxta, prope, ad, secus, in. 2. *Of, from, about, touching, concerning*; de. 3. *For, because of, after, according to*; pro, propter, secundum. 4. *Beside, out of*; e, ex:—1. Be wege *by the way, Mk.* 8, 3. Be þam strande *upon the strand* or *shore, Mt.* 13, 48. Ne be hlafe anum, ac be ælcon worde, *Mt.* 4, 4. 2. Be þam cilde *concerning the child, Mt.* 2, 8. Ahsiað be ealdum dagum, *Deut.* 4, 32. Be hlisan *of* or *about fame, Bt. Titles,* 19, 20 21: *Card.* p. 8. 3. He sette worde be worde *he set word for word, Bt. pref. Card.* p. 2: *pref.* l. 4. 4. Be þam wege *beside the way, Bt.* 40, 5. ¶ Be anfealdum *single.* Be twifealdon *twofold, Ex.* 22, 4. Be þam mæstan *at the most.* Be þam þe *as, Gen.* 3, 6.

Be- [*Ger.* be] is often used as a prefix. When prefixed to verbs, be- frequently expresses an active signification, as behabban to *surround*; begangan *to perform* or *dispatch*, &c. Sometimes be- prefixed indicates no perceptible variation in the sense; as belifan *to be remaining*, or *over* and *above*, begyrdan *to begird* or *gird*, as in sprengan *and* besprengan *to sprinkle*, or *besprinkle.* The same observation will apply to the prefixes a-, for-, ge-, to-, &c. Some words are not now found in their simple state, but only occur with these prefixes; as belifan, gelic, arisan, &c. This preposition is used, with little variety, by all Gothic nations, as *A. S.* by-an, big-an, bycgan, beg-an: *Moes.* bau-an: *Swed.* bo, bo-a, bu-a: *Icel.* by-a, bigg-a: *Al.* big-en, bu-en *Ger.* bau-en: *Dut.* bouw-en, denoting *to prepare, to build, to inhabit, to occupy*, or *possess, to exercise, to practice, to perambulate, to place, to manure, to till, to observe, to worship, to clothe, to repair*; *Jamieson's Herm. Scyth.* p. 57.

BEACEN, beacn, becen, becun [*Frs. v.* beaken: *Dut.* baecke: *Ger.* bake] A BEACON, *a sign, a token*; signum:—*Ps.* 77, 48.

Beacenstan, beacnetorr [beacen *beacon*, stan *stone*, torr *tower*] *A stone whereon the beacon fire was made, a stone* or *tower whereon to set the beacon fire*; specula, pharus:—To beacne torr, *Cd.* 80.

Beacneng, beacnung, bycnung. 1. A BECKONING or *nodding*; nutus:—*Cot.* 139. 2. *A speaking by tropes* or *figures*; tropologia:—*Cot.* 201, *Som.*

Beacne-torr *a beacon-tower*, v. beacen-stan.

Beacnian *to beckon*, v. bicnian.

Beacniendlic *allegorically*, v. bycnendlic.

Bead *a table*, v. bord.

Bead *a prayer*, v. gebed.

Beád *commanded*, v. beodan.

Beada *A counsellor, a persuader, an exhorter* or *intreater*; suasor, *Som.*

Beado, beadow, beadu, beaduw *Battle, war, slaughter, cruelty*; bellum:—*Fr. Jud.* p. 24, 6, 29. It is used in composition as follows—Beadu-lac [lac *a gift*] *play of battle, Beo.* c. 23, l. 9. Beado-mece *or* meca *a sword* or *weapon of slaughter, Beo.* 21, 145. Beadu-mægn *military power, Cd.* 160. Beado-rinc [rinc *a man*] *a soldier, Fr. Jud.* p. 25, 24. Beadurincum wæs Rom gerymed *Rome was conquered by soldiers, Bt. Rawl.* p. 150. Beado-særc [syrc *a garment*] *a war garment, Beo.* 38, 7. Beadu-scearp *sharp in fight, applied to a sword, Beo.* 37, 23. Beado-scrud [scrud *clothes*] *warlike apparel, warlike garment* or *dress, Beo.* 6. Beado-searo [seare *a device, an engine*] *engines* or *weapons of war, snares, Cd.* 170. Beado *or* beaduweorce *warlike operations, Chr.* 938. Beado-wig *holy contest, Bd. Sm.* p. 607, 17, v. wig.

Beæftan *after*, v. bæftan.

Beægþed, beagþed *Dead*; mortuus, *Lye.*

Be-æwnad; *part. Joined in marriage, wedded*; legitimè desponsata:—Beweddod and beæwnad *wedded and united, Chr.* 1051.

Beaftan; *p.* beaft; *pp.* beaftad *To lament*; lamentari, *Lye.*

BEÁG, beg, beah, bæh, beh, es; *m.* [*Frs. v.* beage *fasciola*] 1. *A crown, garland*; corona. 2. *A bracelet, a necklace, collar, jewel to hang about the neck, a ring*; armilla, annulus:—1. To þam beage *to the crown, Bt.* 37, 2. Se beah godes *the crown of good, Id.* 2. *Gen.* 38, 18. ¶ Used in composition as scanc-beagas *shank encirclers, garters, Cot.* 217. Wuldor-beah *a crown of glory, Ps.* 64, 12. Rand-beah *a target, shield* or *buckler.* Beah-gife, beah-gyfa *a crown giver, a munificent rewarder, Chr.* 1038. Beah-hroden *crown-adorned, Fr. Jud.* p. 23, 24. Beahsele *hall of bracelets, Beo.* 17.

Beag *gave way*, v. bugan.

Beagen *both*, v. begen.

Beagian biegan *To crown, to set a garland on*; coronare:—*Ps.* 8, 6, *Som.*

Beagðed *dead*, v. beægðed.

Beah *submitted*, v. bugan.

Beah *a crown*, v. beag.

Beah-gife, beah-gyfa *a bracelet giver*, v. beag.

Beal, bealo, bealu *misery*, v. balew.

O1

O[24c]

O4 Bet [24d]

2 Bát es m. Beo K 420

[25b]

3 Badan Bath, the city of Bath Th. An

[25a]

O[26b]

Beag dl

14 Beáh, beag es ben. bæh

4 Beacen, becen, es; n. a beacen, sign

Be[25b]

O[25c]

Beado[25a]

2 Beado-grima, an; m. a war helmet Beo K 4508

4 Beado-lioma, an; m. a flame, a sword Beo K 3045

5 Beado-rin a warlike undertaking, quarrel; rixa Beo 40 K 496

10 Beadu-serce, an; f. warlike garment, corslet; Beo K 5506

6 Beado-weorc n. a war work

Beo K 4592

7 Beado-weorca an m. a war worker, a soldier Grim # 449, 34

8 Beadu-folm f. warlike hand; a bloody hand; Beo K 1973

3 Beado-hrægl a war garment, a coat of mail; lorica Beo K 1096

9 Beadu-ræs, es; m. rush of battle, a... Th. An

2 Beadon prayed for beden p of biddan

13 Beág-gyfa, an; m. a bracelet giver, a prince Beo K 2197

an m. a ring giver, alluding to bracelet

surrounded with rings; annulis circumdata Beo K 1240

12 Beag dl

17 Beah-hroden adorned with bracelets Th. An

20 Beah-wriða, a bridle, a ring leader; princeps Beo 151, K 4032

15 Beah-gifa, munificus Grim # 450, 4

16 Beah-hord, a treasury; thesaurus Beo 69

Beah-sele, aula Beo K 2354

eah-pego, f. service; annu... distribution ...eo K 4347

bealu; g bealus, bealwes, bealowes

pl. bealwas, bealwas, bealwa, bealwa; f c m. [Fris. bal: bail, bal: Moes. balwains, torment: Icel. bölv, lamentatio: Neb. bli wasting, destruction]

~~evil mischief~~ R. K.

~~3 5. 559~~

Bealwas evils v bealu

1 Bale, evil, mischief; malum, noxa.

2 Wickedness, depravity; pravitas - Chiefly used

2 - 3 Bealo mischief Bt K 559 v. Thl. bealu

~~Bealu; es; m evil, mischief Beo K 559 v. v bealu~~

Bearu byrig cll. * Bearu burh

2 [29a]

Bealu fortium ~~...~~ bale to certainly Beo K 3350: 395: 559

Bealuwa gehwylces of every woe Cd 48 Th p. 61, 9. - 2. Bealowes gast spirit of evil, the devil Cd 228 Th p. 307, 19

Bealo-cwealm deadly death ... Cd 169 K 4525

Bealo-heard mischief deadly hard infensus durus Beo K 2685

Bealo-nið, baleful malice; wickedness; nequitia Beo. 133, K 3513 Gen II 449, 42

Bealo-hycgende evil thinking Beo K 5126

Bealo-sið, es; m

Bealo-spell a baleful story Cd 169 Th p. 210, 5

a destructive path Exodus 816

Bearn-lufu; an. f love of children

~~Bealo~~ ~~...~~ ~~baleful~~

3 [29 b]

4 Bearht [29 c]

Bealu-ben a baleful wound vulnus pestiferum Cd. 154 Th p. 192, 27

6 * Bearhtm, es m brightness glittering, noise; coruscatio, fragor Beo K 3530: 2862

Bearuc-scir, e; Berkshire

Beroc-scir

7 9 Beam [28 a]

6 a pillar - ... beamas twegen two pillars Cd 146 Th p. 183, 20

4 3 Bearw cll. * Bearo, bearu; g bearues, bearu, d. bearue, bearwe, m a grove

Beam - l 12 See * beam

4 Bearhtm instant twinkling Th An

Beam-tun, e; f

5 Bearhtme suddenly subito Beo gl. Jath K Th An p 132, 27

Beamdune at Bampton Chr. 614 Ing p 30, 16

Bears

6 * Bearm, es m a bosom - l. p Moes. * barms m

Bearm [30 a]

11 Beamen [27 b]

7.

2 * barn m

7 [31 a]

7 * Beam-sceado, es m a tree's shade Beo gl

[30 c]

11 Bean [27 c]

... hence the origin of ... see Sir W. Betham's Essay in the Transactions of ...

Bealcan, bealcettan, balcettan [*Frs. v.* balkje: bælc *a belch*] *To* BELCH, *emit, utter, pour out*; eructare:—Swete to bealcetenne *sweet to the stomach, Bt.* 22, 1. Dæg þam dæge bealceð word, *Ps.* 18, 2. Bealcetteð heorte min word god, *Ps.* 44, 1. Bealcettað weleras mine lofsang, *Ps.* 118, 171.

Beald *bold*, v. bald.

Bealdlice, baldlice, ballice; *adv.* BOLDLY, *instantly, earnestly, saucily*; audenter:—*Judg.* 3, 21, 27.

Bealdor *a prince*, v. baldor.

Bealdra *more bold*, v. bald.

Bealdwyrda; *adj.* [bald *bold*, word, wyrd *word*] BOLD, *impudent, saucy in speech* or *language*; audax:—*A saucy jester*; scurra, *Som.*

Bealew *miserable*, v. balew; *adj.*

Bealh *was angry*, v. belgan.

Beallucas *testiculi, Cot.* 163, *Som.*

Bealoful; *adj.* BALEFUL, *dire, cursed, wicked*; pestiferus:—*Fr. Jud.* p. 22, 4, *Mann.*

Bealo-hydig; *adj. Malevolent*; sceleri addictus:—*Beo.* 11, 29.

Bealo-nið *A fatal strife, dangerous contest*; pestiferum odium—*Beo.* 34, 28.

Bealw, bealew *an evil*, v. balew.

BEAM, beom, es; *m.* [*Al.* baum, boum, paum, poum: *Franc.* beam, buom: *Frs.* beam: *Dut.* boom: *Dan.* bom: *Heb.* במה bmh *high*] 1. A BEAM, *post, a stock of a tree, a splint*; trabs, stipes. 2. *A tree*; arbor. 3. *Any thing proceeding in a right line.* Hence, *a ray of light, a sun-beam*; radius. 4. *A trumpet*; tuba *for* byme *which see*:—1. Se beam bið on þinum agenum eagan, *Mt.* 7, 4. 2. Swa great beam on wyda *as a great tree in a wood, Bt.* 38, 2. Lifes beam *the tree of life, Som.* 3. Swilce sunne beam *like a sun-beam, Chr.* 678. 4. *C. Mt.* 24, 31.

Beam-dun [beam *a tree*, dun *a hill*] The name of many places in England, so called from their elevated situation, covered with wood, now corrupted into *Bampton, Chr.* 614.

Beam-fleot [beam *a beam*, fleot *an arm of the sea, an estuary*] The name of places now called *Beamfleet, Beamfled, Hunt., Bamfleet, Benfleet, Essex, Chr.* 897.

Beamian; *pp.* beamed *To shine, to cast forth rays* or *beams like the sun*; radiare, *Som.*

Beam-scead *Tree-shade, the shade of a tree*; arboris umbra:—*Bt. Rawl.* p. 158.

BEAN, bien, [*Plat.* bone: *Ger.* bohne: *Frs. v.* bean: *Dut.* boon: *Dan.* bönne: *Swed.* böna] A BEAN, *all sorts of pulse*; faba, legumen:—*Cot.* 122. Bean pisan *pepper, Cot.* 34.

Bean-belgas, bean-coddas; *pl.* [bean *a bean*, bælg *or* codd *a bag*] *Bean-pods, husks, cods* or *shells*; fabarum sacculi:—*Cot.* 200. Of þam beancoddum, *Lk.* 15, 16.

Beand *a band*, v. bænd.

Beanen; *adj. Beany, belonging to beans*; fabarius:—Beanene melewe BEAN-MEAL, *Herb.* 151, 3. Beanscealas BEAN-SHELLS.

Bear *beer*, v. beor.

Bear *bore*; portavit, v. beran.

Bearanbyrig *Banbury*, v. Beranbyrig.

BEARD, berd [*Plat. Dut.* baard: *Frs. v.* bird: *Ger.* bart *m*: *Dan.* beerd] A BEARD; barba:—*Lev.* 19, 27.

Beardleas; *adj.* BEARDLESS; imberbis. Used as a noun, it denotes those *without a beard, as a youth, stripling*, also *a hawk* or *buzzard*; ephebus, buteo:—*R.* 87.

BEARG, bearug, bearh, berga [*Frs. v.* baerg] *A barrow-pig, a porket*; majalis:—*Elf. gl.* 13.

Bearh *kept*, v. beorgan.

Bearht, bearhtnes *bright*, v. beorht, beorhtnes.

Bearhtm, bryhtm, breahtem, bræhtm, *Brightness, glittering, scintillation*; coruscatio;—Breahtem æfter breahtme *glittering after glittering* or *successive scintillations, Cod. Ex.* 52, a. 10. ¶ Eagan bearhtm *a twinkling of the eye, a moment, Bd.* 2, 13, (used in the dative case as an adverb) *in a twinkling, in a moment, immediately, suddenly.* Bearhtme stopon *in a moment they went, Fr. Jud.* p. 21, 28.

Bearhtm-hwile, byrhtm-hwyle; *adv. A twinkling while, a moment*; oculi nictus tempus:—*Lk.* 4, 5, *Mann.*

BEARM, [*Al. Dan. Swed. Moes.* barm] *A bosom, a lap*; gremium:—On eowerne bearm, *Lk.* 6, 38. Iosep hi nam of þæs fæder bearme, *Gen.* 48, 12, v. bosum, fæþem, greada.

Bearm, -barm-rægl *or* clað *Barm-cloth, a bosom cloth, an apron*; mappula:—*Elf. gl.* p. 61.

Be-arn *occured*, v. be-yrnan.

BEARN, es; *n.* [*Moes.* barn: *Al.* barn, bern: *Icel. Dan.* and *Swed.* barn: *Frs.* barn, bern, born: *Scot.* bairn] 1. A BARN, *child, son, pledge*; filius. 2. *Issue, offspring, progeny*; soboles. 3. *Son of war, a warrior, nobleman, general, hero*; vir, heros:—1. Þys synd Israela bearna naman, *Ex.* 1, 1. Beon mid bearne *gravidum esse, Somn.* 370. Bearna bearn *a son's son, a nephew's son* or *niece's daughter, Cot.* 199. 2. Bearna team *offspring, progeny.* Weðræs beærn *the young of a ram, Ps.* 28, 1. 3. v. beorn.

Bearn-cennan; *p.* de; *pp.* ed; *v. a. To bear* or *bring forth a child, to travail*; parturire:—On sare þu cennyst-bearn, *Gen.* 3, 16.

Bearn-cennung *or* cenning *a child-birth.*

Bearn-eacen, -eacn; *part. Travailing, bringing forth*; pregnans:—Bearneacen wif prowað *a travailing woman suffereth, Bt.* 31, 1. *R.* p. 68 *note.*

Bearn-eacnung *Generation, conception*; genitura, *Som.*

Bearnend *for* byrnende *burning*, v. byrnan.

Bearn-leas, -lest; *adj. Childless*; improles, sine liberis, abortivus, *Gen.* 42, 36.

Bearn-lufu *Love of children, adoption*; adoptio:—On bearn-lufan habban *to take in adoption, Bd.* 15, 19.

Bearn-myrðra *a child-murderer, an infanticide.*

Bearn-team, es [*Scot.* bearntime: bearn *a child*, team *a succession*] *Posterity, generation*; sobolis procreatio:—*Ors.* 1, 14.

Bearo *a grove*, v. bearw.

Bearocscyre, Bearucscyre, Bearwucscire *Berkshire*, v. Barocscire.

Bears *a fish*, v. bærs.

Bearu *a grove*, v. bearw.

Bearug *a barrow-pig*, v. bearg.

Bearw, bearo, bearow, bearuw, es; *m.* A BARROW, *a high* or *hilly place, a wood, a grove, a hill covered with wood*; lucus, nemus:—Bearwas *groves, Cd.* 72. Bearo sette *he planted a grove, Cd.* 136. In bearwe, on bearwe *or* on bearowe *in a wood, Cot.* 109. Wic mid bearuwe ymbsealde *a mansion surrounded with a grove, Bd.* 5, 2, v. beorh.

Beátan he beáteð *or* bet; *part.* beatende, beotiende; *p.* he beot, we beoton; *pp.* beáten; *v. a.* To BEAT, *strike, strike with the hands, to vapour, threaten*; percutere:—Agynð beatan, *Mt.* 24, 49. He bet hine selfne *he strikes himself, Past.* 64. Hwy beatst þu me? *Jn.* 18, 23. Þa Balaam beot þone assan, *Num.* 22, 23. Gefelde ic me beotiende and wyrpende *I felt myself beating, and turn-*

ing or *struggling and writhing as a person does in recovering from a fit, Bd.* 5, 6, v. beotende.
Beatere A BEATER, *fighter, champion;* pugil:—*Elf. gl.* 9, 8.
Beaw *A bee, or hornet;* œstrum: —*R.* 22, v. beo, hyrnet.
Bebaðod *bathed,* v. baðian.
Bebban-burh, Bebban-buruh, Bcben-burh, Bæbban-burh, [Bebba *the name of a man,* burh *a castle:* hence Bebbæ castrum] *Bamborrow* or *Bamborough Castle* in Northumberland. On Bebban-burh *at Banburg, Chr.* 642.
Bebead *offered,* v. bebeodan.
Bebedded; *part. Betrothed, espoused;* desponsatus, *Som.*
k Bebeodan, gebeodan; *part.* bebeodende, he bebyt; *imp.* bebeod; *p.* bebead, hi bebudon; *pp.* beboden [be, bod *a command*] 1. *To give a by-command* or *a gentle command,* but generally *to command, order;* mandare. 2. *To offer, give up, commend, promise;* offerre, promittere: —1. He hys englum bebyt, *Lk.* 4, 10. 2. Lac bebeodan *to offer sacrifice, Cd.* 138. On handa þine ic bebeode gast minne, *Ps.* 30, 6, v. beodan, bodian.
Bebeodend *A master;* præceptor:—*Lk.* 5, 5.
Bebeodendlic gemet, beodendlic gemet *the imperative mood.*
Beber *a beaver,* v. befer.
Bebiddan *to command,* v. biddan.
Bebindan; *p.* bebond *To bind in* or *about;* inligare:—*Bd.* 3, 11.
Bebirged *buried,* v. birgan.
Beblonden *died;* tinctus, v. blonden.
l Bebod, es; *plu.* u, a [as the *Dutch* bod, *or* ge-bod] *A command, mandate, decree, order;* mandatum:—*Mk.* 12, 28, v. bod.
Bebod *command thou;* beboden *commanded, commended,* v. bebeodan.
Beboht *sold,* v. bebycgean.
Bebond *bound,* v. bebindan.
Beboren-innihte *Born within a county, free of a country, native;* municipales:—*Cot.* 136.
Bebr *A cup;* poculum, *Som.*
Bebroken *broken, consumed,* v. brecan.
Bebrugdon *they pretended,* v. brægan.
Bebugan *To dwell, occupy, inhabit, surround, go over, to penetrate;* incolere:—*Cd.* 190.
m Bebycgean *or* bebygan; *part.* bebycgende, *or* bebycende; *p.* beboht *To sell, to set,* or *put to sale;* vendere:—On gold bebycgean *to sell for gold, Bd.* 2, 12, *Sm.* p. 514, 39.

Bebyran *To bring, bring to;* inferre:—*L. Ethelb.* 18, *Mann.*
Bebyrde *Garnished with nails, set with spikes;* clavatus:—*Cot.* 49, *Som.*
Bebyrgean, bebyrgian, bebyrian, bebyrigean; *p.* de; *pp.* ed; *v.a. To bury;* sepelire: —*Gen.* 50, 5, 6, v. byrian.
Bebyrignys, bebyrigednes, se; *f. A burying;* sepultura:—*Bd.* 1, 15.
Bebyt *commends,* v. bebeodan.
Béc *books,* v. boc.
Becæfed, becefed; *part. Barbed, trapped, decked;* phalerata:—*Cot.* 84, v. ymb-cæfed, cæfed.
Becarcan; *v. To take care of;* accurare, *Lye.*
Becc [*Beck* is used in the north of England for *a mountain stream, a small rivulet,* v. burne: *Dut.* beek *f: Icel. Norw.* beckr: *Franc.* bec] *A brook, a rivulet,* A BECK or *small rapid stream;* torrens, rivulus, *Som.*
-becc, -bec, -beck, used for the name of places, or as a termination to the names of places, denotes their situation to be near *a brook* or *river, Chr.* 1140, *Ing.* p. 370, 4.
n Becca [*Plat.* bikke] A BECK, *pick-axe, mattock;* ligo, marra: —*Elf. gl.* 25.
Bece *a beech,* v. boc.
Beceapian, he becypð, becipð; *p.* beceapode; *pp.* becyped *To sell;* vendere:—*Mt.* 10, 29: *Ex.* 21, 7: *Ps.* 104, 16, v. ceapian.
Becefed *barbed,* v. becæfed.
Becen *a beacon,* v. beacen.
Becen; *adj.* BEECHEN, *made of beech;* fagineus:—*R.* 45.
Beceorfan; *p.* becurfe; *pp.* beceorfen *To* BECARVE, *cut off, to cut* or *pare away;* amputare:—*Bd.* 1, 7.
Beceorian *to complain,* v. ceorian.
Becerrad, becierd, becierred *turned, given up,* v. becyrran.
Becinga *Beckingen,* v. Blecinga.
Becipð *sells,* v. beceapian.
o Beclæmed; *part.* [*Dut.* belymd] BECLAMMED, *glued to* or *together, emplastered, plastered over;* glutinatus, *Som.*
Beclænsod *cleansed,* v. clænsian.
Becleaped, becleopod, beclyped; *part.* YCLEPED, *called, named, accused;* vocatus:——*L. Pol. Cnut.* 28, v. clypian.
Beclyppan; *pp.* beclypt *to clip, embrace,* v. clyppan.
Beclysan; *p.* de; *pp.* d, ed, od; *v. a. To close in, to enclose, to shut in;* concludere:—*Jos.* 10, 18.
Becn *a beacon,* v. beacen.
Becnan *to beckon,* v. bicnian.
Becnawan *to know,* v. oncnawan.

Becnend, es [*part. from* bicnian *to beckon*] *A sign,* BEACON, *a token, guide;* index, *Som.*
Becnodon *beckoned, p. of* bicnian.
p Becniendlice; *adv. Allegorically* or *by parable;* allegoricè, *Som.,* v. beacneng.
Becnyndlic; *adj. Allegorical;* allegoricus:—*Bd.* 5, 23.
Becnyttan; *v. a. To knit, bind* or *tie, enclose;* ligare:—*Bd.* 3, 10.
Becom *happened,* v. becuman.
Becorfen; *part.* [be, curfen *from,* ceorfan *to carve*] *Cut off, beheaded;* truncatus:—Becorfen wæs heafde, *Bd.* 1, 27.
Becrafian *to crave,* v. crafian.
Becreopan, gecrupan; *sub. indef.* becrupe, gecrupe; *pp.* becropen *To bring secretly, to creep;* irrepere:—He sie becropen on carcern *he should be secretly led to prison. Bt. Rawl.* p. 187, 24. He sie on carcerne gebroht, *Bt.* 37, 1, *Card.* p. 288, 20.
Becuman, he becymð; *p.* becom, becwom, becuom, hi becomon; *pp.* becumen; *v. n.* 1. *To go* or *enter in, to meet with, to come to, to come together;* ingredi. 2. *To come, to happen, to fall out, to befal;* evenire:—1. He becom on sceaþan, *Lk.* 10, 30. 2. Oft becymð se anweald þisse worulde to swiðe godum monnum *often cometh the power of this world to very good men, Bt.* 39, 11. Þæm godum becymð anfeald yfel *to the good happens unmixed evil, Bt.* 39, 9.
Becun *a beacon,* v. beacen.
q Becunnan *To assay, prove, try;* experiri, *Som.*
Becwæþan; *p.* he becwið, hi becwædon *To* BEQUEATH, *to give by will;* legare:—Ic wylle þat ealle þa mynstra and þa cyrican þa wæron giuene and becweþene *I will that all the ministers and churches that were given and bequeathed, Chr.* 694.
Becwom *fell; p. of* becuman.
Becwyddod; *part. Laid aside, deposited;* depositum:—*R.* 14.
Becyme A BY-COMING, *an event* or *coming suddenly upon;* eventus:—*Bd.* 4, 29.
Becymð *happens,* v. becuman.
Becyped *sold; pp. of* beceapan.
Becypð *sells,* v. beceapan.
Becyrran; *p.* becyrde; *pp.* becerrad, becierred, becierd; *v. a. To turn to, to give up, to deliver, betray;* vertere, transferread:—*Chr.* 1011, v. cerran.
Bed; *n.* [*Dut. Icel.* bed: *Frs. v.* bead: *Moes.* badi: *Al.* bedd, bedde] A BED, *couch, pallet, tick of a bed, a bed in a garden;*

ϕ1 es: m

ϕ2 Bebyht commanded from
~~v behealdan~~ ^be beodan

)1 es: m

)3 ...

~~Be~~ byrgan to bury
– l. 4 v. birgan

O7 [31c]

ϕ4

)5 es: m

O2 [32x]

Bebeorgan to defend
~~oneself~~ oneself, ~~to~~
~~be cautious~~; sese
defendere, ~~cavere~~ cavere
Beo K 3490: 3513
+ [31 b]

O2

Be-bicgan, be-bohte
to buy; ... emere Beo
K 3594

bicgan to buy
surround ... and ^ V bicgan,
bygan

bycgean to sell.
Som says also, to
buy, emere v. ...
be-bicgan

ϕ3

ϕ1 es; ~~xx~~

~~1 Bedælan~~ to entirely divide ~~to deprive~~
Th. An. Bed ql in dæl

~~2 Bedæle~~ partly, but little; paululum?
Th. An

ϕ3 Bedan-ford-scir, e; f
[Hord. Bedefordsire.
Brom. Beddefordschire]
Bedfordshire. Hi
hæfdon ofergan
Bedanford-scire
they had overrun
Bedfordshire Chr.
1011 Ing. 186, 30 — 6, 6

ϕ4 5 q f? Sup

~~3 Bedd-redda~~ Bedd-ryda, an; m
one who is bedridden
clinicus. Elfgl. 9 C/[33d]
Vit Swith; B

O 7 q f

ϕ2 Bedypan to bedip. dip Th. An.

~~3 Beféran~~ v. a. To go over, travel over
Th. An q beferan

~~4 Befæstan~~ to puts in trust. Som v befæstan

stratum, lectus:—To þinum bedde, *Gen.* 16, 2. Hi þa in asendan þat bed, *Mk.* 2, 4, v. wyrt-bed.

Bed *asked*, v. biddan.

Bedan *to offer*, v. beodan.

Bedælan, ed [*Dut.* bedeelen] *To divide;* separare, v. dælan.

Bedanford *Bedford*, v. Bedicanford.

Bedan-heafd *Bedwin in Wiltshire*, *Chr.* 675.

Bedbeer, bedber *A bed, hammock;* grabatus:—*C. Jn.* 5, 8, 12.

Bedbolster *A pillow, bolster;* plumaceus:—*R.* 27, *Lye.*

Bedclyfa, beddclyfa, bedclyofa, bedcleofa, bedcofa; *m. A bedchamber, closet;* cubile hominis:—Gang into þinum bedclyfan, *Mt.* 6, 6.

Bedcofa *a bed-chamber*, v. bedclyfa.

Bedd *a bed*, v. bed.

Bed-dagas *prayer days, Rogation days.*

Beddclyfa *a chamber*, v. bedclyfa.

Beddern, bedern, beodern: *n.* [bed *a bed;* ern *a place*] *A place where beds are made, a chamber;* cubiculum. In reference to the Roman manner of reclining on couches, *a dining room*, *Elf. gl.* 20, *Som.*

Beddian; *v., To go to bed, to rest,* sternere:—*Elf. gr.* 28.

Bedding, beding; *f.* BEDDING, *straw;* stratum:—*R.* 111: *Lps.* 6, 6.

Beddreaf *bed-clothes*, v. bedreaf.

Beddredda beddrida; *part.* BEDRIDDEN; clinicus:—*Elf. gl.* 9.

Beddrest, bedrest *The place of rest, a bed;* lectus:—*Cd.* 102: 129.

Bedeahlian *to hide*, v. bediglian.

Bedeaht *covered*, v. bediglian.

Bedeled *deserted*, v. bedælan.

Bedelfan; *p.* bedielf; *pp.* bedelfen; *v. a.* [*Dut.* bedelven: be, delfan *to dig*] *To dig in* or *around, to bury, inter;* circumfodere:—Oð ic hyne bedelfe, *Lk.* 13, 8. Bedielf hyt on eorðan, *Mt.* 25, 18.

[Be]delfing; *f. A laying bare, exposing;* ablaqueatio:—Niðerwart treowes delfing *exposing the lowest part of the tree or the roots, R.* 50.

[Be]den *prayed; pp. of* biddan.

[Bed]erices weorð [Bederices *Beric's*, weorð *a town* or *residence*] *St. Edmund's Bury* in [S]uffolk.

[Bede]rn *a dining room*, v. beddern.

[Bedf]eld, bedfelt *A bed-covering, coverlet;* lodix:—*R. Ben.*, *Som.*

[Bedh]us [gebed *a prayer*, hus *a house*] *A chapel, an oratory, a place for prayer;* oratorium:—*Fulg.* 43, *Lye.*

Bedicanford, Bedanford BEDFORD:—Æt Bedicanforda *at Bedford.* The *dat.* of ford ends in -a as well as -e, *Chr.* 571.

Bedician; *v. a.* [*Dut.* bedyken: *Frs. v.* bedykje] *To* BEDIKE, *to mound, to fortify with a mound;* aggere munire:—Bedicodon þa burh utan *they embanked the city without, Chr.* 1016.

Bedidrian *to deceive*, v. bedydrian.

Bedicodon, *for* bedicodon *trenched; p. of* bedician.

Bediglian, bedihlian, ic bedihlige: *pp.* bediglod, bedihlod, *or* bedeaht; *v.a. To hide, cover, conceal, keep close* or *secret;* abscondere:—Ne þu hine bediglige, *Deut.* 13, 8, v. hydan.

Bediglincg *A hiding* or *keeping close, a concealing;* occultatio, *Som.*

Bedihlian *to hide*, bedihlad, bedihlud *for* bedihlod, v. bediglian.

Beding; *f.* 1. BEDDING, *a covering of a bed;* stramentum, lectisternium. 2. *A bed;* lectus:—1. *Elf. gl.* 20. 2. Gyf ic astige on bedinge. *Ps.* 131, 3.

Bediped, bedypt *dipped, died;* tinctus, v. bedyppan.

Bedofen *drowned*, v. dufian.

Bedolfen, *for* bedelfen *buried; pp. of* bedelfan.

Bedrædenne *An assignment, ordinance* or *appointment;* assignatio, *Som.*

Bedreaf, es; *m. Bed-clothes, bedding;* lodix:—*R. Ben.* 55.

Bedreda, bedrida *bedridden*, v. beddredda.

Bedrest *a bed*, v. beddrest.

Bedrifan; *p.* bedráf; *pp.* bedrifed, bedrift, bedrifen [*Plat.* bedriven: *Dut.* bedryven: *Dan.* bedrive] *To drive, thrust in* or *upon, to compel, constrain* or *enforce one to do a thing, to follow;* cogere:—*Bd.* 1, 14.

Bedrog *suffered, endured*, v. dreogan.

Bedroren; *pp. Deceived, deluded, bereaved, deprived;* deceptus:—*Cd.* 26.

Bedruncen; *part. Absorbed, imbibed;* imbibitus:—*Medic. ex. quad.* 2, 8.

Bedþen [bed *a bed*, þen *for* þegn *a servant*] *A chamberlain, a servant who has the care of a chamber;* lecti minister:—*R.* 27.

Bedtid BEDTIDE, *bed time;* lecti adeundi tempus:—*R.* 95.

Bedu *fortitude*, v. byld.

Bedul; *adj. Prayerful, suppliant;* petitiosus:—*R.* 101.

Bedulfon *fortified*, v. bedelfan.

Bed-warift *A curtain;* cortina, *Mann.*

Bedydrian, bedidrian; *p.* de; *pp.* ed, od *To deceive, transfigure, charm, enchant;* decipere:—*Gen.* 44, 15.

Bedydrung *A deceit, deceiving;* deceptio, *Som.*

Bedyppan; *p.* bedypte, hi bedypton; *pp.* bediped; *v. a. To dip, immerse;* mergere:—Se þe bedypð on disce his hand, *Mt.* 26, 23.

Bedyrnde, bedyrned *hidden, concealed*, v. dyrnan.

Be-ebbed *be-ebbed, dried as the shore is upon an ebb*, v. ebban.

Beel *a pile*, v. bæl.

Beeodon *dwelt*, v. began.

Beer *a bier*, v. bær.

Befællen *befallen*, v. befeallan.

Befæstan, gefæstan; *p.* de; *pp.* ed; *v. a. To commend, commit, deliver, teach, put in trust, betroth;* committere:—Þæt þu befæstest min feoh, *Mt.* 25, 27.

Befæsting *an entrusting*, v. fæsting.

Befæðman *To embrace (with the arms);* ulnis amplecti:—*Cd.* 163.

Befalden *folded*, v. fealdan.

Befangen *taken*, v. befon.

Befaran; *p.* befór, beferde, hi beferdon; *pp.* befaren; *v. a.* [be, faran *to go*] *To go round, to travel through, to surround, pass over, go among;* peragrare:—*Ex.* 14, 9.

Befealden *enfolded*, v. feallan.

Befeallan, he befylð, befelh; *p.* befeol, befeoll, befealde; *pp.* befeallen. 1. To BEFAL, *happen;* accidere. 2. *To fall, cast down;* dejicere. 3. *To incline* or *tend to, to apply one's self vigorously, to try;* operam dare:—1. *Gen.* 15, 12. 2. An of þam ne befylð on eorðan, *Mt.* 10, 29. 3. Þilcum wordum heo him befelh, *Gen.* 39, 10.

Befeastan *to trust*, v. befæstan.

Befeastnad, ud, ed *betrothed*, v. befæstan.

Befeht *taken*, v. befon.

Befehð *includes*, v. befon.

Befellen *inclined*, v. befeallan.

Befeng *took*, v. befon.

Befeol *befel; p. of* befeallan.

Befeold *enfolded; p. of* fealdan.

Befeollan *to fill*, v. befyllan.

Befeore *before*, v. beforan.

Befer *a bearer*, v. beofer.

Beferde *surrounded*, v. befaran.

Befest *betrothed*, v. befæstan.

Befician; *v. To deceive, to go round;* decipere:—*Off. Episc.* 8.

Befiled *defiled*, v. befylan.

Befilgende *following*, v. befylgan.

Beflæ *skinned*, v. beflean.

[a] **Beflagen flæc** *The bowels*; viscera:—*R.* 75, *Lye.*

Beflean; *p.* beflog; *pp.* beflæ *To flay, to skin,* or *take off the skin,* or *bark*; decorticare:—*Cot.* 62.

Befleogan; *p.* ic befleoh, we beflugon; *pp.* beflogen *To flee, flee away, escape*; effugere:—*Bd.* 3, 10.

Befoerde *fell,* v. befaran.

Befoh *contain,* v. befon.

Befolen *filled,* v. befyllan.

Befón, ic befóh, befó, he befehð; *p.* he befeng, we befengon; *pp.* befangen, befongen, befoen, befeht; *v. a.* 1. *To encompass, surround, take, ensnare*; capere. 2. *To apprehend, seize, to take hold of*; deprehendere. 3. *To receive, contain, embrace, entertain*; recipere:—1. Þat hig woldon þone Hælend on his spræce befon, *Mt.* 22, 15. 2. Þa ne mihton hig hys word befon, *Lk.* 20, 26. 3. Ne mihte befon, *Jn.* 21, 25. Ic befoh hit mid feaum wordum *I contain it in a few words, Solil.* 3, v. fon.

Befongen *contained*; *pp. of* befon.

Befor *a beaver,* v. beofer.

[a] Beforan; *prep. dat. acc.* [be *by, proximity,* foran *fore,* as æt foran] BEFORE; ante, coram:—Be foran þe, *Ps.* 38, 7. Þa Ealdormen heredon hig beforan him, *Gen.* 12, 15. Hwa ne wafað þæs, þat þa steorran scinað beforan þam monan, and ne beforan þære sunnan *who wonders not at this, that the stars shine before the moon, and not before the sun? Bt.* 39, 3.

Beforancwede *foretold,* v. cwæþan.

Beforangestihtiende *fore-ordaining,* v. gestihtan.

Beforleage *Beverley,* the name of a town in Yorkshire, *Som.*

Befotigan; *To cut off the feet*; pedes abscindere, *Som.*

[b] Befrinan, befrynan *to ask*; *p.* ic befran, hi befrunon, v. frinan.

Beftan *after,* v. bæftan.

Be fullan *to the full, perfectly full,* v. full.

Befylan, gefylan; *pp.* befyled, gefylod, befiled, befyld [be, ful *foul*] *To* BEFOUL, *pollute, defile, make filthy*; inquinare:—*Somn.* 168.

Befylgan; *part.* befilgende; *sub.* befulge [be, fylgean *to follow*] *To follow, pursue*; insequi, insistere:—*Bd.* 5, 19.

Befyllan; *pp.* befylled, befolen *To fill, fill up*; adimplere:—*Bd.* 1, 27.

Befylð *falls,* v. befeallan.

Beg *a crown,* v. beag.

Begalian; *To charm, enchant*; incantare:—*Herb.* 86, 4, *Som.*

Begán, ic begá, he begæð; *p.* ic, he begde, beeóde, we beeódon; *pp.* begangen [be, gan *to go*] 1. *To go over, to perambulate*; perambulare. 2. *To follow after, to practise, exercise, take in hand, endeavour, to be diligent about, observe, use, study, occupy, dwell*; exercere, colere:—1. Ic ferde geond þas eorðan and hi beeode *I walked through* [*over*] *the earth, and perambulated it, Thw. Hep. Job.* p. 164, 16. Se þe æcer begæð *he who goes over the land, a farmer, Elf. gr.* 7. 2. He begæð unmætas, *Deut.* 21, 20. Bega þe sylfne to arfæstnysse *exercise thyself in* or *devote thyself to piety,* 1 *Tim.* 4, 7, v. bigan.

Began *began,* v. beginnan.

Begang, bigang, bigong, bigeng [be, gang *a step, proceeding*] *An undertaking, business, exercise, reverence, religious worship*; negotium, cultus:—Bigong hire æfæstnysse *the service of her religion, Bd.* 2, 9: *Jos.* 23, 7.

Beganga, begenga, bigonga, bigenga, bigengea, an; *m. An inhabitant, a dweller, a cultivator, an observer, a benefactor, worshipper*; incola, cultor:—Be ærran bigengum *of the first inhabitants, Bd.* 1, 1. Þearfena bigenga *a benefactor of the poor, Bd.* 3, 14.

[d] Begangan, hi begangeð [be, gangan *to go,* v. began] *To go to* or *after, to attend, lie near, surround, worship*; sequi, observare, incumbere:—Begangan his gebedu *to attend his prayer, Bd.* 3, 16. Begangan wæccan *to attend watch, Bd.* 3, 17. Cartaina wæs mid sæ utan begangen *Carthage was outwardly surrounded by sea, Ors.* 4, 13. Forligru ne begange *should not follow adultery, L. Cnut.* 7.

Begannes [beginnan *to begin*] *The calends, the first day of the month*; calendæ:—*Cot.* 202.

Beg-beam, beig-beam [begir *a berry,* beam *a tree*] *The mulberry tree, the blackberry bush, a tree bearing berries, a bramble*; morus:—*Lk.* 20, 37, *Mann.*

Begea *of both*; *gen. of* begen.

Begean *to bend,* v. bugan.

Begeaten *obtained*; *pp. of* begytan.

Begemed *taken care of, governed*; *pp. of* begyman.

BE'GEN, bá; *gen.* begra, begea; *dat.* bám; *acc.* bá; *pron.* [*Plat. Dut.* beide; *Ger.* beyde: *Ottf.* bethe, bediu: *Tat. Moes.* ba, bai: *Dan.* begge: *Norse,* bathum] BOTH; ambo:—Hig feallað begen on ænne pytt, *Mt.* 15, 14. Heora begra eagan wurdon geopenode, *Gen.* 3, 7. Hyra begea nest, *Fr. Jud.* 11, 5.

Begende *taking care,* v. began.

Begengas *inhabitants,* v. beganga.

[e] Begeond, begeondan, beiundan; *prep. acc. adv.* [be *by,* geond *yonder*] BEYOND; trans, ultra:—Fram begeondan Jordanen, *Mt.* 4, 25. Begeondan sæ *beyond sea, Bd.* 5, 19. ¶ Feor begeondan *far beyond, Elf. gr.* 38, v. geond.

Begeotan, he begyt; *p.* begeát, hi beguton; *pp.* begoten [*Dut.* begieten: be *by,* geotan *to pour*] 1. *To pour out, to cast upon, to sprinkle, cover*; aspergere. 2. *To obtain, acquire*; obtinere:—1. Mid blode begoten *sprinkled with blood, Chr.* 734. 2. *Lye,* v. begitan.

Beger *a berry,* v. berga.

Begetan *to get,* v. begitan.

Begeten *seized,* or begetan *to seize,* v. begitan.

Begetende *seeking out,* v. begitan.

Begehineð *honour,* v. *gehineð.*

Begetn *taken,* v. begitan.

Beggen *both,* v. begen.

Begierdan *to begird,* v. begyrdan.

Begietan *to get,* v. begitan.

Begiman *to govern*; præesse, v. gyman.

Begimen *watching*; observatio, v. begymen.

[f] Begiming; *f. An invention, a device*; adinventio:—*Ps.* 105, 36, *Som.*

Beginnan, anginnan; *p.* began; *pp.* begunnen; *v. a.* [*Plat. Dut. Ger.* beginnen: *Dan.* begynde: *Swed.* begynna] *To begin*; incipere:—Noe þa began to wircenne þat land, *Gen.* 9, 20.

Begiondan *beyond,* v. begeond.

Begir *a berry,* v. berga.

Begitan, hi begytað; *part.* begitende; *p.* begeat; *pp.* begeten, begetn; *v. a.* [be, getan *to get*] *To* GET, *obtain, acquire, to seek out, examine*; obtinere:—Ælc mod wilnað soðes godes to begitanne *every mind wishes to get the true good, Bt.* 24, 2. Mihton eaðe begitan, *Ors.* 3, 4. He begeat ealle þa east land *he obtained all the east country, Ors.* 3, 11.

Begleddian, ic begleddige; *p.* de; *pp.* od *To dye cloth, to stain, corrupt*; inficere:—*Ps.* 105, 36.

Begnagan *To* BEGNAW, *gnaw*; corrodere:—*Martyrol.* 9. *Jul.*

[g] Begne; *f. An ulcer, a carbuncle*; carbunculus;—Seo blace begne *the black ulcer, R.* 64.

Bega of both ~~gen~~ pl. of begen

2 Begán, begangan; p beeode To cultivate, till apply to Th. An. ~~a~~ ~~my~~ Dict. in began

Befón to contain, comprehend, clothe Th. An   of O

4 Begeotan to sprinkle moisten Th. An. v J.B. begeotan

5 Begang, bigenges, m Th. An Begong Bes. pl. in gan

Beforan Th. An

~~Bege sincit Ex. p 70, 39 for beage pincgum from beah a crown & binc ll or rather be & gepinc wh. see~~

~~5 Begirdan~~ to begird p de Th. Ælfr. v begyrdan ~~Begirde begirded Bt. v. begyrdan~~

Befulan to defile pollute, disdain; polluere An v befylan

O 3 Begen [33i]

Begnornian, p ode
pp od To lament
to mourn; lamentari
Beo K 6350 v Beorl gnorn

Be-gong ~~cultus~~ a course
~~what Beo 2?~~ Beo K 721 v begang
~~Grn II 720, 36~~

6 Begroren Cd. Th. Index

2 Begrynian, p ede
ed to ensnare Th. An

Begyded dl. * begylded

7 Begylded gilded Som
v pp of gyldan

3 Begytan, p begeat to
beget, obtain Th. An
Z begitan

for behet:
5 Beheot promised
threatened pp of
behatan Th. An

6 Behidan p behidde
pp behid to hide
Th. An v hydan

2 Behofan to
require; indigere
Beo K 5291

8

5 Behold beheld v
behealdan

~~4 Behelan Beo gl~~

4 Behelan Th. etc

7 Behreafian to bereave
plunder Th. An
v bereafian

Begodian; *pp.* od [be, godian *to benefit*] *To benefit, crown;* coronare:—*Ps.* 5, 15.

Begongan *to exercise,* v. began *or* begangan.

Begongn *dwelt,* v. began.

Begongyn *exercised,* v. began.

Begoten *covered,* v. begeotan.

Begra *of both,* v. begen.

Begrindan [be, grindan *to grind*] *To destroy, rob, spoil;* privare:—*Cd.* 75.

Begrípan; *pp.* ed, en; *v. a.* [be, gripan *to gripe*] *To* GRIPE, *chasten, chide;* increpare:—*Ps.* 15, 7, v. gripan.

Begroren... *Shivering, quaking, dreading;* horrens, stridens:—*Cd.* 214.

Begrornian *To lament, to grieve for;* mœrere:—*Cd.* 13, v. gnornian.

Begryned *ensnared, entrapped.*

Begunne, begunnen *begun,* v. beginnan.

Begyded *gilded,* v. gildan.

Begyman, begíman; *part.* begemende; *p.* de; *pp.* ed; *v. a.* *To take care of, to keep, govern, regard, observe, attend;* observare, v. gyman.

Begymen, begimen *care, regard, observation, shew, pomp;* observatio:—Mid begymene, μετα παρατηρησεως, *with shew* or *pomp, Lk.* 17, 20.

Begyrdan; *p.* de; *pp.* ed, *or* begyrd; *v.a.* [be, gyrdan *to gird*] . *To* BEGIRD, *surround;* cingere. 2. *To clothe;* vestire. . *To defend, mound, fortify;* munire:—1. Begyrdað eower ...ndenu, *Ex.* 12, 11. 2. *Bd.* . 7. 3. *Bd.* 1, 5.

...ytað *shall obtain,* v. begitan.

... *a crown,* v. beag.

...abban, he behabbað, behaeð, behæfeð; *p.* behæfod, hi ...hæfdon; *pp.* behæfed, be...æft; *v. a.* [be *by, near,* habban *have*] 1. *To compass, encompass, surround;* cingere. *To restrain, detain;* detinere:—1. Þine fynd behab... þe, *Lk.* 19, 43. 2. Hi ...hæfdun hine, *Lk.* 4, 42.

...fednes, se; *f. A detention, e;* conservatio:—¶ Behæ...es fæsten *sparingness, parsimony, Cot.* 191, v. fæst-hafolnes.

...ft *held,* v. behabban.

...s [be *by, near,* hæse *command*] *A self-command, vow, promise.* Hence our *behest;* votum:—He fela behæsa behet *many vows made, Chr.* 1093, ...ehat.

...ige *vows,* v. behatan.

...st *shall vow,* v. behatan.

...lan wið *or* from *To mind, ...d, regard;* cavere:—*C. R.* 7, 15, v. behealdan.

Behangian [be, hangian *to hang*] *To* BEHANG, *to hang round;* dependere:—Behangen beon mid bellum *to be [behung] hung round with bells, Past.* 15, 3.

Behát gehát, es; *n.* [be *by,* hat v. hatan *to command,* from *Plat.* hete *a command:* hence in *Chaucer* we have behete, behote, behest *a promise,* v. behæs] *A vow, a promise;* votum:—Þu behat behætst, *Deut.* 23, 21. He gehat gehet *he vowed a vow, Bd.* 3, 27. Ic sende behat, *Lk.* 24, 49.

Behátan, þu behætst, he behæt; *p.* behet, geheht, we beheton; *pp.* beháten, geháten *v. a.* [be *by,* hatan *to call, command*] *To vow, promise;* vovere:—Behat hy beheton *they vowed a vow.* Gehatað Drihtne, *Ps.* 75, 11. Þa behet he mid aðe, *Mt.* 14, 7. ¶ *With* wedd *to give a pledge.* God behet us wedd *God gave us a pledge, Deut.* 5, 2.

Behawian *To see, see clearly;* videre:—Behawa þonne þat þu ut ado þat mot *see then clearly* [τοτε διαβλεψεις] *that thou take out the mote, Mt.* 7, 5.

k Beheafdian; *p.* dode; *pp.* dod; *v. a.* [be *by,* heafd *head*] *To* BEHEAD; decollare:—*Mt.* 14, 10.

Beheafdung, e; *f.* A BEHEADING; decollatio, *L. Athel. Menol.*

Behealdan; *p.* beheold, behold, beheld, behilt, hi beheoldon; *pp.* behealden; *v. a* [be *near,* healdan *to hold, observe*] 1. *To* BEHOLD, *see, look on;* aspicere. 2. *To observe, consider, beware, regard, mind, take heed, to mean, signify;* observare:—1. Beheald þa tunglu *behold the stars, Bt.* 39, 13. 2. Heora æ to behealdenne *their laws to observe, Ors.* 3, 5. Hwæt þat swefen beheold, *Gen.* 41, 8.

l Beheawan; *pp.* beheawon [be, heawian *to hew*] *To hew* or *cut off, make smooth;* amputare:—Beheawon heafde *to cut off the head, Bt. Rawl.* p. 151.

Behefe, behefnes [be, hefe *heavy*] *Gain, advantage, benefit,* BEHOOF; lucrum, *Som.*

Behefe, behefu; *adj. Necessary, behoveful;* necessarius:—Þe behefe synt, *Lk.* 14, 28. ¶ Behefe þing *necessary things, necessaries, C. R. Ben.* 46.

Behegian *To* BEHEDGE, *hedge around;* circumsepire, *Lye.*

Beheld *beheld,* v. behealdan.

Behelian; *p.* behelede, ode, hi beheledon; *pp.* beheled, geheled, behelen; *v. a.* [be, helan *to cover*] *To* HELE, *hill* or *cover, cover over, obscure, hide,* condere:—Wurdon þa behelede ealle þa duna, *Gen.* 7, 19. Se heofen mot þat leoht behelian *the heaven may obscure the light, Bt.* 7, 3.

m Behem, Beme, Behemas *Bohemia,* a country in the east of Germany. Behemas *the Bohemians, Ors.* 1, 1.

Beheofian *to bewail,* v. heofian.

Beheold *beheld,* v. behealdan.

Beheonan; *prep. dat.* [be *by,* heona *hence*] *On this side, close by;* cis, citra:—¶ Git beheonan *or* get behionan *yet nearer, Elf. gr.* 38.

Beheowan *to amputate,* v. beheawan.

Behet *promised,* v. behatan.

Behicgan *to confide,* v. hicgan.

Behid *hid,* v. behydan.

Behilt *beheld,* v. behealdan.

Behindan; *prep. acc.* and *adv.* BEHIND; pone:—Behindan þe *behind thee, Bt.* 36, 2, v. hindan.

Behionan *on this side,* v. beheonan.

Behlad *covered,* v. hlidan.

Behlæstan *to load a ship,* v. hlæstan.

Behleapan; *pp.* en. *To leap upon* or *in, to fix;* insilire:—Behleapen beon *to be fixed, settled, Past.* 46, 5, *Som.*

n Behlehan *to laugh at, deride,* v. hlihan.

Behlidan *covered; p. of* hlidan.

Behófian, heo behófað; *p.* behofode; *pp.* behófen; *v. a.* [*Plat.* behoven: *Dut.* behoeven: *Ger.* behufen: *Dan.* behöve: *Swed.* behöfwa] *To* BEHOVE, *to be fit, to have need of, to need;* decere. *Impersonally, it behoveth, it concerns, it is needful* or *necessary;* oportet, interest:—Mycel wund behofað mycles læcedomes *a great wound has need of a great remedy, Bd.* 4, 25. We behofiað hlafes, *C. R. Lk.* 9, 2. Þat ealle Godes cyricean syn well behofene *that all God's churches be well supplied* or *well provided with all they have need of, L. Edm.* 5.

Behoflic; *adj. Behoveful, needful;* necessarius:—Behoflic wære, *Bd.* 5, 5, *Sm.* p. 618, note 3. Behoflic is *is necessary, C. Mk.* 11, 3: *Lk.* 18, 1.

Behogadnes, se; *f. Use, custom, practice;* exercitatio:—*Cot.* 114, *Som.*

Behogian *to be anxious, solicitous, wise, very careful,* v. hogian.

Behorsed *horsed;* equo impositus, v. gehorsad.

o Behreosað *rush down,* v. hreosan.

Begnornian, p ode; pp od To lament &c. to mourn; for lamentare Beo K 6350 v Beo gl — gnorn

2 Beggong a course Beo K 721 v bigang

6 Begroren Cd. Th Index

2 Begrynian, p ede pp ed to ensnare Th. An

7 Begyded dl. * begylded

7 Begylded gilded Som v H of Gildan

3 Begytan, p begeat to beget, obtain Th. An v begitan

4 Behelan Beo gl

5 Beheot for behet: promised threatened pp of behatan Th. An

6 Behidan p behidde pp behid to hide Th. An v hydan

2 Behofian to require: indigere Beo K 5291

8

5 Behold beheld v behealdan

4 Behelan Th. An

7 Behreafian to bereave plunder Th. An v bereafian

Begodian; *pp.* od [be, godian *to benefit*] *To benefit, crown;* coronare:—*Ps.* 5, 15.

Begongan *to exercise*, v. began *or* begangan.

Begongn *dwelt*, v. began.

Begongyn *exercised*, v. began.

Begoten *covered*, v. begeotan.

Begra *of both*, v. begen.

Begrindan [be, grindan *to grind*] *To destroy, rob, spoil;* privare:—*Cd.* 75.

Begrípan; *pp.* ed, en; *v. a.* [be, gripan *to gripe*] *To* GRIPE, *chasten, chide;* increpare:—*Ps.* 15, 7, v. gripan.

egroren *Shivering, quaking, dreading;* horrens, stridens;—*Cd.* 214.

egrornian *To lament, to grieve for;* mœrere:—*Cd.* 13, v. gnornian.

gryned *ensnared, entrapped.*

gunne, begunnen *begun*, v. beginnan.

gyded *gilded*, v. gildan.

gyman, begíman; *part.* begemende; *p.* de; *pp.* ed; *v. a.* *To take care of, to keep, govern, regard, observe, attend;* observare, v. gyman.

gymen, begimen *care, regard, observation, shew, pomp;* observatio:—Mid begymene, ιετα παρατηρησεως, *with hew* or *pomp*, *Lk.* 17, 20.

gyrdan; *p.* de; *pp.* ed, *or* begyrd; *v.a.* [be, gyrdan *to gird*] . *To* BEGIRD, *surround;* cingere. 2. *To clothe;* vestire. . *To defend, mound, fortify;* unire:—1. Begyrdað eower ndenu, *Ex.* 12, 11. 2. *Bd.* 7. 3. *Bd.* 1, 5.

ytað *shall obtain*, v. begitan.

a crown, v. beag.

abban, he behabbað, behað, behæfeð; *p.* behæfod, hi hæfdon; *pp.* behæfed, beft; *v. a.* [be *by, near*, habban *have*] 1. *To compass, enpass, surround;* cingere. *To restrain, detain;* detie:—1. Þine fynd behab- þe, *Lk.* 19, 43. 2. Hi æfdun hine, *Lk.* 4, 42.

fednes, se; *f. A detention,* ; conservatio:—¶ Behæes fæsten *sparingness, parsiy*, *Cot.* 191, v. fæst-hafolnes.

ft *held*, v. behabban.

s [be *by, near*, hæse *comd*] *A self-command, vow, ise.* Hence our *behest;* vo- :—He fela behæsa behet *any vows made*, *Chr.* 1093, hat.

ge *vows*, v. behatan.

t *shall vow*, v. behatan.

an wið *or* from *To mind, d, regard;* cavere:—*C. R.* , 15, v. behealdan.

Behangian [be, hangian *to hang*] *To* BEHANG, *to hang round;* dependere:—Behangen beon mid bellum *to be* [*behung*] *hung round with bells*, *Past.* 15, 3.

Behát gehát, es; *n.* [be *by*, hat v. hatan *to command*, from *Plat.* hete *a command:* hence in *Chaucer* we have behete, behote, behest *a promise*, v. behæs] *A vow, a promise;* votum:—Þu behat behætst, *Deut.* 23, 21. He gehat gehet *he vowed a vow*, *Bd.* 3, 27. Ic sende behat, *Lk.* 24, 49.

Behátan, þu behætst, he behæt; *p.* behet, geheht, we beheton; *pp.* beháten, geháten *v. a.* [be *by*, hatan *to call, command*] *To vow, promise;* vovere:—Behat hy beheton *they vowed a vow.* Gehatað Drihtne, *Ps.* 75, 11. Þa behet he mid aðe, *Mt.* 14, 7. ¶ *With* wedd *to give a pledge.* God behet us wedd *God gave us a pledge*, *Deut.* 5, 2.

Behawian *To see, see clearly;* videre:—Behawa þonne þat þu ut ado þat mot *see then clearly* [τοτε διαβλεψεις] *that thou take out the mote*, *Mt.* 7, 5.

k Beheafdian; *p.* dode; *pp.* dod; *v. a.* [be *by*, heafd *head*] *To* BEHEAD; decollare:—*Mt.* 14, 10.

Beheafdung, e; *f.* A BEHEADING; decollatio, *L. Athel. Menol.*

Behealdan; *p.* beheold, behold, beheld, behilt, hi beheoldon; *pp.* behealden; *v. a* [be *near*, healdan *to hold, observe*] 1. *To* BEHOLD, *see, look on;* aspicere. 2. *To observe, consider, beware, regard, mind, take heed, to mean, signify;* observare:—1. Beheald þa tunglu *behold the stars*, *Bt.* 39, 13. 2. Heora æ to behealdenne *their laws to observe*, *Ors.* 3, 5. Hwæt þat swefen beheold, *Gen.* 41, 8.

l Beheawan; *pp.* beheawon [be, heawian *to hew*] *To hew* or *cut off, make smooth;* amputare:—Beheawon heafde *to cut off the head*, *Bt. Rawl.* p. 151.

Behefe, behefnes [be, hefe *heavy*] *Gain, advantage, benefit,* BEHOOF; lucrum, *Som.*

Behefe, behefu; *adj. Necessary, behoveful;* necessarius:—Þe behefe synt, *Lk.* 14, 28. ¶ Behefe þing *necessary things, necessaries*, *C. R. Ben.* 46.

Behegian *To* BEHEDGE, *hedge around;* circumsepire, *Lye.*

Beheld *beheld*, v. behealdan.

Behelian; *p.* behelede, ode, hi beheledon; *pp.* beheled, geheled, behelen; *v. a.* [be, helan *to cover*] *To* HELE, *hill* or *cover, cover over, obscure, hide,* condere:—Wurdon þa behelede ealle þa duna, *Gen.* 7, 19. Se heofen mot þat leoht behelian *the heaven may obscure the light*, *Bt.* 7, 3.

m Behem, Beme, Behemas *Bohemia*, a country in the east of Germany. Behemas *the Bohemians*, *Ors.* 1, 1.

Beheofian *to bewail*, v. heofian.

Beheold *beheld*, v. behealdan.

Beheonan; *prep. dat.* [be *by*, heona *hence*] *On this side, close by;* cis, citra:—¶ Git beheonan *or* get behionan *yet nearer*, *Elf. gr.* 38.

Beheowan *to amputate*, v. beheawan.

Behet *promised*, v. behatan.

Behicgan *to confide*, v. hicgan.

Behid *hid*, v. behydan.

Behilt *beheld*, v. behealdan.

Behindan; *prep. acc.* and *adv.* BEHIND; pone:—Behindan þe *behind thee*, *Bt.* 36, 2, v. hindan.

Behionan *on this side*, v. beheonan.

Behlad *covered*, v. hlidan.

Behlæstan *to lead a ship*, v. hlæstan.

Behleapan; *pp.* en. *To leap upon* or *in, to fix;* insilire:—Behleapen beon *to be fixed, settled*, *Past.* 46, 5, *Som.*

n Behlehan *to laugh at, deride*, v. hlihan.

Behlidan *covered; p. of* hlidan.

Behófian, heo behófað; *p.* behofode; *pp.* behófen; *v. a.* [*Plat.* behoven: *Dut.* behoeven: *Ger.* behufen: *Dan.* behöve: *Swed.* behöfwa] *To* BEHOVE, *to be fit, to have need of, to need;* decere. *Impersonally, it behoveth, it concerns, it is needful* or *necessary;* oportet, interest:—Mycel wund behofað mycles læcedomes *a great wound has need of a great remedy*, *Bd.* 4, 25. We behofiað hlafes, *C. R. Lk.* 9, 2. Þat ealle Godes cyricean syn well behofene *that all God's churches be well supplied* or *well provided with all they have need of*, *L. Edm.* 5.

Behoflic; *adj. Behoveful, needful;* necessarius:—Behoflic wære, *Bd.* 5, 5, *Sm.* p. 618, note 3. Behoflic is *is necessary*, *C. Mk.* 11, 3: *Lk.* 18, 1.

Behogadnes, se; *f. Use, custom, practice;* exercitatio:—*Cot.* 114, *Som.*

Behogian *to be anxious, solicitous, wise, very careful*, v. hogian.

Behorsed *horsed;* equo impositus, v. gehorsad.

o Behreosað *rush down*, v. hreosan.

Behreowsian, ic behreowsige; *part.* igende *to repent*, v. hreowan.

Behreowsung, e; *f. A lamenting, repentance, penitence;* pœnitentia:—*Elf. gr.* 33.

Behrincged, behringed; *part.* [be, hrincg *a ring*] *Enclosed in a ring, encircled, surrounded;* circumdatus:—Behringed beon *to be surrounded, Past.* 21, 5.

Behropende; *part.* [*Plat.* beropen: *Dut.* beroepen: *Ger.* berufen; be, hreopende *calling*] *Vexing, molesting, troubling by calling upon;* sugillans:—*Lk.* 18, 5.

Behrumig; *adj. Swarthy, sooty;* fuliginosus:—*Martyr.*3, *April, Lye.*

p **Behrumod**; *part. Bedaubed, dirtied;* cacabatum:—*Cot.*45: 189, v. besciten.

Behwearf *A change, an exchange;* commutatio:—*Ps.* 43, 14.

Behweorfan, behwerfan; *p.* behwearf; *pp.* behworfen *To turn, spread about, return, weave, prepare, provide;* vertere:—Hig behwurfon *they spread about, Num.* 11, 32. Behworfen *woven, L. Edg. can.* 33, *Wilk.* p. 84, 53. Ic wolde þe behwerfan utan *I would wish to prepare thee, Bt.* 34, 4, v. hweorfan.

Behwon *whence*, v. hwona.

Behwurfon *spread about*, v. beweorfan.

Behwylfan *to overwhelm*, v. ahwylfan.

Behwyrfan *To treat, direct, exercise, practice;* tractare:—*Coll. monast. Lye.*

Behyd *hid*, v. hydan.

q **Behydan**; v. *To take off the hide, skin;* excoriare, *Som.*, v. behyldan, æthide.

Behydelice, behydiglice; *adv. Carefully;* solicitè:—*Bd.* 1, 27.

Behydig; *adj. Careful, vigilant, wary, watchful, solicitous, anxious;* solers:—*Bd.* 5, 20, *Som.*, v. hydeg.

Behydignys, se; *f. A desert, a wilderness, where one may carefully hide, cautiousness;* desertum:—*Ps.* 28, 7.

Behyldan *To put off, to skin;* excoriare:—He het hy behyldan, *Ors.* 4, 6.

Behyped; *part. Surrounded with a hoop, surrounded, encompassed;* circumdatus:—*Bd.* 3, 12.

r **Behyring**, e; *f. A hiring, a letting out to hire;* locatio:—*R.* 13.

Behyðelice; *adv. More sumptuously;* sumptuosius:—*Cot.*186. Behyðlic *sumptuous, Lye.*

Beigbeam *a bramble*, v. begbeam.

Beinnan *within*, v. binnan.

Beiundan *beyond*, v. begeond.

Bela *lividness*, v. balew.

Beladian, ic beladige; *p.* ode; *pp.* od *To clear, excuse;* excusare, v. ladian.

Beladung *an excuse*, v. ladung.

Belædan; *p.* belædde; *pp.* belæd, beled; *v.a. To bring, lead by, mislead, lead;* seducere:—Þu belæddest us on grin *thou hast mislead us into a snare, R. Ben.* 7. Belæd beon *to be impelled, R. Ben.* 64, *Lye*, v. lædan.

Belæfde *remained*, v. belifan.

Belænde *disinherited*, v. belandian.

Belæðed; *part. Loathed, detested;* exosus, *Som.*

Belæwa *a betrayer*, v. læwa.

Belæwan, læwan; *p.* belæwde; *pp.* belæwed; *v. a. To* BELAY, *beway, betray;* tradere:—He hyne wolde belæwan, *Mt.* 26, 15, 16.

Belæwing, e; *f. A betraying, treason;* proditio, *Som.*

Belaf *remained; p. of* belifan.

Belagen beon *to be destroyed*, v. belicgan.

Belamp *happened*, v. belimpan.

Belandian; *p.* belænde, belende, hi belandedon; *pp.* od; *v. a. To deprive of land, to confiscate, disinherit;* terris privare:—Se cyng belænde þone eorl *the king deprived the earl of his land, Chr.* 1112. Wearð Eadgar belandod *Edgar was deprived of land, Chr.* 1091. Opposed to gelandian *to inherit.*

Belcentan *to belch*, v. bealcan.

t **Belde**, beldo *Boldness, rashness;* audacia, *Som.*

Beleac *shut in*, v. belucan.

Belean, lean; *p.* beloh *To forbid, reprove, denounce;* reprehendere:—*L. Edg.* 57.

Belecgan; *imp.* belege, belecge; *p.* belede; *pp.* beled; *v. a.* [*Plat. Dut.* beliegen: *Ger.* belügen: be *by*, lecgan, legan *to lay*] *To lay by* or *on one side, to impose, falsify,* BELIE, *accuse falsely, forge, counterfeit;* mentiri, falsò culpare:—Gif man sacerd belecge *if one belie a priest, L. Cnut.* 5, *Wilk.* p. 128, 27, 40, 43. Gif man mid fæhþe belecge *if any one accuse of deadly feud*, p. 128, 46.

Beled *brought*, v. belædan.

Belegde *surrounded*, v. belicgan.

Belene. 1. *Herb henbane;* caliculаris herba. 2. *A kind of sweet cakes* or *dainty meat;* laterculus, *Som.*

Beleoran *to pass over*, v. leoran.

Beleosan; *p.* beleas; *pp.* beloren [be, leosan *to loose*] *To let go, to deprive of, to destroy;* amittere:—Leohte beloren *deprive of light, Cd.* 5, v. forleosan.

Beleð, beled *imposed, taxed with*, v. belecgan.

Belewa, belewend *a betrayer*, v. læwa.

u **Belewite** *simple*, v. bilewite.

Belflyse [bell *a bell*, flys *a fleece*] *The* BELL-WETHER'S FLEECE, *a sheep that carries the bell;* tympani, *i. e.* ducis gregis tintinnabulum gestantis vellus, *Som.*

Belg *a bulge*, v. bælg.

BELGAN, abelgan, gebelgan, he bylgð; *p.* bealg, bealh, we bulgon; *pp.* bolgen, gebolgen, gebylged [*Plat.* verbolgen: *Dut.* belgen: *Ger. Al.* balgen: *Old Ger.* balg *anger*] *To be angry, displeased;* indignari:—Ne belge wið me, *Gen.* 18, 30. Þa bealh he hyne, *Lk.* 15, 28. Gebealh hine, *Lk.* 13, 14, v. abelgan.

Belhringes beacn *a sign by bell ringing.*

Belhus, bellhus A BELL-HOUSE, *a steeple, a clock-house, a bell-tower;* clocarium, campanile:—*Cot.* 210, *Mann.*

Belicgan, hi belicgað *or* belið; *p.* belæg, belegde, we belagon; *pp.* belagen; *v. a.* [be *by*, licgan, ligan *to lie*] *To lie* or *extend, by* or *about, to surround, encompass, destroy;* circumdare:—*Jos.* 7, 9. Beligan uton *to lie around, Cd.* 12.

Beliden *deprived;* privatus:—*Fr. Jud.* 12.

v **Belifan**; *part.* belifiende; *p.* belaf, belæfde [be, læfan *to leave*] *To remain, abide, to be left;* superesse:—Ne se rysel ne belifð oð morgen, *Ex.* 23, 18, v. bidan.

Belig *a bag*, v. bælg.

Beligan utan *to go about*, v. belicgan.

Belimp *an event*, v. gelimp.

Belimpan, limpian; *p.* belamp, hi belumpon; *sub.* belumpe; *pp.* belumpen [be, limpian *to regard*] *To concern, regard, belong, pertain, appertain, agree;* curare, pertinere:-Ne belimpð to þe, *Mk.* 4, 38. Hwæt limpeð þæs to þe *what does it concern thee, Bd.* 1, 7. Hwæt belimpð his to þe *what of it belongs to thee, Bt.* 14, 2. Hit belimpð to þære spræce *it agrees with thy argument, Bt.* 38, 2, v. limpian.

w **Belisnian**, belistnian; *p.* ode; *pp.* od; *v.a.* [be *from*, lustnian *for* lustan *to lust*] *To evirate, emasculate, castrate;* castrare. *Part.* belisnod, belistnod *emasculated, a castrated man.* Used as a noun, *a eu-*

~~Beirnan~~

1 Beladigend, es; m one who makes excuses, a defender; excusator Ben Elfgl. 23

4 Beládung Th. An

6 Belǽfan to leave from belifan ... 347

[35a]

Besyrwen ~~deprived~~ deprived Bes K 5520 v. hreowan

7 to enrage, make angry, be indignant Th. An in belgan

8 Behō token, sign, ... f

...hydd hid ... 4,22 v hydan

...hýdan to hide, conceal Th. An

...hýdan

[35b]

Beleaf left Th. An, for belef of belifan

Belifon remained ... of belifan

9 to happen, endure Th. An

...lt beholds, ...ves Th. An v ...ldan

f

[illegible]

Bell dl. +

~~2~~ Belle; an ~~m~~ n? f a bell [36c]

~~2 Belle, an; f Th. an~~ A bell

Ben; a ~~Attenne~~ d. ac A wound vulnus Beo K. 5465: 5893 ~~to top of~~

~~3~~ 3 Bén, es; ~~f~~ A prayer ~~Th. an~~ g.

~~3~~ Ben-geát es; n a wound's gate or opening Beo K ~~2235~~ 2235

~~4~~ Bell sounded p of bellan

5 Bellan [36 h]

~~7~~ Belóge reprehend subj. of beleán Th. an

5 [37a].

4 Swa þu bena eart so thou a petitioner art, as thou askest Beo K

~~5~~

[37d]

~~6~~ Beo, beoan, bean g. pl. beoena, beond f. ~~Th. an~~ a bee

pl. nom. beoan, bean, beon gen I 667,24

6

7

~~7~~ 7 Bend, e; f a band, vinculum Beo K 1947 v bænd (also bend, es: m)

~~2~~ 5 Beod, es: m a table Ps. Th. 22,6

6 Beodan; p ic bead, þu bude, we budon Th [38a]

~~Benemnan; p de~~

~~6~~ Be-nemnan; p de to engage; ~~allowance~~ Beo K 2188 Beo gl

[37c]

~~7~~ 8 Benn-dl. + Benne of or to a wound; g. dl. ac of ben v. Spl.

5

nuch, *Elf. gr.* 9. Soðlice synd belistnode þe of hyra modor innoðum cumað, and eft synt belistnode þa men þe man belistnað and eft synd belistnode þe hig sylfe belistnodon for heofona rice, *Mt.* 19, 12, v. afyran.

ɛlið *surrounds*, v. belicgan.

ELL, bella, an [*Plat.* belle: *Dut.* bel] A BELL, *church-bell, a small bell;* campana:—Cyricbell *a church-bell.* Hleoþor heora bellan *the sound of their bell, Bd.* 4, 23: *Sm.* p. 595, n. 40. ¶ Litel belle *a little bell;* tintinnabulum. Mucel belle *a large bell;* campana.

ɛllan; *part.* bellende; *p.* bell; *v. n.* [*Ger.* bellen: *Swed.* böla] *To* BELLOW, *to make a hollow noise, to roar, bark;* boare:—Bell egsan hweop *a cry of fear resounded, Cd.* 148.

llhus *a steeple*, v. belhus.

locen, belocyn *shut up*, v. belucan.

ogen *deceived*, v. leogan.

oh *forbade*, v. belean.

one *henbane*, v. belene.

oren *deprived*, v. beleosan.

T, [*Dan.* baelte: *Icel.* belti: *at.* balteus] A BELT, *girle;* balteum:—*Cot.* 25, v. yrdel.

ican, he belycð; *p.* beleác, belucon; *pp.* belocen; *v. a.* *Dan.* lukke: be, lucan *to lock*] *lock up, enclose, shut, shut , store;* obserare:—And þær ne belucan *and therein to k up, Bt.* 1. Seo duru wæs locen, *Mt.* 25, 10.

mpe *concern;* pertineret, v. limpan.

ne *henbane*, v. belene.

cð *locks*, v. belucan.

ted; *part. deceived, C. Mt.* 16, v. beswicod.

cyd *maimed, mangled, beded;* truncatum:——*Cot.*

egan; *p.* ade; *v. a. To al-, inveigle, seduce;* procare: belytegade Greace *he ald Greece, Ors.* 3, 7.

a trumpet, v. byme.

nan; *p.* hig bemændon; *To* BEMOAN, *lament for, il;* lugere:—*Deut.* 34, 8.

an *found; perf. of* beme- v. metan.

cud *Maimed, beheaded;* atus:—*Somn.* 289.

Stringed instruments; bar- —*Cot.* 27.

Bohemians, v. Behem.

n *mourned*, v. myrnan.

a trumpeter, v. bymere.

n; *p.* bemæt, hi bemætan; meten; *v. a.* [be *by*, me *mete*] *To measure by, to*

find out, perceive, esteem, consider; invenire:—*Ors.* 3, 7: 4, 6, v. metan.

Bemiþan *to conceal*, v. miþan.

Bemurcnian, bemurcian *to murmur, murmur greatly*, v. murcnian.

Bemyldan [*Plat.* bemulmen: *Dut.* bemullen: hence our English word bemoil *to bemire*] *To bury, inter, hide* or *put under ground;* inhumare: *Cot.* 101, *Som.*

a Ben, bene, e; *f.* [*Plat.* beën: *Dan.* bon: *Icel.* bón, baen: *Heb.* בן bn *between, a person* or *thing coming between, mediation*, v. gebed] *A praying, prayer, petition, an intreaty, a deprecation, supplication, demand.* Hence in *Chaucer* bone and our BOON; precatio:—Þin ben is gehyred, *Lk.* 1, 13. Ic underfeng þine bene, *Gen.* 19, 21. Hi heom þæra bena forwyrndon *they gave to them a denial of their requests, Ors.* 2, 2. Micelra bena dæg, *Martyr.* 25. *April.*

Bena *A petitioner, demander;* rogator:—Hi bena wæron *they were demanders* or *they demanded, Ors.* 3, 11. Hence bena wesan *to demand.*

Benacan *to make naked*, v. genacian.

b Benæman, beniman, benyman; *p.* benam; *pp.* benemed, benemd, benumen; *v. a.* [be *by*, niman *to take:* hence *Chaucer's* benimmeth *for* bereaveth] 1. *To deprive, take away;* auferre. 2. *To stupify,* BENUMB; stupefacere:—1. Ne meahte hi þæs landes benæman *they could not take away the lands, Ors.* 1, 10. 2. *Som.*

Benc *a bench*, v. bænc.

Benc-sweg *a noise of benches, convivial noise.*

Bend *a band*, v. bænd.

Bend *bound*, v. bindan.

Bendan; *part.* bendende; *v. a.* [bænd *a band, a bow*] *To* BEND, *incline* or *lean;* flectere:—Bendende bogan, *Ps.* 77, 12, v. bugan.

Bene *a prayer*, v. ben.

Beneced *naked*, v. benacan.

Benemd, benemed *taken away*, v. benæman.

Beneotan [be, neotan *to enjoy*] beneotan aldre *or* feore *to take from the enjoyment of life, to take away life, to kill, Cd.* 50: 89, *Lye.*

Beneoð, beneoðan *beneath*, v. benyðan.

Beniman *to take away*, v. benæman.

Beniuða *beneath*, v. benyðan.

c Benn [*Norse*, Mann] 1. *A man;* homo. 2. *A wound;* vulnus:—1. *Cd.* 167. 2. *Cd.* 9, *Mann.*

Benotod *noted*, v. genotian.

Bensian, boensian; *part.* ende; *p.* ode; *pp.* od [ben *a prayer*, sian *or* sigan *to fall down*] *To fall down in prayer, to pray, intreat in prayer;* orare:—*Bd.* 3, 12, *Sm.* p. 537, note 20.

Bentiid *f.* [ben *a prayer*, tid *time*] *Prayer-time, rogation-days;* rogationum dies:—*Menol.* 144.

Bentiþe, bentigþe; *adj.* [ben *a prayer*, tiþa *obtained*] *Easy to be obtained by prayer, exorable, successful;* deprecabilis:—Hi swyðe bentiþige wæron, *Chr.* 883, v. tiþa.

Benugan, hi benugon [*Plat.* vernögen: *Dut.* genoegen: *Ger.* vergnügen] *To enjoy;* oblectare:—Gif hi þæs wuda benugon *if they enjoy* [*have enjoyment of*] *the woods, Bt.* 25. Be nuge, *Hickes's Epist. Diss.* vol. ii. p. 55, 32.

Benum, benumen *deprived, benumbed*, v. benæman.

Benyman *to deprive*, v. benæman.

d Benyðan; *adv.* [be, nyðan *neath*] BENEATH, *below, under;* infra:—Ne nan wuht benyðan *nor any thing beneath, Bt.* 36, 5, v. niðer.

BEO, beaw; *plu.* beon; *f.* [*Dut.* bye, bie *f*: *Ger.* biene *f*: *Al.* bie, bien: *Not.* bine: *Dan. Icel.* bie: *Swed.* bi] A BEE; apis:—Swa swa seo beo sceal losian *as the bee shall perish, Bt.* 31, 2: *Ps.* 117, 12.

Beo *I am* or *shall be;* sum, ero, *be thou;* sis, v. beon. ¶ Beo hit swa *be it so* or *so be it.*

Beo-bread, beon-bread *bee-bread, a honey-comb.*

Beoce *a beech*, v. boc.

Beo-ceorl, beo-cere *a* BEE-CEORL, *a bee-farmer* or *keeper.*

Beod *a table, Ps.* 22, 6, v. bord.

Beodan; *p.* he bead, bude, bád, hi budon; *pp.* boden; *v. a.* [*Plat.* beden: *Dut.* bieden: *Ger.* bieten: *Moes.* buidan: bod *a command*] *To command,* BID, *will, offer, enjoy;* jubere:—Þas þing ic eow beode, *Jn.* 15, 17. He bead Iosepe þat he bude, *Gen.* 45, 17: 5, 2. His boda beodan, *Cd.* 27, v. bebeodan, biddan, bodian.

Beodas; *plu. The scales of a balance;* lances, *Som.*

e Beod-bolla *A table-bowl, a cup, bowl;* cupa, *Som.*

Beod-clað [*Plat. Dut.* beddeklede] 1. A BED-CLOTH, *coverlet, blanket, bed-clothes;* lodix. 2. *A table-cloth, carpet, hanging;* gausape, *Som.*

Beodende *commanding*, v. beodan.

Begnornian, p ode; pp od To lament, to mourn; lamentari
Beo K 6350 v Beod gnorn

Begong a course Beo K 721 v begang
Gen II 720, 36

Begroren Cd. Th. Index

2 Begrynian, p ode. pp ed to ensnare Th. An

Begyded dl. * begylded

7 Begylded guilded Som pp of gildan

3 Begytan, p begeat to beget, obtain Th. An
v begitan

5 Beheot promised threatened pp of behatan Th. An

6 Behidan p behidde pp behid to hide Th. An v hydan

4 Behofan to require; indigere Beo K 5291

8

Behold beheld v behealdan

4 Behelan Beo gl

4 Behelan Th. An

7 Behreafian to bereave plunder Th. An
v bereafian

Begodian; *pp.* od [be, godian *to benefit*] *To benefit, crown;* coronare:—*Ps.* 5, 15.

Begongan *to exercise,* v. began or begangan.

Begongn *dwelt,* v. began.

Begongyn *exercised,* v. began.

Begoten *covered,* v. begeotan.

Begra *of both,* v. begen.

Begrindan [be, grindan *to grind*] *To destroy, rob, spoil;* privare:—*Cd.* 75.

Begripan; *pp.* ed, en; *v. a.* [be, gripan *to gripe*] *To* GRIPE, *chasten, chide;* increpare:—*Ps.* 15, 7, v. gripan.

Begrorenn *Shivering, quaking, dreading;* horrens, stridens:—*Cd.* 214.

h Begrornian *To lament, to grieve for;* mœrere:—*Cd.* 13, v. gnornian.

Begryned *ensnared, entrapped.*

Begunne, begunnen *begun,* v. beginnan.

Begyded *gilded,* v. gildan.

Begyman, begiman; *part.* begemende; *p.* de; *pp.* ed; *v. a. To take care of, to keep, govern, regard, observe, attend;* observare, v. gyman.

Begymen, begimen *care, regard, observation, shew, pomp;* observatio:—Mid begymene, μετα παρατηρησεως, *with shew* or *pomp, Lk.* 17, 20.

Begyrdan; *p.* de; *pp.* ed, or begyrd; *v.a.* [be, gyrdan *to gird*] 1. *To* BEGIRD, *surround;* cingere. 2. *To clothe;* vestire. 3. *To defend, mound, fortify;* munire:—1. Begyrdað eower lendenu, *Ex.* 12, 11. 2. *Bd.* 1, 7. 3. *Bd.* 1, 5.

Begytað *shall obtain,* v. begitan.

Beh *a crown,* v. beag.

Behabban, he behabbað, behafað, behæfeð; *p.* behæfod, hi behæfdon; *pp.* behæfed, behæft; *v. a.* [be *by, near,* habban *to have*] 1. *To compass, encompass, surround;* cingere. 2. *To restrain, detain;* detinere:—1. Þine fynd behabbað þe, *Lk.* 19, 43. 2. Hi behæfdun hine, *Lk.* 4, 42.

[Be]hæfednes, se; *f. A detention, care;* conservatio:—¶ Behæ[f]ednes fæsten *sparingness, parsimony, Cot.* 191, v. fæst-hafolnes.

[Be]hæft *held,* v. behabban.

[Beh]æs [be *by, near,* hæse *command*] *A self-command, vow, promise.* Hence our *behest;* votum:—He fela behæsa behet *many vows made, Chr.* 1093, [v.] behat.

[Beh]etige *vows,* v. behatan.

[Beh]etst *shall vow,* v. behatan.

[Beheal]dan wið or from *To mind, [att]end, regard;* cavere:—*C. R.* [Lk]. 7, 15, v. behealdan.

Behangian [be, hangian *to hang*] *To* BEHANG, *to hang round;* dependere:—Behangen beon mid bellum *to be* [*behung*] *hung round with bells, Past.* 15, 3.

Behát gehát, es; *n.* [be *by,* hat v. hatan *to command,* from *Plat.* hete *a command:* hence in *Chaucer* we have behete, behote, behest *a promise,* v. behæs] *A vow, a promise;* votum:—Þu behat behætst, *Deut.* 23, 21. He gehat gehet *he vowed a vow, Bd.* 3, 27. Ic sende behat, *Lk.* 24, 49.

Behátan, þu behætst, he behæt; *p.* behet, geheht, we beheton; *pp.* beháten, geháten *v. a.* [be *by,* hatan *to call, command*] *To vow, promise;* vovere:—Behat hy beheton *they vowed a vow.* Gehatað Drihtne, *Ps.* 75, 11. Þa behet he mid aðe, *Mt.* 14, 7. ¶ *With* wedd *to give a pledge.* God behet us wedd *God gave us a pledge, Deut.* 5, 2.

Behawian *To see, see clearly;* videre:—Behawa þonne þat þu ut ado þat mot *see then clearly* [τοτε διαβλεψεις] *that thou take out the mote, Mt.* 7, 5.

k Beheafdian; *p.* dode; *pp.* dod; *v. a.* [be *by,* heafd *head*] *To* BEHEAD; decollare:—*Mt.* 14, 10.

Beheafdung, e; *f.* A BEHEADING; decollatio, *L. Athel. Menol.*

Behealdan; *p.* beheold, behold, beheld, behilt, hi beheoldon; *pp.* behealden; *v. a* [be *near,* healdan *to hold, observe*] 1. *To* BEHOLD, *see, look on;* aspicere. 2. *To observe, consider, beware, regard, mind, take heed, to mean, signify;* observare:—1. Beheald þa tunglu *behold the stars, Bt.* 39, 13. 2. Heora æ to behealdenne *their laws to observe, Ors.* 3, 5. Hwæt þat swefen beheold, *Gen.* 41, 8.

l Beheawan; *pp.* beheawon [be, heawian *to hew*] *To hew* or *cut off, make smooth;* amputare:—Beheawon heafde *to cut off the head, Bt. Rawl.* p. 151.

Behefe, behefnes [be, hefe *heavy*] *Gain, advantage, benefit,* BEHOOF; lucrum, *Som.*

Behefe, behefu; *adj. Necessary, behoveful;* necessarius:—Þe behefe synt, *Lk.* 14, 28. ¶ Behefe þing *necessary things, necessaries, C. R. Ben.* 46.

Behegian *To* BEHEDGE, *hedge around;* circumsepire, *Lye.*

Beheld *beheld,* v. behealdan.

Behelian; *p.* behelede, ode, hi beheledon; *pp.* beheled, geheled, behelen; *v. a.* [be, helan *to cover*] *To* HELE, *hill* or *cover, cover over, obscure, hide;* condere:—Wurdon þa behelede ealle þa duna, *Gen.* 7, 19. Se heofen mot þat leoht behelian *the heaven may obscure the light, Bt.* 7, 3.

m Behem, Beme, Behemas *Bohemia,* a country in the east of Germany. Behemas *the Bohemians, Ors.* 1, 1.

Beheofian *to bewail,* v. heofian.

Beheold *beheld,* v. behealdan.

Beheonan; *prep. dat.* [be *by,* heona *hence*] *On this side, close by;* cis, citra:—¶ Git beheonan or get behionan *yet nearer, Elf. gr.* 38.

Beheowan *to amputate,* v. beheawan.

Behet *promised,* v. behatan.

Behicgan *to confide,* v. hicgan.

Behid *hid,* v. behydan.

Behilt *beheld,* v. behealdan.

Behindan; *prep. acc.* and *adv.* BEHIND; pone:—Behindan þe *behind thee, Bt.* 36, 2, v. hindan.

Behionan *on this side,* v. beheonan.

Behlad *covered,* v. hlidan.

Behlæstan *to load a ship,* v. hlæstan.

Behleapan; *pp.* en. *To leap upon* or *in, to fix;* insilire:—Behleapen beon *to be fixed, settled, Past.* 46, 5, *Som.*

n Behlehan *to laugh at, deride,* v. hlihan.

Behlidan *covered; p. of* hlidan.

Behófian, heo behófað; *p.* behofode; *pp.* behófen; *v. a.* [*Plat.* behoven: *Dut.* behoeven: *Ger.* behufen: *Dan.* behöve: *Swed.* behöfwa] *To* BEHOVE, *to be fit, to have need of, to need;* decere. *Impersonally, it behoveth, it concerns, it is needful* or *necessary;* oportet, interest:—Mycel wund behofað mycles læcedomes *a great wound has need of a great remedy, Bd.* 4, 25. We behofiað hlafes, *C. R. Lk.* 9, 2. Þat ealle Godes cyricean syn well behofene *that all God's churches be well supplied* or *well provided with all they have need of, L. Edm.* 5.

Behoflic; *adj. Behoveful, needful;* necessarius:—Behoflic wære, *Bd.* 5, 5, *Sm.* p. 618, note 3. Behoflic is *is necessary, C. Mk.* 11, 3: *Lk.* 18, 1.

Behogadnes, se; *f. Use, custom, practice;* exercitatio:—*Cot.* 114, *Som.*

Behogian *to be anxious, solicitous, wise, very careful,* v. hogian.

Behorsed *horsed;* equo impositus, v. gehorsad.

o Behreosað *rush down,* v. hreosan.

Behreowsian, ic behreowsige; *part.* igende *to repent*, v. hreowan.

Behreowsung, e; *f. A lamenting, repentance, penitence;* pœnitentia:—*Ælf. gr.* 33.

Behrincged, behringed; *part.* [be, hrincg *a ring*] *Enclosed in a ring, encircled, surrounded;* circumdatus:—Behringed beon *to be surrounded, Past.* 21, 5.

Behropende; *part.* [*Plat.* beropen: *Dut.* beroepen: *Ger.* berufen; be, hreopende *calling*] *Vexing, molesting, troubling by calling upon;* sugillans:—*Lk.* 18, 5.

Behrumig; *adj. Swarthy, sooty;* fuliginosus:—*Martyr.* 3, *April, Lye.*

p Behrumod; *part. Bedaubed, dirtied;* cacabatum:—*Cot.* 45: 189, v. besciten.

Behwearf *A change, an exchange;* commutatio:—*Ps.* 43, 14.

Behweorfan, behwerfan; *p.* behwearf; *pp.* behworfen *To turn, spread about, return, weave, prepare, provide;* vertere:—Hig behwurfon *they spread about, Num.* 11, 32. Behworfen *woven, L. Edg. can.* 33, *Wilk.* p. 84, 53. Ic wolde þe behwerfan utan *I would wish to prepare thee, Bt.* 34, 4, v. hweorfan.

Behwon *whence*, v. hwona.

Behwurfon *spread about*, v. beweorfan.

Behwylfan *to overwhelm*, v. ahwylfan.

Behwyrfan *To treat, direct, exercise, practice;* tractare:—*Coll. monast. Lye.*

Behyd *hid*, v. hydan.

q Behydan; *v. To take off the hide, skin;* excoriare, *Som.*, v. behyldan, æthide.

Behydelice, behydiglice; *adv. Carefully;* solicitè:—*Bd.* 1, 27.

Behydig; *adj. Careful, vigilant, wary, watchful, solicitous, anxious;* solers:—*Bd.* 5, 20, *Som.*, v. hydeg.

Behydignys, se; *f. A desert, a wilderness, where one may carefully hide, cautiousness;* desertum:—*Ps.* 28, 7.

Behyldan *To put off, to skin;* excoriare:—He het hy behyldan, *Ors.* 4, 6.

Behyped; *part. Surrounded with a hoop, surrounded, encompassed;* circumdatus:—*Bd.* 3, 12.

r Behyring, e; *f. A hiring, a letting out to hire;* locatio:—*R.* 13.

Behyðelice; *adv. More sumptuously;* sumptuosius:—*Cot.* 186. Behyðlic *sumptuous, Lye.*

Beigbeam *a bramble*, v. begbeam.

Beinnan *within*, v. binnan.

Beiundan *beyond*, v. begeond.

Bela *lividness*, v. balew.

Beladian, ic beladige; *p.* ode; *pp.* od *To clear, excuse;* excusare, v. ladian.

Beladung *an excuse*, v. ladung.

Belædan; *p.* belædde; *pp.* belæd, beled; *v. a. To bring, lead by, mislead, lead;* seducere:—Þu belæddest us on grin *thou hast mislead us into a snare, R. Ben.* 7. Belæd beon *to be impelled, R. Ben.* 64, *Lye*, v. lædan.

Belæfde *remained*, v. belifan.

Belænde *disinherited*, v. belandian.

s Belæðed; *part. Loathed, detested;* exosus, *Som.*

Belæwa *a destroyer*, v. læwa.

Belæwan, læwan; *p.* belæwde; *pp.* belæwed; *v. a. To* BELAY, *bewray, betray;* tradere:—He hyne wolde belæwan, *Mt.* 26, 15, 16.

Belæwing, e; *f. A betraying, treason;* proditio, *Som.*

Belaf *remained; p. of* belifan.

Belagen beon *to be destroyed*, v. belicgan.

Belamp *happened*, v. belimpan.

Belandian; *p.* belænde, belende, hi belandedon; *pp.* od; *v. a. To deprive of land, to confiscate, disinherit;* terris privare:—Se cyng belænde þone eorl *the king deprived the earl of his land, Chr.* 1112. Wearð Eadgar belandod *Edgar was deprived of land, Chr.* 1091. Opposed to gelandian *to inherit.*

Belcentan *to belch*, v. bealcan.

t Belde, beldo *Boldness, rashness;* audacia, *Som.*

Beleac *shut in*, v. belucan.

Belean, lean; *p.* beloh *To forbid, reprove, denounce;* reprehendere:—*L. Edg.* 57.

Belecgan; *imp.* belege, belecge; *p.* belede; *pp.* beled; *v. a.* [*Plat. Dut.* beliegen: *Ger.* belügen: be *by*, lecgan, legan *to lay*] *To lay by* or *on one side, to impose, falsify,* BELIE, *accuse falsely, forge, counterfeit;* mentiri, falsò culpare:—Gif man sacerd belecge *if one belie a priest, L. Cnut.* 5, *Wilk.* p. 128, 27, 40, 43. Gif man mid fæhþe belecge *if any one accuse of deadly feud*, p. 128, 46.

Beled *brought*, v. belædan.

Belegde *surrounded*, v. belicgan.

Belene. 1. *Herb henbane;* calicularis herba. 2. *A kind of sweet cakes* or *dainty meat;* laterculus, *Som.*

Beleoran *to pass over*, v. leoran.

Beleosan; *p.* beleas; *pp.* beloren [be, leosan *to loose*] *To let go, to deprive of, to destroy;* amittere:——Leohte beloren *deprive of light, Cd.* 5, v. forleosan.

Beleð, beled *imposed, taxed with*, v. belecgan.

Belewa, belewend *a betrayer*, v. læwa.

u Belewite *simple*, v. bilewite.

Belflyse [bell *a bell*, flys *a fleece*] *The* BELL-WETHER'S FLEECE, *a sheep that carries the bell;* tympani, *i. e.* ducis gregis tintinnabulum gestantis vellus, *Som.*

Belg *a bulge*, v. bælg.

BELGAN, abelgan, gebelgan, he bylgð; *p.* bealg, bealh, we bulgon; *pp.* bolgen, gebolgen, gebylged [*Plat.* verbolgen: *Dut.* belgen: *Ger. Al.* balgen: *Old Ger.* balg *anger*] *To be angry, displeased;* indignari:——Ne belge wið me, *Gen.* 18, 30. Þa bealh he hyne, *Lk.* 15, 28. Gebealh hine, *Lk.* 13, 14, v. abelgan.

Belhringes beacn *a sign by bell ringing.*

Belhus, bellhus A BELL-HOUSE, *a steeple, a clock-house, a bell-tower;* clocarium, campanile:—*Cot.* 210, *Mann.*

Belícgan, hi belicgað *or* belið; *p.* belæg, belegde, we belagon; *pp.* belagen; *v. a.* [be *by*, licgan, ligan *to lie*] *To lie* or *extend, by* or *about, to surround, encompass, destroy;* circumdare:—*Jos.* 7, 9. Beligan uton *to lie around, Cd.* 12.

Beliden *deprived;* privatus:—*Fr. Jud.* 12.

v Belifan; *part.* belifiende; *p.* belaf, belæfde [be, læfan *to leave*] *To remain, abide, to be left;* superesse:—Ne se rysel ne belifð oð morgen, *Ex.* 23, 18, v. bidan.

Belig *a bag*, v. bælg.

Beligan utan *to go about*, v. belicgan.

Belimp *an event*, v. gelimp.

Belimpan, limpian; *p.* belamp, hi belumpon; *sub.* belumpe; *pp.* belumpen [be, limpian *to regard*] *To concern, regard, belong, pertain, appertain, agree;* curare, pertinere:-Ne belimpð to þe, *Mk.* 4, 38. Hwæt limpeð þæs to þe *what does it concern thee, Bd.* 1, 7. Hwæt belimpð his to þe *what of it belongs to thee, Bt.* 14, 2. Hit belimpð to þære spræce *it agrees with thy argument, Bt.* 38, 2, v. limpian.

w Belisnian, belistnian; *p.* ode; *pp.* od; *v. a.* [be *from*, lustnian *for* lustan *to lust*] *To evirate, emasculate, castrate;* castrare. *Part.* belisnod, belistnod *emasculated, a castrated man.* Used as a noun, *a eu-*

~~Benirnan~~

Ꝑ-1 Beladigend, es; m one who makes excuses, a defender; excusator, Ben Elfgl. 23

Ꝑ4 Beládung Th. An

5 Belǽfan, to leave from, p. de belifan v Rask Gr § 347

2 Befroren ~~robbed~~ deprived Bes K 5520 v hreosan

Ꝑ7 [35 a] To enrage, make angry; be indignant Th. An in belgan

Behó token, sign, O 3 & f proof? Th An

O [35 b]

hydd hid Mk 4. 22 v hydan
-chýdan to hide
conceal Th. An
hydan

6 Beleaf left Th An pret belifan, for belaf

8 Belifon remained p. pl of belifan

Ꝑ9 to happen, conduce Th. An

-elt beholds,
-ves Th. An v
-aldan

-f

-z

Ben ... Rask Gr Th ... flaw ... K 966

(Bill dl. +)

2 Belle, an; m? f a bell [36c]

~~2 Belle, an; f Th. an~~ A bell

3 2

Ben, e; f A wound vulnus Beo K 5465; 5843

Ben-geát es; n a wound's gate or opening Beo K 2235

3 Bén, es; f A prayer ~~Th. an~~

4 Bell sounded p of bellan

5 Bellan [36 b]

Belóge reprehend subj. of belean Th. an

5 [37a]

4 Swa þu bena eart so thou a petitioner art, as thou askest Beo K

[37d]

6 Beo, beoan, bear g. pl beoena, beona f. Th. an a bee

pl. nom. beoan, bean, beon Gen I 647, 26

5

6

7

also bend, es; m

7 Bend, e; f a band vinculum Beo K 1947 v bænd

2 5 Bead, es: m a table L. Th 22, 6

6 Beodan; p gic bead, þu bude, we budon Ettm [38a]

~~Be-nemnan; p de~~

Be-nemnan; p de To engage; ~~[illegible]~~ Beo K 2188 Beo gl

[37c]

8 Benn-dl. + Benne of or to a wound; g. d. ac of ben v. spl.

5

nuch, Ælf. gr. 9. Soðlice synd belistnode þe of hyra modor innoðum cumað, and eft synt belistnode þa men þe man belistnað and eft synd belistnode þe hig sylfe belistnodon for heofona rice, *Mt.* 19, 12, v. afyran.

Belið *surrounds*, v. belicgan.

Bell, bella, an [*Plat.* belle: *Dut.* bel] A bell, *church-bell, a small bell;* campana:—Cyric-bell *a church-bell.* Hleoþor heora bellan *the sound of their bell, Bd.* 4, 23: *Sm.* p. 595, n. 40. ¶ Litel belle *a little bell;* tintinnabulum. Mucel belle *a large bell;* campana.

ellan; *part.* bellende; *p.* bell; *v. n.* [*Ger.* bellen: *Swed.* böla] *To* bellow, *to make a hollow noise, to roar, bark;* boare:—Bell egsan hweop *a cry of fear resounded, Cd.* 148.

ellhus *a steeple*, v. belhus.

elocen, belocyn *shut up*, v. belucan.

elogen *deceived*, v. leogan.

eloh *forbade*, v. belean.

elone *henbane*, v. belene.

eloren *deprived*, v. beleosan.

LT, [*Dan.* baelte: *Icel.* belti: *Lat.* balteus] A belt, *girdle;* balteum:—*Cot.* 25, v. gyrdel.

úcan, he belycð; *p.* beleác, i belucon; *pp.* belocen; *v. a.* *Dan.* lukke: be, lucan *to lock*] *To lock up, enclose, shut, shut up, store;* obserare:—And þær ne belucan *and therein to ck up, Bt.* 1. Seo duru wæs elocen, *Mt.* 25, 10.

impe *concern;* pertineret, v. limpan.

ne *henbane*, v. belene.

cð *locks*, v. belucan.

rted; *part. deceived, C. Mt.* 16, v. beswican.

scyd *maimed, mangled, beheaded;* truncatum:—*Cot.* 0.

egan; *p.* ade; *v. a. To allure, inveigle, seduce;* procare: belytegade Greace *he allured Greece, Ors.* 3, 7.

a trumpet, v. byme.

man; *p.* hig bemændon; *To* bemoan, *lament for, wail;* lugere:—*Deut.* 34, 8.

tan *found; perf. of* bemetan, v. metan.

icud *Maimed, beheaded;* catus:—*Somn.* 289.

Stringed instruments; bar-:—*Cot.* 27.

Bohemians, v. Behem.

n *mourned*, v. myrnan.

a trumpeter, v. bymere.

n; *p.* bemæt, hi bemætan; emeten; *v. a.* [be *by*, mete] *To measure by, to find out, perceive, esteem, consider;* invenire:—*Ors.* 3, 7: 4, 6, v. metan.

Bemiþan *to conceal*, v. miþan.

Bemurcnian, bemurcian *to murmur, murmur greatly*, v. murcnian.

Bemyldan [*Plat.* bemulmen: *Dut.* bemullen: hence our English word bemoil *to bemire*] *To bury, inter, hide* or *put under ground;* inhumare: *Cot.* 101, *Som.*

a Ben, bene, e; *f.* [*Plat.* beën: *Dan.* bön: *Icel.* bón, baen: *Heb.* בן bn *between, a person* or *thing coming between, mediation*, v. gebed] *A praying, prayer, petition, an intreaty, a deprecation, supplication, demand.* Hence in *Chaucer* bone and our boon; precatio:—Þin ben is gehyred, *Lk.* 1, 13. Ic underfeng þine bene, *Gen.* 19, 21. Hi heom þæra bena forwyrndon *they gave to them a denial of their requests, Ors.* 2, 2. Micelra bena-dæg, *Martyr.* 25. *April.*

Bena *A petitioner, demander;* rogator:—Hi bena wæron *they were demanders* or *they demanded, Ors.* 3, 11. Hence bena wesan *to demand.*

Benacan *to make naked*, v. genacian.

b Benæman, beniman, benyman; *p.* benam; *pp.* benemed, benemd, benumen; *v. a.* [be *by*, niman *to take:* hence *Chaucer's* benimmeth *for* bereaveth] 1. *To deprive, take away;* auferre. 2. *To stupify,* benumb; stupefacere:—1. Ne meahte hi þæs landes benæman *they could not take away the lands, Ors.* 1, 10. 2. *Som.*

Benc *a bench*, v. bænc.

Benc-sweg *a noise of benches, convivial noise.*

Bend *a band*, v. bænd.

Bend *bound*, v. bindan.

Bendan; *part.* bendende; *v. a.* [bænd *a band, a bow*] *To* bend, *incline* or *lean;* flectere:—Bendende bogan, *Ps.* 77, 12, v. bugan.

Bene *a prayer*, v. ben.

Beneced *naked*, v. benacan.

Benemd, benemed *taken away*, v. benæman.

Beneotan [be, neotan *to enjoy*] beneotan aldre *or* feore *to take from the enjoyment of life, to take away life, to kill, Cd.* 50: 89, *Lye.*

Beneoð, beneoðan *beneath*, v. benyðan.

Beniman *to take away*, v. benæman.

Beniuða *beneath*, v. benyðan.

c Benn [*Norse*, [illegible]] 1. *A man;* homo. 2. *A wound;* vulnus:—1. *Cd.* 167. 2. *Cd.* 9, *Mann.*

Benotod *noted*, v. genotian.

Bensian, boensian; *part.* ende; *p.* ode; *pp.* od [ben *a prayer*, sian *or* sigan *to fall down*] *To fall down in prayer, to pray, intreat in prayer;* orare:—*Bd.* 3, 12, *Sm.* p. 537, note 20.

Bentiid *f.* [ben *a prayer*, tid *time*] *Prayer-time, rogation-days;* rogationum dies:—*Menol.* 144.

Bentiþe, bentigþe; *adj.* [ben *a prayer*, tiþa *obtained*] *Easy to be obtained by prayer, exorable, successful;* deprecabilis:—Hi swyðe bentiþige wæron, *Chr.* 883, v. tiþa.

Benugan, hi benugon [*Plat.* vernögen: *Dut.* genoegen: *Ger.* vergnügen] *To enjoy;* oblectare:—Gif hi þæs wuda benugon *if they enjoy* [*have enjoyment of*] *the woods, Bt.* 25. Be nuge, *Hickes's Epist. Diss.* vol. ii. p. 55, 32.

Benum, benumen *deprived, benumbed*, v. benæman.

Benyman *to deprive*, v. benæman.

d Benyðan; *adv.* [be, nyðan *neath*] Beneath, *below, under;* infra:—Ne nan wuht benyðan *nor any thing beneath, Bt.* 36, 5, v. niðer.

Beo, beaw; *plu.* beon; *f.* [*Dut.* bye, bie *f*: *Ger.* biene *f*: *Al.* bie, bien: *Not.* bine: *Dan. Icel.* bie: *Swed.* bi] A bee; apis:—Swa swa seo beo sceal losian *as the bee shall perish, Bt.* 31, 2: *Ps.* 117, 12.

Beo *I am* or *shall be;* sum, ero; *be thou;* sis, v. beon. ¶ Beo hit swa *be it so* or *so be it.*

Beo-bread, beon-bread *bee-bread, a honey-comb.*

Beoce *a beech*, v. boc.

Beo-ceorl, beo-cere *a* bee-ceorl, *a bee-farmer* or *keeper.*

Beod *a table, Ps.* 22, 6, v. bord.

Beodan; *p.* he bead, bude, bád, hi budon; *pp.* boden; *v. a.* [*Plat.* beden: *Dut.* bieden: *Ger.* biethen: *Moes.* buidan: bod *a command*] *To command,* bid, *will, offer, enjoy;* jubere:—Þæs þing ic eow beode, *Jn.* 15, 17. He bead Iosepe þat he bude, *Gen.* 45, 17: 5, 2. His boda beodan, *Cd.* 27, v. bebeodan, biddan, bodian.

Beodas; *plu. The scales of a balance;* lances, *Som.*

e Beod-bolla *A table-bowl, a cup, bowl;* cupa, *Som.*

Beod-claþ [*Plat. Dut.* beddeleed] 1. A bed-cloth, *coverlet, blanket, bed-clothes;* lodix. 2. *A table-cloth, carpet, hanging;* gausape, *Som.*

Beodende *commanding*, v. beodan.

Beodendlic gemet *the imperative mood*, v. bebeodendlic.
Beodern *a chamber*, v. beddern.
Beod-fers [beod *a table*, fers *a verse*] *A song or hymn sung during meal-time;* ad mensam carmen, hymnus:—*Dial.* 1, 19, *Mann.*—Beod-gereordu [beod *a table*, gereord *a feast*] *A table meal, a feast;* convivium:—*Cd.* 74.—Beod-hrægel, beod-reaf [beod *a table*, hrægel *or* reaf *clothing*] *a table-cloth*, v. bedreaf.
Beod-sceat, beod-scyte *A table-cloth, table-napkin, hand-towel;* mantile:—*Cot.* 136, *Som.*
Beod-wist [beod, wist *food*] *Food placed on a table, board, a table;* mensa:—*Lps.* 22, 6, *Mann.*
BEOFER, beber [*Plat. Dut.* bever: *Ger.* biber: *Dan.* bæver: *Swed.* bafwer] A BEAVER; castor:—*Elf. gr.* 8.
Beofian *to tremble*, v. bifian.
Beofton *lamented*, v. beaftan.
Beofung, e; *f. A trembling, a quaking;* tremor:—¶ Eorð-beofung *an earthquake*, v. eorð-beofung, bifung.
Beogang *A swarm of bees;* examen, *Som.*
Beogol, beogul; *adj. Agreeing, consenting, bending wholly to;* consentiens, *Som.*
Beohata, behata [behat *a vow*, a v. 1f] *One who promises or vows, an undertaker, surety;* sponsor:—Bald beohata. Moses is so called because he *encouraged* the desponding Israelites, *Cd.* 156, *Mann.*
Beolone *henbane*, v. belene.
Beom *a beam*, v. beam.
Beo-moder *a bee-mother, queen-bee.*
BEO'N, to beónne; *part.* beónde, ic beó, þu bist, byst, he byð, bið, we ge hi beóð, beó; *sub. indef.* ic þu he heo hit beó, we beón; *imp.* beó þu, beóð, beó we; *v. n.* [*Plat. Fries.* ik bin: *Dut.* ik ben: *Ger.* ich bin: *Franc.* ich bim: *Moes.* ik im: by, bye *an habitation, a place to be or exist in*] *To* BE, *exist, become;* esse, fieri:—Se beam bið on þinum agenum eagan, *Mt.* 7, 4. Gyf þar mare byð, þat bið of yfele, *Mt.* 5, 37. Buton God beo mid hym, *Jn.* 3, 2. Nyllege beon swa swa hors *be unwilling to become as a horse, Ps.* 31, 11, v. eom of which beo is often the future tense.
Beon-bread *bee-bread*, v. beo-bread.
Beon-broð, perhaps *mead, a drink of water and honey mingled and boiled together;* melicratum:—*L. M.* 2, 24.
Beonde *being*, v. beon.

Beongewyrhtum *freely, undeservedly;* sponte, *Som.*
BEOR, bear [*Plat.* beer: *Frs. v.* biar: *Dut. Ger. Al.* bier: *Icel.* bioor: *Norse*, bior: *from* bere *barley, quod.* v.] 1. BEER, *nourishing or strong drink;* cerevisia. 2. *Metheglin, drink made with honey and water*, as if derived from beo *a* BEE; hydromelum:—1. He ne drincð win ne beor, *Lk.* 1, 15. 2. *Cot.* 117, *Som.*
Beora *a grove*, v. bearw.
Beoran *to bear*, v. beran.
Beorcan; *part.* beorcende, he byrcð; *pp.* byrce; *v. n.* [*Icel.* barki *the throat*] *To* BARK; latrare:—Hund byrcð *a dog barketh, Elf. gr. Som.* p. 24, 8.
Beorce *a birch tree*, v. birce.
Beorcen *birchen*, v. bircen.
Beordan, -ige [æge *an island*, beordana *of birds*] BARDNEY in Lincolnshire, *Som.*
Beorende *brought forth*, v. beran.
Beorg *a refuge*, v. beorh.
Beorgan, he byrgð: *p.* bearh, we burgon; *imp.* beorh þu; *pp.* borgen; *v. a.* [*Plat.* bargen: *Dut. Ger.* bergen: *Dan.* bjerge: beorg *a refuge*] 1. *To protect, shelter, defend, fortify, keep, preserve, save;* munire. 2. When wið follows *to fortify, guard or provide against, to avoid;* præcavere, vitare:—1. Beorgan his sawle *to save his soul, L. Cnut.* 7. Beorh þinum feore, *Gen.* 19, 17. 2. Þat preostas beorgan wið ofer druncon *that priests avoid* [*keep from over-drinking*] *drunkenness, L. Edg.* 57, *Wilk.* p. 87, 28.
Beorgford, Beorhford [beorh *a hill*, ford *a ford;* collis ad vadum] BURFORD in Oxfordshire, *Lye.*
BEORH, gebeorh, beorg; *gen.* beorges; *dat.* beorge; *plu. nom. acc.* beorgas; *gen.* beorga; *dat.* beorgum; *m.* [*Plat.* barg *m*: *Dut. Frs. Ger. Swed.* berg *m*: *Al. Franc.* berg, perg: *Moes.* bairg: *Dan.* bjerg *n*: *Icel. Norse*, biarg *n.*] 1. *A hill, mountain;* collis. 2. *A rampart, citadel, fortification, defence, refuge;* munimentum. 3. *A heap,* BURROW *or barrow, a heap of stones, a place of burial;* tumulus, v. bearw. 1. Ælc munt and beorh byð genyðerud, *Lk.* 3, 5. Æt þæm beorge þe man Athlans nemneð, *Ors.* 1, 1, *Bar.* p. 14, 30. Se beorh endað *the mountain endeth, Bar.* p. 15, 15. 2. To gebeorge *for the defence, Chr.* 189, *Ing.* p. 9, 13. Þu eart beorg min, *Ps.* 58, 19. 3. Worhton mid

stanum anne steapne beorh him ofer, *Jos.* 7, 26.
Beorh-hleoð, -hlið [beorh *a mountain*, hleoð *a top*] *A mountain's top, the summit of a mountain;* montis jugum:—Under beorh-hleoðum *under the mountain's top, Cd.* 98. Beorh-hliðu, *Cd.* 166.
BEORHT, birhtu, birihto [*Al. Franc.* breht: *Moes.* bairht: *Norse*, biart] *Brightness, a glistening, light, sight;* lux, v. beorhtnes. Onfeng þam beorhte hire eagena *received the sight* [*full sight, sparkling*] *of her eyes, Bd.* 4, 10, *Sm.* p. 578, 2. ¶ An eagan beorht *in the glance of an eye, Bd.* 2, 14, *Sm.* p. 516: note 20, v. bearhtm.
Beorht, bryht; *adv.* BRIGHT, *light, clear, lucid, splendid, excellent;* lucidus:—Eall þin lichama bið beorht, *Mt.* 6, 22.
Beorhte, beorhtlice; *adv. Distinctly, clearly, lucidly;* clare:—He beorhtlice eall geseah, *Mk.* 8, 25. Þonne seo sunne beorhtost scineð *when the sun shines brightest, Bt.* 9, *Card.* p. 40, 2.
Beorhtnhwile *in a glance*, v. bearhtm-hwile.
Beorhtian *To shine, glitter;* clarere:—*Bd.* 3, 19, *Lye.*
Beorhtnes, byrhtnes, se; *f.* [beorht *bright*] BRIGHTNESS, *clearness, splendour;* splendor:—Godes beorhtnes hym ymbescean, *Lk.* 2, 9: *Ps.* 89, 18, v. beorht.
BEORMA, an; *m.* [*Plat. Dut.* barm *m*: *Ger.* barme *f*: *Dan. Swed.* baerma] BARM, *leaven, yeast, froth;* fermentum:—Hit is gelic þam beorman, *Lk.* 13, 21, v. andbita.
Beormas; *plu. The Beormas*, a people dwelling east of the white sea, and of the river Dwina. The northern writers call them Byarmians; the Normans and Swicons had intercourse with them through the Newa, and the lake Ladoga; *Forster.* Þa Finnas him þute, and þa Beormas spræcon neah an geþeode *he thought* [illi videbatur] *the Finns and the Beormas spoke nearly the same (one) language, Ors.* 1, 1: *Bar.* p. 22, 29.
BEORN, es; *m.* [*Norse*, bearn, beorn, biarn, biorn from *Norse* beorn *a bear*, the most ferocious beast in the north, as the lion is in the south: hence princes and heroes had their names composed with beorn, or with the names of other fierce animals as ulfur *or* wulfur *a wolf*]

ϕ1

X Beód-geneat, es. m. table or domestic servant. Bosk 683

ϕ2 [40a]

ϕ2 [39a]

X Beorh-ham-stede; es; m Berk hampstead, Herts Chr. 1066 Ing. p. 264.

◯ 4 [42a]

2 Beorhnys, se f A rampart, citadel munimentum Som

Bin, Lye, bright

2a Beorht, adj

3 Beorc, e; f a birch tree

3

rhtian make a noise; strepere Bos. K. 2315

cohaka-Grim II 496, 39

◯ 7 [40b]

5

3 Beorhtlice Brightly clearly; clare, lucide Som

◯ 4 Beorme, an; f [42b] barm Th. Anl.

4

4 Beorh save, imp of beorgan

◯ 5 [41a]

Beorh l 5 Frs * birgh m.

l 6 Moes * bairgs m

◯ 1 bairgs m

◯ 6 [42c]

Lorming it is m as in mgl Dict

5 7 Beorn, es; m

[* Dan Swed. Icl. biörn m a bear

but Plat Dut Ger Dan Swed Sp baron n a nobleman, one free born Old baro, bar superior, dou v 236 other more

Φ 1

Beorn-cyning, es; m king of men Beo K 4291

Φ 2

Φ 3 Beoten for beoton beaten, p. pl. of beátan Th. An

Beotian To promise vow, threaten Ps. Th.

Φ 5 Beotlic threatening Th. An

Beotnes dl.

Beót-word a threatening word - threat minæ Beo K 5016 187 Grim II 535, 4

Beran-byrig dl

Bd 2.2 menace; intentare minari Som. Lye

Beran-beorh, g. burge; d byrig; f. Banbury

At Beranbyrig at Beranburg Chr. 556 Ing 24, 13

O 3 [45a]

Φ 8 Bepæcestre an; f

Bereafigend, es; m robber, spoiler Th. Apol [part of bereafian]

Φ 9

Beor-sele, es; m a beer hall, Cd 170 Th. p 214, 2

Beor-scealc, es, m a beer servant; Qui cervisiam ministrat Beo K 2481

Beor-þegu, e; f a beer service; cerevisiae ministratio Beo K 1228

Φ 2 Beordre-cwelmas nativitate mortui Manns.

O 6 [44] [44b]

O 1 Gyldan berenne kyrtel

Beót, es; n threat, promise, - to make On beot with threatening. Th. An Beo K 159

1. *A prince, nobleman, chief, general;* princeps. 2. *A man;* vir: (This word is chiefly used by poets):—1. Se beorn *the king, Cd.* 97: 176. Beorna beah gyfa *bracelet giver of Barons* or *a rewarder of heroes, Chr.* 938, *Ing.* p. 141, 10. 2. Beornes blode *with man's blood, Bt. Rawl.* p. 158: 182: 190. Beornas geonge *young men, Cd.* 184. Beorna selost *best of men,* 162. Observe the distinction between bearn *a child,* beorn *a man,* and burne *a brook,* used as a termination in the names of places.

eorna *a coat of mail,* v. byrn.

eorneð *burns,* beorndon *burnt,* v. byrnan, bærnan.

ornica rice, *or* mægð *the kingdom* or *province* BERNICIA, or *of the Bernicians.* BERNICIA, that part of Northumbria which lies between he river Tee and the Scottish ea or frith:—Oswio þone ðerne dæl Norðan-hymbra ces hæfde, þat is Beornicia *swi possessed the other part 'the Northumbrian kingdom, at is Bernicia, Bd.* 3, 14, *.* p. 539, 34.

nicas; *plu. The Bernicians;* rnicii:—*Chr.* 678.

n-wiga *A man;* homo:—*nol.* 430, *Mann.*

ys, se; *f. A defence;* munentum, *Lye,* v. beorh.

cipe *a feast,* v. gebeorscipe.

el, es [beor *beer, strong k,* or beor, gebeor *a guest, a seat*] *A hall of beer, a for feasting, a house, hall, sion, palace;* convivii aula: ttað on beorsele *they sit he feasting hall, Hicks's* vol. i. p. 135, 28.

inig *a publican,* v. bærsu-

A BIRTH; nativitas:— beorðre, *Cot.* 87.

e-þynenu [beorð *a birth, a maid*] *A midwife;* tatis ministra, *Som.*

to shine, v. beorhtian.

a hall, v. bere-tun.

[wic *a village* or *resi-* Beornica *of the Berni-* Berniciorum vicus] CK *on Tweed, Som.*

nde *deceiving,* v. bysm- bysmerian.

byst, bysting [*Plat. Frs.* byist: *Dut.* biest: stmilch] BIESTINGS, *milk of a cow after* colostrum:—Byst, þicce meolc *biest, thick milk, R.* 38, *Lye.*

t *A threatening, peril, torment;* commina-

tio:—Þen in þam beote wæron, *Cd.* 187, *Mann.*

Beot *beat;* verberavit, v. beatan.

~~Beot given, delatum:—Lye says pp. of beodan, Cd. 132.~~

Beoð, beoðan *are;* sunt, v. beon.

Beo-þeof *a thief* or *stealer of bees.*

Beotende, beotiende, beotigende *beating, threatening,* v. beatan.

Beotlice; *adv. In a beating,* or *threatening manner, threateningly;* minaciter:—*Jos.* 8, 10.

~~Beotne invited; pp. of beodan or biddan.~~

Beotung, gebeotung, e; *f.* A BEATING, *thumping, vapouring, threatening, raging;* verberatio:—Beotunge dædum gefyldon [*they*] *followed the threatening with deeds, Bd.* 1, 15, *Sm.* p. 483, 39.

Beo-wyrt [beo *a bee,* wyrt *a plant*] BEE-WORT, *balm-mint;* apiastrum:—*Cot.* 12.

Bepæcan; *part.* bepæcende; *p.* bepæhte; *pp.* bepæht; *v. a.* [be *by,* pæcan *to deceive*] *To deceive, entice, seduce, draw away;* decipere:—Seo Nædre bepæhte me, *Gen.* 3, 13: *Mt.* 2, 16.

Bepæcestre; *f. She who deceives, flatters* or *entices, a harlot;* pellex:—*Elf. gr.* 28.

Bepæcung, e; *f. Lewd practice;* lenocinium, *Som.*

Bepæht *deceived,* v. bepæcan.

Beprenan, beprewan *To wink;* nictare:—*Bt.* 18, 3, *Card.* p. 100, 21.

BERA [*Plat.* baar: *Dut.* beer: *Ger.* bär: *Al.* bero: *Norse,* biura: *Heb.* בעיר boir *a brute animal,* from בער bor *to devour*] A BEAR; ursus:—*Elf. gl.* 13.

Berædan; *p.* bæredde [be *by,* hreddan *to rid*] *To rid from, to deliver;* liberare:—*Bt. Tit.* 1. *Card.* p. iv. 2, v. ahræddan.

Ber-ærn *a barn floor,* v. ber-ern.

Beræsan [be, hreosan *to rush*] *To rush upon, to overthrow;* irruere:—*Gen.* 14, 15.

BERAN, beoran, aberan, geberan, he byrð; *p.* bær, bear; *pp.* boren, geboren; *v. a.* [*Plat.* bören: *Dan.* bære: *Franc.* bar *fruit*] 1. *To* BEAR, *produce, bring forth;* fructum edere. 2. *To carry, bear, offer, support, suffer, endure;* portare. 3. *To excel, surpass;* præcellere:—1. Ælc god tryw byrð gode wæstmas, *Mt.* 7, 17. Mæg beoran wæstmas, *Mt.* 7, 18. Hio bereð sunu, *R. Mt.* 1, 21. Rachel gebær Beniamin, *Gen.* 35, 19. 2. On handum hi berað þe, *Ps.* 90, 12. Man aberan ne mæg, *Mt.* 23, 4. Hi ne magon nan earfoða aberan *they cannot bear any troubles, Bt.* 39, 10, *Card.* p. 348, 16. 3. *Cd.* 178, v. geberan. ¶ Beran forð *Ex.* 22, 13: beran ut; *Colloq. Monast. to carry out,* v. ætberan.

Beran-byrig [*Hunt.* Beranbyri, Banbyry] BANBURY, *Oxfordshire, Chr.* 556.

Berbena, berbine [*Lat.* verbena or herbenæ, herba *an herb*] *Vervain;* verbena, peristereon:—*Herb.* 67, *Som.*

Berbyz *wether sheep;* verveces, *Lye.*

Berc *a birch tree,* v. birce.

Berd *a beard,* v. beard.

Bere *a bear,* v. bera.

Bere *a bed,* v. bær.

BERE, es; *m.* [Old *English,* beere, bere, and bere-corne בר br *corn,* or ברה br∉ *to feed,* v. beor] *Barley;* hordeum:—Þa het he him bere sæd bringan *then told he them to bring barley seed, Bd.* 4, 28, *Sm.* p. 605, 36.

Bereafian, bereafigean, ic bereafige; *p.* bereofode; *pp.* bereafod, berofen; *v. a. To* BEREAVE, *seize, spoil, take away;* eripere:—Heo hit ne mæg bereafian *she cannot bereave it, Bt.* 5, 3, *Card.* p. 18, 19. Hu mæg man hys fata hyne bereafigean, *Mt.* 12, 29: *Mk.* 3, 27.

Berecan *to cover,* v. recan.

Bereccan *to defend, justify, answer,* v. recan.

Bere-corn [bere *barley,* corn *a grain*] A GRAIN OF BARLEY; hordei granum:—*L. Athel. W.* p. 63, 33.

Berecræs, beregræs [bere *barley,* cerse *cress* or græs *grass*] *Barley grass, a farrago;* hordei gramen, farrago:—*Elf. gl. Som.* p. 67, 58.

Bered *vexed,* v. gebered.

Beredian *To promise;* spondere: *Elf. gr. Som.* p. 29, 10.

Bereflór, berenflór A FLOOR FOR BARLEY, *a barn floor;* hordei area:—*Lk.* 3, 17.

Bere-gafol *barley-rent, a tribute of barley.*

Bere-hlaf *barley-loaf.*

Beren; *adj. Barley, made of barley;* hordeaceus:—*Jn.* 6, 9, 13, v. berern.

Beren; *adj.* [bera *a bear*] *Belonging to a bear, ursine;* ursinus:—An beran fel *one bearskin, Ors.* 1, 1, *Bar.* p. 23, 26.

Berende; *part. Fruitful, bearing;* ferax:—*Ps.* 127, 3, v. beran.

Berenedon *they lighted up;* accenderunt, v. bærnan.

Bereowsian *to repent*, v. behreowsian.

Bereowsung *penitence*, v. behreowsung.

Berern, beren, bern, es; *plu.* bernas *or* bernu [bere *barley, corn*, ern *a place*, contracted into bern *a barn*, *Mt.* 3, 12.] A BARN; horreum:–He feormað hys berenes flore, *Lk.* 3, 17: 12, 18, 24. On his bern, *Mt.* 3, 12: 13, 30.

v **Bere-sæd** *barley-seed, barley*, v. bere.

Bere-tun, beor-tun, berewic [beor *beer* or bere *barley, corn*, tun *an enclosure, a place shut in*, or wic *a village*] *A court-yard, a corn farm, a grange, a corn village*, BARTON; villa frumentaria:—*C. Mt.* 3, 12, *Som.*

Berewe A BARROW, *wheelbarrow*; vectula, *Som.*

Berewic *a corn village*, v. beretun, beorwic.

Berga *a pig*, v. bearg.

BERGA, beria, an; *plu.* bergen, berien, berigen [*Plat.* bere: *Dut.* bere, berrie, beyre: *Ger.* beere: *Dan.* bær: *Icel.* ber: *Franc.* bar *fruit*: *Heb.* בָּר br *fruit*] *A grape*, BERRY, *blackberry, a stone of a grape* or *berry*; uva:—Et þæra bergena, *Deut.* 23, 24.

w **Berg-ælfen** *mountain-elves*; oreades, v. ælf.

Bergan *to taste, avoid, take care*, v. onbirian.

Bergen, berien *berries*, v. berga.

Berghamstyde, *perhaps* BERHAM, *near Canterbury, L. With. pref.*

Bergyl *a sepulchre*, v. byrgel.

Berh *for* bearh *shunned*; vitavit.

Berht-hwile *a moment*, v. bearhtmhwile.

Berhtm-hwat *a quick glance*, Berhtm hwate ligetu, *Cd.* 192, *Lye*, v. bearhtm.

Berhtnad *brightened*, *Som.*

Berhtr *brighter*, v. beorht.

Beria *a grape*, v. berga.

x **Beridan**, he berit; *p.* berad; *pp.* beriden; *v.a.* [*Dut.* beryden: be, ridan *to ride*] 1. *To ride round, to surround, besiege*; perequitare. 2. *To ride after, to pursue*; persequi:—1. Þat he his gefan beride *that he besiege his enemy*, *L. Alf.* 38, *W.* p. 43, 36. 2. Þa berad mon þat wif *then they pursued the wife*, *Chr.* 901, *Ing.* p. 125, 14.

Berig *a city*, v. burg.

Berig-drenc [berga *a berry*, drenc *drink*] *Drink made of mulberries*; diamoron:—*R.* 12, *Lye.*

Berigea *a surety*, *L. Hloth.* 6, *W.* p. 8, 25, v. byriga.

Beri-geblæ *hooks*, *Cot.* 93.

Berigen *berries*, v. berga.

Berindan; *p.* de [be *off*, rind *the bark*] *To bark, peel* or *strip off the bark*; decorticare:—*Cot.* 62.

Beriowsian *to repent*, v. behreowsian.

y **Bern** *a barn*, v. berern.

Berne *burn*, v. byrnan.

Bernes, bernet, berning *a burning*, v. bærnes.

Berofen *bereaved*, v. bereafian.

Berowan *To row*; remigare, *Chr.* 897, v. rowan.

Berowsian *to repent*, v. behreowsian.

Berst *loss*, v. byrst.

BERSTAN, he byrst; *part.* berstende; *p.* he bærst, hi burston; *pp.* borsten [*Plat.* barsten: *Dut. Ger.* bersten: *Al.* burstan: *Dan.* briste] *To* BURST, *break, fail, fall*; frangere, decidere:—Gif him að burste, *L. Edw.* 3. Wægas burston, *Cd.* 167. Þa burston þa weallas, *Jos.* 6, 5: *Ors.* 1, 7.

Bersting, e; *f.* A BURSTING, *a rent*; ruptura:—*R.* 12.

z **Berþen** *a burthen*, v. byrþen.

Berð-ling *a child*, v. hyse-berðling.

Berthwile *a moment*, v. bearhtmhwile.

Berumad *bedaubed*, v. behrumad.

Berwe *a grove*, v. bearw.

Berypan; *p.* berypede, hi berypton; *pp.* beryped, berypt. *To spoil*; spoliare:—*Bt. Rawl.* p. 152, 27, v. rypan.

Berywan *to repent*, v. hreowan.

Besacen *questioned*, v. sacan.

Besæh *beheld*, v. beseon.

Besænct *sunk*, mersus.

Besæncan *to sink*, v. sencan.

Besæt, besæton *besieged*, v. besittan.

Besæwð *sows*, v. sawan.

Besanc *sank*, v. sincan.

a **Besargian** *to lament*, v. sargian.

Besargung *a sorrowing*, v. sargung.

Besarigende *condoling*; besarigod *grieved*, v. besargian, sargian.

Besawe *looked*; besawen *seen*, v. beseon.

Besceadenne *clothed*, v. sceadan.

Bescearon *cut*, v. besceran.

Besceat *shot*, v. besceotan, sceotan.

Besceawian. 1. *To consider*; considerare, v. sceawian *to shew*. 2. *To look round*; circumspicere:—1. *Mt.* 6, 28. 2. *Mk.* 3, 5.

Besceawigere, besceawere *A beholder*; spectator, *Som.*

Besceawod *seen*; *pp. of* besceawian, v. sceawian.

Besceawodnes, se; *f. A seeing, vision, sight*; visio:—*Ps.* 9, 11.

b **Besceoren** *shorn*, v. besceran.

Besceotan *to shoot*, v. sceotan.

Besceran, besciran, ic bescere, he bescyrð; *p.* bescear, scær, he bescyrede, hi bescearon; *pp.* bescoren, bescered, bescyred. *To shear off, to shave, to take away, to deprive, remove, deceive*; attondere:—Hy eall heora heafod bescearon *they all shave their heads*, *Ors.* 4, 11. Bescoren preost *attonsus clericus*, *Bd.* 5. 13. Man ne mot hine besciran, *Judg.* 13, 5. Ic bescired beo fram tun-scire, *Lk.* 16, 4, v. sceran.

Bescirugga *degradings*, v. bescyrung.

Besciten *bedaubed*, v. behrumod.

Bescofen *thrust off*, v. bescufan.

Bescoren *shorn*, v. besceran.

Bescreadan *to cut off*, v. screadan *to shred*.

c **Bescrepen** *shaved*; *pp. of* bescreopan *from* be, screopan *to scrape*.

Bescrifen; *part. Confessed, that hath undergone confession*; confessus, *Som.*

Bescufan, he bescyfð; *p.* besceaf, hi bescufon; *pp.* bescofen; *v.a. To thrust, cast, hurl* or *throw off, to precipitate*; detrudere:—*Ors.* 1, 12: *Mk.* 5, 13.

Bescutun *sent*; *pp. of* besceotan, v. sceotan.

Bescyldigan *to accuse*, v. gescyldgian.

Bescylian, þu bescylst *To look upon, to regard*; intueri:—*Bt.* 38, 5.

Bescyre *should shave*, v. besceran.

Bescyred *deprived*, v. besceran.

d **Bescyrednes**, se; *f. An abdication, a casting off, depriving*; abdicatio:—*Cot.* 14, *Som.*

Bescyrð *deprives*, v. besceran.

Bescyrung, bescyrug, e; *f.* [be *from*, scerung *from* sceran *to tonsure* or *consecrate*] *A deposing, degrading, putting from holy orders*; exauctoratio, *Som.*

Bescyt *injects*, v. sceotan.

Beseald *furnished*, v. syllan.

Besecgan [be, secgan *to answer*] *To defend*; defendere:—*Bd.* 5, 19, v. bereccan.

Be self-wille BY SELF-WILL, *willingly*, *Som.*

Besem *a besom*, v. besm.

Besencan *to sink*, besencte *sunk*, v. sencan.

Besengan; *p.* hi besengdan; *pp.* besenced *To singe, burn*; ustulare:—*C. Mt.* 13, 6: *Ors.* 2, 7.

e **Beseon**, hi beseoð; *imp.* beseoh, besæh; *p.* he besawe, beseah, hi besawon [be *by, near, about*, seon *to see*] *To look about*; circumspicere:—*Mk.* 9, 8. Also *to see, behold*; videre: as seon,

Berþ-estre, an; f

O 7 v. ebl. ~~berie~~

O 1 he besayh. p. pu besciet; we bescuton

O 1 [45 b]

What is produced a child

Bearn

b

~~Beorpling~~, cd; m

Ic berne I burn; ardeo

pu byrnst, he burneþ

Beo K 5134

ardet v. byrnan

Elfgr. 33 Som. 38, 5

Beorh

Bearn; m. a swine, hog, barrow hog; porcus Som. R 16. Mk 5, 11 Lye

2 Berstan to evade, escape from, as aet berstan Th. An

O [46 c]

O [46 a]

Berg a hill; mons Som. v. beorg ~~[illegible]~~

beorh

Berian to bare, make naked; nudare Beo K 2478

Berie, berge, an; f ~~[illegible]~~ v. win berie

O Q. Berige, berge

~~[illegible]~~ -dl

O Bescawian, ede

Heed to consider; contemplar

Mone B. 36 v.

~~[illegible]~~ bescea wian

Berende bearing

breeding; foetuosus

Ben Lel v. beran

~~Byrgel~~ -dl *

Byrgels, es; m. A sepulchre Th. An

byrgels

3 Besargian * to condole with, to compassinate Th. An

O 2 Bescyrian to ~~spoil~~, deprive, spoil; privare:

bescyrigan ne

4 Besceah looked about, viewed p. of beseon

4 privare Som

v. besceran

– Q 3 4 above.

6 Besceadd sprinkled shewered, shed; Som. spersus Som.

O 5 ~~Besencean~~ v. a ~~to sink~~

~~Th An~~

* Besceaden clothed

abscondere; privare Beo K 5844 v saegdan

Besorgian to sorrow for pode pphad the appal v sorgian

bestymed reeked circumfusus Beo K 967 v bestemed Beo yk in be-styman

()1 x

2 x Beswaelan to burn, consume, ppd ed Beo 6047 v swelan

3 x

1 x Beslagen cut off Cd Th p121,15 v slean

x Besloh bereft Cd p.4,17 v beslean

O 4

() 7 Besm [46 d]

2 Bestandan to stand on, occupy Th An

x Besmired besmeared Ben v besmyred

3 Beswingan to p beswang, we beswung bt to with p Th An v. swingan

() 4 Besmitan; p he besmat, we besmiton bt to pollute defile Th. An

() 4 Besyrwian to ensnare Th. An.

x Be-smitian, p pode phad to forge Beo K 1543 v smitian

5 x Besyrian p ode phod to ensnare th Apol v besyrwan

Besnydede
Be ... pede
cut off, deprive; Beo K 5844 v snidan

geseon, *Ps.* 10, 5. (For a full explanation v. seon).

Beseten, besetten, *beset*, v. besittan.

3esettan; *p.* besette; *v. a.* [be *by*, settan *to set*] *To set near, to place, own, possess;* collocare;—*Ps.* 68, 42, v. settan.

ieshriuen *confessed*, v. bescrifen.

esidian *by the side, well*, v. sid, sidelice.

esilfred, be-sylfren *without silver* or *money*, *Ben.*

esincan *to sink*, v. sincan.

esingan *To utter enchantments, to enchant, charm;* excantare incantationibus:—*Herb.* 93, 2.

sining *A bending;* sinuatio:—*R.* 100.

sio *regard*, v. beseon, seon.

sið *A scandal, an offence;* candalum, *Som.*

sittan; *p.* besæt, hi besetton; . *a.* [be *by, near*, sittan *to sit*] . *To sit round, surround,* ESET, *besiege;* circumdare. . *To possess;* possidere:—1. at he hine inne besitte *that enclose him within, L. Alf.* 3, *W.* p. 43, 46. 2. *Bd.* 2, 1, besettan.

wian; *p.* ede; *pp.* ed. *To w together, to join;* jungere: Besiwed feþergeweorc, *Cot.* 5.

agen, beslegen *cut off*, v. an.

ean *to beat*, v. slean.

gen *slain*, v. beslagen.

p; *adj. Sleepy, drowsy;* nnolentus, *Som.*

pan *to be sleepy*, v. slepan.

pan; *p.* he beslepte. *To* , and with the preposition *on, upon, to slip* or *put on, impose;* imponere:—Hu g geoc he beslepte on ealle *heavy a yoke he imposed on Bt.* 16, 4, *Card.* p. 88, 23.

besma, besem [*Plat.* bes- *Ger.* besen: *Frs. v.* byiz-] A BESOM, *a broom, rods,* ; scopæ.—Mid besmum mod, *Lk.* 11, 25: *Mt.* 12, Besman *with rods, Ors.* 2, 3.

an, he besmitað; *pp.* bes- [be, smitta *smut*] *To* UT, *defile, dirty, pollute, minate;* inquinare:—Þæt besmitan mæge, *Mk.* 7, *Jn.* 18, 28.

nys, se; *f. Dirtiness,* TINESS, *filthiness, pollu- nfection;* sordes:—*Bd.*

d *besmeared;* interli- —*Cot.* 108.

n *to cut off*, v. snidan.

d *snowed*, v. sniwan *to*

slow, v. solcen.

Besone *soon*, v. sona.

Besorg, besorh; *adj.* [*Frs.* besorge: *Dut. in Kilian* besorghsaem: be *by, near;* sorh, sorg *care*] *Anxious, careful, dear, beloved;* solicitus:—*R. Ben.* 72. Besorgost *most beloved, Bt.* 29, 2.

Besorgod *anxious*, v. sorgian.

Besorh *anxious*, v. besorg.

Bespanan; *p.* bespón, bespeón; *pp.* bespanen. *To entice;* persuadere:—*Ors.* 1, 2, v. spanan.

Besparrad *shut*, v. sparran.

Bespeon, bespon *induced; p. of* bespanan, v. spanan.

Besprecan, we besprecað, besprycð; *p.* bespræc; *pp.* besprecen, bespræcen [be *by*, sprecan *to speak*] *To speak to, to tell, pretend, plead, speak against, to complain, charge, accuse, impeach;* obloqui:—Cristene Romana bespryćð *Christians tell Romans, Ors.* 2, 4. Hu ge besprecað *why complain you, Ors.* 1, 10. Hit bespræcen bið, *L. Ethel.* 9: *Ors.* 1, 12.

Besprengan *to besprinkle*, v. sprengan.

Bespryćð *tell*, v. besprecan.

Bespyrige, bespirige *enquires, from* bespirian, v. spirian.

Best; *adv. sup.* [*Plat. Dut. Ger.* best, beste: *Frs. v.* beast: *the Ger. adj.* bass *good*, has the *comp.* besser *better*, and *sup.* beste *best*] BEST, *most;* optime:—Þe helpes best behofað *who most wants help, L. Cnut.* 66, *W.* p. 143, 31.

Besta; seo, þæt beste *the* BEST, v. betst.

Bestæl *stole*, obrepsit; *p. of* bestelan, v. stelan.

Bestæpan *to step*, v. steppan.

Bestandan *to stand by; pp.* bestanden *stood by*, v. standan.

Bestefnde *called*, v. stefnian.

Bestelan *to steal away*, v. stelan.

Bestemed, bistemed *steamed, smeared:*—Rod blode bistemed *the cross smeared with blood, Cod. Ex.* 23, *b.* 21: *Cd.* 166, *Mann.*, v. steman.

Bestingan *to inject*, v. stingan.

Bestiran, hi bestyredon [be *by*, stiran *to stir*] *To heap up;* aggerare:—*Bd.* 3, 2, v. stiran.

Bestred *strowed*, v. stredan.

Bestreddon *heaped up;* aggeraverunt, v. bestiran.

Bestreowian *to bestrew*, v. streowian *to strew.*

Bestridan, gestridan [be *by*, stræd *a stride*] *To* BESTRIDE; conscendere:—Bestridan hors *to bestride a horse, Lye.*

Bestroden; *part. Brought into the treasury;* infiscatus:—*Cot.* 108, v. strynan.

Bestrudon *spoiled*, v. strudan.

Bestrypan *To strip, rob, spoil;* spoliare:—Bestrypan widuwan, *Off. Episc.* 8.

Bestryþedon *heaped up*, v. bestiran.

Bestrywed *bestrewed*, v. stredan.

Bestungen *injected*, v. stingan.

Bestyredon *heaped up*, v. bestiran.

Bestyrmian *To* BESTORM, *to storm;* agitare:—*Bt.* 3, 2, v. styrmian.

Besueþian, bisueþan, besweþan [be, sueþe *a swathe* or *band*] *To* SWATHE, *to bind;* ligare:—*C. Jn.* 19, 40.

Besuncen *sunk, pp. of* besincan, v. sincan.

Beswac *deceived*, v. beswican.

Beswæled SWEALED, *consumed.*

Beswapan; *p.* -sweop; *pp.* -swapen, -swapyn [be, swapan *to sweep*] *To clear up, to persuade, to make clean, to clothe;* suadere:—*Bd.* 2, 12: *Ps.* 103, 2.

Beswemde *beswum; p. of* beswimman.

Besweop *clothed; p. of* beswapan.

Besweþan *to swathe*, v. besueþian.

Beswic, biswic, bigswic *Deceit, a deceiving, an offence, a scandal;* fraus:—*L. Edw.* 1, v. geswic, *Som.*

Beswican, -cian, ic beswice, he beswicð; *p.* beswác, beswicede, -ode, -ade, hi beswicon; *pp.* beswicen; *v. a.* [be *by*, swican *to deceive*] *To deceive, weaken, escape, offend;* decipere:—*Ors.* 1, 12: *Deut.* 30, 17. Scandalizare, *Mt.* 18, 6: *Jn.* 6, 61.

Beswicenda *A deceiver, harlot;* pellex:—*Cot.* 170, *Lye.*

Beswimman; *p.* beswemde. *To swim, to swim about;* natare:—*Bt.* 37, 4.

Beswincan *to labour*, v. swincan.

Beswuncon *laboured; p.* beswuncen *worn; pp. of* beswincan, v. swincan.

Beswungen *beaten*, v. swingan.

Besyled; *pp.* [be, sylian *to soil*] SOILED, *stained;* maculatus:—*Bt.* 16, 4.

Besylfrede *silvered*, BESILVERED, v. sylfrene.

Besyrod *ensnared*, v. syrwan.

Besyrpan *to take hold of, Ben.*

Besyrwan *to ensnare*, v. syrwan.

BET, bett, abet; *adv. irr. comp. of* wel [*Plat.* bet] BETTER; melius:—Þa axode he to hwylcon timan hym bet wære, *Jn.* 4, 52. Þat se hwæte mæge þy bet weaxan *that the wheat may grow the better, Bt.* 23. His horse bett wurde *his horse should be better, Bd.* 3, 9.

Bet *beats;* ferit, v. beatan.

Beta, bete [Ger. bete f.] BEET, *a herb that bears burs;* personacia:—*Cot.* 28, *Som.*

Betæcan; *p.* betæhte, hi betæhton, betahten; *pp.* betæht, betaht; *v.a.* [be *by,* tæcan *to teach, to shew*] 1. *To shew;* ostendere. 2. *To* BETAKE, *impart, deliver to, commit, put in trust;* impertire. 3. *To send, to follow, pursue;* mittere:—1. v. tæcan. He eow betæcð mycele healle, *Lk.* 22, 12. 2. He betæhte him hys æhta, *Mt.* 25, 14: *Gen.* 9, 2. 3. Betæcan cildru on scole *to send children to school, Obs. Lunæ,* 4, 10. Mid swiftum hundum ic betæce wildeor *with swift hounds I pursue wild beasts, Colloq. Monast.*

p Betæcung, e; *f. A betaking;* traditio, *Som.*

Betæht *given up; pp. of* betæcan.

Betaht *betrothed,* v. betæcan.

Betahten *committed; p. of* betæcan.

Betan, gebetan ic bete; *p.* bette; *sub.* he bette; *v.a.* [*Plat.* betern: *Dut.* beteren: *Moes.* botan: bet *better,* or bot *amends*] 1. *To make better, to improve, amend, repair, restore;* emendare. 2. Joined with fyr *to mend* or *repair a fire, to light* or *make a fire, to kindle;* focum reparare. (In this sense böten is used in low German at the present day. Böt füer *make the fire,* or böt wat in *(literally) light something in, put* or *light some fire.* So in *Frs.* fyoer boete *struere focum*). 3. *To remedy, to make amends, compensate;* compensare:—1. Þat he bette *that he should improve, Bd.* 5, 13: *Ex.* 21, 22. 2. Þa het he betan micel fyr *then ordered he a great fire to be lighted, Ors.* 6, 32, *Bar.* p. 234, 17. 3. Ic hit bete *I will remedy it, Deut.* 1, 17.

q Beteldon *deceived,* v. betilldon.

Betellan; *p.* betealde; *v. a.* [be, tellan *to tell*] *To speak about, to answer, excuse, justify, clear;* excusare:—Þat he moste hine betellan *that he might answer him, Chr.* 1051. Godwine betealde hine *Godwin cleared himself, Id.* 1052.

Beteon *to accuse, bequeath,* v. teon.

Betera, betra; *m.* betere, betre; *f. n. adj. comp. of* gód [*Plat. Dut.* beter: *Icel.* betri: *Dan.* bedre: *Ger.* besser] BETTER; melior:—Þat hy wæron beteran þegnas *that they were better thanes, Ors.* 4, 9, *Bar.* p. 161, 19. Þa betran tida *the better times, Bar.* p. 161, 13. To beteran tide *to a better time, Bd.* 3, 14: *Mt.* 12, 12: 18, 6. Hit is betre *it is a better* [*thing*], *Bt.* 38, 7: 29, 1, v. gód, bet *well.*

r Beterian *to be better,* v. betrian.

Beterung *a bettering,* v. betrung.

Betesta *best,* v. betst.

Beþæht *covered,* v. þeccan.

Beþæarfeð *is needful,* v. beþearfan, þearfan.

Beþeaht *covered,* v. þeccan.

Beþearfan *to want,* v. þearfan.

Beþeccan *to cover, cloak,* v. þeccan.

Beþencan *To consider,* BETHINK, *remember;* considerare:—*Lk.* 15, 17: *Elf. T.* p. 35, v. þencan.

Beþen [beþen *bathed*] *A fomentation, embrocation;* fomentum:—Mid beþenum *with fomentations, Bd.* 4, 32.

Beþerfað *is needful,* v. þearfan.

Beþian *to bathe,* v. baþian.

s Beþied *made prosperous; pp. of* beþian, v. baþian, *Som.*

Beþige, beþyge *cherish,* v. baþian.

Beþing, e; *f. A fomentation, an assuaging* or *nourishing medicine;* fomentum:—*Bd.* 4, 32.

Beþoht, -te, -ton *bethought,* v. þencan.

Beþorfte *need, didst need, Bt.* 33, 4, v. þearfan.

Beþridian, þrydian; *p.* ede; *pp.* ded, dad; *v. a.* [*q.* be *by,* tredan *to tread*] *To surround, beset, circumvent, force, pillage, destroy;* circumdare:—Þat hine man wolde beþridian *that they would surround him, Ors.* 6, 36: 2, 5; redigere:—On his geweald beþrydan sceolde *would force into his power, Ors.* 3, 7.

t Beþurfon *have need,* v. þearfan.

Beþwean *to wash,* v. þwean.

Beþwyr; *adj.* [be, þwir *wicked*] *Perverse, depraved;* depravatus:—*Cot.* 63.

Beþyddon *opened, spread,* v. þydan.

Betiene *shut, conclude;* betiened *shut,* v. betynan.

Betihan *to shut, blame,* v. betynan, teon, *Lye.*

Betiht *blamed,* v. teon.

Betihtlad, betyhtlad *accused.*

Betilldon, beteldon, *for* betældon *deceived,* v. tælan.

Beting *a cable,* v. bæting.

u Betl *a beetle,* v. bitel.

Betnes, se; *f.* [bet *better*] *Satisfaction, amends, recompence;* satisfactio:—*L. Can. Edg. conf.* 9.

Betoce *The herb betony;* herbæ genus ad vomicam:—*L. M.* 1, 39.

Betogen; *part.* [be, teogan *to pull, draw*] 1. *Pulled over, drawn over;* obductus. 2. *Accused, impeached;* accusatus:—1. Heora scyldas wæron betogene mid hydum *their shields were covered with hides, Ors.* 5, 7. 2. Þe oft betogen were þyfþe *who oft was accused of theft, L. In.* 37. ¶ Betogen cræt *a close carriage.*

Betogennes, se; *f. An accusation;* accusatio, *Som.*

v Betræppan [be, treppan *to trap*] *To* BETRAP, *to entrap;* circumvallare:—*Chr.* 992.

Betre *better,* v. betera.

Betredan *to tread upon,* v. tredan.

Betrian, beterian; *p.* ode; *pp.* od [*Plat. Dut.* beteren] *To be better, to excel, to make better, to grow better;* meliorare:—*Elf. gr.* 25, v. betan.

Betrung, beterung, e; *f.* [*Dut.* betering *f*: *Ger.* besserung *f.*] A BETTERING, *amending;* emendatio:—Hit wære heora betrung *it was their amendment, Bt.* 38, 7.

Betrymian; *p.* ede; *pp.* ed [be, trymian *to fortify*] *To besiege, environ;* circumdare vallo:—*Lk.* 19, 43: 21, 20.

w Betst, betest; *adj. sup. def.* se betesta, seo, þæt beteste; *pos.* gód [*Plat. Dut.* best, beste: *Ger.* beste: *Icel.* bestr] BEST, *the best, first;* optimus, primus:—Þa þing þe ge betst ongelifað *the things which ye believe are best, Bd.* 1, 25, *Sm.* p. 487, n. 12. Scipio, se besta Romana witena *Scipio, the best of the Roman senators, Ors.* 5, 4. Se beteste *the best, Cot.* 153. Moises clipode þa betst borenan, *Lev.* 9, 1: *Gen.* 50, 7: *Deut.* 5, 23. He sealde þæt betste hors *he gave the best horse, Bd.* 3, 14.

Betst; *adv. sup. of* wel BEST, *most;* optimè;—Þæt betst licað *that pleases best, Bt.* 18, 2. Ic him betst truwode *I most trusted them, Bt.* 2, *Card.* p. 6, 3. Albinus wæs betst gelæred *Albinus was most learned, Bd. pref. Sm.* p. 471, 23.

Bett *better,* v. bet.

Bette *corrected; p. of* betan.

Betugon *shut in, drew; p. of* beteogan, v. teogan.

x Betuh, betux *betwixt,* v. betwuh.

Betuxsittan [betux *between,* sittan *to sit*] *To insert, interpose, to set, put* or *bring in;* interserere, *Som.*

Betweonan *between, among,* v. betwynan.

Betweonum *between,* v. betwynan.

Betwih-ligan *to lie between, Bd.* 1, 27.

Betwion; *adj.* [be *by,* twam, twæm; *dat. of* twa *two*] *Double, twofold;* duplex:—*Ps.* 108, 28.

q bete Som, Mone.
Betz [47c]

Betæcan to assign appoint the apol

1 Bd 4, 32 Sm p 611,20 note q es in

Betan [47 d]

4 Betimbrian to build h. adeph ad
Beo Kb312 v timbrian

5 Bet. lic adj Excellent
eximius Bold was bet. lic the spouse was excellent Beo K 3846
~~Bewand turned to 10 th p 140, 34~~

1 Betweoh between th
v betwuh

2 Betweox betwixt
v betwuh

3 Betoce [47e]

6 Betwinan between
v. betwynan

4 Betwix betw
Ben v betwuh

2 Bewrîtan, to write, ... Ben.

( ) bewyndan ... [illegible] (to wind) Cd 205, Th p 253, 26.

3 Bewitan, to watch

... he bewiste

* to instruct, to act as a tutor to Th. an

3 Bewitian, bewiste to provide Bes K ... 3590

( ) 1

7 Bewendan to turn Th. ... Beworht

v bewendan

7 Beworht worked round, surrounded Bes K 6316 p of be-wyrcan

2 ~~Bewarian to defend Th. an v bewarian~~

4 Bewarian to defend Som v bewarian

3 Bewarigan To ward off Cd. 127 Th p 35, 31 v warian

( ) 1 Bewrigen covered v bewreon

( ) 1 Bewende turned v wendan

Beworcan to encompass Th. an

5 Beweorpan to cast beat Th. an v weorpan

Betwuh, betwy, betwih, betwyh, betweoh, betweohs, betweox, betwux, betwuxt; *prep. dat. acc.* [be *by,* twa *two*] BETWIX, BETWIXT, *among; inter*:—Þæt wæs betwuh Arabia and Palestina *that was between Arabia and Palestine, Ors.* 1, 3. Betweohs, *Ex.* 34, 10. Betwih, *Bd.* 4, 9. Betwyh him *among them, Bt.* 39, 12. Betweox eow *among you, Mt.* 20, 26. Betwux wulfas, *Lk.* 10, 3. Betwux wifa bearnum, *Lk.* 7, 28: 11, 51. Betwuxt, *Nat. Greg. S.* p. 11, 14.

twuh-bruwum *between the eyebrows.*

twux-alegednes, se; *f.* [be-wux *between,* alecged *laid*] *An interposition, interjection*:—nterjectio mæg beon gecweden betwuxalegednyss on Enlisc *an interjection may be* lled *betwuxalegednes in Engh, Elf. gr. Som.* p. 48, 3.

vux-aworpennys *an interjection.*

rux-cuman *to come between, happen.*

rux-gearcud *left, omitted.*

y, betwyh *among, Bt.* 39, 12. Betwyh þas þing *between se things in the mean while, ilst, Bd.* 1, 27, v. betwuh.

yh-geset *interposed.*

yh-gonging *going between, iding.*

rnan, betweonan, betweoa; *prep. dat.* [be *by,* twæm; *of* twa] BETWEEN, *among;* r:—Him betwynan *among* , *Mt.* 9, 3: *Jn.* 16, 17. Ge að lufe eow betwynan, 13, 35. Þa gewearð hi betweonum *then settled between them, Ors.* 6, 30. reonum *is sometimes sepa*. Be sæm tweonum *for* eonum sæm *between seas,* 63: 170. It is also used rbially. Ne si lang fæc onum *be not a long space* en, *Bd.* 4, 9.

betwixt *betwix, betwixt,* wuh.

sendan *to send between.*

accused, v. betogen.

accuses, v. teon.

; *part.* betynde; he be- *p.* betynde, hi betyn- *mp.* betyn, betiene; *pp.* d, betiened; *v. a.* [be, o *hedge*] 1. *To enclose,* n, *close, shut up, stop, ide;* sepire. 2. *To end, finish;* finire:—1. Beine, *Mt.* 21, 33: *Mk.* 12, ine betyndon *they en*hem, *Bd.* 4, 26. Hy n Janes duru *they clos*ors of Janus, Ors.* 6, 7. Betynde, *Ors.* 5, 14. 2. Þus þat word betynde *thus the speech ended, Bd.* 4, 9. ¶ Betynan inne *to enclose within, L. Alf.* 21. Utan betynde *shut out, Ors.* 4, 5, v. tynan.

a Betyran [be, tyr *tar*] *To* BETAR, *to smear over, to stain a dark colour;* pice liquida inficere: —*Æqu. vern.* 2.

Betyrnan hy *they turned.*

Be-ufan *above,* v. bufan.

Be un-gewyrhtum *freely;* sponte, *Som.*

Be-utan *from without,* v. butan.

Bewæfan; *p.* bewæfde; *pp.* bewæfed, bewefen; *v. a.* [be, wæfan *to cover*] *To befold, to cover round, to cover, hide;* induere:—Heo nam hyre wæfels and bewæfde hig, *Gen.* 24, 65. Bewæfed *clothed, Mk.* 14, 51.

b Bewæg utan *surrounded,* v. wægan.

Bewæht *disappointed,* v. bepæcan.

Bewæpnian; *p.* nde; *pp.* nod [be, wæpen *a weapon*] *To take away arms, to disarm;* armis spoliare:—*L. Polit. Cnut.* 57.

Bewand *wrapped up,* v. windan.

Bewarenian, bewarian *To keep, defend;* custodire:—*L. Eccl. Cnut.* 26, v. warian.

Bewarnian *to beware, warn,* v. warnian.

c Beweallen *cooked,* v. weallan.

Bewealwiað *wallow,* v. wealwian.

Beweardian *to ward, keep,* v. weardian.

Bewearp *has cast; p. of* bewyrpan.

Beweddian; *p.* ede; *pp.* ed, od. *To espouse, wed;* spondere:—*Ex.* 21, 9, v. weddian.

Beweddung *a wedding,* v. weddung.

Bewefen *covered; pp. of* bewæfan.

Bewegde, beweht *disappointed, Ps.* 131, 11, v. biwægan.

Bewendan *to turn,* v. wendan.

d Bewepan *to bewail,* beweopon *wept,* bewopen *bewailed,* v. wepan.

Beweran *to pour out.*

Bewerenes, se; *f.* [bewered *or* beweren *forbidden*] *A forbidding;* prohibitio:—*Bd.* 1, 27, *Resp.* 9.

Bewerian *to defend, restrain.*

Bewerigend *a defender.*

Bewerod *restrained,* v. werian.

Bewerung, e; *f.* [*Plat. Dut.* bewering] *A defence, a fortification;* tutamen:—Bewerung strang *a strong defence, Scint.* 64.

e Bewician *to encamp,* v. wician.

Bewicode *defended.*

Be wille *willingly.*

Bewimmen *A niece;* neptis, *Som.*

Bewindan; *p.* bewand, hi bewundon; *pp.* bewunden; *v. a.* [*Dut.* bewinden: be *about,* windan *to wind*] *To enfold, to wrap or wind about, embrace, entwine, extend;* involvere:—Josep bewand hyne mid clænre scytan, *Mt.* 27, 59: *Lk.* 2, 7.

Bewiste *governed, presided,* v. bewitan.

Bewitan; *p.* he bewiste, we bewiston; *pp.* bewiton: *v. a.* [be *near,* witan *to know, see, take care of*] 1. *To overlook, watch over, superintend, preside, govern, command;* præesse. 2. *To keep, preserve, administer;* custodire:—1. Þe ealle his þing bewiste, *Gen.* 24, 2: 39, 4. Ne miht þu lencg tun-scire bewitan, *Lk.* 16, 2. 2. Ealle gesceafta motan heora gewunan bewitigan *all creatures may keep their custom, Bt.* 7, 3: *Ors.* 2, 2.

f Bewlat *beheld, saw,* v. wlitan.

Bewlatunga *Shows, sights, pageants;* spectacula, *Som.*

Bewopen *bewailed.*

Beworht *employed, worked, built; pp. of* bewyrcan, v. wyrcan.

Beworpen *cast; pp. of* bewyrpan, v. weorpan.

g Bewræcon *wreaked revenge, pursued,* v. wrecan.

Bewrencan [be *about,* wrenc *deceit*] *To deceive;* occultis machinationibus circumvenire: —*Moral. præcpt.* 34.

Bewreon *to cover; p.* þu bewruge, hi bewreogon *covered, surrounded; pp.* bewrigen, bewrogen *covered, hidden, overwhelmed,* v. wreon.

Bewrigennes, se; *f. A hiding, keeping close* or *concealing;* occultatio, *Som.*

Bewriðan *To bind, retain; pp.* bewriðen *retained,* v. wriðan.

Bewrogen *covered; pp.* bewreon, v. wreon.

Bewruge *protected; p. of* bewreon, v. wreon.

h Bewunden *wrapped;* bewundon *tied* or *wound about,* v. bewindan.

Bewurpon,-an *threw, cast around,* ic bewurpe, v. bewyrpan, weorpan.

Bewyddod in sceat *pledged in money, pledged,* v. weddian.

Bewylewan *to wallow;* bewylewad *rolled, wallowed.*

Bewyrcan; *pp.* beworht. *To work, build, work in, engrave*:—Bewyrc on golde *engrave in gold,* v. beworht, wyrcan.

Bewyrpan *to cast, throw,* v. weorpan.

Be-yrnan; *p.* be-arn; *pp.* beurnen [be *by,* yrnan *to run*] *To run by, to come in, occur, incur;* percurrere:—An wundor me nu on mod be-arn *one wonder now* [*runs by me into the mind*] *occurs to me, Dial.* 1, 10, *Wan. Cat.* p. 154, 3. He ne be-arn on leasunga synne *he incurs not the sin of* [*leasing*] *lying, Dial.* 1, 2: *Æqu. vern.* 4.

Bezera, bezere *a baptist*, v. bædzere.

i Bi *by, near, concerning*, v. be.

Biatian *to threaten*, v. beatan.

Biblioþece, an; *f.* 1. *A library;* bibliotheca. 2. *The Bible;* biblia:—1. *C. R. Ben.* 50. 2. Se saltere ys an boc on þære biblioþecan *the psalter is one book in the Bible, Elf. T.* p. 14, 15: 15, 9.

Bibod *commanded*, v. bebod.

j Bi bread *honey-comb, Bt. R.* p. 166, 27, v. beo bread.

Bibugan *to flee away.*

Bibycgong, e; *f.* [be, bycg *from* bycgan *to buy*] *A selling away;* venditio, *Som.*

Bicce, bice; *f.* [*Ger.* betze, petze: *Icel.* bykkia *f.*] A BITCH, *a female of the canine kind;* canicula:—Biccan meolc *bitch's milk.*

Biccen; *adj. Belonging to a bitch;* caninus, *Som.*

Bicerran *to pass by*, v. cerran.

Bicgencgere *an inhabitant*, v. beganga.

Bicnian, bicnigan, beacnian, becnan, he bicneð, bycneð; *part.* becnende, becniende; *p.* bicnode, hi bicnodon, becnodon; *v.a.* [beacn *a beacon*] 1. *To* BECKON, *nod;* annuere. 2. *To shew, signify, form;* demonstrare:—1. He wæs bicniende hym, *Lk.* 1, 22. Þa bicnodon hi to his fæder, *Lk.* 1, 62: 5, 7. 2. Niht bycneð, *Ps.* 18, 2. Hi becnodon mid eagum *they indicate* [*shew*] *with their eyes, Ps.* 34, 22. He sceal mid bellan bicnigan þa tida *he shall with bells shew the times, L. Can. Eccl. Wilk.* p. 155, 10. Bycnað eage *formeth an eye, Ps.* 93, 9.

k Bicnung *a sign*, v. beacneng.

Bicwide *a proverb*, v. bigcwid.

Bídan, abídan, anbídan, gebídan, geanbídian, he bídeð, bit; *p.* bád, gebád, bed, we bidon; *pp.* biden, gebiden [*Plat. Dut.* beijden, beijen, verbeijen: *Moes.* beidan: *Norse*, ad biida: *Icel.* bygd *an habitation. Sax.* bye *or Pers.* اباد abad *a dwelling*, byan *to dwell*, byde *dwelt:* hence byd *or* bid] *To* BIDE, *abide, wait, remain, tarry, expect;* manere:—Utan we well þære tide bidan *we desire well to wait the time, Bd.* 4. 24. Wolde þær anbidian, *Gen.* 12, 10. Þat he gebit *that he waits, Bt.* 38, 3. Hig gebidun his, *Lk.* 8, 40. We oþres sceolon abidan, *Mt.* 11, 3. Gebidað her, *Mt.* 26, 38.

l Biddan, abiddan, gebiddan, ic bidde, þu bitst, he bit, bitt, we biddað; *p.* bæd, gebæd, we bædon; *imp.* bide; *pp.* beden, gebeden; *v. a.* [*Plat. Dut.* bidden: *Frs.* bidde: *Al.* bedan: *Moes.* bidgan: *Dan.* bede: bed, gebed *a prayer*] 1. *To ask, pray, intreat, beseech;* petere. 2. *To* BID, *command, demand, require, enforce, compel;* præcipere:—1. We biddað *we ask, Elf. gr.* 33. Ic bidde þe min Drihten, *Gen.* 19, 18. Þonne we us gebiddað *when we pray, Bt.* 41, 2. Biddan þæs þe he bæd *to pray that which he prayed, Bt.* 35, 6. Abiddað hine *ask him, Id.* 42, *Card.* p. 392, 15. He bitt sibbe, *Lk.* 14, 32. 2. Þu bitst me, *Ex.* 33, 12. Bide his me eft, *Gen.* 43, 9. Hi læton bædan mycele fyrde *then they permitted to order a large army. Chr.* 1051, *Ing.* p. 228, 9. ¶ This verb is used with fram *from, of, as* Bide þu fram me *ask of me, Ps.* 2, 8. Ic bæd fram Drihtne 26, 7: 20, 4. With to *to. To pray to.* Gebiddað him þær to, *Ex.* 32, 8. Ic me to him gebidde *I worship him, Bd.* 1, 7.

m Bidde *a prayer*, v. gebed.

Biddende *praying*, v. biddan.

Biddere *A suiter, petitioner;* procus:—*Cot.* 191, *Som.*

Bidende *waiting for*, v. bidan.

Bideped *bedipped, dyed*, v. bedypan.

n Biecn *a beacon, wonder*, v. beacen.

Biegan *to crown*, v. beagian.

Bieh *a crown*, v. beag.

Bielde *Steadiness, constancy;* constantia:—*Cot.* 56, v. belde.

Bien *a bean*, v. bean.

Biencodd *beanpod*, v. beanbelgas.

Bierhte, bierhtu *a flash of lightning.*

Bierm *a bosom*, v. bearm.

Biernende *burning, for* byrnende, v. byrnan.

Biesen *an example*, v. bysen.

Biesenian *to set an example*, v. bysnian.

Bieter *bitter*, v. biter.

Bieternes *bitterness*, v. biternes.

Bietl *a beetle;* malleus, v. bytl.

Bifærende *passing by;* biferdon *passed by*, v. befaran.

o Bifgende, bifigende *trembling, trembling with a fever*, v. bifian.

BIFIAN, bifgean, beofian; *part.* bifiende; *p.* byfode, hi bifodon [*Plat. Dut.* beven: *Frs.* beefje: *Swed.* bäfwa: *Dan.* baeve: *Icel.* bifa] *To tremble, shake, wave;* tremere:—Þa wudas bifodon *the woods shook, Bt.* 35, 6. Deð hig bifian *or* bifgean, *Ps.* 103, 33: *Elf. T.* p. 37, 10.

Bifleon; *part.* bifleonde [be *by,* fleon *or* fleogan *to fly*] *To escape, to pass by* or *under, to go away privately;* subterfugere:—*Cot.* 192.

Biflitum *A wave;* fluctus:—*Cot.* 87.

p Bifolen *for,* befolen *filled; pp. of* befyllan.

Biforan *before*, v. beforan.

Bifung *A trembling, shaking;* tremor:—*Ps.* 47, 5, v. beofung.

Bifylc [be *by, near,* fylc *or* folc *people*] *A neighbouring people, province,* or *region;* provincia adjacens:—*Bd.* 3, 14, *Mann.*

Big *of, by, near*, v. be.

Big *a crown*, v. beag.

Bigæð *cultivates, practises*, v. began.

Bigan, bigean, bigangan, anbigan, gebigan; *p.* bigde, gebigde, hi bigdon, begdon; *pp.* biged, gebiged; *v. a.* [*Plat.* bögen: *Dut.* buigen: *Frs.* boagje, booghe: *Ger.* beugen: *Dan.* böje: *Swed.* böja: *Icel.* bogna: *q.* bi, gan *to go, or* boga *a bow*] *To bow, bend, worship, subdue, reduce, turn back;* incurvare:—Bigean ure cneowe *to bow our knees, Bd.* 3, 2: *Gen.* 27, 29. Bygdon byra cneow, *Mt.* 27, 29. Þone soðan God ic symle bigange *the true God I only worship, Bd.* 1, 7. Hit abegdon *(they) subdued it, Chr.* 1073, *Ing.* p. 278, 23. Ealle leoda gebigan to geleafan *to reduce all nations to the faith, Elf. T.* p. 30, 6, v. began, begangan, bugan.

Bigang *worship, tillage*, v. begang.

q Bigangan *to worship*, v. bigan.

Bigcwid, bicwid [be, big *by;* cwid *a saying*] *A bysaying, byword, proverb, fable, tale;* proverbium, fabula:—*Deut.* 28, 37, v. bigspell.

BIGE, byge, es; [*Frs.* bôage; *Plat. Dut.* boog, *m. a bow: Ger.* bogen, *m. an arch: Dan.* bue] 1. *A turning, corner, bending, angle, bay, bosom;* flexus. 2. *Exchange, buying, commerce;* commercium:—1. Þærnan bige næs, *Num.* 22, 26. To anes wealles byge *at a corner of a wall, Ors.* 3, 9, *Bar.* p. 115, 18. 2. Wið ure bige hæbban *to have commerce with us, L. Alf. Guth.* 5. ¶ Bige limes *a breaking of a limb, Fulg.* 19.

Bige *buy*, v. bycgan.

p19 ○2 Biddan [49b]

○1x Moes bidjan

2 Bibaeged [illegible] [illegible] ○3

○ Io biege [illegible] [illegible] emasses [illegible] th an p109, 23

7 See top of p 54

3 Biegan [illegible]

p109, 23 [illegible] [illegible]

4 See Margin of col 1

5 Began to beg th [illegible] or bigegan

[illegible] to beclip [illegible]

beclyppan
[illegible]cnian [48h]

4 Bedylt shut up [illegible]

2 Beigean [illegible]

○ Bu biegodest [illegible]

Big [illegible] 4720, 24

[illegible] to desire

7 [50c]

Bilge Bolds had udax. Tom Th

5 Bihæfdian to behead Th. an v. Behæfdian

Bilewitnyss meekness Th an v bilehwitnes

1 Bigenceare, es: m Th. an

3 Bihlæman — l gedeire gehæfte

2 *Biggeng, es: m *tillage culture Th. an

6 Bihidilice heedfully anxiously Th. an v behydilice
See top of page 55

8 [51a]

3

Biggengenne for be- gangenne ~~going~~ ~~over~~ ~~exercising~~ Th. an v begangan to exercise

4

0 [51d]

5 [54a]

7 Bil a bill, beak Th. an [51 b]

See outer margin of p 55

Bigd bugs Th. an v bygan

1 Bilewit [52a]

Binne, an, f? a bine v bin

Bigean *to bend*, v. bigan.
Bigegnes, se; *f. An endeavour, a colony;* studium:—*Dial.* 1,10.
Bigels *An arch, vault, roof;* arcus:—*Elf. gr.* 19.
Bigen *bought, for* bugen, v. bugan.
igencere, *A worker;* operator:—*Collog. Monast., Lye.*
igencg, bigeng *worship, observation*, v. begang.
igenga *an observer*, v. beganga.
igeondan *beyond*, v. begeond.
igeongende *passing by;* præteriens.
gerdel *a purse*, v. bigyrdel.
ggan *to worship;* biggende *worshipping*, v. bigan.
ggen *an observation*, v. begang.
ggencere *a worker*, v. bigencere, beganga.
geng *undertaking*, v. begang.
gengc *exercise*, v. begang.
gyrdel *a treasury*, v. bigyrdel.
hydig, bighydiglic *anxious*, v. behydig.
hydilice *diligently*, v. behydelice.
eofa, bileofa, an [big, bi *for*, *f life] Provision by which life maintained, food, victuals;* ctus:—To bigleofan *for food*, *n.* 6, 21, v. bigwist, wist.
eofan; *part.* ende; *p.* ede; . ed. *To nourish, feed, sup-t;* cibare, *Som.*
es, se; *f. A bending, bow-;* flexio:—*Bd.* 5, 3.
ng *exercise*, v. begang.
nga *a cultivator*, v. beganga
n *an example*, v. bysn.
æc, e; *f. A by-speech, deing;* supplantatio, *Lye.*
ell, bispell, es; *plu.* bigspell, spelle, bigspellu; *n.* [big, bi spell *a history*] *A parable, y, fable, comparison, pro-, pattern, example;* para- :——Þæs sawendan big-l, *Mt.* 13, 18. Mid biglum, *Mt.* 13, 34. Bispell ære sunnan, *Bt. Tit.* 6, . p. 4, 19. We nu sculon ga bisna and bispell rec*ve now should many exam- nd fables* [*comparisons*] *ce, Bt.* 35, 5. Gehyr sum ll *hear an example, Id.*
-boc *a book of parables.*
dan *to stand by* or *near, ort.*
deceit, v. beswic.
food, victuals, v. biwist, fa.
[be, gyrdel *a girdle*] *le,* and as girdles were carry money, hence a *ublic purse, a treasury;* accus, fiscus:—Ne feoh rum bigyrdlum, *Mt.* Kinges gafoles biger-del *the purse of a king's tribute, a treasury, Elf. gl. Som.* p. 69.
Bihealdan *To hold, occupy;* tenere:—*Cod. Ex.* 57, a. 10, *Mann.*
Bihelan *to cover*, v. behelian.
Biheonan *on this side*, v. beheonan.
Bihlæman, bihlemman; *v. a.* [be, hlemman *to sound*] *To rage, roar, dash together, to mix with force so as to produce a noise;* fremere, confundere:—Þa grimman goman bi-hlemmeð *gnashes the grim* [*gums*] *jaws, Cod. Ex.* 97, b. 11. Bi-hlæmeð scre gesceafte *mixes pure elements, Cod. Ex.* 20, b. 9, *Mann.*
Bihydig *careful*, v. behydig.
Bii *near*, v. be.
BIL; *g. d.* bille; *pl. g.* billa; *d.* billum [*Plat.* biel *n*: *Dut.* byl *m*: *Ger.* beil *n*: *Swed.* bila *f*: *Dan.* bile *c*: *Norse*, bula: *Pers.* بيل bil *a pickaxe*] *Steel, any instrument made of steel, such as a* BILL, *knife, sword;* chalybs, flax, ensis. (Hitherto this word has only been found in poetry):—Hi ne bill rude gesawan *they, the blood-red sword, never saw, Bt. R.* p. 158, 84. Abrægd bille *drew sword, Cd.* 142. Blæd forbræcon billa ecgum *shed blood with the edges of swords, Cd.* 210. Billum abreotan *with swords to destroy, Cd.* 153. ¶ Bill-gesleht *bill-clashing, Walton's Poet, by Price,* vol. i. p. 96, 13: *Chr.* 938, *Ing.* p. 144, 6. Bil-swaðu *bill-swathes, sword-paths, wounds, Cd.* 160.
w Bilage [bi *by, near*, lagu *a law*] A BYE-LAW; lex privata:—*Chr. W. Thorn.* an. 1303.
Bilcettan *to belch*, v. bealcan.
Bile A BILL, *beak of a bird, the horn of an animal, a proboscis, the fore part of a ship;* rostrum, acisculum:—Ylpes bile *an elephant's proboscis, R.* 18.
Bile *a bile*, v. byl.
Bilehwit *simple*, v. bilewit.
x Bilehwitlice; *adv. Honestly;* simpliciter:—*Bd.* 5, 13.
Bilehwitnes, bilwetnes, bylewitnes, se; *f. Mildness, simplicity, innocence;* simplicitas:—Se God wunað simle on þære hean ceastre his anfealdnesse and bilewitnesse *God dwells always in the high city of his unity and simplicity, Bt.* 39, 5: *Ors.* 1, 2.
Bilened *inhabited, Som.*
Bileofa *food*, v. bigleofa.
Bileoran; *p.* orde. *To pass over;* transire:—*Ps.* 89, 4, v. leoran.
Bileouene *victuals*, v. bileofa.
Bilewit, bilehwit, belewit, bilwit; *adj.* [bile *the beak*, hwit *white*, referring to the *beaks* of young birds, then to their nature, *Junius*] *Innocent, simple, mild, gentle, sincere, honest, merciful;* mitis:—Beoð bilewite swa culfran, *Mt.* 10, 16. Ic eom bilewite, *Mt.* 11, 29.
y Bilibban [bi *by*, libban *to live*] *To live by* or *upon, to sustain, support;* sustentari:—Neotena meolc hi mæst bilibbað *they mostly live on the milk of cattle, Som.* Ealle cwice wihta bilibbað *all living beings are supported, Ors.* 2, 1.
Biliden *deprived*, v. beleosan.
z Bilifen *food*, v. bigleofa.
Bilig *a bag, Ps.* 118, 83, v. bælg.
Bilið [*Dut. Kil.* beeld, beld, bild: *Ot.* belidi, bild: *Wil.* bilethe: *Chaucer*, blee: hence to know one by the *blee*, by the *bill* or *look*] *An image, a representation, resemblance, likeness, pattern, example;* imago, *Som.*
Bill *steel*, v. bil.
Bilocen *locked up*, v. belucan.
Bilode *having a bill, nib* or *snout;* rostratus, *Som.*
Biloren *deprived*, v. beleosan.
Bil-swaðu *wounds, Cd.* 160, v. bil.
Bilwetnes *innocence*, v. bilehwitnes.
a Bilwit *mild*, v. bilewit.
Bilyhte; *adj. Melancholic, choleric;* biliosus, *Som.*
Bime *a trumpet*, v. byme.
Bimyldan *to bury*, v. bemyldan.
BIN; *g. d.* binne [*Frs.* bin: *Dut.* binne, ben] *A manger, crib,* BIN, *hutch, rack;* præsepe:—Heo hyne on binne alede, *Lk.* 2, 7, 16.
Bin *am;* sum, v. beon.
BINDAN, gebindan, ic binde, þu bindst, he bint, we bindað; *p.* band, he bunde, we bundon; *pp.* bunden; *v. a.* [*Plat. Dut. Ger.* binden: *Moes.* bindan, gabindan: *Dan.* binde: *Swed. Icel. Norse*, binda] 1. *To* BIND, *tie;* ligare. 2. *To pretend;* fingere:—1. Hig bindað byrþena, *Mt.* 23, 4. He band hine, *Gen.* 42, 24. He geband his sunu, *Gen.* 22, 9. Ne mihte gebindan, *Mk.* 5, 3: 6, 17. 2. *C. R. Lk.* 24, 28.
b Bindele, an; *f. A binding, tying, fastening with bands;* vinculis constrictio:—Be mannes bindelan *concerning* [*the*] *binding* [*putting in bands*] *of a man, L. Alf. Pol.* 31.
Bindende *binding*, v. bindan.
Bi-niotan *To pursue, enjoy;* assequi, *Mann.*
Binnan, binnon, be innan *within;* intus:—*Bt.* 1, 1, *Card.* p. 4, 17: *Jn.* 11, 30: *Mt.* 2, 16: *Ors.* 4, 11.
Binne *a manger*, v. bin.

Bio *I am, may be, shall be;* sum, sim, ero:—Mt. 9, 21: *Bt.* 40, 5: 33, 4, v. beon.
Bio bread *honey-comb, Bt.* 23.
Biodan *offer;* offerant:—*Bt.* 25, v. beodan.
Biom *I am, shall be;* sum, ero:—v. beon.
Bior *beer,* v. beor.
Biorg *a defence,* v. beorh.
Biorhto *brightness, Bt.* 41, 1, v. beorht.
Bioð *They are, may be, shall be;* sunt, sint, erunt, v. beon.
Biotian *To threaten;* intentare:—*Cot.* 108.
Biotul *a beetle, staff,* v. bytl.
Biowyrt *beewort;* apiastrum, v. beowyrt.
Birce, byrc [*Plat.* barke *f*: *Frs.* byirk: *Dut.* berkeboom *m*: *Kil.* berck: *Ger.* birke *f*: *Dan.* birk *m. f*: *Swed.* björk] *A birch tree;* betula:—*Cot.* 165.
Bircen, beorcen; *adj.* Birchen, *belonging to birch;* betulaceus, *Som.*
Bird *a bird,* v. brid.
Birden-meto *heavy;* onerosa:—*Prov.* 27, *Lye.*
Birele *a cupbearer,* v. byrle.
Bireð *beareth, for* byrð, v. beran.
Birgan, birgean, byrigan, byrigean, bebyrgan; *p.* de; *pp.* ed, bebirged, gebyrged; *v. a.* [*Dut.* bergen *to cover up: Al.* bergen: *Ot.* giborgan: beorh, beorg *a hill*] To bury; sepelire:—Þær hine man birgde: þær wæs Isaac bebirged, *Gen.* 49, 31. Alyf me ærest byrigean minne fæder, *Lk.* 9, 59: *Gen.* 23, 6.
Birgen, byrgen, byrigen, byrigels, e; *f. A burial place, sepulchre, tomb, grave;* sepulchrum:—Hat nu healdan þa byrgene, *Mt.* 27, 64, 66. Wæs niwe byrgen, *Jn.* 19, 41, 42: 20, 1, 4: *Gen.* 23, 2, 6, 9.
Birginceg *A tasting;* gustatio, *Ben.*
Birgnes *a taste,* v. byrignes.
Birhtu *brightness,* v. beorht.
Birian *to bury;* birgde *buried,* v. birgan.
Birig *a city, Deut.* 14, 27, v. burh.
Birigan *to bury,* v. birgan.
Birighman *a city officer, an overseer of temples, Som.*
Biriging *a tasting,* v. birgincg.
Birihto *brightness,* v. beorht.
Birilian, birlian, byrlian *To draw, bear;* haurire:—*C. R. Jn.* 2, 8, 9.
Birist *bearest,* vehis, *for* berist, *Bt. R.* p. 181, v. beran.
Birne *a coat of mail,* v. byrne.
Birned *burned, armed,* v. bærnan, byrnan.
Bisæc *a bag,* v. sæc. codd.

Bisæcan [be *by,* sæcan *to seek*] *To be present, to go to;* adire—*L. Edg.* 62.
Bisceop, biscop, es; *m. A bishop, prelate, high-priest;* episcopus:—Þa astyredon þa bisceopas þa menegu, *Mk.* 15, 11: *Lev.* 8, 7. Twegen bisceopas *two bishops, Bd.* 4, 5, *S.* p. 573, 31. ¶ Yldesta bisceop, *Ors.* 5, 4. Heah biscop *an archbishop,* v. arcebisceop. Efenhada biscop *a co-bishop, Gr. Dial.* 1, 5.
Bisceopdóm, es; *m.* [bisceop *a bishop,* dom *judgment*] *The judgment of a bishop, excommunication, the province of a bishop;* episcopi judicium, *vel* provincia:—Þæs bisceopdomes wyrðe *worthy of the bishop's judgment* or *excommunication, Bd.* 4, 5, v. bisceoprice.
Bisceophád, biscophád, es; *m.* [bisceop *a bishop;* had *hood, head*] Bishophood, *episcopacy;* episcopatus:—*Bd.* 3, 21, *S.* p. 551, 40: 4, 5, *S.* p. 573, 28. On biscop hade *in (his) episcopacy, during the time of being bishop,* 4, 6, *S.* p. 574, 2, 3.
Bisceop-hyrde, biscophyrede, bisceop-hyred *A bishop's shepherd* or *clergy;* episcopi familia:—*Cot.* 44, *Som.*
Bisceopian, biscopgan; *pp.* bisceopod. *To exercise the office of a bishop, to oversee, visit, confirm;* visitare, confirmare:—*L. Can. Eccl.* 18, *W.* p. 155, 51.
Bisceoplic, biscoplic; *adj. Bishoplike, episcopal, belonging to a bishop;* episcopalis:—*Bd.* 2, 15.
Bisceopod *bishoped, confirmed,* v. bisceopian.
Bisceoprice, bisceopscyre, bisceopdóm, es; *m.* [bisceop *a bishop,* rice *a region,* scyre *a share,* dóm *a province*] A bishopric, *diocese, province of a bishop;* episcopi provincia:—Bisceoprice, *Bd.* 2, 7, *S.* p. 509, *n.* 8. He onfeng his agenre ceastre biscop scire or biscopdom *he received the bishopric of his own city, Bd.* 3, 7, *S.* p. 530, 10, *n.* 10, 3, 21. Adrifen wæs of his bisceopscire *was driven from his bishopric,* 4, 13.
Bisceopsetl, bisceopstol, biscopseld, biscopseðl, es; *n.* [bisceop *a bishop,* setel *a seat*] *A bishop's residence, see, seat;* sedes episcopalis:—He Bisceop setl onfeng *he received the bishop's see, Bd.* 1, 26: 3, 7.
Bisceop þenung *a bishop's duty, service,* v. þegning.
Bisceop-wyrt, biscep-wyrt Bishop's-wort, *bishop's-weed, vervain;* verbena:—*Cot.* 166: *Herb. tit.* 1. ¶ Bisceopwyrt þe læsse *betony,* betonica.
Biscop, biscop-dóm, biscop-hád, biscop-rice, v. bisceop.
Biscopgan *to confirm,* v. bisceopian.
Biscop heafod lin *a bishop's head linen, an ornament which bishops wore on their heads, a mitre, R.* 64: *Elf. gl.* p. 69, *Mann.*
Biscop-rocc *A bishop's rocket;* dalmatica:—*Somn.* 84.
Biscopwite, es; *n. A bishop's fee for visiting, procuration;* episcopo debita:—*Chr.* 675, *Ing.* p. 51, 13.
Biseah *looked about,* v. beseon.
Biseg, byseg, bisgung, e; *pl.* bysgu; *f.* [*Dut.* bezig] *Business, occupation, employment, utility;* occupatio:—For þæm bisgum *for the occupations, Bt. Card. pref.* p. ii. 7, 8. Of þissum bisegum *from these occupations, Bt.* 33, 4, *Card.* p. 206, 14: *Rawl.* p. 180. Mid his modes bisgunga *with his mind's anxiety, Bt.* 35, 1.
Bisegung *employment,* v. biseg.
Bisen *an example,* v. bysn.
Bisen *blind, C. Mt.* 9, 27: 11, 5, v. blind.
Bisencan *to sink,* v. sencan.
Bises *A leap year;* bissextile:—*Menol.* 61, v. bissexte.
Biseted *set,* v. settan.
Bisgan, bysgian; *pp.* hi bisgodan; *v. a.* [*Frs.* bysgje] *To occupy;* occupare:—*Bt. pref. Card.* p. ii. 8: *Rawl.* p. 183, v. abysean.
Bisg, bisgung *occupation,* v. biseg.
Bisleasung *vanity, Ps.* 102, 13, v. leasung.
Bism *a besom,* v. besm.
Bismær word *a reproachful word, L. Hloth. W.* p. 9, 2, v. bismer.
Bismer, bismor, bysmer, bysmor [be, smere *fat, grease*] *Filthiness, pollution, abomination, disgrace, infamy, mockery, reproach, contumely, blasphemy;* abominatio, opprobrium:—Hi amyrdon heora folc on bysmore *they defiled their people with filthiness, Elf. T.* p. 15, 21. Mid þam bismre *by the disgrace, Ors.* 6, 30: *Deut.* 28, 29: *Ps.* 88, 34. Ge gehyrdon his bysmer, *Mk.* 14, 64.
Bismeriend *A deceiver;* illusor: *Prov.* 11, 4, v. bysmrian.
Bismerlic, bismorlic; *adj. Disgraceful, dirty, unpleasant;* turpis:—Mid þam bismerlicestan aðe *with the most disgraceful oath, Ors.* 4, 3: 1, 7: *L. Can. Edg.* 20. On þone bis-

o l2 Ittg. 21

om q

ón to be Th. An v beon

1 Bisárgeidan to lament, deplore Th. An

D

d. es. n s birth

afol v gebyrd

anty s byrgean

al in ofl

eaced for

fod bereaved

re afain

n. l2. e; f

d of birth

a bennan virg

2 ato Deut

27.

k]

v. byrne

O 2 8 e

Bisqua, e f

Bisgumgebunden with sorrows bound, Laboribus vinctus Beo K 3483

O 2 Bisey [55 e] v bysig

2 Bisgu, e f Business, occupation, labour; negotium, labor Beo K

3 Bisgung, e f occupation

2 Biseo, for

beseo see Th. An v beseon

3 Bisettan to beset, cover over Th. An

Bisgian to busy, occupy Th. An

5 Bisig busy Th. Apol sup bysig activus Beo K 559

7 5 Bismerful shameful, blasphemous Th. An

8 6 Bismerian to mock, scorn v ymbsmerian

9 7 Bismorleod defamatory verses, satire; libel carmen invectivum

⊙1[57e]

2 Blacern-es; n a candlestick O[57f]

1 Bismorian to mock, insult, ill treat, th. v. ~~bysmerian~~ bismrian

2 Bisnian to give example ~~th. an~~ exemplum Som v bysmian

fera bere

8

3 Bistalcian to stalk march proceed th an v. stealcian

Bisurcan to deceive Ben v beswican O3[58a]

5 4 Bisy body ~~x~~ Lith. apol

sup bisig

3 Biwerian to defend th. an v bewerian

Blác-hleor pale faced, fare Som th. an

(6,7) 6 swa swa bita ~~sicut~~ sicut bucellas Ps 147.6 o7 Anlige bita singularis ferus Ps 79,14

O9[56h]

3 Blæd ~~euta~~ fruit branch th. an

4 Blædes: m glory prosperity life, blast th. an Beo gl.

O3 Blæd [58 b &c]

Bite, es; m A bite: morsus Beo K 4115

O1 Biwyrd a byword Som v biword

10 Biter-l 2 * Moes O5 [57d] bautr: Icel bitr

merlicostan eard *in the most unpleasant province, Ors.* 3, 11.
Bismernes, e; *f. A polluting;* pollutio, *Som.*
n Bismerung *blasphemy,* v. bysmerung.
Bismiriende *Deriding;* insultans:—*Dial.* 2, 1.
Bismor *a disgrace,* v. bismer.
Bismorful; *adj. Dreadful;* horrendus, *Lye.*
Bismorlic *disgraceful,* v. bismerlic.
Bismorlice; *adv. Disgracefully, indecently;* probrose:—Bismorlice plegan *to play immodestly, Elf. Can.* 35.
Bismrian *to mock,* v. bysmerian.
o Bisn *an example,* v. bysn.
Bisnung, gebysnung, e; *f. An example;* exemplum:—*Elf. T.* p. 5, 15.
Bispell *a fable,* v. bigspell.
Bisseno *a parable,* v. bigspell.
Bissexte, bises *A leap year;* bissextus:—*Menol.* 61: *Bd.* 5, 23, *S.* p. 648, 19.
Bist *art, shall be;* es, eris:—*Bd.* 5, 19, v. beon.
Bistemed *steaming,* v. bestemed.
Bisueþan *to swathe,* v. besueþian.
Bisuic *deceit,* v. beswic.
Bisuic-falle *a pitfall,* v. feall, *Som.*
Biswic *deceit,* v. beswic.
Biswicol, beswicul; *adj. Deceitful;* dolosus:—*L. Eccl., W.* p. 176, 29.
p Bit, bitt *asks,* v. biddan.
Bita, bite, an; *m.* [*Plat.* bet, *m*: *Frs. v.* byt: *Dut.* beet *m*: *Heb.* פת pt *a part, bit*] 1. A BIT, *morsel, piece, fragment, a* BITE; frustrum. 2. *Any thing that bites, an animal;* ferus:—1. Æfter þam bitan, *Jn.* 13, 27: *Ps.* 147, 6. Mid bitum *with bites, Ors.* 1, 7. Banes bite *a bit or fragment of bone, L. Ethelb.* 36, *W.* p. 5, 5. Canceradle, þat is bite *a cancer, that is a biting disease, Herb.* 44. 2. *Ps.* 79, 14.
Bítan; ic bíte, he bít; *part.* bitende; *p.* bát, hi biton; *pp.* biten [*Plat.* bieten: *Dut.* byten: *Swed. Icel.* bita: *Norse,* byta] *To* BITE; mordere:—Byton hyne lys *lice bit him.* Bat fræclice *bit fiercely, Gr. Dial.* 1, 4.
Bite *a bit,* v. bita.
Bitel, bitela, betl; *m.* A BEETLE; blatta:—Þa blacan betlas *the black beetles, Cot.* 141, *v. l.*
Bitende *biting,* v. bitan.
BITER; *adj.* [*Plat. Dut. Dan. Swed. Ger.* bitter: *Moes.* baitrs] BITTER, *sharp, horrid;* amarus:—*Ps.* 63, 3, v. aterlic.
Biterian, abiterian; *p.* de; *pp.* od, gebitered. *To make bitter, sharp;* acerbare:—*Past.* 54, 5. Sealdon gebiterod win, *Mk.* 15, 23.
Biterlice, bittyrlice; *comp.* or; *adv.* BITTERLY; amare:—He weop biterlice, *Mt.* 26, 75: *Bd.* 4, 25, *S.* p. 600, 29.
Biternys, bitternes, se; *f.* BITTERNESS; amaritudo:—Genemned Mara, þat ys biternys, *Ex.* 15, 23.
Bið *is, shall be;* est, erit, v. beon.
Bitl *a mallet,* v. bytl.
Bitmælum, *piecemeal, by bits,* v. mæl.
Bitol *a bridle, Ps.* 31, 12, v. bæte.
Bitolden; *part.* 1. *Estimated, reckoned, numbered;* recensitus. Wuldre bitolden, *Cod. Ex.* 64, b. 13, *from* tellan *to reckon.* 2. Bitolden *cleansed;* purgatus:—Torne bitolden *purified from anger, Cod. Ex.* 15, b. 11: 64, a. 1, *from* teallan *to cleanse, Mann.*
Bitst *prayest,* v. biddan.
Bitt *What affords a bite, food;* herbitum:—*R.* 60, *Lye.*
Bitt *asks,* v. biddan.
Bitte *A bottle, bouget;* uter, v. byt.
Bitternes *bitterness,* v. biternys.
r Bitterlice *bitterly,* v. biterlice.
Bituihu *A foul tetter* or *scab running over the face;* mentagra, *Som.*
Biuundun *bound, for* bewundon, v. bewindan.
Biwægan; *p.* de; *v. a. To disappoint;* frustrari:—*Ps.* 131, 11, *Lye.*
Biwærlan *to pass by,* v. wærlan.
Biwered *forbidden,* v. werdan.
Biwist [be, wist *food*] *Food, provision;* commeatus:—Þat is heora biwist *that is their provision, Bt.* 17: *L. Can. Edg.* 3.
Biwitigan *to preside,* v. bewitan.
Biwoedded *wedded,* v. beweddian.
Biword, biwyrd, es; *n.* [be *by,* word *a word*] A BYEWORD, *proverb;* proverbium:—*Cot.* 157.
Biwritan [be *by,* writan *to write*] *To write after, by,* or *out of, to copy;* postscribere, *Pref. in Past. Lye.*
s Bixen; *adj. Belonging to box,* BOXEN; bucceus:—*R.* 26, v. box.
BLA'C, blæc, bleac; *def.* se blaca; *adj.* [*Plat.* blak *ink: Swed.* black, blek *bleak: Dan.* blek *ink.* The word generally used in Saxon and other Gothic tongues for *black* is swart, but blac is sometimes found, v. blæc *ink*] BLACK, *dark, opaque, dusky, pale, pallid;* niger, pallidus:—Ne might ænne locc gedon hwitne oððe blacne, *Mt.* 5, 36. He hæfde blæc feax *he had black hair, Bd.* 2, 16. Se mona mid his blacan leohte *the moon with her pale light, Bt.* 4.
Blacberian A BLACKBERRY, *mulberry;* vaccinium:—*R.* 47.
Blacern, blæcern, blecernæ, e; *n.* [*Plat. Dut.* blaker, blic *bright, light,* ærn *a place*] *A candlestick, lantern, light, candle, lamp;* lucerna:—Bærnað eower blacern *light your candle, Bd.* 4, 8: *Ps.* 17, 30: *Elf. gl.* 19.
Blacesnung *Ardent desire;* flagrantia:—*Cot.* 87, *Ben.*
Blac-hrem *a raven,* v. hrem.
Blacian, ablacian *To* BLACKEN, *grow black, dark, pale;* pallere:—*Elf. gr.* 26, 35.
Blacþa *the leprosy,* v. blæcþa.
t Blacung; *f. Paleness, wanness;* pallor:—*Lps.* 67, 14.
Blad *a branch,* v. blæd.
Blæc [*Plat.* blak *n.* This word properly signifies *black ink* only; but, in low German, they say, rood and grön blak *red and green ink: Dut. Kil.* black: *Al.* black: *Dan.* blæc *n*: *Swed.* bläck *n*: *Icel.* blek] *Ink;* atramentum:—Þat hi habba blæc and boc fel *that they have ink and parchment, L. Can. Edg.* 3.
Blæcan, blæcean, ablæcan [*Dut.* bleeken: *Swed.* bleka] *To* BLEACH, *to fade;* pallidum colorem inducere:—Ne mæg ne sunne blæcan *can be bleached by no sun, Bd.* 1, 1, *S.* p. 473, 20. n. 20.
Blæcbergen *A blackberry;* vaccinium, *Lye.*
Blæce *Paleness;* pallor, *Som.*
Blæcern *a candle, Bd.* 4, 8, v. blacern, [blæc *ink,* ærn *a place*] *A place for ink, an inkhorn.*
Blæc-gym *a black fossil, called jet, Bd.* 1, 1.
Blæco *paleness, Cot.* 157, *leprosy,* v. blacung, blæcþa.
Blæc-teru *black-tar, tar, naphtha, a sort of bituminous fluid, Som.*
Blæcþa, blæcðrust *Leprosy;* vitiligo:—*Cot.* 221.
u BLÆD, bled; *g.* es; *d.* e; *pl. nom. ac.* a; *d.* um [*Frs. v.* bled: *Plat. Swed. Dan. Dut. Icel.* blad *n. a leaf: Ger.* blatt *n. a leaf: Al.* blæd *fruit: Slav.* plot blod *fruit*] 1. A BLADE, *that which springs forth,* as *a shoot, branch, leaf, product, fruit, corn;* germen, v. brord. 2. *A blast, blowing, breath, spirit, life, mind;* spiritus. 3. *Fruit, enjoyment, faculty, gift, reward, benefit, honour,*

glory; fruitio:—1. Bleda wyrta, *Ps.* 36, 2. Se sumor gearwað bleda *the summer prepares shoots, Bt.* 39; 13. On þæs beames bledum *on the branches of the tree, Cd.* 200. Ælc twig þe blæda ne byrð, *Jn.* 15, 2. Hærfest bryngð ripa bleda *harvest brings ripe fruit, Bt.* 39, 13: 34, 10. Balsames blæd *fruit of balsam, Cot.* 48. 2. Mare blæd windes *a greater blast of wind, Bd.* 4, 3. Gastes blæd *inspiration;* spiritûs flatus, *Cd.* 224. His blæd forleosan *to lose his life, Fr. Jud. Thw.* p. 22, 16. On his blæde geseah *considered in his mind, Cd.* 205. 3. Tires blæd *victory's reward, Cod. Ex.* 25, b. 11. Godes þegna blæd *God's servants' reward, Cod. Ex.* 18, a. 17. Gastes bled *the spirit's gift, Cd.* 227. Þæs blædes, *Cod. Ex.* 38, b. 16. Hi Judea blæd forbræcon billa ecgum *they destroyed the Jews' glory with the edge of swords, Cd.* 210. Wæs heora blæd micel *was their glory great, Cd.* 1.

Blæd *a cup,* v. bledu.

Blæddre *a bladder,* v. blædr.

Blæd horn *a blast horn, a trumpet.*

BLÆDR, blædra, bleddra; *pl.* u, an [*Plat.* bladder *f*: *Dut.* blader *Ger.* blatter *f*: *Al.* blater: *Swed.* bläddra: *Icel.* bladra *f.*] A BLADDER, *a pustule, blister;* vesica:—Eall folc wæs on blædran *all people were in blisters, Ors.* 1, 7. ¶ Blædran-adl, -sare, -wærce *a disease or pain in the bladder;* vesicæ dolor.

Blæge A BLAY, *bleak* or *fresh-water sprat;* gobio:—*R.* 101.

Blæ-hæwen, blæhwen; *adj.* [bleo *blue,* hæwen *hued*] *Of a blue hue, bluish, violet* or *purple colour;* cæruleus:—*Lev.* 8, 7.

Blæsan *To blow;* flare, *Lye.*

Blæse *a blaze,* v. blase.

Blæsere *a burner,* v. blasere.

BLÆST [*Plat.* blas, blast: *Frs. v. Ger.* blast *m*: *Dan.* blaest *c.*] A BLAST, *blasting, burning;* flatus, adustio:—Bæð-weges blæst *a sea blast* or *breeze, Cd.* 158. Fyres blæst *a fire's burning, Cod. Ex.* 22, a. 16.

Blæstan *To puff;* insufflare, *Som.*

Blæstbelg *bellows,* v. blastbelg.

Blæt *A bleating, a bleat like a sheep;* balatus, *Som.*

Blætan; *v. n.* [*Frs. v.* blæte] *To* BLEAT; balare:—Scæp blæt *a sheep bleats, Elf. gr.* 24, 9.

Blætesnung, blætesung, e; *f. A flaming, blazing, sparkling;* flagrantia:—*Ps.* 76, 18.

Blæwen *Light blue;* perseus:—*R.* 80, *Bex.*

Blæwð *blows, Bt. Rawl.* p. 156, v. blawan.

Blan *ceased,* v. blinnan.

Bland [*Norse,* blanda *to pour out*] *A mixture, confusion;* mixtio:—*Hicks.* vol. i. p. 120, 55. Cantilenæ mixtura, *Mann.*

Blanden-feax *yellow haired,* v. blonden-feax.

BLASE, blæse, blysa [*Dut.* blaas] *Any thing that makes a* BLAZE, *a torch, manifestation;* fax:—*Jn.* 18, 3.

Blasere, blisier, es; *m. An incendiary, a burner;* incendiarius:—Be þam blaserum *concerning the incendiaries, L. In.* 77. Þa blisieras *incendiaries, L. Athel.* 6.

Blast-belg [*Dut.* blaasbalg *m*: *Ger.* blasebalg *m*: *Dan.* blæsebælg *c.*] *A blast bag, bellows;* follis:—*Cot.* 86.

BLAT; *sup.* blatast; *adj.* [*Plat. Ger.* platt: *Dut.* plat] *Broad;* latus:—Blatast benna *broadest of wounds, Cod. Ex.* 19, a. 12.

Blate; *adv. Widely, every where;* late:—*Bt. Rawl.* p. 159, 176.

Blatende *Widening, swelling;* expandens, *Mann.*

BLAWAN, ablawan, geblawan; ic blawe, he blæwð; *p.* bleow, gebleow, hi bleowon; *pp.* bláwen. *To* BLOW, *breathe,* flare:—Ge geseoð suðan blawan, *Lk.* 12, 55. Þa bleow he on hi, *Jn.* 20, 22. Bleowun windas, *Mt.* 7, 25, 27. Blewað *blow ye, Ps.* 80, 3. Ne blawe man byman, *Mt.* 6, 2. Blowiað, *Ps.* 147, 7. Blawen is on smiððan *is blown on a forge, Prov.* 27.

Blawennys, se; *f. A blowing,* or *puffing up, a windy swelling;* inflatio, *Som.*

Blawer *A blower;* conflator:—*Past.* 37, 3.

Blawung, ablawung, e; *f. A blowing;* flatus:—*Jud.* 7, 16.

Bleac, bleaca *black, bleak,* v. blac.

Bleað, bleaþe *blithe,* v bliþe.

Blec *black,* v. blac.

Blecernæ *a candle,* v. blacern.

Blecingaeg *Bleckingen,* a province in the south of Sweden, *Ingram's Ang.-Sax. Lect.* p. 64, 2: *Ors.* 1, 1, *Bar.* p. 26, 6.

Blecte *glittered,* v. blican.

Bled, bleda *a bowl,* v. bledu.

Bled *fruit, a branch, herb,* v. blæd.

BLEDAN [*Plat.* bloden: *Dut.* bloeden: *Ger.* bluten: *Dan.* blöde: *Swed.* blöda] *To* BLEED, *draw blood;* phlebotomare:—Se bledenda fic *the bleeding fig or disease, Wanley's Cat.* p. 305, 4: *L. M.* 4, 145, b. *Lye.*

Bleddr *a bladder,* v. blædr.

Bled horn *a trumpet,* v. blæd horn.

Bledsian; *pp.* bledsod *to bless,* v. bletsian.

Bledsung *a blessing, Ben.*

Bledu, blæd *A bowl, viol, cup, goblet;* patera:—*Elf. gl.* 21.

BLEGEN [*Plat.* bleien *f*: *Dut.* blein *f*: *Dan.* blegne] A BLAIN, *blister, bile* or *ulcer;* pustula:—On þa blacan blegene *over the black bile, Wan. Cat.* p. 304, 52: p. 305, 11: *L. M.* 1, 58, v. poc.

BLENDAN; *p.* blonde [*Plat.* blendern: *Dan.* blende: *Icel.* blanda] *To* BLEND, *mix, mingle;* miscere, *Som.*

Blendian, he blent; *pp.* geblend; *v. a. To* BLIND; cæcare:—Se dæg blent hiora eagan *the day blinds their eyes, Bt.* 38, 5, v. ablendan.

BLEO, bleoh, blio, bleow, es, s. *A colour, hue,* BLEE, *complexion, beauty;* color:—Hwites bleos swa cristalla, *Num.* 11, 7. Seolocenra brægla mid mistlicum bleowum *of silken garments of* [*with*] *various colours,* [*blooms*], *Bt.* 15. ¶ Anes bleos *of one colour, R.* 79. Mislices bleos *of a different* or *mixed colour, Elf. gl.* 11. Mislic bleo *a different hue, R.* 79.

Bleo *Blue* or *azure colour;* coeruleus, *Som.*

Bleo-craft BLEE CRAFT, *the art of embroidering, Som.*

Bleofæstnys, se; *f. That which gives pleasure from its colour, pleasure, delight;* deliciæ, jucunditas:—*Ps.* 138, 10.

Bleofag, bleofah [bleo *a colour;* fag *changeable*] *Changing colour, varying hue;* versicolor:—*Cot.* 115: *Somn.* 33.

Bleoh *a colour,* v. bleo.

Bleoread, bleoreod; *adj.* [*Plat.* blaurood: *Dut.* blaauwrood: *Ger.* blaurod: *Dan.* blaaröd] BLUE RED, *purple, myrtle coloured;* cæruleo-ruber:—*Cot.* 135, v. musfealu.

Bleo-stæning *coloured stone-work* or *pavement, Mosaic work, Cot.* 131.

Bleoton *sacrificed,* v. blotan.

Bleow *a colour,* v. bleo.

Bleow *blew,* flabat; hi bleowun *they blew,* flabant, *p. of* blawan.

Blere. 1. *A gem, a kind of marble;* onyx. 2. *Bald;* calvus:—1. *Cot.* 28. 2. *Som.*

Bletcæd *blessed, consecrated,* v. bletsian.

BLETSIAN, gebletsian; ic bletsige, gebletsige; *part.* bletsigende; *p.* bletsode, gebletsode; *pp.* gebletsod; *v. a. To* BLESS, *consecrate;* benedicere:—Ic hig gebletsige and of hire ic þe forgife sunu þone ic wylle bletsian, *Gen.* 17, 16:

Blanca see mon

Blanca, blonca an; m [old Ger. blonc plan= chaz a pale horse]

A horse; equus: On blancum on horses, Beo. 67 K 1705.

Blad [Moes blands mixtio: Icl. bland n mixtura [60 b] a mixture, etc [60 c]

2 Blæd tail (of a seal) Than v. spl Blæd, e; f

Blæd-agende, glory having, glorious famous Beo 1012 K 2020 in agan 2 Cd-47 Th p 60, 14 see opposite print. Margin [58 d]

Blæd-dæg a prosperous day Cd 11 Th p 13, 9

Blætesnung a flaming Som v blætesnung

[59 a] [59 b] [59 c] [59 d]

[17 a 3]

Blēáte, destroyed, deadly deletus.- Beo p 210 K 5643

Bleata drinc potus lethalis Cod Ex 47.

2 [61 b] Blættian

Blēd-dæg fruit Grim H 496, v blæd dæg

3 [61 a] see fort opp 58

Blēd, e; f Grm I 642, 28

Slow, sluggish; Cod Verc i 406 Slowly; segniter 206 Thk 206, 17 Thorpe has a mistake Beo

underfed

A Copy of this page sent to the Printer Octr 6th 1837

Blód-egesa, an; m a bloody storm Cd 166, Th p 208, 3

Blísa A torch; fax Som v blyse, blase

Blód-fág blood stained Beo K 4116

Blis-gerefa incendiary Som blasere

Blód-hreów blood-cruel, bloody Beo K 3436

Bliccettan to shine fulgere Som

Blíd-tian v. margin

Blíd th. an Blíðe Beo gl. alle = Grimm 772, 34

Blíð-mód; cheerful minded kind, well disposed Cd 86 Th p 108, 2

Q 3

O 7 [62 a]

2, 3. He bletsode hig, *Mk.* 10, 16: *Mt.* 14, 19. He wæs gebletsod *he was consecrated, Chr.* 795, *Ing.* p. 81, 19. He wæs gebletsod to cinge, *note o.*
Bletsing boc *a blessing book, Som.*
Bletsung, e; *f.* A BLESSING; benedictio:—*Ps.* 3, 8: 36, 27.
c Blewað *blow,* v. blawan.
Blewan *to flourish,* v. blowan.
Blican, he blicð; *p.* blác, hi blicon; *pp.* blicen; *v. n.* [*Plat.* blekken: *Dut.* blinken: *Frs.* bleackjen *Japicx*: *Ger.* blicken: *Swed.* blicka: *Icel.* bika *splendeo*] *To shine, glitter, dazzle, amaze*; fulgere. Used only by poets:—Blicð þeos beorhte sunne *this bright sun glitters, Cd.* 38: 149: *Jdth.* 11: *Bt. R.* p. 183, 38, *Som.*
BLICE [*Dut.* blik *m*: *Ger.* blick *m*: *Dan.* blink *c.*] *The white, a whiteness, shining*; albor, candor:—Banes blice *the whiteness* or *shining of a bone, L. Ethelb.* 35, *W.* p. 5, 3.
Blicette *quivered, glittered, Cot.* 178, *Lye.*
Blicettung, blycytting; *f. A coruscation, shining*; coruscatio:—*Vps.* 76, 18, *Lye.*
BLIN, *g.* ne; blinnende, *g.* an; *f.* [Hence the old English word blin, used by *B. Jonson* as a noun, *thus* withouten blin *without ceasing, Sad. Shepherd, A.* 2, s. 6] A BLIN, *ceasing, rest, intermission*; intermissio:—Butan blinne, *or* butan blinnendan *without ceasing, Bd.* 5, 12.
BLIND; *adj.* [*Plat. Dut. Dan. Ger.* blind: *Frs. v.* blyn: *Al.* blind, blint: *Moes.* blinda, blinds: *Icel.* blindr: *Norse,* blinde] BLIND; cæcus:—Hig synt blinde and blindra latteowas, *Mt.* 15, 14: *Ps.* 145, 6. ¶ Blind slite *a blind or inward wound, Herb.* 4, 2. Blind netel *a dead nettle*; lanium, *Elf. gl.* 15. Blind þearm *blind intestine*; coecum intestinum. Blinda mann *a* [parasite]; palpo, *Elf. gr.* 36.
[Blin]dan *to blind,* v. blendian.
[Blin]dlice; *adv.* BLINDLY, *rash*[ly]; temere:—Hu blindlice [he]nige sprecað *how blindly* [ma]ny *speak, Ors.* 1, 10.
[Blind]nes, se; *f.* BLINDNESS; [cæc]itas:—*Mk.* 3, 5.
[Blinn]an, ablinnan, geblinnan; [ic b]linne, he blinð, we blin[nað]; *p.* blan, blonn, we blun[non]; *pp.* blunnen. *To* BLIN, *cease, leave off*; cessare:—[R]omane blunnun ricsian [on B]reotene *the Romans ceased* [to ru]le *in Britain, Bd.* 1, 11, [S. p.] 480, 13: *Ps.* 36, 8.

Blinnes *rest,* v. blin.
Blio *colour, beauty,* v. bleo.
Bliotan *sacrificed,* v. blotan.
Bliowende *flourishing, for* blowende, v. blowan.
a BLIS, blys, se; *f.* BLISS, *joy, gladness, exultation, pleasure*; lætitia:—Ne seo hehste blis nis on þam flæsclicum lustum *the highest bliss is not in the fleshly pleasures (lusis), Bt.* 33, 1: *Ps.* 29, 6. Blisse wana *a deficiency of bliss, Bt.* 24, 4: *Bd.* 4, 3: *Jud.* 16, 27: *Ps.* 31, 9.
Blisier *an incendiary,* v. blasere.
Blissian, geblissian; ic blissige, þu blissast, he blissað, we blissiað; *part.* blissiende, blissigende: *p.* blissode, we blissodon; *v. n.* 1. *To rejoice, exult, to be glad, merry*; gaudere. Blissiað mid me, *Lk.* 15, 9: *Mt.* 5, 12: 25, 23. Ge woldon geblissian, *Jn.* 5, 35. Hi blissedon, *Bd.* 5, 12, *S.* p. 628, 34: *Ps.* 31, 14. 2. *v. a. To make to rejoice, to exhilarate*; lætificare:—Ic eow geblissige, *Mt.* 11, 28: *Ps.* 20, 6: 42, 4: 45, 4. Exultare, *Ps.* 13, 11: 46, 1: 91, 4, v. bliðsian.
Blissung, blisung, e; *f. A triumphing, exultation*; exultatio:—*Ps.* 64, 13.
BLIDE; *adj.* [*Plat.* blied, bleide: *Dut. Frs.* blyde, bly: *Dan. Swed.* blid: *Icel.* blidr: *Ot.* blida] 1. *Joyful, merry, cheerful, pleasant,* BLITHE; lætus. 2. *Single, simple, kind*; simplex. 3. *Luxurious, effeminate, lascivious*; luxuriosus:—1. Beo bliðe þu goda þeow, *Mt.* 25, 21. Þa wæs Jethro bliðe, *Ex.* 18, 9. Hig bliðust wæron, *Jud.* 16, 27. 2. *C. Mt.* 6, 22: 10, 16: 21, 5: *Bd.* 3, 22. 3. Hi eac bliðran gewurdon *they also were more effeminate, Ors.* 2, 5.
f Bliðeheort, bliðheort *merry hearted, Cd.* 10.
Bliðeheortnys *merry heartedness, Som.*
Bliðelice; *comp.* or; *adv. Gladly, joyfully, willingly*; alacriter:—Hyne bliðelice onfengc, *Lk.* 19, 6. Bliðelicor *more gladly, Bd.* 5, 14: *Gen.* 46, 30.
Bliðnys, se; *f. Joyfulness, a leaping for joy, exultation*; exultatio:—*Ps.* 99, 2.
Bliðsian; *p.* bliðsode, we bliðsodon. *To be glad, blithe, merry*; lætari:—*Past.* 49, 5: 50, 2.
Bliðust *very merry,* v. bliðe.
BLO'D, es; *n.* [*Plat. Icel.* blood *n*: *Frs. v. Dut.* bloed *n*: *Ger.* blut *n*: *Al.* bluat, bluot, pluat, plut: *Moes.* bloth: *Dan. Norse,* blod] BLOOD; sanguis:—Þines broþor blod clypað up to

me, *Gen.* 4, 10. Mid his eame blode *with his uncle's blood, Ors.* 2, 2: *Ps.* 13, 6: 49, 14. ¶ Dead blod *clotted blood, Cot.* 163.
g Blód dolg, blod dolh *a blood wound, a wound* or *scar after bleeding, Som.*
Blód dryncas *blood sheddings, blood shed, Mann.*
Blódes flownys *a bloody issue, Som.*
Blód forlæten *let blood.*
Blód-geotan *to pour out* or *shed blood.*
Blódgeote *a shedding of blood,* v. blodgyt.
Blódgeotende *shedding blood, bloodthirsty.*
Blódgewod *blood stained, Som.*
Blódgita *A shedder of blood*; sanguinis effusor:—*Lps.* 5, 7.
Blódgyte, es; *m. A blood shedding, bloodshed*; sanguinis effusio:—Þær wæs se mæsta blodgyte *there was the greatest bloodshed, Ors.* 4, 2. Wæron þa mæstan blodgytas *there were the greatest blood sheddings, Ors.* 3, 9. Butan blodgyte *without bloodshed, Bd.* 1, 3. *A red cloud*; nubes sanguinea.
Blódhræcan *to reach* or *spit blood, Som.*
h Blód hræcea *spitting of blood, Som.*
Blódig; *adj.* [*Dut.* bloedig: *Frs. v.* bloedick] BLOODY; sanguineus:—Þa hwettað hyra blodigan teð *who whet their bloody teeth, L. Eccl., W.* p. 174, 9. ¶ Blodig utsiht *a dysentery, R.* 11.
Blódlæs *bloodless,* v. blodleas.
Blódlæsw *a blood letting.*
Blódlætan *to let blood.*
Blódlætere *a blood letter.*
Blódleás; *adj.* BLOODLESS; exanguis:—*Elf. gr.* 9, 28.
Blódmonað *November,* v. blotmonað.
Blód-read *blood-red.*
Blód-ryne *a running of blood,* v. blodyrnende.
Blód-seax, blód-sex *a blood-knife, a lancet,* v. æder-seax.
Blódseten *a stopping of blood, Som.*
Blódsiht, blodutsyð *a flowing of blood.*
Blód-wanian *to diminish blood.*
Blódwite *Blood*; sanguis:—*Lps.* 15, 4, *Lye.*
Blód-wyrt *Bloodwort, knotgrass*; polygonum.
Blódyrnende *a running of blood.*
Bloedsan *to bless,* v. bletsian.
Bloestbælg *bellows,* v. blast-belg.
Bloma, an [*Plat.* blome *f*: *Dut.* bloem *f*: *Ger.* blume: *Swed.* blomma: *Icel.* blómi *m.* blom *n.* The Germans, in mineralogy, use the expression *eisen* or *eisern blume*] *Metal, a mass,*

⊙1 [57 e]

2 Blacern, es; n a candlestick ○ [57 f]

○7

1 Bismorian to mock, insult, ill treat, v Th. Lu bysmerian bismrian

2 Bisnian to give example Th. Lu exemplum praebere Som v bysnian

8

3 Bistalcian to stalk, proceed, march Th. Lu v. Stalcan

Biswican to deceive Ben v beswican ○3 [58 a]

4 5
5.4 Bisy busy Th. Apol sup. bisig

3 Biwerian to defend Th. An v bewerian

2 Blac-hleor pale-faced, fair Th. An Som

(6,7) 6 swa swa bita sicut buccellas Ps 147.6
7 Anlige bita singularis ferus Ps 79,14

○9 [56 h]

3 Blæd fruit branch Th. An

4 Blæd, es; m glory, prosperity, life, blast Th. An Beo gl.

4 Bite, es; m A bite; morsus Beo K 4115

○1 Biwyrd a byword Som v biword

○3 Blæd [58 b Ke]

7 10 Biter-l 2 Moes ○5 [57 d]
baitr: Icel bitr

merlicostan eard *in the most unpleasant province, Ors.* 3, 11.
Bismernes, e; *f. A polluting;* pollutio, *Som.*
Bismerung *blasphemy*, v. bysmerung.
Bismiriende *Deriding;* insultans:—*Dial.* 2, 1.
Bismor *a disgrace*, v. bismer.
Bismorful; *adj. Dreadful;* horrendus, *Lye.*
Bismorlic *disgraceful*, v. bismerlic.
Bismorlice; *adv. Disgracefully, indecently;* probrose:—Bismorlice plegan *to play immodestly, Elf. Can.* 35.
Bysmrian *to mock*, v. bysmerian.
Bysn *an example*, v. bysn.
Bysnung, gebysnung, e; *f. An example;* exemplum:—*Elf. T.* p. 5, 15.
Bigspell *a fable*, v. bigspell.
Bigspell *a parable*, v. bigspell.
Bissexte, bises *A leap year;* bissextus:—*Menol.* 61: *Bd.* 5, 3, *S.* p. 648, 19.
Bist *art, shall be;* es, eris:—*Bd.* 5, 19, v. beon.
Bistemed *steaming*, v. bestemed.
Biswe*þan* *to swathe*, v. besuedan.
Biswic *deceit*, v. beswic.
Biswic-falle *a pitfall*, v. feall, *Som.*
Biswic *deceit*, v. beswic.
Biswicol, beswicul; *adj. Deceitful;* dolosus:—*L. Eccl., W.* p. 6, 29.
Bitt *asks*, v. biddan.
Bite, bite, an; *m.* [*Plat.* bet, *m:* ... *s. v.* byt: *Dut.* beet *m: Heb.* ... pt *a part, bit*] 1. A BIT, *morsel, piece, fragment, a* BITE; *morsum.* 2. *Any thing that bites, an animal;* ferus:—1. ...ter þam bitan, *Jn.* 13, 27: ... 147, 6. Mid bitum *with ...s, Ors.* 1, 7. Banes bite *a ... or fragment of bone, L. ...elb.* 36, *W.* p. 5, 5. Cancer... , þat is bite *a cancer, that biting disease, Herb.* 44. ...*Ps.* 79, 14.
...ic bíte, he bít; *part.* bi...e; *p.* bát, hi biton; *pp.* ...n [*Plat.* bieten: *Dut.* by... *Swed. Icel.* bita: *Norse,* ...] *To* BITE; mordere:—... n hyne lys *lice bit him.* ... fræclice *bit fiercely, Gr.* 1, 4.
...*bit*, v. bita.
...tela, betl; *m.* A BEETLE; ...:—Þa blacan betlas *the beetles, Cot.* 141, *v. l.*
... *biting*, v. bitan.
... *adj.* [*Plat. Dut. Dan. Ger.* bitter: *Moes.* baitrs] ...R, *sharp, horrid;* ama... *Ps.* 63, 3, v. aterlic.
..., abiterian; *p.* de; *pp.* od, gebitered. *To make bitter, sharp;* acerbare:—*Past.* 54, 5. Sealdon gebiterod win, *Mk.* 15, 23.
Biterlice, bittyrlice; *comp.* or; *adv.* BITTERLY; amare:—He weop biterlice, *Mt.* 26, 75: *Bd.* 4, 25, *S.* p. 600, 29.
Biternys, bitternes, se; *f.* BITTERNESS; amaritudo:—Genemned Mara, þat ys biternys, *Ex.* 15, 23.
Bið *is, shall be;* est, erit, v. beon.
Bitl *a mallet*, v. bytl.
Bitmælum, *piecemeal, by bits*, v. mæl.
Bitol *a bridle, Ps.* 31, 12, v. bæte.
Bitolden; *part.* 1. *Estimated, reckoned, numbered;* recensitus. Wuldre bitolden, *Cod. Ex.* 64, b. 13, *from* tellan *to reckon.* 2. Bitolden *cleansed;* purgatus:—Torne bitolden *purified from anger, Cod. Ex.* 15, b. 11: 64, a. 1, *from* teallan *to cleanse, Mann.*
Bitst *prayest*, v. biddan.
Bitt *What affords a bite, food;* herbitum:—*R.* 60, *Lye.*
Bitt *asks*, v. biddan.
Bitte *A bottle, bouget;* uter, v. byt.
Bitternes *bitterness*, v. biternys.
Bitterlice *bitterly*, v. biterlice.
Bituihu *A foul tetter* or *scab running over the face;* mentagra, *Som.*
Biuundun *bound, for* bewundon, v. bewindan.
Biwægan; *p.* de; *v. a. To disappoint;* frustrari:—*Ps.* 131, 11, *Lye.*
Biwærlan *to pass by*, v. wærlan.
Biwered *forbidden*, v. werdan.
Biwist [be, wist *food*] *Food, provision;* commeatus:—Þat is heora biwist *that is their provision, Bt.* 17: *L. Can. Edg.* 3.
Biwitigan *to preside*, v. bewitan.
Biwoedded *wedded*, v. beweddian.
Biword, biwyrd, es; *n.* [be *by*, word *a word*] A BYEWORD, *proverb;* proverbium:—*Cot.* 157.
Biwritan [be *by*, writan *to write*] *To write after, by,* or *out of, to copy;* postscribere, *Pref. in Past. Lye.*
Bixen; *adj. Belonging to box,* BOXEN; bucceus:—*R.* 26, v. box.
BLA'c, blæc, bleac; *def.* se blaca; *adj.* [*Plat.* blak *ink: Swed.* black, blek *bleak: Dan.* blek *ink.* The word generally used in Saxon and other Gothic tongues for *black* is swart, but blac is sometimes found, v. blæc *ink*] BLACK, *dark, opaque, dusky, pale, pallid;* niger, pallidus:—Ne might ænne locc gedon hwitne oððe blacne, *Mt.* 5, 36. He hæfde blæc feax *he had black hair, Bd.* 2, 16. Se mona mid his blacan leohte *the moon with her pale light, Bt.* 4.
Blacberian A BLACKBERRY, *mulberry;* vaccinium:—*R.* 47.
Blacern, blæcern, blecernæ, e; *n.* [*Plat. Dut.* blaker, blic *bright, light,* ærn *a place*] *A candlestick, lantern, light, candle, lamp;* lucerna:—Bærnað eower blacern *light your candle, Bd.* 4, 8: *Ps.* 17, 30: *Elf. gl.* 19.
Blacesnung *Ardent desire;* flagrantia:—*Cot.* 87, *Ben.*
Blac-hrem *a raven*, v. hrem.
Blacian, ablacian *To* BLACKEN, *grow black, dark, pale;* pallere:—*Elf. gr.* 26, 35.
Blacþa *the leprosy*, v. blæcþa.
Blacung; *f. Paleness, wanness;* pallor:—*Lps.* 67, 14.
Blad *a branch*, v. blæd.
Blæc [*Plat.* blak *n.* This word properly signifies *black ink* only; but, in low German, they say, rood and grön blak *red and green ink: Dut. Kil.* black: *Al.* black: *Dan.* blæc *n: Swed.* bläck *n: Icel.* blek] *Ink;* atramentum:—Þat hi habba blæc and boc fel *that they have ink and parchment, L. Can. Edg.* 3.
Blæcan, blæcean, ablæcan [*Dut.* bleeken: *Swed.* bleka] *To* BLEACH, *to fade;* pallidum colorem inducere:—Ne mæg ne sunne blæcan *can be bleached by no sun, Bd.* 1, 1, *S.* p. 473, 20. n. 20.
Blæcbergen *A blackberry;* vaccinium, *Lye.*
Blæce *Paleness;* pallor, *Som.*
Blæcern *a candle, Bd.* 4, 8, v. blacern. [blæc *ink,* ærn *a place*] *A place for ink, an inkhorn.*
Blæc-gym *a black fossil, called jet, Bd.* 1, 1.
Blæco *paleness, Cot.* 157, *leprosy*, v. blacung, blæcþa.
Blæc-teru *black-tar, tar, naphtha, a sort of bituminous fluid, Som.*
Blæcþa, blæcðrust *Leprosy;* vitiligo:—*Cot.* 221.
BLÆD, bled; *g.* es; *d.* e; *pl. nom. ac.* a; *d.* um [*Frs. v.* bled: *Plat. Swed. Dan. Dut. Icel.* blad *n. a leaf: Ger.* blatt *n. a leaf: Al.* blæd *fruit: Slav.* plot blod *fruit*] 1. A BLADE, *that which springs forth,* as *a shoot, branch, leaf, product, fruit, corn;* germen, v. brord. 2. *A blast, blowing, breath, spirit, life, mind;* spiritus. 3. *Fruit, enjoyment, faculty, gift, reward, benefit, honour,*

glory; fruitio:—1. Bleda wyrta, *Ps.* 36, 2. Se sumor gearwað bleda *the summer prepares shoots, Bt.* 39, 13. On þæs beames bledum *on the branches of the tree, Cd.* 200. Ælc twig þe blæda ne byrð, *Jn.* 15, 2. Hærfest bryngð ripa bleda *harvest brings ripe fruit, Bt.* 39, 13: 34, 10. Balsames blæd *fruit of balsam, Cot.* 48. 2. Mare blæd windes *a greater blast of wind, Bd.* 4, 3. Gastes blæd *inspiration;* spiritûs flatus, *Cd.* 224. His blæd forleosan *to lose his life, Fr. Jud. Thw.* p. 22, 16. On his blæde geseah *considered in his mind, Cd.* 205. 3. Tires blæd *victory's reward, Cod. Ex.* 25, b. 11. Godes þegna blæd *God's servants' reward, Cod. Ex.* 18, a. 17. Gastes bled *the spirit's gift, Cd.* 227. Þæs blædes, *Cod. Ex.* 38, b. 16. Hi Judea blæd forbræcon billa ecgum *they destroyed the Jews' glory with the edge of swords, Cd.* 210. Wæs heora blæd micel *was their glory great, Cd.* 1.

Blæd *a cup,* v. bledu.

Blæddre *a bladder,* v. blædr.

Blæd horn *a blast horn, a trumpet.*

BLÆDR, blædra, bleddra; *pl.* u, an [*Plat.* bladder *f: Dut.* blader *Ger.* blatter *f: Al.* blater: *Swed.* bläddra: *Icel.* bladra *f.*] A BLADDER, *a pustule, blister;* vesica:—Eall folc wæs on blædran *all people were in blisters, Ors.* 1, 7. ¶ Blædran-adl, -sare, -wærce *a disease or pain in the bladder;* vesicæ dolor.

Blæge A BLAY, *bleak or fresh-water sprat;* gobio:—*R.* 101.

Blæ-hæwen, blæhwen; *adj.* [bleo *blue,* hæwen *hued*] *Of a blue hue, bluish, violet* or *purple colour;* cæruleus:—*Lev.* 8, 7.

Blæsan *To blow;* flare, *Lye.*

Blæse *a blaze,* v. blase.

Blæsere *a burner,* v. blasere.

BLÆST [*Plat.* blas, blast: *Frs. v. Ger* blast *m: Dan.* blaest *c.*] A BLAST, *blasting, burning;* flatus, adustio:—Bæð-weges blæst *a sea blast* or *breeze, Cd.* 158. Fyres blæst *a fire's burning, Cod. Ex.* 22, a. 16.

Blæstan *To puff;* insufflare, *Som.*

Blæstbelg *bellows,* v. blastbelg.

Blæt *A bleating, a bleat like a sheep;* balatus, *Som.*

Blætan; *v. n.* [*Frs. v.* blæte] To BLEAT; balare:—Scæp blæt *a sheep bleats, Elf. gr.* 24, 9.

Blætesnung, blætesung, e; *f. A flaming, blazing, sparkling;* flagrantia:—*Ps.* 76, 18.

Blæwen *Light blue;* perseus:—*R.* 80, *Ben.*

Blæwð *blows, Bt. Rawl.* p. 156, v. blawan.

Blan *ceased,* v. blinnan.

Bland [*Norse,* blanda] *A mixture, confusion;* mixtio:—*Hicks.* vol. i. p. 120, 55. Cantilenæ mixtura, *Mann.*

Blanden-feax *yellow haired,* v. blonden-feax.

BLASE, blæse, blysa [*Dut.* blaas] *Any thing that makes a* BLAZE, *a torch, manifestation;* fax:—*Jn.* 18, 3.

Blasere, blisier, es; *m. An incendiary, a burner;* incendiarius:—Be þam blaserum *concerning the incendiaries, L. In.* 77. Þa blisieras *incendiaries, L. Athel.* 6.

Blast-belg [*Dut.* blaasbalg *m: Ger.* blasebalg *m: Dan.* blæsebælg *c.*] *A blast bag, bellows;* follis:—*Cot.* 86.

BLAT; *sup.* blatast; *adj.* [*Plat. Ger.* platt: *Dut.* plat] *Broad;* latus:—Blatast benna *broadest of wounds, Cod. Ex.* 19, a. 12.

Blate; *adv. Widely, every where;* late:—*Bt. Rawl.* p. 159, 176.

Blatende *Widening, swelling;* expandens, *Mann.*

BLAWAN, ablawan, geblawan; ic blawe, he blæwð; *p.* bleow, gebleow, hi bleowon; *pp.* blawen. To BLOW, *breathe,* flare:—Ge geseoð suðan blawan, *Lk.* 12, 55. Þa bleow he on hi, *Jn.* 20, 22. Bleowun windas, *Mt.* 7, 25, 27. Blewað *blow ye, Ps.* 80, 3. Ne blawe man byman, *Mt.* 6, 2. Blowiað, *Ps.* 147, 7. Blawen is on smiððan *is blown on a forge, Prov.* 27.

Blawennys, se; *f. A blowing,* or *puffing up, a windy swelling;* inflatio, *Som.*

Blawer *A blower;* conflator:—*Past.* 37, 3.

Blawung, ablawung, e; *f. A blowing;* flatus:—*Jud.* 7, 16.

Bleac, bleaca *black, bleak,* v. blac.

Bleað, bleaþe *blithe,* v bliþe.

Blec *black,* v. blac.

Blecernæ *a candle,* v. blacern.

Blecingaeg *Bleckingen,* a province in the south of Sweden, *Ingram's Ang.-Sax. Lect.* p. 64, 2: *Ors.* 1, 1, *Bar.* p. 26, 6.

Blecte *glittered,* v. blican.

Bled, bleda *a bowl,* v. bledu.

Bled *fruit, a branch, herb,* v. blæd.

BLEDAN [*Plat.* bloden: *Dut.* bloeden: *Ger.* bluten: *Dan.* blöde: *Swed.* blöda] To BLEED, *draw blood;* phlebotomare:—Se bledenda fic *the bleeding fig* or *disease, Wanley's Cat.* p. 305, 4: *L. M.* 4, 145, b. *Lye.*

Bleddra *a bladder,* v. blædr.

Bledhorn *a trumpet,* v. blædhorn.

Bledsian; *pp.* bledsod *to bless,* v. bletsian.

Bledsung *a blessing, Ben.*

Bledu, blæd *A bowl, viol, cup, goblet;* patera:—*Elf. gl.* 21.

BLEGEN [*Plat.* bleien *f: Dut.* blein *f: Dan.* blegne] A BLAIN, *blister, bile* or *ulcer;* pustula:—On þa blacan blegene *over the black bile, Wan. Cat.* p. 304, 52: p. 305, 11: *L. M.* 1, 58, v. poc.

BLENDAN; *p.* blonde [*Plat.* blendern: *Dan.* blende: *Icel.* blanda] To BLEND, *mix, mingle;* miscere, *Som.*

Blendian, he blent; *pp.* geblend; *v. a.* To BLIND; cæcare:—Se dæg blent hiora eagan *the day blinds their eyes, Bt.* 38, 5, v. ablendan.

BLEO, bleoh, blio, bleow, es, s. *A colour, hue,* BLEE, *complexion, beauty;* color:—Hwites bleos swa cristalla, *Num.* 11, 7. Seolocenra hrægla mid mistlicum bleowum *of silken garments of* [*with*] *various colours,* [*blooms*], *Bt.* 15. ¶ Anes bleos *of one colour, R.* 79. Mislices bleos *of a different* or *mixed colour, Elf. gl.* 11. Mislic bleo *a different hue, R.* 79.

Bleo *Blue* or *azure colour;* coeruleus, *Som.*

Bleo-craft BLEE CRAFT, *the art of embroidering, Som.*

Bleofæstnys, se; *f. That which gives pleasure from its colour, pleasure, delight;* deliciæ, jucunditas:—*Ps.* 138, 10.

Bleofag, bleofah [bleo *a colour;* fag *changeable*] *Changing colour, varying hue;* versicolor:—*Cot.* 115: *Somn.* 33.

Bleoh *a colour,* v. bleo.

Bleoread, bleoreod; *adj.* [*Plat.* blaurood: *Dut.* blaauwrood: *Ger.* blaurod: *Dan.* blaaröd] BLUE RED, *purple, myrtle coloured;* cæruleo-ruber:—*Cot.* 135, v. musfealu.

Bleo-stæning *coloured stone-work* or *pavement, Mosaic work, Cot.* 131.

Bleoton *sacrificed,* v. blotan.

Bleow *a colour,* v. bleo.

Bleow *blew,* flabat; hi bleowun *they blew,* flabant, *p. of* blawan.

Blere. 1. *A gem, a kind of marble;* onyx. 2. *Bald;* calvus:—1. *Cot.* 28. 2. *Som.*

Bletcæd *blessed, consecrated,* v. bletsian.

BLETSIAN, gebletsian; ic bletsige, gebletsige; *part.* bletsigende; *p.* bletsode, gebletsode; *pp.* gebletsod; *v. a.* To BLESS, *consecrate;* benedicere:—Ic hig gebletsige and of hire ic þe forgife sunu þone ic wylle bletsian, *Gen.* 17, 16:

Blanca See main

Blanca (blonca) an; m [Old Ger. Mong, plan-chaz a pale horse]

A horse; equus: On blancum on horses. Beo. 67 K 1705.

Bland [Moes blands mixtio: Icel. blandn mixtura [60b] a mixture, etc [60c]

Bleo

Blæd tail (of a seal.) Than v. Spl Blæd, e; f

glory having, glorious agende, famosus K 2020 in again

Blæd-dæg a prosperous day Cd 11 Th p 13,9

2 Cd-47 Th [60, 14]

Margin [58d]

Blatesnung a flaming Som v blatesneeng

[59a]

[59b]

[59c]

[17a 3]

Bleáte, destroyed, deadly deletus. - Beo p 210 K 5643

Bleata drinc potus lethalis Cod Ex 47.

2 [61b] Blessian

sluggish d Vect i 406 vol I

Blæd-dæg fruit Gen-H 490, v blæd-dæg

3 [61a] see foot of p 58

sly; segniter 206, 17 Thorpe has mistake Beo

Bléd, e; f Gen-I 642,28

A Copy of this page sent to the Printer Octr 6th. 1837

C

~~Blód-egesa, an; m a bloody storm Cd 166, Th p 208, 3~~

~~Blísa A torch; fax Som v blysa, blase~~

~~Blódfág blood stained Beo K 4116~~

~~Blis gerepan incendary ... Lindisf ... elusere~~

~~Blód-hreów blood-cruel, bloody Beo K 3436~~

~~Blicettan to shine fulgere Som~~

~~Blid-tian v. margin~~

C 1 Blid Th. an Blidel ~~...~~ Beo gl. ... = Grmtt 772, 34

Q 3

2 Blidemód, kind, cheerful minded ~~friend~~ well disposed ~~Th. An~~: Cd 86 Th p 108, 2

O 7 [62 a]

2, 3. He bletsode hig, *Mk.* 10, 16: *Mt.* 14, 19. He wæs gebletsod *he was consecrated, Chr.* 795, *Ing.* p. 81, 19. He wæs gebletsod to cinge, *note o.*

Bletsing boc *a blessing book, Som.*

Bletsung, e; *f.* A BLESSING; benedictio:—*Ps.* 3, 8: 36, 27.

Blewað *blow*, v. blawan.

Blewan *to flourish*, v. blowan.

Blican, he blicð; *p.* blác, hi blicon; *pp.* blicen; *v. n.* [*Plat.* blekken: *Dut.* blinken: *Frs.* bleackjen *Japicx*: *Ger.* blicken: *Swed.* blicka: *Icel.* bika *splendeo*] *To shine, glitter, dazzle, amaze;* fulgere. Used only by poets:—Blicð þeos beorhte sunne *this bright sun glitters, Cd.* 38: 149: *Jdth.* 11: *Bt. R.* p. 183, 38, *Som.*

lice [*Dut.* blik *m*: *Ger.* blick *m*: *Dan.* blink *c.*] *The white, a whiteness, shining;* albor, candor:—Banes blice *the whiteness* or *shining of a bone, L. Ethelb.* 35, *W.* p. 5, 3.

icette *quivered, glittered, Cot.* 178, *Lye.*

icettung, blycytting; *f. A coruscation, shining;* coruscatio:—*Vps.* 76, 18, *Lye.*

in, *g.* ne; blinnende, *g.* an; [Hence the old English word blin, used by *B. Jonson* as a noun, *thus* withouten blin *without ceasing, Sad. Shepherd, A.* 2, s. 6] A BLIN, *ceasing, rest, intermission;* intermissio:—Butan blinne, *or* bu blinnendan *without ceasing, Bd.* 5, 12.

nd; *adj.* [*Plat. Dut. Dan.* r. blind: *Frs. v.* blyn: *Al.* ind, blint: *Moes.* bliuda, nds: *Icel.* blindr: *Norse,* nde] BLIND; cæcus:—g synt blinde and blindra teowas, *Mt.* 15, 14: *Ps.* 5, 6. ¶ Blind slite *a blind inward wound, Herb.* 4, 2. nd netel *a dead nettle;* lam, *Elf. gl.* 15. Blind þe *blind intestine;* coecum stinum. Blinda mann *a* site; palpo, *Elf. gr.* 36. an *to blind*, v. blendian. ice; *adv.* BLINDLY, *rash*temere:—Hu blindlice ige sprecað *how blindly* y *speak, Ors.* 1, 10. es, se; *f.* BLINDNESS; tas:—*Mk.* 3, 5. n, ablinnan, geblinnan inne, he blinð, we blin *p.* blan, blonn, we blun *pp.* blunnen. *To* BLIN, *cease, leave off;* cessare: mane blunnun ricsian reotene *the Romans ceased* le *in Britain, Bd.* 1, 11, 480, 13: *Ps.* 36, 8.

Blinnes *rest*, v. blin.

Blio *colour, beauty*, v. bleo.

Bliotan *sacrificed*, v. blotan.

Bliowende *flourishing, for* blowende, v. blowan.

e BLIS, blys, se; *f.* BLISS, *joy, gladness, exultation, pleasure;* lætitia:—Ne seo hehste blis nis on þam flæsclicum lustum *the highest bliss is not in the fleshly pleasures (lusis), Bt.* 33, 1: *Ps.* 29, 6. Blisse wana *a deficiency of bliss, Bt.* 24, 4: *Bd.* 4, 3: *Jud.* 16, 27: *Ps.* 31, 9.

Blisier *an incendiary*, v. blasere.

Blissian, geblissian; ic blissige, þu blissast, he blissað, we blissiað; *part.* blissiende, blissigende: *p.* blissode, we blissodon; *v. n.* 1. *To rejoice, exult, to be glad, merry;* gaudere. Blissiað mid me, *Lk.* 15, 9: *Mt.* 5, 12: 25, 23. Ge woldon geblissian, *Jn.* 5, 35. Hi blissedon, *Bd.* 5, 12, *S.* p. 628, 34: *Ps.* 31, 14. 2. *v. a. To make to rejoice, to exhilarate;* lætificare:—Ic eow geblissige, *Mt.* 11, 28: *Ps.* 20, 6: 42, 4: 45, 4. Exultare, *Ps.* 13, 11: 46, 1: 91, 4, v. bliðsian.

Blissung, blisung, e; *f. A triumphing, exultation;* exultatio:—*Ps.* 64, 13.

BLIDE; *adj.* [*Plat.* blied, bleide: *Dut. Frs.* blyde, bly: *Dan. Swed.* blid: *Icel.* blidr: *Ott.* blida] 1. *Joyful, merry, cheerful, pleasant,* BLITHE; lætus. 2. *Single, simple, kind;* simplex. 3. *Luxurious, effeminate, lascivious;* luxuriosus:—1. Beo bliðe þu goda þeow, *Mt.* 25, 21. Þa wæs Jethro bliðe, *Ex.* 18, 9. Hig bliðust wæron, *Jud.* 16, 27. 2. *C. Mt.* 6, 22: 10, 16: 21, 5: *Bd.* 3, 22. 3. Hi eac bliðran gewurdon *they also were more effeminate, Ors.* 2, 5.

f Bliðeheort, bliðheort *merry hearted, Cd.* 10.

Bliðeheortnys *merry heartedness, Som.*

Bliðelice; *comp.* or; *adv. Gladly, joyfully, willingly;* alacriter:—Hyne bliðelice onfengc, *Lk.* 19, 6. Bliðelicor *more gladly, Bd.* 5, 14: *Gen.* 46, 30.

Bliðnys, se; *f. Joyfulness, a leaping for joy, exultation;* exultatio:—*Ps.* 99, 2.

Bliðsian; *p.* bliðsode, we bliðsodon. *To be glad, blithe, merry;* lætari:—*Past.* 49, 5: 50, 2.

Bliðust *very merry*, v. bliðe.

BLO'D, es; *n.* [*Plat. Icel.* blood *n*: *Frs. v. Dut.* bloed *n*: *Ger.* blut *n*: *Al.* bluat, bluot, pluat, plut: *Moes.* bloth: *Dan. Norse,* blod] BLOOD; sanguis:—Þines broþor blod clypað up to me, *Gen.* 4, 10. Mid his eame blode *with his uncle's blood, Ors.* 2, 2: *Ps.* 13, 6: 49, 14. ¶ Dead blod *clotted blood, Cot.* 163.

g Blód dolg, blod dolh *a blood wound, a wound* or *scar after bleeding, Som.*

Blód dryncas *blood sheddings, blood shed, Mann.*

Blódes flownys *a bloody issue, Som.*

Blód forlæten *let blood.*

Blód-geotan *to pour out* or *shed blood.*

Blódgeote *a shedding of blood*, v. blodgyt.

Blódgeotende *shedding blood, bloodthirsty.*

Blódgewod *blood stained, Som.*

Blódgita *A shedder of blood;* sanguinis effusor:—*Lps.* 5, 7.

Blódgyte, es; *m. A blood shedding, bloodshed;* sanguinis effusio:—Þær wæs se mæsta blodgyte *there was the greatest bloodshed, Ors.* 4, 2. Wæron þa mæstan blodgytas *there were the greatest blood sheddings, Ors.* 3, 9. Butan blodgyte *without bloodshed, Bd.* 1, 3. *A red cloud;* nubes sanguinea.

Blódhræcan *to reach* or *spit blood, Som.*

h Blód hræcea *a spitting of blood, Som.*

Blódig; *adj.* [*Dut.* bloedig: *Frs. v.* bloedick] BLOODY; sanguineus:—Þa hwettað hyra blodigan teð *who whet their bloody teeth, L. Eccl., W.* p. 174, 9. ¶ Blodig utsiht *a dysentery, R.* 11.

Blódlæs *bloodless*, v. blodleas.

Blódlæsw *a blood letting.*

Blódlætan *to let blood.*

Blódlætere *a blood letter.*

Blódleás; *adj.* BLOODLESS; exanguis:—*Elf. gr.* 9, 28.

Blódmonað *November*, v. blotmonað.

Blód-read *blood-red.*

Blód-ryne *a running of blood*, v. blodyrnende.

Blód-seax, blód-sex *a blood-knife, a lancet*, v. æder-seax.

Blódseten *a stopping of blood, Som.*

Blódsiht, blodutsyð *a flowing of blood.*

Blód-wanian *to diminish blood.*

Blódwite *Blood;* sanguis:—*Lps.* 15, 4, *Lye.*

Blód-wyrt *Bloodwort, knotgrass;* polygonum.

i Blódyrnende *a running of blood.*

Bloedsan *to bless*, v. bletsian.

Bloesthælg *bellows*, v. blast-belg.

Bloma, an [*Plat.* blome *f*: *Dut.* bloem *f*: *Ger.* blume: *Swed.* blomma: *Icel.* blómi *m.* blom *n.* The Germans, in mineralogy, use the expression *eisen* or *eisern blume*] *Metal, a mass, lump;* metallum, massa:—*Cot.* 135. Bloma oððe dah, (*Dut.* bloem *a flower* or *flour, meal*), *Bloom, Elf. gl.* p. 25. Isenes bloman *a lump* or *wedge of iron, Som.*

Blon, blonn *Ceased;* cessavit, v. blinnan.

Blonde *mingled*, v. blendan.

Blonden *Dyed, coloured;* tinctus, *Som.*

Blonden-feax [*Dut.* blond-haar, *light* or *flaxen hair: Dan.* guulagtig-haar *yellowish hair:* blandet haar *mixed hair.* The German blond is *light, clear,* in reference to the colour of the face or hair, in opposition to brown; "Blonde *d. i.* hell-braune gelbliche haare. Die blonde Ceres, wegen der gelblichen ähren" *Blond, that is, light brown yellowish hair. The yellow Ceres, from the yellowish ears; Adelung*] *Yellow haired, golden haired;* flavicomus:—*Cd.* 107. Beorn blonden-feax *the fair haired youth, Chr.* 938, *Ing.* p. 144, 5. The lad with flaxen hair, *Mr. Turner. Mr. Price* translates it, Bairn blended-haired, and adds "blonden feax is a phrase which, in Anglo-Saxon poetry, is only applied to the advanced in life, and is used to denote that mixture of colour which the hair assumes on approaching or increasing senility," *Walton's Poetry,* vol. i. p. xcvi. n. 20.

BLOSMA, blóstma, blosa, an [*Frs. v.* bloeisem: *Dut.* bloei, bloesem *m: Kil.* blosem, bloemsel: *Ger.* blume *f.*] A BLOSSOM, *bloom, flower;* flos:—Ic geseah blosman. Æfter þam blosmum, *Gen.* 40, 10. Swa swa blosma aceras swa blewð, *Ps.* 102, 14: *Bt.* 5, 2. Blostman, *Cot.* 124.

Blosmbær, blosmbærende, blostmberende *blossom bearing.*

Blosmian *to blossom,* v. blostmian.

Blostmbærende *blossom bearing,* v. blosmbær.

Blostmian *To* BLOSSOM, *blow;* efflorere:—*Bd.* 4, 3, v. growan.

BLOT, blotung, geblot *A sacrifice;* sacrificium:—He to blote gedyde *he gave for a sacrifice, Ors.* 1, 8: *Bar.* p. 43, 14: 5, 2. Swilc geblot *such a sacrifice, Bar.* p. 43, 18. He his agene sunu to blot acweald *he killed his own son for a sacrifice, Som.* v. offrung.

Blótan, ablotan, geblotan: ic blote, he blét; *p.* bleot, we bleoton; *pp.* blóten; *v. a.* [*Moes.* blotan: *Norse,* blota] *To sacrifice, to kill for a sacrifice;* immolare:—Hi blotan meahtan *they might sacrifice, Ors.* 2, 2. Bliotan, *Ors. title,* 4, 4, p. 5, and blotton, 4, 4: *Bar.* p. 138, 20, *for* bleoton.

Blot-hræcung *a spitting of blood, Lye.*

Blotmonað, es; *m.* [blot *a sacrifice,* monað *month*] *November,* the month of sacrifice, so called because at this season the heathen Saxons made a provision for winter, and offered in sacrifice many of the animals they then killed. In an account of the Saxon months, it is thus described. Se monað is nemned on Leden Novembres, and on ure geþeode blotmonað, forþon ure yldran þa hi hæþene wæron, on þam monðe hy bleoton á, þat is þæt hi betæhton and benemdon hyra deofolgyldum þa neat þa þe hi woldon syllan, *Hickes's Thes.* vol. i. p. 219, v. 376.

Blotsm *a blossom,* v. blosma.

Blotsm bær, blotsmberende *blossom bearing, Som.*

Blotsmian *To blossom;* florere:—*Bd.* 4, 3, v. blowan.

Blotspiung, e; *f.* [blod *blood,* spiwing *spewing*] *A throwing up of blood;* hæmoptois:—*R.* 10.

Blotung *a sacrifice,* v. blot.

BLOWAN, geblowan, blewan; ic blowe, we blowað; *p.* blowede; *v. n.* [*Plat.* blöen: *Dut. Frs.* bloeyen: *Ger.* blühen: *Ot.* bluen, blyen] *To* BLOW, *flourish, bloom, blossom;* florere:—Hi blowað swa swa hig eorðan, *Ps.* 71, 16: 91, 13. Hio grewð and blewð *it grows and blossoms, Bt.* 33, 4: *Ps.* 27, 10: 102, 14. Blowan *to blossom,* is sometimes used in Saxon instead of blawan *to blow;* and thus, blowan was occasionally used by the Saxons as the present English, *to blow.* We say *to blow as the wind,* and *to blow* or *blossom as a flower,* v. blawan.

Blowiað *shall blow;* flabit, v. blawan.

Blycyttind *a glittering, for* blycyttung, v. blicettung.

Blydnys *Joyfulness;* exultatio, *Ben.*

Blys *joy,* v. blis.

Blysa *a torch.* Blysige *a little torch,* v. blase.

Bóc, boc-treow [*Plat.* bök, book *f: Dut.* beuke *f: Ger.* buche *f. Al.* buache: *Dan. Norse,* boeg c.] *A beech-tree, a tree bearing acorns,* or *mast, like beech;* fagus;—*R.* 45: æsculus, *Cot.* 165.

Bóc; *g. d. ac.* béc, bóc; *pl. nom. ac.* béc; *g.* bóca; *dat.* bócum; *f.* [*Plat.* book *n: Frs. Dut.* boek *n: Ger.* buch *n: Moes. Swed. Icel.* bok *f: Dan. Norse,* bog c. All these words have evidently the same origin. *Wormius, Saxo, Junius, &c.* suppose that as boc denotes *a beech-tree,* as well as *a book,* in the latter case it was used in reference to the material from which the Northern nations first made their books. *Wormius* infers, that pieces of wood, cut from the beech-tree, were the ancient Northern books, *Lit. Run.* p. 6. *Saxo-Grammaticus* states, that Fengo's ambassadors took with them letters engraved in wood, [literas ligno insculptas] because that was formerly a celebrated material to write upon, *Lib.* iii. p. 52: *Turner's Hist. Ap.* b. ii. ch. 4, n. 25, vol. i. p. 238. Thus the *Lat.* liber, and *Greek* βιβλος *a book,* took their origin from the materials of which books were made. *Liber* originally signified the inner bark of a tree, and βιβλος or βυβλος, *an Egyptian plant,* [Cyperus papyrus, *Lin.*] which, when divided into lamina and formed into sheets to write upon, was called παπυρος, hence papyrus *paper. Martinius, Stiernhielmius, Wachter, Adelung, &c.* rather derive buch, boc &c. from bügen *to bend* or *fold in plaits;* referring to the folded leaves of the parchment. Thus distinguishing these books from their folds, as the ancient *volumina* were denominated from being in rolls, or rolled in the form of cylinders. At the Council of Toledo, in the eighth Century, a book is denominated *complicamentum,* that which is folded. In still earlier times, even one fold of parchment was denominated a book, and *Ker.* calls a letter puah, and *Not.* brief puoch, LITERALLY *a letter book*] A BOOK, *a volume, a writing, index;* liber:—Ic wrat boc *I wrote a book, Bd.* 5, 23. Adilga me of þinre bec, *Ex.* 32, 32, 33. Swa he þa boc unfeold, *Lk.* 4, 17, 20: *Deut.* 31, 26. Ða bec befon, *Jn.* 21, 25. On þæra cininga bocum *in their king's books, Elf. T.* p. 21, 1: 23, 19: 40, 4. On þære bec *in this book, Elf. T.* 24, 25.

λ Blod [v margin ✗] ⊙ Sec. l 4, ✗ ¶* Moes. boka f.

]

62 d]

me, an cd th. p 0 1 [63a]

ton

margin

blossum [v margin

ostme, an

m cd 221 th. p

25 v blosma

strugeld (Days

consent devoted

a, the gal 0 2

flowers,

a. Som 0 3 [63b]

e]

f]

O1

Bóc-cist, e; f
a book-chest, book-case Th. a pol

~~Bóc-stæf~~, es; m a
letter Beo ÿl n stæf

Bóc-stæf

Bodig, es; m a body

Bocholta Hem. Coden
Dipl. XLII

O2 [64 e]

O3

O 1 Bóc-skin kind
or part of book
Th. An

O 2 see suppl. to dyn. &
Th. An for lat. def

Boca bedæled *deprived of books, Elf. T.* p. 2, 3. On fif bec *in five books, Bd.* 5, 23. Þis is seo boc Adames, mægrace, *Gen.* 5, 1: *Mt.* 5, 31. Bocas *indexes, lists, calendars with the names of saints.* ¶ Feower Cristes bec *four books of Christ, the four gospels, Elf. T.* p. 24, 22. Boca streon, *or* gestreon *a treasury of books, or* boc gestreon *a book-treasury, a library.* Godspelboc *gospels.* Pistolboc *epistles.* Mæsseboc *a missal.* Sangboc *a hymn book.* Handboc *a manual, L. Can. eccl., W.* p. 156, 18.

Bóc *baked;* coxit: bocon coxerunt, v. bacan.

ɜócæceras *book-land, freehold,* v. boc-land.

ɩócas *indexes;* indigitamenta, v. boc.

óca streon *a library,* v. boc.

ócce *a beech,* v. boc.

óc-cest *A tavern;* taberna:—*R.* 17, *Ben.*

ɔócræft, es; *m.* [bóc *a book;* cræft *art, science*] *Book learning, learning, literature;* literatura:—Boetius wæs in boceræftum se rihtwisesta *Boe'ius, in book learning, was the nost wise, Bt.* 1. Þara bocræfta *of the knowledge of let-ers, of literature, Greg. pref.* 2.

:ere, es; *m. A writer, scribe, ıstructor;* scriptor:—An bocere *a scribe, Mt.* 8, 10. Hwæt e þurh boceras geleornode *hat he learned through inructors, Bd.* 4, 24.

·fel *A skin prepared for books, 'rchment, vellum;* charta permeńa:—Þæt hi habba blæc d bocfel *that they have ink d parchment, L. Can. Edg.* 3, . p. 82, 37.

gestreon *a book-treasury, a 'ary, Bd.* 5, 21, v. boc.

ɼihamand *a book-coverer, a k-binder, Lye.*

ıord *a book-hoard, a library 'eceptacle for books, papers, Som.*

us *a book-house, library, Lye.*

ı; *pp.* bocod, bocude. *To ;* inscribere:—*Heming.* ²8, v. gebocian.

d, es; *n. Book-land, land by a charter* or *writing, 'rom all fief, fee, service or* (such as was formerly :hiefly by the nobility, and ninated allodialis, and ı we now call *freehold*); ex o sive charta possessa terra codicillaris:—Þe boclande cyrican hæbbe : *his freehold has a church,* ɼ. 2, *W.* p. 76, 37: *L.* ², *W.* p. 49, 4, 6. Se mon boclande hæbbe *the man has a freehold, L. Alf.* 37, *W.* p. 43, 22, 23: *Bd.* 2, 3: 3, 24. Hæfde Romanum to boclande gesealde *Romanis per testamentum tradiderat, Ors.* 5, 4: *Bar.* p. 184, 12. Boclandes, *Cot.* 83, v. folcland *and* land.

Boc-lare *book learning, learning.*

Bóc-leaf *the leaf of a book, a charter, Som.*

Bócleden *book latin, latin,* v. leden.

o Bóclic; *adj.* BOOK-LIKE, *biblical, bookish, relating to books;* biblicus:—On boclicum larum *in book learning, Nat. S. Greg. Elf. pref. Elstob.* p. 5, 3.

Bócod *booked,* v. bocian.

Bócrædere, es; *m. A reader of books, a reader;* lector:—*Cot.* 126.

Bócræding *book reading, reading,* v. ræding.

Bócread *book red, vermilion,* (so named, because of old it was much used in ornamenting books); minium:—Of bocreade, *ex minio, Cot.* 75, 176.

Bóc-scamul *a reading desk* or *seat, Som.*

Bóc-stæf *a letter, character, an epistle,* v. stæf.

Bócsum; *adj.* [*Frs.* boegsum: *Kil.* ghe-boogh-saem] *Obedient, flexible,* BUXOM; obediens, *Som.*

Bócsumnes, se; *f. Obedience, pliantness,* BUXOMNESS; obedientia, *Som.*

Bóc-tæcing, boc-tale *book teaching, a book of decrees, writings, the scriptures, holy writ, the bible, Som.*

Bóc-treow, *a beech-tree,* v. boc.

Bócude *written,* v. bocian.

Bocung, e; *f.* A BOOKING, *a setting down in a book;* inscriptio, *Som.*

BOD, bebod, gebod, es; *pl.* u, o, a; *n.* [*Dut.* gebod *n*: *Ger.* gebot *n*: *Dan. Swed.* bud *c*: *Plat. Frs.* gebod *n*: *Icel.* bod] *A command, commandment, precept, mandate, an edict, order, message;* jussum:—Þæt is þæt mæste bebod, *Mk.* 12, 28, 29, 30, 31: *Mt.* 15, 3, 6. Bod, *C. Mt.* 22, 36. Gemyndig his bebodes *mindful of his command, Bd.* 4, 26, *S.* p. 600, 15. Þa gebodu, *Ors.* 6, 10. Þa hi þæt gebod gehyrdon, *Mt.* 2, 9.

p Boda, an; *m.* [*Frs. Dut.* bode: bod *an order;* a, v. 1e.] 1. *A messenger.* Hence we retain the word BODER, in the same sense; nuncius, *Som.* 2. *A preacher;* præco:—1. Þa bodan us færdon, *Deut.* 1, 28: *Lk.* 9, 52: *Bt.* 36, 1, *Card.* p. 266, 6. 2. Se soþa boda *the true preacher, Bd.* 2, 2, *S.* p. 502, 31, v. ar.

Bodare, bodere *A teacher, a master;* præceptor:—*C. R. Lk.* 9, 33.

Bodian, bodigean, bebodian, gebodian; ic bodige; *part.* bodiende, bodigende; *p.* bodede, hi bodedon, -udon; *pp.* boded, -od, -ud, geboden, -dod; *v. a.* [*Dut.* bieden, gebieden] 1. *To command, order;* mandare. 2. *To deliver a precept* or *command, to publish, tell, announce, proclaim, preach;* annuntiare. 3. *To come with a command, to propose, offer, engage in;* offerre:—Bebodian is only used in the first sense; bodian and bodigean are generally used in the second, and gebodian in the first and third:—1. Bedod *command thou, Ps.* 67, 31. Geboden, *R. Ben.* 5. 2. Ic eom asend þe þis bodian, *Lk.* 1, 19. Geboden *told, L. Athel.* 20, *W.* p. 60, 7. Bodiað, *Ps.* 18, 1: 43, 1. Ic bodige, 9, 14: *Mk.* 1, 45. Ongan bodigean *began to publish, Mk.* 5, 20. Se þat laðspell æt ham gebodode *who related the sad story at home, Ors.* 2, 4. Ongan se Hælend bodian, *Mt.* 4, 17: *Mk.* 1, 14: *Ps.* 2, 6: *Bd.* 5, 9. 3. Geboden *offered, Chr.* 755, *Ing.* p. 71, 15: *L. Alf.* 5, *W.* p. 36, 8: *Bd.* 2, 20, *S.* p. 521, n. 10, v. beodan, bebeodan.

Bodig, [*Heb.* בדי bdi *limbs; f.*] 1. *Bigness* or *height of body, stature;* statura. 2. *The trunk, chest* or *parts of the chest, as the back-bone;* truncus corporis. 3. *The body;* corpus:—The whole body is generally denoted by lic *or* lichoma, and the chest and members by bodig:—1. Lang on bodige, *Bd.* 2, 16. On bodige heah *tall in stature, Bd.* 3, 14. 2. *Cot.* 163. 3. *Past.* 35, 3, *Som.*

q Bodigean *to preach,* v. bodian.

Bodlac, es; *pl.* es; *m. A decree, ordinance;* decretum:—*Chr.* 1129, *Ing.* p. 359, 21.

Bódscipe, gebodscipe, es; *m.* [bod *a command,* scipe] *A message, an embassy, a commandment;* nuntium:—*Cd.* 27.

Bodung, e; *f. A preaching, publishing, divulging;* prædicatio:—Æt Ionam bodunge *at Jonah's preaching, Lk.* 11, 32.

Boec *a book,* v. boc.

Boensian *to intreat,* v. bensian.

Boetende *bettering, mending, gaining,* v. betan.

Boetes, boeties *Bootes, Charles's*

wain, *the constellation lying nearest the north pole*; bootes:—*Bt.* 39, 3, *Card.* p. 328, 27, *R.* p. 193.

Bo'ga, boh, an; *m.* [*Plat.* bagen *m*: *Dut.* boog *m*: *Ger.* bogen *m*: *Swed.* båge: *Icel.* bogi *m*: *Norse*, boge] 1. *Any thing curved, a bow, an arch, a corner*; arcus, angulus. 2. *Any thing extended and curved, a bough of a tree, a branch, an arm, a tail, horn, proboscis*; armus, ramus:—1. Ætcowð min boga *Gen.* 9, 14. 2. Se swiðra boh, *Lev.* 7, 32: *Ex.* 29, 22: *Lk.* 13, 19. Diploma, *Elf. gl.* 8.

Bogan *To boast*; jactare:—*Scint.* 46, *Lye.*

Bogean, bogen *rosemary*, v. boþen.

Boge-fodder *a bow-case.*

Bogeht; *part.* [bog *a bow*; eht *pursued from* ehtan] *Crooked, bent, difficult*; arcuatus:—Bogehte woeg, *C. Mt.* 7, 14.

Bogen *rosemary*, v. boþen.

Boge-net *a bow-net.*

Boge-streng *a bow-string.*

Bogetung, e; *f. A bending, a crook*; anfractus:—*Cot.* 18.

Bogh *a bow*, v. boga.

Bogodon *inhabited*; incoluerunt, *p. of* bugian.

Boh *an arm, a shoulder, branch*, v. boga.

Boh scyld *a shoulder shield.*

Bohte *bought*; emit, v. bycgan.

Bohtimbru *The materials of buildings*; materiæ ædificiorum:—*Solil. pref. Lye.*

Bol *A sleeping room*; dormitorium, *Ben.*

Bolca *the decks of a ship*; *from* balc.

Bold *a village, house, bolt*, v. bolt, botl.

Bold *bold*; audax, *in proper names*, v. bald.

Boldgetal, boldgetæl [bold *or* bolt *a dwelling*; getal *an order or a course*] *A dwelling place, street, habitation, house*; domicilium:—*L. Alf. pol.* 33, *W.* p. 42, 24, 25, 26.

Bolgen *displeased, pp. of* belgan.

Bolla, an [*Dan.* bolle: *Swed.* bål: *v.* fat] *Any round vessel, cup, pot,* BOWL, *a measure*; vas:—*Jdth.* 10, *Thw.* p. 21, 17. ¶ Heafod bolla *the skull, or brain pan, Som.*

Bolstar, bolster, bolste [*Dut. Kil. Al.* bolster] A BOLSTER, *a pillow for the head*; cervical:—His heafod onhylde to þam bolstre *laid his head on* [*to*] *the pillow, Bd.* 4, 24, *S.* p. 599, 6.

Bolt, bold, es; *pl.* boltas A BOLT, *a warlike engine to throw bolts, arrows, &c. a house*, v. boll; catapulta:—*Cot.* 45, *Som.*

Bolttimbru *materials of buildings*, v. bohtimbru.

Bonc selma *a bedstead, a side of a bedstead, Som.*

Bond *bound*; ligatus, *Som.*

Bonda, an; *m.* [bond *bound, one bound by rules, from* bindan *to bind*] *A husband, an householder, a master of a family*; maritus:—Se bonda sæt *the husband dwelt, L. Cnut.* 70, *W.* p. 144, 40: 74, *W.* p. 145, 42.

Bonde-land *Land held under restrictions*, or *on conditions, copyhold*; tributaria terra:—*Chr.* 775, *Ing.* p. 75, 14.

Bondwyrt, bonwyrt *a sort of plant, Som.*

Booc-hord *a library*, v. boc-hord.

Bor [*Plat.* baar: *Dut.* boor *f. a bore* or *an instrument with which holes are made*: *Dan. Swed.* bor *n.*] *A lancet, a surgeon's* or *barber's instrument, a* BURIN, or *graving tool*; scalprum:—*Cot.* 63.

-bor *bearing*; ferens, v. bær.

Bora, an; *m.* [bor *from* beran *to bear, carry*; a, v. 1e] *One who bears, a bearer, supporter*; gestator. This word is only used in compounds, and in the termination has the same meaning as the *Lat.* fer, ger, lator:—Cæg-bora *A key bearer*; claviger, *Cot.* 41: 173: *Elf. gr.* 8. Soð-bora *a truth bearer, a prophet, Chr.* 975: *Gib.* p. 123, 29. Swyrd-bora *a sword bearer, a soldier*; ensifer. Wæpen-, *or* wæpn-bora *a weapon bearer*; armiger, *R.* 51: *Elf. gl.* p. 63. Tacn-bora *a standard bearer*; signifer, *R. & Elf. gl.* v. bær.

Boran, boren *born*; latus, v. beran.

Bord, beod, es; *m.* [*Plat.* boord *n*: *Frs.* boed: *Kil.* berd, bred *n*: *Moes.* baurd: *Swed.* bräde, bord: *Norse*, brod] 1. A BOARD, *plank, table*: hence our word *to board, to receive at table, to live in a house*; tabula, mensa, v. bred. 2. *A ship, a house*; navis. 3. *A border, boundary, bank, shield*; margo:—1. Of aheawenum bordum *of planed boards, Gen.* 6, 14. Borda gefeg *a joining of boards, R.* 26. Ða gebroðru æt beode sæton *the brothers sat at table, Bd.* 3, 2. Bord, *Ps.* 68, 27. 2. *Cd.* 71. 3. Innan bord and ut *at home and abroad.* Innan bordes and utan bordes, *Past. pref.* Famig bordon *with foaming banks, Bt. Card.* p. 400, 6: *R.* p. 188: *Jdth.* 11.

Borda *A list, line*; lesta:—*Cot.* 120: 84, *Ben.*

Bord-hreoþa *A board covered with a raw hide, a buckler, warlike engine*; testudo:—*Cd.* 149, v. hreoþa.

Bord-þaca, bord-þeaca *Board thatch, a warlike engine, a cover* or *roof of a house, a snare*; testudo, laquear:—Bord weall *boarded walls, Chr.* 938, *Ing.* p. 141, 17.

Boren *born, pp. of* beran.

Borennys, se; *f. Birth, nativity*; partus, *Som.*

Borg, borge *to a surety*, v. borh.

Borgas *sureties*, v. borh.

Borges bryce *a breaking* or *breach of a suretyship*, or *pledge*, v. borh-bryce.

Borg-gylda *an usurer*; fœnerator.

Borg-hand *a surety*, v. borh-hand.

Borgian; he borgað [*Plat. Dut. Ger.* borgen: *Dan.* borge: *Swed.* borga: borh *a pledge*] *To* BORROW, *lend*; mutuari:—Þe wille æt þe borgian *who will borrow of thee, Mt.* 5, 42: *Ps.* 36, 22.

Borgiend [*part. of* borgian *to lend*] *An usurer*; fœnerator:—*Ps.* 108, 10.

Borgi-lefde *A promise*, or *bond of appearance before a judge, at a day appointed, a pawn* or *pledge*; vadimonium, pignus, *Som.*

Borg-wed *any thing given in pledge, a promise, Lye.*

Borh; *g.* borges; *d.* borge; *ac.* borh; *pl. nom. ac.* borgas; *g.* a; *d.* um; *m.* [*Plat.* borge *m*: *Dut.* borg *m*: *Ger.* bürge *m*: perhaps from the same root as beorh *a city, a refuge* or *a defence*] 1. *A security, pledge, loan, bail*; foenus. 2. *A person who gives security, a surety, bondsman, debtor*; fidejussor, debitor:—Bail was taken by the Saxons from every person guilty of *theft, homicide, witchcraft, &c.*; indeed, every person was under bail for his neighbour. It is generally thought, that the borh originated with King Alfred, but the first time we find it clearly expressed, is in the Laws of Edgar, v. *Turner's Hist. of A.S. Bk.* vi. *Append.* 3, *Ch.* 6, vol. ii. p. 499:—1. Ic wille, þæt ælc mann sy under borge ge binnan burgum ge butan burgum *I will that every man be under* [*borh*] *both within cities and without cities, L. Edg. Sup.* 12, *W.* p. 80, 45, 47: *Edg.* 6, *W.* p. 78, 23; fidejussio. On his agenon borge *on his own*

Sep 27th 1837

Slume heowun para treowa bogas Mk 21,8; Mk 11,8; Hæfð mycele bogas Mk 4,32

On bogum in gelfe

Ulegra bogum in bending of bough derie

On his boughs On his bogum

Cd 30 Th p 40,26; 151, Th p 188,21; 167 Th p 209,12

Bogan [65a]

on hys bogum Lk 13,19; Mt 13,32

Bendað heora bogan Ps Th 36,13 — Bogan heora beo gebrocen Ps 36,16. Nim pinne bogan Gen 27,3 — Ic Leowð min boga on pam wolcnum Gen 9,14

2 Bona, an; m A slayer occisor Beo 16 K 352

○7 [67a]

3 Bon-gar telum mor-tiferum Beo K 4057 a fatal spear

4 Bont for band bound v bindan

○8 [67c] Swed borr m

5 Bora, an; m A ruler bearer

Rices boran states rulers, or rulers of (the) state Cd 224 Th p 296,10

Bold, es; n A house, hall, palace; domus, atrium Beo K 1987 Cd 216 Th p 273,19

3 baurd n

Bord-hæbbende shield having or bearing, Beo K 5785 shields

○2 es; n Th. an Bord-weal, board wall, shield; Mic's Walth vol I p LXXXIX, 4 also note

Borgen saved ptp of beorgan Borg

○8 [69d]

Borga

Bord-weall shield wand; lignum clypei Beo K 2486

a shouting branch Elfgr 35 Som 38,49 v bog

empty minded Wrath of mind or Cd 183 Th p 228,26

9 Bord, es; m?

○ [68a]

○7 Bord up-ahof shield up raised Cd 156 Th p 193,28

○8

...ho, es; m A shoulder ... shoot, branch, bough ... stipes, propago ... mynet bone swyðran Ex 29,22 — Lev 7,32

...k a balk th an balk, beam, a ridge, ridge of earth; trabs, ... shakum inter sulcos eminens

... an; m ... Boran ofer ... to bear over balks ... can; gestare super ... ram Beo Conyb.

... p 88,3; Beo K 460 ... d-agende possessing a ... Beo K 6218

... gen-mod; superb ... : Beo K 1411

... la, an; m Th An [66a]

Bolstar, bolstr Bolster, of ... hes; n. a bolster

[66c]

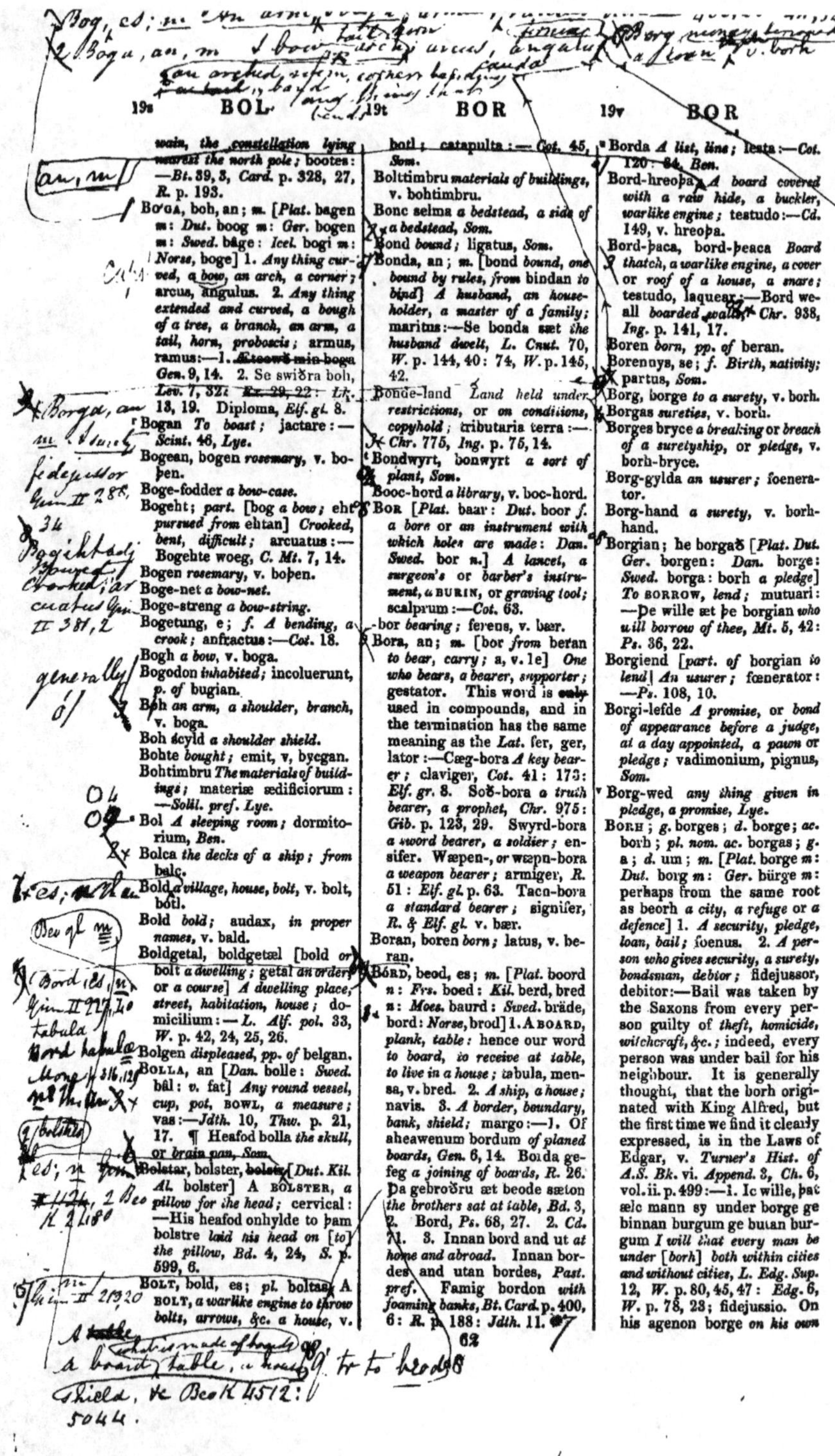

wain, the constellation lying nearest the north pole; bootes:—*Bt.* 39, 3, *Card.* p. 328, 27, *R.* p. 193.

BOGA, boh, an; *m.* [*Plat.* bagen *m*: *Dut.* boog *m*: *Ger.* bogen *m*: *Swed.* båge: *Icel.* bogi *m*: *Norse,* boge] 1. *Any thing curved, a bow, an arch, a corner*; arcus, angulus. 2. *Any thing extended and curved, a bough of a tree, a branch, an arm, a tail, horn, proboscis*; armus, ramus:—1. Ic teowe min boga *Gen.* 9, 14. 2. Se swiðra boh, *Lev.* 7, 32: *Ex.* 29, 22: *Lk.* 13, 19. Diploma, *Elf. gl.* 8.

Bogan *To boast*; jactare:—*Scint.* 46, *Lye.*

Bogean, bogen *rosemary,* v. boþen.

Boge-fodder *a bow-case.*

Bogeht; *part.* [bog *a bow*; eht *pursued from* ehtan] *Crooked, bent, difficult*; arcuatus:—Bogehte woeg, *C. Mt.* 7, 14.

Bogen *rosemary,* v. boþen.

Boge-net *a bow-net.*

Boge-streng *a bow-string.*

Bogetung, e; *f. A bending, a crook*; anfractus:—*Cot.* 18.

Bogh *a bow,* v. boga.

Bogodon *inhabited*; incoluerunt, *p. of* bugian.

Boh *an arm, a shoulder, branch,* v. boga.

Boh scyld *a shoulder shield.*

Bohte *bought*; emit, v, bycgan.

Bohtimbru *The materials of buildings*; materiæ ædificiorum:—*Solil. pref. Lye.*

Bol *A sleeping room*; dormitorium, *Ben.*

Bolca *the decks of a ship*; *from* balc.

Bold *a village, house, bolt,* v. bolt, botl.

Bold *bold*; audax, *in proper names,* v. bald.

Boldgetal, boldgetæl [bold *or* bolt *a dwelling*; getal *an order or a course*] *A dwelling place, street, habitation, house*; domicilium:—*L. Alf. pol.* 33, *W.* p. 42, 24, 25, 26.

Bolgen *displeased, pp. of* belgan.

BOLLA, an [*Dan.* bolle: *Swed.* bål: *v.* fat] *Any round vessel, cup, pot,* BOWL, *a measure*; vas:—*Jdth.* 10, *Thw.* p. 21, 17. ¶ Heafod bolla *the skull, or brain pan, Som.*

Bolstar, bolster, bolste [*Dut. Kil. Al.* bolster] A BOLSTER, *a pillow for the head*; cervical:—His heafod onhylde to þam bolstre *laid his head on* [*to*] *the pillow, Bd.* 4, 24, *S.* p. 599, 6.

BOLT, bold, es; *pl.* boltas A BOLT, *a warlike engine to throw bolts, arrows, &c. a house,* v. botl; catapulta:—*Cot.* 45, *Som.*

Boltimbru *materials of buildings,* v. bohtimbru.

Bonc selma *a bedstead, a side of a bedstead, Som.*

Bond *bound*; ligatus, *Som.*

Bonda, an; *m.* [bond *bound, one bound by rules, from* bindan *to bind*] *A husband, an householder, a master of a family*; maritus:—Se bonda sæt *the husband dwelt, L. Cnut.* 70, *W.* p. 144, 40: 74, *W.* p. 145, 42.

Bonde-land *Land held under restrictions,* or *on conditions, copyhold*; tributaria terra:—*Chr.* 775, *Ing.* p. 75, 14.

Bondwyrt, bonwyrt *a sort of plant, Som.*

Booc-hord *a library,* v. boc-hord.

BOR [*Plat.* baar: *Dut.* boor *f. a bore* or *an instrument with which holes are made*: *Dan. Swed.* bor *n.*] *A lancet, a surgeon's* or *barber's instrument, a* BURIN, or *graving tool*; scalprum:—*Cot.* 63.

-bor *bearing*; ferens, v. bær.

Bora, an; *m.* [bor *from* beran *to bear, carry*; a, v. 1e] *One who bears, a bearer, supporter*; gestator. This word is only used in compounds, and in the termination has the same meaning as the *Lat.* fer, ger, lator:—Cæg-bora *A key bearer*; claviger, *Cot.* 41: 173: *Elf. gr.* 8. Soð-bora *a truth bearer, a prophet, Chr.* 975: *Gib.* p. 123, 29. Swyrd-bora *a sword bearer, a soldier*; ensifer. Wæpen-, or wæpn-bora *a weapon bearer*; armiger, *R.* 51: *Elf. gl.* p. 63. Tacn-bora *a standard bearer*; signifer, *R. & Elf. gl.* v. bær.

Boran, boren *born*; latus, v. beran.

BÓRD, beod, es; *m.* [*Plat.* boord *n*: *Frs.* boed: *Kil.* berd, bred *n*: *Moes.* baurd: *Swed.* bräde, bord: *Norse,* brod] 1. A BOARD, *plank, table*: hence our word *to board, to receive at table, to live in a house*; tabula, mensa, v. bred. 2. *A ship, a house*; navis. 3. *A border, boundary, bank, shield*; margo:—1. Of aheawenum bordum *of planed boards, Gen.* 6, 14. Borda gefeg *a joining of boards, R.* 26. Þa gebroðru æt beode sæton *the brothers sat at table, Bd.* 3, 2. Bord, *Ps.* 68, 27. 2. *Cd.* 71. 3. Innan bord and ut *at home and abroad.* Innan bordes and utan bordes, *Past. pref.* Famig bordon *with foaming banks, Bt. Card.* p. 400, 6: *R.* p. 188: *Jdth.* 11.

Borda *A list, line*; lista:—*Cot.* 120: 84, *Ben.*

Bord-hreoþa *A board covered with a raw hide, a buckler, warlike engine*; testudo:—*Cd.* 149, v. hreoþa.

Bord-þaca, bord-þeaca *Board thatch, a warlike engine, a cover* or *roof of a house, a snare*; testudo, laquear:—Bord weall *boarded wall, Chr.* 938, *Ing.* p. 141, 17.

Boren *born, pp. of* beran.

Borennys, se; *f. Birth, nativity*; partus, *Som.*

Borg, borge *to a surety,* v. borh.

Borgas *sureties,* v. borh.

Borges bryce *a breaking* or *breach of a suretyship,* or *pledge,* v. borh-bryce.

Borg-gylda *an usurer*; foenerator.

Borg-hand *a surety,* v. borh-hand.

Borgian; he borgað [*Plat. Dut. Ger.* borgen: *Dan.* borge: *Swed.* borga: borh *a pledge*] *To* BORROW, *lend*; mutuari:—Þe wille æt þe borgian *who will borrow of thee, Mt.* 5, 42: *Ps.* 36, 22.

Borgiend [*part. of* borgian *to lend*] *An usurer*; fœnerator:—*Ps.* 108, 10.

Borgi-lefde *A promise,* or *bond of appearance before a judge, at a day appointed, a pawn* or *pledge*; vadimonium, pignus, *Som.*

Borg-wed *any thing given in pledge, a promise, Lye.*

BORH; *g.* borges; *d.* borge; *ac.* borh; *pl. nom. ac.* borgas; *g.* a; *d.* um; *m.* [*Plat.* borge *m*: *Dut.* borg *m*: *Ger.* bürge *m*: perhaps from the same root as beorh *a city, a refuge* or *a defence*] 1. *A security, pledge, loan, bail*; foenus. 2. *A person who gives security, a surety, bondsman, debtor*; fidejussor, debitor:—Bail was taken by the Saxons from every person guilty of *theft, homicide, witchcraft, &c.*; indeed, every person was under bail for his neighbour. It is generally thought, that the borh originated with King Alfred, but the first time we find it clearly expressed, is in the Laws of Edgar, v. *Turner's Hist. of A.S. Bk.* vi. *Append.* 3, *Ch.* 6, vol. ii. p. 499:—1. Ic wille, þæt ælc mann sy under borge ge binnan burgum ge butan burgum *I will that every man be under* [*borh*] *both within cities and without cities, L. Edg. Sup.* 12, *W.* p. 80, 45, 47: *Edg.* 6, *W.* p. 78, 23; fidejussio. On his agenon borge *on his own*

On boguni in gelfe

heora boguni in bending of down deroti

On his bogum

Cd 30 Th p 40, 26: 151, Th p 188, 21: 167 Th p 209, 12

[65a]

-thys boguni Lk ,19: Mk 13, 32

-endad heora bogan Ezek. 36, 13 - Bogan heora bid gebroc- en Ez 36, 16. Nim -inne bogan Gen 7, 3 - Aleowd min boga on pam wolcnum Gen 9, 14

-es; m. A shield root branch, bough, bows stipes, propago ramus pone thyoran 29, 22 - Lev. 7, 32 my gode boh

: a brook th. an the beam, a ridge, ridge of earth; tratis elum inter sulcos eminens n; m

Beran ofor to bear over balks n, gestane super m Beo. Cay. p 88, 3 Beo K 460 gende prosting Beo K 6218

-mód, super p 79: Beo K 1411

an; m V. an [68a]

lstar. bolstr olster, of n. a bolster

Sept 27th 1837

Slume heowun para treowa bogas Mk 4, 8; Mk 11, 8: Hæfð mycele bogas Mk 4, 32

2 Bona, an; m A slayer occisor Beo 16 K 352

7 [67a]

3 Bon-gar telum mor- tiferum Beo K 4057 a fatal spear 3.

Bont for band bound v bindan 8 [67c] Swed borr m

5 Bora, an; m A ruler, bearer

Rices boran states rulers, or rulers of (the) state Cd. 224 Th p 296, 10

Bold, es; n A house, hall, palace, domus, atrium Beo K 1987 Cd 216 Th p 273, 19

3 baurd n

angry minded wrath of mood or Cd 183 Th p 228. 26

9 Bord, es; m? [68a]

7 Bord up-ahof shield up raised Cd 156 Th p 193, 28

8

1 a Bord-hæbbende shield having or bear ing, Beo K 5785 shields

2 -es; m th. an Bord-weal, board wall, shield; Mics Walth vol I p LXXXIX, 4 also note

4 Borgen saved pp of beorgan Borg

8 [69d]

Borga

Bord-wudu shield wood; lignum clypei Beo K 2486

a shooter branch Ezk 31.5 Sam 38. 49 v bog

O1[69e]

O2[69f] O2[70b]

3 Bot; i.e. a compensation etc. O3[71a]

[69g]

O7 O 1* Her is seo bot here is the remedy or spell Grim Myth Sup CXXVII

X Brac Adversarius Ben

O6[71b]

X Borsnung corruption; ie Sprecking corruption for Ben v brosnung

O 2* Boruct-waru, i.e. boructuarii O7. [70a]

O1 esi m

security, Ethelr. 1, *W.* p. 103, 26. Gif þu feoh to borh gesylle *if thou give money on loan, Alf. eccl.* 35, *W.* p. 31, 42. 2. Se borh *the surety, L. Edg.* 6, *W.* p. 78, 22, 26. Be borges andsæce *concerning a denial of a bail, L. In.* 41, *W.* p. 21, 17. Sette getreowe borgas *shall appoint true sureties, L. Ethel.* 1, *W.* p. 103, 11, 47; p. 102, 33, 34, 35: *L. Edw.* 6, *W.* p. 49, 40, 43; p. 50, 1. Ge asecað eowre borgas *ye shall search out your debtors, L. eccl.* 42, *W.* p. 194, 28. ¶ Borhes ealdor *a head borough* or *borsholder, Som.*

Borh-bryce, es; *m.* [borh *a pledge,* bryce *a breaking*] *A pledge breaking, a violation of a bail;* fidejussionis violatio:—Be borh-bryce *concerning a pledge breaking, L. Alf.* 3, *W.* p. 35, 12, 13: *L. In.* 31, *W.* p. 20, 2: *L. Alf.* 1, *W.* p. 34, 51.

Borh-fæstan, geborhfæstan [borh *a surety;* fæst *fast*] *To fasten* or *bind by pledge,* or *surety;* fidejussione obligare:—Man borhfæst þam cyninge ealle þa þægnas *they bound by oath all the thanes to the king, Chr.* 1051, *Ing.* p. 228, 33.

[B]orh-hand, borhond, borhoe *a pledge by the hand, a pledge, surety, security.*

[B]orhigenda [borh *a loan;* agenda *a possessor*] *An usurer;* foenerator:—*Lps.* 108, 10, *Lye.*

[Bo]rhoe, borhond *a surety,* v. borh-hand.

[Bo]rhleas; *adj. Void of security;* [fi]dejussore carens:—*L. Const.* [W]. p. 117, 52.

[Bor]h-wed *any thing given in* [pl]*edge, Som.*

[Bor]an [*Plat.* baren: *Frs. v.* bo[r]je: *Dut.* boren: *Kil.* boo[re]n: *Ger.* bohren: *Dan.* bore: [Sw]*ed.* bora, bor *an instru*[men]*t to make a hole*] *To* BORE, [*m*]*ake a hole;* terebrare:— [*Elf.*] *gl.* 25. Wyrm þe boraþ [...]*w a worm that perforates* [...]*d, R.* 23, *Lye.*

[...]e *openly, plainly,* v. bær-[...]

[...]*urned, p. of* byrnan.

[...] *bursted, pp. of* berstan.

[...]ware *A people inhabiting* [...]*t of Germany;* Boructu-[...] *Ger. antiq.* l. 3, c. 13, [...]iver.

[...] borynde *or* berende *from* [...] *to bear*] *Bearing;* fæ-[...] —*Ps.* 77, 76.

[...]m, Bosenham [Forte a [...]sumptum, *Som.*] BOSE-[HAM o]r BOSHAM *in Sussex:*— [Bo]sanham *at Bosham, Chr.* 1049, *Ing.* p. 220, 8: p. 221, 4: 1051, p. 231, 12.

Bosg, bosig, bosih [*Dan.* baas: *Swed.* bås *n*: *Icel.* bás] *An ox* or *cow-stall, where the cattle stand all night in winter, a* BOOSE, as it is now called by the common people in the mid-land and Northern counties. It is now more generally used for the upper part of the stall where the fodder lies—They say "you will find it in the *cow's boose,*" that is, in the place for the *cow's food;* præsepe:—*C. R. Lk.* 13, 15.

x Bósum, bosm, es; *m.* [*Plat.* bosem, bossem, bussem *m*: *Dut.* boezem: *Ger.* busen *m*: *Tat.* buosum: *Not.* buosem] 1. *The space included by the folding of the arms, the* BOSOM, *lap;* gremium. 2. *A fold in clothes, an assemblage of folds,* such as were formed about the breast in the loose dress of the ancients, especially when the arms were closed, *a concavity,* a collection of clouds irregularly folded together. In this sense, the word is chiefly used in composition; sinus, sinus velorum:—1. Ic hig bære on minum bosume, *Num.* 11, 12. Do þine hand on þinne bosum, *Ex.* 4, 6, 7: *Ps.* 34, 16. 2. Segel-bosmas *the bosom, bending* or *bowings of the sails,* v. bearm, fæþem, greada.

Bót [*Plat.* bute *f*: *Dut.* boete *f*: *Swed.* bot *c*: *hence our* to boote, *Chaucer's* boote *a help, remedy*] A BOOT, *compensation paid to an injured party, a redressing, recompence, an amends, a satisfaction, an offering, remedy, a cure, an assistance, a correction, reparation, restoring, renewing, repentance;* compensatio, emendatio, reparatio:—For bote his sinna *for a redressing of his sins, Bd.* 4, 25, *S.* p. 599, 32: 5, 13, *S.* p. 632, 13. Bringaþ anne buccan to bote *bring a kid for an offering, Lev.* 4, 23, 28: *L. Alf.* 49, *W.* p. 34, 3: *Bd.* 1, 27, *S.* p. 489, 9. ¶ To bote *to boot, with advantage, moreover, besides.*

Botelos *bootless;* sine emendatione, v. botleas.

Boþen *Rosemary, darnel;* rosmarinus:—*Herb.* 81. Boþen, Lolium and oðra lyþra cynne *the darnel* [*q* bromus mollis, *Lin.*] *and other injurious kinds, R.* 100.

y Botl *An abode, a dwelling, mansion, house, hall;* domus:—Þær wæs þa cyninges ealdor botl *there was the king's royal dwelling, Bd.* 2, 11, *S.* p. 511, 18. Pharao eode into his botle, *Ex.* 7, 23: *Mt.* 26, 3: *L. In.* 67, 68, *W.* p. 25, 21. ¶ Cynelec botl *a kingly dwelling, a palace, R.* 81. Botlgestreon *household property, Cd.* 52. Botlweard *or* botlwerd *one who hath the care of a house, a house-steward, Elf. gr.* 9, 28.

Botleas; *adj.* BOOTLESS, *unpardonable, what cannot be remedied, recompensed* or *expiated;* inexpiabilis:—Þonne is þat botleas *then is that unpardonable, L. Cnut. eccl.* 2, *W.* p. 127, 26: *pol.* 61, *W.* p. 143, 11.

Botm [*Plat.* böhn: *Dut.* bodem *m*: *Frs.* boem: *Ger.* boden: *Swed.* bötten: *Icel.* botn [A BOTTOM; fundum:—Tunnan botm *a tun* or *tub's bottom, a drum, R.* 25. Scipes botm *a ship's bottom, R.* 83.

Botwyrð; *adj. Pardonable, expiable, that may be atoned for;* emendabilis:—Æt botwyrþum þingum *among pardonable things, L. Cnut.* 3, *W.* p. 127, 52.

z Boung *a bragging, boasting,* v. bogan.

Box, boxtreow [*Dut.* bux: *Span.* box] *The* BOX-TREE; buxus: —*Elf. gl.* 17.

Box; *pl.* buxa [*Plat.* büsse, büske *f*: *Ger.* büchse *f*: *Dan.* bosse] A BOX, *a small case* or *vessel with a cover;* pyxis:—Hundteontig boxa *a hundred boxes, Jn.* 19, 39: *Mt.* 26, 7. ¶ Sealfbox *a salve-box, Mk.* 14, 3.

Bracan [*Frs.* brake: *Dut.* breken] *To* BREAK, *bruise* or *bray in a mortar;* conterere:—Beon æle bracene *to be beaten up with oil, Lev.* 6, 21, v. brecan.

Brac-hwile *a glance while, a moment,* v. bearhtm-hwile.

Bracigean *To dress, mingle* or *counterfeit with brass;* ærare, *Som.* v. bræsian.

Bra'd; *comp.* ra, re; *sup.* ost; *adj.* [*Plat. Frs. Dut.* breed: *Ger.* breit, brad: *Moes.* braid: *Dan. Swed.* bred: *Icel.* breidr] BROAD, *large, vast;* latus:—Twelf mila brad *twelve miles broad, Bd.* 1, 3, *S.* p. 475, 19. Mid bradum handum *with open hands, Mt.* 26, 67. Bradre and bradre *broader and broader, Ors.* 2, 5. Bradost, *Ors.* 1, 1: *Ps.* 118, 96.

a Brád-æx *a broad axe.*

Brádanford [brad *broad,* ford *a ford*] *Bradford in Wilts:*—Æt Bradan-forda be Afene *at Bradford by Avon, Chr.* 652.

Brádanrelic, Brádunreolic, Brádanreige *The Flat Holms, an island in the mouth of the Severn*:—*Chr*. 918, *Ing*. p. 132, 19.

Brád-hlaf, bræd-hlaf *a biscuit, parched* or *baked bread, Som.*

Brádiande nider *or* brædende niðer *tending downwards, Ors.* 5, 10, *Bar*. p. 192, 17, v. brædan.

Brádnis, e; *f.* BROADNESS, *extension, surface*; latitudo, superficies:—Þære eorðan brádnis wæs adruwod, *Gen*. 8, 13: 1, 2: 2, 6, v. bred.

Brád-þistel *a thistle with long leaves, sea-holm, sea-holly*; eryngium:—*Cot*. 212.

Bræc *breeches, pl. of* broc.

Bræc *broke*, fregit, *p. of* brecan.

Bræccæ, braccæ *breeches*, v. bræc, broc.

Bræc-coþu, bræcceoþu *the breaking disease, falling sickness.*

Bræchme *A noise, rustling, cracking*; strepitus, *Som.*

Bræcseoc, bræcseoc-man *A frantic man, lunatic, one troubled with the falling sickness*; phreneticus:—*Bd*. 4, 3.

b Bræcseocnes *Epilepsy*; epilepsia:—*Som.*

BRÆD, bred [*Plat.* breede *f*: *Dut.* breedte *f*: *Ger.* breite *f*: *Dan.* brede c.] 1. BREADTH, *width*; latitudo. 2. *That which is spread, a table, victuals, a rumour, falsehood, fiction*; mensa, fucus:—1. Fiftig fæðma on bræde, *Gen*. 6, 15. On brædo *in breadth, Bd*. 1, 1. 2. Butan bræde *without falsehood, L. Edw*. 1.

Bræd *broad*; latus, v. brad.

Brædan, gebrædan; *p.* brædde, bræd, gebræd, hi bræddon; *pp.* bræded, gebrædd; *v. a.* [*Plat.* breden: *Kil.* breeden: *Ger.* breiten] 1. *To make broad, extend, spread, draw out, stretch out, melt, pave, board*; dilatare. 2. *To spread a report, to publish, pretend*; propalare. 3. *To spread before the fire, to roast*; torrere, v. gebrædan:—1. Þat hi his naman brædan *that they spread his name, Bt.* 30, 1: *Lps*. 118, 32: *Bd*. 2, 7. His handa wæs brædende *was spreading his hands, Ors*. 4, 5. Gebræded mid stane *paved with stone*. 2. Gebræde he hine seocne *he pretended himself sick*, i. e. *that he was sick, Chr*. 1003, *Ing*. p. 176, 26.
a 3. Flesc on fyre gebrædd *flesh roasted* or *broiled on a fire, Herb*. 60, 3, v. tobrædan, abredian.

Bræde *roasted meat, a table, Som.*

Brædednes, se; *f. Width*; latitudo:—*Lps*. 117, 5.

Brædels *A carpet*; stragulum:—*R*. 4.

Brædene [*Flor.* Bradene: so called from its size] BREDON *Forest, near Malmsbury, Wilts., Chr*. 905.

c Bræding, e; *f. A spreading*; ampliatio:—*Bt*. 19.

Bræding-panne *a frying-pan.*

Bræd-isen [bræd, isen *iron*] *A scraping* or *graving tool, file*; scalprum:—*Cot*. 173.

Brædnys *broadness*, v. bradnis.

Bræd-panne *a frying-pan.*

Brægd *bent*; strictus:—*Cod. Ex.* 19, a. 8, v. bredan.

Brægdan; *pp. of* brædan *to spread*; dilatare.

Brægden *deceit*; brægd *fiction, Lye*, v. bræd.

BRÆGEN, bragen, es [*Plat.* brägen *n*: *Frs. Dut.* brein: *Kil.* breghe, breghen] *The* BRAIN; cerebrum:—Bregenes adl *the brain's disease, L. Md*. 2, 27.

Bræhtm *a glimpse*, v. bearhtm.

Bræmas *sea water*, v. brym.

Bræmbel-brær *a bramble brier*, v. bremel.

Brær, brer *A brier*; tribulus, *Som.*

Bræs BRASS; æs:—*Elf. gr.* v. ar.

Bræsen, bresn; *def.* se bræsna; seo, þæt bræsne; *adj.* 1. *Brasen, made of brass*; æreus. 2. *Strong, powerful*; fortis:—1. *Elf. gr*. 5. 2. Se bræsna weard *the strong ward* or *protector, Cd*. 196.

Bræsian *To mix, cover*, or *counterfeit with brass*; ærare:—*Elf. gr*. 36.

d Bræsna *strong*, v. bræsen.

Bræstlung *creaking*, v. brastlung.

Brætan *To change, alter*; mutare:—Ne bræt na his hiw *changes not his hue, H. in die Paschæ*, p. 5, *Som.*

BRÆÐ *An odour, a scent, smell good* or *bad, a savour*, BREATH; odor:—Þære wynsumnysse bræð, *Gen*. 8, 21. Mid þam bræðe ofsmorod *smothered with the smell, Ors*. 6, 32, v. æðm.

Brætmælum *by little and little, by piecemeal, Som.* v. mæl.

BRÆW, breaw, bregh, es; *m.* A BROW, *an eyebrow, eyelids*; palpebra:—*Ps*. 10, 5.

Bragen *the brain*, v. brægen.

Bran *burned*; ardebat:—*Cd*. 162, *q.* barn *from* byrnan *to burn.*

BRAND, brond [*Plat. Dut. Ger. Dan. Swed.* brand *m*: *Old Latin*, branda: *Norse*, brandr: *Franc.* brandon] 1. A BRAND, *a torch*; titio. 2. *Metaphorically from its shining, a sword*; ensis: as *Franc.* brandon: *Norse*, brandr: *Ital.* brando; hence the *Eng.* to BRANDISH:—1. *R*. 30. 2. *Hicks*. i. p. 192, c. 2, l. 16: *Gr. Fr. Theot*. p. 93, c. 2, l. 18, *Mann.*

Brand-isen, brand-red [*Dut. Kil.* brandüser, brandroede] *A branding iron* or *rod, a tripod*; andena, tripes:—*R*. 10: *Cot*. 13, *Som.*

Branwyrt *A blackberry*; vaccinium:—*R*. 39.

e Brassica *colewort, cabbage, Som.*

Brastl *a noise*, v. brastlung.

Brastlian; *part.* brastliende, brastligende [*Ger.* prasseln, brasseln: *Swed.* prassla] *To* BRUSTLE, *crackle, make a noise, burn, burst asunder*; crepare:—*Æqu. vern*. 43, *Som.*

Brastlung, brastl [*Ger.* gebrassel *or* geprassel *n*: *Swed.* prassel *n*.] *A crackling, crashing*, BRUSTLING, *creaking, burning, breaking*; crepitus:—Hig tobræcon þa bucas mid micelre brastlunge, *Jud*. 7, 20. Brastlung treowa *a creaking of trees, Elf. gr*. 1, 10: *Greg*. 1, 2.

Bratt *A cloak*; pallium, *Som.*

Braue [*Icel.* bref *a brief*, or *diploma*] *A letter*, BRIEF; literæ, *Lye.*

Breác *was discharging*; *p. of* brucan.

Breacan *to break*, v. brecan.

Bread, breod [*Plat. Dut.* brood *n*: *Ger.* brod *n*: *Ot.* brot: *Franc.* broud: *Dan. Swed.* bröd *n*: *Icel.* braud] *A bit, fragment*, BREAD; panis:—*C. R. Jn*. 13, 27, 30.

Breahtm *a shining, a moment*, v. bearhtm.

Breahtmung *a noise*, v. brehtnung.

Breard *a brim, height, top*, v. brerd.

Breaw-ern *A place for putting off clothes*; apodyterium:—*R*. 55, *Lye.*

Breawas *the eyebrows*, v. bræw.

Brec *breeches*, v. broc.

Brec *gain, profit, necessity*, v. bryce.

BRECAN, abrecan; þu bricst; *p.* bræc, gebræc, hi bræcon; *pp.* brocen, gebrocen; *v. a.* [*Plat. Dut.* breken: *Frs.* brekke: *Ger.* brechen: *Ot.* brechen: *Moes.* brikan: *Dan.* bräkke: *Swed.* bråka: *Heb.* פרק prq] *To* BREAK, *vanquish, overcome, weaken, open, move, excite, produce*; frangere:—Bræc þa hlafas, *Mt*. 14, 19: *Jn*. 19, 32. Þu bricst, *Ps*. 2, 9: *Chr*. 851, *Ing*. p. 92, 19: *Ors*. 2, 4. Movere. Ongan he hine brecan *began to excite himself, Chr*. 1003,

01

* ~~Bradenu~~
Brædenu, e; f
bræd broad, denu a
valley,] Bredon etc

0]

~~2~~ Brad panne, an f
a frying pan b. ~~[illegible]~~
~~[illegible] panne [illegible]~~

2 Brasilian; l 5 x cre-
pares
O [73c]

3 Bragen*es; n.
the brain, etc
O [72a]

(Bræd, bred-dl.)
Brædo, see Margin

O4 [72b]
O5 [72c]

O3 [73d]
O4 [74a]
O5 [74b]

2 Brædd lumbi
Ben

3 [71c]

O6 [72d]

3
8

O7 ~~[73a]~~ [73a]

O6 [75a]

2 Brand, brond
es; m ~~[illegible]~~ & Norse
brandr m: Fr. brandon
m ~~[illegible]~~] a torch, etc
O [73b]

Brecda broken, fractus Beo K340

Brego m a prince; princeps Beo K 848: 3905

Brego-róf princely eminent Beo K 3847

Brego-weard, es; m a ruler guard, a lord; ruler; regis custodes, regii satellites Cd 131 Th p 166, 13:

Brehtnian l 2 ore: spare

Bremesbyrig-dl

Bremes. burh, g -burge, - d. byrig

Bransbyrig. Æt Bremesbyrig at Bromsb. Chr 910 Ing p 128, 15 v. Breman-burh

Breost-cearu, e f pectoris cura Cod Ex 81 b

Breóst-gewæde es; n breast clothing a coat of mail Beo K 2422: 4319

Breast-weorðung e; f breast ornament Beo K 5093

Breost-wylm, es; m breast flood, ... Beo K 3750

Brember a bramble Cd 142; Th p 177, 12 Index

Breotone Th. An v Brytten Britain

Breawant

O1 O4 [75b] O3 [75c] O5 [76a] O2 [76c] O4 [76e] O2 [77a] O4 [77b] O5 [77c]

Ing. p. 176, 26. Prodesse, Bd. 4, 22.

Brecing, e; f. A BREAKING; fractio:—R. Lk. 24, 35.

Bred; pl. bredu *A surface, plank,* BOARD, *table, a small table;* superficies:—On bradan brede *in a broad surface,* Bt. 18, 1: Deut. 9, 9, v. bradnys. ¶ Lytle hus of bredan *a small house of tables, eating houses,* R. 55. Breda þiling, *or* flor to þerscenne *a joining of planks or floor for thrashing,* R. 55.

Bred *deceit,* v. bræd.

Bred *broad,* v. breden.

Bredan, bregdan; he brit; *p.* bræd, brægd, hi brudon, brugdon; *pp.* broden, brogden, brægd [*Plat. Dut.* breiden: *Frs.* breydje: *Icel.* bregd: *Franc.* breydan] *To weave, bend, fold,* BRAID, *knit, to gripe, lay hold of, draw out;* plectere, distringere:—Ic brede me max *I weave for myself nets, Col. Monast. Elf. gr.* 28, 5. Handum brugdon, *Cd.* 93. Mundum brugdon, *Jdth.* 11: *Th. Hep.* p. 24, 38. *Griped or drew with hands.* Of his brægd bogan *from his bent bow, Cod. Ex.* 19, a. 8.

Bredan 1. *To nourish, cherish, keep warm;* fovere. 2. *To roast;* assare, v. weormian:—1. *Cot.* 86. 2. *Som.*

Bredbure *a bed-chamber,* v. brydbur.

Breden, bred, bræd *broad;* latus, v. brad.

Bredende; *adj.* [*part. of* brædan *to pretend*] *Deceitful, cunning, crafty;* dolosus:—*Ors.* 5, 7: *Bar.* p. 188, 27.

Bredguma *a bridegroom,* v. brydguma.

Brediponne, bredingpanne *a frying-pan,* v. brædpanne.

Bred-isern *a graving iron,* v. brædisen.

reg eagan *the brow of the eye, the eyebrow.*

regd, bregda *fear, terrible, dread,* v. broga, bregnes.

egdan *to knit,* v. bredan.

egden *taken away, drawn out,* v. bredan.

egean, gebregan; *p.* de, hi regdon; *pp.* ed; *v. a.* [broga ear] *To give fear, to frighten, rrify;* terrere:—Sume wif bregdon, *Lk.* 24, 22. Ne o ge gebregede, *Lk.* 21, 9, *t.* 5, 12.

en *the brain,* v. brægen.

en-ford, Brent-ford [*Hunt.* Brendeford; *D.* Brenford: Ford *the ford,* Brent *the r Brent*] BRENTFORD in ddlesex, situate where the river Brent flows into the Thames, *Chr.* 1016.

Bregh *a brow,* v. bræw.

Bregnes, se; *f.* 1. *Fear, terror, dread;* terror. 2. *A scarecrow, bugbear;* terriculum:—1. *Ps.* 87, 17. 2. *Som.*

BREGO, bregu, [*Norse,* brage] A word chiefly used by poets, denoting *a governor, ruler, lord, prince, king;* imperator, rex:—Se beorna brego *a leader of men, Jdth.* 12, p. 25, 11. Norðmanna bregu *the leader of North men, Chr.* 938. Brego engla *the ruler of angels, Cd.* 9. Bregomoncynnes *ruler of mankind, Bt. R.* p. 174. Babilone brego *the king of Babylon, Cd.* 187: 131.

Bregyd *for* breged *frightened,* v. bregean.

Brehtm *a moment,* v. bearhtm.

Brehtnian *To make a noise* or *crackling;* crepere:—*Cot.* 202, *Som.*

Brehtnung, breahtnung, e; *f. A noise, a clattering, a cracking;* convolatus:—*Cot.* 49, *v.l.*

BREM, brym; *comp.* bremra; *sup.* brymust; *def.* se brema; seo, þæt breme; *adj. Renowned, famous,* BRIM, *notable;* celebris:—Se brema ealdor *the famous prince, Jdth. Thw.* p. 22, 10. Þe Romana brymuste *the most renowned of Romans, Ors.* 2, 2. Breme Babilone weard *the famous Babylonian guard, Cd.* 177. Gregorius breme in Brytene *Gregory renowned in Britain, Menol.* 77. Ben tiid bremu *famous prayer tide* or *time, Menol.* 144.

Breman, abreman, gebreman; *p.* de; *pp.* ed; *v. a. To celebrate, solemnize, make famous, have in honour;* celebrare:—Þæt hie þat halige geryne breman mægen *that they may celebrate the holy sacrament, L. Eccl.* 4, *W.* p. 178, 27. Abremende *celebrating, Cod. Ex.* 13, *a. l.* He wold gebreman þa Judeiscan *he would honour the Jews, Som.*

Brembel *a bramble.* Brembelæppel *a thorn apple,* v. bremel.

Brembel-brær *a bramble brier,* v. bræmbel-brær.

Brembr *a bramble,* v. bremel.

Breme *famous,* v. brem.

BREMEL, brembr, bræmbelbrær, brembel, es; *m.* [*Plat.* brummelberen *f*: *Dut.* brummel *m*: *Ger.* brombeere: *Dan.* brambaer *n*: *Swed.* brombår] *A brier, a blackberry bush,* BRAMBLE, *a thistle, tormenting, mulberry tree;* tribulus, vepres, morus, rubus fructicosus, *Lin*:—Betwux þam bremelum, *Gen.* 22, 13. Þornas and bremelas, *Gen.* 3, 18.

Bremelþyrna *a bramble thorn, a bramble bush,* v. bremel.

Bremen *solemn,* v. brem.

Bremesbyrig BRAMSBURY, *or Bramsby, Lincolnshire, Chr.* 910, v. Brunanburh.

Bremman [*Dut.* brommen: *Frs.* brimme] *To rage, roar;* fremere:—*R. Jn.* 11, 48.

Bremra *more illustrious,* v. brem.

Brengan *to bring,* v. bringan.

Brengnes, se; *f. An offering;* oblatio:—*Ps.* 39, 9.

Brenning *A burning;* crematio, *Som.*

Breod *bread,* v. bread.

Breord *a brim,* v. brerd.

BREOST, [*Plat. Dut.* borst *f*: *Ger.* brust *f*: *Moes.* brusts: *Dan.* bryst c: *Swed.* bröst *n*: *Icel. Norse,* briost] *The teats which contain milk, the* BREAST, *mind;* pectus, ubera:—He beot hys breost, *Lk.* 18, 13. Þa breost *the breasts, Lk.* 11, 27. ¶ Breostban *the breastbone, Ben.* Breost-bedern *the breast-chamber, the inmost thoughts, the mind, R.* 73: *Elf. gl.* p. 71. Breost-beorh, breost-geborh *a breast defence, breast-plate, Som.* Breost-cofa *the breast chamber, the mind, the breast, Bt. R.* p. 160.—Breost-gehygd *a breast thought, Cd.* 64. Breostgeþanc *a breast thought, the mind, Cd.* 192.—Breost-hord *a mind hoard, a mind, Cd.* 79. Breost-line *a breast cloth, the stomacher, Cot.* 89.—Breost-loca *the breast enclosure, Cd.* 180.—Breost-net *a breast net, Cd.* 154.—Breost-rocc *a breast clothing;* thorax, *Cot.* 163: *R.* 63: *Elf. gl.* p. 68, v. rocc. Breost-warc *a breast pain, the asthma, short windedness, Som.* Breost-weall *breast works, ramparts* or *parapets made breast high, Cot.* 199, *Som.*—Breost-wylmas *breast warmth, the breast, teats, udders, Ps.* 21, 8.

Breotan; *v. a. To bruise;* conterere:—Hergas breotað, *Cod. Ex.* 14, b. v. brytan, abreotan, tobrittan.

Breoten, Breoten-ealond *Britain,* v. Bryten.

Breoton, *perhaps* beorton, *or* beortun *a hall, Mann.*

Breoton *Britain,* v. Bryten.

Breotone-lond *Britain's land.*

Brer *a briar,* v. brær.

Brerd, breard, briord *A brim, margin, rim, top of a pot or vessel, a shore, bank, brink;* labrum, ora, margo:—Oð þone brerd *to the brim, Jn.* 2, 7.

Bres *brass,* v. bræs.

Bresne *brazen, strong*, v. bræsen.

Bretenan mere *the British mere or lake, a name of a place, Welshpool, Som.*

Bretene *Britain*, v. Bryten.

Breð *breath*, v. bræð.

Breðer *to a brother*; fratri, v. broðor.

Bretland *Britain*, v. Bryten.

Brettas *Britons*, v. Bryt.

Brettnere *A steward*; dispensator, *Lye.*

Bret-walda *ruler of Britons.*

Brew *an eyebrow*, v. bræw.

Bric *a bridge*, v. brycg.

Brica *A breaker*; ruptor, *Som.*

BRICE, gebrice, bryce, es; *m.* [*Plat.* bräk *m*: *Dut.* breuk *f*: *Ger.* bruch *m*: *Dan.* braek, brök: *Icel.* brekt: *Swed.* bråk] *A rupture, breaking, fragment, fracture, violation*; ruptura:—On hlafes brice, *Lk.* 24, 35: *Bd.* 3, 2. Þæs borges bryce *a violation* or *infraction of the pledge* or *security, L. Alf. pol.* 3, *W.* p. 35, 15, v. borh-bryce.

Brice *use, service*, v. bryce.

Bricg *a bridge*, v. brycg.

Bricg-bot *repairing of a bridge.*

Bricge, Brigge, Brycge [*Sim. Dunel.* Brige: *Hovd.* Briges: *Brom.* Brugges, Brugge, Bruggenorth: *Mat. West.* Brigges] *Bruges, Bridgenorth, Shropshire, Chr.* 912, *Ing.* p. 129, 16: 1037, *Ing.* 210, 7. ¶ Bricge begeondan sæ *Bruges in Flanders, Som.*

Bricg-geweorc *a mending of a bridge*:—Bricge-gewurce, *L. Ethel.* Brycg-geweorc, *Heming.* p. 104, *Lye. Turner's Hist. of A. S. app. No.* 4, c. 3, vol. ii. p. 536.

Bricg-stow, Bric-stow, Bristow [*Ord. Vit.* Brichstou.—Brycg *a bridge*, stow *a place, or* stol *a seat*] BRISTOL *in Gloucestershire*, and *Somersetshire*:—To Bricg-stowe *to Bristol, Chr.* 1088, *Ing.* p. 298, 35.

Briest *shalt eat*; edis, v. brucan *and shalt break*; confringes, v. brecan.

Bricsade *profited*; profuit, v. brycian.

Brid *a bride*, v. bryd.

BRID; *g.* briddes; *m.* [*Plat.* brod, brot *f*: *Dut.* broed *n*: *Ger.* brut *f.*] *The young of any bird* or *animal, a* BROOD; pullus:—Turtlah setæ briddas heora, *Ps.* 83, 3: *Lk.* 2, 24: *Lev.* 1, 14. Earnes brid *an eagle's young, Cod. Ex.* 59, a.

Bridal *a marriage feast*, v. brydeala.

Brid-bed *a bride bed*, v. bryd.

Brid-bletsung *a marriage blessing.*

Bridbur *a bedchamber*, v. brydbur.

Briddas *broods*, v. brid.

Bridel, bridels *a bridle*, v. bridl.

Bridel-þwangas *the bridle, reins.*

Bridestung *The herb pimpernel*; bipenella, pampinella, *Som.*

Bridgifte *a marriage feast.*

Bridgifu, bridgifa *a dowry, marriage portion, espousals, Som.*

Bridguma *a bridegroom*, v. brydguma.

BRIDL, bridel, brydel, brydyls, es; *m.* [*Dut.* breidel *n*: *Old. Frs.* bridel] A BRIDLE; frænum:—Gewealdleþer þara bridla *a governing leather*, or *rein of the bridle, Bt.* 21. Brydel-þwangas *bridle thongs* or *reins, Coll. Monast*: *Bt. R.* p. 167: 185: *Bd.* 3, 9, *S.* p. 533, n. 34. ¶ Bridles midl *a bridle's middle, a bit, Elf. gl. Som.* p. 59.

Bridlac *a marriage, amusement*, v. brydlac.

Bridlian *To* BRIDLE, *curb, rule*; frænare, *Som.*

Brig *a bridge*, v. brycg.

Briht *bright*, v. beorht.

Briht-hwile *a glance*, v. bearhtm.

Brihtlice *brightly*, v. beorhte.

Brihtmen *Broken meat, crumbs, scraps, fragments of the table*; fragmenta, *Som.*

Briig *pottage*, v. briw.

Brim *the sea*, v. brym.

Brim-flod *a sea-flood, deluge*, v. brymflod.

Brim-hengest *a sea-horse, a ship.*

Brim-hlæste *the sea's burdens, merchandise, rewards, fishes, Lye.*

Brimsa *A gad-fly*; tabanus:—*Cot.* 160, *Lye.*

Bring, es; *m. That which is brought, an offering, a sacrifice, company*; sacrificium:—*Cd.* 158. Bringas *holocausta, Ps.* 50, 20.

BRINGAN, brengan, gebringan; he bringð, bryngað; *p.* brohte; *pp.* gebroht, brungen; *v. a.* [*Plat. Ger.* bringen: *Frs.* bringe: *Dut.* brengen: *Ker.* pringan: *Isid.* bibringan: *Ott.* bringan: *Will.* bringon: *Moes.* briggan, pronounced bringan: *Dan.* bringe: *Swed.* brenga] *To* BRING, *adduce, lead, produce, bear, carry*; ferre:—Ne mæg gebringan *cannot bring, Bt.* 32, 1: *Ps.* 28, 1: 40, 3. Seo eorðe westmas bringð *the earth produces fruit, Bt.* 33, 4. Mot brengan blosman *may bring blossoms, Bt.* 7, 3. Þær wæs gebroht win *there was wine brought, Chr.* 1012: *Lev.* 1, 2: 32, 24. ¶ To wife broht *to wife brought, married, Bd.* 3, 7: 4, 19.

Briord *a brim*, v. brerd.

Briosa *an ox-fly, a bee, breeze*; tabanus, *Som.* v. brimsa.

Brist *carriest*, vehis *for* berist, *from* beran.

Bristl *a bristle*, v. byrst.

Bristniende, *perhaps for* britniende, brittende *or* bryttende *breaking*; frians, v. brytan.

Brit *knit*; plectit, v. bredan.

Brittanie, Brittonie BRITAIN, v. Bryten.

Brittian *to dispose*, v. bryttian.

Brittisc *British*, v. Bryttisc.

Brittnera *a manager*, v. brytta.

BRIW, es; *m.* [*Plat.* bree, brie *m*: *Frs. Dut.* bry *m*: *Ger.* brey *m*: *Wel.* briw *a fragment, morsel. Huloet*, in the reign of Edward VI., calls it "browesse, *made with bread and fat meat.*" In Yorkshire it is now called breaw. In the north of England a brewis is a thick piece of bread soaked in a pot *of boiling fat, salted beef*] BREWIS, *the small pieces of meat in broth, pottage, frumenty, &c.*; jusculum:—*Elf. gr.* 9, 46. Briwas niman, *Somn.* 205, v. cealer-briw.

Briwan; *pp.* browen. *To brew*; coquere cerevisiam, *Som.*

Bróc; *pl.* bréc, bræc; *pl.* bréc, bræc [*Plat.* brook, büx *f*: *Frs. Dut.* broek *f*: *Ger.* bruch *m*: *Isid.* brucha: *Dan.* brog *c*: *Swed.* brackar, böxor *f*: *Irish,* broages: *Ital.* brache: *Fr.* braies: *Lat.* bracca: *Grk.* βρακα: *Armor.* brag. In the north of England breeks: *Heb.* ברך brc *a knee, dress covering the knee*] *The* BREECHES, *a girdle*; femoralia:—*Elf. gl.* 20: *R. Ben.* 55.

Broc [*Dan.* brok *m*: *Irish,* broc: *Corn. Wel.* brock] A BROCK, *gray* or *badger, a lizard*; grumus:—*Elf. gl.* 13, *Som.*

Broc; [*Frs.* brok *a fragment, from* brocen *the pp. of* brecan *to break* or *burst forth*] 1. *A spring*, BROOK, *rivulet*; latex, torrens. 2. Broc, gebroc, broh *metaphorically, that which violently breaks from the body* or *mind*: hence *affliction, misery, tribulation, adversity, a disease, malady, sickness*; afflictio, morbus:—1. Se broc *the brook, Bt.* 6. 2. God nyle nan unaberendlice broc him ansettan *God wishes not to put on them any unbearable affliction, Bt.* 39, 10. Mid heardum broce *with severe* [*hard*] *affliction, Bt.* 39, 11. Brocu *afflictions, Lye.*

Broc *An inferior horse, a jade*; caballus, equus vilior:—And secen him broc on on-rade *and sought a horse for him to ride on, L. Md.* 2, 6, *Som.*

Bresme-dl × Bresen
strang v bræsen

O 2

O 3 O

O 5 [77d] (Brice)

Bridgifter dl
Bred-gifta nom.
g. ac; d. um. f;
only pl. Nuptials th-
apol.
Bridgifu, brydgifu
dowry etc

O 4 [78b]

O 5
O 6

O 1 g Briose v sfl
brimse

Brittan, part
brittende To crumble
conterere, friare
Som, Ben, Lye
v sfl gebrittan

O 2 [79a]

O 3 [79b]

Bricean to profit
Som, Ben Lye, but
rather bryian
from brecan

Bricge - dl
× Bricge Brig, Brycg
f Bridgenlich ?
at Bricge at
Bridgenorth Ch 912
Ing h 129, 16

Geo com pa to
Bricge she came
thence to Bruges
Chr 1037 Ing 210, 7

6 [78a]

Brim-wylf e f
sea wolf; lupa
marina Beo K 3011

5 Comm Commem.
S. Albani. Lye

Brim-faro a sea-
journey, ocean way,
Cd 190 Th 236, 17

Brim-lade, e f
a sea going; a voyage
navigatio Beo K 2096

Brim-lidend, es; m, brim-man
a seaman Th an Beo gl
O 4 Mr Th says bring
is an error for brim
Cd. Th p 196 noted.

Brim-stream,
es; m the ocean,
streams, the sea
Beo K 3817

Brim-wylm
es; m a sea wave
Beo K 2988

O 5 [81d]

Brim-wisa, an
m a sea ruler, a
sea king Beo K 5855

Bringan v marg
[+ Fri. branga: Swed
bringa]

Bróc, a bróce, d
bréc, pl bréc,
bræc femoralia

See 8 in Margin

O 7 Broc m [80a]
O 8 Broc [80b]
Bróc es m
a brook etc

Broc es; n
affliction misery,
distress
Gm I 643, 25

01

Broðor-wyrt brother wort; herba quaedam strictum pectus et tussim sanans. Ben. Lye

Bront? [Icel. brandr] rostrum navis i.e. aestuans Beo [struck through] K 3210

[81e] 06 07 02 [83a]

[82a]

Streaming, raging, boiling, foaming; aestuans Brontne ceol ladan to lead a foaming keel torrens, Beo [struck through] K 475: Ymb bront ford about the boiling ford ne ford, Beo [struck through] K 1130

Bróc minte, broc-mynte a mint water mint [struck through] v. dpl minte

Brosð breath, th. ae. [struck through] brcost Ic late wrican i well permit (let) to enjoy Cd. 126 th. p 161, 13. Ic bruce Ef 37 Som p 39, 35

Broden-mæl, es; n twisted mark [struck through] Beo K 3231

Broð, es; n. north ... th an 07 [83b]

0 [82b]

07 [81c]

04 [82c]

28 —

Brogden-mæl, es; n twisted sword Beo K 3332

Bróðor l. 8 Maes* brothar m; dl. brother l9 Ir.* brathair m: Wel. brawd m. — l. 30 [struck through] Bróðor-ræden — l. 31 Bróðor-sib — l. 34 Bróðor-pinen — l. 37 Bróðor-wíf

[struck through] Ða hine se broga an-geat when on him the fear fell Beo K 3583

Broh-pred dire calamity Cd. 86, th p. 108, 29

08 [81d]

Broca *a brook*, v. broc.

Broccen, *or* gæten roc [be, roc *a garment*, gæten *a goaten, caprine*] *A garment made of goat or sheep-skins, extending from the shoulders to the loins* melotes:—*R.* 61: *Med. ex. quadr.* 1, 1.

Broce *use*, v. bryce.

Brocen *broken, pp. of* brecan.

Brocian; *p.* ode; *pp.* gebrocod; *v. a.* [broc *affliction*] *To oppress, vex, trouble, afflict, persecute*; opprimere:—Gebetan þe hi þonne brociað *to amend whom they then afflict, Bt.* 39, 11: *Ors.* 2, 4. Næfde se here Angel-cyn gebrocod *the enemy had not destroyed the English nation, Chr.* 897: *Ors.* 4, 1.

Broclic; *adj. Sick, grieved, miserable*; æger.

Broclice; *adv. Sickly, grievously*; ægre, *Som.*

Brocmynt *watermint*, BROOK-MINT [*q.* menta sylvestris, *Lin.*]:—*Herb.* 106, *Som.*

Brocod *sick, broken, afflicted with a rupture, broken in fortune, bankrupt, Som.*

Brocu *troubles*, v. broc.

Brocung *Contrition, sorrow*; contritio, *Som.*

Brod *a brood*, v. brid.

Brod; *adv. Freely, of free cost*; gratis:—*Cot.* 97, 164, *Som.*

Broddetan, brodettan *To tremble, quake, to pant for fear*; tremere:—*Greg.* 2, 25: *Cot.* 154, *Som.*

Brode *A growing together, a congealing, a waxing hard*; concretio:—*Cot.* 55, v. 1, *Som.*

Brodetung *A work, workmanship, fashion, forged tale, a lie*; figmentum:—*Ps.* 102, 13, *Som.* v. bræd.

Brodig; *adj.* BROODY, *brooding*; incubans:—Brodige henne *a broody hen, Bridf.*

Broel [corrupted from the *Lat.* brolium *or* briolium] *A park, warren stored with deer*: hence the BROYL, *a wood in Sussex, belonging to the Archbishop of Canterbury*; vivarium, *Som.*

ROGA, an; *A prodigy, monster, trembling, fear, terror, horror, dread*; monstrum:—Ænig ɔþer broga *any other prodigy, Bt.* 36, 1: *Ps.* 87, 17: *Past.* 7, 2. Butan brogan *without* read, *Lev.* 26, 6.

h *misery*, v. broc.

ht *Bird-lime*; viscum, *Som.*

ıte *brought*; attulit, v. brinn.

ı BROOM, *what is made of* ɔom, *a broom, besom*; myɑ, scopæ:—*Ælf. gl. Som.* p.

ndun [brom *broom*, dun *a hill*] *The name of a place, L. Const. Ethel. W.* p. 117, 41.

Brom-fæsten *a broom-field, a field, a close* or *wood of broom, Som.*

Brond *a torch*, v. brand.

Brooc *a brook*, v. broc.

BRORD, es; *m. A prick* or *point, the first blade* or *spire of grass, corn, &c. a herb*; punctus, frumenti spicæ, herba:—*Cot.* 157. Ne furþan brordas *not even herbs, Bd.* 4, 28, v. blæd.

Brosnian; *p.* ode; *pp.* od. *To corrupt, rot, perish*; corrumpere:—Lichoma brosnian ne mihte *the flesh could not corrupt, Bd.* 4, 19.

Brosniende, brosniendlic, brosnigendlic; *adj. Corruptible, perishable*; corruptibilis:—*Bt.* 16, 1.

Brosnung, e; *f. A corruption*; corruptio:—*Ps.* 29, 11.

Brostlung *a crackling*, v. brastlung.

Brotene *Britain*, v. Bryten.

Broð BROTH; jus:—*Ælf. gl.* 21.

Broð *a scent*, v. bræð.

Bróðer *a brother*, for broðer and its compounds, such as broðerlic, v. broðor and its compounds.

Bróðerscipe Godes, *or* lufe *Christian love*; caritas.

BRO'ÐOR, bróðer, bróður; *nom. g. ac.* bróðor; *d.* bréðer; *pl. nom. ac.* gebroðra, bróðra, u; *g.* bróðra; *d.* bróðrum; *m.* [*Plat. Dan. Swed. Nors.* broder *m*: *Dut.* broeder *m*: *Ger.* bruder *m*: *Ot.* bruader: *Will.* bruoder: *Moes.* brothar, brothr: *Arm.* breur: *Sclav.* bratr: *Irish* bratha: *Sans.* bhrâtre: *Pers.* برادر bradr:—*Avenar* thinks it is derived *from* ברית brit, *an agreement*; fœdus] A BROTHER; frater:—Hwær is þine broðor, *Gen.* 4, 9. Þines broðor blod clypað, *Gen.* 4, 10: *Mt.* 5, 23. Gemang broðrum *among brethren, Jn.* 21, 23: *Mk.* 10, 29, 30: *Ps.* 21, 21: 48, 7. Ge synt ealle gebroðru, *Mt.* 23, 8: *Gen.* 13, 8. ¶ Geboren broðer *Germanus frater, Greg.* 2, 13. Broðor-bana *a brother slayer, Cd.* 75. Broðor-cwealm *the murder of a brother, Cd.* 49. Broðor gefædred *a brother on the father's side.* Broðor gemædræd *a brother on the mother's side* Broðor-gyld, *or* broðor rædden, broðor-had *a brotherhood, Cd.* 153. Broðor-sib *brotherhood, Cot.* 100. Broðor-slaga *a murderer of a brother, Ælf. gl.* 26. Broðor-þinen *a midwife, Gen.* 38, 28. Broðor-sunu *a brother's son, Cd.* 86. Broðor-wif *a brother's wife, Bd.* 1, 27, *resp.* 5.

Bróðorlic, bróðerlic; *adj.* BROTHERLY; fraternus:—*Bd.* 4, 22: *Ælf. gl.* 5.

Bróðorlicnys, se; *f. Brotherlyness, brotherhood*; fraternitas, *Som.*

Bróður, *Mt.* 4, 21:—Broðra broðru, *Jn.* 7, 3, 10, v. broðor *a brother.*

Browen *brewed, cooked, Som.* v. briwan.

Brucað *enjoy*, v. brucan.

Brúcan; þu bricst, he bryceð, we brucað, brycað; *p.* breác, we brucon; *pp.* brocen, gebrocen [*Plat.* bruken: *Frs. c.* bruke: *Dut.* bruiken: *Ger.* brauchen: *Will.* gebruchan: *Swed.* bruke: *Chaus.* broke, browke: bryce *use*] *To use, eat, enjoy, bear, discharge, profit*; uti, frui:—Ne bricst *usest not, Deut.* 28, 30. Þu bricst þines hlafes, *Gen.* 3, 19: *Jn.* 4, 9: *Bd.* 4, 4, 19, 22, v. brycian.

Brucing *A function, an occupation, enjoyment*; functio, *Som.*

Brudon *for* bræddon *spread*; dilatarunt:—*Cd.* 154, v. brædan.

Brugdon *laid hold of, drew*; strinxerunt, v. bredan.

BRUN; *adj.* [*Plat.* bruun: *Frs.* bruen: *Dut.* bruin: *Ger.* braun: *Dan. Swed.* brun: *Fr.* brun: *Ital.* bruno: *Low. Lat.* brunus. *Wach.* says from bærnan *or* byrnan *to burn, from the colour produced in burning*] BROWN; fuscus:—*Cd.* 146: *Bt. R.* p. 189: *Cot.* 86.

Brunan-burh, Brunnan-burh, [*Ethelw.* a contemporary calls it Brunandune: *D. Sim.* Weondune, Ethrunnanwerch, Brunnan byrge: *M. Will.* Brunsford: *Ingul.* Brunford in *Northumbria*: *Hunt.* Brumesburh, Brunesburh, Brunesburh, Bruneburh: *Hovd.* Brunnanburg, Brumenburh: *Brom.* Brunneburyh] *The place where the famous battle of Athelstan was fought,* in the year A.D. 938. *Camden* thought this place was at Ford, near Bromeridge, in Northumberland. *Gibson* mentions, that in Cheshire there is a place called Brunburh. *Mr. Turner* says, I observe that the VILLARE mentions a Brunton in Northumberland. *Dr. Ingram* selects Brumby, Lincolnshire, *Chr.* 938, *Ing.* p. 141, 15, v. Bremes-byrig.

Brunbaso [brun *brown*, baso *pur-*

ple] *A purple colour, a purple* or *scarlet garment;* ostriger:—*Cot.* 145. Þy brunan oððe þy brun basewan, *Cot.* 183.

ᵃBruneþan *A disease;* erysipelas cerebri:—*L. M.* 1, 4, *Som.*

Brunewyrt *Brown-wort water-betony, spleen-wort, miltwast;* scrophularia minor:—*Herb.* 57, *Som.*

Brungen *Brought;* latus, v. bringan.

Brun *a brook,* v. burn.

Bruun *red, brown, Lye, q.* brun.

Bruwa *a brow,* v. bræw.

Bryc *a bridge,* v. brycg.

Bryce *a violation, infraction,* v. brice.

Bryce, brice, broce, es; *m.* [*Plat.* bruuk *m*: *Frs.* brek: *Dut.* gebruik *n*: *Ger.* brauch *m*: *Dan.* brug *n*: *Swed.* bruk *n.*] *Use, the occupation or exercise of a thing, profit, advantage, fruit;* usus, commodum:—Gehiwade wæron mennisces bryces *were made for man's use, Bd.* 3, 22: *Deut.* 4, 19. Gif þat owiht bryce wæs *if that were any advantage, Bd.* 5, 14, *S.* p. 634, 8, n. Lænes landes bryce *advantage of lands, loan, fruit, rent, Cot.* 92.

Brycg, bricg, bryc, brygc [*Plat.* brügge *f*: *Dut.* brug *f*: *Frs.* brigge: *Ger.* brücke *f*: *Swed.* brygga *f.*] A bridge; pons:—Þæt he ne myhte to þære brycge cuman *that he could not come to the bridge, Ors.* 2, 5, *Bar.* p. 76, 1, p. 71, 27, p. 75, 30: 6, 30, *Bar.* p. 231, 9.

Brycg-bot *a repairing of a bridge,* v. bricgbot.

Brycg-geweorc *repairing of a bridge,* v. bricg-geweorc.

Brycgstow *Bristol,* v. Bricgstow.

Brycian; p. bricsade. *To profit, do good;* prodesse:—He his geferum brycian gymde *he took care to do good to his companions, Bd.* 5, 9. Him sylfum bricsade *benefited himself, Bd.* 5, 13, v. brucan.

Bryc𝔡 *uses;* utitur, v. brucan.

Bryd, brid, e; *f.* [*Frs.* breid: *Dut.* bruid *f*: *Ger.* braut *f*: *Not.* prud: *Moes.* bruth: *Dan. Swed. Norse,* brud: *Icel.* bruda] A bride, *wife, woman;* sponsa:—Ferdun ongean þa bryde, *Mt.* 25, 1. Adames bryd *Adam's wife, Cd.* 10: 26. Me Sarran bryde laste beddreste gestah, *Cd.* 129: *Bt. R.* p. 160, 3.

Bryd-bed *a bride-bed.*

Bryd-bur *a bedchamber.*

Bryde *A drawing out;* extractio:—*L. Alf. pol.* 34, v. brædan.

Bryd-eala, bryd-ealo *A bride-ale, bride* or *marriage feast;* nuptiale convivium, *Som.*

Þær wæs þat bryd-eala
Mannum to beala
There was that bride-ale
The source of man's bale.
Chr. 1075, *Ing.* p. 280, 19.

Brydel *a bridle,* v. bridl.

Bryde laste *a bride foot, a step.*

Brydelica gewrit *A play;* drama, *Som.*

Brydel-þwangas *bridle-reins,* v. bridl.

ᵃBryden wah *a broad wall,* v. breden.

Brydgifa *espousals,* v. bridgifu.

Bryd-guma *a bridegroom, suiter;* sponsus, procus:—*Mt.* 9, 15: *Ps.* 18, 5. ¶ Brydguma broþor *a bride-groom's brother.*

Brydlac *a marriage gift, bride-laces.*

Brydleoð *a marriage song.*

Brydlic; *adv. Bridal;* nuptialis:—*C. Mt.* 22, 12.

Brydlofa, brydlopa, brydloppa *a marriage, a marriage feast.*

Brydræst *a bride bed,* v. brydbed.

Brydreaf *a nuptial garment.*

Brydsang *a marriage song.*

Brydþingas *marriage affairs.*

Brydyls *a bridle,* v. bridl.

Brygc *a bridge,* v. brycg.

Bryht *bright,* v. beorht.

Bryhtm *a glance,* v. bearhtm.

Brym, brim; *pl.* brimu, bræmas [*Icel.* brim *n.*] *The sea;* salum, mare:—On þam bradan brime *on the broad sea, Cod. Ex.* 55, a. 7. Ofer brad brymu *over broad seas, Cd.* 100: *Menol.* 539. ¶ Brym-flod *a deluge, R.* 115. Brym-stream *or sæ the sea, R. Mt.* 8, 18.

Bryme *famous,* v. brem.

ᵃBrym-flod *a deluge,* v. brym.

Brymme, es; *m.* A brim, *brink, an edge, a border, lip of a pot, and such like;* ora, margo:—Bremmas sæs *the borders* or *shores of the sea, a strait, Hymn. Som.*

Brym-stream *or sæ the sea,* v. brym.

Brymuste *most famous,* v. brem.

Bryne, byrne, es; *m. A burning, scorching, heat, fire;* incendium:—Þa brynas þara husa *the burnings of their houses, Bd.* 1, 19: *Deut.* 9, 22. ¶ Bryne-adl *a burning disease, a fever, Cot.* 92.—Bryne-gield *a burnt-offering, Cd.* 140.

Bryne Brine, *salt liquor;* salsugo:—*R.* 33.

Brynga𝔡 *bringeth;* ferat, v. bringan.

Bryrd *grieved;* compunctus, *q. from* bryrdan *to goad,* v. onbryrdan.

Bryrd-dæg *passion-day.*

Bryrdnys *sorrow,* v. onbryrdnys.

Bryrð *ruleth;* gubernat:—*Bt. R.* 167, v. prose, c. 25, where welt, from wealdan *to govern,* answers to bryrð in the poetry.

Brysan; p. de; *pp.* brysed, brysyd, gebrysed. *To bruise;* conterere, *Som.*

ᵃBryt *A nymph;* nympha:—*R.* 88.

Bryt, Brit, Bret; *g.* Bryttes; *m.* [*Wel.* brith, brit *of divers colours, spotted: Heb.* ברד brd *hence the pl.* ברדים brdim *spots, spotted with colours*] A Briton, *whether in Great Britain* or *Bretagne;* Britannus:—Ærost wæron bugend þyses landes Bryttas *the first inhabitants of this land were Britons, Chr. Ing.* p. 1, 6: 2, 10: *Chr.* 457, *Ing.* p. 15, 19: *Bt.* 1, 16. Brytta ealond *the island of Britons.* Brytta þeode *the nation of Britons, Bd.* 1, 34: 3, 10.

Bryta *an author,* v. brytta.

Brytan *to break,* v. bryttian.

Brytednys, se; *f. A breaking, a bruising;* contritio, *Som.*

Bryten, Bryton, Brytene, Bryteneland, Brytland, Breoten, Breotene, Breoten-ealond, Breoton, Bretene, Brotene, Brittanie, Brittene, Brittonie, Bryttene [*from* Bryt because of their painted bodies. *Bochart* says, the *Grk.* βρεταγνικη is the Punic ברת־אנך brt-ank *the land of tin*] Britain; Britannia, Cambria:—Brytene igland is ehta hund mila lang *the island Britain is eight hundred miles long, Chr. Ing.* p. 1, 1. Maximus, se Casere on Bryten londe geboren *Maximus, the Emperor, was born in the land of Britain, Chr.* 381, *Ing.* p. 11, 9. Breoton (Brytene C.) is Ealond þæt wæs iu geara Albion haten *Britain is an island that was formerly called Albion, Bd.* 1, 1, *S.* p. 473, 8: 2, 1: *Ors.* 6, 30: *Bar.* p. 228, 16. ¶ Bryten-ricu *British empire, Menol.* 446. Bryten-walda, Bryten-wealda *a British ruler* or *king, Chr.* 827.

Brytford (Bryt *a Briton,* ford *a ford*] Britford, *near Sarum, Wiltshire, Chr.* 1065, *Ing.* p. 253, note *a.*

Bryþen *the herb Britannica,* or *spoon-wort.*

Brytian *to profit,* v. bryttian.

Brytnedon *enjoyed,* v. bryttian.

Brytnere *a distributor, possessor,* v. brytta.

ᵃBrytofta *Espousals;* sponsalia:—*R.* 87.

Bryton, Brytonland *Britain,* v. Bryten.

Brytsan; *g.* brytsena; *d.* bryt-

X Brún-ecg brown edged spoken of a sword Th. An

Brún-fág brown coloured Beo K 5225

X Brún-wyrt brown wort

X Breord an compu gere Beo

O 3

X Brycg, bricg e; f. a bridge Th. An.

O [84 b]

O x 2 Som p. 623, 33

7 [84 c]

4

X Bryde lust a bride's step

O 1 [85 a]

O 2 [85 a]

... A 530 ... brown wort

X Bryden ... from Th. An.

O [85 a]

O 7 [85 b]

X Brym, es; m, the sea Th. An

O [86 a]

O 8 [86 b]

X Brymel v margin

O 7 Brymhusthe

O 9 [86 c]

X Bryne léoma a fire's flame Beo K 4621

X Bryne-wylm, es m. a fire wave, Beo K 4647

X 10 Bryngat

O Bryten, Bryten ... Brittain Bd 1, 10 Som p 480, 2 ... 1, 10 Som p 480, 7 12

O X Bryte ... Britain Th. An.

X Bryten, Bryton, Breoten, Breoton, e; f. Britain Brytene ealand Britain island Chr. ... Gesohte Brytene sought Britain Id p 2, 24

Bisse (f) ... Brytene Bd 1, 1 ... p 473, 34 — On Breotone in Britain Bd 1, 7 Som p 475, 31 — Ealre Breotone of all Britain Bd 5, 33 Som p 645, 5

O 1 Bd 5, 9 note line 33.

X 2 See ...

Bryd-ealo te. bryd-ealu Th. An. bride ale, marriage feast Som

O3

X7 Bryttene g. d. ac
of Bryten Britain

X Brytta, an m
the dispenser Beo gl.
l 1. dl – [Norse briotr] l 7. dl – Norse Gullbrǫtar

O6
O8 [88c]

O Brytta [87d]

O1 Brytte, es; m Briton
th. an.

O5 [87c]

X Brittisn l 3 dl – [Norse
briota, brytta a fragment]

O bid m L m' Grainp 149

O1 adj-

O7 [87e]

~~O4 [88a]~~

O [89g]

X6 Búr, es; m a
bedchamber Beo K 278

O4 [92c]
O8 [88b]

O1 se byrn-wiga
bágan sceolde
the warrior must bow
submit Beo K. 5832

X Burge saved p. sub
of beorgan

O2 Búgan to inhabit th. an
v ruan

X Bûhd for bygd bows th. an from
búgan.

O4 Bulentsan herba
genus ad psoras
S. M. 1, 47 Som

O5

X Búan inhabit
Cd 35. th p 45, 32.
209. th p 259, 18

O4 Bunden-stefna
navis, prora ligua-
lis compacta Beo
143 v Beo gl in stefn

3 Búne, an f. A cup
poculum th. an. Beo K 5547

O Burad for gebyrad
befits th. gn.
v. gebyrian

O10 Burg, mæg. burg
e. ft. A relation,
family, cognatio
Beo K 5769

senum; pl. [from brytan to break] Broken parts, fragments; fragmenta:—Fulle þæra brytsena, Mt. 14, 20: Mk. 8, 8: Jn. 6, 13.

Brytene Britain, v. Bryten.

Brytta, bryta; m. [Norse, brio-tur] A dispenser, an author, a bestower, a possessor, lord, prince; dispensator, dominus:—Lifes brytta life's lord, Lord of life, Cd. 6: Jdth. p. 22, 33, 36. Goldes brytta [Norse, Gullbriotur] dispenser of gold, Cd. 138.

Bryttas, Britta of Britons, v. Bryt.

Bryttian, bryttigan, brytan; hi bryttigað; p. bryttade, we bryttedon; v. a. [Norse, brio-ta. brytta a fragment] To divide into fragments, dispense, rule, use, employ, occupy, possess, enjoy. (A word used by poets); dispensare frustatim, gubernare, frui:—Land bryttade ruled the land, Cd. 62. Mihton mægyn bryttigan might use force, Cd. 4. Sculon welan bryttian shall enjoy wealth, Cd. 99. Woruld bryttade enjoyed the world, Cd. 62.

Bryttisc, Brittisc; adj. British; Britannicus:—Chr. Ing. p. 1.

a Bryttwealas Britons.

Bu both, v. ba, begen.

Búan, gebugian; ic búe, he byð; p. ic búde, we búdon; pp. gebún [Plat. boen: Dut. bouwen to till: Ger. bauen: Ott. Will. buen: Moes. bauan, gabauan: Dan. boe: Icel. búa: Swed. bo.—bu, bye an habitation] To inhabit, dwell, to cultivate, till; habitare, colere:—He let heo buan he let them inhabit, Cd. 13. He bude on East-Anglum he dwelt among the East-Angles, Chr. 890: Ors. 1, 1.

Buc, es; m. [Dut. bak a wooden bowl: Dan. bak c: Swed. bak m. Chaucer writes boket; in some parts of England, as in Cheshire, a pail for water is now called a bouk: hence with the Danish postpositive article -et bouket bucket] A BUCKET, flagon, vessel or water-pot, pitcher; lagena:—Elf. gl. 22. Hydria. Tobræcon þa bucas, Jud. 7, 20, 21.

Buc a stag, buck, v. bucca.

Bucc A cheek, a part of a helmet; buccula:—Cot 25, Lye.

Bucca, an; [Plat. buck m: Dut. Frs. bok m: Ger. bock m.] An he-goat, a BUCK; hircus:—Bringað anne buccan, Lev. 4, 23: Ps. 49, 10, 14. Buccan beard a goat's beard, Cot. 174. Buccan horn buck's horn, the sign Capricorn, Æqu. vern.

Buccingaham, mmes; m. [Hunt. W. Bukingeham: Brom. Bukyngham: Bucen or becen beechen; ham a village, says Camd. from the number and size of the beech trees.—bæc, v. boc a beech, ing, ham] BUCKINGHAM:—To Buccingahamme to Buckingham, Chr. 918. ¶ Buccingahamscir Buckinghamshire, Chr. 1010.

b Buce [Plat. buuk: Dut. buik m: Kil. beuck, buyck m: Ger. bauch m: Al. buh, buch: Swed. buk: Dan. bug: Chau. bouke the trunk of the human body. In the north of England they say bouk, bowk for the bulk, the size, the body of a tree] A solitary and secret place, the belly; secessus, venter:—Cot. 215.

Bucen beechen, v. becen.

Búde commanded; præcepit, offered; obtulit, hi budon, v. beodan.

Búde dwelt; habitavit, v. buan.

Buend One dwelling, an inhabitant, a farmer; incola, agricola:—Buendra leas void of inhabitants, desolate, Cd. 5, v. buan.

Bufan, bufon; prep. d. [Plat. baven: Dut. boven, contracted from be-oven or by-oven: be by; ufa, ufan above] Above, used in opposition to under; super:—God totwæmde þa wæteru þe wæron under þære fæstnisse fram þam þe wæron bufan þære fæstnisse, Gen. 1, 7.

Bufan, bufon, abufan, be-ufan; adv. Above, before, beyond, moreover; supra:—Swa we her be-ufan cwædon as we here above said, L. Athel. 3, W. p. 63, 24. Swa abufan sædan before [before above] said, Chr. 1090: Bd. 4, 22: Past. 8, 1, v. ufa.

Bufancweþen before-said, aforesaid, above-said.

Bugan both, v. begen.

Búgan, begean, abúgan, gebugan; p. ic beáh, beag, we bugon; imp. bug, buh; pp. bugen, bogen, gebogen; v. a. [Plat. bögen: Frs. c. buge: Frs. boege: Dut. buigen: Ger. biegen: Dan. böje neut.—boga a bow] To BOW, bend, to give way, recede, flee, submit, yield; flectere:—Þat ic bugende uncnytte, Mk. 1, 7. Heo wæs abogen, Lk. 13, 11. Heora cneo begean scolden should bow their knee, Bd. 3, 17, S. p. 544, 39. Abeah, Jn. 8, 6: Gen. 28, 12. Þu wylt þyder bugan, Gen. 19, 21: Ex. 21, 13: Num. 25, 2. Hi bugon þa to þam, Jos. 9, 27: 11, 19: Chr. 1013. Hi gebugon to Josue, Jos. 10, 4.

Bugend, bugigend A dweller; habitator:—Chr. Ing. p. 1, 6.

c Búgian, gebugian, to bugianne; p. hi bugodon, bogodon, gebudon; pp. gebuen. To inhabit, incolere:—Bt. 17: 18, 1: Ors. 1, 10: Elf. T. p. 21, 13, v. buan.

Bugunde bowing, v. bugan.

Buh avoid, v. bugan.

Buhsomnes obedience, v. bocsumnes.

Bul A stud, boss, brooch; bulla:—Cot. 26.

Bulberende Bearing bulbs; bulbaceus, Som.

Bulgian To bellow; admugire: Martyr. 17, Jan.

Bulgon Were angry; indignati sunt, v. belgan.

Bulluca A calf, a young bull, a BULLOCK; vitulus:—Scint. 54.

Bulot, bulut, bolot A herb, toadstool, mushroom, an excrescence found at the roots of oaks; herba:—L. Md. 2, 58, Som.

Bun A sort of cup; carchesium, poculi genus:—Jdth. 10.

Bunda A farmer, steward, father; villicus:—L. Cnut. 8.

Bunda Bundles; fasciculi.

Bunde Bound; vinxit:—bunden bound; ligatus, v. bindan.

Bune A cane, reed, pipe, flute; fistula, Som.

Bune, bunna Bologne in France; Bononia:—Chr. 893.

d Buoftalmon Wild chamomile; buphthalmus:—Herb. 140.

Bur, [Al. bauer: Norse, bur] A BOWER, cottage, dwelling, an inner room, storehouse; conclave, casa:—Lps. 26, 9: R. 27. ¶ Cumena bur a guest-house, Bd. 4, 31, v. burh.

Burcg a city, v. burh.

Burcote A bed, couch, a bed-chamber, den; cubile:—Past. 16, 1.

Burge of a city, v. burh.

Burgaman A citizen; civis:—Deut. 1, 16.

Burgan to protect, v. beorgan.

Burgate; pl. burgatu A gate to a dwelling, a door, a porch; porta, fores:—Jud. 16, 3.

Burgbete, burgbote a repairing of cities, v. burh, bot.

Burgbrice house-breaking, v. burhbrice.

Burge-bisceop the bishop of the city.

Burgendaland The land of Burgundians, an island in the west of the Baltic sea, Borringholm or Bornholm, Ors. 1, 1.

Burgendas The Burgundians; Burgundiones, Som.

O3

X7 Bryttene y. dæl of Bryten Britain

X Burge saved p. sub of beorgan

O2 Bŷgan to inhabit th. an v. buan

X Brytta, an m a dispenser Beo gl.

l 1. dl- [Norse briotur] l 7. dl- Norse Gulldrôtar

O8 [880]

O6 Brytta [87d]

O1 Brytte, es; m Briton th. an

X Buhd for byhd bows from bûgan.

O5 [87c]

X Britt... l 3 dl- [Norse briota, brytta a fragment]

O4 Bulentsan herba genus ad psoras L. M. 1, 47 Som

O5

O n bid ... 149 O1 adj-

O7 [87e]

X Bûn inhabit Cd 35, th p 45, 32- 209, th p 259, 18

O4 Bunden-stefna navis prora lignis compacta Beo 143 v Beo gl in stefn

O4 [88a]

O [89g]

X Bûne, an f. A cup poculum th. an. Beo K 5547

X Bûr, es; m a bedchamber Beo K 278

O Burœd for gebyrad befits th gn-

v. gebyrian

O4 [92c]

O8 [88b]

O1 be byrn-wiga bûgan sceolde the warrior must bow submit Beo K 5832

O10 Burg, mæg-burg e. f. A relation, family; cognatio Beo K 5769

senum; pl. [from brytan to break] Broken parts, fragments; fragmenta:—Fulle þæra brytsena, Mt. 14, 20: Mk. 8, 8: Jn. 6, 13.

Brytene Britain, v. Bryten.

Brytta, bryta; m. [Norse, briotur] A dispenser, an author, a bestower, a possessor, lord, prince; dispensator, dominus:—Lifes brytta life's lord, Lord of life, Cd. 6: Jdth. p. 22, 33, 36. Goldes brytta [Norse, Gullbriotur] dispenser of gold, Cd. 138.

Bryttas, Britta of Britons, v. Bryt.

Bryttian, bryttigan, brytan; hi bryttigaδ; p. bryttade, we bryttedon; v. a. [Norse, briota, brytta a fragment] To divide into fragments, dispense, rule, use, employ, occupy, possess, enjoy. (A word used by poets); dispensare frustatim, gubernare, frui:—Land bryttade ruled the land, Cd. 62. Mihton mægyn bryttigan might use force, Cd. 4. Sculon welan bryttian shall enjoy wealth, Cd. 99. Woruld bryttade enjoyed the world, Cd. 62.

Bryttisc, Brittisc; adj. British; Britannicus:—Chr. Ing. p. 1.

Bryttwealas Britons.

Bu both, v. ba, begen.

Búan, gebugian; ic búe, he byδ; p. ic búde, we búdon; pp. gebún [Plat. boen: Dut. bouwen to till: Ger. bauen: Ott. Will. buen: Moes. bauan, gabauan: Dan. boe: Icel. búa: Swed. bo.—bu, bye an habitation] To inhabit, dwell, to cultivate, till; habitare, colere:—He let heo buan he let them inhabit, Cd. 13. He bude on East-Anglum he dwelt among the East-Angles, Chr. 890: Ors. 1, 1.

Buc, es; m. [Dut. bak a wooden bowl: Dan. bak c: Swed. bak m. Chaucer writes boket in some parts of England, as in Cheshire, a pail for water is now called a bouk: hence with the Danish postpositive article -et bouket bucket] A BUCKET, flagon, vessel or water-pot, pitcher; lagena:—Elf. gl. 22. Hydria. Tobræcon þa bucas, Jud. 7, 20, 21.

… a stag, buck, v. bucca.

…c A cheek, a part of a helmet; buccula:—Cot 25, Lye.

…ca, an; [Plat. buck m: Dut. …s. bok m: Ger. bock m.] … he-goat; a BUCK; hircus: Bringaδ anne buccan, Lev. 23: Ps. 49, 10, 14. Bucca beard a goat's beard, Cot. … Buccan horn buck's horn, sign Capricorn, Æqu. vern.

Buccingaham, mmes; m. [Hunt. W. Bukingeham: Brom. Bukyngham: Bucen or becen beechen; ham a village, says Camd. from the number and size of the beech trees.—bæc, v. boc a beech, ing, ham] BUCKINGHAM:—To Buccingahamme to Buckingham, Chr. 918. ¶ Buccingahamscir Buckinghamshire, Chr. 1010.

Buce [Plat. buuk: Dut. buik m: Kil. beuck, buyck m: Ger. bauch m: Al. buh, buch: Swed. buk: Dan. bug: Chau. bouke the trunk of the human body. In the north of England they say bouk, bowk for the bulk, the size, the body of a tree] A solitary and secret place, the belly; secessus, venter:—Cot. 215.

Bucen beechen, v. becen.

Búde commanded; præcepit, offered; obtulit, hi budon, v. beodan.

Búde dwelt; habitavit, v. buan.

Buend One dwelling, an inhabitant, a farmer; incola, agricola:—Buendra leas void of inhabitants, desolate, Cd. 5, v. buan.

Bufan, bufon; prep. d. [Plat. baven: Dut. boven, contracted from be-oven or by-oven: be by; ufa, ufan above] Above, used in opposition to under; super:—God totwæmde þa wæteru þe wæron under þære fæstnisse fram þam þe wæron bufan þære fæstnisse, Gen. 1, 7.

Bufan, bufon, abufan, be-ufan; adv. Above, before, beyond, moreover; supra:—Swa we her be-ufan cwædon as we here above said, L. Athel. 3, W. p. 63, 24. Swa abufan sædan before [before above] said, Chr. 1090: Bd. 4, 22: Past. 8, 1, v. ufa.

Bufancweþen before-said, afore-said, above-said.

Bugan both, v. begen.

Búgan, begean, abúgan, gebugan; p. ic beáh, beag, we bugon; imp. bug, buh; pp. bugen, bogen, gebogen; v. a. [Plat. bögen: Frs. c. buge: Frs. boege: Dut. buigen: Ger. biegen: Dan. böje neut. —boga a bow] To BOW, bend, to give way, recede, flee, submit, yield; flectere:—Þat ic bugende unenytte, Mk. 1, 7. Heo wæs abogen, Lk. 13, 11. Heora cneo begean scolden should bow their knee, Bd. 3, 17, S. p. 544, 39. Abeah, Jn. 8, 6: Gen. 28, 12. Þu wylt þyder bugan, Gen. 19, 21: Ex. 21, 13: Num. 25, 2. Hi bugon þa to þam, Jos. 9, 27: 11, 19: Chr. 1013. Hi gebugon to Josue, Jos. 10, 4.

Bugend, bugigend A dweller; habitator:—Chr. Ing. p. 1, 6.

Bugian, gebugian, to bugianne; p. hi bugodon, bogodon, gebudon; pp. gebuen. To inhabit; incolere:—Bt. 17: 18, 1: Ors. 1, 10: Elf. T. p. 21, 13, v. buan.

Bugunde bowing, v. bugan.

Buh avoid, v. bugan.

Buhsomnes obedience, v. bocsumnes.

Bul A stud, boss, brooch; bulla:—Cot. 26.

Bulberende Bearing bulbs; bulbaceus, Som.

Bulgian To bellow; admugire: Martyr. 17, Jan.

Bulgon Were angry; indignati sunt, v. belgan.

Bulluca A calf, a young bull, a BULLOCK; vitulus:—Scint. 54.

Bulot, bulut, bolot A herb, toad-stool, mushroom, an excrescence found at the roots of oaks; herba:—L. Md. 2, 58, Som.

Bune A sort of cup; carchesium, poculi genus:—Jdth. 10.

Bunda A farmer, steward, father; villicus:—L. Cnut. 8.

Bunda Bundles; fasciculi.

Bunde Bound; vinxit:—bunden bound; ligatus, v. bindan.

Bune A cane, reed, pipe, flute; fistula, Som.

Bune, bunna Bologne in France; Bononia:—Chr. 893.

Buoftalmon Wild chamomile; buphthalmus:—Herb. 140.

Bur [Al. bauer: Norse, bur] A BOWER, cottage, dwelling, an inner room, storehouse; conclave, casa:—Lps. 26, 9: R. 27. ¶ Cumena bur a guest-house, Bd. 4, 31, v. burh.

Burcg a city, v. burh.

Burcote A bed, couch, a bed-chamber, den; cubile:—Past. 16, 1.

Burge of a city, v. burh.

Burgaman A citizen; civis:—Deut. 1, 16.

Burgan to protect, v. beorgan.

Burgate; pl. burgatu A gate to a dwelling, a door, a porch; porta, fores:—Jud. 16, 3.

Burgbete, burgbote a repairing of cities, v. burh, bot.

Burgbrice house-breaking, v. burhbrice.

Burge-bisceop the bishop of the city.

Burgendaland The land of Burgundians, an island in the west of the Baltic sea, Borringholm or Bornholm, Ors. 1, 1.

Burgendas The Burgundians; Burgundiones, Som.

Burgeteld *A tilt* or *covering of a tent, a tent;* tentorium:—*Jdth.* 10, 12.

Burge wearð *a multitude of a city*, v. burh-wered.

Burg-runan *the fairies of the mountains*, beorg *a mountain*, *Som*, v. burhrunan.

Burgscipe *citizenship*, v. burhscipe.

Burgstal, burgstol [Beorg *a hill;* stal *a seat, dwelling*] BORSTAL, BURSTAL, &c. *the name of places built on a hill.*

Burgum *to cities*, v. burh.

Burgwaru *city-men, citizens*, v. burhwaru.

Burgweallas *the city walls*, v. burhweal.

Burh *a surety*, v. borh.

BURH; *g.* burge *f. d.* byrig; *pl. nom. ac.* byrig; *g.* burga; *d.* burgum; *f.* [*Plat.* borch *f*: *Dut.* burgt *f*: *Dan. Swed. Icel.* borg *m. n.*] 1. *A town, city*, what are now called cities were anciently called burhs; urbs. 2. *A fort, castle;* castellum. 3. *Court, palace, house;* curia:—1. He gesawe þa burh, *Gen.* 11, 5: 13, 12. Binnan burgum *within a city*, *L. Edg. Sup. W.* p. 80, 46. Roma burh *the city Rome*, *Bd.* 1, 11. 2. *Ors.* 3, 1. 3. *Som.* ¶ Æfter burgum *through cities, openly, publicly*, *Bt. R.* p. 155: 195. Burg, or the modern bury, denotes *a city*, as Canterbury, &c.

Burhbote *a repairing of cities.*

Burhbrice *A breaking into a city, a burglary, house-breaking;* urbis violatio:—*L. In.* 45: *Alf. pol.* 36.

Burh-ealdor *An elder of a city, a mayor, governor;* præfectus urbis:—*Elf. gr.* 14: 9, 55.

Burh-fæstan *A city-fastness, a fort, fortress, citadel, defence;* arx:—*Cd.* 80.

Burhg *a city*, v. burh.

Burhgeat, burhgata *A city-gate;* porta urbis:—*Jos.* 2, 5.

Burhgemot A BURGMOTE, *a meeting of townsmen, corporation;* urbis comitia:—*L. pol. Edg.* 5: *L. Cnut.* 15.

Burh-gerefa *A city reeve, governor, bailiff;* prætor, præfectus:—*R.* 6: Curiales 8.

Burhgeweardas *the borough-wards* or *keepers*, v. burhweardas.

Burh-leod *A town's people, a citizen;* civis:—*Ors.* 3, 7.

Burh-loca *a locking of a city, a gate.*

Burh-man *A town's man, citizen;* civis:—*Nathan* 1.

Burh-ræden, burh-ræddenn *Freedom of a city;* municipatus:—*Cot.* 128, v. burhscipe.

Burh-riht *The civil law;* jus civile, *Som.*

Burh-runan *The fates, furies, fairies;* parcæ:—*Cot.* 92.

Burh-sæta *A dweller in a city, a citizen;* civis, *Som.*

Burh-scipe. 1. A BOROUGHSHIP, *freedom of a city*, also *boundary of a city;* municipatus urbis, territoria. 2. *A free borough, an incorporate city* or *town;* municipium:—1. *Elf. T.* p. 7. 2. *Elf. gr.* 10: *Jos.* 13.

Burh-scyre *A borough liberty, city boundary, lying within a city's bounds;* territorium:—*Cot.* 148.

Burh-setan *citizens*, v. burhsæta.

Burhsita *one free of a city, a citizen*, v. burh-sæta.

Burhsittend, es, *A citizen;* civis: *Lk.* 15, 15: *Cd.* 106.

Burh-spræc *civil or courtly speech, polite behaviour, urbanity.*

Burh-staþel *a dwelling in a borough, a mansion, house, Som.*

Burh-sted, -styd *A city;* urbs:—*Cd.* 50.

Burh-waru; *g. d.* e; *ac.* e, *or* u; *pl. nom. ac.* e; *g.* a; *d.* um; *f. The population of a city, population;* cives:—Ælc burhwaru wæs bugende to him, *Jos.* 11, 19. Seo burhwaru abeah *the population submitted*, *Chr.* 1013. Yldest burhwara *eldest of the population, governors*, *R.* 8. Burhware gefeoht *a civil war*, *R.* 55: *Chr.* 1012.

Burhwealdan *citizens.*

Burh-weall *a city wall, a wall.*

Burh-weardas *borough-wards, watches* or *keepers.*

Burh-wit; *adj. Courtlike, civil;* urbanus:—*R.* 8.

Burig *a city*, v. burh.

BURNE, an; *f.* [*Plat. Dut. Kil.* born] A BOURN, *stream, brook, river;* torrens, rivus:—Ofer þa burnan Cedron, *Jn.* 18, 1. Ofer burnan, *Ex.* 7, 19: 8, 5: *Bd.* 3, 1. ¶ As a prefix or termination to the names of places, burn denotes that they were situate near a stream: hence in the modern names of places we find bourne, brown, braun, bran: thus, Winterbourne, Swinburn, Brownsover.

Burne *burned*, v. byrnan.

Bur-priche *A parish, diocese;* parœcia, *Som.*

Bur-reaf *hangings for a chamber, tapestry.*

Burste, burston *broken, bursted*, v. berstan.

Bur-þegn, bur-þen *a chamberlain, steward.*

Burug, buruh *a city*, v. burh.

Buruhwaru *the people of a city*, v. burhwaru.

Buruh-weordas *citizens.*

Buta, bute *except, but*, v. butan.

Buta, bute *both*, v. batwa.

Bûtan, bûton, bûtun; *prep. d.* [*Plat.* butèn: *Frs. c.* buten: *Dut.* buiten] *Without, except;* sine, absque, præter:—Butan leahtre, *Mt.* 12, 5. Buton wifum and cildum, *Deut.* 20, 14. Butun geongum litlingum, *Gen.* 50, 8: *Lev.* 4, 21. ¶ Butan æ *without law, an outlaw.* Butan wite *without punishment.* Butan gearnungum *without cost, freely.*

Butan, buton, butun; *conj.* BUT, *unless, except;* nisi:—Buton þat hit sy ut-aworpen, *Mt.* 5, 13: *Bt.* 34, 10.

Bute *but*, v. butan.

Bute *both*, v. batwa.

Buter, butera, [*Frs.* buter, boeter: *Plat.* botter: *Dut.* boter *f*: *Ger.* butter *f.*] BUTTER; butyrum:—*Elf. gl.* 21.

Buter-flege *a butterfly.*

Butericas *bottles*, v. buteruc.

Buterstoppa *a butter-vessel.*

Buteruc, butruc *A flagon, bottle;* flasco, uter:—*Gen.* 21, 15.

Butes-carlas *sailors*, v. butsecarlas.

Bûton *but, without*, v. butan.

Butruc *a bottle*, v. buteruc.

Butse-carlas [bates carlas, *i. e.* bat sæ carlas] *Seamen, sailors;* nautæ:—*Chr.* 1066.

Butte *a butt for wine*, v. byt.

Butting-tun, BUTTINGTON, *the name of a town in Monmouthshire. Somner* thinks it was so called because it was butting or near the river Severn, on Sæferne staþe.

Buttor-fleoge [*Plat.* better-flege: *Dut. Kil.* boter-vilege] A BUTTERFLY; papilio:—*R.* 22.

Butu, butwu *both*, v. batwa.

Butun *but, without*, v. butan.

Buuc [*Plat. Ger.* backe *f.*] *A cheek;* bucca, *Som.*

BY, bye [*Dan.* bye *a town, village: Swed. Icel.* by *an habitation, a village*] *A dwelling, habitation;* habitatio:—*C. Mk.* 5, 3. Hence, by and bye in the termination of the names of places.

By *by*, v. be.

Byan *to inhabit*, v. buan.

BYCGAN, gebigan, gebicgan; io bycge; *p.* bôhte, gebohte; *imp.* byge, bige; *pp.* geboht; *v. a. To buy, procure;* emere:—Bige þa þing, *Jn.* 13, 29. Hig woldon bycgan, *Mt.* 25, 10. Gebigð þone æcer, *Mt.* 13, 44. Gebicgan frið *to procure peace*, *Past.* 59, 2.

1 Bur-geteld, es. n
a bower-tent Th. an

4 Burgh a city Th. an
v burh

Burgon saved p. pl.
of beorgan

3 Burgeweall es,
m. a town wall
Th. an

Burge-weard a city's
guard Cd 180 Th p
226, 19 v burh-weardas

1 Butan l 11 Butan
* gearnungum

) 7 [41b & 90 d] O 3, es; m

O 5 [92a] [from
pwean to
anoint]

1x Im
butearan in butter
Grimm Myth. Sup. CXXXI

Burh-stede, es m
Im . . f. B
a city place, locus
urbis Beo K 4524

Burh-wela, an m
city wealth, wealth of a city
Beo K 6194

Burigan to bury Th. an
v birgan

3 Burh Peterborough
Th. an

3 Burigen a sepulchre Th. an
v birgen

2 Buter-gepweor, butter:
ointment butter Th. an

Buterice, es; m. A
leather bag, or bottle; uter
Th. an

* Buttingtune, es m
Buttington

O [91a]

Burna, an m
a stream Grm. III
387, 25, but? as pa
burnan is f

Butyre, an; f Butter
Th. an

O 5 [92d]

5 Burst a bristle Th. an
v byrst
140 Th. p 182, 3

7 Burh-hleoð a
mountain . . . Cd
v beorh-hleoð

O 7

xx . . . a city's enclosure, a city; urbis septum, . . .
Beo K 3852

. . . Beo . . . K 3852
Gram II 506, 17

~~01~~

~~2~~

~~01~~

0 3 [95d]

0 4 [95e]

4

Byrd ? ~~Heavy~~; gravis Beo K 5316

0 9 [55c]

0 1 [96f]

0 7 [93c]

~~0~~ 015

0 8 [93e]

3 Byġspaec 1 40, 10

4 × Byrga of sureties ~~ticket~~ Thes I p 135, 8 ~~also~~ for berga

0 9 [94a]

pl. of borh

0 4 Byldt [94b]

4 Byhd bows Th. an from bigan

0 8 [94c]

0 9

(a)

2 × Byldan to build, supply, furnish; instruere Beo K 2182

0 10 [94e]

0 11 [95a]

0 12

8 8 { 0 3

3 Byrdan sustinere Beo

2 Byrdinge

I Ger. Bucht a creek, bay, inclosure Dan Icel bugt Th. p 133 n 4c d]

0 5 [95f]

3 2 Byre, es; m Ason, child Th. An Sec Stopps

0 2 Byre, es m An event time ? Th. An ~~ll~~

4 × Byrel es; m ~~a butler~~ Beo K 2316 v ~~byrle~~

3 Ex. Cd 25 Th p 33, 12 see No 7 below

4 Byrelian, pode lle od To serve as a butler; pincerna agere Beo gl.

7 Byrdan to bury Beo K 891 v birgan

4 Byrgels see opposite

0 9 Byrging, ~~of~~

~~0 10~~ 5 Byrht-hwile a moment v ~~birht~~ brihthwile

2 × Byrig, e; f a city civitas Beo ~~byrig~~ K 2395, 4937 Gm II 466, 22 Th. p 92, 1 Dative pl 186, 26 Dative vol I p 175. K 4937

a corslet

2 × Byrne, an f a coat of mail

× Byrn - hom, es m coat of mail Beo

× Beo gl in ham

× Byrn - wigend es; m. a soldier in armour Th An

Byrgan [96a]

0 7

2 × Byrnet gilde burnished ... , ...

3 × Byrst, e; f Th. An

0 [96g]

0 5 [97a]

Bycge *A bitch*; canicula:—*R.* 21.

Bycgene *A buying*; emptio, *Som.*

Bycnað, bycneð *beckoneth, forms*, v. bicnian.

Bycnendlic; *adj. Allegorical, mystical*; allegoricus:—*Bd.* 5, 23.

Bycniendlic gemet *the indicative mood.*

Bycnung *A figure, trope*; figura: —*Bd.* 5, 23, v. beacneng.

Byd *commanded*, v. biddan.

Bydel, es; *m.* [*Dut.* pedel: *Ger.* pedell *m.*] A BEADLE, *crier, officer*; præco, nuncius:—Se bydel þe sende, *Lk.* 12, 58. Het bydelas beodan, *Ex.* 32, 5.

BYDEN. 1. *A bushel*; modius. 2. *Barrel, tun, butt*; dolium: —1. *Mk.* 4, 21: *Lk.* 11, 33. 2. *R.* 49: *Cot.* 64: 174.

Bydle *a worshipper.*

Bye *an habitation*, v. by.

Byffan, abyffan; *part.* byfigende. *To mutter*; mutire:—*Cot.* 134, v. bifian.

Byfor *a beaver*, v. beofer.

Bygan *to buy*, v. bycgan.

Bygdon *bowed*; byge *bow*, v. bigan.

Byge *a corner, bay*, v. bige.

Bygendlic; *adj. Bending, flexible*; flexibilis:—*Bd.* 4, 30.

Byggan *To build*; ædificare, *Som.*

Byg-spræc *a beguiling in speech, a supplanting.*

Byht; *m. A corner, extremity of a country, boundary*; angulus: —*Cd.* 100.

Bying *an habitation*, v. by.

BYL, es; *m.* [*Frs. c.* bule: *Pers.* آبله able] A BILE, *blotch, sore*; carbunculus.—*Cot.* 183.

BYLD, gebyld, bylde, byldo [*Ott.* beldida] *Constancy, boldness*; constantia:—*Bd.* 1, 7.

Byldan; *pp.* gebylded. *To confirm, animate, encourage*; confirmare:—*Bd.* 3, 18: *Menol.* 477.

Bylehwit *simple*, v. bilewit.

Bylehwitnes *simplicity*, v. bilehwitnes.

Bylewit *merciful*, v. bilewit.

Bylg *a bulge, bag*, v. bælg.

Bylgean *To bellow*, mugire:—*Martyr.* 17, *Jan.*

Bylges-lege [*Hov.* Biligesleage: *a ley or field of beans*] *The name of a place*, BISLEY, *in Gloucestershire, Som.*

Bylgð *is angry*, v. belgan.

Bylig *bellows*, v. bælg.

Byllinc *A cake*; collyrida:—*Cot.* 208.

Bylwet, bylwit *simple*, v. bilewit.

Bylwetlice; *adv. Simply*; simpliciter:—*Ors.* 1, 2.

BYME, an; *f. A trumpet*; tuba: —Byman sweg wæs gehired, *Ex.* 19, 16. Þære byman sweg, v. 19: *Ps.* 46, 5: *Cd.* 148.

Bymere, bymesangere; *m. A trumpeter*; tubicen:—*Elf. gl.* 6.

Bymian *To sound* or *play on a trumpet*; tuba canere:—*R.* 114: *Lps.* 80, 3.

Byndel [*Plat. Ger.* bündel *m*: *Frs. Dut.* bundel] *A bundle, band*; fascia, *Som.*

Bynland [byen *from* byan] *Inhabited country*; terra habitata:—*Ors. pref.*

Byoð *are, shall be*, v. beon.

Byr, es; *m. An offspring, a son*; filius:—*Cd.* 62.

Byrc *a birch*, v. birce.

Byrc-holt *a birch-holt*, or *grove.*

Byrcð *barks*, v. beorcan.

Byrd *A birth*; nativitas, v. gebyrd.

Byrdæg, byrtid *a birth-day*, v. gebyrd.

Byrden *a burden*, v. byrðen.

Byrdest, se byrdesta *The first-born, most noble, rich*; genere primus, præstantissimus:—*Ors.* 1, 1.

Byrdicge *A weaver's tool*; plumaria:—*Cot.* 161.

Byrdnes *quality, birth*, v. gebyrd.

Byre *A time, an event*; tempus, eventus:—Oð þone byre *to the time, Chr.* 1013, *Mann.*

Byre *a bear, son*, v. bera, byr.

Byrel *a butler*, v. byrle.

Byren; *adj. Belonging to a bear*; ursinus:—*R.* 21.

Byreð *belongs*; pertinet.

Byrg *a city*, v. burh.

Byrga *a pledger, creditor*, v. byriga, borh.

Byrgan; byrgeð; *p.* þu byrgdest, he gebyrgde. *To taste*; gustare, v. onbirian.

Byrgan *to bury*, v. birgan.

Byrgea, an *a reconciler, trustee, a surety*, v. byriga.

Byrged *buried*, v. birgan.

Byrgels, byrgen *a burial, tomb*, v. birgen.

Byrgen *a tomb*, v. birgen.

Byrgen-leoð *a tomb-ode, an epitaph.*

Byrgen-stow *a burial place, cemetry.*

Byrgere *A burier, sexton*; vespillo:—*Cot.* 155.

Byrging *A burying, the act of burying*; sepultura:—*In.* 20.

Byrging *a taste, tasting*, v. onbyrging.

Byrgð *protects*, v. beorgan.

Byrht *bright*, v. beorht.

Byrhtmhwyle *in a moment*, v. bearhtmhwile.

Byrhtnes, byrhto, byrhtu *brightness*, v. beorhtnes.

Byri *a berry, city*, v. berga, burh.

Byrig *to a city, cities*, v. burh.

Byrig *A berry, an enclosure where mulberry and other fruit-trees are set*; bacca, *Lye.*

Byriga, byrigea, berigea, byrgea, an; *m. A surety*; fidejussor:—He him byrigan gesealdne hæbbe *he has given him sureties, L. Hloth.* 10, *pr.* Byrigean geselle *should give a surety, Id.* 8, v. borh.

Byrigean; *p.* de *to bury*, v. birgan.

Byrigels, byrigen *a sepulchre*, v. birgen.

Byrigen-stow *a burying-place.*

Byrig-leoð *an epitaph*, v. birgen.

Byrigman, byriweard *A city officer*; ædilis:—*Elf. gr.* 14.

Byrignes, birgnes, se; *f.* 1. *A burial*; sepultura. 2. *A taste*; gustus:—1. *Bd.* 4, 11. 2. Mid byrignesse þæs wæteres, *Bd.* 5, 18, v. onbyrging.

Byriweard *a city guard*, v. byrigman.

Byrle, byrel, es; *m. A butler, cup-bearer*; pincerna:—Egypta cynges byrle, *Gen.* 40, 1. Bewiste his byrlas, *Gen.* 40, 2, 20, 21, 23. Yldest byrla *the eldest of butlers, the head butler, Elf. gl.* p. 79.

Byrlian *to draw*, v. birilian.

Byrn, byrna, byrnhoma *A garment of mail, a coat of mail*; lorica:—*L. In.* 55.

Byrna *a torrent*, v. burn.

Byrnan; þu byrnst, he byrnð, we byrnað, byrne; *p.* barn, hi burnon; *pp.* burnen, geburnen; *v. n.* [*Plat. Ger.* brennen *v. a.* and *n*: *Dut.* branden, burnen, bernen *v. a.* and *n*: *Franc.* brinnan *v. n.* *Dan.* brænde: *Swed.* brinna *v. n.*] *To* BURN, *to be on fire*; ardere:—He barn on geleafan, *Bd.* 4, 27. Syn leoht-fatu byrnende, *Lk.* 12, 35: *Ex.* 10, 13: *Deut.* 9, 15.

Byrne *a burning*, v. bryne.

Byrnendra *more burning.*

Byrnhoma *a coat of mail*, v. byrn.

Byrn-wiga, byrn-wiggend *A soldier clothed in armour*; loricatus miles:—*Jdth.* p. 21, 13.

Byrs *A graving-iron, a file*; scalprum, *Som.*

Byrst [*Frs.* boarstel: *Dut.* borstel *m.*] *A bristle*; seta:—Swynene byrst *swine's bristles, Herb.* 52, 2.

Byrst, berst *A loss, defect*; damnum:—*Ex.* 22, 6, 12.

Byrst *burst*, v. berstan.

Byrð *bears*, v. beran.

Byrðen, berðen A BURTHEN, *load, weight, fagot*; onus, fascis:—*Mt.* 11, 13: *Elf. gr.* 9, 32.

Byrðene-dæl *a share of a burthen, a portion.*
Byrðere *A porter;* portarius, *Som.*
Byrðor *A breed;* fœt[illegible] ¶ Byrðor-þinene, byrðþ[illegible] *a midwife, Som.*
Byrðr *Born;* partus:—*Bd.* 1, 27.
Byrð-þinen *a birth servant, a midwife.*
Byrðyn *a burthen,* v. byrðen.
Byseg *business,* v. biseg.
Bysen *an example,* v. bysn.
Bysenian *to give an example,* v. bysnian.
Bysenung *an example,* v. bysn.
Bysgian *to occupy, busy, employ,* v. bisgan.
Bysgu *occupation,* v. biseg.
Bysmere *a deceiver;* bysmernes *deceit,* v. bismer.
Bysmerian, bysmrian; *p.* ode. *To deride, reproach, blaspheme, revile, defame;* irridere, deridere:—He bysmerað hy, *Ps.* 2, 4: *Mt.* 27, 39: *Gen.* 39, 14, 17.
Bysmernunga *blasphemies.*
Bysmor *infamy,* v. bismer.
Bysmorfull *deceitful,* v. bismerlic.
Bysmorlice *disgracefully.*
Bysmorode *mocked,* v. bysmerian.
Bysmor-spræc *disgraceful speech, blasphemy.*
Bysmr *disgrace,* v. bismer.
Bysmrian, bysmrigenne: *p.* ode; *pp.* -od. *To deride,* v. bysmerian.
Bysmrung *deceit, derision,* v. bismer.
Bysn, bysen, bisn, e; *f. An example, pattern, model, resemblance, similitude, precept, command;* exemplum:—He bysne gegearwade *he gave an example, Bd.* 4, 27. Be sumere bisene *by some example, Bt.* 22, 2: *Cd.* 30, 32.
Bysnian; *p.* ode; *pp.* od. *To give or set an example or pattern;* exemplum dare:—Þa bisnodon *these set an example, Bt.* 39, 11: *L. Can. Edg.* 52: 66.
Bysnung *an example,* v. bisnung.
Byssene *an example,* v. bysn.
Byst *A loss;* dammum, *Ben.*
Byst *biestings,* v. beost.
Byst *art;* es, eris, v. beon.
Byt, te; *pl.* bytta [*Frs.* butte] *A bottle, flagon,* butt, *tun;* uter, dolium:—Þa bytta beoð to brocene, *Mt.* 9, 17. On ealde bytta *into old bottles, Mt.* 9, 17. On bytte *into a bottle, Ps.* 32, 7: *Jos.* 9, 5.
Byt *commands,* v. biddan.
Byter, byternys *bitterness,* v. biternys.
Byð *inhabits,* v. buan.
Byðne *a keel,* v. bytne.
Bytl, bitl, biotul [*Plat.* betel m.] A beetle, *hammer;* malleus:—*Jud.* 4, 21.
Bytla *A hammerer, builder;* ædificator:—*Cod. Ex.* 34, b.
Bytlian; *p.* ode. *To build;* ædificare:—*Cd.* 90.
Bytling, bytlung, e; *f. A building, edifice;* edificium:—*Solil. pref.*
Bytne *The keel or bottom of a ship;* carina:—*Cot.* 32.
Bytta *bottles,* v. byt.
Bytte-hlid *a lid of a butt.* Bytt-fylling *a filling of bottles.*

C

C and cc are often changed into *h* or *hh* before *s* or *ð*, and especially before *t*; as strehton *they stretched,* for strecton *from* streccan. Ahsian *for* acsian, *or* axian *to ask;* sehð *for* secð *seeks, from* secan *to seek.* In words immediately derived from Saxon, *k* is frequently substituted for the Saxon *c*, as cyng *a king;* cyn *kin,* or *kindred.* Sometimes *q* or *ch;* as cwen *queen;* cild *a child.*
Cac [*Frs.* kak] *Dung, ordure;* stercus.—Cachus *a privy;* latrina, *Som.*
Cæbestr *a halter,* v. cæfester.
Cæder-beam *a cedar-tree.*
Cæfed *embroidered, Som.*
Cæfester, cæfli *A halter, headstall;* capistrum:—*Cot.* 31, 38.
Cæg, cæga; *ac.* cæge; *pl. ac.* cægia; *f.* [*Frs.* cay: cayce *a small key, Japicx.*] A key:—Stæf-cræfte is seo cæg þe þæra boca andgytt unlycð *grammar is the key that unlocketh the knowledge of books, Elf. pref. gr. Som.* p. 1: *Lk.* 11, 52: *Mt.* 16, 19. ¶ Cægbora, cæg-hiorde *a bearer or keeper of keys.* Cægloc, cæg-loca *a lock, L. Cnut.* 74.
Cæggian *To lock, shut fast;* obserare, *Som.*
Cælan, celan, calian [*Plat.* kölen: *Ger.* kühlen: *Dut.* koelen: *Frs.* koelje: hence *Chauc.* kele] *To* cool, *to make cool, to refresh;* algere, refrigerare:—Þonne him cælð, *Hexaem: Cot.* 113: *Bt.* 26, 2.
Cælc *chalk,* v. cealc.
Cælc, cælic *a cup,* v. calic.
Cæle A keel *or bottom of a ship;* carina, *Som.*
Cælf *a calf,* v. cealf.
Cæmban [*Frs.* kyimme: *Dut.* kammen] *To* comb; pectere:—*Elf. gr.* 28.
Cæmpa *a soldier,* v. cempa.
Cænnan *to know,* v. cennan.
Cænne *a profession,* v. canne.
Cænned *Born;* natus, v. cennan.
Cænnestre, *f. One who has borne, a mother, dam;* genitrix, *Som.*
Cænryn *a generation,* v. cynnryn.
Cæpe-hus [cepa *a merchant,* hus *a house*] *A storehouse;* armarium:—Ælces cynnes cæpehus, *R.* 109.
Cæppe, cappa A cap, *cape, cope, hood;* pileus, cucullus:—*Elf. gl.* 19: *R.* 27.
Cærcærn *a prison,* v. carcærn.
Cærcian *to chirk, chirp,* v. cearcian.
Cæren *A sort of wine;* defrutum:—*Cot.* 66.
Cærfille *Chervil;* cerefolium:—*R.* 43.
Cærse Cress; nasturtium:—*Elf. gl.* 16.
Cæs *chose,* v. ceosan.
Cæster *a city,* v. ceaster.
Caf; *comp.* ra, re; *sup.* est, ost; *adj. Quick, sharp, nimble, swift;* acer, celer:—*Elf. T.* p. 33: *Bt.* 34, 7.

¹Bysmorlic dismaeful than v vismorlic
O4 Bysmerlice dispiteful. V. an v vismorlice

O4

O4 [97d]

42 Bysi
¹Bysig busy Th. An v Bisc. bisig
52 Bysmer infamy Th an v. bismer
2 Bysgung employment; negotium Som. v biseg
3 Bysi, bysig Busy employed, occupied. Som

O7

¹Bytme, an; f a keel of a ship; carina Beo. ₄l in ceol

O1

Cædmon
memoir of Soc Archaeology vol 24 p 341

O2q

[7a]

²Cæge, an f a key
O Higuninse flodon þæt loc and cægan
they unlocked the lock & key Nic 14 Thw p 7, 11

O2 [1d]
O3 [2c] Cærsa an; m. v
O4 [2b] cressa

Cæg, e; f. A key Som

²a Cæge a key Som v cæg

²Cæster gefera an A fellow citizen Som

O3 [1b]
O4 [1c]

O5 [3a]

Byrðene-dæl *a share of a burthen, a portion.*
Byrðere *A porter;* portarius, *Som.*
Byrðor *A breed;* fœtura. ¶ Byrðor-þinena, byrðþinen *a midwife, Som.*
Byrðr *Born;* partus:—*Bd.* 1, 27.
Byrð-þinen *a birth servant, a midwife.*
Byrðyn *a burthen,* v. byrðen.
Byseg *business,* v. biseg.
Bysen *an example,* v. bysn.
Bysenian *to give an example,* v. bysnian.
Bysenung *an example,* v. bysn.
Bysgian *to occupy, busy, employ,* v. bisgan.
Bysgu *occupation,* v. biseg.
Bysmere *a deceiver;* bysmernes *deceit,* v. bismer.
Bysmerian, bysmrian; *p.* ode. *To deride, reproach, blaspheme, revile, defame;* irridere, deridere:—He bysmerað hy, *Ps.* 2, 4: *Mt.* 27, 39: *Gen.* 39, 14, 17.
Bysmernunga *blasphemies.*
Bysmor *infamy,* v. bismer.

Bysmorfull *deceitful,* v. bismerlic.
Bysmorlice *disgracefully.*
Bysmorode *mocked,* v. bysmerian.
Bysmor-spræc *disgraceful speech, blasphemy.*
Bysmr *disgrace,* v. bismer.
Bysmrian, bysmrigenne: *p.* ode; *pp.* -od. *To deride,* v. bysmerian.
Bysmrung *deceit, derision,* v. bismer.
*Bysn, bysen, bisn, e; *f. An example, pattern, model, resemblance, similitude, precept, command;* exemplum:—He bysne gegearwade *he gave an example, Bd.* 4, 27. Be sumere bisene *by some example, Bt.* 22, 2: *Cd.* 30, 32.
Bysnian; *p.* ode; *pp.* od. *To give* or *set an example* or *pattern;* exemplum dare:—Þa bisnodon *these set an example, Bt.* 39, 11: *L. Can. Edg.* 52: 66.
Bysnung *an example,* v. bisnung.
Byssene *an example,* v. bysn.
Bysst *A loss;* damnum, *Ben.*

Byst *biestings,* v. beost.
Byst *art;* es, eris, v. beon.
Byt, te; *pl.* bytta [*Frs.* butte] *A bottle, flagon,* BUTT, *tun;* uter, dolium:—Þa bytta beoð to brocene, *Mt.* 9, 17. On ealde bytta *into old bottles, Mt.* 9, 17. On bytte *into a bottle, Ps.* 32, 7: *Jos.* 9, 5.
Byt *commands,* v. biddan.
Byter, byternys *bitterness,* v. biternys.
Byð *inhabits,* v. buan.
Byðne *a keel,* v. bytne.
Bytl, bitl, biotul [*Plat.* betel *m.*] A BEETLE, *hammer;* malleus:—*Jud.* 4, 21.
Bytla *A hammerer, builder;* ædificator:—*Cod. Ex.* 34, b.
Bytlian; *p.* ode. *To build;* ædificare:—*Cd.* 90.
Bytling, bytlung, e; *f. A building, edifice;* edificium:—*Solil. pref.*
Bytne *The keel* or *bottom of a ship;* carina:—*Cot.* 32.
Bytta *bottles,* v. byt.
Bytte-hlid *a lid of a butt.* Byttfylling *a filling of bottles.*

C

*C and cc are often changed into *h* or *hh* before *s* or *ð*, and especially before *t;* as strehton *they stretched,* for strecton *from* streccan. Ahsian *for* acsian, *or* axian *to ask;* sehð *for* secð *seeks, from* secan *to seek.* In words immediately derived from Saxon, *k* is frequently substituted for the Saxon *c,* as cyng *a king;* cyn *kin,* or *kindred.* Sometimes *q* or *ch;* as cwen *queen;* cild *a child.*
Cac [*Frs.* kak] *Dung, ordure;* stercus.—Cachus *a privy;* latrina, *Som.*
Cæbestr *a halter,* v. cæfester.
Cæder-beam *a cedar-tree.*
Cæfed *embroidered, Som.*
Cæfester, cæfli *A halter, headstall;* capistrum:—*Cot.* 31, 38.
Cæg, cæga; *ac.* cæge; *pl. ac.* cægia; *f.* [*Frs.* cay: cayce *a small key, Japicx.*] A KEY;—Stæf-cræfte is seo cæg þe þæra boca andgytt unlycð *grammar is the key that unlocketh the knowledge of books, Elf. pref. gr. Som.* p. 1: *Lk.* 11, 52: *Mt.* 16, 19. ¶ Cægbora, cæg-hiorde *a bearer* or *keeper of keys.* Cægloc, cæg-loca *a lock, L. Cnut.* 74.
Cæggian *To lock, shut fast;* obserare, *Som.*
Cælan, celan, calian [*Plat.* kölen: *Ger.* kühlen: *Dut.* koelen: *Frs.* koelje: hence *Chauc.* kele] *To* COOL, *to make cool, to refresh;* algere, refrigerare:—Þonne him cælð, *Hexaem: Cot.* 113: *Bt.* 26, 2.
Cælc *chalk,* v. cealc.
Cælc, cælic *a cup,* v. calic.
Cæle A KEEL or *bottom of a ship;* carina, *Som.*
Cælf *a calf,* v. cealf.
Cæmban [*Frs.* kyimme: *Dut.* kammen] *To* COMB; pectere:—*Elf. gr.* 28.
Cæmpa *a soldier,* v. cempa.
Cænnan *to know,* v. cennan.
Cænne *a profession,* v. canne.

Cænned *Born;* natus, v. cennan.
Cænnestre; *f. One who has borne, a mother, dam;* genitrix, *Som.*
*Cænryn *a generation,* v. cynnryn.
Cæpe-hus [cepa *a merchant,* hus *a house*] *A storehouse;* armarium:—Ælces cynnes cæpehus, *R.* 109.
Cæppe, cappa A CAP, *cape, cope, hood;* pileus, cucullus:—*Elf. gl.* 19: *R.* 27.
Cærcærn *a prison,* v. carcærn.
Cærcian *to chirk, chirp,* v. cearcian.
Cæren *A sort of wine;* defrutum:—*Cot.* 66.
Cærfille *Chervil;* cerefolium:—*R.* 43.
Cærse CRESS; nasturtium:—*Elf. gl.* 16.
Cæs *chose,* v. ceosan.
Cæster *a city,* v. ceaster.
Caf; *comp.* ra, re; *sup.* est, ost; *adj. Quick, sharp, nimble, swift;* ácer, celer:—*Elf. T.* p. 38: *Bt.* 34, 7.

O 4

62 Bysi
1 Bysig busy Th. An
v Besf. bisig

52 Bysmer infamy
Th an v. bismer

2 Busgung employment negotium
Som. v biseg

3 Bysi, bysig Busy
employed occupatus Som

Cædmon
mem. of Soc
Archaeolog vol 24
p 341

[1 a]

Cæg. e; f. A key
Som

1 Bysmorlic dis- graceful Th. an v bismorlic

O 4 Bysmerlice disgracefully Th. an
v bismorlice

O 4 [97 d]

O 7

O 29

2 Cæge, an f a key
Hi geninnon flodon
þæt loc and cægan
they unlocked the lock
key Nic 14 Thw
p 7, 11

2a Cæige a key Som v
cæg

O 3 [1 b]

O 4 [1 c]

1 Bytme, an; f a
keel of a ship, carina
Bea. gl in ceol

O 1

O 2 [1 d]

O 3 [2 c] Cærsa
an; m. v

O 4 [2 b] cressa

3 Cæster gefera an
A fellow citizen Som

O 5 [3 a]

○1

☞ Alt Cantwara-burghe B. Seo is sweden at &c

Cantwara-burh ge dll

1 Cantwara burh, g-burge, burhge d. byrg, byri, byri Canterbury, cta burh

○2 {the Chaldea city}

3 Caldea-burh, g. burge, -d. byrg ff. Babylon

○2 [3d] ...

○3 [4a]

○4 [4d]

5 Camb; es: m a comber

○ [4e]

○6 [4f]

○7 [5a]

○ [5b] ...

6 Camp, es: m fight an m Beo gl

○ Cancelleude laughing, ...

○ Canceteung; ... f a laughing, scintillation, etc

○ [5d]

○ Candel, condel, es; m a candle &c Beo ... gl.

○2 q canna

○ [6e]

○3 q m

1

2

3 Capitol* medik, an; f early mass

○4

○ gehafher hoade th. an

○2 [6d]

○3 q

4 Carcern, es; m carcern [carc, ern a place] a prison

5 Carfull, l 2 solicitous

○2 to care, be solicitous th. an

○7 [7a]

6 Carl, es; m a male chiefly ... before ... to denote the male ... as ... v. next pg

Cafertun, cafortun [*i. e.* mycel, and rum heall, *R.* 109.] 1. *A large* and *roomy hall;* atrium. 2. *A vestibule, an entrance, inclosure before a house, an inclosure;* vestibulum, conseptum ante ædes:—1. *Jn.* 18, 15, *Bd.* 3, 11. 2. An lytel cafertun, *Bt.* 18, 1.

Caflice; *adv. Quickly, hastily, stoutly, manfully, valiantly;* velociter, viriliter:—*Num.* 31, 6.

Cafnys *a hastening,* v. cafscype.

Cafortun *a hall,* v. cafertun.

Cafscype *A quickness;* velocitas:—*R. Ben.* 5.

Cal *A herb, wild cole-wort;* arboracia, lapsana:—*R.* 44, v. cawl.

Calc *A shoe, little shoe, sandal;* calceus, sandalium:—*Mk.* 6, 9.

Cald *cold,* v. ceald.

Cald *called, Lye.*

Caldea byrig *the city of Chaldea, Babylon, Som.*

Calf *a calf,* v. cealf.

Calfian *To* CALVE; vitulum edere, *Som.*

Calian *to cool, to grow cold,* v. cælan.

CALIC, cælic, calc; *m.* [*Plat. Dut.* kelk *m*: *Ger.* kelch *m.*] *A cup,* CHALICE, *goblet;* calix:—*Mt.* 26, 28: *Ps.* 22, 7.

Calla [*Icel.* kall, karl] *A man:*—Hilde calla *a man of war, a general, Cd.* 156, *Lye.*

CALO; *adj.* [*Dut. Kil.* kael, kaluwe] CALLOW, *bald, without hair;* calvus:—*Elf. gr.* 9, 3.

Caluer-clim, caluer-clympe *a skull,* v. calwer.

Caluw [illegible], v. calo.

Calwa *A disease which causes baldness;* alopecia:—*Cot.* 12.

Calwer, calwere *A skull, a place for burial, a bald place on the top of the head;* gabalacrum, calvaria, calva:—*Cot.* 96, *Som.*

CAMB [*Frs.* kaem: *Dut.* kam] A COMB, *crest;* pecten:—*Elf. gl.* 27. ¶ Camb helmes *crest of a helmet, R.* 53.—Camb on hætte, *or* on helme *a crest on the hat* or *helmet;* crista:—*Cot.* 46.

Cambiht *Combed;* cristatus, *Som.*

Camell *A camel;* camelus:—*C. R. Mk.* 1, 16.

Cammec, cammoc, cammuc, commuce *Maiden weed, hog fennel* or *rest harrow, cammock;* peucedanum:—*Herb.* 96. Gohina, *Cot.* 160.

CAMP; comp, gecamp, es; *m.* [*Plat. Dut.* kamp *m. a combat, a field: Dan. Swed.* kamp *m. a battle: Ger.* kampf *m. a fight*] A CAMP, *contest, war;* certamen:—*Bd.* 3, 2.

Campdóm, camphád *Warfare;* militia:—*Scint.* 29, 1: *Bd.* 2, 7.

Campian *to fight, encamp,* v. compian.

Camp-sted *a place for encamping, a camp.*

Camp-wered, camp-werod *Men in camp, an army, soldiers;* exercitus:—*Bd.* 2, 5.

Cananeisc *A Canaanite, Gen.* 9, 18.

Can *know; is able, can;* þu canst *thou knowest,* v. cunnan.

Cancelere *A chancellor;* cancellarius:—*Chr.* 1093.

Cancer-adl *a cancer-disease, a canker,* v. bita.

Cancere, cancre A CANCER, *disease, an animal, a crab;* cancer, tam morbus quam animal, *Som.*

Cancer-hæbern, cancer-hædern *a hole for fish* or *crabs, a hole in a wound, a cave, den, Som.*

Cancetung, cancettende *A laughing, giggling;* cachinnus:—*L. Eccl.* 21: *Cot.* 58, v. ceahhetung.

Cancre *a canker,* v. cancere.

Candel, es [*Icel.* kindir *m. fire: Norse,* kindil: *Pers.* قنديل kandeel *a candle*] A CANDLE; candela:—*Elf. gl.* 19.

Candel-bora A CANDLE-BEARER, *a subdeacon, a clerk;* acolythus:—*Cot.* 203.

Candel-leoht *candle-light.*

Candelmæsse CANDLEMAS, the mass at the feast of purification which, in the Romish church, was celebrated with many lighted candles, *L. Const.* p. 114.

Candel-snytels *candle-snuffers.*

Candel-stæf, candel-sticca *A candle-staf* or *stick;* candelabrum:—*Mt.* 5, 15.

Candel-treow *a candlestick with branches, a candlestick.*

Candel-twist *a pair of snuffers.*

Candel-weoc *a wick of a candle, a torch.*

Candel-wyrt CANDLE-WORT, *an herb;* fromos:—*R.* 44.

Cann *Know;* scio, v. cunnan.

Canna, canne [*Frs.* kanne] A CAN, *cup;* crater:—*R.* 24.

CANNE, cænne [*Ger.* künde *f*: *Dut. Kil.* konne, kunne] *A profession, knowledge, cognizance, notice;* professio, notitia:—*L. Hloth.* 16. ¶ Canne riht *a right to take notice, Som.*

Canon, es; *m.* 1. A CANON, *a rule;* regula, canon. 2. *A canon* or *prebendary;* canonicus:—1. Canones boc, *Bd.* 4, 24: *L. Edw. Guth.* 2. *Som.*

Canondóm *a canonship, office of a canon, Som.*

Canoneclic; *adj. Canonical;* canonicus:—*Horæ Can.* p. 1.

Canonias, canonicas *canons,* v. canon.

Cantelcap, canterkæpp, es; *m.* CANTEL-COPE *a sort of priest's garment;* caracalla:—*Chr.* 1070.

Cantere *A singer;* cantor, *Som.*

Cantic; *m. A song;* canticum:—*Deut.* 31, 19.

Cantwara burhge, Cantwaræ burg, Cantwara buruh, Cantwara byrig CANTERBURY, *Rochester:*—Cantwara burhge B'. seo is cweden æt Hrofesceastre, *Bd.* 4, 5, *S.* p. 572, 13.

Cantwara-mægðe *the county of Kent, men of Kent.*

Cant-waras *Kentish men, L. Hloth.* 16: *Bd.* 1, 15.

Capelein, capellan *A chaplain;* capellanus:—*Chr.* 1099.

Capitel, *or* capitol mæssa *early mass.*

Capitol, capitul, capitula, an; *m. A chapter;* capitulum:—On þam ende þises capitulan *in the end of this chapter, Bt.* 32, 2.

Cappa [*Plat. Ger. Dan.* kappe *f*: *Swed.* kappa *f*: *Dut.* kap *f*: *Icel.* kápa *f.*] *A cap, cope, priest's garment,* v. cæppe.

Capun [*Plat.* kapuhn, kapphaan *m*: *Dut.* kapoen *m. a hen*: *Dan. Swed. Icel.* kapún *m.*] A CAPON; gallinaceus:—*R.* 39.

Cár, cára *care,* v. cáru.

Carc CARK, *care;* cura, *Som.* v. car.

Carcern, carcærn [*Moes.* karkara] *A prison, a house of correction, a quarry in which prisoners were compelled to work;* carcer:—He sie on carcerne gebroht *he is brought to prison, Bt.* 37, 1, *Card.* p. 288, 20.

Carclif *Agrimony;* agrimonia:—*Elf. gl.* 16.

Care *care,* v. caru.

Cárefull *careful, Ps.* 39, 23, v. carfull.

Carendre *A people of Germany, the Sclavi.* Carenthani, *or* Carentani, their country is now the Dutchy of Carinthia *or* Cærnthen:—*Ors.* 1, 1, *Foster's notes.*

Cárfull; *adj.* CAREFUL, *anxious, curious;* solicitus:—*Elf. gl.* 23.

Carfullice; *adv.* CAREFULLY; solicite:—*L. Alf.* 35.

Cárfulnys, se; *f.* CAREFULNESS, *curiosity;* solicitudo:—*Hom. pasc.* p. 13.

Cárian *to take care, heed, to be anxious,* v. cearian.

Carited *Charity;* caritas:—*Chr.* 1137, *Lye.*

CARL [*Frs.* keerl: *Dut.* karel] 1. *Charles;* carolus. 2. *A male;* masculus:—1. Carles wæn *Charles's wain;* arctos, *Equ. vern.* 30, 5. 2. Carl cat *a he-cat.* Carl fugol *a male bird, Som.*

Cárleás; *adj. Careless, reckless, void of care, free;* improvidus, securus:—*Cd.* 151.

Cárleásnes, carleast *Security,* CARELESSNESS; securitas:—*R.* 89.

Carl-man *a countryman,* v. ceorl.

CARR *A rock,* SCAR, *north country* CARROCK; rupes, scopulus:—*C. Mk.* 8, 24. Hence Scarborough derives its name, says *Ray.*

Carrum *The place of a naval engagement, near Charmouth, Dorsetshire, Chr.* 840.

Carta *Paper;* charta:—*Somn.* 59, *Lye.*

Cartaina, cartaine *Carthage;* Carthago:—For to Cartaina *went to Carthage, Ors.* 4, 10, *Bar.* p. 168, 6. Cartainan, *Ors.* 4, 13, *Bar.* p. 175, 23. On Cartaine, *Ors.* 4, 6, *Bar.* p. 160, 27.

Cartaine; *pl. g.* Cartaina; *d.* um. Cartinense, Cartinensis *The Carthaginians;* Carthaginenses:—Gewinn Romana and Cartaina *a battle of the Romans and Carthaginians, Ors.* 4, 13, *Bar.* p. 174, 23. Amilcor Cartaina cyning, *Ors.* 4, 7, *Bar.* 153, 26. Terrentius se mæra Cartaina sceop *Terence the best poet of the Carthaginians, Ors.* 4, 10, *Bar.* p. 168, 29.

CARU, cearu; *g. d. ac.* e; *pl.* a; *g.* ena; *d.* um; *f.* [*Moes.* car, cara: *Ir.* car: *Wel.* cûr *anxiety*] CARE; cura:—Nys þe nan caru, *Lk.* 10, 40. On þises lifes carum, *Lk.* 21, 34: 8, 14.

Cásere, es; *m. Cæsar, an emperor;* imperator:—Fram þam Casere Augusto, *Lk.* 2, 1. ¶ Caseres wif, Caseres cwen *an empress, R.* 68.

Cásering, e; *f. A Cæsaring, a coin with an emperor's image, a coin;* drachma:—*C. Mt.* 17, 24.

Cáserlic; *adj. Cæsar-like, imperial;* imperialis, *Som.*

Casern *An empress;* Augusta:—*Ors.* 6, 11.

Cassuc; *f. A kind of bind weed;* cassuta:—*L. Md.* 1, 62.

Castel; *n. A town, village,* CASTLE; villa, oppidum:—Farað on þat castel, *Mt.* 21, 2.

Casul *A cassock, short cloak;* birrhus, *Som.*

Casyr *Cæsar,* v. Casere.

CAT [*Plat. Dut.* kat *f*: *Ger.* katze *f.*] A CAT; cattus, muriceps:—*Elf. gl.* 13.

Cattes-mint *cat-mint.*

Cauertun *a hall,* v. cafertun.

Cawel-wyrm *a cole-worm,*

CAWL, cawl-wyrt, cawel, caul, ceawel, es; *m.* [*Frs.* koal: *Dut.* kool *f.*] 1. COLE, *colewort;* brassica, *Lin.* 2. *A basket;* corbis:—1. Wild cawel *wild cole, Herb.* 129. 2. Heora cawlas afylled *filled their baskets, Ors.* 4, 8, *Bar.* p. 158, 12.

CEAC, ceaca [*Plat.* keef *f*: *Dut.* kaak *f*: *Swed.* kek, kak *m*: *Heb.* חך chk *a palate*] A CHEEK, *jaw;* gena:—*Ps.* 31, 12. Ceacena swyle *a swelling of the jaws* or *cheeks.*

Ceac *A basin, pitcher;* sextarius, urna:—Þweala ceaca and calica, *Mk.* 7, 8.

Ceacban *the cheek-bone.*

Ceace *A trial, proof;* exploratio, *Som.*

Ceæro *be careful, willing,* v. carian.

CEAF, cef; *pl.* ceafu; *n.* [*Plat. Dut.* kaf *n.*] CHAFF; palea:—Þat ceaf he forbærnð, *Lk.* 3, 17: *Mt.* 3, 12.

Ceafertun *a hall,* v. cafertun.

Ceafes *an harlot,* v. cyfes.

Ceafl, es; *m. A bill, beak, snout;* in the plural *jaws, cheeks;* rostrum:—*Cot.* 184. His ceaflas to tær, *Elf. T.* p. 13, 26.

Ceafor, ceafyr, [*Ger.* käfer *n.*] A CHAFER, *beetle;* bruchus, scarabæus:—*Ps.* 104, 32.

Ceahhetan *To laugh, giggle;* cachinnari:—*Bd.* 5, 12.

Ceahhetung *A loud laughter;* cachinnatio:—*Bd.* 5, 12.

CEALC [*Plat. Ger. Dan. Swed.* kalk *m*: *Dut.* kalk *f*: *Icel.* kalk *n*: *Wel.* calc: *Corn.* kalch: *Ir.* cailk] CHALK, *a stone;* calx:—*Ors.* 6, 32. Calculus, *Cot.* 31.

Cealca-ceaster *The chalk city. Camden* thinks it is Tadcaster, in Yorkshire.

Cealc-hyðe *The name of a place, Challock, Chalk, in Kent, Chr.* 785.

Cealc-stan *chalk-stone, chalk.*

CEALD, cald; *adj.* [*Plat.* kold: *Frs.* kald: *Dut.* koud: *Ger.* kalt] COLD; frigidus:—*Bd.* 3, 9.

Cealer-briw *droppings of roasted meat.*

CEALF, celf, es; *pl.* cealfru; *n.* [*Plat. Dut.* kalf *n.*] A CALF; vitulus:—He genam an fætt cealf, *Gen.* 18, 7. He ofsloh an fætt celf, *Lk.* 15, 27. ¶ Cealfa-hus *a calf-house, R.* 1.

Cealf-adl *a calf-disease, a sort of disease.*

Cealfian *to calve,* v. calfian.

CEAP, es; *m.* [*Frs.* keap: *Dut.* koop *m*: *Ger.* kauf *m*: *Icel.* kaup] 1. *Cattle;* pecus. 2. *Saleable commodities, price, sale, bargain, business;* pretium, negotium:—1. His neahgebures ceap *his neighbour's cattle, L. In.* 40. Ceapes cwilde *murrain of cattle, Chr.* 897. 2. Deopum ceapum gebohte us *bought us at a great* [*deep*] *price, L. In.* 57. Sume wæron to ceape gesealde *some were sold at a price, Nath.* 8: *Gen.* 41, 56. Ceap awyrigend *a detestable business, Somn.* 158.

Ceap-cniht *a hired servant, a slave.*

Ceap-dæg *A bargaining* or *market-day.* ¶ Ceap-dagas *the Nones,* or *stated times when the common people came to market, R.* 96.

Ceap-ealeðe *the ale-selling place, an ale-house.*

Ceap-gyld *bargain money, price of what is stolen* or *lost.*

Ceapian; *p.* ceapode, hi ceapodun; *pp.* ceapod [*Plat. Dut.* koopen: *Frs.* keapje: *Ger.* kaufen *to buy*: *Moes.* kaupon] *To bargain, chaffer, trade, to contract for the purchase* or *sale of a thing, to buy;* emere, negotiari:—Ceapiað oð þat ic cume, *Lk.* 19, 13: *Mt.* 21, 12. Mihte yð geceapian, gif ænig man ceapode *might easily buy, if any one bargained, Ors.* 5, 7, *Bar.* p. 188, 12. ¶ Syllan to ceape *to sell,* v. cepa. Hence the name of places remarkable for trade, such as *Cheapside, Chippenham.*

Ceaping, e; *f. A buying, merchandise;* emptio:—*L. Athel.* 24.

Ceaplas *cheeks, whelps, Som.* v. ceafl.

Ceápman, cypman, cypeman, nes; *m.* [*Plat. Dut.* koopman *m*: *Ger.* kaufmann *m.*] A CHAPMAN, *merchant, marketman;* mercator:—*L. Alf.* 30: *L. In.* 25.

Ceap-sceamul *a toll-booth, custom-house, tradesman's stall.*

Ceapscipa *a merchant ship, a ship of burden* or *trade.*

Ceapsetl *a tradesman's booth, stall* or *shop.*

Ceapstow *A market-place, a market;* forum:—*Bd.* 2, 1, 3. Hence the name of *Chepstow.*

Ceapstræt *a street* or *place for merchandise, a market.*

Ceapung, e; *f. Business, trade, traffic, commerce;* negotium:—*Ps.* 90, 6: negotiatio, *L. Athel.* 13.

O merchandise þælic þes ceapes (he) shall have ... of the merchandise
L Edw. Guth 7
W p 52, 36

O [13a]

O [13b]

Ceallian, to call vocare dicere Th. An

Ceap, es; m; a purchase; Fr. Achis Beo Th 4826

Centræ Calmaria Cot 42: 168. inter ea quæ pertinent ad mensam. Frigidarium L. M. I, 39, 44

O 8 [8a]

O 4 [9d]

O 5 [10a]

Céáca, ceca, an; m a cheek, jaw; mala, maxilla Grim III 401, 9

Som Lye

O 4

O 6 [10b]

ceap ale, pelu

5 * Ceap-ealedelu, an ale selling place

1 Cartaina

Ceachetung a retching, Som V ceahhetung

O 5 [14a]

Ceacbora Ankilus Cot 13 Lye

O 7 [11b]

O 8 [11c] Ceator, es; m [coty]

O 9 [11d] ceaferas Th Ps 104, 30

O 10 [12a]

6 [8b]

O 11 [12b]

O 7 V

7 [8c]

Cealc-hyd; e; f [Hunt Cealcide: West Chalcha = the] Chalk, Kent etc

O 12 [12c]

9 [8d]

Ceap-scip, es; n a merchant ship

O 13 [12d]

0

13 Ceaf, ceif, es; n [coty]

11

D [9a]

Ceat, cattes, m Grim III p 341, 24

Ċega a key-dl. 07

Cear anxious, careful Cd 214
[Th 360, 2] anxious; [curis pressus.

Cear-bend ~~vinculum~~ ~~[illegible]~~, anchora ~~[illegible]~~
Gru # 485, 19 v ~~[illegible]~~ oncearbend

4 Cearian [14b]
5 [15a]

Cear-sid iter difficile Beo 179

Cearu, e f care Beo K 2607 v caru

Cear-wylm, es; m a care wave Beo K 561

6 [15b]
7 [15c]

Ceaster-buend es; m a city dweller, a citizen Beo K 1529

Ceaster-ǽsc A sort of ash Quoddam fraxini genus, sylvestri contrarium, et hortensis dicendum, Som. Helleborus N-Lye

Ceaster-gewaru, -ware, -waras, pl m ~~ware~~, e; f pl. ceaster-wera towns men, citizens ~~Th An~~

3 Cedelc

3 Ceclum tortellis Cd 191
Cecil, an; f a cheek Lye Gru III 401, 9 v Ceaca

Ceca. an m or

Cetheing caught ~~[illegible]~~ Cd. Bt 16, 2 Card 78, 21
v ~~cachetthung~~ Cetung
3 v ceaca
[16a]
4 Cellod keeled ~~[illegible]~~ resembling the bottom of a ship
Cetung, e; f A cooling refreshing refrigeratio Som
6 Cemeargode medicatus Lps 65, 14
Cene es m n, res; ~~[illegible]~~ Keen Beo K 4111
[16c]
1 a churl, freeman Th. An Beo 4l
2 Cennan, p cende; pp cenned Th An
[17b]
4

Hentingas men of Kent v ~~[illegible]~~ East-centingas
Cesh
3 [18a]
[18b]
Ceocung, e; f ruminatio Ben
2 Ceol, es; m a ship Beo K 76 a keel was byme
7 [18d]
Campa [16b]
2 Engel het, pæt treow ceorfan an angel bade that tree be hewed Cd 200, Th 248, 11
8 [19a]

Ceapung-gemot *a meeting for trade, a market.*

Ceapung-þing *a buying, setting a price, saleable.*

Ceara *care thou,* v. carian.

Cearcern *a prison,* v. carcern.

Cearcetung, e; *f. A gnashing, grinding, crashing noise, as of the teeth;* stridor, *Som.*

Cearcian; *part.* cierde (hence *Chaucer, to chirke, chirking,* and our *chirp*) *To chatter, creak, crash, gnash;* stridere :—*Elf. gr.* 26.

Ceare *with care:* cearena full *full of cares,* v. caru.

Cearfan *to carve,* v. ceorfan.

Cearian, carian; ic cearige, þu cearast, he cearað; *p.* ode; *pp.* od. *To take care, heed, to be anxious;* curare :—Ne ceara þu *care not thou, Cd.* 104: *Mt.* 6, 34.

Cearig; *adj. Careful, pensive, wary,* CHARY, *anxious, grieving;* solicitus, cautus :—*Cd.* 101.

Cear-sorge *sorrowful care, anxiety.*

Cearung, e; *f. Pensiveness, anguish of mind, a complaint;* solicitudo, *Som.*

CEAS [*Fries.* case] *a quarrel;* lis:—*L. Athel.* 18. *Pr.* v. ceast.

Ceás *chose; p.* of ceosan.

Ceasega *A chooser;* elector :—*Cd.* 151.

Ceasnes, se; *f. Election, choice;* electio, *Som.*

Ceast *Strife, contention, murmuring, sedition, scandal;* lis :—*Alf. eccl.* 18.

Ceaster, cester; *g.* ceastre; *pl.* ceastra; *f.* [From *Lat.* castrum.] The names of places ending in -caster and -chester were probably sites of a castrum, *a fortress,* built by the Romans; the Saxon word is burh, *Gen.* 11, 4, 5.] *A city, fort, castle, town;* urbs, castellum :—Ne mæg seo ceaster beon behyd, *Mt.* 5, 14. On þære hean ceastre *in the high city, Bt.* 39, 5: *Mt.* 28, 11. Se Hælend embfor ealle burga and ceastra, *Mt.* 9, 35.

Ceaster-gewara, -wara *townsmen, citizens.*

Ceaster-wyrhta *An embroiderer;* polymitarius: — *Cot.* 156.

Ceastfull; *adj. Full of contention, tumultuous;* tumultuosus :—*Scint.* 28.

Ceastra *cities,* v. ceaster.

Ceat *A thing;* res :—*Cot.* 100.

Ceatta, *cheats;* circumventiones, *Lye.*

Ceáw *chewed,* v. ceowan.

Ceawel *a basket,* v. cawl.

Cedelc, cedeleac *The herb mercury;* mercurialis :—*Herb.* 84.

Ceder-beam, -triw *a cedar-tree,* v. cæder-beam.

Cef *chaff,* v. ceaf.

Cega *a key,* v. cæg.

Cegan, acægan *To call, name;* vocare :—*R. Mt.* 2, 7.

Cehettung *a laugh.*

Ceke *a cheek,* v. ceac.

Celan *To chill, to be very cold;* algere:—*Bd.* 1, 27. *resp.* 8, v. cælan.

CELE *Chillness, a very great coldness;* algor :—*Bt. R.* p. 175.

Celender, cellendre *The herb coriander;* coriandrum :—*R.* 43.

Celeþonia *The herb celendine;* chelidonia, *Som.*

Celf *a calf,* v. cealf.

Celing, e; *f. A refreshing;* refrigerium, *Som.*

Cellas *Cells;* cellæ, *Lye.*

Cellendre *coriander,* v. celender.

Celment-man, celmert-mon, *an hired servant.*

Celnes, gecelnys, se; *f.* COOLNESS, *air;* refrigerium :—*Ps.* 65, 11: Opposed to hætu.

Cemb, cemde *That which is combed, tow, hards;* stupa :—*Cot.* 192.

Cemban; *p.* de. *To comb;* pectere :—*Elf. gr.* 28, v. cæmban.

Cemes *A coat, surplice;* camisia:—*Cot.* 31.

CEMPA, an; *m.* [*Dut.* kemper, *m: Ger.* kämpfer *m.*] *A soldier, warrior,* CHAMPION, *a novice, a young soldier;* miles :—Ælcon cempan anne dæl, *Jn.* 19, 23. Twa hund cempena *two hundred of soldiers;* manipulus, *R.* 7. ¶ Cempena yldest *first, chief of the soldiers, a commander;* tribunus militum, *Ors.* 4, 6.—Cempena riht *military law.*

CEN; *adj.* [*Dut.* koen: *Ger.* kühn] KEEN, *fierce, bold, warlike;* acer :—*Bt. R.* p. 162. audax, *Past.* 33, 4.

Cene-helm *a crown,* v. cynehealm.

Cene-setel *a king's seat, a throne,* v. cyne-setl.

Cenesta *keenest,* v. cene.

Cenlice; *adv.* [*Dut. Kil.* koenlick: *Ger.* kühnlich] *Keenly, boldly, courageously, notably;* animose :—*Elf. T.* 15.

CENNAN; *part.* -nende, -nynde; *p.* cende; *pp.* cenned, gecenned. *To bring forth;* parere :—*Gen.* 2, 7: 18, 13. Cennynde wif *eniza mulier, Bd.* 1, 27.

Cennestre *one who has borne, a mother,* v. cænnestre.

Cenning, e; *f. Birth, a producing;* partus :—Þære cenninge tima, *Gen.* 25, 24. Cenning tid, *Gen.* 38, 27: *Lk.* 1, 57.

Cennynde *producing,* v. cennan.

Cennys *birth,* v. cenning.

Cenost *keenest,* v. cene.

Cent *The county of* KENT; Cantium :—*Bd.* 3, 15.

Centaure *A centaur;* centaurus, *Som.*

Centauria *The herb centaury;* centauria :—*L. Md.* 2, 8.

Centisc; *adj.* KENTISH, *belonging to Kent;* Cantianus :—*Chr.* 999.

Cent-land KENT LAND, *Kent, Bd.* 2, 3.

Cent-rice *the kingdom of Kent, Som.*

CEO A CHOUGH, *a fowl of the genus corvus, a jay, crow, jackdaw;* cornix :—*Elf. gr.* 9, 64.

Ceoca *a cheek,* v. ceac.

Ceod *a cod, purse,* v. codd.

Ceofl *a basket,* v. cawl.

Ceol, ciol; *m. A ship, small bark or vessel, a keel;* navis, carina :—*Cot.* 33, *Som.*

Ceola, *A little cottage, a cabin;* stega, *Som.*

Ceolas *the jaws.*

Ceoles-ige CHELSEA, *on the bank of the Thames, Middlesex; Somner* says "insularis olim et navibus accommodata, ut nomen significat."

Ceolr *or* þrot A COLLAR *or* THROAT; guttur :—*Lps.* 149, 6.

Ceor *A bondman;* verna, *Som.*

Ceorf-æx *a cutting axe.*

CEORFAN, aceorfan, he cyrfð; *p.* cearf, hi curfon; *pp.* acorfen; *v. a.* [*Plat. Dut.* kerven: *Ger.* kerben] *To* CARVE, *cut, engrave, amputate, kill;* secare :—Mid stanum ceorfende, *Mk.* 5, 5. Curfon þone ram eall to sticcon, *Lev.* 8, 20.

Ceorfinc-isen *a marking or searing-iron;* cauterium :—*Scint.* 9.

Ceorian, ciorian, ic ceorige; *p.* ode. *To murmur, complain;* murmurare :—*Num.* 21, 5: *Elf. gr.* 29.

CEORL, es; *m.* [*Plat.* keerl *m: Dut. Kilian.* caerl *m: Ger.* kerl *m: Dan. Swed. Icel.* karl *m: a man, a fellow*] *A countryman,* CHURL, *husbandman, a man, husband;* rusticus, vir, maritus :—Ceorla cyng *a king of the commons, Chr.* 1020. Ealdan ceorlas wilniað *old men wish, Bt.* 36, 5. Clypa þinne ceorl, *Jn.* 4, 18, 19, 20. ¶ *A free man,* as opposed to þeow *a slave, Ors.* 4, 3, *Bar.* p. 138, 1. Twegra ceorla ealdor *elder,* or *more honourable of two Ceorls, a Duumvir, Som.*

Ceorl-boren *Country born, commons, low born,* opposed to þegen-boren *noble born* :—*L. Wal.* 5.

Ceorl-folc *common people.*
Ceorlian; *p.* ode [ceorl *a husband*] *To take a husband, to marry;* nubere:—Spoken of a woman, and opposed to wifian *to take a wife, Mt.* 22, 30.
Ceorlic, ceorlisc, cirlisc, cyrlisc; *adj.* CHURLIKE, *rustic, common;* vulgaris:—Ceorlisc folc *common people, R.* 87. Ceorlisc-hlaf *common bread, R.* 66.
Ceorlstrang fæmne *a rough woman;* virago.
Ceortes-ig *Cerot's island, Chertsey, in Surrey*:—*Bd.* 4, 6.
Ceorung, e; *f. A murmuring, complaint;* murmuratio.—*Num.* 17, 5.
Ceósan, aceósan, geceósan; ic ceóse; þu, he cyst, gecyst; *p.* ic, he ceás, geceás; þu cure, we curon, acuron, gecuron: *sub.* he ceóse; *pp.* gecoren, acuren. [*Plat.* kösen: *Dut.* Ger. kiesen] *To* CHOOSE, *elect, select;* eligere:—Þat se cyning him ceose sumne wisne man, *Gen.* 41, 33. Þa gecuron hig, *Mt.* 13, 48. In Bisceopes hade wæs gecoren *was chosen to bishophood, episcopacy, Bd.* 4, 23. Feawa gecorene, *Mt.* 22, 14.
Ceosel, ceosl [*Dut. Kil.* kesel] *Gravel, sand;* glarea, sabulum. Hence the sand-hill in Dorsetshire is called CHESIL.
Ceosl-stan *sand-stone.*
Ceosol *The ventricle, a cottage;* ventriculus, *Lye.*
Ceosung *a choosing,* v. aceocung.
CEÓWAN, he cywð; *p.* ceáw, hi cuwon: *pp.* geceowen [*Plat. Dut.* kaauwen: *Ger.* kauen] *To* CHEW, *eat;* ruminare:—*Lev.* 11, 3: manducare, *Elf. T.* p. 42.
Ceowel *a basket,* v. cawl.
Ceowung *A chewing;* ruminatio, *Som.*
Cepa *A chapman, merchant;* mercator:—*Bt.* 15. ¶ Syllan to cepe *to sell.* Cepena þinga gewrixle *commerce, R.* 16, v. ceap.
CEPAN; *p.* cepte. *To go about, endeavour, make an attempt, betake oneself to, seek after, catch at, heed, regard, catch,* KEEP; captare, observare, tenere:—Ne nanes fleames cepan *nor to make an attempt of any flight, Elf. T.* p. 36, 18. Ic cepte *I endeavoured, Mod. confit.* I. Cepan his mæles *to keep the time of his meals.* Þe cepað *who observe, Elf. T.* p. 28, 3.
Cepe-cniht *a bought servant, a slave,* v. ceap-cniht.
Cepeman, cepman *a merchant,* v. ceapman.

Cepestow *a market,* v. ceapstow.
Cepeþinc *Hire, reward;* merces, *Lye.*
Cepeþing *A saleable thing, what is for sale;* res venalis:—*Bd.* 2, 1.
Cepinc, ceping *Traffic, merchandise;* negotiatio:—*C. Mt.* 22, 5.
Cepla *a basket,* v. cawl.
Cepman *a chapman,* v. ceapman.
Cepsceamol *A stall;* telonium: —*Jn.* 8, 20, v. ceapsceamul.
Cepsetl *a stall,* v. ceapsetl.
CER, cier, cyr, re; *f.* [*Plat.* keer *f*: *Dut. Frs.* keer *m.*] *A turn, bending, space of time, season, occasion, business;* versio, flexus, vices:—*Past.* 4, 1: *Cd.* 166. Æt oðrum cerre *at another turn* or *time, Bt.* 35, 2. Æt anum cierre *at one time, Past.* 61, 2. Æt sumum cyrre, cerre or cierre *at the same turn* or *time, when, Lk.* 22, 32.
Cerdis-cesford *Cerdic's ford, Chardford, Hants. Chr.* 508.
Cerdis-cesleag, Cerdicesleah, *Cerdic's ley* or *field, Cheardesley, Bucks, Chr.* 527.
Cerdices ora *Cerdic's shore, Cerdickshore, Norfolk, Chr.* 495.
Cerene, cyrin. 1. *Boiled wine;* sapa. 2. *An earthen vessel;* vas fictile. 3. *A churn;* sinum:—1. *Guthl. Vit.* c. 16. 2. and 3. *Som.*
Cerfe *shall separate,* v. ceorfan.
Cerfille *chervill,* v. ceruille.
Cerian *to murmur,* v. ceorian.
Cerlice *The herb carlock* or *charlock;* rapum sylvestre:—*L. Md.* 1, 39.
Cernan *To churn;* agitare butyrum, *Som.*
Cerran, acerran, gecyrran, gecerran; *p.* cerde, cyrde, cirde, gecerde, gecirde, gecyrde, hi cyrdon; *pp.* acyrred, gecerred, gecirred, gecyrred [*Dut.* keeren] *To turn, avert, return, pass over* or *by;* vertere, reverti:—On woh cerde *turned into an error, deviated, Cot.* 61: *Jn.* 6, 66: *Gen.* 38, 22. Cirrað to fremdum godum, *Deut.* 31, 20: *Ps.* 89, 3. Ic gecyrre on min hus, *Mt.* 12, 44. Gecerrað þat folc, *R. Lk.* 23, 5. Gecerre hine *let him turn, Bt.* 35, 1. Gecerred from wind, *C. Lk.* 7, 24.
Cerre *with a turn,* v. cer.
Cerrednys *a turning,* v. acyrrednes.
Cerse [*Dut.* korst *m.*] CRESS; nasturtium:—*Herb.* 21.
Ceruille *chervill,* v. cærfille.
Cese *a cheese,* v. cyse.
Cese-lib, cyslib *milk curded, curding;* coagulum, *Som.*
Cesol *a cottage,* v. ceosol.

Cest *a chest,* v. cyst.
Cester *a city,* v. ceaster.
Cete *A cabin, cellar;* cella:—*R.* 108.
Cetel, cetil, cetl *a kettle,* v. cytel.
Cetel-hrum *kettle-soot, Som.*
Cetereht *A cataract, flood-gate;* cataractum. CATTERICK, *near Richmond, Yorkshire, Som.*
Chece *a cheek,* v. ceac.
Chid *chid:* chidan *to chide,* v. cidan.
Chieke *the cheek,* v. ceac.
Chinne *the chin,* v. cyn.
Chinteð *the chin* or *fore-teeth,* v. cintoð.
Chor A CHOIR, *dance;* chorus: —*Elf. gl.* 19. Chor-gleow, *Lps.* 149, 3.
Chorl *a churl,* v. ceorl.
Christen *a Christian,* v. cristen.
Cicel *A morsel, a little mouthful;* buccella:—*Cot.* 26, *Som.*
Cicen; *pl.* cicenu [*Dut.* kuiken] A CHICKEN; pullus:—*Elf. gl.* 12. Henne mid cicenum *a hen with chickens, Somn.* 122. ¶ Cicena mete *chicken's meat, chick-weed;* alsine:—*Elf. gl.* 15.
Cicene *a kitchen,* v. cycene.
Cicle *a morsel,* v. cicel.
Cid, cyd *Strife, chiding, contention;* contentio:—*Somn.* 305.
Cidan; *p.* cidde, hi cedun; *pp.* cidd. *To contend, strive, quarrel,* CHIDE, *brawl;* increpare: —*Ex.* 21, 18: *Lk.* 4, 35.
Cidde *told,* v. cyðan.
Cider [*Dut.* cider] CIDER; vinum pomarium, *Lye.*
Ciding, cydung A CHIDING; increpatio:—*Ors.* 4, 12: *Ps.* 103, 8.
Ciele *cold, Cot.* 88, v. cile.
Cielf *a calf,* v. cealf.
Ciellan; *pl. Vessels for drink, wooden tankards, leather bottles;* obbæ:—*Dial.* 1, 5, v. cyll.
Ciepe *an onion,* v. cipa.
Ciepe-mon *a merchant,* v. ceapman.
Cierlisc *a rustic,* v. ceorlic.
Ciern *a churn,* v. cerene.
Cierre *in a turn,* v. cer.
Ciest *a chest, choice,* v. cyst.
Cifes *a harlot,* v. cyfes.
Cifes-gemanna *fornication;* concubinatus:—*L. Can. Edg.* 21.
Cigan *to call, call upon,* v. cygan
Cignis, se; *f. A name, naming;* nomen, *Som.*
Cilct *chalked;* calce illitus, *Som.*
CILD, es; *pl.* cild, *sometimes* cildru; *n.* A CHILD, *infant;* infans:—Aris and nim þat cild, *Mt.* 2, 13, 14. Þat cild wixð and gewurð eft cnapa and eft syþðan cniht *the child*

UN

O1 cote, calla Elf gl. Som 78 col 2, v cote –

charlike, free born Bas gl

O1 [20a]

Netrekt

child a child, v cild

chór es; m. chogri, quir th nullcl

O2 [19b]

Dat kiegen –

cnocl ices ford, es; m cnapl

cian tracie

O5 [22b]

O8

O3 [21a]

O8 Cocel [19c]

O7

O6 [22c]

9 [20b]

O4 [21b]

O7 [22d]

tir kauen

O5 [21c]

O6 [21d]

11 cepe from cepa or cep, scepe, ceap

10 [20c]

2 fleames flean to take flight

O7 [21e]

[48ab cild 22e]

C3 arts cildra

O3 [24c]

O1

[Icel. kofi m
tugurium Cd [49a 1] [24e]

O1 [24f]

O7 Cip, A tent, booth, stall; taber-naculum Som.

Ciste a band of soldiers Cd. 154. Th. p. 192.

Cite a city: cirkulige Suppl.

Cild-clāð, es; m A child-cloth, a swaddling cloth Th. An.

Cipan to sell, Th. An. v cypan

Ciptun, cirice, an; f church Th. An.

Cistwæcce, an; f weeks of penitence Ben. v cyswuce

Cild-cradol, es; m a child-cradle Th. An.

O [25b]

Cīdan to make known Th. An. v cydan

Cildes, scrud, es; n a child's clothing garment, the toga robe or cloak worn by noblemen's children till they were 17 years old; prætexta Lye v. cild

O9

Cille of a bottle Som. v Byt

O8 Ciowung chewing

O10 ruminatio Ben. v cywung

[28d]

Cilddnige Caledonia Hickes Th. 75. Lye

O5 [17a] C 23e]

cyric-dom

O7 [28c]

O6 [23g]

Cin of kin Th. An. v cyn

Ciricliсe Churchlike, ecclesiastical, Th. An.

O9 [28e]

Ciricean a church, Bd. 3, 17, S. 543, 32, Sorcirice

509, 9a cyrice

Cina v cyn

O7 [42a]

O [27a]

Ciric-tun, es; m a churchyard

Cin-berg A covering of the chin, visor Cd 151, Th p. 188, 28

Cirman to make a noise, cry out Th. An. v cyrman

O10 [29a]

O2 q m

O8 [26a]

Cirran to return Th. An. v cerran

Cinca king Som. Ben. v cyng

O9 [26b]

Cirs-treow a cherry tree v cyrs-treow

Cinean to gape, yawn, hiare Ben.

Clæn-heort clean or pure hearted; mundus corde

O4 Cinn a kin, race, Th. An. v cyn

Ciser-æppel, es m a kind of

Cinedom a kingdom Som. Ben. v cynedom

Cine-stol a metropolis Som. Ben. v cyne-stol

Cining, cining a kingdom Ben. cyng

Cinehelm a crown Som. Ben. v cynehealm

grows, and then becomes a boy, and afterwards a young man, Hom. Sax. ¶ Mid cild beon, weorðan, *or* wesan *to be with child.*—Cilda hyrd *a schoolmaster.*—Cilda trog *or* cradelas *a cradle, Elf.gr.*13.—Cilda mæsse dæg CHILDERMAS DAY, *innocents' day.*—Cild-claðas *swaddling-clothes, Lk,* 2, 7.

Cild-fostre *a child-fosterer, a nurse, Som.*

Cildgeong, cildgeongman *An infant;* infans:—*C. R. Ben.* 49, 70.

Cildhád CHILDHOOD, *infancy;* infantia:—*Mk.* 9, 21.

Cild-hama *the womb.*

Cildisc *childish, puerile,* v. cildlic.

Cildiugoð *childhood.*

Cildiung-wif *a child-bearing woman.*

Cildlic, cildisc; *adj. Childish, puerile;* infantilis:—*Bd.* 4, 8.

Cildru *children,* v. cild.

Cildsung *Childishness;* puerilitas, *Som.*

Cile *Cold, coldness;* frigus:—*Gen.* 8, 22, v. cyl.

Cilferlamb, cilforlamb *A female lamb;* agnus femina:—*Lev.* 5, 6.

Cilian *to cool,* v. colian.

Cilic *Hair-cloth;* cilicium:—*C. Mt.* 11, 21.

Cill, cille *a leather bag,* v. ciellan.

Ciltern [ceald *cold,* ern *place*] *The* CHILTERN, *high hills in Buckinghamshire, Som.*

Cim, cim-stanas *The base of a pillar;* bases, *Som.*

Cimbal, cimbala *A cymbal;* cymbalum:—*Elf. gl.* 20: *Greg.* 1, 9.

Cimbing *a joint, conjunction.*

Cime *a coming,* v. cyme.

CINA, cyna, cinu an. *A chink, fissure, vault;* rima:—Ic geseah ane lytle cynan, *Bt.* 35, 3.

Cinan *To gape, to break into chinks;* hiare, dehiscere, *Som.*

Cinban *chin-bone.*

Cincg *a king,* v. cyng.

Cincung *great laughter.*

Cind *a kind, nature,* v. gecynd.

Cine *A commander of four men, or a fourth part of an army;* quaternio:—Cine oððe feower manna ealdor, *Elf. gl.* 8.

Cine *a cleft,* v. cina.

Cinelic *of the same kind,* also *kingly,* v. cynelec.

Cinene, cinende *gaping,* v. cinan.

Cing *a king,* v. cyning.

Cingestun *Kingston,* v. Cyngestune.

Cinlic *gaping,* v. cina.

Cinn *a kind, the chin,* v. cyn.

Cinntoð *a front tooth, a grinder.*

Cio *a chough, a sort of crow,* v. ceo.

Ciol *a ship,* v. ceol.

Ciolæn, ciolon [*Dut.* keel: *Kil.* keele kele] *The throat;* guttur:—*Ps.* 13, 5: 113, 15.

Ciorian *to complain,* v. ceorian.

Ciorl *a rustic,* v. ceorl.

Cipa, cipe *An onion, scallion;* cepa, ascalonium:—*Cot.* 12.

Cipeleac *A leek;* cipus:—*Cot.* 55.

Cipp *A coulter, harrow;* dentale:—*R.* 1.

Cipresse *the cypress-tree;* cupressus, *Som.*

Ciptum *brought,* v. ceapian.

Circ, circe, ciric, cyric, cyrice, an [*Dut.* kerk] A CHURCH, *temple:* ecclesia:—In circan bebyrged wæs *was buried in a church, Bd.* 2, 7, *S.* p. 509, 5: *Elf. gl.* 18. The first Anglo-Saxon churches were built of wood, *Bd.* 3, 25: 3, 4. Cyric is sacerdes æwe *the church is the priest's wife, Off. Reg.* 8. *Ors.* 2, 2. ¶ Cyricean ealdor *an elder of a church, a churchwarden.*

Circe-wic *A church dwelling, monastery;* monasterium:—*Chr. Gib.* p. 240, 23.

Circlic *circular, like a church, ecclesiastical; Elf. T.* 22.

Circol, circul *A circle, the zodiac, a sphere;* circulus, *Som.*

Circol-wyrda *a juggler, a fortune-teller, Som.*

Circul *a circle,* v. circol.

Circul-adl *the shingles, wolfs-hunger;* zona, curcilla:—*L. Md.* 1, 36.

Circul-cræft *knowledge of the sphere, of astrology,* or *mathematics, Som.*

Ciric *a church,* v. circ.

Ciric-grið *the church's peace.*

Ciric-sceat *church-scot, payment made to the church.*

Cirictun *A church-yard;* cœmeterium:—*L. Can. Edg.* 26.

Circ-wæccean *church-watches, vigils.*

Cirisbeam *A* CHERRY-*tree;* cerasus, *Som.*

Cirlisc *rustic,* v. ceorlic.

Cirm *a charm, crashing,* v. cyrm.

Cirnel *a kernel,* v. cyrnel.

Cirpsian; *p.* siede; *pp.* sied. *To crisp, curl;* crispare, *Som.*

Cirpslocces *crisped* or *curled locks, Som.*

Cirrede *turned, changed,* v. cerran.

Cirspan *to crisp,* v. cirpsian.

Cis; *adj.* [*Dut.* kies, koos] *Choice, nice in eating;* fastidiosus in edendo:—*Herb.* 8, 2.

Ciser-æppla *a kind of dried figs;* caricæ:—*Cot.* 38.

Cisilstan *sand-stone,* v. ceoslstan.

Cisnes *choiceness, niceness,* v. ceasness.

Cissa-ceaster [*Cassa's city*] CHICHESTER, *Sussex:*—*Chr.* 895: *L. Athel.* 14.

Cist *chooses,* v. ceosan.

Cist *goodness,* v. cyst.

Cist *election, choice, a band of soldiers,* v. cyst.

Ciste, *A chest;* cista:—*Cod. Ex.* 1. *b,* v. cyst.

Cisten-beam *A chesnut-tree;* castanea:—*R.* 46.

Cistmælum *earnestly, Som.*

Cite *a city, Som.*

Citelan [*Frs.* kitelje] *To tickle;* titillare, *Som.*

Citelung *a tickling.*

CID, es; *m. A young tender shoot of a herb* or *tree, from the root upwards, a germ, sprig, blade;* festuca:—Ofer gærsa ciðas, *Ex.* 32, 2. Forhwi ælc sæd to ciðum and wyrtrumum weorðe *why should every seed turn to germs and roots, Bt.* 34, 10.

Ciðere *A reprover, chider;* reprehensor, *Som.*

Ciðfæst *rooted, growing, Som.*

Citil *a kettle,* v. cytel.

Claded *clad,* v. gecladed.

Clæcleas, clacleas *free, Cot.* 104.

Clæfer-wyrt *Clover, small clover;* trifolium minus:—*L. Md.* 1, 30.

Clæfra; *pl. Violets, gilliflowers;* violæ:—Reade clæfra *marigolds;* calthæ. Hwite clæfra *white violets* or *stock-gilliflowers,* violæ albæ, *Som.*

Clæg [*Frs.* klai] CLAY; samia terra:—*R.* 56.

Clæghangre [*from its clayey situation*] CLAY-HANGER, or *Clayhonger, Suffolk, Chr.* 1016.

Clæia; *adj.* CLAYEY; argillaceus, *Lye.*

Clæmende *hardening, Cot.* 145.

Clæmian [*Frs.* kliemje] *To* CLAM, *smear, anoint;* linere:—*Gen.* 6, 14.

Clæmming, e; *f. A blotting, daubing, smearing, hardening;* litura, oblimatio:—*Elf. gr.* 47, *Som.*

CLÆN; *adj.* 1. CLEAN, *pure;* mundus. 2. *Chaste, innocent;* castus, innoxius:—1. Wit clæn, *Ps.* 74, 7. Clæne nyten, *Bd.* 4, 24: *Lev.* 23, 22. 2. Clæne oððe heofonlic *unmarried, Elf. gr.* 9, 49. Þu bist clæne, *Deut.* 23, 22: *Gen.* 44, 10.

Clænan *To clean;* purificare:—*L. Can. Edg.* 22.

Clæne; *adv.* CLEAN, *entirely;* penitus:—*Ors.* 4, 1.

Clængeorn *a desire of purity.*

Clænehlaf *corn, bread, Som.*

Clænlic *pure, cleanly,* v. clæn.

Clænlice *purely, cleanly;* puré, *Som.*

Clænnes, se; *f. Cleanness, chas-*

tity, modesty; puritas:—Ps. 17, 22, 26.

Clænsere A cleanser, purifier, priest; purgator, Som.

Clænsian, aclænsian, geclænsian; p. ede; pp. ed [Frs. klinsgje] To CLEANSE, purify, make clean; mundare:—Clænsa me, Ps. 18, 13. Þu myht me geclænsian, Mt. 8, 2.

Clænsnige cleanse, free from blame; purget:—L. Ethel. 10, W. p. 106, 25.

Clænsung, geclænsung, e; f. A cleansing, purifying, expiation; emundatio:—Mk. 1, 44: Lev. 1, 4.

Clæppette should palpitate, v. clappan.

Clæppetung, e; f. The pulse; pulsus:—R. 76.

Clæsnung purifying, v. clænsung.

Clam, es, or mes; m. 1. What is clammy, mud, clay; lutum. 2. A poultice, plaister; plasma. 3. A bandage, what holds or retains as a net, fold, prison; vinculum:—1. Ex. 1, 14. 2. Herb. 22. 3. Bt. R. p. 152, v. clom.

Clane clean, v. clæn.

Clansung cleansing, v. clænsung.

Clappan To CLAP, move, palpitate; palpitare, Som.

Clasnung a chastisement, a cleansing.

Clate A bur, sticking to man's clothes; blitum:—Cot. 24.

CLAD, es; m. CLOTH; in the pl. clothes, garments; pannus, vestimenta:—Bt. 17: Mt. 9, 16: Gen. 37, 29.

Clað-sceara a pair of shears, Som.

Clatrung, e; f. Any thing that makes a clattering, a drum, rattle; crepitaculum:—Cot. 51.

Claustr, clauster, cluster A cloister; claustrum:—Elf. gl. 2[illegible].

CLAW; pl. clawa, clawu [Frs. klou: Plat. Ger. klaue f: Dut. klauw m.] A CLAW, talon, hook, pincers; ungula:—Ps. 68, 36: Lev. 11, 3, 4.

Clawian To CLAW; scalpere:—Elf. gr. 28.

Clawung, e; f. A pain, the gripes; tormina:—L. Md. 2, 32.

Cleadur A clatter, drum, rattle; crepitaculum, Som.

Cleafan dens, v. cleofa.

Cleafan To cleave asunder; findere, Som.

Cledemuð [the mouth of the river Cleddy] GLADMOUTH, CLEDMOUTH, South Wales, Chr. 921.

Clem a plaister, v. clam.

Clene Serene, clear; serenus:—Cd. 213, Lye.

Cleofa, an That which is cloven, a cleft, a chasm, den, chamber; cubile:—Bd. 4, 9.

Cleofesho A famous place for Anglo-Saxon councils, perhaps Abingdon, Berks.

Cleofian to cleave, v. clifian.

Cleopian; part. ende, igende; p. ude. To cry, call; clamare:—Bt. 3, 4, v. clypian.

Cleopigend, cleopend A vowel; vocalis, Som.

Cleopung a cry, v. clypung.

Cleot a clout, v. clut.

Cleow, cleowen a clew, v. cliwe.

Clepan To cry out; clamitare:—Prov. 1, Lye.

Clepeþa A clawing; scalpurigo:—Past. 2, 6.

Clepung a calling.

Clerc, cleric, cleroc, es; m. [Lat. clericus] A CLERK, priest; clericus:—Chr. 963: L. Can. Edg. 4.

Cleric-hád, cleroc-hád priesthood.

Clesnung a cleansing, v. clænsung.

Clibbor A burden, load; onus:—Menol. 473.

Clicta chalk washed.

Cliewe a clue, v. cliwe.

CLIF, clyf; pl. u [Frs. klif: Dut. klip m: Ger. klippe f.] 1. A CLIFF, rock, steep descent; clivus, rupes. 2. A bed, nest; cubile:—1. Ors. 1, 1: 5, 4. 2. Bd. 3, 23.

Clife The herb agrimony, a bur; agrimonia, lappa:—Cot. 118. Smæl clife the small bur, Som.

Clifhlep, clifhlyp a cliff-leap, right down, under foot; pessum:—Cot. 155.

Clifian, onclifian, cliofian; p. ode [Plat. Dut. kleven: Ger. kleben to adhere; Plat. klöven: Dut. klooven. Frs. klieven to split] To CLEAVE, adhere; adhærere, findere:—Hi willað clifian on þæm monnum they will cleave to the men, Bt. 16, 3. Woldon hi on þam clifian, Id. To þære lifre clifiað, Lev. 1, 8. Clifode, Lk. 10, 11.

Clifig, clifiht; adj. Cliffy, steep; clivosus:—R. 8.

Clifrian; part. rende. To claw, scratch; scabere:—Elf. gr. 28.

Clifstanas rough stones, rocks; cautes:—Cot. 44.

Clifwyrt Maiden-hair, water-wort, fox-glove; agrimonia:—Clif or Clyfwyrt, sume man hatað foxes-clife, sume ea wyrt cliffwort some men call fox-glove, some water-wort, L. Md. p. 1, 15.

CLIMAN, climban; pp. clumben [Plat. Dut. Ger. klimmen] To CLIMB; scandere:—Chr. 1070.

Clingan To wither, pine, to CLING or shrink up; marcescere:—Elf. gr. 35, Som.

Cliof a cliff, rock, v. clif.

Cliofian To cleave; adhærere:—Bt. 16, 3, v. clifian.

Cliofung, e; f. A CLEAVING; sectio:—R. 62, Lye.

Cliopian; part. cliopende; p. hi clioppadon. To cry, call, Bd. 4, 19, v. clypian.

Clipode called, v. clypian.

Clipur [Dut. klepel] A CLAPPER; nolæ malleus:—W. Cat. p. 109.

Cliroc a clerk, priest, v. clerc.

Clistun, CLIST or CLYST, near Exeter, Devon. Chr. 1001.

CLIWE, an; n. [Frs. klyoumen] A CLEW, any thing that is globular, a bottom of thread, ball; glomus:—Elf. gr. 20: Past. 35, 5.

Cloccan [Frs. klakke] To CLUCK, sigh; glocire, Som.

Clofeshooh Abingdon, v. cleofesho.

Clofen cloven, separated, Som.

Clofþunc clove-tongue, v. clufþung.

Clofwyrt a fox-glove, v. clifwyrt.

CLOM, mes; m. [Frs. klem] A band, bond, clasp, bandage, chain, prison; vinculum, carcer:—Under clommum under bonds, Cod. Ex. 120, b. 13: Chr. 942. Helle clommas the chains of hell, Cd. 19.

Clough a cleft of a rock, or down the side of a hill, Som.

Clow a clue, v. cliwe.

Clucga [Plat. Dut. Frs. klok f: Ger. klocke f.] A bell, CLOCK; campana:—Bd. 4, 28.

CLUD, es; m. [Plat. kloot m: Dut. kluit f: Ger. kloss m: hence the Eng. clod] A rock, stone, a little hill, hillock; rupes, collis:—Ors. 3, 9: 6, 3: Bt. 34, 10.

Clúdig; adj. Rocky; saxosus:—Ors. 1, 1.

Clufe An ear of corn, a clove of garlic; spica, Som.

Clufiht cliffy, v. clifig.

Clufþung The herb crow-foot, clove-tongue; herba scelerata:—Herb. 9.

Clufwyrt Cliff-wort; batracion:—Herb. 10, v. clifwyrt.

Clugga a bell, v. clucga.

Clumian To keep close, to press, cover, murmur, mutter; comprimere, mussitare:—Bd. de Sapi. [illegible], W. Cat. p. 30.

Clusa, an [Frs. klues] A prison, narrow passage, CLOSE; carcer:—Ors. 3, 7: 6, 36.

Cluster a cluster, bunch, v. clyster.

Cluster a cloister, v. claustr.

Cluster-loc a cloister, v. claustr.

Clut A little cloth, CLOUT, a plait, seam; pittacium, lamina:—Elf. gl. 20.

O1 clea ungula Ben
~~clea~~

O1 [29b]

Clænlice cleanly Ben
v clænlice

Clionode balarius ... Som Lye

02 [29c]

Clite the ~~...~~ herb
agrimony Som, Ben v
clife

O[31b] Clif, es; n a rock &
~~...~~
a bed, couch
Clifa v bedclyfa
v also cleafa

3 [30a]

O1 the cleaver, or
sticker, bur y.

4 [30b]

5 [30c]

... scear; e f forfex Som
Clauster, cluster, clyster
es; n a cloister inclosure

6 [31a]

Cledemuda, an; m f
~~gladmouth~~

Cleafa an; m
radu, cellar, thiam v supl.
~~cleofa~~, clyfa

~~cledemuda, an m gladmuth~~

Cleaf ~~...~~ clove
split separated p
of ~~clufan~~ clufan
v. ~~...~~ supl.

Clifian. C6 (findere)
dl-findere

Clænsian to purify
Som v clænsian

Climban; p clamb
pp we clumbon to
climb Th. An v climan

O1

Clipian to call
Th. An. v cleopian

Clipung a calling Som
v clypung

[32a]

Clita, a plaister
poultice; plasma,
malagma Som

06 [32b]

Clofen cloven, separated.
v supl clufan

Egr glocke [22a
Ger glocke

Cluggé, an f
a clock, bell
Th. An

07 [32c]

Clufan, he clyfð
p cleáf we clufon
pp clofen
to cleave, split
Rask's Gr § 250

Clufon cleave, split
v clufan

...

Clyfa an; m. a
room, cellar Th. An
v. cleafa

O2

X clyft cleaves, splits
v. clyf. ~~klifan~~ clufan

X military follower Th. An

3 Clynegan pulsare
Ben.

O4 Is a clyppige to be ~~...~~ 17,3 O2

2 Clypigende, es m.
One calling, or crying
Th. An

X Clypigende crying
Th. An

O78

X Cneord solers Ben

~~Cnibberes. burh. Burgcastle~~

~~Cneo~~
8 Cneo-holen tongue
laurel Som v cneow-holen

X Cniht-wesende
Being a boy, a
boy; puer. Bee
42 K 1065

3 Cnidan to cast down Som
v cnysan

3 Cnosel, ~~et~~ g. cnosles
m. a race, family Cd
~~...~~ 50, Th p 64, 12:
83 Th p 104, 4

O3 → inclosure Th. An
O5 [21 a 4]

X Cnittan to knit Som
v cnytan

X Cnyht a boy Som
cniht

O8

~~Cnyssan to marr~~

2 Cnysean, hedes ??
to beat. Bee K 2636
? to strike, dash Th. Apol.

O9 Cnyt, cnytt knit
tied Som v cnytan

O10

Cnabe Grein vol.
p. 31 r
knabe

X Cneow-sib
3 ~~Cneow-sib~~ g. ~~...~~ bef
relationship, a race
Cd. 161. Th p 200, 13

Cneow ~~...~~ wærc knee
pain; genuum dolor
Som.

X Cneow-wyrste genicul Ben. Tye

O4 Cnif [21 a 5] A 75

Clyferfot *cloven-footed.*

Clyfigenide adl *a joint-disease, the gout, Som.*

Clylle *A sign;* signum:—*Fulg.* 22.

Clympre *Metal;* metallum:—*Cot.* 132.

Clyna, clyne *Metal, a mass, lump, wedge;* metallum:—*R.* 51.

Clypenes *a clipping,* v. clypnys.

Clypian, cleopian, ic clypige; *p.* clypode, geclypode, hi clypodon, clypon; *pp.* geclypod; *v. a.* [*Plat. Ger.* klaffen: *Dut.* klappen] *To speak, speak aloud, to call, say;* loqui, clamare:—*Mk.* 10, 47: *Lk.* 5, 32. Manega synt geclypode, *Mt.* 20, 16.

Clypiendlic, clypigendlic; *adj. Vocative, calling, vocal;* vocalis, vocativus:—Clypiendlic gebigednes *a vocative case, Elf. gr.* 7.

Clypnys, clypenes, se; *f.* A CLIPPING, *an embrace;* amplexus:—*Bd.* 3, 24.

CLYPPAN, beclyppan; *p.* de; *pp.* ed *or* clypte, beclypte [*Plat. Ger.* klappen] *To embrace, clasp,* CLIP, *make much of, love, admire;* amplecti:—*Bd.* 4, 24: *Gen.* 29, 13: *Mk.* 9, 36.

Clypung, e; *f. Articulation, speaking out, the forming of words, a cry;* eloquium, clamor:—Se muð dryfð ut þa clypunge, and seo lyft bið geslagen mid þære clypunge, *Elf. gr.* 1, 5, *Som.* p. 2, 34: *Ps.* 17, 8. Clypunga *the calends.*

Clysing, clysung, e; *f. That which is closed, a period, closing, conclusion, cloister;* periodus, claustrum:—Periodus is clysing, oððe geendung þæs ferses, *Elf. gr.* 51, *Som.* p. 51, 20.

Clyster; *pl.* clystru. A CLUSTER, *a bunch, a branch;* racemus:—*R.* 47: *Gen.* 40, 10.

Clysung *a cloister,* v. clysing.

Clyþa *A plaister, salve, poultice;* plasma:—*Elf. gr.* 9: *Gl.* 7: *Herb.* 51, 2, v. clam.

Clywen *a clue,* v. cliwe.

Cnædan *to knead,* v. cnedan.

CNÆP, cnæpp [*Plat. Dut.* knoop *m.*] *A top, cop,* KNOP, *button;* jugum:—Uppan þæs muntes cnæp, *Ex.* 19, 20: *Lk.* 4, 29: *Numb.* 14, 44.

Cnæpling [*Dut.* knaaplyn: *Fland.* knapelinck] *A stripling, youth;* adolescens:—*W. Bd.* p. 377.

CNAPA, cnafa, an; *m.* [*Plat. Dut.* knaap *m*: *Ger.* knabe *m*: *Old Eng.* knave] *A boy, servant, young man;* puer:—He betæhte hys cnapan and se cnapa hit ofsloh, *Gen.* 18, 7: 21, 19: 39, 10: *Ps.* 85, 15.

Cnáwan, he cnæwð; *p.* cneow; *pp.* cnáwen. *To* KNOW; noscere, v. oncnáwan.

Cnáwing *Knowledge, a knowing;* cognitio, *Som.*

Cnear *A ship, a narrow ship, galley;* navis:—Cnear on flot *the ship on float, Athelst. Vict. Chr.* 938. Nægled on cnearrum *in nailed ships, Id.*

Cneatung, e; *f. A debate, an inquiry, a search;* disputatio, scrutinium:—*Scint.* 14.

Cnedan, gecnedan; *pp.* cneden [*Dut.* kneden] *To* KNEAD, *ferment;* subigere:—*R. Lk.* 13, 21.

Cneo *a generation,* v. cneores.

Cneoehte *Knotty;* geniculatus:—*L. Md.* 1, 64.

Cneoferis-burh *Burgcastle, Suffolk; Bd.* 3, 19, v. Cnobheres-burh.

Cneoholen *A herb;* ruscus:—*Cot.* 165.

Cneoht *a boy,* v. cniht.

Cneomagas *relations,* v. mæg.

Cneordlæcan, gecneordlæcan *To study, take care;* studere, *Som.*

Cneordnys, se; *f. Diligence, care, affection;* cura, *Som.*

Cneores, cneorys, cneornys, cneowres, se; *f. A generation, family, stock;* tribus:—Of þisse wirestan cneoresse, *Deut.* 1, 35: *Gen.* 2, 4: 6, 9. Cneorisse boc, *Mt.* 1, 1.

Cneorim *a generation.*

Cneorisn *family, generation,* v. cneores.

Cneornys, cneorys *a generation,* v. cneores.

CNEOW, es; *n.* [*Plat.* knee: *Dut. Ger.* knie *f*: *Moes.* kniw] A KNEE, *relationship;* genu:—*Mt.* 27, 29. ¶ Binnan cneowe *within relationship, L. Edw. Guth.* 11. Cneow hweorban *the whirl-bone of the knee, Som.*

Cneow-wærce *pain in the knees, Som.*

Cneow-holen, cneow-holm KNEEHOLM, *knee-hulver, tongue laurel;* ruscus:—*Cot.* 165: victoriola, *Herb.* 59.

Cneowian, gecneowian; *p.* ede *To bow the knee, to kneel;* genuflectere:—*Pref. R. Conc.*

Cneowmagas *relations,* v. mæg.

Cneowrim, cneowres *a generation,* v. cneores.

Cneow-sibbe *relationship.*

Cneowung, e; *A kneeling;* genuflectio:—*Bd.* 3, 17.

Cnidan *To beat;* cædere:—*R. Mt.* 21, 35.

Cnif [*Frs.* knyf: *Plat.* knief *c*: *Dan.* kniv *c.*] A KNIFE; culter, v. sex.

CNIHT, cneoht, es; *m.* [*Plat. Dut. Ger.* knecht] *A boy, youth, attendant, servant.* Hence the modern knights of a shire are so called because they serve the shire; puer, servus:—Lytel cniht *a little boy, Bd.* 4, 8: *L. In.* 7: *Gen.* 24, 64: *Lk.* 7, 7: 12, 45. Moises sende cnihtas, *Ex.* 24, 5. ¶ Cnihtcild *a boy, a male-child, Bd.* 4, 8.—Leorning cniht *a learning attendant, a disciple.*

Cnihthád *The period between childhood and manhood, youth, boyhood,* KNIGHTHOOD; pubes:—*Elf. gr.* 9, 28: *Bd.* 5, 14.

Cniht-iuguð *Youth, boyhood;* juventus:—*Bridfr.*

Cnihtlic; *adj. Boyish;* puerilis:—*L. Guth.* 2.

Cnihtwisa *youthwise, youthlike,* v. monwisa.

Cnobheres-burg *Burgcastle, Suffolk;* urbs Cnobheri:—*Bd.* 3, 19: *Bd.* 3, 19.

Cnocian *to knock,* v. cnucian.

Cnodan; *pp.* gecnoden. *To give, attribute;* tribuere:—*Past.* 17, 3.

CNOLL, es; *m.* [*Plat.* knull *m*: *Dut.* knol: *Kil.* knolle: *Ger.* knollen] A KNOLL, *a hill, top, cop, summit;* cacumen:—*Gen.* 8, 5: *Jud.* 16, 3, v. cnæp.

Cnosl, es; *m. A race, progeny;* proles:—*L. Alf.* 9.

Cnotta [*Frs.* knotte: *Plat. Dut.* knobbel *m*: *Kil.* knutte *n*: *Ger.* knoten *m.*] A KNOT, *a fastening, knitting;* nexus:—*Elf. gr.* 21.

Cnotted *knotted.*

CNUCIAN, cnuciað; *part.* ende, gende; *pp.* gecnocod, gecnuced. *To* KNOCK, *beat;* pulsare:—*Mt.* 7, 7, 8: *Lk.* 11, 10.

Cnucl [*Plat.* knökel *m*: *Dut.* knokkel *m*: *Ger.* knöchel *m.*] A KNUCKLE, *joint;* articulus, *Som.*

Cnyll [*Dut.* knal] A KNELL, *a sound of a bell;* signum campanæ:—*R. Ben.* 48.

Cnyllan, cnyllsan; *p.* de; *pp.* ed. *To* KNELL, *sound a bell;* pulsare, campana signum dare:—*R. Ben.* 48: *C. Lk.* 11, 9.

Cnysan, cnyssan; *pp.* gecnysed. [*Plat.* knösen: *Frs.* knieze: *Dut.* kneuzen] *To break down, weaken, beat, calumniate;* premere:—*Ors.* 3, 1: *Ps.* 118, 122.

Cnysung, cnyssung, e; *f. A striking, stroke;* ictus:—*Elf. gr.* 1, 4, *Som.* p. 2.

CNYTAN, cnyttan; *pp.* gecnyt [*Plat.* knütten] *To tie, bind,* KNIT; nectere, ligare:—*Elf. gr.* 36.

Cnyttelsa *the sinews, nerves, Som.*

Cóc, es; *m.* [*Plat. Frs. Dut.* kok *m*: *Ger.* koch *m.*] A COOK;

O2

O he gecyrd to cytan advertebat ad tugurium v Som. in cyte

Cod, e; f A disease, malady, plague morbus Som th. an

powerful th. an

Creca-rice es; n the domain of the Greeks Greece th. v Greceland

O3 [48a 4]

O2

O4

Counel or cawel a basket, corbis Som v cawl

Cradel, cradol es; m

Cradol-cild a cradle child, an infant infans e cunabilis, puer a lacte nondum depulsus Lup 5, 14

Crœft es; m also Crœft, e; f Beo

Crœt, es; n; pl. cratu, a cart

Creopend, es; m a creeping thing, reptile th. an

Crœc a chariot Som v crœt.

Crahettan crocitare Ben

O2

Crang died v. sup cringan

Cringan; p crang, we ge hi crungon to die Cd. 167 Th. 208, 11 Beo K 1264.

Crata of wagons cratu wagons pl of crœt

Crawe. an; f a crow

kaate] A COT, *cottage, den, cave, bed, couch;* casa, spelunca:—To his cotan, *L. Cnut.* 74. He hæfde cytan, *Bd.* 3, 17, *S.* p. 543, 24: 5, 12, *S.* p. 630, 42. To þeofa cote, *Mt.* 21, 13: *Ors.* 3, 9, *Bar.* p. 117, 17.

Coða, coðe *A disease, sickness, pestilence;* morbus:—Swile coðe com on mannum *such a disease came on men, Chr.* 1087.

Coðlice *truly,* v. cuðlice.

Cotlyf; *pl.* cotlyfa. *A little village;* villula:—*Chr.* 963.

Cotsæta *An inhabitant of a cottage, a cottager;* casæ habitator, *Som.*

Cott *a bed,* v. cota.

Cottuc *Mallows;* malva, *Som.*

Coxre *a quiver,* v. cocer.

CRABBA, an; [*Plat. Ger.* krabbe *f: Dut.* krab *f.*] A CRAB, *crawfish, a sign of the zodiac;* cancer:—*Elf. gl.* 12: *Æqu. vern.* 7.

Cracettan *To croak;* crocitare: —*Dial.* 2, 8.

Cradel, cradl, cradul, A CRADLE; cunabulum:—On þam cradele, *L. Cnut.* 74: *Cot.* 208.

Cræcetung, e; *f. A croaking;* crocitatio:—Cræcetung hræfena *the croaking of ravens, Guth.* 6.

Cræfian *to crave,* v. crafian.

CRÆFT, es; *m.* [*Plat. Dut.* kracht *f: Ger.* kraft] 1. CRAFT, *contrivance, art, skill, trade, employment, workmanship;* ars, artificium. 2. *Strength, power;* vis, potentia. 3. *Talent, ability, faculty, excellence, virtue;* facultas, virtus:—1. Mid ænige cræfte *by any contrivance, Bt.* 39, 4. Ælces cræftes andweorc *the materials of every art, Id.* 17. 2. Mid eallum hiora cræftum *with all their powers, Ors.* 1, 13. Sunnan cræftas *the sun's powers, Bt.* 41, 1. 3. Þæt mine cræftas ne wurden forgitene *that my talents might not be forgotten, Id.* 17. Se wer is cræfta full *the man is full of virtues, Id.* 40: 36, 5. Wið þære sawle cræfta ænne *with one of the faculties of the soul, Id.* 32, 1. ...antian cræftas on mode *to ...unt virtues in the mind, Id.* 27, 38, 5. ¶ Ator-cræft *the art of poisoning.*—Boc-cræft *book-craft, literature.*—Dream-cræft *the art of music.*—Dry-cræft *the art of magic.*—Galdor-cræft *incantation.*—Læce-cræft *the art of medicine.*—Leoð-cræft *poetry.*—Rim-cræft *arithmetic.*—...-cræft *navigation.*—Stæf-cræft *letter-craft, grammar.*—...gel-cræft *astronomy.*—

Wicce-cræft *witchcraft.*—Wig-cræft *the art of war.*

Cræfta *An artist, a craftsman, workman;* artifex:—*Elf. gr.* 10.

Cræftan *To exercise a craft, to build;* architectari:—*Elf. gr.* 36.

Cræftega, cræftica, cræftiga *An architect, a workman;* artifex: —*Bt.* 39, 5, v. cræfta.

Cræftgast *most skilful.*

Cræftica *a workman,* v. cræftega.

Cræftig; *adj. Ingenious, skilful,* CRAFTY; ingeniosus, peritus: —*Bt.* 36, 6: 39, 10.

Cræftiga *a workman,* v. cræftega.

Cræftiglice; *adv. Workmanlike, craftily;* artificiose:—*Bd.* 4, 19.

Cræftigra *more skilful,* v. cræftig.

Cræftleas; *adj. Artless, innocent, simple, inexpert;* innocens:—*Elf. gr.* 10.

Cræftlic; *adj. Workmanlike, artificial;* artificialis:—*Bridfr.*

Cræftlice; *adv. Cunningly,* CRAFTILY; affabre:—*R.* 99.

Cræftsearo *An instrument of war, a device, stratagem;* machina, *Som.*

Cræft-wyrc *Workmanship;* artificium:—*Scint.* 29.

Cræn *a crane,* v. cran.

Cræsta A CREST, *tuft, plume;* crista, *Som.*

CRÆT, crat; *pl.* cratu [*Plat.* kare, karet *f: Ger.* karre *f.*] *A chariot,* CART; currus:—He hæfde cratu, and ridende men, *Gen.* 50, 9: *Deut.* 11, 4. Twægra horsa cræt *a chariot or cart drawn by two horses, Som.*

Cræthors *a cart horse.*

Crætwæn *a wain, chariot.*

Cræwð *crows,* v. crawan.

CRAFIAN, becrafian *To ask,* CRAVE, *implore;* petere:—*L. pol. Cnut.* 67: *Chr.* 1070.

Crammian; *pp.* crummen, accrummen [*Dut.* krammen] *To* CRAM, *stuff;* farcire:—*Elf. gr.* 30.

CRAN [*Dut.* kraan *f.*] A CRANE; grus:—*Elf. gr.* 9, 33.

Cranc-stæf *a weaver's instrument.*

Crang *Dead, killed;* mortuus, *Mann.*

Crangan, gecrangan; *p.* hi crungon [*Dut.* krenken: *Ger.* kranken] *To submit, crush, die, perish;* occumbere, perire:—*Cd.* 167. Hettend crungon *the enemy crushed* [*cringed*], *Chr.* 938.

Cranohawe *a crane hawk.*

Crape *should creep,* v. creopan.

Crat *a waggon,* v. cræt.

CRAW, crawe [*Frs.* krie: *Plat. Dut.* kraai *f: Ger.* krähe *f.*] A CROW, *a Cornish chough, a jay;* cornix:—*Ps.* 146, 10.

Crawan, ic cráwe, cræwð; *p.* creow, hi creowon; *pp.* cráwen [*Plat.* kreien: *Dut.* krayen: *Ger.* krähen] *To* CROW *as a cock;* cantare instar galli: —*Mt.* 26, 34, 74: *Mk.* 14, 30.

Crawan-leac *Meadow-saffron;* hermodactylus:—*R.* 44.

Creaca, Creacisc; *adj. Grecian;* Græcus:—*Ors.* 1, 10. Creaca land *Greece, Id.* 1, 1.

Creacanford, v. Creccanford.

Cread *A company, troop;* turma: —Cread-cnearr *a ship's company, a crew, Lye.*

Crecas *the Greeks,* v. Grecas.

Crecca A CREEK, *bay, wharf;* crepido, *Som.*

Creccagelade, Cregelade [*F.* Criccelade: *Hunt.* Criklade] CRICKLADE, CREEKLADE, *Wilts., Chr.* 905.

Creccanford, Crecganford, Creacanford [*Hunt.* Creganford *the ford of the river Crec* or *Craye*] CRAYFORD, *Kent, Chr.* 457.

Crecisc *Grecian,* v. Creaca.

Creda, an; *m. The creed, belief;* symbolum fidei:—¶ Se læsse creda *the less* or *Apostle's creed.*—Se mæsse creda *the sacrament* or *Nicene creed.*

Cregelade, v. Creccagelade.

Crencestre, crencistre; *f. female weaver, a spinster;* textrix:—*Wynfl. Test.*

CREOPAN, he crypð; *p.* creap, hi crupon; *pp.* cropen [*Plat.* krupen: *Frs.* kroepe: *Dut.* kruipen] *To* CREEP, *crawl;* repere:—*Bt.* 36, 4: *Ors.* 1, 7. ¶ Creopende cyn *creeping kind, a reptile, Gen.* 1, 25.

Creopere; *m.* [*Plat.* krüper *m: Dut.* kruiper *m.*] A CREEPER, *cripple;* serpens, clinicus, *Som.*

Creopung, e; *f.* A CREEPING, *stealing;* obreptio:—*Cot.* 144.

Creow *crew,* v. crawan.

Crepel; *m. A little creeper* or *crawfish;* cancellus:—*Prov.* 7.

Cressen *cresses,* v. cærse.

CRICC, cryc [*Frs.* krik: *Plat. Dut.* kruk *f: Ger.* krücke] A CRUTCH, *staff;* baculus:—*Ps.* 22, 5: *Bd.* 4, 31.

Cridian-tun [*Fr.* Cridiatun, Credon *the river Credon;* tun *a town*] *Kirton* or CREDITON, *Devon, Chr.* 977.

Crisma, an. *Chrism, holy oil used in baptism by the Romish church, a white vesture in which children were clothed after baptism;* chrisma:—*L. Alf. Guth.* Under crisman *clothed in albs* or *white, Bd.* 5, 7: 2, 14. ¶ Crism-halgung *consecrating the chrism, W. Cat.* p. 121.

Crismen *Balsam;* balsamum:— *Cot.* 140.

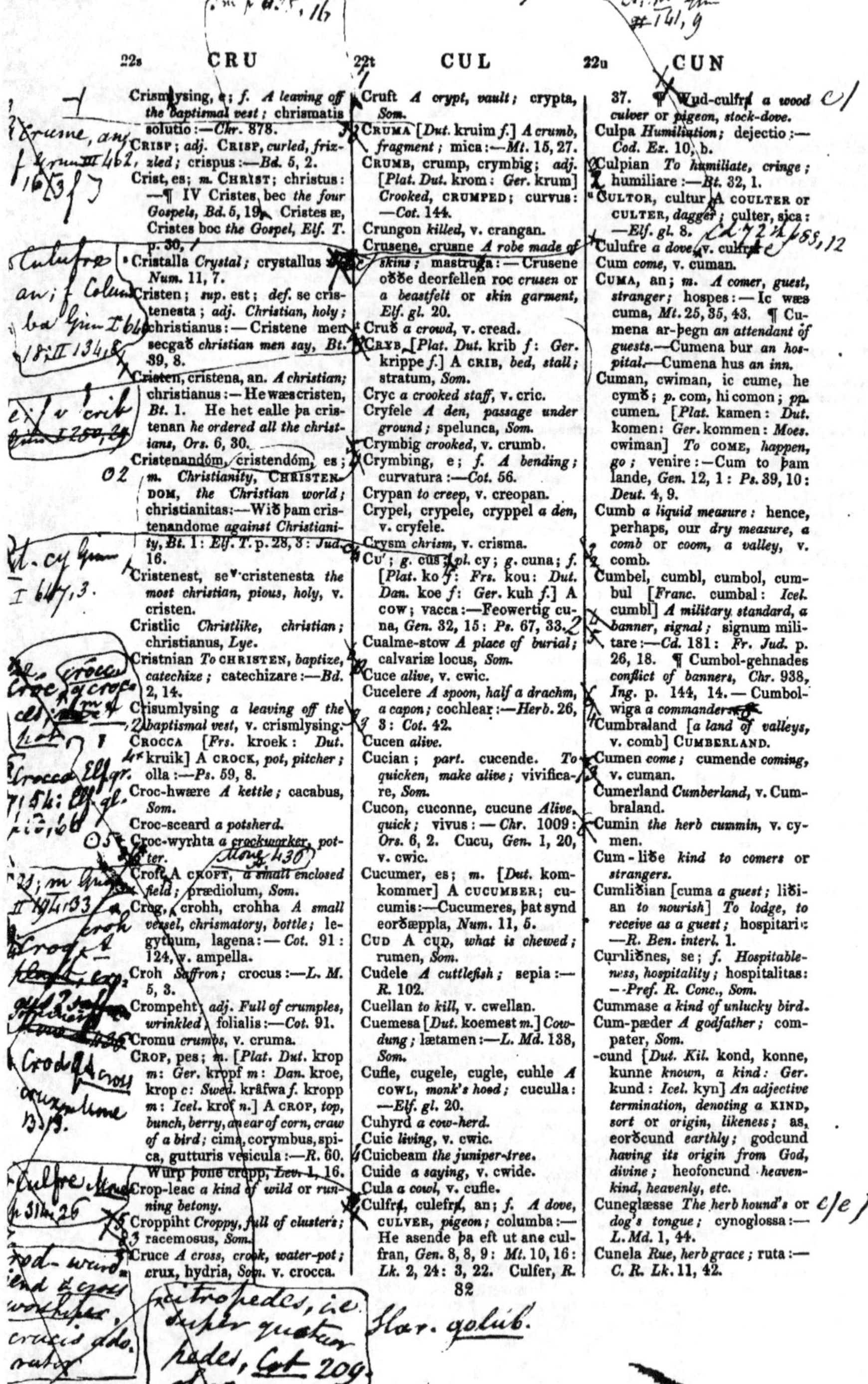

Crismlysing, e; f. A leaving off the baptismal vest; chrismatis solutio:—Chr. 878.
Crisp; adj. Crisp, curled, frizzled; crispus:—Bd. 5, 2.
Crist, es; m. Christ; christus:—¶ IV Cristes bec the four Gospels, Bd. 5, 19. Cristes æ, Cristes boc the Gospel, Elf. T. p. 30, 1.
Cristalla Crystal; crystallus:—Num. 11, 7.
Cristen; sup. est; def. se cristenesta; adj. Christian, holy; christianus:—Cristene men secgað christian men say, Bt. 39, 8.
Cristen, cristena, an. A christian; christianus:—He wæs cristen, Bt. 1. He het ealle þa cristenan he ordered all the christians, Ors. 6, 30.
Cristenandóm, cristendóm, es; m. Christianity, Christendom, the Christian world; christianitas:—Wið þam cristenandome against Christianity, Bt. 1: Elf. T. p. 28, 3: Jud. 16.
Cristenest, se cristenesta the most christian, pious, holy, v. cristen.
Cristlic Christlike, christian; christianus, Lye.
Cristnian To christen, baptize, catechize; catechizare:—Bd. 2, 14.
Crisumlysing a leaving off the baptismal vest, v. crismlysing.
Crocca [Frs. kroek: Dut. kruik] A crock, pot, pitcher; olla:—Ps. 59, 8.
Croc-hwære A kettle; cacabus, Som.
Croc-sceard a potsherd.
Croc-wyrhta a crockworker, potter.
Croft A croft, a small enclosed field; prædiolum, Som.
Crog, crohh, crohha A small vessel, chrismatory, bottle; legythum, lagena:—Cot. 91: 124, v. ampella.
Croh Saffron; crocus:—L. M. 5, 3.
Crompeht; adj. Full of crumples, wrinkled; folialis:—Cot. 91.
Cromu crumbs, v. cruma.
Crop, pes; m. [Plat. Dut. krop m: Ger. kropf m: Dan. kroe, krop c: Swed. kråfwa f. kropp m: Icel. krof n.] A crop, top, bunch, berry, an ear of corn, craw of a bird; cima, corymbus, spica, gutturis vesicula:—R. 60. Wurp þone cropp, Lev. 1, 16.
Crop-leac a kind of wild or running betony.
Croppiht Croppy, full of clusters; racemosus, Som.
Cruce A cross, crock, water-pot; crux, hydria, Som. v. crocca.
Cruft A crypt, vault; crypta, Som.
Cruma [Dut. kruim f.] A crumb, fragment; mica:—Mt. 15, 27.
Crumb, crump, crymbig; adj. [Plat. Dut. krom: Ger. krum] Crooked, crumped; curvus:—Cot. 144.
Crungon killed, v. crangan.
Crusene, crusne A robe made of skins; mastruga:—Crusene oððe deorfellen roc crusen or a beastfelt or skin garment, Elf. gl. 20.
Cruð a crowd, v. cread.
Cryb [Plat. Dut. krib f: Ger. krippe f.] A crib, bed, stall; stratum, Som.
Cryc a crooked staff, v. cric.
Cryfele A den, passage under ground; spelunca, Som.
Crymbig crooked, v. crumb.
Crymbing, e; f. A bending; curvatura:—Cot. 56.
Crypan to creep, v. creopan.
Crypel, crypele, cryppel a den, v. cryfele.
Crysm chrism, v. crisma.
Cu; g. cus; pl. cy; g. cuna; f. [Plat. ko f: Frs. kou: Dut. Dan. koe f: Ger. kuh f.] A cow; vacca:—Feowertig cuna, Gen. 32, 15: Ps. 67, 33.
Cualme-stow A place of burial; calvariæ locus, Som.
Cuce alive, v. cwic.
Cucelere A spoon, half a drachm, a capon; cochlear:—Herb. 26, 3: Cot. 42.
Cucen alive.
Cucian; part. cucende. To quicken, make alive; vivificare, Som.
Cucon, cuconne, cucune Alive, quick; vivus:—Chr. 1009: Ors. 6, 2. Cucu, Gen. 1, 20, v. cwic.
Cucumer, es; m. [Dut. komkommer] A cucumber; cucumis:—Cucumeres, þat synd eorðæppla, Num. 11, 5.
Cud A cud, what is chewed; rumen, Som.
Cudele A cuttlefish; sepia:—R. 102.
Cuellan to kill, v. cwellan.
Cuemesa [Dut. koemest m.] Cow-dung; lætamen:—L. Md. 138, Som.
Cufle, cugele, cugle, cuhle A cowl, monk's hood; cuculla:—Elf. gl. 20.
Cuhyrd a cow-herd.
Cuic living, v. cwic.
Cuicbeam the juniper-tree.
Cuide a saying, v. cwide.
Cula a cowl, v. cufle.
Culfre, culefre, an; f. A dove, culver, pigeon; columba:—He asende þa eft ut ane culfran, Gen. 8, 8, 9: Mt. 10, 16: Lk. 2, 24: 3, 22. Culfer, R. 37. ¶ Wud-culfre a wood culver or pigeon, stock-dove.
Culpa Humiliation; dejectio:—Cod. Ex. 10, b.
Culpian To humiliate, cringe; humiliare:—Bt. 32, 1.
Cultor, cultur A coulter or culter, dagger; culter, sica:—Elf. gl. 8.
Culufre a dove, v. culfre.
Cum come, v. cuman.
Cuma, an; m. A comer, guest, stranger; hospes:—Ic wæs cuma, Mt. 25, 35, 43. ¶ Cumena ar-þegn an attendant of guests.—Cumena bur an hospital.—Cumena hus an inn.
Cuman, cwiman, ic cume, he cymð; p. com, hi comon; pp. cumen. [Plat. kamen: Dut. komen: Ger. kommen: Moes. cwiman] To come, happen, go; venire:—Cum to þam lande, Gen. 12, 1: Ps. 39, 10: Deut. 4, 9.
Cumb a liquid measure: hence, perhaps, our dry measure, a comb or coom, a valley, v. comb.
Cumbel, cumbl, cumbol, cumbul [Franc. cumbal: Icel. cumbl] A military standard, a banner, signal; signum militare:—Cd. 181: Fr. Jud. p. 26, 18. ¶ Cumbol-gehnades conflict of banners, Chr. 938, Ing. p. 144, 14.—Cumbol-wiga a commander.
Cumbraland [a land of valleys, v. comb] Cumberland.
Cumen come; cumende coming, v. cuman.
Cumerland Cumberland, v. Cumbraland.
Cumin the herb cummin, v. cymen.
Cum-liðe kind to comers or strangers.
Cumliðian [cuma a guest; liðian to nourish] To lodge, to receive as a guest; hospitari:—R. Ben. interl. 1.
Cumliðnes, se; f. Hospitableness, hospitality; hospitalitas:—Pref. R. Conc., Som.
Cummase a kind of unlucky bird.
Cum-pæder A godfather; compater, Som.
-cund [Dut. Kil. kond, konne, kunne known, a kind: Ger. kund: Icel. kyn] An adjective termination, denoting a kind, sort or origin, likeness; as, eorðcund earthly; godcund having its origin from God, divine; heofoncund heavenkind, heavenly, etc.
Cuneglæsse The herb hound's or dog's tongue; cynoglossa:—L. Md. 1, 44.
Cunela Rue, herb grace; ruta:—C. R. Lk. 11, 42.

X wudsculfre a
waad....

X Crucethus crucet
house, a box used
for punishment;
Cruceterum, id est,
cista, quae erat brevis
et angusta et depressa
Crucethus, þæt is in
an ceste þæt was
scort ⁊ naru ⁊
undep Chr 1137
Ing p. 366, 21

X culter culter, culter, es, m
a coulter etc

...be, f a crib Som
...crib

Cristen, es; m Th. An
cristena an m a
christian.

O 2 Two articles

X Crymbing-dl; cf

O 4 [48 a 7]

Cucon, cucen,
cucun, cucu
alive etc

...roc a pot Th. An

Crocc-hring ... cucon

Abreccan anne
roccan to break
a pot Ps Th 2, 9

se crocc-wyrhta
the potter Ps Th 2, 9

Cu-cealf a cow calf
vitula Som.

Cumble a wound
... Som

Cumena, of guests
g. pl of cuma

Cumen-hus, an inn
R. 58 v cuma

cumbel cumbul
2 Cumbol, es, n
a banner Th. An

Cumbor, es; n a
sign Beo K 2037 ...
cumbol

Cumbra-land

4 Cumer-land
es; m [Dun cumbre
land: Hunt. Hovd.
Brom Cumberland
Cund a land cumbe
of valley 1.] Cumber
land Chr 945 Ing
p. 147, 25: 1000 Ing
173, 17

...meaning ...
Som

4 [43 a 5]

...ow balationes Cot 2, 3 ... Lye

...uc, e; f? a crock
...tch; Th. An

4 Culfre, an f. a
dove Th. An

O1 Cud dón to make Brown Som

O1 Sweord his cwake gladium suum vibrabit Ps. 7, 13 Tram

2 Cwatbricg, e; f etc L. 4 + Æt Cwatbrcge be Sæfern. &c

3 Cwealm-beale m mortal bale; noxia mortalis Beo K 3876

4 Cwealm-dreor es; m slaughter gore Cd 47 Th 60, 22.

5 Cwealm-prea deadly penalty, fatalis ultio Cd. 116 Th p 151, 12

2 Cunned crafty; callidus Ben v cunnian

O3

O3 Se rica cunnode georne the chief proved earnestly Cd. 137, Th p 172, 19

4 Cwaccan; pcwehte hi cwehton pp cweht to quake, shake, vibrate brandish; vibrare; se deofol cwecede his sword Ps Th 7, 12

Cwecesond Aurispus Cot 21 Ben Lye

4 Cunt hearc earth smoke or fumatory; fugnaria Som

5 Curon chose v. cure from closan Cd 155 Th 193, 9

7 Cwelca colocynthus hundes cwelca Cot 34 Lye. Cwelcan Ben

Cwelmes wyrhta m a man's slayer; homicida Som

4 Cursan To torment punish; plectere Som Ben

2 Cwalu, e; f death Cd 184 Th 229, 30

cwemung

O7

3 Cuslippe Som

2 familiar, domestic certain, evident Th. Apol

Cwelmyd mortificatus Wrt voc 19 Lye

4 Cwemnes complacitior Ben Lye

Cwene an; f a common woman a harlot meretrix Lup 1, 11 Hic. Th 102, 26

8 Cwen, e; f a queen, woman, put before nouns to se

O4

Cunelle *chervil;* cerefolium, *Som.*

CUNNAN, ic can, þu cunne *or* canst; he can, we ge hi cunnon; *p.* ic cuðe, þu cuðest, we ge hi cuðon, gecuðon; *pp.* cuð, gecuð [*Plat. Dut. Ger.* kennen: *Moes.* kunnan] 1. *To* KEN, *know, know how;* scire. 2. *To know how to do, have power, to be able;* posse:—1. Cunne ge Laban? Hig cwædon, þæt hig hine cuðon, *Gen.* 29, 5. Hwanon cuðest þu me, *Jn.* 1, 48: *Bt.* 7, 1. Þæt ne sy cuð and open, *Lk.* 8, 17: 16, 15. Het is cuð *it is known, clear, evident, Greg.* 2, 22. 2. He ne can ongitan *he cannot understand, Bt.* 39, 2, *Card.* p. 328, 9. He eow axað hwæt ge don cunnon, *Gen.* 46, 33. ¶ Cuð doen, gecuðne gedon *to make known.*

Cunnere *A tempter;* tentator:—*C. Mt.* 4, 3.

CUNNIAN, acunnian, gecunnian; *p.* ode; *pp.* ed, od; *v. a. To enquire,* CON, *search into, to prove, try;* probare:—Mot ic nu cunnian *may I now enquire?* Cunna swa þu wille *enquire as thou wilt, Bt.* 5, 3: *Ps.* 138, 1: *Bd.* 3, 2. Ge cunnian hwylc heora swiftost hors hæfde *to try which of them had the swiftest horse, Bd.* 5, 6.

Cunning, e; *f. Experience,* CUNNING; experientia, *Som.*

Cuople *A coble, small ship;* navicula:—*C. Mt.* 8, 13.

Cupp, cuppa A CUP; poculum:—*Æthelf. Test.*

Cure, curon *chose; p. of* ceosan.

Curmealle, curmelle *Centaury;* centauria:—Curmealle seo mære *the greater centaury, Herb.* 3. Curmelle seo læsse *the less centaury, Herb.* 36.

[C]urs A CURSE; maledictio:—On ænigne man curse asettan, *Offic. Episc.* 3.

[C]ursiam *incense,* v. cursumbor.

[C]ursian *To* CURSE; maledicere:—*Ps.* 36, 23: *Chr.* 1137.

[C]ursumbor *frankincense, incense,* v. recels.

[C]ursung, e; *f.* A CURSING, *curse, torment, hell;* maledictio:—*Ps.* 108, 16.

[Cu]sc; *adj.* [*Dut.* kuisch: *Ger.* keusch: *Al.* chusca, kusgi] CHASTE, *modest, pure, clean;* castus, purus:—

[Cu]sceote [*Lancashire,* cowshot] *A ringdove;* palumbus, *Som.*

[Cu]slippa, cusloppe A COWSLIP; [v]erbascum:—*R.* 42.

[Cwid]er *Resin;* mastix, resina:—[*R*]. 48.

[Cuð] *known, certain; pp. of* cunnan.

[CUÐ]A, an, *One known, an acquaintance, a familiar friend, a relation;* notus, cognatus:—*Ps.* 54, 14: *Lk.* 1, 58: 2, 44. Ne clypa þine cuðan, *Lk.* 14, 12.

Cuðe, cuðon *knew, was able; p. of* cunnan.

Cuðelic, cuðlic; *adj. Known, certain;* notus, *Som.*

Cuðelice *certainly,* v. cuðlice.

Cuðemen *relations,* v. cuða.

Cuðian; *p.* ude. *To know, regard;* innotescere:—*Ps.* 143, 4.

Cuðlætan *To enter into friendship, make peace;* societatem facere, *Som.*

Cuðlice, cuðelice; *comp.* or; *adv. Certainly, truly, indeed;* certo:—*Bd.* 2, 12: 3, 22.

Cuðnes, se; *f. Knowledge, acquaintance;* scientia:—*Scint.* 38.

Cuðnoma *A sirname;* cognomen, *Som.*

Cuðomen *relations,* v. cuða.

Cuðon *knew; p. of* cunnan.

Cuðra, cuðre *more sure; comp. of* cuð.

Cuðudyst *regardedst,* v. cuðian.

Cuwon *chewed,* v. ceowan.

CWACIAN; *part.* ende [*Plat.* quakkeln] *To* QUAKE, *tremble;* tremere:—*Ps.* 17, 9: *Ors.* 2, 5.

Cwacung, e; *f.* A QUAKING, *trembling;* tremor:—*Ps.* 2, 11.

Cwæde, cwæden *said,* v. cwæðan.

Cwæle *a violent death,* v. cwale.

Cwælm *death,* v. cwealm.

Cwæman *to please,* v. cweman.

Cwæn *a queen,* v. cwen.

Cwærtern *a prison,* v. cwertern.

Cwæstednys *a trembling,* v. cwacung.

Cwæðan, cweðan, acwæðan, ic cweðe, þu cwyst, he cwyð; *p.* ic cwæð, cwæðe *or* cwæde, þu cwæde, he cwæð, we cwædon; *sub.* cweðe; *imp.* cweð þu, cweðað *or* cweðe ge; *pp.* gecweden [*Moes.* cwithan.—cwyðe *a speech,* v. cwede] 1. *To say, speak;* dicere. 2. *To provoke,* or *excite by speaking;* provocare:—1. Abraham him cwæð to, ic cwæðe on minum geþance, *Gen.* 20, 11: 31, 1. Se witega gecwæð, *Mt.* 24, 15: *Gen.* 21, 2: *Mt.* 3, 3. 2. Brutus gecwæð anwig *Brutus provoked a duel, Ors.* 2, 3.

Cwale, cwalu [*Dut.* kwaal *f*: *Plat. Ger.* quaal *f.*] *A quelling with weapons, a violent death, slaughter, death;* cædes:—*Bd.* 2, 12.

Cwanian [*Plat. Dut.* kwynen: *Moes.* cwainon] *To languish, to be weary, faint, mourn;* languere, lugere:—*Cd.* 220.

Cwanta-wic *Canterbury,* v. Cantwara.

Cwartern *a prison,* v. cweartern.

CWATAN; *p.* cwehte, hi cwehton; *pp.* cweht. *To shake, move, brandish;* quatere, movere:—*Mt.* 27, 39: *Mk.* 15, 29.

Cwatbricg [*Fabio. Æthelw.* Cantbricge: *M. West.* Quantebridge: *Flor. Wig.* Quatbrig] CAMBRIDGE:—Cwatbricge be Sæfern, *Cambridge, on the Severn, Gloucestershire, Som.*

Cwead *Dung, filth;* stercus:—*Ps.* 112, 6.

Cwealm *to kill,* v. cwellan.

CWEALM, es; *m.* [*Plat.* qualm *m*: *Dut.* kwalm *m.*] *Death, destruction, pestilence, contagion, slaughter;* nex:—*Lk.* 21, 11: *Ex.* 5, 3.

Cwealm-bære *death bearing, deadly.*

Cwealmbærnes, cwelmbærnys, se; *f. Destruction, ruin;* exitium:—*Elf. gr.*

Cwealmnys, cwylmnys, se; *f. Torment, pain, anguish;* cruciatus:—*Bd.* 1, 7.

Cwealm-stow *a place of execution.*

Cwearn *a mill,* v. cwyrn.

Cweartern *a prison,* v. cwertern.

Cweccung, e; *f. A disturbance;* commotio:—*Lps.* 43, 16.

Cwede *a saying,* v. cwide.

Cweden *said,* v. cwæðan.

Cwehte *moved,* v. cwatan.

Cwelan *to die,* v. acwelan.

CWELLAN, acwellan, cwealan, cwoellan, acwoellan, acwillan, þu cwelst; *p.* cwealde, cwalde; *pp.* cweald, cwelled, cweld, acwolen, acweald, aquald; *v. a.* [*Plat. Ger.* quälen: *Dut.* kwellen] *To kill, slay,* QUELL; trucidare:—*Ex.* 8, 26: 29, 16: *Bt.* 13, *Card.* p. 60, 1.

Cwellere [*Plat. Ger.* quäler *m*: *Dut.* kweller] *A killer, manslayer,* QUELLER, *tormentor;* carnifex, spiculator:—*Mk.* 6, 27: *Bd.* 1, 7.

Cwelm *destruction,* v. cwealm.

Cwelmbærnys *destruction,* v. cwealmbærnes.

Cwelmende *destroying,* v. cwellan.

Cwelmian *to kill,* v. cwylman.

Cweman, gecweman; *p.* de. *To please, delight, satisfy;* placere:—*Ors.* 1, 12: *Mk.* 15, 15.

Cweming, e; *f. A pleasing;* placentia, *Som.*

Cwemnys, se; *f. A satisfaction; an appeasing, a mitigation;* satisfactio:—*Bd.* 1, 27: *Resp.* 8.

CWEN [*Al.* quena: *Dan.* kone *f*: *Icel.* kona, kuenna: *Moes.* quino *a woman*] *A woman, wife, wife of a king, a* QUEEN; uxor, regina:—Abrahames cwen *Abraham's woman, wife, Cd.* 103: *Ors.* 3, 11. Þes Caseres cwen *a wife of a Cæsar, an empress.* Suð-dæles cwen, *Mt.* 12, 42: *Lk.* 11, 31.

Cwencan *to quench*, v. acwencan.
Cwen-fugol *a female* or *hen bird*.
Cwen-hiord, cwen-hyrd *a keeper of females, one fit to wait upon queens, a eunuch*.
Cwen-land *the country of the Vandals*:—Be norðan Sweon ofer þa westen nu is Cwenland, *Ors*. 1, 1.
Cwen-sæ *the sea of the Vandals*.
Cweoc *quick, alive*, v. cwic.
Cweorn *a mill*, v. cwyrn.
Cweorn-bil *the iron supporting a mill*.
Cweorn-stan *a millstone*, v. cwyrnstan.
Cweornteð *mill-teeth, grinding teeth*.
Cwertern, cweartern, cwiertern, cwærtern *A prison*; carcer:—*Mt*. 5, 25: *Lk*. 3, 20.
Cweðan *to say*, v. cwæðan.
Cweðað *lament*, v. cwiðan.
Cweðe *say*, v. cwæðan.
Cweðe ge *say ye*, v. cwyst.
Cwic, cwuc, cuic, cucu, cucon; *adj*. [*Plat. Frs*. quik, quek: *Dut*. kwik] Quick, *active, not dead, living*; vivus:—Se iunga wæs cwices modes, *Ors*. 2, 1. Cuic wæter *or* cwic wella, *C. Jn*. 4, 10: *Bd*. 1, 14. ¶ Cwicælmessa *a living sacrifice, an oblation*.—Cwic-feoh *living property, cattle*.
Cwicbeam *A wild ash, wicken-tree* or *wich-tree, sedge-bushes, juniper-tree*; juniperus:—*Cot*. 109, *Som*.
Cwiccan; *pp*. od, ud [*Plat*. queken: *Dut*. kweeken: *Icel*. kuikna] *To* quicken, *make alive*; vivificare, *Som*.
Cwice [*Plat*. quek, quik: *Dut*. kweek gras *n*.] *Quick growing grass, couch-grass, quitch-grass*; gramen:—*Herb*. 79.
Cwicfyr *a quick fire, fire of brimstone*.
Cwichelmes-hlæwe [*F*. Cuicelmeslawe: *Hovd*. Cwickelmelow] Cuckamsley Hill, *Berkshire, Chr*. 1006.
Cwicseolfor *quicksilver*.
Cwicsusl, es; *m*. *Burning sulphur*; ignis sulphureus:—¶ Cwicsusles ealdor *the chief of burning brimstone, the devil, Nicod*. 26.
Cwic-treow *the hawthorn-tree*; crespinus, tremulus:—*R*. 47.
Cwicu *alive*, v. cwic.
Cwicwihta *living creatures*.
Cwide, cwyde, cwyðe, es; *m*. *A speech, saying, command, sentence, testament, argument, doctrine*; dictum:—Eower cwide stande, *Jos*. 2, 21. Ealda cwidas *old sayings, proverbs, Bt*. 14, 3. Cwidas don *to make wills, Somn*. 234.
Cwidboc *a book of proverbs*.

Cwiddigan; *p*. hi cwydodon. *To speak*; dicere:—Hearm cwiddigan, *Bt*. 18, 4: *Chr*. 1085.
Cwiddung, cwyddung, e; *f*. *A saying, report, speech*; sermunculus:—*Bt*. 18, 4.
Cwidol *evil tongued*, v. cwydol.
Cwidræden *an agreement*, v. ræden.
Cwiertern *a prison*, v. cwertern.
Cwiferlice; *adv*. *Anxiously*; sollicite:—*C. R. Ben*. 64.
Cwildbær; *adj*. *Plague bearing, pernicious, injurious*; perniciosus:—*Scint*. 53.
Cwildbærlice; *adv*. *Destructively, pestilently*; pestifere:—*Scint*. 8.
Cwilde-flod *the destruction flood, deluge*.
Cwiman *to come*, v. cuman.
Cwinod *wasted*, v. cwanian.
Cwið, cwiða [*Moes*. cwith] *The womb*; matrix:—*R*. 76.
Cwiðan; *p*. we cwiðdun. *To speak* or *moan in grief, mourn, lament*; lamentari, plangere:—Wope cwiðan *with weeping to lament, Cd*. 48: *Mt*. 11, 17: *Ps*. 77, 69.
Cwiðendlic; *adj*. *Proper, peculiar, natural*; genuinus:—*Cot*. 96.
Cwoaðan *to say*, v. cwæðan.
Cwoellan *to kill*, v. cwellan.
Cwom *came*, v. cuman.
Cwuc, cwuca *alive*, v. cwic.
Cwyddung *a saying*, v. cwiddung.
Cwyde *a speech*, v. cwide.
Cwydele *An inflamed swelling*; varix:—*R*. 76.
Cwydeleás; *adj*. *Speechless, intestate*; intestatus:—*L. Pol. Cnut*. 68.
Cwydodon *said, reported*, v. cwiddigan.
Cwydol; *adj*. *Ill tongued*; maledicus:—*Bd*. 1, 23.
Cwydræden *an agreement*, v. gecwidrædden.
Cwylan *to die*, v. acwelan.
Cwyld [cweld *killed, from* cwellan] *Slaughter, destruction, pestilence, plague*; clades, lues:—*Ps*. 1, 1. ¶ Cwyld *or* cwylttid *a dead time*: as we say, *the dead time of night*.
Cwylman, cwelmian, gecwylman; *p*. de, hi cwelmdon; *pp*. ed. [*Plat. Ger*. quälen] *To kill, torment, crucify*; trucidare:—*Ps*. 36, 15: *Bd*. 5, 2. Mid anum slæge gecwylman *to kill with one blow, Coll. Monast*.
Cwylmbære *death bearing, pernicious*.
Cwylmd *killed*, v. cwylman.
Cwylmende, cwylmigende *tormenting, crucifying*, v. cwylman.

Cwylmincg, cwylming, e; *f*. *A cross*; crux:—*Mt*. 10, 38.
Cwylmnys *torment*, v. cwealmnys.
Cwylt-tyd *dead time*, v. cwyld.
Cwyna *a wife*, v. cwen.
Cwyrn, cweorn, [*Plat*. queeren *f*: kweern *f*: *Moes*. cwairn] *A mill, a hand-mill*, quern; mola:—*Mt*. 24, 41: *Num*. 11, 8.
Cwyrn-burne *a mill-stream*.
Cwyrn-stan, cweorn-stan *a millstone*.
Cwysan; *p*. de; *pp*. ed [*Plat*. quesen: *Frs*. queaze] *To crush*, quash, *shake, bruise, squeeze, burst asunder*; quassare, terere:—*Ælf. gr*. 28.
Cwyst þu, cwyst þu la, cwyst tu la *sayest thou? whether it is so?* used in questions, as num in *Latin*:—Cwyst þu eom ic hyt? *Mt*. 26, 22, v. cwæðan.
Cwyð *says*, v. cwæðan.
Cwyðað *lament*; cwyðdende *lamenting*, v. cwiðan.
Cwyðe *a saying*, v. cwide.
Cwyþele *an inflamed swelling*, v. cwydele.
Cy *cows*, v. cú.
Cycen *a chicken*, v. cicen.
Cycene [*Dut*. keuken: *Frs*. koaken] *A kitchen*; culina:—*R*. 107.
Cydde *said, told*; *p. of* cyðan.
Cydung *a chiding*, v. ciding.
Cyf, cyfe [*Ger*. kufe] *A tun, vessel, hogshead, bushel*; dolium:—*Mt*. 5, 15.
Cyfes, ceafes, cefes; *f*. [*Wil*. keuese: *Dut. Kil*. kebs, kefs] *A concubine, handmaid*; pellex, ancilla:—*Elf. gr*. 28: *Gen*. 21, 12.
Cyfesdeboren *base-born*.
Cyfeshád [*Dut. Kil*. kebedom; keuisdom] *Whoredom, adultery*; pellicatus:—*Cot*. 186.
Cygan, cygean, cigan, acigan, gecegan, gecygan; *p*. de; *pp*. ed; *v.a*. 1. *To call, invite, call upon, invoke, intreat*; vocare, invocare. 2. *To call together, assemble*; convocare:—1. *Ps*. 98, 6: 104, 15. Ic gecyge, *Ps*. 114, 2. Gecygde, *Ps*. 73, 19. 2. *Bd*. 4, 23: *Ælf. gr*. 22.
Cyging *a calling*.
Cygling, cyðling, *A relation*; cognatus:—*R. John* 18, 26, v. cuða.
Cyl, cyle; *m*. [*Frs*. kyeld] *Cold, coolness*; frigus:—*Ps*. 147, 6.
Cyldfare *a carrying of children*.
Cyle *A well*; puteus:—*Ors*. 1, 1.
Cylene A kiln, *an oven*; culina:—*Cot*. 45.
Cylenisc; *adj*. *Like a kiln*; fornaceus, *Som*.
Cylew *spotted*.

Cwenas, -a; m pl. the inhabitants of Cwen-land, the vandals; Vandalæ, Ors 1,1.

O7

Cwenlic Queen, like, ~~regal~~ reginalis Bea K 3877

Cwedol. See 1st Marg. opposite

Cwic + l 6 cwic + well

l 8 Cwic-ælmesse

Cwic-æht living property, ~~[illegible]~~ or cattle; vivens capital

Cwic-lifigende living Cd. 65 Th 79,14

Cwichelmes-hlæw, es; m etc

[illegible]c-feoh living cattle; pecus [illegible] im Æ 638.3

[C]wic-suslen sulphurous, fiery Th. apol

~~bwild, e; f destructio~~

Cwid, es; m a saying dictum Gen III 481,36 v. cwide

Cwid, l 1 ~~[illegible]~~ + cwithus uterus, ~~vulva~~, ~~[illegible]~~

Cworpen crapulatus Ben

Cwyc living & alf pol. 10 W. p 37, 24 v cwic

Cwyldbærlice Death bearing, deadly pestifere Ben

8 Icel. quern, quörn, a hand mill

Cyf[illegible], e; f

Cyfes, e; f a concubine

O9

Cyfes-boren (cyfes a concubine, base born Th. an

Cyle, es; m cold, chill; Frandulitan celes ante faciem frigoris. Ps Th 147,6

Cyld cold v cyle

~~cyl~~ cyle

Nympe cyle excell chille Cd. 220 Th 285,10

Cylle, es; m a leather bottle or bag ; uter? Th. An

Cyla guttates Ben

Cymed herbe genus ad tussim valens; Lull 1,15,16

Chamedris Som

Cymlic advantageous, comely; commodus Bev K 76

Cynde natural kind Cd 132 Th p 167, 26

Cyne by nature Cd. 83. Th p 104, 16

~~Cyne-bearn a royal offspring, regia proles~~

~~Cyne-bend a royal band, a crown; diadema~~

~~Cyne-be~~ Cyne-cyn a royal race genus regium Bd. 1,25

Cynedomas the office & dignity of magistrates; fasces, sceptrum Cot 84 Som Lye

Cynehelmode crowned coronatus Som

corp. Jox Bt. p 68,23

Cynende, adj yawning gaping ~~hiulcus Lye~~ hiulcus Cot 401 Lye v cinean

Cyne-róf royal, noble, renowned Th. An

Cyne-prym, mes; m a Kingly Ghost Cd. 209, Th p 260,8

Cyne-wise [illegible] 417, 11

Cyng-bán, cin-bán, chin bone jaw bone Th. An v cin-ban

Cyngestun

Cyninges-tún, es; m Kingston [illegible] Th. An —

Cyning-rice a kingdom

Cyning-gierda a diadem vitta regalis Som

Cynn a race Cd 63, Th p 76, 13 v cyn

Cynestre a mother Som v. cannestre

Cyn-recenne a genealogy pedigree; genealogia Som v. cynryn

Cyppenham, es; m Chippenham

Cyppe-ping merchandise Som v cype-ping

Ic wylle cypan volo vendere Th. An p 116,5

Cyppelac cippus Cot 55 Ben, Lye

Cyppemannarihtthe law of merchandise; lex Rhodia mercatoria Cot 103 Som Lye

Cypsed compedibus Ben

Cyr a time Th An v cer

Cyrce, an; f a church v ~~circe~~ ~~circe~~ v cyrice

Cyre, es, m will choice, ~~[illegible] Th. An~~

Cyre-að, es; m the oath ~~[illegible]~~ by the witnesses, proposed by the plaintiff & chosen by the defendant; electum juramentum, quod quis cum aliquot conjuratoribus a majore numero selectis praestabat. Lye - L. Athel g W p 58, 12

Cyrice

Cyren new wine Cot 62. v awilled

Cyle-wearte, cyle wyrt *Sour sorrel*; oripilatum:—*Cot.* 216.

Cyline, cyline-heorð *a kiln*, v. cylene.

Cyll *A bottle, barrel, flagon*; uter:—*Ors.* 2, 4, v. ciellan.

Cyln *a kiln*, v. cylene, ast.

CYME *A coming, an approach*; adventus:—*Bt.* 39, 13.

Cymen, cymene, cymyn *Cummin*; cuminum:—*Mt.* 23, 23.

Cymð comes, v. cuman.

CYN [*Plat. Moes.* kinn *n*: *Frs. Dut.* kin *f.*] *The* CHIN; mentum:—*Elf. gl.* 2.

CYN; *g.* cynnes [*Dan.* kjön *n*: *Swed.* kynne *n.* kön *n. a kind*: *Icel.* kyn *n*: *Old Ger.* kunne *a kind, generation*] KIN, *kindred, lineage, race, posterity, tribe, nation, people, kind, sort*; cognatio, progenies, genus:—Cyne cynnes *of royal race*, *Bt.* 38, 1: *Ors.* 1, 5. La nædrena cyn, *Mt.* 3, 7: 17, 21: *Mk.* 7, 26. ¶ Fisc-cyn *fish-kind*.

Cyn; *adj.* *Akin, suitable, fit, proper*; congruus:—Þæt is cyn *that is proper*, *Bt.* 33, 1. Swa cynn was *as was suitable* or *fit*, *Bt.* 35, 4.

Cyna *a cleft*, v. cina.

Cynd, cynde *nature, kind*, *Bt.* 35, 4, v. gecynd.

Cyne; *adj.* *Kingly, regal, royal, princely*; regius, regalis:—He wæs cyne cynnes *he was of royal lineage*, *Bt.* 38, 1. Cyne bearn *or* cyne cyn *royal offspring*, *Bd.* 1, 25.

Cynebænd *a royal crown, a diadem*.

Cynebot *a king's compensation* or *recompense*.

Cynebotl *A kingly dwelling, a palace*; palatium:—*Elf. gl.* 27.

Cynedóm, cyningdóm; *m.* *A royal dominion, kingdom, realm*; imperium, regnum:—*Bd.* 1, 3: *Ors.* 4, 5.

Cyneg *a king*, v. cyning.

Cynegeard, cynegyrd *A royal wand, sceptre*; sceptrum:—*R.* 68.

ynegewæd *a king's clothing, a purple robe*.

ynegyld *a king's compensation*, v. cynebot.

ynegyrd *a sceptre*, v. cynegeard.

nehád *A royal state* or *condition, dignity*, KINGHOOD; regia dignitas:—*Pref. Greg.*

nehealm, cynehelm, es; *m.* *A crown, diadem*; diadema:—*Mt.* 27, 29: *Jn.* 19, 2, 5.

nelec, cynelic, cynellic; *adj.* [*Plat. Ger.* königlich: *Dut.* koninklyk] *Regal, royal*; regalis:—Cynelic botl *a royal dwelling*, *Bd.* 1, 5.

Cynelice; *adv.* *Royally*; regie:—*Past.* 16, 5.

Cynelicnys, se; *f.* *Royalty, as shewn in the deportment, a kingly likeness*; regia dignitas:—*Bd.* 3, 14.

Cynellic *kingly*, v. cynelec.

Cynemæresford [*F.* Kimeresford.—Cyne *royal*; mære *famous*; ford *a ford*] *Kempsford, Gloucestershire*, *Chr.* 800.

Cynerice [*Plat. Ger.* königreich *n*: *Dut.* koningryk *n.*—cyne *royal*, rice *a region*] *A royal region* or *possession, a kingdom, realm*; regnum:—*Ors.* 3, 7.

Cynerofe *royal, noble*.

Cynescipe *kingship, royalty*.

Cynesetl, cenesetel *A royal seat, a throne*; imperii sedes, *Ors.* 3, 7: *Ex.* 11, 5.

Cynestol [cyne *royal*, stol *a seat, stool*] *A royal dwelling, chief city, a capital*; urbs regia:—*Bt.* 1: *Ors.* 3, 9.

Cynestræt *a royal street* or *road*.

Cynet KENNET, *Wiltshire*, *Som.*

Cynewise, cynewisa *A republic, commonwealth*; respublica:—*Ors.* 4, 4: *Bd.* 1, 3.

Cynewiððe *A royal wreath, a diadem*; redimiculum:—*Cot.* 185.

Cyngestun *the king's town*, KINGSTON.

CYNING, cyng, cynge, cynig, cyneg, cyninc, cyninge, es; *m.* [*Plat. Ger.* könig *m*: *Dut.* koning *m*: *Dan.* konge *m*: *Swed.* kung, konung *m*: *Icel.* konungr *m*] A KING, *ruler, prince*. Anglo-Saxon kings were elected in the witenagemot on the death of the preceding sovereign, *Turner's Hist.* b. viii. c. 1; rex:—Melchisedech wæs cyning, *Gen.* 14, 18. Se Judea cyning, *Mt.* 2, 1, 2. Eart þu cyning, *Jn.* 18, 37. Þu eart Israhela cyng, *Jn.* 1, 49: *Ors.* 1, 8. ¶ Cyninga bec *histories* or *chronicles of things done from year to year*.—Cyninga seod *the king's purse, exchequer*.—Cyninges botl *or* Cyninges heal *a king's dwelling, a palace*, *Bd.* 2, 14.

Cyning-cynn *royal race*.

Cyningdóm *a kingdom*, v. cynedom.

Cyningrice *kingdom*, v. cynerice.

Cynnas *sorts, nations*, v. cyn.

Cynnreccennis, se; *f.* *A reckoning of relationship, a genealogy*; genealogia:—*Cot.*

Cynnryn, cynryn, cynren, cænryn, es; *pl.* u. [cyn *kin, relationship*; ryne *a course*] *A family course, parentage, generation*; generatio:—La ge nædrena cynnryn, *Mt.* 12, 34: *Gen.* 11, 27: *Bt.* 38, 1. On cynrynes cynrynum, *Ps.* 71, 5.

Cyp *A beam, timber, measure*; trabs:—*R. Ben.* 2: *H. Mt.* 5, 15.

Cypa, an [*Plat.* kipe, küpe *f. a basket*—ceap] 1. *A factor, merchant, trader*; negotiator. 2. *What a merchant has his goods in, a basket*; cophinus:—1. *Gen.* 37, 28. 2. *Lk.* 9, 17, v. ceap.

Cypan; *p.* cypt, þu cyptest, we ge hi cypton, ciptun. *To sell*; vendere:—*Ps.* 43, 14: *Jn.* 2, 16: *Gen.* 47, 20. ¶ Cypende, *Mt.* 25, 9, v. ceapian.

Cypecnihtas *bought servants, slaves*.

Cypeman *a merchant*, v. ceapman.

Cypera *a sort of fish*.

Cyperen; *adj.* *Coppery, belonging to copper*; æreus:—*Ps.* 17, 36. Cyperen hwer *a copper ewer* or *vessel*, *R.* 26.

Cypeþing *a saleable thing, merchandise*.

Cypince, cypingce *A bargaining, setting a price*; negotiatio:—*R.* 81.

Cypinga *A market*; forum:—*Elf. gr.* 13.

Cypman, cyppman *a merchant*, v. ceapman.

Cyppanhamme CHIPPENHAM, *Wilts.*, *Som.*

Cyran *to turn*, v. cerran.

Cyrc *a church*, v. circ.

Cyrce-weard *a churchwarden*, v. cyrc-weard.

Cyrc-halgung *hallowing* or *consecrating a church*.

Cyrc-þingere *a priest*.

Cyrc-weard, cyrc-werd, cyricweard, es. *A churchwarden*; sacri scriniarius:—Cyrcewardes þenung *a churchwarden's duty*, *Greg.* 1, 5.

Cyrde, cyrdon *returned*, v. cerran.

Cyre [*Plat.* küür, kor *f*: *Dut.* keur *f.*] *A turn, choice, will, pleasure*; flexus, arbitrium:—Agenne cyre *own* or *free will*, *S. de Epiph.*, v. cer.

Cyren-ceaster, Cyrn-ceaster CIRENCESTER, *Cicester, Gloucestershire*:—*Ors.* 5, 12: 6, 9.

Cyrf *A cutting off, an instrument to cut with*; abscissio, ferrum abscissionis:—*C. R. Ben.* 40.

Cyrfæt *A gourd*; cucurbita:—Wylde cyrfæt *or* hwit wingeard; *brionia*, *R.* 44.

Cyric *a church*, v. circ.

Cyric-byrig [*Hunt.* Cereburih: *Brom.* Cyrebury] *The Church city*, CHIRBURY, *Salop*:—*Chr.* 915, Ing. 130, 15.

7

Cylle, es; m a leather bottle or bag uter? Th. An

Cylu gestatus Ben

Cymed herbe genus ad Tussim valens; S. Ll. 1,15,16

Chamædris Som

Cymlic advantageous, comely; commodus Beo K 76

Cynde natural, kind Cd 122 Th. p 167, 26

Cyne by nature Cd. 83. Th. p 104, 16

~~Cyne-cwen a royal offspring, regia proles~~

~~Cyne-bend a royal band, a crown; diadema~~

~~Cyne-be~~ Cyne-cyn a royal race genus regium Bd 1,25

Cynedomas the office & dignity of magistrates; fasces, sceptrum Cot 84 Som Lye

Cynehelmode crowned coronatus Som

O corsp Fox Bt. p 68,23

Cynende, adj yawning gaping hiulcus Cot 401 Lye v cinean

O2

Cyne-rof royal, noble, renowned Th. An

Cyne-prym, mes; m a kingly host Cd. 209, Th p 260,8

O2 Cynewide Hom II 417, 11

Cyng-bân, cingban, chin bone jaw bone Th. an v cin-ban

Cyngestun

Cyninges-tun, es; m Kingston Thanes

Cyning-rice a kingdom

Cyning-gierda a diadem tænia regalis Som

Cynn a race Cd 63, Th p 76,13 v cyn

Cynnestre a mother Som v. cænnestre

Cyn-recenne a genealogy pedigree; genealogia Som v. cynryn

Cyppanham, es; m Chippenham

Cyppe-ping merchandise Som v cype-ping

(S) Ic wylle cyppan volo vendere Th. An p 110,5

Cyppeleac cippus Cot 55 Ben, Lye

O 7 Cyppe-man-na-riht the law of merchandise; lex Rhodia mercatoria Cot 103 Som Lye

Cypsed compeditus Ben

Cyr a time Th. An v cer

Cyrce, an; f a church v ~~circe~~ cyrice

Cyre, es, m will choice,

Cyre-að es; m the oath sworn by the witnesses, proposed by the plaintiff & chosen by the defendant; electum juramentum, quod quis cum aliquot conjuratoribus a majore numero selectis præstabat. Lye – L. Athel W p 58,12

Cyrice

Cyren new wine Cot 62. v awilled

Cyle-wearte, cyle wyrt *Sour sorrel;* oripilatum:—*Cot.* 216.

Cyline, cyline-heorð *a kiln,* v. cylene.

Cyll *A bottle, barrel, flagon;* uter:—*Ors.* 2, 4, v. ciellan.

Cyln *a kiln,* v. cylene, ast.

CYME *A coming, an approach;* adventus:—*Bt.* 39, 13.

Cymen, cymene, cymyn *Cummin;* cuminum:—*Mt.* 23, 23.

Cymo comes, v. cuman.

CYN [*Plat. Moes.* kinn *n: Frs. Dut.* kin *f.*] *The* CHIN; mentum:—*Elf. gl.* 2.

CYN; *g.* cynnes [*Dan.* kjön *n: Swed.* kynne *n.* kön *n. a kind: Icel.* kyn *n: Old Ger.* kunne *a kind, generation*] KIN, *kindred, lineage, race, posterity, tribe, nation, people, kind, sort;* cognatio, progenies, genus:—Cyne cynnes *of royal race, Bt.* 38, 1: *Ors.* 1, 5. La næddrena cyn, *Mt.* 3, 7: 17, 21: *Mk.* 7, 26. ¶ Fisc-cyn *fish-kind.*

Cyn; *adj. Akin, suitable, fit, proper;* congruus:—Þæt is cyn *that is proper, Bt.* 33, 1. Swa cynn was *as was suitable* or *fit, Bt.* 35, 4.

Cyna *a cleft,* v. cina.

Cynd, cynde *nature, kind, Bt.* 35, 4, v. gecynd.

Cyne; *adj. Kingly, regal, royal, princely;* regius, regalis:—He wæs cyne cynnes *he was of royal lineage, Bt.* 38, 1. Cyne bearn *or* cyne cyn *royal offspring, Bd.* 1, 25.

Cynebænd *a royal crown, a diadem.*

Cynebot *a king's compensation* or *recompense.*

Cynebotl *A kingly dwelling, a palace;* palatium:—*Elf. gl.* 27.

Cynedóm, cyningdóm; *m. A royal dominion, kingdom, realm;* imperium, regnum:—*Bd.* 1, 3: *Ors.* 4, 5.

Cyneg *a king,* v. cyning.

Cynegeard, cynegyrd *A royal wand, sceptre;* sceptrum:—*R.* 68.

Cynegewæd *a king's clothing, a purple robe.*

Cynegyld *a king's compensation,* v. cynebot.

Cynegyrd *a sceptre,* v. cynegeard.

Cynehád *A royal state* or *condition, dignity,* KINGHOOD; regia dignitas:—*Pref. Greg.*

Cynehealm, cynehelm, es; *m. A crown, diadem;* diadema:—*Mt.* 27, 29: *Jn.* 19, 2, 5.

Cynelec, cynelic, cynellic; *adj.* [*Plat. Ger.* königlich: *Dut.* koninklyk] *Regal, royal;* regalis:—Cynelic botl *a royal dwelling, Bd.* 1, 5.

Cynelice; *adv. Royally;* regie:—*Past.* 16, 5.

Cynelicnys, se; *f. Royalty, as shewn in the deportment, a kingly likeness;* regia dignitas:—*Bd.* 3, 14.

Cynellic *kingly,* v. cynelec.

Cynemæresford [*F.* Kimeresford.—Cyne *royal;* mære *famous;* ford *a ford*] *Kempsford, Gloucestershire, Chr.* 800.

Cynerice [*Plat. Ger.* königreich *n: Dut.* koningryk *n.*—cyne *royal,* rice *a region*] *A royal region* or *possession, a kingdom, realm;* regnum:—*Ors.* 3, 7.

Cynerofe *royal, noble.*

Cynescipe *kingship, royalty.*

Cynesetl, cenesetel *A royal seat, a throne;* imperii sedes, *Ors.* 3, 7: *Ex.* 11, 5.

Cynestol [cyne *royal,* stol *a seat, stool*] *A royal dwelling, chief city, a capital;* urbs regia:—*Bt.* 1: *Ors.* 3, 9.

Cynestræt *a royal street* or *road.*

Cynet KENNET, *Wiltshire, Som.*

Cynewise, cynewisa *A republic, commonwealth;* respublica:—*Ors.* 4, 4: *Bd.* 1, 3.

Cynewiððe *A royal wreath, a diadem;* redimiculum:—*Cot.* 185.

Cyngestun *the king's town,* KINGSTON.

CYNING, cyng, cynge, cynig, cyneg, cyninc, cyningc, es; *m.* [*Plat. Ger.* könig *m: Dut.* koning *m: Dan.* konge *m: Swed.* kung, konung *m: Icel.* konungr *m.*] A KING, *ruler, prince.* Anglo-Saxon kings were elected in the witenagemot on the death of the preceding sovereign, *Turner's Hist.* b. viii. c. 1; rex:—Melchisedech wæs cyning, *Gen.* 14, 18. Se Judea cyning, *Mt.* 2, 1, 2. Eart þu cyning, *Jn.* 18, 37. Þu eart Israhela cyng, *Jn.* 1, 49: *Ors.* 1, 8. ¶ Cyninga bec *histories* or *chronicles of things done from year to year.*—Cyninga seod *the king's purse, exchequer.*—Cyninges botl *or* Cyninges heal *a king's dwelling, a palace, Bd.* 2, 14.

Cyning-cynn *royal race.*

Cyningdóm *a kingdom,* v. cynedom.

Cyningrice *kingdom,* v. cynerice.

Cynnas *sorts, nations,* v. cyn.

Cynnreccennis, se; *f. A reckoning of relationship, a genealogy;* genealogia:—*Cot.*

Cynnryn, cynryn, cynren, cænryn, es; *pl.* u. [cyn *kin, relationship;* ryne *a course*] *A family course, parentage, generation;* generatio:—La genædrena cynnryn, *Mt.* 12, 34: *Gen.* 11, 27: *Bt.* 38, 1. On cynrynes cynrynum, *Ps.* 71, 5.

Cyp *A beam, timber, measure;* trabs:—*R. Ben.* 2: *H. Mt.* 5, 15.

Cypa, an [*Plat.* kipe, küpe *f. a basket*—ceap] I. *A factor, merchant, trader;* negotiator. 2. *What a merchant has his goods in, a basket;* cophinus:—1. *Gen.* 37, 28. 2. *Lk.* 9, 17, v. ceap.

Cypan; *p.* cypt, þu cyptest, we ge hi cypton, ciptun. *To sell;* vendere:—*Ps.* 43, 14: *Jn.* 2, 16: *Gen.* 47, 20. Cypende, *Mt.* 25, 9, v. ceapian.

Cypecnihtas *bought servants, slaves.*

Cypeman *a merchant,* v. ceapman.

Cypera *a sort of fish.*

Cyperen; *adj. Coppery, belonging to copper;* æreus:—*Ps.* 17, 36. Cyperen hwer *a copper ewer* or *vessel, R.* 26.

Cypeþing *a saleable thing, merchandise.*

Cypince, cypingce *A bargaining, setting a price;* negotiatio:—*R.* 81.

Cypinga *A market;* forum:—*Elf. gr.* 13.

Cypman, cyppman *a merchant,* v. ceapman.

Cyppanham CHIPPENHAM, *Wilts., Som.*

Cyran *to turn,* v. cerran.

Cyrc *a church,* v. circ.

Cyrce-weard *a churchwarden,* v. cyrc-weard.

Cyrc-halgung *hallowing* or *consecrating a church.*

Cyrc-þingere *a priest.*

Cyrc-weard, cyrc-werd, cyricweard, es. *A churchwarden;* sacri seriniarius:—Cyrcewardes þenung *a churchwarden's duty, Greg.* 1, 5.

Cyrde, cyrdon *returned,* v. cerran.

Cyre [*Plat.* küür, kor *f: Dut.* keur *f.*] *A turn, choice, will, pleasure;* flexus, arbitrium:—Agenne cyre *own* or *free will, S. de Epiph.,* v. cer.

Cyren - ceaster, Cyrn - ceaster CIRENCESTER, *Cicester, Gloucestershire:*—*Ors.* 5, 12: 6, 9.

Cyrf *A cutting off, an instrument to cut with;* abscissio, ferrum abscissionis:—*C. R. Ben.* 40.

Cyrfæt *A gourd;* cucurbita:—Wylde cyrfæt *or* hwit wingeard; *brionia, R.* 44.

Cyric *a church,* v. circ.

Cyric-byrig [*Hunt.* Cereburih: *Brom.* Cyrebury] *The Church city,* CHIRBURY, *Salop:*—*Chr.* 915, *Ing.* 130, 15.

Cyrice *a church*, v. circ.

Cyric-frið, cyric-grið *church-peace, right of sanctuary.*

Cyric-halgung *church hallowing, dedication.*

Cyriclic, circlic; *adj. Like a church, ecclesiastical;* ecclesiasticus:—*Bd.* 2, 20.

Cyric-rena *church robbery, sacrilege.*

Cyric-sceat *church scot, a payment made to the church.*

Cyric-þen *a minister of the church.*

Cyric-þenung, e; *f. Church-service, the liturgy;* liturgia:—*Can. Edg.* 50.

Cyricweard *a churchwarden*, v. cyrcweard.

Cyricweccan *churchwatches, vigils.*

Cyrin *a churn*, v. cerene.

Cyring-ceaster *Cirencester*, v. cyren-ceaster.

Cyrlisc *rustic, rural*, v. ceorlic.

Cyrliscnys, se; *f.* CHURLISHNESS, *clownishness, rudeness;* rusticitas, *Som.*

CYRM, cirm *A noise, shout, uproar, crashing;* clamor, strepitus:—*Cd.* 109.

Cyrman *To cry out;* clamare:—*Cd.* 166.

Cyrn *a churn*, v. cerene.

Cyrnceaster *Cirencester*, v. Cyren-ceaster.

Cyrnel, cyrnl; *pl.* a, u [*Plat. Ger.* kern *m.*] A KERNEL, *grain, an indurated gland;* nucleus, toles:—*Cot.* 96.

Cyrran *to turn*, v. cerran.

Cyrre *in a time*, v. cer.

Cyrre *turn*, cyrred *turned*, v. cerran.

Cyrs-treow *A cherry-tree;* cerasus:—*R.* 46.

Cyrtel [*Franc.* kyrtel: *Ger.* kittel *m*: *Dan.* kiortel c: *Swed.* kjortel *m*: *Icel.* kióll *m. a cloak*: *Moes.* kintila] *A woman's gown, a vest, mantle,* KIRTLE; tunica:—*C. Mt.* 5, 40. Berenne cyrtel *a bear-skin mantle.*

Cyrtenlice; *adv. Notably, solemnly, cunningly;* subtiliter:—*Scint.* 38.

CYSE, es; *m.* [*Plat.* kese *m*: *Dut.* kaas *f*: *Ger.* käse *m*: *Ir.* cais: *Wel.* caws] A CHEESE; caseus:—Tyn cysas *ten cheeses*, *L. In.* 70, *W.* p. 25, 40.

Cysefæt *a cheese-vat.*

Cyslib *milk curded*, v. ceselib.

Cysp *a fetter*, v. cosp.

Cyspan; *pp.* gecypsed. *To bind; fetter;* compedibus constringere:—*Ps.* 78, 11: *Bt. R.* p. 190, *Card.* p. 403, 17.

Cyssan, ic cysse; *p.* cyste; *pp.* gecyssed; *v. a.* [*Plat. Dut. Ger.* kussen: *Dan.* kysse: *Icel.* kyssa] *To* KISS; osculari:—*Mt.* 26, 48, 49.

CYST, cist, cest [*Plat.* kiste *f*: *Dut.* kist *f.*] A CHEST, *coffer, sheath, casket;* capsa:—*Lk.* 7, 14: *Bd.* 2, 3.

Cyst *chooses*, v. ceosan.

Cyst; *pl.* a [*Frs.* kiste] 1. *Election, choice;* electio. 2. *What is chosen for its excellence, magnificence, fruitfulness, goodness;* bonitas:—1. Nu ic þe cyst abead *now I have offered thee a choice*, *Cd.* 91. 2. On eallum cystum *in all excellencies*, *Bt.* 38, 5. Þa cysta gedoð þa leof-tæle *excellencies make them estimable*, *Id.* 13. Þæs landes cysta *the land's fruitfulness*, *Chr.* 449.

Cystbeam *a chestnut-tree.*

Cystelice; *adv.* [*Plat. Ger.* köstlich: *Dut.* kostelyk] *Munificently;* largiter:—*Elf. gr.* 38.

Cystig; *adj. Munificent, liberal, good;* munificus:—*Elf. gr.* 9: *Past.* 20.

Cystignes, se; *f. Bountifulness, goodness, munificence;* liberalitas:—*Cot.* 119.

Cystleás; *adj. Fruitless, reprobate;* reprobus:—*Cd.* 48.

Cystlic *munificent*: cystlice *munificently.*

Cys-wuce *cleansing week, purification.*

Cyta A KITE; milvus:—*R.* 37.

Cyta *a cottage*, v. cot.

Cytel, cetel [*Plat. Dut.* ketel *m.*] A KETTLE, *a brazen or copper pot, cauldron;* cacabus:—*Elf. gl.* 21.

Cytere *A harp;* cithera:—*Ps.* 56, 11.

CYÐ *A region, place, situation, knowledge;* patria, situs naturalis:—Þæt wæteres agnu cyð is on eorðan, *Bt.* 33, 4, v. cyððe.

Cyðan, gecyðan, ic cyðe, he cyð; *p.* cyðde, cydde, gecydde, gecyðde; *pp.* cyðed, gecyðed; *v. a. To make known, call, declare, relate, tell, announce, show;* annuntiare:—God wolde gecyðan, *Bd.* 1, 33: *Gen.* 20, 23. Johannes cyð, *Jn.* 1, 15: 17, 26. Gecyð me, *Ps.* 101, 24. Cyðað eft me, *Mt.* 2, 8. Heo arfæstnisse cydde, *Jos.* 6, 17.

Cyðer, cyðr *A witness, messenger;* testis:—*Mk.* 14, 63: *Ps.* 26, 18.

Cyðling *a relation*, v. cygling.

Cyðnes, cyðnys, gecyðnes, se; *f. A witness, testimony, testament;* testimonium:—*Mk.* 14, 57: *Lk.* 22, 20.

Cyððe, gecyððe, cyð; *f. Notice, knowledge, kindred, alliance, a country, region;* notitia, cognitio, patria:—*Bd.* 5, 13. On hiora agenre gecyððe *in their own country*, *Bt.* 27, 3. On heora agenre cyððe, *Bd.* 27, 4.

Cywð *chews*, v. ceowan.

Cywung *A chewing;* ruminatio:—*R.* 99.

Cyric-wreóde a diadem crown, garland; diadema sertum, corona Som

Cyrfel i.e. Gitel stigul; paxillus R. 29 Lye

Cyricean v Suzon Th. An

Cyric-bót the repairing of a church; ecclesiæ instauratio Som

Cyric-hád ordo ecclesiasticus L. athel

Cyric-sang a church song, hymn, psalm cantus in ecclesia

Cyric-sangere a church singer cantator

Cyric-sócn church refuge, sanctuary immunitas ecclesiæ

Cyric-tun a church churlish Th. apol

Cyrm, es, m A cry scream

Cyric-wædas church vestments garments Som

Cyrlic the ... Mone A 418 v cedelc

Cyrpsian to crisp v curl Ben v cirpsian

Cyrtelice subtiliter Ben

Cyrtenlæcan venus-tare R. 99 Lye

Cyrtenlic festivus Lye

Cyrnel granum Ben

Cysel-stan calculus silex Ben v cisil-stan

Cyser-æppla caricæ Ben v ciser-æppla

Cysil-stan glarea Ben v cisil-stan

Cyse sticca cheese formaticum ...

caseus Som

Cystel castanea Lye

Cystbeam castanea Lye v cystbeam, cystbeam

Cyric-boc a church book liber ecclesiasticus Ben

Cyric-bryce a breaking into a church ecclesiæ irruptio

Cys adj (Fr. Xis,] Pure, clean purus, mundus

cyswiced tis

Cys-gerunn [gerunnen run together, congealed hence curd, junket] cheese Th. An

[24 a 4]

Cyric-song ecclesiastica cantio Bd 2, 20

Cyst, e, f choice excellence etc

Cyss, es n. a kiss; osculum Bos gl v coss

Cystleán adj. with excellence, excellently; egregie Bos K 1727 v cyst

Cystlice bountifully

Cyst-wæce, ...

Cyte, an, f a spot v cote Th. An cytel cyte a little cottage tuguriolum He gecyrde to sumes hyrdes cytan He turned to a certain shepherd's cottage Som

Cyð, cyðð. Knowledge

Cyric-mangung, -mangung ecclesiæ negotium L. Const. Ethelw. p. 108, 23; L. Lup. W p. 121, 10

Cypere, es, m a martyr, witness Th. An

Cyðung, e, f Consideration; enumeratio Ben v cyþung, ceowung

Cyððe, gecyððe of knowledge v cyð Bos K 1653

cyððe

Dæl, es; m A part

Dæl, es; n: pl. dalu a valley
Dr. B's notes to Oros.
p 11: Ch III § 2. 28 f–29 d
þæs dæles se [dæl] the part of
the valley. Oros. AS. text p 27, 29 a–d:
Ch Bk I Ch III § 2 line 29

se dæd-hwata (g. hwates)

Dæd-hwæt, dæd bold, quick, active, bold, fortis; Cd 191 Th p 238, 12

Dæg-dæd a day deed Cd 169 Th p 212, 18

Dæg-scip, a ship, a ... filtris; Ben Cot 173 Lye

Dæg-feorm; e f Food for a day, unius diei firma Æthel. Test. Lye

Dæg-leohta the ... daylight, the light of day Cd 216 Than 275, 3

Dæg-red es; n early dawn ...

Dæd-berende ... death bearing; pestifer Som

Dæd-beta One repenting, a penitent; poenitens Grein II 452, 1

Dæg-hræfen g hræfnes m a day raven Book 4998

... of ...; virtutes ... Beo 23 ... K 527 Grein II 452, 2: 496, 30

a great deed

Dæd-weorc a deed feat; facinus Cd 170 Thp 214, 27

Dæft convenient, mild, accommodus, mitis Ben

Dæftlice conveniently; commode, opportune Som Ben

Dæges by day, die

Dæg-hwil the space of day; ... Beo ... K 54 Grein II 451, 19

Dæg-leoð a day song ... Grein II ...
... leohta in Cd Th 275, 3.

Dægmete A ... colored stone; agapis Som Cot 15 Lye

Dægmæl ... morning day ... morning

Dæg-rim aurora Grein II 452, 38 Cd 57 K 60, 1;

Dægsan stan, es m Dauston

Dægscade by day or in the day time; interdiu ... S. M. 1, 63. Som

Dæg-sceald, es; m a day shield, a cloud, umbraculum Cd 146 Th p 182, 22

... expenses ... expendu ... K 33: 64 Ex ... Cot ... expensa ... Ben

... dayproud ... Grein II ... Elf. Gl. p 56 ... daily

... Th. Un

Dæg-woma a day shot, a cloud Cd 160 Th 199, 26

Dæl on dwelde gedwylde sank into error Th Cd 2, 82 lapsus est in errorem Lye

Dæl-æx, e; f A large axe for cleaving wood; dolabra Som Ben

Dæges and nihtes die et nocte ... K 1, ...

Dæl-mælum in parts, piece meal Elf ... 38 ... mæl

Dæma [25 a 3]

Dælnimend, dæl nemend es; m, participium a participle Elf ...

Dælnimendlic participial; par... ... Som

Dæl-nimung a partaking Som

Dæn-mearc, e f Denmark ... Dænmarc ... Chr 1070 Ing p 275, 25

Dæn-merce, an f Denmark ... Dænmearcen Chr 1070, Ing p 275, 16 1075 Ing 283, 2

D

D is sometimes changed into ð, as Ic wurde, *or* Ic wurðe:—Ic wearð *I was*, þu wurde *thou wast.*

D and t are often interchanged, as mette *met*, for metde.

Nouns ending in d or t are generally feminine, as gebyrd *birth*; gecynd *nature*; miht *might*; æht *possession*; gymelyst *carelessness.*

A word terminating with ed, d (*Icel.* at, t: *Ger.* et, t) indicates that a person or thing is furnished or provided with that which is expressed by the root, and is usually considered as a participle, although no verb may exist to which it can be assigned; such words have, therefore, generally ge prefixed to them; as gehyrned *horned*; gesceod *shod, Rask's Gr. by Mr. Thorpe*, §. 326.

The proper termination of the perfect participle is ed, but it is often found in ad, od, ud and yd. When the letters *t*, p, c, h, x and s, after another consonant, go before the infinitive an, the vowel before the terminating d is not only rejected, but d is changed into t; as from dyppan *to dip* would be regularly formed dypped *dipped*, contracted into dyppd, dyppt, and dypt *dipped.*

…a [*Dan.* daa *m. a deer*] *A doe*; dama:—*Elf. gl.* 13.

…ag, dag *any thing that is loose, dagling, dangling, Som.*

…D, e; *f.* [*Plat. Dut.* daad *f*: *Frs.* died] A DEED, *an action*; actio, factum:—*Elf. gr.* 11: …*s.* 63, 10. ¶ Dæd weorc *deed-work, a famous work*, …*l.* 170.

…-bana *an evil-doer, perpetrator.*

…betan; *part.* ende. *To make amends, give satisfaction, to be penitent, to repent*; maleficium …pensare, pœnitere:—*Elf.* … 38.

…t *An amends-deed, repentance, penitence*; pœnitentia; …ficii compensatio:—He …ð him dædbote *he teacheth him repentance, L. Can.* … *pœnt.* 3. Doð dædbote, …3, 2, 8, v. behreowsung.

Dædbotnys, se; *f. Penitence*; pœnitentia:—*Scint.* 9.

Dæd-fruma *first actor* or *labourer.*

Dæd-hata *hateful deed.*

Dædlean *a deed-loan* or *reward, a recompence.*

Dædlic; *adj. Deedlike, active*; activus:—Dædlice word *a verb active, Elf. gr.*

Dæd-róf *deed-famed, illustrious, valiant.*

Dæfe *fit, convenient, Som.*

DÆG, dag, dah, dogor, es; *m.* [*Frs.* dei: *Plat. Dut.* dag *m*: *Ger.* tag *m*: *Moes.* dags] 1. A DAY; dies. 2. *The time of a man's life*; tempus vitæ humanæ:—1. God het þæt leoht dæg, *Gen.* 1, 5. Se þridda dæg, *Gen.* 1, 13. 2. On þreora monna dæg *in three men's days* or *lives, Bd. app.* p. 771, 45. ¶ On dæg *in the day, by day.*—To dæg *to-day.*—Dæg ær *the day before.*—On ærran dæg *on a former day.*—Oðre dæg *another day.*

Dæges ege *a daisy.*

Dæghwamlic; *adj. Daily*; quotidianus:—*Lk.* 11, 3, v. dæglic.

Dæghwamlice; *adv. Daily*; quotidie:—*Mt.* 14, 49.

Dægian *to shine*, v. dagian.

Dægla *secret, unknown*, v. degle.

Dæglic; *adj.* [*Plat.* dagelick: *Dut.* dagelyksch] *Daily*; quotidianus:—*Bd.* 4, 25.

Dæg-mæl *A day division, divider, a dial, a clock*; horologium:—*Elf. gl.* 21. Dægmel-sceawere *an inspector*, or *observer of a dial, clock* or *time, a soothsayer, Elf. gl.* p. 56, 70.

Dægred [*Dut.* dageraad *m*: *Frs.* deirend.—dæg *day*, hræd *early*: *Som.* says, read *red*] *Early dawn, morning*; matutinum:—*Lk.* 24, 1: *Ps.* 29, 6. ¶ On dægred *in the dawn*, or *morning, Jn.* 8, 2.

Dægredlic; *adj. Of the morning*; matutinus:—*Lps.* 129, 6.

Dæg-rim, dæirim *a number of days, a course of days, age.*

Dægsan-stan *the stone of Degsa*, DAUSTON, or *Dalston, Cumberland.*

Dægsteorra *the day star.*

Dægþerlic; *adj. Daily, diurnal*; diurnus:—*Ser. Nat. Dom.*

Dægþern *a day's space.*

Dægtima *day time.*

Dægweorc *a day's work.*

Dæi, dæig *a day*, v. dæg.

Dæi-rim *a course of days*, v. dægrim.

DÆL, es; *m.* [*Plat. Dut.* deel *n*: *Ger.* theil *m.*] 1. *A part, portion*, DEAL; pars. 2. *A portion of a sentence, a word*; verbum:—1. Hi heora god on swa manige dælas todælað *they divide their good into so many parts, Bt.* 33, 2: *Lk.* 15, 12. Þæs iglandes mycelne dæl *a great deal of the island, Chr.* 189. 2. *Elf. gr.* 2. ¶ Be dæle *in part, partly.*—Sume dæle *in some part, partly.*—Some dæl *some deal, some part, a little, Gen.* 43, 11.

Dælan, bedælan, gedælan; *p.* de; *pp.* ed; *v. a.* [*Plat. Dut.* deelen: *Ger.* theilen] *To divide, separate, distribute, bestow, deal, dispense*, DOLE, *judge*; dividere, distribuere:—Ic scyle gedælan *I shall separate, Solil.* 8. Bedæled, *Gen.* 27, 45. Gedæled *deprived, made destitute, Solil.* 14.

Dæledlice *by itself, apart*, v. gedæledlice.

Dælend, dælere, es. *A dealer, divider, distributor*; divisor:—*Lk.* 12, 14.

Dæling *A dividing, parting*; partitio, *Som.*

Dæl-leas; *adj. Portionless, deficient*; expers:—*R.* 18, 90.

Dælniman [*Dut.* deelnemen] *To take part, to participate*; participare:—*Elf. gr.* 5.

Dælnimend *A taker of a part, a partaker*; particeps:—*Ps.* 118, 63: *Bd.* 3. 11.

Dælnimendnes, dælnimung, dælnœmeng, e; *f. A participation, portion*; portio:—*Ps.* 121, 3.

Dæma *A judge*; judex:—*Ex.* 21, 23.

Dænas *The Danes*; Dani:—Dæna lag *the law of the Danes, Som.*

Dæn *a valley*, v. den.

Dære *a loss*, v. dar.

Dærenta, Deorwent *the river Darent, Darwent, Derwent*:—

Dærenta-muð, Dertamuða *the mouth of the river Darwent*, DARTMOUTH, *Kent, Chr.* 1049, v. deorwent.

8 Dǽl, es; m A part

Dæl, es; n: pl. dalu a valley
Dr B's note, to Oros
p 11: Ch III § 2. 28 f-29 d
þæs dæles se [dǽl] the part of
the valley. Oros. Ab. text p 27, 29 a-d:
Ch Bk I Ch III § 2 line 29

day time
expenses
a daily
repast

Dæd-hwæt, lœd, quick, active, bold, fortis; Cd 191 Th p 238, 12

Dæg-dæd a day deed Cd 169 Th p 212, 18

Dæg-feorm; e f Food for day, unless dæi formed the Test Lye

Dæg-leohta the daylight, light of day Cd 216 Th an 275, 3

Dæd-berende, leath bearing, mother Som

Dæd-béta, one repenting a penitent; poenitens Grein II 452, 1

Dæg-hræfen g hræfnes m a day raven Book 4998

Dæd-weorc a deed feat; facinus Cd 170 Th p 214, 27

Dægmete A safron coloured stone; agapis Som Cot 15 Lye

Dægred-sang morning song

Dæg-rime aurora Grein

Dægscade by day or in the day time; interdiu C M 1, 63. Som

Dæg-sceald, es; m a day shield, a cloud umbraculum Cd 146 Th p 182, 22

Dæg-woma a day spot, a cloud Cd 160 Th 199, 26

Dǽl or dwilde gedwylde sank into error Th Cd 2, 22 lapsus est in errorem Lye

Dæl-æx, e, f A large axe for cleaving wood, dolabra Som Ben

Dæl-mælum in parts, piece meal Elf gr 38 p. mǽl

Dæm al [25a 3]

Dǽlnimend, dæl-nimend es; m, participium a participle Elf gr

Dǽlnimendlic participial; participialis Som

Dæl-nimung a partaking Som

Dan-mearc, e f Denmark Chr 1070

Dan-merce, an f Denmark Chr 1070, Ing p 275, 1075 Ing 283, 2

D

D is sometimes changed into ð, as Ic wurde, *or* Ic wurðe:—Ic wearð *I was*, þu wurde *thou wast*.

D and t are often interchanged, as mette *met*, for metde.

Nouns ending in d or t are generally feminine, as gebyrd *birth*; gecynd *nature*; miht *might*; æht *possession*; gymelyst *carelessness*.

A word terminating with ed, d (*Icel.* at, t: *Ger.* et, t) indicates that a person or thing is furnished or provided with that which is expressed by the root, and is usually considered as a participle, although no verb may exist to which it can be assigned; such words have, therefore, generally ge prefixed to them; as gehyrned *horned*; gesceod *shod*, *Rask's Gr. by Mr. Thorpe*, §. 326.

The proper termination of the perfect participle is ed, but it is often found in ad, od, ud and yd. When the letters t, p, c, h, x and s, after another consonant, go before the infinitive an, the vowel before the terminating d is not only rejected, but d is changed into t; as from dyppan *to dip* would be regularly formed dypped *dipped*, contracted into dyppd, dyppt, and dypt *dipped*.

Da [*Dan.* daa *m. a deer*] *A doe*; dama:—*Elf. gl.* 13.

Daag, dag *any thing that is loose, dagling, dangling*, *Som.*

Dǽd, e; *f.* [*Plat. Dut.* daad *f*: *Frs.* died] A deed, *an action*; actio, factum:—*Elf. gr.* 11: *Ps.* 63, 10. ¶ Dæd weorc *a deed-work, a famous work*, *Cd.* 170.

Dæd-bana *an evil-doer, perpetrator.*

Dædbetan; *part.* ende. *To make amends, give satisfaction, to be penitent, to repent*; maleficium compensare, pœnitere:—*Elf. T.* p. 38.

Dædbot *An amends-deed, repentance, penitence*; pœnitentia; maleficii compensatio:—He tæceð him dædbote *he teacheth him repentance*, *L. Can. Edg. pœnt.* 3. Doð dædbote, *Mt.* 3, 2, 8, v. behreowsung.

Dædbotnys, se; *f. Penitence*; pœnitentia:—*Scint.* 9.

Dæd-fruma *first actor* or *labourer.*

Dæd-hata *hateful deed.*

Dædlean *a deed-loan* or *reward*, *a recompence.*

Dædlic; *adj. Deedlike, active*; activus:—Dædlice word *a verb active*, *Elf. gr.*

Dæd-róf *deed-famed, illustrious, valiant.*

Dæfe *fit, convenient*, *Som.*

Dæg, dag, dah, dogor, es; *m.* [*Frs.* dei: *Plat. Dut.* dag *m*: *Ger.* tag *m*: *Moes.* dags] 1. A day; dies. 2. *The time of a man's life*; tempus vitæ humanæ:—1. God het þæt leoht dæg, *Gen.* 1, 5. Se þridda dæg, *Gen.* 1, 13. 2. On þreora monna dæg *in three men's days* or *lives*, *Bd. app.* p. 771, 45. ¶ On dæg *in the day, by day.*—To dæg *to-day.*—Dæg ær *the day before.*—On ærran dæg *on a former day.*—Oðre dæg *another day.*

Dæges ege *a daisy.*

Dæghwamlic; *adj. Daily*; quotidianus:—*Lk.* 11, 3, v. dæglic.

Dæghwamlice; *adv. Daily*; quotidie:—*Mt.* 14, 49.

Dægian *to shine*, v. dagian.

Dægla *secret, unknown*, v. degle.

Dæglic; *adj.* [*Plat.* dagelick: *Dut.* dagelyksch] *Daily*; quotidianus:—*Bd.* 4, 25.

Dæg-mæl *A day division, divider, a dial, a clock*; horologium:—*Elf. gl.* 27. Dægmel-sceawere *an inspector*, or *observer of a dial, clock* or *time, a soothsayer*, *Elf. gl.* p. 56, 79.

Dægred [*Dut.* dageraad *m*: *Frs.* deired.—dæg *day*, hræd *early*: *Som.* says, read *red*] *Early dawn, morning*; matutinum:—*Lk.* 24, 1: *Ps.* 29, 6. ¶ On dægred *in the dawn*, or *morning*, *Jn.* 8, 2.

Dægredlic; *adj. Of the morning*; matutinus:—*Lps.* 129, 6.

Dæg-rím, dæirím *a number of days, a course of days, age.*

Dægsan-stan *the stone of Degsa*, Dauston, or *Dalston, Cumberland.*

Dægsteorra *the day star.*

Dægþerlic; *adj. Daily, diurnal*; diurnus:—*Ser. Nat. Dom.*

Dægþern *a day's space.*

Dægtima *day time.*

Dægweorc *a day's work.*

Dæi, dæig *a day*, v. dæg.

Dæi-rim *a course of days*, v. dægrim.

Dǽl, es; *m.* [*Plat. Dut.* deel *n*: *Ger.* theil *m.*] 1. *A part, portion*, deal; pars. 2. *A portion of a sentence, a word, verbum*:—1. Hi heora god on swa manige dælas todælað *they divide their good into so many parts*, *Bt.* 33, 2: *Lk.* 15, 12. Þæs iglandes mycelne dæl *a great deal of the island*, *Chr.* 189. 2. *Elf. gr.* 2. ¶ Be dæle *in part, partly.*—Sume dæle *in some part, partly.*—Sume dæl *some deal, some part, a little*, *Gen.* 43, 11.

Dælan, bedælan, gedælan; *p.* de; *pp.* ed; *v. a.* [*Plat. Dut.* deelen: *Ger.* theilen] *To divide, separate, distribute, bestow, deal, dispense*, dole, *judge*; dividere, distribuere:—Ic scyle gedælan *I shall separate*, *Solil.* 8. Bedæled, *Gen.* 27, 45. Gedæled *deprived, made destitute*, *Solil.* 14.

Dæledlice *by itself, apart*, v. gedæledlice.

Dælend, dælere, es. *A dealer, divider, distributor*; divisor:—*Lk.* 12, 14.

Dæling *A dividing, parting*; partitio, *Som.*

Dæl-leas; *adj. Portionless, deficient*; expers:—*R.* 18, 90.

Dælniman [*Dut.* deelnemen] *To take part, to participate*; participare:—*Elf. gr.* 5.

Dælnimend *A taker of a part, a partaker*; particeps:—*Ps.* 118, 63: *Bd.* 3. 11.

Dælnimendnes, dælnimung, dælnœmeng, e; *f. A participation, portion*; portio:—*Ps.* 121, 3.

Dæma *A judge*; judex:—*Ex.* 21, 23.

Dænas *The Danes*; Dani:—Dæna lag *the law of the Danes*, *Som.*

Dæn *a valley*, v. den.

Dære *a loss*, v. dar.

Dærenta, Deorwent *the river Darent, Darwent, Derwent*:—Dærenta-muð, Dertamuða *the mouth of the river Darwent*, Dartmouth, *Kent*, *Chr.* 1049, v. deorwent.

Dærst, darst, an. *Leaven, dross;* fermentum:—*C. Mt.* 13, 33.

Dæðbana *procurer of death,* v. dædbana.

Dafenlicnys, gedafenlicnes, se; *f. A fit time, opportunity;* opportunitas:—*Ps.* 9, 22.

Dafnað *becomes,* v. gedafnian.

Dag *a day,* v. dæg.

Dagian, dægian [*Plat. Dut.* dagen: *Ger.* tagen] To DAWN, *to become day;* lucescere:—*Bd.* 4, 9.

Dagung, e; *f. A dawning, day-break, dawn;* aurora:—On dagunge þæs dæges *in the dawn of the day, Bd.* 4, 8.

Dah *a day,* v. dæg.

Dah [*Frs.* dai: *Dut.* deeg *f.*] DOUGH; farinaria:—*Elf. gl.* 25, v. bloma.

Dahle *hid,* v. digle.

Dal *a separation,* v. gedal.

Dalamensan *The Dalmatians;* Dalmati:—*Ors.* 1, 1.

Dalc, dolc *A buckle, bracelet, trifle;* spinther, fibula:—*Elf. gr.* 9, 18: *Jos.* 7, 21.

Dalf *dug;* p. *of* delfan.

Dap-fugel *the dip fowl,* or *diver.*

Darað, dareð, daroð, *A dart, weapon;* telum:—Darað hæbbende, *Cod. Ex.* 66, b. 17. Dareða laf *relic of darts, Chr.* 938, *Price's Walt.* p. 97, 16.

Darst *leaven,* v. dærst.

DARU, dære, e; *f.* [*Dut. Kil.* dere, deyre] *Hurt, damage;* damnum:—Hwelc is mare daru *what is a greater hurt, Bt.* 29, 2: *Bd.* 3, 2, *S.* p. 525, 17.

Deacon, diacon *A deacon, levite;* levita:—*Ex.* 4, 14.

Deaconhád, diacontiad *Deaconhood, deaconship;* diaconatus, *Bd.*

Deád, died; *adj.* [*Frs.* dead: *Plat. Dut.* dood] DEAD; mortuus.

Deádbære, deaðbær, deadbærlic, deadberend, deaðberend, *adj. Death-bearing, deadly, mortal, destructive;* mortifer:—*Mk.* 16, 18.

Deádblod *dead blood, congealed blood.*

Deádian *to die,* v. adeadan.

Deádlic; *adj. Deadly, mortal;* mortalis:—*Ors.* 3, 8.

Deádlice *deadly,* v. deaðlic.

Deádlicnys, deaðlicnes, se; *f.* DEADLINESS, *mortality;* mortalitas:—*Bd.* 3, 23.

Deád-rægl *clothing of the dead, a shroud.*

Deád-spring, es; *m. A malignant ulcer, carbuncle;* carbunculus:—*Herb.* 9, 2.

DEAF; *adj.* [*Frs.* deaf: *Plat. Dut.* doof] DEAF; surdus:—*Ps.* 37, 14. Deaf corn *deaf* or *barren corn, Past.* 52, 9.

Deaflice *properly,* v. gedefelice.

Deag, deah *A colour,* DIE; color:—*R. Ben.* 55.

Deagan; *p.* de; *pp.* ed. *To* DIE, *colour;* tingere, *Som.*

Deagle *hidden, obscure,* v. digle.

Deaglenes *solitariness,* v. digelnes.

Deagol *obscure,* v. digle.

Deagollice *obscurely,* v. digelice.

Deagolnes *hiding-place,* v. digelnes.

Deagung, e; *f. A dying, colouring;* tinctura:—*Elf. gr.* 28.

Deáh *be good,* v. dugan.

Deah *a die,* v. deag.

Deahla *hidden,* v. digle.

Deal, dealle; *adj. Deficient, wanting, deprived;* carens:—*Cd.* 89. Fugel feðerum deal *a bird wanting,* or *deficient in feathers, Cod. Ex.* 59, l. 14. Eorlas æscum dealle *men wanting ships, Id.* 106, a. 17.

Dear, þu dearst, durre, we durron; *p.* þu dorstest, he dorste, durste, we ge hi dorston [*Plat.* dörven: *Frs.* dôare: *Dut.* durven: *Kil.* derren: *Ger.* dürfen] *To* DARE, *presume;* audere:—Ne dear ic hám faran, *Gen.* 44, 34: *Cd.* 40. Gif he dear *if he dare, L. In.* 17. Gif ic biddan dear, *Ex.* 32, 30. Hwæðer þu durre gilpan *whether thou dare boast, Bt.* 14, 1: *Bd.* 1, 27, *Resp.* 5, *Nicod.* 12. Hwæðer he winnan dorste *whether he durst fight, Ors.* 4, 11. Þæt hi swa don ne dorsten *that they durst not do so, Bt.* 39, 11.

Dearnenga, dearnunga, deornunga, dernunga; *adv. Secretly, privately;* clam, occulte:—*Deut.* 13, 6.

Dearrlic; *adj. Daring, rash;* temerarius, *Som.*

Dearrscipe *Rashness, presumption;* temeritas, *Som.*

DEAÐ, es; *m.* DEATH; mors:—Se deað cymð, *Bt.* 8, *Card.* p. 38, 19. Deaðes lið *article of death, the point of death.* Deaðas *spirits, ghosts, Cot.* 134.

Deaðbær, deaðberend *deadly,* v. deadbære.

Deaðbernys, se; *f. Death, destruction, pestilence;* pernicies:—*R. Lk.* 21, 11.

Deað-godas *death-gods, spirits, ghosts,* v. deað.

Deaðlic, deadlic; *adj. Deadly, mortal;* mortalis:—*Bd.* 24, 2.

Deaðlicnes *mortality,* v. deadlicnys.

Deaðscufa *Death;* mors:—*Lps.* 6, 5.

Deaðscyld *A death-fault, a capital offence;* capitale crimen:—*L. Cnut. pol.* 40.

Deaðscyldig; *adj. Death-guilty, condemned;* damnatus:—Deaðscyldig man, *L. Cnut. pol.* 41.

Deað-sted, *a death-place, a sepulchre.*

Deað-þenunga *funeral services, funerals.*

Deað-wyrda *death-events, fate.*

DEAW, [*Plat.* dau *m*: *Dut.* dauw *m.*: *Ger.* thau *m.*] DEW; ros:—*Ps.* 132, 3. Deaw drias *dew of the field, Cd.* 188.

Deaw-wyrm [*Frs.* dauw-wyirm] *a ring-worm, tetter.*

Deawian *To* DEW, *bedew;* rorare, *Som.*

Deawig; *adj.* DEWY; roscidus:—*Cd.* 93.

Decan, gedecan *to cover,* v. þeccan.

Ded *dead,* v. dead.

Defenas, Denas *the people of Devonshire, Chr.* 823.

Defenascire, Defanscire, Defnascyre [*Hunt.* Deuenesire, Dauenescyre: *Kil.* Devenschyre] DEVONSHIRE, *Chr.* 851.

Defre; *adj. Timely, seasonable;* tempestivus, *Som.*

Deg *profits;* prodest, v. dugan.—Deg *a day,* v. dæg.—Deg *a colour,* v. deag.

Degelice *secretly,* v. digelice.

Degle, dægl *secret, unknown,* v. digle.

Degollice, degullice *secretly,* v. digelice.

Degolnys, degulnes *solitude,* v. digelnes.

Dehtnung *a disposing,* v. dihtnung.

Deira rice *the kingdom of Deira,* v. deora mægð.

Delan *to divide,* v. dælan.

DELFAN, adelfan, he dylfð; *p.* dealf, dielf dalf, hi dulfon; *sub.* dulf; *pp.* dolfen, gedolfen [*Dut.* delven] *To dig,* DELVE; fodere, effodere:—He dealf deopne, *Lk.* 6, 48. Gif se delfere þa eorðan ne dulfe, *Bt.* 40, 6: *Gen.* 21, 30.

Delfere *A digger;* fossor:—*Bt.* 40, 6.

Delf-isen *A digging-iron, spade;* fossorium:—*Cot.* 90.

DEM, mes. *Hurt, damage, loss, slaughter, disease;* damnum, strages:—*Ors.* 6, 14: *Bt. R.* 5, 3, note n. Be þæs demmes ehte, *Ex.* 22, 5.

DEMA, doema, an; *m. A judge, an umpire;* judex:—Se unrihtwisa dema cwyð, *Lk.* 18, 2, 6.

Déman; *p.* démde, gedémde; *pp.* gedémed; *v. a. To* DEEM,

X
2

1 Dæd death. Th. An v dead

3 Dædberend mortal
v deadbor[illegible]

4 Daga, dagas, dagum
dagas of, to days the pl. of d. ac of dæg

5 Dæg what is spread
Som v daag
Offa
L.M 3, 59

Dage dough v dah

7 Dægian [25a 4]
8 Dah [25a 5]

11 Dalas parts
Dæl [illegible] Cd. 16
Th. p. 20, 8 v dæl

2 Dalo, e; f a den,
caverna. On þas
deopan dalo into this
deep den Cd. 22, Th
p 27, 21

6 Danegeld Danegelt
Danish tribute; tributum
Danicum Som

Dar, e f Destruction
injury Th. An v daru

7 [25a 6]
Darad &c es; m loss
Dead

16 Dead-reagl a hearse
cloth, pall; pallium sepulchrale

~~Dead-pe[illegible]~~
~~[illegible] K 471~~

19 Dead-sweltan to suffer
death, to die; mortem
pati; mortem obire
Som

1 Deafe, deafes Deaf
ness; Surditas Som

deaþwyrmed

2 Deagged troubled
with the gout; poda-
gricus R. 77 Lye

3 Deag-lg Ftrum
Cot 146 & Fuchs 88

4 Deapung, e; f a dipping
immersio Som

Deare loss; damnum Som. Ben
v. daru

14 Dead-dæg, es; m
death day, day of
death Beo K 372 Lye

Dead-den, nes a
death's den Cod.
Ex 122

5 Deare dark
dearc
6 Dearn hidden Rask
v & dyrn

Dead-cwylmnend
mortificatus L.P.S 78
Lye

Dead-drep death swoon
Cd 167 Th 209, 6

8 Dead-bana a man
slayer homicida
Dead-beam es; m
a death tree, tree of
death; Cd 30. Th p.
40, 13 mortis arbor

10 Dead-bed, y-bed
m A death bed, mortis
lectus Beo 215 K 598

Dead-cwealm (cwealm
slaughter) Death,
massacre, slaughter
mors Beo 126, K 3338.
129, K 3422
internecio

Deades (par better) Lye
88

Dead-fæg death colour
ed, discoloured by death
morte discolor Beo K
1693

Deagelican to hide
Bed gl v deglian

Dead-stedes m
a death place Cd 172
Th p 212

Dead-werig death
weary Beo K 4245

2 Dead-wyrd e; f death
Cot 82 Lye

Dead-wic es; m
a death residence
a sepulchre Beo K
2557

Dean, es; m

Ded-bot penitence
Som v dæd-bot

4
3 Defenisc of Devon
shire; Devoniensis Som

5 Dehter daughter Som
v dohtor

6 Deira, wald, Deiraweald
Delfes, es; m & delving
digging Th. An

the wood of Deira; now
Beverley, Deiorum
silva, vel saltus Som

~~Dead-dæg death day~~
~~day of death, mortis~~
~~dies Beo 16 K 372~~

Dead-reaf death garment
or spoil, pillage, booty
exuviae Som

17 Dead-scua shade of
death, death; mortis umbra
Beo 14 K 314
Cd. 77

~~Dead-rwe [illegible]~~
~~walk, [illegible]~~
~~Beo 27 K 2851~~

Dead-betecan morti
tradere Med Confut. 1 Lye

Deme, es; m a judge; judex Bec K 360.

Demere, es; m A judge; judex Som

Den, es, m a valley, plain

Dene, a den v. denu

Denum loss Ors 2, 4 Bar p 67, 11

v. dem

Den-bæra places yielding mast for fatting hogs; valles nemorosæ et glandiferæ porcis pascendis et saginandis idoneæ Som

Dene-mearc, Denmark Chr 1046 Ing p 178, 28 1035 Ing p 207, 18

Deng-in dengum in nobelibus Hoov. 13.

Den-mearc, ...

1119 Ing 360, 30

Of Denemarcan Chr 1070 Ing p 273, 11. To Denmearcan to Denmark Chr 1075 Ing p 280, 30 : 1085 Ing 288, 11 : 1087 Ing p 296, 33

Denn [21 a, 3]

Densc Danish ll. an v Denisc

Deofe perfectus Ben

Deofol-scinna devels dæmonia Som.

with pone dene Gen 13, 18

Deog, e; f Dye; tinctura Bed K 1603

Deogol secret Bec K 549 v dygel

Deople secret, latens Som. Ben v deahla

Deop deep, great, profound magnus, profundus deop leanu a great reward Cd 153, Th 191, 31 : 167, Th 209, 29 : 169, Th 210, 20

Den-seta an m an inhabitant of a valley v sæta

Deorlinges; m a darling

Deorwurde, deorwyrde diorwurde, es, m. n f precious ll. an

Dere damage Som v daru

Derfan to labour Lye v deorfan

Deoradmagð, Dera-mægð by Lrein p 1480 pl

Deoraby-scir, e; f. Derbyshire Mid Deoraby scire with Lindesia Chr. 1065, Ing 253, 13

Deorc-græg dark grey; furvus Som, R 80 Cot

Deor-cyn, es, n a kind of beast Th. An

Deor-fald a park hortus cervorum Som

Deor-hege a hedge against deer, or wild beasts; sepimentum Som

Deor-tun deer-hay

judge, think, examine, consider, doom, condemn; judicare, censere:—Þam ilcan dome þe ge demað, eow bið gedemed, *Mt.* 7, 2: *Bd.* 1, 27, *Resp.* 9. Pilatus gedemde urne Drihten to deaðe, *Ors.* 6, 3, *Bar.* p. 212, 6. Dugeðum demað *by virtues judge, Cd.* 82.

Demman [*Dut.* dammen: *Ger.* dämmen] *To* DAM, *stop water;* obturare flumen, *Som.*

Demmes *of loss,* v. dem.

Denamearc DENMARK; Dania, Dacia:—*Ors.* 1, 1.

Dencgan *To knock, ding;* tundere, *Som.*

a Dene *a valley,* v. denu.

Dene; *g.* dena; *d.* denum; *pl. The* DANES; Dani:—*L. Alf. and Guth.*

Denisc; *adj.* DANISH; Danus:—*L. Alf. Guth., Chr.* 787.

Denisces burn DENISESBURN, *the river Denis:—Bd.* 1, 3, *Sm.* p. 720, 28.

Densæta *a mansion in a valley, Lye.*

DENU, e; *pl.* dena; *g.* denena; *d.* denum; *f. A plain, vale, dale, valley,* DEN; vallis:—Wið þone dene Mamre, *Gen.* 13, 18. Ælc denu byð gefylled, *Lk.* 3, 5. It is often used as the termination of the names of places situate in a *plain* or *valley,* as *Tenterden, &c.*

Deofl *the devil,* v. deofol.

Deoflegyld *idolatry,* v. deofolgeld.

Deoflic; *adj. Devilish;* diabolicus:—*Nicod.* 29.

DEOFOL, deoful, dioful; contracted to deofl, es; *d.* e; *pl.* deofla, u; *m.* [*Plat.* düvel *m*: *Dut.* duivel *m*: *Ger.* teufel *m.*] *The* DEVIL; diabolus:—Þæt he þone deofol adrife, *Mk.* 7, 26: *Mt.* 9, 33, 34: 13, 19: *Ps.* 108, 5.

Deofol-cræft *Devil-craft, the black art, witchcraft;* dæmoniaca:—*Bd.* 1, 25.

Deofol-dæd *a devil-deed, wickedness.*

Deofolgeld, deofolgelt, deofolgyld, deoflegyld, deofulgyld, gedeofulgeld [deofol, gild *tribute, worship*] *Idolatry, sacrifice to devils, an idol, an image of the devil;* idolatria, idolum:—*Bd.* 1, 7: *Cot.* 118.

Deofolseoc *devil sick, a demoniac;* dæmoniacus:—*Mt.* 9, 32.

Deofolseocnys, se; *f. Devil sickness, possessed with the devil;* dæmonium:—*Mt.* 8, 28.

Deofolwitga *A devil-prophet, soothsayer, wizard;* vates diabolicus:—*Cd.* 178.

Deoful *the devil,* v. deofol.

Deofulcund; *adj. Devil kind,* or *likeness, diabolical;* diabolicus:—*Fr. Jdth.* 10.

Deofulgyld *idolatry,* v. deofolgeld.

Deop *the deep, the sea,* v. dypa.

DEÓP, diop; *adj.* [*Plat.* deep: *Frs.* dyip: *Dut.* diep: *Ger.* tief] DEEP; profundus:—Þes pytt is deop, *Jn.* 4, 11. Deop wæter *deep water.* Diop sæs, *Ps.* 64, 7.

o Deóplic; *adj. Deep;* profundus:—*L. Can. Edg.* 10.

Deóplice, dioplice; *comp.* or *Deeply, profoundly;* profunde:—Deoplice þu sprycst *thou speakest profoundly, Coll. Mon. Sol.* 1: *Bt.* 5, 3.

Deópnys, diopnys, se; *f.* [*Plat. Dut.* diepte *f.*] DEEPNESS, *profoundness, an abyss, mystery;* profunditas, abyssus:—*Ps.* 41, 9. On hellican deopnysse *in the hellish abyss, Nicod.* 24.

Deópþancol *deep-thinking, contemplative, Lye.*

DEÓR, es; *n.* [*Plat.* deert *n*: *Dut.* dier *n*: *Ger.* thier *n*: *Will.* diur] *An animal, all sorts of wild animals, a wild beast,* DEER: feræ:—Ofer þa deor, *Gen.* 1, 26: 1, 24, 25. ¶ To þam deorcynne *to the wild beast kind, Bt.* 38, 1.—Rede deor *red deer.*—Deor-fald, deor-frið, deor-tun *a deer-field, a park, an enclosure for deer.*—Deor-net *a beast-net, hunting-net, R.* 84.—Deor-fellen roc *a deer-skin garment.*

Deor, dior *dear, beloved, precious, high in price,* v. dyre.

Deoraby, Deorby [*Hunt.* Dereby; *E.* Derebi.—deor *a deer, beast;* by *an habitation*] DERBY, *Chr.* 918.

Deora mægð, Dera mægð, Deora rice, Deira ric *the province* or *kingdom of Deira, being part of Northumbria, situate between the Tyne and Humber, Bd.* 3, 1, v. Beornica.

Deorboren; *comp.* ra; *sup.* est; *adj. High born, noble;* illustri familia natus:—*L. In.* 33.

Deorc, deorcfull; *adj.* DARK; tenebrosus:—*Lk.* 11, 34. Deorcfull wæg *a dark way, Scint.* 59.

Deorcung, e; *f. Twilight,* crepusculum:—*Elf. gl.* p. 75.

Deoreð-sceaft *a dart shaft, a spear,* v. darað.

DEORFAN, gedeorfan, hi dyrfð; *p.* hi durfon, gedurfon; *pp.* gedyrfed [*Plat. Dut.* derven: *Ger.* derben] *To labour, perish, to be in difficulty, danger;* laborare, perire:—Þearle ic deorfe *I labour too much, Coll. Mon.* Gedurfon heora scipa *their ships perished, Ors.* 4, 6.

Deór-frið *a deer-park,* v. deor.

Deorham [deor *a wild beast,* ham *home, dwelling*] DURHAM, *Gloucestershire, Chr.* 577. *Dereham, Norfolk, Id.* 799.

Deorhyrst DEERHURST, *Gloucestershire, Chr.* 1053.

Deoriende *hurting,* v. derian.

Deorling, deorlinge, derling, diorling, dyrling, es; *f.* A DEARLING, *darling, minion, favourite;* unice dilectus:—*Bt.* 27, 2.

p Deormod *dear mind, beloved;* according to *Lye, sad.*

Deornunga *secretly,* v. dearnenga.

Deorwent *the river Derwent, Bd.* 2, 9, *S.* p. 511, 18: 4, 29, p. 607, 11, v. Dærenta.

Deorwurð, deorwyrð, diorwurð; *adj.* [deor *dear,* weorð *worth*] *Precious, dear, of great worth, value;* pretiosus:—An deorwyrðe meregrot, *Mt.* 13, 46: *Bt.* 10.

Deorwyrðnes, se; *f. Preciousness, precious things, a treasure;* res pretiosa:—*Bt.* 7, 4.

Deoul *the devil,* v. deofol.

Dépan *to dip, baptize,* v. dyppan.

Deprobane *Taprobane, an island in the Indian ocean:—Ors.* 1, 1, *Bar.* p. 15, 13.

Dera mægð *the province of Deira, Bd.* 2, 14, v. Deora.

Deregað *injure,* v. derian.

DERIAN, ic derige, hi deregað, derað; *part.* iende, igende; *p.* gederede; *pp.* gedered [*Dut.* deren: *Frs.* deerje: *Lancashire,* to deere] *To injure, hurt, harm, annoy;* nocere:—Þæt þu me ne derige, *Gen.* 21, 23: *Bt.* 7, 3.

Deriendlic, derigendlic; *adj. Injurious, noxious, hurtful;* nocivus:—*Fulg.* 20.

Derling *a darling,* v. deorling.

Dern-geligr, dern-gelegerscip *a secret lier, adultery.*

Dernunga *secretly,* v. dearnenga.

Derodin *Scarlet dye;* coccus:—*Past.* 45, 4, 6.

Derung, e; *f.* [*Dut.* deering] *An injuring, harming;* læsio, *Som.*

Deð *does,* v. don.

Diabul *the devil,* v. deofol.

Diacon *a deacon,* v. deacon.

Diacontiad *deaconship,* v. deaconhad.

Dic [*Plat.* diek *m*: *Dut.* dyk *m. a mound: Ger.* deich *m.*] A DIKE, *mound, bank; Som.* says *a ditch, trench, moat;* agger, fossa:—*Bd.* 1, 5: *Chr.* 1016, *Ing.* p. 197, 15.

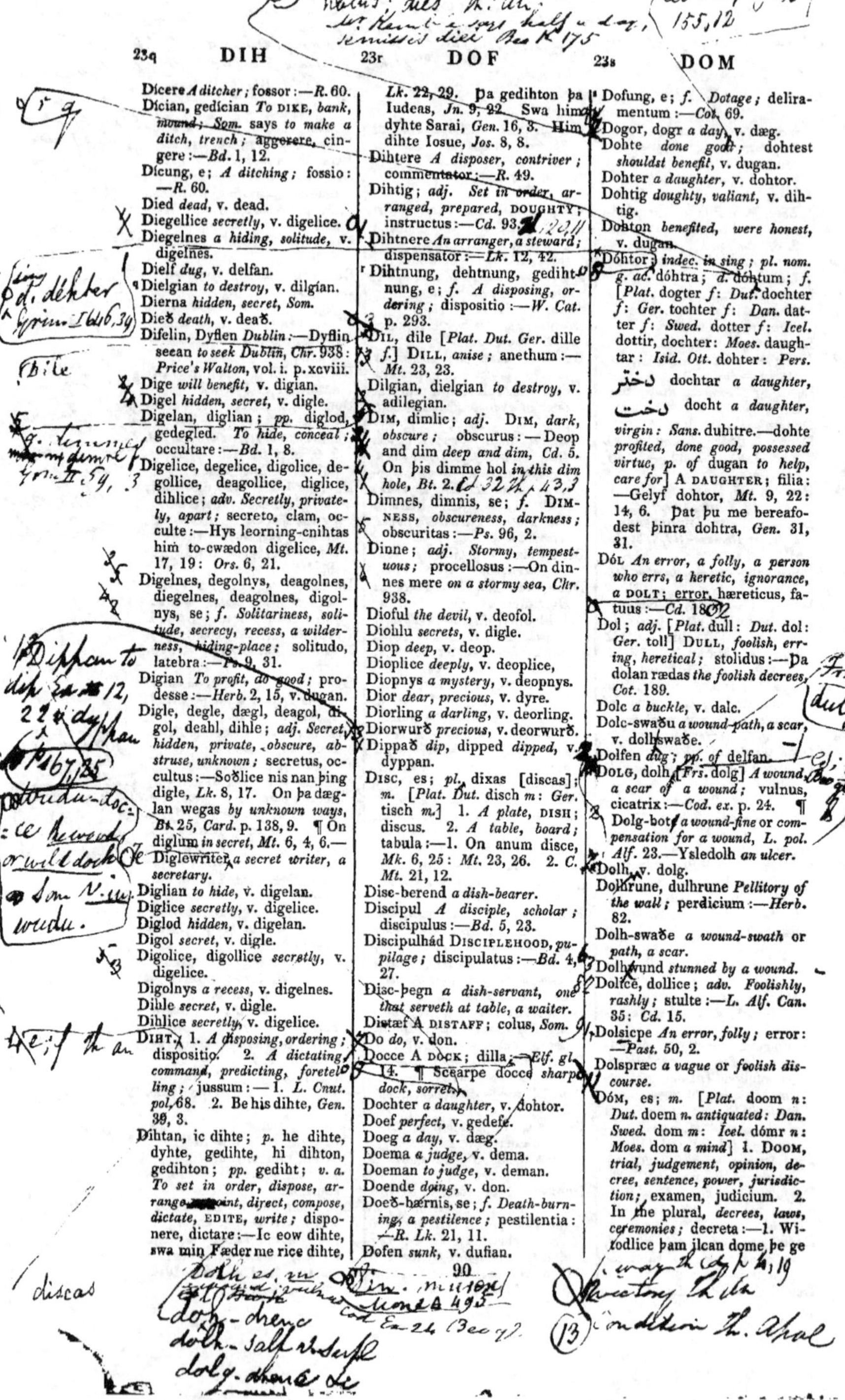

Dicere *A ditcher;* fossor:—*R.* 60.

Dician, gedician *To* DIKE, *bank, mound; Som.* says *to make a ditch, trench;* aggerere, cingere:—*Bd.* 1, 12.

Dicung, e; *A ditching;* fossio:—*R.* 60.

Died *dead,* v. dead.

Diegellice *secretly,* v. digelice.

Diegelnes *a hiding, solitude,* v. digelnes.

Dielf *dug,* v. delfan.

Dielgian *to destroy,* v. dilgian.

Dierna *hidden, secret, Som.*

Dieð *death,* v. deað.

Difelin, Dyflen *Dublin:*—Dyflin seean *to seek Dublin, Chr.* 938: *Price's Walton,* vol. i. p. xcviii.

Dige *will benefit,* v. digian.

Digel *hidden, secret,* v. digle.

Digelan, diglian; *pp.* diglod, gedegled. *To hide, conceal;* occultare:—*Bd.* 1, 8.

Digelice, degelice, digolice, degollice, deagollice, diglice, dihlice; *adv. Secretly, privately, apart;* secreto, clam, occulte:—Hys leorning-cnihtas him to-cwædon digelice, *Mt.* 17, 19: *Ors.* 6, 21.

Digelnes, degolnys, deagolnes, diegelnes, deagolnes, digolnys, se; *f. Solitariness, solitude, secrecy, recess, a wilderness, hiding-place;* solitudo, latebra:—*Ps.* 9, 31.

Digian *To profit, do good;* prodesse:—*Herb.* 2, 15, v. dugan.

Digle, degle, dægl, deagol, digol, deahl, dihle; *adj. Secret, hidden, private, obscure, abstruse, unknown;* secretus, occultus:—Soðlice nis nan þing digle, *Lk.* 8, 17. On þa dæglan wegas *by unknown ways, Bt.* 25, *Card.* p. 138, 9. ¶ On diglum *in secret, Mt.* 6, 4, 6.—Diglewriter *a secret writer, a secretary.*

Diglian *to hide,* v. digelan.

Diglice *secretly,* v. digelice.

Diglod *hidden,* v. digelan.

Digol *secret,* v. digle.

Digolice, digollice *secretly,* v. digelice.

Digolnys *a recess,* v. digelnes.

Dihle *secret,* v. digle.

Dihlice *secretly,* v. digelice.

DIHT. 1. *A disposing, ordering;* dispositio. 2. *A dictating, command, predicting, foretelling;* jussum:—1. *L. Cnut. pol.* 68. 2. Be his dihte, *Gen.* 39, 3.

Dihtan, ic dihte; *p.* he dihte, dyhte, gedihte, hi dihton, gedihton; *pp.* gediht; *v. a. To set in order, dispose, arrange, appoint, direct, compose, dictate,* EDITE, *write;* disponere, dictare:—Ic eow dihte, swa min Fæder me rice dihte, *Lk.* 22, 29. Þa gedihton þa Iudeas, *Jn.* 9, 22. Swa him dyhte Sarai, *Gen.* 16, 3. Him dihte Iosue, *Jos.* 8, 8.

Dihtere *A disposer, contriver; commentator:*—*R.* 49.

Dihtig; *adj. Set in order, arranged, prepared,* DOUGHTY; instructus:—*Cd.* 93.

Dihtnere *An arranger, a steward;* dispensator:—*Lk.* 12, 42.

Dihtnung, dehtnung, gedihtnung, e; *f. A disposing, ordering;* dispositio:—*W. Cat.* p. 293.

DIL, dile [*Plat. Dut. Ger.* dille *f.*] DILL, *anise;* anethum:—*Mt.* 23, 23.

Dilgian, dielgian *to destroy,* v. adilegian.

DIM, dimlic; *adj.* DIM, *dark, obscure;* obscurus:—Deop and dim *deep and dim, Cd.* 5. On þis dimme hol *in this dim hole, Bt.* 2.

Dimnes, dimnis, se; *f.* DIMNESS, *obscureness, darkness;* obscuritas:—*Ps.* 96, 2.

Dinne; *adj. Stormy, tempestuous;* procellosus:—On dinnes mere *on a stormy sea, Chr.* 938.

Dioful *the devil,* v. deofol.

Diohlu *secrets,* v. digle.

Diop *deep,* v. deop.

Dioplice *deeply,* v. deoplice,

Diopnys *a mystery,* v. deopnys.

Dior *dear, precious,* v. dyre.

Diorling *a darling,* v. deorling.

Diorwurð *precious,* v. deorwurð.

Dippað *dip,* dipped *dipped,* v. dyppan.

DISC, es; *pl.* dixas [discas]; *m.* [*Plat. Dut.* disch *m*: *Ger.* tisch *m.*] 1. *A plate,* DISH; discus. 2. *A table, board;* tabula:—1. On anum disce, *Mk.* 6, 25: *Mt.* 23, 26. 2. *C. Mt.* 21, 12.

Disc-berend *a dish-bearer.*

Discipul *A disciple, scholar;* discipulus:—*Bd.* 5, 23.

Discipulhád DISCIPLEHOOD, *pupilage;* discipulatus:—*Bd.* 4, 27.

Disc-þegn *a dish-servant, one that serveth at table, a waiter.*

Distæf A DISTAFF; colus, *Som.*

Do *do,* v. don.

Docce A DOCK; dilla:—*Ælf. gl.* 14. ¶ Scearpe docce *sharp dock, sorrel.*

Dochter *a daughter,* v. dohtor.

Doef *perfect,* v. gedefe.

Doeg *a day,* v. dæg.

Doema *a judge,* v. dema.

Doeman *to judge,* v. deman.

Doende *doing,* v. don.

Doeð-bærnis, se; *f. Death-burning, a pestilence;* pestilentia:—*R. Lk.* 21, 11.

Dofen *sunk,* v. dufian.

Dofung, e; *f. Dotage;* deliramentum:—*Cot.* 69.

Dogor, dogr *a day,* v. dæg.

Dohte *done good;* dohtest *shouldst benefit,* v. dugan.

Dohter *a daughter,* v. dohtor.

Dohtig *doughty, valiant,* v. dihtig.

Dohton *benefited, were honest,* v. dugan.

Dóhtor; *indec. in sing; pl. nom. g. ac.* dóhtra; *d.* dóhtum; *f.* [*Plat.* dogter *f*: *Dut.* dochter *f*: *Ger.* tochter *f*: *Dan.* datter *f*: *Swed.* dotter *f*: *Icel.* dottir, dochter: *Moes.* daughtar: *Isid. Ott.* dohter: *Pers.* دختر dochtar *a daughter,* دخت docht *a daughter, virgin: Sans.* duhitre.—dohte *profited, done good, possessed virtue, p. of* dugan *to help, care for*] A DAUGHTER; filia:—Gelyf dohtor, *Mt.* 9, 22: 14, 6. Þat þu me bereafodest þinra dohtra, *Gen.* 31, 31.

DÓL *An error, a folly, a person who errs, a heretic, ignorance, a* DOLT; error, hæreticus, fatuus:—*Cd.* 180.

Dol; *adj.* [*Plat.* dull: *Dut.* dol: *Ger.* toll] DULL, *foolish, erring, heretical;* stolidus:—Þa dolan rædas *the foolish decrees, Cot.* 189.

Dolc *a buckle,* v. dalc.

Dolc-swaðu *a wound-path, a scar,* v. dolhswaðe.

Dolfen *dug; pp. of* delfan.

DOLG, dolh [*Frs.* dolg] *A wound, a scar of a wound;* vulnus, cicatrix:—*Cod. ex.* p. 24. ¶ Dolg-bote *a wound-fine* or *compensation for a wound, L. pol. Alf.* 23.—Ysledolh *an ulcer.*

Dolh, v. dolg.

Dolhrune, dulhrune *Pellitory of the wall;* perdicium:—*Herb.* 82.

Dolh-swaðe *a wound-swath* or *path, a scar.*

Dolhwund *stunned by a wound.*

Dolice, dollice; *adv. Foolishly, rashly;* stulte:—*L. Alf. Can.* 35: *Cd.* 15.

Dolsicpe *An error, folly;* error:—*Past.* 50, 2.

Dolspræc *a vague* or *foolish discourse.*

DÓM, es; *m.* [*Plat.* doom *n*: *Dut.* doem *n. antiquated: Dan. Swed.* dom *m*: *Icel.* dómr *n*: *Moes.* dom *a mind*] 1. DOOM, *trial, judgement, opinion, decree, sentence, power, jurisdiction;* examen, judicium. 2. In the plural, *decrees, laws, ceremonies;* decreta:—1. Witodlice þam ilcan dome þe ge

Dirling a darling Son v deorling

Dirn-licgend, es; m a secret lier, an adulterer Som v dyrn ...

Dirodin scarlet dye Lye v derodin

Dirstelice boldly Som v dyrstelice

Dirstig bold Som v dyrstig

Disgung, e; f

Dotage, vtadness; deliratio Som

Disig foolish Som v dysie

Dieude lactantes R Mt 21.16 Lye

... es; m Th. Apol

Dile

Dile salve sealf; dile salve; medicamentum ex aneto confectum Cot 208 Lye

Diegel, digle, a degle f A secret Th. An

Dim-gende dim, ... obscure Som v dim

Diegellice secretly v diegelice

Dim-hof a dark house, a cave Som Elf gr 13. Som

Diegel-writere es; m a secret writer, a secretary Som. Ben

Dimme ado Dimly

Ding ding, fimus; als. fallow land Som

Dol-gilp, es; m foolish boasting, vain glory Beo K 1012

Dingiung, e; f A dunging; stercoratio Ben Lye

Dolg dolh, es; m

Dolg-bot

Dolg-drenc a wound drink ... tisanes for wounds

Dolh-wund wounded ... a wound ... ed

Ding dung Ben Lye v dung

Dolle foolish ... tus Beo K 5288

Dinor a penny, denarius Som

Dolg-sealf a wound salve ... emplastrum

Digneras folles Cot 93

Dollice foolishly Cd 15 Th 19.22

Diobul the devil Som v deofol

Dolscape

Dol-scapa, an m a mischievous man Beo K 952

Dinung, e; f A dinning, tingling; tinnitus Ea... rena dinung tingling of ears Lye

Dolgende decrepit ... ely old; decrepitus Som Ben

Diogol secret Lye v digle

Diolu secrets Som v diohle

Dolsmeltas Heap. pan ... Lanid R. 4 Lye

Diogollice secretly Lye v digelice

Diop ... ouste ...

Dior dear ... Som

Diwian to hurt Som v derian.

O 4

O 2

Don A little fallow deer damula ~~dom~~ Cot 68 Lye

Donleca practicus Cot 149 Lye

Dream-healdend es, pleasure keeper, ~~gaudii servator~~ Beo K 2455

Dom questio R Jn 3, 25 Lye

v dóm

Doonde laturi Cot 197 Lye

O 3

Drecan t. drehte (dreahte) ... pp. drecht vex ... Th cu

O 7

Dóm-cadig blessed with power Cd 63 Th 75, 29 — ~~Dóm-leas power less~~

O 3 Cd 218 Th p 279, 3

O 2

Dorlæcan a sort of locusts; attaci Som

Drefliende & Saft-iende Rheumaticas ~~Cot~~ R 77 Lye

~~Dóm-weorþian a place~~

Dot does v dón

Dómian, to dómige, ... give judgement, to exalt glorify; ~~....~~ gloriam tribuere extollere ~~Bo~~

Dracan eardigað dragons dwell Cd 215 Th 270, 30

Dracan gipsum Cot 97 Lye

Dracan blod Dragons blood; sanguis draconis cinnabaris Cot 210 Lye

Dregende drying Som Ben v. drigan

Anmanias pec domige Hannemiah thee glorify Cd 192 Th p 241. 4.

Dómlice adv. powerfully effectually bountifully; cum potestate, ad arbitrium Jdth p 26, 10

Drehte vexed p of dreccan v. &c.

Drenc es m. drink, drench Beo gl v drinc

Pec domige thee exalt 192 Th p 239, 17

Drefan, drefe p af ~~....~~ ~~.... Som, Ben~~ v. of... ... v. of... ... Lye

O 5

O 6

Dreog modesty Ben v gedreog

Dóm-leas powerless dishonourable Beo K 5775 Cd 218 Th p 279, 3

O 7

Dræfde ~~vect~~ vectus Drægende vehens Ben

O 9

... dolg-drenc ...

demað, eow bið gedemed, *Mt.* 7, 2. Æfter eowrum agnum dome *according to your own judgement*, *Bt.* 14, 2. Domes dæg, *Mt.* 10, 15. Syn hi Bisceopes dome scyldig *they are liable to the Bishop's sentence*, i. e. *excommunication*, *Bd.* 4, 5. 2. Þis syndon þa domas *these are the laws*, *L. Ethelb. tit.* *Bd.* 4, 18.

-dóm [in *Dut. Dan.* -dom: *Ger.* -thum: *Icel.* -dómr] as the termination of nouns is always masculine, and denotes *power, authority, property, right, office, quality, state, condition*; as cyngdom *a king's power, office, &c. a kingdom*; freodom *freedom*; haligdom *holiness*; wisdom *wisdom*; i. e. *the state or condition of being free, holy, wise.*

† Dóm-bóc DOOM-BOOK, *a book of decrees* or *laws*; liber judicialis:—*L. Ethelst.* 5.

Dóm-dæg *judgement-day*:—*L. Can. eccl.* 25.—*for* domes dæg *day of judgement*, v. dom.

Dómere *A judge*; judex:—*Past.* 18, 2.

Dóm-ern, e; n. *A judgement-place, a court-house, town hall*; prætorium:—*Mt.* 27, 27.

Dóm-fæst *fast* or *just judgement, just judging*.

Dóm-fæstnes *integrity of judgement*.

Dóm-hus *A house of justice, a town hall*; prætorium:—*R.* 55.

Dómige; *adj.* *Bringing judgement, just, powerful*; justus, potens:—Metod domige *O just Creator!* Creator justus, *Cd.* 182.

Dómlic; *adj.* *Judicial*; judicialis:—*Elf. gr.* 28.

Dómne *A lord*; dominus:—*Bd.* 2, 3.

Dóm-setl *A judgement-seat, a tribunal*:—*Mt.* 26, 19.

Dóm-settend *One sitting in judgement, a judge, a lawyer*; jurisconsultus:—*Cot.* 113.

DÓN, gedón; ic dó, þu dést, he déð, we dóð; *imp.* dó þu; *p.* ic dyde, þu dydest, he dide, dyde, gedyde, we dydon; *pp.* gedón; *v. a.* [*Plat.* doon: *Dut.* doen: *Ger.* thun] *To* DO, *make, cause*; agere, facere:—Ealle þa þing, þe ge wyllen þat men eow don, doð ge him þat sylfe, *Mt.* 7, 12. Hwi dest þu wið me swa, *Gen.* 12, 18. Gedoð eow selfe wyrsan *you make yourself worse*, *Bt.* 14, 2. Ne miht ænne locc gedon, *Mt.* 5, 36. Þæt gefeoht wæs gedon *the battle was done*, *Ors.* 3, 9. He to blote gedyde *he made a sacrifice*, *Ors.* 1, 8.

¶ Don fram *or* of *to take from, depart*, *Ps.* 17, 23.—Lif don *to live*, *Bd.* 4, 23.—Don to witanne *to do to wit, to make to know* or *understand*.

Donafeld *Tanfield, near Rippon, Yorkshire*; Campodunum:—*Bd.* 2, 14.

Donua *The river Danube*; Danubius, *Som.*

Dooc *The south wind*; notus, *Som.*

Dop-ened [ened *a duck*] *A dipping-duck, a moorhen, fenduck*; fulica:—*R.* 36.

Dopettan, doppettan *to sink*, v. dyppan.

Dop-fugel [*Dut.* doopvogel *m.*] *A dipping-fowl, a water-fowl, a moorhen*; mergus, *Som.*

Dora *a door*, v. duru.

Dora *A drone, locust, a mule*; fucus, burdo:—*R.* 22, *Som.*

Dorce-ceaster, Doreceaster, Dorces-ceaster DORCHESTER, *Oxfordshire, situate on the river Frome, just before its entrance into the Isis*:—*Chr.* 639.

Dorm-ceaster, [by the Britons called Cair-Dorm, by *Antoninus* Durobrivæ, from the passage over the water; and the Anglo-Saxons, for the same reason, called it Dornford] *Dornford* or *Dorgford, in Huntingdonshire, on the river Nen*, *Som.*

Dorsætas; *pl.* *The inhabitants of Dorsetshire*:—*Chr.* 837.

Dorste, dorsten *durst*, v. dear.

Dorwit-ceaster *Canterbury*; Dorobernia:—*Chr.* 604.

Drabbe [*Frs.* drabbe] *Dregs, lees,* DRAB; fæces, *Som.*

Draca, *A dragon*; draco:—*Ps.* 103, 28.

Dracentse, dracontian *Dragonwort*; dracontium:—*Herb.* 15.

DRÆD DREAD, *fear*; timor:—*Mt.* 25, 25.

Dræf *A driving out, an expulsion*; expulsio:—*L. In.* 68, v. draf.

Dræge A DRAG; tragula:—Dræge-net *a* DRAG-NET, *R.* 1.

Dræn *a drone*, v. dran.

Dræne *a drink*, v. drinc.

Draf A DROVE, *herd*; armenta:—*Chr.* 1016.

Dráf *drove*; *p. of* drifan.

Dragan, he drægð; *p.* drog, dróh, drógon; *pp.* dragen. *To* DRAG, *draw*; trahere:—*Chr.* 1127. Drogon me *drew me*, *Past.* 66, 2.

Dran, dræn A DRONE; fucus:—*Chr.* 1127.

Dranc *drunk*; *p. of* drincan.

Dreah *did*; *p. of* dreogan.

DREAM, dryr, es; *m.* 1. *Joy, gladness, mirth, rejoicing*; gaudium, jubilum. 2. *What causes mirth, instruments of music, music, harmony, melody, song*; organa, melodia:—1. Fele dreamas *many joys*, *Cd.* 144: 187: *Ps.* 46, 5. 2. On sealum we ahengon dreamas ure, *Ps.* 136, 2: *Bt.* 16, 3. ¶ Woda dream *mad rejoicing, madness*, *Ors.* 3, 6.

Dream-cræft *the art of music, music*.

Dreamere *A musician*; musicus:—Gedeð se dream cræft þat se mon bið dreamere, *Bt.* 16, 3.

Dreamleás; *adj.* *Joyless, sad*; mæstus:—*Cd.* 202.

Dreamlic; *adj.* *Harmonious, joyous*; harmonicus:—*Ps.* 103, 35.

Dreamnes, se; *f.* *A singing*; cantio:—*Ps.* 136, 3.

Dream-swinsung *mirth harmony, harmony*, v. swinsung.

Drearung, e; *f.* *A distilling*; distillatio:—*Cd.* 191.

Dreas *soothsayers*, v. dry.

DRECAN, drecean, dreccean; *p.* drohte, we drohton, drehton; *pp.* drecced, gedrecte, gedreht. *To trouble, vex, grieve, oppress*; turbare, vexare:—Hwi drecst þu, *Mk.* 5, 35: *Ps.* 93, 5. Uneaðe gedreht *greatly afflicted*, *Ors.* 3, 3: *Mt.* 15, 22.

Dreccing, e; *f.* *Tribulation*; vexatio, *Som.*

DREFAN, gedrefan; *p.* de; *pp.* gedrefed. *To* DRIVE, *vex, disturb, trouble, offend*; expellere, conturbare:—*Ps.* 3, 1. Forhwon drefst me, *Ps.* 41, 6. Drefde, *Chr.* 964: *Ps.* 59, 13. Swa hwa swa gedrefð *whosoever shall offend*, *Mk.* 9, 42.

Drefing, e; *f.* *A disturbing*; conturbatio:—*R.* 5.

Drege *dry*, v. drig.

Drehnigean *To drain*; percolare:—*Mt.* 23, 24.

Dreman, dryman; *p.* de. *To rejoice, to play on an instrument*; jubilare:—Dremað Gode Iacobes, *Ps.* 80, 1. Drymað Gode, *Ps.* 46, 1.

Drenc *a drink*, v. drinc.

Drencan, drencean; *p.* þu drenctest, hi drencton, gedræncte; *pp.* gedrenced; *v. a.* [*Dut.* drenken: *Ger.* tränken] *To give to drink*, DRENCH; aquare, potum *vel* potionem dare:—*Ps.* 59, 3: 35, 9.

Drenc-cuppe, drenc-fæt *a drinking-vat, a cup*.

Drenc-horn *a drinking-horn*.

Drenc-hus *a drinking-house*.

Drén-flod, drence-flod *a drenching-flood, the deluge*.

Dreng, *A soldier, a man*; miles:—*Glast.* p. 570.

Drenge *a drink*, v. drinc.

Dreogan, ic dreoge, þu drygast, drigast, he dryhð; *p.* dreah, hi drugon; *pp.* drogen [*Plat.*

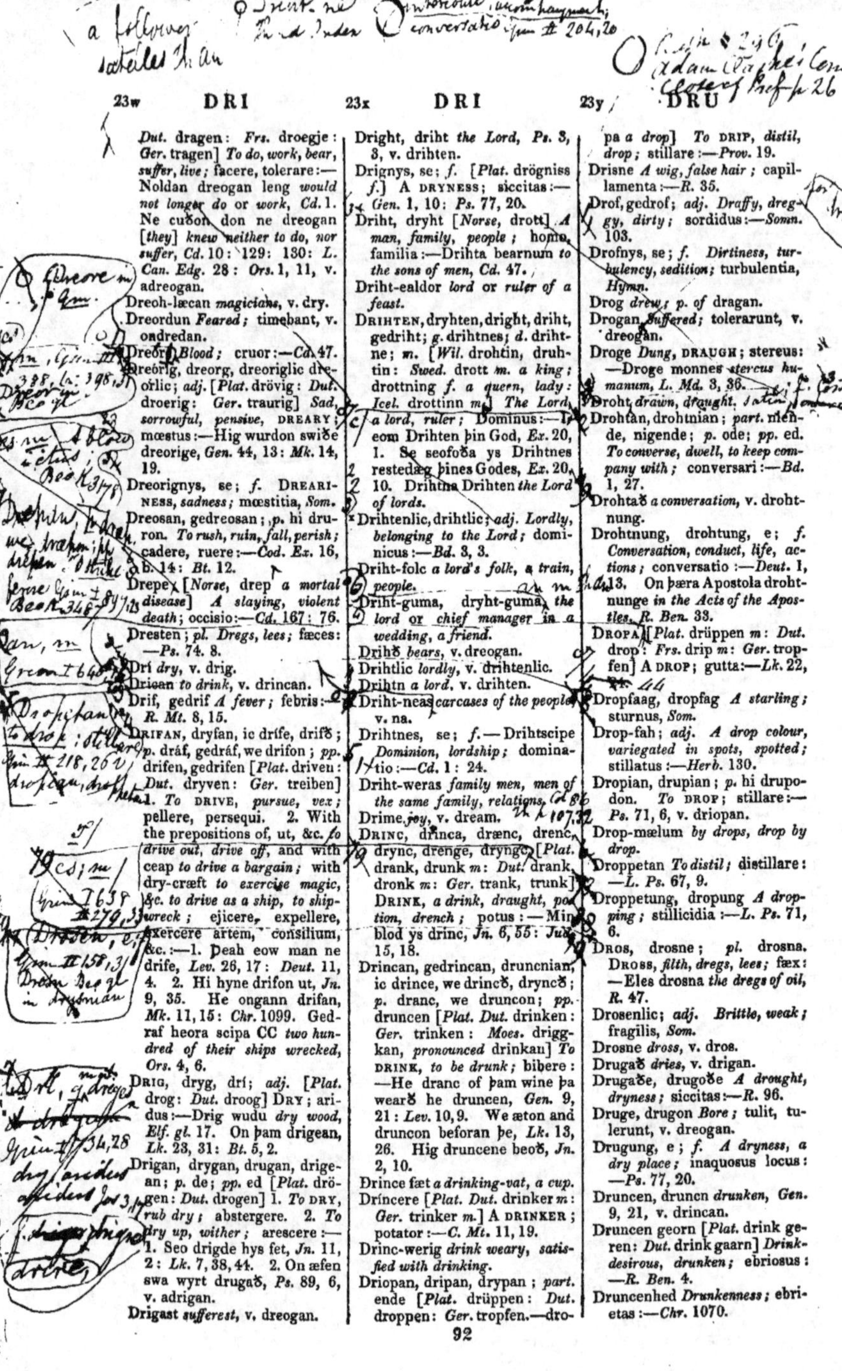

Dut. dragen: *Frs.* droegje: *Ger.* tragen] *To do, work, bear, suffer, live;* facere, tolerare:—Noldan dreogan leng *would not longer do or work, Cd.* 1. Ne cuðon don ne dreogan [*they*] *knew neither to do, nor suffer, Cd.* 10: 129: 130: *L. Can. Edg.* 28: *Ors.* 1, 11, v. adreogan.

Dreoh-læcan *magicians,* v. dry.

Dreordun *Feared;* timebant, v. ondredan.

Dreor *Blood;* cruor:—*Cd.* 47.

Dreorig, dreorg, dreoriglic dreorlic; *adj.* [*Plat.* drövig: *Dut.* droerig: *Ger.* traurig] *Sad, sorrowful, pensive,* DREARY; mœstus:—Hig wurdon swiðe dreorige, *Gen.* 44, 13: *Mk.* 14, 19.

Dreorignys, se; *f.* DREARINESS, *sadness;* mœstitia, *Som.*

Dreosan, gedreosan; *p.* hi druron. *To rush, ruin, fall, perish;* cadere, ruere:—*Cod. Ex.* 16, b. 14: *Bt.* 12.

Drepe [*Norse,* drep *a mortal disease*] *A slaying, violent death;* occisio:—*Cd.* 167: 76.

Dresten; *pl. Dregs, lees;* fæces:—*Ps.* 74. 8.

Dri *dry,* v. drig.

Drican *to drink,* v. drincan.

Drif, gedrif *A fever;* febris:—*R. Mt.* 8, 15.

DRIFAN, dryfan, ic drife, drifð; *p.* dráf, gedráf, we drifon; *pp.* drifen, gedrifen [*Plat.* driven: *Dut.* dryven: *Ger.* treiben] 1. *To* DRIVE, *pursue, vex;* pellere, persequi. 2. With the prepositions of, ut, &c. *to drive out, drive off,* and with ceap *to drive a bargain;* with dry-cræft *to exercise magic,* &c. *to drive as a ship, to shipwreck;* ejicere, expellere, exercere artem, consilium, &c.:—1. Þeah eow man ne drife, *Lev.* 26, 17: *Deut.* 11, 4. 2. Hi hyne drifon ut, *Jn.* 9, 35. He ongann drifan, *Mk.* 11, 15: *Chr.* 1099. Gedraf heora scipa CC *two hundred of their ships wrecked, Ors.* 4, 6.

DRIG, dryg, drí; *adj.* [*Plat.* drog: *Dut.* droog] DRY; aridus:—Drig wudu *dry wood, Elf. gl.* 17. On þam drigean, *Lk.* 23, 31: *Bt.* 5, 2.

Drigan, drygan, drugan, drigean; *p.* de; *pp.* ed [*Plat.* drögen: *Dut.* drogen] 1. *To* DRY, *rub dry;* abstergere. 2. *To dry up, wither;* arescere:—1. Seo drigde hys fet, *Jn.* 11, 2: *Lk.* 7, 38, 44. 2. On æfen swa wyrt drugað, *Ps.* 89, 6, v. adrigan.

Drigast *sufferest,* v. dreogan.

Dright, driht *the Lord, Ps.* 3, 3, v. drihten.

Drignys, se; *f.* [*Plat.* drögniss *f.*] A DRYNESS; siccitas:—*Gen.* 1, 10: *Ps.* 77, 20.

Driht, dryht [*Norse,* drott] *A man, family, people;* homo, familia:—Drihta bearnum *to the sons of men, Cd.* 47.

Driht-ealdor *lord* or *ruler of a feast.*

DRIHTEN, dryhten, dright, driht, gedriht; *g.* drihtnes; *d.* drihtne; *m.* [*Wil.* drohtin, druhtin: *Swed.* drott *m. a king;* drottning *f. a queen, lady: Icel.* drottinn *m.*] *The Lord, a lord, ruler;* Dominus:—Ic eom Drihten þin God, *Ex.* 20, 1. Se seofoða ys Drihtnes restedæg þines Godes, *Ex.* 20, 10. Drihtna Drihten *the Lord of lords.*

Drihtenlic, drihtlic; *adj. Lordly, belonging to the Lord;* dominicus:—*Bd.* 3, 3.

Driht-folc *a lord's folk, a train, people.*

Driht-guma, dryht-guma, *the lord* or *chief manager in a wedding, a friend.*

Drihð *bears,* v. dreogan.

Drihtlic *lordly,* v. drihtenlic.

Drihtn *a lord,* v. drihten.

Driht-neas *carcases of the people,* v. na.

Drihtnes, se; *f.*—Drihtscipe *Dominion, lordship;* dominatio:—*Cd.* 1: 24.

Driht-weras *family men, men of the same family, relations.*

Drime, *joy,* v. dream.

DRINC, drinca, dræne, drenc, drync, drenge, drynge, [*Plat.* drank, drunk *m*: *Dut.* drank, dronk *m*: *Ger.* trank, trunk] DRINK, *a drink, draught, potion, drench;* potus:—Min blod ys drinc, *Jn.* 6, 55: *Jud.* 15, 18.

Drincan, gedrincan, druncnian, ic drince, we drincð, dryncð; *p.* dranc, we druncon; *pp.* druncen [*Plat. Dut.* drinken: *Ger.* trinken: *Moes.* driggkan, *pronounced* drinkan] *To* DRINK, *to be drunk;* bibere:—He dranc of þam wine þa wearð he druncen, *Gen.* 9, 21: *Lev.* 10, 9. We æton and druncon beforan þe, *Lk.* 13, 26. Hig druncene beoð, *Jn.* 2, 10.

Drince fæt *a drinking-vat, a cup.*

Dríncere [*Plat. Dut.* drinker *m*: *Ger.* trinker *m.*] A DRINKER; potator:—*C. Mt.* 11, 19.

Drinc-werig *drink weary, satisfied with drinking.*

Driopan, dripan, drypan; *part.* ende [*Plat.* drüppen: *Dut.* droppen: *Ger.* tropfen.—dropa *a drop*] *To* DRIP, *distil, drop;* stillare:—*Prov.* 19.

Drisne *A wig, false hair;* capillamenta:—*R.* 35.

Drof, gedrof; *adj. Draffy, dreggy, dirty;* sordidus:—*Somn.* 103.

Drofnys, se; *f. Dirtiness, turbulency, sedition;* turbulentia, *Hymn.*

Drog *drew; p. of* dragan.

Drogan *Suffered;* tolerarunt, v. dreogan.

Droge *Dung,* DRAUGH; stereus:—Droge monnes *stercus humanum, L. Md.* 3, 36.

Droht *drawn, draught.*

Drohtan, drohtnian; *part.* niende, nigende; *p.* ode; *pp.* ed. *To converse, dwell, to keep company with;* conversari:—*Bd.* 1, 27.

Drohtað *a conversation,* v. drohtnung.

Drohtnung, drohtung, e; *f. Conversation, conduct, life, actions;* conversatio:—*Deut.* 1, 13. On þæra Apostola drohtnunge *in the Acts of the Apostles, R. Ben.* 33.

DROPA [*Plat.* drüppen *m*: *Dut.* drop: *Frs.* drip *m*: *Ger.* tropfen] A DROP; gutta:—*Lk.* 22, 44.

Dropfaag, dropfag *A starling;* sturnus, *Som.*

Drop-fah; *adj. A drop colour, variegated in spots, spotted;* stillatus:—*Herb.* 130.

Dropian, drupian; *p.* hi drupodon. *To* DROP; stillare:—*Ps.* 71, 6, v. driopan.

Drop-mælum *by drops, drop by drop.*

Droppetan *To distil;* distillare:—*L. Ps.* 67, 9.

Droppetung, dropung *A dropping;* stillicidia:—*L. Ps.* 71, 6.

DROS, drosne; *pl.* drosna. DROSS, *filth, dregs, lees;* fæx:—Eles drosna *the dregs of oil, R.* 47.

Drosenlic; *adj. Brittle, weak;* fragilis, *Som.*

Drosne *dross,* v. dros.

Drugað *dries,* v. drigan.

Drugaðe, drugoðe *A drought, dryness;* siccitas:—*R.* 96.

Druge, drugon *Bore;* tulit, tulerunt, v. dreogan.

Drugung, e; *f. A dryness, a dry place;* inaquosus locus:—*Ps.* 77, 20.

Druncen, druncn *drunken, Gen.* 9, 21, v. drincan.

Druncen georn [*Plat.* drink geren: *Dut.* drink gaarn] *Drinkdesirous, drunken;* ebriosus:—*R. Ben.* 4.

Druncenhed *Drunkenness;* ebrietas:—*Chr.* 1070.

Dreor-fah blood stained Beo K 964

Drenican to drench Ben v drencean

Dreorig bloody; cru entus Beo K 2833

Dre, dri-creeft &c

Driht, dryhten a company 124 a band of 34 Th p 169, 24 soldiers Beo K 236

-1 Ic ageat dreor I shed gore or blood 2 Cd 49 Th 63, 12

3 Dreorig-mod sad of mind

Dreorlice sadly mournfully Th an

Dreorlice drearily mournfully Th an

Dreas saccharum Som v dreas

3 Drencen-georn a drinkard; vinolentus Som

Drif mirra Cd 131 Lye

... an p. dreef

An: Beo gl. Driftan, pellere

Drias a pusture; ager pascuus

deaw-dreas dew of the field Lye - Mr Thorpe reads deaw-drihas dew-drops Cd 185 Th p 293, 17

Drenc-fat, es; n a drinking vessel Beo K 4606

Drihten, drihtman a lord protector Th an

Drihten, weard guardian lord Cd 201 Th p 289, 24

Driht-man a regulator of a wedding Som

Driht-guma

Drihtscipe, es; m Dominion, lordship; dominatio Cd 24 Th p 31, 14. Beo III K 2939

Driht-sele, a royal hall, a hall, regia aula, vel sedes Beo K 964 1527

Driht, a tribe i Theologian Som

Drinc, drenc, es; m drink

Drincet-lean praemia bibendi honoraria - L Cnut pol 78 Som

Drinc-laf or Drenc-lagu drink law; assisa potus Som Lye

Drof-denn a den or arvalter where droves of cattle are fed; armentorum aule Som

Draf-man a drove man, cattle keeper drof mannus Som

Drohtad a sojourn 80 Th p 109, 6 Beo gl

7 His swat was swylce blodes dropan Lk 22, 44 - Dropena drearung a falling of drops Cd 41 Th p 238, 3: 213 Th 265, 23

Dropfah stronius Cot 176

3 Dropsag sternus Ben

Dror gore Lye v dreore

Drencen [illegible] Entru
Cot. 24 Luc.

2 Dreencensu[illegible] [illegible] drunkenness; [illegible]
Som

3 Drunc[illegible] vare man ebriu[illegible] 17, 8 [illegible]

4 Dresiurg[illegible] [illegible] a ryfen [illegible] Som

5 ryht [illegible], w a noble [illegible] Beo K 4065

6 [illegible] lordly [illegible]

7 Dryhtere [illegible] a [illegible], dominus
8 Som. Ben Lye

9 [illegible]

10 [illegible]

16 Drync [illegible] Som

11 Dryne-werig drink [illegible] temulentus Som Ben
drinc-werig

12 Dryp[illegible] a drop
[illegible] drops

13 Dryre blood Cod. Ex. 56 a v dreor
[illegible] sunk, morsus
Ben v [illegible]

O

Dryht-madm es: m lordly treasure Beo K 5681

To subside, [illegible] septare; Luce drey [illegible] side (the) [illegible] settled Beo K 3262

O1 Dryn mas Augusta pomeis [illegible] Cd [illegible] p 5, 34 — August [illegible] [illegible] heryad the [illegible] 170 Th p 213, 2 — Dugada rum bonorum gaudium Cod Ex 60, 1

3 Dugu[illegible] with [illegible] twenty, [illegible]

O7 Dy[illegible] Cd 85 Th p 17, 33
v duged

2 Duth-rune [illegible] [illegible] Som v doth-rune

O8

3 Dumle ongerytanus Cot 23 Ben Lye
47

4 Dun-scrafes m a mountain cavern Cod Ex 56 Beo [illegible] [illegible]

5 [illegible] fixed, [illegible] [illegible] Dut dun [illegible]

8

[illegible] chats Som [illegible]

3 Dyreteas [illegible] worthless [illegible] value Ben Lye
17, 83

O4

2 Lust es, in Th An

5 Dust-wencg (dust-drink) [illegible] against the jaundice [illegible] 3, 12 Som Lye

6 4 Dudhama, Dud, hamor papyrus R 43.

O3

24 Dwelan, to deceive, decipere Beo K 3465

O9

Druncennes, se; *f.* DRUNKENNESS; ebrietas:—*Lk.* 21, 34.
Druncn *drunken,* v. druncen.
Druncnian *to be drunk,* v. drincan.
Druncon *Drunkenness;* ebrietas:—*L. Edg.* 57, *W.* p. 86, 29.
Drupodon *distilled,* v. dropian.
Druron *fell,* v. dreosan.
DRY, es; *m. A magician, sorcerer;* magus:—Þa cwædon þa dryas, *Ex.* 8, 19.
Dry-cræft, es; *m. Magical art, magic, sorcery;* ars magica:—*Ex.* 7, 11.
Dry-cræftig *skilful* or *crafty in magic, magical.*
Dryfan *to drive, vex,* v. drifan.
Dryg *dry,* v. drig.
Drygan *to dry up,* v. drigan.
Dryht *people,* v. driht.
Dryhten *a lord,* v. drihten.
Dryht-guman *friends,* v. driht-guma.
Dryman *to rejoice,* v. dreman.
Dryme *a song,* v. dream.
Drymen *magicians, sorcerers.*
Dryncð *drink;* bibunt, v. drincan.
Drync, dryngc *drink,* v. drinc.
Drypan, drypte *to drip,* v. driopan.
Drymian; *p.* de. *To make sad, to be made sad, to mourn;* lugere:—*Cd.* 144.
Dryslic; *adj. Fearful, terrible;* terribilis:—*R.* 116.
Drysnian, adrysnian; *pp.* gedrysned, od. *To put out, quench, extinguish;* extinguere:—Leoht-fat is gedrysnod *a lamp is put out, Som.*
DUBBAN [*Icel.* ad dubba *to strike:* hence the phrase ad dubba til riddara is in *Swed.* sla en til riddare *to strike one a knight*] *To strike,* DUB, *create;* percutere, creare:—Dubban to ridere *to dub or create a knight, Chr.* 1085.
Dufedoppa *A pelican;* pelicanus:—*L. Ps.* 101, 7.
DUFIAN; *p.* dyfde; *pp.* dofen. *To sink,* DIVE, *immerge;* immergere:—*L. In.* 78, v. gedufian.
DUGAN, digian; *part.* dugende; he deáh, deg, dige, dyge; *p.* dohte, duhte, þu dohtest, we dohton; *v. ir.* [*Plat.* dögen: *Dut.* deugen: *Frs.* dôge: *Ger.* taugen] *To profit, avail, care for, help, be good for, to be virtuous, good, honourable, noble;* valere, probus esse:—Ne dohte *could not help, Chr.* 1006. Ne dohte him *care not for him, Bt.* 29, 2. Gif se nedeah *if he be not good, Id.* 27, 2. Gif hi dohton *if they were honourable, Id.* 18, 3. Eall dugende beon, *L. Can. eccl.* 15, *W.* p. 155, 38.

Dugeð, dugoð, duguð, e; *f.* [*Plat.* dögt *f*: *Dut.* deugd *f*: *Ger.* tugend *f.*] 1. *Advantage, gain, happiness, prosperity, health, riches, goods, accommodation, enlargement;* commodum. 2. *Excellence, virtue, probity, fortitude, magnanimity, power, honour;* virtus. 3. *Nobility, senate, government;* nobilitas:—1. Woruld dugeðum *with worldly advantages, Cd.* 92. Fram duguðe *from happiness, Id.* 49. 2. Seo duguð þæs wlites þe on gimmum bið *the excellence of the beauty which is in gems, Bt.* 13: 10: *Ors.* 1, 12. Duguða helm *a crown of virtues, Cd.* 216. 3. Macedonia duguðe *the nobility of the Macedonians, Ors.* 3, 11. Eall seo dugoð of Angelcynnes þeode, *Chr.* 1016. Se cining mid eallum his dugoðe *the king with all his nobility, Id.* 626.
Dugeð, dugoð, duguð; *adj. Good, virtuous, honourable;* bonus, probus, *Mann.*
Dugoðe-ealdor *a magistrate.*
Duguð-gifu *liberality.*
Duhte *did good,* v. dugan.
Dulf, dulfon *dug,* v. delfan.
Dulmuna *Long ships;* longæ naves:—*Ors.* 1, 10.
DUMB; *adj.* [*Dut.* dom: *Moes.* dumbs: *Heb.* דומה dume] DUMB, *mute;* mutus:—*Mt.* 12, 22.
Dumnys, se; *f.* DUMBNESS, *speechless;* loquendi impotentia, *Som.*
Dun DUN, *a colour partaking of brown and black;* fuscus:—*Cot.* 141.
DUN, e; *f.* [*Plat. Ger.* düne *f*: *Dut.* duinen m. pl: *Dan.* dynerne *f. pl*: *Frs.* dune *f*: *Celt. Bret.* tun *f.*] *A mountain, hill,* DOWNS; mons:—Þæt wæter was ofer þa hehstan duna, *Gen.* 7, 20. On þisse dune, *Deut.* 1, 6. On þære dune, *Gen.* 31, 54: *Mt.* 24, 3. Duna swioran *tops of hills, Juga. Cot.* 114. ¶ Of dune, adune *down, downward,* v. of. dune, adun.
Dun; *adj. Mountainous, hilly;* montanus:—Farað oðrum to feld landum, and dun landum, *Deut.* 1, 7.
Dunelfen; *pl. Down* or *mountain-elves, fairies.*
Duneward, duneweard *downward, Som.*
Dunfalu, dunfealu *Tawny colour;* color cervinus:—*R.* 79.
Dung [*Frs.* dong] DUNG; fimus:—*H. Lk.* 13, 8.
Dunholm [Dun *a hill,* holm *water, an island.*—*F.* Dunhelm: *Brom.* Durem] DURHAM:—*Chr.* 1072.

Dunlændisc, dunlandisc *mountainous,* v. dun; *adj.*
Dunnian *To make of a dun* or *a dark colour, to obscure, darken;* obscurare:—Se mona þa beorhtan steorran dunniað *the moon obscures the bright stars, Bt.* 4.
Dunsætas *mountaineers.*
Dunstræt *a hilly road.*
Dunsaluie, duntæhte *mountain-sage.*
Dunung *A noise;* crepitus, *Som.*
Duolan *to err,* v. dwolian.
Dureward *a door-ward, a door-keeper.*
Durfon *tried,* v. deorfan.
Durre, durron *dare,* v. dear.
Durste *durst,* v. dear.
Durstodl *a door-post.*
DURU, dyr; *g.* e; *d.* e, a, an; *ac.* a; *pl.* dura; *f.* [*Plat.* dör *f*: *Dut.* deur: *Frs.* dôar *f*: *Ger.* thür *f*: *Moes.* daur: *Dan.* dör: *Swed.* dôr *f*: *Frs.* doar, doare: *Icel.* dyr *n*: *Grk.* θυρα: *Wel.* dôr: *Pers.* در dur: *Sans.* dura] A DOOR, *gate;* ostium:—Seo duru wæs belocen, *Mt.* 25, 10. Of þære dura, *Mt.* 26, 71. To þære duran, *Mk.* 1, 33.
Durustod *a door-stead, a door-post.*
Duruþinen; *f. A female door-keeper;* ancilla ostiaria:—*Jn.* 18, 17.
Dust; *n.* DUST; pulvis:—*Mk.* 6, 11: *Lk.* 10, 11.
Dua *a dove, pigeon, Som.*
DWÆS, dwes; *adj.* [*Plat.* dwas: *Dut.* dwaas: *Moes.* dwala] *Dull, foolish, blockish;* hebes, stultus:—*Elf. gl.* 7.
Dwæscan *to extinguish,* v. adwæscan.
Dwæsnes, dwesenys, se; *f. Dulness, foolishness;* stupiditas:—*R.* 88.
Dwala *an error,* v. gedwola.
Dwas-liht [*Dut.* dwaal-licht *n.*] *A false light;* ignisfatuus, *Som.*
Dwelian, dwolian, gedweligan; ge dweligeað dwelegað; *part.* dweligende; *p.* dwealde gedwealde; *pp.* gedweled, gedweald [*Plat. Dut.* dwalen: *Frs.* dwylje] 1. *To err, mistake;* errare. 2. *To deceive, mislead, to lead into error;* seducere:—1. v. n. Soðlice swyðe ge dweligeað, *Mk.* 12, 27, 24: *Deut.* 13, 5: *Bt.* 36, 5. 2. In an active sense, gedweligan is generally used. Me nan man gedweligan ne mæg *no man can mislead me, Bt.* 33, 3, *Card.* p. 196, 1. Þe men gedwelað, *Bt.* 32, 3.

Occasionally dwelian is used in an active sense. Þu me dwelige *thou deceivest me, Bt.* 35, 5. Ic þe dwealde, *Id.*

Dweorg, dwerg, dweorh [*Plat.* dwarf *m*: *Dut.* dwerg *c.*] *A dwarf;* nanus:—*R.* 114.

Dwes *dull,* v. dwæs.

Dwesenys *dulness,* v. dwæsnes.

Dwild *A deception, spectre;* error, spectrum, *Lye.*

Dwimeru, dwimora; *pl. Ghosts, spectres;* spectra, *Som.*

Dwimorlic; *adj. Visionary;* tanquam per visum, *Som.*

DWINAN, adwinan, ic dwine, he dwinð; *p.* dwán, we dwinon; *pp.* dwinen [*Plat.* dwinen: *Dut.* verdwynen] *To pine, fade,* DWINDLE, *waste away, vanish, extinguish;* tabescere:—*Herb.* 2, 4, 17.

Dwola *an error,* v. gedwola.

Dwoleman, dwolman *darkness, chaos; ac. of* dwolma.

Dwolian *to err,* v. dwelian.

Dwollic; *adj. Erring, heretical;* hæreticus:—*L. Alf. Can.* 33.

Dwollice; *adv. Erroneously;* hæretice:—*Hexaem.* 20.

Dwolma *A chaos, a chasm, gulph;* chaos, hiatus:—*Lk.* 16, 26: *Bt. R.* p. 156, 5.

Dwolu *an error,* v. gedwola.

Dwolung, e; *f. Dotage;* deliramentum:—*Cot.* 69.

DYDAN *To die, kill;* mori, occidere:—*L. pol. Cnut.* 42, *W.* p. 140, 45, v. adydan.

Dyde *did; p. of* don.

Dyde A DEED, *an action:* facinus:—*Ors.* 5, 2.

Dyderian, dydrian *To deceive, delude;* illudere:—*Bt.* 35, 5.

Dyderunga *delusions, Som.*

Dydrung *A pretence, deceit;* simulatio:—*Col. mon.*

Dyfde *dived,* v. dufian.

Dyfene *Desert, reward;* meritum:—*C. R. Ben.* 2.

Dyfing *a diving, Som.*

Dyg *a day,* v. dæg.

Dyge *does good,* v. dugan.

Dyhte *arranged,* v. dihtan.

Dylfð *digs,* v. delfan.

Dynan; *p.* dynde. *To* DIN, *make a noise;* strepere:—*Jdth.* 10.

Dynan *To* DINE, *feed;* depascere:—*Ps.* 79, 14.

DYNE, gedyn A DIN, *noise;* sonus, fragor, strepitus:—Se dyne becom, *Cd.* 223: 221: 222.

Dyngan; *pp.* gedynged [*Ger.* düngen] *To* DUNG, *manure;* stercorare, *Som.*

Dynige; *f. Mountainous places;* montana:—*L. M.* 3, 8.

DYNT, es; *m. A stroke, stripe, blow,* DINT; ictus; percussio:—*Bt.* 38, 2: *Chr.* 1012.

Dyorlic; *adj. Beastlike, brutal;* belluinus:—*Mod. Con.* 1.

Dypa, deop, an *The* DEEP, *sea;* profundum:—Teoh hit on dypan, *Lk.* 5, 4.

DYPPAN, dippan; ic dyppe, we dippað; *p.* dypte; *pp.* dypt; *v. a.* [*Plat.* dippen, dopen: *Frs.* dippe: *Dut.* doopen] *To* DIP, *immerge, baptize;* immergere:—Dyppe his finger, *Lev.* 4, 17. Dippað ysopan sceaft, *Ex.* 12, 22.

Dyr *a door,* v. duru.

Dyran *To hold dear, love;* carum habere:—*Cd.* 14.

DYRE, deor, dior; *adj.* [*Plat.* dür: *Dut.* dier] DEAR, *beloved, precious;* charus, dilectus, pretiosus:—Se wæs hym dyre, *Lk.* 7, 2: *Gen.* 44, 5. Deore wæs he Drihtne urum *dear was he to our Lord, Cd.* 14. Deor he hit seld *he sold it dear, R.* 35.

Dyrfð *is in danger,* v. deorfan.

Dyrling *a darling,* v. deorling.

Dyrn *hidden, secret,* v. dyrnan.

Dyrnan, gedyrnan; *p.* dyrnde hi dyrndon; *pp.* dyrnen, dyrne, dyrn, bedyrned, gedyrned; *v. a. To hide, secrete;* occultare:—Ne mihte Iosep hyne leng dyrnan, *Gen.* 45, 1. Þat hit hym næs dyrne, *Lk.* 8, 47: *Ors.* 5, 10. Gedyrneð *shall hide, L. In.* 17: 36.

Dyrne-geligre *secret lying, adultery,* v. geligre.

Dyrn-gewrita *Secret writings, books whose authors are not known, the apocryphal books;* apocrypha:—*Cot.* 10.

Dyrnlicgian *To lie secretly, to fornicate;* fornicari:—*Ps.* 105, 36.

Dyrra *dearer,* v. dyre.

Dyrran *to dare, Som.* v. dear.

Dyrstelice, gedyrstelice, dyrstlice; *adv. Boldly;* audacter:—*Mk.* 15, 43.

Dyrstig, gedyrstig; *adj. Daring, bold, rash;* audax:—*Nicod.* 12: *Bd.* 2, 6.

Dyrstignes, gedyrstignes, dyrstnes, se; *f. Boldness, presumption, rashness;* audacia, temeritas:—*Past.* 13, 2.

Dyrstlæcan; *pp.* gedyrstlæht. *To dare;* audere:—*Chr.* 796.

Dyrstlice *boldly,* v. dyrstelice.

Dyrstnes *boldness,* v. dyrstignes.

Dyrwurðre *more precious,* v. deorwurð.

Dysegað *is foolish,* v. dysian.

Dyselic *foolish,* v. dyslic.

Dysi, dyslic, dyselic, dysig, dysg; *adj.* [*Plat.* düsig: *Dut.* duizelig] *Foolish, weak,* DIZZY, *ignorant, erring, blasphemous;* stultus:—Þa dysige men, *Bt.* 33, 3. Dysgum monnum *by ignorant men, Bt.* 33, 4: *Deut.* 32, 21.

Dysian, he dysegað; *part.* ende, gende. 1. *To be foolish, to talk or act foolishly;* ineptire. 2. *To blaspheme;* blasphemare:—1. *Bt.* 5, 2. 2. He dysegað, *Mk.* 2, 7.

Dysig; *n. An error, ignorance, a folly;* error, stultitia:—Hu frecendlic þat dysig is *how dangerous the error is, Bt.* 32, 3. Gif God abrit þat dysig, *if God remove the ignorance, Id.* 39, 3.

Dysigdóm *Foolishness, ignorance;* imperitia:—*Pref. R. Conc.*

Dysignes, dysines, se; *f. Folly,* DIZZINESS, *blasphemy;* stultitia:—*Bd.* 2, 5: *Mk.* 7, 22.

Dyslic, dyselic *foolish, absurd,* v. dysi.

Dyslice; *adv. Foolishly;* stulte:—*Gen.* 31, 28.

Dystig; *adj.* DUSTY; pulverulentus, *Lye.*

Dystiga [*Plat.* dust] *Dustiness;* pulverulenta:—*Cot.* 183.

DYTTAN; *p.* de; *pp.* ed. *To* DIT, *close or shut up;* opprimere, occludere:—*Lk.* 11, 53.

Dyttan *To howl;* ululare:—Wulf dytt *a wolf howls, Elf. gr.*

Dyxas *dishes, platters,* v. disc.

2 Dweorg. dweorh
pl. es; m a dwarf

7 Dweorgmerce, a [illegible] Som. [illegible] Lye pennyroyal
v gedwymer
4 Dweorge-dwostle pudding [illegible] the herb pennyroyal Herb 49 Lye
3
6 Dwostle, pulegium Bez

7 Dyne thunder Cd 222 Th p 289, 7, 27

Dyrstelice boldly daring; audax Som

7 Dyrste, for dearste dorste durst p. of dear
2 Dyrsting-panne [illegible] [illegible] Lye
Dyrwyrde precious v Sahl deorwurde
7
5 dyrwyrdeth an p 109, 23.

5 Dwis stupid Som
v dwæs

Dwolma [illegible]

6 Dwyld sin Th An

7 Dwyrge-dwostle pudding grass v dweorge dwostle Elfr 16 Lye

19 Dŷr, deor. dior dear precious Th An
21 Dyre adv dearly care Beo K 460?

1 Dysig adj foolish Th An dise

9 Dyderung, e; f. transfiguration, phantom, delusion transfiguratio, illusio Som v dydrung 7.

2 Dydest didst p. of don
Dygel hidden; secret
5 Dygle adv deeply Cd
178 Th p 224, 2 v digle
6 Dyglice secretly Som v diglice

21
3 Dyrne adv secretly, clam Beo K 3755 secretus Beo K 2714 v diegol shl

1 Dyst dust Som v dust
Dydhomar, dydhomer a [illegible], sorcery, cutting; [illegible] Som

18 Dynian. p ede; pp. od to make a din, to rush; [illegible] strepere; irruere (See Grim officile in MS.) Jud. dynede Jdth 10 Th Apl 131, 45 [illegible] Chr 938, v Price's Walton vol I p XCI note
* Feld dennode secga [illegible] swate the field resounded with warriors blood, athlete [illegible] Dr. v p 142, 5

Dygol hidden Som v digle
Dygylnes secrecy Som v diegelnes
Dyhle hid, covered Som v digle
10 Dyhtnere a steward Som v dihtnere
11 Dyle a dill Som v Sahl dile
Dylsta, an f Matter corruption, tabum, sanies pl. M 2.29: 1.31. Som

13 Dylstihte purulent, mattery; suppurate, Som oss [illegible] L. M 1, 29 Som
15 Dym dim Som v dim
17 Dynerae folles R 106 Lye
20 Dyra. wudu [illegible] Deirorum sylva Bd. 5.2
22 Dyrn. hæmend adulterer, fornicator [illegible]

Transferred to p 103

Eofores rude tugd. dami rubra genus, a feris forsan gratum S. M. 2, 4 Som

1 Eofor-heafod caput apri Beo 161

2 Eafor-spreot a boar spear Beo 109 v eofor-spreot

3 Eagan-bræhtm a twinkle of an eye

Eagan-bregh an eye-brow; palpebra Som

Eagan-breoht a moment of time v Eagan-bryhtm

Eagan-spind see Strenger

Eag-ece eye-ach Som

Eagena of eyes v eage

Eages-prince the twinkling of an eye Som

10 Eag-flea a web or white spot in the eye; albugo Som

Eag-hyle the eye

Eag-sealf eye-salve collyrium Som

R. 12 Eage

12 Eag-seaung, eag-siowing a disease of the eye; glaucoma Som Eye

Eah, eah-hringas, eah-sihl, eah-mist v. eage, eag-hringas

2 Ead-hredig exulting in prosperity or success Th. An

3 Eadesburh, -g, burge, d-byrig; f. Eddesbury

4 Eadiglic happy

5 Eadiglice Happily; feliciter, beate Beo K 199

Eadmedlice humbly Th. An

2 Ead-modian dignari Greins II 585, 22

3 Eadmodlic adj humble respectful; humilis Som

(ead opmunion)

1 Eadnys, se; f Happiness; felicitas Hickes Thes I p 135, 8

Eadulfes-nas

Eærfodu tribulation

Eafor-fearn Oak-fern wall-fern, radiolus Som

For the compounds of eah see eag etc

an eye

Eadmundes-burh, g. -burge, d.-byrig St Edmundsbury Chr 1047

Eacen increased, Bosk 394 Cd 179 Th p 224, 14 v. eacan

Eacen increased, quick Cd. 132 Th p 167, 15

Eacne conceived Cd. 123; Th p 157, 16 v. eacnian

E is often interchanged with ea, as ceaster, and cester *a burgh, fortified town;* eahta and ehta *eight.*

-e in the termination of nouns denotes a person, as hyrde *a herd, from* hyrdan *to guard.* The vowel -e is also used to form nouns denoting inanimate objects, as cyle *cold;* cwyde *a saying, testament;* bryce *a breach;* wlite *beauty.* These are mostly derived from verbs, but when derived from adjectives they are feminine, as rihtwise *justice.*

Ea'; *indeclin. in the sing.* but eas is sometimes found in g; *pl.* eá; *d.* eán; *f.* [*Plat. Ger.* aue *f: Dan.* aa *f: Icel.* á, aa *f: Per.* aw *f.*] *Running water, a stream, a river, water;* fluvius, aqua:—Seo feorðe ea ys gehaten Eufrates, *Gen.* 2, 14. On feower ean, *Gen.* 2, 10. Be þære ea, *Gen.* 41, 3: *Bd.* 3, 24. Flod and yrnende ea *flowing and running water.*

Eác, ec; *conj.* [*Plat. Dut.* ook: *Frs.* eak: *Ger.* auch: *Moes.* auk: *Swed.* och.—the *Saxon* eac is evidently the *imp. of* eacan *to add, increase*] *Also, likewise, and, moreover;* etiam, quoque:—*Mt.* 11, 9. ¶ Eac swa, eac swilce *so also, also, moreover, very like, even so.*—Þæt ger wæs fram Cristes hider-cyme þæt syxte eac feower tigum *that year was from Christ's advent the sixth and fortieth:* literally, *the sixth add or increase by forty, Bd.* 1, 3. *Card.*

Eaca, an; *m. An addition,* EEKING *usury, advantage;* additamentum:—*Bt.* 38, 3. ¶ To eacan *besides, moreover.*—Þæt wæs to eacan oðrum unarimedum yfium *that was besides other innumerable evils:* literally, *in or for, addition to, &c. Bt.* 1.—To eacan himselfum *besides himself:* literally, *in addition to, Bt.* 26, 2.

Eacan *to eke;* eacen *increased, added, augmented,* v. ecan.

Ea-cerse *Water-cress;* nasturtium aquaticum:—*L. M.* 1, 38.

Eacnian; *part.* iende, igende; *pp.* eacnen, eacne. *To conceive, to be pregnant, to bring forth;* concipere, parturire:—*Ps.* 7, 15: *Ex.* 21, 22, v. geeacnian.

Eacnung *a conceiving, conception,* v. geeacnung.

Ead, es *A possession, prosperity, happiness;* possessio:—*Cd.* 21: 79: *Ors.* 3, 11. Ead hreðige *elated with prosperity, Fr. Jud.* 11, 8.

Eadeg *happy,* v. eadig.

Eaden *given up, conceded, granted.*

Eades-byrig *Eddesbury* or *Edisbury, Cheshire:*—*Chr.* 913.

Eadga, eadge *happy,* v. eadig.

Eadig, eadeg, eadiglic; *adj. Happy, blessed, rich, perfect;* beatus:—*Mt.* 5, 3—11: *Bt.* 35, 4.

Eadigan; *pp.* geeadigen. *To bless, enrich;* beatificare, *Lye.*

Eadigli *happy,* v. eadig.

Eádignes, se; *f. Happiness;* beatitudo:—*Bt.* 40, 4.

Eadlean *a reward,* v. edlean.

Eadleannung, e; *f. Proper recompence, remuneration, retribution;* retributio:—*Ps.* 54, 22.

Eadmed, eadmet *Humility;* humilitas:—*L. pol. Elf.* 1.

Eadmeddan; *p.* de. *To humble;* humiliare:—*Ps.* 74, 7.

Eadmod; *adj. Humble, meek, mild;* humilis:—*Mt.* 11, 29.

Eadmodan; *pp.* ge-eadmoded. *To humble;* humiliare:—*Ps.* 17, 29.

Eadmodlice, ge-eadmodlice, eadmolice; *adv. Humbly, submissively;* humiliter:—*Ps.* 130, 3.

Eadmodnes, se; *f. Humbleness, humility, humanity;* humilitas:—*Ps.* 9, 13.

Ea-docca *a water-dock.*

Eador *a hedge, dwelling,* v. edor.

Eadulfes-nesse *Ædulph's ness* or *nase, Walton, on the Nase, Essex:*—*Chr.* 1049, *Ing.* p. 220, 24.

Eældian *to grow old,* v. ealdian.

Eællenge; *interj. Behold;* en, ecce:—*Ps.* 53, 4.

Eærdung *A tabernacle;* tabernaculum:—*Ps.* 59, 6.

Eærfoðian; *pp.* ge-eærfoðod. *To trouble;* tribulare:—*Ps.* 12, 5.

Eærfoðness *difficulty, trouble,* v. earfoðnys.

Eærpung *A harping, harp;* cithara:—*Ps.* 32, 2, v. hearpa.

Eæðmod; *adj. Mild;* mitis:—*Ps.* 24, 10.

Ea-flod *a flowing of water, a river.*

Eafor, eofor, efor, efyr, es; *m.* [*Ger.* eber *m.*] *A boar, a wild boar;* aper:—*Bt.* 38, 1.

Eafora, eafera, eafra, eofera, aforà, afera, an [afaran *to go out*] *That which is gone out, a progeny, issue, offspring, successor, heir, son;* proles, successor, filius:—*Bt. R.* p. 189.

Eafora Noes *Noah's son, Cd.* 76: 99.

Eág-æpl *apple of the eye, Som.*

Eágan-bryhtm *the twinkling of an eye,* v. bearhtm.

Eágan-wean *A ring-worm, tetter;* impetigo:—*R.* 73.

Eá-gang *a water-course.*

Eág-duru, eag-þyrl, egþyrl, ehþyrl *An eye-door, a window;* fenestra:—*Jos.* 2, 15: *Martyr.* 12. *Jan.*

Ea'ge, ege, an; *n.* ægh, eah [*Frs.* eag, eeg: *Plat. Dut.* oog *n: Ger.* auge *n.*] *An* EYE, *a quickness;* oculus, acies:—*Mt.* 5, 29.

Eág-hringas *the eyebrows.*

Eágh-þyrl *a window,* v. eágdura.

Eág-hyll *the eye-hill, eyebrow.*

Eágor-stream *a water-stream, water.*

Eág-seung *eye-seeing, eye-sight, Som.*

Eág-þyrl *a window,* v. eágdura.

Eág-wrætt *eye-wreck, a pain of the eye.*

Eág-wyrt *Eye-wort, eye-bright;* ocularia:—*L. Md.* 3, 3.

Eah *an eye,* v. eáge.

Eahe *chief,* v. heah.

Eah-stream *a river,* v. ea-stream.

Eahta, ehta *Eight;* octo:—Eahta dagas, *Lk.* 9, 28, v. æhta.

Eahta-teoða, seo, þæt, e; *adj. The eighteenth;* decimus octavus:—*Ors.* 6, 2.

Eahtatig *eighty.*

Eahta-tyne EIGHTEEN; octodecim:—*Jud.* 3, 14.

Eahte *estimation, worth,* v. æht.

Eahteða, eahteoða *eighth,* v. eahtoða.

Eahtnes *persecution,* v. ehtnes.

Eahtoða, eahteða, ehtoða, ehteða, seo, þæt, e; *adj. The eighth;* octavus:—On þære eahtoðan wucan, *Mt.* 12, 1. Se eahteða *or* ehtoða *the eighth, Ex.* 22, 30.

Eahtung *A price, an estimation;* æstimatio, *Som.*

Eal *all,* v. eall.

Eal *an awl*, v. æl.

Eala, hela; *interjec.* [*Dut.* hela: *Frs.* hyla] *O! alas! Oh!* Eala ge næddran, *Mt.* 23, 33, 37. ¶ Eala eala *very well.*—Eala gif *Oh if, I wish!*—Eala þæt *Oh, that!*—Eala hu *Oh, how!*

Eala *ale*, v. aloð.

Ealand, ealond, igland, iglond, iggað; *n.* [*Plat. Dut. Ger.* eiland *n.*—ea *water;* land *land*] *An* ISLAND; insula:—Claudius Orcadas þa ealand geþeodde to cynedome *Claudius added the Orkney islands to the empire*, *Bd.* 1, 3, *Sm.* p. 475, 7, 13: *Bt.* 15: 38, 1. Þæt igland þe man Ii nemnað *the island which they call Hii*, *Chr.* 560. Igland lac bringað *the islands offer gifts*, *Ps.* 71, 10: 96, 1.

Eala-scop *an ale-shop, ale-house.*

Ealað *ale*, v. aloð.

Ealc *each*, v. ælc.

Ealcynn *all kinds, universal.*

EALD, æld; *comp.* yldra; *sup.* yldest, se yldesta, seo þæt yldeste; *adj.* [*Plat.* old: *Frs.* ald, aeld, eald: *Dut.* oud: *Ger.* alt] OLD, *ancient;* vetus, senex:—Ic eom nu eald, *Lk.* 1, 18. On eald dagum *in old times*, *Bd.* 4, 27.

Eald-cwen *an old queen, an old woman.*

Ealder *an elder*, v. ealdor.

Ealdermen *aldermen*, v. ealdorman.

Eald-fæder, es; *m.* [*Ger.* ältervater *m.*] *A grandfather;* avus:—*Elf. gl.* 3. Eald-eald-fæder *a great grandfather.* Ealdfæderas *ancestors*, *Gen.* 15, 15.

Ealdhlaford *an old* or *ancient lord.*

Ealdian; *p.* -ode; *pp.* ge-ealden [*Plat.* oldern: *Ger.* ältern] *To grow* or *wax old;* senescere:—*Jn.* 21, 18: *Gen.* 18, 12.

Ealdlic; *adj.* [*Ger.* ältlich] *Old, senile;* senilis:—*Elf. gr.* 9, 28.

Eald-moder [*Ger.* ältermutter *f.*] *A grandmother;* avia:—*R.* 91.

Ealdnys, se; *f.* OLDNESS, *age;* vetustas:—*Elf. gr.* 5.

Ealdóm, [*Dut.* ouderdom: *Ger.* alterthum] *Old age;* ætas, vetustas:—*Ors.* 2, 4.

Ealdor *life*, v. aldr.

Ealdor, eoldor, aldor; *g.* ealdres; *d.* ealdre; *pl.* ealdras; *m.* [*Plat.* elder *m*: *Ger.* alter *m.*] 1. *An* ELDER, *parent, author, head of a family;* senior, pater familias. 2. Because societies, in early times, were governed by ELDERS or *the aged:* hence, *a ruler, governor, prince;* princeps:—1. *Lev.* 4, 15. His aldor, læg *his parent lay*, *Cd.* 76. Þystra ealdor *author of darkness;* tenebrarum auctor, *Bd.* 2, 1, *S.* p. 501, 16: 1, 27, *Resp.* 8, *S.* p. 493, 3. Hiredes ealdor, *Mt.* 21, 33. 2. Nichodemus wæs Iudea ealdor, *Jn.* 3, 1: *Mt.* 9, 18. Hundredes ealdor *a governor of an hundred, a centurion*, *Mt.* 8, 5. ¶ Ealdor-apostole *chief of the apostles*, *Bd.* 4, 18.—Ealdor-biscop *an archbishop*, *Bd.* 2, 13.—Ealdor-bold, ealdor-botl *a royal village*, *Bd.* 2, 9.—Ealdor-burh *a metropolis*, *Bd.* 1, 13.

Ealdordóm, aldordóm, alderdóm, es; *m.* *Authority, magistracy, principality;* principatus:—*Ps.* 138, 16: *Bd.* 4, 28. Ealdordomas *signs of office;* fasces, *R.* 6.

Ealdor-duguð, aldor-duguð *the chief magistrate, a magistrate.*

Ealdor-gedal *separation from life, death.*

Ealdorlic, aldorlic; *adj.* *Principal, chief, excellent;* principalis:—*Elf. gr.* 9, 28.

Ealdorlicnes, se; *f.* *Principality, authority;* authoritas:—*Bd.* 1, 27, *Resp.* 7.

Ealdorman, aldorman, ælderman; *pl.* ealdormen, [*Ger.* älterman *m.*—hence is our ALDERMAN] *An elderman, a senator, nobleman.* An ealdorman, though inferior to an etheling, was the superior of the thegn, and the highest officer in the kingdom; he was the chief of a shire, and attended the witena gemot, *Turner's Hist. of A. S.* b. viii. c. 7; præfectus, princeps:—*Ors.* 1, 12: *Mk.* 6, 21: *Bt.* 10.

Ealdornere *a refuge*, v. aldornere.

Ealdor-scype *eldership, supremacy.*

Ealdor-þegn, aldor-þægn, *the principal thane* or *servant.*

Ealdr, &c. Contracted from ealdor *an elder, parent, governor.*

Ealdr *life*, v. aldr.

Eald-riht *an old right.*

Eald-Seaxan *The old Saxons, the old German Saxons,* [to distin]guish *them from the Anglo-English Saxons:*—*Bd.* 5, 10.

Ealdung, e; *f.* *Old age;* senectus:—*Ors.* 4, 8.

Ealdur *a prince*, v ealdor.

Ealdwif *an old wife* or *woman.*

Ealdwita *an elder, a senator.*

Eale *ale*, v. aloð.

Eal-geador *altogether.*

Ealgian *To defend;* defendere:—*R. Ben.* 64.

Ealh *a temple*, v. heal.

Ealh-sted *a palace*, v. alh-sted.

Eal-hus *an ale-house.*

EALL, eal, al, all, æl; *adj.* [*Plat. Ger.* aller, alle, alles: *Dut.* al, alle, alles] ALL, *whole;* omnis, totus:—Eall þin lichama bið beorht, *Mt.* 6, 22, 23. God geseah ealle þa þing, *Gen.* 1, 31. ¶ Ealle ætsomme *all in a sum, altogether*, *Bd.* 2, 26.—Mæst ealle *most of all, almost all.*—Ealle gemete, eallum ge metum *by all means, altogether*, *Bd.* 1, 27, *Resp.* 9.—Ealne wæg *always*, *Bt.* 38, 4.—Ealle wæga, ealles *in all ways, of all, fully, altogether*, *Bd.* 4, 11.

Eallenga, eallinga *altogether*, v. eallunga.

Eallic *all, catholic*, v. allic.

Ealling *altogether*, v. eallunga.

Eallneg, eallnig; *adv.* *Always;* semper:—*Bt.* 38, 4.

Eallreord *barbarous*, v. ælreord.

Eall-ruh *all rough.*

Eall-swa, ælswa, ealswa; *adv.* [*Plat. Ger.* also, so: *Frs.* alsa: *Dut.* alzoo] ALSO, *so, likewise, even as, even so;* etiam, sic:—Þa cwæð he eall swa, *Mt.* 21, 30: 15, 28. ¶ Eall swa eft *so often.*—Eall swa miceles *for so much, at that price.*

Eallunga, eallenga, eallinga, eallnunge; *adv.* ALL ALONG, *altogether, entirely, quite, indeed, at all, assuredly, utterly, absolutely, excessively;* omnino:—Þæt ge eallunga ne swerion, *Mt.* 5, 34. God ne eallinga ne adiligað eow, *Deut.* 4, 31.

Ealmæst, ælmæst; *adv.* [*Plat. Ger.* allermeist: *Dut.* allermeest] ALMOST; fere, pene:—*Chr.* 1091.

Ealo, ealod, ealoð *ale*, v. aloð.

Ealo-gewearc *ale-work, brewing.*

Ealond *an island*, v. ealand.

Ealo-wæg *an ale-way, a drinking, an entertainment.*

Eal-sealf *The herb, called the oak of Jerusalem;* ambrosia, *Som.*

Eal-seolcen *All-silken;* holosericus.

Eal swa *also*, v. eall swa.

Ealteawe *good*, v. æltæw.

Ealu *ale*, v. aloð.

Ealu-clyfa *an ale-house*, v. ealhus.

Ealu-sceop *An ale-brewer, a brewer;* cerevisiarius, *Som.*

Ealwalda *all powerful*, v. ælwalda.

Ealwerlice; *adv.* *All manly, liberally, freely;* prorsus viriliter:—*Ps.* 50, 19.

Eal-gylden all gilded Beo K 2216

O 3

Ealde-lāfe; f old inheritance a sword Beo K 1584

Eald-fæder a father Beo K 743

Ealda an old man Th apol.

Ealddōm es. m. Old age Th an

Eald-hettende es. m. an old persecutor Th an

Ealad-wyrt ale-wort cerevisia musteum Som

Eald-swered worn out wrestail old trifles, vetustus R Ban 57 Grein II 676, 28

Eald-spell es; n an old speech, or discourse, a tale, a fable Ath 39.4

Eald-metod, old or ancient creator Beo K 1883 Grein II 629, 19

Ealde-leodwita, an m an historian; historicus Som v. supl Eald-writere

Eald-Seaxe the Old Saxons v Eald-Seaxan

Eald-writere an old writer, an antiquarian Som

Eale-gafol, eale-gauel tribute & excise of ale Som

Ealepe-tun an alehouse; taberna Som

A 251

Eal-gearo all prepared all good web Beo K 154

Eal-gōdwebbe all of silk; holosericum Cot 96

Ealifer Jack in the hedge, samsons; alliaria Som

Eall-cyn every kind Som

Ealle-offrung whole offering; holocaustum R. 35. Lye

Ealond, es n water land, an island 4662

Eal-nihte all night pernoctus rectus R. Ben 72 Lye

Ealu-fæt an ale vat, lacus Som

Ealder-dugud; f. aristocracy

Edesbiri Brom Edesbury Aldesbury Cheshire of the forest of Delamere

Aldesbyrig al Eddlesbury Chr 913 Ing 130, 11

Eadmundes-burh; f. ... Edmunds-bury, Bury Suffolk

On sce Eadmundes byrig ... St. Edmunds bury Chr 1108 Ing 330, 19

Eadulfes nesse, ...

O 4 → 11 2

... Grein II 629, 2

Ealdor-leas princeless Beo K 30 lifeless Beo K 3173

O 7

Eal-iren all iron tota ferreus Beo K 4760

Ealh-stede es m habitation a palace Ealh sted ... 258, 11 v. Spl alh-stede

Eal-lang all along long Beo K 3414

2 Mid ealle with all, wholly than

Ealles of all wholly Th an

Eald-gesīd, es: m an old companion Beo K 1700

Eald-gestreon old treasure Beo K 2761

Ealo (see mearu 13

Ealo-benc, e; f an ale bench Beo K 2051: 5729

Ealo-gal an ale drinker ... 109, 72 ...765, 19

Ealdrebolla claustrum R 72

Ealo-wæge, e; f an ale cup Beo 956; 985

... or Naze, a ... of ... Walton on the Naze, Essex

To Eadulfesnæsse Chr 1049 Ing p 220, 24

Eald-mynster Old minster; vetus monasterium, opposed to Niwe mynster at Winchester Chr 1042

17

O7 [44 a 2]

trouble; difficulty
molestia. Sal.
Ben

~~difficult~~

Ean-feald
Ean ~~one~~, Som v an,
anfeald &c

2 Eapel, eaples, m
an apple Cd 172 Th 290,7
v ~~apel~~ Supl apel difficult

Earban pulse vetches
Som v earfan

Earfete ~~[illegible]~~
Som
Earberlice uneathely Som
Eard
O1 a dwelling Cd 217 Th 277,14
O1 Weardad eardas
Th 103,11 to dwell

Ear-clæsnend, es; m
an ear cleanser, a little
finger v eare-finger

Ear-copu parotidæ
R. 11.

2 Eard-lufe, an Enemy-love
beloved country, patria dilecta
R 13 Beo Th Gen II 506,22
eardigean to dwell
Cd. 121 Th 156, 19 v eardian

12 Eardung-hus a dwelling house
or abiding place, habitationis
domus Bd, 4,28

Eard-stapa, an m. an
earth stepper, a man
Cod Ex 766
a kind of fruit

Earfan vetches; ervum
L. Ml 1,8

Earce-bord ark board
the ark Cd 70 Th 84,26

Earfod-fera difficult
to be passed; difficulter
transitus — Earfod-
læte diffic. emissu —
Earfod-recce diff.
~~Earfod-~~ narratu
— Earfod-rime diff
~~[illegible]~~ numeratu Lye
Gen II 550, 9
— Earfod-sid a painful
journey Cd 172 Th 189,5
Earfod-prage, a troublesome time
laborium [illegible] Beo R 564

Eargeat a ravenous
bird; harpa Som v
earn-geat

Ear-loccas the fore
locks, hair drawn over
the forehead; antiæ Som
6)

11 3 Ear-hring, es; m
an ear ring; inauris
O — trymat gyldene
7) earhringas Ex 32,2

8 Earm-gegirelan bracelets
dextralia Cot. 63

Earm-hreod armlike
Gen II 667, 17 Dial 1,2

(8)

Earm-boga an elbow
10)

O1
sceapen
Earm-sceapen miserable
made
~~[illegible]~~, a
wretch Beo R 2702

Earfod-hawe difficilis
visu Lye

2 Ear-muða, an m
earmouth
(?) 4)
numerator Lye

O5

5 3 Ear-ring an ear
ring Som v. Supl
ear-hring

(7)

9 4 Eard-dyne an
earth-quake Som v
Supl. eord-dyne
10 Eard-styring
or earth quake Som
11 Ear-wreon an
ear ring Som, Ben

3 Eale of, with alc v. supl eadu

Ealwiht *every creature*, v. ælwiht.
Eam *am*; sum, *for*, eom, v. wesan.
Eam, es; *m.* [Still used in Lancashire, *Som. Plat. Dut.* oom *m*: *Frs.* iem: *Ger.* ohm *m.*] *An uncle*; avunculus:—*Gen.* 28, 2: *Ors.* 2, 2, *Bar.* p. 62, 26.
Eanian; *part.* eanigende; *pp.* eanod, ge-ean. *To* YEAN, *bring forth as an ewe*; eniti, parturire:—*Gen.* 33, 13.
Eapl *an apple*, v. æpl.
Ear *before*, v. ær.
Ea'r, æhher, æchir, es; *n.* [*Plat. Dut.* aar *f*: *Frs.* ier: *Ger.* ähre *f.*] *An* EAR *of corn*; spica:—Hig ongunnun pluccian þa ear, *Mt.* 12, 1. Seofon ear, *Gen.* 41, 5: *Mk.* 4, 28.
Eare *an ark*, v. arc.
Earcnan-stan *a pearl*, v. eorcnan-stan.
Eard, *m.* [*Plat.* eerde *f*: *Dut.* aarde *f*: *Frs.* ierde: *Ger.* erde *f.*] 1. *Native soil, province, country*; patria. 2. *Earth, station, region, situation*; terra, natura:—1. He com to his earde, *Mt.* 13, 54, 57. 2. To his agenum earde *to his own region*, *Bt.* 33, 4, *Card.* p. 202, 29: 34, 10, 11, v. eorðe.
Eard-begenga, eard-biggeng, eard-biggend *an earth-dweller, an inhabitant.*
Eard-begengnes *an abode, habitation.*
Eard-biggend, v. eard-begenga.
Earde-fæst *earth fast, settled, fixed.*
Eardian, ærdian; ic eardige; *p.* eardode; *pp.* geeardod. *To dwell, inhabit, rest*; habitare:—Abram eardode þa on þam lande Chanaan, *Gen.* 13, 12: *Mk.* 4, 32.
Eardigendlic; *adj. Inhabitable*; habitabilis:—*Bd.* 4, 28.
Eardung, ærdung, e; *f. An habitation, a dwelling, tabernacle*; habitatio:—*Ps.* 18, 5; 75, 2.
Eardung-stow, ærdung-stow *a dwelling-place, a tent, tabernacle.*
Ea're, an; *n.* [*Frs.* ear: *Plat. Dut.* oor *n*: *Ger.* ohr *n.*] *An* EAR *of an animal*; auris:—Þæs eare sloh Petrus of, *Jn.* 18, 26. Wurdon his earan ge-oponode, *Mk.* 7, 35. On hys earan, *Mk.* 7, 33. And hys eare of-aceaf, *Mk.* 14, 47.
Eáre-finger *ear finger, little finger.*
Eárelipprica *the flap of the ear.*
Earendel *The day-star*; jubar:—*Cod. Ex.* 9, b.
Earfednyme *an heir*, v. yrfenuma.

Earfeð, earfoð, gearfoð, earfoðlic; *adj. Hard, difficult, troublesome, uneasy*; difficilis:—Swiðe earfoð *very difficult*, *Bt. Pref*: *Bt.* 39, 4, *Card.* p. 332, 5: *Cd.* 9.
Earfeða; *pl. nom. ac.* gearfoðu; *g.* earfoða. *A difficulty, suffering, woe, trouble*; difficultas:—On miclan earfeðan, *Ors.* 3, 7, *Bar.* p. 97, 27. He sceal geþolian manige gearfoðu *he shall suffer many troubles*, *Bt.* 31, 1, *Card.* p. 172, 6. Earfoða dæl *a deal of sufferings*, *Cd.* 9, 33.
Earfoð læran *difficult to be taught, dull.*
Earfoðlic *difficult*, v. earfeð.
Earfoðlice; *adv. With difficulty, hardly*; ægre:—*Mk.* 10, 23, 24.
Earfoðlicnes, earfoðnys, earfoðnes, se; *f. Difficulty, necessity, trouble, pain*; difficultas:—*Dial.* 2, 35.
Earg; *adj.* [*Dut.* erg] *Inert, idle, weak, timid, evil, wretched*; ignavus, miser:—*Ors.* 6, 36: 2, 2, *Bar.* p. 63, 15, 18.
Ear-gebland *the sea*, v. æragebland.
Ear-gespreca *an ear-speaker, a whisperer.*
Eargian, æargian *To be slothful, dull, idle*; torpescere:—*Ors.* 4, 13.
Eargra, earha *weaker*, *Bt.* 26, 2, *Card.* p. 144, 15: *Cd.* 27, v. earg.
Eargscipe, earhscipe *Idleness, sloth*; ignavia, *Lye.*
Earh; *adj. Swift, fleeing through fear, timorous, weak*; fugax:—*Elf. gr.* 9, 60, v. earg.
Earh-fere *a quiver for arrows.*
Earhlice, arhlice; *adv. Fearfully, timidly, disgracefully*; trepide, remisse:—*Gen.* 20, 4: *Jud.* 4, 18.
Ea-risc *a water-rush, bulrush.*
Earlæppe *an ear-lap, the lower part of the ear.*
Earm, arm, es; *m.* [*Frs.* earm: *Dut.* arm *m.*] *An* ARM; brachium:—*Ps.* 88, 21.
Earm, ærm, arm; *adj.* [*Frs.* earm: *Plat. Dut. Ger.* arm] *Miserable, wretched, helpless, poor, mean*; miser:—*Mk.* 12, 42, 43: *Bt.* 39, 2. Earmost, *Bt.* 38, 2.
Earm-beag *an arm-ring, a bracelet.*
Earm-boge *an arm-bow, elbow.*
Earm-heorta *poor hearted, cowardly.*
Earmian *To commiserate, grieve*; misereri:—*Chr.* 1086.
Earming, erming, ... [*Dut.* armoede *f*: *Ger.* armuth *f.*] *Poverty, misery, the miserable*; miseria:—*Elf. T.* p. 37, 2: *Bt.* 34, 8.
Earmlic; *adj.* [*Plat. Ger.* armlich: *Dut.* armelyk] *Miserable, wretched*; miser:—*Bd.* 3, 13: *Chr.* 1086.
Earmlice; *adv. Miserably, wretchedly*; misere:—*Bd.* 1, 12, *S.* p. 481, 21. Earmlicor *more miserably*, *Bd.* 5, 14.
Earm-scanca *arm-bones.*
Earm-strang *arm-strong.*
Earm-swið *arm-powerful, strong.*
Earmð, [*Frs.* earmte] *Misery, poverty*; miseria:—*Bt.* 48, 2.
Ear-muð [*sea-mouth*] YARMOUTH, *in Norfolk*, *Lye.*
Earn, es; *m.* [*Frs.* earn: *Dut.* aarn] *An eagle*; aquila:—*Mt.* 24, 28. Earn-cyn *eagle kind*, *Lev.* 11, 13.
Earn *a cottage*, v. ærn.
Earngeap *A vulture*; vultur:—*R.* 38.
Earnian, ærnian, geearnigan, geærnian, gearnian; p. ...de; *pp.* geearnod: *v. a.* [*Plat.* aren, inaren: *Ger.* erndten, einerndten] *To* EARN, *merit, deserve, get, attain, labour for*; mereri:—Þæt he earnað *that he earns*, *Bt.* 37, 2: *Mt.* 21, 43. Hie magon geearnigan *they can deserve*, *Bt.* 13, *Card.* p. 60, 21: 35, 6.
Earnung, geearnung, e; *f.* [*Plat.* arendte *f*: *Ger.* erndte *f.*] *An* EARNING, *a desert, reward, means of obtaining, good turn, compassion*; meritum:—On godra monna geearnunga *in good men's deserts*, *Bt.* 39, 2, *Card.* p. 326, 1. Earnunga *yearning*, *Ps.* 102, 4: 24, 7.
Earp *a harp*, v. hearp.
Ear-plætt *a blow on the ear.*
Ears *podex*, v. ærs.
Earsod *Backward*, ARSED; tergosus:—*R.* 77.
Ear-spinl *an ear-ring.*
Ears-þirl *anus.*
Earð *thou art*; es, v. eom.
Earð *the earth*, v. eorðe.
Ear þan *before that*, v. ær.
Earðling *a farmer*, v. yrðling.
Ear-wigga *An* EARWIG *or worm*; vermis auricularis, *Som.*
Ea-spring *a water spring, a fountain.*
East; *d.* eastan. [*Frs.* east: *Plat. Dut.* oost *f*: *Ger.* osten *m.*] *The* EAST; oriens:—Þæt is þrittiges mila lang east and west, *Bd.* 1, 3. Eastan *or* be eastan *in the east*, *Gen.* 12, 8. Se morgensteorra cymð eastan up *the morning star cometh in the east*, *Bt.* 39, 13. ¶ Eastinne *in the east*.—East-rihte *east right, by or near the east*.—Eastweard, east-werd *toward the east*, *Bt.* 18, 1.—East-weg

7)

trouble; difficulty molestia. Sal. Ben

Oz [44 a 2]

Ear-feald

Earn one, Som v an. anfeald &c

2 Eapel, geaples, m an apple Cd 1 ... 200,7 v æppel supl apel difficile

3 Earban pulse vetches Som v earfan

Earfede ... fable

5 Earfedlice uneasily Som

Eard a dwelling Cd 217 ... 277,14

Weardat eardas ... 103,11 to dwell

Ear-clæsnend, es; m an ear cleanser, a little finger v eare-finger

Ear-copu parotidæ R. 11.

2 Eard-lufe, an ... love beloved country patria dilecta ... R 1377 Bos ... Gn II 506,22

10 Eardigean to dwell Cd. 121 ... 156,19 v eardian

Eardung-hus a dwelling house or abiding place, habitatio domus Bd. 4,28

Eard-stapa, an m an earth stepper, a man ... Cod Ex 766

a kind of ...

12 Earfan ... vetch; ervum ... Md 1,6

difficult

Earce-bord ark board the ark Cd 70 ... 84,26

O1

Earfod-fere difficult to be passed; difficiles transitu — Earfod-lære difficult ... — Earfod-recce diff. Earfod-... narratu — Earfod-rime diff numeratu Lye Gn II 550,9

— Earfod-sid a painful journey ... 72 ... 89,5

Earfod-træg ... a troublesome time laborum ... R 564

3 Eargeat a ravenous bird; harpa Som v earn-geat

Ear-loccas the fore locks, hair drawn over the forehead; antiæ Som

3 Ear-hring, es; m an ear-ring; inauris

twymat gyldene earhringas Ex 32,2

Earm-geafetan bracelets dextralia Cot 63

3 Earm-heort merciful ... Gn II 667,17 Deal 1,2

Earm-boga an elbow

10)

sceapen

Earm-sceapen miserable made poor; a wretch Bos R 2702

Earfod-hawe difficilis visu Lye

Ear-muda, an m earmouth

O5

5 Ear-ring an ear ring Som v. supl ear-hring

7

Eard-dyne an earth-quake Som v supl eord-dyne

Eard-styrung or earth quake Som

Ear-wreon an ear ring Som, Ben

3 Eale of, with ... v supl eadu

Ealwiht *every creature,* v. ælwiht.

Eam *am;* sum, *for,* eom, v. wesan.

EAM, es; *m.* [Still used in Lancashire, *Som. Plat. Dut.* oom *m: Frs.* iem: *Ger.* ohm *m.*] *An uncle;* avunculus:—*Gen.* 28, 2: *Ors.* 2, 2, *Bar.* p. 62, 26.

Eanian; *part.* eanigende; *pp.* eanod, ge-ean. *To* YEAN, *bring forth as an ewe;* eniti, parturire:—*Gen.* 33, 13.

Eapl *an apple,* v. æpl.

Ear *before,* v. ær.

EA'R, æhher, æchir, es; *n.* [*Plat. Dut.* aar *f: Frs.* ier: *Ger.* ähre *f.*] *An* EAR *of corn;* spica:—Hig ongunnun pluccian þa ear, *Mt.* 12, 1. Seofon ear, *Gen.* 41, 5: *Mk.* 4, 28.

Earc *an ark,* v. arc.

Earcnan-stan *a pearl,* v. eorcnan-stan.

EARD, *m.* [*Plat.* eerde *f: Dut.* aarde *f: Frs.* ierde: *Ger.* erde *f.*] 1. *Native soil, province, country;* patria. 2. *Earth, station, region, situation;* terra, natura:—1. He com to his earde, *Mt.* 13, 54, 57. 2. To his agenum earde *to his own region, Bt.* 33, 4, *Card.* p. 202, 29: 34, 10, 11, v. eorðe.

Eard-begenga, eard-biggeng, eard-biggend *an earth-dweller, an inhabitant.*

Eard-begengnes *an abode, habitation.*

Eard-biggend, v. eard-begenga.

Earde-fæst *earth fast, settled, fixed.*

Eardian, ærdian; ic eardige; *p.* eardode; *pp.* geeardod. *To dwell, inhabit, rest;* habitare:—Abram eardode þa on þam lande Chanaan, *Gen.* 13, 12: *Mk.* 4, 32.

Eardigendlic; *adj. Inhabitable;* habitabilis:—*Bd.* 4, 28.

Eardung, ærdung, e; *f. An habitation, a dwelling, tabernacle;* habitatio:—*Ps.* 18, 5: 75, 2.

Eardung-stow, ærdung-stow *a dwelling-place, a tent, tabernacle.*

EA'RE, an; *n.* [*Frs.* ear: *Plat. Dut.* oor *n: Ger.* ohr *n.*] *An* EAR *of an animal;* auris:—Þæs eare sloh Petrus of, *Jn.* 18, 26. Wurdon his earan ge-oponode, *Mk.* 7, 35. On hys earan, *Mk.* 7, 33. And hys eare of-acearf, *Mk.* 14, 47.

Eáre-finger *ear finger, little finger.*

Eárelipprica *the flap of the ear.*

Earendel *The day-star;* jubar:—*Cod. Ex.* 9, b.

Earfednyme *an heir,* v. yrfenuma.

Earfeð, earfoð, gearfoð, earfoðlic; *adj. Hard, difficult, troublesome, uneasy;* difficilis:—Swiðe earfoð *very difficult, Bt. Pref: Bt.* 39, 4, *Card.* p. 332, 5: *Cd.* 9.

Earfeða; *pl. nom. ac.* gearfoðu; *g.* earfoða. *A difficulty, suffering, woe, trouble;* difficultas:—On miclan earfeðan, *Ors.* 3, 7, *Bar.* p. 97, 27. He sceal geþolian manige gearfoðu *he shall suffer many troubles, Bt.* 31, 1, *Card.* p. 172, 6. Earfoða dæl *a deal of sufferings, Cd.* 9, 33.

Earfoð læran *difficult to be taught, dull.*

Earfoðlic *difficult,* v. earfeð.

Earfoðlice; *adv. With difficulty, hardly;* ægre:—*Mk.* 10, 23, 24.

Earfoðlicnes, earfoðnys, earfoðnes, se; *f. Difficulty, necessity, trouble, pain;* difficultas:—*Dial.* 2, 35.

EARG; *adj.* [*Dut.* erg] *Inert, idle, weak, timid, evil, wretched;* ignavus, miser:—*Ors.* 6, 36: 2, 2, *Bar.* p. 63, 15, 18.

Ear-gebland *the sea,* v. ærageblond.

Ear-gespreca *an ear-speaker, a whisperer.*

Eargian, eargian *To be slothful, dull, idle;* torpescere:—*Ors.* 4, 13.

Eargra, earha *weaker, Bt.* 26, 2, *Card.* p. 144, 15: *Cd.* 27, v. earg.

Eargscipe, earhscipe *Idleness, sloth;* ignavia, *Lye.*

Earh; *adj. Swift, fleeing through fear, timorous, weak;* fugax:—*Elf. gr.* 9, 60, v. earg.

Earh-fere *a quiver for arrows.*

Earhlice, arhlice; *adv. Fearfully, timidly, disgracefully;* trepide, remisse:—*Gen.* 20, 4: *Jud.* 4, 18.

Ea-risc *a water-rush, bulrush.*

Earlæppe *an ear-lap, the lower part of the ear.*

EARM, arm, es; *m.* [*Frs.* earm: *Dut.* arm *m.*] *An* ARM; brachium:—*Ps.* 88, 21.

EARM, ærm, arm; *adj.* [*Frs.* earm: *Plat. Dut. Ger.* arm] *Miserable, wretched, helpless, poor, mean;* miser:—*Mk.* 12, 42, 43: *Bt.* 39, 2. Earmost, *Bt.* 38, 2.

Earm-beag *an arm-ring, a bracelet.*

Earm-boge *an arm-bow, elbow.*

Earm-heorta *poor hearted, cowardly.*

Earmian *To commiserate, grieve;* misereri:—*Chr.* 1086.

Earming, erming, [struck] [*Dut.* armoede *f: Ger.* armuth *f.*] *Poverty, misery, the miserable;* miseria:—*Elf. T.* p. 37, 2: *Bt.* 34, 8.

Earmlic; *adj.* [*Plat. Ger.* armlich: *Dut.* armelyk] *Miserable, wretched;* miser:—*Bd.* 5, 13: *Chr.* 1086.

Earmlice; *adv. Miserably, wretchedly;* misere:—*Bd.* 1, 12, *S.* p. 481, 21. Earmlicor *more miserably, Bd.* 5, 14.

Earm-scanca *arm-bones.*

Earm-strang *arm-strong.*

Earm-swið *arm-powerful, strong.*

Earmð, [*Frs.* earmte] *Misery, poverty;* miseria:—*Bt.* 48, 2.

Ear-muð [*sea-mouth*] YARMOUTH, *in Norfolk, Lye.*

EARN, es; *m.* [*Frs.* earn: *Dut.* aarn] *An eagle;* aquila:—*Mt.* 24, 28. Earn-cyn *eagle kind, Lev.* 11, 13.

Earn *a cottage,* v. ærn.

Earngeap *A vulture;* vultur:—*R.* 38.

Earnian, earnian, geearnigan, geærnian, gearnian; *p.* ode; *pp.* geearnod: *v. a.* [*Plat.* aren, inaren: *Ger.* erndten, einerndten] *To* EARN, *merit, deserve, get, attain, labour for;* mereri:—Þæt he earnað *that he earns, Bt.* 37, 2: *Mt.* 21, 43. Hie magon geearnigan *they can deserve, Bt.* 13, *Card.* p. 60, 21: 35, 6.

Earnung, geearnung, e; *f.* [*Plat.* arendte *f: Ger.* erndte *f.*] *An* EARNING, *a desert, reward, means of obtaining, good turn, compassion;* meritum:—On godra monna geearnunga *in good men's deserts, Bt.* 39, 2, *Card.* p. 326, 1. Earnunga *yearning, Ps.* 102, 4: 24, 7.

Earpa *a harp,* v. hearpa.

Ear-plætt *a blow on the ear.*

Ears *podex,* v. ærs.

Earsod *Backward,* ARSED; tergosus:—*R.* 77.

Ear-spinl *an ear-ring.*

Ears-þirl *anus.*

Earð *thou art;* es, v. eom.

Earð *the earth,* v. eorðe.

Ear þan *before that,* v. ær.

Earðling *a farmer,* v. yrðling.

Ear-wigga *An* EARWIG *or worm;* vermis auricularis, *Som.*

Ea-spring *a water spring, a fountain.*

EAST; *d.* eastan. [*Frs.* east: *Plat. Dut.* oost *f: Ger.* osten *m.*] *The* EAST; oriens;—Þæt is þrittiges mila lang east and west, *Bd.* 1, 3. Eastan *or* be eastan *in the east, Gen.* 12, 8. Se morgensteorra cymð eastan up *the morning star cometh in the east, Bt.* 39, 13. ¶ Eastinne *in the east.*—East-rihte *east right, by or near the east.*—Eastweard, east-werd *toward the east, Bt.* 18, 1.—East-wæg east way, towards the east, Cd. 174.

East, eastern, easten, eastan; *adj.* EAST, EASTERN, *easterly, ori*entalis:—East-Angel, East-Engles *East-Angle, East-Angles, Bd.* 5, 23. ¶ Ðonne cymð easterne wind *then cometh an eastern wind, Cd.* 17.—East-Francan *East-Franks.*—East folc *eastern people.*—East-land *east country, Gen.* 29, 1.—East-rice *an eastern kingdom, Ors.* 2, 1. — East-Seaxan, East-Seaxe *East-Saxons.*—Easten wind *east wind, R.* 54.—East-an-suðan wind *south east wind, Bd.* 4, 3. — Eastan-norðan *north east.*

East-Angel, East-Engle, East-Englas, East-Englan *the* EAST-ANGLES, *Chr.* 449.

Eastan-norðan *north eastern,* v. east; *adj.*

East-dæl, east-dele *an eastern part, the east.*

Easten *eastern,* v. east.

East-Engle *The East-Angles,* v. East-Angel.

Easter, eoster, eastro, eastron [*Ger.* ostern *f.* From the goddess Eostre, whose festivities were in April, *Bd. de Temp. Rat. Works,* vol. ii. p. 81.] EASTER, *the feast at Easter, the passover;* pascha:—Æfter twam dagum beoð eastro, *Mt.* 26, 2. Wæron eastron, *Mk.* 14, 1. Ðat þu eastron ete, *Mk.* 14, 12.

Easter, Eastor, easterlic; *adj. Easter;* paschalis:—On easter æfen, *Mt.* 28, 1. Eastor dæg *Easter day, Bd.* 5, 23. Easter tide *Easter tide* or *time, Bd.* 5, 23. Easter fæsten or Easterlic freols *Easter feast, Lk.* 2, 42. Easter-monað *Easter month, April.*

East-ern *an eastern place, in the east,* v. east; *adj.*

East-Francan *the East-Franks,* or *Frenchmen, Som.* v. east.

East-inne *within the east, in the east.*

East-ric *east kingdom, eastern empire.*

East-rihte *east right, towards* or *in the east.*

East-Seaxe *The East-Saxons, people of Essex:*—Of Eald-Seaxum comon East-Seaxan *from the Old Saxons come the people of Essex, Chr.* 449, v. seax.

Ea-stream *a water stream, a river, Cd.* 12.

East-weard, east-werd *eastward, in the east,* v. east.

EAÐ; *comp.* eáðere, eáðre, éðre; *sup.* eáðost; *adj.* [*Chau.* eth, eyth] *Easy, ready, gentle, mild, meek, soft;* facilis:—Hwæðer is eðre to secgenne, *Mk.* 2, 9: *Lk.* 5, 23. Eaðere, *Mk.* 10, 25.

Eáð bene *an humble intreaty, a deprecation, Som.*

Eáðe, æðe; *comp.* éð; *adv. Easily, readily, soon, perhaps;* faciliter:—Hi mihton eaðe begitan, *Ors.* 3, 4. Ðæt ic eð mæge gebringan *that I may more easily bring, Bt.* 5, 3: 19. ¶ Æðe mæg, eaðe mæg *easily can, perhaps.*

Eáðe-fere *easily trod, easy.*

Eáðelic; *comp.* ra; *adj. Easy, possible;* facilis:—*Mt.* 19, 26, v. eað, æðelic.

Eáðelice, æðelice, eðelice; *comp.* or *sup.* ost, ust; *adv. Easily, remarkably, elegantly;* facile:—Ðæt þu mæge eðelicost cumon *that thou mayest most easily come, Bt.* 41, 5: *Lk.* 22, 6. Eaðelicor *more easily, Lk.* 18, 25.

Eáðfynde *easily found.*

Eáð-gete *prepared.*

Eáð-hylde *easily held, satisfied, content.*

Eáð-lære *easily taught, teachable.*

Eáðmed, eað-mod *an easy mind, humble,* v. eadmod.

Eáðmedan *To adore;* adorare:—*Ex.* 24, 1.

Eáðmet, -ta [*Dut.* ootmoed *m.*] *Humility, submission;* humilitas:—*Bt.* 12.

Eáðmod *humble,* v. eaðmed.

Eáðmodian *To obey;* obedire:—*R. Mk.* 4, 14.

Eáðmodlice; *adv.* [*Plat.* odmodiglik: *Dut.* ootmoediglyk] *Humbly;* humiliter:—*Bt.* 42.

Eáðmodnes, se; *f. Humility;* humilitas:—*Bt.* 12.

Eatogeð *eighth,* v. æhta.

Eaufæst *pious,* v. æfest.

Eaufæstnys *piety,* v. æfestnes.

Eaw *an ewe,* v. eowu.

Eawan; *p.* de; *pp.* ed. *To shew, manifest;* ostendere: — *Bd.* 2, 6.

Eawesclice; *adv. Openly;* palam:—*Bd.* 3, 19.

Eawfæst *pious,* v. æfest.

Eawfæstnys *religion,* v. æfestnes.

Eawla OH! v. eala.

Eawunga, eawunge; *adv. Openly, publicly;* palam: — *Ps.* 49, 3.

Ea-wylm *a well of water,* v. æwelm.

Eax *an axe,* v. æx.

EAX, æx, e; *f.* [*Plat. Dut.* as c: *Ger.* achse *f.*] *An axis, axle-tree;* axis:—Neah þam norðende þære eaxe *near the north end of the axis, Bt.* 39, 3. Sio eax welt ealles þæs wænes *the axle-tree regulates all the waggon, Bt.* 39, 8.

Eaxan-ceaster, Exan-ceaster, Execester [Ex, exa *the river Ex,* ceaster *a city*] EXETER, *Devon., Chr.* 876.

Eaxan-minster *The minster on the river Ex,* AXMINSTER, *Devon., Som.*

Eaxan-muð *the mouth of the river Ex,* EXMOUTH, *Devon., Chr.* 1001.

Eaxl; *pl.* exla, eaxla [*Ger.* achsel *f.*] *A shoulder;* humerus:—On his exla, *Lk.* 15, 5: *L. Ethelb.* 39.

Eaxl-clað *a shoulder cloth, a scapular.*

Ebal-san [ebul *evil;* secgan *to speak*] *To blaspheme;* blasphemare.

Ebban, de; *pp.* æbbad, beebbed, geebbed [*Plat. Dut.* ebben] *To* EBB; recedere:—Ðæt wæter wæs geebbod, *Chr.* 897.

EBBA, an; *m.* [*Plat. Dut. Ger.* ebbe] *An* EBB, or *receding of water;* recessus aquarum:—Ðæs ebban *of the ebb, Bt.* 21, v. æbbung.

Ebolsung *blasphemy.*

Ebreisc; *adj. Hebrew, belonging to Jews;* Hebræus:—*Elf. T.* p. 7.

Ebul *Evil;* malum, *Lye.*

Eburðring *the celestial sign Orion, Som.*

Ebylgnes, se; *f. Anger, indignation;* ira: — *Ps.* 29, 4, v. æbylgð.

Ec *also,* v. eac.

Ecan, æcan, ican, ycan, ycean, geícean; he ecð, we ecað; *p.* he ecte, ycte, ihte, geichte, hi icton, geihton; *pp.* geeced, geiced, geict, geiht [eaca *an addition*] *To* EKE, *increase, add;* augere:—Ge ecað eowre wædle *ye increase your want, Bt.* 26, 2. Ecte *he prolonged, Bt.* 12. Mæg ican, *Lk.* 12, 25. He ihte *increased, Ex.* 9, 34. Heo ongan geicean *she began to increase, Cd.* 56.

ECE, éccelic, écelic; *def.* se eca; *adj. Eternal, perpetual, everlasting;* æternus:—Ðys ys soðlice ece lif, *Jn.* 17, 3: 12, 50. On þam ecan setle *on the eternal seat, Bt.* 4.

Ece *an ake,* v. æce.

ECED, æced, æcced, aisil, es [*Plat.* etig *m*: *Dut.* edik, eek *m*: *Ger.* essig *m.*] ACID, *vinegar;* acetum:—Ða stod an fæt full ecedes, *Jn.* 19, 29.

Eced-fæt, æced-fæt *an acid vat, a vinegar-vessel.*

Ecelice; *adv. Eternally, ever;* perpetuo:—*Ps.* 23, 9.

Ecenys *eternity,* v. échys.

Ecer *an acre,* v. æcer.

ECG [*Frs.* ich: *Plat.* ekse *f.*] 1. *An edge, a sharpness;* acies.

Eastan from the east th au

Eastcentingas East Kentians or men of East Kent Cantii Orientalis incolæ Chr. 1009 Ing p 183, 17

Easter, pl eastra Easter th an

Easterlic adj Easter th an v easter

Ea-sted, es; n A rivers bank th an

2 East-folc people of the east Som

Eat-ben, e; f an humble

2 Ea-þyrl an eye hole window v eag-þyrl

~~seadest most~~ easily th an

Easten from the east Cd 27, th 35, 16

Eadost most easily

Eatol terrible Beo K 495

Eatole Italy Som

Eatol-waru Italians Itali Som

Eawian to shew v eawan

Him eawde Bd 2.6 ... p 508, 24 Beo gl

Eaxan-muda, an m Exmouth, etc

Eaxel, e; f; a shoulder Beo gl

Eaxl-gestella an; m a shoulder or arm companion, a bosom friend; comes, qui est a latere Beo 101 K 2652: 129 K 3426 Grim II 146, 32 v stealla

2 Ebere-morð mani-fest, or notorious murder manslaughter; homicidium manifestum Som

Ebolsan to blaspheme blasphemare Som

Ebylgan to be angry; irasci Ben

3 Ecan [34 a 9]

3 Eberþring v eofor þring

4 [24 a 8]

East-suð south east Som

East-weg, es m east way Cd 174. th 220, 11

Eatan to eat Som v etan

Ecg-bana an m a sword killer Beo K 2526

Ecg-clif es n a sea cliff Beo K 5781

Ecg-hete es m war hate

~~Efen-gemæcca consortia~~

~~jure æqualis~~ Ecg lye

Efen-gesceaft an even creature

Efen-gefeormian to sup

Eged edæd, a warped

Ecilma

Ecelma

Ecilmeht, one who had gout in his feet, podagricus Som

Eg-sotlice

Edderne

Edcerre, es; m a return

Edcwelm

pleasure

coolness

Eddyse

Edcer-bryce a hedge breaking Som v edor bryce

Edre a vein v æddre

es; m a tumult

Ed-hwyrft reditus Beo K 2562 Grm II 758, 20

Edignes happiness Som v eadignes

Edisc-weard a park ward a keeper Som vivarii custos Cot 26 Lye

Edicung young Som v ed-geong

Edlæht renewed v ed-læcan

~~Ed-wendan to~~ ~~Beo K 2~~

bellicum odium ... war or savage courage Beo K 1185

Ecg-præc, es

Efen-hebban

Efen-herian to praise together; collaudare Som

Efen-herenis, a praising together K 331 Som

Efen-læcestre, an imitator; imitatrix Som

Efen-læcung, a imitating; imitatio; comparatio Som

Efen-metan to make equal, compare Som

Efen-mete even meat

Efen-niwe

Efen-swedylic, consubstantial Som

~~Efen-peowa, an m a fellow servant~~ Matt 18, 28, 29 v Efen-þeow

Edlesende

Edlesende Som v ed-lesende

Edmeleu holy service or ceremonies; sacra orgia Som

Ed-mod mild, obedient Ben v eadmod

Edneow

Cd 7 Th p 10, 25 v ed-niw, &c.

Edulf-staf

Ed-wendan

Cd 223

v edcer

Edwyrþan to amelio rate; meliorari to un warp Lye

Efen-læcung; a ... imitatio Th Ak

Efen-rice, esm of equal power; æqualis potentia, equipollens Bd. 5, 10 equal sorrow compassion Lye

Efen-sarig even or equally sorry; æque tristis; compassus Gr. Dial

Efen-sarignys

Efen-bwære agreeing; concors Lye

Edulf-staf a staff, support; sustentaculum Cd. 55 Th p 68, 16 Grm II 525, 21

Efen-cesten the herb mercury; mercurialis Som, Ben Lye

Efen-nu even now; etiam nunc, ecce Ben pref Lye

~~Efen-ceasterwaran fellow citizens~~

Efen, cristen, a fellow Christian Lye v emn

treasure Beo K 557

Ed-nescafe, a reverse

Ed-neowung a renewing

Efen even Som v efen

Efen-læfte the herb mercury Som v efen-cesten

Efen ... Grm II 635, 19 & 653, 1&2

Efen-beorhte even bright or equally bright

Efen-dyre alike or equally dear; æque charus Som Lye L. Alf. Guth. 2

Efen-gemæcca a companion; consort Grm II 635, 20

Efen-had esm evenhood, evenness conditio æqualis

Efen-hæftling a co-captive Mann

Efen-heafod es m co-manipulares

Efen-hlytta, a consort; consors

Efen-þeow a fellow servant Grm II 635, 23

~~Efen-wyrhta~~ ~~a coworker~~

Efen-yrfeweard a coheir Grm II 635, 24

1. Applied to the mind also, a quickness, ability; acumen, acies animi:—1. On swurdes ecge, Lk. 21, 24. Billa ecgum with edges of swords, Cd. 210. 2. Cd. 162, Mann.

Ecg-plega *play of swords, battle.*

Ecg-wal *swords' wail, slaughter.*

Ecnys, écenys, se; *f. Eternity, everlasting;* æternitas:—Bt. 42. ¶ On ecnysse *for ever,* Mk. 3, 29.

Ec-soð *but truly, but also.*

E'd [ead *happiness*] *Safety, security, happiness;* salus, asylum:—Ed monne *safety of men, the ark,* Cd. 70, Mann. Some think éd signifies *a renewing, restoration, regeneration;* renovatio: then ed monne might be translated, *regeneration of men.*

Ed-, prefixed to words, denotes *anew, again,* as the Latin re. Edniwan *to renew, to make new again;* renovare.

-ed used as a termination of *pp.* v. 23. *h.*

Ed-cenning *Regeneration;* regeneratio:—Mt. 19, 28.

Edcer, edcir, edcyr, *A return;* reditus:—Edcir þære adle *a return of the disease,* Past. 33, 7.

Ed-cuceþa *revived.*

Ed-cucian; *p.* geedcucude; *pp.* geedcucod. *To re-quicken, revive;* reviviscere:—Dial. 1, 12.

Ed-cwide *a relation, retelling.*

Ede *a flock,* v. eowed.

Eder *a hedge,* v. edor.

Edergong [ed *again,* gong *going*] *Away, journey, return;* via, reditus:—Cod. Ex. 22, b. 9.

Ed-geong, ed-gung *young, growing young again.*

Ed-gift *a re-giving, restitution,* Lye.

Ed-growung *a re-growing.*

Ed-gyldend *a remunerator, rewarder.*

Edisc, *A park,* EDISH or *aftermath;* vivarium, fœnum serotinum:—Cot. 207.

Edisc-hen *an edish hen, a quail.*

Ed-læcan; *p.* edlæhte; *pp.* geedlæht. *To repeat, renew;* repetere, Som.

Ed-læcung, e; *f. A repetition;* repetitio:—L. Eccl. 21.

Ed-leænan, ed-leanian, geed-leanian. *To reward, recompence, renew, remit;* retribuere:—Ps. 77, 22.

Ed-leænung *a rewarding,* v. ed-leanung.

Ed-lean, ead-lean, æd-lean, es; *n.* [ed *or* ead; lean *a loan*] *A reward, recompence, requital, retribution;* præmium:—Edleanes dæg, Lk. 4, 19. Þæt edlean, Bt. 3, 4.

Edleanian *to reward,* v. edleænan.

Ed-leanung, ed-leænung, e; *f. A rewarding, recompence;* retributio:—L. Ps. 102.

Ed-lesende, edlesendic; *adj. Reciprocal, relative;* relativus, Som.

Ed-lesung, e; *f. A relation, relating;* relatio, Som.

Ed-modian *to be humble, to obey,* v. eadmodan.

Ed-niw; *adj. New, again new;* novus:—Jud. 10, 6.

Ed-niwan; *adv. Anew, again;* de novo, denuo:—Jn. 3, 3.

Ed-niwian, ge-edniwian; *part.* igende; *p.* de; *pp.* ud, ed. *To make new again, to renew;* renovare:—Þu edniwast ansine eorðan, Ps. 103, 31.

Ed-niwung, e; *f. A renewing, reparation, renovation;* reparatio:—Bd. 1, 27, Resp. 1.

Edo *a flock,* v. eowed.

EDOR, eader, es; *m. A hedge, fence, a place enclosed by a hedge, a fold, dwelling, house;* sepes, domus, tecta:—Gif friman edor gegangeð *if a freeman forcibly enter a dwelling,* L. Ethelb. 30. Under edoras *under a dwelling,* Cd. 112: 114.

Edor-bryce, edor-breche *a fence-breaking, house-breaking.*

Edorcan *to chew, ruminate, consider,* v. eodorcan.

Edre, edre *a drain for liquids,* v. æddre.

Edrecan *to ruminate,* v. eodorcan.

Edrecedroc *The covering for what is chewed, the dewlap;* rumen:—Cot. 169.

Ed-rine *A meeting;* occursus:—Ps. 18, 7.

Edroc *A consideration;* ruminatio:—R. 99.

Ed-sceft, ed-sceaft, æd-sceaft *A new creation, new birth;* regeneratio:—Bt. 34, 10.

Ed-staþelian, ge-edstaþolian; *p.* de; *pp.* od. *To establish again, re-establish, restore;* restabilire:—Jos. 6, 25.

Ed-staþelig; *adj. Firm, strong;* firmus:—Jos. 6, 26.

Ed-staþelung, e; *f. An establishing again, a re-establishment, a renewing;* reparatio:—R. Ben. 36.

Ed-þingung *a reconciliation.*

Ed-wielle *A whirlpool, dizziness;* vortex aquæ:—Cot. 86.

Ed-wihta *a reproach,* Mann. v. edwit.

Ed-winde *a winding again, a vortex.*

Edwist, ædwist, ætwist; *f. Being, subsistence, existence, essence, substance;* substantia:—Gen. 7, 4.

Edwistlic; *adj. Existing, subsisting, substantial, substantive;* substantialis:—Ic eom, is edwistlic word *I am, is the substantive* [*existing*] *verb,* Elf. gr.

Ed-wit, ædwit *Reproach, disgrace, blame, contumely;* opprobrium:—Ps. 14, 4: 21, 5.

Ed-witan, ædwitan, ætwitan; *p.* hi edwioton; *pp.* ædwitod, edwited. *To reproach, blame, upbraid;* exprobrare:—Bd. 5, 13.

Edwitfullice; *adv. Disgracefully;* probrosum:—Cot. 195.

Efalsian *to blaspheme.*

Efalsung *blasphemy.*

Efel *evil, bad,* v. yfel.

Efeleac *An onion, a scallion;* cepe, Som.

EFEN, æfen; *adj.* [*Plat. Dut.* effen, even: *Ger.* eben] EVEN, *equal;* æquus, Som.

Efen *an evening,* v. æfen.

Efen-, in composition, denotes *even, equal,* represented by co-, con-, com-, *as*

Efen-bisceop *a co-bishop.*

Efen-bliesian *to congratulate.*

Efen-ceaster-waran *co-citizens.*

Efen-cuman *to convene, to assemble together.*

Efen-eald *coeval, of the same age.*

Efen-ece *coeternal.*

Efen-ehð *Evening;* vesper:—Chr. 894, Ing.

Efen-feola *so many, as many.*

Efen-gefeonde *rejoicing together.*

Efen-gelic *like, coequal.*

Efen-læcan, geefen-læcan; *part.* ende; *p.* efen-læhte. *To be equal, like, to imitate;* imitari:—Mt. 6, 8.

Efenlic; *adj. Even, equal;* æqualis:—Bd. 4, 17.

Efenlice; *adv.* EVENLY, *alike;* æque:—Bd. 3, 23.

Efenlicnes, se; *f. Evenness, equality;* æqualitas:—Past. 17, 9.

Efen-mære *equally large.*

Efen-niht *even night, equinox.*

Efennys, efynnis, se; *f.* EVENNESS, *equality;* æqualitas:—Ps. 10, 8.

Efen swa *even so, even as.*

Efen-þrowian *to suffer together, to compassionate, commiserate.*

Efer-wic, Eofer-wic, Eofor-wic, Euer-wic, Euor-wic, Eoferwic-ceaster [ea-ure-wic *castrum ad vel secus aquam* URE, Som.] *York;* Eboracum:—Chr. 189, &c.

Efese *Eaves of a house, a brim, brink;* margo:—L. Ps. 101, 8.

Efesham, Eofesham, Euesham [*H.* Evisham: Efes *a brim;* ham *a dwelling, residence on the bank of a river*] *Evesham, Worcestershire,* Chr. 1054.

Efesian *to shave*, v. efsian.
Efestan *To hasten, assemble*; properare:—*Bd.* 2, 2.
Efesung, e; *f. A polling, rounding, shearing, compassing*; tonsura:—¶ Efesung-sceara *a pair of scissors* or *shears.*
Efeta, efete *An* EFT, *a newt, lizard*; lacerta:—*Elf. gl.* 14.
Efin, efn, efna *even*, v. efen.
Efnan, æfnan *To perform*; perpetrare:—*Cd.* 181.
Efne, æfne, eofne; *interj. Lo! behold! truly!* en! ecce!—*Mt.* 17, 3.
Efne-cuman *to convene*, v. efencuman.
Efne-geceigan *to assemble, convoke.*
Efnes, se; *f. Equity, justice*; æquitas:—*Ps.* 118, 75: 142, 12.
Efn-esne *a fellow servant.*
Efne-spedilic *of the same substance, consubstantial.*
Efn-lic *equal*, v. efenlic.
Efn-ling *A consort, an equal, a fellow*; consors:—*Ps.* 44, 9.
Efolsian *to blaspheme*, v. ebalsan.
Efolsung *blasphemy*, v. ebolsung.
Efor *a boar*, v. eafor.
Efor-wicingas; *pl. The people of York, Chr.* 918.
Efosode *shaved*, v. efsian.
Efre *ever*, v. æfer.
Efsian, efesian, afesian; *p.* efsode, efosode; *pp.* geefsod. *To cut in the form of eaves, to round, shear, shave*; tondere:—Man ne mot hine efsian, *Jud.* 13, 5: *Lev.* 19, 27.
Efsiend, efsigend *A shaver, barber*; tonsor, *Som.*
Efsod *shaved*, v. efsian.
Efst *a hastening, speed, Lye.*
Efstan, æfstian; *part.* efstende; *imp.* efst; *p.* efste, hi efston. *To hasten, make haste to go, to strive*; festinare:—Þa efste he, *Lk.* 19, 6: *Ps.* 106, 18.
Eft *again, back, afterward*, v. æft.—In composition it has the same effect as the Latin re-, retro-.
Eft-agyfan *to give back*; reddere, *i. e.* re-dare.
Eft-betæht, æft-beteht *re-assigned, re-delivered, given back.*
Eft-cierran *to return.*
Eft-cuman *to come back.*
Eft-edwitan *to reprove, upbraid again.*
Efter *after*, v. æfter.
Efter-filginc *a following after, a pursuing.*
Efter-genga *a successor*, v. æftergenga.
Eft-gecigan, eft-gecigean, *to recall, call back.*
Eft-gelæt *bring back*, v. gelædan.
Eft-gelic *again like, in like manner, likewise, accordingly.*

Eft-hweorfan *to turn back, return.*
Eft-lesing *redemption.*
Eft-oncnawan *to know again.*
Eft-ongen-bigan *to untwist again, to unwreathe.*
Eft-sittan *to sit again, reside.*
Eft-sona; *adv.* [eft *after*; sona *soon*] EFTSOONS, *soon after, again, a second time*; iterum:—*Mk.* 10, 1.
Eft-spellung *a recapitulation.*
Eft swa micel *even so much*; eft swa miceles *for so much, at that price, Som.*
Eft syððan *after that, furthermore.*
Eftyr *after*, v. æfter.
Efyngelic *even like, alike, equal, coequal.*
Efynnis *evenness, equity*, v. efennys.
Efyr *a boar*, v. eafor.
Egbuend, egbugend *An inhabitant, a dweller*; incola:—*Chr.* 973.
EGE, æge, eige; *m. Fear, terror, dread*; timor:—And beo eower ege, *Gen.* 9, 2. Ege drihtnea, *Ps.* 18, 10, v. egesa.
Ege; *g.* egan; *pl. nom.* egan; *g.* egna *an eye*, v. eage.
Egean *to harrow* or *break clods.*
Ege-full, ege-ful; *adj. Fearful, terrible, dreadful*; terribilis:—Mære God and mihtig and egefull, *Deut.* 10, 17: *Bt.* 18, 2.
Egehealdan *To hold in fear, correct*; corripere:—*Ps.* 93, 10.
Egeland *an island*, v. ealand.
Egeleas; *adj. Fearless*; impavidus:—*Past.* 36, 1.
Egen *fear*, v. ege.
Egenu *a little round heap*; glomulus, *Som.*
Egenwirht *Hire, wages, a gift*; merces:—*Ps.* 126, 4, *MS. Tr. Cam.*
Egenys, egesfulnes, se; *f. Fearfulness, fear*; timor:—*Ps.* 88, 39.
Egesa *horror*, v. egsa.
Egesful, egesfullic *fearful*, v. egefull.
Egesfulnes *fear*, v. egenys.
Eges-grima, egese-grimma *A witch, sorceress, bugbear*; masca, *Som.*
Egesian, egsian; *p.* geegsode; *pp.* geegsod. *To affright, terrify*; terrere:—*Jud.* 4, 17: 7, 22.
Egeslic; *def.* se egeslica; *adj.* [*Dut.* ysselyk: *Kil.* eyselick: *Ger. Wil.* egeslich] *Fearful, terrible, dreadful*; terribilis:—Ealla hu egeslic þeos stow ys, *Gen.* 28, 17: *Bt.* 35, 6.
Egeslice; *adv. Fearfully*; terribiliter:—*Æqu. Vern.* 43.
Egesung, egsung, e; *f. A threatening, fear, dread*; commina-tio:—*Jud.* 16, *Thw. Hep.* p. 161, 37.
Egeðe *A rake, harrow*; rastrum, *Som.*
Egeðere *A raker*; occator, *Som.*
Eggian *To* EGG, *excite*; excitare, *Lye.*
Eghþyrl *an eye hole, a window*, v. eag-dura.
Eghwelc *all, every*, v. æghwilc.
Egipt, Egypt, *Egypt, an Egyptian*;—Pharao aras and eall Egipta folc, *Ex.* 12, 30. On eallum Egiptalande, *Ex.* 9, 11. Eallum Egiptum, *Gen.* 45, 9.
Egiptisc, Egiptisce, Ægiptisc; *def.* se Egiptiscea; *adj. Belonging to Egypt, an Egyptian*; Ægyptius:—Sum Egiptisc man sloh sumne Ebreiscne, *Ex.* 2, 11. An Egiptisc esne us generede, *Ex.* 2, 19. Se Egyptiscea cyng, *Ex.* 1, 17.
Egiðe *a rake*, v. egeðe.
EGLA, egle; *f. A sprout, tender shoot, the beard of corn, the pricks of a thistle, a thistle, that which pricks, trouble*; festuca, carduus:—Ic ateo þa egle of þinum eage, *Lk.* 6, 41, 42.
Egland *an island*, v. ealand.
Egle *a prick*, v. egla.
Egle; *adj. Troublesome, hateful*; odiosus:—*Basil. R.* 8.
Egle-edwaelle *a channel for water.*
Eglian, eglan, elan; eglað, eglæð, egleð; *p.* eglde, eglede, aglade; *sub.* hi eglion, eglian. *To feel pain, to ail, grieve, trouble, torment*; dolere:—Gif men innan wyrmas eglian *if worms trouble men within, Herb.* 2, 10. It is more frequently used as the Latin dolet, tædet, as, Me egleð *it grieves me*; Me tædet, *L. Edm. pol. in pref. W. p.* 73, 26.
Ego *an eye*, v. eage.
Egonesham [*F.* Eignesham: *Gerv.* Egenesham] *Ensham, Oxfordshire, Chr.* 571, *Ing.*
Egor *Nine ounces* or *inches, a span*; dodrans:—*Cot.* 64, *Som.*
Egor, [*Icel.* ægir *m.*] *The sea, water*; æquor:—¶ Egor stream *water of the sea, Bt. R.* p. 176.
Egsa, ægsa, egesa, an [*Ger. Wil.* egiso] *Fear, horror, dread, what causes fear, a storm, slaughter*; terror:—And beoð hungor and egsan of heofone, *Lk.* 21, 11: *Bd.* 4, 12.
Egsian *to frighten*, v. egesian.
Eg-stream *a dire stream.*
Egsung *a threatening*, v. egesung.
Egða *An instrument to beat out corn*; tribula:—*R.* 2, *Lye.*
Egðe *a rake*, v. egeðe.
Egðer *either*, v. ægðer.
Egþyrl *an eye hole, a window*, v. eag-dura.

to esp out, spring up again; renascitum — Eft-togeten afosus Bd 4,16 — Eft-wendan to turn back; redire C Mk R 1,46 Lye — Eft-gewyrd, Efn-gemetgian comparativi Ps. 48, 12, 21 Lye — Eft-cennis to evenness P 111

1) Efn, on efn, on emn even, over against, e regione contra Beo K 5801

3) Efne even, just; Cd 169 th K 154, 11 v. efen

4) Efne alumen, et stypteria R 41: 56 Lye

5) Efne-eald even old, co-eval R 9 Lye — Efne-gecerran to turn about; convertere C Lk 7, 9 — Efne-gehatrigan to restrain, co-angustare C R Lk 19, 43 — Efne-[illegible] to agree, consentire C R Lk 23, 5 Lye — Efne-spittan to spit together, conspuere C Mk 14, 65 — Efne-gepeccan to think alike, to agree, consentire C Mt 18, 19 — Efne-geponcigan to give thanks together; confunctim gratias agere R Lk 15, 9 — Efne-[illegible] a conspiracy C[illegible] 9, 22 — Efne-pegn a fellow servant C Mt 18, 29 — Efn-licnes, se; f an equality Past 17, Past 17, 9 Lye — Efn-peow a fellow servant Past 29.

Efor-fearn wallfern Herb 85 a Sthl. eafor-fearn — Efor-prote the sow-thistle[illegible]; Scilla Som v. eofor-prote

K 1668

afterwards Cd 169 th 212, 15 v. æfteweard

Eft-ancndwian to restore, save; set there — R Mt 8, 25 Lye — Eft-awacian to reawaken, to revive, resuscitare Bd 5, 12 Lye — Eft-awunende dwelt again, returned; reversus C Lk 8, 55 — Eft-colian to recool; refrigescere C Mt 24, 12 — Eft-cymed

Eft-edniwung a renewing of the kind; regeneratio C Mt 19, 28 — Eft-cyrnan to return Lye Som v cerran — Eft-gan to go again; iterare Ben — Eft-gebicgan to buy again, redimere Som — Eft-foerda again; recessit R Lk 4, 13 — faran Lye — Eft-gebetan to make better again, to restore R Mk 3, 5 Lye — Eft-gecyrran again pursue Bt R 4 F K 46, 13 — Eft-gelangian to send for again, recall Lye — Eft-gemyndian to remind again C Mt 26, 75 Lye — Eft-geniwian to renew again C Mt 17, 11 — Eft-myndig mindful C Jn 12, 16 — Eft-ncnwian to restore C Mk 8, 25 Lye — Eft-rædan to read after Som — Eft-sceawian to look after, to regard C Mt 22, 16 Lye — Eft-selenis a going back; [illegible] Ben — Eft-sid, es; m a renewed journey Beo K 2668

Efn-gedcelan to share alike or evenly Cd 146 th K 183, 22 — Efn-ian to perform Cd 181 th K 227, 7, 13 — 3th Indices

Eft-syne, es; m a return Beo K 5788

Eg huona undique C Mk 1, 45

Egan tabescere — Egbuan to inhabit Ben, incolere Ben — Egere a harrower Som Ben v egepere

Egleswurd Eglesworth Chr 963 v Aglesword

Egor-here water-host Cd 69 th 84, 23

Eft-onfon to take again, recapere Bd 4, 10 Lye

Eft-sellan to give back; retribuere Lye — Eft-sidian to go back; redire Cd 206 th p 255, 31 — Eft-sprytan

Æg-wearde maris custodia
Beo K Apx 480

~~Ellen-seóc~~

Ellen-mærðo, e; f
glory Beo K 1649
2941

1 Ellen-spræc, e; f
a bold speech Th. an

Ellen-þriste boldly
daring Th. an

Ellen-weorces, n
heroic work Beo K 1315

Eldo-gebunden bound
with age, senectute
vinctus Beo K 4218

Elles-hwergen elsewhere
aliorsum Beo K 5176

Elles-hwider to
another place
aliorsum Elf gr 38

O1

Ellor-sīð, es; m
a strange path,
death Beo K 4897

Eller-seóc (g ellen strong)
deadly sick Beo K 4501

El-land, es; n
foreign
land; terra peregrina
Beo K Apx 6034

Elmes-hlaf, es; m an
alms loaf Th. an.

Elmesse, an; f Alms
Th. an. v. Ælmesse

Ellor-gæst, es; m
a strange guest,
stranger Beo K 2697
Ellor-gæst, es; m fiend
spirit a strange spirit Beo K

Elhtan to persecute
Lk 249 Th 24, 25
v ehtan, which should be Ehtan

Elfen, gelfenne
Grim
268.

O 2

Eh-pyrl, es; n
Th. An.

Elnes of strength Cd 47
Th 59, 22

Ehtung; e; f Persecution Th. an.

Elf, e; 1. Æl-elfenne

Elhwelc every Th An v. æghwelc

v. Supl. Ellen

Elne wild-man
Som v

Elseg icy Cd 213 Th 267, 10

Ellebor Hellebore
helleborum Som

Eðe traha R. 1 Lye

O Elotr
Som v elektre

Ele-horn an oil horn Som

Ellen-camp a powerful
contest, a fight; pugna
Grim II 44, 6

Elpan-ban ivory
Som. v elpen-ban

Elesceocche fisclum
R 66 Lye

Elra Strange foreign
peregrinus Beo K 1498

Elesdrisma

Ellen-campian To contend
vigorously, to fight its champions, to fight the combat
pugilare Cot 40

Som, Lye

Ellen-dæd, e; f a powerful, bold or valiant
deed, a good deed;
facinus, praeclarum
facinus Lye Grim II 44, 6 Beo 69 K 1793 Cd 24

Egylt *a fault*, v. ægylt.
Egypte; *nom. pl. The Egyptians; g.* Egypta, Ægypt *Egypt*, v. Egipt.
Egysful *fearful*, v. egesful.
Ehennys, se; *f. Modesty;* pudor, *Som.*
Eher *an ear of corn*, v. ear.
Ehsle *a shoulder*, v. eaxl.
Ehsyne *A face, countenance;* facies, *Som.*
Ehsta *the highest*, v. heh.
Eht *value*, v. æht.
Ehta *eight*, v. eahta.
Ehtan, ehtian; he eht, hi ehtað [æht, eht *property*] 1. *To follow after, chase, pursue;* persequi. 2. *To persecute, annoy, afflict;* infestare:—1. Ne eht he nanre wuhte *he pursues not any thing, Bt.* 42. Hig ehton wild-deor *they chased wild beasts, Coll. Mon.* 2. Þonne hi eow ehtað on þysse byrig, *Mt.* 10, 23: 5, 11.
Ehtend *A persecutor;* persecutor:—*Ors.* 6, 9.
Ehteoða, ehteða *eighth*, v. eahtoðe.
Ehtere, es; *m. A persecutor;* persecutor:—*Mt.* 5, 44.
Ehþyrl *eye hole, a window*, v. eagdura.
Ehtian *To esteem, deem, value;* æstimare:—*Bd.* 5, 6.
Ehting, e; *f. Persecution;* persecutio:—*Ors.* 6, 23.
Ehtnes, eahtnes, se; *f. Persecution;* persecutio:—*Mt.* 5, 10.
Ehtoða, ehtuða *eighth*, v. eahtoða.
Ehtr *a persecutor*, v. ehtere.
Eige *fear*, v. ege.
Eigland *an island*, v. ealand.
Eipe *an assembly*, v. heap.
Eiseg; *adj.* [*Dut.* yzing] *Rough, hard;* ferreus:—*Cd.* 213.
Eisile *vinegar*, v. eced.
El *an eel*, v. æl.
-el, -ol [*Icel.* -ill, -ull] a termination denoting persons, as, Forridel *an outrider;* bydel *a herald.* It denotes also inanimate objects, as, Gyrdel *a girdle;* stypel *a steeple.*
Elæs *hedgehogs, Som.*
Elboga, eleboga, elnboga [*Dut.* elleboog] *An* ELBOW; cubitus:—Fæðm betwuxt elboga and hand-wrist *a fathom is between the elbow and wrist, R.* 72.
Elc *each*, v. ælc.
Elch *An* ELK; alce, *Som.*
Elcian, ælcian; *part.* elcigende. *To put off, delay;* differre:—*Elf. gr.* 25.
Elcor, elcur *otherwise, else*, v. ælcor.
Elcung *a delay*, v. ylding.
Eld *age, time*, v. yld: *fire*, v. æled.

Eldan *to linger*, v. yldan.
Eldas *elders, men*, v. yld.
Eldcung *delay*, v, ylding.
Eldendlic *old like, slow.*
Eldor *a prince*, v. ealdor.
Eldra-fæder *a grandfather.*
Eldran *elders, parents*, v. ealdor.
Eldung *delay*, v. ylding.
Ele *a lamprey*, v. æl.
ELE, æl, es; *m.* [*Dut.* oly] OIL; oleum:—Hund sestra eles *a hundred measures of oil, Lk.* 16, 6:—Æle bracene, *Lev.* 6, 21.
Elebeam, es; *m.* [ele *oil;* beam *a tree*] *An olive-tree;* olea:—An twig of anum elebeame, *Gen.* 8, 11.
Elebeamen *oily.*
Eleberge, eleberia [ele *oil;* berge *a berry*] *An olive, the fruit of an olive;* oliva:—Þat ys elebergena, *Lk.* 22, 39: *Ps.* 51, 8.
Eleboga *an elbow*, v. elboga.
Elebyt [ele *oil;* byt *a bottle*] *An oil vessel* or *cruet, a chrismatory;* lenticula:—*Cot.* 121.
Electre, elehtre *Amber, myrrh;* electrum:—*Elf. gl.* 14.
Ele-fæt *an oil-vat, cruise* or *pot.*
Elehtre *amber*, v. electre.
Elelænd *strange*, v. ellend.
Elelendisca *A stranger;* advena:—*L. Ps.* 17, 47.
Elesealf *oil-salve, sweet balm.*
Ele-treow *an oil-tree, an olive.*
Ele-twig *an olive twig, a small branch of olive.*
ELF, ælf, es; *pl.* ælfas, ælfen [*Plat. Ger.* elf *m: Ger.* alp *m: Dan.* alfe *m: Swed.* elfwa *f: Icel.* álfr *m.* genius] *An* ELF, *a fairy;* lamia:—*Jdth. Thw.* p. 21, 11.
Elfenne *the night-mare*, v. ælfsidenne.
Elian *to trouble*, v. eglian.
Elig, Elige, Helige, Ely, Eligburg. ELY, *Cambridgeshire, Chr.* 673. ¶ Heliga-land, Elige, Eligea *the Isle of Ely.*
Ellarn *an elder-tree*, v. ellen.
Elle *the rest.*
Ellean, v. ellen.
ELLEN; *g.* elne; *f.* [*Norse*, eliun] *Strength, power, valour, courage, fortitude;* vis animi:—Þridde is ellen *the third is fortitude, Bt.* 27, 2: *Cd.* 47.
Ellen, ellarn [*Plat.* elloorn] *An elder-tree;* sambucus:—*Cot.* 165.
Ellend; *adj. Strange, foreign;* exterus:—*Bt. R.* p. 158. In ellende *in foreign land, far, R. Mt.* 21, 33.
Ellen-dun [*Ella's hill*] *Allington, near Amesbury, Wilts., Chr.* 823.
Ellengodnes *zeal*, v. ellenwodnes.
Ellen-læca *a champion.*

Ellen-rof *remarkably strong, powerful, daring, brave.*
Ellen-wodian *to contend valiantly.*
Ellen-wodnes, ellen-godnes, se; *f. Zeal, envy, emulation;* zelus:—*Ps.* 78, 5: 118, 139.
Ellen-wyrt *elderwort, wallwort, danewort.*
Elles; *adv.* ELSE, *otherwise, amiss;* aliter:—Elles næbbe gemede, *Mt.* 6, 1. Na elles *or na hu elles not otherwise, Bt.* 32, 1. No hwit elles *nothing else, Bd.* 2, 14. Elles hwær *elsewhere.* Elles mæst *chiefly.* Elles ofer *from some other place.*
Ellicor *elsewhere*, v. ælcor.
ELLM [*Plat. Dut.* olm *m: Ger.* ulme *f: Dan. Swed.* alm *f: Icel.* almr *m.*] *An* ELM; ulmus:—*L. Can. Edg.* 16.
Ellnung *emulation*, v. elnung.
Ellor; *adv. Elsewhere;* alias:—*Cd.* 79: *Jdth.* 10.
Ellreord elreordig *barbarous*, v. ælreord.
Ellþeod, ellþied *Banishment;* exilium:—*Ors.* 3, 7.
Ellþiodig, ellþeodig; *adj. Foreign, an alien,* peregrinus:—*Cd.* 89.
Ellyn *zeal*, v. elnung.
Elm *an elm*, v. ellm.
Elmihtiga *the Almighty*, v. ælmiht.
Elnboga, elneboga *an elbow*, v. elboga.
Elne *of strength*, v. ellen.
ELNE, alne; *f.* [*Dut.* el *f: Frs.* yelne] *An* ELL, *a measure;* ulna:—Hwylc eower mæg ican ane elne to hys anlicnesse, *Lk.* 12, 25: *Mt.* 6, 27.
Elnian; *p.* ode; *pp.* geelnod. *To strive, endeavour earnestly, contend, emulate;* zelare:—Þa elnode he hine, *Gen.* 48, 2.
Elnung, ellnung, ellyn, e; *f. Zeal, hot emulation, envy;* zelus:—*Ps.* 118, 139.
Elp *an elephant*, v. ylp.
Elpen-ban *an elephant's bone, ivory*, v. ylpen.
Elpen-bænen *made of ivory*, v. ylpen bænen.
Elpend, ylpend, es; *m. An elephant;* elephas:—Hu hy þa elpendas beswican mihton *how they could disperse the elephants, Ors.* 4, 1, *Bar.* p. 134, 9; p. 135, 8. ¶ Elpend-toð *an elephant's tooth.*
Elreord, elreordig *barbarous*, v. ælreord.
-els, a termination of nouns usually masculine; as, scyccels *a cloak, mantle;* wæfels *a coat;* pallium: recels *frankincense;* freols *a festival.*
Elreordignes, se; *f. Barbarous-*

ness, outlandishness; barbaries, *Som.*
Elriord *barbarous,* v. ælreord.
Elsta *eldest,* v. eald.
Elþeodig, elþiodig *foreign,* v. ælþeodig.
Elþeodiglice *abroad,* v. ælþeodelice.
Elþeodignes *a travelling,* v. ælþeodignes.
Elþeodin, elþeodisc *foreign,* v. ælþeodig.
Elþiod *abroad.*
Elþiodig *strange, foreign,* v. ælþeodig.
Elþiodigian *to travel.*
Elys *hedgehogs, Som.*
Em-, in composition, denotes *even, equal;* as efen; also, as emb *about.*
Emb, embe *about, round, around,* v. ymb.
Embegan *to go round.*
Embegang *A going round, circuit;* circuitus:—*R. Conc.* 3.
Embegyrdan *to surround, begird.*
Embeht *an office,* v. ambeht.
Embehtan *to minister, serve.*
Embeht men *servants,* v. ambeht.
Embehtsumnes, se; *f. A compliance, kind attention;* obsequium, *Lye.*
Embe-hydignes, se; *f. Solicitude;* solicitudo:—*C. R. Ben.* 43, *Lye.*
Embene *Amiens, in Picardy,* Ambianum:—*Chr.* 884.
Embe-smeagung *a considering about, experience.*
Embe-þencean *to think about, to be anxious for, careful.*
Embiht *an office,* v. ambeht.
Emblennan *To enclose, press;* circumvallare, *Lye.*
Emblong *at length,* v. ymblong.
Emb-ryne *a running round, a circle,* v. ymb-ren.
Emb-snydan, emsnidan *To cut round, circumcise;* circumcidere:—*Lk.* 2, 21.
Embstemn *by turns.*
Embutan *about,* v. ymbe-utan.
Embwlatian *to consider,* v. ymbwlatian.
Eme *Deceit, fraud;* fraus, *Som.*
Emel *A canker-worm, weevil;* eruca:—*Ps.* 77, 51.
Emertung, e; *f. A tickling, an itching;* prurigo—*R.* 11.
Emet; *pl.* emittan *an ant,* v. æmet.
Emetig *empty,* v. æmti.
Emfeála, emfela *about so much, just so much, L. In.* 78.
Emhydig *anxious,* v. ymbhidig.
Emlang *equally long.*
Emleof *equally dear.*
Emlice, emnelice, emnlice; *adv. Even like, evenly, patiently;* æqualiter:—*Ors.* 2, 1.
Emlicnes, se; *f. Evenness, equality, equity;* æquitas:—*Ps.* 95, 10.
Emn-, Emne-, in composition, *even, equal,* as efen and emb; as Emneþeow, efneþeowa, efenþeowa *an equal* or *fellow servant.*—Emnecristen, efnecristen *a fellow christian.*—Emnescolere, efenscolere *a school fellow.*
Emn:—On emn *opposite, over against, Gen.* 16, 12. Þær on emn, *Gen.* 21, 19: *Jos.* 10, 5.
Emn-æþel *equally noble.*
Emne; *adj. Equal, just;* æquus:—And emne wæga and emne gemetu and sestras, *Lev.* 19, 36.
Emne; *adv. Equally;* æqualiter:—*Bt.*
Emnecristen *a fellow christian,* v. emn.
Emnelice *evenly,* v. emlice.
Emnes *evenness,* v. emnys.
Emnettan *to make even, smooth,* v. emnian.
Emnette *Evenness, level ground;* planities:—*Ors.* 4, 8.
Emnian, ge-emnian. *To equal, to make alike;* adæquare:—*Bt.* 19.
Emniht *equal night, the equinox.*
Emn-land *even land, a plain.*
Emnlice *equally,* v. emlice.
Emn-ræðe [hreðe *cruel*] *equally cruel.*
Emn-sár *equal sorrow, condolence.*
Emn-sarian *to be alike sorry, to condole.*
Emn-sarig, em-sarig *equally sorry, condoling.*
Emnys, emnes, se; *f. Evenness, equity;* æquitas:—*Ps.* 16, 3. ¶ To emnes *opposite to, opposite, over against, Ors.* 1, 1: *Bar.* p. 24, 17, 20.
Emnyttan *to make equal.*
Empire *An empire;* imperium, *Lye.*
Emptian *To* EMPTY; evacuare, *Som.*
Emrene *a circle,* v. ymb-ren.
Emsarig *condoling,* v. emnsarig.
Emsnidan *to circumcise,* v. embsnydan.
Emswapen *clothed;* amictus, *Som.*
Emta *leisure,* v. æmta.
Emtig *empty,* v. æmti.
Emtrymming, e; *f. A fortress, fence;* munimentum, *Som.*
Em-twa *between two.*
Em-wlatian *to look around, to behold, consider,* v. ymbwlatian.
-en is the termination of nouns. A few of these are masculine, as drihten *a lord,* from driht *people;* but many feminine, (corresponding with the *Ger.* -in: *Dan.* -inde) as þinen *a maid servant,* from þen; þeowen *a famale slave, from* þeow; byrgen *a tomb;* sylen *a gift.* Some are neuter; as, mægen *strength;* mæden *a maiden;* midlen *a middle.*
-en, and sometimes -an, is also a termination of adjectives and participles from an, which is from unan *to give, add,*—hence from gold *gold,* is gylden *golden;* stæn *a stone,* stænen *stony;* arisen *risen,* from arisan *to rise;* dolfen *digged,* from delfan *to dig;* witen *known,* from witan *to know.*
Encgel *an angel,* v. engel.
-end, the ending of nouns, denoting the agent; *as,* wegferend *a way-faring man.*
ENDE, geende, ænde, es; *m.* [*Dut.* eind] *An* END; terminus:—Ac nys þonne gyt se ende, *Mt.* 24, 6. Feower endas þyses middangeardes *four* [*ends*] *quarters of this world, Ors.* 2, 1.
Ende, eonde *A sort, part, corner;* species:—*Bd.* 3, 14.
Ende *and,* v. and.
-ende, the termination forming the active participle; as, wegferende *way-faring.*
Endebyrdan, geendebyrdan; *p.* de; *pp.* geendebyrd, geendebyrded. *To set in order, adjust, dispose;* disponere:—*Ps.* 49, 6.
Endebyrdlic; *adj. Belonging to order, ordinal;* ordinalis:—*Elf. gr.*
Endebyrdlice; *adv. Orderly, in order, succession;* successive:—*Bd.* 3, 24.
Endebyrdnes, endebyrnes, se; *f. Order, disposition, method, way, manner, means;* ordo:—*Lk.* 1, 3, 8.
Endeleás; *adj.* ENDLESS, *infinite, eternal;* æternus:—Endeleas wundor, *Bt.* 36, 1.
Endeleaslice; *adv.* ENDLESSLY, *eternally;* infinite, *Som.*
Endeleasnys, se; *f.* ENDLESSNESS, *eternity;* infinitas, *Som.*
Endemæst *endmost, last.*
Endemes, endemest, ændemes, ændemest; *adv. Equally, likewise, in like manner, together;* pariter:—*Bt.* 41, 1.
Endemestnes, se; *f. An extremity;* extremitas:—*R. Ben. interl.* 6.
Endenehst, endenexta, endenihsta; *adj. The nighest end, the last, uttermost;* ultimus:—*Dial.* 1, 12.
Ende-sæta *limits, boundaries.*
Ende-spæc *an endspeech, epilogue.*
Ende-stæf, endstæf *an epilogue, conclusion, destruction.*
Endian *to end,* v. ge-endian.
Endlufon, endleofun, ændlefen,

2 ymnes plane
to ymnes over
against Tr. p. 24

ymnesm ise well

s ymnan

Ymne-scolere,

schoolfellow

3 Ymm-sange

Ymn

volentes

7

near 34 42 Ymm-
geow a fellow servant Lye

Ym-ryht sequence

Ym-sittan to sit round, circumsiste Ben. Lu

Embe-den Embe-doen

circumdare ymniht

3. Ende-byrdnes

embe-hembend circumdat Cot 214

embe-hwyrfan

Embe-stand an to stand
about Lk 12,1 Lye

embe-hwyrft Embe-panc animadversio
Conf. R Conc. Lye

Embene, confessed

Summan to embehemm

Somne to Ymus Cot 88

Endebyrdes orderly
Ælf. Ps 44,41

Endebyrdian to arrange, order them

Ende-dæg the last
day Som Bea K 1268

8 Embe-utstandan to stand without. Lk 14,47

Emb-faran to go about Ælf.

Emb-perte circuitus

Ymnete, emitte

e emb-irn
an encircling iron
a fetter

Beo 60 K 1268;
225, 6066 Grein
II 447, 30

Ende-lean, reward

sufficiens
Beo 128 K 3383
Cd 141 Th 237, 15

umbren bothoma, batha
ma Cot 124 Lye

Embrin. Balus Cot 203

Emtrymming Lidle

Emb-geniete campes
caris. Ps 82, 1 Lye

Emb-rud collar

Emb-

Emb-dan to daghe, envelop
Lye — Emb-settan to set
around, besiege Ps 2,3 Lye

Ende-seta on m
limitis in cola Beo
K 479

Ende-rim a last
number

finis Grein II 447
33 — Beo 132

II 525, 22

Endleof eleven Som

— Emb-tyrnan circum-
sceinen Som — Emb-tryming circumvallatio Lye Som

— Emb-lyllan circumdare Som

On-Engliscum gereorde in the english tongue Thorkel Lauch 364

(3) Endlyft eleventh ?l ar

Endemest endmost; last Som v endemest
2 End-stæf in epilogue, an end, death
Som v ende-stæf

Eorcan-stan es; m cod Ex 124 gen
eorcnan-stan v
Eorclan-stan es; m
Eorcnan-stan a precious stone Beo K 2416 v. l

Enge narrow; augustus Beo K 2819

Englisc-man an english man; D engen

(2) On Englisc e spræce in English speech Ælf. Som 2, 7 On pære Engliscan spræce Bede Ælf S. 12, 13

End-sægan to deliver ... end-segnan

Eord-reste lying on the ground as penitents

Eored-geatwe, an of war apparatus Beo K 5747

2 Engel an angel Som v engel

Eored-men horsemen, cerethi Lye v eorod-man, rad-here

Engla, rac of the English Lawyer jurisdiction L. Cnut pol 14.

3 Ent-cyn, es-cynnes; n Giant kind or race, gigantum genus Num 13, 33 Lye

Eorl th a man Cd 93, Th p 120, 13; 156 Th 194, 15

Eorl-weorod, es n a troop of warriors; virorum turma Beo K 5782

Engle nom ac: g Engla, d Englum pl. The Angles Rask Gr. § 101 see top of p 103

Eodor ... dor-byrce ... v edor ...

(7) Eormen-lâf, e f a great legacy: Beo K 11166

Eofer, e boar m ... Beo K 2217
79, 13 Edor v edor

Eofores-rude v Som
Eofor-lic like a boar Beo K 604
Eofor-spring (see top of p 98

Eofor ... a boar ... apri ... eforen ...
Eofor vale ... Som

Eormen-cyn es; m human race, genus humanum Beo 147 K 1909
Eormen-grund es; m the earth orbis terrarum terra Beo K 1711 Grim Myth p 83

Eormen-leaf malva erratica Mone p 538 Beo gl

Eorm an arm Som v earm

2 Eoh, es; m [that the

A horse; equus Th An He gehleop pone eoh he leapt upon the horse Brythn p 375 K. Beo K p 239 Th An p 126, 46

~~Eormen-lafe ... ~~
~~... antiquæ ...~~
~~... 488, 37~~

endlyuan ELEVEN; undecim:—Mid hira endlufon sunum, *Gen.* 32, 22: *Chr.* 71.

Endlyfta, endlefta, ændlyfta, ællyfta; seo, þæt, -e; *adj. The eleventh;* undecimus:—On þam endlyftan monðe, *Deut.* 1, 3.

Endung, geendung, e; *f. An* ENDING, *end;* finis:—*Mt.* 13, 39.

Ened [*Dut.* eend] *A duck, drake, moorhen;* anas:—*R.* 36.

Engle
Anglen the Angles or Anglo Saxons — inhabitants of a low flat pastureground, synonimous with the appellation Low saxons (Ger. Niedersachsen) The Ger. anger m Swed äng m Dan. engi Icel. engi n Eng. ing have all the signification of a meadow a low pasture ground.

Berks, ...

Engla-land *Angles' land,* ENGLAND:—*Chr.* 597, v. Engle.

Englas *angels, English,* v. engel, Engle.

Engle, Englan, Angle; *pl. nom. ac.* an; *g.* a; *d.* um, an. *Anglen, the Angles, English;* Angli. The denomination of the province and people from which the English derived their being and name. Anglen lies on the south east part of the Duchy of Sleswick, in Denmark. The majority of settlers in Britain, were from Anglen and the neighbourhood, hence this country and people derived their name *England* and *English;* England being derived from Engla land *the land or country of the Angles.*—And of Engle coman East-engle *and from Anglen came East Angles, Bd.* 1, 15, *S.* p. 483, 24. East Engla cyningas *kings of East Angles, Bd.* 2, 15, p. 518, 38. Þæt land þe man Angle hæt *the land which one calls Anglen, Ors.* 1, 1, *Bar.* p. 20, 9. Of Angle comon East Engle, and Middel Angle, and Mearce, and calle Norðymbra *from Anglen came East Angles, Middle Angles, Mercians, and all Northumbrians, Chr.* 449, *Ing.* p. 15, 1. Betweox Wealum and Englum *betwixt Welsh and English, L. Wal.* 2, *W.* p. 125, 21. Betweox Wealan and Englan, *Id.* 2, *W.* p. 125, 27. Tæcean Wealan and Englan, VI Englisce *to teach English and Welsh, six English, Id.* 37. Wealas flugon þa Englan *Welsh fled from the English, Chr.* 473.

...

Entse; *g. pl.* entsena. *A shekel, Jewish money;* siclus:—*Jos.* 7, 21.

Enwintre *a year old,* v. anwintre.

Eode *a flock,* v. eowed.

Eode *went, delivered; p. of* gan.

Eodor *a hedge,* v. edor.

Eodorcan, edorcan *To chew, ruminate;* ruminare:—*Bd.* 4, 24.

Eofel *evil,* v. yfel.

Eofera *a successor,* v. eafora.

Eoferwic *York,* v. Eferwic.

Eofesham *Evesham,* v. Efesham.

Eofet *a debt,* v. eofot.

Eofne *behold,* v. efne.

Eofolsian *to blaspheme,* v. efolsian.

Eofor *a boar,* v. eafor.

Eofora *a successor,* v. eafora.

Eofor-spreot *a boar-spear.*

Eofor-wic *York,* v. Eferwic.

Eofor-wicingas *Yorkists, people of York.*

Eofor-wic-scire *Yorkshire.*

Eofot, eofut, geeofot. *A debt;* debitum:—*L. Alf. pol.* 22.

Eofulsian *to blaspheme,* v. ebalsan.

Eofulsong, eofulsung *blasphemy.*

Eoland *an island,* v. ealand.

Eoldor *an elder, a parent,* v. ealdor.

Eolene, eolone *wild marjorum;* origanum:—*Cot.* 108.

Eolh-sand *Amber;* electrum:—*Cot.* 75.

Eom *I am;* sum, v. wesan.

Eom *to them;* for heom, him.

Eond *yond, beyond,* v. geond.

Eonde *a species,* v. ende.

Eond-liht *beyond light, brilliant.*

Eond-send *overspread,* v. geondsend.

Eonu *moreover, Som.*

Eorcnan-stan, earcnan-stan *A pearl, topaz;* topazion:—*Ps.*

...

chief, leader, general, hero; dux. 2. *An Anglo-Saxon nobleman of the highest rank, about the same as an ealdorman.* He who was in early times styled ealdorman, was afterwards denominated *an earl;* comes:—1. Se eorl wæs æðele *the chief was noble, Cd.* 59: 118. 2. On eorles tune, *L. Ethelb.* 13: *Chr.* 963.

Eorlcund; *adj. Earl kind, noble;* nobilis:—*L. Hloth.* 1.

Eorldóm, es; *m. An* EARLDOM, *the province or dignity of an earl,* the same as ealdordom, v. *Turner's Hist.* b. viii. c. 7; comitis munus:—Ælfgar eorl feng to þam eorldome þe Harold ær hæfde, *Chr.* 1053.

Eorlisc, eorllic; *adj.* EARLISH, *belonging to an earl;* nobilis, *Lye.*

Eormð *poverty,* v. yrmð.

Eornende *running,* v. yrnan.

Eornes, eornest *A duel, combat;* duellum, *Som.*

Eornest *earnest,* v. eornost.

Eornestlice, v. eornostlice.

Eornfullice; *adv. Earnestly;* studiose.

Eornigende *murmuring.*

Eornost, eornest, eornust; *adj.* EARNEST, *serious;* serius:—

¶ On eornoste, on earnust, *Mt.* 5, 18: 13, 17.

Eornostlice; *adv.* EARNESTLY, *truly*; sedulo:—*L. eccl. Cnut.* 15.

Eornostlice; *conj. Therefore, but*; ergo, igitur:—*Mt.* 10, 16.

Eorod *a band*, v. weorad.

Eorodman *A horseman*; eques:—*Bd.* 3, 9.

Eorp *a legion*, v. eored.

Eorre *anger*, v. yrre.

Eorsian *to be angry*, v. yrsian.

Eorsung *anger*, v. yrsung.

EORÐE, eorð, an; *f.* [*Al.* ertha: *Moes.* airtha] EARTH, *ground*; terra:—Seo eorðe hit helt, *Bt.* 33, 4. Sie eorð is ceald, *Id.* Betwux þære cealdan eorðan, *Id.* ¶ Eorðan styrrung, eorð-beofung *an earthquake, Mk.* 13, 8, v. eard.

Eorð-æppel *An earth-apple, a cucumber*; cucumis:—*Num.* 11, 5.

Eorð-ærn *An earth-place, a cave, den*; spelunca:—*Cod. Ex.* 119, b.

Eorð-byre *a heap of earth.*

Eorð-cafer, es; *m. An earth-chafer, a cock-chafer*; taurus:—*R.* 24.

Eorð-cripel, eorð-crypel *An earth-creeper, a snail, paralytic*; cochlea:—*R. Mt.* 11, 3.

Eorð-dyn *Earth din, an earthquake*; terræ motus:—*Chr.* 1060.

Eorð-gemet *Earth-measure, geometry*; geometria:—*Cot.* 95.

Eorð-hele *A heap*; tumulus:—*Ex.* 16, 14.

Eorð-hrocnis *an earthquake.*

Eorð-hus *an earth-house, a den.*

Eorð-ifig, eorð-iuig *earth or ground-ivy.*

Eorðlic; *adj. Earth-like, earthly*; terrenus:—*Jn.* 3, 12.

Eorðling *a farmer*, v. yrðling.

Eorð-rice *earth dominion, kingdom of the earth.*

Eorðtylð *Earth tillage, agriculture*; agricultura:—*Coll. Mon.*

Eorð-tyrefa *earth-turf, turf*, v. turf.

Eorð-wela *Earth-wealth, fertility*; fertilitas:—*Ors.* 1, 5.

Eoryd *a legion*, v. weorad.

Eosol *an ass*, v. assa.

Eoster *easter*, v. easter.

Eota land *Jutland*, v. Iotas.

Eotende *eating, for* etende;—

Eoton *ate, for* æton, v. etan.

Eotole *Italy*;—Eotol-wara *Italians, Bd.* 2, 4.

Eouland *Oeland, an island in the Baltic, Ors.* 1, 1.

Eow *The wild ash, yew-tree*; ornus, taxus:—*R.* 47, v. iw.

Eow *you*; *d. ac. pl. of* þu.

Eow; *interj. Wo! alas!* væ! heu!—*Ps.* 119, 5.

Eowed, eowod, eowde, ewyde, ewede, eode, eld; *n. A flock, herd, fold*; grex:—*Ps.* 77, 57, 76.

Eowena *of ewes*, v. eowu.

Eowend *membrum virile*:—*L. Ælf.* 25.

Eowendende *returning*, v. awendan.

Eower *of you, your, from* þu.

Eowernan *altogether.*

Eowestre *a sheepfold*, v. ewestre.

Eowian *to shew*, v. ywan.

Eowic, eowih *you*; *ac. pl. of* þu.

Eowod *a flock*, v. eowed.

Eowr *your*, v. eower.

Eowðen *The Saxon god Wothen, Woden*; deus Saxonum, *Som.*

Eowu, es; *pl. nom. ac.* eowa *g.* ena; *d.* um; *f.* [*Frs.* ei] *An ewe, a female sheep*; ovis fœmina:—*Gen.* 32, 14: *L. In* 55.

Eowunga *openly*, v. ewunga.

Epegitsung, e; *f. Avarice, covetousness*; avaritia:—*Ps.* 118, 36.

Epistol *A letter*; epistola:—*Ors.* 3, 11.

Epl, eppl *an apple*, v. æpl.

Epse *an asp-tree*, v. æps.

Er *eer, before*, v. ær.

-er, as an adjective termination, v. letter R.

-er, as terminating nouns, v. -ere.

Eran *a shrill sound, the ears*, v. eare.

Erc *an ark, a chest*, v. arc.

Erce-bisceop *an archbishop*, v. arcebisceop, &c.

Erce-hád *Archhood, an archbishop's pall, his dignity, of which the pall was a sign*; pallium, *Som.*

Ercol, es; Erculus *Hercules, Ors.* 3, 9.

-ere, -er, as the termination of many nouns, signifying a person or agent. Some think from wer *a man*, as plegere *a player*; sædere *a sower*; writere *a writer.*

Ered *ploughed, cultivated, eared*, v. erian.

Erest *first*, v. ær, æra.

Eretic; *adj. Heretical*; hæreticus:—*Bd.* 4, 13.

Erfe *an inheritance*, v. yrf.

Erfeð *difficult*, v. earfeð.

Erfeweard *an heir*, v. yrf-weard.

Erfwyrdnes, erfwyrðnes, se; *f. An inheritance*; hæreditas:—*Chr.* 694.

Erhe, erhlice *fearfully*, v. earlice.

Erian, to erigenne, ic erige; *part.* erigende, eregende, ergende; *p.* erede; *pp.* gerod; *v. a.* [ear *an ear of corn*] *To plough, till,* EAR; arare:—Mine æceras ic erige *I plough my fields, Elf. gr.* 15, 51, *Som.* p. 19, 44. He erede mid horsan *he ploughed with horses, Ors.* 1, 1, *Bar.* p. 23, 18.

Eriung, e; *f. A ploughing*; aratio:—*R.* 1, *Lye.*

Erk *an ark, a chest*, v. arc.

Erming *misery*, v. earming.

Erming-stræt [here-man-stræt *via strata militaris, Som.*] *Erming-street. One of the four great Roman roads in Britain, Som.*

Ermð *poverty*, v. yrmð.

Ern *a place*, v. ærn.

Ern *an eagle*, v. earn.

-ern, as a termination, denotes a *place*, v. ærn.

Ernð *Sown land*; seges:—*Bd.* 1, 12, *S.* p. 480, n. 35, v. yrð.

Erra *the former*, v. æra.

Ersc-henn, ærsc-hen *A quail, partridge*; coturnix:—*Ex.* 16, 13.

-es is the termination of the genitive case singular, in the greater part of Saxon nouns. —Cynenges botl *a king's palace.*—Abrahames God *Abraham's God.* In English, e is omitted, but its place is denoted by an apostrophe.

-es is the termination of adverbs in many cases where the noun is not so formed; as nightes *by night, nightly*; nedes *of necessity, necessarily.*

Escesdun *Ashdown*, v. Æscesdun.

Escole *a school.*

Eske *a wooden vessel*, v. æscen.

Esl *a shoulder*, v. eaxl.

ESNE, æsne, es; *m. A man of the servile class, a man, male, servant, youth*; servus, vir:—Se esne hig hamweard lædde, *Gen.* 24, 61. Uton agifan þæm esne his wif *let us give the man his wife, Bt.* 35, 6.

Esnelice; *adv. Manly, valiantly*; viriliter:—*Deut.* 31, 6.

Esol *an ass*, v. assa.

Essian *To waste, consume*; tabescere:—*Ps.* 118, 139.

EST, æst, es; *m.* [*Norse,* aast] 1. *Liberality, munificence, love, favour, devotion*; munificentia. 2. *A banquet, feast, dishes*; epulæ:—1. On Godes est, *L. Can. Edg.* 49. 2. Cyninga estas *banquets of kings, R.* 65: *Lk.* 7, 25.

-est, the termination of the superlative degree, perhaps from est *abundance.*

Estelice; *comp.* or; *adv. Kindly, delicately, daintily*; benigne:—*Ps.* 50, 19.

Ester *easter*, v. easter.

Estfull *full of kindness, kind, delicate.*

Estfullnes, se; *f. Fulness of liberality, devotion*; devotio:—*Past.* 58, 1.

Est-gereht *interpreted.*

Lile examined in Thorpe Cod.

Cd 77.11

Gád or gada – ~~dd~~ in Lye & insert in ~~gadara~~ Gegada

Gefræge in Lye

Gegnunga q. now Dd in Lye Cd 17.3

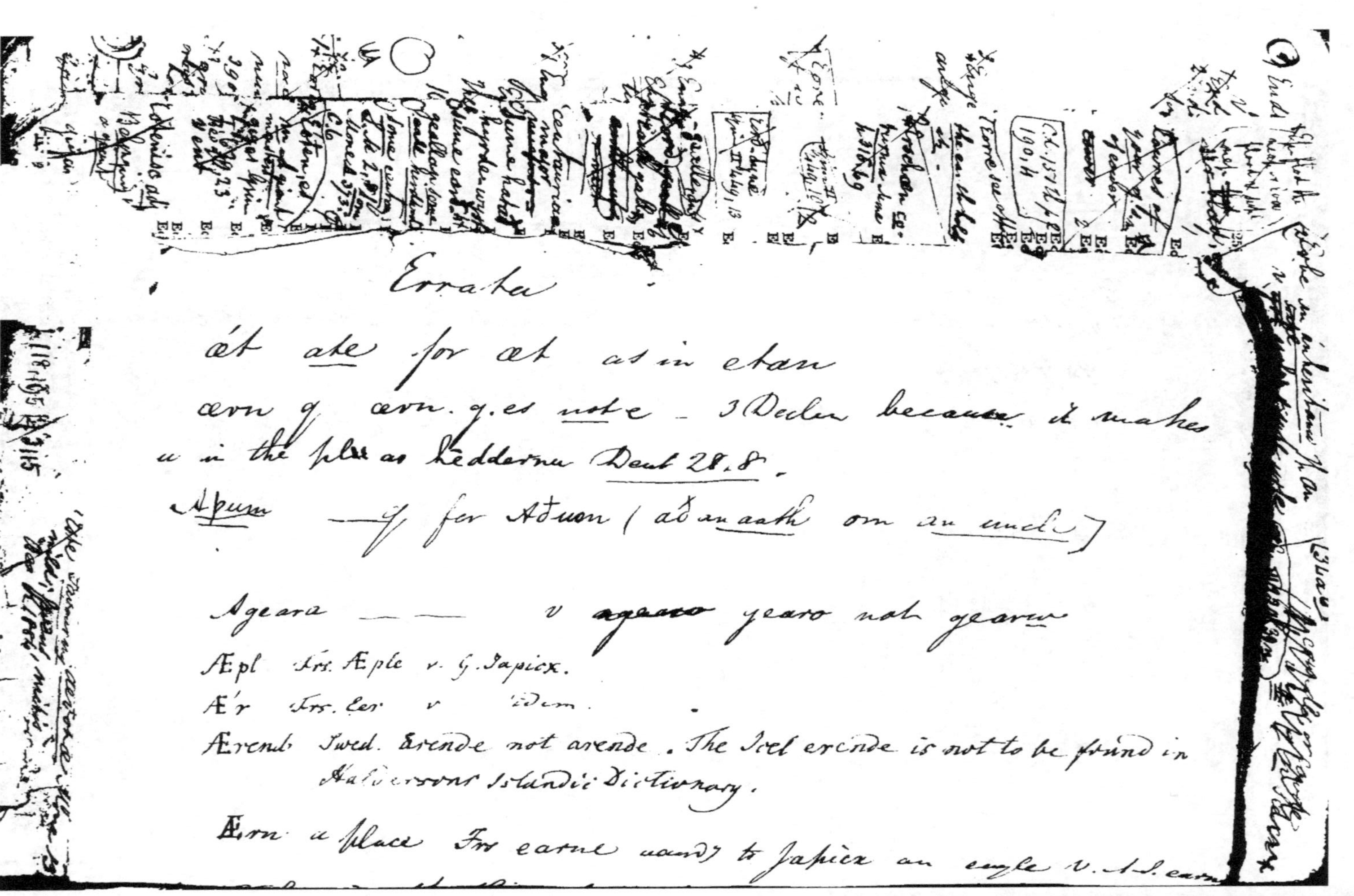

Errata

æt ate for æt as in etan

ærn q. ærn. q. es not e – 3 Decl. because it makes u in the plur. as ǩeddernu Deut 28.8.

Aþum — q. for Aðum (að an aath om an uncle)

Ageara — v ~~agaro~~ gearo not geara

Æpl Frs. Æple v. G. Japicx.

Æ'r Frs. Eer v Idem.

Ærend Swed. Erende not arende. The Icel erende is not to be found in Haldersons Islandic Dictionary.

Ærn a place Frs earne wandy to Japicx an engle v. A. S. earn

Why some Large & other small A.S. Caps –

9 Lyto ¶ of Lyterne earlshipe cowardice som &

Pearsa – read pearsa 53, c 2 –

Errata ... Oct. 21st – 1835

Some chief or radical words are printed larger where Ð are used, because there was no Ð the same size as smaller caps – also Most lines

In the first & 2d sheet þ is often put for ð

Distance from the Press

Preface p VII Note * 1e ... 86 Note ‡ read Note *

XIV l 3 writers read writings ... or a translator of Isidore XV 2, 20

[34ab]
C.L. 157th p
190, 4
centauria
major
Eoten, -es
giant
Eotenisc adj
Belonging to
a giant
gigantdus
II 375, 31
Errata

Easter- mon a ð easter month

Sow Erdling. A bittern, Ardea palustris

Eregend- feow a plough

Mar. /63

11th

15,1

Serena Ben. Lye.

A S

O S faeder

fäder lbhkft

o ad oadygec

B SSF oecd

ג ה ח ד ב

c o, a, d, q, g e, c f. fæder

ge ga

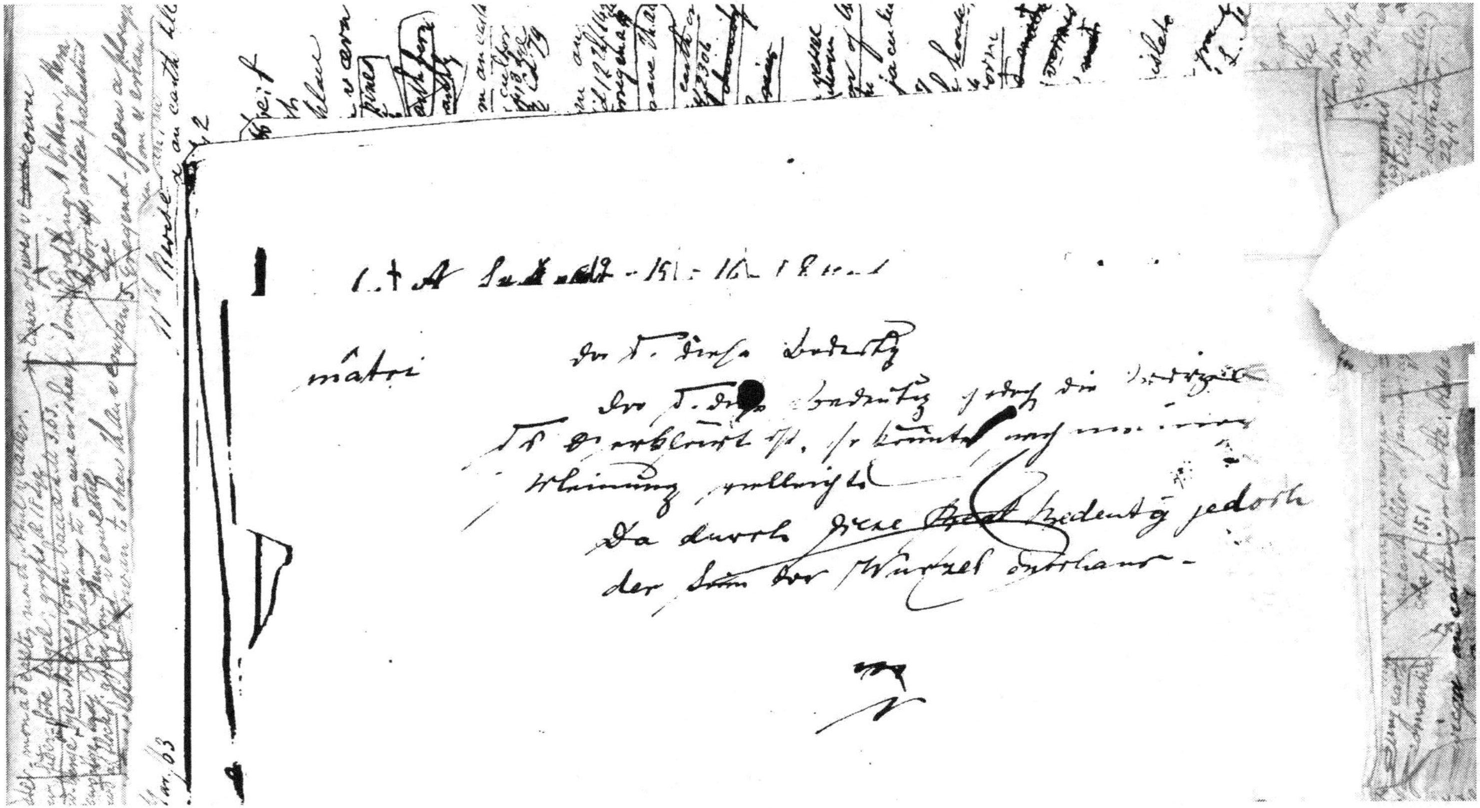
1. + A [illegible] - 151 - 16 18 [illegible]

mâtri   Da d. diese bedeutg

Da d. diese bedeutg jedoch die [illegible]

[illegible] erklärt ist, so konnte man meine

Meinung [illegible]

Da durch diese ~~Bedt~~ bedeutg jedoch

der Sinn der Wurzel durchaus -

mon at easter, month April yeaster.

Cowa of ewes v cowu

Erdling A bittern, hera

ardea palustris

5 Eregend- feorw a plough

11th Revise

an earth [illegible]

place

pines

earth

m an earth

grave

m earth

earth house,

K 2434

a worm

misleto

[illegible] earth [illegible] a battle

or A.Sax.
A.S. A.S. or ~~A.Sa~~ A.Sax. or A.S. or A.S.
O.S. or O.Sax. O.S. or O.Sa Old Saxon in Heliand ed. by Köne

Dan Danish

Frs. Frisic
O.Frs. Ofrs. Old Frisic that is the laws ed. by Richthofen
Ger. German New high ~~German~~ German
Goth. Gothic
Grk Greek

Copy sent

flod the
flood & tide

Eownes of
eower

Cd. 137th pf 190, 4

Eorre see

the earth holds

Ersc

Grim II 449, 10

Grim II 449, 13

centauria major

kyrden

Eten, ed
giant
monsters
Grim
679, 23

Eotenisc adj
Belonging to a giant
gigantic

18, 105 B. 3115

mild, gentle, mitis
Ass K 1884

Mar. 63

11th Revise

Nov. 5th 1862 JB. Transferred to Contracts in Old 8vo 1838. March 31st 1866

† Icl. Icelandic

† NGer.

† Ir.

† MGer. † Mhg. Middle High German

† Lat. Latin

† Nor. Norse

† Lth. Lithuanian

† 3 ONrs. Old Norse, Icelandic

Scottish

Skrt. Sanskrit

† 1 Ofrs. Old Fries.

† Slv. Slavonic

† OGer. 2 Ohg. Old High German

† Swd. Swedish

† OSx. or O.S.

† 4 OSax.

x x x

x x

x

x

x x

eorþe an arhenrau

yrfes t eafl yrfe

pr Alex.

Cawres of
your
of ewer
ewer

CL. 157 ll. p
190 ll.

Eorre see
the earth hol
ch.

Ersch en
terrena
p. 318. 69

Eord-dyne
II 449, 15

-gealla
Eord-geall
Earth-gall
erd-nuss

centauria
major

uma hala
hyrde wy
uma eard
geallan
sall hirder
some cent
L. M. 2, 8
II 373
C. b

Eoten, ed
gian
magnus
gigas Grim
L. 69. 23
Vent

Eotenisc

Belonging
a giant
gigan
II

118 d05 3115

"Eorþe tavinoy" eorþe
mild; furud, micle
Dec 12 1864

Mar. /63

The meaning of ídel in Anglo-Sax + Low German.

Every ~~[illegible]~~ opinion or statement of ~~B[?] Hallline~~ deserves ~~the~~ ~~most careful~~ considerate, ~~examination~~,

I have, therefore, ~~carefully~~ carefully examined the A-S word ídel idle, the result of which is the same as that which I have given in my Dict.

I have not found ~~one~~ one instance in which ídel idle ~~[illegible]~~ is used for Gentleman, or confused with æðel noble or æðeling a nobleman –

The words are quite distinct in AS.

Thorpes A.S. Chronicle 2 vols 8vo

Of Iotum comon Cant wara 7 Wiht wara p 21 Col 1 l 14 –
From the Jutes came the ~~men~~ people of Kent & the ~~men~~ people of Wight p 11
An. CCCC. ~~XLIX~~

of Athelbriht to Cant wara rice p 31 Col 1
Atheberht succeeded to the kingdom of the Kentish ~~men~~ people p. 16

An DC.LXXXVI. Her Ceadwalla 7 Mul Cent 7 Wiht forhergedon p 62
Here Ceadwalla & Mul ravaged Kent & Wight p 35

on Cent p 63 An DC.LXXXVII
in Kent.
Her Cantware gepingedon wid Ine
Her Cant wara gepingoden wid Ine p 66 l 7
Here the Kentish people compounded with Ine p 36

ster - mon a d easter n. e. th Ahul yeaster. Eawa of wes v cowe

ow Fidir - fote figel ; grysts R 18 sye Som Erdling A bittern, Hern

aw - Crede ; Jyewberies, Corhi bacca L.tt 3.63. ardea stellaris, ardea palustris sye

Dowgerige. ladg ... an awe or sheet

cows of flacke ; gres dom See v eowestre Eregend - perow a plough

... ertian to shew th an v cowan in Som v ertan

Mar. /63 Priste ... d an earth tilles

4, 2

... at, e. i f

... sheeh

... & place

... Som v earn

... des pines

... earth ferr

... earthly

... an m an earth

... erre culture

Bos 413 sye

... thely id 79

... 12 4/1420

... terrigena

... grave th.

... on m earth or

Bos K. 2306

... Adamah

... as Gynia

... earthen vessel

... speor of th

... ja cu leg

... 17

... earth hoare,

K 5434

... mouth, vermes

... Som v worte

... tel mislete

... or the gra

... genus L.

... the nayl

... earth, the

... ies ... al band

... 35.

18.2 ...

... weore earth or lic

... orgreth, terrenus, gord styrung

... earth ... 15 sye

... eorth tilia an ...

... eorth tiler ... yer ...

... romantia ... Bos 15, 1

Som

... wiega an earthing or beetle; blatta

wiþ Cantwarum — p 130
with the people of Kent p 39
Cantware, hiere feoh geheton p
the people of Kent promised them money p
ofer hergode calle Cent eastweard
ravaged all Kent Eastward p 130 p 39

Fyrd, e; f [Ger. fahrt f an expedition: faran to go, proceed] An army, chiefly of citizens, the military force of a country &c ~~an expedition~~ Hence Fyrd-craeft military craft or art ~~fyrd-…ung preparation for~~
Compd. Dict.
Fyrd-ung A military expedition
Cnut 79 p 420
vol I

Ine's Laws 51
Land-fyrd Land fyrd
Scyp-fyrd Ship } Cnut's laws 78 Thorpe vol I p 420

(1884) 3115

Mar./63

[The words very similar; thus frequently mistaken]

In Old Saxon, that is [illegible] among the Continental Saxons, from whose ancestors the A.-S. came to England, we find idil, idal idle, & edel or edil noble. Not only in Old Saxon, but in other Low German dialects, as in Dutch we find the same similarity: thus ÿdel, or ydel idle, & adel, edel noble. Thus the Dutch say de groote en kleine adel or edel the greater & lesser nobles, or in our phraseology the Nobility & gentry. [Edel is constantly used in Dutch to indicate the greatest respect, even to the present

Erbe an anhertaunt

Eormes of
year of
of eoder

Eorre see
the earth

Eorðgyne

centaurea
major

Sume ha
hyrdes

Eotenisc
Belonging to
a giant gigan
gigantaeus

Este
mild, gracious
1884

Mar./63

[Sl]ay.- Now, as I think, Bp. Hall was at the Synod of Dordrecht or Dort in Holland, & must have heard the word edel constantly used in addressing Gentlemen. If by Saxon he meant Old-Saxon or Low German, then the word edel or edel noble; may ~~quite rightly~~, but I do not find that idel, if ever used, or mistaken for edel noble, in AS. ~~for a Gentle~~ ~~man~~ or styling a nobleman

March 22nd 1860

have been easily mistaken for ~~ydel~~ idal, idel idle

~~A~~ Idle for Atel
for Dr. Murray
Res. of St Johns
Coll Oxford
March 23rd
1860-

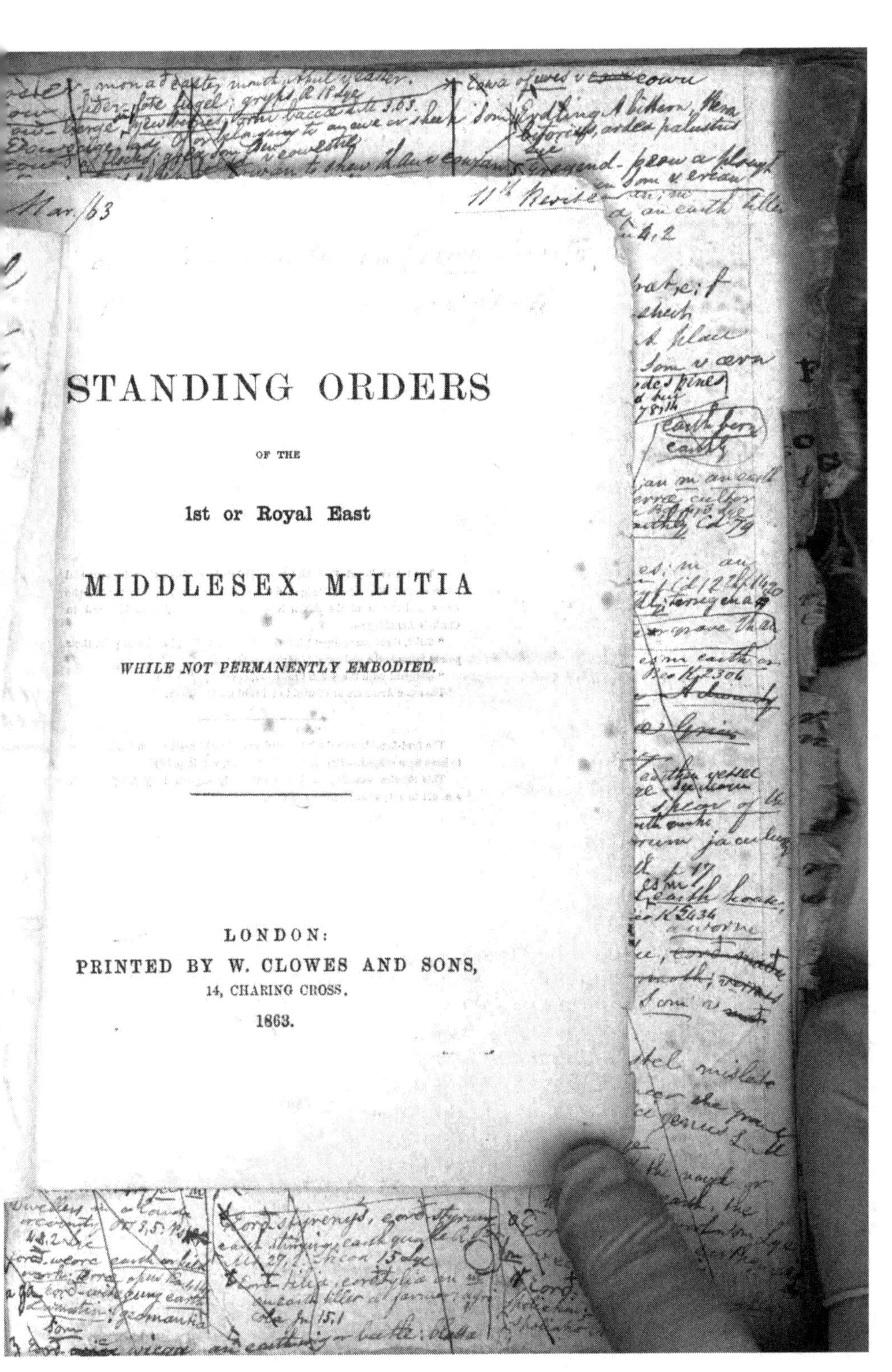

Mar./63

STANDING ORDERS

OF THE

1st or Royal East

MIDDLESEX MILITIA

WHILE NOT PERMANENTLY EMBODIED.

LONDON:
PRINTED BY W. CLOWES AND SONS,
14, CHARING CROSS.
1863.

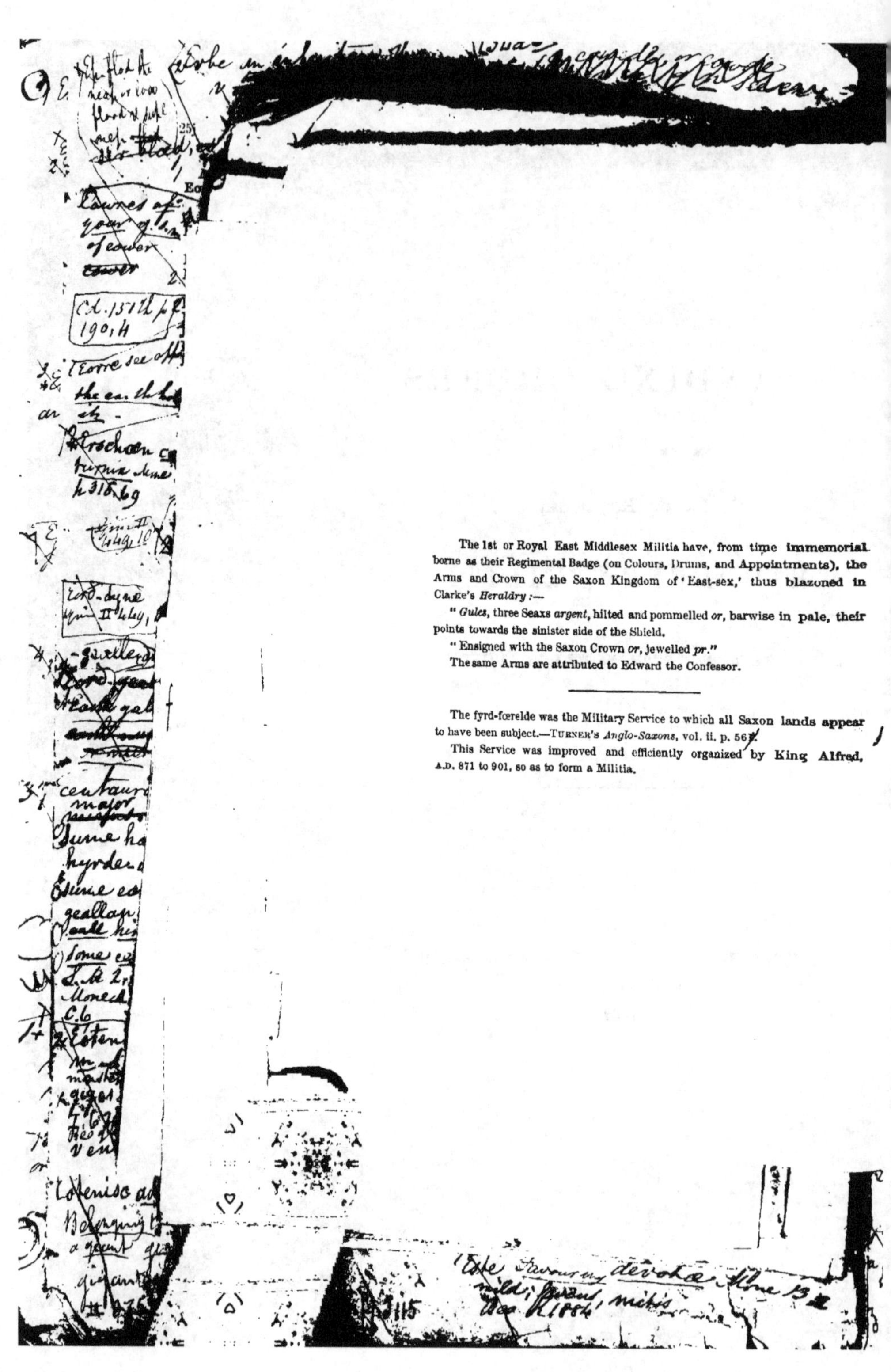

The 1st or Royal East Middlesex Militia have, from time immemorial borne as their Regimental Badge (on Colours, Drums, and Appointments), the Arms and Crown of the Saxon Kingdom of 'East-sex,' thus blazoned in Clarke's *Heraldry* :—

"*Gules*, three Seaxs *argent*, hilted and pommelled *or*, barwise in pale, their points towards the sinister side of the Shield.

"Ensigned with the Saxon Crown *or*, jewelled *pr*."

The same Arms are attributed to Edward the Confessor.

The fyrd-fœrelde was the Military Service to which all Saxon lands appear to have been subject.—TURNER'S *Anglo-Saxons*, vol. ii. p. 56.

This Service was improved and efficiently organized by King Alfred, A.D. 871 to 901, so as to form a Militia.

Cowa of wes v cowu

Eordling A bittern, Ardea stellaris ardea palustris Lye

Eregend- ploughman Som v erian

Eord- tilia, an earth tiller farmer Gen 4.2

Erming-stræt e.f Erming-street

Ern, es, n A place house Th. Som v ærn

Sceap cowdes pines

earth for earth

Eord-bugenga an m an earth dweller

Eord-cund earthly Cd 79

Eord-buend, es m an earth inhabitant

Eord-cund earthly terrigena

an earth house

Eord-cyning, es m earth or world king Beo K p. 304

Grimm Myth

Eorþ-fæt es n an earthen vessel

Esa gescot a spear of the gods

divorum jaculum

Grimm Myth p 47

Eord-reced earth house

Beo K 5434

Eord-mata, earth moth, vermis

Eord- mistel mistletoe

Som visce

Eord-nafel the navel or centre of the earth

Eord-rypnes an earthquake

Eord-hrernis

Eowan to shew Ælf v eowian

Eowed shewn Cdy

202 Th p 250

Geædde hi swa swa cowde

Ps. 77.57

Ps 77. 76

Eord-hnutu an earth nut

Eord-hrernis an earth quake C Mth 27.54

Eord-typewe

Eord-sele an earth dwelling, a cavern

Eord-weall an earth walle, a mound; murus de terra factus

Beo K 5909

Eord-wæstm earthly fruit, fructus terræ Bd 1,14

Eord-styrennys, eord-styrung earth stirring, earth quake

Eord-tilia, eorþtylia an earth tiller a farmer

Eord-mede

Eord-hus an earth house

Eord-beofung, e f earth trembling, earthquake; terræ motus

Eord-cyn

Eord-cyning an earthly king a king

Eord-reste a lying on the ground, prostration

Eord-scræf an earth cave, a cavern

a monster

Beo K 223

1760

Eord-wæstm

Eord-weorc earth work

Eord-wela

2 Ēþelxes ; m, n. ones own residence, or property : allodium etc

3 Ēþel-cyning, es m. a king of his native country

Ēþel-weard ... Cd 90

... 113, 32 ; 91 ... 115, 30

... tafol ... ; m

... Ēþel-[illegible] -rym, mes, m a country's dignity. Cd 79 th ... 98, 23

... Ēþel-turf, e, f native turf or soil Cd 127 th ... 162, 6

Ēþel-riht ... tes patrium Beo th 1640 391

... T 515, 2

2 Ēþel-[illegible] a prince ... Beo K 1226

Ēþyl-stæf family staff, a support Cd 101 th 134, 11

Ēþyl-turf a country, native soil Cd 12, th 14, 26 v sup. ēþel-turf

Ētiewan to shew v ætēowian

Ēþ-ge-syne easy to be seen Beo K 2214

Ēþm v. margin

8 Ētonisc v. margin

Ēþyl-stæf the staff of a family or country, columna patriæ

2 Esttice ...

3 Eþel ... Cd. 16 ...

Eþel-cweorn a mill ... with asses

Ēþ-be-gete easy to be got ... Beo K 3717

Ēþel-wyn, e, f inheritance pleasure possessionum avitarum gaudium Beo K 4981

Facen-staf as (stæf es.) m deeds of treachery Beo K 2030

2)

3 Facen-searo, es, n a deceitful wile Cod Ex 83 ...

Fācan ... fac

Fæcan, p-ade ... ; acquirere ... 253, 11 ...

Flæg ; es, m flaiae plateia ... R. 102

[33a 1]

[23a-2]

follows from the rt. hand corner of p. 104

Eren iron Som v iren

Ǣrend-gewrit a written errand, a letter Som — Ærend

raca a messenger v ærend-raca

Ǣrexna-wong paradise R Lk 23,43 v neorcsen

Yrfe-gewrit a writ of an inheritance, a will

Charter; donationis charta Heming p 120 Lye

Yrfe-land es; n hereditary land Th. An

Eppl yrfe

angry Som v eorre Ben Lye v. edisc

Ete a park, warren; vivarium Ben Lye v. edisc

Esceen an urchin, hedgehog; herinaceus Som

Erpon pe before that Som

Esol, d esle A shoulder Cd 228 Th 307,18

Esceapa a patch; commissura C Lk 5,36 R

Esne-wyrhta an; m A male wright, a workman; mercenarius, operarius

Esol — astasan, L. Alf. pol 39

Est, east, est-dæl east part v east &c

Este ... Chr 1052 Ing 238,9 v easter adj

Ester dag Easter day Som

Est-fullice adv Devoutly; devote Dial 2.16

Edmensker ... III. 475, 33

Ext 21,37

Etonisc Like a giant; gigantean Ben I, 226, 13 v. Epl eotonisc

Eowe ...ovile III 327, ... [34a7]

Eom vapour smell v æþm

Cd 228 Th 309,

Eulne ... fern

fraud, guile Th. An

Facen, es; n deceit, dolus Ben I 643, 31 III 572, 12

Facen-ful ... Ælf gl Som p 77; 52

t-hrinan.
18.
ng.
at last,
glutton
11, 19.
etol.
ss, glut-
fesham.
ty, reli-
p. 28,
brecc.
yrdla.
ovile:
æwisc-
ga open-
yrdla.
Eaxan-
Eaxan-
r.
t deceit,
plex:—
l; dolo-
ceitfully,
— Gen.
dj. De-
sus:—
full.
c fa-

Faag *a varying colour*, v. fag.
Faca *a space*, v. fæc.
Facade *fetched, acquired*, v. feccan.
Facenfulnes *deceitfulness, deceit*, *Som.*
Facen-gecwis *a wicked consent, a conspiracy.*

2 Ǣlexes; m. n. ones own residence, or property: allodium etc

Hitte: arm

Ǣsyl-stæf the staff
a family or county
columna patriae
527, 22

3 Ǣsel an ass Cot. 16
Ǣsel-cweorn
a mill turned
with asses
16 mola asinaria

1 Æt subject

Ǣrd-weall, as; m. an earth wall
or mound of earth Beo K 5909

7 Eorsalxes; m. An ass, asellus La
Th p 173, 25 v ex p 30 Ezel keatton

to be-gete
be gotten
Beo K 3717

Æl-wyrde
inheritance
possessionum
gaudium Beo

Estines, se. *Benignity, kindness;* benignitas:—*Ps.* 64, 12.
Est-land *East-land, east country, the east;* terra orientalis, v. east.
Est-mete *delicate meat, dainties.*
Estra-dæg *easter day,* v. easter.
-estre,-istre,-ystre, are the feminine terminations of nouns of action, same as the Latin -ix and English -ess; *as* læreestre *an instructress;* sangestre *a songstress.*
Estum *with favour, favourably.*
Esuica, esuicnis *deceit,* v. æswic.
Esul *an ass,* v. assa.
Eswic *deceit,* v. æswic.
Eswica, eswice *a hypocrite, heathen,* v. æswica.
[m]Eswician *to offend, scandalize,* v. swican.
Eswicnis, se; *f. Hypocrisy, deceit;* hypocrisis:—*C. R. Mk.* 7, 21.
ETAN, ic ete, þu ytst, he heo yt, ytt, we etað, ete; *p.* ic he æt, þu æte, we ge æton; *sub. indef.* ic ete, we eton; *pp.* eten, geeten; *v. a.* [*Dut.* eten: *Moes.* etan] *To* EAT, *consume, devour;* edere:—Se þe ytt hlaf, *Jn.* 13, 18. Þu ytst wyrta, *Gen.* 3, 18. He æt þa offring hlafas, *Mt.* 12, 4: *Gen.* 3, 1.
Eten *a giant,* v. ent.
Etere, es; *m. An* EATER, *a consumer, devourer;* vorax:—*C. Mt.* 11, 19.
Et-filian *to follow after, adhere.*
Eð *more easily,* v. eáðe.
Eðan *to flow,* v. yðian.

Eðcwide, eðwiðe *a rehearsal,* v. edcwide.
Eðel, oeðel, *A country, native country, soil, region, a place;* patria:—Nan witega nys andfenge on his eðele, *Lk.* 4, 24, v. æðel.
Eðel *noble,* v. æðele.
Eðel-boren *noble born,* v. æðelboren.
Eðel-dream *the happiness of one's country, domestic pleasure, Cd.* 78.
Eðel-eard *a native country.*
Eðelice *easily,* v. eaðelice.
Eðelicnes *easiness,* v. eðnes.
Eðeling *a noble,* v. æðelin.
Eðelinga ig. *The island of nobles, the island of Athelney, Chr.* 878.
Eðel-land *a native land.*
Eðel-leás *countryless, homeless.*
Eðel-meare *a country, limit.*
Eðel-stól, eðel-stow *a chief residence, metropolis.*
Eðem *a smell,* v. æðm.
Eðer *a hedge,* v edor.
Eðfynde *easily found.*
Eðgiende *breathing.*
Eðgung, eðung, e; *f. A breath, inspiration, breathing, vapour, abolishing;* halitus:—*Bd.* 5, 9, *Som.*
Eðhelde, eðhylde *contented, satisfied.*
Eðiende *abounding* v. yðian.
Eðle *in a country,* v. eðel.
Eðnes, eðelicnes, se; *f. Easiness, facility, favour;* facilitas:—*Bt.* 1.
[n]Eðode *Breathed, inspired;* inspiravit.

Eðre *more easy,* v. eað.
Et-hrinan *to touch,* v. æt-hrinan.
Eðða *or;* aut, *R. Mt.* 5, 18.
Eðung *a breath,* v. eðgung.
Eðyl *a country,* v. eðel.
Et nyhstan *at nighest, at last, lastly,* v. neh.
Etol, ettul, ettulman *A glutton;* edax:—*Elf. gr.* 9: *Mt.* 11, 19.
Ettan *to eat,* v. etan.
Ette *meat,* v. æt.
Ettol, ettul *a glutton,* v. etol.
Ettulnys, se; *f. Greediness, gluttony;* edacitas, *Som.*
Euen *even,* v. efen, &c.
Euesham *Evesham,* v. Efesham.
Eufæstnys, se; *f. Sincerity, religion;* religio:—*Elf. T.* p. 28, 11, v. æfestnes.
Euwa *a sheep,* v. eowu.
Ewbryce *adultery,* v. æwbrece.
Ewe *water,* v. ea.
Ewe *marriage,* v. æw.
Ewede *a flock,* v. eowed.
Ewerdla *damage,* v. æfwyrdla.
Ewestre, es *A sheepfold;* ovile:—*Cot.* 7.
Ewisad *clear.*
Ewisenes *shamelessness,* v. æwiscnys.
Ewunga, ewunge, eowunga *openly,* v. eawunga.
Ewyde *a flock,* v. eowed.
Ewyrdlu *damage,* v. æfwyrdla.
Ex *an axe,* v. æx.
Ex *an axis,* v. eax.
Exancester *Exeter,* v. Eaxanceaster.
Exan-muð *Exmouth,* v. Eaxanmuð.
Exla *shoulders,* v. eaxl.

[o]F, B, P, and V, [U] are often interchanged; as lufian *or* luvian *to love;* heuen, heafan *heaven;* euen, efen *even.* [See B.] The Dutch *v* has exactly the sound of the English *f;* thus, for *finger,* the Dutch write *vinger; fish, visch; full, vol; forefather, voorvader.*
Fá *Foelike, unfriendly, hostile;* inimicus;—*Cd.* 4: 114.
Faag *a varying colour,* v. fag.
Faca *a space,* v. fæc.
Facade *fetched, acquired,* v. feccan.

FACEN, facn, fæcn; *d.* e; *pl.* facnu [*Plat.* faxen *m. pl. deceit: Ger.* fatzen *pl. f: Icel.* fyx *cunning*] *Deceit, fraud, guile, wickedness;* fraus:—Facen ne do þu, *Mk.* 10, 19. Mid facne, *Mt.* 26, 4. Facnu, *Mk.* 7, 22. On þam nis nan facen, *Jn.* 1, 47.
Facenfull, facnfull; *adj. Deceitful, crafty;* fraudulentus:—*Ps.* 42, 1.
Facenfulnes *deceitfulness, deceit, Som.*
Facen-gecwis *a wicked consent, a conspiracy.*

Facenleás; *adj. Without deceit, simple, innocent;* simplex:—*Som.*
Facenlic; *adj. Deceitful;* dolosus:—*Ors.* 3, 1.
Facenlice; *adv. Deceitfully, fraudulently;* dolose:—*Gen.* 27, 35.
Facn *deceit,* v. facen.
Facn, fæcn, se facna; *adj. Deceitful, factious:* dolosus:—*Cd.* 23: 214.
Facon *deceit,* v. facen.
Facynfull *deceitful,* v. facenfull.
FADAN, fadian, gefadian; ic fa-

dige, gefadige; *p.* de; *pp.* ed, gefæd. *To set in order, dispose*; ordinare:—*L. eccl. Cnut.* 19, *W.* p. 131, 50: *pol. Cnut.* 2, *W.* p. 133, 45.

Fadung, gefadung, e; *f. A setting in order, disposing, adorning*; dispositio:—*R. Ben.* 18.

Fæc [*Plat.* fack *n*: *Frs.* feck: *Ger.* fach *n*: *Dan.* fag *n*: *Swed.* fack *n.*] *Space, interval, distance, portion of time, suspicion*; spatium:—*Lk.* 24, 13. Twegra dæga fæc *two days' space*, *R. Ben.* 53. Lytel fæc *a little time*, *Elf. gr.* 47. Æfter fæce *afterwards*, *Bd.* 5, 23.

Fæccean *to fetch*, v. feccan.

Fæcele *a torch.*

Fæcn *deceitful, suspicious*, v. facn.

FÆDER, fædyr; *indecl. in sing. pl.* fæderas, ra, um; *m.* [*Plat. Dut.* vader *m*: *Old Frs.* feder, feider *m*: *Ger.* vater *m*: *Isd. Ker.* fater: *Dan. Swed.* fader *m*: *Old Swed.* fódur: *Icel.* fadir *m*: *Pers.* پدر pader, phader: *Sans.* pita.—The *Icel.* fædi, at fæda, *Dan.* föde, *Swed.* föda, signify, generare *to engender*] A FATHER; pater:—Fæder and moder *a father and mother*, *Elf. gr.* 9, 38. Þridda fæder *great grandfather*, *Elf. gl.* 3: *Deut.* 24, 16.

Fædera, an; *m. An uncle, a father's brother*; patruus:—*Bd.* 3, 11, *S.* p. 535, 16. Mines fæderan þridda fæderes broðor *a brother of my uncle's great grandfather.*

Fæderen; *adj. Paternal, belonging to a father*; paternus:—Fæderen-cyn *paternal kind, a father's relation* or *kin*, *Chr.* 755. Fæderen magas, fædern magas *paternal relations*, *R.* 91.

Fæder-eðel, fæder-geard *a paternal region, one's own country.*

Fæder-gestreona *a patrimony.*

Fædering-magas *paternal relations*, v. fæderen.

Fæderleás *fatherless.*

Fæderlic; *adj.* FATHERLY; paternus:—Fæderlice nama *a sirname*, *Elf. gr.* 5.

Fædren *fatherly*, v. fæderen.

Fædyr *a father*, v. fæder.

Fæge; *adj. Dying, fated*; moribundus:—*Fr. Jdth.* 10, 11.

Fægen, fegen, gefagen; *adj.* FAIN, *glad, joyful*; lætus:—*Bt.* 40, 5: *Cd.* 100.

Fægenian *to rejoice*, *Bt.* 30, 1, v. fægnian.

FÆGER *Beauty*; pulchritudo:—Þæs lichoman fæger *the body's beauty*, *Bt.* 32, 2.

Fæger, fægr; *adj.* [*Dan.* faver: *Swed.* fager: *Icel.* fagr *splendid*: *North Eng.* feg *fair*] FAIR, *beautiful*; pulcher:—*Bd.* 1, 7.

Fægere, fægerlice; *adv. Pleasantly, softly, gently, fairly, beautifully*; pulchre:—Fægere he singað *pulchre canit*, *Elf. gr.* 38.

Fægernes, fægernys, se; *f.* FAIRNESS, *beauty*; pulchritudo:—*Ps.* 44, 5.

Fægnian, fagnian, fægenian; ic fægenige; *p.* fagnude, fahnude, hi fahnudon. *To rejoice, exult, to be delighted with, to boast of, to wish for, to flatter*; gaudere:—We fægniað *we rejoice*, *Bt.* 14, 1: *Ps.* 31, 14.

Fægnung, gefægnung, e; *f. A rejoicing, exultation*; exultatio:—*Ps.* 125, 6.

Fægnys *an ornament*, v. fagnys.

Fægr *fair*, v. fæger.

Fægre *slowly*, v. fægere.

Fæhð-bote *feud-boot, compensation for engaging in a feud or quarrel.*

FÆHÐE, fægð [*Plat.* fede, vede, veide: *Dut.* veede *f*: *Frs.* faithe *f. enmity*: *Ger.* fehde *f*: *Dan.* fejde *c*: *Swed.* fejd *f*: *Icel.* fæd *f.*] *Feud, vengeance, enmity, deadly feud, that enmity which the relations of the deceased waged against the kindred of the murderer*; capitalis inimicitia:—*L. eccl. Cnut.* 5: *In.* 74: *Cd.* 67.

Fæigr *fair*, v. fæger.

Fæla *many*, v. fela.

Fælan *to feel*, v. ge-felan.

Fæle; *adj. Faithful, true, steady*; fidelis:—Wæs fæle freond *was a faithful friend*, *Cd.* 130: 135.

Fælga, fælge [*Plat.* falge, felge *f*: *Dut.* velg *f*: *Ger. Dan.* felge *f.*—fæla, fela, *much*; ga from gan *to go*] A FEILY, *a part of the circumference of a wheel*; canthus:—*Bt.* 39, 7.

Fælging *a harrow*, v. fealga.

Fællan *to offend.*

Fælnis *an offence.*

Fæm *foam*, v. fam.

Fæman, famgan [fam *foam*] *To* FOAM or *froth*; spumare:—*Lk.* 9, 39.

Fæmi, fæmig, fæmiht *foamy*, v. famig.

Fæmnan *of a virgin*, v. fæmne.

Fæmnan-hád, fæmn-hád *womanhood, virginity*, *Ors.* 3, 6.

Fæmne, an; *f.* [*Frs.* faem] *A virgin, maid, woman*; virgo:—Þære ylcan fæmnan lichoma, *Bd.* 4, 19, *S.* p. 587, 36: *Mt.* 1, 23: *Gen.* 2, 23: *Cd.* 101.

Fæmnenlic *virginlike.*

Fæmn-hád *virginity.*

Fæn, fænn *dirt*, v. fenn.

Fæna, *a vane, standard*, v. fana.

Fæng-toð *a fang tooth.*

Fæniht, fænlic; *adj.* FENNY, *marshy, dirty, muddy*; palustris, *Som.*

FÆR, fer, for [*Plat.* foor *f*: *Dut.* voer *f*: *Ger.* fuhre *f*: *Ot.* fuara: *Dan.* fören: *Swed.* fora *f*: *Icel.* för *f*: *Pers.* فار far *one going a journey, a fugitive*] 1. *A journey, way,* FARE, *going, a going together, an assembly, a meeting*; iter. 2. *That in which a journey is made, a vehicle, a vessel, ship*; navis:—1. Anes dæges fær, *Lk.* 2, 44. Folces fær *a public way*, *L. Edg.* 14. 2. Þu þæt fær gewyrc, *Cd.* 65. Fær Noes *Noah's ark*, *Cd.* 66.

Fær FEAR; timor:—Fær ongeton *they felt fear*, *Cd.* 166: *Conyb.* p. 195.

Fær; *adj. Void, sudden, intense, horrid*; subitus:—Fær gryre fyres *a sudden dread of fire*, *Cd.* 197. Fær cyle *intense cold*, *Cd.* 2.

Færan *to frighten*, v. afæran.

Færan forð *to go forth, die*, v. faran.

Færbena *A husbandman, peasant*; rusticus:—*L. North. pres.* 50.

Fær-bryne *sudden* or *great heat.*

Færbuja *a colour.*

Færcoðon *supported, from* fercian.

Fær-coðe, fær-cwealm, fær-deað *Sudden sickness* or *death*; repentina ægritudo:—*L. Edg.* 79. Fære-fyll *a sudden fall*, *Cot.* 112.

Færd, færde *an army*, v. fyrd.

Færeld, fareld, es. *A way, a journey, passage, progress, company*; via:—Godes færeldes offrung, *Ex.* 12, 27. Mid eallum his færelde *with all his company*, *Ors.* 4. 6.—Færeld-freols *the passover feast*, *Jos.* 5, 10.—Færesceat *fare-scot, passage money.*

Færeldtu *A passage*; meatus, lustra:—*Cot.* 134.

Færeng *A swooning, trance*; deliquium:—*Cot.* 79.

Færh *a litter, a little pig*, v. fearh.

Færinga, færunga; *adv. Suddenly, by chance*; subito:—*Mk.* 13, 36.

Færlic, fearlic, fyrlic; *def.* se færlica; *adj. Sudden, fortuitous*; subitus:—*Gen.* 19, 19.

Færlice, ferlice; *adv. Suddenly, immediately, by chance*; subito:—*Lk.* 9, 39.

Færm *a supper, feast*, v. feorm.

Færnes, se; *f. A passage, fare*; transitus:—*Bd.* 2, 16.

Færr *A passing, passed*; transitus:—*L. Ps.* 143, 18.

Fers [*Frs.* fers] *Verse, section*; versus, capitulum:—*Elf. pref.* p. 3.

Fær-spell *a sudden message.*

Færst *goest*; færð *goes*, v. faran.

Færð *the mind*, *Bt. R.* p. 192, v. feorh.

12a Fædren-cyn, nes; n paternal race Cod Ex 11. b v fæderen cynn

10 2 Fæc-es; n; pl. facu, g. faca a space etc

3 Fæder-dæd, e; f paternal deed Beo K 4114

4 7 Fæd[illegible] a fathom Som v fæðem

Fælg, fælge a felly Som v ohl felg.

0. 2 Fifta fæder fifth father, the fourth from his father or great grand father's father; atavus. Elf p 3 note

5 7 Fæder-eðel, es; m a fatherland, or country; patria, paterna regio Cod 41, 9 — Fæder-geard, es; m paternal country Cod 50, Th 64, 20

6 11a Fæderlice adv Fatherly Th An

11 Fæder-slaga, a; m a slayer of a father, parricida Grim II 523, 37

11 12 Fæderyn-cyn [illegible] kind Cod 170 Th p 213, 29

12 v fæderen

14 Fægan, he fægde, to paint [illegible] pingere [illegible] Beh [illegible]

2 Fægerlic adj lovely? Th An

4 Fægnian [Sax 1]

3 to fawn Th An

24 Fægn fain, glad Lye fægen

3 Fæhð vengeance Cod 6, 30 fæhð

4 Fæhð, e; f Feud

Ic fæhte geworhte I enmity wrought Cod 42, Th p 55, 27 Beo [illegible]

5 Fæld-ælbynne wrought of the wood handicraftsmen Som

Fæder-rice, es; m a paternal kingdom Cod 220 Th p 283, 22.

Fæder-æðelo, e; f a father-race, nobility or origin, ancestry Beo K 1815

7 Fæderen-cnosl es; n a paternal race L. Alf pol 9.

Fædrunga, an; m my paternal relation Beo K 4251

10)

1 Fæðlamany Som v fela

2 2 Fær, es; n Beo 4b in faran; te fær begeat the expedition came

Fær, es; m (Dolor) Beo K 2130/50 Dolus Beo K 4013

8 Færfyll a sudden fall Cod 112 v 8 in Fær-cod e

4 2 Færan to go Elf gr 30; Lye v faran

5 Fær-cod, e; f sudden sickness

[elfen, ne; f a fairy]

6 2 Færela penetralia Scint 81.

v færnes

7 Færennys, se; f [illegible] [illegible] [illegible]

9 Fær-gripe, es; m a sudden gripe, or an attack Beo K 1469

10 Fær-gryre, es; m sudden horror Beo K 346

15 4 Færnø nuptiæ Ben C. [illegible] 2, 1 Lye

11 12 Fær-nið, es; m sudden mischief Beo K 946

13 Fær-sceaða, an; m a fierce robber Th An

14 Fær-searo, es; n sudden deceit Cod Ex 19 Beo [illegible] searo

Fæsðe
Fær-tyhted bedridden clinicus Som.
[1× fasel
foetus
Færwyrd death Som
for-wyrd
Fæsceaftnes, se; f
poverty, paupertas Lye

Fæder-homa father's covering Cd 111, 1
Fædmende that hath many bendings; sinuosus Som

Fædra an uncle, relation, Som. v fædera

Fæt, fætes, pl. nom. ac. fatu g. a. d. um a vessel
Fætt, Fat, thick pinguis, densus Bo 16 664 v fætt
Fæted fatted, thickened pinguefactus, densatus Bo 16 7665 v fættian
Fætels, es; m a bag
Fæter, feter a fetter
Fæda an army Som v feda
Fæðm, es; m a fathom etc

Fæste-gepuft fast growing Som gepuf
Fæstenes; n fastness, firmament Cd 8 Th 9. 27.

[31a 4]

Fæhð, es; m Bo 16 16 etc

Fah-wyrm a variegated serpent Cd 42. Th 55, 24 v. fag
Fah-mon a foe man, an enemy Som
Fah-wer es; m a foe man Cd 64 Th 78, 19
Fahnys, se; f Enmity, hatred inimicitia Som
Faldung folding

Fæst-hræd bold Lye v fæst-ræd

Færðrade *prepared, bold;* animo paratus:—*Mann.*

Færunga *suddenly*, v. færinga.

Fær-wundr *a great wonder.*

Fæs; *pl.* fæsu. *A fringe, list;* fimbria:—*Ps.* 44, 15.

FÆSL [*Plat. Dut. Kil.* fasel *f*: *Icel.* fædsla] *Food, provision;* victus:—Þær sceal fæsl wesan *there shall be food, Cd.* 65: 67. To fæsle *for food, provision, Cd.* 67.

FÆST, fest; *adj.* [*Plat. Dan. Swed. Icel.* fast: *Dut.* vast: *Ger.* fest] FAST, *firm, constant, fortified, tenacious;* firmus:—*Bd.* 3, 16.

-fæst, as a termination, denotes *fast, very, perfectly, effectually,* as the English *fast asleep, perfectly asleep;* æw-fæst *fast in the law, firm, religious;* soðfæst *fast in truth, true, just;* staðolfæst *steadfast, steady;* unstaðolfæst *unsteady, unsteadfast.*

Fæstan, afæstan; *pp.* gefæst, gefæsted. *To* FAST; jejunare:—*Mk.* 2, 19.

Fæstan *To commend, entrust, commit;* commendare:—*C. Lk.* 23, 46.

Fæste; *adv. Fast, firmly, swiftly;* firmiter:—Fæste belocen, *Jos.* 6. 1. Sticode fæste *stuck fast, Bd.* 2, 13.

Fæsten, [*Plat. Ger.* fasten *f*: *Dut.* vasten *f*: *Dan.* faste *c*: *Swed. Icel.* fasta *f.*] *A fast, fasting;* jejunium:—*Mt.* 17, 21.

Fæsten, [*Plat. Ger.* feste *f*: *Dut.* vest *f*: *Ot.* festi: *Wil.* veste: *Dan.* fæste *n*: *Swed.* fästning *f*: *Icel.* festing *f.*] *A fastness, fortress, bulwark, place of strength, a castle, wall;* munimentum:—*Jos.* 11, 12. Swa swa fæsten *as a fortress, Elf. gl.* Nearo fæsten *narrow fortress, Bd.* 4, 26. —Fæsten-behæfednes *parsimony, niggardliness;* parsimonia, *Cot.* 191.

Fæsten-bryce *fast-break,* BREAKFAST, *Som.*

Fæsten-dæg *fast-day.*

Fæsten-gewerc *fortification work, fortification.*

Fæstennes *fastness, a walled town, Som.*

Fæsten-tid *fast-tide,* or *time.*

Fæster-moder *a fostermother,* v. fostermoder.

Fæstes; *adv. By chance;* forte:—*Cot.* 88.

Fæst-hafod, fæst-hafel, fæst-hafol *fast-having, sparing, having, sordid.*

Fæst-hafolnes, se; *f. Fast-havingness, greediness;* parcitas:—*Past.* 60.

Fæst-hydig *steadfast in mind, Cd.* 67.

Fæsting, e; *f. An entrusting, an act of confidence;* commendatio:—*L. pol. Alf.* 17, v. fæstan.

Fæstingan *To fasten, make firm;* firmare:—*Lev.* 26, 9, v. fæstnian.

Fæstingman *A surety;* fidejussor:—*Heming.* p. 32, 48.

Fæstlic; *adj.* FASTLIKE, *firm;* firmus:—*Cd.* 203.

Fæstlice; *comp.* or; *sup.* ost; *adv. Firmly, fast, quickly;* firmiter:—Hig fæstlice weoxon, *Jud.* 4, 24. Færð micle fæstlicor *goes much more firmly, Bt.* 39, 7, *Card.* p. 338, 23.

Fæst-mod *constant in mind, steady, Ors.* 6, 33.

Fæstmod-staðol *constancy, Off. Episc.* 1.

Fæstn *a fasting,* v. fæsten.

Fæstn *a fortification,* v. fæsten.

Fæstnes, se; *f.* FASTNESS, *fortification, firmness, stability;* propugnaculum:—*Bt.* 32, 3: *Gen.* 1, 6, v. fæsten.

Fæstnian *to fasten,* v. afæstnian.

Fæstnung, e; *f. A* FASTENING, *confirmation;* fixura:—*Jn.* 20, 25.

Fæst-ræd; *def.* se fæst-ræda; *adj.* [ræd *an opinion,*] *Bold, constant, inflexible;* constans:—*Bt.* 19.

Fæst-rædlice; *adv. Boldly, constantly;* constanter:—*Wulfst. Par.* 5.

Fæst-rædnes, se; *f. Fixed state of mind, fortitude, resolution;* fortitudo:—*Bt.* 5, 3.

FÆT, fat, es; d. e; *pl.* fatu, a, um; *n.* [*Plat. Dut.* vat *n*: *Ger.* fass *n*: *Ker.* faz: *Ot.* fazz: *Dan.* fad *n*: *Swed. Icel.* fat *n.*] *A vessel, cup,* VAT; vas:—*Mk.* 4, 27: *Gen.* 40, 11. Fætes botm *a vat's bottom, Cot.* 92.

Fætels, *a small vessel, a bag,* v. fetels.

Fæter, fetor, feotur; *pl.* fætero [*Dut.* veter] *A* FETTER, *band;* compes:—*C. Mk.* 5, 4.

Fætere *light, negligent, Som.*

Fæt-fellere *a vat-filler.*

Fæð *commits;* committit:—*R. Mt.* 5, 32.

FÆÐEM, fæðm, feðm, [*Plat.* fadem, faem *m*: *Dut.* vadem, vaam *f*: *Ger.* faden, fadem, faem *m*: *Ot.* fadom: *Dan.* favn *c*: *Swed.* famn *m*: *Ir.* fead] 1. *A cubit;* cubitus. 2. A FATHOM, *the space of both arms extended;* ulna. 3. *An enclosing of the arms, a grasp, an embrace;* amplexus. 4. *Whatever embraces* or *contains; as the bosom, the lap, an abyss, the deep, an expanse;* sinus, gremium:—1. Fæðm betwuxt elboga and handwrist *a cubit* (*is*) *betwixt the elbow and wrist, R.* 72: *Gen.* 6, 15, 16. 2. *Cot.* 162. 3. On fæðm *in a grasp, Cd.* 4. Widum fæðmum *wide embrace, Cd.* 146. 4. Of fæðme *from the bosom, Cd.* 187. Ofer ealne foldan fæðm *over all the earth's expanse, Cod. ex.* 116, b. 12.

Fæðer *a feather,* v. fyðer.

Fæðmian *To* FATHOM, *embrace;* amplecti:—*Cod. ex.* p. 89.

Fæðmlic; *adj. Bending, winding;* sinuosus:—*Ct.* 202.

Fætian *To* FETCH; adducere, *Lye.*

Fætnys, se; *f.* FATNESS; pinguedo:—*Ps.* 16, 11.

FÆTT, fett; *adj.* [*Plat. Ger.* fett: *Dut.* vet: *Dan.* feed, fedt: *Swed.* fet: *Icel.* feitr, fit.—fedan *to nourish*] FAT, *fatted;* pinguis:—Ofsloh an fætt celf, *Lk.* 15, 27, 23.

Fættian; *pp.* gefætted. *To* FATTEN; pinguefacere:—*Ps.* 64, 13.

Fæx *deceit;* fucus, *Lye.*

Fæx *hair,* v. feax.

FAG, fah; *adj.* [*Dan. Swed.* fager: *Icel.* fagr] *Shining, beautiful, of various colours, dyed;* versicolor:—Fag wyrm *a shining worm, Cd.* 42: *Ps.* 90, 13. Golde fah *shining with gold, Menol.* 491, v. bleo.

Fage *A kind of fish, a flounder;* flessus:—*MS. Tib. A.* 3.

Fagen *glad,* v. fægen.

Fagennian, gefagenian, gefagnian. *To rejoice, to be glad;* lætari:—*Bt.* 14, 1, v. fægnian.

Fagettan *to vary,* v. fagian.

Fagetung *inequality;* inæqualitas, *Som.*

Fagian *To shine, glitter, vary;* variare:—*Bt. R.* p. 164.

Fagmon *a foe man, an enemy.*

Fagnian *to rejoice,* v. fægnian.

Fagnys, se; fagung, e; *f. A variety, an ornament;* varietas:—*L. Ps.* 44, 15: *Dial.* 2, 27.

Fah *of different colours,* v. fag.

FAH, fa, gefah. *A* FOE, *an enemy, enmity, revenge;* inimicus:—Ic eom fah wið god, *Cd.* 215. Sy he fah wið þone cyng, *L. Athel.* 20, *W.* 60, 27.

Fahnodon, fahnude *rejoiced,* v. fagnian.

Fahnys *a rejoicing,* v. fægnung.

Faht *fought,* v. feohtan.

Falæcan *To kill;* interficere:—*L. Athel.* 20.

Falæd, fald, falde, falud. A FOLD, *a sheep-fold, stable;* ovile:—*Jn.* 10, 1: *Gen.* 18, 7.

Fald-gang *fold going, putting sheep in fold to manure the land.* —Fald-gang-penig *fold going money, money paid by a vassal to be free from sending sheep to*

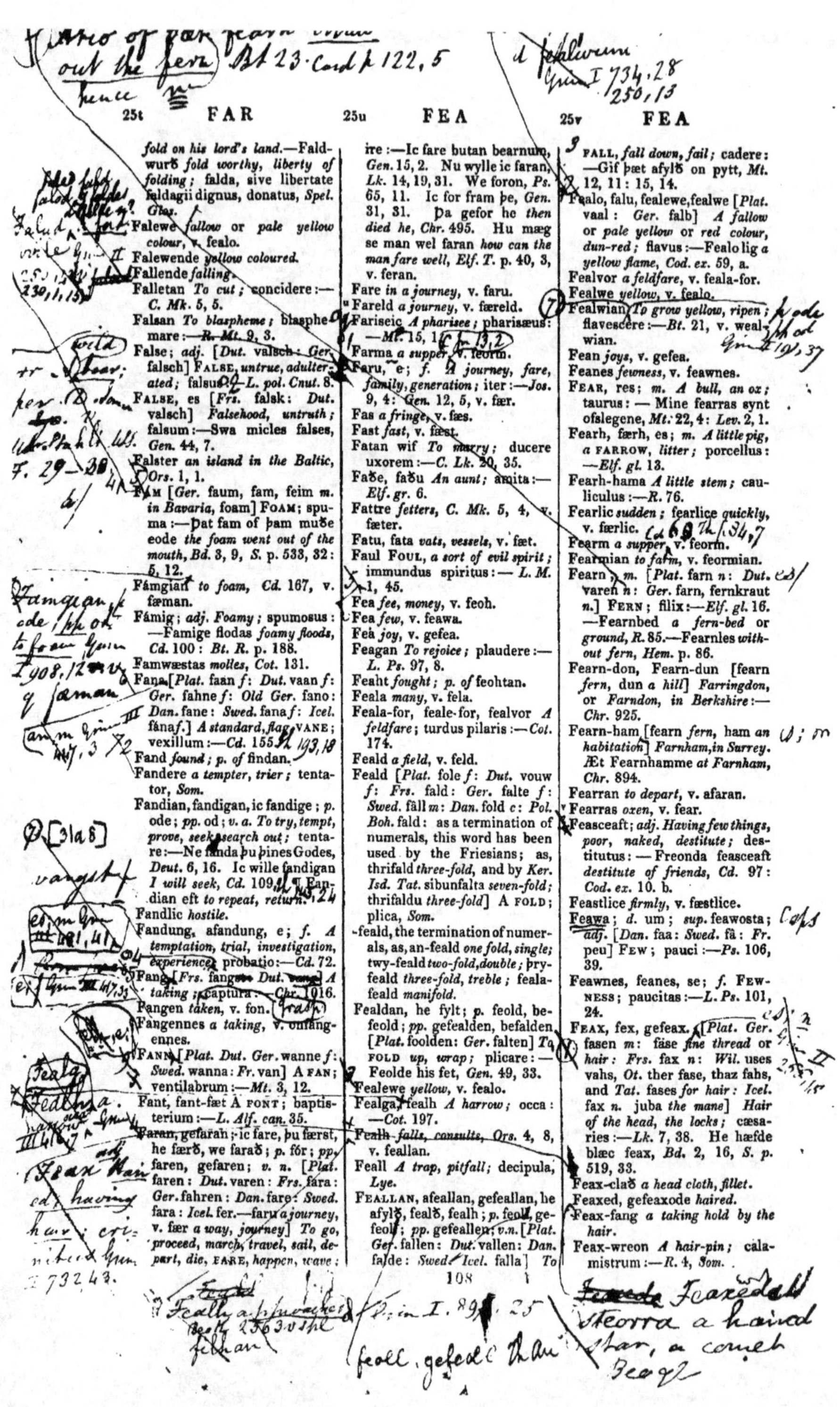

fold on his lord's land.—Faldwurð *fold worthy, liberty of folding;* falda, sive libertate faldagii dignus, donatus, *Spel. Glos.*
Falewe *fallow* or *pale yellow colour,* v. fealo.
Falewende *yellow coloured.*
Fallende *falling.*
Falletan *To cut;* concidere:—*C. Mk.* 5, 5.
Falsan *To blaspheme;* blasphemare:—*R. Mt.* 9, 3.
False; *adj.* [*Dut.* valsch: *Ger.* falsch] FALSE, *untrue, adulterated;* falsus:—*L. pol. Cnut.* 8.
FALSE, es [*Frs.* falsk: *Dut.* valsch] *Falsehood, untruth;* falsum:—Swa micles falses, *Gen.* 44, 7.
Falster *an island in the Baltic, Ors.* 1, 1.
FAM [*Ger.* faum, fam, feim *m.* in *Bavaria,* foam] FOAM; spuma:—Þat fam of þam muðe eode *the foam went out of the mouth, Bd.* 3, 9, *S.* p. 533, 32: 5, 12.
Fámgian *to foam, Cd.* 167, v. fæman.
Fámig; *adj. Foamy;* spumosus:—Famige flodas *foamy floods, Cd.* 100: *Bt. R.* p. 188.
Famwæstas *molles, Cot.* 131.
Fana [*Plat.* faan *f*: *Dut.* vaan *f*: *Ger.* fahne *f*: *Old Ger.* fano: *Dan.* fane: *Swed.* fana *f*: *Icel.* fána *f.*] *A standard, flag,* VANE; vexillum:—*Cd.* 155.
Fand *found; p. of* findan.
Fandere *a tempter, trier;* tentator, *Som.*
Fandian, fandigan, ic fandige; *p.* ode; *pp.* od; *v. a. To try, tempt, prove, seek, search out;* tentare:—Ne fanda þu þines Godes, *Deut.* 6, 16. Ic wille fandigan *I will seek, Cd.* 109. ¶ Fandian eft *to repeat, return.*
Fandlic *hostile.*
Fandung, afandung, e; *f. A temptation, trial, investigation, experience;* probatio:—*Cd.* 72.
Fang [*Frs.* fangst: *Dut.* vang] *A taking;* captura:—*Chr.* 1016.
Fangen *taken,* v. fon.
Fangennes *a taking,* v. onfangennes.
FANN [*Plat. Dut. Ger.* wanne *f*: *Swed.* wanna: *Fr.* van] A FAN; ventilabrum:—*Mt.* 3, 12.
Fant, fant-fæt A FONT; baptisterium:—*L. Alf. can.* 35.
Faran, gefaran; ic fare, þu færst, he færð, we farað; *p.* fór; *pp.* faren, gefaren; *v. n.* [*Plat.* faren: *Dut.* varen: *Frs.* fara: *Ger.* fahren: *Dan.* fare: *Swed.* fara: *Icel.* fer.—faru *a journey,* v. fær *a way, journey*] *To go, proceed, march, travel, sail, depart, die,* FARE, *happen, wave;* ire:—Ic fare butan bearnum, *Gen.* 15, 2. Nu wylle ic faran, *Lk.* 14, 19, 31. We foron, *Ps.* 65, 11. Ic for fram þe, *Gen.* 31, 31. Þa gefor he *then died he, Chr.* 495. Hu mæg se man wel faran *how can the man fare well, Elf. T.* p. 40, 3, v. feran.
Fare *in a journey,* v. faru.
Fareld *a journey,* v. færeld.
Fariseic *A pharisee;* pharisæus:—*Mt.* 15, 1.
Farma *a supper,* v. feorm.
Faru, e; *f. A journey, fare, family, generation;* iter:—*Jos.* 9, 4: *Gen.* 12, 5, v. fær.
Fas *a fringe,* v. fæs.
Fast *fast,* v. fæst.
Fatan wif *To marry;* ducere uxorem:—*C. Lk.* 20, 35.
Faðe, faðu *An aunt;* amita:—*Elf. gr.* 6.
Fattre *fetters, C. Mk.* 5, 4, v. fæter.
Fatu, fata *vats, vessels,* v. fæt.
Faul FOUL, *a sort of evil spirit;* immundus spiritus:—*L. M.* 1, 45.
Fea *fee, money,* v. feoh.
Fea *few,* v. feawa.
Feà *joy,* v. gefea.
Feagan *To rejoice;* plaudere:—*L. Ps.* 97, 8.
Feaht *fought; p. of* feohtan.
Feala *many,* v. fela.
Feala-for, feale-for, fealvor *A feldfare;* turdus pilaris:—*Cot.* 174.
Feald *a field,* v. feld.
Feald [*Plat.* fole *f*: *Dut.* vouw *f*: *Frs.* fald: *Ger.* falte *f*: *Swed.* fâll *m*: *Dan.* fold *c*: *Pol. Boh.* fald: as a termination of numerals, this word has been used by the Friesians; as, thrifald *three-fold,* and by *Ker. Isd. Tat.* sibunfalta *seven-fold;* thrifaldu *three-fold*] A FOLD; plica, *Som.*
-feald, the termination of numerals, as, an-feald *one fold, single;* twy-feald *two-fold, double;* þry-feald *three-fold, treble;* fealafeald *manifold.*
Fealdan, he fylt; *p.* feold, befeold; *pp.* gefealden, befalden [*Plat.* foolden: *Ger.* falten] *To* FOLD *up, wrap;* plicare:—Feolde his fet, *Gen.* 49, 33.
Fealewe *yellow,* v. fealo.
Fealga, fealh *A harrow;* occa:—*Cot.* 197.
Fealh *falls, consults, Ors.* 4, 8, v. feallan.
Feall *A trap, pitfall;* decipula, *Lye.*
FEALLAN, afeallan, gefeallan, he afylð, fealð, fealh; *p.* feoll, gefeoll; *pp.* gefeallen; *v. n.* [*Plat. Ger.* fallen: *Dut.* vallen: *Dan.* falde: *Swed. Icel.* falla] *To* FALL, *fall down, fail;* cadere:—Gif þæt afylð on pytt, *Mt.* 12, 11: 15, 14.
Fealo, falu, fealewe, fealwe [*Plat.* vaal: *Ger.* falb] *A fallow* or *pale yellow* or *red colour, dun-red;* flavus:—Fealo lig *a yellow flame, Cod. ex.* 59, a.
Fealvor *a feldfare,* v. feala-for.
Fealwe *yellow,* v. fealo.
Fealwian *To grow yellow, ripen;* flavescere:—*Bt.* 21, v. wealwian.
Fean *joys,* v. gefea.
Feanes *fewness,* v. feawnes.
FEAR, res; *m. A bull, an ox;* taurus:—Mine fearras synt ofslegene, *Mt.* 22, 4: *Lev.* 2, 1.
Fearh, færh, es; *m. A little pig, a* FARROW, *litter;* porcellus:—*Elf. gl.* 13.
Fearh-hama *A little stem;* cauliculus:—*R.* 76.
Fearlic *sudden;* fearlice *quickly,* v. færlic.
Fearm *a supper,* v. feorm.
Fearmian *to farm,* v. feormian.
Fearn, *m.* [*Plat.* farn *n*: *Dut.* varen *n*: *Ger.* farn, fernkraut *n.*] FERN; filix:—*Elf. gl.* 16.—Fearnbed *a fern-bed* or *ground, R.* 85.—Fearnles *without fern, Hem.* p. 86.
Fearn-don, Fearn-dun [fearn *fern,* dun *a hill*] *Farringdon,* or *Farndon, in Berkshire:*—*Chr.* 925.
Fearn-ham [fearn *fern,* ham *an habitation*] *Farnham, in Surrey.* Æt Fearnhamme *at Farnham, Chr.* 894.
Fearran *to depart,* v. afaran.
Fearras *oxen,* v. fear.
Feasceaft; *adj. Having few things, poor, naked, destitute;* destitutus:—Freonda feasceaft *destitute of friends, Cd.* 97: *Cod. ex.* 10. b.
Feastlice *firmly,* v. fæstlice.
Feawa; *d.* um; *sup.* feawosta; *adj.* [*Dan.* faa: *Swed.* fâ: *Fr.* peu] FEW; pauci:—*Ps.* 106, 39.
Feawnes, feanes, se; *f.* FEWNESS; paucitas:—*L. Ps.* 101, 24.
FEAX, fex, gefeax. [*Plat. Ger.* fasen *m*: fâse *fine thread* or *hair*: *Frs.* fax *n*: *Wil.* uses vahs, *Ot.* ther fase, thaz fahs, and *Tat.* fases *for hair*: *Icel.* fax *n.* juba *the mane*] *Hair of the head, the locks;* cæsaries:—*Lk.* 7, 38. He hæfde blæc feax, *Bd.* 2, 16, *S.* p. 519, 33.
Feax-clað *a head cloth, fillet.*
Feaxed, gefeaxode *haired.*
Feax-fang *a taking hold by the hair.*
Feax-wreon *A hair-pin;* calamistrum:—*R.* 4, *Som.*

Farm food v feorm

Fald-socn the liberty of folding, or of folding sheep Som. Gavelkynd p 135, 27

Falæce foelike hostilis Som

Falu a fallow colour Som v fealo

Fām, es; n foam etc

Fana, an; m a stand etc

Fane the white flower de luce; iris alba L. M 1, 63 Som

Fang, es; m a taking grasp etc

— discovery Cd. 72 Th p 87, 21

Fanne, fe fan etc

Fanel ? fane

Fara, an; m? A traveller; viator Beo K 2925 Beo. ye

Far, e; f A journey, fare Th. An v fær, fare

Fare, es; m A course family; iter familia Th. An Dine fare lædan to lead thy family Cd 83 p 105

Farnes iland on the northcoast

Farnea-dalond insula Farnensis Som

Fær a boar Som v. Sl. eofer

Farmaz

Farod A shore; littus Beo K 3828

Faderman a smith Ben v fædling man

False-pening a bad penny; adulterinus denarius R. 100 Ben

Fast-stow A fast or close place, a fold L. In 70

Fax hair Th An v feax

also a noun

Feala many 2 feala-feald many fold v fela

Fela 3 fealdan to multiply — Feala 4 fealdlice manifold — Feala 5 fealdnes multifying Som

Fealefor a feldfare Som v feala for

Fealo, fealu fallow colour Som v fealo

Feax-nedl a hair needle R 4

Feax-net a hair net R 4

Feallendlic lekeh to fall, ruinous, caducus Som

Fealwe-docce a fallow coloured dock lapathum fulvum Som

Fean to hate; odisse Ben

Fearn, es, n fern

Fea-tid a short time; modicum tempus Ben

Fædem a fathom Th. An v fæðm

Fea-sceaft, e, f misery distress Beo K 1781

Feaw few Th An v feawa

Feax, es; n hair

Feax-facas, feax-facon hair hanging down the fore head; antiæ frontes Som — Feax-fealling falling off of the hair; alopecia — Feax-gerædian to dress the hair — Feax-sceacga a bush of hair, coma — Feax-sceaged comatus

Feld-westen, es; n a field waste, desert; campestris solitudo Deut 1, 1 Lye

Feleferd a centipede Som v feldi-ferd — Felte-fuerc, es; m melancholy L. M 2, 1

strictilis Som — Felnys, ... perdues Bosw

Fel-terre centaurea minor, centaurea, pa smalor fel-terre L. M 2, 8 v

centaurea — Felt-wyrt ... wurma-wyrt

wild marjoram; origanum — Felaw a fellow; Socius Lye — Som — Felt-wyrt gladiolus

Elf gl. 14 Som L — Feloh a harrow Som v Spl. — Femne

feldgr

Fec a space Som v fec — Feld-beo a field bee, locust

Feccan p fehte — attacus Som — Feld-elfen elves of — Feld-ferd a centipede centumpellio Cot 171 Lye

Fecele a torch Som v fecele — Feld-elfen wood nymphs Som — Feld-gongende field ganging or wild beast Som

Feer fever Som — 1 Fage feldas variegated fields Cot 157 Spl 196, 5

a fever Som Cot 88 Som — Feld-hnyder, es; m a field ..., or calf, chit ad cut C R Ben Lye

8 Fefrian to have a fever Som v feferian — 2) Fen-gelad, es n a fen-path Beo K 2717

9 Feging a compting Som v fefegung inca — Feld-more wild carrot; pastinaca erratica Cot 24 Lye

7) Fen-hop, es n a fen dwelling Beo K 1521 — Feld-ruw field rue; ruta sylvestris

Felge, an f. a marsh ... Th 166 — 3) Feoh-ærn a fee place a treasury; gazophylacium Som Lye

4) Fefordrifende having a fever, febricitans R 44 — Feld-swam mushroom, toadstool; fungus Cot 89 Som

6) Fefrian to be sick of a fever febricitare Som — 6) Feoh-gafol, es m Usury; usura Som Grim II 452 — bradigaco Cot 25 Lye

7 Fefer-seoc fever sick, sick of a fever — Feoh-georn covetous, avarus. Som Lye

10 Feing a fight ... v Supl. fang — 5) Feoh-gyft, e f a gift of money, pecuniarum donum Beo Th, K 2046, 2177 — Feoh-gytsung, e f a getting of money, a ... pecuniae amor cupiditas Bd 212 Lye

Fenegas the bowels, intestines; viscerum receptacula Mone B 173 — 7) Feoh-hord, feoh-hus a money hoard or house, a treasury; ærarium Cot 212 — Feoh-læning, e f a money lending, a loan ... fæneratio, hypotheca R. 14 Lye

Feoh-spilling money wasting, profusion, waste; pecuniarum effusio Chr 1096 Lye — Feoh-leasnes, se f want of money, poverty; pecuniae inopia

Feirnes fairness Th an v fægernys — Fen-fixas fen fishes pisces palustres Som — Feolif munificence, Som munificentia Som

9 Fen-freodo a fenny dwelling, habitation paludenosa Beo 66 K 1695 Grim II 452, 36

Feng a span ... Cd 5 — Fen-fugelas fen fowls; aves palustres — 6) Fen-hop, es n a fen

Th Ap. 3 ... Grim II 452, 35 — den, or ... receptacle; paludose Beo 59 K 1521

Fen-hleoþ, es n fen covers ... Beo K 1634 — Fen-land fen land palustris terra Mos 1, 10

12 Fela-hror, strong, dear ... pristus Grim II 731, 17 — Fen-mynte, an f water mint; mentha aquatica Som Lye — Fen-gelad, es n ... fenny way, or road iter paludinaceum Grim II 452, 37 Beo 103 K 2717

Fenol the herb fennel; foeniculum Som — Feolo many Cd 222 Th p 290, 26 v fela

Fen-hleoþ, es n

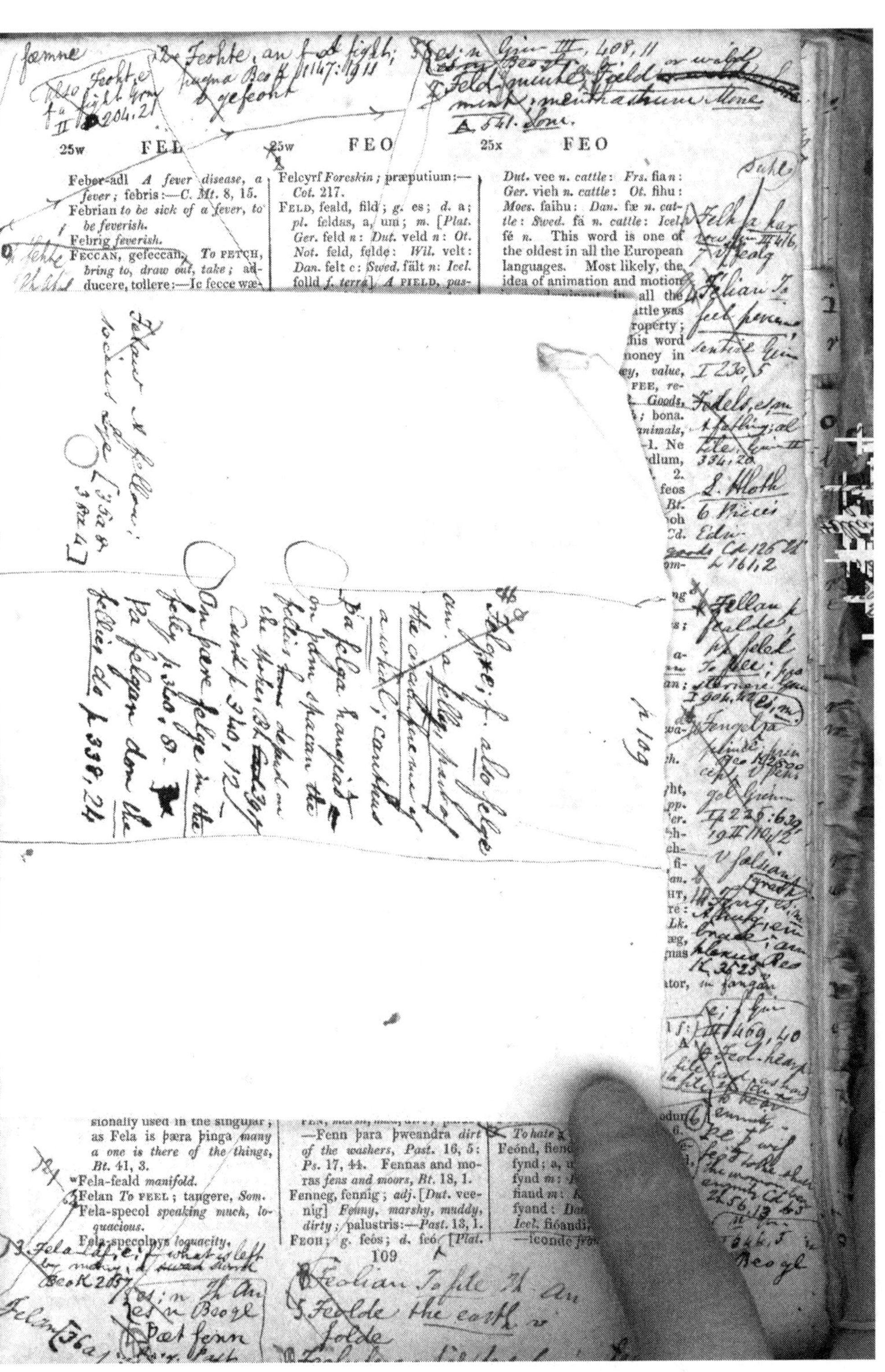

Feber-adl *A fever disease, a fever;* febris:—*C. Mt.* 8, 15.
Febrian *to be sick of a fever, to be feverish.*
Febrig *feverish.*
FECCAN, gefeccan, *To* FETCH, *bring to, draw out, take;* adducere, tollere:—Ic fecce wæ-

Felcyrf *Foreskin;* præputium:—*Cot.* 217.
FELD, feald, fild; *g.* es; *d.* a; *pl.* feldas, a, um; *m.* [*Plat. Ger.* feld *n*: *Dut.* veld *n*: *Ot. Not.* feld, felde: *Wil.* velt: *Dan.* felt c: *Swed.* fält *n*: *Icel.* folld *f. terra*] *A* FIELD, *pas-*

Dut. vee *n. cattle*: *Frs.* fia *n*: *Ger.* vieh *n. cattle*: *Ot.* fihu: *Moes.* faihu: *Dan.* fæ *n. cattle*: *Swed.* fä *n. cattle*: *Icel.* fé *n.* This word is one of the oldest in all the European languages. Most likely, the idea of animation and motion ... all the ... attle was ... roperty; ... his word ... money in ... ey, *value,* ... FEE, *re-* ... *Goods,* ... ; bona. ... *animals,* ... 1. Ne ... dlum, ... 2. ... feos ... *Bt.* ... oh ... *Cd.* ...

sionally used in the singular; as Fela is þæra þinga *many a one is there of the things, Bt.* 41, 3.
Fela-feald *manifold.*
Felan To FEEL; tangere, *Som.*
Fela-specol *speaking much, loquacious.*
Fela-specolnys *loquacity.*

—Fenn þara þweandra *dirt of the washers, Past.* 16, 5: *Ps.* 17, 44. Fennas and moras *fens and moors, Bt.* 18, 1.
Fenneg, fennig; *adj.* [*Dut.* veenig] *Fenny, marshy, muddy, dirty;* palustris:—*Past.* 13, 1.
FEOH; *g.* feós; *d.* feó, [*Plat.*

To hate ...
Feónd, fiend ... fynd; a, ... fynd *m*: ... fiand *m*: ... fyand: ... *Icel.* fióandi ... —feonde fro...

Feld-westen, es; n a field waste desert; campestris solitudo Deut 1, 1 Lye

Feleferd a centipede Som v feld-ferd — Felle-fwercnes, melancholy L. M. 2, 1

atractylis Som — Felnys, se; f Centaurea; þa smalan Cetterre L. M. 2, 8 v centaurea minor

Fel-terre centaurea minor

centaurea — Felt-wyrt

wild marjorum; origanum

Elf gl. 14 Som — Felaw a fellow, socius Lye — Som — Felt-wyrt wurma wyrt

Felch a harrow Som V! L — Fenne

feldga

Fec a space Som v fec — Feld-beo a field bee, locust; attacus Som — Feld-ferd a centipede, centumpellio R 17 Lye

Feccan p felite — Feld-elfen, wood nymphs — Som — Feld-gon

Feer, Pher a fever Cot 88.

Fefrian to have a v fefer-gan

Feging a co... v gefeging inc

Fen-hof... dwelling

Felge, ...

Fefer-adl-fen... fever; febr...

Fefer-gan to ... febricitare

Fefer-seoc fev...

Feing ... v sup

Fenian ... intestines receptacul...

Feoh-spi... washing water

Feirnes fai... v fægerni...

Feng a...

Fen-land fen land paludis terra Bosl, 10 — ... paludre ... Beo 59 R 152

Fen-mynte, an water mint; mentha aquatica Som. Lye — Fen-ælad, -ad fenny way or road iter paludinosum Grm II 452, 37 Beo 103 R 2717

Feolo many Cd 222 Th p 290, 26 v fela

Feber-adl *A fever disease, a fever;* febris:—*C. Mt.* 8, 15.

Febrian *to be sick of a fever, to be feverish.*

Febrig *feverish.*

Feccan, gefeccan, *To* FETCH, *bring to, draw out, take;* adducere, tollere:—Ic fecce wæter, *Gen.* 18, 4: 27, 42: *Lk.* 12, 20.

Fe'dan, afédan, he fet; *p.* fedde; *pp.* feded, fedd [*Plat.* voden: *Dut.* voeden: *Frs.* feda, *Het.* fieden *Jap.*: *Dan.* föde: *Swed.* föda: *Icel.* fódra *to nourish*] *To* FEED, *nourish, bring up, educate;* pascere:—Eower heofonlica fæder hig fet, *Mt.* 6, 26. Hig afedde wæron, *Gen.* 25, 27. We þe feddon, *Mt.* 25, 37.

Fedels *fatlings.*

Feder *a father,* v. fæder.

Feder *a feather,* v. fyþer.

Fedesl *A feeder, provider;* obsonator:—*L. Ethelb.* 12.

Feding; *m. A feeding;* pastio, pabulatio, *Som.*

Fednes, se; *f. Nourishment;* nutrimentum:—*Bd.* 1, 27. *resp.* 9.

Fedra *an uncle,* v. fædera.

Feerlic *sudden;* feer-lice *suddenly,* v. færlic.

Feer-stylt *Astonishment;* stupor:—*C. Mk.* 5, 42.

Fefer, fefor, fefer-adl [*Plat.* feeber *n*: *Ger.* fieber *n*: *Wil.* fieber: *Tat.* fiobar, fieber: *Dan. Swed.* feber *m*: *Pol.* febra] *A* FEVER; febris:—*Mt.* 8, 15. Ælces dæges fefer *an every day* or *quotidian fever.*

Fefer-fuge *feverfew, a herb, R.* 40.

Fefor *a fever,* v. fefer.

Fegan *To join;* jungere:—*Somn.* 128, v. gefegan.

Feger, fegr *fair,* v. fæger.

Fegre *early.*

Feh *money,* v. feoh.

Feh-gerefa, feh-groefa *a money director, a steward.*

Fehst *takest;* fehð *takes,* v. fon.

Fel *a fell, skin,* v. fell.

Fela, [illegible], feala, feola; *adj. indecl.* [*Plat. Dut.* veel: *Ger.* viel: *Ker.* fil, filu: *Moes.* filu: *Icel.* fiöl *for* fiölld, in composition, the same as the *Ger.* viel] *Many, much;* multi:—On feala wisan *in many ways, Col. Mon.* He ongan hig fela læran, *Mk.* 6, 34. Occasionally used in the singular; as Fela is þæra þinga *many a one is there of the things, Bt.* 41, 3.

Fela-feald *manifold.*

Felan *To* FEEL; tangere, *Som.*

Fela-specol *speaking much, loquacious.*

Fela-specolnys *loquacity.*

Felcyrf *Foreskin;* præputium:—*Cot.* 217.

Feld, feald, fild; *g.* es; *d.* a; *pl.* feldas, a, um; *m.* [*Plat. Ger.* feld *n*: *Dut.* veld *n*: *Ot. Not.* feld, felde: *Wil.* velt: *Dan.* felt *c*: *Swed.* fält *n*: *Icel.* folld *f. terra*] *A* FIELD, *pasture, a plain, an open country;* campus:—*Deut.* 34, 8: *Ps.* 103, 9.

Feld-cyric *a field church, a country church; L. eccl. Cnut.* 3.

Feld-hus *a field-house, tent, Som.*

Feld-land *Field-land, a plain;* planities:—*Deut.* 1, 7, opposed to dun *a hill.*

Feldlic; *adj. Fieldlike, country, rural;* agrestis:—On feldlicre stowe, *Lk.* 6, 17.

Feld-wyrt *field wort, gentian.*

Fele *much, many,* v. fela.

Felg, felge *a felly,* v. fælge.

Feligean *to follow,* v. fylgean.

Fell [*Plat. Ger.* fell *n*: *Dut.* vel *n*: *Frs.* fel *n*: *Moes.* fill: *Icel.* felldr *m*: *Icel.* fela *to cover*] *A* FELL, *skin;* pellis:—Cealfes fell, *Ex.* 29, 14. On deora fellum *in beasts' skins, Ors.* 1, 1, *Bar.* p. 23, 21, 25, 26.

Fell; *adj.* [*Frs.* fel] FELL, *cruel, severe;* crudelis, *Som.*

Fell *gall, anger, Som.*

Fellan, fellað; *pp.* gefellen, *To give,* v. sellan.

Fellen *Belonging to a skin, skinny;* pelliceus:—Fellen gyrdel, *Mk.* 1, 6.

Fellen hæt *felt-hat, R.* 18.

Felleread *purple, a purple robe.*

Felnys, se; *f. Cruelty, fierceness;* crudelitas, *Som.*

Felsan *To recompence;* expiare, *Som.*

Felt FELT; pannus, *Som.*

Feltun *An enclosed place, garden, privy, dunghill;* secessus:—Swa swa meox under feltun *as dirt on a dunghill, Bt.* 36, 1.

Fen *a fen,* v. fenn.

Fen-cerse *Fen-cress;* nasturtium aquaticum, *Som.*

Fen-fearn, fenfern *Water-fern;* salvia:—*R.* 42.

Feng, fengon *took,* v. fon.

Fenix *a phœnix.*

Fen-lic *fenlike, marshy.*

Fenn, fen, fæn, fænn, föen, es; *m.* [*Plat. Ger.* fenne *f.* fenn *n*: *Dut.* veen *n*: *Frs.* and fenne: *Moes.* fani *dirtiness*] *A* FEN, *marsh, mud, dirt;* palus:—Fenn þara þweandra *dirt of the washers, Past.* 16, 5: *Ps.* 17, 44. Fennas and moras *fens and moors, Bt.* 18, 1.

Fenneg, fennig; *adj.* [*Dut.* veenig] *Fenny, marshy, muddy, dirty;* palustris:—*Past.* 13, 1.

Feoh; *g.* feós; *d.* feó [*Plat. Dut.* vee *n. cattle*: *Frs.* fia *n*: *Ger.* vieh *n. cattle*: *Ot.* fihu: *Moes.* faihu: *Dan.* fæ *n. cattle*: *Swed.* fä *n. cattle*: *Icel.* fé *n.* This word is one of the oldest in all the European languages. Most likely, the idea of animation and motion is predominant in all the preceding words. Cattle was the first kind of property; and, by bartering, this word came to signify money in general.] 1. *Money, value, price, hire, stipend,* FEE, *reward;* pecunia. 2. *Goods, property, riches, wealth;* bona. 3. *Property in living animals, cattle, sheep;* pecus:—1. Ne feoh on eowrum bigyrdlum, *Mt.* 10, 9: *Gen.* 23, 9. 2. Ne wilniað nanes oðres feos *wish for no other riches, Bt.* 14, 2. 3. Gangende feoh *walking property, cattle, Cd.* 129.

Feoh-bote, *a pecuniary recompence.*

Feoh-fang *a fee taking, taking* [illegible]

Feoh-gestreon *Treasure, riches;* gaza:—*Cot.* 119, *Som.*

Feoh-gyrnes *money, desire, avarice.*

Feoh-gytsere *A covetous man;* avarus:—*Bt.* 7, 4.

Feoh-leas *moneyless.*

Feoh-sceatt *money tribute, wages.*

Feoh-strang *money strong, rich.*

Feoht *a fight,* v. gefeoht.

Feohtan, gefeohtan, he fyht, fiht; *p.* feaht, hi fuhton; *pp.* fohten, gefohten [*Plat. Ger.* fechten: *Ker.* fehtan: *Ot.* fehtanne: *Wil.* in the *p.* vuchton: *Dut.* vechten: *Frs.* fiuchta: *Swed.* fäkta: *Dan.* fegte: *Ir.* fichim] *To* FIGHT, *contend, make war;* pugnare:—Cyning wyle feohtan, *Lk.* 14, 31. He gefeohtan ne mæg, *Lk.* 14, 32. Mine þegnas fuhton, *Jn.* 18, 36.

Feohtere *A fighter;* pugnator, *Lye.*

Feohtlác *a fight.*

Feol [*Frs.* file *f*: *Dut.* vyl *f*: *Plat.* fiel *f*: *Ger.* feile *f.*] *A* FILE; lima:—*Elf. gr.* 27.

Feola *many,* v. fela.

Feoll *fell; p. of* feallan.

Feon *a fen,* v. fenn.

Feon, he feoð; *p.* hi feodon, *To hate;* odisse:—*Ps.* 10, 6.

Feónd, fiend, es; *pl.* fynd, gefynd; a, um; *m.* [*Plat.* fiend, fynd *m*: *Dut.* vyand *m*: *Frs.* fiand *m*: *Ker. Ot.* fiant: *Moes.* fyand: *Dan. Swed.* fjende *m*: *Icel.* fióandi, fiáandi, fiandi *m.*—feonde *from* feon *to hate,* fa,

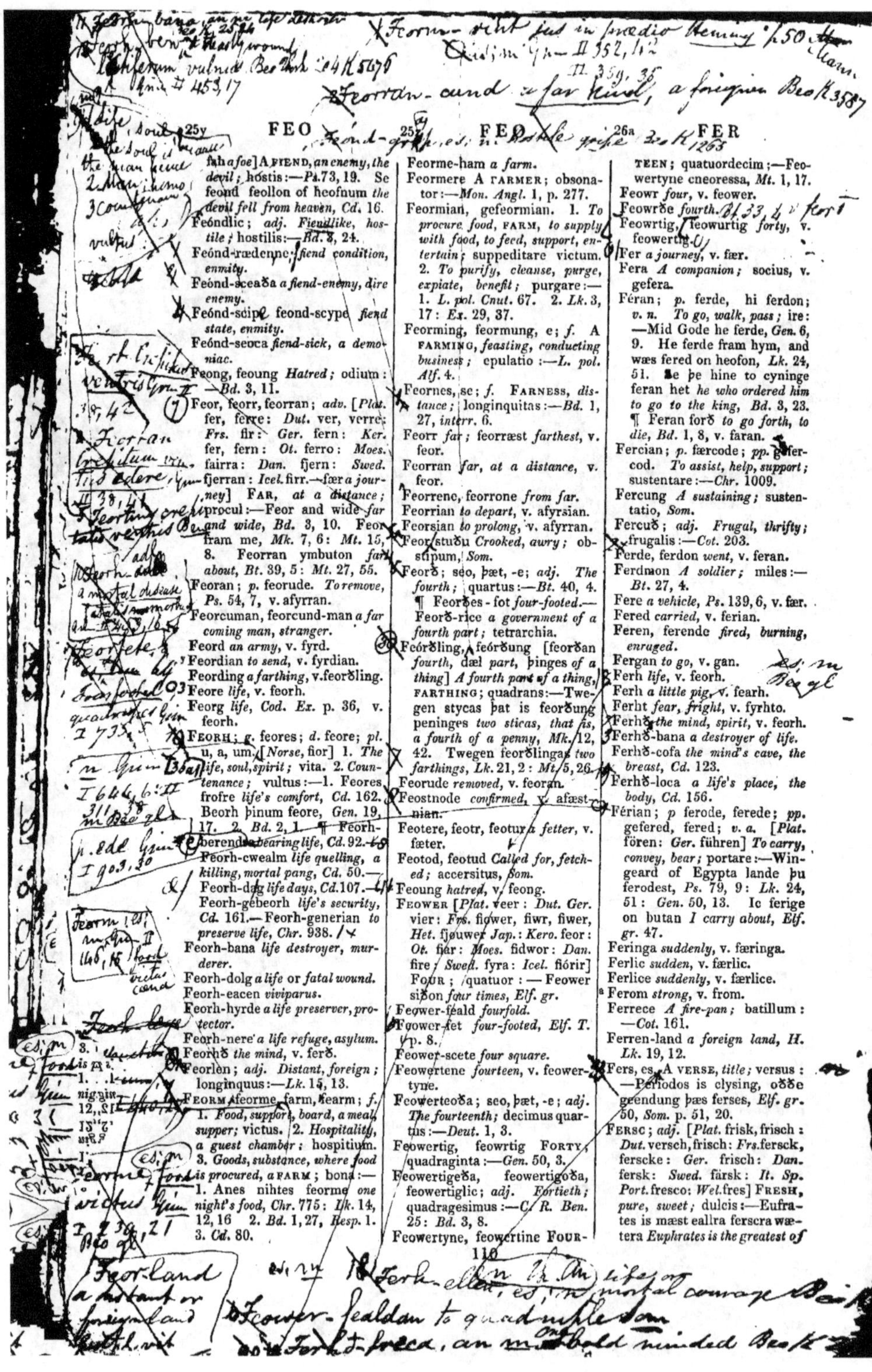

fah a foe] A FIEND, an enemy, the devil; hostis:—Ps. 73, 19. Se feond feollon of heofnum the devil fell from heaven, Cd. 16.

Feóndlic; adj. Fiendlike, hostile; hostilis:—Bd. 3, 24.

Feónd-rædenne; fiend condition, enmity.

Feónd-sceaða a fiend-enemy, dire enemy.

Feónd-scipe, feond-scype fiend state, enmity.

Feónd-seoca fiend-sick, a demoniac.

Feong, feoung Hatred; odium:—Bd. 3, 11.

Feor, feorr, feorran; adv. [Plat. fer, ferre: Dut. ver, verre: Frs. fir: Ger. fern: Ker. fer, fern: Ot. ferro: Moes. fairra: Dan. fjern: Swed. fjerran: Icel. firr.—fær a journey] FAR, at a distance; procul:—Feor and wide far and wide, Bd. 3, 10. Feor fram me, Mk. 7, 6: Mt. 15, 8. Feorran ymbuton far about, Bt. 39, 5: Mt. 27, 55.

Feoran; p. feorude. To remove, Ps. 54, 7, v. afyrran.

Feorcuman, feorcund-man a far coming man, stranger.

Feord an army, v. fyrd.

Feordian to send, v. fyrdian.

Feording a farthing, v. feorðling.

Feore life, v. feorh.

Feorg life, Cod. Ex. p. 36, v. feorh.

FEORH; g. feores; d. feore; pl. u, a, um. [Norse, fior] 1. The life, soul, spirit; vita. 2. Countenance; vultus:—1. Feores frofre life's comfort, Cd. 162. Beorh þinum feore, Gen. 19, 17. 2. Bd. 2, 1. ¶ Feorh-berende bearing life, Cd. 92.—Feorh-cwealm life quelling, a killing, mortal pang, Cd. 50.—Feorh-dæg life days, Cd. 107.—Feorh-gebeorh life's security, Cd. 161.—Feorh-generian to preserve life, Chr. 938.

Feorh-bana life destroyer, murderer.

Feorh-dolg a life or fatal wound.

Feorh-eacen viviparus.

Feorh-hyrde a life preserver, protector.

Feorh-nere a life refuge, asylum.

Feorhð the mind, v. ferð.

Feorlen; adj. Distant, foreign; longinquus:—Lk. 15, 13.

FEORM, feorme, farm, fearm; f. 1. Food, support, board, a meal, supper; victus. 2. Hospitality, a guest chamber; hospitium. 3. Goods, substance, where food is procured, a FARM; bona:—1. Anes nihtes feorme one night's food, Chr. 775: Lk. 14, 12, 16 2. Bd. 1, 27, Resp. 1. 3. Cd. 80.

Feorme-ham a farm.

Feormere A FARMER; obsonator:—Mon. Angl. 1, p. 277.

Feormian, gefeormian. 1. To procure food, FARM, to supply with food, to feed, support, entertain; suppeditare victum. 2. To purify, cleanse, purge, expiate, benefit; purgare:—1. L. pol. Cnut. 67. 2. Lk. 3, 17: Ex. 29, 37.

Feorming, feormung, e; f. A FARMING, feasting, conducting business; epulatio:—L. pol. Alf. 4.

Feornes, se; f. FARNESS, distance; longinquitas:—Bd. 1, 27, interr. 6.

Feorr far; feorræst farthest, v. feor.

Feorran far, at a distance, v. feor.

Feorrene, feorrone from far.

Feorrian to depart, v. afyrsian.

Feorsian to prolong, v. afyrran.

Feorstuðu Crooked, awry; obstipum, Som.

Feorð; seo, þæt, -e; adj. The fourth; quartus:—Bt. 40, 4. ¶ Feorðes-fot four-footed.—Feorð-rice a government of a fourth part; tetrarchia.

Feórðling, feórðung [feorðan fourth, dæl part, þinges of a thing] A fourth part of a thing, FARTHING; quadrans:—Twegen stycas þat is feorðung peninges two sticas, that is, a fourth of a penny, Mk. 12, 42. Twegen feorðlingas two farthings, Lk. 21, 2: Mt. 5, 26.

Feorude removed, v. feoran.

Feostnode confirmed, v. afæstnian.

Feotere, feotr, feotur a fetter, v. fæter.

Feotod, feotud Called for, fetched; accersitus, Som.

Feoung hatred, v. feong.

FEOWER [Plat. veer: Dut. Ger. vier: Frs. fiower, fiwr, fiwer, Het. fjøuwer Jap.: Kero. feor: Ot. fiar: Moes. fidwor: Dan. fire: Swed. fyra: Icel. fiórir] FOUR; quatuor:—Feower siðon four times, Elf. gr.

Feower-feald fourfold.

Feower-fet four-footed, Elf. T. p. 8.

Feower-scete four square.

Feowertene fourteen, v. feowertyne.

Feowerteoða; seo, þæt, -e; adj. The fourteenth; decimus quartus:—Deut. 1, 3.

Feowertig, feowrtig FORTY, quadraginta:—Gen. 50, 3.

Feowertigeða, feowertigoða, feowertiglic; adj. Fortieth; quadragesimus:—C. R. Ben. 25: Bd. 3, 8.

Feowertyne, feowertine FOURTEEN; quatuordecim;—Feowertyne cneoressa, Mt. 1, 17.

Feowr four, v. feower.

Feowrðe fourth.

Feowrtig, feowurtig forty, v. feowertig.

Fer a journey, v. fær.

Fera A companion; socius, v. gefera.

Féran; p. ferde, hi ferdon; v. n. To go, walk, pass; ire:—Mid Gode he ferde, Gen. 6, 9. He ferde fram hym, and wæs fered on heofon, Lk. 24, 51. Se þe hine to cyninge feran het he who ordered him to go to the king, Bd. 3, 23. ¶ Feran forð to go forth, to die, Bd. 1, 8, v. faran.

Fercian; p. færcode; pp. gefercod. To assist, help, support; sustentare:—Chr. 1009.

Fercung A sustaining; sustentatio, Som.

Fercuð; adj. Frugal, thrifty; frugalis:—Cot. 203.

Ferde, ferdon went, v. feran.

Ferdmon A soldier; miles:—Bt. 27, 4.

Fere a vehicle, Ps. 139, 6, v. fær.

Fered carried, v. ferian.

Feren, ferende fired, burning, enraged.

Fergan to go, v. gan.

Ferh life, v. feorh.

Ferh a little pig, v. fearh.

Ferht fear, fright, v. fyrhto.

Ferhð the mind, spirit, v. feorh.

Ferhð-bana a destroyer of life.

Ferhð-cofa the mind's cave, the breast, Cd. 123.

Ferhð-loca a life's place, the body, Cd. 156.

Férian; p ferode, ferede; pp. gefered, fered; v. a. [Plat. fören: Ger. führen] To carry, convey, bear; portare:—Wingeard of Egypta lande þu ferodest, Ps. 79, 9: Lk. 24, 51: Gen. 50, 13. Ic ferige on butan I carry about, Elf. gr. 47.

Feringa suddenly, v. færinga.

Ferlic sudden, v. færlic.

Ferlice suddenly, v. færlice.

Ferom strong, v. from.

Ferrece A fire-pan; batillum:—Cot. 161.

Ferren-land a foreign land, H. Lk. 19, 12.

Fers, es, A VERSE, title; versus:—Periodos is clysing, oððe geendung þæs ferses, Elf. gr. 50, Som. p. 51, 20.

FERSC; adj. [Plat. frisk, frisch: Dut. versch, frisch: Frs. fersck, ferscke: Ger. frisch: Dan. fersk: Swed. färsk: It. Sp. Port. fresco: Wel. fres] FRESH, pure, sweet; dulcis:—Eufrates is mæst eallra ferscra wætera Euphrates is the greatest of

Ferd-wite forisfacta belli Coot Rolf 14 + Lye v fyrd-wite

Ferd-wyrþe a herb L.Ke 1,87 — Fered deluded, delusus Som — Fered gressus S 1216,18 Lye

Fereld a way Lye v fareld — Ferennis se f a trans. migratio Lye v sup færenyss — Feowertig feald fortyfold Som

— Fre-scot fare scot, way money, naulum Rot 138 Lye — Feren-socn a framing bay sibba of 173 v fær

— Feorh-cwealm e f murrain of hogs; lues porcina Som

feorh — lives, in Feorh-cwalu internecies Cd 114

1. Feond-ræs

2. violence Cd 22 Th p 55,35 — Feond-seocnes, se

4) fiend sickness, demonology, morbus daemoniacus

custom

wilderness

Feorwit ... curiosity

Feorwit-georn curious Som

Feorwit-geornes se f curiosity Som v fir.

wet-georn

Feower-wintra of four years Som v winter

vessel Cd 75 Th p 93,12 v far

Feon-land fen land Hr 1070 v fenn

Feored ... Cd Th 130 Lye

Feorh-bealo es m life-bale or mortal affliction Beo 310: K 1149

Feorh-bennum mortal wound ... K 4176

Feorh-adl e f mortal disease, fatalis morbus L M 3,22 Som

Feorh-cere loss of life vitae damnum Ex ... Wiht Ex 13,3

Feorh-hus, es n a life house, the body Th An 27

Feorh-lean life-gift Cd 149 Th p 187,12

Feorran to remove Lye v feorgan

Feorla ... far be it ... absit Som

Feorh-last, es m life's course, life vitae vestigium Beo K 1976

Feorh-sweng ... stroke

Feorh-cleofa ... bosom, the body Cod Ex 42

Beo 186,1 Grein 453,24

Feorh-ge-midla

Feor-weg far way, distance Dob 20,49

Feorh-wund, e f a deadly wound ... vulnus Beo K 1766

propter Hospites Kitchen

5 Feor-begeondan far beyond longe ultra Lye

6 Feor-buendes far dwellers a stranger Beo K 506

3 Feore To widan feore in the wide existence ... for ever ... fere, feorh

Feor-gewitan to ...

Feorh-cyn the living ... Beo K 4526

Feorh-lege es m laying down of life, fate, death fatum, exitium, lethum Beo 20 K 5595 Grein 640,27 II 453,21

genidla, an m. murderer, homicida Beo K 117; 214

... man worthe ... feorme ...

... Þonne þu ... feorme ...

Feorbed a bed for a journey; bajanula R 66

Ferd-faru, e f an hostile expedition Elene 234

Ferd a going, journey; an army v fyrd

Feorh-last life's path, track of life

Ferhd-gleaw prudent minded, sagacious Th. An Jdth 10

Ferhd-cearig soul anxious Cd 104 Th p 133,20

Forloren lost Cd 16 Th p 20,1

a swiðe lytle feorme ... para boca ... the very little ... books

Food & Hospitality; Goods & use advantage

Feorme ... substance Cd 125 Th 161,2

Ulta lædan feoh & feorme to take possession cattle & stores Cd 80 Th p 99,21 — Faran mid feorme to go with substance stock Cd 53 Th p 104,6 — Mid feo & feorme with goods

Ferh-weard, e. f.
life guard Beo
1168

Fersian, fers-wyrcan
to make verses; to ve[illegible]
feare Som

A sore or scab moving in the Body where there is hair
Fic-adl, e. f. Ficus morbus
Lk 3, 48 Som
Fic-leaf a fig leaf Gen 3, 7
Fic-wyrmas figworms vermes ex ficu morbo orti
Lk 3, 48
Fic-treow [illegible] fig tree
ficus [illegible] Th. Anth.
Fic-wyrt, figwort; ficus Ben

Fert mud, spirit, life
[illegible] 145, Th. 180, 25
wide ferd perpetually
v. ferht
3 Feste fast Th. An
v. faste
Ferwatfull anxious; solicitus C. R. 12, 26
v. firwit-georn
Fester-fæder foster father
Fester-bearn fosterling
v. foster
Fester-mon a surety
L. North pres 1 W. p. 98, 20
Fæsten-mon
[illegible] sluggish [illegible]
Fete [illegible] fete
[illegible] fast track
[illegible] Th. An
Feder-homa feather covering, wings;
Dalæ Cd 22 Th p 27, 13
Fetigan to fetch Th. An v. fetian
24 Fett feeds Th. An v. fedan
25 Fettian to contend Th. An v. feohtan
fettode
Som
Feter

Forwernan to refuse Th. An v. for-wyrnan
Fetr[illegible] Ben v. fet
Ferd-wic an army station
v. fyrd-wic
Fifel-cyn; es, n
[illegible] old
fifl n monster, dæmon infestus: Nor. Dan fiœll, fiolle fatuus
A sort of monster; genus monstrorum
Beo. p 11 K 208
See Kembles Beo. p 245
Fifti fifty Th. Apol
fifta of
Fetena of foot soldier
v. feda
Feder-bed a feather bed; 27 culcita
Feder-berende having feathers, feathered
penniger Cat 150 Som
Feder-cræft the art or craft of feather embroidering; ars plumaria Som
Feder-fet four footed
Som v. feower-fet
Feder-geweorc feather work Cat 145
opus plumarium

Fertino fostered [illegible]
Find enemies [illegible] v. fynd
Fier-fet four feet Bk F. p 139, 24 v. feower-fet
Fif-boc, e. f. the five books of Moses: pentateuchus Som
Fif-ceorla alder quinquevir Som
Fif-eged five eyed Som
Fif-fealde
a butterfly; papilio Som
Fif-feald five fold Som
Fif-geara a space of five years Som
Fif-hund five hundred Som
Fif-leaf five leaved grass; quinquefolium Elf. gl 15
Fifta-dohter [illegible] adneptis Som a great grand daughter; adneptis Som
Fifta-fæder fifth father the fourth from the father atavus Elf. gl 3, e.
Fiftig-feald fifty fold Som
Fiftig-sidon fifty times Som

[illegible] freca, an [illegible] minded [illegible]

all fresh waters, [rivers], Ors. 2, 4.

Ferscipe *society, L. Lund.* p. 65; 119, v. geferrǽden.

Icel. fiai] *To hate;* odisse:— *Ps.* 25, 5: 96, 10.

Fic, fíc-æppel, fíc-æppl; *pl.*

Fillende *filling,* v. fyllan.

Film [*Plat.* femel *a thin light coat: Frs.* fimel *skin*] A FILM, *skin, husk;* cuticula, *Som.* rima:—*Cot.* 180.

[*Plat. Ger. Dan.* ut. vin *f*: *Swed.* N; pinna:—*Lev.*

195, *Lye.*

ecker; marsopi- 11.

r. Dan. Swed. fink k *m.*] A FINCH, gilla:—*Cot.* 86.

v. finger.

lan, afindan, þu ð, fint; *p.* fand, fundon; *pp.* ge- len; *v. a.* [*Plat.* *Dut.* vinden: *Ot.* fintan: *Swed.* To FIND, *invent,* e, *order, dispose,* venire:—Hig ne findan, *Mt.* 26, ær fundon *as we* ned, *L. pol. Alf.*

ntion, *a device;* om.

nsiderable, good, erosus:—Findig rn, *Lye.*

g. fingrès [*Plat.* ed. finger: *Dut.* *Isd.* fingro: *Ot.* figger, pronoun- *Icel.* fingr *m.*— from feng *took,* NGER; digitus: ð, *Lk.* 16, 24.

l; *adj. Decayed,* ruptus:— Finie 5.

; *adj. Finny;* -*L. M.* 2, 37. *fins,* v. fin. , *people of Fin-*

ol, finugl FEN- 5.

findan.

v. feoh.

of fian.

. fian.

, *Bt. R.* p. 177,

feond.

fioung.

. feor.

odium:—*Bt.*

ihrer *m*: *Norse,* , *rulers;* and, head or gover- creation, this or *men* or *man-* :—Fira cyn *the* nkind, *Cod. Ex.*

12 Ferh-weard, e. f.
life guard
1266

Forsian, fors-wyrcan
to make verses; versi
facere Som

Fert mind, spirit,
Cd 145. Th p 180, 26

wide ferd perfectum
v. ferht

3 Feste, fast Th An
v. fæste

5 Ferwetfull unsound
deficient C. R. Lk 12, 26
v. firwet-georn

Fetter-bearn foster-child
v. foster

Fester-mon a surety
Nth. prel 1 W p 98, 26
v. fæsten-mon

Feter, es in A fetter; compes Cd 86

Feter-wræsn, e. f. a fetter chain, a fetter; compes Cod. Verc l. 2213

O 3 Fifele [35 a 4]

Fint findeth Mt 7, 8 v. find findan

Feter-homa feather covering, wings
Cd 22 Th p 27, 13.

21 Fetigan to fetch v. fetian

24 Fett feeds Th. An. fetan.
25 Fettian to contend Th. An v. fetian
fettode

Feter-geweorc feather work Cot 145

freed, an ... vbls ... needed

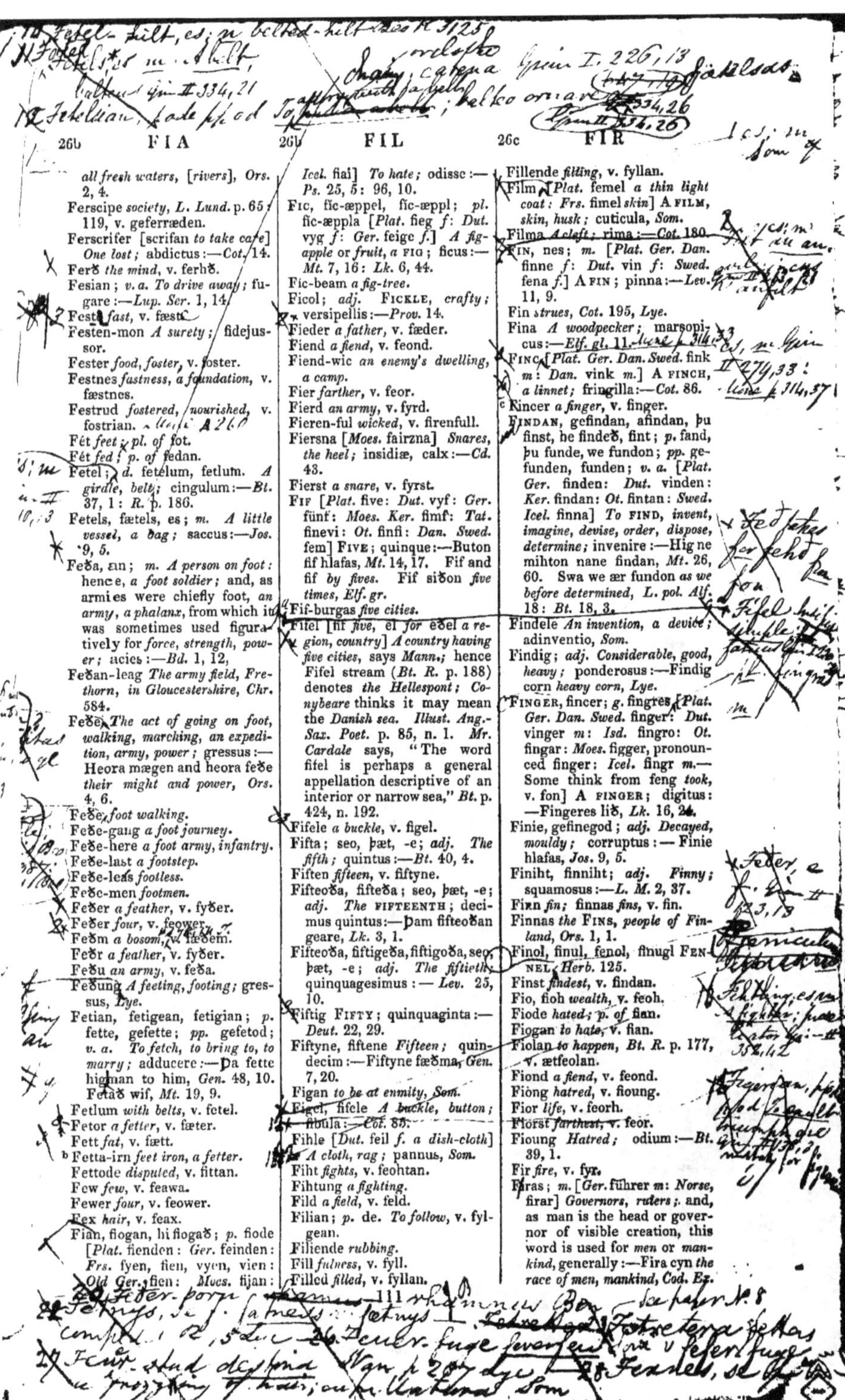

all fresh waters, [*rivers*], *Ors.* 2, 4.
Ferscipe *society*, *L. Lund.* p. 65: 119, v. geferræden.
Ferscrifer [scrifan *to take care*] *One lost*; abdictus:—*Cot.* 14.
Ferð *the mind*, v. ferhð.
Fesian; *v. a. To drive away*; fugare:—*Lup. Ser.* 1, 14.
Fest *fast*, v. fæst.
Festen-mon *A surety*; fidejussor.
Fester *food, foster*, v. foster.
Festnes *fastness, a foundation*, v. fæstnes.
Festrud *fostered, nourished*, v. fostrian.
Fét *feet*; *pl. of* fot.
Fét *fed*; *p. of* fedan.
Fetel; *d.* fetelum, fetlum. *A girdle, belt*; cingulum:—*Bt.* 37, 1: *R.* p. 186.
Fetels, fætels, es; *m. A little vessel, a bag*; saccus:—*Jos.* 9, 5.
Feða, an; *m. A person on foot*: hence, *a foot soldier*; and, as armies were chiefly foot, *an army, a phalanx*, from which it was sometimes used figuratively for *force, strength, power*; acies:—*Bd.* 1, 12.
Feðan-leag *The army field, Frethorn, in Gloucestershire*, *Chr.* 584.
Feðe *The act of going on foot, walking, marching, an expedition, army, power*; gressus:—Heora mægen and heora feðe *their might and power*, *Ors.* 4, 6.
Feðe *foot walking*.
Feðe-gang *a foot journey*.
Feðe-here *a foot army, infantry*.
Feðe-last *a footstep*.
Feðe-leas *footless*.
Feðe-men *footmen*.
Feðer *a feather*, v. fyðer.
Feðer *four*, v. feower.
Feðm *a bosom*, v. fæðm.
Feðr *a feather*, v. fyðer.
Feðu *an army*, v. feða.
Feðung *A feeting, footing*; gressus, *Lye*.
Fetian, fetigean, fetigian; *p.* fette, gefette; *pp.* gefetod; *v. a. To fetch, to bring to, to marry*; adducere:—Þa fette higman to him, *Gen.* 48, 10. Fetað wif, *Mt.* 19, 9.
Fetlum *with belts*, v. fetel.
Fetor *a fetter*, v. fæter.
Fett *fat*, v. fætt.
b Fetta-irn *feet iron, a fetter*.
Fettode *disputed*, v. fittan.
Few *few*, v. feawa.
Fewer *four*, v. feower.
Fex *hair*, v. feax.
Fian, fiogan, hi fiogað; *p.* fiode [*Plat.* fienden: *Ger.* feinden: *Frs.* fyen, fien, vyen, vien: *Old Ger.* fien: *Moes.* fijan: *Icel.* fiai] *To hate*; odisse:—*Ps.* 25, 5: 96, 10.
Fic, fic-æppel, fic-æppl; *pl.* fic-æppla [*Plat.* fieg *f*: *Dut.* vyg *f*: *Ger.* feige *f.*] *A fig-apple* or *fruit, a* FIG; ficus:—*Mt.* 7, 16: *Lk.* 6, 44.
Fic-beam *a fig-tree*.
Ficol; *adj.* FICKLE, *crafty*; versipellis:—*Prov.* 14.
Fieder *a father*, v. fæder.
Fiend *a fiend*, v. feond.
Fiend-wic *an enemy's dwelling, a camp*.
Fier *farther*, v. feor.
Fierd *an army*, v. fyrd.
Fieren-ful *wicked*, v. firenfull.
Fiersna [*Moes.* fairzna] *Snares, the heel*; insidiæ, calx:—*Cd.* 43.
Fierst *a snare*, v. fyrst.
Fif [*Plat.* five: *Dut.* vyf: *Ger.* fünf: *Moes. Ker.* fimf: *Tat.* finevi: *Ot.* finfi: *Dan. Swed.* fem] FIVE; quinque:—Buton fif hlafas, *Mt.* 14, 17. Fif and fif *by fives*. Fif siðon *five times*, *Elf. gr.*
Fif-burgas *five cities*.
Fifel [fif *five*, el *for* eðel *a region, country*] *A country having five cities*, says *Mann.*; hence Fifel stream (*Bt. R.* p. 188) denotes *the Hellespont*; *Conybeare* thinks it may mean the *Danish sea*. *Illust. Ang.-Sax. Poet.* p. 85, n. 1. *Mr. Cardale* says, "The word fifel is perhaps a general appellation descriptive of an interior or narrow sea," *Bt.* p. 424, n. 192.
Fifele *a buckle*, v. figel.
Fifta; seo, þæt, -e; *adj. The fifth*; quintus:—*Bt.* 40, 4.
Fiften *fifteen*, v. fiftyne.
Fifteoða, fifteða; seo, þæt, -e; *adj. The* FIFTEENTH; decimus quintus:—Þam fifteoðan geare, *Lk.* 3, 1.
Fifteoða, fiftigeða, fiftigoða, seo, þæt, -e; *adj. The fiftieth*; quinquagesimus:—*Lev.* 25, 10.
Fiftig FIFTY; quinquaginta:—*Deut.* 22, 29.
Fiftyne, fiftene *Fifteen*; quindecim:—Fiftyne fæðma, *Gen.* 7, 20.
Figan *to be at enmity*, *Som.*
Figel, fifele *A buckle, button*; fibula:—*Cot.* 85.
Fihle [*Dut.* feil *f. a dish-cloth*] *A cloth, rag*; pannus, *Som.*
Fiht *fights*, v. feohtan.
Fihtung *a fighting*.
Fild *a field*, v. feld.
Filian; *p.* de. *To follow*, v. fylgean.
Filiende *rubbing*.
Fill *fulness*, v. fyll.
Filled *filled*, v. fyllan.
Fillende *filling*, v. fyllan.
Film [*Plat.* femel *a thin light coat*: *Frs.* fimel *skin*] A FILM, *skin, husk*; cuticula, *Som.*
Filma *A cleft*; rima:—*Cot.* 180.
FIN, nes; *m.* [*Plat. Ger. Dan.* finne *f*: *Dut.* vin *f*: *Swed.* fena *f.*] A FIN; pinna:—*Lev.* 11, 9.
Fin *strues*, *Cot.* 195, *Lye*.
Fina *A woodpecker*; marsopicus:—*Elf. gl.* 11.
FINC [*Plat. Ger. Dan. Swed.* fink *m*: *Dan.* vink *m.*] A FINCH, *a linnet*; fringilla:—*Cot.* 86.
c Fincer *a finger*, v. finger.
FINDAN, gefindan, afindan, þu finst, he findeð, fint; *p.* fand, þu funde, we fundon; *pp.* gefunden, funden; *v. a.* [*Plat. Ger.* finden: *Dut.* vinden: *Ker.* findan: *Ot.* fintan: *Swed. Icel.* finna] *To* FIND, *invent, imagine, devise, order, dispose, determine*; invenire:—Hig ne mihton nane findan, *Mt.* 26, 60. Swa we ær fundon *as we before determined*, *L. pol. Alf.* 18: *Bt.* 18, 3.
Findele *An invention, a device*; adinventio, *Som.*
Findig; *adj. Considerable, good, heavy*; ponderosus:—Findig corn *heavy corn*, *Lye*.
FINGER, fincer; *g.* fingres [*Plat. Ger. Dan. Swed.* finger: *Dut.* vinger *m*: *Isd.* fingro: *Ot.* fingar: *Moes.* figger, pronounced finger: *Icel.* fingr *m.*—Some think from feng *took*, v. fon] A FINGER; digitus:—Fingeres lið, *Lk.* 16, 24.
Finie, gefinegod; *adj. Decayed, mouldy*; corruptus:—Finie hlafas, *Jos.* 9, 5.
Finiht, finniht; *adj. Finny*; squamosus:—*L. M.* 2, 37.
Finn *fin*; finnas *fins*, v. fin.
Finnas *the* FINS, *people of Finland*, *Ors.* 1, 1.
Finol, finul, fenol, finugl FENNEL, *Herb.* 125.
Finst *findest*, v. findan.
Fio, fioh *wealth*, v. feoh.
Fiode *hated*; *p. of* fian.
Fiogan *to hate*, v. fian.
Fiolan *to happen*, *Bt. R.* p. 177, v. ætfeolan.
Fiond *a fiend*, v. feond.
Fiong *hatred*, v. fioung.
Fior *life*, v. feorh.
Fiorst *farthest*, v. feor.
Fioung *Hatred*; odium:—*Bt.* 39, 1.
Fir *fire*, v. fyr.
Firas; *m.* [*Ger.* führer *m*: *Norse*, firar] *Governors, rulers*; and, as man is the head or governor of visible creation, this word is used for *men* or *mankind*, generally:—Fira cyn *the race of men, mankind*, *Cod. Ex.*

Ferh-weard, e. f.
a life-guard Cd.
1268

Ferscian, fers-wyrcean
to make verses; versi-
facere Som

A sore or scab running in the
body where [illegible]

Fert mind, spirit,
Cd 145. Th. p 180, 20
wrote ferd perfectum
v. ferht

3 Feste fast Th. An.
v. faeste

Ferwet-full anxious
solicitus C. R. Lk 12, 26
v. firwet-georn

Fester-bearn foster-child
v. foster

Fester-mon a surety
S. forth pres 1 W p 98, 26
festen-mon

da sluggish, tired
Fete lasst (fete
fetch fast, trouble)
fast Th. An.

Feter-homa Feathers
covering, wings
Cd 22 Th.
p 27, 13.

Fetigan to fetch
v. Fetian

Fett feeds Th. An
Fettian to contend
Th. An v. fetian
fettode

fetor.
Fetor, -e, f. n. A fetter; compes Cot 86 Lye
Lye Hymn II 161

Feter-wraesn, e. f. a fetter chain,
a fetter; compes Cod. Verc l. 2213
Also gl. in wraesn

() 3 Fifele [35 a 4]

Fint findeth Mt 7, 8 v. find findan

-wer-geweorc feather-work Cot 145 [illegible]

-freca, an [illegible] [illegible] [illegible] 12 [illegible]

all fresh waters, [*rivers*], *Ors.* 2, 4.
Ferscipe *society, L. Lund.* p. 65, 119, v. geferræden.
Ferscrifer [scrifan *to take care*] *One lost;* abdictus:—*Cot.* 14.
Ferð *the mind,* v. ferhð.
Fesian; *v. a. To drive away;* fugare:—*Lup. Ser.* 1, 14.
Fest *fast,* v. fæst.
Festen-mon *A surety;* fidejussor.
Fester *food, foster,* v. foster.
Festnes *fastness, a foundation,* v. fæstnes.
Festrud *fostered, nourished,* v. fostrian.
Fét *feet; pl. of* fot.
Fét *fed; p. of* fedan.
Fetel; *d.* fetelum, fetlum. *A girdle, belt;* cingulum:—*Bt.* 37, 1: *R.* p. 186.
Fetels, fætels, es; *m. A little vessel, a bag;* saccus:—*Jos.* 9, 5.
Feða, an; *m. A person on foot:* hence, *a foot soldier;* and, as armies were chiefly foot, *an army, a phalanx,* from which it was sometimes used figuratively for *force, strength, power;* acies:—*Bd.* 1, 12.
Feðan-leag *The army field, Frethorn, in Gloucestershire, Chr.* 584.
Feðe *The act of going on foot, walking, marching, an expedition, army, power;* gressus:—Heora mægen and heora feðe *their might and power, Ors.* 4, 6.
Feðe *foot walking.*
Feðe-gang *a foot journey.*
Feðe-here *a foot army, infantry.*
Feðe-last *a footstep.*
Feðe-leas *footless.*
Feðe-men *footmen.*
Feðer *a feather,* v. fyðer.
Feðer *four,* v. feower.
Feðm *a bosom,* v. fæðm.
Feðr *a feather,* v. fyðer.
Feðu *an army,* v. feða.
Feðung *A feeting, footing;* gressus, *Lye.*
Fetian, fetigean, fetigian; *p.* fette, gefette; *pp.* gefetod; *v. a. To fetch, to bring to, to marry;* adducere:—Þa fette hig man to him, *Gen.* 48, 10. Fetað wif, *Mt.* 19, 9.
Fetlum *with belts,* v. fetel.
Fetor *a fetter,* v. fæter.
Fett *fat,* v. fætt.
Fetta-irn *feet iron, a fetter.*
Fettode *disputed,* v. fittan.
Few *few,* v. feawa.
Fewer *four,* v. feower.
Fex *hair,* v. feax.
Fian, fiogan, hi fiogað; *p.* fiode [*Plat.* fienden: *Ger.* feinden: *Frs.* fyen, fien, vyen, vien: *Old Ger.* fien: *Moes.* fijan: *Icel.* fiai] *To hate;* odisse:—*Ps.* 25, 5: 96, 10.
Fic, fic-æppel, fic-æppl; *pl.* fic-æppla [*Plat.* fieg *f*: *Dut.* vyg *f*: *Ger.* feige *f.*] *A fig-apple* or *fruit, a* FIG; ficus:—*Mt.* 7, 16: *Lk.* 6, 44.
Fic-beam *a fig-tree.*
Ficol; *adj.* FICKLE, *crafty;* versipellis:—*Prov.* 14.
Fieder *a father,* v. fæder.
Fiend *a fiend,* v. feond.
Fiend-wic *an enemy's dwelling, a camp.*
Fier *farther,* v. feor.
Fierd *an army,* v. fyrd.
Fieren-ful *wicked,* v. firenfull.
Fiersna [*Moes.* fairzna] *Snares, the heel;* insidiæ, calx:—*Cd.* 43.
Fierst *a snare,* v. fyrst.
Fif [*Plat.* five: *Dut.* vyf: *Ger.* fünf: *Moes. Ker.* fimf: *Tat.* finevi: *Ot.* finfi: *Dan. Swed.* fem] FIVE; quinque:—Buton fif hlafas, *Mt.* 14, 17. Fif and fif *by fives.* Fif siðon *five times, Elf. gr.*
Fif-burgas *five cities.*
Fifel [fif *five,* el *for* eðel *a region, country*] *A country having five cities,* says *Mann.;* hence Fifel stream (*Bt. R.* p. 188) denotes *the Hellespont; Conybeare* thinks it may mean the *Danish sea. Illust. Ang.-Sax. Poet.* p. 85, n. 1. *Mr. Cardale* says, "The word fifel is perhaps a general appellation descriptive of an interior or narrow sea," *Bt.* p. 424, n. 192.
Fifele *a buckle,* v. figel.
Fifta; seo, þæt, -e; *adj. The fifth;* quintus:—*Bt.* 40, 4.
Fiften *fifteen,* v. fiftyne.
Fifteoða, fifteða; seo, þæt, -e; *adj.* THE FIFTEENTH; decimus quintus:—Þam fifteoðan geare, *Lk.* 3, 1.
Fifteoða, fiftigeða, fiftigoða, seo, þæt, -e; *adj. The fiftieth;* quinquagesimus:—*Lev.* 25, 10.
Fiftig FIFTY; quinquaginta:—*Deut.* 22, 29.
Fiftyne, fiftene *Fifteen;* quindecim:—Fiftyne fæðma, *Gen.* 7, 20.
Figan *to be at enmity, Som.*
Figel, fifele *A buckle, button;* fibula:—*Cot.* 85.
Fihle [*Dut.* feil *f. a dish-cloth*] *A cloth, rag;* pannus, *Som.*
Fiht *fights,* v. feohtan.
Fihtung *a fighting.*
Fild *a field,* v. feld.
Filian; *p.* de. *To follow,* v. fylgean.
Filiende *rubbing.*
Fill *fulness,* v. fyll.
Filled *filled,* v. fyllan.
Fillende *filling,* v. fyllan.
Film [*Plat.* femel *a thin light coat: Frs.* fimel *skin*] A FILM, *skin, husk;* cuticula, *Som.*
Filma *A cleft;* rima:—*Cot.* 180.
FIN, nes; *m.* [*Plat. Ger. Dan.* finne *f*: *Dut.* vin *f*: *Swed.* fena *f.*] A FIN; pinna:—*Lev.* 11, 9.
Fin *strues, Cot.* 195, *Lye.*
Fina *A woodpecker;* marsopicus:—*Elf. gl.* 11.
FINC [*Plat. Ger. Dan. Swed.* fink *m*: *Dan.* vink *m.*] A FINCH, *a linnet;* fringilla:—*Cot.* 86.
Fincer *a finger,* v. finger.
FINDAN, gefindan, afindan, þu finst, he findeð, fint; *p.* fand, þu funde, we fundon; *pp.* gefunden, funden; *v. a.* [*Plat. Ger.* finden: *Dut.* vinden: *Ker.* findan: *Ot.* fintan: *Swed. Icel.* finna] *To* FIND, *invent, imagine, devise, order, dispose, determine;* invenire:—Hig ne mihton nane findan, *Mt.* 26, 60. Swa we ær fundon *as we before determined, L. pol. Alf.* 18: *Bt.* 18, 3.
Findele *An invention, a device;* adinventio, *Som.*
Findig; *adj. Considerable, good, heavy;* ponderosus:—Findig corn *heavy corn, Lye.*
FINGER, fincer; *g.* fingres [*Plat. Ger. Dan. Swed.* finger: *Dut.* vinger *m*: *Isd.* fingro: *Ot.* fingar: *Moes.* figger, pronounced finger: *Icel.* fingr *m.*—Some think from feng *took,* v. fon] A FINGER; digitus:—Fingeres lið, *Lk.* 16, 24.
Finie, gefinegod; *adj. Decayed, mouldy;* corruptus:—Finie hlafas, *Jos.* 9, 5.
Finiht, finniht; *adj. Finny;* squamosus:—*L. M.* 2, 37.
Finn *fin;* finnas *fins,* v. fin.
Finnas *the* FINS, *people of Finland, Ors.* 1, 1.
Finol, finul, fenol, finugl FENNEL, *Herb.* 125.
Finst *findest,* v. findan.
Fio, fioh *wealth,* v. feoh.
Fiode *hated; p. of* fian.
Fiogan *to hate,* v. fian.
Fiolan *to happen, Bt. R.* p. 177, v. ætfeolan.
Fiond *a fiend,* v. feond.
Fiong *hatred,* v. fioung.
Fior *life,* v. feorh.
Fiorst *farthest,* v. feor.
Fioung *Hatred;* odium:—*Bt.* 39, 1.
Fir *fire,* v. fyr.
Firas; *m.* [*Ger.* führer *m*: *Norse,* firar] *Governors, rulers;* and, as man is the head or governor of visible creation, this word is used for *men* or *mankind,* generally:—Fira cyn *the race of men, mankind, Cod. Ex.*

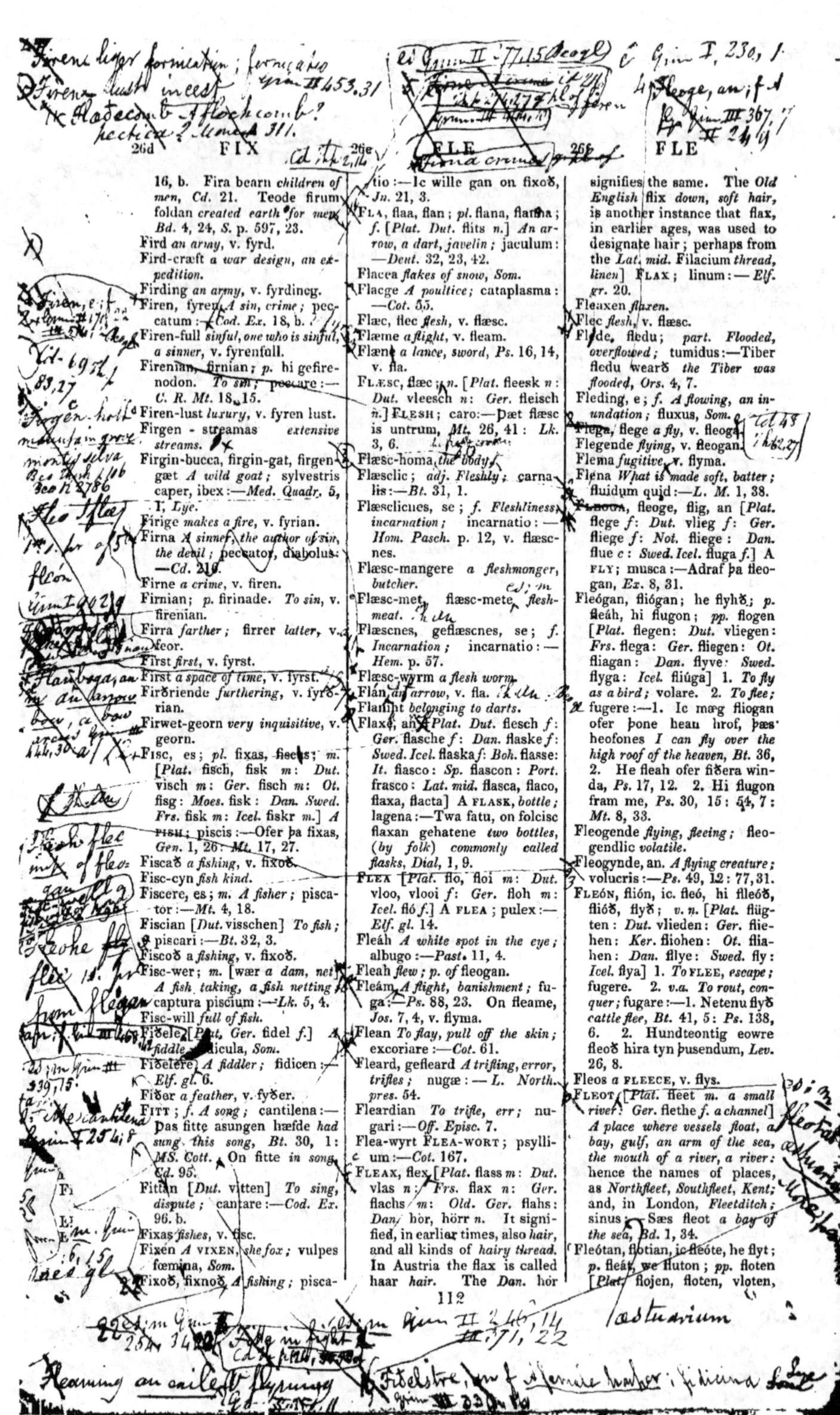

16, b. Fira bearn *children of men, Cd.* 21. Teode firum foldan *created earth for men, Bd.* 4, 24, *S.* p. 597, 23.
Fird *an army,* v. fyrd.
Fird-cræft *a war design, an expedition.*
Firding *an army,* v. fyrdincg.
Firen, fyren *A sin, crime;* peccatum:—*Cod. Ex.* 18, b.
Firen-full *sinful, one who is sinful, a sinner,* v. fyrenfull.
Firenian, firnian; *p.* hi gefirenodon. *To sin;* peccare:—*C. R. Mt.* 18, 15.
Firen-lust *luxury,* v. fyren lust.
Firgen-streamas *extensive streams.*
Firgin-bucca, firgin-gat, firgengæt *A wild goat;* sylvestris caper, ibex:—*Med. Quadr.* 5, 1; *Lye.*
Firige *makes a fire,* v. fyrian.
Firna *A sinner, the author of sin, the devil;* peccator, diabolus:—*Cd.* 216.
Firne *a crime,* v. firen.
Firnian; *p.* firinade. *To sin,* v. firenian.
Firra *farther;* firrer *latter,* v. feor.
First *first,* v. fyrst.
First *a space of time,* v. fyrst.
Firðriende *furthering,* v. fyrðrian.
Firwet-georn *very inquisitive,* v. georn.
FISC, es; *pl.* fixas, fiscas; *m.* [*Plat.* fisch, fisk *m*: *Dut.* visch *m*: *Ger.* fisch *m*: *Ot.* fisg: *Moes.* fisk: *Dan. Swed. Frs.* fisk *m*: *Icel.* fiskr *m.*] A FISH; piscis:—Ofer þa fixas, *Gen.* 1, 26: *Mt.* 17, 27.
Fiscað *a fishing,* v. fixoð.
Fisc-cyn *fish kind.*
Fiscere, es; *m. A fisher;* piscator:—*Mt.* 4, 18.
Fiscian [*Dut.* visschen] *To fish;* piscari:—*Bt.* 32, 3.
Fiscoð *a fishing,* v. fixoð.
Fisc-wer; *m.* [wær *a dam, net*] *A fish taking, a fish netting;* captura piscium:—*Lk.* 5, 4.
Fisc-will *full of fish.*
Fiðele [*Plat. Ger.* fidel *f.*] *A fiddle;* fidicula, *Som.*
Fiðelere, *A fiddler;* fidicen:—*Elf. gl.* 6.
Fiðer *a feather,* v. fyðer.
FITT; *f. A song;* cantilena:—Þas fitte asungen hæfde *had sung this song, Bt.* 30, 1: *MS. Cott.* On fitte *in song, Cd.* 95.
Fittan [*Dut.* vitten] *To sing, dispute;* cantare:—*Cod. Ex.* 96. b.
Fixas *fishes,* v. fisc.
Fixen *A* VIXEN, *she fox;* vulpes fœmina, *Som.*
Fixoð, fixnoð *A fishing;* piscatio:—Ic wille gan on fixoð, *Jn.* 21, 3.
FLA, flaa, flan; *pl.* flana, flanna; *f.* [*Plat. Dut.* flits *n.*] *An arrow, a dart, javelin;* jaculum:—*Deut.* 32, 23, 42.
Flacca *flakes of snow, Som.*
Flacge *A poultice;* cataplasma:—*Cot.* 55.
Flæc, flec *flesh,* v. flæsc.
Flæme *a flight,* v. fleam.
Flæne *a lance, sword, Ps.* 16, 14, v. fla.
FLÆSC, flæc; *n.* [*Plat.* fleesk *n*: *Dut.* vleesch *n*: *Ger.* fleisch *n.*] FLESH; caro:—Þæt flæsc is untrum, *Mt.* 26, 41: *Lk.* 3, 6.
Flæsc-homa *the body.*
Flæsclic; *adj. Fleshly;* carnalis:—*Bt.* 31, 1.
Flæsclicnes, se; *f. Fleshliness, incarnation;* incarnatio:—*Hom. Pasch.* p. 12, v. flæscnes.
Flæsc-mangere *a fleshmonger, butcher.*
Flæsc-met, flæsc-mete *flesh-meat.*
Flæscnes, geflæscnes, se; *f. Incarnation;* incarnatio:—*Hem.* p. 57.
Flæsc-wyrm *a flesh worm.*
Flán *an arrow,* v. fla.
Flanht *belonging to darts.*
Flaxe, an; [*Plat. Dut.* flesch *f*: *Ger.* flasche *f*: *Dan.* flaske *f*: *Swed. Icel.* flaska *f*: *Boh.* flasse: *It.* fiasco: *Sp.* flascon: *Port.* frasco: *Lat. mid.* flasca, flaco, flaxa, flacta] A FLASK, *bottle;* lagena:—Twa fatu, on folcisc flaxan gehatene *two bottles, (by folk) commonly called flasks, Dial,* 1, 9.
FLEA [*Plat.* flo, floi *m*: *Dut.* vloo, vlooi *f*: *Ger.* floh *m*: *Icel.* fló *f.*] A FLEA; pulex:—*Elf. gl.* 14.
Fleáh *A white spot in the eye;* albugo:—*Past.* 11, 4.
Fleah *flew; p. of* fleogan.
Fleám, *A flight, banishment;* fuga:—*Ps.* 88, 23. On fleame, *Jos.* 7, 4, v. flyma.
Flean *To flay, pull off the skin;* excoriare:—*Cot.* 61.
Fleard, gefleard *A trifling, error, trifles;* nugæ:—*L. North. pres.* 54.
Fleardian *To trifle, err;* nugari:—*Off. Episc.* 7.
Flea-wyrt FLEA-WORT; psyllium:—*Cot.* 167.
FLEAX, flex, [*Plat.* flass *m*: *Dut.* vlas *n*: *Frs.* flax *n*: *Ger.* flachs *m*: *Old. Ger.* flahs: *Dan.* hör, hörr *n.* It signified, in earlier times, also *hair,* and all kinds of *hairy thread.* In Austria the flax is called haar *hair.* The *Dan.* hör signifies the same. The *Old English* flix *down, soft hair,* is another instance that flax, in earlier ages, was used to designate hair; perhaps from the *Lat. mid.* Filacium *thread, linen*] FLAX; linum:—*Elf. gr.* 20.
Fleaxen *flaxen.*
Flec *flesh,* v. flæsc.
Flede, fledu; *part. Flooded, overflowed;* tumidus:—Tiber fledu wearð *the Tiber was flooded, Ors.* 4, 7.
Fleding, e; *f. A flowing, an inundation;* fluxus, *Som.*
Flega, flege *a fly,* v. fleoga.
Flegende *flying,* v. fleogan.
Flema *fugitive,* v. flyma.
Flena *What is made soft, batter;* fluidum quid:—*L. M.* 1, 38.
FLEOGA, fleoge, flig, an [*Plat.* flege *f*: *Dut.* vlieg *f*: *Ger.* fliege *f*: *Not.* fliege: *Dan.* flue *c*: *Swed. Icel.* fluga *f.*] A FLY; musca:—Adraf þa fleogan, *Ex.* 8, 31.
Fleógan, flíogan; he flyhð; *p.* fleáh, hi flugon; *pp.* flogen [*Plat.* flegen: *Dut.* vliegen: *Frs.* flega: *Ger.* fliegen: *Ot.* fliagan: *Dan.* flyve: *Swed.* flyga: *Icel.* fliúga] 1. *To fly as a bird;* volare. 2. *To flee;* fugere:—1. Ic mæg fliogan ofer þone heau hrof, þæs heofones *I can fly over the high roof of the heaven, Bt.* 36, 2. He fleah ofer fiðera winda, *Ps.* 17, 12. 2. Hi flugon fram me, *Ps.* 30, 15: 54, 7: *Mt.* 8, 33.
Fleogende *flying, fleeing;* fleogendlic *volatile.*
Fleogynde, an. *A flying creature;* volucris:—*Ps.* 49, 12: 77, 31.
FLEÓN, flíón, ic. fleó, hi fleóð, flióð, flyð; *v. n.* [*Plat.* flügten: *Dut.* vlieden: *Ger.* fliehen: *Ker.* fliohen: *Ot.* fliahen: *Dan.* flye: *Swed.* fly: *Icel.* flya] 1. To FLEE, *escape;* fugere. 2. *v.a. To rout, conquer;* fugare:—1. Netenu flyð *cattle flee, Bt.* 41, 5: *Ps.* 138, 6. 2. Hundteontig eowre fleoð hira tyn þusendum, *Lev.* 26, 8.
Fleos *a* FLEECE, v. flys.
FLEOT, [*Plat.* fleet *m. a small river*: *Ger.* flethe *f. a channel*] *A place where vessels float, a bay, gulf, an arm of the sea, the mouth of a river, a river:* hence the names of places, as *Northfleet, Southfleet, Kent;* and, in London, *Fleetditch;* sinus:—Sæs fleot *a bay of the sea, Bd.* 1, 34.
Fleótan, flotian, ic fleóte, he flyt; *p.* fleát, we fluton; *pp.* floten [*Plat.* flojen, floten, vloten,

Flæsc strǽt, e; f. a flesh street, the shambles; macellum R 55 Lye

Flæc-tawere, es; m. a flesh tawer, or butcher, an executioner R 113 Lye — Flæran earlæppa pinnula R 71 vearlæppa — Flæsc-æt, es; m. Flesh food. R Ben 36 Lye — Flæsc-cypping a flesh selling; a market, macellum R 55 Lye — Flæsc-lic fleshly, carnal Som — Flæsc-hus a flesh house; catasta Cd 121 — a male R 108 — Flæsc-fodan carnes L 12; 118/2 — Flæsc-mete Mt 15, 29 a flesh-maggot a worm Cd 24 Lye — Flæsc-stræt a flesh street, the shambles; macellum R 55 Lye — Flæra flakes of — Flace a — Flæsc-penning a pen — an obelisk Som

fyren-gat

Fire-gat a wild goat

Firen-dæd a sinful or wicked deed Beo 77 K 1995 / 126 K 3337 v fyren-dæd

Fird-werod a phalanx Som — square army of 8000

Flea a flea Som

Fleapan-wyrt float

Fird-secn, e; f. an — Fire-ad — 134, 19

Flede a flow, or flowing Cd 15, 12 — altogether swelled

Firgen-stream a mountain stream Beo 103 K 2718 — 3, 10

Fiorgyn ... Old Norse fiörgyn the earth Beo K p 246

Firgen-beam a mountain tree Beo 167 K 2828

Flæsc-mete, es; m. flesh meat

Fireste, first-hrof — a —

Fleapan-wyrt float grass; gramen fluviatile S. M. 2, 51 — Flenod a cloak; lacerna Ben — Fleog-ryft a fly net Cot 46 — Fleoh-net a fly net, a net to cover a bed, conopeum R 86 Lye

Firgen-gat a mountain goat Ben v supl v fyren-gat

Firnum fearfully Cd 39 Th p 51, 26 v fyrnum

Flane, flan a dart, arrow — Flan-boga a dart bow, a bow Beo K 2865; 3 a

Firwet-geornes, se; f. solicitude — curiositas Ben Cot 60 Lye

Firhted frightened Som

Firmest foremost first Som v fyrmest

Flæsc-cwellere, es; m. a flesh-queller, a butcher, a hangman Som

Flasc, es; m. A flask, leathern bottle; flasco

Fire-scofl a fire shovel; batillum Som

Flæsc-cypping — macellum R 55

Flaxa-fan; m.? a flesh ladle

Fleot-netes; n. a fly net. Th. An

First a rafter, perch; tigillum Som

Fiscnoðes, es; m. a fishing Th. An v fiscoð

Fisc-bryne fish brine, garum R 32 Lye

Fisc-hus a fishing house piscinale R 103 Lye

Fisc-mere A fish pond piscina Som — Fisc-net a fishing net Jn 21, 8 Lye

Fisc-pol a fish pool piscina Lye 18 — Fisc-bryttas pl. little fishes, a multitude of fishes; pisciculi Som

Fisc-wellies; m. a fish well or fish

Fisc-vel full of fishes; piscosus Som

Fisting fistulatio Lye

Fleogende — flying kind

Fiðer-sticca clavus tentorii R 110

Fiðer-berende feather bearing Som

Fiðered feathered Som

Fiðerleas featherless Som

Fiwan to hate odio habere Som

Fixian to fish; piscari Som v fiscian

Firprungnes desire of humanity; desiderium promovendi L. Cnut W p 137

Jene 296

1249 h 143; 22 2 8

Flot-wyrt a creeter plant; herba quaedam vomitoria Som. v. flespan wyrt

Flot-man a sailor, nauta Som. v. flot-man

Flæsclic fleshly Som.

Flæsclicnes, se fleshliness Som. carnalitas Som.

Flesc a fleshe Som.

Flys, fleece

Flic-camb pectica

Flet-gestald es; m a house entrance, vestibule Cd 130 Grim II. 453, 35

Flet-rast e; f home rest Beo K 2483

Flet-werod

Flæsc-fodor flesh's covering what covers the body a house. Hickes Thes I 135, 49

1st Food, pabulum

2 a covering, a case, theca because the capsule or theca is the shell which covers the fruit or grain used for food.

Flygan to put to flight Th. an v. aflygan

Flion to flee Th. an v. fleon

Flie a fly, flea Som. v. flea

Flys a fleece Som. v. flys

Flitcræft the dialectic art, Grim II 516, 35 art of logic; dialectica Som.

Flit stripe; lite jossel Som.

Flet-sittend es; m a palace sitter, one sitting in a palace house or home Beo K 3573

Flod-blac flood pale Cd 167 Th. p 209, 11

Flod-egsa a flood dread Cd 166, Th. p 206, 4

Flod-weard es; m a flood ward Cd 167 Th. p 209, 3

Flod-weg es; m flood way, the sea Cd 147 Th. p 184, 12

Flot, es; m a float

Flet-sittende a sitting on couches in a house or palace band, or guard Beo K 2047

Flet-werod

a large family; domus

96

Flot afloat, at on flot feran to go afloat Th. an

5 Flotan to float Th. an

6 Flot here es; m

Flot-smere fat, scum of a pot, olla pinguedo supernatans Beo K 5175

Flod a flood Th. an v. flod

Fluge pt. of fleogan

Flyht a flight Th. an

Flyma an exile; profugus

Flum a river; flu-men Lye

Folc-agende possessing people Beo K 6221

Folc-beorn, es; m the people's prince, leader, a king Grim II. 453, 44; 486, 3 Beo K 4436

Folc-cyning the people's king, a king; populi rex Cd 95. Th 125, 5

Flod-yð, e; f a flood wave; fluentum Beo K 1078

Floga, an; m A fleer; qui volat Beo

Fnæd es; m pl fnada

Fnæst aspiratus Cd Exon 56 a Mann

Fnæstan puffs. Som.

Foda, fodda, an; m food

Flood a plaice Som. v flec

Foder, fodor; foddor fodres, fodre n.

Fodder-brytta, an; m a food dispenser, fosterer; a ja-bu-tetor

Fofrotad dabes Ben.

K 2728

Fola, an; m A fole; pullus ...

En. m fole wh. be fola Th. an

Folc-bearn e; m a child of the people, a child; populi filius Cd. 84, Th. 105, 28; 100 132, 16.

Dut. vloeden: *Frs.* floeyen: *Ger.* fluten] *To* FLOAT, *swim*; fluctuare:—*Martyr.* 22, *Mar.*
Fleowan *To* FLOW; fluere:—Fleowð meoloc and hunig, *Ex.* 3, 17, v. flowan.
Flere *a floor*, v. flor.
Flering, e; *f.* [*Dut.* vloeren] A FLOORING; contabulatio:—*Gen.* 6, 16.
Flesc *flesh*, v. flæsc.
Flet *Cream*; flos lactis:—*Cot.* 37, *Lye.*
FLET; *g.* tes; *d.* te; *n.* *A dwelling, a habitation of a ceorl,* or *a person of inferior degree, a seat, hall*; area, casa:—Þe þæt flet age *who owns the dwelling, L. Hloth.* 11, 12, 13. Flet gesteald *a fixed habitation, a dwelling place, Cd.* 52: 79.
Flewsa *a flowing.*
Flewð *flows*, v. flowan.
Flex *flax*, v. fleax.
Flicce [*Plat.* flikke, flak, plek m: *Ger.* flicke, fleck *m*: *Dan.* flekke *to cleave, slit*: *Icel.* flicki *n.* *massa carnea*] *A flitch of bacon*; succidia:—*Elf. gl.* 27.
Flicerian, fliceran *To move the wings, flitter, flutter,* FLICKER; motare alas:—*Deut.* 32, 11.
Fliet *a ship.*
Flicte *cream*, v. flet.
Flig *a fly*, v. fleoga.
Fliht *A flight*; volatus:—*Deut.* 32, 1.
Flima *a runaway*, v. flyma.
Flind *Genitrix, Cot.* 98, *Lye.*
FLINT [*Old Ger.* flins *n.*] *A flint*; silex:—*Num.* 20, 10, 11.
Fliogan *to fly*, v. fleogan.
Fliende *fleeing*, v. fleon.
Flionne *to escape.*
FLIT, geflit *Scandal, strife, contention*; scandalum:—*Ps.* 49, 21.
Flitan, ic flíte, he flít; *p.* flát, we fliton; *pp.* fliten, geflíten. *To strive, contend, dispute, quarrel, rebel*; certare:—Hwi flitst þu wið þine nextan, *Ex.* 2, 13: *Bt.* 36, 2.
Flitere *A wrangler, contender*; rabula:—*Cot.* 208.
Flit-georn, flitgern *one desirous of contention, a quarreller.*
Flit-mælum *by strife*; certatim, *Som.*
Floc *a place, a kind of fish.*
FLOCC *m.* [*Dan.* flok *c*: *Swed.* flock *m*: *Icel.* flocky *m.*] A FLOCK, *company, division*; grex:—Se oðer flocc, *Gen.* 32, 8.
Flocc-mælum *by flocks* or *herds, Num.* 2, 34.
Flocende *Complosis, Cot.* 39.
Floc-rade *A riding company, a troop*; turma:—*Chr.* 917.
FLÓD, es; *m.* [*Plat.* flood *f*: *Dut.* vloed *m*: *Frs.* flod *f*: *Ger.* fluth *f*: *Dan.* flod *c*: *Swed.* flod *m*: *Icel.* flod *n.*] 1. A FLOOD, *deluge*; diluvium. 2. *A flowing of water, a river, a wave*; flumen:—1. Þæt flod com, *Mt.* 24, 39. 2. Þæt flod ys todæled on feower ean, *Gen.* 2, 10.
Floda, flode *A place where any thing flows, a channel, sink, gutter*; cloaca:—*Cot.* 44.
Flodlic; *adj.* FLOODLIKE; fluvialis:—*Elf. gr.* 9, 28.
Flod-wæter *flowing water, a river.*
Floege *a vessel, ship.*
Flogen *flown*; *pp.*; v. fleogan.
Flogettan *to flow.*
Floh *That which is flown off, a fragment, piece,* FLAW; fragmen:—Floh stanes *a piece of stone, Cot.* 99.
FLÓR; *f.* [*Plat.* floor: *Dut.* vloer *m*: *Ger.* flur *f*: *Icel.* flór *m.*] A FLOOR, *pavement*; pavimentum:—On þære flore to the floor, *Bt.* 36, 7: *Ps.* 118, 25: *Lk.* 3, 17.
Flota, an. 1. *A floater, a ship*; navis. 2. *A sailor*; nauta:—1. Flota wæs on yðum *a ship was on the waters, Beo.* p. 18. 2. Unrim flotan *numberless sailors, Chr.* 975, *Pr.*
Flotian *to float*; flotigende *floating*, v. fleotan.
Flotman *a floatman, a sailor.*
Flot-scip *a floatship, a light bark.*
Flouing *a flowing, wave.*
FLÓWAN, ic flówe, he flewð; *p.* fleow, gefleow; *v. n.* [*Plat.* fleten: *Dut.* vloeyen: *Ger.* fliessen] *To* FLOW, *issue*; fluere:—Þat land flewð meolece and hunie, *Ex.* 3, 8. Fleow blod ut, *Jn.* 19, 34.
Flowednes, flownes, se; *f.* *A flowing, flux, wave*; fluxus:—*Bd.* 1, 27.
Flox-fote *broad footed.*
Flugol; *g.* flugles; *pl.* fluglas. *One that flies* or *flees, a bird, a runaway*; fugax, volucris:—*Elf. gr.* 9, 60.
Flugon *flew*; *p.* of fleogan.
Flustrian *To plat,* WEAVE; plectere:—*Cot.* 176.
Flycð *for* flyhð *flees*; 3 *s. indef.* of fleogan.
Flygd, flyht A FLIGHT; fuga:—*Nicod.* 26.
Flyht-clað *A joining* or *binding together*; commissura, *Som.*
Flyma, fleam, flema *One who flees, a runaway, vagabond*; profugus:—*Gen.* 12, 16.
Flyman *to banish*, v. aflyman.
Flyming *A banished man*; exul: hence *Noel* says, the Flemings, whose country was wild and strong, and therefore, a receptacle for outlaws, by whom it was inhabited, call their country Flanderland, in Saxon fleondra-land *the land of runaways.*
FLYS, A FLEECE, *wool*; vellus:—*L. In.* 69: *Ps.* 71, 6.
Flyte *Pontonium, R.* 103.
Flyð *flees*, v. fleon.
FNÆD, fnæd, es; *pl. nom. ac.* fnadu; *g.* a; *d.* um *A hem, edge, fringe*; fimbria:—*Mt.* 23, 5.
Fnæst, fnæsta *A puff, blast*; flatus:—*Hexaem.* 4.
Fnæstiað *The wind-pipe*; aspera arteria:—*L. M.* 2, 36.
Fneosung, fnora [*Dut.* fniezing] *A sneezing*; sternutatio:—*R.* 79.
Fo *take*, v. fon.
Foca, an. [*Lat.* focus *a hearth*] *A cake baked on the hearth*; panis sub cinere pistus:—*Gen.* 18, 6.
FODA, fode, an [*Plat.* foder *n.* *fætura*: fodsel *n.* *nourishment*: *Dan.* föde *c*: *Swed.* foda *f*: *Icel.* fódr *n.*] FOOD, *nourishment*; alimentum:—Foda fyres, holt *food of fire, wood, Scint.* 12.
Fodder, foddor, foddur, foder; *g.* fodres; *d.* fodre; *m.* [*Plat.* foder *n*: *Dut.* voeder: *Ger.* futter *n.*] FODDER *for cattle, food*; pabulum:—To þam fodre *to the fodder, Bt.* 14, 2: *Gen.* 42, 27.
Fodnoð *Food, nourishment*; alimentum, *Som.*
Fodre *with food*, v. fodder.
Fodrere *A fodderer*; pabulator:—*Ors.* 4, 1.
Foedende *feeding*, v. fedan.
Foera *a companion*, v. gefera.
Foerde *went*, v. feran.
Foereld *a company, relation*, v. færeld.
Foerðmest, *first.*
Foeð *going on foot*; on foeðe *on foot*, v. feðe.
Foetmen *footmen.*
Fog *an agreement*; conjunctio, v. fegan.
Fogere *A suiter, wooer*; procus, *Som.*
Fóh *take*, v. fon.
Fohlic *what may be comprehended*; comprehensibilis, *Som.*
FOLC, es; *n.* [*Plat.* folk, volk *n*: *Dut. Frs. Ger. Dan. Swed. Icel.* folk *n*: *Isd.* folc: *Ot. Not.* folck] *The* FOLK, *people, common people, multitude, a people, a tribe, family*; populus:—Þat folc, *Lk.* 1, 21. Micel folc *much people, Mt.* 26, 47. Folces man *a man of the people, a common man, Lev.* 4, 27: *Bt.* 30, 1.
Folc-cuð *known to the people, well known, public, celebrated.*
Folc-driht *a company.*
Folc-fry, folc-fryg *free, a freeman.*
Folc-gefeoht *a public battle.*
Folc-gemot *a popular assembly.*

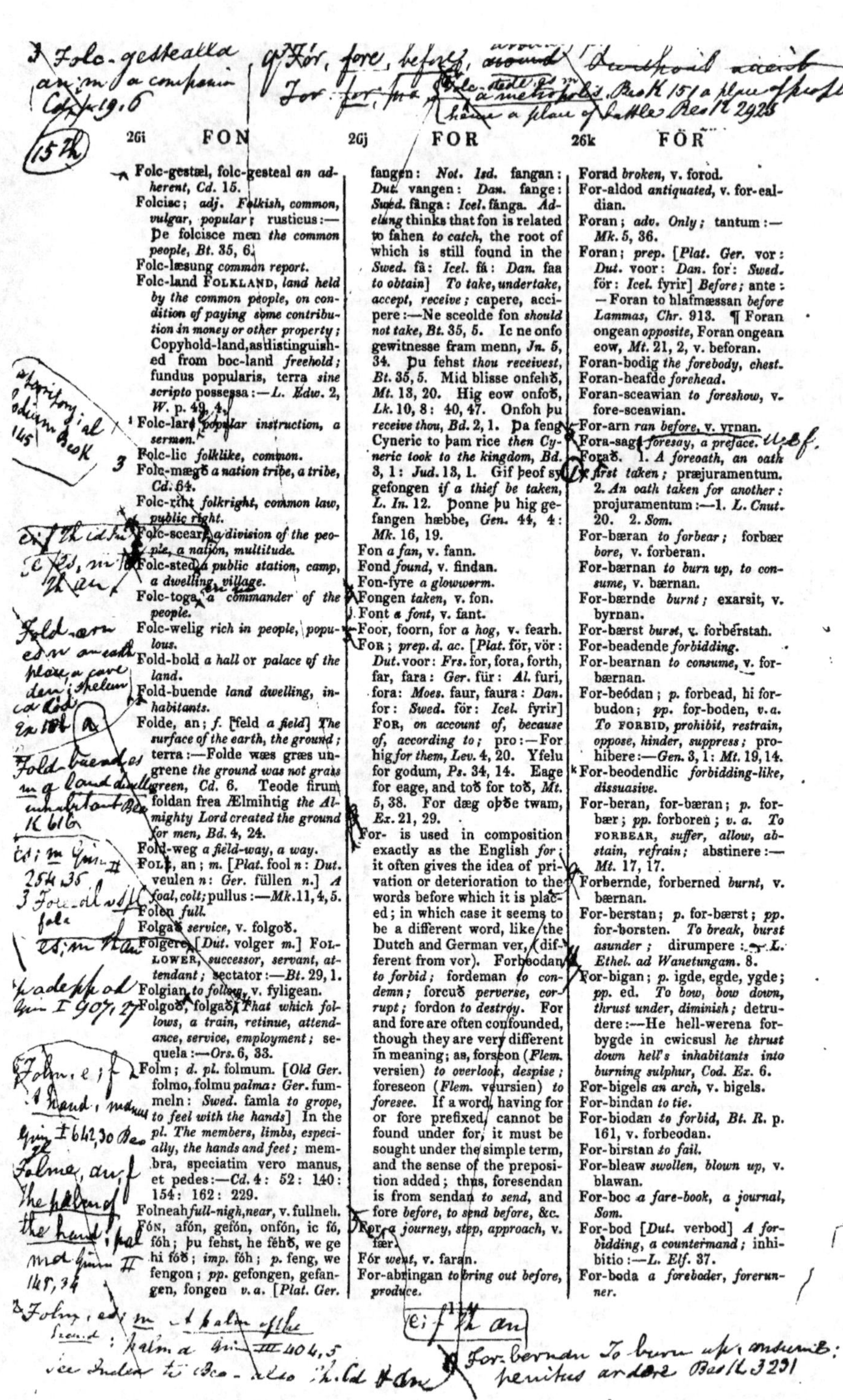

Folc-gestæl, folc-gesteal *an adherent, Cd.* 15.
Folcisc; *adj. Folkish, common, vulgar, popular;* rusticus:—Þe folcisce men *the common people, Bt.* 35, 6.
Folc-læsung *common report.*
Folc-land FOLKLAND, *land held by the common people, on condition of paying some contribution in money or other property;* Copyhold-land, as distinguished from boc-land *freehold;* fundus popularis, terra *sine scripto* possessa:—*L. Edw.* 2, *W.* p. 49, 4.
Folc-lare *popular instruction, a sermon.*
Folc-lic *folklike, common.*
Folc-mægð *a nation tribe, a tribe, Cd.* 64.
Folc-riht *folkright, common law, public right.*
Folc-scearu *a division of the people, a nation, multitude.*
Folc-sted *a public station, camp, a dwelling, village.*
Folc-toga *a commander of the people.*
Folc-welig *rich in people, populous.*
Fold-bold *a hall* or *palace of the land.*
Fold-buende *land dwelling, inhabitants.*
Folde, an; *f.* [feld *a field*] *The surface of the earth, the ground;* terra:—Folde wæs græs ungrene *the ground was not grass green, Cd.* 6. Teode firum foldan frea Ælmihtig *the Almighty Lord created the ground for men, Bd.* 4, 24.
Fold-weg *a field-way, a way.*
Fola, an; *m.* [*Plat.* fool *n*: *Dut.* veulen *n*: *Ger.* füllen *n.*] *A foal, colt;* pullus:—*Mk.* 11, 4, 5.
Folen *full.*
Folgað *service,* v. folgoð.
Folgere [*Dut.* volger *m.*] FOLLOWER, *successor, servant, attendant;* sectator:—*Bt.* 29, 1.
Folgian *to follow,* v. fyligean.
Folgoð, folgað *That which follows, a train, retinue, attendance, service, employment;* sequela:—*Ors.* 6, 33.
Folm; *d. pl.* folmum. [*Old Ger.* folmo, folmu *palma*: *Ger.* fummeln: *Swed.* famla *to grope, to feel with the hands*] In the *pl. The members, limbs, especially, the hands and feet;* membra, speciatim vero manus, et pedes:—*Cd.* 4: 52: 140: 154: 162: 229.
Folneah *full-nigh, near,* v. fullneh.
FÓN, afón, gefón, onfón, ic fó, fóh; þu fehst, he fehð, we ge hi fóð; *imp.* fóh; *p.* feng, we fengon; *pp.* gefongen, gefangen, fongen *v. a.* [*Plat. Ger.* fangen: *Not. Isd.* fangan: *Dut.* vangen: *Dan.* fange: *Swed.* fånga: *Icel.* fánga. *Adelung* thinks that fon is related to fahen *to catch,* the root of which is still found in the *Swed.* få: *Icel.* fá: *Dan.* faa *to obtain*] *To take, undertake, accept, receive;* capere, accipere:—Ne sceolde fon *should not take, Bt.* 35, 5. Ic ne onfo gewitnesse fram menn, *Jn.* 5, 34. Þu fehst *thou receivest, Bt.* 35, 5. Mid blisse onfehð, *Mt.* 13, 20. Hig eow onfoð, *Lk.* 10, 8: 40, 47. Onfoh þu *receive thou, Bd.* 2, 1. Þa feng Cyneric to þam rice *then Cyneric took to the kingdom, Bd.* 3, 1: *Jud.* 13, 1. Gif þeof sy gefongen *if a thief be taken, L. In.* 12. Þonne þu hig gefangen hæbbe, *Gen.* 44, 4: *Mk.* 16, 19.
Fon *a fan,* v. fann.
Fond *found,* v. findan.
Fon-fyre *a glowworm.*
Fongen *taken,* v. fon.
Font *a font,* v. fant.
Foor, foorn, for *a hog,* v. fearh.
FOR; *prep. d. ac.* [*Plat.* för, vör: *Dut.* voor: *Frs.* for, fora, forth, far, fara: *Ger.* für: *Al.* furi, fora: *Moes.* faur, faura: *Dan.* for: *Swed.* för: *Icel.* fyrir] FOR, *on account of, because of, according to;* pro:—For hig *for them, Lev.* 4, 20. Yfelu for godum, *Ps.* 34, 14. Eage for eage, and toð for toð, *Mt.* 5, 38. For dæg oþþe twam, *Ex.* 21, 29.
For- is used in composition exactly as the English *for;* it often gives the idea of privation or deterioration to the words before which it is placed; in which case it seems to be a different word, like the Dutch and German ver, (different from vor). Forbeodan *to forbid;* fordeman *to condemn;* forcuð *perverse, corrupt;* fordon *to destroy.* For and fore are often confounded, though they are very different in meaning; as, forseon (*Flem.* versien) *to overlook, despise;* foreseon (*Flem.* voursien) *to foresee.* If a word, having for or fore prefixed, cannot be found under for, it must be sought under the simple term, and the sense of the preposition added; thus, foresendan is from sendan *to send,* and fore *before, to send before,* &c.
For *a journey, step, approach,* v. fær.
Fór *went,* v. faran.
For-abringan *to bring out before, produce.*
Forad *broken,* v. forod.
For-aldod *antiquated,* v. for-ealdian.
Foran; *adv. Only;* tantum:—*Mk.* 5, 36.
Foran; *prep.* [*Plat. Ger.* vor: *Dut.* voor: *Dan.* for: *Swed.* för: *Icel.* fyrir] *Before;* ante:—Foran to hlafmæssan *before Lammas, Chr.* 913. ¶ Foran ongean *opposite,* Foran ongean eow, *Mt.* 21, 2, v. beforan.
Foran-bodig *the forebody, chest.*
Foran-heafde *forehead.*
Foran-sceawian *to foreshow,* v. fore-sceawian.
For-arn *ran before,* v. yrnan.
Fora-sagu *foresay, a preface.*
Forað. 1. *A foreoath, an oath first taken;* præjuramentum. 2. *An oath taken for another:* projuramentum:—1. *L. Cnut.* 20. 2. *Som.*
For-bæran *to forbear;* forbær *bore,* v. forberan.
For-bærnan *to burn up, to consume,* v. bærnan.
For-bærnde *burnt;* exarsit, v. byrnan.
For-bærst *burst,* v. forberstan.
For-beadende *forbidding.*
For-bearnan *to consume,* v. forbærnan.
For-beódan; *p.* forbead, hi forbudon; *pp.* for-boden, *v. a. To* FORBID, *prohibit, restrain, oppose, hinder, suppress;* prohibere:—*Gen.* 3, 1: *Mt.* 19, 14.
For-beodendlic *forbidding-like, dissuasive.*
For-beran, for-bæran; *p.* forbær; *pp.* forboren; *v. a. To* FORBEAR, *suffer, allow, abstain, refrain;* abstinere:—*Mt.* 17, 17.
Forbernde, forberned *burnt,* v. bærnan.
For-berstan; *p.* for-bærst; *pp.* for-borsten. *To break, burst asunder;* dirumpere:—*L. Ethel. ad Wanetungam.* 8.
For-bigan; *p.* igde, egde, ygde; *pp.* ed. *To bow, bow down, thrust under, diminish;* detrudere:—He hell-werena forbygde in cwicsusl *he thrust down hell's inhabitants into burning sulphur, Cod. Ex.* 6.
For-bigels *an arch,* v. bigels.
For-bindan *to tie.*
For-biodan *to forbid, Bt. R.* p. 161, v. forbeodan.
For-birstan *to fail.*
For-bleaw *swollen, blown up,* v. blawan.
For-boc *a fare-book, a journal, Som.*
For-bod [*Dut.* verbod] *A forbidding, a countermand;* inhibitio:—*L. Elf.* 37.
For-boda *a foreboder, forerunner.*

Folc-gesetnes, se; f a law, or statute of the people; plebiscitum Som
Folc-gesid, es; m a prince
of the people id y bch
p 128, 29
Folc-gestreon, e; f
a public treasure; publicum
commodum Cd 93.
Folc-lar, e; f a more
Th p 119, 17 Folc-getæl number of the people, the populace
Folc-getrum an plebiscitum Cd 154 Th p 192, 9
assembly or knot of people
Cd 93: Th p 119, 29
Folc-cwen, e; f
a popular queen Beo
Folc-gesprang folk, the
turba hominum confer
Ors 3.9
Folc-mære populous
Cd 86, Th p 108, 5
Folc-lagu, e; f folk
a public law; publica lex
Folc-leasung a common or public
Folc-mægen, es; n the peoples
force Cd 160 Th p
199, 31 — Folc-motes,
a popular assembly Som
v folc-gemot — Folc-
rædenne f a popular
law Cd 125 Som
Som v folc-leasung
Folc-man
a common man; a
tie Bd 4, 22
Font bæc baptism Som
Folc-slite, es; m sedition
sedetio Cd 215, Th p
Folc-stow, e; f a public
place Bd 3, 5
Folc-werod, es; n a
multitude of people, a multitude
of people, a multitude;
populi multitudo Cd 171
Th p 215, 2 — Folc-tal, e; f folk reckoning,
genealogy Cd 151, p 201, 29
or Folcleasung
Folc-weras men
of the people, the
people Cd 12 Th p 14, 21;
89, Th p 110, 30
Foging a young youth Som
For before;
prae, coram Th p 114
For for, notwithstanding, too, very Th p
Folc-truma an army, an assembly of people, the people
plebs L. Ps 7, 8 Lye
Forbigean to bow
them v forbigan
Folc a multitude
Lye
For-bærnednes, se; f a burning; ustio
Herb 164, 2 — For-beaban to forbear Som
11 Lye v. for-beran — For-betan
to recompense; compensare Som
For-blawen inflated, puffed up L M 2. 34
v blawan — For-blindad blinded, hardened
Mk 6, 52 Lye.
Folm, e, f a hand, manus, etc
Folm, e; m, acc folme, an; f a palm, an
open hand; palma
Fora-gleawlice
heedfully, cautiously
provide 2 Ben
interl. 3 Ben, Lye
Foran-dæg before
day or dawn Ben
Foran-ryht the
throwing, the tortight Ben 5, 2 Lye
Foran-onsettende, præclusus
Bd 5, 13. Lye
Fora-sceawung consideration
Ben interl
Forbaned a banished
man; exul Som
Foraþ the oath which an
accuser took of freedom
from calumnious
intention, before he
was allowed to
bring an action in
a court of law.
instar juramenti
de calumnia.
Of ægylc man his
gyldan mid foreaþ
fore at let every man
commence his accusation
with his foreaþ, or
freedom from bad
intention L. Athel 23
W p 61, 11 — Ne beo
afre ænig forad forgyfen
there is otherwise never any foreaþ forgiven
L. Cnut pol 20 W p 137,
2 Gif þægen habbe
getrywthe man, to
forathe for hine, þa
swa sy if a thane
have a true man
for a foreoath, be it so
L. Cnut pol 20 W p 137, 6

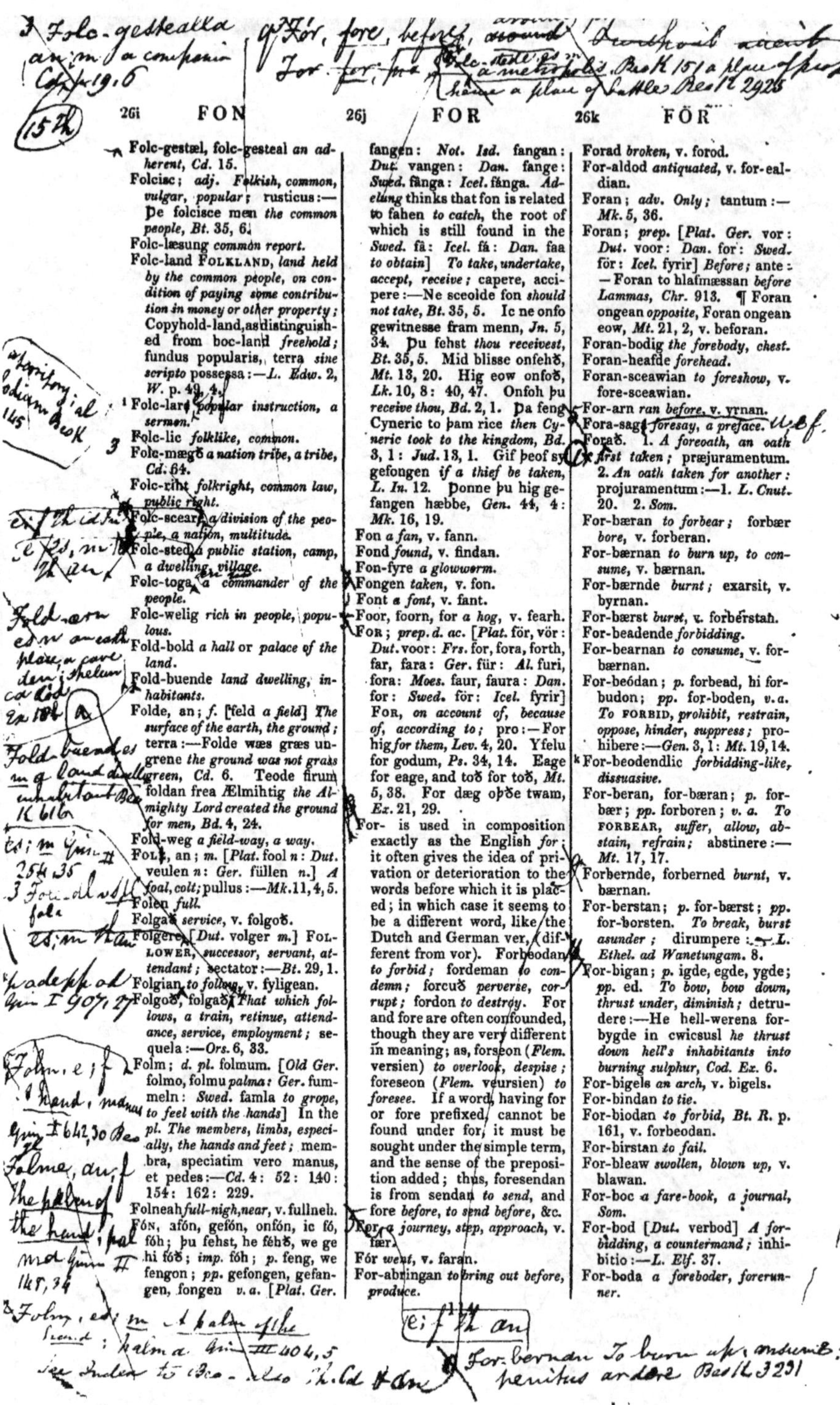

Folc-gestæl, folc-gesteal *an adherent, Cd.* 15.

Folcisc; *adj. Folkish, common, vulgar, popular;* rusticus:—Þe folcisce men *the common people, Bt.* 35, 6.

Folc-læsung *common report.*

Folc-land FOLKLAND, *land held by the common people, on condition of paying some contribution in money or other property;* Copyhold-land, as distinguished from boc-land *freehold;* fundus popularis, terra *sine scripto* possessa:—*L. Edw.* 2, *W.* p. 49, 4.

Folc-lar *popular instruction, a sermon.*

Folc-lic *folklike, common.*

Folc-mægð *a nation tribe, a tribe, Cd.* 64.

Folc-riht *folkright, common law, public right.*

Folc-searu *a division of the people, a nation, multitude.*

Folc-sted *a public station, camp, a dwelling, village.*

Folc-toga *a commander of the people.*

Folc-welig *rich in people, populous.*

Fold-bold *a hall* or *palace of the land.*

Fold-buende *land dwelling, inhabitants.*

Folde, an; *f.* [feld *a field*] *The surface of the earth, the ground;* terra:—Folde wæs græs ungrene *the ground was not grass green, Cd.* 6. Teode firum foldan frea Ælmihtig *the Almighty Lord created the ground for men, Bd.* 4, 24.

Fold-weg *a field-way, a way.*

FOLA, an; *m.* [*Plat.* fool *n*: *Dut.* veulen *n*: *Ger.* füllen *n.*] *A foal, colt;* pullus:—*Mk.* 11, 4, 5.

Folen *full.*

Folgað *service,* v. folgoð.

Folgere [*Dut.* volger *m.*] FOLLOWER, *successor, servant, attendant;* sectator:—*Bt.* 29, 1.

Folgian *to follow,* v. fyligean.

Folgoð, folgað *That which follows, a train, retinue, attendance, service, employment;* sequela:—*Ors.* 6, 33.

Folm; *d. pl.* folmum. [*Old Ger.* folmo, folmu *palma*: *Ger.* fummeln: *Swed.* famla *to grope, to feel with the hands*] In the *pl. The members, limbs, especially, the hands and feet;* membra, speciatim vero manus, et pedes:—*Cd.* 4: 52: 140: 154: 162: 229.

Folneah *full-nigh, near,* v. fullneh.

FÓN, afón, gefón, onfón, ic fó, fóh; þu fehst, he féhð, we ge hi fóð; *imp.* fóh; *p.* feng, we fengon; *pp.* gefongen, gefangen, fongen *v. a.* [*Plat. Ger.* fangen: *Not. Isd.* fangan: *Dut.* vangen: *Dan.* fange: *Swed.* fånga: *Icel.* fánga. Adelung thinks that fon is related to fahen *to catch,* the root of which is still found in the *Swed.* få: *Icel.* fá: *Dan.* faa *to obtain*] *To take, undertake, accept, receive;* capere, accipere:—Ne sceolde fon *should not take, Bt.* 35, 5. Ic ne onfo gewitnesse fram menn, *Jn.* 5, 34. Þu fehst *thou receivest, Bt.* 35, 5. Mid blisse onfehð, *Mt.* 13, 20. Hig eow onfoð, *Lk.* 10, 8: 40, 47. Onfoh þu *receive thou, Bd.* 2, 1. Þa feng Cyneric to þam rice *then Cyneric took to the kingdom, Bd.* 3, 1: *Jud.* 13, 1. Gif þeof sy gefongen *if a thief be taken, L. In.* 12. Þonne þu hig gefangen hæbbe, *Gen.* 44, 4: *Mk.* 16, 19.

Fon *a fan,* v. fann.

Fond *found,* v. findan.

Fon-fyre *a glowworm.*

Fongen *taken,* v. fon.

Font *a font,* v. fant.

Foor, foorn, for *a hog,* v. fearh.

FOR; *prep. d. ac.* [*Plat.* för, vör: *Dut.* voor: *Frs.* for, fora, forth, far, fara: *Ger.* für: *Al.* furi, fora: *Moes.* faur, faura: *Dan.* for: *Swed.* för: *Icel.* fyrir] FOR, *on account of, because of, according to;* pro:—For hig *for them, Lev.* 4, 20. Yfelu for godum, *Ps.* 34, 14. Eage for eage, and toð for toð, *Mt.* 5, 38. For dæg oþðe twam, *Ex.* 21, 29.

For- is used in composition exactly as the English *for;* it often gives the idea of privation or deterioration to the words before which it is placed; in which case it seems to be a different word, like the Dutch and German ver, (different from vor). Forbeodan *to forbid;* fordeman *to condemn;* forcuð *perverse, corrupt;* fordon *to destroy.* For and fore are often confounded, though they are very different in meaning; as, forseon (*Flem.* versien) *to overlook, despise;* foreseon (*Flem.* voursien) *to foresee.* If a word, having for or fore prefixed, cannot be found under for, it must be sought under the simple term, and the sense of the preposition added; thus, foresendan is from sendan *to send,* and fore *before, to send before,* &c.

For *a journey, step, approach,* v. fær.

Fór *went,* v. faran.

For-abringan *to bring out before, produce.*

Forad *broken,* v. forod.

For-aldod *antiquated,* v. for-ealdian.

Foran; *adv. Only;* tantum:—*Mk.* 5, 36.

Foran; *prep.* [*Plat. Ger.* vor: *Dut.* voor: *Dan.* for: *Swed.* för: *Icel.* fyrir] *Before;* ante:—Foran to hlafmæssan *before Lammas, Chr.* 913. ¶ Foran ongean *opposite,* Foran ongean eow, *Mt.* 21, 2, v. beforan.

Foran-bodig *the forebody, chest.*

Foran-heafde *forehead.*

Foran-sceawian *to foreshow,* v. fore-sceawian.

For-arn *ran before,* v. yrnan.

Fora-sagu *foresay, a preface.*

Forað. 1. *A foreoath, an oath first taken;* præjuramentum. 2. *An oath taken for another:* projuramentum:—1. *L. Cnut.* 20. 2. *Som.*

For-bæran *to forbear;* forbær *bore,* v. forberan.

For-bærnan *to burn up, to consume,* v. bærnan.

For-bærnde *burnt;* exarsit, v. byrnan.

For-bærst *burst,* v. forberstan.

For-beadende *forbidding.*

For-bearnan *to consume,* v. forbærnan.

For-beódan; *p.* forbead, hi forbudon; *pp.* for-boden, *v. a.* *To* FORBID, *prohibit, restrain, oppose, hinder, suppress;* prohibere:—*Gen.* 3, 1: *Mt.* 19, 14.

For-beodendlic *forbidding-like, dissuasive.*

For-beran, for-bæran; *p.* forbær; *pp.* forboren; *v. a.* *To* FORBEAR, *suffer, allow, abstain, refrain;* abstinere:—*Mt.* 17, 17.

Forbernde, forberned *burnt,* v. bærnan.

For-berstan; *p.* for-bærst; *pp.* for-borsten. *To break, burst asunder;* dirumpere:—*L. Ethel. ad Wanetungam.* 8.

For-bigan; *p.* igde, egde, ygde; *pp.* ed. *To bow, bow down, thrust under, diminish;* detrudere:—He hell-werena forbygde in cwicsusl *he thrust down hell's inhabitants into burning sulphur, Cod. Ex.* 6.

For-bigels *an arch,* v. bigels.

For-bindan *to tie.*

For-biodan *to forbid, Bt. R.* p. 161, v. forbeodan.

For-birstan *to fail.*

For-bleaw *swollen, blown up,* v. blawan.

For-boc *a fare-book, a journal, Som.*

For-bod [*Dut.* verbod] *A forbidding, a countermand;* inhibitio:—*L. Elf.* 37.

For-boda *a foreboder, forerunner.*

Folc-gesetnis, se; f a law, or statute of the people; plebiscitum Som
Folc-gestod, es; m a ... make of the people Cd 98 ... p 128, 29
Folc-gestreon, es; f a public treasure; publicum ... Folc-lar, e; f a ... commodum Cd 93 Th p 119, 17
Folc-getæl, number of the people, the population Cd 154 Th p 192, 9
Folc-getrum an assembly or host of people Cd 93 Th p 119, 29
Folc-gewin, folk-war ... Folc-lagu, e; f folk or public law; ...
Folc-cwen, e; f a popular queen Beo K 1275
Folc-mære popular Cd 86 Th p 108, 5
Folc-leasung a common or public lie Som v folc-lasung
Folc-mægen ... force Cd 160 Th p 199, 31
Folc-mot, es; m a popular assembly Som v folc-gemot
Folc-reden, ne; f a popular law Som
Folc-stede, es; m a seditious ... Folc-stow ... e; f a public place Bd 3, 5
Font bæd baptism Som
Folc-wer ... a multitude, a multitude of people, a multitude; populi multitudo Cd 171 Th p 215, 2
Folc-tal, e; f folk reckoning; genealogy Cd 161 Th p 201, 29
Folc-weras men of the people, the people Cd 12 Th p 14, 21; 89 Th p 110, 30
Folc-truma, an assembly of people, the people; plebs S. Ps 7, 8 Lye
Folcæ a multitude Lye
For-bærnedness, se; f a burning; ... Herb 164, 2
For-beaban to forbear Som 11 Lye v for-beran
For-betan to recompense; compensare Som
For-blawen inflated puffed up L M 2, 34 v blawan
For-blindad blinded hardened Mk 6, 52 Lye
For-bigean to bow ... v forbigan
Fosing a young ...
For ... before ... ; Goram Th ...
For for, notwithstanding, too, very ...
Fornelm, es; m ... a palm, an open hand; palma

Fora-gleawlice headfully, cautiously provide ... Ben interl. 3 Ben Lye
Foran-dæg before day or dawn Ben
Foran-niht the evening, the twilight Ben ... 2 Lye
Foran-onsettende prælusus Bd 5, 13
Fora-sceawung consideration Ben
Forbaned a banished man; exul Som
the oath which an accuser took of freedom from calumnious intention, before he was allowed to bring an action in a court of law. instar juramenti de calumnia
Ofgange man his ... mid ... fore at ... let every man commence his accusation with his fore-oath, or freedom from bad intention L Athel 23 W p 61, 11 Ne beo ... forað ... there not ... any fore-oath ... L Cnut pol 20 W p 137
Gif ... hæbbe getrywðne man, to forað for hine, ... swa ... if a thane have a true man for a fore-oath, ... L Cnut pol 20 W p 137

Fore-beran praeferre Bd 4, 11 Lye

Fore-beorh an outer work; promurale R 55

Fore-byenung a foretoken Som v fore-becen

Fore-byrdig mild-nitis, Ems[illegible] 's ta[illegible] incert edit. p. 173 Lye

For-cypped praecisus cantic Ezech

Fordaes [illegible] shallows breria [illegible] v. f ford

Ford-bot [illegible] on Thyme; epithymum Som

Fordeadian to kill interficere W[illegible] 112

For-dician to [illegible] with a ditch; fossa obstruere Som

For-brekan to break forbrytan Som v [illegible]

Forbygan he forbygd to bend, break, forbilie v forbigan [illegible]

Fore-cwide to a prediction Som v fore-cwide

Fore-cwedan aforesaid [illegible]

Fore-cwede predicted [illegible]

Fore-cwide [illegible] [illegible] prediction praedicted [illegible] 7 27, 35

For-dimmian to make dim or dark obscurare Som

Fore-cyn a predecessor antecessor Som

Fore-cynren progeny offspring; progenies Cot 145 Lye

3 For-burnen burnt v bernan

For-dittynde closing [illegible] Ps 57, 4 C v for-dyttan [illegible] [illegible] v for. 2[illegible]

Fore-cum to be before or above; praesum [illegible] [illegible]

Fore

Fore-heafod the fore-head; frons [illegible] 727, 27 v for-heafod

Fore-hlutan to bend before; procumbere C R Mk 1, 7

Fore-gegyrded girded about; praecinctus C Lk 12, 35 Lye

Fore-gleoran to pass away; praeterire C Lk 16, 18 Lye

Fore-gengenceaster [illegible] foregoers; predecessors Som

Fore-gesettan to set before; praeponere Bd [illegible] 17

Fore-[illegible] praecessor [illegible] 727

Fore-gepistrat blinded hardened C Mk 6, 52

For-cnidan to break into pieces Som v for-cnidan

For-cwidod capitula Lye

Fore-gewiten over past

Fore-cetywian to [illegible] foreshew Som

praeteritus Som

Fore-gegearwadae [illegible] propositionis R [illegible] Lk 2, 26

Fore-[illegible] praeoccupatio [illegible] 724, 30

Fore-gleaw foreseeing, heedful; providus R Ben 64 Som Lye

Fore-gleawlice headfully, providently R. Ben interl 3. [illegible] Fore-gleawnes, se; f a forecast, providence Som [illegible] Fore-gengend a predecessor Som [illegible] Fore-griffen taken beforehand v for-gripen

Fore-heafod a forehead Som [illegible] forgu-heafod — Fore-irnene

Fore-[illegible] a predecessor Cot 1 Lye [illegible] Fore-irnere a fore[illegible]

For-boden *forbidden*, v. forbeodan.

Forbogen *avoided*, v. forbugan.

For-boren *foreborne, allowed*, v. forbæran.

For-borsten *bursted*, v. for-berstan.

For-brædan, forbredan *To throw down, precipitate;* præcipitare:—*Ps.* 54, 9.

For-brecan; *p.* forbræc, hi forbræcon; *pp.* forbrocen [*Dut.* verbreken] *To break in two, break, bruise;* confringere:—*Jn.* 19, 31, 36.

Forbret *Astraba, R.* 3.

For-brytan; *p.* for-brytte; *pp.* ferbryt, forbrut. *To break in pieces, smash, bruise;* confringere:—*Mt.* 12, 20: *Deut.* 28, 24: *Lk.* 20, 18.

Forbrytednys, se; *f. Bruisedness, sorrow;* contritio:—*Ps.* 13, 7.

For-bugan; *imp.* forbuh; *p.* forbeah, hi forbugon; *pp.* forbogen; *v. a.* [*Dut.* verbuigen] *To bend from, pass by, decline, avoid, shun, eschew;* declinare, præterire:—He ne mihte forbugan, *Num.* 22, 26. He hine forbeah, *Lk.* 10, 31: *Num.* 22, 23.

Forbugennys *An avoiding, eschewing, a declining;* declinatio, *Som.*

For-byrd *Forbearance, patience;* patientia:—*Ors.* 1, 2.

For-byrdigað *Waiteth;* sustinet.

For-byrnan *to burn*, v. byrnan.

Forc [*Plat. Ger.* forke *f*: *Dut.* vork *f*: *Dan.* fork *c. a hay-fork*: *Icel.* forkr *m*: *Wel.* ffwrch, forch: *Bret.* forch *f*: *Sp.* horca *f*: *It.* forca *f.*] A fork; furca:—*R.* 66.

For-ceawan *to chew off, bite off.*

For-ceorfan *To cut* or *carve out, down, off* or *away;* excidere:—*Lk.* 13, 7.

For-cirfst *shalt cut.*

For-clingan; *pp.* forclungen [*Dut.* verslensen] *To shrink up;* marcescere:—*Nath.* 8.

For-cneow *A progeny, race;* progenies, *Lye.*

For-cnidan [*Dut.* versnyden] *To beat* or *break into pieces;* comminuere:—*Ps.* 17, 44.

For-corfen *cut down*, v. forceorfan.

For-cuman [*Dut.* voorkomen] *To fore come, go before, prevent;* prævenire:—*Ps.* 16, 14.

For-cunnan *to tempt*, v. cunnian.

For-cuoeþan; *p.* forcuom, hi forcuoedon. *To reprove*, v. forcwæðan.

For-cursed *cursed.*

For-cuð; *comp.* forcuðera; *sup.* forcuðost; *adj. Perverse, infamous, wicked;* pravus:—*Gen.* 13, 13.

For-cuðlice; *adv. Perversely, across;* perverse:—*Jos.* 10, 24.

For-cwæðan, for-cweðan *To chide, rebuke, speak against;* increpare:—*Bt.* 27, 1.

For-cwysð *shall shake.*

For-cyman *to overcome, bind.*

For-cyrfað *shall cut off*, v. forceorfan.

For-cyrran *to turn again, subvert, avoid.*

Ford, es; *m.* [*Ger.* furt *f*: *Old Ger.* fuert, related to this word is the *Dan.* fjord: *Swed.* fjärd: *Icel.* fiördr *m. a creek, an arm of the sea*: *Lat. mid.* forda] A ford; vadum:—*Gen.* 32, 22.

For-dælan *to deal out, expend.*

For-déman *to judge, condemn, damn.*

For-demednes; *f. Condemnation;* proscriptio:—*Bd.* 1, 6.

For-demman *to shut* or *dam up.*

For-dettan *to shut up*, v. fordyttian.

For-dilgian, fordiligan *to hide, blot out, destroy.*

For-doan *To destroy;* perdere:—*C. Mt.* 11, 13.

For-dón; *p.* fordide, hi fordidon. [*Dut.* verdoen] *To undo, destroy;* perdere:—*Mt.* 10, 28: *Mk.* 3, 6.

For-drencan; *pp.* fordrænct, fordrenct. *To make drunk, intoxicate;* inebriare:—*Gen.* 19, 32, 33.

For-drifan; *p.* fordraf; *pp.* fordrifen. *To compel, drive out, eject, banish;* pellere:—*Bt.* 38, 1.

For-drifene *One driven out, a stranger;* peregrinus:—*Deut.* 10, 18, 19.

For-drigan, fordrugan, fordruwian *to dry up, parch, Jn.* 15, 6.

For-dwilman *to confound.*

For-dwinan, for-duinan [*Dut.* verdwynen] *To vanish* or *dwindle away;* evanescere.—*Herb.* 2, 2.

For-dyttian *to close* or *shut entirely up.*

Fore *an access, journey, going together, an assembly, a sign, vehicle*, v. fær.

Fore *for*, v. for.

Fore *before*, used in composition as the English *fore.*

For-ealdian *to grow* or *wax old.*

Fore-astreccan *to lay* or *stretch out before.*

Fore-að *a foreoath*, v. for-að.

Fore-beacen *A foretoken, prodigy, wonder;* ostensum:—*Mt.* 24, 24.

Fore-beodan *to forbid*, v. forbeodan.

Fore-beon *to be before, to preside.*

Fore-betan *to amend.*

Fore-birig *a vestibule.*

Fore-bodian *To forebode, announce, declare;* annuntiare:—*Ps.* 70, 16.

Fore-breost *forebreast, the breast.*

Fore-bysen *a foremodel, an example*, v. bysn.

Forecennednes, se; *f. A generation;* progenies:—*Lk.* 1, 50.

Fore-ceorfan *to cut off.*

Fore-costigan *to profane.*

Fore-cuman *To come forth, to come before, prevent;* prævenire:—*Ps.* 17, 21.

Fore-cwæðan, fore-cweðan *to foresay, predict.*

Forecyman *To come before, go, proceed;* prævenire:—*Ps.* 58, 10.

Fore-duru, fore-dyru *A foredoor, porch, an entry, hall;* vestibulum:—*Cot.* 190.

Fore-fang, fore-feng *a fore-taking, prevention.*

Fore-fon *to take before, anticipate.*

Fore-gan, foregangan *to go before, precede.*

Fore-geblind *Blinded, hardened;* obcæcatus:—*C. Mk.* 6, 52.

Fore-gehat *a promise, vow.*

Fore-genga, an; *m.* [*Dut.* voorganger *m.*] *A fore-goer, predecessor;* prædecessor:—*Bd.* 2, 7, *S.* p. 509, 6.

Fore-gewitnys *a false witness.*

Fore-gulpon *boasted*, v. gilpan.

Fore-halig *particularly holy, dedicated, one who is so only before others;* hence, *a dissembler.*

Fore-mære; *def.* se fore-mæra; *adj. Fore-great, first, chief, honourable, illustrious, eminent;* primus:—*Bt.* 19, *Card.* p. 106, 22. Hu he fore-mærost seo *how he may be most illustrious, Bt.* 33, 2, *Card.* p. 190, 23.

Foremærnes, se; *f. Greatness, eminence, renown, glory;* claritas:—*Bt. R.* 34, 6.

Fore-meahtig, fore-mihtig *Prepotent, most mighty;* præpotens:—*Cd.* 80: 208.

Fore-mearcod *fore-noted.*

Fore-mearlic *eminent*, v. mærlic.

Fore-munt *a fore-mount, promontory.*

Forene *Before;* ante, citius:—*L. Cnut.* 30, *Lye.*

Fore-rym *A prologue, preface;* prologus:—*C. Mt. Prol.*

Fore-rynel, for-rynel *a fore-runner.*

Fore-sacan; *p.* foresoc. *To forbid;* prohibere:—*C. Mt.* 3, 14.

Fore-sæcgan, fore-secgan; *p.* foresæde; *pp.* foresæden. *To* FORESAY, *speak before, to predict;* prætari:—To þam foresædan ærendracum *to the foresaid messengers, Jos.* 6, 22: *Mk.* 13, 23.

Fore-sceawian *to foreshew, foresee.*

Fore-sceawung, e; *f. A foreshewing, providence.*—Fore-sceawung Godes *God's providence, Bt.* 39, 4.

Fore-secgan *to foresay, predict,* v. foresæcgan.

Fore-sedla *First seats;* primi recubitus:—*C. Mt.* 23, 6.

Fore-seon *to foresee, provide.*

Fore-seonnes *a foreseeing, providence.*

Fore-setnes, for-gesettenes *a thing proposed, intention, a preposition.*

Fore-settan *to set before, place, shut, close in.*

Fore-seuwenes *dishonour,* v. forsewennys.

Fore-singend, es; *m. A foresinger, one who pitches tunes;* præcentor:—*R.* 33.

Fore-sittend *one who sits before, a president.*

Fore-slop *A long robe;* stola:—*C. Lk.* 20, 46.

Fore-smean, fore-smeagean *to premeditate.*

Fore-spæc *a preface,* v. forespræc.

Fore-speca, fore-spræca, fore-spreca *One who speaks for another, a sponsor, an advocate, a patron;* prolocutor:—*Lup. Serm.* 1, 22.

Fore-specen, fore-sprecen; *adj. Fore-spoken;* antedictus:—*Bt.* 37, 2.

Fore-spræc, fore-spæc, fore-sprec, *f. A fore-speech, preface, introduction, defence, excuse, agreement;* præfatio:—*Bt.* 38, 7.

Fore-spræca *an answerer, a sponsor,* v. fore-speca.

Fore-sprec *a preface, an excuse.*

Fore-spreca *an answerer, a sponsor.*

Fore-sprecen *forementioned.*

Fore-stæppan, fore-stæpan, fore-steppan *To step or go before, precede;* præcedere;—*Lk.* 22, 26.

Fore-standan *To stand before, to excel;* præstare:—*Cot.* 149.

Fore-standend *A prelate, bishop;* antistes:—*Elf. gr.* 9, 26.

Fore-steppan *to step before, to precede,* v. fore-stæppan.

Fore-stigan *to go before, to excel.*

Fore-stihtud *fore-appointed* or *ordained,* v. stigan.

Fore-stihtung, foretiohhung *a fore-appointment, Bd.* 4, 29.

Fore-swerian; *p.* foreswore. *To fore-swear, declare before.*

Fore-tacn, fore-tacen, fore-tacnu *a fore-token, presage, sign, wonder.*

Fore-tacnian *to foretoken, foretel.*

Fore-teod *preordained.*

Fore-teohung *predestination,* v. fore-tiohhung.

Fore-þanc *forethought, consideration.*

Fore-þanclice *considerately.*

Fore-þencean *to fore-think, anticipate, forebode, despair, Bt.* 40, 3.

Fore-þinger *An intercessor;* præcator:—*W. Cat.* p. 117.

Fore-þingian *to beg pardon, intercede, defend, Bt.* 38, 7.

Fore-þonc *providence.*

Fore-þystrian *to obscure.*

Fore-tige *A market-place;* forum:—*Mt.* 11, 16.

Fore-timbrigende *building before, shutting up, Bd.* 5, 1.

Fore-tiohhung, fore-teohung, fore-stihtung, e; *f. A fore-appointing, predestination, prescience, providence;* predestinatio:—*Bt.* 39, 4: 40, 5, 6.

Fore-tynd *hedged afore, fore enclosed, Bd.* 5, 1.

Fore-weallas *fore-walls, Cd.* 158.

Fore-weard, fore-wærd, fore-ward, for-ward; *f.* [*Dut.* voorwaarde] A FORE-WARD or *guard, a beginning, condition, an agreement, a compact, bargain;* principium, conditio, pactum:—On foreweardum *in the fore-guardings, in the beginning, Bd.* 5, 2, *S.* p. 914, 24. To þat forewearde *to* or *on the condition, Chr.* 852. On heora forewarde *on their agreement, Chr.* 1091.

Fore-weard; *adj. Forward, fore, early;* primus:—Forweard niht *fore, early night, Bd.* 2, 12. Foreweard heafod *the forehead, Elf. gl.* 1.

Fore-weard, for-weard; *adv.* [*Dut.* voorwaards] FORWARD, *before, first;* primo, præ:—Forweard fremman *first to fulfil, Cd.* 37. On foreweard *on forward, forward, before, Deut.* 28, 13.

Fore-weosan, fore-wesan *To be before, to preside;* præesse:—*Bd.* 1, 34.

Fore-wis *forewise, foreknowing, Cot.* 149.

Fore-witega *a prophet, diviner, Elf. gl.* 41.

Fore-wost *a president, governor, prince.*

Fore-writennes *a proscription, banishment.*

Forf *a treasure.*

For-fang *a seizing, apprehending.*

For-fangen *taken.*

For-faran; *p.* forfor; *pp.* forfaren. *To go away, perish, destroy;* perire:—*L. Edw. Guth.* 11.

For-fleon *to flee away.*

For-fylden *Filled up, stopped, opposed;* obstructus:—*Cot.* 148.

For-gædnes, forgægednys, se; *f. A transgression, prevarication, stubbornness;* præteritio:—*Jos.* 6, 18.

For-gægan *To transgress, prevaricate;* transgredi:—*L. Ps.* 118, 158.

For-gan, for-gangan *To forego, pass by, go away, flee;* præterire:—*Ps.* 72, 7: *Ex.* 12, 23.

For-geatan *to expose, forget.*

For-geldan *to repay, return;* reddere:—*C. Mt.* 12, 36, v. for-gyldan.

For-gemeleasian *To neglect;* negligere:—*L. Athel.* 1.

For-geofan *to forgive,* v. forgifan.

For-gesettenys *a proposition,* v. foresetnes.

For-getan *to forget,* v. for-gitan.

For-gieldan *to recompence, Past.* 63, v. for-gyldan.

For-gifan, for-gyfan; *p.* forgeaf; *pp.* for-gifen. 1. *To* FORGIVE, *remit;* remittere. 2. *To give, grant, supply, impart;* dare:—1. Þe synt þine synna forgyfene, *Lk.* 7, 48. 2. Þæt wif þat þu me forgeafe, *Gen.* 3, 12.

For-gifenlic, forgifendlic; *adj.* FORGIVING, *pardonable, giving, dative; bearable;* remissus:—*Mt.* 11, 22. Forgifendlic gebygednes *a dative case, Elf. gr.* 7.

For-gifennes, for-gyfennes, se; *f.* [*Dut.* vergiffenis *f.*] FORGIVENESS, *indulgence, a grant;* remissio:—*Gen.* 4, 13: *Mt.* 26, 28.

For-gifung *a forgiving.*

For-gitan, for-gytan *to forget, neglect.*

Forgitelnes, forgitennes *forgetfulness.*

For-gnagan *to gnaw* or *eat up.*

For-gnidan *To dash* or *throw down, break;* allidere:—*Lk.* 9, 18: *Mk.* 9, 20.

For-gnidennys, for-gnisednys *Contrition, sorrow;* contritio:—*L. Ps.* 13, 7.

For-grindan; *pp.* forgrunden. *To grind up, pound, bruise, demolish.*

For-gripan [*Dut.* vergrypen] *To take before, prepossess, seize, snatch away;* apprehendere:—*Bd.* 5, 7.

For-gyldan *To recompence, pay for, redeem;* compensare:—*Gen.* 31, 39: *Mt.* 18, 25.

Fore-saegdnes, a fore saying; preface Som.

Fore-sceawere, a provident Bd 4,1 Lye

Fore-saega a fore sayer, prophet, prophetess Spin. II 727, 31

Fore-sceawere, es, m. a provisor Lye

Fore-sendan to send before Lye

Fore-seond, es; m. a foreseer, provisor Bd 4,23

Fore-set fore set, preferred; praepositus R87

Fore-settendlic set or preferred before Som

Fore-settednes, se; f. a proposition, proposition Som

Fore-singan to lead in singing Som

Fore-sittan to preside, preside Som

Fore-spraecan to intercede, to undertake for Som

Fore-steppung a stepping before, anticipation

Fore-stal, a forestalling, interception Som

Fore-steallan, to forestall Som v fore-steallan Som

Fore-stemnian to hinder C Lk 11,52 Ben

Fore-steora the guider or guide of the fore ship or deck Cot 149 Som

3 Fore-steora, a steersman, or master, a pilot Spin II 727, 32

Fore-sced foresaid Man

Fore-sendan to send before, praemittere Elf gr 28

Ben Fore-styltan to astonish Ben v for-styltan

Fore-pincan to fore think, to premeditate, Som v fore-pencean

For-eolice precisely Som

Fore-poncolice fore thinkingly, cautiously Som

For-eldan see No 30 [?] 115

Forenspreca D 35

Prov. 19

For-gemen to neglect v for-gymeleasian

Fore-smeaung premeditation Som

Foreweard forward carly Man

Fore-witegan to foretell, foretel Lye

Fore-witan to fore know Bd 39, 5.

Fore-witol provident Spin II 727, 35

Fore-wyrd added done before pactum Som Spin 727, 35

Fore-wregan to accuse Bd 5, 19

Forfesta very much Man

For-gaegincg transgression, excess Som

Fore-pancul a forethinking, provider Past 41, 5.

Fore-pingraeden, fore-pingung intercession, intercession Bd 4, 13 Lye

For-radon to deshair Bd 4, 11 v for-don

Forgied refoulness, confession Ben

For-gewitnes, se; f a false witness Som

Forgifenes, forgifennes, se; f. an Lev. 25,10

Forgitol (see Mem

For-glendred devoured, Cot 124 ingluttis L 13, 43, 28 Lye

Fore-witol forewise, skilful Lye

Fore-wite a fore wise, skilling Som

Fore-witung a foreknowing, a presage

Fore-word a bargain v for-word

Fore-writan to banish, proscribe Som

Forgolden, recompensed v forgildan

Fore-gymst affliction Cod Ex 32 B. 9, 15 Mann

Forgyfan to forgive v for-gifan

For-gymednes, se; f negligence Som
For-gymeleas [med] id Som.
For-gytan to forget Ben v for-gitan
For-hæfed denied Cd 179. [illegible] 225, 1 [illegible] for-habban, habban one
For-hatena, an m
For-hafa restrain; prohibere Cd 33, 13 [illegible]
For-healden headlong
1 Forheawan; p. forheow to cut down, slay, mangle Th an L. p. 128, 4 [illegible]
For-heold kept back p. of for-healdan

For-hogigendlic contemptible Som
For-hogian
For-hohnes, for-hogednes; se; f. contempt Th an
For-hrædlice suddenly; repente Past 58, 6 Lye

For-ht-leás Fearless bold; impavidus Som
For-ht-leasnys, se; f. Fearlessness, courage fortitudo Som
For-ht-modnes, se f. Faintheartedness; pusillanimitas Som
For-hwæðre however Th an
For-hwerfian to turn change Th an
Cd 5 [illegible] 7, 6
For-hycgande se causing R Jn 5, 45
For-lacan pp. - lacen to give over, to betray Bo H
For-intinyan be cause, for in respect of; qua, propter Som
For-lædend, es; m a misleader, seducer, seductor Som
For-lædc a leek; porrum Ben
For-legernes, se f fornication Som
For-leoran to leave relinquere Th an Bd 26
For-leornes, se; f prævarication Ben

for-leggand
For-licgend, es; m se [illegible] Som
For-liden shipwrecked Th an
For-lidenes, se; f a shipwreck Ben Th an
For-legernes, n fornication Th an Cut 26, 32
For-legis mulier prostituta, meretrix
For-leoran to go before Ben
For-leornian to lose, perdere Som
For-lire a fornicator Som & for-legere
For-lidednes, se f a shipwreck; naufragium Som
For-logen belied, Sup 12, 3 v for-leogan
Forma (se), sed, þæt forme the first, etc. Sup fyrmest

O. G. e. f. a niece

For-gyltan *to become guilty, to commit, Scint., Lye.*
For-gyman, for-gymeleasian *To neglect, pass by, transgress;* negligere :—*Mt.* 22, 5.
For-gyrd *A martingale;* antela, antilena, *Som.*
For-gytel *forgetful.*
For-habban, for-hæbban *To hold in, restrain, abstain, refrain, forbear;* cohibere :—*Bd.* 4, 4: *Lk.* 24, 16.
For-hæfdnes, for-hæfednes, se; *f. Restraint, abstinence;* continentia :—*Bd.* 3, 5.
For-hæfed; *comp.* ra; *sup.* est; *part. adj. Continent, abstemious;* continens :—*Bd.* 4, 3.
For-hælde *an offence.*
For-haten *foretold.*
For-heafod *forehead;* sinciput :—*R.* 69.
For-healdan *To withhold, keep back;* detinere :—*Bt.* 29, 1.
For-healden *Pollution, incest;* incestus :—*Cot.* 105.
For-heardan *to harden.*
For-helan, forhilð; *p.* forhæl; *pp.* forholen. *To hide, conceal, oppose;* celare :—*Gen.* 18, 17.
For-heregian, for-hergian; *p.* ede; *pp.* ed. *To lay waste, destroy, ravage, plunder;* vastare :—*Bt.* 16, 1.
For-hergung, forheriung, e; *f. A molesting, annoyance, trouble;* infestatio :—*Ors.* 2, 4.
For-hicgan, forhigan; *p.* de; *pp.* ed. [hicgan *to endeavour*] *To neglect, reject, despise, condemn;* spernere :—*Jn.* 12, 48.
For-hilð *hides,* v. forhelan.
For-hogan, for-hogian; *p.* ode; *pp.* ed, od. [hogian *to be anxious*] *To neglect, despise, accuse;* negligere :—*Deut.* 9, 23.
For-hogednes, forhogodnes, se; forhogung, e; *f. Contempt, disdain;* contemptus :—*Bd.* 3, 22: *Ps.* 122, 4.
For-holen *concealed, hidden,* v. forhelan.
Forhorwade *Was dirty;* obsorduit, *Hymn.*
For-hradian *to hasten before, prevent, overtake.*
For-hrered *made void.*
Forhspebung *a storm, T. Ps.* 106, 25.
Forht, geforht; *adj. Fearful, timid, affrighted;* timidus :—*Deut.* 28, 65.
Forhtfull *Fearful;* formidolosus :—*Coll. Monast.*
Forhtian, forhtgean; *part.* igende; *p.* ode; *pp.* od. *To fear, dread, tremble, to make afraid, to* FRIGHTEN, *affright;* pavere :—*Ps.* 13, 9: *Jn.* 14, 27: *Deut.* 1, 21.
Forhtiendlic, forhtigendlic; *adj. Timorous, fearful;* meticulosus :—*Cot.* 129.
Forhtlice *Fearfully, tremblingly;* trepide :—*R. Ben. interl.* 5.
Forht-mod *a frighted mind, timid, pusillanimous.*
Forhtnys, fyrhtnis, se; *f. Fear, amazement, terror, dread;* timor :—*Gen.* 27, 33.
Forhtra *more fearful, Cd.* 156.
Forhtung *fear.*
For-hule *concealed,* v. forhelan.
For-hwæga *at least.*
For-hwám *wherefore, why.*
For-hwerfed, v. forhwyrfan.
For-hwi, forhwig *for why, wherefore.*
For-hwon *why.*
For-hwyrfan, for-hwerfan; *p.* ede; *pp.* ed; *v. a. To cast aside, pervert, subvert, deprave, defile;* pervertere :—*Lk.* 23, 14; *Deut.* 27, 17.
For-hygan, forhycgan; *part.* forhyccende. *To despise,* v. forhicgan.
For-hygdelic *Despisable;* contemptibilis :—*L. Ps.* 118, 141.
For-hynan; *p.* de. *To cast behind, hinder, oppress, injure;* impedire :—*Ors.* 6, 1: 4, 10.
For-lædan; þu forlætst; *p.* de; *pp.* ed. [lædan *to lead*] *To mislead, seduce;* seducere :—*Cd.* 32: *Elf. gr.* 47.
For-læge *neglected, disgraced,* v. licgan.
For-læran [*Dut.* verleeren, læran *to learn*] *To mislearn, deceive, seduce;* decipere :—*Num.* 31, 16.
For-lætan; *p.* forlet; *pp.* forlæten. [*Dut.* verlaten] 1. *To let go, permit, suffer;* permittere. 2. *Relinquish, quit, forsake, omit, neglect;* relinquere :—1. *Bd.* 1, 27, *Resp.* 5. 2. *Gen.* 2, 24: *Ps.* 15, 10.
For-lætennys, for-lætnys, se; *f. A leaving, omission, desolation;* prætermissio :—*Bd.* 2, 14: *Ps.* 72, 19.
For-leas *lost; p. of* forleosan.
For-léc *deceived.*
For-legen *fornicated, committed fornication,* v. forlicgan.
For-legennys, forlegnes, se; *f. Fornication;* fornicatio :—*Mt.* 5, 32.
For-legere *An adulterer;* fornicator, *Som.*
For-legis, forlegystre *An adultress;* adultera :—*Past.* 52, 2.
For-leógan; *pp.* od. *To bely;* ementiri, *Som.*
For-leósan, leósan, he forlyst; *p.* ic, he forleas, þu forlure, we forluron; *pp.* forloren. [*Dut.* verliezen] *To lose, let go;* amittere :—Gif he forlyst an of þam, *Lk.* 15, 4. Ic forleas, *Lk.* 15, 9.
Forlet *left,* v. forlætan.
For-letenes *an omission,* v. forlætennys.
For-licgan, for-liggan [licgan *to lie*] *To fornicate, commit fornication;* fornicari :—*Edw. Guth.* 4.
For-ligenys *fornication,* v. forlegennys.
For-liger; *adj. Adulterous;* adulterus :—Forliger cneorys, *Mt.* 12, 39.
For-ligere; *pl.* ru, eru. *A fornicator, fornication; fornicator,* fornicatio, adulter :—*Mt.* 19, 9: 15, 19.
For-liggang *Lupanar, prostibulum, Cot.* 194.
For-ligrian *to fornicate.*
For-longe *for long, long ago.*
For-lor *Destruction;* perditio :—*Ors.* 3, 9.
For-loren *forlorn, lost,* v. forleosan.
For-lorenes, se; *f.* FORLORNNESS, *destruction;* perditio :—*Deut.* 32, 35.
For-losan *to lose,* v. for-leosan.
For-lure *lost; p. of* for-leosan.
For-lustlice; *adv. Willingly, gladly;* libenter :—*Bt.* 22, 2.
For-lyst *loses,* v. for-leosan.
Form; *def.* se forma; seo, hit forme; *adj. Early, first;* primus :—Se forma ys Simon, *Mt.* 10, 2: 22, 25, v. *comp.* furðra; *sup.* fyrmest.
For-mæl, for-mal *An agreement, a treaty;* fœdus :—*L. Ethel.* 1.
For-mærnes, se; *f. Brightness, glory;* claritas :—*Bt.* 34, 6.
For-manega *many.*
For-meltan, for-mylt; *p.* formealt, hi formulton; *pp.* formolton. *To melt, liquefy;* liquescere :—*Cot.* 125.
For-mengan [*Dut.* vermengen] *To join, mingle;* conjungere :—*Past.* 21, 1.
Formest *foremost, first,* v. fyrmest.
For-met *fare-meat, provision for a journey.*
For-molsnian; *pp.* formolsnod, gemolsnod. *To putrify, corrupt, to make rotten;* putrefacere :—*W. Cat.* p. 20.
For-mylt *dissolves,* v. for-meltan.
For-myrðrian *to kill, murder.*
Forn [*Ger.* fore *a trout*] *Turnus piscis, R.* 102.
For-naht *for naught, vain, void, Som.*
Forne; *adv. Before, sooner;* prius :—Forarn Petrus forne, *Jn.* 20, 4. *Prep. for;* pro, propter, *L. Ethelb.* 5.
For-neah, for-nean; *adv. Forenigh, nigh, near, almost;* prope :—*Ps.* 118, 87.
For-nefa, for-nefe *a nephew's son.*

For-niman; *p.* fornam; *pp.* fornumen; *v. a.* *To take away, deform, plunder, destroy, ransack, waste, consume;* consumere:—*Lk.* 9, 54: *Mt.* 6, 16.

For-nydan; *p.* ydde. *To force, compel;* cogere:—*Lup. Ser.* 1.

Forod, forad, forud, often contracted to fród; *adj.* [*Moes.* frods] 1. *Old, ancient, advanced in years;* senex. 2. *Debilitated, enfeebled, weakened, as by age, broken;* debilitatus. 3. *Wise, prudent, provident, as from age;* sapiens:—1. *Cot.* 96. 2. Frod fyrn *debilitated by age, Cd.* 57. Gif se earm bið forod *if the arm be broken, L. Alf.* 40, *W.* p. 45, 26. 3. *Menol.* 34.

For-oft *often, oftentimes.*

Foron *went,* v. faran.

For-pæran, aparan, pæran *To pervert;* pervertere:—*Past.* 39, 3.

For-radian *to go before,* v. forbradian.

For-rædan [rædan *to consult*] *To miscounsel, deceive, seduce;* seducere:—*L. Edw. Guth.* 12.

For-raðe *very quickly.*

For-ridel *an outrider.*

For-rotian *to rot, putrify,* v. rotian.

For-rotadnes, se; *f. Rottenness, corruption;* putredo:—*Elf. gr.* 8.

For-rynel *a forerunner,* v. forerynel.

For-sacan, for-sæcan; *p.* soc; *pp.* socen. *To forsake, withdraw;* detrahere:—*L. pol. Edg.* 8.

For-sæd *foresaid, accused.*

For-sawon *despised,* v. for-seon.

For-scapung *An escaping, an error, a bad action, sin;* perversa actio:—*Ors.* 1, 7.

For-sceaden *separated, dispersed,* v. sceadan.

For-sceaf *cast down,* v. scufan.

For-sceamian *to have shame, to blush, Scint.* 8.

For-sceap *a fault,* v. forscapung.

For-sceapen *transformed,* v. forsceoppan.

For-sceawian *to foreshew, provide.*

For-scending *perplexity, R. Lk.* 21, 25.

For-sceóppan; *p.* forscóp, forsceop; *pp.* forsceapen. [*Dut.* verscheppen] *To re-create, transform, deform;* transformare:—*Bt.* 38, 1.

For-sceotan *to shoot before, anticipate.*

For-scepen *transformed, Cd.* 214, v. for-sceóppan.

For-scip *foreship.*

For-scræncan; *pp.* for-scrænct, forscrenct. *To supplant, press,* v. gescrencean.

For-scrah *Abdicavit, Cot.* 205.

For-scrifan; *p.* hi forscrufon; *pp.* for-scrifen. *To shave or cut away;* corradere:—*Ors.* 5, 4, *Som.*

For-scrincan, scrincan, gescrincan, he forscrinð; *p.* forscranc, we forscruncon; *pp.* forscruncen. *To shrink, wither, contract;* arescere:—Þa sona forscranc þat fic-treow, *Mt.* 21, 19: *Mk.* 4, 6.

Forscunian *to blush, Scint.* 4.

For-scyedgod *vicious, wicked, Som.*

For-scyldigað *condemns;* forscyldigod *condemned, damned,* v. gescyldgian.

For-scyttan *Prævenire, L. Ps.* 48, 10.

For-seapung *an error,* v. forscapung.

For-searian; *pp.* forsearod. *To sear, dry up, wither,* v. searian.

For-secgan *To foresay, missay, pretend, deny;* injuste insimulare:—*L. pol. Cnut.* 15: *Edg.* 4.

For-sendan *to send away.*

For-seón, þu forsihst, forsixst, he forsyhð; *p.* forseáh, forsawe, þu forseage, hi forsawon; *imp.* forseóh; *pp.* forsewen; *v. a.* *To overlook, despise, scorn, neglect;* contemnere:—Se þe þone mannes sunu forsyhð, *Lk.* 9, 26.

For-settan; *p.* forsæt; *pp.* forseten; *v. a.* *To stop, hinder, obstruct, cause delay, neglect;* obstruere:—*Ps.* 21, 11. Hæfdon þone weg forseten, *Ors.* 4, 6.

For-settednys, se; *f.* *That which is set before, an intention, proposition;* propositio:—*Ps.* 77, 2.

For-sewen *despised,* v. forseon.

For-sewennys, foresewennes, se; *f.* *Contempt, dishonour;* contemptus:—*Ps.* 122, 4, 5: *Ors.* 4, 4.

For-singian *to sin against.*

For-sion *to despise,* v. forseon.

~~For-sið *Chlamys, R.* 65.~~

For-sið *death, destruction.*

For-sittan *to mis-sit, to be absent from, L. Athel.* 20.

For-slæhð *breaks.*

For-slagen *beaten, slain.*

For-slawian; *p.* wode. *To be slow, unwilling, to grieve;* pigere:—*Bt.* 10.

For-slean, he forslyhð; *p.* forsloh; *pp.* forslegen, forslagen. *To kill, slay, beat,* v. slean.

For-slitnys *desolation.*

For-soð; *adv.* FORSOOTH, *truly, certainly;* certe:—*Bt.* 14, 3.

For-spanc, forspanceg; *pl.* forspanincga, forspanningcga. *An enticement, allurement.*

For-spanan *to entice, seduce,* v. spanan.

For-speca *a sponsor,* v. forespeca.

For-specen *spoken in vain.*

For-spedian *to forespeed, flourish.*

For-spendan *To forespend, consume;* consumere:—*Ors.* 1, 1.

For-spennestre *A bawd;* lena:—*Elf. gr.* 9, 3.

For-spillan; *p.* de; *pp.* ed. [*Dut.* verspillen] *To spill, lose, destroy, disperse;* perdere:—*Mt.* 16, 25. Darius wolde hine sylfne forspillan *Darius would destroy himself, Ors.* 3, 9, v. spillan.

For-spillednes, se; *f.* *A spilling, perdition, destruction;* perditio:—*Mt.* 7, 13.

For-spreca *a sponsor, advocate,* v. fore-speca.

FORST, frost, [*Dut.* vorst *f.*] FROST; gelu:—*Ps.* 77, 52.

For-stælan *to steal;* forstæl *stole,* v. stelan.

For-stæpan *to step before, go before.*

For-stal *a forestall, a stoppage of the way.*

For-stalian *To* FORESTALL, *hinder;* impedire:—*L. In.* 24.

For-standan, standian, he forstent; *p.* forstód; *pp.* forstanden; *v. a.* 1. *To stand up for, to defend, aid, help, benefit, avail;* defendere, prodesse. 2. *To stand before, preside, understand;* intelligere. 3. *To stand against, to oppose;* impedire:—1. Willað forstandan *will protect, Cd.* 117: *L. In.* 62. Hwæt forstent hit þam *what profits it those, Bt.* 18, 4. 2. Ic mæg forstandan þine acsunga *I can understand thy questions, Bt.* 5, 3, *Card.* p. 18, 7: *Cd.* 37. 3. Engel forstod þone weg, *Num.* 22, 22: *Cd.* 131: 148.

For-stelan *to steal,* v. stelan.

For-stylð *steals,* v. stelan.

For-styltian *to astonish,* v. styltan.

For-styntan *To break, knock;* contundere:—*Cot.* 48, 177.

For-sugian, forsuwian; *pp.* forsugod. *To be silent,* v. forswigian.

For-swælan; *p.* de; *pp.* ed. *To inflame, set on fire, burn;* inflammare:—Seo sunne hyt forswælde, *Mk.* 4, 6.

For-swærian *to forswear,* v. forswerian.

For-swapian *to cast down.*

For-swelgan; *p.* forswealh, we forswulgon; *pp.* forswolgen; *v. a.* [*Dut.* verzwelgen] *To swallow up, devour;* absorbere:—Þa þe wudewena hus forswelgað, *Mk.* 12, 40. Seo eorðe forswealh Daðan, *Deut.* 11, 6.

For-sweltan *to die,* v. sweltan.

For-swerian; *p.* forswor; *pp.* forsworen. *To* FORSWEAR, *to*

For-þastð snawas
cofige the frosts & snows
splendid Cd 192 Th p 239,29

For-rim a preface, prologue
Som v fore-ryn

2 For-rotadnes, -ro-
tednys, -rotadnys
rottenness &c

3 For-sæt delayed p
of for-sittan
Cd 180, Th p 173,10

4 For-scandnes se; f
supplantatio Lye 40,10 Lye
5 For-sceawedlice provide
Prof R Conc Lye

7 For-sceawung providence
contemplation Som
v fore-sceawung

8 For-sceden scathed
Than v supl for-sceadan

For-scones, se; f
contempts Som v
for-sewennys

15 For-sittan to sit before
or around; to oppress Theo
K 3531

For-scildian pp od
to accuse, condemn Th
Apol

2 For-scrifen proscribed, condemned
Cd. 213, Th p 267,5; Book 212

3 For-scyncan to shrink
Ben v for-scrincan

4 For-scamigean to blush
Ben v for-scamian

5 For-scyppan to mis-
create, transform Than
in for-sceoppan

6 For-scytlican duru
vectiferae valvæ

7 For-seawenes, se; f
contempt; contemptus C
R Ben 43

(vgl for sich versehen)
8 For-seon to err, sin
Thorkelin

For-stapan to fore-
step, to precede Ben v
for-steppan, steppan

For-sceadan, p-sceod
For-sceaden to scatter
Than

9 For-settendlic
set before; præpositivus Som
10 For-setnes, se; f
a resolution, contin-
uation Thorkelin 177,2 Ben

11 For-sewenlic con-
temptible Som

12 For-sewestre she
who despises; contemp-
trix Som

16 For-steet inter-
necio Cd 108

17 For-slifen slit
broken Som

18 For-smorod suf-
focated Som

19 For-socen forsaken
Som

20 For-sogen wearied
worn Som

21 For-sorged sad, sorrowful Som

For-spanend, es; m
a seducer Som

2 For-spennend a
whoremonger; leno Som

3 For-spenning an
allurement Som v
for-spanc

4 For-speon urged Cd 18
Th p 22,34

5 For-spon enticed
v for-p of for-spanan

(7) su marge

For-spyllan to destroy
Som v for-spillan

for-stelan
For-stolen stolen
Som prop

For-stondan to benefit
R Sk 9,25 v for-standan

delivered
Cd 225, Th

For-steal a forestay
Som

For-steallan to fore-
stall Som v for-stallian

For-sewend, es; m
a despiser Som

For-stoppan to
stop up Som

For-strogdnys, se; f
presumption V Ps 57,4
v for-trugadnes

For-swapan to
sweep away
Cd 21 Th p 25,9 v forswapan

Forsīd-dl v thl
For-sid

Ford-feredness, i.e. a going forth; transitus, Bd 4,19 Lye. Ford-fleogan to fly forth, Mk #11.

For-swith to lies, Bd 2,31, hoste p. 63

For-swiðan to oppress, reprimere Beds. 50

For-sworcenness, ie. darkness, gviant Bd before Som

For-sworen forswore

For-tearendes, i.e. forth-reaching perfection Som

For-tacn a foretoken Som v fore-tacn

Ford-asledan, passed or gone before Som

Ford-bærst to burst forth Som v berstan

Ford-beseon prospicere Ps 101, 20

Ford-big-faran to pass by Som

Ford-blawan to belch or break out

Ford-clipung a provoking, an appeal Som

Ford-cuman to come forth

Ford-dæges at close of day Som

Ford-fæder forefather Som

Ford-for departure death Som

Ford-faran to bear forth, to depart, die

Ford-ferd borne forth death Th an

Ford-for-c. f. departure death Th an

Ford-fremung promoting Ps 104, 36 Th an

Ford-gangan to go forth Th an Bd 3,19 Lye

Ford-gefaran to go forth Som

Ford-geong a going forth Bd 2

Ford-geornes to seeker

Ford-gestepan to go forth, intrepid Th an

Ford-goten poured forth

Ford-gebrengan to bring forth or to light Bt. 42,7

Ford-gecyggan to call forth Bd 1,16 Lye

Ford-gefaran to go forth Bd 4,27

Ford-acygan provocare Bd 5,14

Ford-aresan to rush forth Ben v forþahresan

Ford-asendan to send forth Ben

Ford-blestan to blow or break forth

Ford-flowan to flow forth Som

Ford-lec promotus, progressus, provectus Som

Ford-gelædan to lead forth Bd 2,12

Ford-gostrode obscur. Ps 104, 26

Forder further Som v further

Ford-ferd goes forth departure, v ford-faran

Ford-rekt directus Lye Bt 30,29

Ford-ryht procedure

Fortuna portenta C R Mt 13,22

Fortiohung providence Lye

Ford-ryneses, in an onward course Cd 12, Th p. 14,8

For-mud Som

Ford-gang

Ford-kom to carry or produce Th an v feon

Ford-gesceaft, of death Book 3498

Ford-geleoran to go forth depart, die Bd 3,25 Lye

Ford-geraht reached forth porrectus Lye v geræcan

Ford-gewitenes departure, de. i.f. profectio Ps 104, 36

Ford-weard forward Th an v ford-weard

For-py therefore Th an v forþi

For-hyrrode very dry, arandus Som

For-tredde trodden; Gen 2,27 Som

Forðedniss continuation

Ford-gesceaft future condition Menol 3 p.54,3

Ford-lædnys. se; f a leading forth, a production; prolatio Bd 4,27 Res 8 Lye

Ford-leorende passing forth Bt 4,17

Ford-locian to look forth Ps 52,3

Ford-lutan to bow down Ps 94,6

Ford-many very rich, wealthy Som

Ford-nihte far in the night v ford-swapan

swear falsely, perjure: pejerare:—*Mt.* 5, 33.

For-swigian; *pp.* forswugod. *To pass over in silence, to dissemble, conceal;* silentio præterire:—*Bt.* 17.

For-swiðe *very great, vehemently.*

For-sworcen *darkened.*

For-sygian, *to conceal,* v. forswigian.

For-tende [fortend *seared, burned*] *Amazons, Scythian women,* so called, because hi fortendon þat swyðre breost *they burnt off the right breast, Ors.* 1, 10.

Forð; *adv.* [færð *goes,* v. faran] FORTH, *thence, further, directly, forward;* inde:—Balaam rad forð, *Num.* 22, 35. ¶ Forð dagas *the forth* or *going out of the day, far in the day.* Forð nihtes *far in the night.*

Forða *because.*

Forð-agan *gone forth, passed, Mt.* 14, 15.

Forð-ahræsan *to rise* or *rush forth.*

Forþám, forþan, forþon, forþambe, forþan þe; *conj.* [*for that which*] *For this reason that, on this account that, because, for that cause, for, therefore,* quoniam, nam:—*Mt.* 5, 3, 4: 6, 25: 14, 2.

Forð-ateon; *p.* forðateah *to draw forth, produce.*

Forðatincg *exhortatio, Pref. R. Conc.*

Forð-aurnen *elapsed, gone, Bd.* 4, 6.

Forð-bæran, forðberan, *to bring* or *carry forth.*

Forð-bæro *bringing forth; procreative:*—*Cd.* 7.

Forð-becoman *to come forth, proceed, Bd.* 1, 27, *resp.* 9.

Forð-boren *born forth, noble born;* opposed to læs-boren.

Forð-bringan *to bring forth, produce, fulfil, accomplish.*

Forð-bylding *an instigation, incitement, Chr.* 999.

Forð-clipian *to call forth, to provoke, Gal.* 5, 26.

~~Forð-cure *preferred, Cd.* 79.~~

Forð-cure *chose, preferred,* v. ceosan.

Forð-cyme *a coming forth, egress, Gen.* 38, 28.

Forð-cyþan *to declare, pronounce, Hymn.*

Forð-don *put forth, protrude, Bd.* 5, 2.

For-þearle *very much, greatly.*

For-þearlice *Shortly, sharply;* districte:—*R. Ben.* 2.

For-þencan *To misthink, disdain, distrust, despair;* diffidere:—*Bt.* 8.

For-þeon *to go* or *proceed before, to excel.*

Forþ-fæderas *forefathers, Elf. T.* p. 7.

Forð-faran *to go forth, depart, die.*

*Forð-fering *a going forth, deceasing, dying.*

~~Forð-fore~~ [fore *went,* v. faran] *A going forth, death;* mors:—He læg æt forðfore, *Jn.* 4, 47.

Forð-forlætenes, se; *f. A free permission, license, a fault;* derelictio:—*Bt.* 5, 1.

Forð-framian *to shoot forth, grow large.*

Forð-gætan *to explain, solve.*

Forð-gan *to go forth.*

Forð-gang *a forth going, progress.*

Forð-geclypian *to call forth, incite, Scint.*

Forð-gelang *Conducing, profitable, available;* conducens:—Forð-gelang beon *to conduce, L. Can. Edg. Poent.* 1.

Forð-genge *a forthcoming, increasing.*

Forð gewat *went forth.*

Forð-gewendan *to go out.*

Forð-gewitan *to go forth, proceed, pass over, depart, die.*

Forð-gyrd, for-gyrd *A tablet, a brooch, a stud on a bridle;* antela, antilena:—*Elf. gl.* 23, *Som.*

Forð-hald *stooping forward.*

Forð-healdan *to hold forth, to hold continually, retain.*

Forð-herge *the front* or *van of an army.*

Forþi, forþy, forþig, forþy þe, forþi þonne; *conj. Therefore, wherefore, for, because;* ideo:—*Bt.* 19: *Jn.* 7, 22.

Forðian, geforðian *To further, aid, assist, advance, perform;* promovere:—*Chr.* 675.

For-þingian *to beg pardon, intercede,* v. fore-þingian.

For-þiofan *to thieve, steal, C. Mk.* 10, 19.

Forð-lædan *to forth-lead, produce.*

Forð-læstan *to fulfil.*

Forð-letan; *pp.* forðleten, forðloten. *To let forth, send forth, emit, to incline, to be prone.*

Forð-lifan *to stand out, appear.*

Forðmest *foremost, first, C. Mt.* 20, 27.

For-þoht *despaired,* v. for-þencean.

For-þon *for that, for,* v. forþam.

For-þoncl *forethoughtful, prudent, R. Mt.* 11, 25.

Forðonloten *Provolutus, Dial.* 1, 8.

Forðor *further,* v. furðor.

For-þræstan; *pp.* ed. *To entirely bruise, break, to be contrite.*

For-þriccan *to tread under, oppress.*

For-þriccednes, se; *f. A pressing, an oppression, distress, anxiety;* pressura:—*Lk.* 21, 25.

Forð-rihte *right forth, down right, distinct, plain, direct;* hence, forðrihte spræce *prose.*

For-þryct *oppressed.*

For-þrysman; *p.* ode; *pp.* ed. *To suffocate, choak, strangle;* suffocare:—*Mt.* 13, 22.

Forð-scencan *to drink to.*

*Forð-scian *to die.*

Forð-scype; *m. A going forth, an expedition;* profectus:—*Bd.* 1, 34.

Forð-sið [sið *a journey*] *death.*

Forð-spownes, se; *f. Profit, gain, advantage;* profectus:—*Bd.* 2, 4.

Forð-stæppan; *p.* stop. *To step forth, proceed;* procedere:—*Mk.* 14, 35.

Forð-steallian *to have a place forward, to happen.*

Forð-swefan *to prevail, profit;* proficere:—*C. Ps.* 88, 22.

Forð-tege forð-tige *a porch, an entrance.*

Forð-tihtincg *an exhortation.*

For-þunden *swollen.*

Forðung, e; *f. A going forth, things necessary for going forth, a provision for travelling;* apparatus:—*L. pol. Cnut.* 10.

Forð-weard *forward,* v. forweard.

Forð-weaxan *to grow* or *break forth.*

Forð-weg [weg *a way*] *a going forth, progress, departure.*

Forð-wesan *to be out.*

Forð-wif *a matron.*

For-þyldian, for-þyldigian, forþyldegian *to bear, endure,* v. geþyldgian.

For-þylmed *obscured.*

Forð-yppan *to publish, lay open.*

Forð-yrnan *to run forth.*

Fortio, fortið *affrights, Bt.* 35, 1, v. forhtian.

For-togen *tugged together, gathered.*

For-togennes, se; *f. A drawing* or *shrinking together;* contractio:—¶ Fortogennesse innan *a contraction within, the cholic, L. M.* 2, 33.

For-tredan, þu fortrydst; *p.* -træd; *pp.* -treden. *To tread upon, tread under foot;* conculcare:—*Mt.* 5, 13, v. tredan.

For-trugadnes, fortruwednes, se; *f. Precipitancy, presumption, arrogance;* præcipitatio.

For-truwian; *p.* de; *pp.* ed. *To be over confident, rash, to presume;* præsumere:—*Bt.* 7, 3.

For-truwung, e; *f. Overconfidence, presumption;* præcipitatio:—*Bt.* 3, 1.

For-trydst *treadest,* v. fortredan.

For-tymbrian *to misbuild, stop up, hinder.*

For-tynan *To shut in, stop, hinder.*

Forud *broken,* v. forod.

Forucred *worn, C. Mt.* 9, 16, v. forwered.

Foruord *A point, jot;* apex:—*C. Mt.* 5, 18.

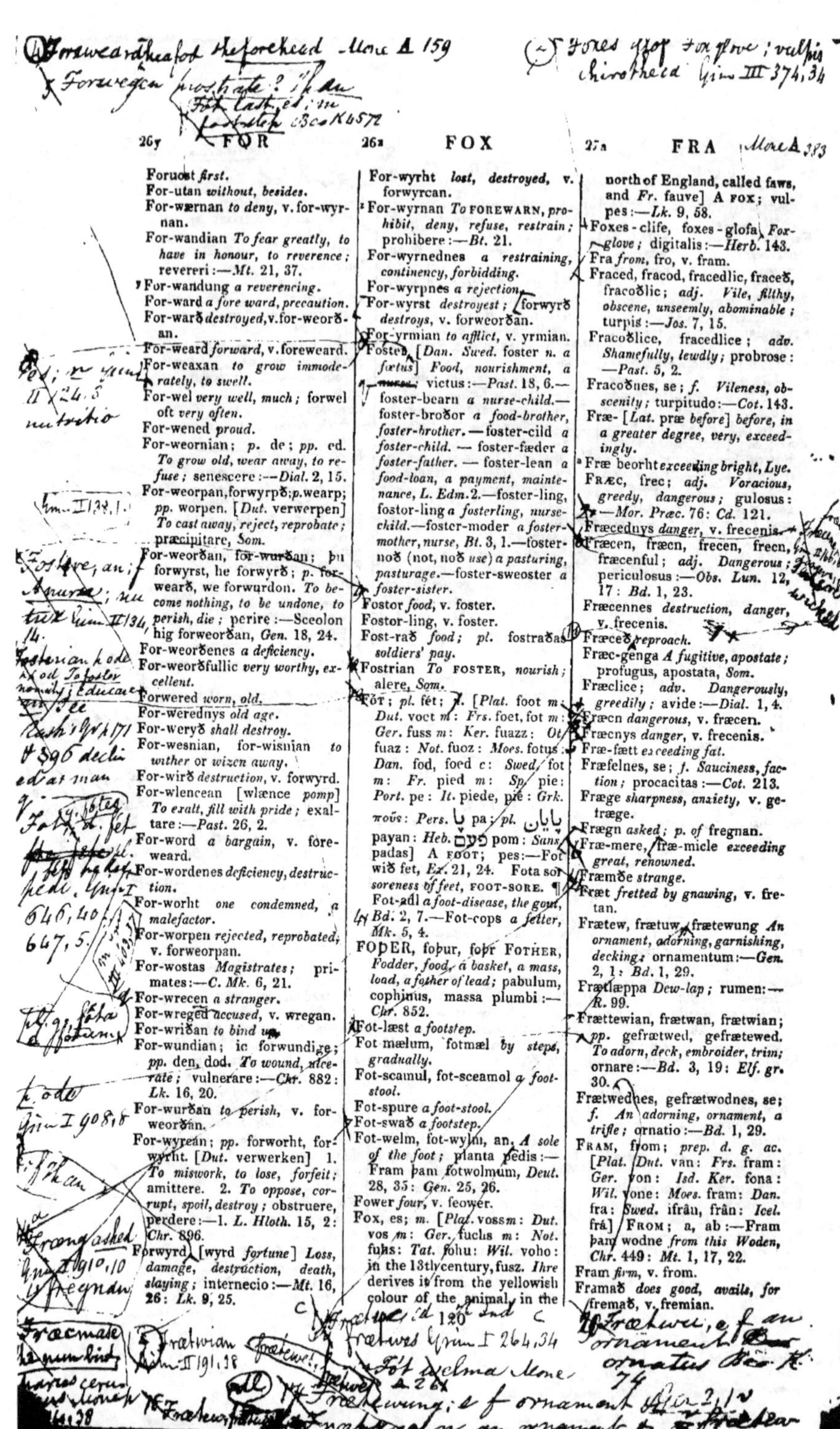

Foruost *first.*
For-utan *without, besides.*
For-wærnan *to deny,* v. for-wyrnan.
For-wandian *To fear greatly, to have in honour, to reverence;* revereri:—*Mt.* 21, 37.
For-wandung *a reverencing.*
For-ward *a fore ward, precaution.*
For-warð *destroyed,* v. for-weorðan.
For-weard *forward,* v. foreweard.
For-weaxan *to grow immoderately, to swell.*
For-wel *very well, much;* forwel oft *very often.*
For-wened *proud.*
For-weornian; *p.* de; *pp.* ed. *To grow old, wear away, to refuse;* senescere:—*Dial.* 2, 15.
For-weorpan, forwyrpð; *p.* wearp; *pp.* worpen. [*Dut.* verwerpen] *To cast away, reject, reprobate;* præcipitare, *Som.*
For-weorðan, for-wurðan; þu forwyrst, he forwyrð; *p.* forwearð, we forwurdon. *To become nothing, to be undone, to perish, die;* perire:—Sceolon hig forweorðan, *Gen.* 18, 24.
For-weorðenes *a deficiency.*
For-weorðfullic *very worthy, excellent.*
Forwered *worn, old.*
For-werednys *old age.*
For-weryð *shall destroy.*
For-wesnian, for-wisnian *to wither* or *wizen away.*
For-wirð *destruction,* v. forwyrd.
For-wlencean [wlænce *pomp*] *To exalt, fill with pride;* exaltare:—*Past.* 26, 2.
For-word *a bargain,* v. foreweard.
For-wordenes *deficiency, destruction.*
For-worht *one condemned, a malefactor.*
For-worpen *rejected, reprobated,* v. forweorpan.
For-wostas *Magistrates;* primates:—*C. Mk.* 6, 21.
For-wrecen *a stranger.*
For-wreged *accused,* v. wregan.
For-wriðan *to bind up.*
For-wundian; ic forwundige; *pp.* den, dod. *To wound, ulcerate;* vulnerare:—*Chr.* 882: *Lk.* 16, 20.
For-wurðan *to perish,* v. forweorðan.
For-wyrcan; *pp.* forworht, forwyrht. [*Dut.* verwerken] 1. *To miswork, to lose, forfeit;* amittere. 2. *To oppose, corrupt, spoil, destroy;* obstruere, perdere:—1. *L. Hloth.* 15, 2: *Chr.* 896.
Forwyrd [wyrd *fortune*] *Loss, damage, destruction, death, slaying;* internecio:—*Mt.* 16, 26: *Lk.* 9, 25.

For-wyrht *lost, destroyed,* v. forwyrcan.
For-wyrnan *To* FOREWARN, *prohibit, deny, refuse, restrain;* prohibere:—*Bt.* 21.
For-wyrnednes *a restraining, continency, forbidding.*
For-wyrpnes *a rejection.*
For-wyrst *destroyest;* forwyrð *destroys,* v. forweorðan.
For-yrmian *to afflict,* v. yrmian.
Foster [*Dan. Swed.* foster *n. a fœtus*] *Food, nourishment, a nurse;* victus:—*Past.* 18, 6.—foster-bearn *a nurse-child.*—foster-broðor *a food-brother, foster-brother.*—foster-cild *a foster-child.*—foster-fæder *a foster-father.*—foster-lean *a food-loan, a payment, maintenance, L. Edm.* 2.—foster-ling, fostor-ling *a fosterling, nurse-child.*—foster-moder *a foster-mother, nurse, Bt.* 3, 1.—foster-noð (not, noð *use*) *a pasturing, pasturage.*—foster-sweoster *a foster-sister.*
Fostor *food,* v. foster.
Fostor-ling, v. foster.
Fost-rað *food; pl.* fostraðas *soldiers' pay.*
Fostrian *To* FOSTER, *nourish;* alere, *Som.*
FŌT; *pl.* fét; *m.* [*Plat.* foot *m*: *Dut.* voet *m*: *Frs.* foet, fot *m*: *Ger.* fuss *m*: *Ker.* fuazz: *Ot.* fuaz: *Not.* fuoz: *Moes.* fotus: *Dan.* fod, foed *c*: *Swed.* fot *m*: *Fr.* pied *m*: *Sp.* pie: *Port.* pe: *It.* piede, pie: *Grk.* πούς: *Pers.* پا pa; *pl.* پایان payan: *Heb.* פעם pom: *Sans.* padas] A FOOT; pes:—Fot wið fet, *Ex.* 21, 24. Fota sor *soreness of feet,* FOOT-SORE. ¶ Fot-adl *a foot-disease, the gout, Bd.* 2, 7.—Fot-cops *a fetter, Mk.* 5, 4.
FOÞER, foþur, foþr FOTHER, *Fodder, food, a basket, a mass, load, a fother of lead;* pabulum, cophinus, massa plumbi:—*Chr.* 852.
Fot-læst *a footstep.*
Fot mælum, fotmæl *by steps, gradually.*
Fot-scamul, fot-sceamol *a footstool.*
Fot-spure *a foot-stool.*
Fot-swað *a footstep.*
Fot-welm, fot-wylm, an, *A sole of the foot;* planta pedis:—Fram þam fotwolmum, *Deut.* 28, 35: *Gen.* 25, 26.
Fower *four,* v. feower.
Fox, es; *m.* [*Plat.* voss *m*: *Dut.* vos *m*: *Ger.* fuchs *m*: *Not.* fuhs: *Tat.* fohu: *Wil.* voho: in the 13th century, fusz. *Ihre* derives it from the yellowish colour of the animal, in the north of England, called faws, and *Fr.* fauve] A FOX; vulpes:—*Lk.* 9, 58.
Foxes-clife, foxes-glofa *Foxglove;* digitalis:—*Herb.* 143.
Fra *from,* fro, v. fram.
Fraced, fracod, fracedlic, fraceð, fracoðlic; *adj. Vile, filthy, obscene, unseemly, abominable;* turpis:—*Jos.* 7, 15.
Fracoðlice, fracedlice; *adv. Shamefully, lewdly;* probrose:—*Past.* 5, 2.
Fracoðnes, se; *f. Vileness, obscenity;* turpitudo:—*Cot.* 143.
Fræ- [*Lat.* præ *before*] *before, in a greater degree, very, exceedingly.*
Fræ beorht *exceeding bright, Lye.*
FRÆC, frec; *adj. Voracious, greedy, dangerous;* gulosus:—*Mor. Præc.* 76: *Cd.* 121.
Fræcednys *danger,* v. frecenis.
Fræcen, fræcn, frecen, frecn, fræcenful; *adj. Dangerous;* periculosus:—*Obs. Lun.* 12, 17: *Bd.* 1, 23.
Fræcennes *destruction, danger,* v. frecenis.
Fræceð *reproach.*
Fræc-genga *A fugitive, apostate;* profugus, apostata, *Som.*
Fræclice; *adv. Dangerously, greedily;* avide:—*Dial.* 1, 4.
Fræcn *dangerous,* v. fræcen.
Fræcnys *danger,* v. frecenis.
Fræ-fætt *exceeding fat.*
Fræfelnes, se; *f. Sauciness, faction;* procacitas:—*Cot.* 213.
Fræge *sharpness, anxiety,* v. geþræge.
Frægn *asked; p. of* fregnan.
Fræ-mere, fræ-micle *exceeding great, renowned.*
Fræmðe *strange.*
Fræt *fretted by gnawing,* v. fretan.
Frætew, frætuw, frætewung *An ornament, adorning, garnishing, decking;* ornamentum:—*Gen.* 2, 1: *Bd.* 1, 29.
Frætlæppa *Dew-lap;* rumen:—*R.* 99.
Frættewian, frætwan, frætwian; *pp.* gefrætwed, gefrætewed. *To adorn, deck, embroider, trim;* ornare:—*Bd.* 3, 19: *Elf. gr.* 30.
Frætwednes, gefrætwodnes, se; *f. An adorning, ornament, a trifle;* ornatio:—*Bd.* 1, 29.
FRAM, from; *prep. d. g. ac.* [*Plat. Dut.* van: *Frs.* fram: *Ger.* von: *Isd. Ker.* fona: *Wil.* vone: *Moes.* fram: *Dan.* fra: *Swed.* ifrån, från: *Icel.* frá] FROM; a, ab:—Fram þam wodne *from this Woden, Chr.* 449: *Mt.* 1, 17, 22.
Fram *firm,* v. from.
Framað *does good, avails, for* fremað, v. fremian.

(4) Forwelmed overwhelmed suffocated Ben
Forwærian, forwerian to wear away destroy

For-wrigen darkened obscurated R Ps 23,5
For-wrecsid captivated Lye
For-wird death C Ps 104

(7)

p 120

Forfot spunge work; xephion Som Herb 47 Lye

Fræcednys frecodnys lessvaleness, pernicies Lye

dear Sir,

I find Mr van Baalen to England & then to Edin

For-wrecan to injure, wreck, banish Bea 35, 21 forwrecan wrecan

For-wrítan to carve, to cut asunder scindere Beo K 5406 v. writan sculpere, carve, ingrave, write, Bea

Fot nom ac; g fotes; d fet; pl nom fet, g fota d fotum; in Gen 164/11

Fræcod a despised despectus Som v fra-cod

Fræced vile Gen 230,4 v fraced

Frecendlic dangerous perilous Som contume Lye

Fræcne adv

Frecnely severely boldly, dangerously audacter

Abrahames ewen fræc fræcne on Sarran abraham's wife spoke fiercely against the damsel Cd 103 Th p 136,22

Fræ-cud despised despectus Som

Fræfele, fræfol saucy, insolent procax Som

Frænne frænnige the bit of a bridle, orea, frænum Som

Frænes, se; vile n 4 Ben

Fræmd foreign fremd

For-swæt a welling of the feet Ben

Fot-wære a foot pain

Fot-gemearc, es; n a foot mark, length of a foot Beo K 6080

Fræ-fellice saucily procaciter Lye

Fræ-fostlice very 178 Lye

Fræ-gian to ascertain asked

28

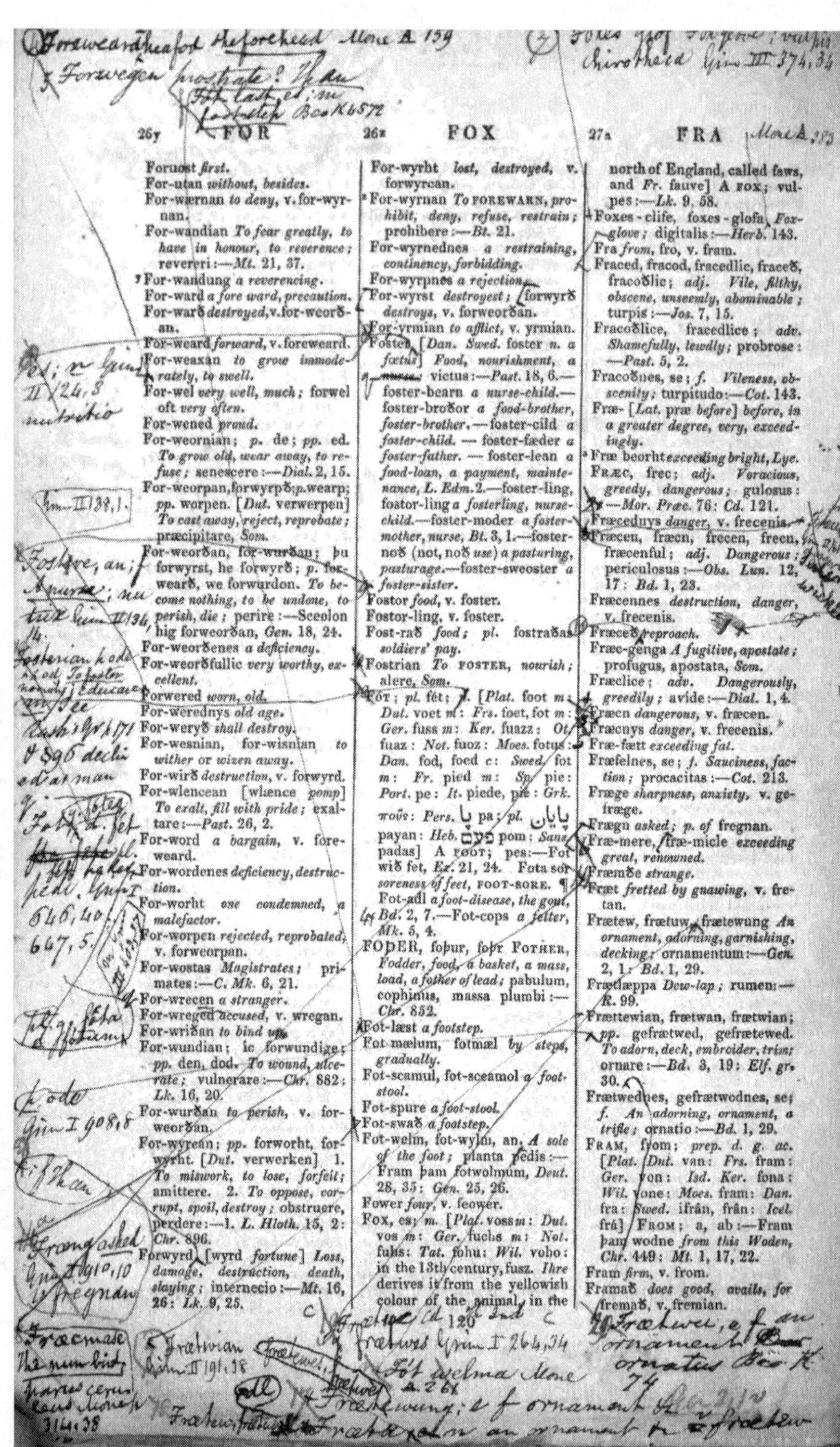

Foruost *first.*
For-utan *without, besides.*
For-wærnan *to deny,* v. for-wyrnan.
For-wandian *To fear greatly, to have in honour, to reverence;* revereri:—*Mt.* 21, 37.
For-wandung *a reverencing.*
For-ward *a fore ward, precaution.*
For-warð *destroyed,* v. for-weorðan.
For-weard *forward,* v. foreweard.
For-weaxan *to grow immoderately, to swell.*
For-wel *very well, much;* forwel oft *very often.*
For-wened *proud.*
For-weornian; *p.* de; *pp.* ed. *To grow old, wear away, to refuse;* senescere:—*Dial.* 2, 15.
For-weorpan, forwyrpð; *p.* wearp; *pp.* worpen. [*Dut.* verwerpen] *To cast away, reject, reprobate;* præcipitare, *Som.*
For-weorðan, for-wurðan; þu forwyrst, he forwyrð; *p.* forwearð, we forwurdon. *To become nothing, to be undone, to perish, die;* perire:—Sceolon hig forweorðan, *Gen.* 18, 24.
For-weorðenes *a deficiency.*
For-weorðfullic *very worthy, excellent.*
Forwered *worn, old.*
For-werednys *old age.*
For-weryð *shall destroy.*
For-wesnian, for-wisnian *to wither* or *wizen away.*
For-wirð *destruction,* v. forwyrd.
For-wlencean [wlænce *pomp*] *To exalt, fill with pride;* exaltare:—*Past.* 26, 2.
For-word *a bargain,* v. foreweard.
For-wordenes *deficiency, destruction.*
For-worht *one condemned, a malefactor.*
For-worpen *rejected, reprobated,* v. forweorpan.
For-wostas *Magistrates;* primates:—*C. Mk.* 6, 21.
For-wrecen *a stranger.*
For-wreged *accused,* v. wregan.
For-wriðan *to bind up.*
For-wundian; ic forwundige; *pp.* den, dod. *To wound, ulcerate;* vulnerare:—*Chr.* 882: *Lk.* 16, 20.
For-wurðan *to perish,* v. forweorðan.
For-wyrcan; *pp.* forworht, forwyrht. [*Dut.* verwerken] 1. *To miswork, to lose, forfeit;* amittere. 2. *To oppose, corrupt, spoil, destroy;* obstruere, perdere:—1. *L. Hloth.* 15, 2: *Chr.* 896.
Forwyrd [wyrd *fortune*] *Loss, damage, destruction, death, slaying;* internecio:—*Mt.* 16, 26: *Lk.* 9, 25.

For-wyrht *lost, destroyed,* v. forwyrcan.
For-wyrnan *To* FOREWARN, *prohibit, deny, refuse, restrain;* prohibere:—*Bt.* 21.
For-wyrnednes *a restraining, continency, forbidding.*
For-wyrpnes *a rejection.*
For-wyrst *destroyest;* forwyrð *destroys,* v. forweorðan.
For-yrmian *to afflict,* v. yrmian.
Foster [*Dan. Swed.* foster *n. a fœtus*] *Food, nourishment, a nurse;* victus:—*Past.* 18, 6.—foster-bearn *a nurse-child.*—foster-broðor *a food-brother, foster-brother.*—foster-cild *a foster-child.* — foster-fæder *a foster-father.* — foster-lean *a food-loan, a payment, maintenance, L. Edm.* 2.—foster-ling, fostor-ling *a fosterling, nurse-child.*—foster-moder *a foster-mother, nurse, Bt.* 3, 1.—foster-noð (not, noð *use*) *a pasturing, pasturage.*—foster-sweoster *a foster-sister.*
Fostor *food,* v. foster.
Fostor-ling, v. foster.
Fost-rað *food; pl.* fostraðas *soldiers' pay.*
Fostrian *To* FOSTER, *nourish;* alere, *Som.*
Fót; *pl.* fét; *m.* [*Plat.* foot *m*: *Dut.* voet *m*: *Frs.* foet, fot *m*: *Ger.* fuss *m*: *Ker.* fuazz: *Ot.* fuaz: *Not.* fuoz: *Moes.* fotus: *Dan.* fod, foed *c*: *Swed.* fot *m*: *Fr.* pied *m*: *Sp.* pie: *Port.* pe: *It.* piede, pie: *Grk.* ποῦς: *Pers.* پا pa; *pl.* پایان payan: *Heb.* פעם pom: *Sans.* padas] A FOOT; pes:—Fot wið fet, *Ex.* 21, 24. Fota sor *soreness of feet,* FOOT-SORE. ¶ Fot-adl *a foot-disease, the gout, Bd.* 2, 7.—Fot-cops *a fetter, Mk.* 5, 4.
FOÞER, foþur, foþr FOTHER, *Fodder, food, a basket, a mass, load, a fother of lead;* pabulum, cophinus, massa plumbi:—*Chr.* 852.
Fot-læst *a footstep.*
Fot mælum, fotmæl *by steps, gradually.*
Fot-scamul, fot-sceamol *a footstool.*
Fot-spure *a foot-stool.*
Fot-swað *a footstep.*
Fot-welm, fot-wylm, an. *A sole of the foot;* planta pedis:—Fram þam fotwolmum, *Deut.* 28, 35: *Gen.* 25, 26.
Fower *four,* v. feower.
Fox, es; *m.* [*Plat.* voss *m*: *Dut.* vos *m*: *Ger.* fuchs *m*: *Not.* fuhs: *Tat.* fohu: *Wil.* voho: in the 13th century, fusz. *Ihre* derives it from the yellowish colour of the animal, in the north of England, called faws, and *Fr.* fauve] A FOX; vulpes:—*Lk.* 9, 58.
Foxes-clife, foxes-glofa, *Foxglove;* digitalis:—*Herb.* 143.
Fra *from,* fro, v. fram.
Fraced, fracod, fracedlic, fraceð, fracoðlic; *adj. Vile, filthy, obscene, unseemly, abominable;* turpis:—*Jos.* 7, 15.
Fracoðlice, fracedlice; *adv. Shamefully, lewdly;* probrose:—*Past.* 5, 2.
Fracoðnes, se; *f. Vileness, obscenity;* turpitudo:—*Cot.* 143.
Fræ- [*Lat.* præ *before*] *before, in a greater degree, very, exceedingly.*
Fræ beorht *exceeding bright, Lye.*
FRÆC, frec; *adj. Voracious, greedy, dangerous;* gulosus:—*Mor. Præc.* 76: *Cd.* 121.
Fræcednys *danger,* v. frecenis.
Fræcen, fræcn, frecen, frecn, fræcenful; *adj. Dangerous;* periculosus:—*Obs. Lun.* 12, 17: *Bd.* 1, 23.
Fræcennes *destruction, danger,* v. frecenis.
Fræceð *reproach.*
Fræc-genga *A fugitive, apostate;* profugus, apostata, *Som.*
Fræclice; *adv. Dangerously, greedily;* avide:—*Dial.* 1, 4.
Fræcn *dangerous,* v. fræcen.
Fræcnys *danger,* v. frecenis.
Fræ-fætt *exceeding fat.*
Fræfelnes, se; *f. Sauciness, faction;* procacitas:—*Cot.* 213.
Fræge *sharpness, anxiety,* v. gefræge.
Frægn *asked; p. of* fregnan.
Fræ-mere, fræ-micle *exceeding great, renowned.*
Fræmðe *strange.*
Fræt *fretted by gnawing,* v. fretan.
Frætew, frætuw, frætewung *An ornament, adorning, garnishing, decking;* ornamentum:—*Gen.* 2, 1: *Bd.* 1, 29.
Frætlæppa *Dew-lap;* rumen:—*R.* 99.
Frættewian, frætwan, frætwian; *pp.* gefrætwed, gefrætewed. *To adorn, deck, embroider, trim;* ornare:—*Bd.* 3, 19: *Elf. gr.* 30.
Frætwednes, gefrætwodnes, se; *f. An adorning, ornament, a trifle;* ornatio:—*Bd.* 1, 29.
FRAM, from; *prep. d. g. ac.* [*Plat. Dut.* van: *Frs.* fram: *Ger.* von: *Isd. Ker.* fona: *Wil.* vone: *Moes.* fram: *Dan.* fra: *Swed.* ifrån, från: *Icel.* frá] FROM; a, ab:—Fram þam wodne *from this Woden, Chr.* 449: *Mt.* 1, 17, 22.
Fram *firm,* v. from.
Framað *does good, avails, for* fremað, v. fremian.

(4) For-welhned overwhelmed suffocated Ben

For-werian, for-wenan to wear away, destroy

For-wrigen darkened obscuratus R Lk 23,45

For-wrecend capitulum Lye

For-wyrd death Cot 104

(7)

For-fot spurge wort; xiphion Som. Herb 47 Lye

fracodnys

Fracodnys, vileness, turpitudo Som Lye

Fot nom ac. g fotes; d fet; pl nom d fet, g fota d fotum

Fracod despi... despectus Som v fra-cud

Fraced vile ... H 230,4 v fraced

Fracendlic ... contume...

Fraclic dangerous

Fraecne adv Fiercely, severely boldly, audacter

Abrahames cwen spraec fraecne on Samnan abrahams wife spoke fiercely against the handmaid Cd 103 Th p 136, 22

Fra-cud Despi... despectus Som

Fraefele, frafol saucy, insolent

Fraene, the bit of a bridle; orea, fraenum Som

Fraenes, se; vile ... Ben

Fraemd foreign Som v fremd

Fraeng asked v fregnan

Fraetennes ... v. fraetennes

p 120

Sir,

I find ... to England & then to Edin...

For-wrecan to injure, wreck, banish Beo 35; 218 v wrecan

For-wrat to carve, to cut asunder v writan

cindere Beo K 5406 V. sculpere, scribere

carve, ingrave; write, Bes yt ...

For-swat a walking of the feet Som

Fot. weard foot ... Som

For-gemearc ... a foot-mark, length of a foot Beo K 6080

Fra-fellice saucily ... Lye

Fraefestlice very hastily Cot 175 Lye

Fraegian to accuse Som

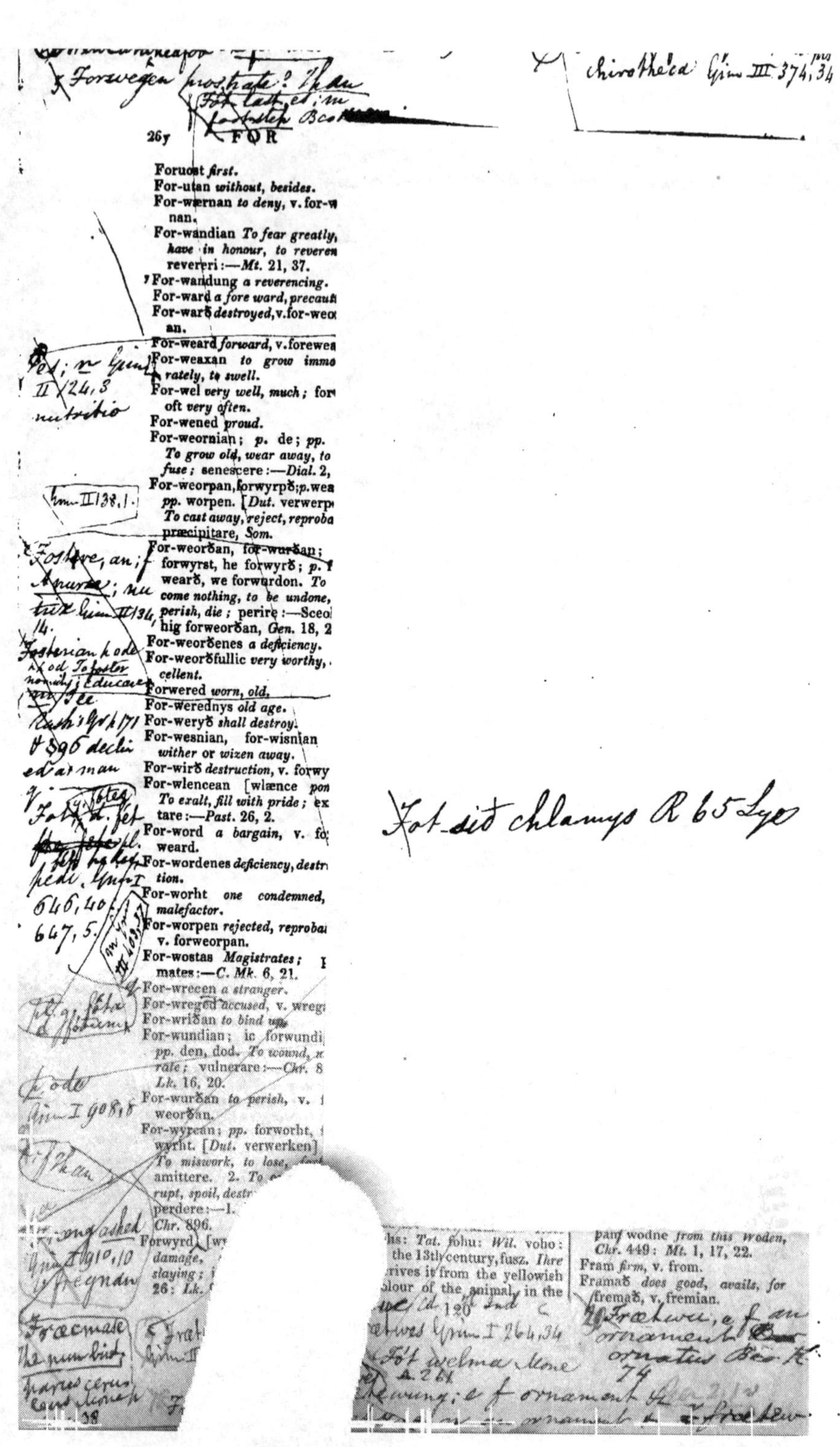

Forwegen prostrate? Than

chirotheca Grim III 374, 34

Foruost *first.*
For-utan *without, besides.*
For-wærnan *to deny,* v. for-w nan.
For-wandian *To fear greatly, have in honour, to reveren* revereri:—*Mt.* 21, 37.
For-wandung *a reverencing.*
For-ward *a fore ward, precauti*
For-warð *destroyed,* v. for-weo an.
For-weard *forward,* v. forewea
For-weaxan *to grow immo rately, to swell.*
For-wel *very well, much;* for oft *very often.*
For-wened *proud.*
For-weornian; *p.* de; *pp. To grow old, wear away, to fuse;* senescere:—*Dial.* 2,
For-weorpan, forwyrpð; *p.* wea *pp.* worpen. [*Dut.* verwerp *To cast away, reject, reproba* præcipitare, *Som.*
For-weorðan, for-wurðan; forwyrst, he forwyrð; *p.* wearð, we forwurdon. *To come nothing, to be undone, perish, die;* perire:—Sceol hig forweorðan, *Gen.* 18, 2
For-weorðenes *a deficiency.*
For-weorðfullic *very worthy,* cellent.
Forwered *worn, old.*
For-werednys *old age.*
For-weryð *shall destroy.*
For-wesnian, for-wisnian *wither or wizen away.*
For-wirð *destruction,* v. forwy
For-wlencean [wlænce pon *To exalt, fill with pride;* ex tare:—*Past.* 26, 2.
For-word *a bargain,* v. fo weard.
For-wordenes *deficiency, destr* tion.
For-worht *one condemned, malefactor.*
For-worpen *rejected, reproba* v. forweorpan.
For-wostas *Magistrates;* mates:—*C. Mk.* 6, 21.
For-wreccen *a stranger.*
For-wreged *accused,* v. wreg
For-wriðan *to bind up.*
For-wundian; ic forwundi *pp.* den, dod. *To wound,* rate; vulnerare:—*Chr.* 8 *Lk.* 16, 20.
For-wurðan *to perish,* v. f weorðan.
For-wyrcan; *pp.* forworht, wyrht. [*Dut.* verwerken] *To miswork, to lose,* amittere. 2. *To* rupt, spoil, destr perdere:—I. *Chr.* 896.
Forwyrd, [wy *damage, slaying;* i 26: *Lk.*

hs: *Tat.* fohu: *Wil.* voho: the 13th century, fusz. *Ihre* rives it from the yellowish olour of the animal, in the

pan wodne *from this woden, Chr.* 449: *Mt.* 1, 17, 22.
Fram *firm,* v. from.
Framað *does good, avails, for* fremað, v. fremian.

Fot-sid chlamys R 65 Lye

(4)

For-welned wrinkled
suffocated Jen
For-werian, for-wernan
[illegible] away destroy
v wernan
For-wandigende
disrespectful [illegible]
For-wealden through [illegible]
voided Som
~~Fraeddad [illegible]~~
For-weosnian to
[illegible] away Som v
for-wesnian

For-wrigen darkened
obscured [illegible] 23,45
For-wregd capitulum Lye
For-wyrd death Cot 104
Lye v for-wyrd
~~[illegible]~~ castigaturus
v for-wyrd [illegible]
For-wyrdendlic
ready to perish Som

For-yldan to put
off v yldan
~~[illegible]~~
For-yrnere, es; m
a forerunner, precursor Som
Foster-land land
given to find food, as
to maintain [illegible] for the
[illegible] Som

(7)

For-fot sponge
[illegible] sephion Som
Herb 47 Lye

fraecednys
Fraecednys, se; f
vileness, [illegible]
~~Som~~ Lye

For-witan to foreknow
know beforehand Th Apol
For-werdan barrain
[illegible] p. 59 8 v forwerd
~~For-werdnes, se; f~~

For-wernan to forewarn Bov 30 Lye [illegible]
For-wernedlice agre,
angusta Ben
For-[illegible] wervd destroys
[illegible] 51,5 [illegible] v forwernan
For-witegan to foretell
For-witig foreknowing Som
For-witignes, se; f
foreknowledge Som
For-wardenlic
lamentable Som
For-wordan to
perish
For-witolnes, se; f
industry [illegible]
2nd Ben

Fostring [illegible] nourishing
offspring, nutritio C
[illegible]
Fot-bret distraba
[illegible]
Elf [illegible] 55
Fot-mael
mecel very great
[illegible] 732, 17
Frae-ofestlice very [illegible]
[illegible] Cot 178
Fot-[illegible] cosp a fetter
Fot-cypsed fettered Som
[illegible]
Fot-mael a foot measure
a step
[illegible] 19
a step [illegible] 509,28
Fot-rap ~~[illegible]~~ ropes
Fot-swaede, es; m
a foot-trace
Fot-[illegible] or paper
Fot-stan, es; m a
foot stone; fulture
R 116
Fra[illegible]lice saucily
[illegible] Lye

Fot nom ac; of fotas, d
fet, pl nom fet, g fota
d fotum ; [illegible] 667,11
Fraced at a despised
despectus Som v frae-cud
Fraeced vile
[illegible] 230,4 v
fraced
Fraecendlic [illegible]
[illegible] v contume
Fraeclic dangerous
Fraecne adv
fiercely, severely
boldly, audacter, dangerously
perniciose
Abrahames cwen
spraec fraecne on
Farman abraham
wife spoke fiercely
against the [illegible]
Cd 103 Th p 136, 22
Fra-cud despised
despectus Som
Fraefele, fra fol
saucy, [illegible] procax Som
Fraene, [illegible]
a riddle; orca, [illegible]
franum Som
Fraecnes, se; vile
ness Ben
Fraend foreign
Som v fremd
Frang asked
fregnan
Fraekennes, se; f
[illegible]
v fraecennis

For-wyrd a wasting
of the feet Son
Fot-ece footache
Fot-gemet a fetters
Som Ben
Fot-sweal a washing
of the feet Son
Fot-waerc foot pain
For-gemaerc, es; n a
foot-mark, length of a
foot Bed R 1080
[illegible]

Fraeofestlice very
hastily Cot 178 Lye
Fraengian to accuse [illegible]

Fraetwung, ... purredan ...

Fraetot ... sauy son v. fraefle

Fram-cynne ...

Gen II 733,9 ...

Fram-cynne; ...

~~Fram-faerldi discessus~~

~~Fram-sid ...~~

~~Fram-scike profectus~~

Franca, an. m. A halbert, pike; lancea; hastile

lancea. Beo p. 92 K 2420. Mid his francan ofsceat Byrhtn. Cd II p 119 note a

Frato, fratohe an ornament, ... dye v fraetwa

Frelah free son v frech

Frécen, d frecne Danger, peril, woe. fercalem ... dalra frecna of all perils Cd 26 ... p 31, 21. Frecne with woe Cd 71, ... 196,20

Frecenisse; ... earth ... woefully

Frecne dangerously Cd 92: 144: 170 v fraecne

Frecnys danger se

... v frecenis ...

Freale bearht ... bright

Frea-rued speedy; ... quick son

... to hear, learn, understand ...

Fraward, perverse ... v froward; perverse son

v. frecenis

Frecne-stig, e. f a dangerous path, a precipice son

Fredan sentire Ben

Frede peace son v. supp fride

Fraefelice saucily v supp fraefellice

Fregan, problema ...

Fremdness, se; f strangeness, a dwelling abroad; peregrinitas son

... 38 Fraetewung ...

Fraegenlic Much spoken ... renowned

celebris ... 155,2

~~Framian to ...~~

Fram-weard, ... averse, perverse, turned away ... son

Fram-wis, ... with ... sapiens Gen II 733, 9

Fram ... began to decline M 2,5 ... adyrran ... to ... 1384, 4

... to do away ... 73,8

... to expell Cd 192 ... ahyldan to decline ... 13,4

... to repel ... 142,4 ... to cut or shear ... son to ...

... to draw ... away son ... to learn ... to rob son Elf gr 28

... to cast away Elf gr 28 ... began to decline son ... fleon to flee from son ... faereld a departure ... abomination son

Fram-scipe es, m ... son

... departure ... to depart son ... to stand off son ... to shake off son ...

Frane ... son v fraene

Freo-bearn a free child Cd 183 ... 230, 26 ... 292,19

Freo-brodor an own brother Cd 160 ... 199,14

Fremde, fremed strange, foreign, alien ...

fraetewung, e f ornament ...

... fraetedon an ornament ...

Freo-burh, ... a free city Beo K ... 1379

Frecennes, se danger son v ...

v. frecenis

Freo-lac a free offering or sacrifice ... 34, 20

Freo-laetan ... libertinus ... 56

Freo-laeta libertus ... 56

Freols-bric ... breaking ... a feast son

Freonda, ... m ...

Freo-drihten, es m a lord, Beo K 1585

... Freogan to love ...

K 1889: 6346

[Freo-halsian Gen II 669,30]

... began ... son

Freo-man ...

... fremian

Frec Bold, fierce audax, improbus Beo K 1771

Freme, an; f ... advantage; commodum Cd 38 ... 22: 59,12

Freme adj ... good ... Beo K 1860; Cd 12 p 13, 29

Adam fundi his wif, freo faegroste Adam found his wife, fairest woman Cd. 23 ... p 29, 28

Fram-gewitan *to depart.*
Framian *to avail,* v. fremian.
Framlice *strongly,* v. fromlice.
Framwisum *Wisely;* sapienter: —*Ps.* 57, 5.
Francan; *g.* Francana, Francna; *d.* Francum. *The Franks;* Franci, Francones: — *Chr.* 780: 854: 885: *Bd.* 1, 25.
Franc-land, Franc-ric *Franks' land, France, Bd.* 1, 25.
Frasian, gefrasian [*Dut.* vragen] *To ask, inquire;* interrogare: —*C. Jn.* 21, 12.
Frea, freo, fri, friga, frigia [*Frs.* fria *m: Ot.* Fro *dominus,* frowa *domina: Moes.* frauja *dominus*] *A lord, master, the goddess Frea;* dominus:—*Cd.* 1: 101: *Bt. R.* p. 171.
Frea-bodian *to speak, declare, L. Ps.* 118, 171.
Frec *a devourer:* hence, *ravenous, greedy,* v. fræc.
Frecednes *danger,* v. frecenis.
Frecelsod *endangered.*
ᵇFrecendlic, frecenlic; *adj. comp.* ra. *Dangerous, perilous;* periculosus:—*Bt.* 38, 3.
Frecene, frecenfull *dangerous,* v. fræcen.
Frecenis, fræcennes, frecennes, frecnes, fræcnys, frecednes, fræcednys, se; *f. Danger, mischief, ruin, destruction;* periculum:—*Bd.* 2, 7: *Ps.* 114, 3.
Freclice; *adv. Dangerously;* periculose:—*Ors.* 4, 8.
Frecn *dangerous,* v. fræcen.
Frecnes *A dormouse;* glis:—*Cot.* 96; *Lye.*
Fréfrian; *part.* igende; *p.* -frede; *pp.* -fred, gefrefred, afroefred; *v. To comfort, console;* consolari:—*Jn.* 11, 19.
Frefriend; *m. The comforter;* paracletus:—*Jn.* 16, 7.
Frefrung, e; *f. Comforting, reconciling, consolation;* consolatio:—*Gen.* 37, 35.
Fregnan, gefrægnan; *p.* frægn, frægin, fræng, we frugnon; *pp.* frugnen, gefrugnen [*Dut.* vragen: *Lancashire,* frayne] *To know by asking, inquire, interrogate;* interrogare: — *Bd.* 2, 1.
Fremd *foreign, strange,* v. fremed.
Fremdian *To alienate, estrange;* alienare:—*R. Ben.* 4.
FREME *Profit, advantage, gain, kindness;* commodum:—*Bt.* 14, 1: *Cd.* 12.
FREMED, fremd, fremð [*Plat.* freemd: *Dut.* vreemd: *Frs.* fremeth: *Ger.* fremd *strange: Ker. Ot. Not.* fremed: *Dan.* fremmet: *Swed.* främmande: *Icel.* framandi *hospes, advena.* —Fram *from afar: Old Eng.* fren, forenne *foreign: Chau.* uses fremde, fremed *strange. Spen.* appears to use fren as a contraction for frenne *a stranger*] *An alien, a stranger, a guest,* used as an adjective, *foreign, strange;* alienus:—Of fremedum, *Mt.* 17, 25, 26: *Ps.* 68, 11. Ac fremdum menn, *Deut.* 23, 20.
Fremfull; *adj. Beneficent, profitable;* beneficus:—*Lk.* 22, 25.
Fremfullice *Effectually, beneficially;* efficaciter:—*R. Ben. interl. Prol.*
Fremfulnes, se; *f. Profitableness, utility;* utilitas:—*R. Ben.* 53.
Fremian; *part.* fremiende, fremigende; *p.* ede [*Dan.* fremme *to forward, promote: Swed.* främja: *Icel.* frama *artes edocere, nomen et famam acquirere*] *To profit, do well, prosper, advance, avail;* prodesse:—Hwæt fremað ænegum menn, *Mt.* 16, 26. Hwæt him his swefn fremion, *Gen.* 37, 20.
Fremman, gefremman; *p.* de; *pp.* ed [*Icel.* fremia: *Celt. Bret.* framma *to join*] *To* FRAME, *form, make, do, effect, execute, benefit;* facere:—Ærest fremman *first to frame, Cd.* 1. Ic hæla gefremme to dæg, *Lk.* 13, 32.
Fremming, fremmincg, e; *f. A framing, an effect, efficacy, power;* fabricatio:—*Elf. gr.* 11.
Fremsum; *adj. Kind, benign, courteous;* benignus:—*Bd.* 3, 6.
Fremsumlice; *adv. Kindly, benign, Bd.* 1, 25.
Fremsumnys, se; *f. Kindness, benefit, liberality;* benignitas: —*Bd.* 1, 27, *Resp.* 8.
Fremð *a guest-stranger,* v. fremed.
Fremðian *to make as an alien, to excommunicate, to curse.*
Fremung, freomung, e; *f. Advantage, profit;* emolumentum, v. freme.
Frencisc; *adj. Belonging to France;* Francus:—*Chr.* 650.
Frend *a friend,* v. freond.
Frendlicre *more kindly, bearable.*
FREÓ, frio, freoh, frig; *adj.* [*Plat. Dan. Swed. Icel.* fri: *Dut.* vry: *Ger.* frey: *Ker.* fri, frig: *Moes.* frya] FREE, *having liberty* or *immunity;* liber, sui juris:—*Bd.* 4, 10: *Ps.* 87, 4.
Freo *a lord,* v. frea.
Freó-bearn *free-born.*
Freó-borh; *g.* freoborges. *A free surety, pledge, bondman.*
Freod, freode *Liberty, affection, good will;* dilectio:—*Cot.* 48.
Freódóm, es; *m.* [*Dut.* vrydom *m.*—freo *free;* dom *power, state*] FREEDOM, *liberty;* emancipatio:—*Bt.* 41, 2: *Bd.* 3, 24.
Freofestlice *Quickly;* propere, *Som.*
Freogan, gefreogan *To free;* manumittere:—*Lev.* 25, 10.
Freóh *free,* v. freo.
Freólic; *adj.* [freo *a lord,* lic *like*] *Liberal, ingenuous, goodly;* liberalis:—*Cd.* 9.
Freólice, friolice; *comp.* or; *adv.* FREELY; libere:—*Ps.* 93, 1: *Bt.* 18, 4.
Freols; *m. A time of freedom, a holy day, a feast, festival;* festum:—*Lk.* 2, 42.
Freols-dæg *a feast-day.*
Freolsdóm *Freedom, liberty;* libertas:—*L. With.*
Freolsgefan *to give a holy day* or *freedom.*
Freols-gear *a feast-year, jubilee.*
Freolsian; *pp.* gefreolsod, gefrylsod [*Ker. Not.* frihalse: *Dan.* frelse *to save: Swed.* frälsa: *Icel.* frelsa *to free*] *To keep holy day, to celebrate, to deliver, free;* celebrare diem festum:—*L. eccl. Cnut.* 17: *Lev.* 25, 2.
Freolslice *Solemnly, freely;* solemniter:—*Bd.* 3, 10.
Freols-tid *a feast-time.*
Freol-stow *a feast-place, banqueting room.*
Freolsung, e; *f. A feasting, celebrating a feast;* solenne: —*Ps.* 73, 5.
Freom *firm, strong,* v. from.
Freómæg *A relation, kinsman;* germanus:—*Cd.* 47.
Freó-man frig-man *Freeman;* liberæ conditionis homo:—*L. Edw. Guth.* 7, 8.
Freomlic; *adj. Firm, strong;* fortis:—*Bd.* 1, 3.
Freomon *a freeman,* v. freoman.
Freomung *profit,* v. fremung.
Freon; *p.* gefreode; *pp.* gefreod [*Plat.* fryen: *Dut.* vryen: *Frs.* fryen *to woo: Ger.* freyen *to free, love: Dan.* frie: *Swed.* fria: *Icel.* fria *to free*] *To* FREE *liberate, love;* liberare:—*Deut.* 15, 12.
Freo-nama *A sirname;* cognomen:—*Bd.* 2, 5.
Freónd, frend, friend; *pl. nom. ac.* frynd, gefrynd; *g.* frynda; *d.* fryndum; *m.* [*Plat.* fründ *m: Dut.* vriend, vrind *m: Frs.* friund *m: Ger.* freund *m: Ker. Ot.* friunt: *Moes.* frionds: *Dan.* frende *m. a kinsman: Swed.* frände *m. a relation: Icel.* frændi *c.*—freonde; *part. of* freon *to love*] A FRIEND;

amicus:—Hwylc eower hæfð sumne freond, *Lk.* 11, 5, 6. Ge synt mine frynd, *Jn.* 15, 14.

Freóndheald *friend inclined, friendly.*

Freóndleás; *adj. Friendless;* absque amicis:—*L. pol. Cnut.* 32.

Freóndleaste *Want of friends, indigence;* indigentia:—*L. pol. Cnut.* 32.

Freóndlic; *adj. Friend-like, friendly;* amicus, benignus:—*Bd.* 5, 14.

Freóndlice; *adv. Like a friend, kindly;* amice:—*Cd.* 76.

Freónd-lufu *friend-love, friendship.*

Freónd-rædenn, freóndræden *A friend-condition, friendship;* amicitia:—*Bt.* 21: *Gen.* 37, 4.

Freóndscipe; *m.* [*Dut.* vriendshap *f.*] *Friendship;* amicitia:—*Bd.* 3, 5.

Freora manna *of freemen; g. pl. of* freo.

Freó-riht *a free-right, common-right, right of a free-man.*

Freót; *m. Freedom, liberty, an enfranchisement, a setting a man free;* libertas:—*L. Edw.* 9.

Freoðan *To rub, froth;* fricare:—*Cod. Exon.* 36.

Freoðe, freoðo, freðo, friðo *Liberty, peace, love;* libertas, amor:—*Cd.* 48.

Freoðian; *p.* ode. *To consider kindly* or *affectionately, to pursue;* amore consulere:—*Bd.* 2, 6.

Fresan *Frisans;* Frisones:—*Bd.* 3, 13.

Fresisc; *adj. Belonging to Friesland, Frisian;* Frisicus:—*Chr.* 897.

FRETAN, he frit, fryt; *p.* fræt, we fræton, freton; *pp.* freten [*Plat.* freten: *Dut.* vreten: *Ger.* fressen: *Ot. Not.* frezzen: *Moes.* fretan, frætan: *Dan.* fraadse: *Swed.* fräta.—This word has, in all dialects, a contemptible meaning. *Ot.* uses it only once in a good sense. Ni frázum sie iz allaz, *Ot. Krist.* iii. 6. v. 56.] *To* FRET, *gnaw, break, eat up, devour;* devorare:—*Deut.* 28, 38.

Fretere *A glutton;* lurco, *Som.*

Freðo *peace,* v. freoðe, frið.

Fretnes, se; *f. A devouring, ravening;* edacitas, *Som.*

Fretol, frettol [*Dut.* vreter *m.*] *A glutton;* edax:—*R.* 88.

Fri, fria *a lord,* v. frea.

Friborges *of a freeman,* v. freoborh.

Fric [*Dut.* vrek *m.*] *A devourer;* devorator:—*C. Mt.* 11, 19, v. fræc.

Fricgean *to ask,* v. fregnan.

Frician *To dance;* saltare:—*Mt.* 11, 17.

Frician *To desire, seek for;* appetere:—*Cd.* 89.

Friclo *An appetite;* appetitus:—*L. M.* 2, 16.

Frico *With interest;* cum usura: *C. Mt.* 25, 27.

Friend *a friend,* v. freond.

Frig *free,* v. freo.

Friga, frigea, frigia *a lord,* v. frea.

Frigan *to free,* v. freogan.

Frig-dæg [*Plat.* freedag *m*: *Dut.* vrydag *m*: *Frs.* fredi *m.*—from Freja, Friga, Frea, *the goddess of love, and the consort of Woden*] *Friga's day,* FRIDAY, *the day on which the heathens worshipped the goddess Friga,* or *Venus;* dies Veneris:—*L. Athel.* 3. On frige-dæg, *Mt.* 4, 11, 22.

Frige *Love;* amor:—*Cod. Ex.* 8, b. 1.

Frigenes, frignys, gefrygnys, se; *f. An asking, a question;* interrogatio:—*Bd.* 5, 13.

Frig-læta *one let free.*

Frigman *a freeman, L. Cnut. pol.* 43.

Frignes, se; *f. Freeness;* libertas:—*Chr.* 796.

Frignian *to inquire,* v. fregnan.

Frignys *a question,* v. frigenes.

Frihtan *To fright, terrify;* terrere, *Som.*

Frihtrung, e; *f. Divination, sooth-saying;* hariolatio:—*Cot.* 21.

Fri-lic *free, liberal, Prov.* 28.

Friman *a freeman, L. Ethelb.* 28.

Frimdie, frimdig; *adj. Inquisitive, asking;* inquisitivus:—*With* beon *To be inquisitive, to ask, require;* requirere:—*Ex.* 12, 31.

Frinan, befrinan, frinð; *p.* fran, we frunon, gefrunon; *pp.* gefrunen; *v. a.* [*Dut.* vragen: *Frs.* fregia: *Plat. Ger.* fragen: *Ker.* frahen: *Isd.* fraghen: *Moes.* fraihnan: *Swed.* fråga, v. fregnan] *To ask, consult;* interrogare:—Hi frunon me, *Ps.* 34, 13. He befran hi, *Mt.* 2, 7: *Ps.* 34, 13.

Frio *free,* v. freo.

Friodóm *freedom,* v. freodom.

Friolice *freely,* v. freolice.

Friolsend, friolsiend *A deliverer, redeemer;* liberator:—*T. Ps.* 69, 7, v. freolsian.

FRIÐ, freðo, es [*Plat.* frede contracted freë *m*: *Dut.* vrede *m*: *Frs.* freda: *Ger.* friede *m*: *Isd.* frido: *Dan.* fred *c*: *Swed.* fred, frid *m*: *Icel.* fridr *m*: *Lat. mid.* fredus.—*from* freon, *or Moes.* frion *to love*] *Peace, love, agreement, league;* pax:—He nam frið wið þat folc, *he made peace with that people, Ors.* 5, 2. Friðes bot *a compensation* or *offering of peace, peace-offering, amends for a breach of the peace, L. pol. Cnut.* 8.—Friðdom *liberty, freedom.*

Frið-bena *a peace-petitioner, refugee.*

Frið-candel *a peace-candle, the sun, Cd.* 118.

Frið-geard *a peace-guard, an asylum.*

Frið-gedal *life* or *spirit-separation, death.*

Frið-gewritu *peace-writing, articles of peace.*

Frið-hus *peace-house, an asylum.*

Friðian; *p.* friðode, gefriðode; *pp.* gefriðod; *v. a.* 1. *To make peace;* pacem ferire. 2. *To protect, defend, keep, deliver, free;* protegere:—1. *L. Ethel.* 1, *W.* p. 104, 21. 2. Eall þat friðian woldon þat he friðode *would protect all that which he protected, Chr.* 921.

Friðleás *peaceless, not included in a treaty of peace.*

Friðlic: *adj. Peaceable;* pacificus:—*L. pol. Cnut.* 2.

Frið-man *a peace* or *league-man, an envoy.*

Friðo *peace, love,* v. freoðe.

Frið-socn, *a peace-refuge, an asylum.*

Frið-stol *a peace-stool* or *seat, an altar, asylum, Chr.* 1006.

Frið-stow *a peace-place, asylum.*

Friðsum, *peace-some, pacific.*

Frocca, frocga *a frog,* v. froga.

Fród *old, prudent, debilitated, broken,* v. forod.

Frófer; *g.* frófre; *f. Comfort, solace, convenience, profit;* solatium:—*Ps.* 17, 1: 31, 9. Frofre sunu *consolation's son, son of consolation; Barnabas, Martyr.* 11. *Jun.*

Frófer-boc *consolation book.*

Frófer-gast *consolation ghost, the Holy Ghost, Jn.* 14, 26.

Frofrian *To comfort;* consolari, *Som.*

Frofrung *A comfort;* consolatio, *Som.*

Froga, frogga, frocca, frocga, frox; *m.* [*Plat. Frs.* pogge *f*: *Dut.* vorsch *or* kikvorsch *m*: *Ger.* frosch *m*: *Not.* frosg: *Mons.* frosk: *Dan.* frõe *c*: *Icel.* froska *f.*] A FROG; rana:—*Ps.* 104, 28.

Frohto *Fearful;* timidi:—*C. Mk.* 4, 40.

FROM, freom; *comp.* ra; *sup.* esta; *adj.* [*Plat.* fraam: *Dut.* vroom: *Frs.* from: *Ger.* fromm: *Dan. Swed.* from: *Icel.* frómr] FIRM, *strong, stout, bold;* strenuus:—*Bd.* 2, 23.

From *A physician;* medicus:—*R. Matt.* 9, 12.

[14a.1]

Freond-lar, e; f friendly counsel

Freond-lāðu, e; f a friendly invitation Beok 2388

Freond-spēdig, f friend-spēd, many friends Cd 105 Th p 140, 29

Freondo-spedig friend-rich, rich in friends, amicorum dives L Ethy 95

(also Frigdæg, el; m)

Freorig Freezing, chilly Th An

Freos captives Cd 174 Th p 220, 4 v free

Freoslice freely Bd Som 1.17 v freolice

Freodo-mund amoris vel libertatis tutela; Abba Leth Lye

Freodo-sceale, es; m a free servant, a minister; manumissi servi Cd 115 Th p 150, 25 : 105 Th p 138, 32

Freoda-peawas, Loving manners, v peaw Cd 4 Th p 4

Freodo-wær, e; f a peace covenant, compact, covenant of love Cd 158 Th 197, 13

Freodo-wong, es; m a large champain, the peaceful plain

Freot-mon a free man Som

Frefrian to adorn Som Ben v frætwian

Fretwung an ornament Som Ben v fræt wrung

Freyndōme an f. female friend; amica Som

Frian to free Ben v freon

Fricca an m a crier Som v frycca

Se frigea a freeman L In 7th Wilk p 26, 16

Frig, e; f the Friga, the wife of Odin, the Venus ... Cd, m.

Frige-dæg, Friga's day, Friday Grimm Myth p 88 Th An

Freodo-burh a peace city, an asylum Beok 1638

Freoscipe es; m ingenuousness Th An

Freodo-gyfa, an m a giver of freedom

Freah-gyfu a free gift, giving freedom Lye

friendly supplicant

Frynde Th An

Freond-geþingu, friends' agreement Th An

Freodo-spēd peaceful rule; great sway Cd 60 Th 1 73, 2

Frind friends pl. v frynd pl. of freond

Friolete one set free Som v frig-læta

Frisca, an m a bittern; bittern

Som

Freodo-wær, e; f a peace compact

Beok 4559

Freodu-webbe, an a peace weaver, or intermediator, a woman Beok 3880 v webba

Friccan to free ... a crier's office Som

Friðdom ... Som

Frið-að an oath of peace Lye - Freoðu a peace breaking Lye - burh a peace city, a city of refuge Lye - gear peace year, year of jubilee Som - gegyld a peace guild, an association Som - geora peace desirous, desirous of peace

Swa deo þe frið socne gesece ad aedes magnas asylum confugerit L. Const Eccl 2 W p 107, 29

Frið-land a land at peace, terra pace ... Cd 1097

Friðlice peaceably Som

Friðu peace ...

Freodo peace v Ll frið

Frið-mæl an agreement, pact Som Grim Æ 509 28

Freodo-tacn a peace token Cd 107 Th p 142, 29

Frittan to feel to ... Cd 48, 14 v fretan

Freoca ... luscinia Cd 121 Lye

ful field Beok 5913

Freodo-webba, an m a peace weaver, peace-maker Cod Vercell 174. Bos gl.

Spring Th An good Beok 41

... pins, bones

amicus :—Hwylc eower hæfð sumne freond, Lk. 11, 5, 6. Ge synt mine frynd, Jn. 15, 14.

Freóndheald friend inclined, friendly.

Freóndleás; adj. Friendless; absque amicis :—L. pol. Cnut. 32.

Freóndleaste Want of friends, indigence; indigentia:—L. pol. Cnut. 32.

Freóndlic; adj. Friend-like, friendly; amicus, benignus :—Bd. 5, 14.

Freóndlice; adv. Like a friend, kindly; amice :—Cd. 76.

Freónd-lufu friend-love, friendship.

Freónd-rædenn, freóndrædenn A friend-condition, friendship; amicitia:—Bt. 21: Gen. 37, 4.

Freóndscipe; m. [Dut. vriendshap f.] Friendship; amicitia: —Bd. 3, 5.

Freora manna of freemen; g. pl. of freo.

Freó-riht a free-right, common-right, right of a free-man.

Freót; m. Freedom, liberty, an enfranchisement, a setting a man free; libertas :—L. Edw. 9.

Freoðan To rub, froth; fricare :—Cod. Exon. 36, 4.

Freoðe, freoðo, freða, friðo Liberty, peace, love; libertas, amor :—Cd. 48.

Freoðian; p. ode. To consider kindly or affectionately, to pursue; amore consulere :—Bd. 2, 6.

Fresan Frisans; Frisones :—Bd. 3, 13.

Fresisc; adj. Belonging to Friesland, Frisian; Frisicus :—Chr. 897.

FRETAN, he frit, fryt; p. fræt, we fræton, freton; pp. freten [Plat. freten: Dut. vreten: Ger. fressen: Ot. Not. frezzen: Moes. fretan, frætan: Dan. fraadse: Swed. fräta.—This word has, in all dialects, a contemptible meaning. Ot. uses it only once in a good sense. Ni frázum sie iz allaz, Ot. Krist. iii. 6. v. 56.] To FRET, gnaw, break, eat up, devour; devorare :—Deut. 28, 38.

Fretere A glutton; lurco, Som.

Freðo peace, v. freoðe, frið.

Fretnes, se; f. A devouring, ravening; edacitas, Som.

Fretol, frettol [Dut. vreter m.] A glutton; edax :—R. 88.

Fri, fria a lord, v. frea.

Friborges of a freeman, v. freoborh.

Fric [Dut. vrek m.] A devourer; devorator :—C. Mt. 11, 19, v. fræc.

Fricgean to ask, v. fregnan.

Frician To dance; saltare :—Mt. 11, 17.

Frician To desire, seek for; appetere :—Cd. 89.

Friclo An appetite; appetitus :—L. M. 2, 16.

Frico With interest; cum usura : C. Mt. 25, 27.

Friend a friend, v. freond.

Frig free, v. freo.

Friga, frigea, frigia a lord, v. frea.

Frigan to free, v. freogan.

Frig-dæg [Plat. freedag m: Dut. vrydag m: Frs. fredi m. —from Freja, Friga, Frea, the goddess of love, and the consort of Woden] Friga's day, FRIDAY, the day on which the heathens worshipped the goddess Friga, or Venus; dies Veneris :—L. Athel. 3. On frige-dæg, Mt. 4, 11, 22.

Frige Love; amor :—Cod. Ex. 8, b. 1.

Frigenes, frignys, gefrygnys, se; f. An asking, a question; interrogatio :—Bd. 5, 13.

Frig-læta one let free.

Frigman a freeman, L. Cnut. pol. 43.

Frignes, se; f. Freeness; libertas :—Chr. 796.

Frignan to inquire, v. fregnan.

Frignys a question, v. frigenes.

Frihtan To fright, terrify; terrere, Som.

Frihtrung, e; f. Divination, sooth-saying; hariolatio :—Cot. 21.

Fri-lic free, liberal, Prov. 28.

Friman a freeman, L. Ethelb. 28.

Frimdie, frimdig; adj. Inquisitive, asking; inquisitivus :—With beon To be inquisitive, to ask, require; requirere :—Ex. 12, 31.

Frinan, befrinan, frinð; p. fran, we frunon, gefrunon; pp. gefrunen; v. a. [Dut. vragen: Frs. fregia: Plat. Ger. fragen: Ker. frahen: Isd. fraghen: Moes. fraihnan: Swed. fråga, v. fregnan] To ask, consult; interrogare :—Hi frunon me, Ps. 34, 13. He befran hi, Mt. 2, 7: Ps. 34, 13.

Frio free, v. freo.

Friodóm freedom, v. freodom.

Friolice freely, v. freolice.

Friolsend, friolsiend A deliverer, redeemer; liberator :—T. Ps. 69, 7, v. freolsian.

FRIÐ, freðo, es [Plat. frede contracted freë m: Dut. vrede m: Frs. freda: Ger. friede m: Isd. frido: Dan. fred c: Swed. fred, frid m: Icel. fridr m: Lat. mid. fredus.—from freon, or Moes. frion to love] Peace, love, agreement, league; pax :—He nam frið wið þat folc, he made peace with that people, Ors. 5, 2. Friðes bot a compensation or offering of peace, peace-offering, amends for a breach of the peace, L. pol. Cnut. 8.—Friðdom liberty, freedom.

Frið-bena a peace-petitioner, refugee.

Frið-candel a peace-candle, the sun, Cd. 118.

Frið-geard a peace-guard, an asylum.

Frið-gedal life or spirit-separation, death.

Frið-gewritu peace-writing, articles of peace.

Frið-hus peace-house, an asylum.

Friðian; p. friðode, gefriðode; pp. gefriðod; v. a. 1. To make peace; pacem ferire. 2. To protect, defend, keep, deliver, free; protegere :—1. L. Ethel. 1, W. p.104, 21. 2. Eall þat friðian woldon þat he friðode would protect all that which he protected, Chr. 921.

Friðleás peaceless, not included in a treaty of peace.

Friðlic: adj. Peaceable; pacificus :—L. pol. Cnut. 2.

Frið-man a peace or league-man, an envoy.

Friðo peace, love, v. freoðe.

Frið-socn, a peace-refuge, an asylum.

Frið-stol a peace-stool or seat, an altar, asylum, Chr. 1006.

Frið-stow a peace-place, asylum.

Friðsum, peace-some, pacific.

Frocca, frocga a frog, v. froga.

Fród old, prudent, debilitated, broken, v. forod.

Frófer; g. frófre; f. Comfort, solace, convenience, profit; solatium :—Ps. 17, 1: 31, 9. Frofre sunu consolation's son, son of consolation; Barnabas, Martyr. 11. Jun.

Frófer-boc consolation book.

Frófer-gast consolation ghost, the Holy Ghost, Jn. 14, 26.

Frofrian To comfort; consolari, Som.

Frofrung A comfort; consolatio, Som.

Froga, frogga, frocca, frocga, frox; m. [Plat. Frs. pogge f: Dut. vorsch or kikvorsch m: Ger. frosch m: Not. frosg: Mons. frosk: Dan. fröe c: Icel. froska f.] A FROG; rana :—Ps. 104, 28.

Frohto Fearful; timidi :— C. Mk. 4, 40.

FROM, freom; comp. ra; sup. esta; adj. [Plat. fraam: Dut. vroom: Frs. from: Ger. fromm: Dan. Swed. from: Icel. frómr] FIRM, strong, stout, bold; strenuus :—Bd. 2, 23.

From A physician; medicus :—R. Matt. 9, 12.

[14a.1]

Frian to free Ben v freo
Fricca an m a crier Som v friccea

Friccan scipe ~~the off~~ a crier's office Lau

~~Freodóm es, m free~~ Som

Freond-lar, e; f friendly counsel
Freond-lāda, e; f a friendly invitation Bes K 2380
Freond-sped, e; f friend-speed, many friends Cd 106 Th p 140, 29
Freondo spedig friend-rich amicorum dives Lebh p 96

Se frigea a freeman L. In 7th Wilh p 26, 16

Frig, e; f the Friga, the wife of Odin, the Venus of the Northern nations ... p ... Cd, m

Frige-dæg Friga's day Grimm Myth p 88 Th. an

als. Frigdæg, es; m

Freorig Freezing, chilly Th. an

Freos cuftures Cd 174 Th p 220, 4 v freo
Freoslice freely Bd Lm 634.17 v freolice
Freodo-mund amoris vel libertatis tutela; Ælbe Tesh Lye
Freodo-sceale, es, m a free servant, a minister; manumissi servi Cd 115 Th p 150, 25 : 105 Th p 138, 3
Freoda peaceable, loving Cd 4 Th 5, 29 manners, v. peace
Freodo-wær, e; f a peace covenant, compact, covenant of love Cd 158 Th 197, 13
Freodo wong, es m a peace-field
Freot-mon a free man Som
Fretwian to adorn Som Ben v frætwian
Fretwung an ornament Som Ben v frætwung
Freondyne an f. a female friend; amica Som Lye

Freodo-burh a peace city, an asylum Bes K 1038
Freodo ... es, m ...
Freodo-gyfa, an m a giver of freedom Lye
Freoll-gyfu freedom Lye

friendly supplicant
Friend Th an
Friend ... beginning Th an
Freodo-sped, e; peaceful rule, glad sway Cd 60 Th p 73, 2
Freond friends ... Th. v freond pl of freond
Frioleta ... Som v frig-lata
Frisea, an m a bittern, butio Som
Fredo-wær, e; f a peace contract Bes K 4559
Freodu webbe, an a peace weaver or contriver, a woman Bes K 3880 v webban

Frid-ad an oath of peace Lye — bree a peace breaking — Lye — burh a peace city, a city of refuge Lye — gear peace year, year of jubilee Som — gegyld a peace guild, an association Som — georn peace deserving, peaceable

vera deo pro frid socne gesete ad deo magnum asylum confugerit Chart Eccl ... p 127, 29
Frid-land a land at peace, terra pace Cd ... 1097
Fridlice ... Som
Fride ... Th 454
Frido peace v fridh
Frid-mal an agreement, pact Bes K Grim II 509 28
Fredo-tacn a peace token Cd 107 Th p 142, 29
Frithan to free, to spare ... v fretan
Frecce ... laicinia ... Cd 121 Lye
... full field Bes K 5913
Fredo-webba, an m a peace weaver, peace treater Cod ... Verc II 174 ... gl.

Spione, th an good Bes K 41
... pins, bones

Froman proferre Ben

2 From-gewitan to go from, depart Bt 33,4 Lye

From-healdan to hold from Lye — From-awendan to turn from Lye Cd 45 Th p. 58, 9

From-lad, e f an escape from a subject Cd 97 Th p. 125, 20

4 From-locciende beon respicere Ben

5 From-weard beon abiturus esse Bt 41,2 Cd p 52, 21

Fremnan v mægen ... p 123

Frumbirdling pube-tenens R 88 Lye

Frum-gyfu an original gift a prerogative R 99 Lye

Fule-treow a perch for a bird, the black alder tree Som

Ful-geare full ready Bt 5,3 Lye

Ful-hræde full soon v ful-rade

Fullan to fill Ben v fyllan

Fugling a fowling Som

Fugolope a fowling Som

Fuhtiond moist Lye

Frum-hrægel es: n a first garment Cd 45 Th p 58

Frum-leoht first light the dawn W Cat p 47 Lye

2 Frum-meolc, e f meolce the first milk, nectar Som

6 Frum-slæp es: m first sleep Cd 77 Th p 9

7 Frum-talu first accusation, prima delatio L Ethelst 67 Som

Frum-wæstmas first fruits Elf gr 13 — Frum-yldo the elders of the first age Som

Fryd-gyld a free guild or society Som

Fryd-georn peaceable Som

Frydgyld an attractive Som

Fryd-gysel, -es hostage of peace

Fryd-mæl an agreement

Fryd peace Cd 74 Th p 91, 16

Fulan-beam the black alder tree ... Som

Ful-fremman to execute accomplish perfect v ful-fremman

Fugel-net a fowl, or bird net Cot 173 Som

Ful-don to fully do satisfacere R Ben 44

Fugel-treow a perch for a bird on which hawks are kept in hawking Som

Full-bryce, es: m plena violatio ... L With 13

Full-endian to make an end complere Grim II 670, 29

Fuhton fought v feohtan

Frum-ræd, es m the first decree L Milk p 119

Frum-sceapen first shaped or formed, first created Kenaen 14

Frum-stiðing first tithing, from dæten C R p 17, 24

Fryse a bittern Som

Ful-berstan rumpi Lye Grim II 670, 28

Ful-don satisfacere Grim II 670, 28

Ful-feastnian to establish, fasten; plane stabilire Somdye

Fulfreolic very free or liberal; valde liberalis Som, Lye

Fullenham: Hunt Fulenham; Dun. Fulanham Brom. Fullenham — fil foul ham home, dwelling

Fulham ... at Fullan-hamme Chr 879: 880

Full-blide full or very glad; per laetus Jud 16, 23

Full-cuð fully known, remarkable Jud p 161

Grim II 652, ...

From *from*, v. fram.
From, FROME; fluvii nomen in agro Dorsetensi, *Som.*
Fromawælted *rolled away, C. R. Lk.* 24, 2.
From-cumen *to be rejected, R. Lk.* 9, 22.
From-cyme *a coming from, a race, progeny.*
From-cyn *a from-kin, progeny.*
Fromian *to be well, strong,* v. fremian.
Fromlic; *adj. Strong, stout;* strenuus:—*Jdth.* 10.
Fromlice, framlice; *adv. Strongly, stoutly, effectually;* strenue:—*Bd.* 5, 7.
Fromscipe; *m. Exercise, use, a proceeding, courage;* exercitatio:—*Bd.* 1, 34.
From-slitnis *desolation, C. Mk.* 13, 14.
From-swican *to withdraw, desert, Cd.* 46.
Fromung, e; *f. A going, journey;* profectio:—*Bd.* 5, 8.
Fronc, Froncland *France, Chr.* 836, v. Francan.
Frost *frost,* v. forst.
Frostig *Frosty;* gelidus, *Som.*
Frouer *A favourer;* fautor:—*Chr.* 1089.
Frox *a frog,* v. froga.
Frugnen *asked,* v. fregnan.
FRUM; *def.* se fruma; *adj.* [*Icel.* frum *n. prima proles*] *Original, primitive, first;* nativus, primitivus:—Frum, in composition, is used with the preceding meanings:—Þone fruman sceaft geþencan *to remember the first creation, Bt.* 30, 2. Fram fruman gesceafte, *Mk.* 10, 6.
Fruma, an; *m.* [*Moes.* fruma] *Beginning, origin, author, founder;* principium:—*Bd.* 1, 13: *Bt.* 39, 13. Æt fruman, *Jn.* 6, 64. On fruman, *Mt.* 19, 4, *at or in the beginning.*
Frum-bearn *first-born.*
Frum-cenned *first-begotten, primitive.*
Frum-cerr *first turn.*
Frum-cneow *a progenitor, Cd.* 161.
Frum-cyn *original kind, race, offspring, seed.*
Frum-gar, frum-gara [frum *first,* gear *a year*] *A patriarch, father of a family, a prince;* patriarcha:—*Cd.* 58: *Jdth.* 11.
Frum-gesceap *first creation.*
Frum-gyld *the first payment made to the kindred of a slain person, in recompence of his murder.*
Frum-heowung *first formation.*
Frumo *the beginning, C. Mk.* 13, 8, v. frum.
Frum-ripan *the first fruit.*
Frum-sceaft *first creation, the creation.*

Frum-sceateas, frum-sceattas *first fruits.*
Frum-spræce *an original speech, a promise, a covenant.*
Frum-stol *a chief seat, mansion-house, a proper residence* or *station.*
Fry *free,* v. freo.
Fryccea *A crier, preacher;* præco:—*Past.* 15, 3.
Frydom *freedom, Bt.* 40, 7, v. freodom.
Frymlic, frymðelic; *adj. Primitive, first;* primitivus:—*Bd.* 1, 26.
Frymð, es; *m. A beginning;* initium:—Of middan geardes frymðe, *Mt.* 25, 34.
Frymðelic *primitive,* v. frymlic.
Frynd, gefrynd *friends,* v. freond.
Frysa *A Frieslander;* Friso:—*Bd.* 5, 9.
FRYSAN; *pp.* gefroren [*Dut.* vriezen] *To* FREEZE; gelare:—*Elf. gr.* 22.
Frysisc *Friesic;* Frisius, *Som.*
Frysland *Friesland;* Frisie:—*Ors.* 1, 1.
Fryt *consumes,* v. fretan.
Fryð *a peace, league,* v. frið.
Fryðing *a making peace.*
Fugel, es; *pl.* fugelas, fuglas; *m.* [*Plat.* fagel, vagel *m*: *Frs.* fugel *f*: *Dut. Ger.* vogel *m*: *Ot. Not.* fogal: *Moes.* fugls: *Dan.* fugl *c*: *Swed.* fogel *m*: *Icel.* fugl *m.*—*from* fleogan *to fly; pp. of* flogen *flown;* hence flug *syncope* fug,-el] *A* FOWL, *bird;* volucris:—*Lk.* 13, 34: *Mt.* 6, 26.
Fugel-cynn *fowl kind, Gen.* 1, 30.
Fugelere, es; *pl.* fugeleras; *g.* a; *d.* an; *m.* [*Dut.* vogelaar *m.*] A FOWLER; auceps:—*Elf. gl.* 6.
Fugeles-wise *fowl-wise, in the manner of a fowl, a dolphin from its swiftness.*
Fugel-hælsere, fugel-hweolere *A soothsayer;* augur:—*R.* 4.
Fugel-hwate *a divination by birds, R.* 48.
Fugelian, fuglian [*Dut.* vogelen] *To fowl, catch birds;* aucupari:—*Elf. gr.* 35.
Fugel-lime *birdlime, Cot.* 194.
Fugel-noð *a fowling, Ethel. privil.*
Fugla *of birds;* fuglas *birds,* v. fugel.
Fuglian *to fowl,* v. fugelian.
Fugol *a bird,* v. fugel.
Fugol-wyll *bird-springing, producing birds, abounding in birds.*
Fugul *a bird,* v. fugel.
Fuhlas *for* fuglas *fowls,* v. fugel.
Fuht; *adj.* [*Plat.* fucht, fuchtig: *Dut.* vocht, vochtig: *Ger.* feucht: *Dan.* fugtig: *Swed.* fuktig: *Icel.* fugt *f. odour*] *Moist;* humidus:—*Herb.* 9, 1.

FU'L, es [*Moes.* fuls] *Foulness, impurity, a fault;* impuritas:—Ne naht fules, *Jud.* 13, 4. Þæs fules gewita *conscious of the fault, Jud. C. L.* 4, *Mann.*
Fúl; *adj.* [*Plat.* fuul: *Dut.* vuil: *Frs.* ful: *Ger.* faul: *Ot.* ful: *Moes.* fuls: *Dan.* fuul *rotten, malicious*: *Swed.* ful *ugly*: *Icel.* fúll *putrid*] FOUL, *dirty, impure, corrupt, guilty;* sordidus:—*Nic.* 27.
Ful-, full-, in composition, denotes the *fulness, completeness* or *perfection* of the meaning of the word with which it is joined, v. full.
Ful-betan *to give full satisfaction.*
Fulbete, fulbot *full satisfaction, Som.*
Ful-boren *full born, noble born.*
Ful-brecan *to violate;* violare:—*L. Cnut.* 2.
Ful-cuð *well-known, public.*
Fule *A stink, foulness;* fœtor, *Som.*
Ful-fealdan *To explain;* explicare:—*Elf. gr.* 24.
Ful-fremed *full* or *quite perfect.*
Ful-fremedlice *perfectly.*
Fulfremednes, se; *f. A perfection;* perfectio:—*Job.* p. 167.
Ful-fremian; *p.* de; *pp.* od. *To perfect, accomplish, fulfil, practice;* perficere:—*Bt.* 35, 6.
Ful-gan, ful-gangan, full-gan; *p.* fulleode. *To go to the full, to accomplish, perfect, fulfil;* perficere:—*Bt.* 39, 2.
Ful-gehende *full nigh, neighbourhood, Som.*
Ful-georne *very well.*
Ful-hare *gray-haired* or *headed.*
Fúlian, befylan, befulan, ic fulige; *p.* fúlode; *pp.* gefúlod. *To* FOUL, *rot, corrupt;* putrescere:—*Ors.* 1, 1.
Fulice *Foully;* sordide:—*R. Ben.* 82.
Full; *adj.* [*Plat.* full, vull: *Dut.* vol: *Frs.* ful: *Ger.* voll: *Ot.* and all the authors of the 8th and 9th century, full: *Moes.* fulls: *Dan.* fuld: *Swed.* full: *Icel.* fullr.—fyll *the full*] FULL, *entire, complete;* plenus:—*Lk.* 6, 38. Full mona *full moon.* Tyn winter full *ten years full or complete, Bt. R.* p. 188. Þar hig wæron seofon dagas fulle, *Gen.* 50, 10.
Full-, *full,* v. ful-.
Fullafreod *a defender.*
Fullan-ham (*A foul* or *dirty habitation, Som.*) FULHAM, *Middlesex.*
Full-betan *to make full satisfaction, Elf. gr.* 37.
Fullere, es; *m.* A FULLER, *bleacher;* fullo:—*Mk.* 9, 3.
Full-fleon *to chase away, rout.*

Full-fremian *to perfect*, v. fulfremian.

Full-fyllan *To fulfil, accomplish*; implere:—*Elf. gr.* 26.

Fullgan, fullgangan *to fulfil*, v. fulgan.

Full-getreow *full true, altogether true.*

Fúllian, fulwian, gefullian, ic fullige, he fullað; *p.* fulode; *pp.* fullod, gefullod; *v. a. To baptize, whiten*; baptizare:—Ic eow fullige on wætere, *Mt.* 3, 11.

Fullian *To fulfil*; exequi:—*Cd.* 106.

Fúllic *foul, base*, v. ful.

Fullice; *comp.* icor; *adv. Fully, perfectly, completely*; plenè:—*Bd.* 2, 3: 4, 25: *Ors.* 2, 5.

Fúllice; *comp.* icor; *adv. Foully, shamefully*; sordide:—*L. Can. Edg. poen.* 42.

Fulligeað *baptize*, v. fullian.

Full-mannod *full manned*, *Bt.* 17.

Full-neh, full-neáh; *adv. Full nigh, near, almost*; prope:—*Bt.* 4.

Fúlnes, se; *f.* FOULNESS; fœtor:—*Bd.* 5, 12.

Fulloc *baptism.*

Full-soð *full sooth, most truly.*

Fulluht, fulwiht, es; *m. A baptism, baptizing*; baptismus:—*Mt.* 21, 25: *Bd.* 1, 27.

Fulluhtere, fulwihtere, es; *m. A baptizer, baptist*; baptista:—*Mt.* 3, 1.

Full-wiht *baptism.*

Full-wyrcan *to accomplish*, v. fulwyrcan.

Fúlnes *foulness*, v. fullnes.

Ful-oft *full oft, very often.*

Ful-rihte *full right, quite right.*

Fultemian *To assist, help*; juvare:—*Past.* 34, 3.

Fulþiclice *very thickly, frequently.*

Fultom *help*, v. fultum.

Ful-truwian *to trust fully in, confide in.*

Fultum, fultom, fultume, fylst, gefylst. 1. *Help, aid, assistance, emolument, favour*; auxilium. 2. *An helper, army, force*; adjutor, copiæ:—1. He asende þe fultum, *Ps.* 19, 2. 2. *Ps.* 17, 2: *Chr.* 913.

Fultumian, gefultumian; *p.* ade; *pp.* od. *To help, assist*; juvare:—*Bd.* 2, 13.

Fultumiend *A helper*; adjutor:—*Bd.* 3, 30.

Ful-wacor *very watchful.*

Ful-wærlic *full wary, cautious.*

Fulwer *A baptist*; baptista:—*Menol.*

Fulwian *to baptize*, v. fullian.

Fulwiht *baptism*, v. fulluht.

Fulwihtere *a baptist*, v. fulluhtere.

Fulwihte *a full mulct* or *fine.*

Fulwihðe *baptism*, v. fulluht.

Fulwon, fulwod *baptized*, v. fullian.

Ful-wyrcan *to finish, accomplish.*

Funde, funden *found*, v. findan.

Fundian, ic fundige; *p.* ode. *To endeavour to find, tend to, strive, go forward*; tendere:—Twegen men fundiað to anre stowe, *two men are going to one place*, *Bt.* 36, 4. Fyr fundige up *fire tends upward*, *Bt.* 34, 11. Þe fundode wið his, *Num.* 22, 6, v. findan.

Fundung *a departure, absence.*

Fur, furh [*Plat.* fore *f*: *Dut.* voore, vore *f*: *Ger. Not.* furche *f*: *Dan.* furre *c*: *Swed.* fåra *m.*] A FURROW; sulcus:—*Bt.* 5, 2.

Furlang, furlung FURLONG; stadium:—*Lk.* 24, 13.

Furðan, furðon, furðum *Also, too, even, indeed, further*; etiam, quidem:—*Mt.* 6, 29.

Furðor, furður; *adv.* FURTHER; ulterius:—*Jos.* 10, 12.

Furðra, seo het furðre; *adj. def.* FURTHER, *greater*; major:—Nis se þeowa furðra þonne his hlaford, *Jn.* 13, 16, v. form.

Furðrung *a furthering*, v. fyrðrung.

Furðum *also, indeed*, v. furðan.

Furðumlic; *adj. Effeminate*; mollis:—*Ors.* 1, 12.

Furður *further*, v. furðor.

Fu's; *adj.* [*Dan.* fuze *to rush violently forth, to hasten on*: *Icel.* fús *pronus*: *Eng.* fuss *a bustle*] *Ready, prompt, quick, willing*; promptus:—Swiðe fus *very quick*, *Elf. T.* p. 30: *Cd.* 8.

Fuslice; *adv. Quickly*; prompte:—*Bd.* 4, 27.

Fyht *a fight*, v. gefeoht.

Fyht *fights*, v. feohtan.

Fyhtling, *A fightling, soldier*; præliator:—*Dial.* 2, 3.

Fyht wite *a fine for fighting.*

Fylc *A company, troop*; agmen.

Fyld, es; *m. A fold, a volume*; volumen, *Som.*

Fylging, e; *f. That which follows, a barrow*; occa:—*Cot.* 143.

Fyligean, fylgean, filian, feligean, folgian, befylgan; *p.* fylgde, filide. *To follow, succeed*; sequi:—Wyle me fyligean, *Mk.* 8, 34. He ne let hym ænig ne fylgean, *Mk.* 5, 37.

Fylignes, se; *f. A following, completing, executing*; successio:—*Bd.* 3, 5.

Fyll, fill [*Ger.* fülle *f*: *Ker.* fullii: *Not.* fulli: *Swed.* fylle *n*: *Icel.* fylli *f.*] *The* FILL *fulness*; plenitudo:—Ge etað to fylle, *Lev.* 26, 5.

Fyll, es; *m.* A FALL, *ruin, destruction*; casus:—*Ors.* 3, 2.

Fyllan; *p.* de; *pp.* gefylled; *v. a.* [*Plat. Dut.* vullen: *Ger.* füllen: *Ker.* fullen: *Isd.* fullan: *Moes.* fulljan: *Dan.* fylde: *Swed.* fylla: *Icel.* filli] *To* FILL, *replenish, satisfy, finish*; implere:—Þu fylst ælc, *Ps.* 144, 17. He fylde hig, *Ps.* 104, 38. Hig fyllde oðende, *Deut.* 31, 30, v. gefyllan.

Fyllan; *p.* fylde; *pp.* gefylled; *v. a.* [*Plat. Dut.* vellen: *Ger.* fällen: *Not. Ot.* fallan: *Dan.* fælde: *Swed.* fälla: *Icel.* fella *from* feoll *fell*; *p. of* feallan *to fall*] *To fell, cut down, destroy*; prosternere:—Fyllan, *Jdth.* 11, p. 24, 18. Seo nædre gefylled wæs *the serpent was destroyed*, *Ors.* 4, 6.

Fylle *a fall, ruin, destruction*, *Som.*

Fylle *Wild thyme*; serpyllum, *Som.*

Fyllen *Omentum*, *R.* 74.

Fylle-seoc *a lunatic.*

Fylle-seocnys *falling sickness, epilepsy, lunacy.*

Fylmen, es. A FILM, *thin skin, prepuce*; præputium:—*Gen.* 17, 11.

Fylnes, se; *f.* A FOULNESS; fuligo:—*Cot.* 83.

Fylst *help, assistance*, v. fultum.

Fylstan, gefylstan *To help, aid*; adjuvare:—*Lk.* 5, 7.

Fylð FILTH, *impurity*; spurcitia:—*Mt.* 23, 27.

Fynd *enemies, an enemy*, v. feónd.

Fynegean, fynigean *To become musty, filthy*; *L. Alf. Can.* 35.

Fynig; *adj. Musty*; mucidus:—*L. Alf. Can.* 35.

Fyr, fyryn, es; *n.* [*Plat.* für, vüer *n*: *Dut.* vuur *n*: *Frs.* fior, fiure *n*: *Ger.* feuer *n*: *Ker.* fuire: *Ot.* fiur: *Isd.* fyor: *Tat.* fuir: *Dan.* fyr *n*: *Swed. Icel.* fyr *m*: *New Guinea*, for: *Fr.* feu *m*: *Grk.* πῦρ] A FIRE, *hearth*; ignis:—Swa scearp andget swa þat fyr *as sharp an understanding as fire*, *Bt.* 39, 4: *Mk.* 9, 44.

Fyr *far*, v. feor.

Fyran *To castrate*, FIRE; castrare:—*Obs. Lun.* 3, v. afyran.

Fyrbeta *One who looks after the fire*; focarius:—*R.* 30.

Fyr-bryne *a fire, burning.*

Fyrclian *To bring upon*; ingerere:—*Chr.* 1106, *Lye.*

Fyr-clómmas *fire-bonds*, *Cd.* 213.

Fyr-cruse *a fire-cruse* or *pot.*

Fyrd, feord; *f.* [*Ger.* fahrt *f. an expedition*; heerfahrt *f. a military expedition*: *Not.* uses faren *to lie in ambush, to lay snares.*—ferde; *p. of* feran *to*

(3)

Full-lyst-y, turiger a foolish; her. secte stultus Herdiem Lye -

2) Full-cades fully or quite easy ... Jacolliane 1318

Full-cuðran ... perfficere 313,23

7 Full-healdan ... fulfilling ... Som v ful-healdan

4 Full-slaw full slow very slow; ... Key 15

5 Fulluht-nama the baptismal name ... Som

7 Ful-neah full nigh, very near Som

6 Full-unrot full or very sorrowful ... 11,1

8 Full-welig fully or ... rich ... 11,1 Full-money

9 Fulnieh fullnigh Som v fulneah

10 Ful-raðe full soon ... L22 ...

16) 13 Fulstan to help Ben v fylstan

14 Ful-stincende foul smelling ... 27

17 Fullumwuld ...

15 Fuldungen highly cel... Ben 73 Lye

18 Fulteam-ledan helpless ... 71,14 Lye

4 Ful-wenest ... Ful-wine ... Ben

4 Ful-fremman perficere ... 670,31 See p 123 Ms.

Ful-wide fullwide, ... 238,12 p 307,24

2 Fulwiht-nama an n the baptismal or christian name Chr 890 Lye v ... fulluht-nama

3 Fulwiht stowe f a baptismal place, a font ... 2114 Lye Som

6 Furh-wudu firewood ... pine tree Som

Furre forth Th ... v ford

X Fyhthung See Tent

Fyllung, e; f perfection finishing v gefyllednes

4 Fuslic ... ready ... paratus Beo K 462

8 Fuse promptly, ... Th An

10 Futi-gend ... mouth Som v ... futi-end

12 Fyl a ... Th An v feol

13 Fyl of fylle, f ... fall ... Beo K ... 2763 ... v fyll, fylle

16 Fyld-elfen ... -elfenne f a field or wood nymph, a ... Lye v ... feld-elfen

17 Fylegan to follow ... 14, ... 1612 v fy... ligean

Ful-worhte fully wrought, perfect Ben

1 Fylle ... a ... falling, slaughter Th ... v fyl, fyll

2 Fyllan to draw ... ... 4,15 Lye

3 Fylled ... filled; ... ciated Ben v fyllen, fell

4 Fylled-flod, ... a high flood or tide ... Mart ... 20 Mart Lye

6 Fyl-werig fell weary; ... Beo K 1918

7 Fyndele invention Ben

8 Fyndan to find Som v findan

4 Fyor life Cd 59 ...

9 Fyne ... Ben v finger Fynger a finger Som v finger

11 Fyr-bad a fire pledge Cd Ex 20.226

12 Fyr-bend, e f fire bound or harden ... Beo K 1457

(7)

Fyr-heard fire harden-ed Beo K 607

Fyrn-wita, an m an old counseller Beo K 424

(7)

Fyrlitec, e; f fear &c

Fyr-leóht, es n a fire-light Beo K 3032

Fyrd-gestealla an m a fellow soldier Cd 93 Th p 19.-

Fyr-spearca an m a fire spark Th an

Fyr-leoma, an m a fire beam Cd 215 Th p 272, 32

Fyrd-gemaca a military companion fellow soldier; commilito Guthl 456, 31

Fyrloca, a fire bond claustrum igneum Cd 214 Th p 268, 20

Fyrst-frost, es; m gelu frost

Fyrd-hom, es, m; An army coat, a coat of mail; lorica Beo K 3007

Fyrd-homa, an m Beo K 3007 Th An p 137, 9 Beo Apx

Fyrn fire igni

Fyrd-searo, es; n army preparation Beo K 462

Fyrdinga in companies or flocks; catervatim Som

Fyr-draca an m a fire serpent or dragon Beo K 5374

Fyrdleas armyless without an army defenceless Chr 894 Ing 115, 11

Fyrd-werod an army host, or phalanx Som

Fyrd wet ephibulenta Cot 212 Lye

Fyrn-gewin, es; n an old contest Beo K 3376

Fyrdung, e; f an army preparation L. Cnut. pol 10. v fyrdinc

Fyrd-wyrde excellent in war warworthy Beo K 2633

Fyren-gab, e; f gaffe

Fyr-tang a pair of tongs Som

Fyr-betal &c

Fyren-licgend, a harlot; meretrix Som

Fyrewitnys, se f curiosity Th An

Fyres-gold the fire god Vulcan Som

Fyrb a firebrand torch; facula Scint ... p 124, 27 Lye Som

Fyr-fear fiery heaven

Fyr-gearwung, e f fire preparation, fuel Cot 89

Fyres-lig, es, m a fire's flame

Fyrgen mountain Beo K 2786 v. firen

Fyrnlic ancient Som v fyrn

Fyrdrungnes, a fastening v firdrungnes

Fyrn-... ancient ... the ancients Beo K 5518

Fyren-pearf, e; f evil need Beo K 28

Fyrgen-holt, es; n a mountain grove Beo K 2780 v firen etc

go, proceed] *An expedition, army, chiefly of citizens;* expeditio:—*L. In.* 5, 1: *Bd.* 1, 3.

Fyrd *a ford,* v. ford.

Fyrderung *A preparation* or *provision for a journey;* expeditionis apparatus, *Som.*

Fyrd-esne *a warlike youth* or *man.*

Fyrd-færelde, fyrd-fare *military expedition* or *service of citizens, inhabitants.*

Fyrd-gesteal *a martial comrade, Cd.* 93.

Fyrd-getrum *a martial band, Cd.* 147.

Fyrdian; *p.* hi fyrdedon. *To go, go out, send, proceed;* ire:—*Chr.* 443.

Fyrdincg, fyrding, firdincg, e; *f. An expedition, army, an army prepared for battle;* expeditio:—*Chr.* 1016: *L. pol. Cnut.* 10: 75: 80.

Fyrdlic *like an army, military.*

Fyrd-man *a military man, a soldier.*

Fyrd-rinc *a man of arms, a warrior.*

Fyrdringnes, se; *f. A promotion;* exaltatio, *Som.*

Fyrdscip *a ship of war, naval expedition.*

Fyrd-timber *a sacrifice.*—Fyrdtruma *an army, Som.*

Fyrdwæn *a travelling wain* or *waggon.*

Fyrd-wic *An army-station, a camp, tent;* castra:—*Gen.* 32, 2.

Fyrd-wite *an army-fine, a fine for leaving the army.*

Fyre-bryne *A burning;* incendium:—*Ors.* 4, 7.

Fyren *a crime,* v. firen.

Fyren; *adj. Fiery, flagitious, wicked;* igneus:—*Gen.* 3, 24.

Fyrenan *To commit adultery, sin;* mœchari:—*Lk.* 18, 20.

Fyren-cylle, fyren-cylne *a fire-kiln, an oven.*

Fyren-dæd *a wicked deed, Cd.* 191.

Fyren-full, firen-ful; *adj. Sinful, unjust, wicked;* iniquus:—Used as a noun, *One who is sinful, a sinner;* peccator, *Ps.* 9, 18: 72, 3.

Fyrenfullnes, se; *f. Luxury, riot;* luxuria, *Som.*

Fyren-gat *a wild goat,* v. firginbucca.

Fyren-lust, firen-lust *Impure pleasure, luxury;* luxuria:—*Bt.* 15.

Fyren-þecelle *an oven.*

Fyres *furz,* v. fyrs.

Fyrest *first,* v. fyrst.

Fyr-faran *to travel far.*

Fyr-fluge *flee far away,* v. fleogan.

Fyrh *a furrow,* v. fur.

Fyrhtnis *fear, trembling,* v. forhtyns.

Fyrhto, afyrhto, fyrhtu *Fear, fright, dread, terror, trembling;* tremor:—*Ps.* 2, 11.

Fyr-hus *a fire-house, chimney.*

Fyrian, firige *To make a fire, give warmth, to cherish;* focum præbere:—*L. Can. Edg.* 14.

Fyrian *To make a furrow, to plough, till;* proscindere aratro:—*Scint.* 32.

Fyrlen; *adj. Far, distant;* longinquus:—*Gen.* 20, 13.

Fyrlic *suddenly,* v. færlic.

Fyrlocan *fire bonds, Cd.* 214.

Fyrme *A feast,* epulæ:—*Jud.* 16, 27.

Fyrmest, formest; *def.* se fyrmesta, seo, þæt fyrmeste, *adj.* FOREMOST, *first, utmost;* primus:—Se þe wyle beon fyrmest *he who will be first, Mt.* 20, 27. Þis ys þæt mæste and þæt fyrmeste bebod, *Mt.* 22, 38. Se fyrmesta and se betesta *the foremost and best, Cot.* 153. Fyrmyste nama *primitive names, Elf. gr.* 5. Swa we fyrmest magon *as the utmost we could, Bd.* 5, 21, v. form.

Fyrmð, fyrmð [*from* feormian *to purify, to procure food.*] 1. *A receiving to food, a reception, an entertainment, a table, harbouring;* receptio ad victum. 2. *A washing, baptizing;* ablutio:—1. *L. In.* 46. 2. *Mk.* 7, 4.

Fyrn *Fire;* ignis:—*Cd.* 216.

Fyrn [*Luther.* firn, fernd: *Al.* forn: *Not.* firnen: *Moes.* fairnja, fairni: *Old Swed.* fyrnas: *Icel.* fyrnd *f.*] *Antiquity, age;* antiquitas:—Frod fyrn *broken with age, Cd.* 57. Fyrn-dagum *with length of days, Cd.* 52.

Fyrn; *adj. Ancient, old, former;* antiquus:—Fyrn geweorc *ancient work, Cod. Ex.* 57, a. 15. In fyrn dagum *in former days, Cd.* 170.

Fyrn, gefyrn; *adv. Formerly, long ago, of old;* olim:—*Mt.* 11, 21: *Cd.* 25.

Fyrnum; *adv. With horror, horribly, intensely;* horribiliter:—Þonne cymð forst fyrnum cald *then cometh frost intensely cold, Cd.* 17.

Fyr-panne *a fire-pan.*

Fyrre *farther;* fyrrest *farthest, Bt.* 39, 7, v. feor.

Fyrs, es; *m. Furze, furze-bushes, brambles;* genista, rhamnus:—*Bt.* 23.

Fyr-scofl *a fire-shovel.*

Fyr-scyan; *p.* yde. *To shade the fire.*

Fyrsian; *p.* syde [*Plat.* versten: *Frs.* versta *to delay:* *Ger.* fristen, fernen: *Icel.* fersta *to delay*] *To put far, remove, separate, drive away;* elongare:—*L. Edw. Guth.* 11, v. afyrsian.

Fyrsn [*Dut.* verzenen; *f. pl. the heels:* *Ger.* ferse *f:* in the south of Germany fersn, versan, fiersen: *Not.* fersenu: *Tat.* fersna] *The heel;* calcaneum:—*Cot.* 38.

Fyr-spearcan *fire-sparks.*

Fyrst, [*Dan.* fyrste *m:* *Swed.* första *m. a prince:* *Plat. Frs.* forst *m:* *Dut.* vorst *m:* *Ger.* fürst *m:* *Ot.* furisto: *Icel.* fyrsti, fursti *m.*—*Plat.* furst, vaste *f. the ridge of a thatched roof:* *Dut. Kil.* vorst *f.* culmen: *Frs.* forst *f:* *Ger.* firste, forste, *f.* forst *m. the ridge of a roof.* In the south of Germany it signifies *a house,* and also *the top of a mountain.*—fyrst *first; sup.* v. feor.] 1. *The first in station, a prince, chief;* princeps. 2. *The first in height, the top, ridge, the inward roof, ceiling of a chamber;* laquear, culmen. 3. *The first entrance, a threshold, door;* limen:—1. Fyrst forð gewat *a prince went forth, Beo.* 3, 43. 2. *Elf. gl.* 20: *R.* 29. 3. *Cot.* 118.

FYRST, first, [*Plat.* ferst *f:* *Frs.* ferst *n:* *Ger. Dan.* frist *f:* *Ker. Mons.* frist *an occasion:* *Ot.* frist: *Swed.* frist *m:* *Icel.* frest *f.*] *A space, time, space of time, respite, truce;* spatium:—Nu binnan litlon fyrste, *Ex.* 17, 4. Wunode mid hire oð þone first *dwelt with her to the time, Bt.* 38, 1, *Card.* p. 300, 31. Æfter litlan fyrste, *Mt.* 26, 73.

FYRST, first, fyrest; *adj.* [*Dan. Swed.* förste: *Icel.* fyrstr.—*sup.* v. feor] FIRST; primus:—*Chr.* 973.

Fyr-stan *a fire-stone, a flint to strike fire with.*

Fyrstan *To give respite;* inducias facere, *Som.*

Fyrste *a torch.*

Fyrstig; *adj. Frosty;* gelidus:—*Bd.* 3, 19.

Fyrst-mearc *a space-mark, a space of time, a respite, setting of the sun.*

Fyr-þolle *an oven.*

Fyrðrian, gefyrðrian; *p.* ede; *pp.* ed. *To further, support, advance, promote, prosper;* provehere:—Friðað and fyrðrað *protects and supports, Bt.* 34, 10.

Fyrðrung *A furthering;* promotio:—*Som.* 166.

Fyr-þung, e; *f. What relates to the hearth, home, domestic af-*

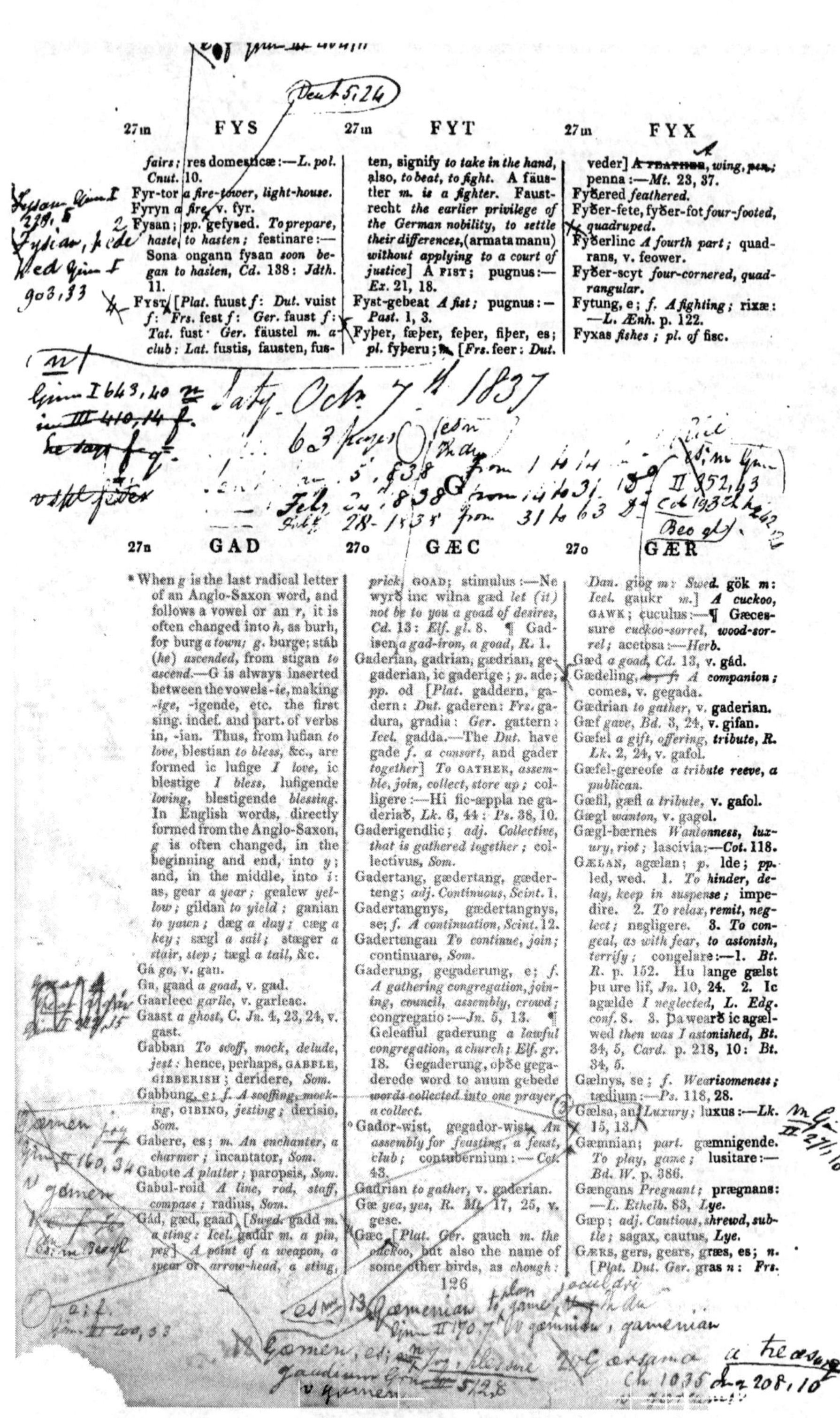

27m FYS — 27m FYT — 27m FYX

fairs; res domesticæ:—*L. pol. Cnut.* 10.
Fyr-tor *a fire-tower, light-house.*
Fyryn *a fire*, v. fyr.
Fysan; *pp.* gefysed. *To prepare, haste, to hasten*; festinare:—Sona ongann fysan *soon began to hasten, Cd.* 138: *Jdth.* 11.
Fyst [*Plat.* fuust *f*: *Dut.* vuist *f*: *Frs.* fest *f*: *Ger.* faust *f*: *Tat.* fust· *Ger.* fäustel *m. a club*: *Lat.* fustis, fausten, fusten, signify *to take in the hand*, also, *to beat, to fight.* A fäustler *m. is a fighter.* Faustrecht *the earlier privilege of the German nobility, to settle their differences,*(armata manu) *without applying to a court of justice*] A FIST; pugnus:—*Ex.* 21, 18.
Fyst-gebeat *A fist*; pugnus:—*Past.* 1, 3.
Fyþer, fæþer, feþer, fiþer, es; *pl.* fyþeru; *m.* [*Frs.* feer: *Dut.* veder] A FEATHER, *wing, pen*; penna:—*Mt.* 23, 37.
Fyðered *feathered.*
Fyðer-fete, fyðer-fot *four-footed, quadruped.*
Fyðerlinc *A fourth part*; quadrans, v. feower.
Fyðer-scyt *four-cornered, quadrangular.*
Fytung, e; *f. A fighting*; rixæ:—*L. Ænh.* p. 122.
Fyxas *fishes*; *pl. of* fisc.

G

27n GAD — 27o GÆC — 27o GÆR

* When *g* is the last radical letter of an Anglo-Saxon word, and follows a vowel or an *r*, it is often changed into *h*, as burh, for burg *a town*; *g.* burge; stáh (*he*) *ascended*, from stigan *to ascend.*—G is always inserted between the vowels -*ie*, making -*ige*, -igende, etc. the first sing. indef. and part. of verbs in, -ian. Thus, from lufian *to love*, blestian *to bless*, &c., are formed ic lufige *I love*, ic blestige *I bless*, lufigende *loving*, blestigende *blessing.* In English words, directly formed from the Anglo-Saxon, *g* is often changed, in the beginning and end, into *y*; and, in the middle, into *i*: as, gear *a year*; gealew *yellow*; gildan *to yield*; ganian *to yawn*; dæg *a day*; cæg *a key*; sægl *a sail*; stæger *a stair, step*; tægl *a tail*, &c.
Gá *go*, v. gan.
Ga, gaad *a goad*, v. gad.
Gaarleec *garlic*, v. garleac.
Gaast *a ghost*, C. *Jn.* 4, 23, 24, v. gast.
Gabban *To scoff, mock, delude, jest*: hence, perhaps, GABBLE, GIBBERISH; deridere, *Som.*
Gabbung, e; *f. A scoffing, mocking*, GIBING, *jesting*; derisio, *Som.*
Gabere, es; *m. An enchanter, a charmer*; incantator, *Som.*
Gabote *A platter*; paropsis, *Som.*
Gabul-roid *A line, rod, staff, compass*; radius, *Som.*
Gád, gæd, gaad [*Swed.* gadd *m. a sting*: *Icel.* gaddr *m. a pin, peg*] *A point of a weapon, a spear or arrow-head, a sting, prick*, GOAD; stimulus:—Ne wyrð inc wilna gæd *let (it) not be to you a goad of desires, Cd.* 13: *Elf. gl.* 8. ¶ Gad-isen *a gad-iron, a goad, R.* 1.
Gaderian, gadrian, gædrian, gegaderian, ic gaderige; *p.* ade; *pp.* od [*Plat.* gaddern, gadern: *Dut.* gaderen: *Frs.* gadura, gradia: *Ger.* gattern: *Icel.* gadda.—The *Dut.* have gade *f. a consort*, and gader *together*] To GATHER, *assemble, join, collect, store up*; colligere:—Hi fic-æppla ne gaderiað, *Lk.* 6, 44: *Ps.* 38, 10.
Gaderigendlic; *adj. Collective, that is gathered together*; collectivus, *Som.*
Gadertang, gædertang, gæderteng; *adj. Continuous, Scint.* 1.
Gadertangnys, gædertangnys, se; *f. A continuation, Scint.* 12.
Gadertengan *To continue, join*; continuare, *Som.*
Gaderung, gegaderung, e; *f. A gathering congregation, joining, council, assembly, crowd*; congregatio:—*Jn.* 5, 13. ¶ Geleafful gaderung *a lawful congregation, a church*; *Elf. gr.* 18. Gegaderung, oþðe gegaderede word to anum gebede *words collected into one prayer, a collect.*
Gador-wist, gegador-wist *An assembly for feasting, a feast, club*; contubernium:—*Cot.* 43.
Gadrian *to gather*, v. gaderian.
Gæ *yea, yes, R. Mt.* 17, 25, v. gese.
Gæc [*Plat. Ger.* gauch *m. the cuckoo*, but also the name of some other birds, as *chough*: *Dan.* giög *m*: *Swed.* gök *m*: *Icel.* gaukr *m.*] *A cuckoo*, GAWK; cuculus:—¶ Gæcessure *cuckoo-sorrel, wood-sorrel*; acetosa:—*Herb.*
Gæd *a goad, Cd.* 13, v. gád.
Gædeling, *m*; *f. A companion*; comes, v. gegada.
Gædrian *to gather*, v. gaderian.
Gæf *gave, Bd.* 3, 24, v. gifan.
Gæfel *a gift, offering, tribute, R. Lk.* 2, 24, v. gafol.
Gæfel-gereofe *a tribute reeve, a publican.*
Gæfil, gæfl *a tribute*, v. gafol.
Gægl *wanton*, v. gagol.
Gægl-bærnes *Wantonness, luxury, riot*; lascivia:—*Cot.* 118.
GÆLAN, agælan; *p.* lde; *pp.* led, wed. 1. *To hinder, delay, keep in suspense*; impedire. 2. *To relax, remit, neglect*; negligere. 3. *To congeal, as with fear, to astonish, terrify*; congelare:—1. *Bt. R.* p. 152. Hu lange gælst þu ure lif, *Jn.* 10, 24. 2. Ic agælde *I neglected, L. Edg. conf.* 8. 3. Þa wearð ic agælwed *then was I astonished, Bt.* 34, 5, *Card.* p. 218, 10: *Bt.* 34, 5.
Gælnys, se; *f. Wearisomeness*; tædium:—*Ps.* 118, 28.
Gælsa, an *Luxury*; luxus:—*Lk.* 15, 13.
Gæmnian; *part.* gæmnigende. *To play, game*; lusitare:—*Bd. W.* p. 386.
Gængans *Pregnant*; prægnans:—*L. Ethelb.* 83, *Lye.*
Gæp; *adj. Cautious, shrewd, subtle*; sagax, cautus, *Lye.*
GÆRS, gers, gears, græs, es; *n.* [*Plat. Dut. Ger.* gras *n*: *Frs.*

Fyrwit curiosity Beo K 4163

Fysan to drive, incite, expell, send forth (arrows) send away Th. An. Gen.

Fysan v. reip[illegible] to hasten, rush Th. An.

Gād a goad ... v gād

Gān [illegible] v gān

v gān ... gān-hwyrft

Fyr-wylm, es; m a fire-wave Beo K 5338

[illegible] hasten; agere, fugare, festinare Th. K Gen. 903, 33

Gādinca Mutinee, fascinum obscoenum a muto, membrum virile; priapus R 22.

Gadrigendlic collective Som v gaderigendlic

Gændung an end, death Som v gesendung

Gān-hwyrft conversio L. M. [illegible] Gān-ryne es; m a meeting L. M. 5 [illegible] v gean-ryne

Gent Ghent Som v supl Gent

Fyder-hama

Fyder four. for fyower, feower.

Gæderstang continued Ben v gaderstang

Gæderstangnys a [illegible] continuation Ben v gaderstangnys

Gæderstangian to continue Som v gaderstangian

Gægnes-burh

Gainsborough Th. An. v Gegnes-burh [gæled]

Gælad a cage to seize or punish. bondmen in; catasta Som

Gældan to pay to depend, suspend Som, Lye Ben v geldan

Gæle saffron; crocus Som v geolo

Gænian to game Som v gamian, gæmnian

Gān yet; adhuc Ben

Oct. 9th 1857

G

5 [illegible] ... Cd 1542 th p 14 ... gamol

Gærs-grene green grene, green Som

Gærst green like grass; herbeus Som

Gærwe millefolium 240 [illegible]

Wæs se gre[illegible] gæst erat teter spiritus

Gæstlipe gæstlipe hospitable i. an [illegible] 71

[illegible] gaule

Gaurue, gauroc, es; m Elf gl 7 p 63 a gavelin [illegible]

Gaffetung, c; f [illegible] derision Ben Som

Gagel, gagolle Gale gale sweet willow or Dutch myrtle [illegible] Som [illegible] mete [illegible]

[illegible] Jdth 12 Lye Th. An

Gafol-cynd Som [illegible] 4, 15 & 41

Gafol-rand a compass [illegible] Som

Gaf-mod lightminded lascivious Th. An Jdth Beo gl. in mód

* gærsum, e; f.

* gærsame; an; f. a treasure etc — v. gersume

Gaf-spræc, e; f lewd speaking; babbling; Som Lye

Gagat-stan, es; m the agate stone Ben. v gagates

Gagul-swillan To gargle; gargarizare Som

[Icel gaflok]

Galdor-galere, es; m a soothsayer Som

Galdor-leod an incantation song, a charm, spell, Som Lye

[Galdrygea an; m an enchanter Som

Gale a nightingale; luscinia Ben

gal-freols, es; m a joyful feast; tuba? calixe Som

Gallue gauls, an oak-apple galla Cot 96 Som Lye

Galscipe madness Cod 18 Th 22, 15 a galscype

Gal-smære light laughing; petulant Ben Lye

Galwan to clap, sport, rejoice; plaudere Som; Ben & gilpan

Gal-wræne luxurious Som Ben

Galsmære facilis Ben

Gal-weala-rice the kingdom of Gaul Som.

Gomen-hof a pleasure porch; [illegible] gaudii Beo 66 Grein 455, 2 — Gomen-wudu a musical instrument; lignum ludi Beo 81. K 2123

6 Gamenung; e; f a gaming; lusus Som Lye

Gamian to game, play, sport; ludere Som v gamenian

Gamian, ode, ode, to game, sport, play; jocari Som

Galdor-galan to inchant, foretell Som

Galdor-galend es; m a soothsayer Ben

Galg-treow, es; n a gallows tree

Galga gallows Beo K 5876

Galg-mód gallows minded Beo K 2554

1 A wife of Assyria Th. An

2 a gait, course, hou[se] of office

gærs, gres, gers, ges n: Moes. gras: Dan. græs n: Swed. gräs n: Icel. gras n.—Heb. גרש grs *to shoot forth, to sprout*] GRASS, *a blade of grass, corn, herb, hay*; gramen:—Ofer gærsa ciðas, *Deut.* 32, 2: *Mk.* 4, 28. ¶ Gærs-hoppa GRASS-HOPPER; cicada, *Ps.* 77, 51.—Gærs-stapa GRASS-STEPPER, *a locust*; locusta, *Mk.* 1, 6: *Ex.* 10, 14.—Gærs-tun *A grass-enclosure, a meadow*; pascuum: hence, GERSTON, now used in Surrey and Sussex, in the same sense.

Gærsuma, an. *Expense, riches, treasure, a premium, fine, an earnest*:—opes:—*Chr.* 1070: 1035.

Gæsne; *adj. Dear, rare*; carus: *Cod. Ex.* 20, a.

Gæst *a guest*, v. gest: also, *a ghost*, v. gast.—Gæst-hus *a guest-house*.

Gæstliðnes, gestliðnes, giestliðnis, angestliðnes, se; *f.* [gest *a guest*, liðenes *kindness*] *Hospitality, entertainment of guests*; hospitalitas:—*Bd.* 4, 5.

Gæt *a gate, Bd.* 3, 11, v. geat.

Gæt *a goat, Cod. Ex.* 26, *a*, v. gat.

Gætan-rocc *a garment made of goat-skin*, v. broccen.

Gæð *goes*, v. gan.

GAF, gegaf; *adj. Base, vile, lewd*; turpis:—*L. Alf. can.* 35.

Gaf *gave*; *p. of* gifan.

Gafel *a tribute, L. Lund.* p. 71, v. gafol.

Gafellic; *adj. Tributary*; tributo sive fisco pertinens:—*Cot.* 85.

Gaflas; *m. pl.* [*Plat. Dut. Dan. Swed.* gaffel *f*: *Ger.* gabel *f*: *Icel.* gaffal *m*: *Bret.* gaolod] *Forks, props, spars of a building, a gallows*; furcæ, patibulum, *Som.*

Gafol, gafel, gæfel, es; *m.* [*From* gaf; *p. of* gifan *to give*, el. The *Eng.* gabel *a tax* seems nearly allied to gafel] *Tax, tribute, rent*; tributum:—*Mt.* 17, 25: 25, 27. ¶ Gafoles manung *a levying of tribute, Cot.* 73.—Gafol-gyld *tribute-money, usury*.—Gafol-gylda, gaful-gylda *a tribute-payer, debtor, usurer*.—Gafol-gyldan *to pay tribute*.—Gafol-hwitel *a tribute cloak, a kind of livery*; saga vectigalis, *Som.*—Gafol-land *tribute-land, land granted* or *demised on condition of paying some contribution in money* or *other property*.

Gaful *a tribute, Elf. gr.* 9, 2, v. gafol.

Gaful-ford [*The tribute ford*] *Camelford, Cornwall, Chr.* 823.

Gagates *The agate* or *jet, a precious stone*; gagates:—Her bið eac gemeted gagates, se stan bið blæc gym *here is also found the agate, the stone is a black gem, Bd.* 1, 1.

Gagol, gægl; *adj.* [*Icel.* gagl] *Lascivious, wanton*; lascivus:—*R.* 106, v. gal.

Gagol-bærnes *wantonness*, v. gægl-bærnes.

GA'L, an. *Lust, lightness, folly*; levitas:—Hyra gal beswac *their folly deceived, Cd.* 18, v. hælga.

Gal; *adj.* [*Plat.* gail: *Dut.* geil: *Dan. Ger.* geil: *Bret.* gadal] *Light, pleasant, wanton, licentious, wicked*; levis, libidinosus:—*Bt.* 37, 4: *Cd.* 209. Galan gastas *wicked spirits, Bd.* 5, 13.

GALAN, agælan; *part.* galende, agælende, he gælð; *p.* gól, we gólon; *pp.* galen, gegalen [*Dan.* gale: *Swed.* gala *to sing*: *Icel.* gala] *To sing, enchant*; canere:—*C. T. Ps.* 57, 5.

Galdere *An enchanter, sorcerer*; augur, v. galere.

Galdor; *pl.* galdru; *g.* galdra. *An incantation, enchantment, a charm*; incantatio:—Þurh heora galdor, *Bd.* 4, 27, *S.* p. 604, 8: *Ex.* 7, 11: *Deut.* 18, 11.

Galdor-cræft *the art of enchanting*.

Galdor-cræftiga *one crafty* or *skilful in enchantments, an enchanter*.

Galdra *of enchantments*, v. galdor.

Galere, galdere, es; *m. An enchanter*; incantator:—*Elf. gl.* 7.

Gal-ferhð *a lustful mind, lustful*.

Gal-full *lustful, luxurious*.

Gal-fullice *lustfully, luxuriously*.

GALGA, gealga, an. [*Plat.* galg, galge *m*: *Dut.* galg *f*: *Frs.* galga *m*: *Ger.* galgen *m*: *Moes.* galga: *Ot.* galgen: *Dan. Swed.* galge *m*: *Icel.* galgi *m.*] *A gallows, gibbet, cross*; crux:—On galgan *on the cross, Cd.* 225.

Galg-mod *gallows-minded, evil-minded, Beo.* 19.

Galileisc *Galilean, Mk.* 14, 70.

Galleas *Gauls, the French, Bd.* 5, 11.

Gallia-rice *the kingdom of Gaul* or *France*.

Galloc *Sowbread*; malum terræ, *Som.*

Galmanho *A Saxon abbey at York, afterwards St. Mary's*.

Galnes, se; *f. Lustfulness, lust, luxury*; lascivia:—*Cot.* 150.

Gal-scype, es; *m.* [gal *lust*, scype *ship*] *Lustfulness, luxury*; luxuria:—*Deut.* 21, 20: *L. Cnut. eccl.* 24.

Galsere *lustful*.

Gal-walas, Gal-wealas *Gauls, Frenchmen, Chr.* 1.

Gamele *old*.

GAMEN [*Frs.* geane *c*: *Icel.* gaman *n.*—The *Moes.* 2 *Cor.* 13, 13, has gaman κοινωνια; but this is not the root, as the stress of the accent is on the second syllable, and in gamen upon the first. The word is connected with gheenen *subridere, Kil.* and γανω, γανος: *Frs.* geane *a public feast*. The *Old Frs.* has the *m*, like *A. S.* Tha dede God use hera en grate gama *then God, our Lord, caused us great joy, Asegabok*, p. 332. H.] GAME, *joy, pleasure, sport, gaming, taunt, scoff*; ludus:—Him macian sum gamen, *Jud.* 16, 27. Ic mæg swegles gamen gehyran *I can hear heaven's joy, Cd.* 32.

Gamenian *To joke, be merry*; joculari:—*Scint.* 55.

Gamenlice; *adv. Sportingly, deceitfully*; jocose:—*Jos.* 9, 3.

Gaming, e; *f.* A GAMING, *playing, gesticulation*; lusus:—*Cot.* 203.

Gamnigende *jesting, joking*, v. gamenian.

Gamol, gamul *old, Lye*:—*a camel, Som.*

Gamol-feax *old, grey* or *flaxen hair*.

Gamol-ferhð *camel spirit, brave, magnanimous*.

GA'N, gangan, ic gá, gange, he gæð, we gáð, gæð; *imp.* gá, gang; *p.* ic eóde, we eódun; *pp.* gán, agæn, agán, gangen; *v. n.* [*Plat. Dut.* gaan, gaen: *Frs.* ga, geán: *Ger.* gehen: *Old Ger.* kan: *Ot. Moes.* gaggan, pronounced gangan: *Dan.* gaa: *Swed.* gâ: *Icel.* gánga: *Heb.* גאה gea *to rise*] *To go, walk, happen*; ire:—Þu gæst on þinum breoste, *Gen.* 3, 14. Ealle hi eodon, *Lk.* 2, 3. He wæs þanon agan *he was gone from thence, Mt.* 26, 39. Þa sæternes dæg wæs agan, *Mk.* 16, 1. Ga or gang hider *come hither, Gen.* 27, 21, 26. Her gæð *comes here, Gen.* 37, 19. Agæð, *Deut.* 13, 2.

Gandis, gandes *the river Ganges, Ors.* 1, 1.

Gandra, ganra, A GANDER; anser masculus:—*Elf. gr.* 9, 18.

Ganet *a fen-duck*, v. ganot.

Gang, gong, es; *m.* [*Dut.* gang] *A journey, step, going, way, path, a passage, drain, privy*; iter:—*Ors.* 2, 4: *Ps.* 139, 5.

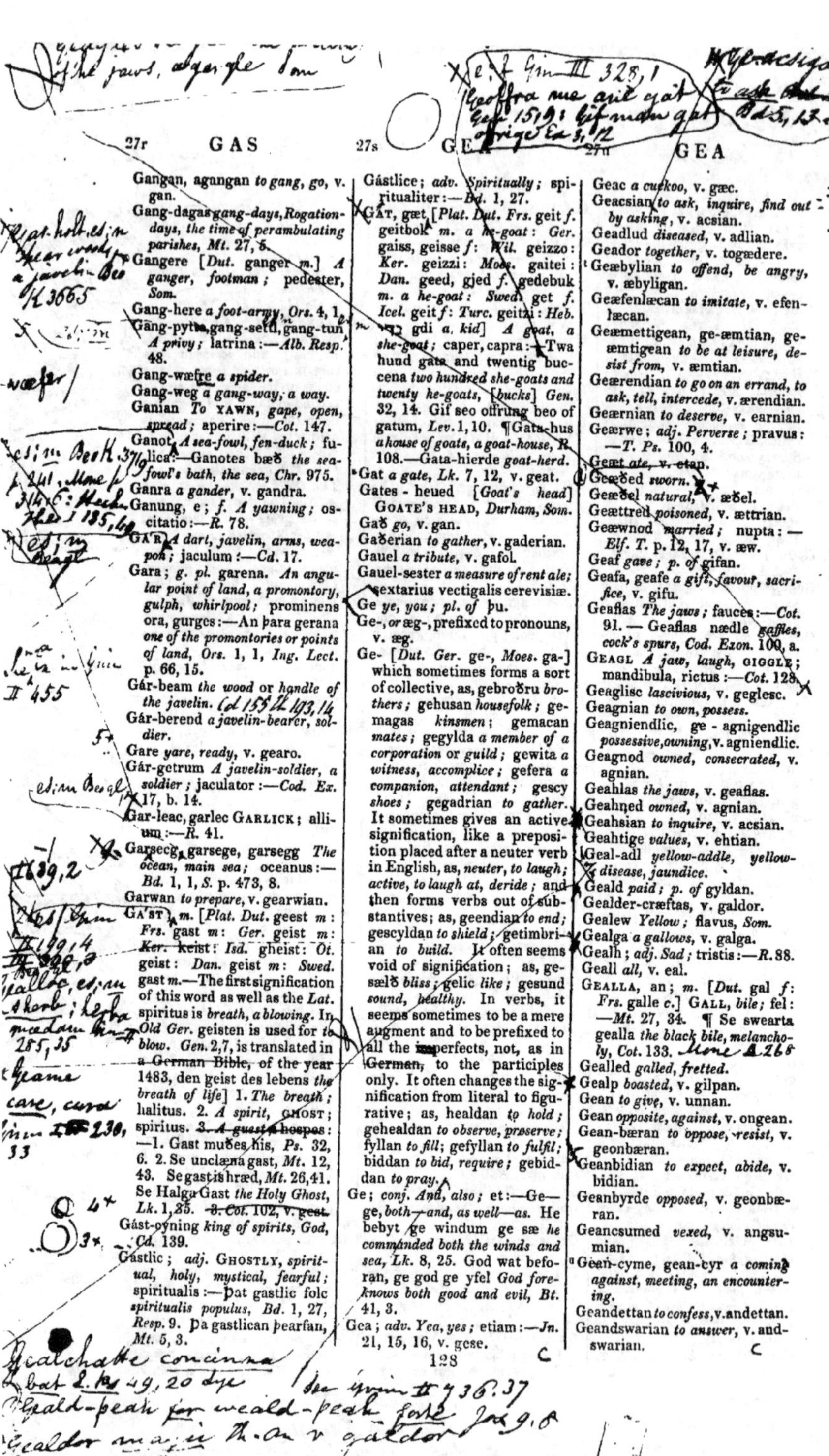

Gangan, agangan *to gang, go*, v. gan.

Gang-dagas *gang-days, Rogation-days, the time of perambulating parishes*, Mt. 27, 8.

Gangere [*Dut.* ganger *m.*] *A ganger, footman*; pedester, *Som.*

Gang-here *a foot-army*, *Ors.* 4, 1.

Gang-pytt, gang-setl, gang-tun *A privy*; latrina:—*Alb. Resp.* 48.

Gang-wæfre *a spider.*

Gang-weg *a gang-way, a way.*

Ganian *To* YAWN, *gape, open, spread*; aperire:—*Cot.* 147.

Ganot *A sea-fowl, fen-duck*; fulica:—Ganotes bæð *the sea-fowl's bath, the sea, Chr.* 975.

Ganra *a gander*, v. gandra.

Ganung, e; *f. A yawning*; oscitatio:—*R.* 78.

GAR *A dart, javelin, arms, weapon*; jaculum:—*Cd.* 17.

Gara; *g. pl.* garena. *An angular point of land, a promontory, gulph, whirlpool*; prominens ora, gurges:—An þara gerana *one of the promontories or points of land, Ors.* 1, 1, *Ing. Lect.* p. 66, 15.

Gár-beam *the wood* or *handle of the javelin.*

Gár-berend *a javelin-bearer, soldier.*

Gare *yare, ready*, v. gearo.

Gár-getrum *A javelin-soldier, a soldier*; jaculator:—*Cod. Ex.* 17, b. 14.

Gar-leac, garlec GARLICK; allium:—*R.* 41.

Garsecg, garsege, garsegg *The ocean, main sea*; oceanus:—*Bd.* 1, 1, *S.* p. 473, 8.

Garwan *to prepare*, v. gearwian.

GAST, *m.* [*Plat. Dut.* geest *m*: *Frs.* gast *m*: *Ger.* geist *m*: *Ker.* keist: *Isd.* gheist: *Ot.* geist: *Dan.* geist *m*: *Swed.* gast *m.*—The first signification of this word as well as the *Lat.* spiritus is *breath, a blowing.* In *Old Ger.* geisten is used for *to blow. Gen.* 2,7, is translated in a German Bible, of the year 1483, den geist des lebens *the breath of life*] 1. *The breath*; halitus. 2. *A spirit,* GHOST; spiritus. 3. *A guest*; hospes:—1. Gast muðes his, *Ps.* 32, 6. 2. Se unclæna gast, *Mt.* 12, 43. Se gast is hræd, *Mt.* 26, 41. Se Halga Gast *the Holy Ghost, Lk.* 1, 35. 3. *Cot.* 102, v. gest.

Gást-cyning *king of spirits, God, Cd.* 139.

Gastlic; *adj.* GHOSTLY, *spiritual, holy, mystical, fearful*; spiritualis:—Þat gastlic folc *spiritualis populus, Bd.* 1, 27, *Resp.* 9. Þa gastlican þearfan, *Mt.* 5, 3.

Gástlice; *adv. Spiritually*; spiritualiter:—*Bd.* 1, 27.

GAT, gæt, [*Plat. Dut. Frs.* geit *f.* geitbok *m. a he-goat*: *Ger.* gaiss, geisse *f*: *Wil.* geizzo: *Ker.* geizzi: *Moes.* gaitei: *Dan.* geed, gjed *f.* gedebuk *m. a he-goat*: *Swed.* get *f.* *Icel.* geit *f*: *Turc.* geitzi: *Heb.* גדי gdi *a. kid*] *A goat, a she-goat*; caper, capra:—Twa hund gata and twentig buccena *two hundred she-goats and twenty he-goats,* [*bucks*] *Gen.* 32, 14. Gif seo offrung beo of gatum, *Lev.* 1, 10. ¶ Gata-hus *a house of goats, a goat-house, R.* 108.—Gata-hierde *goat-herd.*

Gat *a gate, Lk.* 7, 12, v. geat.

Gates - heued [*Goat's head*] GOATE'S HEAD, *Durham, Som.*

Gað *go*, v. gan.

Gaðerian *to gather*, v. gaderian.

Gauel *a tribute*, v. gafol.

Gauel-sester *a measure of rent ale*; sextarius vectigalis cerevisiæ.

Ge *ye, you*; *pl. of* þu.

Ge-, *or* æg-, prefixed to pronouns, v. æg.

Ge- [*Dut. Ger.* ge-, *Moes.* ga-] which sometimes forms a sort of collective, as, gebroðru *brothers*; gehusan *housefolk*; gemagas *kinsmen*; gemacan *mates*; gegylda *a member of a corporation* or *guild*; gewita *a witness, accomplice*; gefera *a companion, attendant*; gescy *shoes*; gegadrian *to gather.* It sometimes gives an active signification, like a preposition placed after a neuter verb in English, as, *neuter, to laugh*; *active, to laugh at, deride*; and then forms verbs out of substantives; as, geendian *to end*; gescyldan *to shield*; getimbrian *to build.* It often seems void of signification; as, gesælð *bliss*; gelic *like*; gesund *sound, healthy.* In verbs, it seems sometimes to be a mere augment and to be prefixed to all the imperfects, not, as in German, to the participles only. It often changes the signification from literal to figurative; as, healdan *to hold*; gehealdan *to observe, preserve*; fyllan *to fill*; gefyllan *to fulfil*; biddan *to bid, require*; gebiddan *to pray.*

Ge; *conj. And, also*; et:—Ge—ge, *both—and, as well—as.* He bebyt ge windum ge sæ *he commanded both the winds and sea, Lk.* 8, 25. God wat beforan, ge god ge yfel *God foreknows both good and evil, Bt.* 41, 3.

Gea; *adv. Yea, yes*; etiam:—*Jn.* 21, 15, 16, v. gese.

Geac *a cuckoo*, v. gæc.

Geacsian *to ask, inquire, find out by asking*, v. acsian.

Geadlud *diseased*, v. adlian.

Geador *together*, v. togædere.

Geæbylian *to offend, be angry*, v. æbyligan.

Geæfenlæcan *to imitate*, v. efenlæcan.

Geæmettigean, ge-æmtian, geæmtigean *to be at leisure, desist from*, v. æmtian.

Geærendian *to go on an errand, to ask, tell, intercede*, v. ærendian.

Geærnian *to deserve*, v. earnian.

Geærwe; *adj. Perverse*; pravus:—*T. Ps.* 100, 4.

Geæt *ate*, v. etan.

Geæðed *sworn.*

Geæðel *natural*, v. æðel.

Geættred *poisoned*, v. ættrian.

Geæwnod *married*; nupta:—*Elf. T.* p. 12, 17, v. æw.

Geaf *gave*; *p. of* gifan.

Geafa, geafe *a gift, favour, sacrifice*, v. gifu.

Geaflas *The jaws*; fauces:—*Cot.* 91. — Geaflas nædle *gaffles, cock's spurs, Cod. Exon.* 100, a.

GEAGL *A jaw, laugh,* GIGGLE; mandibula, rictus:—*Cot.* 128.

Geaglisc *lascivious*, v. geglesc.

Geagnian *to own, possess.*

Geagniendlic, ge - agnigendlic *possessive, owning*, v. agniendlic.

Geagnod *owned, consecrated*, v. agnian.

Geahlas *the jaws*, v. geaflas.

Geahned *owned*, v. agnian.

Geahsian *to inquire*, v. acsian.

Geahtige *values*, v. ehtian.

Geal-adl *yellow-addle, yellow-disease, jaundice.*

Geald *paid*; *p. of* gyldan.

Gealder-cræftas, v. galdor.

Gealew *Yellow*; flavus, *Som.*

Gealga *a gallows*, v. galga.

Gealh; *adj. Sad*; tristis:—*R.* 88.

Geall *all*, v. eal.

GEALLA, an; *m.* [*Dut.* gal *f*: *Frs.* galle *c.*] GALL, *bile*; fel:—*Mt.* 27, 34. ¶ Se swearta gealla *the black bile, melancholy, Cot.* 133.

Gealled *galled, fretted.*

Gealp *boasted*, v. gilpan.

Gean *to give*, v. unnan.

Gean *opposite, against*, v. ongean.

Gean-bæran *to oppose, resist*, v. geonbæran.

Geanbidian *to expect, abide*, v. bidian.

Geanbyrde *opposed*, v. geonbæran.

Geancsumed *vexed*, v. angsumian.

Gean-cyme, gean-cyr *a coming against, meeting, an encountering.*

Geandettan *to confess*, v. andettan.

Geandswarian *to answer*, v. andswarian.

Gangel-wæfre
~~Gangel-wæfre~~ a spider.
araneus Som v gang-wæfre q wæfer

Ge-anegdu anxia
... 18 ~~Som~~ Lye

Ge-aniant
geacnung ...
v ge-ecwan ...
Geac ... ...
item Som v eac
Geacniendlic preg
nant Som ~~v geeacnian~~

Ge-ahtan [illegible]
To appreciate, praise
appretiare, laudibus
efferre Beo K 3764
~~Gangeteld papilio~~
~~Som papilio R 1100~~
~~Lye~~ — Gang-feorr
... a ... former
... Som

Gangan-dæg ...
... p. 164, 23
v. Gangenfeta ... Som
Gang-geteld
~~tent~~ travelling tent,
tent, pavilion; ~~papilio~~
papilio R 10 —
Gang-wuce ...
... ...

Geacsung, e; f.
inquiry; inquisitio
Som v acsung
Geador together
to continue Som
gader tengan

Gataloc tutela Som
Gate-treow gaten
tree ... dog
... ... Som L.M. 1. 136

pg 128

Ge-ahtle, an f? property, riches; possessio,
divitiæ Beo K 735

... me vespera-
... p. XC. 2 ... alc
... ... endlic ...
... ...

... ged coloured,
... coloratus, Som
... eswicod ...
... ... Som
... ...
... ... Som

Ge-ahnian to take as his own, sibi
appropriare, in potestatem reducere Beo
~~to~~ ... in agan
... triumphi ... ...

Ge-aldor ... m a ... Beo K 5883 ... 8, 11
~~enchantment, incantatio~~
~~magica Beo K 6100~~

... branch, a
... cross; patibulum
Beo 218 ... K 529
... gealg treow

... ...
... K 5346
... ...
Geagle lascivious Som
v Geagle
Gealgian to defend
Th. An

... gærsuma
...
Gast-bona ... killer, the devil
~~...~~ interfector Beo K 3
Gen ... 485, 11
Gast-hus
Gast-gedal a sepa
ration from life, death
Cd. 55, ... p 68, 33

... ...
Ge-afored lifted
sublimatus Som
Ge-agenned ad...
Som
Geagle wanton Som
v. geaglisc
Geafol ... meaning
e; f toll or custom
house R ... 2, 14
v ... gafol

Gealt ... mod sad in
mind, gloomy Cd 164
Th ... 230. 8
Geara ... ... 17, 5 ...
Geanbidian to
abide Th. An.
Geane yet ... p 8, 57 ...
~~...~~

Geagl-swile a
swelling Som
~~Geagl~~
Geahnung ... ...
v ahnung

Geahle dentes
molares Beo

Geald ... for
weald perhaps
... ...

paralysis Beo K 428

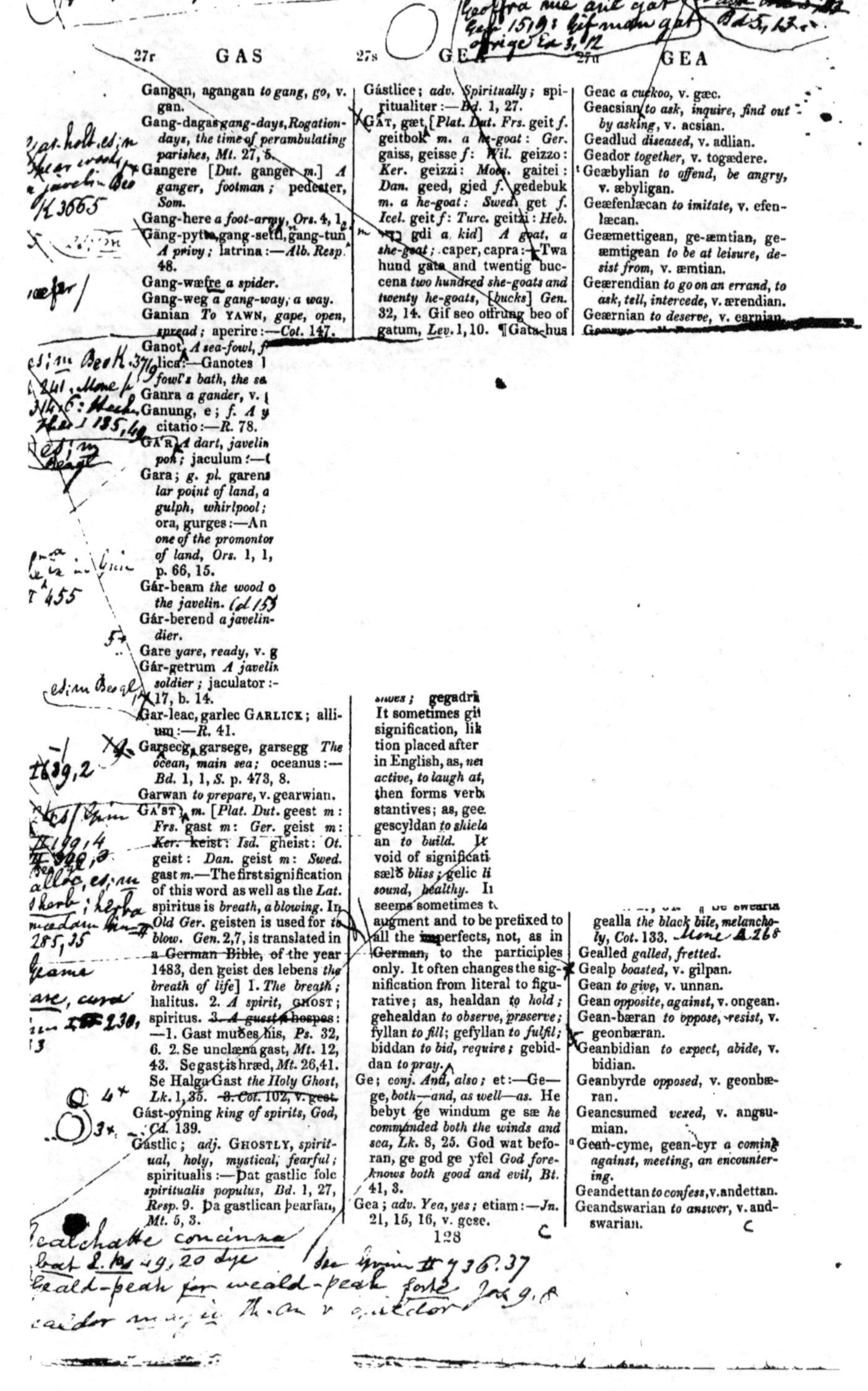

Gangan, agangan *to gang, go*, v. gan.
Gang-dagas *gang-days, Rogation-days, the time of perambulating parishes, Mt.* 27, 5.
Gangere [*Dut.* ganger *m.*] *A ganger, footman;* pedester, *Som.*
Gang-here *a foot-army, Ors.* 4, 1,
Gang-pytt, gang-setl, gang-tun *A privy;* latrina:—*Alb. Resp.* 48.
Gang-wæfre *a spider.*
Gang-weg *a gang-way, a way.*
Ganian To YAWN, *gape, open, spread;* aperire:—*Cot.* 147.
Ganot, *A sea-fowl, f*... lica:—Ganotes ... *fowl's bath, the se*...
Ganra *a gander*, v. ...
Ganung, e; *f. A y*... citatio:—*R.* 78.
GÁR *A dart, javelin*... *pon;* jaculum:—...
Gara; *g. pl.* garena ... *lar point of land, a* ... *gulph, whirlpool;* ora, gurges:—An ... *one of the promontor*... *of land, Ors.* 1, 1, p. 66, 15.
Gár-beam *the wood o*... *the javelin.*
Gár-berend *a javelin-dier.*
Gare *yare, ready*, v. g...
Gár-getrum *A javeli*... *soldier;* jaculator:-... 17, b. 14.
Gar-leac, garlec GARLICK; allium:—*R.* 41.
Garsecg, garsege, garsegg *The ocean, main sea;* oceanus:—*Bd.* 1, 1, *S.* p. 473, 8.
Garwan *to prepare*, v. gearwian.
GÁST, *m.* [*Plat. Dut.* geest *m*: *Frs.* gast *m*: *Ger.* geist *m*: *Ker.* keist: *Isd.* gheist: *Ot.* geist: *Dan.* geist *m*: *Swed.* gast *m.*—The first signification of this word as well as the *Lat.* spiritus is *breath, a blowing.* In *Old Ger.* geisten is used for *to blow. Gen.* 2,7, is translated in a German Bible, of the year 1483, den geist des lebens *the breath of life*] 1. *The breath;* halitus. 2. *A spirit,* GHOST; spiritus. 3. *A guest;* hospes:—1. Gast mudes his, *Ps.* 32, 6. 2. Se unclæna gast, *Mt.* 12, 43. Se gast is hræd, *Mt.* 26,41. Se Halga Gast *the Holy Ghost, Lk.* 1, 35. 3. *Cot.* 102, v. gest.
Gást-cyning *king of spirits, God, Cd.* 139.
Gastlic; *adj.* GHOSTLY, *spiritual, holy, mystical, fearful;* spiritualis:—Þat gastlic folc *spiritualis populus, Bd.* 1, 27, *Resp.* 9. Þa gastlican þearfan, *Mt.* 5, 3.

Gástlice; *adv. Spiritually;* spiritualiter:—*Bd.* 1, 27.
GÁT, gæt [*Plat. Dut. Frs.* geit *f.* geitbok *m. a he-goat*: *Ger.* gaiss, geisse *f*: *Wil.* geizzo: *Ker.* geizzi: *Moes.* gaitei: *Dan.* geed, gjed *f.* gedebuk *m. a he-goat*: *Swed.* get *f. Icel.* geit *f*: *Turc.* geitzi: *Heb.* גדי gdi *a kid*] *A goat, a she-goat;* caper, capra:—Twa hund gata and twentig buccena *two hundred she-goats and twenty he-goats,* [*bucks*] *Gen.* 32, 14. Gif seo offrung beo of gatum, *Lev.* 1,10. ¶Gata-hus

...*shoes;* gegadri... It sometimes gi... signification, lik... tion placed after... in English, as, *ne*... *active, to laugh at,*... then forms verb... stantives; as, gee... gescyldan *to shield*... an *to build.* It... void of significati... sælð *bliss;* gelic *li*... *sound, healthy.* I... seems sometimes t... augment and to be prefixed to all the imperfects, not, as in German, to the participles only. It often changes the signification from literal to figurative; as, healdan *to hold;* gehealdan *to observe, preserve;* fyllan *to fill;* gefyllan *to fulfil;* biddan *to bid, require;* gebiddan *to pray.*
Ge; *conj. And, also;* et:—Ge—ge, *both—and, as well—as.* He bebyt ge windum ge sæ *he commanded both the winds and sea, Lk.* 8, 25. God wat beforan, ge god ge yfel *God foreknows both good and evil, Bt.* 41, 3.
Gea; *adv. Yea, yes;* etiam:—*Jn.* 21, 15, 16, v. gese.

Geac *a cuckoo*, v. gæc.
Geacsian *to ask, inquire, find out by asking*, v. acsian.
Geadlud *diseased*, v. adlian.
Geador *together*, v. togædere.
Geæbylian *to offend, be angry*, v. æbyligan.
Geæfenlæcan *to imitate*, v. efenlæcan.
Geæmettigean, ge-æmtian, geæmtigean *to be at leisure, desist from*, v. æmtian.
Geærendian *to go on an errand, to ask, tell, intercede*, v. ærendian.
Geærnian *to deserve*, v. earnian.

gealla *the black bile, melancholy, Cot.* 133.
Gealled *galled, fretted.*
Gealp *boasted*, v. gilpan.
Gean *to give*, v. unnan.
Gean *opposite, against*, v. ongean.
Gean-bæran *to oppose, resist*, v. geonbæran.
Geanbidian *to expect, abide*, v. bidian.
Geanbyrde *opposed*, v. geonbæran.
Geancsumed *vexed*, v. angsumian.
Gean-cyme, gean-cyr *a coming against, meeting, an encountering.*
Geandettan *to confess*, v. andettan.
Geandswarian *to answer*, v. andswarian.

Gangel - wæfre
~~Gangel-wæfre~~ a spider
arned Som v gang - wæfre q. v. wæfer

Gangende gong
... 164, 23

Gangenfeta agmen Ben

Gang-geteld
~~tent~~ travelling tent,
tent, pavilion; ~~pavilion~~
papilio R 10 —

Gang-wæg
... Septima ...
... ...
... assignata
... 17.

Gar-céne spear bold
Bo Th 3912

Gar-clife grimmy
Som Herb 32.

Gar-fatgan ...
Gar-falcon ...

Gar-cwealm
... spear
... ;
... ; occisio jaculo
heracta Bes. 153 ...

Gar-heap a heap ...
... jaculorum ... Cd. 160 Th. 198, 11

Gar-ræs ...
Gar-secg the sea
... Th 1135 5

Gar-wudu spear-
wood a javelin
Cd 160, Th 198, 20

Garsuma expense Som
v gærsuma

Gast-bona soul killer, ... interfector ... Bes 30
Grein ... 485, 11

3 Gast-hus

4 Gast-gedal a separation from life, death
Cd. 55, Th p 68, 33

Ge-anegden anxia
... 18 ...

Ge-ahtan to ... appreciate ... apprehend laudibus efferre Bes 12 ...
~~Gangeteld papilio~~

~~Som papilio R 110 ...~~
Lye — Gang-ferz
mer a jakes farmer
fimarius Som

Gatalóc tutela Som

Gate-treow Gaten
tree ... dog
berry tree ... Th

Gate-hær, es; n
goats hair ...

Gavelóc a spear ...
v. gafeloc ...
... Cd 160 Th 199, 23

Gar-gewinn ...
... Cd 160 Th 198, 11

Garum-fol ...
... Som
v gearumtol
Cd 160 Th 198, 11

... Bo Th 1026
... Cd 157 ...

Gar-wiga ... spearman, fighter ...

... R 34 ...
... Bes. 39
Gar-...
Gæt-heord goatherd
caprarius Som

Ge-afored lifted
sublimatus Som

Ge-agnod ...
Som ...

Geagle wanton Som
v. geaglisc

Geafol-meaning
ci f toll or custom
house R. Mk 2, 14
v gafol

Geagl-swile a
swelling Som ...
~~Geagl~~
Ge-ahnung owning ...
v ahnung

Ge-acsunga ...
geacnung ...
v ge-edcwan ...
Geac also likewise
item Som v eac
Geaciendlic ...
nant Som ~~v geacnian~~

Geacsung, e; f.
inquiry; inquisitio
Som. v acsung

Geader-tengan
to continue Som —
gader-tengan

Geæftnes ...
... Som ...
... Th. 1. 136

Ge-æfnad ... vespera ...
Cd. ...
... Walton p. ... C. 2 also
Note 5

Ge-æhtendlic that
may be valued; estimable
... Som

Ge-ælged coloured,
tanned, coloratus Som

Ge-æswicod ...
scandalized Som
Geafla ... lever ...
... Som
Gealg-treow
... branch, a
cross; patibulum
Bo 218 ... 529,
~~Gealg-treow~~
Gealge, luxurious Som
v geagle
Gealgian to defend
Th. An

Gealh-mod sad in
mind, gloomy Cd 186
Th 230. 8

Geand-...
... 17, 5 ...

Geanbidjan to
abide Th. An.

Geane yet ... 8, 57 ...

Geahle dentes
molares Ben

Geald for
weald ... perhaps ...

gearewe. millefolium

v. arrow; millefolium Som

Gear-n. [illegible]

5,10

p 150

Ge-aurnen overrun over-run, overtaken Som

v. yrnan

Ge-aworpen cast away Som v. a-weorpan

Ge-anung owning Som v. ahnung

Geare-wita intellect Bt. 38, 9 ; p 130, 9 v gearowita

Gebærd towardliness indoles Som

Gear-hwyrft annus Bo. Lyn II 755, 6

Gebærd-stan calculus, calcesura R 38 Lye

Gebære as in Som & Ben

Geanpingian to acquire Cd 48 Th 162, 5

Gearnung; f Desert merit; [illegible]

Ge-bærmed barmed, leavened Som

Geanwyrde beon to be professed

desert; meritum Som

Gebeacnung; f a speaking by tropes or figures a predicament; categoria Cot 57 Lye

Gearo-foncol ready witted Th An

Geapes around Cd 149 Th p 154, 16

Gebealg anger Som v gebelg

Gebeah bedecked, preserved Som v gebeorgan

Gear-torht yearly bright Cd 76 Th 94, 13

Geapung; f cumulus Bd. 5, 13 B Lye

Gebecan to book Lye v gebocian

Gearowa, an in clothing [illegible]

Gebeenendlic rationally Cot 1 Som

5 Geara-feng arpax lupus R 3, 105

Gearutol, gearutol severe, austere C. Lk 19, 21 Som, Lye

v beeniendlice

6 Geara-gewuned long accustomed Som

Gearwa, made dishes; condimenta S. M 2, 23 Som, Lye

Gebaded compelled Som v biddan gebaded

7 Geare ready Th An; for Geare, gearo

Gebegdnes, gebegednes; se f crooked ness; aduncitas Som

Gearwan-leaf yarrow leaf; millefolium Som

Gearcung-dæges in Goodfriday Som Mt 26, 17

preparation [illegible]

Gebegendlic flexible bowing; flexibilis Som

Gebedigan to pray Lye 5, 9 Som L 622, 21 note

gear-king

Year-cyning-kcon sul; a ruler or king for a year; consul Som. Lyn II, 479, 39

Gear-cunningdon es. [illegible] year keeping the conful shef Som

Geadmodian to humble, to be pleased. Th An

Ge-belh offensio Lyn II 740, 10 v gebelg

Gear-dagas in a day or time, days of yore 99, 36 L 80 Th 99, 36

hear, learn Th. An

Geardlic adj worldly mundialis Som

Geben a prayer; preces offensio Ben

Geare ready Cd 2 Th 3. 26 v gearo

Geardode-domas responsa R 16 Lye

Geandweardod *presented*, v. andweardian.
Geandwyrdan *to answer*, v. andwerdan.

GEARN [*Plat. Dut.* garen *n*: *Frs.* jern *n*: *Ger. Dan. Swed. Icel.* garn *n*: *Ot.* garno] YARN, *spun wool*; pensa:—*Cot.* 85.

Gebæc *a back*; gebæcu *back parts*, v. bæc.
Gebæd *prayed*, v. biddan.
Gebæded *driven, compelled*, v.

yore, of old.
Geare *formerly, certainly*, v. gera.
Gearfoð *difficult*, v. earfeð.
Gearian *to pardon, honour*, v. arian.
Gearlic; *adj. Yearly, annual*; annuus:—*L. Athel.*
Gearlice; *adv. Yearly, quickly*; annuatim, *Cot.*

give to-day, *Id.* 963: 675: 656.
Geatas *the Jutes, the Goths*, v. Iutas.
Geatelod *deformed*, v. atol.
Geatolic *like the Jutes, warlike.*
Geatweard *a gate-ward, doorkeeper.*
Geaxian *to ask after, inquire, hear*, v. acsian.
Gebacen, gebæc *baked*, v. bacan.

Gebegean *To crown, to bend*; coronare:—*C. Ps.* 102, 4.
Gebeged *bowed, constrained*, v. bigan.
Gebelg *Anger, offence*; offensio, *Bd.*
Gebelgan *to be angry, displeased*, v. belgan.
Gebelimpe *the event*, v. gelimp.
Gebend *bound.*

yarrow; millefolium Som Gear- ...
... Rit 5,10
4) ... p150

... Som X Geare-wita intellect

... over-run, overtaken Som v yrnan
... aworpen cast away Som v a-weorpan

6 Geard [... 39a 1]

Gebad abided, Beo ... K 3236 p of bidan

9,39

... cyning-dom ... ... kingdom ... consulship

gear-dag ... a time, days of yore ... 80 Th K 99,36

Geare ready ... Th 6 v geare

... Geadmodian to humble, to be pleased. Th An

3 ... hear, learn Th. An.

Geardlic adj worldly mundialis Som.

... Gearode-domas ... responsa R 116 Lye

... Ge-belh offensio ... II 740, 10 v gebelg

Gebeu ... a ... prayer; preces offensio Ben

Geandweardod *presented*, v. andweardian.

Geandwyrdan *to answer*, v. andwerdan.

Geanede *made one, united*, v. unnan.

Gean-fare *returned*, v. faran.

Geangsumian *to vex*, v. angsumian.

Geanlæcan *To unite, make one, atone;* unire:—*Elf. gr.* 37.

Geanlician *To liken;* assimilare: —*Mk.* 4, 30.

Geanryne *a running against, meeting.*

Geanwyrdan *To arraign, accuse;* convincere:—*Chr.* 1055.

GEAP; *comp.* ra; *adj.* 1. *Crooked, bent;* curvus. 2. *Deceitful, cunning;* fallax:—1. *Cot.* 50. 2. *Gen.* 3, 1.

Geapan *To* GAPE, *open;* pandere: —*Cot.* 158.

Geaplic; *adj. Deceitful;* subdolus:—*Jos.* 9, 4.

Geaplice; *adv. Deceitfully;* procaciter:—*Prov.* 21.

Geapscipe, es; *m. Deceit, fraud, guile;* fraus:—*Jos.* 9, 17.

GEAR, ger, es; *m.* [*Plat. Dut.* jaar *n*: *Frs.* jer *n*: *Ger.* jahr *n*: *Ker.* jar: *Isd.* jaar: *Moes.* jer: *Dan.* aar *n*: *Swed.* år *n*: *Icel.* ár *n.*] A YEAR; annus:—Ðis wæs feorðes geares *this was in the fourth year, Chr.* 46.

Geára, geare, gearwe, gere; *adv.* [gear *a year*] 1. YORE, *formerly, for a long time;* olim. 2. *That which has been known for a long time, is well known:* hence, *well, certainly, enough;* bene:—1. *Bd.* 2, 3. 2. *Bd.* 1, 27, *Resp.* 1: *Lk.* 20, 6.

Geara *Provision, furniture,* GEARS *for horses;* apparatus, v. gearwa.

Gearcian, gegearcian, ic gearcige; *p.* ode; *pp.* ed; *v. a. To prepare, make ready;* parare: —*Ps.* 7, 14: *Gen.* 19, 3.

Gearcung, gegearcung, e; *f. A preparation, preparing;* præparatio:—*Ps.* 9, 41.

Geard, es; *m.* [gird, gyrd *a rod*] A YARD, *enclosure, region, the earth, world, turf, peat;* sepes: —*Mt.* 4, 16: *Chr.* 852. Grene geardas *green regions, places, Cd.* 25: 35.

Gear-daga *yore-days, days of yore, of old.*

Geare *formerly, certainly*, v. geara.

Gearfoð *difficult*, v. earfeð.

Gearian *to pardon, honour*, v. arian.

Gearlic; *adj. Yearly, annual;* annuus:—*L. Athel.*

Gearlice; *adv. Yearly, quickly;* annuatim, *Cot.*

GEARN [*Plat. Dut.* garen *n*: *Frs.* jern *n*: *Ger. Dan. Swed. Icel.* garn *n*: *Ot.* garno] YARN, *spun wool;* pensa:—*Cot.* 85.

Gearnfull; *adj. Anxious;* solicitus:—*Lk.* 12, 11.

Gearnian *to earn, deserve*, v. earnian.

Geáro, gearu, gearow, gearuw, gearw, ageara, agearwa, gare; *comp.* gearor, gearwur; *adj.* YARE, *ready, prepared;* paratus:—Gearo wyrde on gespræce *was ready in speech, Bd.* 5, 2, *S.* p. 615, 29: *Ors.* 5, 14. Ealle mine þing synt gearwe, *Mt.* 22, 4.

Gearo *formerly*, v. geara.

Gearod *clothed*, v. gegyrian.

Gearow *prepared, Ors.* 4, 4, v. gearo.

Gearowita, an; *m. Intellect, understanding;* intelligentia:—*Bt.* 39, 8.

Gears *grass, Deut.* 32, 2, v. gærs.

Gearu *ready, Jn.* 7, 6, v. gearo.

Gearuw *prepared, Bd.* 4, 2, v. gearo.

Gearw *ready, Mt.* 22, 4, v. gearo.

Gearwa *Clothing, preparation;* habitus:—*Cd.* 30.

Gearwe, YARROW; millefolium: —*Elf. gl.* 15.

Gearwe *formerly, well*, v. geara.

Gearwian, agearwian, gearwan, gegearwian, gearwigean, girian, gyrian *To prepare, procure, supply;* parare:—*Jn.* 14, 2: *Ps.* 27, 48.

Gearwung, gegearwung, e; *f. A making ready, preparation;* præparatio:—*Ps.* 64, 10.

Gearwurðod *honoured*, v. arwurðian.

Geascade *asked, inquired, heard*, v. acsian.

Geascung *asking*, v. acsung.

Geasmyred *smeared, anointed*, v. smirian.

Geasyndrod *sundered, separated*, v. asyndrian.

GEAT, gat, gæt, es; *pl.* geatu, gatu; *n.* [*Plat. Dut. Frs. Ger. Dan. Icel.* gat *n. a hole, aperture*] A GATE, *door;* porta:— *Mt.* 7, 13, 14.

Geat *poured out*, v. geotan.

GEATAN; *p.* hi geottan, getton. *To grant, confirm;* concedere:— Ic geate þe *I grant thee, Chr.* 658. Ic Ædgar geate and gife to dæi *I Edgar grant and give to-day, Id.* 963: 675: 656.

Geatas *the Jutes, the Goths*, v. Iutas.

Geatelod *deformed*, v. atol.

Geatolic *like the Jutes, warlike.*

Geatweard *a gate-ward, doorkeeper.*

Geaxian *to ask after, inquire, hear*, v. acsian.

Gebacen, gebæc *baked*, v. bacan.

Gebæc *a back;* gebæcu *back parts*, v. bæc.

Gebæd *prayed*, v. biddan.

Gebæded *driven, compelled*, v. biddan.

Gebælded *animated*, v. bælded.

Gebær; *d. pl.* gebærum. *A bearing, a state* or *habit of body* or *mind, practice, society, fellowship, deportment, demeanour;* gestus:—*Ors.* 1, 12.

Gebæran *to carry, bear, pretend*, v. beran.

Gebærscype *a feast*, v. gebeorscipe.

Gebæte, gebætel *bit of a bridle, a bridle*, v. bæte.

Gebætte *bridled*, v. bætan.

Geban, geben *A proclamation, edict,* BANNS; edictum:—*Elf. gl.*

Gebannan *to proclaim*, v. abannan.

Gebasnian *to expect*, v. basnian.

Gebatad, gebatod *Abated;* mitigatus:—*Cot.* 135.

Gebeacnian *to point out*, v. bicnian.

Gebearscype *a feast*, v. gebeorscipe.

Gebeaten *beaten*, v. beatan.

Gebecnan *to point out*, v. bicnian.

GEBED, gebedd, bead; *pl.* gebedu, gebedo, [*Plat.* bede, bidde *f*: *Dut. Frs.* gebed *n*: *Dut.* bede *f*: *Ger.* gebeth *n*: *Ker.* pet: *Wil.* gebete: *Ot.* gibet] 1. *A prayer, petition, supplication;* oratio. 2. *A command, demand;* mandatum:—1. *Ps.* 34, 16: *Lk.* 6, 12. 2. Gehealdað his gebed, *Ex.* 12, 24.

Gebed-clyfa *a den, C. Ps.* 9, 31.

Gebedda *a bed-fellow, a wife.*

Gebeden *demanded, intreated*, v. biddan.

Gebedgiht *Bed-time;* conticinium:—*R.* 16.

Gebed-hus *a prayer-house, an oratory, house of prayer.*

Gebed-man *a praying man, a supplicant.*

Gebed-rædden *the office of prayer, prayer.*

Gebed-scipe *bed-fellowship, marriage.*

Gebed-stow *a prayer-place, oratory.*

Gebegan *To recline, lie down;* reclinare:—*R. Lk.* 9, 58.

Gebegd *bowed, bent, crooked*, v. bigan.

Gebegean *To crown, to bend;* coronare:—*C. Ps.* 102, 4.

Gebeged *bowed, constrained*, v. bigan.

Gebelg *Anger, offence;* offensio, *Bd.*

Gebelgan *to be angry, displeased*, v. belgan.

Gebelimpe *the event*, v. gelimp.

Gebend *bound.*

Gebeoda *prayers*, v. gebed.
Gebeodan *to command*, v. beheodan.
Gebeón *for* gebeonn, v. gebannan *to proclaim*.
Gebeón *been*, v. beón.
GEBEOR, es; *m. A guest; hospes*:—*Bd.* 3, 10.
x Gebeoran *to bear*, v. beran.
Gebeorc *barked*, v. beorcan.
Gebeorgan *to defend*, v. beorgan.
Gebeorge *for a defence*, v. gebeorh.
Gebeorglic, gebeorhlic; *adj. Defensible, mitigated, bearable, pardonable, cautious, safe*; tolerabilis:—*L. Edg. pol.* 1.
Gebeorh *a refuge*, v. beorh.
Gebeorhlic, v. gebeorglic.
Gebeorhnys, se; *f. A refuge*; refugium:—*C. Ps.* 30, 3.
Gebeorhtian *to glorify*, *Jn.* 17, 5, v. beorhtian.
Gebeorscipe, beorscipe, es; *m.* [beor *beer, strong drink*] *A drinking together, feast, entertainment, banquet*; convivium:—*Mt.* 23, 6.
Gebeot *a threatening*, *Elf. T.* p. 39, 12, v. beot.
Gebeotan *To threaten, try, beat*; minari:—*Ors.* 2, 4, v. beatan.
Gebeotung *a threatening, beating*, v. beotung.
Geberan *to bear*, *Ors.* 4, 1, v. beran.
Gebered *Moved, teased, steeped*; vexatus, maceratus:—*C. Mt.* 9, 36.
Geberhtan *to enlighten*, v. beorhtian.
Gebernan *to light, burn*, v. bærnan.
Gebétan *to make better, amend*, *Bt.* 39, 11, v. betan.
Gebetered *bettered, amended*, v. betrian.
Gebeðod *bathed, washed*, v. baðian.
Gebett *amended*, v. betan.
Gebette *Defended, walled*; muratæ:—*Num.* 13, 20.
Gebettung, e; *f. A bettering, amending, renewing, restoring*; emendatio:—*L. Athel.* 13.
Gebicgan; *p.* gebohte. *To buy*, *Past.* 59, 2, v. bycgan.
Gebicnian *to shew, indicate*, v. bicnian.
Gebicnigende, gebicnigendlic *Indicative, shewing*; indicativus:—*Elf. gr.* 21.
Gebicnung *A presage, prophecy*; præsagium, *Bd.*
Gebídan *to abide, remain, expect*, *Bt.* 38, 3, v. bidan.
Gebiddan, gebidan *to pray, worship, adore*, *Ex.* 32, 8, v. biddan.
Gebigan *to bend, turn*, *Elf. T.* p. 30, v. bigan.
Gebigednys, se; *f. A bending, declining, case*; declinatio:—*Elf. gr.* p. 17, 30.

Gebige [bigan *to bend*] *A case*; casus:—Nemnigendlic *nominative*; gestrinendlic, geagniendlic *genitive*; forgifendlic *dative*; wregendlic *accusative*; clypigendlic *vocative*; ætbredendlic gebige *ablative case*, *Elf. gr.* 7: *Som.* p. 6, 16.
Gebigð *buys*, *Mt.* 13, 44, v. bycgan.
y Gebind *A binding, bundle*; fasciculus:—*R.* 11.
Gebindan *to bind, feign, pretend*, *Ps.* 31, 12, v. bindan.
Gebirað, gebireð *happens, becomes*, v. gebyrian.
Gebirhtan; *pp.* gebirht. *To enlighten, illuminate*; illuminare:—*Bt.* 34, 5, 8.
Gebirigan *to taste*, v. onbirian.
Gebitered *made bitter*, v. biterian.
Geblædfæst; *adj.* [blæd *fruit*] *Fruitful*; fertilis:—*Cd.* 5.
Geblecte *destroyed*; exterminavit:—*C. Ps.* 79, 14.
Geblend *blinded*, v. blendian.
Geblendan; *p.* gebland, geblende, hi geblendon; *pp.* geblanden, geblonden. 1. *To* BLEND, *mix, mingle*; miscere. 2. *To stain, colour, corrupt*; inficere:—1. *Ors.* 4, 8: *Bt. R.* p. 155. 2. *Cot.* 112, v. blendan.
Gebleod *Of different colours, variegated*; versicolor:—*Prov.* 31.
Gebleow *blew*; *p. of* blawan.
Gebletsian; *p.* ode. *To bless, consecrate*, v. bletsian.
Geblinnan; *p.* geblann. *To cease*, v. blinnan.
Geblissian *to rejoice*, *Lk.* 15, 32, v. blissian.
Geblissung *rejoicing*, v. blissung.
Geblodgod; *part. Beblooded, blooded, covered with blood*; cruentatus:—*L. Hloth.* 8.
Geblonden *mixed*, v. geblendan.
Geblot *a sacrifice*, v. blot.
Geblowan *to blow, flourish*, v. blowan.
Gebocian, bocian; *p.* ode; *pp.* od [*Dut.* boeken] 1. *To book, register* or *enter in a book*; libro aliquid donare. 2. *To furnish with books*; instruere:—1. *Chr.* 854. 2. *Elf. ep.* 43.
Gebod *a command*, v. bod.
Gebodian *to command, tell, offer*, *L. Alf. pol.* 5, *Wilk.* p. 36, 8, v. bodian.
Gebodscipe *a commandment*, v. bodscipe.
Geboetan *to improve, amend*, v. betan.
Gebogen *subjected*, v. bugan.
Geboht *bought*, v. bycgan.
z Gebolgen *offended, angry*, v. belgan.
Geboned *like a bone*; osseus.
Geboren *born*, v. beran.
Geborgen *defended, safe*, v. beorgan.

Geborh-fæstan *to determine* or *fasten by a surety*, v. borhfæstan.
Geborsnung *corruption*, v. gebrosnung.
Gebræc *a noise*, *Cd.* 119, v. gebrec.
Gebræc *broke, struck down, destroyed*, v. brecan.
Gebræcseoc *a lunatic*, v. bræcseoc.
Gebrædan, gebrægan *to spread, draw out, pave, pretend, roast*, *Bd.* 5, 20, v. brædan.
Gebrægdas; *plu. m. Deceits, frauds*; fraudes:—*C. Mt.* 13, 22.
Gebrægdnys, se; *f. Craft, deceit*; astus:—*Cot.* 18.
Gebrec, gebræc *A noise, crashing, storm*; fragor:—*Bd.* 5, 1.
Gebredan; *p.* gebræd, hi gebrudon. *To enlarge, spread*, v. gebrædan, bredan.
Gebregan *to frighten*, v. bregean.
Gebreman *to make famous, honour*, v. breman.
Gebrengnis *Food, support*; victus:—*C. R. Mk.* 12, 44.
Gebrice *a breaking*, v. brice.
Gebridlian *to bridle in, restrain*, v. bridlian.
Gebrihted *clear, lucid.*
Gebringan *to bring*, v. bringan.
Gebroc *pain, affliction*, v. broc.
Gebrocad, gebroced, gebrocod *broken, afflicted*, v. brocian.
Gebrocen *broken*, v. brecan.
Gebrocen *exercised, discharged*, v. brucan.
Gebroht *brought*, v. bringan.
Gebroiden *placed.*
Gebrosnad, gebrosnod *corrupted*, v. brosnian.
Gebrosnung, e; *f. A decaying, corruption*; corruptio:—*Ps.* 15, 10.
Gebroðorscipe, es; *m. Brotherhip, brotherhood, fraternity*; fraternitas:—*Ors.* 3, 2.
Gebróðra, gebroðro, gebroðru; chiefly used as the *pl. of* broðor *brethren*, *Mt.* 1, 11.
Gebrotu, gebrote; *pl. Fragments*; fragmenta:—*Lk.* 9, 17.
a Gebrowen *cooked*, v. briwan.
Gebrúcan *to eat*, v. brucan.
Gebrysed *bruised, contrite*, v. brysan.
Gebúgan, he gebyhð; *p.* gebeáh, we gebugon; *pp.* gebogen. *To bow, bend, submit, to bend* or *swerve from, revolt*, *Jos.* 10, 4, v. bugan.
Gebúgian; *p.* gebúde; *pp.* gebúen, gebún. *To dwell, occupy, inhabit*; incolere:—*Bt.* 18, 1, v. búan.
Gebuh *departs from, declines, for* gebug *or* bug, v. bugan.

Gebenlic nunlike; vestalis Som

2 Gebenn an edict Cot 70 Lye v geban

3 Gebeogul flexible afraing; contentious C.R. Mt 5, 25

1) Gebeorge security defence Th. An

5 Gebeorlic safe, secure Th. An

Gebeotian to promise, vow, threaten Th. An

Gebend-wiglere, es; m a wizard; magus R. 4 Lye

Gebere a habit, state Som v gebær

Geberede hit happened it; accidit Bt 16, 2 R p 33 note c

10 Geberian competere C.R Ben 37 Lye

11 Gebesmed besmed bent, cracked; dinsatus Som

12 Gebeten beaten Lye v gebeaten

13 Gebeterung a better ing v gebeterung

14 Gebigean to bend bow Th. A. Leit 62 v bigan

Gebiled that hath bill or mouth; rostratus Som

2 Gebilegan take away Som v gebelgan

Gebeorscipe a feast Som v gebeorscipe

4 Gebired clothed, amictus Ben

5 Gebesgad seized; comprehensus Ben

6 2 Gebesnung, e f. An example, instruction, a lesson exemplum Som

v bisnung

7 Gebit a biting, grinding stridor Lye

Geblaud, commentatio

Bt 104 Lyn #741 2

Geblanden finished, spent; also coloured Som v geblandan

12 Geblegan to destroy exterminare Ben

11 Gebleyenad ulcerated blistered; ulceratus Som

13 Geblohtrescipe a cornrich ambitat 14 Lye

14 Gebolged disdained swollen Som

15 Gebolstrad bolstered up, defended, environed stipatus Som

Gebregan to frighten

Gebregednes fear Som a dreadness

Gebonn a proclamation Som Having p 93 Lye v. gebann

gebann

Gebrocod broiled; decoctus Som

17 Gebonnen proclaimed Cod. Ex p 117, 2 man v gebannan

Gebosmed bosomed sinuatus Cot 185

2 Gebotad bettered emended Chr 1093 v gebetan

3 Gebræc broke Cd 4 stripping v brecan

4 Gebræc, es; m a breaking, crash Th. An fragor fractio Som Cd 119 Th p 154, 24: Bes K 4512

5 Gebrecseocnes, se, f the falling sickness morbus comitialis Som v bræcseocnes

6 Gebrec noise pain Som

Ge brecan to exhibit ... to break small, crumble, friare Som

Gebredde broiled R 24, 42

Gebrengan to bring v gebringan

Ge brot fragment Som ... 4 v gebrot

16 Gebrocseoc-man a frantic man Bd 4, 3 v bræcseoc

Gebrodert taken away; sublatus Som

5 Gebrot a barn keeper; granarius Som

17 Gebrysednes, se a bruising: contusio Som

18 Gebryttan ... to break C. Ps 97, 14 v gebrittian

... kille ... us ... on ... na ... nunc ... tu ... atus ... d ... par

Gebunden bound Som v gebindan

[illegible] inhabited
3 Gebun-land, gebund-land inhabited land ors pref Lye Som

4 Gebard bearded v supl gebyrd

5 Geburnen burned v gebyrnan

~~Gebyrged bound~~

9 Gecend-limu genitalia Lye v gecynd-lim

6 Ge-capitulod headed; capitulatus Lye

6 Gebyldan pp gebyld [Ger bilden] to imagine, design, plan, devise, draw

[illegible] Th. An.
11 Gebylged disdained Som

Gebyrd, e; f also Gebyrdu, e; f Th. An

~~Gebyrdes; n Th. Apol.~~

Gebyrd
Gebyrded bearded Som Lye.

10 Gebyrdlice orderly [illegible] Ben v. endebyrdlice

11 Gebyrdo ~~[illegible]~~ Som [illegible] ~~[illegible]~~

v gebyrd

12 Gebyrelice becom [illegible] equally [illegible] co. [illegible] C Jn 4, 9

14 Gebyr-tid for gebyrd-tid nativity

1 Gebysmrung, e; f A deriding, mocking; derisio Som

2 Gebysnian to give an example C R Ben 45 Lye

[both edcs]

3 Gebytle, aedificium [illegible] II 38, 25

4 Gebytlung, e; f A building edifice; aedificium Som

8 Ge-cealfe, foetus. Som inqalu... Lye Lim II 743, 36

5 Gecance. A mocking stock ludibrium Som.

Gecahhetung, e; f loud laughing; ~~[illegible]~~ cachinnus Som

10 Gecenenys, se; f a delight; delectatio Som.

11 Gecennednys, se; f birth; nativitas Som

v gebatged
12 Gecigan invocare L. Ps. 19, 8 Lye

13 Gecigan to call Th. An v gecygan

14 Gecirred turned Som v gecerran

15 Geclæmian to smear [illegible] with treat[illegible] v clæmian

16 Geclænsung; e f a cleansing [illegible] 1288, 43 v geclænsung

17 Geclibt gathered together; collectus. Hand geclibt a clutched hand fist Som

Ge[illegible] to taste
Gebyrgan p de [illegible] 31, 10

18 Geclyfian to cleave, stick to, adhaerere Herb 166, 1 v supl clifan

19 Geclypian to call Th An Ben Lye Sint 54.60 v clypian

20 Geclyster, es; n A cluster; racemus Cot 24

Gecnilled beaten, sounded, Ancr. 1 v cnyllan

1 Gecnited tied; bound ligatus R Jn 11, 44

2 Gecnosu collisions Cot 49 v gescænednes

4 Gecnucian to knock v ge-cnocian

5 Gecnewan to knead stamp, grind; pinsere, subigere Som

6 Gecnycled knuckled crooked; obuncus, nodosus Som

7 Gecneordlic diligent [illegible]

v gecelfe
7 Gecnyclende knuckling obuncans Cot 146

Gecnyht tied C Jn 11, 44 v gecnitted

Gecnoslnes [illegible] B. 29

8 Gecnyrdnys study [illegible] Th. An v gecneordnys

9 Gecnyordnys diligent study Som v gecneordnys

10 Gecnyrdnys study Quadr 4. v gecneordnys

11 Gecocsnad cooked decoctus Som

20 Gecostnian to tempt prov. - v costnian

21 Gecrincan; p gecranc, we gecruncon to cringe, fall, die Th An Beo K 2419

(18)

Gebundenes, se; *f. An obligation;* obligatio :—*L. Ps.* 124, 5.

GEBUR, es; *m.* [*Plat.* buur *m*: in earlier time *a neighbour, a citizen;* now *a farmer, a peasant*: *Dut. Frs.* boer *m*: *Ger.* bauer *m*: in *Silesia* gebaur *m.* The *Old Franc.* and *Al.* writers designate by puarre, buara *an inhabitant,* and by gibura, giburo *a peasant, a farmer*: *Heb.* בר br *open fields, country.* From the *A.-S.* byan *to inhabit,* buan *to till*] *A husbandman, farmer, countryman,* BOOR; colonus :—*L. In.* 6.

Geburhscipe *a neighbourhood, village.*

Gebycgan *to buy,* v. bycgan.

Gebycnian *to beckon,* v. bicnian.

Gebydan *to abide, wait,* v. bidan, gebidan.

Gebyde, hi gebyedon *inhabited,* v. gebugian.

Gebygle; *adj. Subject, obedient;* subjectus :—Gebygle to donne *to make obedient, Chr.* 1091.

Gebyld *boldness, courage,* v. byld.

Gebyld; *adj. Bold, courageous;* audax :—Gebyld swiðe þurh God, *Jud.* 4, 14.

Gebylded *emboldened, animated,* v. byldan.

GEBYRD; *f.* 1. *A birth, origin, beginning, parentage, family, lineage;* nativitas, origo. 2. *Quality, nature, state, condition, opulence;* qualitas :— 1. Syn ealle men anra gebirda *all men are of one origin, L. Can. Edg.* 13. Be þam gebyrdum *concerning their families, Bt.* 30, 1. 2. By his gebyrdum *by his qualities, nature, Ors.* 1, 1.

Gebyrd; *adj. Birth, natal;* natalis :—On gebyrd dæge, *Mt.* 14, 6.

Gebyreð *bears, produces,* v. beran.

Gebyrgde *tasted,* v. byrgan, onbirian.

Gebyrged *buried,* v. birgan.

Gebyrhte *declared.*

Gebyrian, gebyrigan, gebiran; *p.* ede; *pp.* ed [*Dut.* gebeuren] *To happen, fall out, become, behove, concern, belong to;* often used impersonally. *It behoves, becomes, happens;* accidere, oportere :—Þat hit scyle gebyrian *that it may happen, Bt.* 40, 5.

b Gebyrigednes *a burial,* v. byrignes.

Gebyrmed; *adj.* BARMED, *fermented, leavened;* fermentatus :—*Ex.* 12, 15, 19.

Gebyrnan; *pp.* geburnen. *To burn, consume,* v. byrnan.

Gebyrned, gebyrnod *clothed with armour,* v. byrn.

Gebysgian; *pp.* od. *To occupy,* v. bysgian.

Gebysmerian *to deride,* v. bysmerian.

Gebysnung *an example,* v. bysnung.

Gebytla, gebytlu *Instruments, foundations;* fundamenta :—*Deut.* 6, 10.

Gebytlian *to build,* v. bytlian.

Gecælan *to cool,* v. cælan.

Gecænenis, gecænes *a calling, vocation,* v. gecigednes.

Gecænnan [cænnan *to know*] *To make himself known, to clear, purify;* manifestare :— *L. Hloth.* 2.

Gecafstrod *bridled, restrained,* v. cæfester.

Gecamp *warfare,* v. camp.

Geceapian; *p.* ode; *pp.* ed. *To buy, purchase;* emere :—*Ors.* 5, 7: *Bar.* p. 188, 12: *Gen.* 43, 21.

Gecearfan *To kill, cut off* or *up;* interficere :—*R. Mt.* 3, 10.

Geceas *chose,* v. ceosan.

Gecegan, geceigan, gecigean *to call, to call together, Gen.* 16, 11, v. cyan.

Gecelan *to cool,* v. acolian.

Gecele *an icicle,* v. gicel.

Gecelfe cy *an in-calved cow, a cow great with calf, Gen.* 33, 13.

Gecelnys *coolness,* v. celnes.

Gecenned *begotten, born, brought forth,* v. cennan.

Geceolan *to cool,* v. acolian.

Geceosan *to choose;* geceas *chose,* v. ceosan.

Gecerran; *p.* de; *pp.* ed. *To turn, return, Bt.* 35, 1, v. cerran.

Gecerringc *a turning,* v. cer.

Gecid *strife,* v. cid.

Gecidan; *pp.* en. *To chide,* v. cidan.

Gecigednes, se; *f. A calling, profession;* vocatio:—*Bd.* 5, 12.

Gecind, *a kind, nature, sort, generation, Gen.* 7, 3, v. gecynd.

Gecist *chooses,* v. ceosan.

Gecladed; *adj. Clothed;* vestitus :—*C. Mk.* 5, 15.

Geclænsian *to purify, cleanse,* v. clænsian.

c Geclænsung *a cleansing,* v. clænsung.

Geclæsnian *to cleanse,* v. clænsian.

Gecleofede *cleaved to,* v. clifian.

Geclibs, gecleps, geclebs, geclysp. *A clamour, outcry; clamor* :—*L. Eccl. Alf.* 41.

Geclungne; *adj.* CLINGING; adhærens :—*Cod. Exon.* 59, *a.*

Geclutod; *adj.* [clut *a patch*] CLOUTED, *patched, nailed;* consutus, clavatus :—*Jos.* 9, 5. Gesceod mid gecludedum scon *shod with clouted shoes, Dial.* 1, 4.

Geclypode, *ycleped, called, invited,* v. clypian.

Gecnæw *knowledge, witness.*

Gecnawan, he gecnæwð; *p.* gecneow. *To know, Bt.* 23, v. oncnawan.

Gecnedan, cnedan, cnædan; *pp.* gecneden; *v. a.* [*Plat. Dut.* kneden: *Frs.* knetten, knettjen: *Ger.* kneten: *Dan.* knede: *Swed.* knåda: *Icel.* gnyda] *To mix, mingle, spread, knead;* depsere :—Gecned nu hrædlice þri sestras smedeman, *Gen.* 18, 6. Gecneden sealf *cataplasma, Cot.* 209.

Gecneord *Intentive, diligent;* intentus :—*Bd.* 4, 28.

Gecneordlæcan *to study, be diligent,* v. cneordlæcan.

Gecneordlice; *adv. Diligently;* studiose :—*Hom.* 8. *Jan.*

Gecneordnys, se; *f. Study, diligence;* studium :—*Ps.* 105, 28.

Ge-cneowian *to bend the knee,* v. cneowian.

Ge-cnocian; *pp.* oced, uced. *To knock, beat,* v. cnucian.

Gecnoden *given, dedicated,* v. cnodan.

Gecnyrdlæcan *to study,* v. cneordlæcan.

Gecnysan; *p.* þu gecnysydyst; *pp.* gecnysed. *To beat down, afflict,* v. cnysan.

Gecnyt, ge-cnytt *knitted, fastened, tied,* v. cnytan.

Gecope, gecoplic *fit, proper,* v. coplic.

Gecoren *chosen, select, beloved, Deut.* 3, 25, v. ceosan.

Gecorenes *a choice,* v. corenes.

Gecorfen *carved,* v. ceorfan.

Gecostan *to prove, try,* v. costian.

Gecostnes, se; *f. A trial;* probatio :—*Bd.* 3, 19.

Gecræft *art,* v. cræft.

Gecræftgad *made, fabricated,* v. cræftan.

Gecrangan; *p.* gecrang, gecrong, gecrung. *To die,* v. crangan.

Gecristnad, gecristod *christened,* v. cristnian.

Gecuelled *quelled, killed,* v. cwellan.

d Gecumen *come, derived,* v. cuman.

Gecundelic; *adj. Natural;* naturalis :—*Bt.* 14, 2.

Gecunnian *to try, Bd.* 5, 6, v. cunnan.

Gecure, gecuron *chose;* gecoren *chosen,* v. ceosan.

Gecuð *known,* v. cunnan.

Gecwæðan, gecweðan *to say,* v. cwæðan.

Gecwed, gecwid, gecwyde *a word, command,* v. cwide.

Gecweman *to please, Mk.* 15, 15, v. cweman.

Gecweme; *adj. Pleasant, pleasing, grateful, acceptable, fit;* gratus :—*Gen.* 6, 8: *Jn.* 8, 29.

Gecwemedlic *well pleased.*

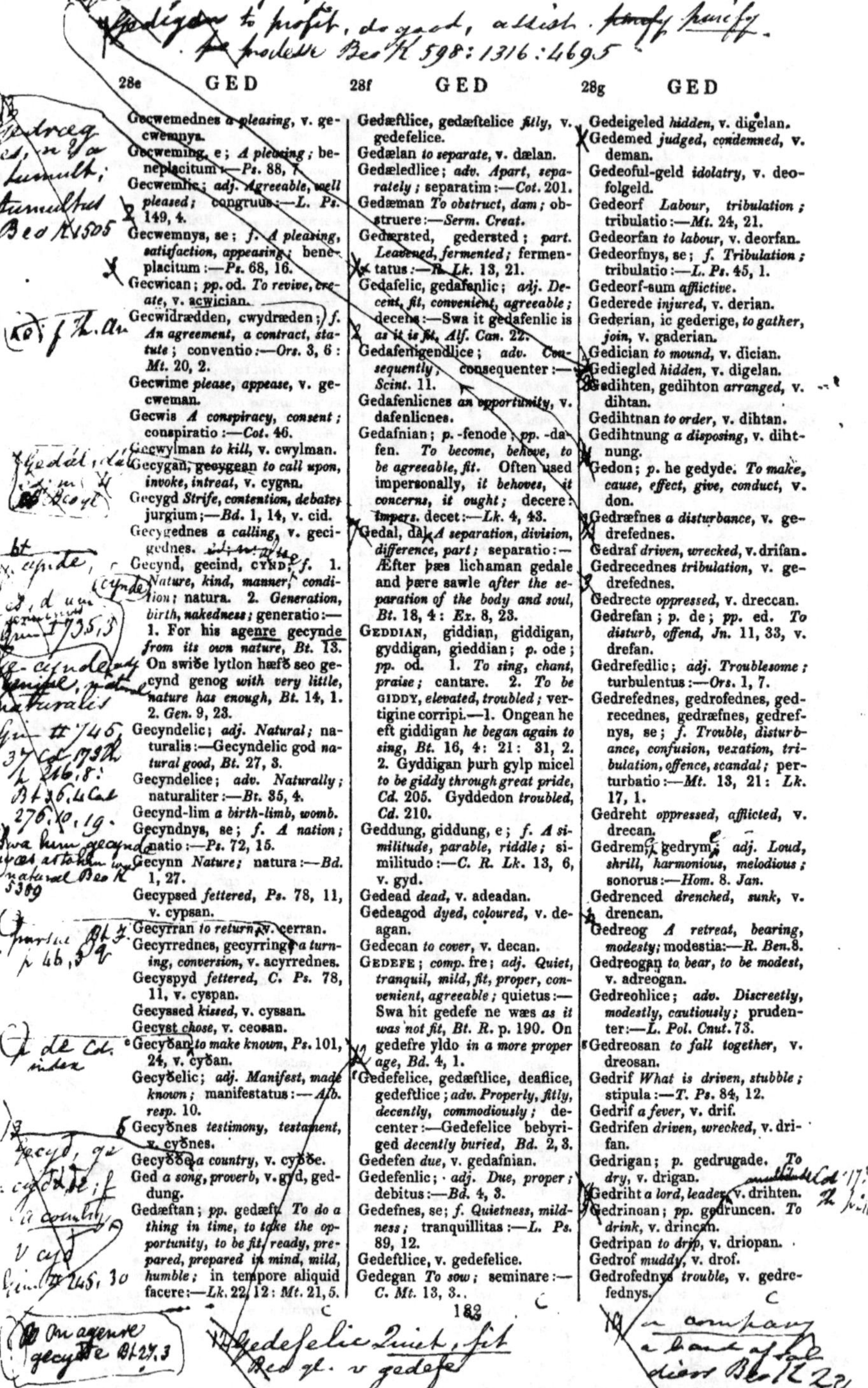

Gecwemednes *a pleasing*, v. gecwemnys.

Gecweming, e; *A pleasing; beneplacitum*:—*Ps.* 88, 7.

Gecwemlic; *adj. Agreeable, well pleased*; congruus:—*L. Ps.* 149, 4.

Gecwemnys, se; *f. A pleasing, satisfaction, appeasing*; beneplacitum:—*Ps.* 68, 16.

Gecwican; *pp.* od. *To revive, create*, v. acwician.

Gecwidrædden, cwydrædden; *f. An agreement, a contract, statute*; conventio:—*Ors.* 3, 6: *Mt.* 20, 2.

Gecwime *please, appease*, v. gecweman.

Gecwis *A conspiracy, consent*; conspiratio:—*Cot.* 46.

Gecwylman *to kill*, v. cwylman.

Gecygan, geeygean *to call upon, invoke, intreat*, v. cygan.

Gecygd *Strife, contention, debate*; jurgium;—*Bd.* 1, 14, v. cid.

Gecygednes *a calling*, v. gecigednes.

Gecynd, gecind, CYND; *f.* 1. *Nature, kind, manner, condition*; natura. 2. *Generation, birth, nakedness*; generatio:—1. For his agenre gecynde *from its own nature*, *Bt.* 13. On swiðe lytlon hæfð seo gecynd genog *with very little, nature has enough*, *Bt.* 14, 1. 2. *Gen.* 9, 23.

Gecyndelic; *adj. Natural*; naturalis:—Gecyndelic god *natural good*, *Bt.* 27, 3.

Gecyndelice; *adv. Naturally*; naturaliter:—*Bt.* 35, 4.

Gecynd-lim *a birth-limb, womb.*

Gecyndnys, se; *f. A nation*; natio:—*Ps.* 72, 15.

Gecynn *Nature*; natura:—*Bd.* 1, 27.

Gecypsed *fettered*, *Ps.* 78, 11, v. cypsan.

Gecyrran *to return*, v. cerran.

Gecyrrednes, gecyrring *a turning, conversion*, v. acyrrednes.

Gecyspyd *fettered*, *C. Ps.* 78, 11, v. cyspan.

Gecyssed *kissed*, v. cyssan.

Gecyst *chose*, v. ceosan.

Gecyðan *to make known*, *Ps.* 101, 24, v. cyðan.

Gecyðelic; *adj. Manifest, made known*; manifestatus:—*Alb. resp.* 10.

Gecyðnes *testimony, testament*, v. cyðnes.

Gecyððe *a country*, v. cyððe.

Ged *a song, proverb*, v. gyd, geddung.

Gedæftan; *pp.* gedæft. *To do a thing in time, to take the opportunity, to be fit, ready, prepared, prepared in mind, mild, humble*; in tempore aliquid facere:—*Lk.* 22, 12: *Mt.* 21, 5.

Gedæftlice, gedæftelice *fitly*, v. gedefelice.

Gedælan *to separate*, v. dælan.

Gedæledlice; *adv. Apart, separately*; separatim:—*Cot.* 201.

Gedæman *To obstruct, dam*; obstruere:—*Serm. Creat.*

Gedærsted, gedersted; *part. Leavened, fermented*; fermentatus:—*R. Lk.* 13, 21.

Gedafelic, gedafenlic; *adj. Decent, fit, convenient, agreeable*; decens:—Swa it gedafenlic is *as it is fit*, *Alf. Can.* 22.

Gedafenigendlice; *adv. Consequently*; consequenter:—*Scint.* 11.

Gedafenlicnes *an opportunity*, v. dafenlicnes.

Gedafnian; *p.* -fenode; *pp.* -dafen. *To become, behove, to be agreeable, fit.* Often used impersonally, *it behoves, it concerns, it ought*; decere: *impers.* decet:—*Lk.* 4, 43.

Gedal, dal; *A separation, division, difference, part*; separatio:—Æfter þæs lichaman gedale and þære sawle *after the separation of the body and soul*, *Bt.* 18, 4: *Ex.* 8, 23.

GEDDIAN, giddian, giddigan, gyddigan, gieddian; *p.* ode; *pp.* od. 1. *To sing, chant, praise*; cantare. 2. *To be* GIDDY, *elevated, troubled*; vertigine corripi.—1. Ongean he eft giddigan *he began again to sing*, *Bt.* 16, 4: 21: 31, 2. 2. Gyddigan þurh gylp micel *to be giddy through great pride*, *Cd.* 205. Gyddedon *troubled*, *Cd.* 210.

Geddung, giddung, e; *f. A similitude, parable, riddle*; similitudo:—*C. R. Lk.* 13, 6, v. gyd.

Gedead *dead*, v. adeadan.

Gedeagod *dyed, coloured*, v. deagan.

Gedecan *to cover*, v. decan.

GEDEFE; *comp.* fre; *adj. Quiet, tranquil, mild, fit, proper, convenient, agreeable*; quietus:—Swa hit gedefe ne wæs *as it was not fit*, *Bt. R.* p. 190. On gedefre yldo *in a more proper age*, *Bd.* 4, 1.

Gedefelice, gedæftlice, deaflice, gedeftlice; *adv. Properly, fitly, decently, commodiously*; decenter:—Gedefelice bebyriged *decently buried*, *Bd.* 2, 3.

Gedefen *due*, v. gedafnian.

Gedefenlic; *adj. Due, proper*; debitus:—*Bd.* 4, 3.

Gedefnes, se; *f. Quietness, mildness*; tranquillitas:—*L. Ps.* 89, 12.

Gedeftlice, v. gedefelice.

Gedegan *To sow*; seminare:—*C. Mt.* 13, 3.

Gedeigeled *hidden*, v. digelan.

Gedemed *judged, condemned*, v. deman.

Gedeoful-geld *idolatry*, v. deofolgeld.

Gedeorf *Labour, tribulation*; tribulatio:—*Mt.* 24, 21.

Gedeorfan *to labour*, v. deorfan.

Gedeorfnys, se; *f. Tribulation*; tribulatio:—*L. Ps.* 45, 1.

Gedeorf-sum *afflictive.*

Gederede *injured*, v. derian.

Gederian, ic gederige, *to gather, join*, v. gaderian.

Gedician *to mound*, v. dician.

Gediegled *hidden*, v. digelan.

Gedihten, gedihton *arranged*, v. dihtan.

Gedihtnan *to order*, v. dihtan.

Gedihtnung *a disposing*, v. dihtnung.

Gedon; *p.* he gedyde. *To make, cause, effect, give, conduct*, v. don.

Gedræfnes *a disturbance*, v. gedrefednes.

Gedraf *driven, wrecked*, v. drifan.

Gedrecednes *tribulation*, v. gedrefednes.

Gedrecte *oppressed*, v. dreccan.

Gedrefan; *p.* de; *pp.* ed. *To disturb, offend*, *Jn.* 11, 33, v. drefan.

Gedrefedlic; *adj. Troublesome*; turbulentus:—*Ors.* 1, 7.

Gedrefednes, gedrofednes, gedrecednes, gedræfnes, gedrefnys, se; *f. Trouble, disturbance, confusion, vexation, tribulation, offence, scandal*; perturbatio:—*Mt.* 13, 21: *Lk.* 17, 1.

Gedreht *oppressed, afflicted*, v. drecan.

Gedrem, gedrym; *adj. Loud, shrill, harmonious, melodious*; sonorus:—*Hom.* 8. *Jan.*

Gedrenced *drenched, sunk*, v. drencan.

Gedreog *A retreat, bearing, modesty*; modestia:—*R. Ben.* 8.

Gedreogan *to bear, to be modest*, v. adreogan.

Gedreohlice; *adv. Discreetly, modestly, cautiously*; prudenter:—*L. Pol. Cnut.* 73.

Gedreosan *to fall together*, v. dreosan.

Gedrif *What is driven, stubble*; stipula:—*T. Ps.* 84, 12.

Gedrif *a fever*, v. drif.

Gedrifen *driven, wrecked*, v. drifan.

Gedrigan; *p.* gedrugade. *To dry*, v. drigan.

Gedriht *a lord, leader*, v. drihten.

Gedrincan; *pp.* gedruncen. *To drink*, v. drincan.

Gedripan *to drip*, v. driopan.

Gedrof *muddy*, v. drof.

Gedrofednys *trouble*, v. gedrefednys.

Gecwemlic proper; gemæne v cwemendlic
gecwylmod killed v gecwylled

Gecydde declared said Som v gecydan
Gecygendlic Appellative appellativus Som

2 Gecwemlice adv agreeably, pleasingly Th. An

3 Gecwedan to say Th. An Ben v cwedan

Gecwide a word Ben v gecwed
Gecwidung an to bicker tricare Ben v [illegible]

Gecynd kind Th. An v cynan

Gecynd controversy Ben v gecynd

Gecyndelic native, a kin Th. An

Gecynd-bóc book of generation Genesis Th. An

Sunnon pæt gecynde intra [illegible] Hickes Diss p 51 Lye

10 Gecyndelic-lim the natural member genitals Som v gecynd-lim

11 Gecyrnad corned; salted sale condition Som

12 Gecyssan to kiss Bos K 3736 v cyssan

13 Gecypnisse cyþan to testify Th. An

Gecwoeme pleasant Lye C R Jn 8,29 v gecweme

Gecwoeden said dictus C Mk 15,17 Lye v gecwadan

Gecwyd a condition Ben v gecwed

Gedafned ought; oportet Th. An v gedafnian

Gedaledness, se f A divorce; divortium; secare

Gedafan to become Som Gen 11 42,37 v gedafnian

Gedafene an to be fitting

Gedafen agreed, due Th. An gedafan, v gedafnian
debitus, decent, conveniens Cot Lye

Gedafsum Agreeing, becoming; conveniens Gen 11 42, 38 Lye

Gecynd-riht natural right Th. 222 — Gecynde spræc native speech v lingua L. 101 Lye

Gedd song, cantilena Som v ged

Gedeaded dead C Mk 7,10 v gedead

Gedeawe dewy Ben v deawig

Gedeof perfect R Mt 5,48 v gedefe

Gededed killed C Lk 23,32 v gedead

Gediernan to lie hid; delitere Cot 65 Lye

Gedrihpa prudentia Lit. Const p 148, 2 Man

Gedrimere a knave, villain; nebulo Som

Gedoefe perfect C Mk 5,48 v gedefe

Gedofen dived, ducked v supl gedafan

Gedelf a digging Th. An v dup delf

Gedeman to judge Th. An v deman

Geden for gedydon corned [illegible] Th p 41.23 v don, geda
Th. An v gedafnian

Gedafenlice adv Fitly, properly, decently Th. An

Gedicht a dictate a dictatum
Gedihtan to order Som Ben v dihtan

Gedreas overthrew Cd 167 Th p 209, 15 v gedreosan

Gedrecan to vex, afflict Th. An v drecan

Gedrencte drowned Cd 167 Th p 209, 16 v of-gedrincan

Gedeaf dived v Lye gedeafan

Gedreog drying, rubbing Th. An p 80, 12

Gedremere melodious; consonus Som

Gedreoh sober sobrius Som

Gedryht a ford, multitude, host Cd 118 Th p 148, 26 v driht
Gedrinc, es m Drink drinking Th. An

Gedritan cacare Med. ex Quadr 11, 9 Ben Lye

citractus Som
Gedruncnian to sink
c. Ke 57 Ben
Ge-dryhta convelitor
... II 7. 5
[40
Ge-dryme consonus
... II ... v. Sh. ge-dreme Ge-dwola

Gedrecen driven Som
gedrefen
Gedufan, p gedeaf ... gedofen ... ge-dofen

Gedufan sceolun must
dive ... 213. ... 266. 34
7 Ge-dwimor ... manifestatio ... 89. 12
8 Gedwimor a phantasy
Elf ... v gedwymer 54
Gedwola an er...
10 Gedwild, es, n Error
heresy v gedwola
11 Gedwimorlic ... in a fantastic or illu...
Som manner Th. An
Gedwola an, m
heretic v gedwolman
15 Gedwollic erroneous
erring; erroneus Som
16 Gedwyld an error
Som v gedwild
17 Gedwyldlic erroneous
Som v suppl gedwollic
18 Gedyppan to dip
Som v dyppan

Ge-dwola
Gedwolda
an error v
Ge-dwola

I worship Th. An
Geeadmettan to worship
adore Th. An v geeadmedan
2 Geeadmedian dignare
... 2. 2 Lye Ben
... Cd. Th 222
Gedwyldlic erroneous Som
Gedwollic
Geeaht added, ad
dictus ... 9
2 Geearwian p de ... to prepare
Th. An
5 Ge-eadmodan
to vouchsafe Th. An
Geedlasan to restore; ...
Ge-edlian to renew;
renovare Som
Ge-edstadelian to
re-establish Th. Apol
v edstadelian
Geedprawen twisted
again; retortus Som
Geeducian
Ge-edwistade brought
... 2. 2
Geefenlæcestre an f
... imitatrix
Geefenhtan Th. An
Geefenlæcing an imitation
imitatio R Conc in Eph
Geefola a little cheek
Som v geaflas
18 Geefstan to hasten
accelerare ... 30. 2

2 Geenegod careful
solicitus Som
3 Geendebrednan to set
in order, Cdk 1. 1 v Lye ge-
ende byrdan

Geearnian to deserve
earn Som v ge-earnian

5 Ge-epian to breathe
spirare id
6 Ge-euenlæcan to
equal ... 36. 1 v ge-efen
læcan
Geedcucian, p ode; pp
od to revive; reviviscere ... 35 Lye Som
Geedlæcan to repeat
repetere ... 9 Lye Ben
v edlæcan
Geedleanend, es m
restituere ... 15. 52
... remunerator
Som
Gefæder a gaffer;
godfather; compater
Som
Gefægen joyful Som
fægen
Gefægerian to adorn
ornare Som
Gefærnyss ... f a trans
migratio Som
Gefangen taken
(prisoner) Th. An
v fon
Gefaran to ex
perience, suffer
Th. Apol

Gefælnysse f. a passage
transmigratio C Mt 1. 12
19 Gedyrstlice rashly
temere Som v dyrstelice
20 Gedyrstnes boldness
c.d. Ben 69 v gedyrstignes
15 Geefesod shaved Som
v geefsod
16 Geefned evened
4.29 v efn

Gedrym *harmonious*, v. gedrem.
Gedrync *drink, drinking together*, v. drinc.
Gedrysned *vanished, extinguished*, v. drysnian.
Gedryt *a lord*, v. gedriht.
Gedufian, dufian, gedyfð; *p.* gedeaf, we gedufon; *pp.* gedofen, gedyfed. *To plunge in water, to duck, sink, dive, be drowned;* mergere:—He wearð gedofen, *Mt.* 14, 30: *Ors.* 1, 7.
Gedurfon *perished*, v. deorfan.
Gedwælan, gedwelan, gedwellan; *p.* gedwealde; *pp.* gedweled. *To deceive*, *Bt.* 33, 3, v. dwelian.
Gedwola, gedweola, gedweolda, gedwild, gedwyld, DWOLA, dwala, an; *m. An error, deceit, imposture, heresy;* error:—Se mennisca gedwola *the human error*, *Bt.* 33, 2. On gedwolan gelædde, *Mt.* 24, 24: *Gen.* 21, 14.
Gedwolen; *adj. Wandering, erroneous;* erraticus:—*Cd.* 91.
Gedwol-goda *false gods, idols.*
Gedwol-man, gedwol-mon *an erring man, an impostor, a heretic.*
Gedwolode *erred, wandered*, v. dwelian.
Gedwolsum; *adj. Erroneous;* erroneus:—*Elf. pref. Gen.*
Gedwol-þing *an erroneous thing, deceit, imposture.*
Gedwymer, gedwimor. 1. *A phantasy, false representation;* phantasma. 2. *A juggler;* præstigiator:—1. *L. pol. Cnut.* 5. 2. *Jud.* 15.
Gedwymorlic; *adj. Like a juggler, illusive;* phantasticus:—*Dial.* 2, 10.
Gedygdan, *for* gedydon, dydon *did, effected, escaped*, *Chr.* 978, v. gedon.
Gedyn *a clang, loud sound*, v. dyne.
Gedynged *dunged*, v. dyngan.
Gedyre *a door-post*, v. duru.
Gedyrfsum *Afflictive;* calamitosus, *Lye.*
Gedyrneð *shall hide; pp.* gedyrned. *Hidden*, v. dyrnan.
Gedyrstelice *boldly*, v. dyrstelice.
Gedyrstig *bold*, v. dyrstig.
Gedyrstigan *To dare, presume;* audere:—*Bd.* 5, 21.
Gedyrstignes *boldness*, v. dyrstignes.
Gedyrstlæcean; *pp.* gedyrstlæht. *To dare*, v. dyrstlæcan.
Gedysig *foolish*, v. dysi.
Gee, geeac *yea, yes*, v. gea.
Geeacnian ic geeacnige; *p.* geeacnode, we geeacnodon; *pp.* geeacnod. *To conceive, to be pregnant, bring forth, produce, add, increase;* concipere:—Elizabeð his wif geeacnode, *Lk.* 1, 24. Þu on innoðe geeacnast, *Lk.* 1, 31. Ic hine bletsige and geeacnige, *Gen.* 17, 20: *Jud.* 4, 1, v. eacnian.
Geeacnung, eacnung, e; *f. A conceiving, conception;* conceptio:—*Gen.* 3, 16.
Geeadmedan, geeaðmedan, he geeadmedeð; *p.* medde, mette; *pp.* moded, met; *v. a.* [ead *happiness;* eað *mild;* mod *mind*] *To be humble, to become humble, adore;* humiliare:—Hine to him geeaðmedde, *Mt.* 8, 2: 18, 4: 23, 12. Geeadmedum þe ealle mægða, *Gen.* 27, 29: *Jud.* 11, 33.
Geeadmoded *humbled*, v. eadmodan.
Geeadmodlice *humbly*, v. eadmodlice.
Geeædleænian, ic geædleænige *to repay, reward*, v. edleænan.
Geeærfoðod *troubled*, v. eærfoðian.
Geealden *grown old*, v. ealdian.
Geealgian *to defend.*
Geeane *yeaned*, *Gen.* 33, 13, v. eanian.
Geeardod *dwelt*, v. eardian.
Geearnian *to earn, deserve*, *Bt.* 13, v. earnian.
Geearnung *merit*, v. earnung.
Geeaðmodad *deigned, vouchsafed.*
Geeawian *to shew.*
Geebalsadon *they blasphemed*, v. ebalsan.
Geebbod *ebbed*, v. ebban.
Geeced, geecte *increased*, *Bt.* 31, 1, v. ecan.
Geedcenned *Regenerated;* regeneratus:—*R. Jn.* 3, 5.
Geedcucude, geedcucod *revived*, v. edcucian.
Geedleanian *to reward, renew, requit*, v. edleænan.
Geedleht *repeated*, v. edlæcan.
Geedniwian *to renew, restore*, *Mt.* 17, 11, v. edniwian.
Geedstaðelung *repairing*, v. edstaðelung.
Geedstaðolian *to restore*, v. edstaðelian.
Geedwyrpen *improved, revived.*
Geefenlæcan *to be like*, *Mt.* 6, 8, v. efenlæcan.
Geefsod *shaved*, *Jud.* 16, 16, v. efsian.
Geegesad *frightened*, v. egesian.
Geegian *to excite*, v. eggian.
Geegled *troubled*, v. eglian.
Geegsode, geegsod *frightened*, v. egesian.
Geeld, geelded *put off*, v. eldan.
Geelnode *contended*, v. elnian.
Geembehtan, geambihtan *to minister*, v. embehtan.
Geemnet *equals*, v. emnian.
Geemnittan *to equal*, v. emnyttan.
Geende *an end*, v. ende.
Geendebyrdan *to set in order*, *Lk.* 1, 1, v. endebyrdan.
Geendian, ENDIAN; *p.* ode; *pp.* od; *v. a. To* END, *finish;* finire:—*Lk.* 14, 30. Ic geendige on heom, *Deut.* 32, 23. Geendode his dagas, *Jud.* 3, 11.
Geendung *an end, finish, death*, *Gen.* 6, 13, v. endung.
Geengd, geenged *anxious, sad*, v. ange.
Geeode *overcome, vanquished, happened*, v. gegangan.
Geeofot *a debt*, v. eofot.
Geeorsod *enraged*, v. yrsian.
Geeowian *to shew, discover*, *Bt.* 39, 8, v. ywan.
Geerod *ploughed*, v. erian.
Gees *geese; pl. of* gós.
Geeten *eaten*, v. etan.
Geeðcucigan *to revive*, v. edcucian.
Gef *if*, *Bt.* 36, 4, v. gif.
Gefa *an enemy*, v. fah.
Gefadian *to set in order;* gefadod, gefæd *arranged, ordered*, v. fadan.
Gefadung *a disposing*, v. fadung.
Gefæde *in order*, v. gefadian.
Gefædren *paternal*, v. fæderen.
Gefægnian *to rejoice*, v. fægnian.
Gefægnung *a joy, an exultation*, v. fægnung.
Gefægon *united*, v. gefegan.
Gefælan *to overturn*, v. afælan.
Gefælsian; *p.* ode. *To recompense, expiate;* expiare:—*Cod. Ex.* 10, a.
Gefær *a journey, going*, *Ps.* 104, 36, v. fær.
Gefæran *To go, to act;* proficisci:—*L. Can. Edg. poen.* 12, v. faran.
Gefærreden, gefærscipe, geferscipe *a society, company, college*, v. geferræden.
Gefæst, gefæsted *fasted*, v. fæstan.
Gefæstan *to commit*, v. befæstan.
Gefæstnian *to fix, fasten, confirm, betroth*, *Ors.* 5, 13, v. afæstnian.
Gefætian *to fetch, send for*, v. fetian.
Gefætnodest *hast fattened;* gefætted *fattened*, v. fættian.
Gefagen *glad*, v. fægen.
Gefagenian, gefagnian *to rejoice*, *Lk.* 1, 14, v. fagennian.
Gefah, gefahmon *an enemy*, v. fah, fagmon.
Gefandod *tried*, v. afandian.
Gefara *a companion*, *Bd.* 1, 15, v. gefera.
Gefaran *to go, proceed, depart, die*, *Num.* 11, 31, v. faran.
Gefe *a gift*, *Bd.* 2, 13, v. gifu.
Gefeá, FEA, an; *m. Joy, gladness, glory, favour;* gaudium:—*Jn.* 3, 29: 15, 11. On gefean *with joy*, *Ps.* 20, 6.

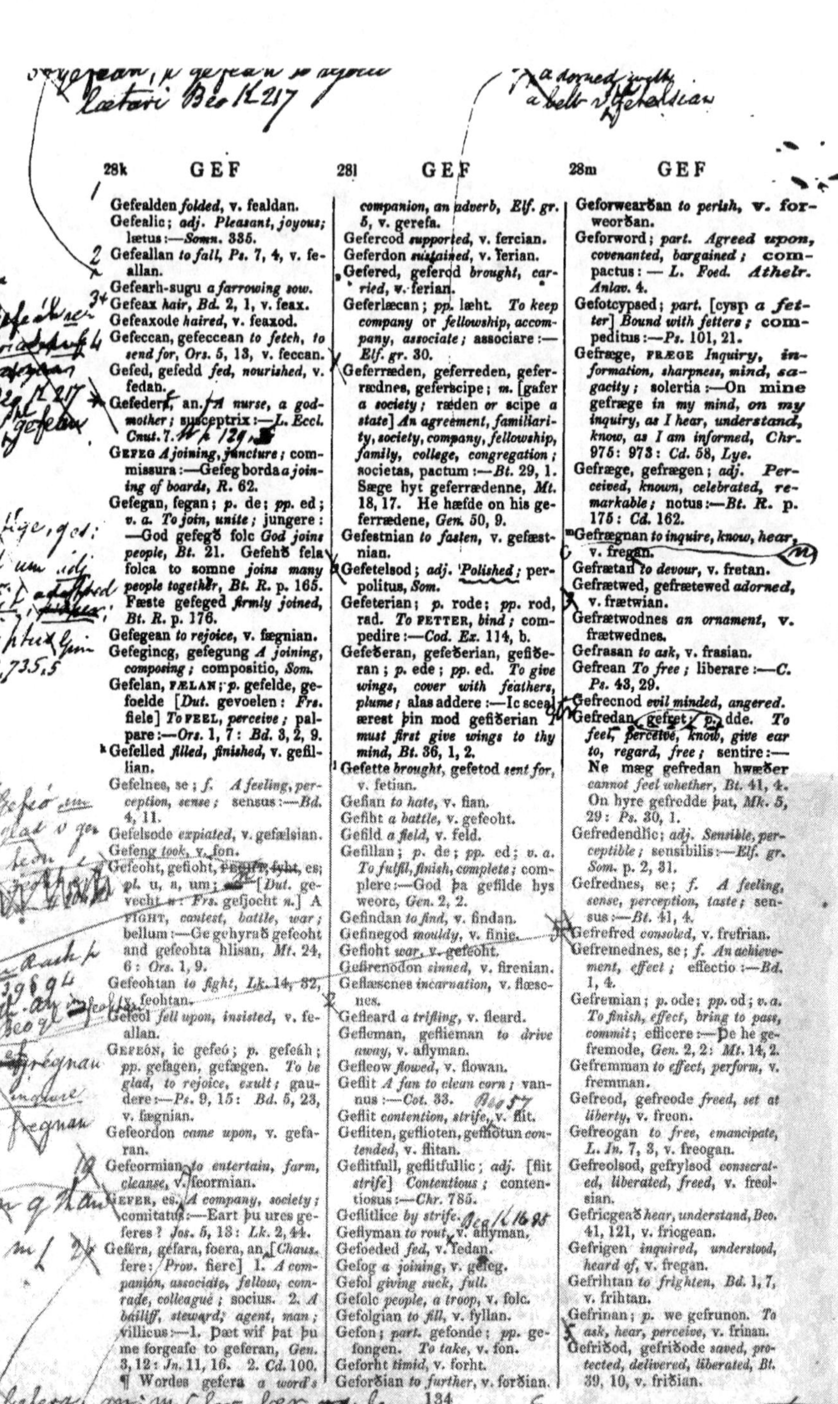

Gefealden *folded*, v. fealdan.
Gefealic; *adj. Pleasant, joyous*; lætus:—*Somn.* 335.
Gefeallan *to fall*, *Ps.* 7, 4, v. feallan.
Gefearh-sugu *a farrowing sow.*
Gefeax *hair*, *Bd.* 2, 1, v. feax.
Gefeaxode *haired*, v. feaxod.
Gefeccan, gefeccean *to fetch, to send for*, *Ors.* 5, 13, v. feccan.
Gefed, gefedd *fed, nourished*, v. fedan.
Gefedera, an. *A nurse, a god-mother*; susceptrix:—*L. Eccl. Cnut.* 7.
GEFEG *A joining, juncture*; commissura:—Gefeg borda *a joining of boards*, *R.* 62.
Gefegan, fegan; *p.* de; *pp.* ed; *v. a. To join, unite*; jungere:—God gefegð folc *God joins people*, *Bt.* 21. Gefehð fela folca to somne *joins many people together*, *Bt. R.* p. 165. Fæste gefeged *firmly joined*, *Bt. R.* p. 176.
Gefegean *to rejoice*, v. fægnian.
Gefegincg, gefegung *A joining, composing*; compositio, *Som.*
Gefelan, FÆLAN; *p.* gefelde, gefoelde [*Dut.* gevoelen: *Frs.* fiele] *To* FEEL, *perceive*; palpare:—*Ors.* 1, 7: *Bd.* 3, 2, 9.
k Gefelled *filled, finished*, v. gefillian.
Gefelnes, se; *f. A feeling, perception, sense*; sensus:—*Bd.* 4, 11.
Gefelsode *expiated*, v. gefælsian.
Gefeng *took*, v. fon.
Gefeoht, gefioht, FEOHT, fyht, es; *pl.* u, a, um; [*Dut.* gevecht *n.*: *Frs.* gefjocht *n.*] A FIGHT, *contest, battle, war*; bellum:—Ge gehyrað gefeoht and gefeohta hlisan, *Mt.* 24, 6: *Ors.* 1, 9.
Gefeohtan *to fight*, *Lk.* 14, 32, v. feohtan.
Gefeol *fell upon, insisted*, v. feallan.
GEFEÓN, ic gefeó; *p.* gefeah; *pp.* gefagen, gefægen. *To be glad, to rejoice, exult*; gaudere:—*Ps.* 9, 15: *Bd.* 5, 23, v. fægnian.
Gefeordon *came upon*, v. gefaran.
Gefeormian *to entertain, farm, cleanse*, v. feormian.
GEFER, es, *A company, society*; comitatus:—Eart þu ures geferes? *Jos.* 5, 13: *Lk.* 2, 44.
Gefera, gefara, foera, an, [*Chaus.* fere: *Prov.* fiere] 1. *A companion, associate, fellow, comrade, colleague*; socius. 2. *A bailiff, steward, agent, man*; villicus:—1. Þæt wif þat þu me forgeafe to geferan, *Gen.* 3, 12: *Jn.* 11, 16. 2. *Cd.* 100. ¶ Wordes gefera *a word's companion, an adverb*, *Elf. gr.* 5, v. gerefa.
Gefercod *supported*, v. fercian.
Geferdon *sustained*, v. ferian.
Gefered, geferod *brought, carried*, v. ferian.
Geferlæcan; *pp.* læht. *To keep company* or *fellowship, accompany, associate*; associare:—*Elf. gr.* 30.
Geferræden, geferreden, geferrædnes, geferscipe; *m.* [gafer *a society*; ræden *or* scipe *a state*] *An agreement, familiarity, society, company, fellowship, family, college, congregation*; societas, pactum:—*Bt.* 29, 1. Sæge hyt geferrædenne, *Mt.* 18, 17. He hæfde on his geferrædene, *Gen.* 50, 9.
Gefestnian *to fasten*, v. gefæstnian.
Gefetelsod; *adj. Polished*; perpolitus, *Som.*
Gefeterian; *p.* rode; *pp.* rod, rad. *To* FETTER, *bind*; compedire:—*Cod. Ex.* 114, b.
Gefeðeran, gefeðerian, gefiðeran; *p.* ede; *pp.* ed. *To give wings, cover with feathers, plume*; alas addere:—Ic sceal ærest þin mod gefiðerian *I must first give wings to thy mind*, *Bt.* 36, 1, 2.
l Gefette *brought*, gefetod *sent for*, v. fetian.
Gefian *to hate*, v. fian.
Gefiht *a battle*, v. gefeoht.
Gefild *a field*, v. feld.
Gefillan; *p.* de; *pp.* ed; *v. a. To fulfil, finish, complete*; complere:—God þa gefilde hys weorc, *Gen.* 2, 2.
Gefindan *to find*, v. findan.
Gefinegod *mouldy*, v. finie.
Gefioht *war*, v. gefeoht.
Gefirenodon *sinned*, v. firenian.
Geflæscnes *incarnation*, v. flæscnes.
Gefleard *a trifling*, v. fleard.
Gefleman, geflieman *to drive away*, v. aflyman.
Gefleow *flowed*, v. flowan.
Geflit *A fan to clean corn*; vannus:—*Cot.* 33.
Geflit *contention, strife*, v. flit.
Gefliten, geflioten, geflotun *contended*, v. flitan.
Geflitfull, geflitfullic; *adj.* [flit *strife*] *Contentious*; contentiosus:—*Chr.* 785.
Geflitlice *by strife.*
Geflyman *to rout*, v. aflyman.
Gefoeded *fed*, v. fedan.
Gefog *a joining*, v. gefeg.
Gefol *giving suck, full.*
Gefolc *people, a troop*, v. folc.
Gefolgian *to fill*, v. fyllan.
Gefon; *part.* gefonde; *pp.* gefongen. *To take*, v. fon.
Geforht *timid*, v. forht.
Geforðian *to further*, v. forðian.
Geforwearðan *to perish*, v. forweorðan.
Geforword; *part. Agreed upon, covenanted, bargained*; compactus:—*L. Foed. Athelr. Anlav.* 4.
Gefotcypsed; *part.* [cysp *a fetter*] *Bound with fetters*; compeditus:—*Ps.* 101, 21.
Gefræge, FRÆGE *Inquiry, information, sharpness, mind, sagacity*; solertia:—On mine gefræge *in my mind, on my inquiry, as I hear, understand, know, as I am informed*, *Chr.* 975: 973: *Cd.* 58, *Lye.*
Gefræge, gefrægen; *adj. Perceived, known, celebrated, remarkable*; notus:—*Bt. R.* p. 175: *Cd.* 162.
m Gefrægnan *to inquire, know, hear*, v. fregan.
Gefrætan *to devour*, v. fretan.
Gefrætwed, gefrætewed *adorned*, v. frætwian.
Gefrætwodnes *an ornament*, v. frætwednes.
Gefrasan *to ask*, v. frasian.
Gefrean *To free*; liberare:—*C. Ps.* 43, 29.
Gefrecnod *evil minded, angered.*
Gefredan, gefret; *p.* dde. *To feel, perceive, know, give ear to, regard, free*; sentire:—Ne mæg gefredan hwæðer *cannot feel whether*, *Bt.* 41, 4. On hyre gefredde þat, *Mk.* 5, 29: *Ps.* 30, 1.
Gefredendlic; *adj. Sensible, perceptible*; sensibilis:—*Elf. gr. Som.* p. 2, 31.
Gefrednes, se; *f. A feeling, sense, perception, taste*; sensus:—*Bt.* 41, 4.
Gefrefred *consoled*, v. frefrian.
Gefremednes, se; *f. An achievement, effect*; effectio:—*Bd.* 1, 4.
Gefremian; *p.* ode; *pp.* od; *v. a. To finish, effect, bring to pass, commit*; efficere:—Þe he gefremode, *Gen.* 2, 2: *Mt.* 14, 2.
Gefremman *to effect, perform*, v. fremman.
Gefreod, gefreode *freed, set at liberty*, v. freon.
Gefreogan *to free, emancipate*, *L. In.* 7, 3, v. freogan.
Gefreolsod, gefrylsod *consecrated, liberated, freed*, v. freolsian.
Gefricgeað *hear, understand*, *Beo.* 41, 121, v. friegean.
Gefrigen *inquired, understood, heard of*, v. fregan.
Gefrihtan *to frighten*, *Bd.* 1, 7, v. frihtan.
Gefrinan; *p.* we gefrunon. *To ask, hear, perceive*, v. frinan.
Gefriðod, gefriðode *saved, protected, delivered, liberated*, *Bt.* 39, 10, v. friðian.

Gefeoht fought Th. An
Geohtan
Gefeallan to fail Th. Spr.
Lye — Ge-fe ax comatus
Grim II 745, 38

Geferan to journey Cd 57 Th p 196, 14 v geferan

Gefangennes, se; f taking, laying hold, apprehension Som

Society; societas Lye

Gefean to rejoice Ps ... geheran to begin

Gefeallice pleasantly Lye

Gefearred to go far off, to withdraw L. Lk 22, 41

Geferian to carry, bear lead Ld 215 Ld 274, 3; Bos K 6208a

Geferaeden fellowship, society, fellowship

Gefeccan to fetch Th. An

Gefeddre; an; f godmother

Gefegednes, se; f figure, shape, a joining; figura, compages Som

12 Gefeg- faest seam or joint fast Cd 65 Th 79, 12

13 Gefeig Agula, manner? Som

14 Gefeinega compages R. 70

15 Gefellendlic, filling up Som v gefillendlic

16 Gefeoll forgetfulness oblivio Som

Gefetian to fetch Bos K 4376 v Th. fetian

Geferscype, es m company, society Th. An

Geforn ... of old Som p gefyrn

Gefetigan to fetch ... v fetian Som

Gefilednes, se; f a completion Som v gefilledness

Gefillenlic filling up completing; completivus Som

Gefindig capable, catchy; capax, Som

Gefiorode for gefiorode Swid ge ...

Gefiperad feathered plumatus v gefiðeran

Geflaeschamian to cover with flesh, to render incarnate Th. An carne obducere S. de fide Cathol Lye

14 Geflea, Trifles; nugae Ben

15 Geflenod hacele a cloak; lacerna R. 1 ...

Gefotrace, fraktio C. Jul 1, 17

18 Gefoldwif gratiosa mulier Bos 9 Lye

Gefor went to faran

Geflitfulnes, se; f contention; contentio Lye

Geflitgeorn contentious Ben 7 l Som

Geflitglip cavilling Cd 45 v. l Lye

Geflitmaelum by strife; certatim contentio; inter ... Ben

Geflogen percussus Hebb 3, 1

Gefreahan to free Cd 8, 30; v gefreogan

Geformian, p geform, made to entertain Cd 127 Th p 162, 24 v geformian

Gefraeggean to accuse; accusare 2 to renowne; renown K. Mk 12, 10 — 2 Cd. Mk 12, 6 Lye

Gefraetewian to fret, adorn Bos K 9? Th an

Gefraegede embraced complexus R. Mk 10, 16

to ode; apod

Gefrefrian to console comfort Th. an

Gefreogynd es m a redeemer; redemptor Som C. M. 17, 49

Gefreogian to a ... v gefreogian

Gefreoted ... fetiafus Cd 81 Lye

Gefrigade embraced L. Mk 10, 16 v gefragede

Gefreodian to free, release

D

Gefryded freed consecrated Som Ben v gefrided

Gegreatod enlarged v greatian

C

Gefullean; ode p ad to veptize Som Ben Th An v fullian

Gegroetan to torment cruciare C Lk 8.28

Gefullumend es, m A helper; adjutor v Th Ai 17.2

Gefylsmend: fulfumend

Gefundian to try, inquire Ben K 490 v fundian

2 To take, capture, gain, get Th An

Geglofed Gloved, having sleeves; manica Fust Lat. 10

Gegearnian mandatum deferre Ben Lye v gearnian

Gefyllung a fullness v gefylednes

Gegered, gegerwed, gegirwed clothed Som Lye v gegereland

Gegimmed set with gems Som v gegymmed

Gegyred adorned Lk 24 Th Ps 39.7

Gegyman to take care of, regard; curare L de M 3,65

Gefylstend es, m A helper; adjutor Som Ben

Gegirla, an; m A garment Th Apol. v gegerela

Gegiuan to desire; deferre Mk 11.24

Gegirwend, es, m One wearing a purple robe praetextatus Som

Gegyrela to clothe clothing Som v gegerela

Gefyrnes, se; A farness, a great distance v antiquity; antiquitas Som

Gegnunga forthwith directly Bo K 65 with Th An p 135.21

Gegn-cwide, es; m a saying again, an answer Bd K 731

Gegn-ryne, a meeting v Ps 58.4 v gean-ryne

Gegladung, e; f a gladdening, delight delectatio Som

Gegienced adorned arranged v gefrencan

Gegendrian to cast down headlong, praecipitare Som

Geglengan to adorn decorate Th An v glengan

Gehabban to have Lye v habban

Gehaeca, an, m A hatchet, mattock, staff; sarmentum Som Cot 93.

Gegaederednes, se; A gathering together; collectio Som

Gegod good Th Sam v gegod

Gegaedrung a gathering Ben v gegaedrung

Gegrame troublesome molestus Som

Bd K 1442

gefyht contentio a fau ... v gefylt

Gefroren *frozen*, v. frysan.
Gefrunon *asked, understood*, v. frinan.
Gefrygnys *a question*, v. frigenes.
Gefrynd *friends*, *Lk.* 23, 12, v. freond.
Gefryðsum, *adj. Safe, fortified;* salvus:—*Ps.* 70, 3.
Gefullan *to fill*, *Ps.* 15, 11, v. fyllan.
Gefullfremman *to perfect*, v. fulfremian.
Gefullod *baptized*, v. fullian.
Gefultumian *to help*, v. fultumian.
n Gefulwian; *pp.* lwad, luhtod. *To baptize*, *Bd.* 5, 6, v. fullian.
Gefunden *found*, v. findan.
Gefungon *took*, v. fon.
Gefylan *to pollute*, v. befylan.
Gefylc [folc *people*] *A troop, people;* turma:—*Jud.* 16. Gefylceo *camps, forts, Past.* 21, 5.
Gefylced *collected as an army.*
Gefylde *cut down*, v. fyllan.
Gefyllan; *p.* de; *pp.* ed; *v. a. To fulfil, accomplish, satisfy;* implere, saturare:—Þus unc gedafenað ealle rihtwisnisse gefyllan, *Mt.* 3, 15. He gefylde hi, *Ps.* 80, 15.
Gefylled *cut down, destroyed*, v. fyllan.
Gefyllednes, se; *f. A fulness, perfection, finishing;* plenitudo:—*Jn.* 1, 16.
Gefyllendlic; *adj. Filling;* expletivus:—*Elf. gr.* 44.
Gefylst *help*, v. fultum.
Gefylsta, an; *m. A helper, an assistant;* adjutor:—*Ps.*17, 2: 27, 9.
Gefylstan *to help*, v. fylstan.
Gefynd *foes, enemies*, v. feond.
Gefyndig; *adj. Capable;* capax:—*Elf. gr.* 9, 60.
Gefyrht, gefyrhted; *adj. Fearing, affrighted, doubting;* timidus:—*Bd.* 1, 7.
Gefyrn *long ago, of old*, *Jos.* 10, 11, v. fyrn.
Gefyrðrian *to promote*, v. fyrðrian.
Gefysed *hastened, prepared*, v. fysan.
Gefystlian; *pp.* lad. *To beat with the fists, to buffet;* pugnis impetere:—*Scint.* 2.
Gefyðered *feathered, winged*, v. gefeðeran.
Gegada, an, gad, gædeling. *A fellow traveller, a companion, associate;* comes:—*Elf. gr.* 27.
Gegaderian *to gather*, v. gaderian.
Gegaderung *a collection*, v. gaderung.
Gegadorwist *an assembly*, v. gadorwist.
Gegæde *A collection, congregation;* congregatio:—*R. Ben. interl.* 2.

Gegæderian *to gather*, v. gaderian.
Gegælen, gegalen *enchanted*, *Ps.* 57, 5, v. galan.
Gegæncg *A society, meeting, an assembly;* cœtus:—*Elf. ep.* 1*st*, 50.
Gegærwan *to prepare*, v. gearwian.
Gegaf *base*, v. gaf.
Gegafelod *Confiscated;* infiscatus:—*Cot.* 108, 194.
Gegan *to go, observe*, v. gegangan.
Gegang *an event, a fate*, v. gegong.
Gegangan, gegan; *p.* geeode. *To go, happen, enter into, overrun, go against with hostile intention, to subdue, overcome;* superare:—Gif friman edor gegangeð *if a freeman forcibly enter a residence, L. Ethelb.* 29, *Pr.*
o Gegealt *keep, hold*, v. gehealdian.
Gegearcian; *p.* ode; *pp.* od. *To prepare*, v. gearcian.
Gegearcung *a preparation*, v. gearcung.
Gegearwian, gegearwigean *to prepare, procure*, v. gearwian.
Gegearwung *a preparation*, *Ps.* 88, 14, v. gearwung.
Gegerela, gegyrela, gegyrla, gerela, gyrla, an. *Clothing, apparel, habit, garment, robe;* amiculum, stola:—Bringað raðe þæne selestan gegyrelan, *Lk.* 15, 22, *Mk.* 12, 38.
Gegerelad, gegerlad; *part. Clothed;* indutus:—*L. Ps.* 92, 1.
Gegladian; *p.* ode; *pp.* od; *v. a. To please, make glad, gladden;* oblectare:—*Ps.* 103, 17.
Geglæncan, geglengcan, geglengan *to adorn, set in order, compose*, v. glengan.
Geglesc; *adj. Lascivious, wanton;* lascivus:—*Bd.* 5, 6.
Geglidan *to glide*, v. glidan.
Gegn, gegnes, v. geng.
Gegnes-burh *Gainsborough, Lincolnshire, Chr.* 1013.
Gegnidan *to rub*, v. gnidan.
Gegnunga; *adv. Plainly, wholly, altogether, certainly, directly;* omnino:—*Cd.* 32.
Gegnysan *to dash against*, *Ps.* 136, 12, v. forgnidan.
Gegodian *to please, enrich*, v. godian.
Gegogud *Relying on;* fretus:—*R. Conc.*
Gegolden; *part. Paid, performed;* præstitus:—*L. In.* 71.
Gegong, gegang *Fate, a falling out, an accident;* fatum:—*Cot.* 48.
Gegongan *to go over*, v. gegangan.
Gegoten *poured out, molten, melted*, v. geotan.
Gegrapian *to grope, touch*, *Bt.* 41, 4, v. grapian.

Gegremian *to irritate, provoke*, v. gremian.
Gegretan; *p.* gegrette. *To greet*, v. gretan.
Gegrewð *grows*, *Bt.* 34, 10, v. growan.
p Gegrin *a snare*, v. grin.
Gegrinan; *pp.* nod. *To ensnare;* illaqueare:—*Prov.* 6.
Gegrind *A grinding or rubbing together, a noise, whizzing, clashing;* fragor:—*Cd.* 95.
Gegrip *a gripe, seizing*, v. gripa.
Gegripan; *p.* grap; *pp.* gripen. *To gripe, seize*, v. gripan.
Gegripennis, gegripnes, se; *f. A taking, seizing, snare;* correptio:—*T. Ps.* 34, 9.
Gegriðian *to make peace*, v. griðian.
Gegrunded *grounded, founded*, v. agryndan.
Gegrundon *ground*, v. grindan.
Gegrundweallian *To ground a wall, to found, lay a foundation;* fundare:—*Ps.* 23, 2.
Gegyddode *sang*, v. geddian.
Gegyfan *to bestow*, v. gifan.
Gegyld *gilded*, v. gylden.
Gegylda, GYLDA, gilda, an; *m. A person who belongs to a guild or corporation, a companion, fellow;* socius:—Healf þæm gegyldan *half to the companion, L. Alf.* 27, *W.* p. 41, 17: *Hickes's Ep. dis.* p. 20, 51, &c.
Gegyldan *to pay*, v. gyldan.
Gegyldscipe *a society*, v. gildscipe.
Gegyltan *To become guilty, to offend;* peccare:—*Ors.* 1, 12.
Gegymmod; *adj. Gemmed, set with gems;* gemmatus:—*Elf. gr.* 43.
Gegyrela, gegyryla *a garment*, v. gegerela.
Gegyrian; *p.* ode; *pp.* od, wed; *v. a. To clothe, put on, adorn, endow;* vestire:—Þu gegyrydist, *C. Ps.* 103, 2. Þone lichoman gegyredon *clothed the body*, *Bd.* 4, 30. Gegyrewod *endowed*, *Bt.* 14, 3.
Gegyrnendlic; *adj. Desirable;* desiderabilis:—*T. Ps.* 18, 11.
Gegyrwan *to prepare*, *Ors.* 1, 7, v. gearwian.
Gehabban *to have*, v. habban.
Gehaccod *hacked, cut*, v. haccan.
Gehada, an; *m. One of the same state, condition;* qui ejusdem status est:—*L. Cnut.* 5, *W.* p. 128, 33, 35, 37.
Gehadian *to ordain, consecrate*, *Bd.* 3, 7, v. hadian.
Gehæftan, HÆFTAN; *pp.* gehæfted, hæfted, gehæfed, gehæfd, gehæft, hæft [*Dut.* hechten: *Frs.* heftje] *To take, take captive, cast into prison, detain, bind;* captare:—Hi gehæftað on sawle rihtwises, *Ps.*

93, 21. Abraham geseah anne ramm be þam hornum gehæft, *Gen.* 22. 13. On ecnesse gehæft *for ever binds, Bt.* 19: *Ex.* 12, 29.
Gehæftednes, gehæftnys, se; *f. A captivity;* captivitas:—*L. Ps.* 125, 5.
Gehæged *hedged,* v. hegian.
Gehælan *to heal, Mt.* 9, 28, v. hælan.
Gehæld *A keeping, regarding;* observatio:—*Bd.* 4, 23.
Gehæled; *comp.* gehæledra, gehældra, gehaldre; *adj. Safe, secure, good;* tutus:— *Bd.* 2, 2.
Gehæman *to cohabit,* v. hæman.
Gehænan *to accuse, C. Jn.* 8, 6, v. gehenan.
Gehæt *made warm,* v. hatian.
Gehætan *To promise;* promittere:—*Bt.* 20.
Gehafa *have, Mt.* 18, 26; *imp. of* habban.
Gehafen *Heaved up, fermented;* tumefactus:— *R.* 66.
Gehal; *adj.* [*Dut.* geheel] *Entire, whole;* integer:—*Bt.* 34, 12.
Gehaldan; *pp.* gehalden. *To keep, hold,* v. healdan.
Gehalding, ~~e; f.~~ *A holding, keeping;* custodia:—*Ps.* 118, 9.
Gehaldre *better,* v. gehæled.
Gehalgian; *p.* ode; *pp.* od. *To consecrate, dedicate, Jn.* 11, 55, v. halgian.
Gehalgung *a consecration, a sanctuary,* v. halgung.
Gehamettan *To appoint a home;* domum assignare:—*L. Athelst.* 2.
Gehât *a promise, vow, Bd.* 3, 27, v. behat.
Gehata *A hater, an enemy;* inimicus:—*Cot.* 74.
Gehatan; *pp.* en. *To promise, vow,* v. behatan.
Gehaten *called,* v. hatan.
Gehaðrian; *p.* erod. *To restrain,* v. heaðerian.
Gehatude *heated, grew warm,* v. hatian.
Gehawade *looked around,* v. hawian.
Gehead *exalted,* v. geheed.
Geheahtendlic; *adj. Eminent;* insignis:—*Pref. Wihtr.*
Geheald *What is held, a territory, keeping, regarding;* custodia:—*Bd.* 5, 21: *Chr.* 1055.
Gehealdan, þu gehiltst, he gehylt; *p.* geheold, gehold; *pp.* gehealden; *v.a.* 1. *To keep, preserve;* custodire. 2. *To observe, regard;* observare:—1. Fiftyne winter geheold *he kept it fifteen years, Chr.* 189. Ic þe geheolde, *Gen.* 20, 6. Þat sæd si gehealden, *Gen.* 7, 3. 2. Gif þu hig gehiltst, *Deut.* 7, 12. ¶ Mid gehealdan *to satisfy, Bt.* 13. Wel gehealden *contented, satisfied, Bt.* 18, 3, v. heald.
Gehealdnys *a keeping,* v. healdnes.
Gehealdsum; *adj. Keeping, stingy, modest, chaste;* parcus:—*Past.* 20.
Gehealdsumnes *a keeping,* v. healdnes.
Gehealgian *to consecrate,* v. halgian.
Gehealtsumnys *captivity,* v. healdnes.
Geheapod *heaped,* v. heapian.
Geheaw *A gnashing;* stridor:—*Cd.* 221.
Geheawan *to hew, cut,* v. heawian.
Gehede *seized.*
Geheed *lifted up.*
Gehefigod, gehefegud, gehefgod, gehefigad *made heavy, troubled, aggravated,* v. hefigan.
Gehelan, ed, god *to hide, conceal, deceive,* v. helan.—*to heal,* v. hælan.
Gehelmian; *p.* ode; *pp.* od [helm *a helmet*] *To crown, crest;* coronare:—*Ps.* 5, 15: 8, 6.
Gehelpan *to assist, preserve, Bt.* 14, 1, v. helpan.
Gehenan *to accuse, R. Lk.* 23, 2, v. hynan.
Gehende; *adj. Neighbouring, next;* vicinus:—On gehende tunas, *Mk.* 1, 38.
Gehende, gehened *humbled, opposed, condemned,* v. hynan.
Gehende; *prep.* d; *adv. Nigh, near at hand;* prope:—Me gehende, *Gen.* 45, 10. Sumor ys gehende, *Lk.* 21, 30.
Gehendnes, se; *f. Nearness;* proximitas:—*Elf. gr.* 5.
Gehentan *to take, pursue, Bt. R.* p. 168, v. hentan.
Geheold *a regard,* v. healdnes.
Geheoran *to hear,* v. hyran.
Geheordnes, geheordung *a custody, keeping,* v. healdnes.
Geheorte, geheorted; *comp.* ra; *adj. Hearted, animated, Mk.* 10, 49.
Geheran *to hear,* v. hyran.
Gehered *praised,* v. herian.
Gehergian *to ravage, afflict, destroy,* v. hergian.
Gehernes, se; *f. A hearing;* auditus:—*Bt.* 41, 4.
Gehet *promised,* v. behatan.
Gehhol *Christmas,* v. geol.
Gehicgan, gehicggan, gehicgean, gehiggan *to study, search out,* v. hicgan.
Gehienan *to humble,* v. hynan.
Gehierstan *to fry,* v. hyrstan.
Gehihtan *to hope, rejoice, increase,* v. hihtan.
Gehilt *a hilt, handle,* v. hilt.
Gehiltst *keepest, Ex.* 34, 6, v. gehealdan.
Gehinan *to oppress,* v. hynan.
Gehindred *hindered,* v. hindrian.
Gehiorað *hear,* v. hyran.
Gehiowian, gehiwian, gehiwan *to form, pretend,* v. hiwian.
Gehiscian *to hate.*
Gehiwung *a pretence,* v. hiwing.
Gehladen, gehlæden *laden; pp. of* hladan.
Gehlænian *to make lean, thin,* v. lænian.
Gehlæst, gehlæsted *loaded,* v. hlæstan.
Gehlaðen *invited,* v. laðian.
Gehleapan *to dance,* v. hleapan.
Gehleat *appointed by lot, ordained,* v. hleotan.
Gehleoð; *adj. Agreeable, harmonious;* consonus:— *Bt.* 1, 25.
Gehleow *a lowing,* v. gehlow.
Gehlid *a lid, covering,* v. hlid.
Gehlidad, gehlyd *covered,* v. hlidan.
Gehlihan, hi gehlogun *to deride,* v. hlihan.
Gehlioran *to pass over,* v. leoran.
Gehlið [hleoð *a top*] *A covering;* tectum:—*Cd.* 36.
Gehlodon *laden,* v. hladan.
Gehlot *a lot, Jos.* 7, 14, 17, v. hlot.
Gehloten *appointed by lot,* v. hleotan.
Gehlow, gehleow *A lowing of beasts;* mugitus:—*Elf. gr.* 1.
Gehlyd, HLYD, hlud [*Frs.* luwd *n.*] *A clamour, muttering, disturbance, noise, tumult;* clamor:—*Mt.* 27, 24.
Gehlyst *hearing,* v. hlyst.
Gehlystan *to listen, obey,* v. hlystan.
Gehlyt *A companion;* consors:—*Ps.* 44, 9.
Gehnad, es *A conflict, fight;* immanitas:—*Chr.* 938, v. gehnæst.
Gehnægde; *part. Subdued, oppressed;* oppressus:—*Bd.* 4, 15, v. hnecan.
Gehnæst, gehnast *A conflict, slaughter;* conflictus:—Æfter þæm gehnæste *after the slaughter, Cd.* 94: *Chr.* 938.
Gehnesctun, gehnescod *softened,* v. hnescian.
Gehoered *heard,* v. hyran.
Gehogode, gehogod *studied, determined, despised,* v. hogian.
Geholen *hidden,* v. helan.
Gehopp *A little bag;* folliculus:—*Cot.* 87.
Gehorsad, behorsud, gehorsud; *part. Behorsed, set* or *mounted on horseback;* equo impositus:—*Ors.* 3, 9: *Chr.* 885, *Ing.* p. 108, 14.

~~Gehæftnian to take Lk 7,5 v gehæftan~~

Gehæftræ cataracte ... 141,9 v supl gehæft

7 Gehalgung ... sancta ... sanctificium Ex 15,17 v gehalgung

Gehænd near Som v gehende

Gehæp apt, fitting Th An

6 Gehæplic ~~fitting~~ Equal, even, like, compar Som Cot 35

7 Gehagian opportune facere aliquid Lye v onhagian

8 Gehalan to feed; pascere C Jn 21,16

9 Gehald regarding Lye v gehald ... ; a holding

11 Gehalian to heal sane; C Mt 18,11 v gehælan

12 Gehalsian to beseech, obsecrare Lye

13 Gehatheortian exardescere R Ben 70 Lye

15 Geheafdod ringed ... Samathracius R 65 Som Lye

16 Geheah high, altus ~~celsitus~~ Som

17 Geheald held, ... ; tutus Som v healdra

Geheowan to form fashion; plasmare ... 118,73

Gehered gehered served ministred C Mt 8,15 v hyran

Geheaterod restrained Bed K 6139 v heaperian

Gehlænsod made lean; tenuatus Som v ge-hlænsian

Gehlænced tortus L Mt 2,55

Geheapian to heap up Prov 28 v heapian

Gehladan to lade, draw haurire C Jn 4,15

Geheded hidden Lye v gehydan

Gehende humbled, humiliatus Bos Lye v v gehende

Geheft gehæfted taken Som v gehæftan

Gehæftræ waterfall cataracte L Ps 41,9 Lye

Geheige A meadow, pratum Som Prov 27 v haga

Gehened condemned Cot 217 R L 276,18 p of gehenan

2 Ge-heort cordatus Lyr II 745,38

13 Gehergian to destroy Som v gehergian

14 Gehering a hearing report; auditio L Ps 111,6

16 Geheaw hewed cut, R Mt 27,60 v geheawan

~~Gehleonian~~ Gehleonian to recline; recumbere C Mt 14,9 v hleonian

12 Gehlid laughter, risus Som

13 Gehliwan to shield ... v hleowan

Gehiwentic Allegorical; simulatorius Cot 17

Gehiwnes a ... v gehywnes

14 Gehiwian to form, to appear Mt 17,2 v gehiowian

Ge-hleode consonus Lyr II 747, ...

Gehlystfull listening ... L Ps ... 15 v gehlyst

Gehefaldad ... Ezek v ... efaldigean

Geheld a keeping Lye v gehæld

15 Gehlyttrad ... defaecatus R 32

16 Gehlyta consors Lyr II 737,2

17 Gehlywan to cherish Scint 43,54 v supl gehliwan

18 Gehneade ... propinquavit C Mk 10,7

19 Gehnyſned bending down; inclinatus L Mt 2,46

20 Gehnescan to make soft R Mt 21,45 v hnescian

Gehoferod ... hunchbacked, gibbosus Som ... Lye

pierced; perforatus Som
2 Geholpen helped
nourished Som v gehelpan
3 Gehorning e. [illegible]
great ancestor Som
Gehorwigende unclean vile; sordidus Som
7 Gehradian [illegible]
[illegible]

9 Gehreean ruid p
of hreosan v
se Rowan
10 Ge-hreccan to tell
publish; edicere
Henning p 404 v
reccan Lye
11 Gehrefian to cover
tegere Som de [illegible]
12 Gehreman to cry
Ps 16, 20 v hreman
13 Gehreohnung [illegible] confessio Cot 17
Lye Ben
14 Gehrepod touched
Gen 6.6 v hrepan
15 Gehreowan to rue
Cd 225 Th p 298, 29 v hreowan
16 Gehrieved ruined,
subrutus Som
Gehusa, an m Domesticus Gm II 7, 27, 2
Gehul christmas Som
gehhol; geol
[illegible] little, small
Ge-newede, modicus
Mt 6.30
Gm II 747, bottom
Gehyryed ruined, dirutus Som
Gehuscipe, es; m house-safe
houseship C Ps 134, 9 v hus-scipe m
hus
21 Gehused housed
Gehused snegl x
housed snail; testudo
R. 23 Ben Lye
22 Gehusled communicated
R. [illegible] 5 v huslian
Gehwaede a little Som
Gehwaede
Gehwaednes sparingness
v gehwaednes
Gehwearfe an exchange
v gehwyrfe

Gehradian to hasten
Bd 1, 16 v hradian
Gehrered ruined
subrutus Ben Som
Gehwearfan, to change
[illegible] Som v hweorfan
Gehwetted whetted
[illegible]
Gehwilc each than
v gehwylc
3 Gehwaede
Gehwilcnys, se; f
Quality; qualitas Som
4 Gehwilum sometime
v hwilum
5 Gehwing a pinnacle
pinnaculum, angulus Som
Gehwit, White; candidus R 65 Lye
Gehwyd [illegible] C. T. 150, 18 Lye
secret place; abditum
Cd 812 Th p 267
Gehwyrfe A translation,
change; translatio Som
10 Gehwyrftman, gehwyrf
man to turn, take;
transferre [illegible] Ors 3, 11 Bar
12242 v hweorfan
guardianship Cd 161
Th 202, 3 A holster, fa
Beo 16 6107
Gehwylan to roar down
declinare L Ps 16, 12 v ahylan
14 Gehylmd, gehylmed
helmeted, covered, shaded
with foliage; galeatus, frondosus Som Cot 89; 97 Lye
Gehyrednes a Keeping
Gehrife, gehrofe st
house, roof; domus, tectus
Som
Gehringed ring C. R Ben
Lye v hringan
Gehrino building; aedificationes
R Mk 13, 2
Gehrised must
R 13, 33
Gehroered commoted Ben
Gehrumpen wrinkled; rugosus Som
Gehrunnen assembled
L Ps 67, 16 v gerunnen
Gehiwed feigned, as
feigned; hypocritical
Th Apol
27 Gehyslacan re
petere Brov 17 Lye
29 Geirmed afflicted
Past 28, 1
30 Geihtnys, se; f an addition; in hl. Spaets Som
Gehyspendlic abominable L Ps 13, 1

Gehwrecan to guide
Ps 89, 19 v gewrecan
Geinseglian to seal
Th Apol
2
2a)
Gewin Drift pleasure
Beo 2 335 v lac
3 Ge-lac. Ludus
Beo 79.
Gelac An a
number
Poetry, numerus
Cot 178 F 8 34 345 Lye
4 Gelacnian p ode
to heal; curare
Ps 27 Lye
5 Gelacod numbered
numerari Deut Som Lye
Gelaehtataen
Gelaeccan
Gelende
Gelandade landed p
of gelandian
L Ps 140, 3 v ge
Gehyrstan To adorn
ornare Cot 60
Gehyrstende
comfortatus; confortatus Som
19 Gehyrsto trappings
Som v hyrst
20 Gehyrsumlice
obediently; obedienter
Som
21 Gehyrtan To encourage; animare
Deut 2, 21 Som
22 Gehyrewed blamed
Som v hyrwan
23 Gehyscan to mock
deride; subsannare
L Ps 79, 7
Gehyspan to mock
Gehyspte mocked
angered v hyspan
Gehyspte

Gehradod *Hastened, prospered;* acceleratus:—*Bd.* 4, 19, v. hradian.

Gehran *touched,* v. gehrinan.

Gehreas *rushed,* v. hreosan.

Gehrec *government,* v. gerec.

Gehremmed *hindered,* v. hremman.

Gehreosan *to rush,* v. hreosan.

Gehrero *banishment,* v. gehrore.

Gehrifede *brought forth,* v. hrif.

Gehrinan, gerinan, HRINAN, ic gehrine; *p.* gehran, hi gehrinon; *pp.* gehrinen. 1. *To touch, to take hold of;* tangere. 2. *To touch with an instrument, to brush, clean, adorn, deck;* verrere:—1. Gehrinen mid adle, *Bd.* 4, 8. 2. Gehrinæd mid besmum, *C. Mt.* 12, 44.

Gehrinenes *a touch,* v. hrinenes.

Gehrist *falls,* v. hreosan.

Gehroden *adorned,* v. hroden.

Gehrore, gehrero, geror *Banishment, exile, a casting away;* exilium:—*Bd.* 4, 7.

Gehroren; *pp. Fallen, forsaken, desolate,* v. hreosan.

Gehrorenes, se; *f. Affliction, ruin;* ærumna:—*L. Ps.* 31, 4.

Gehruron, gehryred, gehriered, gehrored, gehroren *rushed down, destroyed, was desolate,* v. hreosan.

Gehruxl *A noise, disturbance;* tumultus:—*Dial.* 2, 10.

Gehryne *a sacrament,* v. geryne.

Gehrysed *shaken,* v. hrysede.

Gehð *a station, Ex. MS. Conb.* p. 233, v. giht.

Gehugod *studied, intended, purposed,* v. gehogod.

Gehúsan *Housefolk, those of the household;* domestici:—*Mt.* 10, 36.

Gehwa; *m.* gehwæt; *n. g.* gehwæs; *pron. Every one, whoever, who;* quisque, quis:—*Mk.* 15, 24, v. hwa.

Gehwædnes, gehwednes, se; *f. Sparingness, paucity, fewness, subtilty;* parcitas, paucitas:—*Ps.* 101, 24.

Gehwær, gehwar *On every side, everywhere;* undique, ubique:—*Bd.* 2, 1.

Gehwæðer *Both, each, either, doubtful;* uterque, promiscuus:—*Bd.* 5, 7.

Gehwæðeres; *adv. Anywhere, on every side, every way;* undique.

Gehwanon *on all sides, round about.*

Gehwearf *returned,* v. hweorfan.

Gehwearf, gehweorf, gehwyrf *a change,* v. hwearfung.

Gehweled *heated.*

Gehwerfnes *a conversion,* v. gehwyrfednes.

Gehweted *wetted,* v. wætan.

Gehwider *Whithersoever, anywhere, everywhere;* alicubi:—*Bd.* 3, 17.

Gehworfen *returned,* v. hweorfan.

Gehwylc *Each, every one, all, whoever, whatever;* quisque, unusquisque:—*Lk.* 19, 15: *Deut.* 24, 16.

Gehwyrfednes, gehwyrfenes, se; *f. A conversion, change;* conversio:—*Bd.* 1, 26: 4, 5, v. hwearfung.

Gehwyrfð *turns;* [gehwyrfed *turned,* v. hweorfan.

Gehydan, he gehyt; *p.* gehyd, gehydde; *pp.* gehyden, gehe-ded. *To hide,* v. hydan.

Gehydnes, se; *f. An inn;* diversorium:—*Past.* 50, 1.

Gehygd *A thought;* cogitatio:—*Cd.* 221.

Gehyht *a hope, refuge,* v. hiht.

Gehyhtan *to hope,* v. hihtan.

Gehyhtlic; *adj. Seasonable, fit, commodious;* opportunus:—*R. Ben.* 53, v. hihtlic.

Gehyld *Regard, observation, keeping, concealing;* observantia, custodia:—*Bd.* 2, 4.

Gehyldre *Safer;* tutius.

Gehylt *keeps,* v. gehealdan.

Gehynan; *p.* de; *pp.* ed. *To humble, oppress, waste, destroy, Ex.* 1, 10, v. hynan.

Gehyran *to hear, obey,* v. hyran.

Gehyrde *kept, oppressed,* v. hyrdan.

Gehyrned *Horned, covered with horn* or *scales, glazed* or *brightened;* cornutus:—Moises wæs gehyrned, *Ex.* 34, 29, 30.

Gehyrnes, se; *f. A hearing, report;* auditus:—*Mt.* 13, 14.

Gehyrst, gehyrsted *fried, baked,* v. hyrstan.

Gehyrsted *adorned, Bt.* 37, 1, v. hyrstan.

Gehyrsum *obedient,* v. hyrsum.

Gehyrsumian *to obey,* v. hyrsumian.

Gehyrsumnes *obedience,* v. hyrsumnes.

Gehyst *hides,* v. gehydan.

Gehyðelic; *adj. Favourable, seasonable;* opportunus:—*Ps.* 31, 7.

Gehyðnes *opportunity.*

Gehywung *a deception, deceit,* v. hiwung.

Geicean; *p.* geichte, hi geihton; *imp.* geic; *pp.* geiced, geict, gecht. *To add, eke, Cd.* 56, v. ecan.

Geicendlic; *adj. Added to, adjective;* adjectivus:—Geicendlic nama *a noun adjective, Som.*

Geichte, geihton *added; p. of* geicean, v. ecan.

Geilleroeað *Surfeited;* crapulatus:—*Ps.* 77, 71.

Geimpod *grafted,* v. impan.

Geinnian; *pp.* geinnod. *To bring in, include, to fill, supply, charge;* præstare, includere:—Wolde God geinnian þone lyre *God would supply the loss, Ser. Creat.* p. 9: *L. In.* 62. Susle geinnod *with sulphur filled, Cd.* 2. He hæfð geinnod þat ær geutod wæs *he has included what, before was excluded, Cod. Ex.* p. 1.

Geirged *affrighted.*

Gelad *a way, road,* v. lad.

Geladian *to excuse,* v. ladian.

Gelæcean, gelæccean, læccan; he gelæcð; *p.* he gelæhte, læhte, hi gelæhton, gelahton; *pp.* gelæht. *To take, catch, seize, apprehend;* capere, arripere:—Þat hig woldon hine gelæccean and to cyninge don, *Jn.* 6, 15. Hig gelæhton hys hand, *Gen.* 19, 16: *Mk.* 9, 18. Eac menne læhte *also took men, Chr.* 1094: *Gen.* 12, 15.

Gelædan, he gelæt; *p.* gelædde; *pp.* gelæded. *To lead,* v. lædan.

Gelædenlic; *adj. What is easily led* or *beaten out, malleable;* ductilis:—*Ps.* 97, 6.

Gelæfa *permission,* v. leaf.

Gelæfan *to believe,* v. gelyfan.

Gelæfed *left; pp. of* læfan.

Gelæmed *Lamed;* claudus factus:—*L. Ethelb.* 39, v. lam.

Gelænde *lent,* v. lænan.

Gelændð *One accusing, a slanderer;* detrahens:—*C. Ps.* 100, 5, v. getælan.

Gelænged *lengthened, drawn out,* v. langian.

Gelær *Void, empty;* vacuus, *Som.*

Gelæred *Taught, persuaded, learned, skilful;* doctus, v. læran.

Gelærednes, se; *f. Learnedness, knowledge, skill;* eruditio:—Gelærednes to spræcanne, *Bd.* 4, 27.

Gelæstan *to last, continue, follow, perform,* v. læstan.

Gelæswod *fed,* v. læsian.

Gelæte, es; *pl.* gelætu; *n.* [lætan *to let go, leave*] *A going out, ending, meeting;* exitus, occursus:—To wega gelætum *to the meetings of ways, Mt.* 22, 9. Twegra wega gelætu *meetings of two ways, Cat.* 110. Æt þæra wæga gelæte, *Gen.* 38, 21.

Gelæten *let, let go, omitted,* v. lætan.

Gelagod *Lawed, sanctioned by law;* lege sancitus:—*Elf. cp.* 40.

Gelamp *happened; p. of* gelimpan.

Gelandian. 1. *To land, arrive;* accedere ad terram. 2. *To enrich with lands* or *possessions;* terris locupletare:—1. *Som.*

2. Þe gelandod sy *who has lands, L. Lund.* 11. Opposed to be-landian.

Gelang, geleng; *prep.* ALONG *of, owing to, in consequence of*; opera, causa, cujusvis:—Æt þe ys ure lyf gelang *it is along of thee that we live.* Hi sohton on hwon þat gelang wære *they inquired long of whom that was, Bd.* 3, 10. Gif hit on preoste gelange sy *if it be along of the priest, L. Edg. impon. pn.* 44.

Gelangian; *p.* ode; *pp.* od; *v. a. To call for, send for, deliver, liberate*; accersire, vocare, liberare:—Gelangast to þe þine frynd, *Jos.* 2, 18. Gelangode, *Dial.* 2, 3. Gelangod, *Elf. T.* p. 32, 26.

Gelast *Path, duty*; officium:—*L. Lund.* 3, *W.* p. 66, 14, 27.

Gelaðian, ic gelaðige; *p.* ode; *pp.* od. *To invite, bid, desire to come, to assemble, congregate, allure*; invitare, congregare:—Magon we Ioseph to us gelaðian *can we invite Joseph to come to us? Nicod.* 20. Gelaðian to geþeahte *to invite to consultation, R. Ben.* 3: *Lk.* 14, 8, 16: *Jn.* 2, 2. Beforan Roman witan gelaðode *assembled before the Roman senators, Ors.* 3, 6.

Gelaðung, laðung, e; *f. A congregation, church*; congregatio:—On middele gelaðunge or circean ic herige þe, *Ps.* 21, 21: 88, 6.

Gelaured *Of* or *belonging to laurels*; laureus, *Som.*

Geld *a change, society*, v. gild.

Geldan *to pay*, v. gyldan.

Gelde *Yeaned, brought forth*; enixa:—*Cot.* 75.

Gelden *golden*, v. gyldan.

Geleaf *leave, license*, v. leaf.

Geleáfa, an; *m. Belief, faith, confidence*; fides, fiducia:—Þu þone geleafan hæfst *thou hast this belief, Bt.* 5, 3. Habbað geleafan, *Mt.* 14, 27. Geleafan nom *belief adopted, Cd.* 30.

Geleafful, leaful LAWFUL, *believing, faithful, holy*; licitus, fidelis, credulus:—*Ps.* 77, 41. On geleafullum bocum *in lawful* or *holy books, the Scriptures, Elf. T.* p. 13, 22. Geleaffull gaderung, oððe cyrce *a faithful congregation or church, Elf. gl.* 18.

Geleaffulnes *Faithfulness, belief, trust*; fidelitas:—*Elf. gr.* 9, 25.

Geleáfleást, geleáflyst *Want of faith, unbelief, infidelity, unfaithfulness*; incredulitas:—*Deut.* 1, 40.

Geleaflic *What may be believed, credible*; credibilis:—*Ps.* 92, 7.

Geleafsum *Faithful, credible, credulous*; fidelis:—*Bd.* 3, 11: *Ors.* 3, 9.

Geleánian; *pp.* geleanod. *To render, repay, Cd.* 21, v. leanian.

Geleas *false*, v. leas.

Geleast *Carelessness, negligence*; incuria, *Som.*

Geleccan; *p.* geleht, *To wet, moisten*, v. leccan.

Gelecnian *to cure*, v. lacnian.

Geled *laid*, v. lecgan.

Geledd *Malleable, easily beaten out*; ductilis:—*T. Ps.* 97, 6.

Gelefan *to believe*, v. gelyfan.

Gelefde *trusted, allowed*, v. lyfan.

Gelefed *permitted*, v. lyfan.

Gelefenscipe *Permission, excuse*; excusatio:—*C. R. Jn.* 15, 22.

Gelefst *believest, for* gelyfst, v. gelyfan.

Gelegen *laid*, v. lecgan.

Geleht *wet*; *p. of* leccan.

Gelend *rich*, v. gelynd.

Gelenda, gelanda *A man of landed property, a rich man*; dives, *Som.*

Gelengede *prolonged*, v. lengian.

Gelent *approached*, v. gelandian.

Geleofod *lived*; *pp. of* lybban.

Geleofst *believest, for* gelyfst, v. gelyfan.

Geleogan *to lie, falsify*, v. leogan.

Geleoran *to depart, die, permit*, v. leoran.

Geleorednys, se; *f. A departing, passing, emigration*; transitus:—*Mt.* 1, 17.

Geleornian *to learn, read, inquire*, v. leornian.

Geleosian *to lose*, v. losian.

GELESE, gelise, es; *n.* [*Dut.* lezen; *pp.* gelezen: *Frs.* læse *to read*] *Care, study, learning*; studium:—On gelesum haligra gewrita gelæred *learned in the study of the Holy Scriptures, Bd.* 5, 20.

Geleswian *To feed*; pascere:—*C. Jn.* 21, 17.

Gelet *an ending, a meeting*, v. gelæte.

Gelettan; *p.* gelette; *pp.* gelett, gelet; *v. a. To hinder, delay, let*; impedire:—Hi hine magon gelettan, *Bt.* 41, 2, *Card.* p. 374, 24: *Ps.* 77, 35: *Ors.* 2, 4, v. lætan.

GELEW [*Plat. Dut.* geel: *Ger.* gelb: *Dan.* guul: *Swed.* gul]. YELLOW; flavus:—*Somn.* 88.

Gelewan; *p.* geleah; *pp.* gelewed. *To betray, deceive, weaken, injure*; prodere:—Seo wen geleah *that hope deceived, Cd.* 4: *Ex.* 22, 10, 14.

Gelic *like*, v. lic.

Gelice; *adv. Likewise, also, as*; pariter:—*Ps.* 67, 7. Gelice swa swa heo bebead *likewise as she commanded, Bd.* 4, 19. Elpendes hyd wyle drincan wæter gelice an spinge deð *an elephant's hide will imbibe water as a sponge doth, Ors.* 5, 7: *Bar.* p. 189, 29.

Gelicgan *to lie together*, v. licgan.

Gelicgean *To loiter, delay*; cessare:—*Ors.* 3, 11.

Gelician *to please, delight*, v. lician.

Gelicnes, se; *f. A likeness, resemblance, comparison, proverb, resemblance, image*; similitudo, proverbium:—*Ps.* 143, 15: *Lk.* 4, 23.

Gelicung *a liking*, v. licung.

Geliden *sailed, carried*, v. liðan.

Geliefan, gelifan; *p.* gelifde. *To believe*, v. gelyfan.

Geliese *care, learning*, v. gelese.

Gelifdest *believedst, for* gelyfdest, v. gelyfan.

Gelifedlice *lawfully*, v. gelyfedlice.

Geliffæstan *to make alive*, v. liffæstan.

Gelifgean, gelifian *to live*, v. lifian.

Geligery, geligre *A prostitute, a lying with, adultery, fornication*; adulterium:—*Ors.* 1, 2, *Bar.* p. 36, 5, 8.

Geligernes, se; *f. Fornication, adultery*; fornicatio:—*Ors.* 1, 2, *Bar.* p. 36, 2.

Geliht *alighted*, v. onlihtan.

Gelihtan. 1. *To lighten, mitigate, assuage*; alleviare. 2. *To enlighten*; illuminare:—1. *R. Conc.* 2: *L. Can. Edg. de mag.* 1. 2. *R. Mt.* 5, 15.

Geliman; *pp.* ed. *To glue* or *join together, connect*; conglutinare:—Gelimð þa friend togædere *joins the friends together, Bt.* 24, 3. Gelimed fæste to somne *joined fast together, Bt.* 35, 2.

Gelimp, belimp; *m. An event, accident, a chance*; accidens:—*Job.* p. 166.

Gelimpan; *p.* gelamp, gelomp, hi gelumpon; *pp.* gelumpen [limpian *to regard*] *To happen, occur*; evenire:—Gyf hyt gelimpð, *Mt.* 18, 13.

Gelimplic *Fit, seasonable, meet, ordered by fate, fatal*; opportunus:—*Bd.* 3, 19. On tide gelimplicre, *Ps.* 144, 16.

Gelimplice *opportunely*, v. limplice.

Gelioran *to pass over*, v. leoran.

Geliornes *a going, death*, v. geleorednes.

Gelirde *emigrated*, v. leoran.

Gelise *study, learning*, v. gelese.

Gelisian, gelissian *To fail, glide away*; cadere:—*Past.* 57, 2.

Gelisðelicnis, se; *f. Opportunity*; opportunitas:—*T. Ps.* 9, 9.

Geleafnes-word, es; n a confidence, or faith word Bd. K 488

or geleogan

along, neighbouring, belonging to Ge-lang vicenus Bco Lye Gen II 747, 5

Geleah deceived Cd 4 Th p 4, 5 p of ge leogan

Geleahtrian to corrupt to reproach to accuse Ben 61 v leahtrian

Geleafa consent Gen II 741, 26 v geleafa

Geleced to water irrigatus Som

Gelefan p de to believe deliver Cd 218 Th p 279, 31

Geleged laid down & deposited Som

Geliced likened Mt 7, 24

Gelicetan gelicettan To flatter dissemble; dissentan simulare Som Lye

Gelegen gyld days dedicated to Pan, Lupercalia Som

Geladgan To call for asciscere Cot 169 Lye

Geladian, L 1 x p. ode

Gelendian gelendian to land Th ah glandian

Gelic gemaca a compeer Som Elf gr 9, 17

Ge-legere a bed-fellow, concubine concubitus adulterium Gen II 738, 26

Gelatian to delay Lup Som 1. 20 v latian

Geleodode, ap for a countryman; cotizen; populace, cives L In 11 Th 47, 37 v leode

Gelecost a twin Som v gelycost

Geleoma rade radii atius; radii spectatis Lye Dogu v erur 37

Geliht

Geleohtan, p gelihte descend, alight; descendere, desilire Cd wolde gelihtan would descend Cd 222 Th p 291, 16: Dial 1, 2

Gelegan to lie down v gelicgan

Gelegen deceitful mendan Lye

Geleodrian pode pp od To lather; ungere L M 1, 1 Lye

Geleganod mentitus Pau. S. Steph Lye

1 To descend, alight descendere Bd 2, 13 Som p 517, 11: Cd
3 To lighten, alleviate; To alighte illuminare Nic 34 Th p 20, 2 v on lihtan

Gelimpfull liable to accident

Bef Lye

Geleoma A light lumen Lye

Geleaf-hris leaved vices, green twigs Som Cot 93

Geleafleas faith less, incredulous; infidus Som

Geleafnes, sc f Confidence. Shrewdness; fides, Galevtka, sagacitas Bd 3, 9 B. Beo K 488 Bco gl m leafa

Geleweend, es; m A traitor; traditor Som

Gelt gilt; auratus
Sandre

Gelīdan to sail
travere, move
B4192 F p 125, 43
v līdan

Gelocen locked Bosk
5534 v lūcan; belūcan

Gelodwyrt liver
mental; heptaphyl
lon Som Cot 71

Gemagtes: pl. nom
gemagas m A relation
kinsman; cognatus
Cd 91 Th p 114, 14 mæg

Gelutian to lurk
lie hid. Cd 216, Th
p 273, 2 v lutian

Gelyfed delivered
Cd 17 Th p 213, 21
v gelyfan

Gelifan to abide,
remain; manere
Bos K 875

Gemædla the mendes
Ael. M. 35. Som

Gemægnan to mingle
Th. Apol v gemengan

Gemædrian to con
sider Som v gemæd-
rian

Gemæg-fæsth A
plutter; cibo de-
ditus Som

Gemælde said
Cd 37 Th p 49, 10
v gemælan

Ge-mænden
remembered
2190. v gemænan

Gelyhte enlightened
Nic 34 Th p 20, 2
v gelihtan onlihtan
Spl ge-lihtan

Gemænigfealdan
to multiply Th. An
v gemenigfealdan

Gemænigfyld multi
plied, enlarged
Ps 91, 12

Gemænnung, e. f
a communion fellow
ship, familiarity;
communio; contuber
nium Som

Gelomlice often
Th An v gelomelice

Gelyden Multiplicis
peregrina
tionis experientia om
nium terrarum
gnarus. Nathan. Lye

Gelomlice frequently
often; frequenter Som
v gelomelice

9

Ypan to boast
Ps 30, 1 Rawl
p. 66, 21
Gn Ett 183, 10: I 1028 no 345
v. gilpan

Geliðewæhte *appeased*, v. liðewæcan.
Geliðod, geliðegod; *pp.* geliðegode; *p. of* liðian. *To soothe.*
Gelitlian *to diminish*, v. litlian.
Gellet *A large vessel* or *cup*; alveus, poculum majus:—*L. M.* 3, 48.
Gelm *a handful*, v. gilm.
Gelo *Saffron, yellow*; crocus, *Som.*
Geloca, geloce, *behold*, v. locian.
Geloccian *To stroke gently*; demulcere, *Som.*
Gelocian *to look upon*, v. locian.
Geloda *joints of the back*, v. gelyndu.
Gelodan *brothers*; fratres:—*R.* 92, *Lye.*
Geloden *loaden*, v. hladan.
Gelodr *A part of the body about the chest*; pars corporis circa thoracem:—Se maga bið neah þære heortan and þære gelodr *the stomach is near the heart and the gelodr*, *L. M.* 2, 1.
Gelogian; *p.* de; *pp.* od. *To place, dispose, regulate*, v. logian.
GELOMA, loma LOOM, *household-stuff, furniture, utensils, tools*; supellex, instrumenta:—*Bd.* 4, 28.
Gelome, gelomelice; *comp.* gelomlicor; *sup.* gelomlicost; *adv. Often, frequently*; sæpe:—Gelome on gebedum *frequent in prayers*, *Bd.* 4, 11: *Mt.* 9, 14: *Mk.* 7, 3.
Gelomed *Shining*; radiatus:—*Æqu. vern.* 33, *Lye.*
e Gelomelic, gelomlic; *adj. Frequent, general*; frequens:—*Bd.* 2, 7.
Gelomelice *often*, v. gelome.
Gelomlæcan *To frequent, to use often*; frequentare:—Gelomlæcende word *frequentative verb*, *Elf. gr.* 36.
Gelomlæcing, gelomlæcung, e; *f. Frequency, a frequenting, a common resort*; frequentatio:—*Elf. gr.* 36.
Gelomlæcnys, gelomlicnes, se; *f. A frequented* or *public place*; locus condensus:—*Ps.* 117, 26.
Gelomp *happened*, v. gelimpan.
Gelondan *brothers*, v. gelodan.
Gelong *along, on account of*, v. gelang.
Gelostr *A gathering to form matter, impostume*; suppuratio, *Som.*
Geloten dæg oððe ofernon *Later part of the day*; pomeridiana:—*R.* 95.
Gelp, gelpnes *a boasting, glory*, v. gilp.
Gelpð *boasts*, v. gilpan.
Gelsa *Luxury*; luxuria:—*Confes. Pec.*
Gelt *a debt, cause*, v. gylt.

Geludon *descended*, v. ludon.
Gelufad, gelufed *loved, beloved*, v. lufian.
Geluggian *To pull, lug*; vellere, *Som.*
Gelugon *falsified*; *p. of* geleogan.
Gelumpe, gelumpen *happened*, v. gelimpan.
Gelustfullian *to delight, covet*, v. lustfullian.
Gelustfullice *Earnestly, studiously*; studiose:—*Bd.* 2, 13.
Gelustfulling, e; *f. That which delights* or *pleases*; oblectamentum:—*Scint.* 81.
f Gelustfulnys *delight*, v. lustfulnes.
Gelutian *to lie hid*, v. lutan.
Gelycost *A twin*; gemellus:—Didymus, þat is gelicost, *Jn.* 20, 24: 21, 2.
Gelydan *to arrive*, v. gelandian.
Gelyfan, þu gelyfst, he gelyfð, we gelyfað; *p.* gelyfde, we gelyfdon; *pp.* gelyfed; *v. a. To believe, trust*; credere:—Gyf þu gelyfan miht, *Mk.* 9, 23. Ge ne gelyfdon him, *Mt.* 21, 32. He gelyfð on God, *Mt.* 27, 43. Gelyfst þu þysses, *Jn.* 11, 26.
Gelyfedlic; *adj. Lawful*; licitus:—*L. Eccl.* 9.
Gelyfedlice; *adv. With leave* or *licence, assuredly, lawfully, patiently*; patienter, cum licentia:—*Ors.* 2, 5.
Gelymp *an accident*, v. gelimp.
Gelymplicnys, se; *f. Opportunity, occasion*; opportunitas:—*C. Ps.* 9, 9.
Gelynd, gelend, LYND. *Grease, fat, fatness*; adeps:—*Lev.* 3, 10.
Gelyndu *Joints of the backbone*; spondyli, juncturæ vertebrarum:—*R.* 74.
Gelysed *redeemed*, v. alysan.
Gelysednes *redemption*, v. alysednys.
Gelystan *to please, desire*, v. lystan.
Gelysted *pleased*; delectatus:—*Bt. R.* p. 150.
Gelytfullice; *adv. Prosperously*; prospere:—*Ps.* 44, 5.
Gelytlian *to diminish*, v. lytlian.
Gemaad *mad*, v. gemæd.
Gemaca, MACA, gemæcca, gemeca [*Dut.* makker *m.*] A MATE, *an equal, companion, wife*; socius, conjux:—Twegen gemacan, *Gen.* 6, 19: 4, 1: 28, 1.
Gemacene *Like*; similis:—*L. With.*
Gemacian; *p.* de; *pp.* od. *To make, do*, v. macian.
Gemæcca, gemæccea, gemæcga, gemæc *a wife*, v. gemaca.
Gemæclic; *adj. Relating to a wife, conjugal*; conjugalis:—*Scint.* 58.

Gemæcnes, se; *f. A companionship, mixture*; commixtio:—*Bd.* 1, 27, *resp.* 8. *B.*
Gemæd *Troubled in mind, mad*; amens:—Gemæded, *Cot.* 10, 169.
Gemægened *Established, confirmed, strengthened*; confirmatus:—Gemægenad and gestrongad beon *to be confirmed and strengthened*, *Bd.* 4, 16.
Gemægð *Power, greatness*; potentia:—*Bt.* 17.
Gemægð *a family, tribe*, v. mægð.
Gemænan *to mean, intend*, v. mænan.
Gemænan *to mourn*, v. mænan.
Gemænegan, gemængan; *p.* gemænced. *To mix*, v. mengan.
Gemæne, gemænelic, gemænlic [gemana *a company*] COMMON, *general, universal*; communis:—Gemæne win *common labour*, *Bd.* 2, 1. Hwæt is þe and us gemæne *what is common to thee and us*, *Mt.* 8, 29. Ne beo þe nan þing gemæne ongen þysne rihtwisan *ne sit tibi nulla res communis versus hunc justum*, *Mt* 27, 19. Hæbbe him wið Gode gemæne *be it between God and him*; habeat ipsi cum Deo commune, *Bd.*: *L. Cnut. eccl.* 26. Eow gemæne *common to you*, *Jos.* 8, 2. Hi sceoldon habban sunu him gemæne *they should have a son* [*common to them*] *between them*, *Jud.* 13, 3. Gemænelice naman *an appellative* or *common noun*, *Elf. gr.* 9.
h Gemænelice, gemænlice; *adv. Commonly, generally, one amongst another*; communiter, invicem:—Þæt ge lufion eow gemænelice, *Jn.* 15, 12, 17.
Gemænigfyldan; *p.* de. *To multiply, enlarge*; multiplicare:—Þu gemænigfyldest sunu manna, *Ps.* 11, 9: 17, 16. Gemænigfylde beon, *Ex.* 1, 7.
Gemænne *Care, attention, study*, cura:—*Bd.* 2, 7.
Gemænnes, se; *f. A mixing, fellowship*; commixtio:—*Bd.* 1, 27, *resp.* 8. *What is had in common, common pastures*: hence the *Kent* word, mennys.
Gemænscipe *m.* [*Dut.* gemeenschap *f.*] *Communion, fellowship*; communio:—*W. Cat.* p. 49.
Gemænsuman, gemænsumian; *p.* do; *pp.* ed. [*Plat.* sammen gedan *to be married*] *To join, communicate, marry*; communicare, nubere:—*Bd.* 1, 25, *S.* p. 487, 14. Opposed to amansumian *to excommunicate.*
Gemænsumnys, se; *f. A communion, fellowship, sacrament*; communio:—Gemænsumnys

Cristes lichoman and blodes, Bd. 1, 27, resp. 5.

Gemænsumung, e; f. A communion; communio:—R. Ben. 38.

l Gemære, MEARE, es; n. pl. nom. a, o, u [Frs. maren c. canals which bound a district] An end, a MERE, boundary, termination, limit; finis:—Gemære þu settest, Ps. 103, 10. Oð gemære Humbre streamas to the boundary of Humber river, Bd. 5, 23. To þæm gemæran to the borders, Cot. 21. Gemæro eorðan, Ps. 2, 8. Landgemæra land boundaries, land marks.

Gemæred Celebrated, enlarged; divulgatus:—Bd. 3, 10.

Gemærsian; p. ode; pp. od. To praise, v. mærsian.

Gemærsung magnificence, v. mærsung.

Gemæst; adj. Fat; pinguis:—Deut. 32, 15.

Gemæstan to fatten, v. amæstan.

Gemæt Fitted, meet; aptus:—Mod. conf. 1, v. gemet.

Gemætfæst; adj. [mæte modest, fæst fast] Moderate, modest; modestus:—Bd. 1, 16: Bt. 10: 11, 1.

Gemætfæsted Compared; comparatus:—L. Ps. 48, 21.

Gemætfæstnes moderation, temperance, v. gemetfæstnys.

Gemæðegode Bestowed, honoured, given with honour; honoravit, benigne contulit:—Elf. T. p. 4, 11.

Gemæðrian To gratify, honour; honorare:—L. pol. Cnut. 12, 14.

Gemætte dreamed, v. mætan.

Gemagas relations, v. mæg.

Gemagdnes, gemagnes, se; f. Babbling, urgency, importunity; garrulitas, Som.

Gemah, gemagn, gemahlic; adj. Greedy, shameless, wicked, resolute, importunate; procax:—Elf. gl. 28: Ors. 1, 10.

j Gemáh watered, v. mígan.

Gemahlice; adv. Stoutly, importunately; importune:—Dial. 1, 8.

Gemahlicnes, gemahnes, se; f. Importunity, perverseness, dishonesty; importunitas;—Past. 3, 2.

Gemal mægene an assembly, v. mal.

Gemaleca Importunate; importunus:—Cot. 2.

Gemalice; adv. Importunately; importune:—Cot. 189.

Geman The hollow of the hand, sole of the foot; vola:—Cot. 198.

Geman, þu gemanst, we gemunon, gemunan; p. gemunde, gemundon; v.a. To remember; recordari:—Jn. 16, 21, v. gemunan.

Geman care for, regard, v. gyman.

GEMA'NA, an; m. [Plat. meente f: Dut. gemeente f: Frs. mente f: Ger. gemeine f: Not. kemeine: Ot. gimeinda: Dan. gemeene f.] A company, society, association, fellowship, familiarity, commerce, conjunction; consortium, copula:—Bd. 2, 9. Þu mines gemana bruce, Gen. 38, 16.

Gemang, gemong, amang, onmang; prep. d. ac. [gemang a mixture, gemenged mixed; pp. of mengan] AMONG; inter:—Aris gemang hym, Mk. 3, 3: Mt. 10, 16: Jn. 21, 23. ¶ On gemang þam, Jn. 4, 31, or Gemang þam in the mean time, then, Gen. 43, 1.

Gemang A mixture, an assembly, encumbrance, burden; mixtura:—L. With: Ex. 23, 3: Deut. 1, 12.

Gemangnys, se; f. A mingling, confection; commixtio, Som.

Gemangode gained, v. mangian.

Gemannian; pp. gemannod. To man, supply with men, v. mannian.

k Gemanode, gemanod admonished, v. manian.

Gemartyrad [Dut. gemarteld] Martyred, suffered as a martyr; martyr factus:—Hi gemartredan, Ors. 6, 5.

Gemaðel conversation, v. meðel.

Gemdon regarded, gyman.

Gemear an end, v. gemære.

Gemearc, es; m. [Dut. merk n.] A boundary, limit; locus designatus:—Cd. 139.

Gemearcian to describe, appoint, determine, v. mearcian.

Gemearr a boundary, impediment, L. Can. Edg. 16, v. gemære.

Gemearra Bad, wicked; malus:—L. Edw. 1.

Gemeca, gemecca a wife, companion, v. gemaca.

Gemed mad, v. gemæd.

Gememian to honour, moderate, humble, v. medemian.

Gemeder godmother: whence our GAMMER, Som.

Gemedred, gemedren Related on the mother's side, by a mother; a materna parte:—Gemedryda broðor, Gen. 43, 29: Ors. 3, 7.

Gemeldod betrayed, v. meldian.

Geme-leas negligent, v. gymeleas.

Gemeleaslice negligently, v. gymeleaslice.

Gemelest negligence, v. gymeleast.

Gemeltan to melt, v. meltan.

l Gemen care, v. gymen.

Gemencednys, gemencgednys, gemencgnys, gemengednys. A mixture, mixing, mingling together, connexion, copulation; mixtura, admistio.—Gemencgednys þæs gesinscypes admistio conjugalis, Bd. 1, 27. ans. 8. Wifes gemencgnys admistio cum muliere, id.

Gemend a memorial, v. gemynd.

Gemendfull; adj. [gemynd a mind] MINDFUL, memorable, attentive; memor:—Obs. Lun. 7.

Gemenelic; adj. [gemæne common, lic] Common; communis:—L. Pol. Cnut. 10.

Gemengde, gemenged, gemencged, gemenencged, gemengced mixed, mingled, confused, v. mengan.

Gemengung, e; f. A mixing, confusing; mixtura:—Cot. 35.

Gemenigfealdan, gemenigfildan; p. de [menig many, feald a fold, plait] To multiply, increase, extend; multiplicare:—Ex. 32, 13: Gen, 9, 27: 32, 12.

Gemenis, gemenn care, v. gymen.

Gemercad marked out, described, v. mearcian.

Gemere a boundary, v. gemære.

Gemerran to mar, spoil, v. myrran.

Gemet, met, es; n. [gemet; pp. of metan to measure] 1. A measure, size, quantity, limit, bounds; mensura. 2. A manner, way, sort; modus:—1. On þrim gemetum melewes, Mt. 13, 33. And gefylle ge þat gemet eowra fædera, Mt. 23, 32. On þam gemete þe ge metað, Mk. 4, 24: Deut. 25, 15. Gytsung gemet nat avarice knows no bounds, Scint. 25. Gemetta and gewihta measures and weights, L. pol. Cnut. 9. 2. On þat ylce gemet in the same manner, Bd. 4, 24. Ealle gemete by every way, Bd. 1, 27, resp. 5. On þam gemetum, on þam gemete, Ps. 32, 22: 36, 2, 21.

m Gemét; adj. MEET, fit, proper; aptus:—Swa him gemet þinceð as to him seemeth meet, Cd. 140: Bt. R. p. 195.

Gemet met, found, painted; pp. of metan.

Gemet an assembly, v. gemot.

Gemét, gemétte met, found, v. métan.

Gemétednes, se; f. An invention, a discovery; inventio:—L. Ps. 27, 5.

Gemetegod moderated, v. gemetgian.

Gemetegung, gemetgung, metgung, e; f. Measure, limit,

Gemen people Th. an

Gemencged mixed v gemengde

Gemærsan to magnify, honour Th. an

Gemære, es; n. a boundary ... to þæm gemæran to the borders Cot 21. etc

A mixture, collection, assembly; mixtura, collectio, coetus

Ge-mang, es; m. confusio Beo K 3284

Gemenged mixed defiled Cot 181 Th. p 27, v gemengde

Gemanian to exhort Th. an

Gemenig-feald manifold Som

Gemenigfild multiplied Th. an from gemenigfealdan

Gemæred enlarged ... v gemæred

Gemærsian to celebrate Som gemærsian

Gemet, es; n. a measure etc. l. 15, 2 - dl. l 16 in the same measure - l 17 Ealle gemete by ... Gemet a mood

Gemagas relations pl ge-mæg.

Gemearcian to mark, take note Th. an

Gemetan, ... to find meet ... Th. ...

Gemæltic

Gemed. A consent, condescention; consensus, condescensio Som

Gebicnigendlic indicative — bebeodendlic imperative — wiscendlic optative — underþeodendlic subjunctive — ungeendigendlic infinitive Elf gr 21 Som p 23

Ge-mete, es; n a meeting Beo K 1551 v ge-mot

Gemeted discovered v metan

Gemah shameless Som v gemah

Gemetegian to measure, moderate Th. an v gemetgian

[illegible]

D

1 Gemiltsiend, es; m A pitier; miserator Ben

2 Gemindleás mindless mad

3 Gemind-stow a memorial Som v ge-mynd-stow

4 Gemnise those being well, valentibus R Mt 9,12

5 Gemoet found R Mt 12,44 v gemet

1 Gemetgung, e; f Temperance, moderation moderamen Som

2 Gemeting, es m f a meeting; congressus Beo K 3997

Posted in thy ... Feby 27th 1838

3 Gemet-man a moderate man, homo moderatus Beo K 5862 189 Grn # 50, 1, 40

Gemeting a meeting Som v gemeting

6 Gemon remembers Beo K 2371 Grn I 909, 21 v gemunan

7 Gemong a multitude Th An

8 Gemot-ern, es; n a moot-hall, senate house Th An

Gemundig mindful Th An v gemyndig

guidance, moderation, temperance; temperantia :—*Bd.* 3, 5 : *Bt.* 39, 5.

Gemeten *measured, painted*; *pp. of* metan.

Geméteng, *a meeting*, v. gemeting.

Gemetfæst *modest, moderate*, v. gemætfæst.

Gemetfæstlice; *adv. Modestly*; modeste :—*Bd.* 5, 19.

Gemetfæstnys, se; *f. Modesty, moderation, sobriety*; modestia: —*Bd.* 3, 3, 14.

Gemetfæt, es; *n. A measuring vat, a measure*; mensura quævis definita :—An gemetfæt full, þe hig Gomor heton, *Ex.* 16, 16, 33.

Gemetgian, METGIAN, gemetian; *p.* ode; *pp.* od; *v. a. To temper, moderate, regulate, order, govern, restrain*; temperare: —A sceal þæt wiðerwearde gemetgian, *ever must the contrary moderate*, *Bt.* 21, *Card.* p. 114, 18. Se gemetgað þone bridel *he regulates the bridle*, *Bt.* 36, 2, *Card.* p. 270, 22: 39, 8. Se God se þat eall metgað *the God that governs all*, *Bt. R.* p. 165.

Geméting, gemétung, e; *f. Meeting*; conventus :—*Ors.* 4, 9. Fram gemetinge, *Ps.* 15. 4: 63, 2. Gemeting folces *a congregation of folk*, *V. Ps.* 61, 8.

n Gemetlic; *adj. Fit, moderate, modest*; aptus :—*Bt.* 14, 2: 40, 3.

Gemetlice; *adv. Meetly, soberly, modestly*; apte :—*Bd.* 4, 24.

Gemetlicung e; *f. Due, measure, moderation*; moderatio, *Som.*

Gemétnes, se; *f. A discovery, invention*; inventio :—*Bd.* 5, 10.

Gemetod *painted*, v. metan.

Gemetsian *To compare*; comparare :—*T. Ps.* 48, 21.

Gemettan *Eaters*; comestores, *Som.*

Gemetu *Metre, verse*; metrum, *Som.*

Gemiclian; *p.* de; *pp.* od; *v. a.* 1. *To increase, enlarge*; augere. 2. *To praise, extol*; magnificare :—1. *Ors.* 1, 12: *Ps.* 103, 1. 2. Gemicliað hine, *Ps.* 21, 22: 49, 16.

Gemiclung, myclung, e; *f.* [mycel *much, great*] *Greatness, magnificence, glory*; magnificentia :—*Ps.* 144, 5 : 70, 21.

Gemidlian, gemiddlian; *p.* de; *pp.* od [middel *middle*] 1. *To divide, to separate in the middle*; dimidiare. 2. *To keep in the middle, to restrain*; frænare: —1. *C. Ps.* 54, 27. 2. *Scint.* 12: *Past.* 38, 8.

Gemidlige *a bridle*, v. midl.

Gemieltan *to boil thoroughly*, v. gemeltan.

Gemigan *To water*, mingere, v. migan.

Gemilcian *to milk*, v. meolcian.

Gemildscad *Any thing mixed with honey*; mulsus, v. milisc.

Gemildsian *to pity*, v. gemiltsian, miltsian.

Gemilt *Consumed, melted*; absumptus, *Som.*

o Gemiltsian, ic gemiltsige *to pity, pardon*, v. miltsian.

Gemiltsung *mercy*, v. miltsung.

Gemimor *Known, cunning, skilful, expert*; notus :—*Bd.* 5, 20.

Gemimorlice; *adv. Knowingly, by heart, extempore*; memoriter :—*R. Ben. inter.* 13.

Gemineged *mixed*, v. mengan.

Gemind *memorial*, v. gemynd.

Gemindbliðe [bliðe *cheerful*] *A grateful remembrance, a memorial*; memoriale :—*T. Ps.* 101, 13.

Gemindig, gemyndig; *adj. Mindful*; memor :—*Ps.* 8, 5: 110, 5.

Gemindiglicnys, se; *f.* [licnes *likeness*] *A remembrance, memorial*; memoriale :—*Ps.* 101, 13.

Gemittan *to meet, find*, v. metan.

Gemittincg, gemitting, gemittung, e; *f. A meeting, assembly*; congressus :—*Ors.* 4. 6, 8. Wega gemittung *a meeting of ways*, *Lye.*

Gemme A GEM; gemma :—Sweor-gemme *a neck-gem* or *lace*; monile :—*Cot.* 170.

Gemnis, se; *f. Care, anxiety*; cura :—Ne is þe gemnisse *non est tibi curæ*, *C. R. Lk.* 10, 40.

Gemod [mod *mind*] *Of one mind, agreed, plotted*; concors : —*Solil.* 8.

Gemodsumian *To agree*; concordare :—*Past.* 46, 6.

Gemodsumnes, se; *f. An agreement, concord*; concordia :—*Past.* 46, 5.

Gemodþencende [þencende *thinking*] *Agreeing*; consentiens :—*R. Mt.* 5, 25.

p Gemolsnad *Rotten, putrified*; tabefactus : — *R.* 12, v. formolsnian.

Gemolten *molten, melted*, v. meltan.

Gemon, *for* genom *laid hold of, took*, *C. Mk.* 5, 41, v. niman.

Gemong *among*, v. gemang.

Gemonian, ic gemonige; *p.* ode; *pp.* od. *To remind, remember, recollect*; monere, meminisse: —Seo leo gemonð þæs wildan gewunan *the lion remembers the wild manner*, *Bt.* 25, *Card.* p. 136, 16 : *Bd.* 4, 19, v. monian.

Gemonigfealdan; *p.* ode. *To increase, multiply*; amplificare : —*Bd.* 5, 20.

Gemonnad *manned, supplied with men*, v. gemannian.

Gemot; *adj. Agreeing, according*; consentiens :—*R. Mt.* 5, 25.

Gemot; *n.* [gemet; *pp. of* metan *to meet*] 1. *A meeting*, MOTE or MOOT, *assembly, council*; conventus. 2. *A deliberation, consultation, advice, counsel*; consilium :—1. Eall þat gemot sohton lease saga, *Mt.* 26, 59. Þa gesomnedon hi gemot *then summoned they a meeting*, *Bd.* 1, 14, *S.* p. 482, 35. Ær þat gemot sy *ere the meeting is*, *L. Athel.* 20, *W.* p. 60, 7. On þæm gemote, *id.* 2. Hig hæfdon micel gemot, þat hig woldon þone Hælend ofslean, *Mt.* 26. 4. Þa gesamnudun þa ealdras hig and worhtun gemot, *Mt.* 28, 12. ¶ Witena gemot *an assembly of the wise*; (sapientum conventus, *Bd.* 3, 5.) *the supreme council of the Anglo-Saxon nation or parliament.*—The king, the gentry or thegns, knights, bishops and abbots, were members of it. Some were elected. *Mr. Turner* says (*Hist. of A.-S.* b. 8, ch. 14. vol. iii. p. 180) after many years' consideration, I am inclined to believe, that the Anglo-Saxon witena gemot very much resembled our present parliament, in the orders and persons that composed it; and that the members, who attended as representatives, were chosen by classes, analogous to those who now possess the elective franchise.—Synoðlice gemot *a synod*; synodale consilium, *Pref. R. Conc.*—Biscopa gemot *a bishop's meeting*, *Bd.* 1, 14.—Folc gemot *an asbly of the people*, *L. Alf.* 30, *W.* p. 41, 35.—Gemot ærn *a meeting place, a hall*, *Ors.* 5, 12. Gemot man *a senator, preacher*, *Elf. gl.* 5.—Gemot stow *a meeting-place*, *T. Ps.* 25, 4.—Scir gemot *a meeting of a shire*, *Hickes's Dis.* p. 2.

q Gemotod *disputed, discussed*, v. motian.

Gemultan *to melt*, v. meltan.

Gemunan, MUNAN; *p.* de; *pp.* en; *v. a. To remember, call to mind, consider, reflect*; reminisci :—Gemunan his halegan cyðnesse, *Lk.* 1, 72. Gemunað wundra his, *Ps.* 104, 5. Ne bið gemunen naman, *Ps.* 82, 4: 108, 4, v. munan.

Gemund *Meditation*; meditatio, *Som.*

Gemundbyrdan, gemundian; *p.* de [mund *a defence*, byrd *birth*] *To protect life, defend, patronize*; protegere :— *Bt.* 35, 6, *Card.* p. 262, 15: *Cd.* 113.

Gemung, e; *f. A marriage;* nuptiæ:—*R. Mt.* 22, 2, 3.
Gemunglic *Marriagelike, nuptial;* nuptialis:—*R. Mt.* 22, 12.
Gemyltan *to melt,* v. meltan.
Gemynan *to remind, admonish,* v. gemunan.
Gemynd, es; *m. Mind, memory, memorial, commemoration, intention, purpose, consideration;* mens:—*Elf. T.* p. 24. To his gemynde *to his mind, Bt.*35, 1, *Ex.* 17, 14: *Mt.* 26, 13. Þurh modes gemynd *by thought of mind, Cd.* 52. ¶ Gemynd dæg *commemoration day, Bd.* 3, 8. Gemynd drepe *mind's swoon, delirium.*
Gemyndelic; *adj. Belonging to memory, memorable;* memorabilis:—*Bd.* 3, 16.
Gemyndelice; *adv. By memory, without book;* memoriter:—Butan bec, *Deut.* 31, 19.
Gemyndgian, gemyndan; *p.* de, te; *pp.* ded, ted, t. *To remember, commemorate, remind, attend, determine, resolve;* reminisci, attendere, statuere:—Þu gemyndest þa word *thou rememberest the word, Bt.*35, 2, *Card.* p. 244, 24. Gemynted hafað *hath resolved, Bd.* 3, 9. Hæfde gemynt, *Gen.* 18, 33: *Num.* 24, 11, v. myngian.
Gemyndig *Mindful;* memor:—*Bd.* 4, 26, *S.* p. 600, 14.
Gemynt *remembered,* v. gemunan.
Gemyð *mouth of a river,* v. muða.
GE'N, gēna, gien, giena; *adv.* [Frs.jin] *Again, moreover, besides, at length, as yet, hitherto;* iterum:—Þa gen *then again, Cd.* 98: *Bd.* 2, 7.
Genacian, genacodian, benacan; *p.* ode; *pp.* od, nacod, genacod. *To make bare, naked, to strip;* nudare:—*Bd.* 4, 3.
Genæfd *Necessity, need;* necessitas:—*Bt.* 14, 1.
Genægdon *approached,* v. nægde.
Genæged [*Dut.* geneigd *inclined*] *Subdued, humbled;* subactus:—*Mt.* 23, 12.
Genæs, genæson *saved,* v. genesan.
Genæte *oppressed, afflicted,* v. gehnægde.
Genamode *named, called,* v. nemnan.
Genap *Shaded, extinguished, destroyed;* extinxit:—*Cd.* 166.
Gend-geotan; *p.* gendgute. *To pour out fully,* v. geond.
Geneadian *to compel,* v. neadian.
Geneah, geneahe, geneahhe *nigh, sufficient.*—geneahht *sufficiently,* v. neah.
Genealæcan; *p.* læhte; *pp.* læht, we læhton. *To approach, draw near, adhere, hasten;* appropinquare:—Hit to him na to genealæcað, *Ps.* 31, 8: 33, 5. Folce genealæcendum him, *Ps.* 148, 14. Geneolacende, *C.Mt.* 4, 3.
Genealæcnung, e; *f. An approach;* appropinquatio:—*Herb.* 156.
Genear, gener *A refuge, protection;* refugium:—Genear min eart þu, *Ps.* 90, 2: *Ors.* 1, 12.
Genearwod, wad, wot *straightened, vexed, oppressed,* v. nearwian.
Geneat, geneat-mann, es; *m.* [neat, nitan *cattle*] *A cowherd, farmer, bailif, husbandman, vassal, associate, servant;* bubulcus, colonus:—Be cyninges geneate, *L. In. Tit.* 19, 22. Strange geneatas *strong associates, Cd.* 15.
Genec *A light ship, a frigate;* liburnica:—*Cot.* 120.
Genedde, genidde, geniedde, geneded, geniedeed, genided, genied, gened *forced, compelled, urged, invited,* v. nydan.
Genededlic; *adj. Compulsive, coercive;* compulsorius:—*Bd.* 1, 26.
Genefa *a nephew, Ors.* 6, 1, v. nefa.
Genehhe *near,* v. neah.
Genehlice *chiefly,* v. neahlice.
Geneh was, genh wes *adheres, cleaves to;* geneh wade *adhered, C. Mt.* 19, 5.
Genemned, genemnod, genemnd *named,* v. nemnan.
Geneop *destroyed, Cd.* 166, v. genap.
Geneosian; *p.* ode; *pp.* od. *To visit, Ps.* 8, 5, v. neosian.
Geneosung *a visiting, Lk.* 19, 44, v. neosung.
Geneoðerian *to condemn,* v. niðerian.
Gener *a refuge,* v. genear.
Generenes, se; *f. A taking, deliverance;* ereptio:—*Bd.* 4, 22.
Generian; *p.* ode; *pp.* od, ed. *To save, deliver, Ps.* 34, 12, v. nerian.
Generwde *vexed,* v. nearwian.
Genesan he genist; *p.* genæs; *pp.* genesen [*Dut.* genezen] *To heal, to be recovered, saved, preserved;* sanare, servari:—Guðe genæs *saved in battle, Cd.* 94: *Ors.* 4, 8, *Bar.* p. 157, 8.
Genesburuh *Gainsborough,* v. Gegnesburh.
Geneðan; *p.* de. *To subdue, bring under, decline;* subjugare:—Ne dorste he geneðan, *Ors.* 1, 10, *Bar.* p. 48, 15: 41, 8: *Cd.* 170. Nihtes geneðeð, *Bt. R.* p. 169, 16.
Geng, genga *a privy;* latrina; *Cot.* 123, v. gang.
Gengdon *passed,* v. gangan, gan.
Genge A GANG, *flock, company;* grex:—*Chr.* 1070.
Genge *would go,* v. gan.
Genge beon *To prevail;* multum posse:—*Bd.* 3, 12, *Lye.*
Gengyme *A meeting, assembly;* conventus:—*T. Ps.* 63, 2.
Genhlade, genlade *An unloading, a discharging, an arm of the sea, into which a river discharges itself;* exoneratio, brachium oceani, *Som.*
Genian *to yawn,* v. ganian.
Genierede, wod *vexed,* v. nearwian.
Geniht *abundance,* v. genyht.
Genihtlice; *adv. Abundantly;* abunde:—*Cot.* 6.
Genihtsum; *adj. Abundant, plentiful, fruitful;* abundans:—*Bd.* 5, 11.
Genihtsumian; *p.* ode; *pp.* od. *To suffice, abound;* abundare:—*Ps.* 64, 14: 72, 12: 127, 3.
Genihtsumlice; *adv. Sufficiently, abundantly, plentifully;* abunde:—*Ps.* 30, 30: *Bd.* 1, 27, *resp.* 8.
Genihtsumnes, se; *f. An abundance, plenty, sufficiency;* abundantia:—*Ps.* 29, 7: 64, 12.
Geniman; *p.* genam, genom; *pp.* genumen. *To take, obtain, enter into,* v. niman.
Genioman *to take, seize,* v. niman.
GENIP, es; *pl.* u. *A cloud;* nubes:—On þat genip, *Lk.* 9, 34. Of þam genipe, *Lk.*9, 35. And hig ealle gesawon þat þat genip stod, *Ex.* 33, 10: *Ps.* 76, 16.
Genirwed *vexed,* v. nearwian.
Geniðerian, geniðrian; *p.* ode; *pp.* od. *To condemn, Elf. gl.* 28, v. niðerian.
Geniðle, an. *Hatred, enmity;* odium:—Ic onfeng feonda geniðlan *I took the hatred of enemies, Cod. ex.* p. 29: *Jdth.* 11, *Thw.* p. 24, 37.
Geniwian *to renew, Ps.* 50, 11, v. niwian.
Geniwung, e; *f. A renewing, recovering;* renovatio, *Som.*
Genlade *a discharging,* v. genhlade.
Genneahhe *nigh,* v. geneah.
Gennelung, e; *f. Greatness;* magnificentia:—*Ps.* 67, 37.
GENOG, genoh, noh; *adv.* [*Plat. Ger.* genug: *Dut.* genoeg: *Frs.* genoach: *Moes.* ganah: *Al.* ginuoh: *Dan.* nok: *Swed.* nog: *Icel.* gnógr, nóg: *Heb.* נוח nuh, nuch *a rest, from* נח nh *to settle:* in *Hiph. to give rest*] *Sufficiently, abundantly,* ENOUGH; satis, abunde:—Genog sweotol hit is *it is sufficiently manifest.* Genog riht þu segst *rightly enough thou sayest, Bt.* 33, 1. Genoh hit is, *Mk.* 14, 41. Hæfð genoh, *Mt.* 6, 34. Habbon genoh, *Jn.* 10, 10.
Genogan *to multiply;* multiplicare, *Lye.*

15 Gewarn (ran again, arn p of yrnan) a meeting; occursus C. Ps 58,5 Lye

Gemyclian to extol Som gemiclian

2 Gemyltyd melted Som v gemolten

(ch. sast from neolan to ongen of oper, shaver) [Som]

Gemynd-bennimning mindbenumming; lethargia Cot 126

1 Ge-neat 4 socius Bd 22 Th. An

Gemynd-dæg es; m memorations day; commemorationis dies, sive natalis Bd 3,8

Genehe numerous, enough Th. an v geneahhe

Genemnian to name Th. Ipol v nemnan

Gemyndleas adj 1 Mindless, witless, rash; amens, insipiens 2 Forgetful, immemor Som

3 Genende acta Cot, Lye

7 Gemyndleasnes se; f Witlessness, madness; amentia Som

Ge-nehost abounce, ablest; proximae Beok 1582 v neah [29a8]

8 Gemynd-stow memorial; monumentum Som

Generigan, to save Cd 117 Th 152,22

9 Gemynd-wyrde worthy of remembrance, memorable Som

Genægladd nailed [Th.] R Mt 27,22 p of næglian

Geneahhe enough Th. an

Genefan, to dare, audere:

11 Gemynegod remembered; memoratus Som

5 Geneddon dared Beok 1912 v sol nēðan

Genemnan, pode to name Th an v nemnan

Genap clelle, shaded put Genap a cloud Cd 166 Th p 206, 20 v genip

13 Genamian to name Th An v nemnan

Genicelede carved 2 also adj. obscure, Bosw

2 Genidde, genidde genied, geneded, geniede d, geneded compelled, urged invited v genedde

Genierwed distressed Sort v geniervad

Genip, es; n darkness; caligo under the fills darkness Beok 2710

Th. An

Genidla, an m hate enmity; malitia Beogl

Gemyngian to remember, meditate admonish Th. An

V nixis, hrun ...

Geohsa. sgabbinr; singultus Som

3 Geold a payment; Som v gild

3) Geolewiarte. a nightingale; luscinius; R 38 Lye

1 Gemumen taken, p. p. ofgenimen

2 Gezeorrad altogether; quickly citos. Obs. Mir. 10 Lye Som

Gengydda

1) Genyddan pressed Cd 140, Th p 157, 28 v genydan

3)

4 Genyttan To enjoy; uped, od munere fungi: Beo K 6088

5 Geóc, e; f con fort help; consolatio; aux lium Beo K 353

— leccende wetting, moistening; about

sawan to sow about scatter, Cd 188 Th 233, 19

sendan to send, cast about; to overspread

9 Geocre ado Harshly severely; aspere Cd 183 Th p 229, 3 v geoc

1 Geodon for eodon went Th An

12 Geofon-yd, e; f a sea wave Beo K 1025

Geogara afold Him Som

2 Geogara Som

Beus geohhel

Geogud-leorunge; a tithing of young kite foetuum decema Som

Geohol geohol geol; m

1 Geola; Som; m Gr. i. Mytt. XXI

xxiv 10

On pone salteden on the eighth geohhel-dæg bid yule day is the 1 pæs monðes fruma first of the month pe mon nemned wh men name se æftera geola the after yule die octavo a Natr vitalis festo inchoatur mensis, qui dicitur posterior geola vel Januarius Marshall S. Gos p. 521: Junius Etymol. sub yool. Iddon on Latin bedum heo ba pian wolde, butan pam hyhstum symbel nessum & tidum æt Eastrum, & æt Pentecosten, & pys twelfstan dæge ofer geohol raro in calidas latices praeter imminentibus sollemniis majoribus verbi gratia Paschae Pentecostes, Epiphaniae lavari voluerit, on the twelfth day after yule or christmas. Bd 4, 19, Sm p 588, 6. 163, 4 — Junius sub yool fuis, in this passage geohol, gehhel

Geolna A kind of Egyptian stork; ibis R. 38 Lye

Geomor-mód sad minded, sorrowful Beak 4083

Geomrian to sigh; Som v geomerian

2 Geomrung groaning

Geond-geotan to pour out; suffuse

2 Geond-blawan blow upon

— rende turning back

faran to go through

— gang pass over

— geat-geotan pour out suffuse

— lihtan to enlighten

— scenan to seek

— scinan shine

— scrídan to traverse

— secan to seek

— seon to look over

— sprengan to sprinkle

— spurned over

— stregdan to strew over

— to scatter over

— pehtan to look

— wlitan to look

— yrnan to run through

Geong-cempa young soldier Som

Genoh; *g.* es, re, es; *adj. Sufficient, abundant;* abundans:—Dugeða genohra *of abundant blessings, Cd.* 42.

Genohtud, benotod *used, noted,* v. notian.

Gent *Ghent, in Flanders;* Gandavum:—*Chr.* 879.

Gentod *Driven;* pulsus:—*Chr. Gib.* 975, p. 123, 39.

Genycled *Knuckled, crooked;* obuncus, *Som.*

Genydan, he genyt; *p.* de; *pp.* ed. *To compel,* v. nydan.

Genydmagas, genyhemagas *those necessarily related, related by blood.*

Genyht, geniht *An abundance, plenty, sufficiency, fulfilment;* abundantia:—*Bt.* 33, 1, *Card.* p. 186, 18: 35, 3: *Cd.* 90.

Genyhtfull, genyhtsum *plentiful,* v. genihtsum.

Genyman *to take, Ps.* 49, 17, v. niman.

Genyrwian *to narrow, restrain, press, Lk.* 19, 43: *Ps.* 68, 19, v. nearwian.

Genyt *compels,* v. nydan.

Genyðerian, genyðrian; *p.* ode; *pp.* od, ad, ud. *To humble, condemn, Ps.* 17, 29: *Lk.* 6, 37, v. niðerian.

Genyðerung *humility, condemnation,* v. nyðerung.

Geo; *adv.* [*Frs.* ea] *Formerly, of old;* olim:—*Bd.* 1, 1: 4, 3, 4. ¶ Geo ær, geo hwilum, geo dagum, geo gara, geo geara *heretofore, long ago, Bt.* 31, 1.

Geoc; *n.* [*Plat.* juk, jok *n: Dut.* juk *n: Frs.* jok *n: Ger.* joch *n: Per.* [Persian] yogh: *Sans.* yuga] A yoke; jugum:—*Ps.* 2, 3: *Mt.* 11, 29, 30.

Geoc; *adj.* [*Plat. Dut.* gek *foolish: Kil.* gheck: *Ger.* geck *foolish: Moes.* juk] *Rash, violent, troublesome;* præceps:—*Cd.* 183: 205.

Geocan *To keep, save;* servare:—Geoca user *preserve us, Cd.* 188. Geocend *saving, a saviour, Cod. ex.* p. 10, b.

Geocboga *a yoke,* v. geoc.

Geóc; *Safety, help, succour;* salus:—*Bd.* 5, 13. Geoce gefremede *might afford succour, Cd.* 77.

Geocend *a saviour,* v. geocan.

Geocsa, geocsung *A sobbing;* singultus:—*Bt. R.* p. 152: *R.* 99.

Geoc-stecca, geoc-sticca *A bolt of a door, a bar;* obex:—*Cot.* 145.

Geof *a gift, Bd.* 1, 33, v. gifu.

Geoffrian; *p.* ode; *pp.* od. *To offer, sacrifice, Elf. T.* p. 8, 13.

Geofian *to give, Cd.* 26, v. gifan.

Geofon, es. *The sea, deep;* mare:—*Cd.* 171. Geofonhus *a seahouse, Cd.* 66.

Geogelere *A juggler;* præstigiator, *Som.*

GEOGUÐ, geogeð, geogoð, geogað, iuguð; [*Plat.* jögd *f: Dut.* jeugd *f: Frs.* jeucht *c: Ger.* jugend *f.*] Youth, *a youngling, the young;* juventus:—Of minre geoguðe, *Mk.* 10, 20: *Gen.* 8, 24.—Geogað hád *youth, the state of youth, docility.*

Geoguðlic; *adj.* Youthlike; juvenilis:—*Bd.* 5, 6.

Geol, geohol, gehhol, iule [*Dan.* juul: *Swed.* jul: *Icel.* jól: *Norse,* jaul: *Arm.* gouel, gouil *a feast*] Yule, *Christmas;* festum nativitatis Domini:—On geol *at Christmas, L. Alf.* 5, 39. ¶ Se ærra geola *the ere or before yule, December.* Se æftera geola *the after yule, January.* Se monað is nemned on Leden, *Decembris,* and on ure geþeode se ærra geola; *Januarius* se æftera geola, *Cott. Tiberius,* b. 1: *Hickes's Thes.* vol. i. p. 212, 55, v. *Fox, Menol.* p. 59, n. l. 3.

Geolca, gioleca, A yolk: ovi vitellus:—*Serm. in Nat.*

Geoleccan; *v. a. To allure;* blandiri:—Þa hi þe mæst geoleccan *when they most allured thee, Bt.* 7, 2.

Geolewe, geolu, geoluwe, geolwa, geolwe *yellow,* v. gelew.—Geolo-read *yellow red;* croceus.—Geoluhwit *yellow white;* mellinus, color stramineus.—Geolwe-blac *yellow black;* fulvus, *L. M.* 3, 62.—Geoluwe adl, geolwa adl *yellow addle, jaundice;* icterus.

Geolhstor, geolster, *matter, corruption, poison, venom;* sanies: *Bd.* 4, 19.

Geolstru *Full of poison, virulent;* virulentus, *Som.*

Geomeleaslice *carelesly,* v. gymeleaslice.

Geomen *care,* v. gymen.

Geomer, geomor, geomre [*Plat. Dut. Ger.* jammer *m. pity*] Grum, *sad, sorrowful;* querulus, mœstus:—Geomre gastas *sad spirits, Cd.* 4. Þu scealt geomor hweorfan *thou shalt sad depart, Cd.* 48. Geomor-mod *sad minded, Gen.* 27, 34: *Cd.* 40.

Geomerian, geomrian; *p.* ode; *pp.* od. *To grieve, groan, mourn, lament, bewail;* gemere:—*Bd.* 1, 27, *resp.* 9. Se Hælend geomrode on hys gaste, *Jn.* 11, 33, 38. Geomriende, geomrigende, *Mk.* 5, 38: 8, 12: *Gen.* 42, 38.

Geomerung, geomrung; e; *f. A groaning, lamentation;* gemitus:—*Ps.* 6, 6: *Bd.* 1, 13: *Ps.* 30, 12.

Geomian *to take care of,* v. gyman.

Geomorlic *Doleful, afflictive;* querribundo similis:—*Ors.* 4, 5.

Geona, geone *hitherto, through, during, Ps.* 7, 12, v. gen.

Geonan, geonian *to yawn, chatter,* v. gynian.

Geon-bæran; *p.* geonbyrde. *To bear against, oppose, resist;* opponere:—*L. Edw. and Guth.* 6.

Geonc *young, Bt.* 8, v. geong.

Geond, geondan; *prep. ac.* [*Plat.* günner: *Dut.* ginder: *Frs.* gint: *Moes.* jaind.—ge, *Frs.* ond *to, as far as, by*] *Through, over, as far as, after, beyond;* per, ultra:—He gæð geond drige stowa, *Mt.* 12, 43: 14, 35: *Lk.* 19, 1: 21, 12. Geond to þam stane, *Num.* 20, 8. Geond feowertig daga *after forty days, Num.* 13, 22. Fram geondan sæ *from beyond sea, Chr.* 1047, v. begeond.

Geond; *adv. Yond, yonder, thither, beyond;* illuc:—Hider and geond *hither and thither, Bd.* 5, 13. Hyder geond *yonder, Mt.* 26, 36.

Geondettan *to confess, L. Alf.* 14, v. andettan.

Geondfolen *beyond full, filled throughout, Cd.* 2.

Geond-send, geondsended *overspread.*

Geondspettan *to spit or squirt out.*

Geond spregde *poured out;* perfudit:—*Guthl. vit.* c. 6.

Geonduarde *Answered;* respondit:—*C. Mt.* 3, 15.

Geone *through,* v. geona.

Geonetan; *pp.* geonet. *To occupy, fill up, hasten;* occupare:—*C. Lk.* 13, 7: *Cot.* 149.

Geong *a journey, path, C. Lk.* 10, 33, v. gang.

Geong *Sighs;* gemitus:—*Bd.* 1, 13.

Geong, ging, geonc, giung, gung; *def.* se geonga; *comp.* gyngra, geongra; *sup.* gyngest; *adj.* [*Plat.* junk: *Dut.* jong: *Ger.* jung: *Swed. Dan.* ung] Young, *tender;* juvenis:—Þa ic geong wæs *when I was young, Bd.* 4. 19. Se geonga man, *Mt.* 19, 22. Geongra *younger, a younger, one obedient, a servant, vassal.* Geongra weorðan *to be a vassal, Cd.* 15: *Bd.* 4, 23.

Geongerdóm, geongordóm, es; *m. Youngership, minority, subjection, obedience, service;* juvenilis status:—*Cd.* 14: 15: 30: 35.

Geonglic; *adj. Youthful, young;* juvenilis:—*Elf. gr.* 9, 28.

Geonglienys, se; *f. Youth;* juventus:—*Scint.* 32.

Geongling, gungling, es; *m.* [*Dut.* jongeling] *A Youngling, a boy;* juvenis:—*Ælf. gr. pref.*: *R. Mt.* 18, 2.

Geonre *There, yonder;* illuc, *Som.*

Geonung, e; *f.* A YAWNING, *braying, chattering;* oscitatio, barritus:—*Cot.* 95.

GEORN; *adj.* [*Plat.* geern: *Dut.* gaarne: *Frs.* jern: *Ger.* gern: *Dan.* gierne: *Swed.* gerna: *Icel.* giarn] *Desirous, eager, studious, intent, careful, diligent;* cupidus:—Þæs gefeohtes georn *eager for the fight, Ors.* 3, 8. Þat ic seo teonum georn *that I be anxious for mischiefs, Cd.* 27.

Georne; *comp.* or; *sup.* ost, est; *adv. Earnestly, diligently;* diligenter:—Herodes befran hi georne, *Mt.* 2, 7. He geornor wolde sibbe *he more earnestly desired peace, Ors.* 3, 1: *L. Cnut. eccl.* 11, *W.* p. 135, 12. Swa mon geornest mæg *to his utmost;* pro virili.

Geornes, gyrnes, se; *f. Earnestness, diligence, industry, care, endeavour;* solertia:—*Bd.* 3, 6, 11, 17, 23, 28, 30.

Geornest *earnest, vehement, Som.*, v. georne.

Geornfull, geornfullic; *adj. Full of desire, eager, solicitous, anxious, intent:* solicitus:—*Lk.* 10, 41: *Bd.* 2, 1: 5, 11, v. georn.

Geornfullice; *adv. Most anxiously* or *diligently;* studiose:—*Bd.* 5, 13, 20.

b Geornfulnes, se; *f. Diligence, earnestness, zeal, fervour;* solertia:—*Bd.* 3, 7, 23, 30: *L. eccl. Edg.* 5.

Geornian, girnan, gyrnan; *p.* de [georn *eager*] *To desire, study, seek for,* YEARN, *require;* desiderare:—Satanas gyrnde, *Lk.* 22, 31: *Bt.* 18, 2. Þat ge georniað þam þinga *that ye earnestly desire the things, L. Athel. pref., W.* p. 55, 56, 61. Girn þu fram me, *Ps.* 2, 8: *Chr.* 674, *Ing.* p. 52, 2.

Geornlic; *adj. Earnest, diligent;* diligens:—*Ors.* 4, 12.

Geornlice; *adv.* 1. *Diligently, anxiously;* diligenter. 2. *Therefore, on that account;* ergo:—1. *Mt.* 2, 8: *Lk.* 7, 4. 2. *Bd.* 3, 8, *Lye.*

Geornung, gyrning, e; *f.* 1. *An endeavour, industry;* industria. 2. *A petition;* petitio. 3. *Merit, desert;* meritum:—1. *Lye.* 2. *Chr.* 675, *Ing.* p. 50, 30. 3. *R. Conc.* 1.

Georrettan. 1. *To defame, slander;* infamare. 2. *To defile, disfigure, deface;* turpare:—1. *Cot.* 111. 2. *Som.*

Georsod *enraged, L. Ps.* 105, 37, v. geyrsian.

Georst *heath,* v. gorst.

Georstan-dæg *yesterday,* v. gyrstan-dæg.

Geortruwian *to distrust, despair, Bt.* 10, *Card.* p. 44, 28, v. ortruwian.

Georwenan; *pp.* ed [wen *hope*] *To despair, to be out of hope;* desperare:—Georwened *out of hope, desperate;* desperatus:—*Bd.* 5, 14.

Georwyrðed *Disgraced;* traductus:—*Cot.* 171, v. orwurðe.

Geosterlic *yesterday,* v. gysternlic.

c Geot *yet, Bt.* 5, 3, v. gyt.

GEOTAN, he gyt; *p.* geát, get, we guton; *pp.* goten, gegoten; *v. a.* [*Dut.* gieten: *Frs.* jiette: *Plat.* geeten: *Ger.* giessen: *Dan.* gyde: *Swed.* gjuta] *To pour, pour out, shed;* fundere:—He get þat blod, *Lev.* 8, 24. Geat tearas *shed tears;* fundebat lachrymas:—*Bd.* 2, 6.

Geotende *A pouring out, an artery* or *vein;* arteriæ:—*Cot.* 8.

Geotere *A melter;* fusor:—*Ors.* 1, 12.

Geotton *confirmed,* v. geatan.

Geoweorða *Jugurtha, Ors.* 5, 7.

Geoweðan *To subdue;* subjugare, *Som.*

Geoxa, geoxung *a sobbing, hiccup, Cot.* 109, v. geocsa.

Gep *sly, cunning, Scint.* 3, 24, 65, v. geap.

Gepilod *heaped* or *piled up, Ex.* 16, 14.

Geplægde *danced,* v. plægan.

Gepose *The pose, stuffing of the head;* gravedo, dolor capitis:—*Herb.* 46, 1, *Som.*

Geprice *A point* or *comma;* comma, *Som.*

Gepunian *To* POUND, *bray, break;* comminuere:—*Herb.* 100, 3, v. punian.

Gepyndan *To* POUND, *empound, shut in;* circumcludere:—*Past.* 39, 1.

Ger *a year, Lk.* 2, 36, v. gear.

Gerad *invaded,* v. geridan.

Gerad; *n.* [ræd *advise*] *Consideration, account, condition, reason, wisdom, prudence, manner;* ratio, conditio:—Þa he þæt gerad sette, *Mt.* 18, 24. Se hlaford dyhte hym gerad, *Mt.* 25, 19: *Ælf. gr. pref., Som.* p. 1, 33. ¶ On þat gerade, (*Ors.* 1, 12.) On þa gerad (*Bt.* 7, 3, *Card.* p. 32, 16,) *on the condition* or *account.*

d Gerad; *adj. Considered, instructed, learned, skilful, expert, prudent, suited, conditioned;* prudens:—Of geradra worda *from considerate words, Bt.* 2, *Card.* p. 4, 25. Gif ic þe geradne gemete *if I find thee instructed* [*skilful*], *id.* 5, 1. Gerad beon wið his wyrd *to be suited to his fortune, id.* 11, 1. ¶ Þus gerad, swa gerad *such, of such sort, Bt.* 39, 11, *Card.* p. 352, 12.

Geradnes, se; *f. An agreement, a conspiracy;* conjuratio:—*Cot.* 209.

Geradod *quickened, moved, arranged, Bt.* 35, 2, v. hradian.

Geradscipe, es; *m.* [gerad *consideration,* scipe *condition*] *Prudence;* prudentia:—*Bt. R.* p. 183.

Geræc *Opportunity, season;* opportunitas:—*Ps.* 9, 9.

Geræcan; *p.* geræhte; *pp.* geræht; *v. a. To reach, occupy, obtain, earn, seize, lay hold of, reach to, to extend;* attingere, assequi:—Sio fyrd hie geræcan ne mihte *the army could not reach them, Chr.* 895. Þu scealt þine and þine geræcan *thou shalt earn thy sustenance, Cd.* 43: *Chr.* 921. Geræcan tearas of eagum *fundere lachrymas ab oculis, L. Can. Edg. poen. magn.* 3, *W.* p. 97, 27. Geræhte þa burh *seized the city, Ors.* 2, 4.

e Geræd *prudent,* v. gerad.

Geræd *ready, quick, Bd.* 5, 23, *S.* p. 648, 27, v. hræd.

Gerædde, gerædded *arranged, prepared, determined, decreed,* v. rædan.

Gerædde, geræd *read, considered, imagined,* v. rædan.

Gerǽde, gerǽdu, gereda, gerædro. *Trappings;* phaleræ:—*Ælf. gl.* 23.

Gerǽding *Decrees;* consulta:—*Cot.* 59.

Gerǽdnys, se; *f. An ordinance, a decree, purpose, an intention, a resolution;* consultum:—*L. Edg. pol.* 1.

Geræf *Fixed;* fixus:—*L. Alf. pol.* 28.

Geræft *Torn, distracted;* discerptus:—*Bt.* 37, 1.

Geræpan *to bind, Bt. R.* p. 167, v. ræpan.

Geræsde *rushed,* v. ræsan.

Gerǽstan *To rest, sit;* quiescere:—Gerǽstan mid þone Hæland, *C. Mt.* 9, 10, v. ræstan.

Geræwen, geræwud *Set in rows, plaited, embroidered;* segmentatus:—*R.* 63.

Gerafende, gerawende RIFING, *cleaving;* infindens:—*Cot.* 181.

Gerar *A roaring, howling;* boatus, ululatus:—*Martyr.* 10. *Jan.*

Geongor-scipe es; m Youngership, service; servitium

Geon-hweorfende or ing back Som

Geon-hwearfan to turn, bring back Som

Yeonian to yawn v geonan

Geon-smead made manifest, enucleatus

~~Geopenian~~ geopnian, p ode; pp od. act. neut to open Th An

~~Geopenode~~ opened 19.24 v openian

Georman-leaf cormen-letic ~~m~~ malva Cot 201: R.42 v spl cormen-leaf

Geosceaft, e f ... power; poten tia Beo K 2467: 2532

Geonguifrd an, m a spider; aranea Ps Th: 89.10

~~Geonstew dag yester day Som~~

ed. Th p 16 v Baeln ~~scapen~~ scapan v geongor-scipe

~~Geraedigean ne; Tinelu conferre; suffer tare cum aliquo Lye~~

~~Gepicad pitched; picatus Som~~

~~Geplantod planted v plantian~~

~~Gepricud pricked goaded v priccian~~

~~Gerade in order Beo K 1740~~

~~Georned, se.f.~~

~~Gerad spraec, or word prose; sermo solutus, prosa Som. Ben Lye~~

~~Geraed, e f. Housing trapping; phalerae Th An~~

~~spraec, v Gerad, word prose Som v gerad-spraec~~

(a)

~~Geraed-man a prudent man, a counsellor Som~~

~~Geraedad taught instructed, v gerade~~

~~Gerahte reached p of geraecan~~

Gerecan ruet? Cd 224 th p 295, 20 p of hreowan

Gereda Beport? furniture, apparel, apparatus Som

Ge-redra (rotor an rower; oar) socius remigande Grein II 737, 6

Gerethre, gerot-ll

Geretor; gerethres; pl gretraru; in an oar rower; pl rotor

Ger-cyning a year king, consul Lye v Year-cyning

1 Grein dose from roof tectum II 737, 5

Gereccenod explained, interpreted Cd 69 Th p 211, 12 v recan p rehte

Geredu ornaments of a ship; aplustra Som

(Beow 891)

Golde geregnad with gold adorned Beow K 1547

Gerenod seasoned, tempered, mixed; conditus Som

Gereocan to smoke Som v reocan

Gereordan to transact, dispatch, to come to a conclusion; transigere Som

Gereording a meal Th an v gereording

Geres (as of gaers) from [illegible] sedge A fen, marsh; [illegible] lus Som.

Ger-hwamlice yearly; ana annu[illegible] athun Som

Gericod enriched; ditatus Som.

Gerifled, gerifl[illegible] gerefod wrinkled, rivelled; rugatus Som

7

Gerihtaes a right, ceremon[illegible] Th an v riht

Geriht-wise[illegible] es m A teacher of the law, a Sadducee Th an

Gerim-craeft the art of numbers, arithmetic, metre Som v rim-craeft rim-at

10)

Gerinad adorned; ornatus Lye v gerenian

Geras *It became, it ought;* decuit:—*Bd.* 3, 8, 17, v. riseð.

Gerd *A yard, rod, reed, twig, young shoot;* virga, arundo:—*Solil. pref. C. R. Mt.* 9, 7: 12, 20.

Gerdel *a girdle, Prov.* 31, v. gyrdel.

Gere *well,* v. geara.

Gereafod *bereaved, spoiled,* v. reafian.

Gereaht *ruled, explained, guided, corrected,* v. recan.

Gereapan *to bind, Bt. R.* p. 187, v. ræpan.

Gerec, gehrec *Rule, government, direction, exposition, correction;* regimen:—*Bd.* 4, 12.

Gereca *A governor, ruler;* præfectus:—Heah gereca, *Hom. Nat. Greg.* p. 21, 1.

Gerecan, gereccan, gereccean *to tell, say, shew, instruct, explain, define, fix, establish, rule, govern, compel, subdue, Bt.* 11, 2: 20, *Card.* p. 108, 22, v. reçan.

Gereccednys, gerecednys, gerecennes, se; *f. A narration, history, report, an interpretation, a direction, correction, heap;* relatio:—*Ps.* 98, 4. Æfter Matheus gerecednysse, *Mt.* 1, 1, *Lye.*

Gereccelic; *adj. Drawn, extended, firm, steadfast;* strictus, *Som.*

Gereclicle; *adv. Widely, far and near;* extensive:—*Bt.* 35, 4, *Card.* p. 252, 13.

Gerefa, an; *m.* [*Plat.* gräve, greve *m*: *Dut.* graaf *m*: *Frs.* greef *c*: *Ger.* graf *m*: *Dan.* greve *m*: *Swed.* grefwe. The same as gefera *a companion;* from fer, fær *a journey,* ge *together, a travelling together, Wach.*] 1. *A companion, an associate, a fellow;* socius. 2. *A person having a delegated authority, a governor, prefect, commander,* REEVE, *bailiff, agent;* præpositus. A *gerefa* or *reeve* was an officer appointed by the executive power, and in rank inferior to the earl, or ealdorman. There was one in every hyrig; he was a judicial officer and was ordered to judge according to right judgment, and the *domboc* or *book of judgment.* He delivered over offenders to punishment, and was present at the *folcgemot,* where he was to do justice. He was ordered to convene a gemot every four weeks to end lawsuits. He took bail or security in his shire for every one to keep the peace; and if he omitted to take the bail and neglected his duty, he lost his office and the king's friendship, and forfeited to him one hundred and twenty shillings, *Turner's Hist. of the A.-S.* b. 8, ch. 7, p. 225:—1. *Bd.* 4, 1, v. gefera. 2. And se sette gerefan geond eall þat rice, *Gen.* 41, 34: 43, 16: *Mk.* 15, 43. Þa cwæð se gerefa, *Lk.* 16, 3. ¶ *Margrave,* mær-gerefa *finium præpositus.*—*Palsgrave,* palant-gerefa *palatii præpositus, etc.* Our *sheriff* or *shire-reeve, i. e.* scire-gerefa *a governor of a shire.*

Geref-land *Tributary land;* tributarium territorium:—*Cot.* 106.

Geref-mæd *a governor's wages, Heming.* p. 138, v. med.

Geref-scipe *office of a sheriff.*

Gerefscire *Stewardship, a county, shire;* villicatio, locus in quo officium exercetur:—*Lk.* 16, 3.

Geregnian *To dye, stain, colour;* inficere:—*Cot.* 112.

Geregnong *A making up;* confectio:—*Cot.* 44.

Gerehtad *Made whole, set up;* erectus:—*C. Lk.* 13, 13.

Gerehte *Rules;* regit:—*Ps.* 22, 1.—Gerehtest *explainedst,* v. recan.

Gerela *a robe,* v. gegerela.

Gerenian; *pp.* od. *To adorn, enlarge;* ornare:—*Ors.* 3, 8: *Bt.* 14, 3, *Card.* p. 70, 15, 16: 27, 1.

Gerenu *Ornaments;* ornamenta:—*Bt.* 14, 3.

Gereofage *seizes,* v. reafian.

Gereohnung, e; *f. A making up;* confectio:—*Cot.* 171.

Gereonian *To conspire, conjure, adorn;* conspirare:—*Elf. gr.* 47.

Gereonung, e; *f. A conspiracy, confederacy;* conjuratio, *Som.*

Gereord. 1. *Language, speech;* lingua. 2. *A table, food, repast, feast, supper;* mensa, convivium:—1. *Bd.* 1, 1. 2. Æt gereorde, *Mt.* 26, 20: *Mk.* 14, 14: *Lk.* 11, 38. ¶ Gereord-hus *a dining-room, R.* 207, v. reord.

Gereordian; *p.* ode; *pp.* od; *v. a. To refresh, take food, to dine, satisfy;* saturare:—Þat ge eow gereordian, *Gen.* 18, 5: *C. Ps.* 80, 15.

Gereordig-hus *a dining-room.*

Gereordnes, gereordnys, se; *f. A repast, dinner, fullness;* refectio:—*C. Ps.* 22, 2: *Bd.* 4, 28.

Gereordung, e; *f. A dinner, repast;* prandium:—*Ps.* 22, 2.

Gereosan *to fall, Ps.* 9, 33, v. reosan.

Geresp *Convicted;* convictus:—*L. Alf. pol.* 28.

Gerestan; *p.* t; *pp.* ed; *v. a.* 1. *To rest, be at leisure;* quiescere. 2. *To rest, lie with, to cohabit;* coire:—1. Ic me gerest *I rest, Elf. gr.* 28. Gerest þe, *Lk.* 12, 19. 2. Heo nam Balan and sealde Jacobe to gerestan, *Gen.* 30, 4.

Gerestscipe. 1. *Rest, ease;* otium. 2. *A cohabitation;* concubitus:—1. *Som.* 2. *Bd.* 1, 27, *resp.* 8.

Geretan *to refresh,* v. aretan.

Gereðra, [illegible] *a sailor, rower,* an oar, *the colours, Chr.* 891, v. reðra.

Gerian *To clothe;* vestire:—*Bd.* 4, 31.

Gerice *a kingdom, L. Ps.* 67, 35, v. rice.

Geridan; *p.* gerad; *pp.* geriden. *To ride, to ride through* or *over, invade;* equitando peragrare, invadere:—Geridon West Seaxna lond *rode over the West Saxon's land, Chr.* 878. Gerad to Ecgbyrhtes-stane *rode to Brixton, Chr.* 878, *Ing.* p. 105, 12: 1015: 1016. Se cyng let geridan ealle þa land *the king determined to invade all the land, Chr.* 1043, *Ing.* p. 214, 12.

Gerid-men *horsemen, knights.*

Gerif [reafian *to seize*] 1. *A seizing, capture;* raptura. 2. *An impediment, obstacle, a delay;* mora:—1. Gerif fisca *a taking of fishes, R.* 98. 2. *Lye.*

Gerifen *seized,* v. reafian.

Geriht *right, justice, custom, duty, reason, L. pol. Cnut.* 12, v. riht.

Geriht; *adj.* RIGHT, *direct;* directus:—Beoð on gerihte, *Lk.* 3, 5.

Gerihtan *to make right* or *straight, to correct, direct, Jn.* 1, 23, v. rihtan.

Gerihtlæcan, rihtlæcan; *p.* læhte; *pp.* læht. *To justify, correct, direct, rectify, reprove;* corrigere:—Þat hys weorc ne syn gerihtlæhte, *Jn.* 3, 20: *L. Ps.* 36, 24.

Gerihtnes, se; *f. Setting right, correcting;* correctio:—*Bd.* 5, 22.

Gerihtwisian; *p.* ode; *pp.* od; *v. a. To justify;* justificare:—*Lk.* 10, 29: *Mt.* 3, 7.

Gerim *a number, computation, calendar, Ps.* 38, 6, v. rim.

Geriman *to number, Gen.* 13, 16, v. riman.

Gerinan *to touch, Bd.* 3, 12, v. gehrinan.

Gerino *Buildings;* ædificationes:—*R. Mk.* 13, 2.

[illegible] *a harvest, Gen.* 8, 22, v. rip.

Geriped *grown old, ripe*, *Gen.* 18, 12, v. ripian.

Gerisan *To take, seize*; rapere:—*R. Mt.* 11, 12.

Gerisen *A seizing, plunder*; rapina:—On gerisne, *Guthl. vit.* c. 18.

Gerisene, gerysene, gerisn; *adj. Convenient, agreeable, fit, worthy*; congruus:—Gerisene stowe, *Bd.* 1, 26, *S.* p. 488, 19: *Cd.* 9: *Ors.* 4, 6.

Gerisenlic; *adj. Convenient, suitable, fit*; aptus:—*Bt.* 41, 2, *Card.* p. 374, 9.

Gerisenlice; *comp.* or; *adv. Fitly, agreeably*; apte:—*Bd.* 4, 9, *S.* p. 588, 27.

Gerisennes, gerisnes, se; *f. Conveniency, agreeableness, congruity*; convenientia:—*Cot.* 58.

Gerislic *convenient*, *Bd.* 5, 19, v. gerisenlic.

Gerisnian *To agree, accord*; convenire:—*Cot.* 38.

Gerist, ariseð, geriseð *It behoveth, becomes, agrees, suits*; convenit, decet:—Rihtwise gerist, *Ps.* 32, 1: *Bt.* 34, 10: 64, 1.

Geriw *Sorrow, affliction*; ærumna:—*T. Ps.* 31, 4.

Gerlic *Yearly*; annuus:—*Cot.* 18.

Germanie *Germany*; Germania:—*Chr.* 449.

Gernde *Is busy*; satagit:—*Cot.* 178, *q. from* geornian.

Gernwinde *Yern-wind*; conductum [apud textores]:—*Cot.* 39, 161, *Lye.*

Gerora *banishment*, v. gehrore.

Gerosod *Rosy, belonging to roses*; rosaceus, *Som.*

Gerostod *Roasted*; assus, *Som.*

Gerowen *rowed*, v. rowan.

Gers *grass*, v. gærs.

GERST [*Plat.* garste, gast *f*: *Dut.* gerst, garst *f*: *Dan.* byg *n*: *Swed.* bjugg *n*: *Ger.* gerste *f.*] GRIST, *pearled barley*; frumentum quodvis tritum, *Lye.*

Gerum *room, space*, *Bt.* 21, v. rum.

Gerumpen *Rough, wrinkled*; rugosus:—Gerumpenu nædre *cerastes, coluber*:—*Cot.* 38.

Gerunnen *Run together, congealed, joined*; coagulatus:—*Ps.* 67, 16: 118, 70.

Gerwigan *To prepare*; parare:—*Somn.* 204.

Geryman; *p.* de; *v. a. To extend, enlarge, make room, open, lay waste*; dilatare:—Ic geryme, *Ex.* 34, 24. Geryman wæg *to open a way*, *R. Ben.* 59, 71.

GERYNE, gehryne; *pl.* u; *n. A mystery, sacrament*; mysterium:—*Bd.* 1, 27, *resp.* 9: *L. Eccl.* 4, *Wilk.* 178, 27: *Mt.* 13, 11.

Gerynelic *Mystical*; mysticus:—*Bd.* 2, 1.

Gerynelice *Mystically*; mystice:—*Cot.* 131.

Gerypan *to reap* or *mow*, v. ripan.

Gerysene *fit*, v. gerisene.

Gés *geese*, v. gos.

Gesaca *An adversary, accuser*; adversarius:—*Bd.* 2, 2. On gesacum, *Cd.* 4.

Gesadelod *saddled*, *L. pol. Cnut.* 69, v. sadelian.

Gesadod *filled*, *L. Ps.* 103, 18, v. sadian.

Gesæd *said, told*, v. secgan.

Gesæga *A saying, relation*; narratio:—*Bd.* 5, 13.

Gesægan *to say, tell, relate*, *Bd.* 1, 12, v. sægan.

Gesægdnis *A mystery*; mystérium:—*C. Mt.* 13, 11.

Gesæged *Sacrificed*; immolatus:—*Jdth.* 12.

Gesægen *a saying, relation, tradition*, *Bd.* 5, 12, v. sægen.

Gesæhtlad *reconciled*, v. sæhtlian.

Gesælan; *p.* de [sæl *an opportunity*] *To happen, come to pass*; provenire:—Gif hit æfre gesælð *if it ever happen*, *Bt. R.* p. 168.

Gesæld, gesæled *tied, united, sealed*, *Cd.* 37, v. sælan.

Gesælge; *adv. Happily*; fauste:—*Cot.* 89.

Gesælig, gesæli, sælig, gesæliglic, gesællic; *comp.* ra; *sup.* ost; *adj. Happy, prosperous, fortunate*; felix:—*Elf. gr.* 7, *Som.* p. 1, 34. Swiðe gesælige *very* or *most happy*, *Cd.* 1, *Th.* p. 2, 12. Fram gesælgum tidum *from happy times*, *Ors.* 5, 2. Se seo se gesælgosta *who is the happiest*, *Bt.* 26, 1, *Card.* p. 140, 9. Gesæli, *Bt.* 26, 1.

Gesæliglice, gesælilice, gesællice; *adv. Happily*; feliciter:—*Bt.* 11, 1: *Bd.* 5, 19.

Gesælignys, gesælignes, se; *f. Happiness*; felicitas:—*Bd.* 1, 7.

Gesælð *happiness, felicity, wealth, good, advantage*, *Bd.* 26, 1, v. sælð.

Gesæt *sat, sat down*, v. gesittan.

Gesætnys, se; *f.* 1. *A site, situation*; collocatio. 2. *A thing settled, a decree, law*; decretum, *Som.*

Gesætu, gesetu *Seats, dwellings*; sedes:—*Past.* 50, 1.

Gesam, in composition, denotes *together, with*; simul, con, v. sam.

Gesamhiwan *companions*, *Bd.* 1, 27, *resp.* 8, v. hiwan.

Gesamnian *to assemble, collect, unite*, *Bt.* 21, v. somnian.

Gesamnung, gesomnung, samnung, e; *f. A congregation, union, assembly, synagogue, church*; congregatio, synagoga:—On gesamnungum, *Mt.* 23, 6. Þære gesamnunge ealdor, *Lk.* 8, 41.

Gesanco *Suckers*; exugia:—*Cot.* 167.

Gesargod, gesaroged *grieved, afflicted, torn*, *Chr.* 897, v. sargian.

Gesawan; *pp.* gesawen. *To sow*; seminare:—*C. Mt.* 13, 3, v. sawan.

Gesawen *seen*, v. seon.

Gescad *reason, difference*, v. gescead.

Gescadenlice, gescadlice *Separately, distinctly*; separatim:—*Can. Edg. Con.* 3: *Cot.* 198.

Gescadwis, gescadwite *reasonable, intelligent*, v. gesceadwis.

Gescadwislice; *comp.* or; *adv. Wisely, prudently, clearly*; prudenter:—*Ors.* 1, 10.

Gescæft *a creation*, v. gesceaft.

Gescænctest *Thou hast given drink*; potasti:—*L. Ps.* 59, 3.

Gescænednes, gescæningnes, se; *f. A dashing together, a breaking*; collisio:—*Cot.* 59.

Gescænian *to lessen, shake*, v. scænan.

Gescafen *shaven*, v. scafan.

Gescaldwyrt *Groundsel*; senecio:—*Cot.* 174.

Gescamian, ic gescamige *to shame, blush*, *Ps.* 69, 3, v. sceamian.

Gescapa *pudenda*, *Herb.* 94, 4: 102, 1, *Lye.*

Gescapen *formed, created*, v. sceapian.

Gescappennys, se; *f. A formation*; figmentum:—*L. Ps.* 102, 13.

Gescea *A sobbing*; singultus:—*Cot.* 174.

Gesceád *Reason, discretion, prudence, distinction, difference, respect, regard*; ratio:—Gescead agyldað, *Mt.* 12, 36. For hwylcum gesceade *for which reason, wherefore*, *Elf. gr.* 44.

Gesceadan *to separate*, *Cd.* 167, v. sceadan.

Gesceádlice; *adv. Reasonably, rationally*; rationabiliter:—*Bt.* 39, 2, *Card.* p. 244, 3.

Gesceádwis; *adj. Reasonable, intelligent, prudent, cautious*; rationalis:—*Bt.* 41, 2: 42.

Gesceádwislic; *adj. Reasonable*; rationalis:—*R. Ben. interl.* 2.

Gesceádwislice, sceádwislice; *adv. Rationally*; rationabiliter:—*Bt.* 21: 33, 4.

Gesceádwisnes, sceádwisnes, se; *f. Reason, discretion*; ratio:—*Bt.* 33, 4, *Card.* p. 384, 18.

Gevined lēd is vanād upon; complicitar cot 53 Lye

Gevinn labour Ben

Gersene l 1. ✱ gersne

gerysne fit. be

Geryd Lēvis,

aequus, planus

Lye Ben

Gesacan To seek

arguere, ~~increpare~~

increpare BeoK 2001

Gesacu

(1)

(4)

ref 35 th

p 47, 11

5 Gersume expense

Som v gersuma

6

7 Gerumi an to

be large & wide patere

ampliare; Som v

~~rumian~~ rumian

8 Gerumlīcor

more roomy, spa

tiosius BeoK 277

(2)

Geruxl Atumult

noise; tumultus Som

Gerwung a preparation

Lye v gearwung

Gerysed ~~shaken~~ shaken or

~~stirred~~ stirred together,

rystled; concussus

Som cogitatus Lye

5 2 Gesaca, an, m

[saca causa] an adversary

Gnm # 737, 7 BeoK 3546

7 Gesacen An accuser

adversary: accusator

Som

8 Gesacu, e f hos

tility BeoK 1472 v

~~saca~~ saca

~~Gesagan~~

4 Gesælde ~~happened~~

had good fortune,

happened, befell

BeoK 1142: 1773: 2500

p of ~~gesælan~~ gesælan

Gerum roomy, great

cd 188, 7 th

236, 12 v rum

10 Gesætednys a

situation, decree

Bed. lue v gesætnys

gesætnys

Gesceran, to

gescear To cut, to

cut through BeoK

2575: 3052 v sceran

Ges... heawan l. 2

v ✱ hiwa

Gesca, an m

Distaffness, skela

ing; ... tenting

Som

es; m ~~distinct~~ distinct

gescad

distinction

300 24 ... # 740, 17

K 574

(1)

3 Gescad - wyrt

Shade wort, bis

torta L. M 2 53 Lye

Som

4 Gescænd con

founded, reproached

confusus, Som

5 Gescæned beaten

broken; collisus, frac

tus Som v gescænan

6 Gesceap hwīl, e f

appointed time, day of

death BeoK 52

7 Gescead, es; m ~~Boogie~~

~~... scadam~~ v sk

ge-scad

Ge-rund, run

secretum] amicus

Gnm # 737, 6

Geruna a secre

tis, consiliarius

R 7, 113 Lye Ben

Gescādnys se

f Confusio Ben

Gesceorf a gnawing, biting, gnawing; rosio Som

Gesceowan to look around; circumspicere Ben

Gescepan to create Ben v gesceppan

Gesceadded laesus Lye

Gesceapa pudenda Som v gescapa

Gescirpla, an m clothing; vestitus Bensl. v scerp

Gesceat-wyrpe despondit despondere Cot 63 Som Lye

Gesceatwan Som

Gesceldan to shield, protect Som v gescyldan

Gescinco suckers, axungia — Swine's grease; axungia Som Lye v gescinco

Gescynt confounded v gescendan

Gescyndan to shend, put to shame Th an

Gescry ceremonies; caeremonia Som

Gescyldgyspe due, deserved Som v gescyldgian

Gescynd confounded Som v sutil ge-scand

Gescyppan to form Cd 66 Th p 79, 4 v gescyppan

~~Gescead shed~~

10 xvii.20

Gesceaft, SCEAFT, es; *n. m.* 1. *A creation, origin*; creatio. 2. *A created being, a creature*; creatura. 3. *A thing created, an element, the world*; elementum:—1. Fram fruman gesceafte, *Mk.* 10, 6. Gif ge willað þone fruman sceaft geþencan *if you will remember the first origin*, *Bt.* 30, 2, *Card.* p. 170, 18. 2. God is fæder eallra gesceafta *God is the father of all creatures*, *id.* p. 170, 9. Bodiað godspell ealre sceafte, *C. Mk.* 16, 15. 3. On feower gesceafta *into four elements*, *Bt.* 33, 4, *Card.* p. 200, 4: 39, 8.

Gesceamian *to blush, to make ashamed*, *L. Ps.* 6, 10, v. sceamian.

Gesceandnys *confusion*, *Ps.* 68, 23, v. sceonde.

Gesceanian *To shake*; conquassare:—*C. Ps.* 109, 7.

Gesceap, *A creation, forming, shaping*; creatio:—*Bd.* 4, 24, v. gesceaft.

Gesceapen *formed, created*, v. scyppan.

Gesceapenis, se; *f. A creation*; creatio:—*Alb. resp.* 1.

Gesceaplice; *adv. Properly, fitly, well*; apte:—*Bd.* 4, 19.

Gesceapu. 1. *Beauty, form*; forma. 2. *Verenda, pudenda.* 3. *Commands, precepts, destinies*; mandata:—1. *Cd.* 25, *Th.* p. 32, 14. 2. *Gen.* 9, 22. 3. *Cd.* 40, *Th.* p. 52, 12: 76: 136.

Gesceátan, he gescytt; *p.* gesceot, we gesceoton; *pp.* gesceaten [sceat *a part*] *To fall to, give up, divide*; dividere, cedere in partem alicujus:—Hit gescitt to his dæle, *Ex.* 29, 26. Eower earde us gesceote, *Jos.* 9, 8. Hig gesceatað to Aarones dæle, *Ex.* 29, 28.

Gesceaðan *to injure, hurt*, *L. eccl. Cnut.* 26, v. sceaðan.

Gesceawian; *p.* ode; *pp.* od. *To regard*; considerare, v. sceawian.

Gescendan, gescindan, SCENDAN; *p.* de; *pp.* ed; *v. a.* [*Dut.* schenden] *To confound, deprave, defile*, SHEND, *mar, disgrace, defeat*; confundere:—Nylle þu me gescendan, *Ps.* 118, 31. Þu gescendest, *Ps.* 43, 11: 24, 3: 30, 1: *Gen.* 20, 6.

Gescendnys, gescyndnys, se; *f. A confounding*; confusio:—*Ps.* 34, 30.

Gesceod *shod, covered, rendered*, *Mk.* 6, 9, v. sceadan.

Gesceop *created*, v. scyppan.

Gesceortan *To shorten*; deficere:—*C. Jn.* 11, 3.

Gesceot, gescot. 1. A SHOT, *spear, dart, an arrow*; pila, jaculum. 2. A SHOT, *reckoning, lattices, a most sacred place*; symbolum, cancelli gradus ligneus, propitiatorium:—1. Þa wæmna flugon mid swiftum gesceote *tela volabant celeri jactu*, *Jud. c.* 16, p. 162. Nim þin gesceot, *Gen.* 27, 3. 2. Gesceot bæftan þæm heah weofode *a lattice or step behind the high altar*, *R.* 109.

Gesceppan *to create*, *Elf. gr.* 26, v. scyppan.

Gescerian *To bestow, give*; tribuere:—*Cd.* 14, *Th.* p. 17, 12.

Gescerpte *adorned*, *Bt. R.* p. 170, v. gescyrped.

Gescierpan *to sharpen*, *Past.* 35, 1, v. scyrpan.

Gescild *a refuge, shield*, *Ps.* 71, 1, v. scyld.

Gescildnes, se; *f. A protection, defence*; tuitio:—*Bd.* 2, 5: *Gen.* 14, 20.

Gescinan *to shine*, *Bt.* 34, 5, v. scinan.

Gescindan *to confound, deprave, defile*, *Gen.* 20, 6, v. gescendan.

Gescipan *To ship, to go on board a ship, to load*; navem conscendere, in navem imponere:—*Chr.* 893.

Gescippan *to create*, *Elf. gr.* 26, *Som.* p. 29, 16, v. scyppan.

Gescirpan *to sharpen*, *Deut.* 32, 41, v. scyrpan.

Gescod *Shod*; calceatus:—*Somn.* 49, 50.

Gescola *A fellow-debtor*; condebitor:—*Cot.* 208.

Gescomian *to blush*, *Ors.* 4, 12, v. sceamian.

Gescored, gescoren *shorn*, v. sceran.

Gescot; *pl.* gescotu. *An arrow*, *Ors.* 3, 9, v. gesceot.

Gescoten *brought, bestowed*, *Can. Edg.* 7, v. sceotan.

Gescræpe, gescreop *Convenient, meet, fit for, accommodated*; aptus:—Gescræpe on læswe, *accommoda pasturæ*, *Bd.* 1, 1.

Gescreaded [*pp. of* screadan *to shred*] *Cut, pruned*; amputatus:—Gescreaded wingeard *sarpta vinea*, *R.* 99.

Gescrencean, forscræncan, screncan, he gescrencð; *p.* þu gescrenctyst. *To supplant, overturn*; supplantare:—*C. Ps.* 17, 41: *Past.* 2, 6, v. ascrencan.

Gescrencednes, se; *f. A supplanting, an overturning*; supplantatio:—*C. Ps.* 40, 10.

Gescreop *fit for, apt*, v. gescræpe.

Gescrepelice; *adv. Aptly, conveniently, fitly*; apte:—*Bd.* 4, 19.

Gescrif *A reproof, command, ceremony*; censura:—*Cot.* 59.

Gescrifan *to shrive, impose, assign, appoint, prescribe, to impose penance* or *censure*, *Can. Edg. conf.* 2, *W.* p. 87, 13, v. scrifan.

Gescrincan; *p.* hi gescriungon; *pp.* gescrunced. *To shrink, contract*; arescere:—Gescrunced him ealle ædra *contracti erant ei omnes nervi*, *Ors.* 3, 9, v. scrincan.

Gescropelice *fitly, meetly*, v. gescrepelice.

Gescropenys, se; *f. An applying, a fitting, accommodation*; accommodatio, *Som.*

Gescrydan; *p.* gescridde; *pp.* gescryd, ~~gescrydde~~. *To clothe*, *Gen.* 3, 21, v. scrydan.

Gesculdre *The shoulders*; humeri:—*Elf. gl. Som.* p. 71, v. sculder.

Gescy *shoes*, *Mt.* 3, 11, *a shoe*, *Deut.* 25, 9, v. sceo.

Gescyft [scyft *a division*] *Divided, distributed, parted, shifted*; distributus:—*L. Cnut. pol.* 68, *W.* p. 144, 14.

Gescyldan *to shield, protect, defend*, *Ps.* 16, 10, v. scyldan.

Gescyldend *a protector, an avenger*, *Ps.* 8, 3, v. scyldan.

Gescyldgian, bescyldigan, forscyldigan; *p.* hig gescyldgudun; *pp.* gescylgad [*from* scyldig *or* scildi *guilty*] *To be guilty, to find guilty, to catch, condemn, cast away, damn*; reum facere, carpere:—*Lk.* 20, 20.

Gescyldnes, se; *f. A protection, defence, safeguard*; defensio:—*Ps.* 17, 37: *Bd.* 1, 12.

Gescyldru *the shoulders*, v. sculder.

Gescyndnys *a confusion*, *L. Ps.* 43, 17, v. gescendnys.

Gescyppan *to create, form*, v. scyppan.

Gescyred *decreed*, *Cd.* 22, *Th.* p. 27, 28, v. sceran.

Gescyrped, gescyrpt *Sharpened, adorned, decked*; acutus, ornatus:—*Bt.* 28: *Bd.* 2, 13, v. ascyrpan.

Gescyrtan; *p.* gescyrte; *pp.* gescyrte; *v. a.* [scyrt *short*] 1. *To shorten, contract*; abbreviare. 2. *To fail, to be sick*; ægrotare:—1. He gescyrte þa dagas, *Mk.* 13, 20. Þa dagas beoð gescyrte, *Mt.* 24, 22. 2. Gescyrte æger est, *C. Jn.* 11, 3.

GESE, gise, gyse, gæ, gea; *adv.* [*Plat. Dut. Ger.* ja: *Old Frs.* jes: *Dan. Swed.* ja, jo: *Icel.* já: *Moes.* ja, jai: *Ot.* io, ja: *Wel.* ys] YES, *yea*; immo:—Gise, la gese, *yes, oh yes*, *Bt.* 16, 4, v. gea.

Geseagone *to be spoken*, v. secgan.
Geseah *saw*, v. seon.
Geseald *given, sold*, v. gesyllan.
Gesean *to see*, v. seon.
Gesécan, gesecean *to seek, inquire, make for, to advance, Bd.* 1, 23: 4, 19, v. secan.
Gesecednes, se; *f. A search, an inquiry, appeal*; inquisitio, *Som.*
Gesecgan, gesegan, gesecgean; *pp.* gesed, gesegen. *To say, confess, relate, declare, prove, Bd.* 4, 3, v. secgan.
Geseglian *to sail, Ors.* 1, 1, *Bar.* p. 25, 5, v. segelian.
Gesegnian, gesenian *to mark, sign, bless, L. Eccl.* 29, *W.* p. 187, 50, v. senian.
Gesehtodan *settled, Chr.* 1101, v. sehtian.
Gesele *A tabernacle*; tabernaculum:—*T. Ps.* 14, 1, v. sel, sele.
Geselenis *tradition, C. Mk.* 7, 3, v. selenis.
Geselig *happy, Somn.* 188, v. gesælig.
Geselignes *happiness*, v. gesælignys.
Gesellan *to give, C. Mt.* 22, 17, v. syllan.
Geselð *happiness, Chr.* 1009, v. sælð.
Geseman, gesemian; *pp.* gesemod. *To compose, settle, Ors.* 3, 7, *Bar.* p. 100, 28, v. seman.
Gesemen *An agreement, compromise*; reconciliatio:—*L. Hloth.* 10, *W.* p. 8, 49.
Gesencan *to sink*, v. sencan.
Gesene; *adv. Clearly*; manifeste:—*C. Jn.* 11, 14.
Geseon, gesion, ic geseó, þu gesihst, he gesyhð; *p.* geseah, þu gesawe, we gesawon; *imp.* gesyh, geseoh; *pp.* gesawen. *To see*, v. seon.
Geseotu *dwellings, Cd.* 227, *Th.* p. 302, 20.
Gesete *possess*; *imp. of* gesettan.
Geseted, gesetted *placed, C. Mt.* 7, 25, v. gesettan.
Gesetednes, gesetenes, gesetnes, gesettednys, se; *f. Position, foundation, institution, constitution, decree*; positio, fundatio:—Fram middan-eardes gesetednesse, *Mt.* 13, 35: *Mk.* 7, 5: *Ex.* 12, 25, 26: *Bt.* 21, *Card.* p. 114, 31.
Geseten *settled, Cd.* 37, v. gesettan.
Geseten *placed, Ors.* 3, 9, *Bar.* p. 112, 18, v. gesettan.
Geseðan; *pp.* geseðed. *To utter, speak, say, testify, prove, shew, affirm, Bt.* 7, 3, *Card.* p. 30, 4, v. seðan.
Gesetl *a seat, settle, R. Mk.* 12, 39, v. setl.
Gesetnian *To lay wait, to deceive, to have a quarrel against*; insidiari:—*C. Mk.* 6, 19.
Gesettan; *p.* gesette; *pp.* geset, gesett, geseten. *To set, appoint, allay, settle, populate, plant, replace, possess, put, expose, constitute, sanction, provide, Bd.* 3, 8, *S.* p. 532, 16, 38: *Cd.* 21, *Th.* p. 25, 20, v. settan.
Gesetu *seats, Cod. Exon.* 26, a, v. gesætu.
Geseul[illegible] *A servant*; minister:—*C[illegible]t. Canuti.*
Geseupes *The sea*; æquor:—*Cot.* 15.
Gesewenlic *Visible*; visibilis:—*Bt.* 33, 4.
Gesib; *g.* gesibbe; *f.* [sib *peace, a relation*] *One of the same stock* or *tribe, a neighbour, a relation*; cognatus, propinquus:—Þe him gesibbe wæron *who were relations to him, Job.* p. 167.
Gesibbian *to pacify, appease, Bd.* 4, 21, v. sibbian.
Gesiblice; *adv. Peaceably*; pacifice:—*Bt. R.* p. 175.
Gesibling *a relation, R.* 92, v. sibling.
Gesibnes, se; *f. Relationship*; affinitas:—*Cot.* 7.
Gesibsum *peaceable, loving peace, Mt.* 5, 9, v. sibsum.
Gesibsumian *To be reconciled, made at peace*; reconciliari:—*Mt.* 5, 24.
Gesibsumlice *peaceably, Ps.* 34, 23, v. sibsumlice.
Gesibsumnes *concord, agreement, reconciliation, Lev.* 7, 32, v. sibsumnes.
Gesiced *Weaned*; ablactatus, v. asicyd.
Gesicelod, gesiclod, gesyclod, gesiclud. *Become sick, infirm, sick, in danger*; ægrotatus:—*Gen.* 48, 1: *Jn.* 4, 46.
Gesida *Sides*; latera:—*Lev.* 3, 3, v. side.
Gesiehð *sight, Bt.* 5, 3, v. gesiht.
Gesigan *to set as the sun*, v. sigan.
Gesigefæst *Triumphant*; triumphans:—*Cd.* 188, *Th.* p. 234, 8.
Gesigefæsted *Crowned*; coronatus:—*Bd.* 2, 6.
Gesiht, gesihð, gesyhð, gesihtð, gesið. 1. *Sight, view, aspect, respect*; visus. 2. *A vision, apparition*; visio:—1. Þu wast þat gesiht, and gehernes *thou knowest that sight, and hearing, Bt.* 41, 4. Yfel gesyhð, *Mk.* 7, 22. Scearp gesihð *a sharp sight, Elf. gr.* 5: *Lk.* 4, 18: *Cd.* 49, *Th.* p. 63, 20. Of heora gesihðum, *Jud.* 16, 3. Butan gesyhðe *without respect, Bd.* 4, 12. 2. On gesyhðe *in a vision, Ps.* 88, 19. He on þam temple sume gesihðe geseah, *Lk.* 1, 22: 24, 23.
Gesingallicode *Continually*; continuatim:—*V. Ps.* 140, 7, v. singallice.
Gesingan *to sing, C. R. Jn.* 13, 38, v. singan.
Gesinhiwan, gesinhiwode *those joined together, partners, mates, Past.* 52, 8, v. sinhiwan.
Gesinhiwe *Marriage*; conjugium:—*Bd.* 4, 5.
Gesinigan *to marry, R. Lk.* 20, 34, v. sinigan.
Gesinlice *Curiously, strictly*; curiose:—*R. Ben.* 58.
Gesinscipe, es; *m. Marriage, wedlock, matrimony*; conjugium:—*Bd.* 4, 5, 19.
Gesinsciplic; *adj. Conjugal, matrimonial*; conjugalis:—*L. Eccl.* 43.
Gesion *to see, Bt.* 38, 5, v. geseon.
Gesiowed *sewed together*, v. siwian.
Gesirian; *pp.* gesired. *To conspire, deliberate, Past.* 56, 6, v. syrian.
Gesið; *g.* gesiðes; *d.* gesiðe; *m.* [sið *a path*] 1. *A companion, fellow, associate, a partner*; socius. 2. *A president, noble, head*; præpositus:—1. Se gesið ah healf *the companion has half, L. In.* 23, *W.* p. 18, 34. Gesiððas *allies, Cd.* 95, *Th.* p. 124, 23: 91. On gesiððe is *is as a companion, Cd.* 135, *Th.* p. 170, 3. 2. *L. In.* 50, *W.* p. 23, 4: *Bd.* 3, 14.
Gesiðcund *of the same condition, L. In.* 45, *W.* p. 22, 14, v. siðcund.
Gesiðcundlic *Of the same condition, social*; socialis:—*Bd.* 2, 9.
Gesiðman *a companion, ruler, L. In.* 30, v. gesið.
Gesiðscipe, es; *m. A fellowship, society*; comitatus:—*Bd.* 3, 28.
Gesittan; *p.* gesæt. *To sit, possess, inhabit*; sedere:—*Ps.* 126, 3: *Lk.* 7, 36. Gesæton land *inhabited a land, Cd.* 46, *Th.* p. 59, 9.
Gesiwed, gesiwod, gesiuwed *sewed*, v. siwian.
Geslaa, *C. Mk.* 14, 65, v. slean.
Geslagen, geslægen *slain, beaten, forged*, v. slean.
Geslapan *to sleep, Ps.* 67, 14, v. slapan.
Geslefed *Having sleeves*; manicatus:—*R.* 8.
Gesleht, es. *Clashing, slaughter*; cædes:—Bill geslehtes *of sword clashing, Chr.* 938: *Price's Walt.* vol. i. p. xcvi, 21.

(v)

Gesegen, e; f a [illegible] Beo. K 1732

Gesellscipe, m a comrade companion; comes Beo. v. Spl. hond-gesel

Geselda, an m a seat] One sitting the same seat, a companion; qui in eadem transtro sedet, socius Beo K 3963

~~Ge-setla~~ ~~sedes~~ ~~socius~~ a companion ... v. Spl. hond-gesel

Gesend sent; missus L Ps. 33,7 v. sendan

Geseonian [illegible] mark, sign; [illegible] Som Ben. v gesegnian

Geseoc sick Som v. seoc

Geseowid, a little, acorn, zymus ~~hlaf~~ ~~[illegible]~~ ~~panis~~ R 66

Gesgdan (sod true) To confirm; verificare [illegible] in sod

~~Geseowen seen~~ ~~Som~~ v ~~geseon~~

Geseup tasted gustassat L. Mt 27.34 v supan

Geseowen seen ~~[illegible]~~ pp of geseon

Gesib related, of kin, Th. An

— (3)

Gesibsumung, e f Agreement, concord, conciliatio Ben 5) 5 a

6 to sink, submit Beok 5314

5 a Gesiewed ~~[illegible]~~ sewed together Som v gesiwed

(4)

Gesingal-lician condenicare Gm II 669, 46

Gesingian to sin do wrong Th Apol

(2)

Gesirwan to lay snares for Th Apol

(gestegen)

Gesleau, to slay strike. Th. an v sleau

Gesetnes, the text, a position, tradition, law, institute, book. textus, Elne 2. 33 Mk 7,3 R. an v. gesetednes.

Geseagone *to be spoken*, v. secgan.
Geseah *saw*, v. seon.
Geseald *given, sold*, v. gesyllan.
Gesean *to see*, v. seon.
Gesécan, gesecean *to seek, inquire, make for, to advance*, *Bd.* 1, 23: 4, 19, v. secan.
Gesecednes, se; *f. A search, an inquiry, appeal*; inquisitio, *Som.*
Gesecgan, gesegan, gesecgean; *pp.* gesed, gesegen. *To say, confess, relate, declare, prove*, *Bd.* 4, 3, v. secgan.
Geseglian *to sail*, *Ors.* 1, 1, *Bar.* p. 25, 5, v. segelian.
Gesegnian, gesenian *to mark, sign, bless*, *L. Eccl.* 29, *W.* p. 187, 50, v. senian.
Gesehtodan *settled*, *Chr.* 1101, v. sehtian.
Gesele *A tabernacle*; tabernaculum:—*T. Ps.* 14, 1, v. sel, sele.
Geselenis *tradition*, *C. Mk.* 7, 3, v. selenis.
Geselig *happy*, *Somn.* 188, v. gesælig.
Geselignes *happiness*, v. gesælignys.
Gesellan *to give*, *C. Mt.* 22, 17, v. syllan.
Geselð *happiness*, *Chr.* 1009, v. sælð.
Geseman, gesemian; *pp.* gesemod. *To compose, settle*, *Ors.* 3, 7, *Bar.* p. 100, 28, v. seman.
Gesem[illegible] *An agreement, compromise*; reconciliatio:—*L. Hloth.* 10, *W.* p. 8, 49.
Gesencan *to sink*, v. sencan.
Gesene; *adv. Clearly*; manifeste:—*C. Jn.* 11, 14.
Geseón, gesion, ic geseó, þu gesihst, he gesyhð; *p.* geseah, þu gesawe, we gesawon; *imp.* gesyh, geseóh; *pp.* gesawen. *To see*, v. seon.
Geseotu *dwellings*, *Cd.* 227, *Th.* p. 302, 20.
Gesete *possess*; *imp. of* gesettan.
Geseted, gesetted *placed*, *C. Mt.* 7, 25, v. gesettan.
Gesetednes, gesetenes, gesetnes, gesettednys, se; *f. Position, foundation, institution, constitution, decree*; positio, fundatio:—Fram middan-eardes gesetednesse, *Mt.* 13, 35: *Mk.* 7, 5: *Ex.* 12, 25, 26: *Bt.* 21, *Card.* p. 114, 31.
Geseten *settled*, *Cd.* 37, v. gesettan.
Geseten *placed*, *Ors.* 3, 9, *Bar.* p. 112, 18, v. gesettan.
Geseðan; *pp.* geseðed. *To utter, speak, say, testify, prove, shew, affirm*, *Bt.* 7, 3, *Card.* p. 30, 4, v. seðan.
Gesetl *a seat, settle*, *R. Mk.* 12, 39, v. setl.
Gesetnian *To lay wait, to deceive, to have a quarrel against*; insidiari:—*C. Mk.* 6, 19.
Gesettan; *p.* gesette; *pp.* geset, gesett, geseten. *To set, appoint, allay, settle, populate, plant, replace, possess, put, expose, constitute, sanction, provide*, *Bd.* 3, 8, *S.* p. 532, 16, 38: *Cd.* 21, *Th.* p. 25, 20, v. settan.
Gesetu *seats*, *Cod. Exon.* 26, a, v. gesætu.
Geseul[illegible] *A servant*; minister:—*C[illegible]t. Canuti.*
Geseunes *The sea*; æquor:—*Cot.* 15.
Gesewenlic *Visible*; visibilis:—*Bt.* 33, 4.
Gesib; *g.* gesibbe; *f.* [sib *peace, a relation*] *One of the same stock or tribe, a neighbour, a relation*; cognatus, propinquus:—Þe him gesibbe wæron *who were relations to him*, *Job.* p. 167.
Gesibbian *to pacify, appease*, *Bd.* 4, 21, v. sibbian.
Gesiblice; *adv. Peaceably*; pacifice:—*Bt. R.* p. 175.
Gesibling *a relation*, *R.* 92, v. sibling.
Gesibnes, se; *f. Relationship*; affinitas:—*Cot.* 7.
Gesibsum *peaceable, loving peace*, *Mt.* 5, 9, v. sibsum.
Gesibsumian *To be reconciled, made at peace*; reconciliari:—*Mt.* 5, 24.
Gesibsumlice *peaceably*, *Ps.* 34, 23, v. sibsumlice.
Gesibsumnes *concord, agreement, reconciliation*, *Lev.* 7, 32, v. sibsumnes.
Gesiced *Weaned*; ablactatus, v. asicyd.
Gesicelod, gesiclod, gesyclod, gesiclud. *Become sick, infirm, sick, in danger*; ægrotatus:—*Gen.* 48, 1: *Jn.* 4, 46.
Gesida *Sides*; latera:—*Lev.* 3, 3, v. side.
Gesiehð *sight*, *Bt.* 5, 3, v. gesiht.
Gesigan *to set as the sun*, v. sigan.
Gesigefæst *Triumphant*; triumphans:—*Cd.* 188, *Th.* p. 234, 8.
Gesigefæsted *Crowned*; coronatus:—*Bd.* 2, 6.
Gesiht, gesihð, gesyhð, gesihtð, gesið. 1. *Sight, view, aspect, respect*; visus. 2. *A vision, apparition*; visio:—1. Þu wast þat gesiht, and gehernes *thou knowest that sight, and hearing*, *Bt.* 41, 4. Yfel gesyhð, *Mk.* 7, 22. Scearp gesihð *a sharp sight*, *Elf. gr.* 5: *Lk.* 4, 18: *Cd.* 49, *Th.* p. 63, 20. Of heora gesihðum, *Jud.* 16, 3. Butan gesyhðe *without respect*, *Bd.* 4, 12. 2. On gesyhðe *in a vision*, *Ps.* 88, 19. He on þam temple sume gesihtðe geseah, *Lk.* 1, 22: 24, 23.
Gesingallicode *Continually*; continuatim:—*V. Ps.* 140, 7, v. singallice.
Gesingan *to sing*, *C. R. Jn.* 13, 38, v. singan.
Gesinhiwan, gesinhiwode *those joined together, partners, mates*, *Past.* 52, 8, v. sinhiwan.
Gesinhiwe *Marriage*; conjugium:—*Bd.* 4, 5.
Gesinigan *to marry*, *R. Lk.* 20, 34, v. sinigan.
Gesinlice *Curiously, strictly*; curiose:—*R. Ben.* 58.
Gesinscipe, es; *m. Marriage, wedlock, matrimony*; conjugium:—*Bd.* 4, 5, 19.
Gesinsciplic; *adj. Conjugal, matrimonial*; conjugalis:—*L. Eccl.* 43.
Gesion *to see*, *Bt.* 38, 5, v. geseon.
Gesiowed *sewed together*, v. siwian.
Gesirian; *pp.* gesired. *To conspire, deliberate*, *Past.* 56, 6, v. syrian.
Gesið; *g.* gesiððes; *d.* gesiððe; *m.* [sið *a path*] 1. *A companion, fellow, associate, a partner*; socius. 2. *A president, noble, head*; præpositus:—1. Se gesið ah healf *the companion has half*, *L. In.* 23, *W.* p. 18, 34. Gesiððas *allies*, *Cd.* 95, *Th.* p. 124, 23: 91. On gesiððe is *is as a companion*, *Cd.* 135, *Th.* p. 170, 3. 2. *L. In.* 50, *W.* p. 23, 4: *Bd.* 3, 14.
Gesiðcund *of the same condition*, *L. In.* 45, *W.* p. 22, 14, v. siðcund.
Gesiðcundlic *Of the same condition, social*; socialis:—*Bd.* 2, 9.
Gesiðman *a companion, ruler*, *L. In.* 30, v. gesið.
Gesiðscipe, es; *m. A fellowship, society*; comitatus:—*Bd.* 3, 28.
Gesittan; *p.* gesæt. *To sit, possess, inhabit*; sedere:—*Ps.* 126, 3: *Lk.* 7, 36. Gesæton land *inhabited a land*, *Cd.* 46, *Th.* p. 59, 9.
Gesiwed, gesiwod, gesiuwed *sewed*, v. siwian.
Geslaa, *C. Mk.* 14, 65, v. slean.
Geslagen, geslægen *slain, beaten, forged*, v. slean.
Geslapan *to sleep*, *Ps.* 67, 14, v. slapan.
Geslefed *Having sleeves*; manicatus:—*R.* 3.
Gesleht, es. *Clashing, slaughter*; cædes:—Bill geslehtes *of sword clashing*, *Chr.* 938: *Price's Walt.* vol. i. p. xvi, 21.

(V)

Gesegen, i.e. f. a ... Beo K 1732

2) Geselles; m. A comrade ... comes Bo ... hond-gesel

4 Geselda, an m ... a seat] One sitting ... the same seat, a companion; qui in eadem transtro sedet, socius Beo K 3963

1) Ge-setla ... le sedes] socius ... Beo 112. v. Spl hond-gesel

5) Gesend sent; missus L Ps. 33, 7 v. sendan

7 Geseonian pade to mark, sign ... Som Ben v gesegnian

8 Geseoc sick Som v seoc

9 Gesewid, a little learned, acm ... zymus ... R 65

Gesewen seen Som v gesean

4 Geseuh lashed guttasset C. Mt 27, 34 v seupan

2 Gesewen seen ... of geseón

3 Gesib related, of kin. Th. an

(3)

4 Gesibsumung, i.e. f. Agreement, concord, conciliatio Ben 5) 5a

6 to sink, submit Beo K 5314

5a Gesiewed ... sewed together Som v. gesiwed

7)

10 Gesodan (sot true) to confirm; verificare ... in sot

11 Gesetnes, a position, tradition, law, institute, the text textus Mone B. 33 Mk 7, 13 v gesetednes.

Gesingal-lician continuare Gm II 669, 46

Gesingian to sin do wrong Th apol

(6)

Gesirwan to lay snares for Th apol

gestegen

Gesleán, to slay strike. Th. an v sleán

Geslight skilling, slaying; occisio, interfectio Som

2 Geflit-glieve A caviller, wrangler, cavillator Som

3 Gesmerian, to deride [illegible] to smear [illegible] v smerian

4 Gesmiltan to appease Ben v gesmyltan

Gesmirwed smeared Ben v gesmered

5 Gesmyred smeared Ben v gesmered

ge-slyht, e; f. a [illegible] Beo K 4791 v sleiht

Geslyt a bite, slit, rent, morsus, schisma Som

2 Gesmacian demulcere; Jac Lye

Gespreca easy, an affable, to be spoken to, affabilis Som

Gespecan to speak v specan

Gesporian to investigate, inquire Som, Ben Lye v spirian

3 Gespowan, to speed, succeed, speed, v spowan

Gespreca an affable person Som v gespeca

6 Gespringan to rise up Som. v springan

Gest, gist, giest, es m a guest, hospes Bd 1. 27 resp 1: Cd 113 Th p 149, 9: 112 Th p 147, 15 v Stl gæst.

Gesteanan to stone Th an

(2) [Status furtum]

Gestadolian to establish, make good Th apol Ben

3 Lye

(1) Gestence odorus Grimm II 745, 41

Gestened stoned Som v stanan

Gest-heal, gest-healle; f a guest hall. an inn Som v gest-ern

Gestlor a sheer, hallock Som v steor

Gest-feorme hospitality Som

Gesticce a [illegible] Som v gestiht

Gesomnigean to assemble Ben v gesomnian

Gespring, es m a spring Beo K 1689 v spring

7 Gespanian to persuade, suadere Som Ben v spanan

Geslóh *struck*, v. slean.

Gesmæccan *to taste*, *R.*5, v. smæccan.

Gesmead *considered, feigned*, *R.* 100, v. smean.

Gesmeagan *to search, consider*, *Pecc. Med.* 1, v. smean.

Gesmered, gesmirwed, gesmyred, gesmirode *besmeared, anointed*, *Ex.* 29, 29, v. smyrian.

Gesmeðian, smeðian; *p.* gesmeðde; *pp.* gesmeðed; *v. a.* *To make smooth* or *even*, *to soothe, soften*; complanare:—Se ele gesmeð þa wunda *the oil soothes the wounds*, *Past.* 17, 10.

Gesmicerad [smicere *elegant*] *Worked, neatly made*; fabrefactus:—*Cot.* 88, 184.

Gesmiten *Anointed, smeared, smutted*; litus, unctus, *Som.*

Gesmiðed, asmiðod *made, forged*, *R.* 64, v. smiðian.

Gesmyltan [smylt *serene*] *To appease, quiet*; placare:—*Bd.* 5, 1.

Gesnað *cut off*, *C. Mk.* 14, 47, v. snidan.

Gesne *cut off*, v. snidan.

Gesnid *A killing, slaughter*; occisio:—*R. Ben.* 7.

Gesnidan; *pp.* gesniden. *To cut, make even, cut off*, *Ex.* 20, 25, v. snidan.

Gesniðung, e; *f.* *A smoothing, making even*; dolatio, *Som.*

Gesnote *snot*, v. snote.

Gesoc *suck*, *Gen.* 21, 7, v. soc.

Gesod *A boiling, seething*; coctio:—*Elf. gl.* 21.

Gesoden *sodden, boiled*, v. seoðan.

Gesoecan *to seek, follow*, *C. R. Jn.* 13, 37, v. secan.

Gesoht *sought*, v. secan.

Gesome *Unanimous, peaceable*; concors:—*Gen.* 45, 24.

Gesomnian *to assemble*, *Jn.* 11, 52, v. somnian.

Gesomnung *a congregation, church, synagogue, a union*, *Mt.* 4, 23, v. gesamnung.

Gesoð *A soother, flatterer*; parasitus:—*Cot.* 152.

Gesoðfæstad [soð *truth*, fæst *fast*] *Justified*; justificatus:—*C. Mt.* 12, 37.

Gesoðian, ic gesoðige; *p.* ode; *pp.* od. 1. *To prove the truth, to assert*; probare. 2. *To sooth*; assentari:—1. *L. Edw. Guth.* 6. 2. *Som.*

Gespænning *A provocation*; incitamentum, *Som.*

Gespan *The tamarisk tree*; myrica:—*Cot.* 131.

Gespan *A prompting*; suggestio:—*Past.* 53, 7.

Gespannan *to join, span*, v. spannan.

Gesparrade *shut*; clausus:—*C. Mt.* 6, 6, v. sparran.

Gespearn *perched*, *Cd.* 72, v. gespornan.

Gespedan *to prosper, succeed, effect*, *Cd.* 75, *Th.* p. 92, 12, v. spedian.

Gespediglice *Prosperously, successfully*; prospere:—*L. Ps.* 44, 5.

Gespelia, gespeliga *A substitute, deputy, vicar*; vicarius:—*L. Const.*, *W.* p. 147, 13.

Gespellian *to speak, tell*, *C. Lk.* 24, 15, v. spellian.

Gespeon *persuaded, joined*, v. spannan.

Gespeow *prospered*, *Jdth.* 11, v. spowan.

Gesperod *A spearman*; hastatus:—*Elf. gr.* 43.

Gespillan *to waste*, *C. Lk.* 16, 1, v. spillan.

Gespinnan *To stretch out*; extendere:—*C. Mt.* 8, 3.

Gespitted *spit*, *C. Lk.* 18, 32, v. spittan.

Gespon *A persuasion, an artifice*; suasio:—*Cd.* 33, *Th.* p. 45, 2, v. spannan.

Gespon *enticed*, *Chr.* 905, *Ing.* p. 127, 4, v. spanan.

Gespon, gespong *A joining, clasping*; junctio, nexus:—*Cd.* 35, *Th.* p. 47, 17: 19, *Th.* p. 24, 14, v. spannan.

Gesponnen *persuaded*, *Bd.* 3, 21, *S.* p. 551, 5, v. spanan.

Gespornan; *p.* gespearn. *To perch, tread upon, to spurn*, *Cd.* 72, *Th.* p. 87, 33, v. ætspurnan.

Gespræc, gesprec *a speaking, discourse, conversation, advice*, *Bd.* 3, 14. Gespræcu, gesprecu *oracula*, *Cot.* 143, v. spræc.

Gespræc *spake with*, v. sprecan.

Gespræce; *adj.* *Eloquent*; facundus:—*Ex.* 4, 10.

Gespræcelice *Loquelaris*, *Elf. gr.* 47, *Som.* p. 48, 49.

Gesprang *went*, v. springan.

Gesprecen *spoken*, v. sprecan.

Gespredan *To* SPREAD; extendere:—*C. Mt.* 12, 13.

Gesprengan *to sprinkle*, v. sprengan.

Gesprucg *Discord, strife*; seditio:—*Somn.* 171.

Gespryng *a spring*, v. spring.

Gespunnen *Spun*; netus, *Som.*

GEST, gæst, gæst, giest, gist, es; *m.* [*Plat. Dut. Ger. Frs. Moes.* gast *m*: *Ot.* gesto: *Ker.* kasto, kesteo: *Dan.* giest *m*: *Swed.* gäst *m*: *Icel.* giestur *m*: *Böhm.* host: *Pol.* gosc: *Russ.* gost: *Wel.* gwêst] GUEST, *stranger*; hospes:—*Bd.* 1, 27, *resp.* 1.

Gestæflæred *Literate, learned*; literatus:—*Obs. Lun.* 1, 7, 21.

Gestæl, gesteal *An ordinance, establishment, a decree*; constitutio, decretum:—*Cd.* 15, *Lye.*

Gestælan *to accuse*, *Cd.* 21, *Th.* p. 25, 10, v. stelan.

Gestænc *stinking*; odorus:—*Herb.* 154, 1, v. stincan.

Gestæppan *to step*, v. steppan.

Gestærn *a guest-place, an inn.*

Gestæððig *steadfast*, *Bt.* 39, 5, v. stæðig.

Gestæððignys, se; *f.* *Gravity, constancy, maturity*; gravitas:—*Bd.* 3, 15.

Gestah *ascended*, v. stigan.

Gestal *An obstacle, objection*; objectio:—*Cot.* 144.

Gestala *A thief*; fur:—*L. In.* 25.

Gestalian *to steal*, *L. Edw. Guth.* 3, v. stelan.

Gestandan; *pp.* gestanden, gestonden. *To stand, remain, detain, exist, be, urge, attack, seize*, *Bd.* 4, 6, v. standan.

Gestarian *to stare*, *Cod. Exon.* 12, *b*, v. starian.

Gestaðelian, *Bd.* 3, 23, gestaðolfæstan, *Ps.* 20, 11, *to found, establish, confirm, fortify, repair, restore*, v. staðelian.

Gestaðolung, e; *f.* *Firmness*; stabilitas:—*T. Ps.* 103, 6.

Gesteald *A settled place, a station, an abode*; statio:—*Cd.* 4, *Th.* p. 4, 36.

Gestedhors *A stallion*; equus admissarius:—*Bd.* 2, 13.

Gestefnde *fixed*, *Cd.* 8, *Th.* p. 10, 21, v. stefnian.

Gestenc *Odoriferous*; odorus:—*Herb.* 154, 1.

Gestentan *To remind*; admonere:—*Elf. pref. Hom.* p. 5.

Gesteoran, gestioran *to steer, rule, direct*, *Edw. Guth. pref.*, *W.* p. 51, 16, v. styran.

Gesteped *One introduced, a beginner*; initiatus:—*Cot.* 108.

Gestepte *raised*, *Cd.* 158, *Th.* p. 196, 26, v. stepan.

Gestern *a place for guests, an inn.*

Gesthus *a guest-house, an inn.*

Gesticced, gesticode *stuck, pricked, transfixed*, *Bd.* 4, 19, v. stician.

Gestigan *to ascend*, *Cd.* 101, *Th.* p. 134, 22, v. stigan.

Gestihtan; *p.* gestihtade, gestihtode, gestitode; *pp.* gestihtod. *To dispose, order, determine*, *Bd.* 1, 14, v. stihtian.

Gestihtung *a dispensing, disposing*, *Ors.* 2, 1, v. stihtung.

Gestillan, STILLAN; *p.* de; *pp.* ed. 1. *To restrain, stop, stay, keep in*; compescere. 2. *To be quiet, still, mute*; quiescere:—1. Gestillende *restraining*, *Cot.* 34: *Elf. gr.* 24, 33: *C. Ps.* 84, 3. Heht fyrde gestillan *command (the) march to stay*, *Cd.* 156, *Th.* p. 194, 2. 2. Gestildon *rested*, *Lk.* 23, 56.

Gestille *be still*, *Mk.* 4, 39.

Gestilled *stilled*, *Bd.* 3, 9.

Gestincan *To smell, to perceive by the sense of smelling*; odorari:—Sume magon gehyron, sume gestincan *some can hear, some smell*, *Bt.* 41, 5, *Card.* p. 384, 11. Hi lyft gestuncan *they smelled air*, *Bd.* 1, 1, *S.* p. 474, 35.

Gestiðian [styð *a pillar*] *To increase, become stronger*; fortior fieri:—*Guth. Vit.* c. 2.

Gestlið *Hospitable*; hospitalis, *Som.*

Gestliðnes *hospitality*, *Bd.* 1, 7, v. gæstliðnes.

Gestod *stood*, v. standan.

Gestolen *stolen*, v. stelan.

Gestondan, gestonden *detained, confined*, *Bd.* 5, 3, p. 616, 3, v. gestandan.

Gestrandæg *yesterday*; hesternus dies:—*V. Ps.* 89, 4, v. gyrstandæg.

Gestrangian; *p.* ode; *pp.* od; *v. a.* *To strengthen, confirm, establish*; corroborare:—Ic gestrangie *I confirm*, *Coll. Mon.* Bebeod Iosue and gestranga hine, *Deut.* 3, 28. Gestrangod, *Ex.* 1, 7.

Gestredd *spread, sprinkled, seasoned*, v. stredan.

Gestreht *spread*, v. streccan.

Gestreon, gestrion, es; *n.* *Gain, product, emolument, riches, treasure, usury, business*; lucrum:—Gestreones wæstm *mercis fructus*, *Ps.* 126, 4: *Ors.* 5, 13. Beran gestreon *to bring treasures*, *Cd.* 209, *Th.* p. 260, 4. Eorðan gestreona ongenimeð *taketh earth's treasures*, *Cd.* 60, *Th.* p. 73, 22: *Ps.* 54, 11. Mid gestreone, *Lk.* 19, 23: *Ps.* 90, 6: *Bt. R.* p. 150, 44.

Gestreonan, *Cd.* 226.—gestrienan, *L. In.* 27.—gestrionan, *C. Mt.* 18, 15, *to gain, get, acquire, procreate*, *L. In.* 27, v. strynan.

Gestreonde *placed out, hired*, *C. Mt.* 21, 41, v. strynan.

Gestric *strife, mutiny*; seditio:—*Somn.* 159, v. stric.

Gestridan *to stride*, v. bestridan.

Gestrod *Banishment*; proscriptio:—*Cot.* 194.

Gestroden *brought into the treasury*, v. strynan.

Gestrodu *Deceits*; fraudes:—*Bt.* 3, 4.

Gestrudan *plundered*, v. strudan.

Gestrynan *to gain, obtain, get, procreate*, *L. In.* 27, *Roff.*, v. strynan.

Gestrynedlic, gestrynendlic *Producing, genitive*; genitivus:—Gestrynendlic oððe geagniendlic *genitive* or *possessive*, *Elf. gr.* 7, 17.

Gestrynge *A wrestler, champion*; athleta:—Gestrynga plegstow *a place of wrestlers, a theatre*; athletarum locus:—*Cot.* 151.

Gestun *A noise*; strepitus:—Þurh gestun *per turbinem*, *Cot.* 157.

Gestungen *pierced*, *L. eccl.* 21, v. stingan.

Gestyldton *astonished*; *p. of* styltan.

Gestyran; *p.* gestyde; *pp.* gestyred. *To rule, correct, restrain, withhold, remove*, *Bt.* 38, 2: *Cd.* 27, v. styran.

Gesufel *Sifted, fine*; pulmentaris:—*L. Lund.* 8, *W.* p. 68, 36.

Gesugian *to be silent*, *Bt. R.* 18, 4, C, v. swigan.

Gesuirfed *Polished, filed*; politus, *Som.*

Gesund, sund; *adj.* *Sound, healthy, safe*; sanus:—Beo gesund *be healthy*; ave, salve. Beoð gesunde *salvete*, *Elf. gr.* 33, 66. Beon hig ealle gesunde, *Deut.* 20, 11.

Gesund *a swimming, sea*, v. sund.

Gesundelic, gesundlic *Prosperous, successful*; prosperus:—*Ps.* 117, 24: *Bd.* 4, 23.

Gesundfull *full* or *quite sound, prosperous*, *Ps.* 67, 21, v. gesundlic.

Gesundfullian; *p.* ode; *pp.* od. *To make prosperous, to be successful*; prosperare:—*Ps.* 1, 4: 36, 7.

Gesundfullic *Prosperous, successful*; prosperus:—*Bt.* 39, 7.

Gesundfullice; *adv.* *Successfully*; prospere:—*Ps.* 44, 5.

Gesundfulnes, se; *f.* *Soundness, healthiness, prosperity*; sanitas corporis:—*Elf. T.* p. 48, 16: *Bt.* 6.

Gesundig *prosperous*, *Bd.* 5, 1, v. gesundlic.

Gesúndrian, asyndrian; *p.* de; *pp.* od, asindrod. *To separate, divide, sunder*; separare:—*Cd.* 6, *Th.* p. 8, 18: 8, *Th.* p. 10, 26.

Gesundsumlice; *adv.* *Soundly, without loss, peacefully*; pacifice:—*Chr.* 920.

Gesungen *sung, said*, v. singan.

Gesuwian *to be silent*, *Solil.* 16, v. suwian.

Geswæled *lighted, kindled*, *R.* 60, v. swelan.

Geswænced *fatigued, afflicted*, v. swencan.

Geswæpa, geswæpo *Sweepings*; peripsema, sordes:—*Cot.* 149. 169. Geswapa *ruinæ*, *R.* 17.

Geswæs *pretty, sweet*, *Ass. S. Johan.* v. swæs.

Geswæslæcan *to flatter*, *Elf. gr.* 31, v. swæslæcan.

Geswæsnys, se; *f.* *A sweet word, a compliment, an enticement, allurement, a dainty*; blanditia:—*Elf. gr.* 13.

Geswæðrung, e; *f.* *A failing, a want*; deliquium:—Modes geswæðrunga *animi deliquium*, *L. M.* 2, 21, v. sweðerian.

Geswearc *failed*; *p. of* gesweorcan.

Geswearf, gesweorf, geswyrf. *The scum of metals, rust*; spuma metallorum:—Geswearf of seolfre *the scum of silver*, *Med. ex. quadr.* 2, 8.

Gesweccan *To smell*; odorari:—Na Gesweccað, *Ps.* 113, 14, *M.*

Geswefian; *pp.* geswefed, geswefod. *To cast asleep, to lull, appease*; sopire:—*Elf. gr.* 30: *L. Ps.* 3, 5.

Gesweg *a noise*, v. sweg.

Geswel, geswell *A swelling, tumour*; tumor:—*Herb.* 4, 12.

Gesweltan *to die*, *Ps.* 81, 6, v. sweltan.

Geswenc *trouble*, v. geswinc.

Geswencan; *p.* geswencte; *pp.* geswenced. *To fatigue, molest, afflict*, *Lk.* 21, 16, v. swencan.

Geswencednes, geswincednis, geswenctnes, se; *f.* *Sorrow, affliction, tribulation*; afflictio:—*Ps.* 9, 9: *Mk.* 13, 24.

Gesweogode *was silent*, *Bt.* 39, 2, v. swigian.

Gesweopornes, geswiopernis, se; *f.* *Cunning, craftiness, hypocrisy*; astutia:—*C. R. Mk.* 12, 15.

Gesweor *swore*; *p. of* swerian.

Gesweorc, gesworc *A cloud, mist, smoke*; nubes:—*Cd.* 5, *Th.* p. 7, 19: 38, *Th.* p. 50, 12.

Gesweorcan, he geswyrcð; *p.* geswearc, we geswurcon; *pp.* gesworcen. 1. *To fail, leave one, faint*; deficere, deficere animo. 2. *To fail as light, to darken, obscure, thicken*; deficere, caligare:—1. Ic geswearc *excidi*, *V. Ps.* 30, 15. Geswearc se Godes man *the man of God fainted* [*failed*]; defecit Dei vir, *Bd.* 4, 25, *S.* p. 600, 29. Aswearc ure mod, *Jos.* 2, 11. 2. Geswearc *thickened*, *Cd.* 166, *Th.* p. 207, 4.

Gesweorcnes, se; *f.* *Cloudiness, horror, affliction*; horror:—*Eccl.* p. 176.

Gesweorf *the scum of metals, rust*, v. geswearf.

Gesweostor *a sister*, *Cd.* 123, *Th.* p. 157, 16, v. sweoster.

Gesweotolad *manifested*, v. sweotolan.

Geswetan; *p.* geswette; *pp.* geswet, gesweted [swete *sweet*] *To sweeten, season*; condire, indulcorare:—Gesweted win, geswet win *sweetened wine*; indulcoratum vinum, melicraton, *R.* 32: *Herb.* 110, 2. Geswet wæter *sweet water*;

Gest sele a guest hall Beo K 1980 v gest (C hpl.

Geswapen downfall, dregs ruins R 17 v geswapa

Geswealh swallowed 169 th h 210, 9 p of swelgan

Gestuncon stank pl. of stincan

2 Gestyllan to make quiet or still, to appease Som v gestillan

Gestop stepped gone p. of steppan

1 Wel gesund all hail, a salutation Th. Apol

Gesthinan to gain Som v strynan

4 Geswencnes sorrow Som v geswencednes

Gestreon, etc of apes Beo gl in streonan

3 Gesundlic healthy prosperous Th Ap v Gesundelic

3

4 Gesustrenu con sobrini Bow

5 Gesuwian to be silent Ben v gesuwian Bow

Gesweriau to swear Th Apol

1 Gestrynedlic gebigednes a genitive case

Gesworc a cloud
Som v geswearc

Geswiccan recipiscere Ben

Geswencgean laboured scourged pp of swingan

Geswutelung a manifesting v swutelung

Gesweccednes affliction Som v swencednes

Geswincednes, se; f sorrow; tribulatio Ben

Gesybsum peaceable Ben v gesibsum

Gesybsumian to be at peace Ben v gesibsumian

Gesyclod sick Som v gesicelod

Gesylfred silvered covers; argento obductus Som

Gesyn(s)cipas nuptials used generally in the pl like gyfta the a pl v gesinscipe

Geswipperness f craftiness Som v geswipornes

Gesyne visible, Ben K 2511

Geteala well happily Som v teala

Getegd a purse; marsupium Som Ben

Gesynto, c; f health Bed gl in Lund

4

indulcorata aqua, *Herb.* 33, 2: 1, 1, 3.

Gesweðerad, geswiðrad, geswiðrod. *Dispersed, decayed, soothed, mitigated;* mitigatus:—Gesweðerad wæs se swyle *the swelling was (decayed) soothed, Bd.* 5, 3: *Jdth.* 12, v. sweðerian.

Gesweðodest *hast searched;* investigasti:—*T. Ps.* 138, 2.

Geswetton *afflicted;* vexaverunt:—*C. Ps.* 93, 5, v. swencan.

Geswic *an offence, T. Ps.* 49, 21, v. beswic.

Geswícan, geswicean, geswicnan. *To leave off, desist, clear, avoid, cease, to deceive, seduce, Deut.* 32, 26, v. swican.

Geswicenes, se; *f. A ceasing, repentance, an amendment;* cessatio:—Þurh geswicenysse yfeles *by the ceasing of evil;* per cessationem a malo, *Wan. Cat.* p. 2: *Elf. T.* 29.

Geswicneful *laborious,* v. geswincful.

Geswicung, e; *f. A ceasing, an intermission;* cessatio:—*R. Conc. pref. Mon. Angl.*

Geswigean, geswigian *to be silent, keep secret,* v. swigian.

Geswigung *silence, Off. Hom. Chr.* 4, v. swigung.

Geswinc, swinc, geswing *Labour, inconvenience, fatigue, trouble, affliction, torment, temptation, banishment;* labor:—On hyra geswinc, *Jn.* 4, 38. Under tungan his geswinge and sar, *Ps.* 9, 29. On geswince, *Ps.* 54, 2. On minum geswincum, *Lk.* 22, 28. For þam com þis geswinc ofer us, *Gen.* 42, 21. Sum heard geswinc *some hard torment, Cd.* 17, *Th.* p. 20, 30.

Geswincfull, swincfull *Full of labour, difficult, troublesome, wearisome;* laboriosus:—Hit bið swiðe geswincfull *it is very laborious, Past.* 60. Geswincfulran, *Bt.* 14, 1, *Card.* p. 64, 28.

Geswincfulnys, se; *f. Sorrow, affliction;* tribulatio:—*L. Ps.* 33, 6.

Geswiopernís *cunning,* v. gesweopornes.

Geswipe *A scourge, whip;* flagellum, *Som.*

Geswiporlice; *adv. Cunningly;* astute:—*V. Ps.* 82, 3.

Geswipp; *adj. Cunning, crafty;* astutus:—*Bd.* 2, 9.

Geswiria *A sister's son;* sororis filius:—*Cot.* 35.

Geswiðian, geswiðrian; *p.* ode; *pp.* od. *To prevail, strengthen, surmount, conquer, subdue;* prævalere:—Hæfde he þa geswiðed *he had then strengthened, Cd.* 143, *Th.* p. 179, 17. Geswiðde *strong, Cd.* 226, *Th.* p. 300, 29, v. swiðian.

Geswiðrod *subdued,* v. geswiðian.

Geswogen *silenced, dead, Elf. T.* 14, 5, v. geswugian.

Geswogung *Silence, dumbness;* silentium, *Som.*

Geswor *swore;* gesworen *sworn,* v. swerian.

Geswugian; *p.* ede; *pp.* geswogen. *To be silent, Bt.* 18, 4, *Card.* p. 104, 2, v. swigian.

Geswurdod *Armed with a sword;* gladio cinctus:—*Elf. gr.* 43.

Geswuster *a sister, Mk.* 10, 29, v. swuster.

Geswutelian, geswuteligan, swutelian; *p.* ode; *pp.* od. *To declare, publish, make known, to manifest, shew, glorify;* monstrare, publicare:—Geswutelude þa æ, *Deut.* 1, 5. Geswutelige hym me sylfne, *Jn.* 14, 21: 14, 22: 13, 32. Nan þing þat ne sy geswutelod, *Lk.* 8, 17.

Geswyrf *the scum of metals, Herb.* 3, v. geswearf.

Geswyrfan *To file off, to polish;* elimare:—*Cot.* 71.

Geswystréna *of sisters, Bt.* 35, 4, v. swuster.

Geswytelian; *pp.* geswytelod. *To make known, L. Edw.* 3, v. geswutelian.

Gesyd *A place for rolling;* volutabrum:—*R.* 56.

Gesyfled *sifted;* gesyfled hlaf *sifted bread, fine bread,* v. gesufel.

Gesyft *sifted, Ex.* 12, 34. v. siftan.

Gesyhð *sight, Cd.* 188, v. gesiht.

Gesylhð *A plough;* aratrum, *Som.*

Gesyllan *to give, deliver, say, betray, sell, give up, Bd.* 4, 19, v. syllan.

Gesylt *Salted;* sale conditus:—*Mt.* 5, 13.

Gesylð *happiness,* v. gesælð.

Gesymed *loaded, Gen.* 45, 23, v. syman.

Gesyndlic *Prosperous, happy;* prosperus:—*Bd.* 4, 23.

Gesyndred, gesyndrod *separated,* v. syndrian.

Gesynelic *What can be seen;* visibilis:—*Bd.* 3, 19.

Gesyngalian; *p.* ade. *To continue, to hold on, hold together, to be diligent;* continuare:—*C. Ps.* 88, 49.

Gesyngian *to sin, Mt.* 5, 28, v. singian.

Gesynlice *More frequently;* sæpius:—*R. Ben.* 56.

Gesynra *manifest, from* gesyne; *pp. of* seon *to see.*

Gesynto, synto *Health, prosperity, success, advantage, profit;* prosperitas:—*Bd.* 2, 13.

Get, geta *yet, as yet, Bt.* 7, 3, v. gyt.

Get *a she-goat, Somn.* 126, v. gat.

Get *a gate,* v. geat.

Get *poured out,* v. geotan.

Getacnian; *p.* ode; *pp.* od. 1. *To denote by a sign, signify, instruct;* significare. 2. *To witness, seal;* obsignare:—1. *Elf. gr.* 37: *V. Ps.* 118, 27. 2. *Jn.* 3, 33: 6, 27, v. tacnian.

Getacniendlic, getacnigendlic *Bearing a sign, significative, typical;* significativus:—*Hom. Pasch.* p. 11.

Getacnung *a signification, Jud.* 16, v. tacnung.

Getade *Went, was spread;* abiit, diffusus est:—Getade mersung his, *C. Mt.* 4, 24.

Getæcan, getæcnan; *p.* getæhte. *To teach, to shew, declare, assign, Bt.* 34, 9, v. tæcan.

Getæl *a number, reckoning, computation, Mt.* 14, 21, v. getel.

Getælan *to accuse, reprove, compare, Bt.* 10, *Card.* p. 42, 4, v. tælan.

Getæld *a tent, Cot.* 204, v. geteld.

Getælfæst *measurable, L. Ps.* 37, 7.

Getænge *heavy, grievous, Herb.* 11, 12, v. getenge.

Getæse *An advantage;* commodum:—*Cot.* 59.

Getæse; *adj. Meet, convenient;* accommodus:—Getæsost, *Bt. R.* p. 174.

Getæsnes, se; *f. An opportunity, a saving, placing;* commoditas:—*Cot.* 55.

Getal *a number, reckoning, calendar, Deut.* 1, 11, v. getel.

Getalad, getaled *numbered, esteemed, C. Lk.* 12, 7, v. tellan.

Getan, geatan *To* GET; obtinere, *Lye,* v. geatan.

Getang *Lying, prostrate;* prostratus:—*C. R. Ben.* 34.

Getanned *Tanned;* cortice maceratus:—*R.* 17.

Getawa *Instruments;* instrumenta:—*L. Eccl.* 2.

Getawian *to prepare, reduce or bring to, Nathan,* 7, v. tawian.

Getead *drawn, prepared,* v. geteod.

Geteag, geteah *drew, united,* v. teon.

Geteal, geteall *a number, Hymn. Nat. S. Greg.* v. getel.

Geteald *told; p. of* tellan.

Geteald *a tent, Ps.* 51, 5, v. geteld.

Geteama, getyma *An advocate, avoucher, a warranter;* advocatus, qui rei emptæ fidem præstat:—*L. Edw.* 1.

Getecan *to shew, Bt.* 33, 1, v. tæcan.

Getede *enticed, Bt. R.* p. 168, v. teon.

Getegd *bound,* v. getian.

Getehhod *determined,* v. teohhian.

Getel, getæl, geteal, getel, es;

n. 1. *A number, series,* TALE, *reckoning;* numerus. 2. *A course, race, tribe, a book of reckoning;* laterculus:—1. Witodlice agene naman habbað anfeald getel, and nabbað mænigfeald eac sunne, and mona syndon anfealdes geteles, *Elf. gr.* 13, 3. Þas twa getel *these two numbers, Elf. gr.* 13, 3, 5, 12, 14. Þat ilce tigol getel, *Ex.* 5, 18: *Ps.* 39, 8. 2. *Cot.* 31, 37: *R. Mt.* 24, 30.

Getelan *to accuse, reprove, reproach, deride, impute to, to confer, dispute, R. Lk.* 20, 26, v. tælan.

Geteld, getæld, geteald, teld, es; *n. A tent, tabernacle, pavilion,* TILT, *cover;* tentorium:—He sæt on his geteldes ingange, *Gen.* 18, 1. Þæt micele geteld *the great tent.* Aslogan an geteld *erected a tent;* fixerunt tentorium, *Bd.* 3, 17.

Geteldung *A tent, tabernacle;* tabernaculum:—*T. Ps.* 18, 5: 26, 9.

Getelged *Coloured, dyed;* coloratus:—*Cot.* 49, 81, v. tælg.

Getellan *to number, reckon, esteem, consider, Ps.* 89, 13, v. tellan.

Geteman [teman *to teem*] *To lead out, to excite, require;* perducere, provocare:—*L. Hloth.* 7: *L. In.* 35. Geteme *required, provoked.* Hæfdon hie wroht-geteme *they had criminations, Cd.* 2, *Th.* p. 3, 34.

Getemesd, getempsud *Sifted;* cribratus:—Hlafas getemesda *shew-bread, C. Mt.* 12, 4.

Getemian *to tame, Elf. gr.* 36, v. temian.

Getempsud *sifted,* v. getemesd.

Geten *should confirm, Chr.* 675, v. geatan.

Getenge, getænge. 1. *Heavy, grievous, troublesome;* gravis. 2. *Incumbent, happened, occurred, incident, lying, prostrate;* incidens:—1. Cyme hægles scur hefone getenge *cometh a heavy shower of hail from heaven, Cd.* 38, *Th.* p. 50, 14. Þe him getenge wæs *qui illis molestus erat, Ors.* 5, 8: 6, 3. 2. Nan unaberendlic broc getenge *no intolerable misery happened, Bt.* 10. Eorðan getenge *prostrate on the ground;* humi prostratus, *Bt. R.* p. 197.

Getenys, gytenes, se; *f. A procuring, attaining,* GETTING, *instruction, education;* adeptio, institutio:—*Bd.* 3, 22.

Geteod *drawn, prepared, determined, led, educated, finished, decreed, Bd.* 3, 24, v. teohhian.

Geteóde *formed, decreed, Cd.* 182, *Th.* p. 288, 19, v. teode.

Geteohan *to determine,* v. teohhian.

Geteolod *Gained;* lucrifactus:—*W. Bd.* p. 289.

Geteon, getion *to draw, entice, R. Jn.* 21, 6, v. teon, ateon.

Geteorian, geteorigean, ateorian, teorian; *p.* ode; *pp.* od. *To fail, faint, tire, to be weary, to languish;* deficere, languere:—Geteoriað, *Ps.* 17, 39. Geteorode, *Ps.* 38, 14. Þe læs hig on wege geteorian, *Mt.* 15, 32. Geteorigeað, *Mk.* 8, 3. Geteorod bið *fatigatus est, Herb.* 112, 1, v. ateorian.

Geteorung, ateorung, e; *f. A failing, fainting, languishing, tiring;* deliquium:—*Ps.* 118, 53.

Getesa *Convenient;* commodus:—*Solil.* 18.

Getete *pomp, shew, ostentation, magnificence,* v. getote.

Geþæf *Agreeing, content;* consentiens:—*R. Ben.* 7.

Geþæslæcan *To fit, to be fit, to become;* aptare:—*R. Ben. interl.* 2.

Geþæslic *fit, proper, Elf. gr.* 14, v. þæslic.

Geþæt *advice, Bd.* 2, 13, v. geþeaht.

Geþafa, an; *f. A favourer, supporter, helper, assenter, consenter;* fautor, adjutor:—Wolde geþafa wurðan *would be a supporter, Cd.* 22, *Th.* p. 27, 8. Ic eom geþafa *I am an assenter, I grant, Bt.* 35, 2: 38, 2. We sceolon beon nede geþafan *we should necessarily be consenters, Bt.* 34, 12.

Geþafian, geþafigean *to consent, agree, permit, Bd.* 2, 13, v. þafian.

Geþafsum *Agreeing;* consentiens:—*C. Mt.* 5, 25.

Geþafung, þafung, e; *f. Permission, consent, allowance;* permissio:—Geþafung gesyllan, *to give consent, Bd.* 4, 8. Geþafung sealde *gave consent, Bd.* 2, 13.

Geþáh *prevailed, throve,* v. geþeawod.

Geþah *ate, Cd.* 42, *Th.* p. 54, 3, v. þicgan.

Geþanc, es; *m.* [þanc *will*] *Mind, will, opinion, thought;* mens:—Þat geþanc eode on hig, *Lk.* 9, 46. Se Hælend geseah hyra heortan geþancas, *Lk.* 9, 47. Þincð on his geþance *thinks in his mind, R. Ben.* 65.

Geþancian *to thank, L. Lond.* 7, v. þancian.

Geþancmetan *To deliberate, consider;* considerare:—Geþancmeta *deliberate, Cd.* 91.

Geþancol *mindful, R. Lk.* 1, 54, v. þoncol.

Geþang, es. *Departure, leading;* excessus:—*Ps.* 67, 29.

Geþawened *Wetted;* humectatus:—*Bt. R.* p. 176.

Geþeado *Captives;* captivi:—*R. Lk.* 21, 24.

Geþeáh *finished; p. of* þeon.

Geþeah þe *wheresoever.*

Geþeaht, geþæht, þeaht; *f.* 1. *Counsel, thought, consideration, advice, purpose, design, resolution;* consilium. 2. *A council, an assembly;* concilium:—1. Geþeaht syllan *to give advice, Bd.* 4, 25. Butan geþeahte *without purpose, unadvisedly, Bd.* 3, 1. Nime ge ealle an geþeahte *take ye all one design, Nathan.* 6. Þat hie þære geþeahte wæron *that they were of the resolution, Cd.* 182, *Th.* p. 228, 21. 2. Ic ne sæt mid geþeahte ydelnyssa, *Ps.* 25, 1: 21, 15. Geþeahtu *consilia, Somn.* 292.

Geþeaht *covered,* v. þeccan.

Geþeahtendlic; *adj. Consulting, belonging to a consultation;* consultatorius:—Geþeahtendlic ym-cyme *a convention in council, L. With.* p. 10, *pref.*

Geþeahtere *counsellor, Bd.* 5, 19, v. þeahtere.

Geþeahtian *to consult, advise, Ps.* 30, 17, v. þeahtian.

Geþeahting, geþeahtung, e; *f. Counsel, consultation;* consilium:—*Bd.* 4, 25.

Geþearfan *to have need* or *necessity, Mor. præc.* 73, v. þearfan.

Geþeawlice *well, properly, Bd.* 3, 19, v. þeawlice.

Geþeawod *prevailed.* Land-riht geþah *land-right prevailed, Cd.* 161, *Th.* p. 200, 10.

Geþeh *should proceed,* v. þeon.

Geþencan, geþengcan, geþencean *to think, consider, remember, Mt.* 6, 27, v. þencan.

Geþenian *to extend, C. Mt.* 12, 49, v. þenian.

Geþenod *served,* v. þenian.

Geþensum *Obsequious, obliging;* officiosus:—*R. Ben.* 53.

Geþeodan, þeodan, geþyddan, he geþeot; *p.* geþeode, geþeodde; *pp.* geþeoded; *v. a. To join, associate;* adjungere:—Geþeot hine to his wife, *Gen.* 2, 24: *Mt.* 19, 5: *Bt.* 16, 3. Hi hie ne þeodað *they join not themselves.* Hi hie oftost togeþeodað *they oftest join themselves, Bt.* 16, 3, *Card.* p. 86, 30, 31. Geþeoded wæs *was joined, Bd.* 2, 20, *S.* p. 521, 10.

Geþeode; *n. Language, speech, idiom, country, people, society;* lingua:—Ne furþum þat geþeode ne can *nor even knows the language, Bt.* 27, 3. Þat

1) # Seo boc þe ys cnemned on Lyden Numerus, and on Englisc Getel. Num. Ref.

1 Geteled numbered told, for geteald pp of tellan

2 Getemed tamed Som pp v getemian

3 Getemprod tempered mixed Som pp of ~~temprian~~ temprian

2) 4 Getengde went, intened p.p. of g tengan, tengan

4 Getenge [44 a 6] Getinge [4 x ...] ...

1 Geteog es; n Stuff, matters, implements, utensils Th. An

3 Geteon to play (on the organ ... Th. ...

4 Ge-teona; an; m. an enemy ~~a damage~~ ... malum ... 1942

5 Geteonan to irritate

geteond injured, wronged Som Lye v Tynan

6 Geteung, e; f ~~ofer~~ Ofer boc geteung a crick in the back, a cramp, stiffness; tetanus R. 20 Lye

7)

6 Gepenan estimare Ben Lye

5 Gepeahting counsel ~~advice~~ Ben v gepeahting

8)

1 Gepang, gepwang es; m a thong, ... sinew Th. An

2)

3 Gepeahtar an m A counseller, adviser, Th. An

4 Gepeahton to consider Ben v gepeahtian

~~Gepeahton to consider Ben v gepeahtian~~

5 ~~Gepencan ...~~ Gepeo flourish v peon

8 / x Gepeod es n language tongue Th. An

... e; f Th. An

[sent in a boat hence ge-pofta a] One who sits in a boat with you a companion

1 Gepofta ... socius ... II 7, 11 Beo

~~Gepeon~~ to thrive grow Th an v peon

~~gepeodraeden~~, e f society, fellowship, associa... societas, consortium Ben 48

~~Gepogen ... peon~~

?

5 Gepinc ... [illegible] ... v ge-mot

6

Gepind, gepinpenes honour Som ge-pinod

8 Gepiodan to join See v gepeodan

gepyhd grows v ~~gepeon~~ peon

10 Gepuren struck, beaten percussus ? Beo K 2571

2 Gepiot joins v gepeodan

Gepeslic fit, proper Ben v gepaeslic

~~gepoft-raeden~~, e f mutual affection, fellowship; complacitum, consortium Som

2 Gepogen ~~...~~ increased pp of peon

3 Gepone thought, mind See v gepanc

4 Gepraece ~~...~~ rakin..., ~~...~~ Som v gepraec

5 Geprawen ~~...~~ twisted See v geprawen

6 Gepregdan to vex torment ... pregan

4 Geprecced, gepricced, geprycced oppressed, depressed v priccan

8 Gepraecednes oppression violence; oppressio Som v prycnes

Gepregian to blame rebuke; increpare Som.

2 Gepresc ~~...~~ verbera Ben

3 Gepnisced oppressed Ben v gepryced

4 Geprowung, e f a suffering Som v prowing

~~Gepryced~~

Gepryced oppressed Som v gepreced

Gepufe An orchard, a young grove; fruticetum Som

7 Gepugen grown Som v gepogen

8 Gepugon ~~...~~ have pleased Som Rasc p. 13, 22 v peon

9 Gepungen full perfect age, youth Som

Gepewild patience ... 18 on margin

is gerehte on ure geþeode, *Mt.* 1, 23: *Mk.* 5, 41: 15, 22: *Ors.* 1, 1, *Bar.* p. 22, 30.

Geþeodendlic; *adj. Conjunctive, joining;* copulativus:—*Elf. gr.* 44.

Geþeodnes, se; *f. A conjugation, joining, desire, an appetite;* conjunctio:—Worda geþeodnys *a conjugation of verbs, Elf. gr.* 24, 2. To geþeodnesse *to a desire, Bd.* 4, 24.

Geþeofian *To steal, seize;* furari:—Geþeofade, *L. In.* 48. Gif hwa geþeofige *si quis furetur, L. Alf. pol.* 6.

Geþeon *to flourish, thrive, proceed, Elf. gr.* 26, v. þeon.

Geþeowade; *pp.* geþeowed, geþeowod. *Subjugated, enslaved, L. In.* 48, v. þeowian.

Geþersc *A stripe, blow;* verber:—*Dial.* 1, 2.

Geþicgan *to eat, Ors.* 3, 6, v. þicgan.

Geþiedan *To add;* adjicere:—*T. Ps.* 113, 23.

Geþihð *strengthens, Job.* p. 167, v. þeon.

Geþincgan; *pp.* od. *To celebrate, honour;* honorare:—Geþincged *honoured, Menol.* 14.

Geþincð *dignity, merit, L. Lond.* 70, v. geþingð.

Geþincðe *Honoured;* honoratus:—*L. Const.* p. 117.

Geþing, þing, es; *n. A council, an assembly, a thing, deed;* concilium:—Geþinges wyrcan *to form an assembly, Cd.* 197, *Th.* p. 245, 25: *L. In.* 50: 52.

Geþingelic *concerning a council, Cot.* 179.

Geþingian; *p.* ode; *pp.* od. *To intreat, intercede, mediate, to obtain by intreaty, to bargain, agree, implead;* intercedere, pacisci:—*R. Mt.* 5, 24: *L. In.* 22. Swa he þonne geþingian mæge on þa rædene *as he then can agree on the condition, L. In.* 62: 73.

Geþingio *A provision;* apparatio:—*Cot.* 8.

Geþingsceat *price of ransoming.*

Geþingð, geþincð, bege-þincð, *Honour, dignity, merit, excellence, summit, top;* honor:—Be heora geþingðum *by their dignities, Lib. Jud.* p. 161. Gif we willað habban þa miclan geþingðe *if we wish to have the great honour, W. Cat.* p. 2. Geþingðo *honours, Cd.* 23.

Geþinnian *To thin, disperse;* attenuare:—*Bt.* 5, 3.

Geþinoð, geþinð, geþinðenes *honour, dignity, step, Nat. S. Greg.*, v. geþingð.

Geþiode *speech,* v. geþeode.

Geþiogan *to feed, eat,* v. þiegan.

Geþiostran *to obscure, Bt. tit.* 9, v. þiostran.

Geþofta *A companion, comrade, client;* also *affable, courteous;* consors:—*Bd.* 3, 27.

Geþoftian; *p.* ode; *pp.* od. *To associate, to enter into an agreement;* associare:—Geþoftian heom togædere *associare se simul, Ors.* 3, 2.

Geþoftscipe, es; *m. Companionship, a treaty;* consortium, fœdus:—*Past.* 46, 5.

Geþóht, þóht, es; *m.* THOUGHT, *thinking, mind, determination;* cogitatio:—Geþohtas of manegum heortum, *Lk.* 2, 35: *Ps.* 32, 10.

Geþohte *thought,* v. þencean.

Geþolian *to sustain, bear, suffer, forfeit, Cd.* 219, *Th.* p. 281, 17, v. þolian.

Geþonan, geþonne *excellent, perfect, holy, Chr.* 694; *from* geþeon, v. þeon.

Geþorscan *to beat, to strike, R. Mk.* 14, 65, v. þerscan.

Geþracen; *adj. Prepared, decked;* ornatus:—Geþracen hors *ornatus equus, R.* 5.

Geþræsnes, se; *f. Contrition, sorrow;* contritio:—*Bd.* 5, 12.

Geþræstan *to press upon, wear, torment, Bd.* 3, 2, v. þræstan.

Geþrafod *corrected, chastised,* v. þrafian.

Geþrang A THRONG, *crowd;* turba:—*Ors.* 3, 9.

Geþrawen, geþræwen *twisted,* v. þrawan.

Geþread *afflicted,* v. þreatian.

Geþreatian *to urge, chide, compel, afflict, torment, L. Alf. pol.* 25, v. þreatian.

Geþrec, geþræce *A preparation, provision;* apparatus:—*Cot.* 1.

Geþrece, geþrete *A noise;* clangor:—*Cot.* 59.

Geþring *A noise, company, breaking in upon, an entrance;* strepitus:—*Chr.* 975.

Geþringan *to press, throng, constrain, contend, C. R. Lk.* 8, 45, v. þringan.

Geþristian [þrist *bold*] *To dare, presume;* audere:—*Bd.* 1, 7.

Geþristlæcan *To dare, presume, excite;* provocare:—We geþristlæcton *provocavimus, Cot.* 154.

Geþrowian *to bear, suffer,* v. þrowian.

Geþruen, *for* geþrungen *joined, come, Bt.* p. 177.

Geþrungen *come.* Þæra tide is neah geþrungen *to that time [it] is nearly come, Cd.* 116, *Th.* p. 151, 15.

Geþryle *An assembly, a meeting;* frequentia:—For þæs folces geþryle *for the folk's assembly, Hom.* 8, *Cal. Jan.* p. 18.

Geþryscan *To drive, incite;* impellere:—*Past.* 14, 3.

Geþryðed *Forced;* coactus.

Geðtrywð *Faith, integrity;* fides:—*Chr.* 1001, v. getriwð.

Geþuf *Growing, luxuriant;* luxurians:—*Cot.* 123, 198.

Geþuht *seemed,* v. þincan.

Geþuild *patience, C. Lk.* 18, 17, v. geþyld.

Geþun *A noise;* clangor:—*Cot.* 56.

Geþungen *prayed for, obtained, great, excellent, perfect, religious, Bd.* 2, 1, 12, v. þingian.

Geþungenys, geþungennes, se; *f. An increase, gravity, authority;* gravitas:—*Scint.* 55.

Geþungon *worshipped, obtained,* v. þingian.

Geþuog *anointed, washed,* v. þwean.

Geþwænan *To moisten, wet, soften;* irrigare:—Gif þat wæter hi ne geþwænde *if the water moisten it not, Bt.* 33, 4.

Geþwær, þwær *Agreeing, consonant, accordant, mild, humble;* consonus, mansuetus:—*Bt.* 33, 4: *Ps.* 36, 11.

Geþwærian, geþwerian, geþweorian; *p.* ode, ede; *pp.* od. *To agree, consent, conform, to make suitable, to adapt;* consentire:—Gyf twegen of eow geþwæriad, *Mt.* 18, 19: *Bt.* 39, 8.

Geþwærlæcan *To agree;* concordare:—*Alb. resp.* 47.

Geþwærlic *agreeing, Fulg.* 33, v. geþwær.

Geþwærlice; *adv. Constantly, gently, mildly;* constanter:—*Bd.* 4, 17.

Geþwærnes, se; *f. Concord, agreement, mildness;* mansuetudo:—*Ps.* 44, 6: *Bd.* 4, 23.

Geþweorian [þweor *bad*] *To become bad, corrupt, to be spoiled;* depravari, rancidus fieri:—Butere geþweor ælc *butyrum depravatur omne, Coll. Monast.*

Geþwin *Torment;* tormentum:—*Cd.* 33, *Th.* p. 43, 26.

Geþwit *cut off,* v. þwitan.

Geþyddan *to join, associate, Bd.* 1, 26, v. geþeodan.

Geþyld *Patience, resignation;* patientia:—Gehafa geþyld on me, *Mt.* 18, 26. On geþylde, *Lk.* 8, 15: *L. In.* 6.

Geþyldelice; *adv. Patiently, quietly;* patienter:—*Bd.* 1, 7.

Geþyldgian, geþyldian, *for* þyldian. *To be patient, to bear patiently, endure;* pati:—*Mt.* 18, 29.

Geþyldig; *adj. Patient, quiet;* patiens:—*Ps.* 36, 9.

Geþyldiglice; *adv. Quietly;* patienter:—*Pass. S. Steph.*

Geþylmod *a patient mind, patience.*

Geþylmodnes, se; *f. Patience;* patientia:—*Off. Hom. Christ.*

Geþynd *A knot, tumour;* tuber:—*Herb.* 46, 4.

Getian, þu getihst, he getit, getið; *pp.* getiged, getigged, getegd. To TIE, *bind, finish;* ligare, constringere:—Gyt gemetað assan folan getiged, *Lk.* 19, 30: *Mt.* 21, 2: *Mk.* 11, 2: *Gen.* 6, 16.

Getidan, getydan; *p.* de. *To betide, happen;* contingere:—Þe getide, *Jn.* 5, 14. Getideð oft *happened oft, Bt.* 33, 2.

Getiht *persuaded,* v. teon.

Getilian *to cure, Bt.* 5, 3, v. tilian.

Getillan, atillan *To touch, practise, attain to, to appertain;* attingere:—*Job.* p. 165, 15.

Getimbernes, se; *f. A building;* ædificatio:—*Bd.* 4, 7.

Getimbre; *pl.* getimbro. *An edifice, a building;* structura:—*Bd.* 3, 8.

Getimbrian, getimbrigean *to make of wood, to build, to build up, to instruct, define, Bd.* 2, 3, v. timbrian.

Getimbrung, timbrung, e; *f.* 1. *An edifice, a structure, building;* ædificatio. 2. *A definition;* definitio:—1. *Mt.* 24, 1: *Mk.* 13, 1. 2. *Cot.* 69.

Getimian, getymian *To happen, to fall out;* accidere:—*Lib. Jud.* 5.

Getincge *A condition, state;* conditio:—*Bd.* 1, 7.

Getingce, getinge *Pleasantness of speech, eloquence;* lepor, *Som.*

Getingce, getinge; *adj. Pleasant, eloquent, talkative, rhetorical;* lepidus, facundus:—*Elf. gr.* 47.

Getingelic; *adj. Pleasant in speech, affable, eloquent;* lepidus, affabilis:—*Cot.* 179.

Getingnys, se; *f. Eloquence, ease of speech;* facundia:—Dumbum he forgeafe getingnysse *to the dumb he gave eloquence, Serm. Creat.* p. 14: *Elf. T.* p. 17.

Getiode *determined, decreed.*

Getiohhan, geteohan *to judge, determine, decree, Ps.* 40, 9, v. teohhian.

Getion *to draw, Bt.* 38, 1, v. teon.

Getiorian *to tire, grow weary, Bt.* 16, 5, v. geteorian.

Getitelod *Entitled, noted by the title;* intitulatus:—*Elf. T.* p. 17, 13.

Getiðian, getyðian, getygðian *to grant, give, afford, perform,* v. tiðian.

Getoge *Contraction, cramp;* contractio:—Sina getoge *a contraction of sinews, Med. Quad.* 6, 20.

Getogen *drawn out, risen, instructed, finished, Bd.* 2, 9, v. teon.

Getorfode *covered,* v. torfian.

Getote *Pomp, splendour;* pompa:—*R. Ben.* 7.

Getrahtnian *to treat, explain, C. Mt.* 1, 23, v. trahtian.

Getredan *to tread under foot, C. Mt.* 7, 6, v. tredan.

Getregian *To disregard, despise;* despicere:—Þu ne getregedest *thou despisedst not, Te Deum.*

Getreminc *A fort, fortress;* munimentum:—*Prov.* 12.

Getreowe, getrewe *true, faithful, Gen.* 42, 33, v. getrywe.

Getreowfull; *adj. Faithful;* fidus:—*Ps.* 18, 8.

Getreowfullice; *adv. Faithfully;* fideliter:—*Ps.* 11, 6.

Getreowian, getriowian *to trust, confide, to make another to trust, to persuade, to clear, to be confederate with, to conspire, Bd.* 31, 1, v. treowian.

Getreowleás *unfaithful, perfidious, Bd.* 3, 24, v. treowleas.

Getreowleásnes, se; *f. Infidelity, perfidy;* perfidia:—*Bd.* 1, 8.

Getreowlic, getriowlic, treowlic *Faithful;* fidelis:—*Ps.* 110, 7.

Getreowlice; *adv. Faithfully;* fideliter:—*Bd.* 3, 23.

Getreowð *a covenant, treaty, Ex.* 2, 24, v. treowð.

Getricce *A custom;* consuetudo:—*R. Ben.* 61.

Getriowan, getriwan *to trust, confide, L. Alf. pol.* 17, v. getrowian.

Getriowe *true, prepared, R. Lk.* 12, 40, v. getrywe.

Getriowlice, getriwlice, getrywlice *faithfully, L. Ps.* 11, 6, v. getreowlice.

Getriwð, getrywð *truth, faith, Lup.* 50, 7, v. treowð.

Getrucian *to diminish, truck, H. Jn.* 2, 3, v. trucian.

Getrudend, es; *m. A seizer;* raptor:—*Cot.* 170.

Getrugian *to confide,* v. treowian.

Getrugung, e; *f. A certainty, defence, refuge;* confidentia:—*V. Ps.* 88, 18.

Getrum *A knot, band;* nodus:—*Cd.* 147, *Th.* p. 184, 6.

Getruma *a soldier, a troop of soldiers, Chr.* 871, v. truma.

Getrumian *to recover, to gain strength, Ps.* 79, 16, 18, v. trumian.

Getruwa *confidence,* v. truwa.

Getruwian, getruwigeað *to trust, confide,* v. getreowian.

Getruwung *a confidence, C. Ps.* 88, 18, v. getrugung.

Getrymian *to establish, confirm, strengthen, encourage, found, fortify, dispose, set in order, bring forward, Bd.* 36, 1, v. trymian.

Getrymnes *exhortation, persuasion, Bd.* 1, 33, v. trymenes.

Getrywe, getreowe, treowe, triwe; *adj.* TRUE, *faithful;* fidelis:—Forþam þe þu wære getrywe, *Mt.* 25, 21: 24, 45: *Bd.* 3, 13.

Getrywie *shall justify, L. In.* 34, v. treowian.

Getrywleás *perfidious, Dial.* 2, 14, v. treowleás.

Getrywsian *to justify, L. Edw.* 6, v. treowian.

Gette *yet, C. Mt.* 17, 5, v. get.

Getucod *punished,* v. tucian.

Getwæfan *To dote, rave, fail;* desipere, deficere mente:—Mod getwæfde *deprived of courage, Cd.* 4, *Th.* p. 4, 14. Ferhð getwæf *the soul fails, Cd.* 148, *Th.* p. 185, 8.

Getwæman *to separate, divide, Mt.* 19, 6, v. twæman.

Getweode *doubted;* getweogan *to doubt,* v. tweogan.

Getweonode *doubted,* v. tweogan.

Getwifealdad *doubled,* v. twifealdan.

Getwinne *Twins;* gemini, gemelli:—*Cot.* 78.

Getwisan *Twins, kinsmen;* gemini, germani:—*Gen.* 38, 27.

Getyd *Skilful, learned;* peritus:—Getydesta *most skilful, Bd.* 5, 20.

Getyd, getyde, getydde *instructed, taught, shewn,* v. tyan.

Getydnes, se; *f. Learning, skill, knowledge, education;* eruditio:—*Bd.* 4, 27.

Getyhted *persuaded,* v. teon.

Getyhtled, getyhtlod *accused, L. Athel.* 7, 22, 23, v. teon.

Getyma *an avoucher, L. Edw. Guth.* 4, v. geteama.

Getyme *A team, yoke;* jugum:—Ic bohte an getyme oxena, *Lk.* 14, 19: *Job.* 164.

Getynge *talkative, V. Ps.* 139, 12, v. getingce.

Getyrfian; *pp.* getyrfed. *To cover;* obruere:—*Dial.* 1, 4.

Getyrige *shouldest grow weary, Bt.* 40, 5, v. geteorian.

Geuferan; *pp.* geuferad, geuferod. *To exalt, elevate, increase;* exaltare:—*R. Ben.* 7: *L. Ps.* 36, 37.

Geunarian *To dishonour, despise;* despicere:—*Ors.* 1, 5. Syn geunarode, *Ps.* 34, 4.

Geunclænsian *To make unclean, to dirty;* fœdare:—*Ors.* 2, 2.

Geunlibba, geunlibbe *what destroys life, the art of poisoning,*

Gepyldum with patience, patiently; patienter Beo K 3409

~~Gepywe befitted~~
~~the ... ratus ... Beo K ...~~
3 ~~Gepywe~~ Custom,
fashion, manner;
mos, Som Beo K 1659

Getogennes, se i f. A convulsion; the cramp
says + moves, the jerates, x om officious convulsio Som

6 Getigian To tie than
gebian
to tie ... ; getiggd
... 745, 14
5 Getigian to tie than v getian getigan
Getiged bound,
vinctus Som v getian, getigian
... getigode granted Cl. 131 th p 166, 23
5 Getihtlad accused
pp of tihtlian
(10)

Getrymnian, getrymnian to confirm, encourage
than v getrymian
~~Getrywe ... 2657~~
~~Getrymminc~~
~~Getrewian to ..~~

Getton, to get
getton confirmed Som
v getan

3 Ge-twæfan to divide, separate; separare; dividere
God meg getwæfan
God may separate Beo K 953 Beo d in twa

4 Getwyan ... hesitate ...

~~Getintregod~~
Getintregod punished, tortured
pp of tintregian
2 Getirged Consitute, broken
v tirian.

2 Getrifulad stamped, broken Som
v trifelan

3 Getrimman To build; edificare
Som Ben

4 Getrimminc es, establishing Som v trymming

5 Getrynnes, se f. A conjunction, joining; conjunctio
Som
6 Getwysan to twist, torquere Ben
7 Getyddrian To cherish; to nourish forth young; parere Som than
8 Getyht exercised practised; exercitatus Som

1 Getym, es; n a team, yoke than

6 Getrywd faithfulness Som
v getreowd

10 Getymian to happen ... v getimian
11 Getypian to appear Ben v getypian
12 Geol Christmas
Som v geol
13 Geonc young than
v geong
14 Geunga a young man; juvenis Som

in wealdan

Gewæht weary, troubled; fessus Som

Gewealdes of one's will, willingly; sponte Bes gl see in geweald

(18) Gewrotlian to sadden, cast down Th an

Gewæmmodlice corruptly; cor. rupte Lye

Gewæmman to pollute, sully Th Apol v gewemman

Gewænan to turn Th Apol v gewendan

Gewændan to turn Th Apol v gewendan

Ge-waden gone, passed, sailed Bev K 439 v wadan

Gewæscen washed Som v wæscan

Gewunlitigad defamed dishonoured; dedecoratus Som

Gewæde a garment Som

Geweald power, potestas Som v geweald

Gewæde

Gewæder the weather coelum Som v weder

Ge-wand modesty, bashfulness, verecundia Lye # 74, 9 Som

Gewæfast that hath given earnest; sub. aratus Som

Gewæterian to water Th An v ge-waterian

Gewæcednes, sef frailty, weakness; fragilitas Som

Gewæda fords, shallows; vada, brevia Som

Gewef a weaving, texture Som v weft

Ge-wæde es; n clothing, garment; vestimentum Bes K 581

Gewegan to go out, Bes K 4796

Gewæge A weight, pondus Som

Gewealcen rolled Som v wealcan, wealc

(l)ro; moore

14 Geweald, geweald, geweald, e. f; aldo m es; n; in power, etc

[illegible] Train

sorcery; veneficium:—*Ex.* 22, 18.

Geunnan *to give, grant, bestow, Bt.* 29, 2; *pp.* geunnen *granted, given, R. Ben. interl.* 6, v. unnan.

Geunne *a concession, gift, L. Cnut. eccl.* 2, v. unne.

Geunret, geunrot *sorrowful, Mt.* 14, 9, v. unrot.

Geunretan *To be sorrowful, sad, sorry for;* contristare:—*Mk.* 6, 26.

Geunrotsian, geunrotsigean *To be sorrowful, contrite, sorry for, to grieve, to offend;* contristare:—Þat we hi ne geunrotsigeon, *Mt.* 17, 27. Gast geunrotsod, *T. Ps.* 50, 18.

Geunsoðian *To disprove, refute, to prove false;* refellere:—*Cnut.* 15.

Geunstillian *To disquiet, disturb;* inquietare:—*Bd.* 4, 5.

Geunþwærian *To disagree, differ;* dissentire:—*Elf. gr.* 37.

Geuntreowsian; *p.* ode; *pp.* od [untreowsian *to deceive*] *To be offended;* scandalizari:—Þeah þe hig ealle geuntreowsion, ic næfre geuntreowsige, *Mt.* 26, 33.

Geuntrumian; *p.* ode; *pp.* od. *To weaken, to make weak, to be sick;* infirmare, ægrotare:—Hi geuntrumiað, *Ps.* 9, 3. Geuntrumod, *Ps.* 17, 38: 108, 23: *Jn.* 6, 2.

Geunwurðod *dishonoured,* v. unweorðian.

Geurnan *ran, occurred,* v. yrnan.

Geuðe *gave, granted, Chr.* 959; *p. of* unnan.

Geutian *to eject,* v. utian.

Geutla *an outlaw, Chr.* 1055, v. utlaga.

Geutlagode *outlawed,* v. utlagian.

Geutode *ejected,* v. utian.

Gewacan *to grow weak,* v. awacian.

Gewæcan, gewæcean, gewæcian; *p.* we gewæhton; *pp.* gewæced, gewæged, gewæct, gewæht. *To affect, trouble, vex, afflict;* affligere:—Mid deaðe hi gewæceað, *Mk.* 13, 12. Gewæcte mid hungre *confecti fame, Bd.* 4, 13: *Ps.* 37, 8. Mid hungre gewæhte, *Jud.* 6, 2. We synd to deaðe gewæhte *we are vexed to death, C. R. Ben.* 11.

Gewædod *Fitted up, prepared;* apparatus, instructus:—*Chr.* 992.

Gewædu *clothes, Bd.* 1, 6, v. wæd.

Gewægan; *pp.* gewæged. 1. *To carry, bear;* advehere. 2. *To weigh down;* deprimere:—1. *Bd.* 3, 16. 2. *Bt. R.* p. 152.

Gewægnian *To be frustrated, deceived, disappointed;* frustrari:—*Cot.* 83.

Gewæled *Troubled;* vexatus:—*R. Mt.* 9, 36.

Gewæltan *To cast* or *fall down;* provolvere:—Gewælten cneum *provolutus genibus, C. Mt.* 17, 14.

Gewæmnednes, se; *f. A corruption;* corruptio:—Anes wordes gewæmnednys *a corruption of a word, a barbarism;* barbarismus, *Som.*

Gewæmnod *armed, Elf. T.* 36, 22, *q.* gewæpnod, v. gewæpnian.

Gewænian, gewenian, wænian, wenian; *p.* ode; *pp.* od; *v. a.* 1. *To* WEAN, *accustom, reconcile, to reconcile to a loss, to detach;* assuescere, ablactare. 2. *To allure, incite* or *seduce, to study;* excitare:—1. Þat cild wearð gewened, *Gen.* 21, 8. Gewenede hine sylfne *he accustomed himself, Elf. T.* p. 34, 19. 2. Fram Gode gewenian *to seduce from God, Job.* p. 165. Hi gewenedon *they allured, Bt.* 25.

Gewæpnian, gewepnian; *p.* ode; *pp.* od, ud. *To arm;* armare:—*Elf. gr.* 24, 36: *Lk.* 11, 21.

Gewærdan, gewerdan *To damage, hurt, strike;* nocere:—Gif hwa gewerde *if any one hurt;* si quis læserit, *L. Alf. eccl.* 18, 26, *W.* p. 31, 3.

Gewær *wary, cautious, C. Mt.* 10, 17, v. wær.

Gewærelæht *Reminded, admonished;* commonefactus:—*Alb. resp.* 44.

Gewæsc *A rising* or *swelling of water;* alluvio:—*R.* 100, 110.

Gewætan, gewetan *to wet, to make wet, Past.* 43, 1, v. wætan.

Gewæterian, gewætrian *to water, irrigate, Past.* 18, 5, v. wæterian.

Gewand *rolled,* v. windan.

Gewanian *to diminish, lessen, cut off, Gen.* 8, 1, v. wanian.

Gewaran *citizens, inhabitants, Nat. S. Greg.* v. waru.

Gewardod *Seen;* visus:—Þat he sy gewardod fram him *ut videatur ab illo, R. Ben. interl.* 49.

Gewarenian *beware, Bt.* 7, 2, v. warnian.

Gewarnian *to admonish, warn, defend, Bd.* 2, 5, v. warnian.

Gewat *departed; p. of* gewitan.

Gewealc, gewilc *A rolling, motion, an attack;* volutatio, impetus:—Yða gewealc *a rolling of waves, Cd.* 166, *Th.* p. 206, 21: *Chr.* 973, *Ing.* p. 162, 11.

Geweald, anweald, angeweald, gewald, es; *m.* 1. *Power, strength, might, efficacy;* potestas. 2. *Empire, rule, dominion, government, subjection;* imperium. 3. *Will, purpose, accord;* voluntas, intentio:—1. Gif mon oðrum þa geweald forslea *if one, the powers of others destroy:* Þat he nage geweald *that he have not power, L. Alf. pol.* 40. He is geweald hafað *he hath his power, Cd.* 30, *Th.* p. 40, 7. 2. He wæs of Herodes anwealde, *Lk.* 23, 7. Þu scealt wesan on gewealde *thou shalt be in subjection, Cd.* 43, *Th.* p. 56, 30. 3. His gewealdes *of his will, accord;* sponte sua, *L. Alf. eccl.* 13. Brech unwealdes, bete gewealdes *unwittingly offend, wittingly amend, Spel. Glos.* v. anweald.

Geweald, geweald-leðer, geweald-leðer *a power-leather, a rein, Ps.* 31, 12: *Bt.* 21, *Card.* p. 116, 1.

Gewealda *Pudenda, Herb.* 5, 5.

Gewealden *commanded, governed; pp. of* wealdan.

Geweallod, geweallode *Walled, fortified;* muro cinctus, munitus:—*Num.* 13, 29.

Geweallen *boiled; pp. of* weallan.

Gewearmede *warmed,* v. wearmian.

Gewearnian *to admonish, avoid, Bd.* 1, 14, v. warnian.

Gewearð *was, was made,* v. weorðan.

Geweaxan *to grow, grow up, Gen.* 38, 11, v. weaxan.

Gewed *A raging, madness;* furor insanus:—*Bd.* 2, 20.

Gewedan *To clothe, put on;* vestire:—Geweded, *R. Mk.* 1, 6.

Geweddad *wedded,* v. weddian.

Geweddian *To weed;* herbis noxiis purgare:—*Cot.* 178, 188.

Gewefen *woven,* v. wefan.

Gewegen, gewehgen *carried,* v. wægan.

Geweldan *to rule, restrain, Past.* 17, v. wealdan.

Geweled *Joined, united;* copulatus:—Geweled togadære, *Lup.* 1, 15.

Gewelgian, geweligan; *p.* ode; *pp.* od, ad. *To enrich, make wealthy, endow, to wax rich;* locupletare:—*Ps.* 64, 9. Ic gewelegode, *Gen.* 14, 23. Gewelgad, gewelgod, gewelegod, *Bd.* 1, 25.

Gewelhwær *Every where;* ubique:—*Menol.* v. 58.

Gewemman, gewæman, wemman; *p.* de; *pp.* ed; *v. a.* [wom, wæm *a stain*] *To stain, calumniate, profane, to make impure, to defile, vitiate, corrupt by fornication;* corrumpere:—*Ps.* 118, 121. Ne moð þe ne gewemð, *Lk.* 12, 33. Eagan bregh wemde *dirtied the brow of the eye, Bd.* 4, 32, *S.* p. 611, 18. Gyf rihtwisnys nim hi wemmað (*M. Ps.* gewemað), *Ps.* 88, 31. Þam temple gewemmað, *Mt.* 12, 5. Hi gewemmede synd, *Ps.* 13, 2: *Bd.* 2, 12.

Gewemmednys, se; *f. Profligacy, collusion;* prævaricatio:—*Elf. T.* p. 34, 16: *Ps.* 100, 3.

Gewemming, gewemmincg *A corruption, violation, profanation;* corruptio:—*Nicod.* 10.

Gewénan *to hope, think, esteem, note, T. Ps.* 30, 31, v. wenan.

Gewendan; *p.* gewende; *pp.* gewended, gewend. *To go, depart, turn, change, translate, return, Cd.* 22, *Th.* p. 27, 34, v. wendan.

Gewened *Inclined;* proclivis:—*Ex.* 32, 22.

Geweng *the cheek, Lk.* 6, 29, v. weng.

Geweorc, geworc, es; *n.* [weorc work] 1. *A work;* opus. 2. *A fort, fortress, workmanship;* arx, figmentum:—1. *Bd.* 1, 23. 2. *Scint.* 62: *Cot.* 85, 128.

Geweorht, gewyrht [worht *that which is done,* v. wyrcan] *Work, deed, merit, desert;* meritum:—*Bd.* 4, 6. ¶ Be gewirhton, be gewyrhtum, be geweorhtum *deservedly, worthily, justly, Gen.* 42, 21. Buton gewyrhtum, butan gewyrhton *without desert, undeservedly, Jn.* 15, 25.

Geweorht *finished, for* geworht; *pp. of* wyrcan.

Geweorhta, gewyrhta *a workman, L. Const.* p. 115, v. wyrhta.

Geweorðan *to be, to be made, Jn.* 3, 9, v. weorðan.

Geweorðian, gewurðian, gewyrðian *to honour, dignify, adorn, distinguish, celebrate, to be worthy, endowed, Bt.* 14, 3, v. weorðian.

Geweoton *went, departed,* v. gewitan.

Geweredlæht, gewerodlæht. *Sweetened, made sweet;* indulcoratus:—*Scint.* 64.

Gewergod *wearied,* v. werian.

Gewerian *to keep, defend, protect, cover, clothe, Elf. gr.* 28, v. werian.

Gewesan *To soak, dissolve, subdue;* macerare:—Gewesed mid ecede *soaked in acid, Herb.* 115, 3.

Gewexan *to grow, grow up, Bt.* 35, 4, v. weaxan.

Gewican; *p.* gewicode. *To give way, depart, retire;* cedere, recedere:—To hwy driht gewic þu? *Ps.* 9, 22: *Dial.* 2, 14, v. wican.

Gewician *to dwell, lodge, encamp, Ors.* 1, 4, v. wician.

Gewider, gewidor *the air, weather, a tempest, Bd.* 5, 9, v. weder.

Gewidlian *to defile, profane, R. Mk.* 7, 15, v. widlian.

Gewidmærsian *to publish, spread abroad, divulge, defame, Mt.* 1, 19, v. widmærsian.

Gewife *Fortune, destiny;* fatum:—*Cot.* 88.

Gewifode, gewifod *taken a wife, married,* v. wifian.

Gewiglung, wigelung, e; *f. Deceit, juggling, enchanting, bewitching;* error:—*L. Can. Edg.* 16.

Gewiht *A weight;* pondus:—Be fullon gewihte, *Gen.* 23, 16. Twegra ponda gewiht *two pounds' weight, R.* 59.

Gewil, gewill; *n. A will, wish;* voluntas:—On yfelra manna gewill *to evil men's wish, Bt.* 4, *Card.* p. 12, 13, v. willa.

Gewilc *a rolling, motion, Ps.* 88, 10, v. gewealc.

Gewillsum *desirable, Ps.* 105, 23, v. willsum.

Gewilnian *to wish, desire, expect, Mt.* 5, 28, v. wilnian.

Gewilnigendlic, gewilniendlic, gewilnindlic *Desirable;* desiderabilis:—*Ps.* 105, 23.

Gewilnung *a wish, desire, choice, appetite, Lk.* 22, 15, v. willnung.

Gewin *labour, contest, battle, sorrow, agony, Cd.* 15, *Th.* 19, 23, v. win.

Gewind, gewynd [windan *to bend*] *A winding, circuit, spiral shell, a scroll, an ascent;* circuitus, cochlea:—*R.* 49, 55.

Gewinde *a wind, Bd.* 3, 16, v. wind.

Gewinful *Full of labour;* laboriosus:—*Bd.* 2, 2.

Gewinna *an enemy, a rival, Bd.* 1, 12, v. winna.

Gewinnan *to win, acquire, obtain, fight, conquer, Cd.* 21, *Th.* p. 26, 6, v. winnan.

Gewinnfullic *Laborious, difficult;* laboriosus:—*Bd.* 1, 12, 23.

Gewinnfullice; *adv. Laboriously, with difficulty;* laboriose:—*Bd.* 3, 14.

Gewinstow *a battle-place, a place to contend in, a theatre.*

Gewintrad, gewintred *Grown to full ripeness* or *size, old age;* adultus:—*L. In.* 38: *Ors.* 6, 31.

Gewiorðþan *to be, Bt. R.* p. 164, v. weorðan.

Gewirht *A deed;* facinus:—*Elf. T.* p. 4, 24.

Gewis, gewisse; *adj. Certain, sure, knowing, foreknowing;* certus:—*Bd.* 5, 22. On gewissum tidum *at certain times, R. Ben. interl.* 48. Of gewissum intingan *of certain causes, R. Ben. interl.* 63. Þurh gewis andgit *through certain knowledge, understanding, Bt.* 41, 5, *Card.* p. 384, 6.

Gewiscan *to wish, Bt.* 38, 2, v. wiscan.

Gewiscednys, se; *f. An adoption;* adoptio:—*R. Ben. interl.* 2.

Gewiscendlic *Optative, wishing, desirable;* optativus:—Gewiscendlic gemet *optative mood, Elf. gr.* 21.

Gewiscing, e; *f. Adoption, wishing;* adoptio:—*R. Ben.* 2.

Gewisfullice; *adv. Knowingly, expertly;* scienter:—*Greg. pref. lib.* 2, *Dial.*

Gewisian, gewissian *to instruct, inform, direct, command, govern, Jos.* 3, 7, v. wisian.

Gewislice, wislice; *adv.* 1. *Wisely, certainly, undoubtedly;* sapienter. 2. *To wit, truly, especially, besides;* videlicet:—1. He wislice and wyrde, *Mk.* 12, 34. Swiðe gewislice *certainly, Elf. T.* p. 17, 22. 2. *Elf. gr.* 38, 44: *Lk.* 10, 42.

Gewissung, gewisung *direction, instruction, command, Elf. T.* p. 12, v. wissung.

Gewistan *To banquet, rejoice, be merry;* epulari:—*Lk.* 12, 19.

Gewistfullian, gewistlæcan *to feast, rejoice, Lk.* 15, 23, 24, v. wistfullian.

Gewit, wit; *g.* gewittes; *n.* 1. *The mind, genius, intellect, sense;* ingenium. 2. *Knowledge, instruction, wisdom, prudence;* scientia:—1. Of þam gewitte *from the mind, Bt.* 39, 5, *Card.* p. 336, 14. Hit ne mæg his gewittes bereafien *cannot bereave it of its understanding, Bt.* 5, 3, *Card.* p. 18, 18: *Cd.* 14, *Th.* p. 16, 29: 203, *Th.* p. 252, 1. 2. *Lk.* 1, 77: *Bt.* 8.

Gewita, an; *m. A witness, an accomplice;* testis:—*Lk.* 24, 48.

Gewitan; *pp.* gewiten. *To understand, Cd.* 123, *Th.* p. 157, 13, v. witan.

Gewítan, he gewít; *p.* gewát, we gewiton; *pp.* gewiten. *To pass over, to go, depart, withdraw, go away, retreat, retire, die;* transire, discedere:—Gyf ne mæge gewitan, *Mt.* 26, 42. Gewitan of worulde *to depart from the world, to die, Somn.* 217. Gewat se dæg forð, *Lk.* 9, 12: *Mt.* 24, 35. Gewiten, *Bd.* 3, 12.

Gewitednes, gewitenes, se; *f. A departure;* discessio:—*Bd.* 4, 24.

Gewis prudent skilful thapol

Gewen hope Som v wen

Gewemnesde [illegible] contaminated Som

Gewenian To allure, entice, incline illicere Som

Geweorcan to work make do Th an v weorcan

Geweorpan to throw Lye v weorpan

Geweox increased v weaxan

Geweorpe throw cast; jactus Som

Gewepan to weep Lye v wepan

Gewepnian To arm; armare Som v gewæpnian

Gewerdan to damage, hurt Som

Gewesan to be Lye v wesan

Gewet an moisten Lye v wætan

Gewidor the weather Som v sube gewedder

Gewis-selig Fortunate Lucky; fortunatus Som

Gewilc A rolling, tossing, motion, commotio; motus Ps 88, 10 Som v geweale

Gewilcumian To salute, to be welcome; salutare, opportune advenire Lye

Gewird Corrupted depraved; vitiatus Som

Gewirdelic His-torical; historicus Som.

Gewitan onfleam sceacan to begin in flight to withdraw to begin to fly, Jdth p 25, 34. Tid gewat sceacan time began to pass away Cd 8 Th p [illegible] Heo þe fle-on gewat she then be gan to flee Cd 103 Th p 136, 23

Gewildan to wield Th an v gewealdan

Gewindan to wind, revolve Th an v windan

Gewiofies n, the Way wefts; subtegmen Bos [illegible] 1387

Geweordan, geweordan v impers, with ac of person. To agree, settle, seem good or fitting, to be agreed. Th an

Gewisnys, se; f certitudo Bos

Gewistfull rich, costly; lautus Som

Gewistfullung, e; riches, abundance; divitiæ Som

Gewistlæcan to feast Lk 15, 24 v gewistfullian

I [illegible] to proceed, begin, in wh sense it seems to be employ in the follow g examples where Lye supposes it to be pleonastic Gewitan him þa gangan, Pær ic þa incipere illis tunc ire, they began then to go Cd 40 Th p 53, 8

1?

1 Gewitendnes a departure Sye v gewitednes

Gewitenes, se f a witness, departure, death, Th an v Gewitnes

(k- weold ink wealdan)
Gewyldan to rule govern Th an v wealdan

3 Gewleced made warm Som v gewlacod

1 Gewomian to defile Sye v gewemman

5 Gewopen wept for lamented Som [struck] v wepan

Gewregendlic accusative, Gewregendlic gebiged nes the accusative case Som

2 Gewrehte accused v wrehte, wrecan

3 Gewrigen covered pp of [struck] wrigan

4 Gewrinclod wrinkled Som v wrinclian

5 Gewringan to wring Sye v wringan

6 Gewrixled exchanged Cd Th p 22.3 v wrixlan

7 Gewroeged accused Cd Mt 27,10 v ge-wregan

8 Gewunnen conquered Som v gewinnan, winnan

Gewynd a circuit Sye v gewind

Bos R 5310

Gewyrht a design a deed custom a desert Th an v gewirht

Gewyrhtum Deservedly Buton gewyrhtum undeservedly Th an

Gewyrhto merits Cd 196 Th 244.7

Gewurdlod spoken Som v wordlian

Gewyht a weight Som wiht

Gewylc a rolling Som v gewilc

5 Gewyldor a ruler Som v wealdend

Gewylled boiled Som v weallan

8 Gewyrged cursed Som v wyrgian

Gewyrht wrought made Som v ge-wyrcan

Gewyrhta an m. fellow labourer Som v wyrhta

Gewyrnled warned Som v wearnian

16 Gewyrms purulence festered Som v gewyrms

17. Gewyrtod wine mixed wine Som hyppocras

Gewitendlic; *adj. Ready to fall, transitory;* deciduus:—*Past.* 46, 5.

Gewitig *knowing, wise, intelligent, Solil.* 2, v. gewittig.

Gewitleás; *adj. Witless, ignorant, foolish, mad;* inscius:—*Elf. gr.* 47.

Gewitleast, gewittleast *Folly, madness, phrensy;* stultitia:—*Elf. T.* p. 32, 24.

Gewit-loca *a container of intelligence, the mind;* intelligentiæ clausura:—*Bt. R.* p. 166.

Gewitnes *witness, testimony, knowledge, Mk.* 1, 44, v. witnes.

Gewitnian *to punish, Elf. gr.* 27, 28, v. witnian.

Gewitodlice *as, truly, T. Ps.* 57, 1, v. witodlice.

Gewitscipe, es; *m. A testimony, witnessing;* testimonium:—*Bd.* 1, 27, *resp.* 6.

Gewitseoc *mind-sick, a lunatic, demoniac, Elf. gl.* 9.

Gewitseocnes, se; *f. Insanity;* insanitas, *Som.*

Gewittig, gewitig; *adj. Wise, knowing, conscious;* intelligens:—*L. Cnut. pol.* 74: *Bt.* 36, 5.

Gewlacod *made warm,* v. wlacian.

Gewlæt, gewlæten *Defiled, debased;* fœdatus:—*Bt.* 37, 4.

Gewleht *Made warm;* tepefactus:—*Herb.* 19, 6: 80, 3.

Gewlenced *Lifted up, enriched;* elatus:—*Heming.* p. 104, v. wlænce.

Gewlitegian *to form, adorn, Ps.* 94, 5, v. wlitigan.

Gewló *Adorned;* ornatus:—*Cd.* 85, *Th.* p. 107, 14.

Gewod *waded, pervaded,* v. wadan.

Gewoested *Desolated, destroyed;* vastatus:—*C. Mt.* 12, 25.

Gewon *deficient, wanting,* v. won.

Gewonian *to lessen, V. Ps.* 88, 44, v. wanian.

Geworc *work, Ps.* 91, 4, v. geweorc.

Geworden *been, done, made,* v. weorðan.

Geworht *wrought, built,* v. wyrcan.

Geworpan *to cast, Bd.* 4, 13, v. weorpan.

Geworðan *to be, to be made, C. Jn.* 3, 19, v. weorðan.

Gewræc *wreaked,* v. wrecan.

Gewræstan *To writhe, twist, join;* intorquere:—*Cot.* 4.

Gewræðan [wræð, wrað *wrath*] *To trouble, vex;* infestare:—*Somn.* 242.

Gewraðian; *p.* ode. *To be angry with one;* succensere:—*Chr.* 1070.

Gewrecan *to wreak, avenge, revenge, Cd.* 64, v. wrecan.

Gewregan; *p.* de; *pp.* ed. *To accuse, Mk.* 3, 2, v. wregan.

Gewreot *scripture, Bd.* 4, 23, v. gewrit.

Gewreðede *Supported;* sustinuit:—*Bd.* 4, 31, *B,* v. wræðian.

Gewrid; *pl.* gewrido. *A little heap, a place where shrubs grow;* glomulus:—*Cot.* 95.

Gewring *Drink, beer;* sicera, potus:—*Alf. gr.* 21.

Gewrit, es; *pl. nom. ac.* u; *g.* a, ena; *d.* um; *n. A writing, treatise, scripture, a letter, an inscription;* scriptura:—Ne rædde ge þis gewrit, *Mk.* 12, 10, 16. Þis gewrit *this treatise, Elf. T.* p. 1, 1, 18, 22. ¶ Halig gewrit *holy writ* or *scripture.* Ofer gewrit *over writ, superscription, title.* Riht gewrit *right writing, orthography.*

Gewrítan; *p.* gewrát; *pp.* gewriten. *To write, to give* or *bestow by writing, Ps.* 39, 11, v. writan.

Gewritere *a writer, T. Ps.* 44, v. writere.

Gewriðan *to bind, restrain, tie, tie together, L. Ps.* 34, 6, v. wriðan.

Gewrixl *a change, interchange, vicissitude, turn, course, Bt.* 21, *Card.* 114, 20, v. wrixl.

Gewroht *wrought, finished,* v. wyrcan.

Gewrungen *bound, tied together, heaped up,* v. wringan.

Gewuldorbeagan, he gewuldorbeagað; *p.* þu gewuldorbeagodest; *pp.* gewuldorbeagod [wuldor *glory,* beag *a crown*] *To crown with glory, to crown;* coronare:—*Ps.* 8, 6: 102, 4.

Gewuldrian; *p.* ode; *pp.* od. *To glory, boast, extol, glorify;* gloriari:—Gewuldriende, *C. T. Ps.* 48, 6. Gewuldrod, gewuldrud, gewuldrode beoð, *Ps.* 48, 6: 73, 5: *Jn.* 7, 39: 14, 13.

Gewuna, wuna, an; *m. A custom, manner, use, rite;* consuetudo:—Æfter gewunan *after the custom, Lk.* 1, 9: 2, 27, 42. Of gewunan *from custom, R. Ben. interl.* 7. Ofer mine gewunan *beyond my custom, Elf. T.* p. 43, 7. Swa hit gewuna is *as it is a custom, Ors.* 3, 3.

Gewundian; *p.* ode; *pp.* ed, od. *To wound, Mk.* 12, 4, v. wundian.

Gewundorlæcan *To make wonderful;* mirificare:—*Ps.* 16, 8.

Gewunelic, gewunolic *Accustomed, wonted;* consuetus:—Þam folce wæs gewunelic, *Jud.* 7, 8.

Gewunelice; *adv. According to custom, ordinarily, commonly;* ritè:—Swiðe gewunelice *very commonly, Elf. T.* p. 17.

Gewunian; *p.* ode; *pp.* od. *To inhabit, remain, abide, to be* WONT, *accustomed;* manere, consuescere:—Sceoldon his þegnas gewunian *his followers must inhabit, Cd.* 220, *Th.* p. 284, 24. Swa his mod ær swiðor to þam woruld sælðum gewunod wæs *as his mind very early to worldly prosperity had been accustomed, Bt.* 1, *Card.* p. 4, 16. Swa swa he gewunude, *Mk.* 10, 1.

Gewunsum *pleasant, Bt.* 31, 1, v. winsum.

Gewurde *was,* v. weorðan.

Gewurms, gewurmsmed *Full of matter, suppurated;* purulentus:—*Cot.* 185, v. wurmsig.

Gewurðan *to be, to become,* v. weorðan.

Gewurðian *to honour,* v. weorðian.

Gewyder *the weather, a storm, Ors.* 3, 3, v. weder.

Gewyldan, he gewylt; *p.* gewylde, we gewildon; *pp.* gewyld; *v. a. To tame, subdue, conquer, take hold of;* domare:—Hyne nan man gewyldan ne mihte, *Mk.* 5, 4. Gewylt eow, *Deut.* 31, 3. Hi gewildon synd *dominati sunt, Ps.* 105, 38. He gewilde þe, *Gen.* 3, 16. Gewildað, *Gen.* 1, 28. Gewylde man hine *prehendat aliquis eum, L. Cnut. pol.* 23. Gewild, gewyld *subdued, taken;* captus, *Elf. T.* p. 42. Ic beo gewyld, *Jud.* 16, 7.

Gewyld *power, Jud.* 3, 15, v. geweald.

Gewyled *Joined, connected;* copulatus:—*Lup.* 1, 15.

Gewylwed *Wallowed, rolled;* volutatus:—*Dial.* 2, 2.

Gewyrc. 1. *A working, a work;* operatio, opus. 2. *The art of making any thing of earth;* plastice:—1. *Cd.* 65, *Th.* p. 79, 11: *Cd.* 65, *Th.* p. 79, 6. 2. *Cot.* 186.

Gewyrcan, gewyrcean *to work, do, make, prepare, build, celebrate, Cd.* 39, *Th.* p. 51, 31, v. wyrcan.

Gewyrd *condition, fate, destiny, fortune, prediction, Ors.* 3, 9, v. wyrd.

Gewyrdelice; *adv. Excellently, worthily;* præstanter:—*Elf. T.* p. 17.

Gewyrdlian *To hurt, injure;* nocere:—*Bd.* 3, 16.

Gewyrfed *turned,* v. hweorfan.

Gewyrpan *To convert, turn again, recover;* recuperare:—Gewyrpte *recuperaverat, Bd.* 3, 13.

Gewyrsmed *putrid,* v. gewurms.

Gewyrð *is, is become, shall be,* v. weorðan.

Gewyrðian *to honour,* v. weorðian.

Geycan *To add, eke*; addere: —To geyc *adjicies, Ps.* 60, 6. Geycte *added, Bd.* 1, 12. Geyht *added*; auctus, v. ycan.

Geyde *subdued, conquered, Chr.* 617, *from* geeode, v. gegan.

Geyflian *To injure, weaken, grow sick*; malefacere, infirmare: —Gif hine mon geyflige *if one injure him, L. Alf. pol.* 2, *W.* p. 35, 5. Lazarus wæs geyflod, *Jn.* 11, 2. Geyflod mid fræcepo *affectus contumeliis, C. Mt.* 22, 5.

Geypped, geypte *opened, revealed, Ors.* 3, 6, v. yppan.

Geyrfweardian *to inherit, L. Ps.* 24, 14, v. yrfweardian.

Geyrgd, geyrged *Terrified, affrightened*; territus: — *Jos.* 2, 9, 24: 8, 6.

Geyrmed *afflicted, W. Bd.* p. 168, v. yrmian.

Geyrnan *to run, go back, arise*, v. yrnan.

Geyrsian; *pp.* geyrsudd, georsod. *To irritate*, v yrsian.

Gibed *a petition, Lk.* 23, 24, v. gebed.

Gibeged *bowed, constrained*, v. gebeged.

Gibeldan *To adorn with images*; iconibus ornare: — *Cod. Cott. end of Evang. D. Jn.*

Gibered *Teased, vexed*; vexatus: —*C. R. Mk.* 5, 15.

GICEL [*Plat.* ishekel, istakke, in the diminutive, istäkel, in *Ditmarshen*, isjäkel: *Dut.* yskegel: *Ger.* eiszakken: *Swed.* ispigg: *Dan.* jistap *m.*—Gicel, cel *or* col *cold, what is cold* or *congealed*; hence isesceł *or* gicel *a drop of ice*] *An icicle*; stiria:—Ises gicel *glacialis stiria, R.* 16.

Gicenes, se; *f. An itch, or burning in the skin*; prurigo:—*Cot.* 156.

Gicþa *An itching, scab, tetter, ring-worm*; pruritus, scabies: —*R.* 11: *Herb.* 21, 2.

Giddian, gieddian; *p.* ode. *To sing*, v. geddian.

Gidig; *adj.* GIDDY; vertiginosus, *Som.*

Gield *a payment, offering, substitute, place, society*, v. gild.

Gieldan *to yield, pay, give, worship, Bt.* 41, 3, v. gildan.

Giellan *to yell, shriek, Cod. Exon.* 106, b, v. gyllan.

Gielp *presumption, Cd. Th.* p. 2, 27, v. gilp.

Gielso *care, trouble*; solicitudo: —*C. Mt.* 13, 22.

Giemeleás, giemeleáslic, giemeliest, giemelist. *Careless, Past.* 15, 1, v. gymeleas.

Gien, giena *again, still, yet*, v. gen.

Gieran *to prepare*, v. gearwian.

Gierstandæg *yesterday*, v. gyrstandæg.

Gierwan *to prepare, Cod. Exon.* 119, b, v. gearwian.

Giest *a guest, Cd.* 112, v. gest.

Giestliðnis *entertainment, Cd.* 112, v. gæstliðnes.

Giet, gieta *yet, Cd.* 29, v. get.

Gif, gyf; *conj.* [*imp. of* gifan *to give*] *If, when, though*; si: —Gyf cyning his leode to him gehateð *if the king call his people to him, L. Ethelb.* 2, *W.* p. 2, 1. Gif seo wyrd swa hweorfan *if the fortune be so to change, Bt.* 4, *Card.* p. 12, 12.

Gifa *gifts*; *nom. ac. pl. of* gifu.

Gifan, gyfan, geofian, he gifð; *p.* geaf, gæf, gaf, we geafon; *pp.* gifen. *To give*; dare:— Hwæt gifst þu me, *Gen.* 15, 2. Gyfan cystelice *to give costly, liberally, Elf. gr.* 31. Hit gæf wæstm his, *Ps.* 66, 5.

Gifende *Gives in marriage, is married*; nubit:—*Cot.* 216.

Gifer *A lurcher, devourer, glutton*; ambro:—*R.* 88.

Giferlice; *adv. Covetously, greedily*; avide:—*Bd.* 3, 9.

Gifernes, se; *f. Greediness, avarice, gluttony*; aviditas: — Þat ilce yfel þæs gifernesse *that same evil of greediness, Bt.* 35, 6, *Card.* p. 264, 1: *L. Can. Edg. conf.*

Gifeðe *Given, granted*; datus: —Gifeðe weorðan *or* beon *to be given*; dari:—*Cd.* 83, *Th.* p. 103, 31: 101.

Giffæst *Able to receive, capacious*; capax:—*Cot.* 57.

Gi-fian, fian *To hate*; odisse:— Gifiað þat leht *hates the light, R. Jn.* 3, 20.

Gifian *To give, grant*; dare:— Him cynelice gifode *he royally granted*; eum regio more donavit, *Chr.* 994. Giffigende massere, *Can. Edg.* 14, *W.* p. 83, 35.

Gifl *A time for eating*; cibi accipiendi tempus:—Æfen gifl *a supper, Past.* 1, 2.

Gifoelde *felt*, v. gefelan.

Gifol, giful *Generous, bountiful, liberal*; largus:—*Bt.* 38, 3.

Gifr, gifra, gifre; *adj.* [*Icel.* gifur] *Greedy, covetous, voracious, anxious, desirous*; avidus:—Ic eom swiðe gifre *I am very anxious, Bt.* 22, *Card.* 118, 15: *Elf. gl.* 28: *Lk.* 16, 14.

Gifta *nuptials, marriage, dowry, Ex.* 22, 17, v. gyfta.

Giftelic *Belonging to a wedding*; nuptialis:—*Cot.* 139.

Gifð *gives*, v. gifan.

GIFU, gyfu, geof, geafu, e; *pl. nom.* a, *g.* ena; *f.* [*Plat. Dut. Dan.* gave *f*: *Ger.* gabe *f*: *Ker.* gaba, geba, keba: *Isd.* gheba: *Ot.* geba: *Moes.* giba: *Swed.* gåfwa *f*: *Icel.* gáfa *f.*] *A gift, grace, favour*; donum: —Godes gyfu wæs on him, *Lk.* 2, 40. Corban, þat is on ure geþeode, gyfu, *Mk.* 7, 11. Þam he geaf micle gife *to them he gave a great gift, Bt.* 41, 2, *Card.* p. 374, 14. Gifum growende *with gifts flourishing, Cd.* 5, *Th.* p. 6, 13. We onfengon gyfe for gyfe, *Jn.* 1, 16. ¶ To gife *or* gifum *gratis, Gen.* 29, 15.

Gigant *A giant*; gigas:—*C. Ps.* 18, 6: 32, 16. Gigant mægas *giant progeny*; gigantes genere, *Cd.* 64, *Th.* p. 76, 36.

Gign *A youth, young man*; juvenis:—*C. R. Mt.* 14, 51: 16, 5.

Gihrinan *To cover, clothe*; tegere:—*Cod. Cott. end of Evan. Jn.*

Giht, gihð, geht, gyte. *Time, staying, station, refuge*; tempus, mansio, statio, refugium. *Manning* thinks gyhð is from gehyht, hiht *a refuge*:—Gihðum healdeð *in refuge hold, Cd.* 169, *Th.* p. 212, 5. Gehðum hremig *in a querulous station, Ex. MS. Conb.* p. 233, n. —Gyte-sal *an apartment, Jdth.* 10, 6.—Gebed-giht *bed-time, R.* 16.—Sun-giht *solstice, Martyr.* 24, *Jun. Wan.* p. 107.

Gilæccan *to take, seize, R. Mk.* 14, 48, v. gelæccan.

GILD, gield, geld, gyld; [*Plat. Dut. Ger.* geld: *Moes.* gild: *Icel.* gilldi *n.*] 1. *A payment of money, an exchange, a compensation, turn, fold, tribute*; tributum. 2. *A* GUILD, *society*, or *club where payment was made for mutual support, like our benefit societies*; fraternitas. 3. *A payment to God, worship, service, sacrifice, offering*; cultus:—1. *Chr.* 1013. IX gylde forgylde *recompence* 9 *fold, L. Ethelb.* 4. 2. On gilde *in a society, Hickes's dis. epis.* 20. 3. On Abeles gield *on Abel's offering, Cd.* 47, *Th.* p. 60, 6: 137, *Th.* p. 172, 11: *Bd.* 2, 1.

Gilda *a companion, fellow*, v. gegylda.

Gildan *to pay, restore, requite, Ex.* 22, 9, v. gyldan.

Gildan; *p.* gildede; *pp.* gilden, gylden; *v. a.* To GILD; deaurare:—Se abbot gildede þat mynstre *the abbot gilded the minster, Chr.* 1052, *Ing.* p. 240, 4: 1070.—Gilden, *Lev.* 8, 9.

Gildeneburh [*The golden city*, so called because Abbot Leofric gilded the monastery] *Peterborough, Chr.* 1052: 1064.

Gild-ford, Gyldford, Guldeford [Gild *a fraternity*; ford *a ford*:

Gewyrtun A garden
stus ~~Som~~ Sye
Gewyscan to wish
Som v gewiscan.
Gewyslice wisely
[illegible] an
Som v gewislice
Gewyderod
withered, dry Som
Geyht [illegible]
[illegible]
[illegible], increased
[illegible] v geycan
Som
Geyferan to [illegible]
[illegible] v giferan
Gyldan to trifle
[illegible]; tricari Som
v gildan
Gicelig Sye, old
Jacidlis Som
Gidd a song, an lay [illegible]
Som v gydd
Giddung a [illegible] Som v geddung
[illegible] a goddess [illegible]
v gyden
Giefa a giver
Som v gyfa
Giefu a gift Som
v gifu
Gieman to [illegible]
[illegible] Som v gy[illegible]
man
Gien an abyss
Sye v gin
Gierd a yard Som
v gyrd

Gierela clothing
Som v gyrela
Gieman to [illegible]
[illegible] Som v gyman
Giesthus an inn Som v gesthus
Gitsian to desire
for Som v gitsian
[illegible] of a gift
Som v gifu
Gift a gift
Som v gyfta
Gift-bur, es m
a bride chamber
Som
Gifthus a bride house, wedding Som
Giftlead a marriage song Som
Gihamian To cover
[illegible] Sye
Gifr-adj. Gifra, gifre [illegible]
~~[illegible]~~ v gifer
Gif-sceat, es m a gift
donum. Beo K 753
[illegible] II 522, 43
Giftelic marriage
~~[illegible]~~ Som
Giftig marriageable
Som v supl giftelic

Giftian to be given in marriage
Som.
Gifule bountiful,
liberalis Som
Gig a giffin Som
gice, geocsa
Giksa a sobbing
Som v Supl geohsa
Gihsung a sobbing
Som ~~[illegible]~~
Gif-stol, es m
a gift seat, a throne
Beo K 334
v gifer
Gilden gylden golden
adj an

Gimmian to bud; blom; gemmare Som

Gilp-sceapa an; m a glorious host Cd -- Th p 6.

Gilp-cwide boasting saying arrogantia Beo 50 Grim II 513, 38 Beo K 1273

Gilpgeornes vain glory Som vana gloria

Gilt a fault Som v gylt

Gild, gilk, gilde Som a gylte

Giltend a debtor Som v gyltend

Gimæcca a mate Som v gemæcca

Geman to take governm. to care of Som v gyman

Gin-fæsten very fast glorious Cd 169 Th p 211, 10

Gind-geotan to pour out v geond &c

Gilp-hlæden pride laden, proud Beo K 1729

Ginnne an f a disable female formally attendant Th an &c

Ginnis, se; f A space or distance of place, intercapedo Som

Gioc a yoke, also rash Som v geoc

Giscapu decree Sum Lye

Gistlipe hospitable Th an a Subst gestlipe

Gioht-hád Som v geogu-hád

Giornlice diligently Lye v geornlice

Giotan to g... v getan

Girdl a girdle Som v gyrdel

Girela clothing Som v gyrla

Girnes, appetite, ... Som v gyrnes

Girstan-dæg yesterday Som v gyrstandæg

Gisldu, a giving of hostages or pledges ... dato

Gist-bur a guest dwelling Ben v gest

Gid-corn ... gith; gith corn Som v gyth

(3)

Domesd. Gilda ad vadum] GUILDFORD, *a town in Surry, on the river Wey, Lye.*

Gildscipe *a guildship, society, L. Can. Edg.* 9, v. gild.

Gileofful *faithful, C. R. Lk.* 12, 42, v. geleafful.

Gillester, gillestre *Phlegm*; pituita:—*L. M.* 1, 72.

Gillinga, Gillinga-ham GILLINGHAM, *in Dorsetshire, on the river Stour, Chr.* 1016.

GILM, es; *m.* A YELM, *a handful of reaped corn, bundle, bottle;* manipulus:—Eowre gilmas stodon, *Gen.* 37, 7.

Gilp *Powder, dust;* scobs:—*Cot.* 181.

GILP, gelp, gielp, es; *m.* [*Icel.* geip] *Glory, ostentation, pride, boasting, arrogance, vain glory, haughtiness;* gloria, ostentatio:—Gilpes þu girnest *of glory thou desirest, Bt.* 32, 1, *Card.* p. 176, 23. Gielp micel *great presumption, Cd. Th.* 2, 27. Hu unnyt se gilp bið *how useless is the boast, Bt.* 30, 1, *Card.* p. 168, 13.

p Gilpan, gylpð; *p.* gealp, we gulpon; *pp.* golpen. *To glory, boast, desire earnestly;* gloriari:—Gif þu gilpan wille, gilp Godes *if thou wilt glory, glory in God, Bt.* 14, 1.

Gilpgeornesta *most desirous of glory, Bd.* 1, 34.

Gilplice; *adv. Proudly, vauntingly;* arroganter:—*Cot.* 1.

Gilpna *A boaster;* jactator:—*Past.* 20: 33, 1.

Gilp-word *a glorious word, a proverb, a proud word*

GILTE A GILT, *a young female pig;* suilla:—*R.* 20.

GIM, gym, *g.* gimme; *f.* A GEM, *jewel;* gemma:—Gim cynn *a gem kind, a gem, Bt. R.* p. 159. Se stan bið blæc gym *the stone is a black gem, Bd.* 1, 1. Gimma wlite *beauty of gems.* On gimmum *in gems, Bt.* 13. Þæt æreste gim cynn is þæt blac and grene, bute togædere gemenencgede geaspis haten. Oðær is saphyrus, se is sunnan gelic, and on him stadað swilce gildene steorran. Smaragdus ys swiðe grene. Sardonix is blode licost *the first gem-kind is the black and green, both together mingled, called geaspis. The other is saphyrus, which is like a sun; and in it stand like golden stars. Smaragdus is very green. Sardonix is likest blood, Cotton. MS. Tib. A.* III. p. 99.

Gimelist *careless,* v. gymeleast.

Gimerc; *pl.* gimerca. *A sign;* signum:—*C. R. Mk.* 16, 17, v. gemearc.

q Giming, gymung, e; *f. A marriage;* nuptiæ:—*Bd.* 3, 24: *Cot.* 140.

Gimrecan; *p.* hi gimrecede. *To take care of;* curare:—*Bt. R.* p. 158.

Gimrodor *A precious stone;* draconites, dracontia:—*Cot.* 63.

Gimstan, gymstan *a gem-stone, a gem.*

Gimwyrhta, gymwyrhta *a gem-worker, jeweller.*

GIN [*Icel.* gin *n. rictus, oris diductio*] *A gap, an opening, abyss;* hiatus:—Garsecges gin *ocean's expanse, Cd.* 163, *Th.* p. 205, 3.

Gin; *adj. Gaping, lying open, spacious, ample;* hians, amplus:—Beligeð uton ginne rice *encompasseth ample realms, Cd.* 12, *Th.* p. 15, 7: *Jdth.* 9, 11.

Gin, in composition, increases the sense of the word; as, fæst *fast,* ginfæst *very* or *most fast.*

Ginan *to yawn, Cot.* 23, v. gynian.

Gind *beyond, Ors.* 4, 8, v. geond.

Ginfæst *Very fast* or *lasting, ample;* firmissimus:—Onfon ginfæstum gifum *receive very fast gifts, Cd.* 141, *Th.* p. 176, 28: 169, *Th.* p. 211, 10.

Ging *young, tender;* gingra *younger;* gingast *youngest, Cd.* 176, v. geong.

Gingra, an; *m. A younger, disciple;* discipulus:—*Cd.* 224, *Th.* p. 297, 24: 225, *Th.* p. 298, 11.

Ginian *to open, yawn, Gr.* 2, 26, v. gynian.

Ginsta *for* gingsta *youngest,* v. geong.

Ginung *A yawning;* hiatus:—*Cot.* 23.

Gio *formerly, Bt.* 16, 1, v. geo.

Giocþa *a scab, Past.* 11, 5, v. gicþa.

Gioful *liberal,* v. gifol.

Giofulnes, se; *f. Munificence, liberality;* munificentia:—*Past.* 44, 2.

r Gioguð, giagoð, giogað *youth,* v. geoguð.

Gioleca *the yolk of an egg, Bt. R.* p. 178, v. geolca.

Giolu *yellow,* in composition, *as,* gioluread an *yellow red, &c.* v. geolewe, &c.

Giomor *sad, Bt. R.* p. 152, v. geomer.

Giond *through, over, beyond,* and in composition, v. geond.

Gionetan *to occupy, C. Lk.* 13, 7, v. geonetan.

Giong *young, Ors.* 2, 4, v. geong.

Giongor *a younger, servant, Cd.* 21, v. geong.

Giongorscipe *youngership, service, Cd.* 14, v. geongordom.

Giornan *to beg, desire,* v. geornian.

Giornan, hi giorndon *to run, rush on, C. Lk.* 5, 1, v. yrnan.

Giornis, se; *f. Importunity, earnestness;* importunitas:—*C. R. Lk.* 11, 8.

Giostordoeg *yesterday, C. Jn.* 4, 52, v. gyrstandæg.

Giowian *to ask, R. Mk.* 11, 24, v. giuan.

Gird *a staff, Ex.* 4, 2, v. gyrd.

Giren, girn *a snare, V. Ps.* 17, 6, v. grin.

Girian; *p.* þu giredost. *To prepare, Ps.* 146, 8, v. gearwian.

Girnan *to yearn, seek for, require, Ex.* 21, 22, v. geornian.

Girran, gyrran *To chatter, prate;* garrire:—*Elf. gr.* 36.

Girwan *To prepare;* parare:—*Jdth.* 9, v. gearwian.

Giscian *To sob, sigh;* singultire:—*Bt.* 2.

Gise *yes, Bt. R.* p. 16, 4, v. gese.

Gisedla *A sitting down to meat;* discubitus:—*R. Mk.* 12, 39.

Gisel; *g.* gisles; *d.* gisle; *m. A pledge, hostage;* obses:—Gislas sealdon *gave hostages;* obsides dederunt, *Chr.* 876: 894. To gisle gesealde *in obsidem traditus, Bd.* 3, 24.

s Gislian; *p.* ode, ade; *pp.* od. *To give hostages* or *security;* obsides dare:—He gislode, *Chr.* 1016. Ða þægenas gislodon *the thanes gave hostages, Chr.* 1013.

GIST [*Plat.* gäst, jest *m*: *Dut.* gist, gest *f*: *Ger.* gäscht, gischt *m*: *Icel.* jastr *n. nugarum strepitus:* ysting *f. coagulatio: Lat. mid.* gesta, gistum] YEAST, *barm, froth;* spuma cerevisiæ:—*Herb.* 21, 5.

Gist, es; *m. A guest, Cd.* 113, v. gest.

Gist *a storm,* v. yst.

Gist-burh *a guest-house, a bedchamber, T. Ps.* 18, 5.

Gist-hus, gyst-hus *a guest-house, an inn.*

Git *yet, you two,* v. gyt.

Giþode *subdued,* v. þeowian.

Giþreatian *to reprove, R. Jn.* 16, 8, v. þreatian.

Gitsian *to desire,* v. gytsian.

Gitsunc, gitsung *desire, Bt. R.* p. 159, v. gytsung.

Gitugon *conspired,* v. teon.

Giu, giw *A griffin:* gryps.—*Cot.* 159.

Giuan; *p.* giude. *To give, ask, require;* petere:—*R. Mk.* 6, 22.

Giuli *yule, Christmas,* v. geol.

Giululing *August;* sextilis, [illegible]; but *Som.* and *Ben.* say *July;* quintilis.

Giung *young, Bd.* 4, 32, v. geong.

Giwedo *Clothes;* vestimenta:—*R. Mk.* 11, 8.

Gimmian to bud, bloom; gemmare Som

Gielp-sceapa an; in a glorious deed Cd Th p 6.

Gilp-cwide boasting saying arrogantia Beo 50 Grm II 513, 38 Beo K 1273

Gilpgeornes vain glory Som v and Gloria

Gilt or fault Som v gylt

Gild gild, gilded Som a gylte

Giltend a debtor Som v gyltend

Gimæcca a mate v gemæcca

Geman to take care of Som v gyman

Gen-fæsten very fast or glorious Cd 169 Th p 211, 10

Gind-geotan to pour out v geond

Gilp-hlæden pride laden, proud Beo K 1729

Ginnge an f A disaple female

Ginnis, se; f A space or distance of place, intercapedo Som

Gioc a yoke, also rash Som v geoc

Giscapu decree Lye

Gistlipe hospitable Th an a subst gæst-lipe

Gioht-had youth B 1395 Som v gehoð

Giornlice diligently Lye v georn-lice

Giotan to get v getan

Girdl a gerdle Som v gyrdel

Girela clothing Som v gyrela

Girnes, se; f appetite, greediness Som v gyrnes

Girstan-dæg yesterday Som v gyrstandæg

Gisldu, gisl-had a giving of hostages or pledges; obsidium dat. Som

Gist-bur a guest dwelling an inn Ben v gest

Gid-corn the de Githe Som v gyth; githago-corn

(3)

Domesd. Gilda ad vadum] GUILDFORD, *a town in Surry, on the river Wey, Lye.*

Gildscipe *a guildship, society, L. Can. Edg.* 9, v. gild.

Gileofful *faithful, C. R. Lk.* 12, 42, v. geleafful.

Gillester, gillestre *Phlegm;* pituita:—*L. M.* I, 72.

Gillinga, Gillinga-ham GILLINGHAM, *in Dorsetshire, on the river Stour, Chr.* 1016.

GILM, es; *m.* A YELM, *a handful of reaped corn, bundle, bottle;* manipulus:—Eowre gilmas stodon, *Gen.* 37, 7.

Gilp *Powder, dust;* scobs:—*Cot.* 181.

GILP, gelp, gielp, es; *m.* [*Icel.* geip] *Glory, ostentation, pride, boasting, arrogance, vain glory, haughtiness;* gloria, ostentatio:—Gilpes þu girnest *of glory thou desirest, Bt.* 32, 1, *Card.* p. 176, 23. Gielp micel *great presumption, Cd. Th.* 2, 27. Hu unnyt se gilp biꝺ *how useless is the boast, Bt.* 30, 1, *Card.* p. 168, 13.

Gilpan, gylpꝺ; *p.* gealp, we gulpon; *pp.* golpen. *To glory, boast, desire earnestly;* gloriari:—Gif þu gilpan wille, gilp Godes *if thou wilt glory, glory in God, Bt.* 14, 1.

Gilpgeornesta *most desirous of glory, Bd.* 1, 34.

Gilplice; *adv. Proudly, vauntingly;* arroganter:—*Cot.* 1.

Gilpna *A boaster;* jactator:—*Past.* 20: 33, 1.

Gilp-word *a glorious word, a proverb, a proud word.*

Gilte A GILT, *a young female pig;* suilla:—*R.* 20.

GIM, gym; *g.* gimme; *f.* A GEM, *jewel;* gemma:—Gim cynn *a gem kind, a gem, Bt. R.* p. 159. Se stan biꝺ blæc gym *the stone is a black gem, Bd.* 1, 1. Gimma wlite *beauty of gems.* On gimmum *in gems, Bt.* 13. Þæt æreste gim cynn is þæt blac and grene, bute togædere gemenencgede geaspis haten. Oꝺær is saphyrus, se is sunnan gelic, and on him stadaꝺ swilce gildene steorran. Smaragdus ys swiꝺe grene. Sardonix is blode licost *the first gem-kind is the black and green, both together mingled, called geaspis. The other is saphyrus, which is like a sun; and in it stand like golden stars. Smaragdus is very green. Sardonix is likest blood, Cotton. MS. Tib. A.* III. p. 99.

Gimelist *careless,* v. gymeleast.

Gimerc; *pl.* gimerca. *A sign;* signum:—*C. R. Mk.* 16, 17, v. gemearc.

Giming, gymung, e; *f. A marriage;* nuptiæ:—*Bd.* 3, 24: *Cot.* 140.

Gimrecan; *p.* hi gimrecede. *To take care of;* curare:—*Bt. R.* p. 158.

Gimrodor *A precious stone;* draconites, dracontia:—*Cot.* 63.

Gimstan, gymstan *a gem-stone, a gem.*

Gimwyrhta, gymwyrhta *a gem-worker, jeweller.*

GIN [*Icel.* gin *n. rictus, oris diductio*] *A gap, an opening, abyss;* hiatus:—Garsecges gin *ocean's expanse, Cd.* 163, *Th.* p. 205, 3.

Gin; *adj. Gaping, lying open, spacious, ample;* hians, amplus:—Beligeꝺ uton ginne rice *encompasseth ample realms, Cd.* 12, *Th.* p. 15, 7: *Jdth.* 9, 11.

Gin, in composition, increases the sense of the word; as, fæst *fast,* ginfæst *very* or *most fast.*

Ginan *to yawn, Cot.* 23, v. gynian.

Gind *beyond, Ors.* 4, 8, v. geond.

Ginfæst *Very fast* or *lasting, ample;* firmissimus:—Onfon ginfæstum gifum *receive very fast gifts, Cd.* 141, *Th.* p. 176, 28: 169, *Th.* p. 211, 10.

Ging *young, tender;* gingra *younger;* gingast *youngest, Cd.* 176, v. geong.

Gingra, an; *m. A younger, disciple;* discipulus:—*Cd.* 224, *Th.* p. 297, 24: 225, *Th.* p. 298, 11.

Ginian *to open, yawn, Gr.* 2, 26, v. gynian.

Ginsta *for* gingsta *youngest,* v. geong.

Ginung *A yawning;* hiatus:—*Cot.* 23.

Gio *formerly, Bt.* 16, 1, v. geo.

Giocþa *a scab, Past.* 11, 5, v. gicþa.

Gioful *liberal,* v. gifol.

Giofulnes, se; *f. Munificence, liberality;* munificentia:—*Past.* 44, 2.

Gioguꝺ, giagoꝺ, giogaꝺ *youth,* v. geoguꝺ.

Gioleca *the yolk of an egg, Bt. R.* p. 178, v. geolca.

Giolu *yellow,* in composition, *as,* giolureadan *yellow red, &c.* v. geolewe, &c.

Giomor *sad, Bt. R.* p. 152, v. geomer.

Giond *through, over, beyond,* and in composition, v. geond.

Gionetan *to occupy, C. Lk.* 13, 7, v. geonetan.

Giong *young, Ors.* 2, 4, v. geong.

Giongor *a younger, servant, Cd.* 21, v. geong.

Giongerscipe *youngership, service, Cd.* 14, v. geongordom.

Giornan *to beg, desire,* v. geornian.

Giornan, hi giorndon *to run, rush on, C. Lk.* 5, 1, v. yrnan.

Giornis, se; *f. Importunity, earnestness;* importunitas:—*C. R. Lk.* 11, 8.

Giostordoeg *yesterday, C. Jn.* 4, 52, v. gyrstandæg.

Giowian *to ask, R. Mk.* 11, 24, v. giuan.

Gird *a staff, Ex.* 4, 2, v. gyrd.

Giren, girn *a snare, V. Ps.* 17, 6, v. grin.

Girian; *p.* þu giredost. *To prepare, Ps.* 146, 8, v. gearwian.

Girnan *to yearn, seek for, require, Ex.* 21, 22, v. geornian.

Girran, gyrran *To chatter, prate;* garrire:—*Ælf. gr.* 36.

Girwan *To prepare;* parare:—*Jdth.* 9, v. gearwian.

Giscian *To sob, sigh;* singultire:—*Bt.* 2.

Gise *yes, Bt. R.* p. 16, 4, v. gese.

Gisedla *A sitting down to meat;* discubitus:—*R. Mk.* 12, 39.

Gisel; *g.* gisles; *d.* gisle; *m. A pledge, hostage;* obses:—Gislas sealdon *gave hostages;* obsides dederunt, *Chr.* 876: 894. To gisle gesealde *in obsidem traditus, Bd.* 3, 24.

Gislian; *p.* ode, ade; *pp.* od. *To give hostages* or *security;* obsides dare:—He gislode, *Chr.* 1016. Þa þægenas gislodon *the thanes gave hostages, Chr.* 1013.

GIST [*Plat.* gäst, jest *m*: *Dut.* gist, gest *f*: *Ger.* gäscht, gischt *m*: *Icel.* jastr *n. nugarum strepitus:* ysting *f. coagulatio: Lat. mid.* gesta, gistum] YEAST, *barm, froth;* spuma cerevisiæ:—*Herb.* 21, 5.

Gist, es; *m. A guest, Cd.* 113, v. gest.

Gist *a storm,* v. yst.

Gist-burh *a guest-house, a bedchamber, T. Ps.* 18, 5.

Gist-hus, gyst-hus *a guest-house, an inn.*

Git *yet, you two,* v. gyt.

Giþiode *subdued,* v. þeowian.

Giþreatian *to reprove, R. Jn.* 16, 8, v. þreatian.

Gitsian *to desire,* v. gytsian.

Gitsunc, gitsung *desire, Bt. R.* p. 159, v. gytsung.

Gitugon *conspired,* v. teon.

Giu, giw *A griffin:* gryps:—*Cot.* 159.

Giuan; *p.* giude. *To give, ask, require;* petere:—*R. Mk.* 6, 22.

Giuli *yule, Christmas,* v. geol.

Giululing *August;* sextilis, Mensis; but *Som.* and *Ben.* say *July;* quintilis.

Giung *young, Bd.* 4, 32, v. geong.

Giwedo *Clothes;* vestimenta:—*R. Mk.* 11, 8.

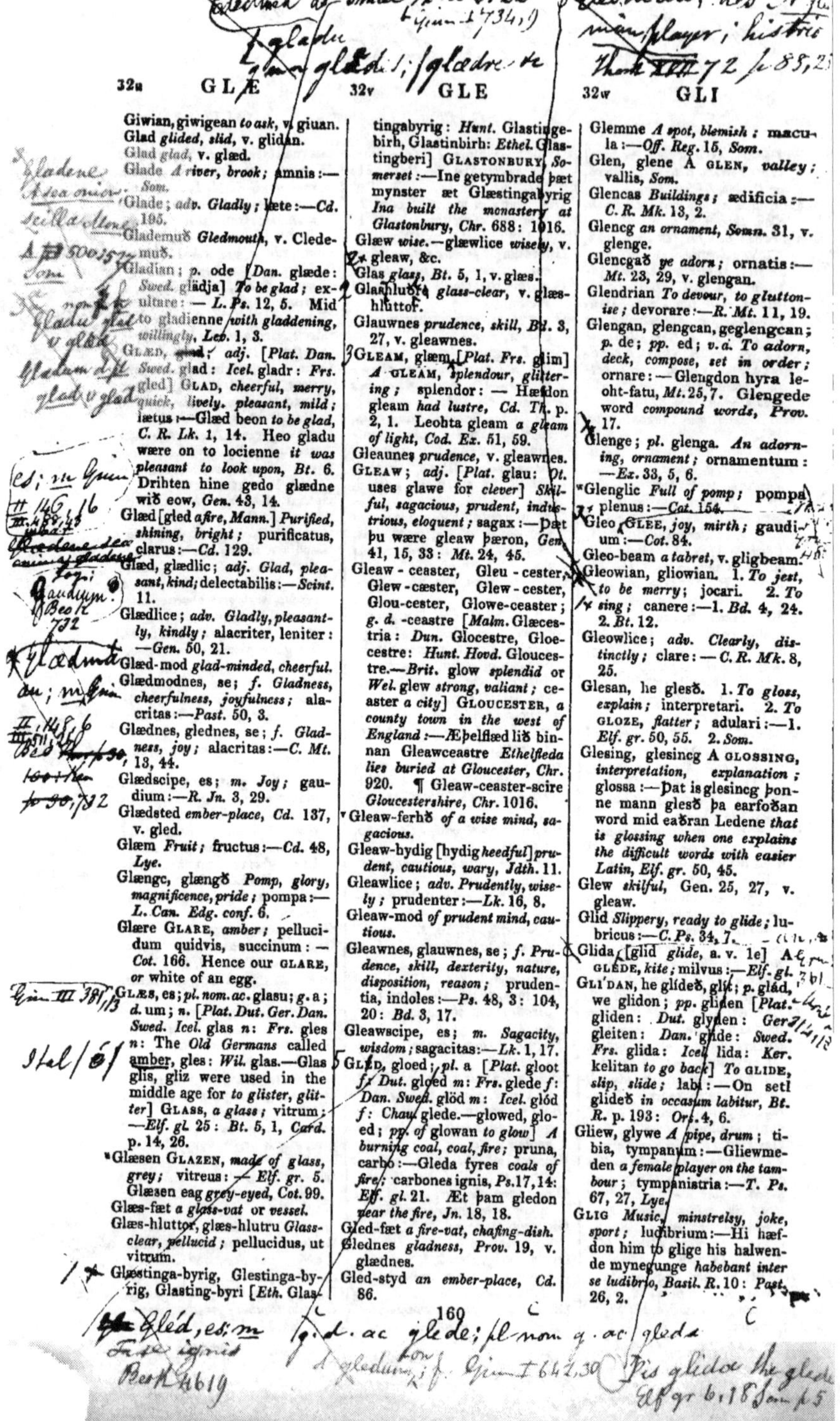

Giwian, giwigean *to ask*, v. giuan.
Glad *glided, slid*, v. glidan.
Glad *glad*, v. glæd.
Glade *A river, brook;* amnis:—*Som.*
Glade; *adv. Gladly;* læte:—*Cd.* 195.
Glademuð *Gledmouth*, v. Cledemuð.
Gladian; *p.* ode [*Dan.* glæde: *Swed.* glädja] *To be glad;* exultare: — *L. Ps.* 12, 5. Mid to gladienne *with gladdening, willingly, Lev.* 1, 3.
GLÆD, glæd; *adj.* [*Plat. Dan. Swed.* glad: *Icel.* gladr: *Frs.* gled] GLAD, *cheerful, merry, quick, lively. pleasant, mild;* lætus:—Glæd beon *to be glad, C. R. Lk.* 1, 14. Heo gladu wære on to locienne *it was pleasant to look upon, Bt.* 6. Drihten hine gedo glædne wið eow, *Gen.* 43, 14.
Glæd [gled *afire, Mann.*] *Purified, shining, bright;* purificatus, clarus:—*Cd.* 129.
Glæd, glædlic; *adj. Glad, pleasant, kind;* delectabilis:—*Scint.* 11.
Glædlice; *adv. Gladly, pleasantly, kindly;* alacriter, leniter:—*Gen.* 50, 21.
Glæd-mod *glad-minded, cheerful.*
Glædmodnes, se; *f. Gladness, cheerfulness, joyfulness;* alacritas:—*Past.* 50, 3.
Glædnes, gladnes, se; *f. Gladness, joy;* alacritas:—*C. Mt.* 13, 44.
Glædscipe, es; *m. Joy;* gaudium:—*R. Jn.* 3, 29.
Glædsted *ember-place, Cd.* 137, v. gled.
Glæm *Fruit;* fructus:—*Cd.* 48, *Lye.*
Glængc, glængð *Pomp, glory, magnificence, pride;* pompa:—*L. Can. Edg. conf.* 6.
Glære GLARE, *amber;* pellucidum quidvis, succinum:—*Cot.* 166. Hence our GLARE, *or white of an egg.*
GLÆS, es; *pl. nom. ac.* glasu; *g.* a; *d.* um; *n.* [*Plat. Dut. Ger. Dan. Swed. Icel.* glas *n*: *Frs.* gles *n*: The *Old Germans* called amber, gles: *Wil.* glas.—Glas glis, gliz were used in the middle age for *to glister, glitter*] GLASS, *a glass;* vitrum;—*Elf. gl.* 25: *Bt.* 5, 1, *Card.* p. 14, 26.
*Glæsen GLAZEN, *made of glass, grey;* vitreus:—*Elf. gr.* 5. Glæsen eag *grey-eyed, Cot.* 99.
Glæs-fæt *a glass-vat* or *vessel.*
Glæs-hluttor, glæs-hlutru *Glass-clear, pellucid;* pellucidus, ut vitrum.
Glæstinga-byrig, Glestinga-byrig, Glasting-byri [*Eth.* Glastingabyrig: *Hunt.* Glastingebirh, Glastinbirh: *Ethel.* Glastingberi] GLASTONBURY, *Somerset:*—Ine getymbrade þæt mynster æt Glæstingabyrig *Ina built the monastery at Glastonbury, Chr.* 688: 1016.
Glæw *wise.*—glæwlice *wisely*, v. gleaw, &c.
Glas *glass, Bt.* 5, 1, v. glæs.
Glashluttor *glass-clear*, v. glæshluttor.
Glauwnes *prudence, skill, Bd.* 3, 27, v. gleawnes.
GLEAM, glæm [*Plat. Frs.* glim] A GLEAM, *splendour, glittering;* splendor: — Hæfdon gleam *had lustre, Cd. Th.* p. 2, 1. Leohta gleam *a gleam of light, Cod. Ex.* 51, 59.
Gleaunes *prudence*, v. gleawnes.
GLEAW; *adj.* [*Plat.* glau: *Ot.* uses glawe for *clever*] *Skilful, sagacious, prudent, industrious, eloquent;* sagax:—Þæt þu wære gleaw þæron, *Gen.* 41, 15, 33: *Mt.* 24, 45.
Gleaw - ceaster, Gleu - cester, Glew - cæster, Glew - cester, Glou-cester, Glowe-ceaster; *g. d.* -ceastre [*Malm.* Glæcestria: *Dun.* Glocestre, Gloecestre: *Hunt. Hovd.* Glouces-tre.—*Brit.* glow *splendid* or *Wel.* glew *strong, valiant;* ceaster *a city*] GLOUCESTER, *a county town in the west of England:*—Æþelflæd lið binnan Gleawceastre *Ethelfleda lies buried at Gloucester, Chr.* 920. ¶ Gleaw-ceaster-scire *Gloucestershire, Chr.* 1016.
*Gleaw-ferhð *of a wise mind, sagacious.*
Gleaw-hydig [hydig *heedful*] *prudent, cautious, wary, Jdth.* 11.
Gleawlice; *adv. Prudently, wisely;* prudenter:—*Lk.* 16, 8.
Gleaw-mod *of prudent mind, cautious.*
Gleawnes, glauwnes, se; *f. Prudence, skill, dexterity, nature, disposition, reason;* prudentia, indoles:—*Ps.* 48, 3: 104, 20: *Bd.* 3, 17.
Gleawscipe, es; *m. Sagacity, wisdom;* sagacitas:—*Lk.* 1, 17.
GLED, gloed; *pl.* a [*Plat.* gloot *f*: *Dut.* gloed *m*: *Frs.* glede *f*: *Dan. Swed.* glöd *m*: *Icel.* glód *f*: *Chau.* glede.—glowed, gloed; *pp.* of glowan *to glow*] *A burning coal, coal, fire;* pruna, carbo:—Gleda fyres *coals of fire;* carbones ignis, *Ps.* 17, 14: *Elf. gl.* 21. Æt þam gledon *near the fire, Jn.* 18, 18.
Gled-fæt *a fire-vat, chafing-dish.*
Glednes *gladness, Prov.* 19, v. glædnes.
Gled-styd *an ember-place, Cd.* 86.
Glemme *A spot, blemish;* macula:—*Off. Reg.* 15, *Som.*
Glen, glene A GLEN, *valley;* vallis, *Som.*
Glencas *Buildings;* ædificia:—*C. R. Mk.* 13, 2.
Glencg *an ornament, Somn.* 31, v. glenge.
Glencgað *ye adorn;* ornatis:—*Mt.* 23, 29, v. glengan.
Glendrian *To devour, to gluttonise;* devorare:—*R. Mt.* 11, 19.
Glengan, glengcan, geglengcan; *p.* de; *pp.* ed; *v. a. To adorn, deck, compose, set in order;* ornare:—Glengdon hyra leoht-fatu, *Mt.* 25, 7. Glengede word *compound words, Prov.* 17.
Glenge; *pl.* glenga. *An adorning, ornament;* ornamentum:—*Ex.* 33, 5, 6.
*Glenglic *Full of pomp;* pompa plenus:—*Cot.* 154.
Gleo, GLEE, *joy, mirth;* gaudium:—*Cot.* 84.
Gleo-beam *a tabret*, v. gligbeam.
Gleowian, gliowian. 1. *To jest, to be merry;* jocari. 2. *To sing;* canere:—1. *Bd.* 4, 24. 2. *Bt.* 12.
Gleowlice; *adv. Clearly, distinctly;* clare:—*C. R. Mk.* 8, 25.
Glesan, he gleső. 1. *To gloss, explain;* interpretari. 2. *To* GLOZE, *flatter;* adulari:—1. *Elf. gr.* 50, 55. 2. *Som.*
Glesing, glesincg A GLOSSING, *interpretation, explanation;* glossa:—Þat is glesincg þonne mann gleső þa earfoðan word mid eaðran Ledene *that is glossing when one explains the difficult words with easier Latin, Elf. gr.* 50, 45.
Glew *skilful*, Gen. 25, 27, v. gleaw.
Glid *Slippery, ready to glide;* lubricus:—*C. Ps.* 34, 7.
Glida, [glid *glide*, a. v. 1e] A GLEDE, *kite;* milvus:—*Elf. gl.*
GLI'DAN, he glideð, glit; *p.* glad, we glidon; *pp.* gliden [*Plat.* gliden: *Dut.* glyden: *Ger.* gleiten: *Dan.* glide: *Swed. Frs.* glida: *Icel.* lida: *Ker.* kelitan *to go back*] *To* GLIDE, *slip, slide;* labi:—On setl glideð *in occasum labitur, Bt. R.* p. 193: *Ors.* 4, 6.
Gliew, glywe *A pipe, drum;* tibia, tympanum:—Gliewmeden *a female player on the tambour;* tympanistria:—*T. Ps.* 67, 27, *Lye.*
GLIG *Music, minstrelsy, joke, sport;* ludibrium:—Hi hæfdon him to glige his halwende mynegunge *habebant inter se ludibrio, Basil. R.* 10: *Past.* 26, 2.

Gitswan to wash
vare Ben

Gitsere greedy man
v gytsere

Gladung, e f A
gladdening, exhila
ratio, gratulatio
Som

Glappa, an f A bur
Lappa. Rask's Gr thp
p 189 — or Glappe, an
f? th. An

Glaeow wide;
prudent; v gleaw

Glad glad Som
glade gladly; late
glad Beo K 116

Gladene a sea
onion v gladene

Glaengcan, ornare Todorn
Lye

Glaeng Hickes' Thes
I p 135, 13. Gram
Runes 218, v 712.
Gleo, es, m Joy; glee
song; Beo K 4205
Gleo-craeft music
musica
Gleo-dream, es; m
joy, jubi
Beo K 6037
glee song
Gleo-gaman jubi
latio Grim
II 456, 9

Glaedlic Easy
tale pleased, mild
placabilis Som

Gleawlic skilful,
cunning Th. An

Glewnes prudence
v gleawnes

Gledlice gladly
Som. v gladlice

Glidiende Totter
ing, likely to fall
nutabundus Som

Glie glee; gau
dium Som

Gled sinc es; m fire
gettrum Treasure
Beo K 4042

Glaestinga-burh
g-burge. de. bvrig
the Glastonbury tel

Glaestinga-ea Grim II 451, 6

Glysung a glossing
catechus? glossa
Som v glesung

4+ God, es; m God,
Bens

God es; m An
idolum
Besgl

Glysung, e.f.
A glossing, a making
a gloss; glossatio. Som

1 Glig-gamen mer
ements, gamboli;
joci Som

Glyw-beam
a tabret Som v
glig-beam

Glyw-meden
a glee maiden, a
female minstrel Ben
v in gliew

Glioda a glede
kite; Som v glida

Gnagan to gnaw
Som v. gnagan

Glitmian To glitter
coruscare Bes
Gling 5512

2 Gnedlice sparingly
Ben v gnedelice

5 Gliw-stafas wisdom
Besgl

Gliwere es; m
A fawner, flatterer;
parasitus Som

3+ Gnorn, es m Grief,
distress
sorrow; moeror Bes
2 5343

3+ phanatically

6 Glóden A mari
gold; Caltha Som

7 Glodian To make
gentle, to tame;
mansuefacere
Som

Gleto A glutton Th An

Glyd a glede
Som v glida

Glyffa scraped, polished,
filed; interrasilis
Som

Gnyrran to
gnash; stridere
Som

Glig-beam *A timbrel, tabret;* tympanum:—*Ps.* 80, 2: 150, 4.

Glig-cræft *the art of amusing, minstrelsy, mummery.*

Glig-georn *One desirous of sport, a jester, buffoon;* joci amans: —*Off. Episc.* 3.

Gligman, gliigman, gliiman, gliman; *g.* -mannes; *pl.* -men; *m. A musician, minstrel,* GLEEMAN, *player, buffoon;* histrio, joculator:—It was in the character of a gleeman or joculator that Alfred visited the Danish camp. These persons were not only valued, but well rewarded in their day. Edmund, son of Ethelred, gave a villa to his gleeman. In Doomsday-book, Berdic, a *joculator* of the king, possessed three villas in Gloucestershire, *Mr. Turner's Hist. of A.-S.* b. vii. ch. 7, vol. iii. p. 61.

Gliowian *to sing, Bt.* 12, v. gleowian.

Glioword, es; *n.* [gleo *mirth,* word *word*] *A song;* cantilena:—*Bt. R.* p. 156.

Glisian, glisnian *To* GLISTEN, *glow, shine;* micare:—Glisnað *coruscat, Cott. MS. Otho. B.* 10, v. *Hickes's Thes.* vol. i. p. 135.

Glitenan, glitinian *To* GLITTER, *glisten, shine;* coruscare:—His reaf wurdon glitiniende, *Mk.* 9, 3.

Glitenung, e; *f. A flash of lightning;* coruscatio:—Mid glitenungum, *Ps.* 143, 8.

Gliw. 1. *A jester;* mimus. 2. *Repartees, drollery;* facetiæ: —1. *Cot.* 132, 214. 2. Winsum gliw *jocundæ facetiæ, R.* 115.

Gliw-beam *a timbrel, Ps.* 149, 3, v. glig-beam.

Gliw-bleoðriend *following music, musical.*

Gliwian, glywian *To joke, jest, to play on an instrument;* jocari:—Ne ænige wisan gliwige *nec ullo modo scurram agat, L. Can. Edg.* 58.

Gloed *a fire, R. Jn.* 18, 18, v. gled.

Gloed-scof *a fire-shovel, warming-pan, Som.*

Glof *a cliff,* as cliof, v. clif.

Glomung, glommung, e; *f. Twilight;* crepusculum, *Som.*

Glowan *To glow like a coal of fire;* candere, *Som.*

Glydering, glyderung, e; *f. What glides away, a vision, an illusion;* visio:—*Cot.* 84.

Glywe *a pipe, L. Ps.* 146, 11, v. gliew.

Glywian *to play on an instrument, Ps.* 67, 27, v. gliwian.

Gnád *rubbed; p. of* gnidan.

GNÆT, gnat; *g.* gnættes; *m.* [*Plat.* gnid *f. a small kind of gnat: Ger.* gnatze *f. the itch*] GNAT; culex:—*Mt.* 23, 24. Gnættas, *Ex.* 8, 16, 17: *Ps.* 104, 29.

GNAGAN, he gnægð; *p.* gnóh, we gnógon; *pp.* gnagen [*Plat.* gnauen: *Dut.* knagen, knaauwen: *Ger.* nagen: *Dan.* gnave, nage: *Swed.* gnaga, nagga: *Icel.* gnaga, naga] *To* GNAW, *bite;* rodere:—*Elf. gr.* 28: *Cot.* 131.

Gneðelice; *adv. Sparingly;* parce:—*Dial.* 1, 7.

Gneðen, gneðn *Moderate, temperate, modest, low;* frugalis, modestus:—*Cot.* 129: *Bd.* 5, 19.

Gneðenes, gneðnes, se; *f.* 1. *Frugality, care;* parcimonia. 2. *A failing, want;* defectus: —1. *Cot.* 81, 149. 2. Gneðnes hwætes *defectus tritici, Martyrol.* 28, *Apr.*

GNI'DAN, gegnidan, he gnít; *p.* gnád, we gnidon; *pp.* gniden, gegniden [*Plat.* gnittern, kniittern: *Dut.* kneuzen: *Dan.* gnide: *Swed.* gnida: *Icel.* gny'a] *To rub, break, rub together, comminute;* fricare, comminuere:—Mid hyra handum gnidon, *Lk.* 6, 1. Gnid swiðe smale to duste *rub very small, to dust, Herb.* 1, 2.

Gnidill [*Plat.* gniedel *m.* gniedelsteen *m. a stone to polish or to rub with:* gnideln *v. to polish*] *A pestle;* pistillum, *Som.*

Gniding *A rubbing;* frictio, *Som.*

Gnorn *Discontent, a grudging;* mœstitia:—*Cd.* 111.

Gnorne; *adj.* [*Plat.* gnurrig, knurrig, gnarrig: *Dut.* knorrig: *Frs.* gnorrich: *Ger.* knurrig: *Dan.* knurren, knarvorn: *Swed.* knarrig: *Icel.* gnudd *n.* knurr *n.*] *Sorrowful, sad, dejected, complaining;* mœstus: —Gylp wearð gnornra *want grew sadder, Cd.* 166. Gnornword *sad words, Cd.* 37.

Gnornian, ic gnornige, þu gnornast, hi gnorniað; *p.* ode; *pp.* od. *To grieve, murmur, groan, lament;* mœrere:—Scyle ymb þat gnornian *ought about that to grieve, Bt.* 40, 3. Ferde gnornigende *went away sorrowing, Mk.* 10, 22: *Elf. gr.* 33: *Bd.* 2, 12.

Gnorning, gnornung, e; *f. Grief, lamentation, mourning;* mœstitia:—Þeos gnornung *this grief, Bt.* 5, 3: 7, 2: *Bd.* 1, 13.

Gnyrn *a grudging,* v. gnorn.

GOD, es; *m.* [*Plat. Dut. Frs.* God *m*: *Ger.* Gott *m*: *Dan. Swed. Icel.* Gud *m*: *Moes.* Goth: *Ot.* Got: *Pers.* خدا choda: *Hindoo.* khoda, codam.—There is a beauty in the name appropriated by the Saxon and German nations to the Deity which is not equalled by any other, except his most venerated Hebrew appellation יהוה yewe, with points Jehovah, or יה ye, with points Jah, *the existence, subsistence, he who exists of himself absolutely and independently,* 'Ο ΩΝ. In A.-S. God both signifies *God* and *good:* but man is used to denote man and wickedness, sin, v. man. The Saxons call him God, which is literally *the good;* the same word signifying both the Deity, and his most endearing quality. For those qualities which the Gothic nations considered the best and most attractive, v. guð] 1. GOD; Deus. 2. In the *pl. the heathen gods, idols;* divi, dii:— 1. Weolde gód þat þat he is, þat ic hate God *good directed whatever is, that I call God, Bt.* 35, 2. An God ys gód, *Mt.* 19, 17. Nys nan man gód, buton God ana, *Lk.* 18, 19. Hu gód Israhel God, *Ps.* 72, 1. Her is Godes lamb, *Jn.* 1, 29. Enoch ferde mid Gode, *Gen.* 5, 24. 2. Drihten sylf ys Goda God, mære God, and mihtig, and egefull, *Deut.* 10, 17. Hig worhton him gildene godas, *Ex.* 32, 31: 23, 32: *Jn.* 10, 34, 35. ¶ Godfæder GODFATHER. — Godgelda *a sacrifice.*—God-gildlice *an enthusiast.*—God-gyld *an altar.* — God-moder *a* GODMOTHER.—Godsibb *a maker of peace with God, a gossip, a sponsor.*—Godspell *the Gospel,* v. in its alphabetical order.— Godspræce *an oracle, a counsel.*—God-sunu *a* GODSON.— God-wræca *one banished from God, a wicked wretch.*—Godwræcnis *wickedness, a dreadful deed.*

Gód; *pl.* gód; *g.* góda; *n.* GOOD, *goods, property;* bonum, bona, facultates:—The phrases, to góde, *Ors.* 6, 8; on nanum góde, *Ors.* 6, 30; shew that when used as a noun, gód is inflected as a noun. Hi þæt gód forlætað *they the good forsake, Bt.* 37, 3, *Card.* p. 296, 12, 16. Of his hlafordes gódum, *Gen.* 24, 10. Æt þam heahstan góde *to the highest good, Bt.* 32, 1.

Gód; *def.* se góda; *comp.* betera; *sup.* betest, betst: *adj.* GOOD; bonus:—Þæs gódan godnes bið his agen gód *the goodness of the good is his own good, Bt.* 37, 3, *Card.* p. 294, 18. Gód mann soðlice of gódum goldhorde bringð gód forð, *Mt.* 12, 35.

b Goda *a Goth, Bt. R.* p. 151, v. gota.

God-æpple *A quince apple;* cydonium:—*Cot.* 34, 93.

Godcund [cund *a kind, sort*] *Divine, sacred, godly;* divinus:—*Bd.* 1, 1: *L. Edm. pref.*

Godcundlice; *adv. Divinely, from heaven, by inspiration;* divinitus:—Þeah he se godcundlice gesceadwis *though he be divinely rational, Bt.* 14, 2: *Bd.* 4, 3, 24.

Godcundnys, se; *f. Divine nature, Deity, Divinity;* Deitas:—*Bt.* 34, 4.

Gode hwile *a good while, a long time.*

Godera, goddera *better, Chr.* 1066, v. gód.

Gode-wæbb, god-webb GOODWEBB, *any kind of fine cloth, purple, scarlet silk;* bona textura, purpura:—*Bd.* 3, 2: *Cd.* 171.

Godgundnys *Divinity, Elf. T.* p. 25, v. godcundnys.

Godian, gegodian; *p.* ede; *pp.* gegodod. *To do good, benefit, delight, enrich, endow, cure;* prodesse:—*L. Cnut. pol.* 11. Godede þat mynstre *enriched the minster, Chr.* 963.

God-leás; *adj. Godless, goodless;* sine Deo, infaustus:—*Bd.* 3, 1.

Godlec, godlic *Godly, godlike, goodly;* pulcher, divinus:—Godlecran stol *a diviner throne, Cd.* 15. Godlice geardas *goodly courts, Cd.* 35.

Godmundingaham [mund, or munding *defence, protection,* ham *an habitation, a home, a protecting home of the gods*] GODMUNDHAM, (*Lye* says, Goodmanham, between Pocklington and Beverley) a place a little to the east of York, beyond the river Derwent, where a famous Witena-gemot was convened by Edwin, king of Northumbria, in A.D. 625, to consider the propriety of receiving the Christian faith. The speeches were so much in favour of Christianity, that the creed was at once received; these speeches are particularly worthy of notice, *Bd.* 2, 13. *Mr. Turner's Hist. of A.-S.* b. iii. ch. 7, vol. i. p. 344—347, *and Elements of Anglo-Saxon Gr.* p. 283.

Gódnes, se; *f.* GOODNESS; bonitas:—*Bt.* 38, 4: 37, 3: *Ps.* 36, 3: *Elf. gr.* 5.

Godspedig *rich in good, Cd.* 48.

God-spell, es, ys; *n.* [spell *a history, speech, declaration*] GOSPEL; Dei verbum, evangelium:—Þat godspell *the gospel, Mk.* 13, 10. Godspellys angyn, *Mk.* 1, 1: *Mt.* 24, 14: *Mk.* 1, 15: 8, 35: 13, 10: *Bd.* 5, 9, 11.

Godspellere, es; *m. An evangelist, a gospeller;* evangelista:—*Chr.* 84: 90: *Bd.* 4, 3.

Godspellian *To preach glad tidings* or *the gospel;* evangelizare:—*Elf. gr.* 24.

Godspellic; *adj. Like the gospel, evangelical;* evangelicus:—He godspellice lare lære *he evangelical doctrine taught, Bd.* 3, 19.

Gol *A song;* cantilena:—Golgydæst *most harmonious, Bt. R.* p. 156.

Gol *sang,* v. galan.

GOLD, es; *n.* [*Plat. Ger. Ot. Moes.* gold *n*: *Ker.* cold: *Wil.* guold: *Dut.* goud *n*: *Dan. Swed.* guld *n*: *Icel.* gull *n*: *Tart.* goltz.—Gelew *yellow: Ar.* [Arabic] gla *to be clear, bright*] GOLD; aurum:—*Mr. Turner* says, "my belief is, that gold was used in an uncoined state, in the payments of the Anglo-Saxons, as no gold coins have reached modern times," *Hist. of A.-S. ap. No.* 2, vol. ii. p. 470. Þeah Balac me sille goldes an hus full, *Num.* 22, 18. Þat templ þe þæt gold gehalgað, *Mt.* 23, 17: *Gen.* 2, 12, 13, 6. ¶ Gold-bleoh [bleoh *colour*] *a gold colour;* auricolor.—Gold-burh *a golden city.*—Goldes-brytta *a bestower of gold, a lord.*—Gold-fæt *a gold-vessel.*—Gold-fel, gold-fyld *golden-skin, gold-leaf.*—Gold-finc *a goldfinch, a bird.*—Gold-fynger *the gold-finger, ring-finger.*—Gold-gyfa *a giver of gold;* auri dispensator, *Jdth.* 12.—Gold-hilted *gold-hilted, having a gold handle.*—Gold-hold *gold-hold, a treasury, R.* 109.—Gold-hord *gold-hoard, a treasury, Gen.* 43, 23.—Gold-hord-hus *a privy, R.* 107.—Gold-læfra *gold-leaf, Cot.* 207. Gold-mæstling *latten* or *copper metal;* aurichalcum, *Elf. gr.* 8.—Gold-sele *a golden* or *splendid hall, Beo.* 11, 11.—Gold-smið *goldsmith, Gen.* 4, 22.—Gold-wine *a liberal friend, munificent chief, Beo.* 17, 95.

d Gold *an idol, Cd.* 182, v. gyld.

Golden *golden,* v. gylden.

Golden *paid, requited, Cd.* 55, v. gildan.

Goldhordian *To treasure up, to hoard;* thesaurizare:—Goldhordiað eow soðlice goldhordas on heofenan, *Mt.* 6, 20.

Golfetung *A mock, taunt;* subsannatio:—*L. Ps.* 78, 4.

Gol-gydæst *very poetical, harmonious, tuneful.*

GOMA, an [*Ger.* gaumen *m*: *Not.* giumo: *Swed.* gom *m*: *Icel.* gómr *m. gums*: *Dut.* gom *f*: *Ger.* gummi *n*: *Fr.* gomme: *Sp.* goma: *It.* gomma *resin*] 1. *The gums of the mouth, the jaws;* palatum, fauces. 2. *Gum, resin;* resina:—1. *Elf. gr.* 9, 71: *Ps.* 68, 4. 2. ¶ Gom-teð *gum-teeth.*

Gombon *Obedience, homage, tribute;* obedientia:—*Cd.* 93.

Gomel, gomol *old,* v. gamol.

Gomen *game, sport,* v. gamen.

Gomol-feax *grey-haired,* v. gamol.

Gond *yond, beyond,* v. geond.

Gondfaran *to go beyond* or *over.*

Gondsmeagan *To examine fully;* discutere:—*Bd.* 4, 3.

Gong *a journey, path, step, Mk.* 1, 3, v. gang.

Gongan *to go, Bd.* 25, v. gangan.

Good *good, Bt.* 35, 3, v. gód.

Goodnes *goodness, Bt. R.* p. 174, v. godnes.

Gor. 1. GORE, *clotted blood;* tabum. 2. *Dirt, mud, dung;* fimus:—1. *Ex.* 29, 14. 2. *Herb.* 9, 3.

Gorst, gost GORSE, *furze, a bramble, bush;* erica, rubus:—On gorste, *Lk.* 6, 44. Juniper þat is gorst *juniperus est rubus, L. M.* 1, 31. Ofer þone gorstbeam, *Mk.* 12, 26.

GÓS; *g.* góse; *pl. nom. ac.* gés, gees; *g.* gósa; *d.* gósum [*Plat.* goos *f*: *Dut. Ger.* gans *f*: *Dan.* gaas *f*: *Swed.* gås *f*: *Icel.* gás *f*: *Bret.* gwaz, goaz *f*: *Wel.* gwyz: *Russ.* gus] A GOOSE; anser:—Hwite gos *white goose, Elf. gl.* 11. Græg gos *a grey goose, Cot.* 99. Gose innelfe *goose's giblets;* anseris exta. Gés, gees *geese;* anseres, *L. In.* 70.

Gos-hafoc, gos-fuc *Goshawk, goosehawk;* aucarius:—*R.* 36.

f Gost *gorse, R.* 47, v. gorst.

Gota, Goda [v. guð *war*] A GOTH; Gothus:—Gotena cyning *a king of Goths, Bd.* 1, 11.

Gotende *pouring out.*—Goten *shed,* v. geotan.

Got-land GOTHLAND; Gothia:—*Ors.* 1, 1.

Goung *A sighing, sobbing, mourning;* gemitus:—*Bd.* 1, 27, *resp.* 8.

~~Gāte~~
Gōd good [Bt 12 2]

God-bot, e; f Atone[ment] for an offence against God; Som; godcund-bot, e; f recompense to the church

× God-æppel, es; a quince apple

God-bearn a child; puer lus[tricus] Ben Wulfst Paren 4

God-borh, g- borges m a divine surety; Dei fidejussor L. Alf pol 29

Godful full of good ...

god-webb [2 g u 1]

Gold-fah gold ornamented / adorned Beo K 613

Gold-siowode gold sewed; auro textus Cot 178 Ben

Gold-hroden ~~...~~ gold adorned Beo K 1221

Gold-hwæte gold greedy; auri avidus Beo K 6143

Gold-maðm, es m a gold treasure Beo K 4824

~~Gold-weard, es; m a gold~~

Gold-wlanc gold proud Beo K 3758

Godspell Ælf ... p 26. 4

Godspellic evangelical, gospel

Godcund-lareow es; m A divine teacher a divine; theologus Som

Gōd-don to do good Som

Gode a goad; Som v gād

Godgund divine C R. Ben 62. Som v godcund

Gafol a tax ~~...~~ Mann v gafol

possession of gold Beo K 6492

Gold-æht (æht property) treasury; thesaurus Beo 294

Gold-þeof gold thief auri fur ... D 45 ... L. Alf pol. 9

Gongel-wæfre (gongel wæfre) an; A spider; phalangium Som

Gomele-lāfe; f old inheritance; a sword Beo K 5123

Goldsele a gold hall; a treasure house Beo K 1423

Godes-scalc a servant of God,

God-fremmende doing good Beo K 595

Gombon-u ...

× Gombe, an; f [Plat gambra f a tax] A tax, tribute; homage; vectigal. Scolde gomban gyldan should pay tribute Beo K 21

Sceoldon gomban gieldan sh'd pay homage Cd. 93 Th 119 11

Gomen-wudu pleasure wood, a harp Beo K 4234

Gong-stol, es; m A close-stool; lasanum, scaphium. Som

Godweresang harmonia Ben

Gomen-wað e pleasure path Beo K 1702

Gota, Goda an; m a goth Bt 1, 1

v commencement; Tyrocinium due
v Grab a grave. Bye
v graf

1 Græs-groen grass green
grassineus Som

1 Grad es; m. 2t
step &c Th An

2 Græfere a graver
Som v græfere

2 Græc, es. m
A Greek Th An
v Grecas

Great-wyrt
emetic herb L. M.
Som v Supl. Great-wyrt

Grām, es m. Rage
furor Beo 2d

3

4 Grame Fiercely Th
An

4 Gramian to anger
provoke; irritare Som
v græmian

5 Gramscipe es; m
Anger, wrath; ira
Som

Grædig greedy,
Grædighes &c v
grædig &c

Græft a graven
image Som v
græft

Grene
Grn. I 735,20

5 Græg, græg
Som v græg

Leo, þæt grene
52 Gren, green &c
Th An

Grante brycg,
Grante-brycg, Gran
tan-brycg, e; f
Cambridge &c

Gramum Fiercely fiercious
[illegible] Beo K 842

Grene ær, gr
ær green oar;
latten or copper
metal; aurical,
cum Som Cot 14,
Som

2

3 / x Græg-hama
1 Coat line Grn. II 632,41

4 Græg-hiw, es; m
a grey hue; ferrugo
Som

5 Græg-mæl
grey marked, grey
spotted Beo K 5360

Grad, an. A GRADE, *step, order;* gradus, ordo:—Blod com uppon þam gradan and of þam gradan on þa flore *blood came upon the step and from the step on the floor, Chr.* 1083: *L. With. W.* p. 12, 48.

Græat *great, R.* 39, v. great.

Grædan, grætan [*Dut.* kryten *to cry: Frs.* greta *to complain: Moes.* creitan: *Dan.* græde: *Swed.* gråta: *Icel.* græta: *Wel.* grydian: *Sp. Port.* gritar: *It.* gridar] *To cry, call upon, to lament;* clamare, flere:—Græt se lareow *clamat prædicator, Past.* 63. Ic græde swa gos *clamo sicut anser, Cod. Exon.* p. 106, b.

Græde, es; *m. Grass, a herb;* gramen:—Grædas *gramina, Cot.* 95.

Grædelice, grædiglice, grædilice; *adv.* GREEDILY, *covetously;* avidè:—*Cot.* 104.

Grædig; *adj.* 1. GREEDY, *covetous,* avidus. 2. As a noun, *a devourer;* vorator:—1. *Cot.* 104: *Scint.* 46. 2. *R.* 88.

Grædignes, se; *f.* GREEDINESS, *covetousness, a ravening;* aviditas:—*Scint.* 30.

Græf, graf [*Plat. Dut.* graf *n*: *Frs.* græf *n*: *Ger.* grab *n*: *Ot.* grap: *Not.* grab, crab: *Dan.* grav *c*: *Swed.* graf *m*: *Icel.* gröf *f. scrobs: Rus.* grob] 1. A GRAVE, *sepulchre, den, cave;* tumulus. 2. *A graver, an iron pen;* stylus. 3. *A* GROVE; lucus:—1. *L. Ethelb.* 22: *L. Cnut. eccl.* 13. 2. *Elf. gl.* 8. 3. *Cot.* 89, 183.—Græf-hus *grave-house.*—Græf-sæx *a pen-knife, an instrument to carve with;* scalpellum, graphium, *Elf. gl.* 8.

Græfa, an; *m. Coal;* carbo fossilis:—*Chr.* 852.

Græfere, grafere, es; *m. A graver, an engraver;* sculptor:—*Elf. gl.* 8.

Græft *Carved, cut, a thing carved, a carved* or *graven image;* sculptile:—*Deut.* 5, 8: *Elf. gl.* 8. Græftas *sculptilia, L. Ps.* 96, 7: 105, 19.

Græg GREY; glaucus:—*R.* 79.

Græg-hama *A grey cricket, grasshopper;* cicada:—*Hickes's Thes.* p. 192.

Græg-hwæte *grey wheat, bread-corn.*

Græmian, gramian *to irritate, provoke, L. Ps.* 73, 11, 18, v. gremian.

Græp *A grip, furrow, ditch;* sulcus, *Som.*

Græs *grass, Cot.* 98.—Græshoppa *a grasshopper,* v. gærs, &c.

Grætan *to cry out, L. Mk.* 15, 13, v. grædan.

Grætta GRITS, *groats, bran;* farina crassior, furfur, *Som.*

Graf *a grave, den, Solil.* 9, v. græf.

Grafan he græfð; *p.* gróf, agróf, we grófon; *pp.* grafen, agrafen [*Plat. Dut.* graven: *Frs.* grewa: *Ger.* graben: *Dan.* grave: *Swed.* grafwa: *Icel.* grafa] *To* GRAVE, *engrave, carve, dig;* sculpere:—Mid Godes handa agrafene, *Ex.* 31, 18: *Lev.* 26, 1: *Deut.* 27, 15: *Ps.* 77, 64. Grof æfter golde *dug after gold, Bt. R.* p. 159, 5.

Grám, grom; *adj.* [grama *anger*] 1. *Furious, fierce, angry, offended, incensed, hostile;* furiosus. 2. *Troublesome;* molestus:—1. Þam folce gram, *Deut.* 1, 37. Gram him *incensed with him, Cd.* 16: *Bt.* 35, 6. 2. Ne beo þu me gram, *Lk.* 11, 7. Þeos wuduwe me is gram, *Lk.* 18, 5.

GRAMA, an [*Plat. Ger.* gram *m*: *Dut.* gramschap *f*: *Frs.* gram: *Dan.* gram *c*: *Icel.* gramr *m.*] 1. *Anger, rage, fury, indignation, wrath;* ira. 2. *Trouble;* molestia. 3. *Injury;* injuria:—1. Ic ondred his graman, *Deut.* 9, 19: *Ps.* 6, 1. Mid graman, *Gen.* 19, 25. 2. *Somn.* 262. 3. *Scint.* 78.

Gramatisc-cræft *the art of grammar.*

Gram-bære *bearing anger, angry.*

Grámlice; *adv. Angrily, fiercely;* iratè:—*Cd.* 210.

Grámulic *Furious;* furiosus:—*Jud.* 4, 2.

Grand *ground; p. of* grindan.

Granian; *p.* ude [*Plat.* grienen: *Ger.* grannen, greinen: *Dan.* grine: *Frs. Swed.* grina] *To* GROAN, *lament;* gemere:—*C. Ps.* 77, 69.

Granta-brycge, Grantebrycge, Grantan-brycge [*Hunt.* Grantebrige: *Dunel.* Grantabric, Granthebrige, Grantebryge: *Hovd.* Grauntebrigge] CAMBRIDGE, *a county town and famous university, Chr.* 875, 921. ¶ Granta-brycg-scire *Cambridgeshire, Chr.* 1010.

Granta-ceaster GRANTCHESTER, *a village near Cambridge.*

Granung, e; *f.* GROANING, *lamentation;* gemitus:—*L. Eccl.* p. 176.

Grap *a gripe, grasp, Beo.* 6, 133, v. gripa.

Grap *grasped; p. of* gripan.

GRAPIAN, gropian, gegrapian, ic grapige; *p.* ode; *pp.* od. [Composed of ge and rapian *to reap, gather: Dut.* rapen. The Friesians have the old frequentative verb grabbelge. *Plat.* grabbelen. The Persians have their گرفتن griften *to take: Ger.* greifen *to gripe,* v. gripan. *H.*] *To* GROPE, *touch, feel;* palpare:—Þystro swa þicce þat hig grapion, *Ex.* 10, 21. Grapiað and geseoð, *Lk.* 24, 39.

Grasian *To graze;* gramine vesci:—*Somn.* 36.

GREADA *A bosom;* sinus, gremium:—On Habrahames greadan, *Lk.* 16, 22, 23, v. bearm, bosm.

GREAT [*Plat. Dut.* groot: *Frs.* great, grat, grad: *Ger.* gross] GREAT, *large, thick;* magnus:—Greate hagol stanas, *Jos.* 10, 11. Great beam *a large tree, Bt.* 38, 2.

Greatian *To* GREATEN, *to become great* or *large;* grandescere:—*Past.* 11, 4.

Greatnes, se; *f.* GREATNESS; magnitudo:—*R. Ben.* 55.

Grecas, Græcas; *g.* a; *d.* um, *The Greeks;* Græci:—*Bd.* 4, 31.

Grecisc, Greccisc; *adj. Greek, Grecian;* Græcus:—Greccisc gereord *Greek language, Bd.* 5, 8. Ic leornige Grecisc *I learn Greek, Elf. gr.* 36.

Grec-land, Greca-land *Greek land, Greece;* Græcia:—*Ors.* 1, 1.

Gredig *greedy, Cd.* 213, v. grædig.

Gremetunc, gremetung, e; *f. A raging, roaring, murmuring;* fremitus:—*Prov.* 19.

Gremian, gegremian; *p.* ede; *pp.* gegremed; *v. a.* 1. *To irritate, provoke, exasperate;* irritare. 2. *To blaspheme, revile, curse;* blasphemare:—1. Ge gremedon, *Deut.* 9, 7, 8. 2. Hyne gremede, *Lk.* 23, 39.

Grena-wic, Grene-wic [grene *green;* wic *a village, bay*] GREENWICH, *near London, Chr.* 1013: 1014: 1016.

GRENE; *adj.* [*Plat. Dan. Swed.* grön: *Dut.* groen: *Frs.* gren: *Ger.* grün: *Ot.* gruan: *Not.* gruan: *Icel.* grænn] GREEN, *flourishing;* viridis, virens:—Sæte ofer þæt grene hig, *Mk.* 6, 39. Grene gærs, *Cot.* 32. On grenum treowe, *Lk.* 23, 31. Grene tacne *with a green sign, Cd.* 157.—Gren-hæwen *green* or *azure colour, Cot.* 53.

Grenian *To become green, to flourish;* virescere:—*Bt. R.* p. 164.

Grennes, se; *f.* GREENNESS; viriditas:—*Bd.* 3, 10.

Grennian, grinnian, ic grennige; *p.* ode. *To grin, to make a face, to be angry, to grunt;* ringere:—Grenniendum welerum hleahter forð-bringan *ringenti-*

bus labiis risum proferre, Scint. 55.

Grennung, grinnung, e; *f.* GRINNING; rictus, *Som.*

Greofa, greoua *A pot;* olla:—*Cot.* 146, 173.

GREOT [*Plat.* grut, gruus *n*: *Dut.* gruis *n*: *Frs.* grjues *n*: *Ger.* grus *m*: *Not.* grieze *f*: *Old Ger.* krieze: *Dan. Swed.* grus *n*: *Icel.* griót *n*: *Wel.* grut] GRIT, *sand, dust, earth;* pulvis:—Þu scealt greot etan *thou shalt eat dust, Cd.* 43. On greot gefeoll *in terram decidit, Jdth.* 12.

Greow, *grew; p.* growan.

Grep *a furrow, burrow,* v. græp.

GRE'TAN, he grét; *p.* grette; *pp.* gretten, gegret; *v. a.* [*Plat.* gröten: *Dut.* groeten: *Frs.* groetjen: *Ger.* grüssen: *Ot.* gruozan. *Ihre* thinks from grið, the *Old Frs. Icel.* grid *peace, a wishing peace,* being the oldest manner of saluting. The common people in Sweden and Norway now salute one another with Gud's fred *the peace of God*] 1. *To* GREET, *bid welcome, salute, call out, take leave, bid farewell;* salutare. 2. *To approach, admit, touch, know carnally;* appropinquare:—1. Ongunnon hyne þus gretan, *Mk.* 15, 18. Hilde gretten *battle* [*greeted*] *hailed, Cd.* 151: *Bd.* 2, 12. 2. He ne grette hi, *Mt.* 1, 25: *Bd.* 3, 17: *Cd.* 154.

k Greting, gretung, e; *f.* A GREETING, *salutation;* salutatio:—*Lk.* 1, 29, 44.

Gretta *grit, dust,* v. greot.

Grette *knew,* v. gretan.

Greue *greve, governor,* v. gerefa.

Grewð *grows, Bt.* 34, 10, v. growan.

Griellan, grillan *To provoke, excite to anger;* provocare:—*Past.* 40, 4.

Grig-hund *a greyhound, Cot.* 173.

GRIM; *adj.* [*Old Plat. Ger.* grimm: *Not.* crimmi: *Wel. Isd.* grimmi: *Dut.* grimmig: *Frs.* grimme: *Dan.* grim *ugly,* grum *cruel: Swed.* grym: *Icel.* grimmr: *It.* grimo *morose: Sp.* grima *fright*] *Sharp, bitter, dire, savage, cruel,* GRIM, *horrible;* acer, immanis:—*Bd.* 1, 14: 3, 14: *Ors.* 1, 2. Grimmost *most cruel, Cd.* 184, v. grim.

Grima *A witch;* venefica, *Som.*

Grimena, grimenæ *A caterpillar;* eruca, bruchus:—*Ps.* 104, 32.

Grimetan *to roar, rage, Ps.* 103, 22, v. grymetan.

Grimetung *a raging, roaring,* v. grymetung.

Griming *A witchcraft;* veneficium, *Som.*

Grimlic *Grim, sharp, severe, bloody;* atrox:—*Lup.* 1, 1.

Grimman *To rage;* fremere:—*Cd.* 37.

Grimnes, se; *f.* GRIMNESS, *fierceness, cruelty;* ferocitas:—*Cot.* 1.

Grimsian *To rage, to be cruel;* sævire:—*Bd.* 1, 7.

l Grimsung *Roughness;* asperitas:—*Past.* 17, 11.

Grin, gegrin, giren, girn; *pl.* grinu. A GRIN, *snare;* laqueus:—*Ps.* 34, 9: *Lk.* 21, 35.

GRINDAN, grine, he grint; *p.* grand, we grundon; *pp.* grunden, gegrunden [*Plat. Dut.* gruizen *to bruise: Frs.* grunen, grusen *to grind in small pieces: Dan.* gryned *gritty.* It appears to be allied to *A.-S.* rendan, hrendan: *Ir.* rannan, rannaim: *Wel.* rhannu: *Bret.* ranna *to divide: Dan.* gryned signifies *grit, groats* or *gritty,* grytte *to grind* or *bruise by a mill*] *To* GRIND, *bruise, gnash;* molere:—Twa beoð æt cwyrne grindende, *Mt.* 24, 41. Hi grundon mid toðum heora, *Ps.* 34, 19.

Grindel, es; *m. A hurdle, lattice-work, grating;* crates:—Geslægene grindlas greate *forged large gratings, Cd.* 19.

Grindere *A grinder;* molitor, *Som.*

Grind-toðas *grinding teeth, the grinders, Som.*

Grinnian *to grin,* v. grennian.

Grinu, grionu *More greedily;* avidius:—*R.* 79: also, *a colour;* color, *Cot.* 79.

Griopan *to lay hold of,* v. gripan.

Griosn *A pebble stone;* calculus:—*Prov.* 20.

Gripa, gripe, gegrip, grap, an; *m.* [*Plat. Dut.* greep *f*: *Frs.* gryp, greep: *Ger.* griff *m*: *Dan.* greeb, greb *c*: *Swed.* grepe *m*: *Icel.* greip *f.*] A GRIPE, *grasp, laying hold of, a handful;* manipulus:—Berende gripan heora, *Ps.* 125, 8. Se gripe þære hand *the gripe of the hand, R.* 72.

Gripan, gegripan, he gripð; *p.* gráp, we gripon; *pp.* gripen; *v. a.* [*Plat.* grapsen, gripen: *Dut.* grypen: *Ger.* greifen: *Ker.* criffan: *Ot.* greipon: *Not.* greiffon: *Wil.* griphen: *Dan.* gribe: *Frs. Swed.* gripa: *Icel.* greipa: *Grk.* γριπευειν, γριπιζειν: *Heb.* גרף grp *to wrap, gripe,* אגרף agrp *what is wrapped together, a fist, gripe*] *To* GRIPE, *grasp, seize, lay hold of, apprehend;* rapere:—Syrwð þat he gripe þearfan, *Ps.* 9, 22. Gripað lare, *Ps.* 2, 12. Ic gegripen beo, *Ps.* 17, 31.

m Gripennis *Captivity;* captivitas, *Som.*

Grislic, agrisenlic, angrislic; *adj.* GRISLY, *horrible, dreadful, horrid;* horridus:—*Bd.* 5, 2: *Ps.* 88, 8.

Grist *grist, a grinding;* molitura:—*R.* 50, v. gryt.

Grist-bitan *to gnash the teeth.*

Grist-bitung *a gnashing of teeth, a raging.*

Gristle GRISTLE; cartilago:—*R.* 72.—Gristl-ban *gristle bone.*

Gristra *Belonging to corn, a baker;* cerealis, pistor:—*R.* 50.

GRID [*Old Frs.* grid *f*: *Icel.* grid *n*: *Chau.* grith *peace*] *Peace;* pax:—*L. Cnut. eccl.* 2: *Chr.* 1004.—Grið-brec, grið-brice *a breaking of peace, L. Cnut. eccl.* 14.

Griðian, gegriðian; *p.* ode; *pp.* od. 1. *To make peace,* or *a treaty;* pacificare. 2. *To defend, protect;* tueri:—1. Griðede mid þone here *he made peace with the army, Chr.* 1016. 2. *Chr.* 1093: *L. Cnut. eccl.* 2, 4.

Griðleás *Peaceless, without peace* or *protection;* pacis expers:—*Lup.* 1, 5.

Gritta *Grit, bran;* furfur:—*Elf. gr.* 9, 22.

Groen *green, C. R. Lk.* 23, 31, v. grene.

Groetan *to greet;* groeting *a greeting,* v. gretan, greting.

Grof *carved,* v. grafan.

Grom, grum *fierce, Cd.* 97, v. gram, grim.

Grome; *adv. Fiercely, furiously;* furiose:—*Cd.* 64.

Gropian *to grope, Elf. gr.* 24, v. grapian.

n Grornað *grieves,* for gnornað, v. gnornian.

Grot [greot *dust*] *A particle, an atom;* particula:—Nan grot rihtwisnesse *no particle of wisdom, Bt.* 35, 1. Nan grot andgites *no particle of sense, Bt.* 41, 5.

Groue *a grove,* v. græf.

GROWAN, gegrowan, agrowan, he gréwð; *p.* greow, we greowun; *pp.* grówen [*Plat.* groien, grojen: *Dut.* groeyen: *Dan.* groe *v. n*: *Swed.* gro *v. n*: *Icel.* gróa] *To* GROW, *increase, spring, sprout, spring up;* crescere:—Þat sæd growe, *Mk.* 4, 27: *Elf. ep.* p. 28, 84. Greowan þa land and blostmodan *the fields grew and blossomed, Bd.* 4, 3: *Gen.* 1, 11.

Grownes, se; *f. Growth, increase, a germ, flower, herb;* incrementum, germen:—*Bd.* 3, 23.

1 Grimetan to roar Th. An v grymetan

Grim-lic Cruel; sævus Beo K 607

Grimme Cruelly sæviter Beo K 6020

3 Grim-spring a malignant ulcer, a bile; chironium ulcus Som

Gripend, es; m A griper, seizer; captor Som

2 Gripennes, gripnes, se; f captivity &c m

3 Grisle, gristle Som v gristle

Grist-bitian to gnash with the teeth Th. an

5 Grið, es; (m?) peace &c. Th. Sax n

Grillan to provoke Grim II 58, 9 v grillan

2)

3 Greótan to lament mourn; lamentari Beo K 2684 v grætan

6 Groepe a privy, ditch; latrina Som v grep

Gron-wisc the herb Stork-bill; Jacus Mastorius Som

4 Great-wyrt an enula campana Som v the great-wyrt

[gegrip]

Grípa, an; m A gripe handful; manipulus, Ps. 105, 8

Gripe, gripes; es m A gripe taking hold of; arrepto Beo K 2289

Grim-helm, esim. A grim or masked helmet, helmet, visor; larva (Beo K 666) Cd 151, Th p 188, 27: 160 Th p 198, 29 Grim II 499, 26

5 Gripe covetous, greedy; avidus Som

6 Gripode wrinkled Som v gerifod Lye ge-rifled

7 Gripull apt to take, receive & hold, holding fast; capax, tenax Som

~~Gryrlic Beo. v gryrelic~~

2 Grystlic grisly, horrible ~~Som~~ v gristle

3 Grystle gristle ~~Ben~~ gristle

1 Grim grim, dire v. grim

2 Grim-heort grim or stern hearted Beo 127 K 3362. Grim II 657, 17

3 ~~Grund-buend es m ground inhabiting, an inhabitant Beo K 2005~~

derius

1 Gryð & peace v grið &c

Grydian to pacify

~~Th~~ an v griðian

~~Grund-bedd ...~~

Gud-searu, e f war-accoutrements; militaris armatura Beo K 2416

Gud-sele battle hall Beo K 880

Gud-sweord, es; n a war sword Beo K 4303

Gylpan gloried, boasted. Perf. of gilpan

Gymeleas ... to forget; oblivisci Ben

Grund-weallan to lay a foundation, to found

es; m snare

11 Gryn ~~...~~ Som Beo K ~~...~~ 1853 v grin

4 Grund-hyrde, es m an abyss keeper Beo K 4268

Grund-stanas ground stones, rubbish; rudera Som

Grund-wyrm a part of the earth Cod Ex 86, 17

Gut, tes; m the gut, in pl. bowels, viscera; vet. sinus, a ... viscerum receptacula Som B. 178

7

Gum-feða; an, m a troop; turma Beo K 2802

Gum-man a famous man, a man Beo K 2050

Grund-sewelige the groundsel; senecio Som Grim II 456, 13

8

Grund-wyrgen, ne f a sea wolf, siren, monstrum maris Beo 115 Grim II 456, 15 K 3036

1 Gyfu gumena byð gleng liberality is men's ornament Hickes Thes I 135, 13.

a war maiden, soldier

Gud-beorn es; m hero Beo K 626

Gud-deað a war death, mors Beo 168

~~Gud-fana a military standard~~

Grymman to roar v grimman

Gryre-geatwe, an f terrific apparatus, warlike apparatus Beo K 645

a horrid guest

Gryre-gæst monstrum Beo K 5116

Gryre-leoð a terrifying song Beo K 1565

a dreadful sound

17 Gryre-seo ... horrendus Grim II. 456, 21 Beo K 2923

Gum-cyst (cystes magnificence) bounty, liberality; munificentia Beo K 2971 Cd 85, Th 106, 10

Gum-dream human joy, life; gaudium vita Beo 184 K 2934

Gum-stol es; m a throne, thrones Beo K 3900

~~Gud-floga war-flier~~

Gud-floga, an a war flying animal, a dragon draco Beo K

Gud-leod es; m war song, cantilena Beo K 3043

11 Gud-rinc es; m a warrior, a hero Beo K

Gud-rof war famous Beo K 1209

Gud-scearu

15 Gudfreo eager for battle

Gud-helm, es; m war helmet Beo K 5946

Gud-horn a war horn Beo K 2863

2460

Grunan. 1. *To consider, ruminate;* ruminare. 2. *To grunt;* grunnire:—1. *Scint.* 12. 2. *Elf. gr.* 22.

GRU'ND, es; *m.* [*Plat. Ger. Dan. Swed.* grund *m*: *Not.* grund: *Dut.* grond *m*: *Frs.* gruwn *c*: *Russ.* grunt] GROUND, *earth, foundation, depth, the deep, abyss;* solum, fundus:—Grundas *fundi, Cot.* 83. On sæs grund, *Mt.* 18, 6. On þam grundum *in profundis, Bd.* 5, 14: *Ps.* 129, 1: *Lk.* 8, 31: *Ps.* 68, 2: *Cd.* 5: 18.

Grunden *ground; pp. of* grindan.

Grunde-swelge, -swelige, -swilige, -swulie. GROUNDSELL; senecio:—*Herbal.* 77.

Grundleás, grundleáslic GROUNDLESS, *bottomless, boundless, immense, unbounded, interminable, endless;* fundo carens, immensus:—*Bt.* 7, 4: *Past.* 53, 6.

Grundlinga, grundlunge; *adv. From the bottom, ground* or *root;* funditus:—*Elf. gr.* 38, *Som.*

°Grundsopa *Gristle;* cartilago:—*Cot.* 32, *Som.*

Grundweall, es; *m. A ground-wall, foundation;* fundamentum:—*Lk.* 6, 48, 49. Grundweallas, *Ps.* 17, 9, 17.

Grund-welan *earth's riches, Cd.* 46.

Grundwong *a region, country, Beo.* 35.

Grut. 1. *Meal of wheat* or *barley* GROUT; far. 2. *Wort, new ale;* condimentum cerevisiæ. 3. A GROT, *dungeon, abyss;* abyssus:—1. *Cot.* 93. 2. *Som.* 3. *Som.*, v. gryt.

Grymetan, grimetan; *p.* ede, ode. *To roar, rage, clash, grunt, cry out;* fremere:—Forhwon grymetydon *quare fremuerunt, C. T. Ps.* 2, 1. Eaforas grymetedon *boars grunted, Bt.* 38, 1. Grymetode, *Cd.* 162.

Grymetung, grimetung, e; *f. A murmuring, fretting, roaring;* murmur, fremitus:—*Cot.* 134.

Grymme; *adv. Bitterly;* acerbe:—*Cd.* 4.

Grynd *an abyss, Cd.* 220, v. grund.

Gryndan *to ground, Cot.* 68, v. agryndan.

GRYRE [*Plat.* grüsung *f*: *Ger.* graus *m*: *Dan.* grue *c*: *Pol.* groza] *Horror, terror, dread, shrieking;* horror, stridor:—Mid grimme gryre *with grim horror, Cd.* 55: *Bd.* 4, 27: *Lup.* 3, 12: 5, 7.

Gryrelic; *adj. Horrible, roaring;* horrendus:—*Cot.* 102.

Gryrende *Gnashing;* stridens.

Grystlung, e; *f. A gnashing;* stridor:—*Lk.* 13, 28.

GRYT, grytta, grut [*Plat.* grüt *f*: *Dut.* grut, gort *f*: *Frs.* grôat *n*: *Ger.* grütze *f*: *Dan.* gröd, gryn *c*: *Swed.* gryt *n.* gröt *m*: *Icel.* grión *n.*] GRIT, *fine flour, mill-dust;* furfur, pollis:—Hwæte grytta *tritici furfur, R.* 50.

Gryð *peace*, v. grið.

Grytte *A spider's web;* aranea:—*V. Ps.* 89, 10.

Gu *if*, v. gif.—Gu *formerly;* quondam:—*R. Mt.* 5, 27.

Guast *a spirit, C. Mt.* 1, 18, v. gast.

Gudæda *Old deeds;* antiqua gesta:—*Cod. Exon.* 64, a.

Gugeldoppe *a water-hen*, v. fugeldoppe.

Gugoð *a youth, L. Ps.* 70, 6, v. geoguð.

Gulde, guldon *paid, Bt.* 39, 1, v. gyldan.

Gum, prefixed to words, denotes *excellence, eminence,* as gum-cysta *choice, precious;* pretiosus:—Gum-cystum god *in wealth abundant;* rebus pretiosis abundans, *Cd.* 85.—Gum-rinc *a chieftain, prince, patriarch, Cd.* 75, *Som.*

GUMA, an; *m.* [*Ot.* goma *m.* *homo; Krist.* 1, 27, 27: *Icel.* gumi *m.* primipilus: *Wel.* gwr: *Old. Eng.* gom *a man.* In the compound *Eng.* word *bridegroom*: *Plat.* brögam: *Dut.* bruidegom: *Frs.* bredgome: *Ger.* bräutigam: *Dan.* brudgom: *Swed.* brudgum, it signifies *the bride's man.*] *A man;* vir:—Guman God wurðedon *men worshipped God, Cd.* 187, *Th.* p. 232, 14. Gumena baldor *chief of men, Cd.* 128.

Gum-cynn *Mankind;* humanum genus:—*Cd.* 64.

Gumena *of men*, v. guma.

Gumenian; p. ode. *To play, sport;* alludere:—Þa Gregorius gumenode to þam naman *tum Gregorius allusit circa nomen ejus, Nat. Greg.* p. 16, v. gamenian.

Gum-rice *a kingdom, Cd.* 180.

Gum-rinc *a brave man, a prince, leader.*

Gum-þeod *human race, Cd.* 12.

Gund *Matter, corruption;* pus:—*L. M.* 1, 4.

Gung *young, Bd.* 4, 25, v. geong.

Gungling *a youngling*, v. geongling.

Guona *wanting, C. Mt.* 19, 20, v. wana.

GUÐ [Uþr, udr *rage, the fury in battle, the highest god, Odin*: *Icel.* gudur, guwr *battle,* bellona: *Icel.* Gud *God*: *Moes.* Guth, Goth *God;* ytas, gytas *ravenous warriors, the Jutes*: O'dr *violent,* furiosus: *Icel.* Odin *the most fierce in battle,* the highest god of the Scandinavians, because he was the first and most heroic of their leaders in war. Woden *the god of war,* adored by the German nations; in other dialects godan. Gotnar *warlike, valiant men*: *Icel.* Gautr *the highest god, Odin.* The name of the Goths implies *brave warriors.* The name of *God* is justly also derived from *good;* but not after the usual mode of thinking, because he is *kind* and *beneficent;* but, because he is *furious* and *destructive.* It is a common error of etymologists to attribute to the savages, who composed our words, the ideas of a civilized age. *Good* and α-γαθ-ος are the same word. The first notion of αγαθος is that of being *quick* and *vigorous.* Αγαθοι ανδρες are *Goths,* and gotnar *stout men.* A coward was called κακος. Αριστος comes from αρης, *virtus* from *vis.* When bravery in battle was the first of virtues, and cowardice the meanest of vices, evil and good were indicated by words implying these notions. The intrepid man alone was deemed worthy to be obeyed as judge or commander, and adored as God. The Persians give a further proof of my assertion, for خدا Choda is not only *God,* but *a lord, commander. H.*] *War, battle, fight;* bellum:—*Jdth.* 11: *Bt. R.* p. 150. Guðe *in battle, Cd.* 94.—Guð-bil *a war-bil, a sword, Beo.* 35.—Guð-bord *a warlike board, a shield, Cd.* 128.—Guð-byrne *a coat of mail, Beo.* 5.—Guð-cyning *a warlike king, Cd.* 97.—Guð-cyste *a war-tribe, Cd.* 160.—Guð-fana, guð-fona *a war-vane, a standard, Ors.* 4, 1.—Guð-flan *a war-dart, Cd.* 95.—Guð-freca *a warrior, Beo.* 34.—Guð-gemot *war-mote* or *assembly, Cd.* 95.—Guð-gewædu *war-garments, Beo.* 3.—Guð-hafoc *a war-hawk, a kite.*—Guð-herge *a hostile band, Cd.* 92.—Guð-lac *warfare.*—Guð-myrce *hostile frontier, Cd.* 145.—Guð-plega *war-sport, war, Cod. Ex.* 16, a. 11.—Guð-ræs *a warlike attack, Beo.* 34.—Guth-sceorp *war-clothing, Jdth.* 12.—Guð-searo *arms, armour, Beo.* 3.—Guð-spell *war-tidings, Cd.* 97.—Guð-þræc *war-force, Cd.* 93.—Guð-þreat *a war-host, Cd.* 151.—

Guð-weard *a war-guard.* —Guð-wiga *a warrior, Beo.* 28. —Guð-win *battle, Beo.* 37.

Guton *shed,* v. geotan.

Gycel-stan *Ice-stones, hail;* crystallus:—*L. Ps.* 147, 6.

Gyd, ged, gid, des; [v. geddian *to sing*] *A song, verse, elegy, proverb, parable;* cantilena:—*Bd.* 3, 12, *S.* p. 537, 27, 30: *Bt. R.* p. 152.

Gyddian; *p.* ode. *To sing, Cd.* 97, v. geddian.

Gyddigan, hi gyddedon *to be giddy, troubled,* v. geddian.

Gydene; *f. A goddess;* dea:—Sceolde bion gydene *should be a goddess, Bt.* 38, 1, *Card.* p. 300, 20: 35, 6.

Gydenlic *Nunlike, vestal;* vestalis:—*Cot.* 179.

Gyf *if, Jn.* 3, 12, v. gif.

Gyfa *A giver, bestower;* dator:—*Chr.* 1038.

Gyfe *grace, a gift, Lk.* 1, 30; *ac. of* gifu.

Gyfl *Fruit;* fructus:—*Cod. Exon.* 45, a.

Gyfta, gifta; *no sing. pl. nom. g. ac.* a; *d.* um, on, an; *f:* seo gyft, is also found. *The price of a woman, nuptials, dowry, marriage;* nuptiæ:—Þe macode hys suna gyfta, *Mt.* 22, 2. Þas gifta synt gearwe, v. 8. To þam giftum, v. 3, 24, 38. Be þære giftan mæðe *according to the dowry of a virgin, Ex.* 22, 17. Gif seo gyft forð ne cume *if the dowry come not forth, L. In.* 31. ¶ Gyft-hus *a wedding or feasting-room, Mt.* 22, 10.—Gyft-leoð *a marriage song.*—Gyft-lic *nuptial, belonging to a marriage, Mt.* 22, 12.

Gyftigean *To give in marriage;* nuptum dare:—*Mk.* 12, 25.

Gyfu *a gift, grace, Lk.* 2, 40, v. gifu.

Gyfung, e; *f. A consent;* consensus:—*Bd.* 1, 27.

Gyhð *a refuge, Cd.* 169, v. giht.

Gyl *shine;* gyl sunne *let the sun shine, Hymn.*

Gylað, gelamp *Happened;* attigisset:—*Cot.* 184.

Gyld *a payment, turn, place, fold, as two-fold, an idol,* v. gild.

Gylda *a companion,* v. gegylda.

Gyldan, gildan, geldan, gegyldan, he gylt; *p.* geald, we guldon; *pp.* golden; *v. a. To pay, restore, requite, give, render,* YIELD, *worship;* reddere:—Gylde þæm Cynge *pay to the king, L. Ethel.* 1, *W.* p. 103, 32. He ne meahte mine gife gyldan *he could not my gift repay, Cd.* 22, *Th.* p. 27, 5: 141, *Th.* p. 176, 31. Gilde twifealdon, *Ex.* 22, 9, 12. Þat he hit gilde, *Ex.* 14: *Bt.* 40, 7. Ne gylt he gafol, *Mt.* 17, 24. Ælc gulde *each should render, Bt.* 39, 1, *Card.* p. 321, 15. Geld þæt þu aht to geldanne, *C. Mt.* 20, 8. Gyldan sceolde *must worship, Cd.* 183, *Th.* p. 229, 5.

Gylden, gilden, gegyld; *def.* se gyldena, gyldna; *adj. Golden, gilded;* aureus:—Þær is geat gylden *there is a golden gate, Cd.* 227, *Th.* p. 305, 19. An gylden celf, *Ex.* 32, 8. Se gyldna þræd *the golden thread, Cot.* 26. To þam gyldnan gylde *to the golden idol, Cd.* 182, *Th.* p. 228, 18. Læfr gylden *leaf-gold, R.* 58: *Lev.* 8, 9.

Gylding-wecg *A gold mine, a vein of gold;* aurifodina:—*Cot.* 16, 167, *Som.*

Gyld-sester *A measure belonging to a gild;* sextarius:—*Mon. Angl. I.* 277.

Gyllan, giellan; *p.* gylede [*Plat. Dut.* gillen *shriek: Dut.* galmen *to sound: Frs.* galljen: *Ger.* gällen *to sound: Ger.* gal, gall *a sound: Ker.* calm: *Ot.* galm: *Icel.* gella] *To make a harsh noise, to* YELL, *roar, shriek, scream, chirp;* stridere, fremere:—Gesceod gyllende gryre *shed yelling horror, Cd.* 167, *Th.* p. 208. Ic gielle swa hafoc *I shriek as a hawk, Cod. Ex.* 106. b. Gylleð græg-hama *a cricket chirps, Hickes's Thes.* p. 192.

Gylm *a handful,* v. gilm.

Gylp *pride, glory, Cd.* 4, v. gilp.

Gylp, and its compounds, v. gilp, &c.

Gylt, es; *m.* [*Dan.* gjæld *debitum: Icel.* giald *n: Chalta,* in the Salic laws, signifies *a fine, amercement.* Gelte has the same meaning in the Schwabenspiegel, or laws of Swabia. The *Ger.* gelten, in earlier times, not only signified *to pay,* but when there was no restitution, to be obliged to submit oneself to punishment] GUILT, *crime, sin, fault, debt;* delictum:—Forgyf us ure gyltas, *Mt.* 6, 12: *Ex.* 32, 35: *Deut.* 9, 21: *Ps.* 18, 13. Debitum, *Mt.* 18, 27, 32.

Gylt *pays, Mt.* 17, 24, v. gyldan.

Gyltend, es; *m. A debtor, an offender;* debitor:—*Mt.* 6, 12.

Gylte GELT, *gelded;* castratus, *Som.*

Gyltig; *adj.* GUILTY; reus:—*Mt.* 23, 18.

Gyltlic-spræce *blasphemy, Mt.* 26, 65.

Gym *a gem,* v. gim.

GYMAN, begyman, begiman; *p.* gymde; *pp.* gymed, gegymed. 1. *To take care of, attend, regard, observe, preserve, keep;* curare. 2. *To govern, rule;* regere:—1. Ic gyme min wedd, *Lev.* 26, 42, 43. Arna ne gymden *honorem non curarunt, Cd.* 113: *Mt.* 16, 6. Hi gymdon *they observed, Mk.* 3, 2: *Lk.* 6, 7. 2. Satan het hine gyman *Satan bade him rule, Cd.* 18, *Th.* p. 22, 25, 31: *Lk.* 3, 1. ¶ Don gyman *to have care, to regard, Ors.* 3, 9, *Bar.* p. 115, 20.

Gymeleás; *adj. Careless, negligent, wandering, straying;* negligens:—Gymeleas feoh *straying cattle, L. Eccl. Elf.* 42.

Gymeleasian *To neglect, be careless, despise;* negligere:—*Bd.* 4, 27.

Gymeleaslice, gemeleaslice; *adv. Carelessly;* negligenter:—*R. Ben.* 44.

Gymeleasnys, se; *f. Carelessness;* negligentia:—*Bd.* 3, 27.

Gymeleást, gimelist, gemelest; *f. Carelessness, negligence;* negligentia:—*Bd.* 3, 17: *Bt.* 5, 1.

Gymen, gyming, gemen; *f. Care, heed, solicitude, diligence, superintendence;* cura:—Gymene do se Abbod *curam gerit abbas, R. Ben. interl.* 27: *Chr.* 26: *Bd.* 2, 1.

Gymend, es; *m. A governor;* gubernator:—*Scint.* 32.

Gymung *a marriage, Bd.* 3, 24, v. giming.

GYNAN *To* GAIN; lucrari:—*W. B.* p. 398.

Gynd *beyond, L. Edm.* v. geond.

Gyngra *younger,* v. geong.

Gynian, ginian; *p.* ode; *pp.* od. [*Plat.* janen: *Dut.* geeuwen: *Ger.* gähnen: *Old Ger.* ginon, geinon: *Icel.* gin, gina.—gin *an opening*] *To* YAWN, *gape, chatter;* hiare:—*Elf. gr.* 24: *Ors.* 3, 13. Gyniendum muðe *with open mouth, Dial.* 2, 25.

Gynnan [*from* gan *to go,* v. beginnan] *To begin;* incipere:—*Scint.* 22.

Gypes-wic [*Dunel.* Gippeswic: *Gerv.* Gipeswich: *Kni.* Ypeswich.—The river Gipping *from* geap *winding,* wic *a village, residence*] IPSWICH, *the chief town of Suffolk, Chr.* 591: 593.

GYR. 1. *A fir tree;* abies. 2. *A marsh;* palus:—1. Gyrtreow, *R.* 46. 2. Gyran, gyras *marshes, Lye,* v. gyrwa.

GYRD, gird, gyrda, gyrde, geard [*Dut.* gaard, *f: Frs.* gerd *f: Ger.* gerte *f: Ker. Not. Kerta. Isd.* gardea: *Ot.* gertu, garde, gurda: *Dan.* gaard *c: Swed.* gärd: *Icel.* girdi *n.*] *A staff, rod,*

...ed-sceaþa, an m ... ar enemy, BeoK 4630

Guð-geweorc, es; n battle work, BeoK 1349

~~... a shield Bat. Fins ... in war ...~~

Guð-oma, an m ... tear in the bowels ... BeoK 2164 Som v oma Ist

[illegible]

Gycenys an itch v gicenes

Gyddunge ... parabola Som song riddle, poetry th an

Gyden, e; f gydene ... f A goddess th an

Gyfan to give v gifan

Gyfetes ~~[illegible]~~ a capacity th an v gifeþas

~~Gyfu~~ a gift th ... v gifu

Gygand, es; m a giant th an v gigant

Gyldan to gild Som v gildan

~~gylden~~ ~~gelden~~ ... v gylden

(1) He sceolde gomban gyldan he must tribute pay BeoK 21

~~Gylp-georn-wan glorious Som v gilp~~

Gylp-spræc, e; f a boasting speech BeoK 4955

Gyld-ræden, e; f a guildship, society club Som

...den of a wild beast, lustrum Som

Gylian to yell, cry th an v gyllan

Gylpgeorn-wan ... striving Som

Gylpð boasts v gilp han

Gylpword a bold word th an v gilp-word

Gyltan to make or prove guilty; reum facere Som

Gyman [51a 1]

Gym-cynn gem kind, a topaz Som v gim

Guð-werig wær weary BeoK 3171

Gyfen, es; n the sea Beo ... in ... geofon

Gym-stan a precious stone Som

Gym-wyrhta a gem maker, lapidary Som v gimwyrhta

Gynd-leccincg that waterth, irrigous Som

Gyrd, e; f a yard, rod, switch th an (gird)

Gyrdel-bred writing tables, so called as hanging from the girdle; pugillares, Cot 173 Som

Gyrdel-hring, es; m a latchet, lace, garter; ligula Som

~~Gyrd clothes~~

Gyrdenlic pertaining to a guest hospitalis Som

Gyst-hus a guest room an inn Som v gest-hus

~~Gyrnendlice desirable; desiderabilis Som v geornlice~~

Gyrnian to yearn Som ~~gyrnan~~, ~~geornian~~

Gyrwe-fen

Gystel cistus, herba sic dicta Som

Gysel a hostage Th an v gisel

Gyst-ern es; n a guest chamber Th an v ~~gyst~~ gestærn

Gyst-sal es; n a guest saloon or hall Judith 10 Th an v gyst-sele

Hain count, hold, detain Th an

2 hacele hacele
1 Hacele Th an, f a garment Gm II 118, 1

~~Gystran yesterday; pertaining to yesterday; Som~~

~~nius 2 Gystran-niht yester night, v Beow 2667 gyrstan~~

~~Gyd-corn the herb spurge; lacteris Som gyd-corn~~

Gyd-rife the gum of the herb ~~la~~ laserwort; laser Som

Posted the Index Feby 28th 1838

measure, YARD, *rood;* virga:—Næbbe ge gescy ne gyrde, *Mt.* 10, 10. Þæt næs ne an gyrde landes *that there was not a rood of land, Chr.* 1085, *Ing.* p. 289, 31: *Ex.* 4, 2, 4. Gyrde-landes *yard land, measured land;* virgata terræ, *L. In.* 67, *W.* p.25, 15, 16.—Gyrdwite *pain bringing rod, Cd.* 143.

v Gyrdan, he gyrt; *p.* gyrde; *pp.* gyrded [*Plat. Dut.* gorden: *Ger.* gürten: *Ot.* gurten: *Ker.* curtan: *Moes.* gaurdan: *Dan.* giorde: *Swed.* gjorda: *Icel.* girda] *To* GIRD, *bind round;* cingere:—Þu gyrdest þe, *Jn.* 21, 18. Gyrde sweorde *girded with a sword, Cd.* 138: *Lev.* 8, 7. Oþer þe gyrt *another shall gird thee, Jn.* 21, 18.

Gyrdel, gyrdels, gerdels [*Plat. Dut.* gordel *m*: *Frs.* gerdel *f. Ger.* gürtel *m*: *Dan.* giord *c*: *Swed.* gjord *f*: *Icel.* girding *f.*] A GIRDLE, *belt, purse;* cingulum:—*Elf. gr.* 19: *Ps.* 108, 18. Ne feoh on hyra gyrdlum, *Mk.* 6, 8, v. belt.

Gyrian; *p.* gyrede. *To prepare, Ps.* 64, 7, v. gearwian.

Gyrla *clothing, garment,* v. gegerela.

Gyrmian *To roar;* rugire:—*L. Ps.* 37, 8.

Gyrnan; *p.* de. *To yearn, desire, require, Mk.* 11, 24, v. geornian.

Gyrne *diligently, Chr.* 1083, v. georne.

Gyrnes *industry, labour, desire, Bd.* 3, 11, v. geornes.

Gyrning *a yearning, desire, endeavour, Ps.* 9, 41, v. geornung.

Gyrran *to chatter, Elf. gr.* 36, v. girran.

Gyrretynde *Roaring;* rugiens:—*L. Ps.* 21, 11.

Gyrstan-dæg, gestran-dæg [*Plat. Dut.* gisteren: *Ot.* gesteren: *Ger.* gestern: *Moes.* gistradagis: *Lat.* hesternus] YESTERDAY, heri:—*Jn.* 4, 52.

w Gyrwa, gyrwe, gyrwe fenn. *A marsh, moor, fen;* palus, locus palustris:—*Elf. gr.* 9, 33. Gyrwalond *marshy land, Bd.* 4, 6.—Gyrwa mægð *a country of marshes,* Gyrviorum, *sive palustrium provincia, Bd.* 3, 20.—Girvii, so called from gyr, *a marsh.*

Gyrwan *to prepare,* v. gearwian.

Gyse *yes, Mt.* 17, 25, v. gese.

Gyst *a guest,* v. gest.

Gysternlic-dæg *yesterday,* v. gyrstan-dæg.

Gystigan *To lodge, to abide as a guest;* hospitari:—*Scint.* 47.

Gyst-sele *a guest-hall, Cd.* 169.

Gyt *ye, you;* vos:—*Mt.* 5, 19.

GYT, get, geot; *adv.* [*Grk.* ἔτι *yet,* from ἔτει the *d.* of ἔτος *a year: Heb.* עוד oud, changed to out, yt, from עד od, *a continuance, duration, beyond, further;* or from giht, gyte *time,* as in the compound gebed-giht *bed-time*] YET, *hitherto, moreover, still, as yet;* adhuc:—Hys tid ne com þa gyt, *Jn.* 7, 30. Gyt ma *yet more.* Gyt swiðor *yet rather, Elf. gr.*

Gyt *pours out;* git *poured out, Lev.* 1, 16, v. geotan.

Gytan *to get,* v. getan.

Gyte, es; *m.* [gyt *pours out,* from geotan] *An overflowing, a shedding;* inundatio:—Blod gyte *bloodshed, Cd.* 75. On þæra witegyna blodes gyte, *Mt.* 23, 30.

Gytenes *a getting, obtaining knowledge, Bd.* 4, 23, v. getenys.

Gyte-sal *an apartment,* v. giht.

Gyte-stream *A catarrh;* rheuma:—*R.* 105.

Gytsere, es; *m. A miser, a rapacious man;* avarus:—Gitsunga þæs gitseres *desires of the miser, Bt.* 16, 3, *Card.* 86, 9. Gytseras, *L. Cnut. pol.* 74.

Gytsian *To covet, desire, lust after;* concupiscere:—Gytsiende, gytsigende *coveting, Cd.* 42: *Ps.* 100, 6: *Bt.* 26, 2: *Ps.* 61, 10.

Gytsung, gitsung, e; *f. A desire, craving, lust, covetousness, avarice, rapacity, usury;* concupiscentia:—Unriht gytsung, *V. Ps.* 118, 36. He ne mæg þa grundleasan gitsunga afyllan *he cannot the boundless desires fill, Bt.* 16, 3, *Card.* 86, 8: 7, 3.

H

x H is sometimes used for g; v. 27n.

To monosyllables ending in a vowel, the *Anglo-Saxons* sometimes add an *h*, corresponding to the *Icel.* and *Swed. g*; as, feoh *money, Icel.* fé: slóh *he beat, Icel.* sló, slóg: *Swed. Dan.* slog; seah *he saw, Icel.* sá, ság: *Swed.* sag: *Rask's Gram.*

Ha ha, he he. *An interjection of laughter;* interjectio ridentis, *Som.*

Haal-stan *a fire-stone, a crust,* v. hal-stan.

Haam *a long linen vesture which priests wore, a surplice,* v. hama.

HABBAN, hæbban, ic habbe, hæbbe, þu hæfst, hafast, he hæfð, hafað, we habbað, hafiað; *p.* hæfde, we hæfdon; *imp.* hafa, habbað, habbe ge; *pp.* hæfed, hæfd; *v. a.* [*Plat. Dut.* hebben: *Frs.* habbe, ha: *Ger. Ker.* haben: *Moes.* haban: *Dan.* have: *Swed.* hafwa: *Icel.* hafa] *To* HAVE; habere, tenere:—Þat hi hine habban sceoldon *that they should have him, Bt.* 3, 1. Foxas habbað holu, *Mt.* 8, 20. Ic þis leoð asungen hæfde *I had sung this lay, Bt.* 3, 1. Ic hæbbe fordon, *Ex.* 10, 2. Hig habbað him gegoten an gylden celf, *Ex.* 32, 8.

Haccan; *pp.* gehaccod [*Plat. Dut.* hakken: *Ger.* hacken: *Dan.* hacke: *Swed.* hacka: *Frs.* hacher.—acas *an axe,* v. æx] *To* HACK, *cut, hash;* concidere:—*Cot.* 93, *Lye.*

Hacela, hacele, hæcile, hæcla. 1. *A habit for a man of war, a cloak, mantle;* chlamys, pallium, sagum. 2. *A coat, cassock;* lacerna. 3. *An under garment, a shirt;* subucula, capsula:—1. *R.* 65: *Ors.* 5, 10. 2. Mæsse hacele *a mass* or *monk's garment.* Preostes hacele *or* hæcla *a priest's garment, Cot.* 126. 3. *Cot.* 39: 164, *Som.*

Hacine *Pusta, R.* 33.

y Hacod, es; *m.* [*Plat.* heket *m*: *Ger.* hecht *m*: *Mons.* hæcid: *Lat. mid.* hacedus] *A pike, mullet, hakot,* HAKEDS, *a large sort of pike;* lucius piscis:—*Mugil: Elf. gl.* 12.

HA'D, es; *m.* [*Ger.* haupt *n. a head, person*: *Dut.* hoofd *n. Frs.* haved, haud *n*: *Dan.* hoved *c*: *Swed.* hufwud *n*: *Icel.* höfud *n. a head*: *Icel.* hæd *f. height.—Plat.* hood *m. a hat, degree, dignity,* v. hæt, for the other cognate words] 1. *A person, form, sex;* persona, sexus. 2. *Habit, dress;* habitus. 3. *State, order, degree;* ordo, gradus:—1. Þu ne besceawast hanes mannes had, *Mt.* 22, 16. Ana God on hadum efnespedelicum *one God in three persons;* unus Deus in tribus subsistentiis, *Bd.* 4, 17. Æghwæðeres hades *of both sexes;* utriusque sexus, *Bd.* 7. 2. Þone æfestnesse had underfeng *took the habit of religion;* religionis habitum suscepit, *Bd.* 4, 11. 3. Had oferhogedon halgan lifes *despised a state of holy life, Cd.* 188. Butan halgum hadum *out of holy orders, Bd.* 1, 27: *Resp.* 1. Biscopes oððe oþera hada *a bishop's* or *other degrees, Bd.* 2, 5. Hades man *a man of degree* or *orders, Elf. gr.* 11. Heahlic had *highest degree, L. Const.* p. 110. ¶ Had-bote *a recompence for violation of holy orders.*—Had-breca *a violator of holy orders.*—Had-bryce *a violation of holy orders.*—Had-grið *peace of holy orders, L. Const.* p. 111.

-hád [*Plat. Dan.* hed: *Dut.* heid: *Ger.* heit, keit] *Head, hood.* At the end of words it denotes, *the person, form, sex, quality, state, condition:*—Werhád, manhád *manhood.* Wifhád *womanhood.* Cildhád *childhood.* Weoroldhád *secular state* or *habit.* Broðorhád *brotherhood.* Preosthád *priesthood.*

a Haderung, e; *f.* [had *a person,* arung *an honouring*] *The respect of persons;* personarum acceptio, *Som.*

Hadian, gehadian, ic hadige; *p.* ode; *pp.* ed; *v. a. To ordain, consecrate, give holy orders;* ordinare:—Bisceopas hadian *to consecrate bishops, Bd.* 2, 8.

Hading, hadung, e; *f. Ordaining, consecration;* ordinatio:—*Nat. Greg.* p. 22.

Hador *A convexity, an arch;* arcus:—Under heofones hador *under heaven's arch, Beo.* 6, 83.

Hador, hadre; *sup.* hadrost; *adj.* [*Ger.* heiter: *Old Ger.* hedro: *Icel.* heidr: *Moes.* haize *light*] *Clear, bright;* serenus:—On hadrum heofone *in serene sky, Bt.* 9.

Hadrian *To restrain;* angustare, *Lye.*

Had-swæpe *a bridemaid,* v. heorð, &c.

Hæbban *to have, move,* v. habban.

Hæbbendlic *Fit, handsome, able;* habilis:—*Elf. gr.* 9, 28.

Hæbbenga *A restraining;* cohibitio, *Som.*

Hæbern *A crab, scorpion;* nepa, cancer, *Som.*

Hæca *A bar* or *bolt of a door, a* HATCH; pessulus, *Som.*

Hæcce *A cloak;* pallium:—*Chr.* 1070.

Hæccla, hæcla, hæcile *a cloak, mantle, shirt,* v. hacela.

Hæced, hæcid, *a pike,* v. hacod.

Hæcewoll *A collector;* exactor:—*R.* 8.

Hædern *A cellar, buttery;* cellarium, *Som.*

a Hæfd *head,* v. heafod.

Hæfde *had; p. of* habban.

Hæfe [*Dut.* hef, heffe *f. the lees: Ger.* hefen *f.*—heafian *to heave*] *Leaven;* fermentum:—*Mk.* 8, 15.

Hæfe [*Hunt. Heve*] *Heefeld* or *Heugh, in Northumberland,* a place where Bertfrith fought with the Picts, *Chr.* 710.

Hæfed, hæfd *had; pp. of* habban.

Hæfednes, se; *f. Abstinence;* retentio, *Som.*

Hæfeg, hæfig *heavy, Bt.* 31, 1, v. hefig.

Hæfeldan HELVETIANS; Helvetii:—*Ors.* 1, 1.

HÆFEN [*Plat. Dut.* haven *f*: *Ger.* hafen *m*: *Dan.* havn *c.*—In *Plat.* havenung, hävenung signify, *a place sheltered from wind and rain:* and the *Old Ger.* heiman *to cover*] A HAVEN; portus:—*Chr.* 1031.

Hæfen-blæte, hæfen-bleat *a haven screamer, a seagull, hawk.*

Hæfenleás *Poor, needy;* inops:—*L. Ps.* 11, 5.

Hæfen-least *Poverty, want;* necessitas:—*L. Ps.* 48, 27.

HÆFER; *g.* hæferes, hæfres; *m. A he-goat;* caper:—*Cot.* 32.

Hæfer-bite *a pair of pincers.*

Hæfer-blæte *the bleating of a goat.*

Hæfern *a crab, Cot.* 39, v. hæbern.

Hæfig *heavy,* v. hefig.

Hæfignes *heaviness,* v. hefignes.

HÆFT, es; *m.* [*Dut. Frs. Ger.* heft *n*: *Dan.* hæfte *n*: *Swed.* häfte *n*: *Icel.* hefti *n.*—*captio, captivitas,* is in *Frs.* hefte *f*: *Ger.* haft *f*: *Icel.* haft *n.*] 1. A HAFT, *handle;* manubrium. 2. *A holding, captivity, bonds;* captio. 3. *One held, a captive, slave;* captivus:—1. *Elf. gl.* 24. 2. *Ps.* 123, 5. Of hæftum *from bonds, Cd.* 225. 3. Hæftas ne willað wurðigean *captives will not worship, Cd.* 182: 187.

b Hæftan; *pp.* hæfted, hæft. *To take, Bt.* 11, 1, v. gehæftan.

Hæftedóm *Captivity;* captivitas:—*Bt. R.* p. 188.

Hæftencel, hæftincle *What may be bought;* emptitius:—*Cot.* 74.

Hæftene *Captivity, custody;* captivitas:—*Chr.* 1095.

Hæfting *A holding, seat, possession;* possessio:—*Nicod.* 27.

Hæftling, es; *m. A captive;* captivus:—Beoð hæftlingas, *Lk.* 21, 24.

Hæftned, hæftnod, hæftnyd [*Plat. Dut.* hechtnis *f*: *Frs.* hefte *f*: *Ger.* haft *f.*] *The state of being bound, custody, captivity, slavery;* captivitas, custodia:—*Ps.* 67, 19: 123, 5.

Hæftneð, hæftnoð *What takes* or *holds, a prison,* also *confinement, custody;* custodia:—Het on hæftneðe gebringan *ordered to be brought into prison, Chr.* 1095. On hæftneðe wæs *was in custody, Chr.* 1101. Hæftnoð, *Somn.* 58.

Hæftnian, hi hæftniað *To take, lay hold of, capture;* captare:—*L. Ps.* 93, 21, v. gehæftan.

Hæftnung, heftning, e; *f. A taking, captivity;* captio:—*Ps.* 13, 11: 34, 9.

Hæg *a hedge, defence,* v. hege.

HÆGEL, hagal, hagel, hagul; *g.* hægles; *m.* [*Plat. Dut. Ger. Not.* hagel *m*: *Frs.* heil *c*: *Dan.* haggel, hagel, hagl *n*: *Swed.* hagel *n*: *Icel.* hagall *m.* hagl *n.*—So called from its globular form: *Heb.* עגל ogl *round,* אגל agl *a drop, from* גל *to roll*] HAIL; grando:—Hæglas and snawas *grandines et nives, Bt.* 39, 13: *Ps.* 17, 14: 77, 52: 104, 30.

c Hægelan *To hail;* grandinare, *Lye.*

Hæges, se; *f.* [*Plat. Dut.* heks *f*: *Ger.* hexe *f*: *Frs. Dan.* hex *f*: *Swed.* hexa: *Icel.* hagr *clever*] A HAG, *witch, fury, fiend;* larva, furia, *Som.*

Hægsteald, heahsteald [*Plat.* hagestolt *m*: *Ger.* hagestolz *m*: *Old Ger.* hagastult: *Icel.* hagstædr *temperate*] 1. *A bachelor, virgin, novice;* cœlebs, tyro. 2. *One high in dignity, a youth, prince;* princeps:—1. *Cot.* 42, 45: *Scint.* 77. 2. *Cd.* 151: 160.

Hægtes *a fury, R.* 112, hæges.

Hægþorn, hagaþorn HAWTHORN; alba spina:—*R.* 48.

Hæh *A hole, den;* fovea, *Som.*

Hæh-sedlan *a pulpit,* v. heh, &c.

Hæl [*Icel.* heill *n.*] *An omen, a guess, conjecture;* omen, *Som.*

Hæl *whole, health, Lk.* 18, 9, v. hælu, *Som.*

Hælan, gehælan; *p.* hælde; *pp.* hæled; *v. a.* [hæl *health*] 1. *To* HEAL, *cure;* sanare. 2. *To preserve, keep;* servare:—

Hæcce, es; m A hook, crook, pastoral staff Th an

2 Hæcele
Grm II 118, 2 v hacele
pacele

2 Hæft-mece, es; m a hilted sword
Beo K 2913

es m
Hadorycas Lup 16, 14

Hægl-scur, es; m hail shower, grandinis imber Cod Ex 81 b v Beo gl scur

Hadelice Personally; personaliter Som

2 Hador, es, m Serenity calmness; serenitas Beo K 822

Hador serene, bright Beo K 988

Hæft, es; m captive captivus Beo gl C 182 Beogl

Hæftes; m A band; vinculum Beo

Hadre Serenely; serene Beo K 3142

Hebban To heave move, lift v hebban hebban

(1)

(1) ... here maire
hætó ... [illegible] med
[illegible] 17, 3.
Ham ... a dwelling, home, an
v ham

(1) Hæle, es; m. A brave man, a man
[illegible] K 1431

(2) Hæleð, es; m. A brave man, hero,
a man; homo larvatus,
heros, pugil, vir. Beo
K 103

(3) Hæleð-helm, es m
galea larvata id K
[illegible] 29 Bos gl

(2)

(1)

(4)

(1) Hælsera haruspices
aruspicium Ben

(3)

(5)

(2)

(3)

2 Hærlice Nobly,
generously bravely
Tha[illegible]

3 Hær-scearde
a falling off of the
hair; alopecia
L M. 1, 13
Som

(4)

1. Hælað untrume, *Mt.* 10, 8. Untrume gehælan, *Lk.* 9, 2: *Gen.* 50, 20. 2. Earm heora ne hælð hig, *Ps.* 43, 4. Sweord min ne hælð me, v. 8.

Hælan *to conceal*, *Ors.* 6, 33, v. helan.

Hæl-bære *health-bearing*, v. halbære.

Hæle *of health*, v. hælu.

Hæle, hælo, hæleð, es; *m.* [*Norse*, at hæla *to laud;* hence, halur *one praised, an eminent man*] *A brave man, chief, hero, a man;* heros, vir:—Frod hæle *a sage hero*, *Cd.* 62. Gleawferhð hæle *a sagacious man*, *Cd.* 112. Boitius se hæle hatte *the man was called Boetius;* Boetius hic vir vocatus est, *Bt. R.* p. 151: *Menol.* 98. Hæleðas heardmode *heroes firm*, *Cd.* 15: 59. Mid þam hæleðum *with the men*, *Cd.* 112.

d Hælend, es; *m.* [hælende *healing*] *The healer, saviour;* salvator:—Þu nemst hys naman Hælend. He soðlice hys folc hal gedeð fram hyra synnum, *Mt.* 1, 21.

Hælettung, e; *f.* *A greeting;* salutatio:—*C. R. Mt.* 23, 7.

Hælfter; *d.* hælftre; *pl.* hælftra [*Plat.* halter *m*: *Dut.* halster, helster *m*: *Ger.* halfter *f*: *Mon.* halftro.—hals, hæls *the neck*] HALTER, *headstall;* laqueus, capistrum:—*C. Ps.* 31, 12.

Hælga, [se. *The*] *light;* levis:—*Bt.* 37, 4.

Hælig *holy*, v. halig.

Hæling [*Ger.* heilung *f.*] *Healing;* sanatio:—*Nicod.* 10.

Hæll, hælla *a hall*, v. heal.

Hælm, halm *haulm, stubble*, v. healm.

Hælnes *Wholeness, health;* salus:—*Past.* 36, 1.

Hælo *health*, v. hælu.—*a man*, v. hæle.

Hælsere, hælsend *A soothsayer, diviner;* aruspex:—*Cot.* 190, *Som.*

Hælsian *to foretel*, *Cot.* 14, 17, v. halsian.

Hælsung *a divination*, *Cot.* 11, v. halsung.

Hælð [*Dan.* helse, hilse *f*: *Swed.* helsa *f*: *Icel.* heilsa *f.*—hælð *what healeth* or *makes hale*] HEALTH; sanitas:—*Scint.* 13.

HÆLU, hælo, hæl; *g.* hæle; *pl.* hæla; *g.* hælena; *d.* um; *f.* [*Plat. Dut. Frs. Dan.* heel *whole*: *Ger.* heil: *Moes.* hails: *Swed.* hel: *Icel.* heil *f. health*] *Healing, health, cure, safety, salvation;* salus:—Ys hæl geworden, *Lk.* 19, 9. Ic hæla gefremme, *Lk.* 13, 32. Hæle-gewit *salutis scientia*, *Lk.* 1, 77. Hæle horn *salutis cornu*, v. 69. Hælo beadan *salutem dicere*, *C. Mt.* 5, 47.

e Hæm *top*, *L. In.* 61, v. healm.

Hæman, gehæman; *p.* de; *pp.* ed [*Old Ger.* hemmen *to cover*, tegere.—hama *a cover*] *To lie with, cohabit, to commit fornication* or *adultery;* carnaliter cognoscere:—Gif ænig man hæme mid oðres wife, *Deut.* 22, 22: *L. Alf. pol.* 10: 11.

Hæmdo *A marriage;* nuptiæ:—*C. R. Jn.* 2, 1.

Hæmed *A lying with, cohabiting;* coitus:—Heora hæmed rihtan *coitus suos emendare*, *L. Cnut. pol.* 52.—Unriht-hæmed *an improper cohabiting, adultery*, *Jn.* 8, 4.—Hæmed-ceorl *a husband.*—Hæmed-gemana *marriage*, *Cot.* 129.—Hæmed-gifta *dowry*, *Cot.* 102.—Hæmed-scipe *marriage.*—Hæmed-þing *a cohabitation, propagation*, *Bt.* 34, 11.—Hæmed-þingian *to cohabit*, *L. Alf. pol.* 18.—Hæmed-wif *a matron, wife*, *Cot.* 136.

Hæmere *A fornicator;* concubinus, *Som.*

Hæmeð *A marriage, marriage-song;* hymenæus:—*R.* 9.

Hæn *a hen*, v. hen.

Hænan *To stone;* lapidare:—Wylle ge me hænan, *Jn.* 10, 32, v. hynan.

Hæn-belle, hænne-belle *hen-bell, hen-bane*, *Herbal.* 5, 1.

Hænep [*Plat.* hemp, hennep *m*: *Dut.* kennep, hennip *f*: *Ger.* hanf *m*: *Dan.* hamp *c*: *Swed.* hampa *f*: *Icel.* hanpr *m*: *Pers.* قنب kunib. Most likely the plant, and its *Greek* and *Lat.* name *cannabis*, were brought over at the same time from its native country, the East Indies] HEMP; cannabis:—*Herb.* 27, 115.

Hæn-fugul *a hen fowl*, v. hen, &c.

f Hængene *A cage, stall;* catasta, *Som.*

Hænð *want*, *Bt.* 11, 1, v. henð.

Hæp *Fit;* aptus:—*Coll. Monast.*

Hæplic *Equal*, also *a compeer;* compar:—*Cot.* 35, *Som.*

Hæpmælum *by heaps*, v. heapmælum.

HÆPS, [*Plat. Ger. Dut. Dan.* häspe, hespe *f*: *Swed.* haspa *m*: *Icel.* hespa *f*: *Dut.* gesp *a buckle*: *Lat. mid.* haspa] A HAPSE, *hasp;* sera:—*Elf. gl.* 19.

Hæpsian *To hapse, hasp, lock;* sera includere:—*Elf. gr.* 37.

Hær *here*, v. her.

HÆR, her [*Plat. Dut. Ger. Dan.* haar *n*: *Frs.* heer, her, hier *n*: *Wil.* har: *Tat.* haru: *Swed.* hår *n*: *Icel.* hár *n.*] HAIR; crinis, pilus:—Mid oluendes hærum, *Mk.* 1, 6: *Mt.* 3, 4. Nostrela hær *hair of the nostrils*, *R.* 16.

Hæra, hera, an; *m.* [*Icel.* hæra *f*: *Fr.* haire *f.*] *Cloth made of hair, sackcloth;* cilicium:—Þu slite hæran mine, *Ps.* 29, 13. Ic scrydde mid hæran, *Ps.* 34, 15. On hæran and on axan, *Mt.* 11, 21.

Hære *an army*, *Ex.* 14, 23, v. here.

Hærean-fagol *A hedge-hog;* herinaceus:—*Ps.* 103, 19.

Hærfest, hærfest, harfest, herfest; *m.* [*Plat.* harfst *m*: *Dut.* herfst *f*: *Ger.* herbst *m*: *Not.* herbist.—*Wach.* derives it from ar *yearly produce*, and fest from fon *to take*] HARVEST, *autumn;* messis:—Þat se hærfest sie welig on wæstmum *that the harvest is abundant in fruits*, *Bt.* 14, 1: 21: *Ps.* 73, 18. ¶ Hærfest-wæta *autumn wet*, *Ors.* 3, 3.—Hærfest-monað, harfest-monað *harvest-month, September*, *Elf. gr.* 9, 18.

g Hærelof *A report, common fame;* rumor, *Som.*

Hæren *Made of hair;* cilicius:—*L. Ps.* 68, 14.

Hærenes, se; *f.* 1. *Praise;* laus. 2. *An assembly, troop, army;* congregatio:—1. *Bd.* 3, 19. 2. *Som.*

Hærg *a temple*, v. hearge.

Hæriht *Hairy;* crinitus:—*Cot.* 186.

HÆRING, hæringc, herinc, es; *m.* [*Plat.* hering *m*: *Dut.* haring *m*: *Ger.* häring *m*: *Icel.* hæringr *m*: *Fr.* hareng *m.*] HERRING; halec:—Hwæt fehst þu on sæ? Hæringcas *what catchest thou in the sea? herrings*, *Colloq. Mon. MS. Cot. Tib. A.* iii. p. 60: *Elf. gl.* 12.

Hærlic *Laudable;* laudabilis:—*Bt. R.* p. 151: 161.

Hærn *A full tide, ebbing and flowing water;* æstus:—*Cot.* 81.

Hær-nædl *hair-needle.*

Hærnes *The brain;* cerebrum:—*Chr.* 1137.

Hærðan *Testiculi, pudenda virilia*, *Elf. gl.* 2: *L. Alf. pol.* 40.

Hærung HEARING; auditus, *Som.*

HÆS, [*Plat.* hete *n*: *Dut.* eisch *m*: *Ger.* geheiss *n. m*: *Old Ger.* till the 15th century hasse, haiss] *A command, behest, precept, wages;* mandatum:—Be his hlafordes hæse, *Gen.*

24, 10: *Ex.* 18, 23. Ciningesi hæs *king's behest*, *Cd.* 6: 161: *Elf. T.* 34, 2.

Hæsel *A hat*, galerus, *Som.*

Hæsere *An instructor*; præceptor, *Lye.*

HÆSL [*Plat.* hassel *f*: *Dut.* hazelaar *m*: *Ger.* hasel *f*: *Mon.* hasal: *Dan. Swed.* hassel *m*: *Icel.* hasl *n.*] HAZEL; corylus:—¶ Hæsl-nutu *hazel-nut*, *R.* 45, 47.—Hwit-hæsl *white hazel*, *R.* 45.

Hæste [*Lat.* æstus] *A raging of the sea* or *fire*; æstus maris, *vel* solis:—*Cot.* 69: 113.

Hæstingas, Hestingas, Hæstinga-ceaster, Hæstingaport [*Flor.* Hestinga: *Hunt. Hovd.* Hastings: *Lat.* Hastingæ.—hæste *a raging*] HASTINGS, *Sussex, one of the Cinque Ports*, *Chr.* 1011: 1066.

Hæswalwe *A hawk, buzzard*; astur, *Som.*

HÆT [*Plat.* hood *m*: *Dut.* hoed *m*: *Frs.* hod *m*: *Ger.* hut *m*: *Mon.* huoth: *Ker. Swabenspiegel*, hut: *Dan.* hat *c*: *Swed.* hatt *m*: *Icel.* hattr *m.*] 1. HAT; pileus. 2. *A mitre, an ornament for the head*; mitra, tiara:—1. *Ors.* 4, 10. 2. *Cot.* 131, 189.

Hæt *commands*, *Bt.* 41, 3, v. hatan.

Hæta *heat*, v. hætu.

Hætan; *p.* gehæt; *v. a.* *To heat, make hot*; calefacere:—*L. In.* 78, v. hatian.

Hætero, hæteru *Clothing, apparel*; vestitus:—Mid his hætron *cum vestitu suo*, *Ex.* 21, 4. Se hund to tær his hæteru *canis dilaceravit vestitum ejus*, *Som.*

HÆÐ [*Plat. Dut. Frs. Ger.* heide *f.*] HEATH, *thyme*; erica, thymus:—*R.* 46: 48.—¶ Hæð-berge *heath-berry*.—Hæð-feld *heath-field*, *Bt.* 16, 1.

Hæð-cole [hæt *a hat*, col *cool*] *A cover to keep the head cool, a cap, mitre, helmet*; cassis, galea:—*Cot.* 32, 36, *Som.*

Hæðe, Hæðeby, Haitabi [æt *at, by*; hæð *heath, by the heaths*; so called from the heath which abounds in the neighbourhood] HADDEBY, once called Haithaby, a town situate on the south of the small river Schle, and opposite to Schleswig. Though Haddeby is nearer the mouth of the river, it is now eclipsed by Schleswig:—Of Sciringes heale, he cwæð þæt he seglode, on fif dagan, to þæm porte þe mon hæt æt Hæðum, se stent betwuh Winedum, and Seaxum, and Angle, and hyrð in on Dene *he said that he sailed, in five days, from Sciringes to the port which they call Haddeby, which stands between the Winedæ, Saxons, and Angles, and is obedient to the Danes*, *Ors.* 1, 1, *Bar.* p. 25, 12. Þa twegen dagas ær he to Hæðum come him wæs on þæt steor-bord Gotland, and Sillende, and iglanda fela, on þæm landum eardodon Engle ær hi hider on land comon *for two days ere he came to Haddeby, on the starboard was Jutland, Sealand, and many islands, on which lands the Angles dwelt before they came hither (England)*, *Id. Bar.* p. 25, 20.

Hæðen *A Sardonian garment*; mastruca.

Hæðen, heðen [*Plat. Dut.* heiden *m*: *Ger.* heide *m*: *Ot.* heithiner: *Moes.* haithns] HEATHEN, *gentile, pagan*; ethnicus:—Þæt wif wæs hæðen, *Mk.* 7, 26: *Jn.* 12, 20: *Bd.* 1, 7.—Hæðen-cynn *a heathen kind*.—Hæðen-cyning *a heathen king*, *Cd.* 174.—Hæðendóm *heathenism*.—Hæðen-gyld *heathen-worship, idolatry*, *Elf. T.* p. 7.—Hæðen-man *a heathen man*.—Hæðen-scype, heðenscype *heathenism*, *L. Cnut. pol.* 5: *Chr.* 634.

Hæðenisc; *def.* se hæðenisca; *adj.* HEATHENISH; ethnicus: —*Ors.* 3, 3.

Hæðennes, se; *f.* HEATHENISM; gentilismus:—*Bd.* 1, 26.

Hæt-heortnys *hot-heartedness, rage*, *Ps.* 6, 1, v. hat.

Hæð-feld *a heath-field*, v. hæð.

Hæð-feld, Heat-feld [*Bd.* Hedtfeld: *Hunt.* Hatfeld: *Brom.* Hatfeld.—hæð *heath*; feld *a field*] *Bishop's* HATFIELD, *Herts.*, *Chr.* 680.

Hæðna, heðne *heathen*, v. hæðen.

Hæð-stapa *heath-stepper, an insect found among heath*, *Cod. Ex.* 87, a.

Hæðung, e; *f.* HEATING; calefactio:—*Serm. Fid. Cath.*

Hæting *calipatum*, *Cot.* 168.

Hæto *heat*, *Bt.* 33, 4, v. hætu.

Hætol *hot, furious*, v. hetol.

Hætron *clothing*, v. hætero.

Hætt *calls*, v. hatan.

Hættian *To pull the skin over a man's ears*; capillum cum cute detrahere, *Som.*

HÆTU, hæto; *g.* hæte; *d.* e; also *nom.* hæte; *g.* hætan; *f.* [*Plat. Dut.* hitte *f*: *Frs.* hjitte: *Ger.* hitze *f*: *Wil.* hizza: *Not.* hizzo: *Dan.* hede: *Swed.* hetta *f*: *Icel.* hita *f.* hiti *m*: *Heb.* חתת hte *to keep fire alive*] HEAT; calor:—Cile and hæte, *Gen.* 8, 22. On þære hætan, *Gen.* 18, 1. On þyses dæges hætan, *Id.*: *Mt.* 20, 12: *Cd.* 21: 187: *Bt.* 33, 4: 34, 10. Mid monegum hætum *cum multis fervoribus scilicet animi*, *Bd.* 2, 12.

Hæued *a head*, *Chr.* 1137, v. heafod.

Hæwen *A grey, tawny, blue* or *sky colour* or *hue*; glaucus, fulvus, cæruleus:—*Cot.* 96, *Som.*

Hafa *have*; hafast *hast*; hafað *hath*; hafedon *obtained*, v. habban.

Hafecere, es; *m.* *Hawker*; auceps:—*L. Can. Edg.* 64.

Hafen *raised*; *pp. of* hebban.

Hafenes, se; *f.* *Fermentation*; fermentatio:—*Ex.* 12, 19.

Hafenleás *poor*, v. hæfenleás.

Hafenleast *need, want*, *W. B.* p. 245, v. hæfenleast.

Hafettan *To applaud, rejoice*; plaudere:—*Elf. gr.* 28: *Ps.* 96, 8.

HAFOC, hafuc, es; *m.* [*Plat.* havik, haafk, haak *f*: *Dut.* havik, *m*: *Frs.* hauck *m*: *Ger.* habicht *m*: *Dan.* hög *m*: *Swed.* hök *m*: *Icel.* haukr *m*: *Fin.* haucka] A HAWK, *falcon, bird of prey*; accipiter:—*Menol.* 482. ¶ Hafoc-cynn *hawk-kind*, *Lev.* 11, 13.

Hafud-land *headland, a promontory.*

HAGA, hagen; *pl.* hagan [The *Ger.* hag *m*: *Swed.* hage *m.* hägn *n.* signify not only *a hedge* and *an inclosed field* or *space*, but also in earlier times *a house*] A HAY, *hedge, haw, a small quantity of inclosed land, a dwelling-house*; agellus, domus:—Nigan and XX hagena syndon *novem et viginti prædia sunt*, *Mon. Ang.* I, 258, v. hege.

Hagal, hagol, hagul *hail*, *Ps.* 17, 14, v. hægel.

Hagal-scur *hail-shower*, *M. Ps.* 104, 30.—Hagol-stan *hailstone.*

Hagan *Haws, fruit of the white thorn*; mora spinæ albæ:—*R.* 47: *Cot.* 99.

Haga-þorn *hawthorn*, v. hægþorn.

Hagian *to be at leisure*, v. onhagian.

Hagol, hagul *hail*, v. hægel.

Hagolan *To* HAIL; grandinare: —*Ors.* 3, 5.

Hagustald, Hagusteald, Hagustaldesea, Hagustaldes-ee, Hagustaldes-ham, Hagustald-ee [*Dun.* Hestaldesham, Hestaldeshige: *Ric.* Hestaldasham:

mail hood worn under the helmet

× Hafela, hafala, heafola, heafula, an n. the head caput Beo K 3227 : 2743
× the mail hood worn under the helmet, probably any head dress Beo K p 248 Glos : — Beo p 53 K 1337 : 2654 &c hafala Beo K 886. heafola 5319 : 5319.

5 × Hæte, an f heat Th An

× Hæste adj violent hot, hasty; ardens, violentus. Hence hæstne hand in a violent manner Beo K 2069 : Cd 110 Th p 146, 2

Hæðen gold heathen gold Beo K 4547 treasures Beo 170 Grein II 46. 8

× Hæste adv Furiously; violenter Cd 69 Th p 84, 11

Hæter ardens Beo 97.

1 Seo hæwene lyft the blue air Cd 166 Th p 207, 33

3 Hafenian to hold made of wood manu tollere Beo K 3146

5 × Haga, an; m Hage, es m Shaw, hedge Th. an: Beo 96

× Haga a hedge Beo v haga

8 Hagol. scur a hail shower Beo v scur

7 × heath stepper, a stag Beo K 2735 Beo 19l

Hagustald

hagu-sund, sagan-
sund-AL + 1V margin

Hali holy H apol
v haliq

háliq ol6 -haligra
* manna

(9)

Halan pascere Ben

3 Halga, an m A
saint H dn

Gerv. Hestoldesham: Kni. Exseldesham.]—Some say from heage-steald a high place; others from hægsteald a bachelor, a residence of priests] Hexham, Northumberland, Chr. 681: 685: 766: 780: 806.

l Hagu-swind, eaganswind The cheek; mala, Som.

Hál; def. se hala; adj. [hæl health] Healthy, sound, WHOLE, safe.—Used in salutation, as hail, be healthy; sanus, salvus, salvus sis:—Hwæðer hira fæder wære hal, Gen. 43, 27: Jn. 5, 9, 14: Bd. 4, 25: Mk. 2, 17. Hal wes þu Iudea cyning salvus sis tu, Judeorum rex, Mt. 27, 29: Lk. 1, 28. Hale wese ge salvi sitis vos, salvete, Mt. 28, 9. Wesað hale valete, Cot. 184. ¶ WASSAILE, wassail bowl, wæs hal be whole, healthy; sis salvus. Haldon, hal gedon to make whole, to heal; sanum reddere, Lk. 19, 10. Þin geleafa þe hale gedyde, Mk. 5, 34. Gedo me halne, Mt. 14, 30.

Hal a hole, den, Ps. 16, 13, v. hol.

Hala-ferðe a breathing-hole, L. M. 1, 1.

Halbære Health-bearing, wholesome; salutaris:—Scint. 32, 78.

Hald, halde bending, inclining, stooping, v. heald.

Haldan to hold, tame, C. Mk. 5, 4, v. healdan.

Halech holy, Chr. 890, v. halig.

Haleg holy, Mk. 13, 11, v. halig.

Haleging consecration, v. halgung.

Haletta, an; m. A hero, an eminent man; heros, vir egregius:—Ic Beda sende gretan þone leofastan cyning and halettan Ceoluulf ego Beda, mitto salutem dilectissimo regi et viro egregio Ceolwlfo, Bd. pref. Somner says halette a greeting, saluting, wishing of health: hence he would translate Ic sende gretan and halettan I send greeting and health.

m Halettan To salute, greet; salutare:—Bd. 2, 12.

Halette a greeting, saluting, v. haletta.

Halettung, e; f. A greeting, salutation; salutatio:—C. R. Mt. 23, 7.

Halewend healthful, v. halwend.

Half half, Bd. 4, 26, v. healf.

Hal-fæst qui potest sanare, R. Ben. 46.

Half-clungu half frozen or clung.

Halga holy, Mk. 1, 24, v. halig.

Halgian, gehalgian; p. ode; pp. od; v. a. [halig, halg holy] To HALLOW, consecrate, dedicate; sanctificare:—Halgian Bisceop to consecrate a bishop, Bd. 1, 27, resp. 6: Lev. 8, 12.

Halgo-land A district belonging to the province of Nordland, in Norway, lat. 66°. 40'., now written HALIGELAND or HALGELAND, Ors. 1, 1.

Halgung, gehalgung, e; f. A HALLOWING, consecration, ordination; sanctificatio:—Bd. 1, 27, resp. 6: Ex. 29, 22.

Halian to become well, v. hælan.

Halic holy, Bd. 1, 27, v. halig.

Halidóm holiness, Cat. p. 33, v. haligdóm.

Hali-ern a sacred place, sanctuary, Ex. 29, 30.

Hálig, often contracted in the cases whose terminations begin with a vowel, as in def. se hálga, seo hálge, but not when it begins with a consonant; as, haligra man of holy men [Plat. helig, hillig: Frs. helga, helick, hillig: Dut. Ger. heilig: Dan. hellig: Swed. helig: Icel. heilager.—hal sound, safe, ig] HOLY; sanctus, sacer:—Þæt halige gewrit, Jn. 17, 12. He spræc þurh his halegra witegena muð, Lk. 1, 70. Mid halgum þeowdome, L. Can. eccl. 20, W. p. 156, 5.—Halig-dag holy day.—Halig ealond holy island, Lindisfarne, in Northumberland.—Halig-Gast Holy Ghost.—Halig-monað holy month, September.—Halig-munt holy mount.—Halig-ryft the veil of the temple.—Halig-wæter holy water.

n Haligan To consecrate, to become whole; sanescere:—Bd. 4, 22, S. p. 591, 10.

Haligdóm, es; m. [dóm jurisdiction] 1. A sanctuary; sanctuarium. 2. A sacrament, sacred things, relics; res sacræ, sacramentum. 3. Holiness; sanctimonia:—1. To þæs halig domes dura, Ex. 21, 6: L. Ps. 73, 8: 77, 75. 2. Þurh haligum haligdom Drihtnes lichaman and blodes per sacrosanctum sacramentum Domini corporis et sanguinis, W. Cat. p. 79. Hwæt se haligdom is þe her on þisum halgan mynstre is quænam reliquiæ sunt quæ hic in hoc sancto monasterio sunt, Cart. Antiq. in Mon. Ang. I. 223. On þam haligdome swerian per reliquias jurare, L. Const. Ethel. p. 117, 20. 3. Som.

o Halig-monað, es; m. [Franc. uuintu-manoth, herbst-monat: Dan. fiskmanet: Swed. host-monat: Icel. addrata manudr. —halig holy, monað month] September; Septembris:—Halig-monað or harfæst-monað the holy month or harvest-month, Hic. Thes. I. p. 215. Septembres fæers September fierce, Menol. F. 331. On þæm nigoðan monðe on geare bið xxx daga, se monað hatte Leden Septembris, and on ure geþeode halig-monað, for þon þe ure yldran þa þa hi hæþene waron on þam monðe hi guldon hiora deofol geltun, Hic. Thes. I. p. 219, 37.

Halignes, halines, se; f. 1. HOLINESS, holy things; sanctitas. 2. A sacred place, sanctuary, asylum; locus sacer:—1. Lk. 1, 75: Elf. gr. 5. 2. L. Ps. 12, 17: Lup. 5. On halignysse his, Ps. 95, 6.

Haligung the king's evil, v. hals, &c.

Halines holiness, Chr. 642, v. halignes.

Halm stubble, C. R. Lk. 3, 17, v. healm.

Halpenig halfpenny, H. Lk. 12, 6.

Hals a neck.—Halsado a napkin, neckhandkerchief.—Hals-bearh, halsbeorg a protection of the neck, a brigandine, breastplate.—Hals-boc a neck-book, phylactery, Cot. 213.—Halscod a napkin, R. Jn. 11, 44.—Halsfæst stiff necked, stubborn, C. 102.—Halsfang neck-catch, pillory, L. With. W. 11, 29.—Halsgang a running sore, or scrofulous humour in the neck, R. 115.—Halswurðung a supplication, Cd. 171, v. heals.

p Halsere a soothsayer, v. hælsere.

Halsian, healsian, alisian, alsian, hælsian, ic halsige; p. ode; pp. od; v. a. [heals, hals the neck] To beseech, implore, conjure, adjure, prove, try, augur; obsecrare:—Ic halsige þe, Mt. 26, 63: R. Mk. 5, 7. He halsode Israhela bearn, Ex. 13, 19.—Interrogare, Ps. 10, 5, 6.—Augurari. On wigbede to halsienne in altari ad augurandum, Cot. 17.

Halsiendlic importunate, Som.

Halsiendlice; adv. Importunately, earnestly; importunè:—Greg. 1, 2.

Hal-stan The hard shell, hull or crust of a thing; crusta:—Cot. 191.

Halsung, se; f. A praying, supplication, deprecation, augury, divination; obsecratio, adjuratio, exorcismus:—On halsungum in precibus, Lk. 2, 37. Halsunga doð preces faciunt, Lk. 5, 33. On halsunge in auspicium, Bd. 2, 9: L. Cnut. eccl. 4.

Hals-wyrt A daffodil; narcissus, Herbal. 56; epicurcum, Elf.

gl. 15; sinfitus albus, Herbal. 127; auris leporis, R. 81.

Haltsumnys custody, v. healdnes.

Halwend, halwendlic, halewend; adj. [hæl health, wendan to turn] Health-bearing, healthful; salubris:—Bd. 1, 1.

Halwendlice; adv. Healthfully; salubriter, Som.

Halwendnes, se. Healthiness, health; salubritas:—Bd. 1, 1.

Ham a skin, covering, v. hama.

HAM, hamm, hom; pl. hamma [Plat. Dut. ham f: Frs. hamme f: Old Ger. hamm f.] The HAM, back part of the knee; poples:—Elf. gl. 2: R. 75.

HAM, es; m. [Plat. ham: Frs. ham, hem n: Ger. heim n: Ot. heime: Moes. haim: Dan. hiem n: Swed. hem n: Lat. mid. hama.—Old Ger. hemmen to cover: Chald. חמה hme to protect] 1. A HOME, house, dwelling; domus. 2. A village, town, farm, property; prædium, villa. The terms hof, hiwa, ham, hyd, hide appear to be synonymous:—1. Þa he ham com, Mt. 9, 28. Woldon hamas findan would find homes, Cd. 166. Hig cyrdon ealle ham, Jn. 7, 53. Þa Noe ongan ham staðelian then Noah began to found a house, Cd. 75. Æt ham at home, Mk. 9, 33: Lk. 9, 61. 2. Forbærndon feala oðra godra hama burnt many other good towns, Chr. 1001. Ciptun ealle hira hamas vendebant omnia prædia sua, Gen. 47, 20. On hira hamon in possessionibus suis, Gen. 48, 6.—Ham-færeld, hamfærelt a journey home, Ors. 3, 11.—Hamfæst an inhabitant, Bt. 18, 2, 3.—Hamfare protection, freedom, L. Henr. 1, 80, v. hamsocn.—Ham-ferian to carry home, Cot. 8, 196.—Ham-scir the office of an edile; officium ædilis, Cot. 71.—Ham-sittend an inhabitant.—Ham-socn protection, v. in alphabetical order.—Ham-stede homestead.—Ham-weard homeward, hamweardes homewards, Gen. 24, 61.—Ham-weorud neighbours, neighbourhood, Bd. 3, 10.—Ham-wyrt homewort, houseleek, L. M. 1, 1, 40.

-ham, -hom, as a termination, denotes a covering, form. Feðerhom a feather covering, a wing, Cd. 22. Wuldor-ham a glorious covering, a garb of glory, Cd. 190. In the names of places, ham denotes a home, dwelling, village.—Ham-ton home-town, Buckingham, &c.

Hama, homa, an; m. [Plat. Dut. Ger. hemd n: Frs. hemeth n: himþd: South. Ger. hemat: Not. hemide a coat: Dan. ham a skin, coat: Icel. hams a skin] A skin, covering, shirt, surplice; cutis, tegmen, camisia:—R. 76: Cot. 31.

Hama [Plat. hemken, ehme f: Ger. heime f.] A grasshopper, cricket; cicada, gryllus:—R. 37: Cot. 39, 96.

Hamacgað Grows strong; convalescit, Lye.

Hamelan To hamstring, to cut the hamstrings; poplites scindere, Som.

Hamer a hammer, v. hamor.

Hamere A staff by which the pilot directs the rowers; portisculus:—Cot. 158, 202.

Hamod Covered, clothed; indutus, Som.

Hamor a hammer; hamora of hammers, strikers, swords, Chr. 938, v. hamur.

Hamorwyrt HAMMERWORT; parietaria:—L. M. 1, 25.

Hamsocn, hamfare [Plat. heemsöken to visit: Frs. hamsekene, hemsekene a searching, and an attack of a house: Ger. heimsuchen to afflict, visit. Its antiquated signification is burglary, and any violation or injury done to the owner of the house or his inmates: Dan. hiemsöge: Swed. hemsöka to afflict: Icel. heimsókn, visitatio, invasio hostilis: Lat. mid. hamsoca.—ham home, socn liberty, protection] 1. Protection from assault in one's own house; domûs immunitas. 2. The privilege of lords of manors to hold a court, and impose a fine for a breach of that immunity, a breaking of the peace; facultas dominis maneriorum concessa inquirendi de immunitatis istius infra maneria sua violatione. Sæpius tamen in vet. L. L. pro ipsa violatione seu infractione juris accipitur. Ut in L. Edm. 6: Cnut. 12, 59.—Hamsocna est, vel Hamfare, si quis præmeditate ad domum eat ubi suum hostem esse scit et ibi eum invadat, Hamsocna judicatur:—Unworhtre hamsocne infecta invasio, Text. Roff. p. 44.

Ham-tun [ham a dwelling, tun a fence; habitatio vallo circumsepta] Used both for SOUTHAMPTON, Chr. 994, Ing. p. 170, 31; and also NORTHAMPTON, Chr. 917, Ing. p. 130, 28.—Hamtunscire HAMPSHIRE, Chr. 755, Ing. p. 69, 7: 860, for Northampton, v. Norðhamtun.

Hamtun-port Northampton, Lye.

Hamula A steersman; proreta:—Chr. 1039.

Hamur, hamer, hamor, homer. A HAMMER; malleus:—Hamera lafum with relics of hammers, Chr. 938. Homera lafe relics of hammers, Beo. 39, 18: Cot. 135.

HANA, an; m. [Plat. Dut. haan m: Ger. hahn m: Salic laws, chana: Ot. hano: Moes. hana: Dan. Swed. hane m: Icel. hani m.] A cock; gallus:—Ne crǽwð se hana to dæg, Lk. 22, 34, 60: Mk. 14, 30, 68, 72.—Han-cred, han-cræd, a cock crowing.

HAND; g. e; d. a; ac. hand; pl. nom. ac. a; d. um; f. [Plat. Dut. Ger. Swed. hand f: Frs. hond f: Ker. Ot. hant: Moes. handus: Dan. haand c: Icel. hönd, hand f: Tart. handa] HAND; manus:—He æthran hyre hand, Mt. 8, 15. Of ure feonda handa alysede, Lk. 1, 74. Hyre handa gegripenre manu ejus prehensa, Mk. 1, 31. ¶ On hand agan to give up into the hands, to yield, Ors. 3, 11. Lætan to hande elocare in possessionem, Chr. 852. Hand on hand syllan to be idle; manum in manu ponere, L. Edw. 9. Swiðra hand a right hand. Winstra hand a left hand.—Hand-beafton have lamented; planximus, C. Lk. 7, 32.—Hand-bell a hand-bell.—Hand-boc a manual.—Hand-bred hand's breadth, Elf. gr. 8.—Hand-clað a hand-cloth, towel.—Hand-copse a hand-copse, hand-cuffs, Ps. 149, 8.—Hand-cræft a hand-craft, a handicraft, L. Can. Edg. 11.—Hand-cræftig mechanicus.—Hand-cwyrn a hand-mill; mola trusatilis, Jd. 16, 21.—Hand-dæd handy work.—Hand-dæda a deed-doer, L. Ethel. 5.—Hand-fæstan to pledge one's hand.—Hand-fæstnung, handfæstung an assurance, Cot. 136.—Hand-full a handful, Ex. 9, 8.—Hand-gang, hand-gong a giving up, R. 112.—Hand-gecliht the fist; manus collecta.—Hand-gesceaft formed by the hand, a creature, Cd. 23.—Hand-geweorc handy work, Deut. 4, 28.—Hand-gewinn handy labour, Bd. 4, 4, 28.—Hand-gewrit a hand-writing, R. 13.—Hand-grið pax manu data, L. Edw. Guth. 1.—Hand-hamer hand-hammer Cot. 135.—Hand-hrægl a hand-cloth, R. 30.—Hand-hwil a moment.—Hand-hwyrft a turning of the hand, a moment.—Hand-lean a reward, recompence, Cd. 143.—Hand-lin hand-linen, a handkerchief,

Hám-weorðung; e f home dignity; honour to the home Beo Th 5391

Halwend-fut hal-wende; halwendlic healing, salutary

Hamor; es; m Beo gl

Hamcred Grim II, 421, 33

Hamsocn; e f home protection – etc

Hand-bana one who kills with his hand a murderer, qui manu interficit Beo Th 915 Grim II 485, 14

Hand-bred a hands breadth Hand-bred es; n a palm of the hand Th An

Hand-dæd creatura Grim II 491, 2

Hand-gestealla socius Beo Th 4333

Hand-gripe; es m hand gripe grasp Beo K 1921

~~4 Hand-ræcgh~~ com

1 Hand-preost hand priest sacellanus ~~Æl~~ 68 Som

(4) ~~Hand-spere~~ ~~wæter~~ a hand-spear, a ~~javelin~~ Beo ~~K~~ 1965

5 Hand-stocas ~~manicæ~~ manicæ

~~Hand-wyrm~~ ~~hand-worm, a swelling at the root of the nails; paronychia Lye II 61,30~~

~~Hange~~

(5) Hangian; ic hangige pode; pp. od. v. 69

(5) ~~Hangian ic~~ þæt ic geseah wlitig hangian eald sweord eacan ut ego viderem pulchrum pendere antiquum ensem obductum squama Beo Thork XXIV, 23 p 125 – G Cot hangode cyrothecam suspendit Beo XXVIII 240 Thork p 156 – Phil Mem p 384

~~Hand-scalu, -scolu~~ a troop, company Beo K 2034: 3922

3 Hand-sceag cidaris Cot 39. 3a Hand-scyldig manu reus L. Cnut W. p 111

1 Hare-fot the hare's foot lagopus ~~Lye~~ II 422,10 v hara

Hare-hune the herb horehound, marrubium ~~Lye II 422, 10~~ Herb Lye II 425

7 Hangian to hang suspendere Beo K v hon

8 Hange mons Ben

9 Hasewe (5 Haswe) culufre

Hát hat, es, m heat, fervour Beggl. an v hæte

K 5207

5 Hát hot 13 Hát-heort hot-hearted

Hata, an; m A hater; osor Beo gl

~~Hát-heort~~

Hara, an; m a hare etc

1 Hatter, y hattre adj raging, furious pestiferus, ~~venenatus~~ ~~virulentus~~ Beo K 5042 v atter pl ~~atter~~ atter

~~Haaro~~

2 Hauoc a hawk Lye v hafoc

Head lifted up sublimatus Som

2 Heafde had, for hafde p of habban

(3)

(7)

~~Heafod~~

4 Heáfod-beorh, es m a head defence, a helmet Beo K 2054

napkin, *Cot.* 132.—Hand-lin *manualis, Elf. gl.* 19.—Hand-lunga *forthwith, Greg.* 1, 9.—Hand-mægen *the power of hand, Cd.* 14. —Hand-mitta *pondus pendens quatuor scrupula.*—Hand-plega *hand-play, Cd.*95.—Hand-rof *famous hand;* manibus insignis, *Cd.* 155.—Hand-sceaft *a creature.* —Hand-sceate *a hand-sheet, handkerchief, napkin.*—Hand-seax *a short sword, cutlass.*—Hand-selen *a putting into another's possession.*—Hand-syllan *to deliver up.*—Hand-þegen, hand-þeng, hond-þeng *one always at hand, a servant, a domestic, Cd.* 224. —Hand-þweal *hand-bason.* —Hand-weard *hand-ward, at hand, ready, Ors.* 2, 4.—Hand-weorce *a hand-work, workmanship, handiwork, Cd.* 167.—Hand-worhte *hand-worked, finished, Mk.* 14, 58.—Hand-wyrm *hand-worm, R.* 24. —Hand-wyrst *a cubit;* cubitus, *Som.*

Handa *hurt, Gen.* 4, 23, v. anda.

Handle A HANDLE; manubrium :—*Cot.* 167.

Handlian *To handle, feel;* tractare, palpare :—Gif min fæder me handlað, *Gen.* 27, 12.

Hangian, ic hangige : *v. n.* [*Plat. Dut.* hangen *v. a*: *Frs.* henghia *v. a*: *Ger.* hangen, hängen: *Ker. Ot.* hangen: *Dan.* hænge, hange: *Swed.* hänga: *Icel.* hánga: *Wel.* hongian] *To hang down, to* HANG; pendere, dependere: —*Elf. Gr.* 26, 118, *Som.* p. 29, 11. Of dune hangian *to hang from a mountain;* de monte dependere, *Som.* Þe mid him hangode, *Lk.* 23, 39.

Hannes, *highness,* v. heahnes.

HAR [*Icel.* hæra: *Heb. Chal. Syr. Arab.* חוּר hur *white*] HOAR, *hoary, grey-haired;* canus :—Har hæð *hoar heath, Cd.* 148 : 151 : 154. Of clife harum *de clivis canis, Bt. R.* p. 155.

Hara, haran [*Plat. Ger.* hase *m*: *Dut.* haas *m*: *Dan. Swed.* hare *m*: *Icel.* heri *n.* hieri *m.*] HARE; lepus :—*R.* 19. Haran-hige *the herb haresfoot, Herbal.* 62. —Haran-wyrt, hare-wyrt *hare-wort.*—Hare-fot *the herb hare-foot.*—Hare-mint *hare-mint, R.* 42.—Hare-wyrt *hare-wort.*

Hara-hune, hare-hune *Horehound;* marrubium : —*Herb.* 46 : *R.* 43.

Haran *an estuary, Chr.* 1066, v. hærn.

Haran *To spare;* parcere :—*M. Ps.* 77, 55.

Haran-spræcil, haran-spræcol, haran-sprecel *wild burrage;* ecius :—*L. M.* 1, 38.

Harat [*Icel.* hérad *a tribe*] *An assembly;* cœtus, *Lye.*

Hardnys, se; *f.* [heard *hard*] HARDNESS; durities :—*Lev.* 26, 19.

Harfest *harvest,* v. hærefest.

Harian *To become grey, hoary, mouldy;* canescere :—*Elf. gr.* 26.

Harm *harm,* v. hearm.

Harnes, se; *f.* HOARINESS; canities :—*Prov.* 20.

Harra *a lord,* v. hearra.

Harung, e; *f.* 1. *Greyness, hoariness;* canities. 2. *Old age;* senium :—1. *Elf. gr.* 12. 2. *L. Ps.* 60, 19.

Harwæng, harweng, harwelle *Hoary, grey;* canus, *Som.*

Harwengnes *hoariness,* v. harnes.

HAS [*Plat.* heserig : *Dut.* heesch: *Old Fl.* heersch : *Ger.* heisch: *Old Ger.* heis : *Swed.* hees: *Dan.* hæs : *Icel.* hás] HOARSE; raucus : — Hase gewordene synd goman mine, *Ps.* 68, 4.

Hasæton *Pilots;* gubernatores : —*Chr.* 1052, *Ing.* p. 234, 6.

Hasegian, hasian *To be hoarse;* raucere :—*Elf. gr.* 30.

Hasnys, se; *f.* HOARSENESS: raucedo :—*Elf. gr.* 9; 3.

Haswe. 1. *Livid, a sad colour mixed with blue, russet;* lividus. 2. *Dry, rough, rugged;* aridus, ariditate asper : —1. Haswe culufre *a livid dove, Cd.* 72. 2. Haswe here-stræta *rugged army roads, Cd.* 157.

Hat [hætu *heat*] *Hot, fervent;* calidus, fervidus :—*Bd.* 1, 1. Hat-heort *hot-hearted, Greg.* 1, 9.—Hat-heortnes *hot-heartedness, enthusiasm, Mk.* 3, 21. —Hat-wend *hot, Cd.*146.

HÁTAN, he hæt, we hátað; *p.* het, heht, we heton; *imp.* hát, hátte þu, hátton ge; *pp.* háten, geháten; *v. a.* [*Plat.* heten: *Dut.* heeten: *Frs.* heta : *Ger.* heissen : *Moes.* haitan : *Dan.* hede, hedde : *Icel.* heita] 1. *To call, name, have for a name;* vocare. 2. *To command, ordain, promise;* jubere :—1. God het þa fæstnisse heofenan, *Gen.* 1, 8. Ne hat þu, *Gen.* 17, 15. Hu ne hatte hys modor, Maria? *Mt.* 13, 55. Þæt we heretoha hatað, Boetius wæs haten, *Bt.* 1, *Card.* p. 2, 17. 2. He hæt fealdan þat segl *he commands to fold the sail, Bt.* 41, 3. Hat me, *Mt.* 14, 28.

Hate *hate, L. Ps.* 51, 1, v. hete.

Haþoliðan *vena axillaris, L. M.* 2, 51.

Hatian, ic hatige; *part.* hatigende; *p.* ode; *v. n.* 1. *To become or be hot;* æstuare. 2. *To* HATE; odisse : — 1. Hatode heorte min, *C. T. Ps.* 38, 4. 2. Ne mæg middan-eard eow hatian, ac he hatað me, *Jn.* 7, 7.

Hatigendlic *Hateful;* odiosus, *Som.*

Hatlice *hardly,* v. heardlice.

Hatol *Hateful;* odiosus :—*Prov.* 14, 30.

Hátte *call, command,* v. hátan.

Hatte-fagol *a hedgehog, M. Ps.* 103, 19.

Hatung, e; *f.* HATING, *hatred;* odium :—Ge beoð on hatunge, *Mt.* 10, 22: *Lk.* 21, 17.

Hauelest *poverty,* v. hæfenleast.

Hawad *Cloven;* fissus, *Som.*

Hawe *A view, aspect, sight;* visus :—*Bt.* 33, 4.

Hawere *An inspector, a favourer;* spectator, fautor, *Som.*

Hawian; *p.* gehawade. *To view, look on, regard;* spectare :—Hawa nu mildelice *look now mercifully, Bt.* 4.

He; *pron.* [*Plat.* he : *Dut.* hy : *Frs.* hi : *Ger. Ot.* er : *Isd.* ir, and other old writers of Southern Germany, her: *Dan. Swed.* han: *Icel.* hann: *Heb.* היא eia] HE; or indefinitely, *some one, any one;* is, ille : — He wæs rihtwis, *Mt.* 1, 19.

Hea, heach *high, Ex.* 6, 6, v. heah.—Hea-deor *a roebuck, stag, Chr.* 1086. — Hea-deor-hunta *a hunter of stags, Æthelst. Test.* — Hea-dor-hund *a staghound.*

Heabur-eahg [heah *high,* burh *a town, &c.*] HABROUGH *or* EGBOROUGH *island, Yorkshire, Chr.* 686.

HEAF, es; *m. A groan, mourning;* ululatus :—*Cd.* 2.

Heafd *a head,* v. heafod.

Heafd-bolstal *capitale, C. R. Ben.* 67.

Heafde *with a head, Ps.* 39, 11, v. heafod.—Heafdehte *headed;* capitatus : — Heafde - peninc *head-penny.* — Heafde-weard *head-ward;* tribunus.

Heafdian; *pp.* od. *To behead,* v. beheafdian.

Heafian *to mourn,* v. heofian.

Heafig *heavy,* v. hefig.

Heáfod; *g.* heáfdes; *d.* heáfde; *pl.* heáfdu; *n.* [The cognate words, v. hád] A HEAD; caput: —On heafde boc gewriten is, *Ps.* 39, 11. Smyra þin heafod, *Mt.* 6, 17.—Heafod-ædre *the head vein.* — Heafod-beah *a crown, Bt.* 37, 2.—Heafod-bolla *a skull;* heafod-bollanstow *Golgotha.* — Heafod-bolster *a pillow, R.* 70. — Heafod-burh *head borough, a metropolis, Ors.* 4, 6.—Heafod-clað, *head-cloth, a handkerchief, R.*64.—Heafod-cyric, *a head-church, mother-church, L. Cnut. eccl.* 3.—Heafod-ece *head-ach.* — Heafod-fæder *a patriarch.* — Heafod-foreweard *a forehead, L. Eccl.* 29.—Heafod-frætewnes *a head-ornament, head-pin, Cot.* 65.—Heafod-gemaca *an equal, a mate, fellow, Bd.* 4, 22.—Heafod-gewæd *a veil, Gen.* 20, 16. —Heafod-gim *the eye, Cod. Ex.* 27, a. 20.—Heafod-gylt *head-guilt, a capital offence, Off. Reg.* 3. — Heafod-hær *hair of the head, R.* 70.—Heafod-briefðo *scabies, L. M.* 2, 30.—Heafod-leahter *a capital offence, Off. Reg.* 15. — Heafod-leás *head-less, Elf. gr.* 26.—Heafod-maga *a chief relation, prince, Cd.* 78: 60.—Heafod-man *a head-man, general, leader, prince, Num.* 1, 16.—Heafod-mynster *a mother-church.* — Heafod-pann *head-pan, skull, Golgotha, Mt.* 27, 33.—Heafod-port *a chief port, Chr.* 1087. — Heafod-rice *a monarchy, Ors.* 2, 1.—Heafod-sare *a head-sore.*—Heafod-sien *power of sight.*—Heafod-slæge *an ornament for the head, Cot.* 50. — Heafod-stede, heafod-stol, heafod-stow *a capital, metropolis.* — Heafod-swima *a head-swimming*; vertigo, *Cd.* 76.—Heafod-wærc *a head-sore, Cot.* 209.—Heafod-wisa *a chief ruler, Cd.* 79.—Heafod-wylm *capitis fervor, æstus, L. Md.* 1, 1.

Heafodlic, heafudlic; *adj. Capital, chief;* capitalis:—Heafodlicu ricu *capitalia regna, Ors.* 2, 1.

Heafodling *A fellow, mate;* coæqualis:—*C. Mt.* 11, 16.

Heafre *a heifer, Lev.* 3, 1, v. heahfore.

Heaf-sang *an elegy, Cot.* 118.

Heaftling *a captive,* v. hæftling.

Heafuc *a hawk,* v. hafoc.

Heafud *a head, top, C. Lk.* 16, 17, v. heafod.

Heag *a hedge, R. Mt.* 21, 33, v. hege.

Heag *high, Bt.* 35, 4, v. heah.—Heag-engel *an archangel.*

Heago-steald, Heago-stealdes-ea, *Hexham. Bd.* 5, 23, v. Hagustald.

a HEAH, heag, heach, hea; *comp.* hyrra, hyra; *sup.* hyhst, hehst; *adj.* [*Plat. Dut.* hoog. *Frs.* hoech: *Ger.* hoch: *Isd. Ot.* hoh: *Moes.* hauhs: *Dan.* höj: *Swed.* hög: *Icel.* háa: *Heb.* גאה agg, *from* גג gag *the roof of a house*] HIGH, *lofty, noble, excellent;* altus, sublimis: — Heah in bodige, *Bd.* 3, 14. Ofer þa hehstan duna, *Gen.* 7, 20. Heahran on heofonum *higher in heaven, Cd.* 15. On hean earme, *Ex.* 6, 6. Swiðe heage astigan, *Jos.* 8, 20.—Heah-bisceop *an archbishop, Bd.* 2, 3.—Heah-boda *an archangel, Cod. Exon.* p. 12, b.—Heah-burh *a metropolis, Bt.* 1. —Heah-bytlere *a master-builder, an architect.*—Heah-cining *the high king, God, Cd.* 6.—Heah-cræft *architecture.* — Heah-cræftiga *an architect, Bd.* 5, 21.—Heah-ealdor *a chief ruler of the synagogue, Mk.* 5, 38.—Heah-ealdorman *a patrician, Bd.* 1, 13. — Heah-engel *an archangel, Bd.* 5, 2. —Heah-fæder *a patriarch, Bd.* 1, 34.—Heah-gerefa *high-sheriff, Chr.* 778.—Heah-gesamnung *archisynagogus, Mk.* 5, 22.—Heah-græfte *high-graved, much engraved, Cot.* 7.—Heah-had *high order, high degree, Off. Reg.* 11.—Heah-heort *high of heart, proud, Cd.* 202.—Heah-læce *a chief physician, Cot.* 3. — Heah-land-rica *a justice of peace, Cot.* 114. —Heah-lareow *an abbot, prior, prelate, Cot.* 4.—Heah-mod *proud.* — Heah-run *one who prophesies or divines, Cot.* 171. —Heah-sacerd *a chief priest, Mk.* 14, 1.—Heah-sæ-þeof *a notable pirate;* archipirita, *Cot.* 9, 171.—Heah-sangere *a* b *leader of a choir, Bd.* 4, 18.—Heah-setl *high settle, a throne, Bt.* 37, 1.—Heah-þungen, *illustrious, famous, Ors.* 1, 1.—Heah-tid, *a festival, Bd.* 4, 19.—Heah-torras *the Alps.*

Heahfore, heafre A HEIFER; vaccula: — Fæt heah-fore *a fat heifer, R.* 22.

Heahlic *high,* v. healic.

Heahmodnes, se; *f. Pride;* superbia, *Som.*

Heahnes, heanes, heannes, hannes, se; *f.* 1. HIGHNESS, *height, top, an end, a pinnacle, a fortress;* celsitudo, culmen. 2. *Excellence;* excellentia:—1. Þrittig fæðma on heahnisse, *Gen.* 6, 15. Of eorðan heahnesse oð heofones heahnesse, *Mk.* 13, 27. 2. *Bd.* 2, 16: 3, 13.

Heahsteald, heahstald *a youth, virgin; R. Mt.* 1, 23, v. hægsteald.

Heahþo *height, excess, Cot.* 60, v. heaðo.

Heal *An angle, a corner;* angulus, *Som.*

Heal, alh, hæll [*Dut.* hal *f: Ger.* halle *f: Moes.* alh: *Swed.* hall *m: Lat. mid.* hala: *Icel.* höll *f.*] A HALL, *place of entertainment, palace, an inn, a house;* d aula, cœnaculum: — Healle, *Mt.* 9, 23: *Mk.* 14, 15: *Bd.* 2, 13. Hæleð in healle *men in hall, Cd.* 210.

Healand *weighty,* v. healede.

Heald [*Plat.* helden, halden, hellen *to incline: Dut.* hellen *to hang or lean over: Frs.* halda, hilda, helde *f. a declivity: Ger.* halde *f: Old Ger.* haldo, halda: *Dan.* held *c: Icel.* halla *inclinare aliquid*] *Inclined, bowed down;* propensus, incurvatus:—Þider heald *thither inclined, Bt.* 24, 4. Of dune healde *downwards inclined, Bt.* 41, 6.

c HEALDAN, he hylt, we healdað; *p.* heold; *pp.* healden; *v. a.* [*Plat.* holden, holen: *Dut.* houden: *Frs.* halde: *Ger.* halten: *Ker. Ot. Wil.* haltan: *Isd.* haldan: *Dan.* holde: *Swed.* hålla: *Icel.* hallda.] 1. *To* HOLD, *secure, fasten, keep;* tenere. 2. *To regard, observe, watch, take heed of, to tend, feed;* observare, pascere:—1. Þe healdað *te servabunt, Gen.* 12, 12. Hig heoldon þa wifmenn to life, *Num.* 31, 15. 2. Heald þa beboda, *Mt.* 19, 17. Healdað and wyrceað, *Mt.* 23, 3. Hat nu healdan þa byrgene, *Mt.* 27, 64. Þat he heolde, *Lk.* 15, 15: *Jn.* 21, 15, 16.

Healdend, es; *m. One who keeps, a preserver, general, prince;* dux: — Beheafdod healdend ure, *Jdth.* 12.

Healdnes, gehealdnys, gehealdsumnes, haltsumnys, geheordnes, gehealtsumnes, se; *f. A keeping, custody, captivity, regarding, chastity, observance;* observatio:—*Bd.* 2, 4.

Healede *Weighty;* ponderosus: *Past.* 11, 7.

HEALF, half [*Plat. Dut. Swed.* half: *Ger. Ot. Moes.* halb: *Dan.* halv: *Icel.* halfr] HALF, *part, side;* dimidium, pars:—Ic healde þa swiðran healfe, *Gen.* 13, 9. Ic sylle healfe mine æhte, *Lk.* 19, 8. On hwilce healfe *on which side, Cd.* 91.—As a numeral it is generally placed after the ordinal, which it diminishes by half; that is, one half must be taken from the number expressed. Oðer healf hund *one hundred and fifty, Gen.* 8, 3. Þridde healf *two and a half.* Þridde healf hund *two hundred and fifty, Num.* 16, 2. Gilde six healf marc *pay five and a half marks, L. Const.* p. 118.—Healf-clypiend, healf-clypigend, healf-clypigendlic *a semi-vowel, Elf. gr.* 2.—Healf-cuce, healf-cwic *half alive, Ors.*

ealdor, l 16 + Heafod-
mynster a mother church
cyrice l 35 + Heafod
mæg, es; m a chief relation
a ... l 40
+ Heafod-panne, an f a head-pan skull

2 Heafod-gerim
es; n a chief num-ber
the beauty highest of the
a ... th. An

3 Heafod-segen, es
m head ornament Beo
K 4300

4 Heafod-weard, es, m
a chief guard a king th. An
Beo K 5814

5 + Heafod-sola un; m
a border of the head,
tegmen capitis
Beo K 5319
Lin II 17, 232
hafela

8 Heage, high. th. An

9 Heago-spind the
cheeks v supl
hagu-spind

+ Heah high. l 32 + Heah-gesamnung, e; f
l 39 + Heah-loce es; m
2 Heah-fæsten sum;
munimen castrum R 54 —

3 Heah-flod high flood
malina R 105 — 4 Heah-
freols a high or great feast
summa festivitas L Pol Cnut 44 —
Heah-gerefa high
marshal Som —

5 6 Heahlice highly
Som v healice
7 Heah-sele a high hall
Beo K 1294
8 Heah-sittende
alte sedens Pref R.
Conc. Lye
9 Heah-stede, es
m a high place
Beo K 567

6 Heafud-bald That hath
a high forehead, bald
frontosus Som
+ Heafud-hrægel a
long garment flowing from head
to feet; capite de-
pendens vestis Som

(7)

1 Heal-ærn, es n
a hall place, a hall
Beo K 155

2 Heale a hook
wyrtea
Som v hylca

5 Heah-gestreon
high treasure
Beo K 4598

7 + Healf half, e; f
a half, side, divis
th. An: Beo K 1593

Heal-þegn, es, m
a hall thane Beo K
282

Heal-gamen, es; n
hall-game or pleasure
Beo K 2125

2 Healic,
high, sublime Th An

2 Heal-wudu hall
wood, boarding,
floor Beo K 2635

Heard-hicgende
hard or brave think-
ing, brave Beo K 793

(2)

Heall-dl,

Healle, an f.
[illegible]

Of 2 hall v the heal

2 Hean-burh, g
burge, d. byrig

(4)

5 Heanra, an f.
[illegible]
vielgus. Ben.

Heara hair, ...
v hear

(4)

4 a

5 Heals-gebedda a
bedfellow; consors tori
Beo K 126

6 Heal-sittend, es; m
a hall sitter, one
who sits in a hall Beo
K 4026

Hearg, e f.

1 Hearg, es, m
idol; idol-temple
Grimm ... gd.
in 40 Beo K 349
Heargas templa Bd 2, 13
Smith 516, 39: 517, 11, 12.

4 Hearg-træf(tra) m
an idol's tent or temple
in
Beo 1 7, K
349

... Healle ... f
also Beo gl III 427, 10

3, 9.—Healf-eald *middle aged.* —Healf-heafod *the fore part of the head.*—Healf-hund *semicanis;* cynocephalus, *Cot.* 209. —Healf-sester *semi-sextarius, Cot.* 131. — Healf-tryndel *a hemisphere, R.* 49.

Healfunga; *adv. By halves, in parts;* dimidiatim, ex parte: —*Past.* 31, 1.

Healh-stan *a crust,* v. halstan.

Healic, healig; *def.* se healica; *adj. Highest, most high, chief, remarkable;* summus, præcipuus:—Se healica God, *Gen.* 14, 19, 20. Healic gemot *principalis conventus, panegyris, Elf. T.* p. 15. Healice *of importance;* magni momenti. Swa oft swa ænig þincg healices *so often as any thing of importance, R. Ben.* 3.

Healice, hehlice; *adv.* HIGHLY, *chiefly, perfectly;* altè, præcipuè: — Healice intimbred *perfectly built, Bd.* 5, 9, 19. Healicost and swiðost *præcipuè et maximè, R. Ben.* 33.

Healig *high, proud, Cd.* 15, v. healic.

Heall *a hall,* v. heal.

Heallic; *adj. Belonging to a hall or palace;* aulicus:—*Cot.* 194.

Heall-reaf, heall-wahrift *tapestry, Wulfar. Test.*

HEALM, halm, hælm, hielm, es; *m.* [*Plat. Dut. Ger. Not. Dan. Swed.* halm *m*: *Icel.* hálmr *m.*] 1. HAULM, *stubble, straw;* culmus. 2. *A helmet;* galea: —1. *Ex.* 5, 7. Healm-streaw *haulm-straw, stubble, Ps.* 82, 12. Healmes laf *a leaving of straw, stubble, R.* 59. 2. *Elf. T. Lye.*

e Healma *a helm, R.* 104, v. helma.

Healp *assisted; p. of* helpan.

Healran *to weigh,* v. heoloran.

HEALS, hals [*Plat. Dut. Frs. Ger. Not. Ot. Rab. Moes. Dan. Swed. Icel.* hals *m*: *Ker.* halsa: *Chau.* halse] *The neck;* collum, cervix: — *Cd.* 19. ¶ Heals-bec *neck-book, phylactery, Mt.* 23, 5.—Heals-fang *a neck-catch, pillory, L. With. W.* p. 11, 18, 23.—Heals-gund *the king's evil.*—Heals-mægeð *beloved damsels, Cd.* 98, *Th.* p. 130, 6.—Heals-mene, healsmyne *a neck-chain;* monile, torquis, *Gen.* 41, 42.

Healsed *A hood, hooded, covered with a hood;* caputium:—*Cot.* 170.

Healsian *to beseech, Bt.* 22, 2, v. halsian.

Healstan *a crust,* v. halstan.

Healsung *a beseeching, Bd.* 1, 25, v. halsung.

HEALT [*Frs.* halte: *Dan. Swed.* halt: *Icel.* halltr.—The *imp.* of the *A.-S.* healdan: *Ger.* halten] HALT, *lame;* claudus: —*Mt.* 18, 8.

Healtian; *p.* de; *pp.* od. *To* HALT, *to be lame;* claudicare:—*Bd.* 5, 22. Healtedon *claudicaverunt, Ps.* 17, 47.

Heamol, heamul *Frugal, thrifty;* frugi:—*Cot.* 86.

Heamstede [ham *home,* stede *a place, dwelling-place*] HAMSTEDE, *Finchamstead, Berkshire, Chr.* 1103.

Heán; *pp.* head. *To raise, exalt, elevate;* evehere:—*Bd.* 2, 4.

HEAN; *def.* se heana, seo þæt heane; *adj.* [*Frs.* hana *the offender and also the offended, Het: Frs.* hena *to hurt, damage*] *Poor, needy, humble, mean, worthless;* pauper, humilis: — Demað þam rican swa þam heanan, *Deut.* 1, 17. Swa rice swa heane, *Bd.* 3, 5.

f Hean *high,* v. heah.

Hean-byrig HANBURY, *Huntingdonshire, Chr.* 675.

Heandifa *Rocks, steep hills* or *banks;* rupes, *Som.*

Heanes *highness, Bd.* 1, 1, v. heahnes.

Heanlic; *def.* se heanlica. *Poor, vile;* pauper:—*Bt.* 11, 1.

Heanlic; *adj.* [hean *to elevate*] *High, lofty, excellent, famous;* excellens:—*Ors.* 2, 5.

Heanlice; *adv. Basely, meanly;* turpiter:—*Ors.* 3, 10.

HEAP [*Plat.* hoop, hope, hupe, hupen, hupel *m*: *Dut.* hoop *f*: *Frs.* heap: *Ger.* haufe *m*: *Wil. Not.* huffo: *Dan.* hob *c*: *Swed.* hop *m*: *Icel.* hópr *m.*] 1. A HEAP, *pile;* acervus. 2. *Men standing close together, a legion, troop;* legio, turma: —1. On heap bið gesamnod *in a heap be collected, Cot.* 136. 2. *Cot.* 39, 128, 196. ¶ Heapum *in heaps, by crowds, Cd.* 189.

Heap *a hip, bush,* v. hiop.

Heapian; *p.* geheapode; *pp.* geheapod. *To* HEAP, *pile up;* acervare:—*Lk.* 6, 38.

Heapmælum, hæpmælum; *adv. In heaps, by troops, bands, companies;* acervatim, per turmas:—*Num.* 1, 3: *Bd.* 1, 15.

Heapung, e; *f.* A HEAPING; cumulatio:—*Bd.* 5, 13.

Hear *hair,* v. hær.

Heár *high, proud, Cd.* 122, *Th.* p. 156, 26, v. heah.

Hearch *a temple, an idol, Lev.* 20, 2, v. hearge.

HEARD [*Plat.* hard, harde: *Dut.* hard: *Frs.* hird: *Ger.* hart: *Ker. Ot.* harto: *Moes.* hardus: *Dan.* haard: *Swed.* hård: *Icel.*
g hardr] HARD; durus:—Þu eart heard mann, *Mt.* 25, 24: *Jn.* 6, 60. ¶ Heardra *harder, Bd.* 3, 5. — Heard-heawa *a chisel;* scalprum, *Som.*—Heard-heort *hard-hearted, Ex.* 33, 3, 5.—Heard-heortnis *hard-heartedness, Deut.* 31, 27.—Heard-mod *stern, cruel, Cd.* 15.—Heard-nebba *hard-nibbed, a bill of a rapacious bird.* — Heard-ræd *steadfast, Cd.* 107.—Heard-sæld *misfortune,* v. heard-sælð.—Heard-sælig *unhappy, Bt.* 31, 1.—Heard-sælnes *misfortune, Ors.* 3, 5.—Heard-sælð *a hard lot, an unhappiness, misfortune, misconduct, Bt.* 18, 3.—Heard-stan *hard stone,* v. hwit, &c.

Heard *a shepherd, leader, Bt. R.* p. 188.—Heard-man *a herdsman,* v. hyrde.

Heard *an herd,* v. heord.

Hearde; *sup.* heardost; *adv. Severely, greatly;* durè:—Þis folc nu heardost ondræt *this people now most dreads, Bt.* 36, 2.

Heardian *To* HARDEN; durescere:—*Elf. gr.* 35, 37, v. aheardian.

Heardlic *Hard, cruel;* durus:—*L. Const. W.* p. 148, 29.

Heardlice; *comp.* heardlicor; *adv.* HARDLY, *immoderately, hastily, quickly;* duriter:—*Bd.* 4, 25: *Gen.* 42, 8: *Elf. T.* p. 34, 22.

Heardnes, se; *f. Hardness;* durities:—*Mt.* 19, 8: *Mk.* 10, 5.

Heardra *A sort of fish, a miller's thumb, a mullet;* cephalus, mugil:—*R.* 102: *Elf. gl.* 12.

Heardwendlice; *adv.* [wend *a turn*] *Severely, stiffly, rigidly;* severè:—*Bd.* 4, 25.

Hearepa *a harp, Bt.* 35, 6, v. hearpa.

Hearge, hærg, hearh, hearhg, hearch, es; *m.* 1. *A temple, church, an altar;* templum. 2. *An idol;* idolum:—1. *Bd.* 2, 13: *Ors.* 3, 9. 2. *Ex.* 34, 15: *Lev.* 26, 1, 30. ¶ Heafodlice hearge *capitale templum;* capitolium:—*Cot.* 49.

h Hearge *Hercules, Cot.* 102, 193.

Hearh, hearhg *a temple, Bd.* 2, 13, v. hearge.

Hear-loccas *hair-locks, Som.,* v. hær.

Hearm *an arm, Ps.* 88, 11, v. earm.

HEARM, es; *m.* [*Ger. Dan. Swed.* harm *m. grief, offence: Icel.* harmr *m. grief*] HARM, *hurt, damage, calamity:* damnum: —*L. Cnut. pol.* 45, 73. Hearmes swa fela *of calumny so much, Cd.* 27: 37: 38: *Bt.* 41, 3.—Hearm-cwedan, hearm-cweð-

2 Hand-scalu, -scolu
of a troop, company
Beo K 2634. 3922

3 Hand-sceag cidaris
Cot 39. 3 Hand-scyldig
manu reus L. Const
W. p 111

1 Hand-preost friend
priest sacellanus
Æ 68 Som

4 Hand-spore
a light stun
Beo 1965

5 Hand-stocas
manicæ

1 Hare-fot the hares foot
Lagopus
Som II, 422, 10 v hara

2 Hare-hune the herb
horehound; marrubium
Som II 422, 10 Hare
L 425

1 Hatter, y hattres
adj Raging, poison
pestiferous, virulent
Beo K 5042
v atter pl attor

2 Hauoc a hawk
v hafoc

[Head lifted up
sublimatus Som

1 Hand-wyrm
hand-worm, a
swelling at the
root of the nails;
paronychias Som
II 61, 30

5 Hangian; ic hangige
p ode; pp od. v. 69

7 Hangan to hang
suspendere. Beo
v hon

8 Hange mons Ben

9 Hæswe L 5 Hæswe & caluffe

Hát as m
heat, fervour
Beogl stan v hætu
K 5207

5 Hát hot L 3 & Hat-
heort hot hearted

Hata, an; m A
hater; osor Beo gl

Hára, an; m a hare
eh

5 þæt ic
geseah
wlitig hangian eald
sweord eacan ut
ego viderem pulchrum
pendere antiqua ontem
obductum squama
Beo Thork X XIV. 23
p 125 - Gl of hangode
apothecam suspendit
Beo XXVIII 240 Thork
p 156 Phil Mem p
387

2 Heafde had, pers
hafde p of habban
(3)

(7)

Heafod-beorh, e
a head defence, a
helmet Beo K
2054

napkin, *Cot.* 132.—Hand-lin *manualis*, *Elf. gl.* 19.—Hand-lunga *forthwith*, *Greg.* 1, 9.—Hand-mægen *the power of hand*, *Cd.* 14.—Hand-mitta *pondus pendens quatuor scrupula.*—Hand-plega *hand-play*, *Cd.* 95.—Hand-rof *famous hand;* manibus insignis, *Cd.* 155.—Hand-sceaft *a creature.*—Hand-sceate *a hand-sheet, handkerchief, napkin.*—Hand-seax *a short sword, cutlass.*—Hand-selen *a putting into another's possession.*—Hand-syllan *to deliver up.*—Hand-þegen, hand-þeng, hond-þeng *one always at hand, a servant, a domestic*, *Cd.* 224.—Hand-þweal *hand-bason.*—Hand-weard *hand-ward, at hand, ready*, *Ors.* 2, 4.—Hand-weorce *a hand-work, workmanship, handiwork*, *Cd.* 167.—Hand-worhte *hand-worked, finished*, *Mk.* 14, 58.—Hand-wyrm *hand-worm*, *R.* 24.—Hand-wyrst *a cubit;* cubitus, *Som.*

Handa *hurt*, *Gen.* 4, 23, v. anda.

Handle A HANDLE; manubrium:—*Cot.* 167.

Handlian *To handle, feel;* tractare, palpare:—Gif min fæder me handlað, *Gen.* 27, 12.

Hangian, ic hangige: *v. n.* [*Plat. Dut.* hangen *v. a*: *Frs.* henghia *v. a*: *Ger.* hangen, hängen: *Ker. Ot.* hangen: *Dan.* hænge, [illegible]nge: *Swed.* hänga: *Icel.* hánga: *Wel.* hongian] *To hang down, to* HANG; pendere, dependere:—*Elf. Gr.* 26, 118, *Som.* p. 29, 11. Of dune hangian *to hang from a mountain;* de monte dependere, *Som.* Þe mid him hangode, *Lk.* 23, 39.

Hannes, *highness*, v. heahnes.

HAR [*Icel.* hæra: *Heb. Chal. Syr. Arab.* חור hur *white*] HOAR, *hoary, grey-haired;* canus:—Har hæð *hoar heath*, *Cd.* 148: 151: 154. Of clife harum *de clivis canis*, *Bt. R.* p. 155.

Hara, [illegible] [*Plat. Ger.* hase *m*: *Dut.* haas *m*: *Dan. Swed.* hare *m*: *Icel.* heri *n.* hjeri *m.*] HARE; lepus:—*R.* 19. Haran-hige *the herb haresfoot*, *Herbal.* 62.—Haran-wyrt, hare-wyrt *hare-wort.*—Hare-fot *the herb hare-foot.*—Hare-mint *hare-mint*, *R.* 42.—Hare-wyrt *hare-wort.*

Hara-hune, hare-hune *Hore-hound;* marrubium:—*Herb.* 46: *R.* 43.

Har[illegible] *an estuary*, *Chr.* 1066, v. hærn.

Haran *To spare;* parcere:—*M. Ps.* 77, 55.

Haran-spræcil, haran-spræcol, haran-sprecel *wild burrage;* ecius:—*L. M.* 1, 38.

Harat [*Icel.* hérad *a tribe*] *An assembly;* cœtus, *Lye.*

Hardnys, se; *f.* [heard *hard*] HARDNESS; durities:—*Lev.* 26, 19.

Harfest *harvest*, v. hærefest.

Harian *To become grey, hoary, mouldy;* canescere:—*Elf. gr.* 26.

Harm *harm*, v. hearm.

Harnes, se; *f.* HOARINESS; canities:—*Prov.* 20.

Harra *a lord*, v. hearra.

Harung, e; *f.* 1. *Greyness, hoariness;* canities. 2. *Old age;* senium:—1. *Elf. gr.* 12. 2. *L. Ps.* 60, 19.

w Harwæng, harweng, harwelle *Hoary, grey;* canus, *Som.*

Harwengnes *hoariness*, v. harnes.

HAS [*Plat.* heserig: *Dut.* heesch: *Old Fl.* heersch: *Ger.* heisch: *Old Ger.* heis: *Swed.* hees: *Dan.* hæs: *Icel.* hás] HOARSE; raucus:—Hase gewordene synd goman mine, *Ps.* 68, 4.

Hasæton *Pilots;* gubernatores:—*Chr.* 1052, *Ing.* p. 234, 6.

Hasegian, hasian *To be hoarse;* raucere:—*Elf. gr.* 30.

Hasnys, se; *f.* HOARSENESS: raucedo:—*Elf. gr.* 9, 3.

Haswe. 1. *Livid, a sad colour mixed with blue, russet;* lividus. 2. *Dry, rough, rugged;* aridus, ariditate asper:—1. Haswe culufr[illegible] *a livid dove*, *Cd.* 72. 2. Haswe here-stræta *rugged army roads*, *Cd.* 157.

Hat [hætu *heat*] *Hot, fervent;* calidus, fervidus:—*Bd.* 1, 1. Hat-heort *hot-hearted*, *Greg.* 1, 9.—Hat-heortnes *hot-heartedness, enthusiasm*, *Mk.* 3, 21.—Hat-wend *hot*, *Cd.* 146.

HATAN, he hæt, we hátað; *p.* het, heht, we heton; *imp.* hát, hátte þu, hátton ge; *pp.* háten, geháten; *v. a.* [*Plat.* heten: *Dut.* heeten: *Frs.* heta: *Ger.* heissen: *Moes.* haitan: *Dan.* hede, hedde: *Icel.* heita] 1. *To call, name, have for a name;* vocare. 2. *To command, ordain, promise;* jubere:—1. God het þa fæstnisse heofenan, *Gen.* 1, 8. Ne hat þu, *Gen.* 17, 15. Hu ne hatte hys modor, Maria? *Mt.* 13, 55. Þæt we heretoha hatað, Boetius wæs haten, *Bt.* 1, *Card.* p. 2, 17. 2. He hæt fealdan þat segl *he commands to fold the sail*, *Bt.* 41, 3. Hat me, *Mt.* 14, 28.

x Hate *hate*, *L. Ps.* 51, 1, v. hete.

Haþoliðan *vena axillaris*, *L. M.* 2, 51.

Hatian, ic hatige; *part.* hatigende; *p.* ode; *v. n.* 1. *To become or be hot;* æstuare. 2. *To* HATE; odisse:—1. Hatode heorte min, *C. T. Ps.* 38, 4. 2. Ne mæg middan-eard eow hatian, ac he hatað me, *Jn.* 7, 7.

Hatigendlic *Hateful;* odiosus, *Som.*

Hatlice *hardly*, v. heardlice.

Hatol *Hateful;* odiosus:—*Prov.* 14, 30.

Hátte *call, command*, v. hátan.

Hatte-fagol *a hedgehog*, *M. Ps.* 103, 19.

Hatung, e; *f.* HATING, *hatred;* odium:—Ge beoð on hatunge, *Mt.* 10, 22: *Lk.* 21, 17.

Hauelest *poverty*, v. hæfenleast.

Hawad *Cloven;* fissus, *Som.*

Hawe *A view, aspect, sight;* visus:—*Bt.* 33, 4.

Hawere *An inspector, a favourer;* spectator, fautor, *Som.*

Hawian; *p.* gehawade. *To view, look on, regard;* spectare:—Hawa nu mildelice *look now mercifully*, *Bt.* 4.

He; *pron.* [*Plat.* he: *Dut.* hy: *Frs.* hi: *Ger. Ot.* er: *Isd.* ir, and other old writers of Southern Germany, her: *Dan. Swed.* han: *Icel.* hann: *Heb.* הִיא eia] HE; or indefinitely, *some one, any one;* is, ille:—He wæs rihtwis, *Mt.* 1, 19.

Hea, heach *high*, *Ex.* 6, 6, v. heah.—Hea-deor *a roebuck, stag*, *Chr.* 1086.—Hea-deor-hunta *a hunter of stags*, *Æthelst. Test.*—Hea-dor-hund *a stag-hound.*

Heabur-eahg [heah *high*, burh *a town*, &c.] HABROUGH *or* EGBOROUGH *island*, *Yorkshire*, *Chr.* 686.

y HEAF, es; *m. A groan, mourning;* ululatus:—*Cd.* 2.

Heafd *a head*, v. heafod.

Heafd-bolstal *capitale*, *C. R. Ben.* 67.

Heafde *with a head*, *Ps.* 39, 11, v. heafod.—Heafdehte *headed;* capitatus:—Heafde-peninc *head-penny.*—Heafde-weard *head-ward;* tribunus.

Heafdian; *pp.* od. *To behead*, v. beheafdian.

Heafian *to mourn*, v. heofian.

Heafig *heavy*, v. hefig.

Heáfod; *g.* heáfdes; *d.* heáfde; *pl.* heáfdu; *n.* [The cognate words, v. hád] A HEAD; caput:—On heafde boc gewriten is, *Ps.* 39, 11. Smyra þin heafod, *Mt.* 6, 17.—Heafod-ædre *the head vein.*—Heafod-beah *a crown*, *Bt.* 37, 2.—Heafod-bolla *a skull;* heafod-bollanstow *Golgotha.*—Heafod-bolster *a pillow*, *R.* 70.—Heafod-burh *head borough, a metropolis*, *Ors.* 4, 6.—Heafod-clað, *head-cloth, a handkerchief*, *R.* 64.—Heafod-cyric, *a head-church, mother-church, L. Cnut. eccl.* 3.—Heafod-ece *head-ach.* — Heafod-fæder *a patriarch.* — Heafod-foreweard *a forehead, L. Eccl.* 29.—Heafod-frætewnes *a head-ornament, head-pin, Cot.* 65.—Heafod-gemaca *an equal, a mate, fellow, Bd.* 4, 22.—Heafod-gewæd *a veil, Gen.* 20, 16. —Heafod-gim *the eye, Cod. Ex.* 27, a. 20.—Heafod-gylt *head-guilt, a capital offence, Off. Reg.* 3. — Heafod-hær *hair of the head, R.* 70.—Heafod-brieſðo *scabies, L. M.* 2, 30.—Heafod-leahter *a capital offence, Off. Reg.* 15. — Heafod-leás *headless, Elf. gl.* 26.—Heafod-maga *a chief relation, prince, Cd.* 78; 60.—Heafod-man *a head-man, general, leader, prince, Num.* 1, 16.—Heafod-mynster *a mother-church.* — Heafod-pann *head-pan, skull, Golgotha, Mt.* 27, 33.—Heafod-port *a chief port, Chr.* 1087. — Heafod-rice *a monarchy, Ors.* 2, 1.—Heafod-sare *a head-sore.*—Heafod-sien *power of sight.*—Heafod-slæge *an ornament for the head, Cot.* 50. — Heafod-stede, heafod-stol, heafod-stow *a capital, metropolis.* — Heafod-swima *a head-swimming;* vertigo, *Cd.* 76.—Heafod-wærc *a head-sore, Cot.* 209.—Heafod-wisa *a chief ruler, Cd.* 79.—Heafod-wylm *capitis fervor, æstus, L. Md.* 1, 1.

Heafodlic, heafudlic; *adj. Capital, chief;* capitalis:—Heafodlicu ricu *capitalia regna, Ors.* 2, 1.

Heafodling *A fellow, mate;* coæqualis:—*C. Mt.* 11, 16.

Heafre *a heifer, Lev.* 3, 1, v. heahfore.

Heaf-sang *an elegy, Cot.* 118.

Heaftling *a captive,* v. hæftling.

Heafuc *a hawk,* v. hafoc.

Heafud *a head, top, C. Lk.* 16, 17, v. heafod.

Heag *a hedge, R. Mt.* 21, 33, v. hege.

Heag *high, Bt.* 35, 4, v. heah.—Heag-engel *an archangel.*

Heago-steald, Heago-stealdesea, *Hexham. Bd.* 5, 23, v. Hagustald.

a HEAH, heag, heach, hea; *comp.* hyrra, hyra; *sup.* hyhst, hehst; *adj.* [*Plat. Dut.* hoog. *Frs.* hoech: *Ger.* hoch: *Isd. Ot.* hoh: *Moes.* hauhs: *Dan.* höj: *Swed.* hög: *Icel.* háa: *Heb.* גאג agg, *from* גאג gag *the roof of a house*] HIGH, *lofty, noble, excellent;* altus, sublimis: — Heah in bodige, *Bd.* 3, 14. Ofer þa hehstan duna, *Gen.* 7, 20. Heahran on heofonum *higher in heaven, Cd.* 15. On hean earme, *Ex.* 6, 6. Swiðe heage astigan, *Jos.* 8, 20.—Heah-bisceop *an archbishop, Bd.* 2, 3.—Heah-boda *an archangel, Cod. Exon.* p. 12, b.—Heah-burh *a metropolis, Bt.* 1. —Heah-bytlere *a master-builder, an architect.*—Heah-cining *the high king, God, Cd.* 6.—Heah-cræft *architecture.* — Heah-cræftiga *an architect, Bd.* 5, 21.—Heah-ealdor *a chief ruler of the synagogue, Mk.* 5, 38.—Heah-ealdorman *a patrician, Bd.* 1, 13. — Heah-engel *an archangel, Bd.* 5, 2. —Heah-fæder *a patriarch, Bd.* 1, 34.—Heah-gerefa *high-sheriff, Chr.* 778.—Heah-gesamnung *archisynagogus, Mk.* 5, 22.—Heah-græfte *high-graved, much engraved, Cot.* 7.—Heah-had *high order, high degree, Off. Reg.* 11.—Heah-heort *high of heart, proud, Cd.* 202.—Heah-læce *a chief physician, Cot.* 3. — Heah-landrica *a justice of peace, Cot.* 114. —Heah-lareow *an abbot, prior, prelate, Cot.* 4.—Heah-mod *proud.*— Heah-run *one who prophesies* or *divines, Cot.* 171. —Heah-sacerd *a chief priest, Mk.* 14, 1.—Heah-sæ-þeof *a notable pirate;* archipirita,

b *Cot.* 9, 171.—Heah-sangere *a leader of a choir, Bd.* 4, 18.— Heah-setl *high settle, a throne, Bt.* 37, 1.—Heah-þungen, *illustrious, famous, Ors.* 1, 1.— Heah-tid, *a festival, Bd.* 4, 19.—Heah-torras *the Alps.*

Heahfore, heafre A HEIFER; vacca: — Fæt heah-fore *a fat heifer, R.* 22.

Heahlic *high,* v. healic.

Heahmodnes, se; *f. Pride;* superbia, *Som.*

Heahnes, heanes, heannes, hannes, se; *f.* 1. HIGHNESS, *height, top, an end, a pinnacle, a fortress;* celsitudo, culmen. 2. *Excellence;* excellentia:—1. Þrittig fæðma on heahnisse, *Gen.* 6, 15. Of eorðan heahnesse oð heofones heahnesse, *Mk.* 13, 27. 2. *Bd.* 2, 16: 3, 13.

Heahsteald, heahstald *a youth, virgin; R. Mt.* 1, 23, v. hægsteald.

Heahþo *height, excess, Cot.* 60, v. heaðo.

Heal *An angle, a corner;* angulus, *Som.*

Heal, alh, hæl [*Dut.* hal *f*: *Ger.* halle *f*: *Moes.* alh: *Swed.* hall *m*: *Lat. mid.* hala: *Icel.* höll *f.*] A HALL, *place of entertainment, palace, an inn, a house;* aula, cœnaculum: — Healle,

d *Mt.* 9, 23: *Mk.* 14, 15: *Bd.* 2, 13. Hæleð in healle *men in hall, Cd.* 210.

Healand *weighty,* v. healede.

Heald [*Plat.* helden, halden, hellen *to incline: Dut.* hellen *to hang* or *lean over*: *Frs.* halda, hilda, helde *f. a declivity: Ger.* halde *f*: *Old Ger.* haldo, halda: *Dan.* held *c*: *Icel.* halla *inclinare aliquid*] *Inclined, bowed down; propensus,* incurvatus:—Þider heald *thither inclined, Bt.* 24, 4. Of dune healde *downwards inclined, Bt.* 41, 6.

c HEALDAN, he hylt, we healdað; *p.* heold; *pp.* healden; *v. a.* [*Plat.* holden, holen: *Dut.* houden: *Frs.* halde. *Ger.* halten: *Ker. Ot. Wil.* haltan: *Isd.* haldan: *Dan.* holde: *Swed.* hålla: *Icel.* hallda.] 1. *To* HOLD, *secure, fasten, keep;* tenere. 2. *To regard, observe, watch, take heed of, to tend, feed;* observare, pascere:— 1. Þe healdað *te servabunt, Gen.* 12, 12. Hig heoldon þa wifmenn to life, *Num.* 31, 15. 2. Heald þa beboda, *Mt.* 19, 17. Healdað and wyrceað, *Mt.* 23, 3. Hat nu healdan þa byrgene, *Mt.* 27, 64. Þat he heolde, *Lk.* 15, 15: *Jn.* 21, 15, 16.

Healdend, es; *m. One who keeps, a preserver, general, prince;* dux: — Beheafdod healdend ure, *Jdth.* 12.

Healdnes, gehealdnys, gehealdsumnes, haltsumnys, geheordnes, gehealtsumnes, se; *f. A keeping, custody, captivity, regarding, chastity, observance;* observatio:—*Bd.* 2, 4.

Healede *Weighty;* ponderosus: *Past.* 11, 7.

HEALF, half [*Plat. Dut. Swed.* half: *Ger. Ot. Moes.* halb: *Dan.* halv: *Icel.* halfr] HALF, *part, side;* dimidium, pars:— Ic healde þa' swiðran healfe, *Gen.* 13, 9. Ic sylle healfe mine æhte, *Lk.* 19, 8. On hwilce healfe *on which side, Cd.* 91.—As a numeral it is generally placed after the ordinal, which it diminishes by half; that is, one half must be taken from the number expressed. Oðer healf hund *one hundred and fifty, Gen.* 8, 3. Þridde healf *two and a half.* Þridde healf hund *two hundred and fifty, Num.* 16, 2. Gilde six healf marc *pay five and a half marks, L. Const.* p. 118.—Healf-clypiend, healf-clypigend, healf-clypigendlic *a semi-vowel, Elf. gr.* 2.—Healf-cuce, healf-cwic *half alive, Ors.*

Heafod, l. 16 + Heafod-cyrice, an; f. a mother church l. 35 + Heafod-mæg, es; m. a chief relation, l 40 + Heafod-panne, an; f. a skull

2 Heafod-gerim es; n. a chief number the best & highest of the army Th. An

3 Heafod-segen, es m. head ornament Beo K 4300

4 Heafod-weard es; m a chief guard a king Th. An Beo K. 5846

7 Heafod-fola an; m. a cover of the head, tegmen capitis Beo K 5319

hafela

8 Heage, high. Th. an

9 Heago-spind the cheeks v. hago-spind

Heah high, l. 32 + Heah-lace es; m l. 39 + Heah-gesamnung, e; f. a synagogue

2 Heah-fæsten summum castrum R 54

3 Heah-flod high flood malina R 105 + Heah-freols, a high or great feast, summa festivitas L Pol Cnut 44

Heah gerefa high marshal Som

5 Heahlice highly Som v. healice

7 Heah-sele, a high hall Beo K 1296

8 Heah-sittende, alte sedens Bref R. Conc. Lye

9 Heah-stede, es m. a high place Beo K 567

Heafud-bald That hath an high forehead, bald from the forehead Som

Heafud-hrægel a long garment flowing to the feet: capite dependens vestis Som

7

10

1 Heal-ærn, es n a hale place, a hall Beo K 155

2 Heale a hook Som v. hylca

5 Heah-gestreon high treasure Beo K 4598

7 + Healf, half, e; f a half, side, divided Th. An: Beo K 1593

x Heal-þegn, es; m a hall thane Beo K 282

1 Heal-gamen, es; n hall sport game or pleasure Beo K 2125

2 Healic, 7+ High, sublime Th An

2 Heal-wudu hall wood, boarding, floor Beo K 2635

1 Heard-hicgende hard or brave thinking, brave Beo K 783

(2)

(2)

3 Heall-dl,

1 Healle, of a hall v Spl heal

2 Heau-burh, g burge, d. byrig

(4)

5 Heanra, an f. vulgus. Ben.

Hear hair, v hear

4)

2 Hearg, e f D

1 Hearg, es; m idol; idolum Beo K 349
Heargas templa Bd 2,13
Lrth 516,30; 517,11,12

4+ Hearg-træf, es; n an idol's tent or temple is Beo 175, K 349

4a

5 Heals-gebedda a bedfellow; consors tori Beo K 126

6 Heal-sittend, es; m a hall sitter, one who sits in a hall Beo K 4026

heall a te heallum f III 427, 18 also Beo gl

an, hearm-cwidian, hearm-cwedelian *to calumniate, slander, Bt.* 18, 4.—Hearm-cwiðele *a calumniator, R. Mt.* 5, 44.—Hearm-cwyde *a malediction, Cd.* 29.—Hearm-fullic *damni plenus, Somn.* 117. — Hearm-heortnes *a murmuring, muttering, Cot.* 187.—Hearm-loca *hell*; damnatorum claustrum, *Cd.* 5.—Hearm-plega *contention, strife, Cd.* 90.—Hearm-scearu *vengeance, punishment, Cd.* 38.—Hearm-spræce *harm-speaking, slander.* — Hearm-spræcol *calumnious.*—Hearm-spræcolnys *a slandering.* — Hearm-stæf *a writ of evil, a sentence, Cd.* 45.—Hearm-tan *a germ of evil, Cd.* 47.

Hearma *A sling for to support a wounded arm*; mitella:—*Cot.* 130.

Hearmian *To* HARM; lædere:—*Somn.* 91.

Hearming HARMING; læsio, *Som.*

Hearmlic; *adj. Hurtful, noxious*; damnosus:—*Hexaëm.* 18.

Hearpa, hearepa, earpa, an; *m.* [*Plat. Dut.* harp *f*: *Ger.* harfe *f*: *Old. Ger.* harphe: *Ot.* harpha: *Dan.* harpe *f*: *Swed. Icel.* harpa *f.*] A HARP; lyra:—*Bd.* 4, 24. Hearpa, *Ps.* 56, 11. Mid hearpan, *Ps.* 80, 2.—Hearp-nægl *harp-nail*; plectrum, *R.* 71.— Hearp-sang *harp-song, R.* 34.—Hearp-sleg *a harp, L. Ps.* 96, 6.

Hearpene *A nightingale*; aëdon:—*Cot.* 19.

Hearpere, herpere, es; *m.* A HARPER; citharædus:—Þæs hearperes wif *the harper's wife, Bt.* 35, 6.

Hearpestre *A female harper*; citharistria:—*R.* 114.

Hearpian; *p.* ode; *pp.* od. *To* HARP; citharizare:—*Bt.*35, 6.

Hearpung, e; *f.* HARPING; citharæ pulsatio:—*Bt.* 35, 6.

Hearra, an; *m.* [*Plat.* heer *m. particularly a clergyman*: *Dut.* heer *m*: *Ger.* herr *m. Isd.* herr: *Ot. Wil.* herro: *Dan. Swed.* herre *m*: *Icel.* herra, heri, harri *m. a king.* — hearra, heahra; *comp. of* heah *high*] *A lord, master, leader*; dominus:—Hearran to habbane *to have a lord* or *superior, Cd.* 15. Wið his hearran *against his master, Cd.* 14, 30.

Hearre *a hinge, Elf. gl.* 22, v. heor.

Hearste-panna *A frying-pan*; sartago, v. hyrsting.

Hearsumian *to obey, Bd.* 1, 6, v. hyrsumian.

Hearð *a hearth*, v. heorð.

Heart-hama *the heart-covering, caul, Ex.* 29, 22.

Hearwian *To cool*; refrigerare:—*Prov.* 29, *Lye.*

Heat *heat*, v. hætu.

Heatfeld *Hatfield, Herts., Chr.* 675, v. Hæðfeld.

Heaþerian; *p.* geheaþorade, we heaþorodon, v. *To restrain*; cohibere:—*Bt.* 39, 5.

Heaðo, heaðu, heoðo, heahðo, *Top*, HEIGHT, *excess*, also *high*; culmen, altitudo: *Cot.* 60.—Heaðo-lind *a high banner, Chr.* 938.—Heaðo-rinc *a chieftain, Cd.* 154.—Heaðo-welm, heaðo-wylm *excess of heat, intense heat* or *anger, Cd.* 17: 149: *Menol.* 25.

Heaþungen *illustrious, R. Ben.* 7, v. heah, &c.

Heaw *hue, colour, Ps.* 44, 3, v. hiw.

Hea-waldas *nobles, rulers.*

HEAWAN, geheawan, he heaweð; *p.* heow, geheow; *pp.* heawen, geheawen; *v. a.* [*Dut.* houwen; *Plat. Ger.* hauen: *Ot. Not.* houuen: *Lat. mid.* houare.—hiw, heaw *a form*] 1. *To* HEW, *carve, cut, beat*; secare. 2. *To cut off, cut, dig, thrust, spur*; fodere:—1. *Bd.* 4, 11, *Cd.* 224. 2. Heow þat hors mid þam spuran *thrust the horse with the spurs, Elf. T.* p. 36, 25: *Mt.* 21, 8.

Heawan *to shew, Bd.* 5, 2, v. ywan.

Heawgas *images, Ps.* 134, 15, v. hearge.

Heawi-grei HUE-GREY, *sky colour*; color glaucus, *Som.*

HEBBAN, þu hefest, he hefð; *p.* hóf, ahóf, we hófon; *imp.* hefe, *pp.* hafen, hefen, heafen, ahafen; *v. a.* [*Plat.* heven: *Dut.* heffen: *Frs.* hefa: *Ger.* heben: *Ker.* heffan: *Ot.* heffen: *Isd.* hepfan: *Winsbeek.* haben: *Moes.* hafjan: *Dan.* hæve: *Swed.* häfwa: *Icel.* hefia] *To* HEAVE, *elevate, raise*; elevare:—Ic hebbe to heofena mine hand, *Deut.* 32, 40. Hebbað upp eowre eagan, *Jn.* 4, 35.

Hebel, hebeld *The thread of the shuttle*; licium, *Som.*

Hebel-geard *A weaver's shuttle*; liciatorium, *Som.*

Heben *heaven, Bd.* 4, 24, v. heofon.

Heben-hus *The chief beam of a house*; lucunar.

Heber *a goat*, v. hæfer.

Hecen *A kid*; hædus:—*Somn.* 4.

Hecga-swind *The eye-lid, cheek*; gena:—*R.* 71.

HEDAN; *p.* we heddon [*Plat.* höden, hoën: *Dut.* hoeden: *Frs.* hoda, huda: *Ger.* hüten, hüthen: *Dan.* hyte, hytte: *Swed.* hålla: *Icel.* hallda: The *Ger.* halten, hüten, hüthen are closely related. In the South, particularly in Austria, the pasture ground is called *halte*, and a herd *halter*] *To* HEED, *take care of, attend*; cavere, curare:—*Off. Episc.* 3. Heden his *caveant ab eo, L. In.* 74, v. healdan *to keep.*

Hed-clað *ventrale, Med. ex. Quadr.* 4, 14.

Hedd-ern, hed-ern. *A cellar, granary, barn, hiding-place*; horreum:—Heddernu, *Deut.* 28, 8. Nabbað hig heddern, *Lk.* 12, 24: *Bd.* 3, 8, *S.* p. 532, 19.

Heddon *heeded*, v. hedan.

Heder *a hedge, covering, house*, v. edor. — Heder-bryce *a hedge*, or *house-breaking, Som.*

Hef *Sorrow*; luctus:—*C. R. Ben.* 37.

Hefe *heave*; *imp. of* hebban.

Hefe, es; *m. A weight, pile, heap*; pondus:—*Prov.* 20.

Hefed *a head, Chr.* 1137, v. heafod.

Hefeg *heavy, Bt.* 31, 1, v. hefig.

Hefegode *made sad, Bd.* 4, 3, v. hefigan.

Hefeld *The thread of the shuttle*; licium:—*R.* 110, *Som.*

Hefeld-gyrd *A weaver's shuttle*; liciatorium:—*Cot.* 120.

Hefelic *heavy, afflictive, Elf. Epist.* 32, v. hefilic.

Hefelice; *adv. Heavily, painfully*; graviter, ægre:—*Mt.* 13, 15.

Hefel-þræd *A thread*; licium:—*Jud.* 16, 9: *Cot.* 193.

Hefen *heaven*, v. heofon.—Hefen-waru *dwellers in heaven.*

Hefetime, hefigtyme *Heavy, troublesome*; molestus:—*Num.* 11, 10.

Hefia *Scarcely, hardly*; vix:—*C. Lk.* 9, 39.

HEFIG, hæfig, hæfeg [*Plat.* hevig *great*: *Dut.* hevig *violent*: *Frs.* heftich: *Ger. Dan.* heftig *vehement*: *Ot.* hebig: *Not. Tat.* hevig: *Swed.* häftig: *Icel.* höfgr *heavy.*—The idea of gravity being prevalent in this word, it has a relation to the *A.-S.* hefð *heaves, from* hebban, *Moes.* hafjan: *Old Ger.* heffan, hepfan: *Dut.* heffen, heven: *Plat.* heven: *Ger.* heben *to heave*] 1. HEAVY, *weighty*; gravis. 2. *Afflicted*; afflictus:—1. Hig bindað hefige byrðena, *Mt.* 23, 4. Hefigeran þære æ *graviora legis, Mt.* 23. 2. *Ps.* 4, 3: 34, 15.—Hefig-mod *a heavy mind, sad, T. Ps.* 54, 3.

Hefigan, hefigean, *p.* hefegode, gehefegode; *pp.* hefigod, gehefegod. *To make heavy* or

Hele-wah, e; m
heelwall than

( )

Hel-dore, e; f

Hefon heven, hefon-
-trice &c v heofon &c

(1)

Hege-clife, Hege-rife
Hege-ryfe Hege-trife

Hai-reve, clavers,
broadleaved Burweed;
Lappa minor,
xanthium, see
Smith's Flora vol III p 136
S. M 3, 8: 1, 24 Som
Ben, Lye.

(1)

(2)

(5) Hel-dl. Helde
an, f. v Held, e; f.

6 Helle-hæft, es; m
a hell captive Beo. K
1564.

(4)

Hel-runa, an m
a hell sorcerer
Beo K 324

6 Helle-run, e; f
hell mystery

3 Helle
Dut. hel: Ger hell,
clear, eminent, an eminent
man; clarus; Beo K
3628 for hæle a
brave man

4 Hell-bend, e; f a
hell bond Beo K 6140

5 Helle-gast a hell-
or fiend spirit Beo K 2548

5 Hell-heorte, unhal
hearted, astonished
exanimatus Som

1027

3 Hell-sceaþa, an, m
a hell miscreant the
Beo gl in scaþa

2 Hell-raden, ne; f
fidelity

Bt. 37, 4.

hielm m: Icel. hiálmr: Lat. mid. helmus: It. elmo: Fr. heaume.—from helan to cover. The old Suab. poets wrote heln, and it signified any kind of covering, a roof, &c.] 1. The top or head of any thing, crown; culmen, corona. 2. A helmet, protection, defender; galea, præsidium:—1. Oð þone helm to the top, Bt. 34, 10: Mk. 15, 17. 2. Elf. gr. 43. Gasta helme to the protector of spirits, Cd. 86: 216: 219.

HELMA, healma [Plat. Dut. Ger. helm: rudder or rather the head or handle of the rudder, which often has the form of a helmet] HELM, rudder; gubernaculum navis:—Bt. 35, 4.

Helmiht Full of branches; frondosus:—Cot. 75, 198.

Helo health, v. hælu.

HELP, helpe [Plat. Dut. hulp f: Frs. help: Ger. hülfe f: Ker. helfa: Ot. helpha: Not. helfa c: Dan. hielp c: Swed. hielp m: Icel. hiálp f.] HELP; auxilium:—Ors. 3, 2.

Helpan, gehelpan, he hylpð; p. healp, we hulpon; pp. holpen. To HELP, assist, preserve; adjuvare:—L. Cnut. pol. 66. Þat wif eowrum life geheolp, Jos. 6, 22: Lk. 5, 36.

Helpend-bær Help-bearing, succouring; opifer:—Cot. 148.

Helpendlic Helping, profitable; auxiliaris, Som.

Helrun, helrynegu One possessed with a spirit of prophesying; python:—R. 113.

Hel-spura, hell-spura, an; m. A heel, footstep; calcaneum:—C. Ps. 48, 5: 55, 6.

Helt a hilt, handle, v. hilt.

Helur a turning of the balance, Cot. 26, v. helerung.

Hem HEM; margo:—R. 28.

Hemeðo marriage, Cot. 198, v. hæmeð.

Hemleac, hemlyc HEMLOCK; cicuta:—R. 43.

Hemming A shoe made of rough hide; pero:—Cot. 155.

HEN, hæn, henn; g. henne; f. [Plat. hen, häne f: Dut. hen f: Frs. hoyn f: Ger. henne: f: Not. henna: Dan. höne f: Swed. höna f: Icel. hæna f.] A HEN; gallina:—Seo henn, Mt. 23, 37. ¶ An henne æg a hen's egg, Bd. 3, 23.—Hen-fugel hen fowl, Herb. 4, 10.

Henan to humble, hinder, oppose, v. hynan.

Hencgen a prison, v. hengen.

Henep hemp, v. hænep.

Heng, hengon hung, v. hon.

Henge-clif hanging-cliff, R. 101.

Hengen, hencgen [Plat. Ger. henge f.] A prison, house of correction; ergastulum:—Hengen witnuncg prison punishment, L. Const. Ethel. W. p. 111, 31.

Hengest [Plat. Dan. Swed. hingst m: Dut. Ger. hengst m: Böhm. hynst: Frs. hanxt m. In Münster, Westphalia, hangst signifies a horse, in general also Dan. hest and Swed. häst, but the Plat. hingst: Dut. Ger. hengst are only used for a stallion. The Icel. hengla f. signifies a steril, meager creature; animal effœtum et macrum, corresponding with the A.-S. hengest] A gelding, a horse, jade; cantherius, caballus:—Cot. 41, Som.

Hengest-dun, Hengestes-dun [Hunt. Hengistentune] HENGIST'S DOWN, Hengston hill, Cornwall.

Henise A treading, trampling; calcatio:—C. Lk. 10, 19.

Henne-belle henbane, Herb. 5, 1, v. hæn-belle.

Heno [Icel. hana] Behold; en, ecce, Lye.

Henon from hence, v. heona.

Henon-forð henceforth, C. Ps. 118, 8, v. heona.

Hentan, gehentan [Icel. henda to lay hold of: Chauc. hent took.—hunta a hunter] To make diligent search, to prosecute, pursue, hunt after, take; recuperandi studio insequi:—Þat he mote hentan æfter his agenan, L. Cnut. pol. 18.

Henð, henðo, henðu, hienð, hynð; d. henðe, hænðe [henð from henan to humble] Loss, damage, misfortune, punishment, injury, poverty, hinderance; damnum:—Henðo geþoliað shall suffer punishment, Cd. 222. Hynðo ne woldon þolian injury would not endure, Cd. 160, Th. p. 198, 16: Bt. R. p. 166. Mid henðe with poverty, Bt. 11, 1, Card. p. 48, 5.

Heo; pron. nom. s. f. [Plat. se: Dut. zy: Ger. sie: Ker. Ot. si, sie: Moes. si: Dan. hun: Swed. hon: Icel. hún] She; illa:—Heo cwæð, Gen. 3, 13. ¶ Heo dæg this day, Cd. 30.

Heodor-hund a stag-hound, v. hea, &c.

Heof Lamentation; luctus:—Ors. 2, 4: Ps. 29, 13.

Heofd a head, W. B. p. 168, v. heáfod.

Heofelic Sorrowful; funebris, Som.

Heofen heaven, Lk. 16, 17, v. heofon.—Heofen-cund celestial, Bt. 5, 1.

Heofen-feld [cœlestis campus] HEFENFELD, in Northumberland, Bd. 3, 2.

Heofen-hæbbend one having a bow, an archer.

Heofen-hrof an arched roof, Cot. 119.

Heofenlic heavenly, Gen. 24, 3, v. heofonlic.

Heofesham Evesham, v. Efesham.

Heofian, beheofian; p. ode; pp. od; v. n. To mourn, lament; lugere:—Heofodon lamentaverunt, Lk. 8, 52. Ge heofiað and wepað, Jn. 16, 20. Heofigende, Ps. 34, 17. Heofiende, Bt. 2.

Heofing, heofincg Heaving, lamentation, mourning; luctus:—Jac. 4, 9: Scint. 55.

Heofne to heaven, v. heofon.

Heofod elevated, the head, Ps. 3, 3, v. heafod.—Heofod-burh head-borough, a metropolis, Hom. Nat. Greg. p. 34.—Heofod-weard head-ward; principalis custodia, Jdth. 12.

Heofod, &c. that is, with its other compounds, v. heafod, &c.

Heofon, heofen, heofun, hiofon; g. heofones, heofnes; d. heofone, heofne; pl. heofonas, heofenas; m. [Plat. heven m.—hafen, heafen what is elevated; pp. of hebban to raise] HEAVEN; cœlum:—Heofon and heofuna heofun, Deut. 10, 14. He geseah opene heofonas, Mk. 1, 10. Þa tunglu heofnes the stars of heaven, Bt. 39, 13. Heofenas, Gen. 2, 1.—Heofon-beacn heavenly beacon, Cd. 148.—Heofon-beorht heavenly bright, Cd. 190.—Heofon-candel heavenly candle, the sun, Cd. 148.—Heofon-col heaven's coal, heat of the sun, Cd. 146.—Heofon-cund celestial, Cod. Ex. 33, b.—Heofon-ligende one leading a heavenly life, a virgin, bachelor.—Heofon-rice kingdom of heaven, Bd. 4, 24.—Heofon-timber heavenly frame, Cd. 8.—Heofon-torht heavenly bright, Cd. 146.—Heofon-tungol; cœli sidus, phœbus, Bt. R. p. 183.—Heofon-waras heavenly inhabitants, Ors. 3, 5.—Heofon-wered heavenly host.

Heofone, an; f. Heaven; cœlum:—Gen. 1, 1, 14, 17, v. heofon.

Heofon-heah heaven-high, very high, Cd. 202.

Heofonisc; adj. Heavenly; cœlestis:—Ors. tit. 3.

Heofonlec, heofonlic, heofenlic; def. se heofonlica, seo þæt, -e; adj. Heaven-like, HEAVENLY; cœlestis:—Swa deð min se heofonlica Fæder, Mt. 18, 35.

1 Heofonlic-hlaf m
heavenly bread, man-
na Som

2 Heof-sang an elegy
~~song of~~ a mourning song Som

3 Heold, e. f. Shold,
shelter lurking places, a
lair; latebra. Se
wudu-beam wild-deor
scylde, eallum heolde
the forest tree wild beasts
shielded, for all a shelter
Sd 200 Lup 247, 30

4 Heolfre-dl. Heolfer,
g. heolfres, d. heolfre
in gore &c Beo. gl.

5)

6 Heolster adj (Dark
obscure ~~gloomy~~ Th an

7 Heolster-cofa an m
a shady dwelling, se-
cret-place Cod Ex
56 b Beo gl

8 Heonon-weard
henceward, back-
ward, going back
Cd 71, Th p 86, 15

9)

10 Heorre ~~[illegible]~~ heorres m
a hinge Beo K 1991

1 Also Heorde, an f?
a troop, company;
grex Beo K 5856
v heord

~~Heorot-berg-dl~~

1 Heord-clæfer,
clæfre: f

2 ~~Heorot-berie, -berge~~
an f

2 Heord-raeden, e. f
custody, charge Th an

3 Heoro mild gentle Beo K 2744
hyra

4 ~~Heoro swang~~
Heoro-hocyht
fiercely hooked,
saviter aduncus
Beo 2875

5 Heorot-brembel e
hurtle-berry Som v
heorot-berge

14 Heorra an m a lord Th
an v hearra

1 Heoro-wearh es; m
a beast, monster
lupus, monstrum
Beo 97 K 2534

15 Heort hearted,
spirited; animosus
Som blid-heort
glad hearted Beo
K 3601 v blide
~~Heortele~~

16 Heort-clæfre e f
Germander; ~~[illegible]~~
~~[illegible]~~ cha.
madrys Som

17 Heoft-[illegible], an
[illegible]

1 Heort-wærc
heart pain Som
Lye

2)

3)

4 ~~Heorlafre-dl~~
Heoru indeed;
saltem, quidem
Th an

5 Heoro-dreor es; m
sword blood
sanguis effusus Beo
K 9[illegible]

Heoro-drync sm
sword or deadly drink
Beo K 4711
Grm II 460, 43

6 Heoro-dreorig
sword bloody Beo
K 1864

8 Heoro-grim
sword cruel Beo
K 3127

10 Heoro-sweng
a sword swing;
ensis vibratio Beo
K 3179

11 Heoro-wearh, es
m severe or bloody
wolf Beo K 2534

7 ~~Here~~ Here ~~here~~, now
Som
here, v her

fire, v. hloð; exercitus:—Se cyning sende hys here to, *Mt.* 22, 7. Hergas on helle *multitudes in hell*, *Cd.* 145, *Th.* p. 180, 16. ¶ Inghere *an army of natives.* — Uthere *an army of foreigners.* — Gangend-here *infantry.*—Ridende-here *cavalry.* — Here-beacen, here-beacn *a watch-word, a beacon.*—Here-beorgan *to harbour.*—Here-berga *a station* or *standing where the army rested in their march, a harbour*, *Chau.* herborow, *Som.* —Here-byma *a war-trumpet*, *Cd.* 147.—Here-bymere *a war-trumpeter.* — Here-byrigan *to harbour.*—Here-cist *a warlike band*, *Cd.* 151.—Here-farg *a predatory excursion of a foreign army.*—Here-feoh *booty*, *Ors.* 3, 7.—Here-folc *military men*, *Jdth.* 11.—Here-fong *a bone-breaker;* ossifragus, *Elf. gl.* 11.—Here-fugolas *war-birds*, *Cd.* 150. — Here-gang *an irruption, attack*, *Bd.* 1, 14, *B.* Here-geat *a heriot*, v. more in alphabetical order. — Here-geold, here-gyld *a military tribute*, *Chr.* 1040. —Here-hand *a hostile hand*, *Bd.* 4, 26.—Here-huð, here-hyð *plunder, prey*, *Bd.* 4, 16.—Here-mæcg *a principal man, a leader*, *Cd.* 114. — Here-man *a soldier*, *C. Jn.* 18, 3. — Here-pað, her-pað *an army-path*, *Cd.* 174. — Here-reaf *plunder, spoil*, *Jos.* 7, 21.—Here-rinc *hostilis consiliarius*, *Bt. R.* p. 152.—Here-stræt *a military way*, *Cd.* 157.—Here-team *the conduct of an army, spoil*, *Cd.* 97: 98.—Here-teama, here-tema *a leader of an army*, *L. In.* 15.—Here-þreat *an army-band, an army, a company*, *Cd.* 170.—Here-þrym *an army-band, an army*, *Cot.* 94. — Here-tyma *a martial leader*, *Cd.* 205.—Here-wæða *a leader of an army*, *Jdth.* 11.—Here-wisa *a general, martial leader*, *Cd.* 160. — Here-wop *army-cry*, *Cd.* 166. — Here-word *military fame*, *Chr.* 1009, *Cot.*—Here-wosa *hostile band*, *Cd.* 5.— Here-wulf *war-wolf, destroying army*, *Cd.* 94.

Hered; *comp.* ra. *Praised*, v. herian.

Hereford, Hereford-port [here *an army*, ford *a ford*] *The city of* HEREFORD, *Chr.* 918.—Herefordscyre [scire *a share, division*] *Herefordshire*, *Chr.* 1051.

Heregas *armies*, v. here.

Here-geat [*from* geotan *to pour out, to give*] *military apparatus, weapons, armour*, what was given of old to the lord of the manor to prepare for war. Now it denotes the best horse, cow, &c. given to the lord of the manor at the death of the tenant, called a HERIOT; militaris apparatus, armamentum.

Heregendlice; *adv. Commendably;* laudabiliter:—*Bd.* 1, 27, *resp.* 8.

Heregung, hergung, e; *f. An invasion, inroad;* incursio:—*Jos.* 10, 40, v. heregang *in* here.

Herelic; *def.* se herelica; *adj. Warlike;* militaris:—Þa herelican *res militares*, *Cot.* 47.

Herenes, se; *f.* 1. *Praise, worship;* laus, cultus. 2. *Obedience;* obsequium:—1. *Bd.* 3, 27: 4, 24. Herenes Godes *worship of God*, *Bd.* 4, 14. 2. He him to herenysse geteah *he brought them to obedience*, *Bd.* 3, 24, v. hyrnes.

Herenitig *An expedition;* expeditio:—*Cot.* 73.

Heretoga, heretoha, an; *m.* [here *an army*, teon *to lead*] *A general, consul, duke;* exercitûs ductor, consul:—Of þe forðgæð se heretoga, *Mt.* 2, 6. Þa heretohan hi woldon utadrifan *the consuls they would expel*, *Bt.* 16, 1. Þa wæs sum consul, þat we heretoha hatað *then was a certain consul that we call* Heretoh, *Bt.* 1.

Herewian, herwian *To despise;* contemnere:—We herewiað us selfe *we despise ourselves*, *Bt.* 13, *Card.* p. 60, 26. Herwdon me *aspernabantur me*, *V. Ps.* 21, 6.

Here-wic, Her-wic [here *an army*, wic *a residence*] *A place where an army encamps, or is in garrison, a station, camp:* hence the name of HARWICH, *Essex;* militaris vicus, castra:—*Cd.* 97: *Cot.* 48.

b Herfest *harvest*, *Elf. gl.* 10, v. hærfæst.

Hergadan *captives.*

Hergan, hergean *to praise*, v. herian.

Hergað, hergeað [here *an army*, gað, gæð *from* gan *to go*] *An irruption, invasion, destruction;* direptio:—*Chr.* 894.

Herge, hergh *a troop, an army, a depopulation*, *Cd.* 145, v. here.

Herge *An image, idol, altar, temple;* simulachrum, templum:—To þam herige *to the idol*, *Cd.* 181: *Ors.* 3, 7.

Hergendlic, herigendlic; *adj. Praise-worthy;* laudabilis:—*V. Ps.* 117, 14.

Hergian, herian, gehergian; *p.* ode; *pp.* od [*Ger.* heren: *Not.* herron: *Dan.* herge, hærje: *Swed.* härja: *Icel.* heria *arma circumferre.*—here, herge *an army*] *To act as an army, plunder, ravage, waste, afflict, vex, destroy;* vastare:—He hergode æghwar *he plundered every where*, *Chr.* 1009. Hi wurdon þa gehergode, *Jud.* 10, 8. Ongan herian *began to vex*, *Cd.* 102.

Hergionge, hergoð *an invasion*, *Jud.* 16, p. 162, v. hergað.

Hergung *an invasion*, *Bd.* 1, 11, v. here, &c.

Herian, hergan, hergean, ic herige, herge, we herien, herigen; *part.* heriende, herigende; *p.* ede; *pp.* hered, gehered; *v. a.* [*Ger.* ehren: *Dut.* eeren.—here *fame*] *To praise, commend;* laudare:—Herigað drihten *praise the Lord*, *Cd.* 214: 187. Heredon hig beforan him, *Gen.* 12, 15: *Ps.* 17, 4: *Lk.* 2, 20.

c Herige *an army*, v. herge.

Herigean *to praise*, v. herian.

Herigendlic *laudable*, v. hergendlic.

Herinc, hering *a herring*, v. hæring.

Hering, herung, e; *f. Praise, commendation, favour, emulation;* laus:—*Bt.* 27, 3: 30, 1.

Hering-man *a hearing-man, a subject*, *Som.*

Herm-bealow *noxious*, *Cd.* 228, v. hearm.

Hern *a horn*, v. hyrne.

Hernis, se; *f. A tax, tribute;* census:—*R. Mt.* 17, 25.

Hernise *A mystery;* mysterium:—*C. Mk.* 4, 11.

Hernisse *obedience*, *Bd.* 3, 30, v. hyrnes.

Her-pað *a military way*, *Jdth.* 12, v. here, &c.

Herpere *a harper*, *Gen.* 4, 21, v. hearpere.

Herra *for* heora, hira *of them.*—herra *for* hehra *higher*, v. heah. —*a master, lord*, v. hearra.

Hersta *A fagot, fire-brand;* cremium:—*V. Ps.* 101, 4.

Herstan *to fry*, *Elf. gr.* 28, v. hyrstan.

Hersting-hlaf *a bread-crust*, *Cot.* 45.

Hersum *obedient*, v. hyrsum.

Hersumian *to obey*, *C. Mk.* 4, 41, v. hyrsumian.

Hersumnes *obedience*, v. hyrsumnes.

Herð-belig [hærðan *testiculi*, belig *venter*] *viscus, scrotum*, *Cot.* 163.

Herung *praise, favour, emulation*, *Ps.* 110, 10, v. hering.

Herwendlic; *adj. Despicable;* contemptibilis:—*Cot.* 37.

Herwian *to despise*, v. herewian.

d Herwic *a camp*, v. herewic.

(4)

1r Hete-nīd, es; m hateful malice Beo K 303

Hete-swenge, es; m a hated stroke; hostilis ictus Beo K 4445

Hete-þanc, es m a hateful thought, enmity Beo K 1945

(4²)

4 Het-were, pl m [hete ~~hated~~ hated] hated men, enemies Beo K 5827

5

Heabenlic heavenly Th. an v heofonlic

a)

Hia they Beo K 2714 v hi

Hierde-bóc the Pastoral book; ~~the~~ Pastoralis liber Som

~~Hyg od~~

Hig O! Th. an

5')

Hige-pihtig mind ~~brave brave~~ strong brave minded; fortis animo Beo K 1486

~~Hyge-sorh, e; f mental mind sorrow Beo K 4651~~

2

Hige-þrym mind ~~strength~~ courage Beo K 675

Higscipe *Familyship*; familiæ status:—*Bt.* 21.

Higð *An endeavour*; nisus, *Som.*

Hih *high*, v. heah.

Hihsend *Hissing*; subsannans, *Lye.*

HIHT, hyht, gehyht *Hope, expectation, refuge, joy, exultation*; spes:—*Ælf. gr.* 12 Gaudium, *T. Ps.* 46, 1.

i Hihtan, gehihtan, ic hihte, we hihten, gehyhtað; *p.* ic gehihte, hihte; *pp.* gehyten. 1. *To hope, trust*; sperare. 2. *To rejoice, exult*; exultare. 3. *To increase*; augere:—1. Ic hihte on God, *Ps.* 68, 4: 30, 18. Þeoda gehyhtað, *Mt.* 12, 21. 2. Muntas gehihtað, *Ps.* 113, 6: 117, 18. 3. He gehihte folc his, *Ps.* 104, 22. Hihte, *M. Ps.* 104, 22.

Hihtful, hyhtful; *adj. Full of joy, pleasant*; gaudii plenus:—*Cd.* 45.

Hihð *height*, *T. Ps.* 55, 3, v. heaðo.

Hihtleás; *adj. Joyless, hopeless*; gaudio vacuus, *Som.*

Hihtlic, hyhtlic; *adj. Joyous, glad, exulting, hopeful, desirable, sublime*; jucundus, sublimis:—*Cd.* 95: 8.

Hihtlice; *adv. Gladly, diligently*; studiose:—*L. Eccl.* 4.

Hii *the island Hy*, v. Ii.

Hila, hi *Alas*; heu, *Som.*

Hilan *To hill, conceal*; tegere:—Hilð *conceals*, *Bt.* 27, 1, v. helan.

Hilc *a turning*, *Cot.* 18, v. hylca.

HILDE [*Icel.* hilldur *f.*] *A battle, fight*; pugna:—Hilde-grædige *greedy of battle*, *Cd.* 150: 155. *Menol.* 481.—Hilde-calla *a man of war*, *Cd.* 156.—Hilde-leoð *a military song*, *Jdth.* 11.—Hilde-nædran *military serpents, arrows*, *Jdth.* 11.—Hilde-rinc *a soldier*, *Æthelst. Epinic. Chr.* 938.—Hilde-sweg *battle crash*, *Cd.* 93.—Hilde-þræc *martial violence*, *Cd.* 98.—Hilde-wulfas *soldiers.*

Hilde *affection*, v. hyld.

Hil-hama *A grasshopper*; cicada:—*R.* 37.

HILL, hyll, es; *m.* [*Plat.* büll, hövel *m*: *Dut.* heuvel *m*: *Ger.* hügel *m*: *Dan.* höj *c*: *Icel.* höll *m. tumulus*: *Icel.* hvoll *m.*] A HILL, *mountain*; collis, mons:—*C. Ps.* 71, 3: *R. Lk.* 23, 30.

j Hil-song *A timbrel, drum*; tympanum:—*T. Ps.* 150, 4.

Hilt, gehilt, holt, hylt, an. HILT, *handle*; capulus:—Þa hiltan, *Jud.* 3, 22.—Hiltleás *without a handle*, *R.* 62.

Him *to him, or them*; illi, illo, illis; *d. s.* and *pl. of* he.

Himming *a shoe*, v. hemming.

Him-self HIMSELF; ipse:—*Gen.* 18, 7.

Hina *A domestic, servant*; domesticus:—*Cd.* 107.—Hina-ealdor, hina-ealdor *the good man of the house*, *Bd.* 3, 9.—Hine-man *a farmer.*

Hinan *hence*, *Bt. R.* p. 156, v. heona.

Hindan *behind*; post:—*Ors.* 6, 36.

Hind-beri, hind-berig HINDBERRY, *raspberry*; fragum, acinus:—*Cot.* 72, 91.

Hind-cealf, hind-calf *A little hind, hind-calf*; hinnulus:—*R.* 19.

Hinde, hynd A HIND; cerva:—*Chr.* 1086.

Hinder-geape, hinder-gep *versutus*, *R.* 84: *Coll. Monast.*

Hinderling [hinder *remote*, ling *a pattern*] *Not like the original*; a prototypo prorsus abhorrens, *Lye*:—*Wilk. L. A.-S.* p. 208.

Hinder-scipe, es; *m. Naughtiness, negligence*; nequitia, *Som.*

Hind-hele, hind-heleðe, hind-heolað, hind-heoleðe, hind-hioleðe, HIND-HEEL; pæonia:—*Elf. gl.* 16.

Hindrian; *pp.* gehindred [*Plat. Dut.* hinderen: *Frs.* hindera *Ger.* hindern: *Not.* hintern: *Dan.* hindre: *Swed. Icel.* hindra] *To* HINDER; impedire:—*Chr.* 1003.

k Hindweard HINDWARD; a retro:—*L. Alf. pol.* 32.

Hine *him*; illum, se; *ac. s. m. of* he.

Hi-ne *is it not, are they not*; nonne:—*Ps.* 13, 8.

Hine *a domestic*, v. hina.

Hine-weard INWARD; intrinsecus:—*C. R. Mt.* 7, 15.

Hin-gong *A departure*; abitus:—*Cod. Exon.* 30, b.

Hingrian, hyngrian; *p.* ede; *pp.* od [*Dut.* hongern: *Plat. Ger.* hungern: *Not.* hungeren: *Moes.* huggrian, *pronounce* hungrian: *Dan.* hungre: *Swed.* hungra: *Icel.* húngrar.—hunger *hunger*] *To hunger*; esurire:—Hingriað esuriunt, *Mt.* 5, 6: *Lk.* 6, 21. Hingriende, *Cot.* 83. Hingrende, *Cod. Exon.* 27a. Hingrigende, *Mt.* 25, 37. Also used impersonally, Me hingrað *I hunger*, *Elf. gr.* Hine hingrede *he was hungry*, *Lk.* 4, 2.

Hinoð *the bowels*, *Ps.* 50, 11, v. innoð.

Hinsið, hinnsið *Death, destruction, horrour*; mors, perditio:—*Cd.* 33: *Jdth.* 10.

Hio, heo *She*; illa; *nom. s. f. of* he.—hio *is used for* he, hi, &c.

Hiofon *heaven*, *Bt.* 33, 4, v. heofon.

Hiofonlic *heavenly*, *Bt.* 33, 4, v. heofonlic.

Hiolstr *a den*, v. heolster.

Hiom, heom, him *Them*; illis; *d. pl. of* he.

Hion; *f.* [*Swed.* hinna: *Dan.* hinde] *A membrane*; cuticula:—*L. Ethelb.* 37.

Hion, him *To him*; illi; *d. s. of* he.

Hiona, hionan, hionon *hence*, *Bt.* 36, 2, v. heona.

Hiop, heap, heop A HIP, *the fruit of the dogrose, a bush, bramble*; rosæ sylvestris bacca, rubus:—Brer þe hiopon on-weaxð *a brier which beareth hips*, *L. M.* 1, 38. Heop-brymel *a hip-bramble*, *R.* 64.

l Hior *a hinge*, *Bt.* 34, 7, v. heor.

Hiora, heora, hira *Of them*; illorum; *g. pl. of* he.

Hiord, hiored *a herd*, *Cot.* 167, v. heord.

Hiort *a heart*, v. heorte.

Hiorð *hearth*, *Cot.* 20, v. heorð.

Hiow *a hue*, *Cd.* 14, v. hiw.

Hioweslice *familiarly*, *Bd.* 5, 2, v. heowæslice.

Hipe *a hip.*—hipes-ban *hip-bone*, v. hype.

Hiran *to hear*, v. hyran.

Hird, hirde *a shepherd*, v. hyrde.

Hird-clerc *a domestic chaplain.*

Hirdelic; *adj. Pastoral*; pastoralis, *Som.*

Hirdnys *a prison*, *Gen.* 42, 17, v. hyrdnes.

Hirdwendlic *familiar, contemptible*, *Cot.* 37.

Hire *an army*, *Gen.* 14, 17, v. here.—hire *usury*, v. hyre.

Hired, hyred, es [hyred *pp. of* hyrian *to hear, obey, &c.*] 1. *A family, household*; familia. 2. *A palace, court*; palatium. 3. *An army, a host, crew, an assembly, convent*; exercitus:—1. *Gen.* 12, 17: *Mt.* 24, 45: *Lk.* 2, 4: 12, 42. 2. *Ors.* 6, 30: *Chr.* 1085. 3. *Lk.* 23, 11.—Hired heofona *host of heaven*, *Cd.* 221.—Hiredes-ealder, *Mt.* 21, 33.—Hiredes-fæder, *Mt.* 10, 25.—Hiredes-hlaford *master of the family*, *Elf. gl.* 5.—Hiredes-modor *a mistress.*—Hired-gerefa *exconsul*, *R.* 6.—Hired-man *a domestic*, *Gen.* 50, 7.—Hired-wifman *a maid servant*, *Wulfar. Test. Hicks's Thes. Dis. Ep.* p. 54.—Hired-wist *familiarity*, *Scint.* 78.

m Hirniende *attonitus.*

Hirsum *obedient*, *Ex.* 24, 7, v. hyrsum.

Hirsumian *to obey*, v. hyrsumian.

Higscipe *Familyship;* familiæ status:—*Bt.* 21.
Higð *An endeavour;* nisus, *Som.*
Hih *high,* v. heah.
Hihsend *Hissing;* subsannans, *Lye.*
HIHT, hyht, gehyht *Hope, expectation, refuge, joy, exultation;* spes: — *Ælf. gr.* 12. Gaudium, *T. Ps.* 46, 1.
i Hihtan, gehihtan, ic hihte, we hihten, gehyhtað; *p.* ic gehihte, hihte; *pp.* gehyten. 1. *To hope, trust;* sperare. 2. *To rejoice, exult;* exultare. 3. *To increase;* augere:—1. Ic hihte on God, *Ps.* 68, 4: 30, 18. Þeoda gehyhtað, *Mt.* 12, 21. 2. Muntas gehihtað, *Ps.* 113, 6: 117, 13. 3. He gehihte folc his, *Ps.* 104, 22. Hihte, *M. Ps.* 104, 22.
Hihtful, hyhtful; *adj. Full of joy, pleasant;* gaudii plenus:—*Cd.* 45.
Hihð *height, T. Ps.* 55, 3, v. heaðo.
Hihtleás; *adj. Joyless, hopeless;* gaudio vacuus, *Som.*
Hihtlic, hyhtlic; *adj. Joyous, glad, exulting, hopeful, desirable, sublime;* jucundus, sublimis:—*Cd.* 95: 8.
Hihtlice; *adv. Gladly, diligently;* studiose:—*L. Eccl.* 4.
Hii *the island Hy,* v. Ii.
Hila, hi *Alas;* heu, *Som.*
Hilan *To hill, conceal;* tegere:—Hilð *conceals, Bt.* 27, 1, v. helan.
Hilc *a turning, Cot.* 18, v. hylca.
HILD [*Icel.* hilldur *f.*] *A battle, fight;* pugna:—Hilde-grædige *greedy of battle, Cd.* 150: 155. *Menol.* 481.—Hilde-calla *a man of war, Cd.* 156.—Hilde-leoð *a military song, Jdth.* 11.—Hilde-nædran *military serpents, arrows, Jdth.* 11.—Hilde-rinc *a soldier, Æthelst. Epinic. Chr.* 938.—Hilde-sweg *battle crash, Cd.* 93.—Hilde-præc *martial violence, Cd.* 98.—Hilde-wulfas *soldiers.*
Hilde *affection,* v. hyld.
Hil-hama *A grasshopper;* cicada:—*R.* 37.
HILL, hyll, es; *m.* [*Plat.* hüll, hövel *m*: *Dut.* heuvel *m*: *Ger.* hügel *m*: *Dan.* höj *c*: *Lat.* höll *m. tumulus*: *Icel.* hvoll *m.*] A HILL, *mountain;* collis, mons:—*C. Ps.* 71, 3: *R. Lk.* 23, 30.
j Hil-song *A timbrel, drum;* tympanum:—*T. Ps.* 150, 4.
Hilt, gehilt, holt, hylt, an. HILT, *handle;* capulus:—Þa hiltan, *Jud.* 3, 22.—Hiltleás *without a handle, R.* 52.

Him *to him, or them;* illi, illo, illis; *d. s.* and *pl. of* he.
Himming *a shoe,* v. hemming.
Him-self HIMSELF; ipse:—*Gen.* 18, 7.
Hina *A domestic, servant;* domesticus:—*Cd.* 107.—Hina-ealdor, hina-ealdor *the good man of the house, Bd.* 3, 9.—Hine-man *a farmer.*
Hinan *hence, Bt. R.* p. 156, v. heona.
Hindan *behind;* post:—*Ors.* 6, 36.
Hind-beri, hind-berig HINDBERRY, *raspberry;* fragum, acinus:—*Cot.* 72, 91.
Hind-cealf, hind-calf *A little hind, hind-calf;* hinnulus:—*R.* 19.
Hinde, hynd A HIND; cerva:—*Chr.* 1086.
Hinder-geape, hinder-gepe *versutus, R.* 84: *Coll. Monast.*
Hinderling [hinder *remote,* ling *a pattern*] *Not like the original;* a prototypo prorsus abhorrens, *Lye*:—*Wilk. L. A.-S.* p. 208.
Hinder-scipe, es; *m. Naughtiness, negligence;* nequitia, *Som.*
Hind-hele, hind-heleðe, hind-heolað, hind-heoleðe, hind-hioleðe. HIND-HEEL; pæonia:—*Ælf. gl.* 16.
Hindrian; *pp.* gehindred [*Plat. Dut.* hinderen: *Frs.* hindera: *Ger.* hindern: *Not.* hintern: *Dan.* hindre: *Swed. Icel.* hindra] *To* HINDER; impedire:—*Chr.* 1003.
k Hindweard HINDWARD; a retro:—*L. Alf. pol.* 32.
Hine *him;* illum, se; *ac. s. m. of* he.
Hi-ne *is it not, are they not;* nonne:—*Ps.* 13, 8.
Hine *a domestic,* v. hina.
Hine-weard INWARD; intrinsecus:—*C. R. Mt.* 7, 15.
Hin-gong *A departure;* abitus:—*Cod. Exon.* 30, b.
Hingrian, hyngrian; *p.* ede; *pp.* od [*Dut.* hongern: *Plat. Ger.* hungern: *Not.* hungeren: *Moes.* huggrian, *pronounce* hungrian: *Dan.* hungre: *Swed.* hungra: *Icel.* húngrar.—hunger *hunger*] *To hunger;* esurire:—Hingriað esuriunt, *Mt.* 5, 6: *Lk.* 6, 21. Hingriende, *Cot.* 83. Hingrende, *Cod. Exon.* 27a. Hingrigende, *Mt.* 25, 37. Also used impersonally, Me hingrað *I hunger, Ælf. gr.* Hine hingrede *he was hungry, Lk.* 4, 2.
Hinoð *the bowels, Ps.* 50, 11, v. innoð.
Hinsið, hinnsið *Death, destruction, horrour;* mors, perditio:—*Cd.* 33: *Jdth.* 10.

Hio, heo *She;* illa; *nom. s. f. of* he.—hio *is used for* he, hi, &c.
Hiofon *heaven, Bt.* 33, 4, v. heofon.
Hiofonlic *heavenly, Bt.* 33, 4, v. heofonlic.
Hiolstr *a den,* v. heolster.
Hiom, heom, him *Them;* illis; *d. pl. of* he.
Hion; *f.* [*Swed.* hinna: *Dan.* hinde] *A membrane;* cuticula:—*L. Ethelb.* 37.
Hion, him *To him;* illi; *d. s. of* he.
Hiona, hionan, hionon *hence, Bt.* 36, 2, v. heona.
Hiop, heap, heop A HIP, *the fruit of the dogrose, a bush, bramble;* rosæ sylvestris bacca, rubus:—Brer þe hiopon on-weaxð *a brier which beareth hips, L. M.* 1, 38. Heopbrymel *a hip-bramble, R.* 64.
l Hior *a hinge, Bt.* 34, 7, v. heor.
Hiora, heora, hira *Of them;* illorum; *g. pl. of* he.
Hiord, hiored *a herd, Cot.* 167, v. heord.
Hiort *a heart,* v. heorte.
Hiorð *hearth, Cot.* 20, v. heorð.
Hiow *a hue, Cd.* 14, v. hiw.
Hioweslice *familiarly, Bd.* 5, 2, v. heowæslice.
Hipe *a hip.*—hipes-ban *hip-bone,* v. hype.
Hiran *to hear,* v. hyran.
Hird, hirde *a shepherd,* v. hyrde.
Hird-clerc *a domestic chaplain.*
Hirdelic; *adj. Pastoral;* pastoralis, *Som.*
Hirdnys *a prison, Gen.* 42, 17, v. hyrdnes.
Hirdwendlic *familiar, contemptible, Cot.* 37.
Hire *an army, Gen.* 14, 17, v. here.—hire *usury,* v. hyre.
Hired, hyred, es; [hyred *pp. of* hyrian *to hear, obey,* &c.] 1. *A family, household;* familia. 2. *A palace, court;* palatium. 3. *An army, a host, crew, an assembly, convent;* exercitus:—1. *Gen.* 12, 17: *Mt.* 24, 45: *Lk.* 2, 4: 12, 42. 2. *Ors.* 6, 30: *Chr.* 1085. 3. *Lk.* 23, 11.—Hired heofona *host of heaven, Cd.* 221.—Hiredes-ealder, *Mt.* 21, 33.—Hiredes-fæder, *Mt.* 10, 25.—Hiredes-hlaford *master of the family, Ælf. gl.* 5.—Hiredes-modor *a mistress.*—Hired-gerefa *exconsul, R.* 6.—Hired-man *a domestic, Gen.* 50, 7.—Hired-wifman *a maid servant, Wulfar. Test. Hicks's Thes. Dis. Ep.* p. 54.—Hired-wist *familiarity, Scint.* 78.
m Hirniende *attonitus.*
Hirsum *obedient, Ex.* 24, 7, v. hyrsum.
Hirsumian *to obey,* v. hyrsumian.

(1) v hyse

2 Hiwgende dissemb-
ing Som v hiwian

(3

3 Hiwisc family Idea

(4 Gm I p 235
* Hláfdige

Hiwes any Shape,
colour hue &c
1 Ælc stæf hæfþ preo
þing, nomen, figura,
potestas þ is nama,
& hiw & miht — Hiw,
hu he gesceapen bið
each letter has 3 things a
name, form + power. Hiw
Form (to show it is formed
Elf gr. 2 Som p2 44

(2

Hlænian to
make lean Som v
lænian
Hlænnes lean
ness Som v lænis

(1)

2+ Hwa
þæm hlæste on-fenge
who received the freight Beow
104

(4)

T Hlæw, hlaw + es; m
a heap barrow
+ grave, etc
Ofer þone hlæw
ridon Gm. Myth. Spl
CXXVI

ét icapan 214.41 + Hiw hyaw mannes Grimm

Hirwnes *contempt, T. Ps.* 118, 141, v. hyrwnes.

His, hys, *his, of him;* illius; *g. s. m. of* he.

Hiscan *To reprove;* exprobrare: *L. Ps.* 32, 10.

HISE, hyse [*Plat.* he, heken: *Ger.* er: *Dan. Swed.* han: *Icel.* hann] *A male;* mas, masculus:—Hise-cild, hyse-cild, hyse-rinc *a male child, Ors.* 1, 10: *Gen.* 17, 10, 12.

Hispan *to deride, Ps.* 2, 4, v. hyspan.

Hispanie, Ispanie *Spain;* Hispania:—*Chr.* 1087.

Hissæpe *Cedria, Lye.*

Hit, hyt [*Plat.* het, idt, et: *Dut.* het: *Ger.* es: *Isd.* izs: *Moes.* ita: *Dan.* det, dette: *Swed.* thet, det: *Icel.* thad *or* that] *It;* id. *nom. ac. s. n. of* he:—Ic hit eom *it is I, Gen.* 27, 24.

Hitan *to eat, Lev.* 7, 25, v. ytan.

Hið *a haven, port,* v. hyð.

Hiðende *destroying, Cot.* 95, v. hyðian.

Hiðer *hither,* v. hider.

Hiðfull *Hateful;* odiosus:—*Scint.* 1.

Hiu, heo *she;* illa; *nom. s. f. of* he.

Hiu, *hah;* hei, *Lye.*

Hiu *hue, hew, Lk.* 3, 22, v. hiw.

HIW, heaw, hiwe, hyew, es. [*Plat.* hau *m: Dut.* houw *m: Frs.* hei *f: Ger.* hieb *m.*] 1. *A form, fashion, face, appearance;* species, forma. 2. HUE, *colour;* color:—1. On oðrum hiwe, *Mk.* 16, 12. Wlitig on hiwe, *Gen.* 12, 11. Heofones hiw, *Mt.* 16, 3. 2. Ælces hiwes *of every colour, Bd.* 1, 1. Anes hiwes *of one colour, Elf. gr.* 49.

n Hiwa, an; *m.* [*Icel.* hión: *Swed.* hion] *A family,* in the *pl. persons of the same family, domestics, servants;* familia, domestici:—Heora hiwan eall *all their domestics, Cd.* 133, *Th.* p. 168, 10. To hire hiwun, *Gen.* 39, 14. Mid hira hiwun, *Ex.* 1, 1. To þinum hiwun, *Mk.* 5, 19, v. hiwen.—Hiw-gedal *a separation of a family, a divorce, Mt.* 5, 31.

Hiw-cuð *known to a family, familiar, R.* 115.

Hiw-cuðlice; *adv. Familiarly;* familiariter:—*Bd.* 5, 2.

Hiwcuðrædnes, se; *f. Acquaintance, intimacy;* familiaritas: —*R.* 116.

Hiwen *Servants;* domestici:—Hiwenu beþurfon *domestici indigent, Gen.* 42, 33, v. hiwa.

Hiwere, es; *m.* [hiw *a form*] *One who puts on a form, a hypocrite, a fabricator, an inventor, a fowler;* simulator, fabricator, auceps:—*Elf. gl.* 25, *Prov.* 6.

Hiw-gedal *a divorce,* v. hiwa.

Hiwian, hywan, gehiwan; *part.* hiwigende; *p.* ode; *pp.* od, gehiwod; *v. a.* 1. *To form, fashion, shape, hew, transform;* formare. 2. *To feign, pretend, counterfeit;* simulare:— 1. Þe hiwode eage, *C. Ps.* 93, 9. Þu hiwodest me, *C. Ps.* 138, 4. Sio godcunde fore teohhung eall þing gehiwað *the divine Providence fashions every thing, Bt.* 39, 6. 2. Hiwigende lang gebed, *Lk.* 20, 47. Þeah hit gehywod wære *though it were pretended, Job.* p. 166.

o Hiwing, hiwwing, gehiwung *a pretence, Num.* 12, 8, v. hiwung.

Hiwisce *A family;* familia:—Æt hiwisce *per familias, L. In.* 44.—Hiwisc-fæder *a master of a family, C. Lk.* 13, 25.

Hiwislice; *adv. Familiarly;* familiariter, *Som.*

Hiwleás; *adj. Without form, deformed;* deformis:—*Elf. gl.* 3.

Hiwleasnes, se; *f. Deformity, foulness;* deformitas, *Som.*

Hiwlic; *adj.* [hiw *a form*] *Assuming a form, beautiful, figurative;* formosus, figurativus: —*Somn.* 101, 244.

Hiwlic; *adj.* [hiwa *a family*] *Relating to a family;* matronalis:—*Cot.* 129.

Hiwræden, e; *f.* [hiwa *family,* ræden *state, condition*] *A house, family, tribe;* familia:—To þam sceapum Israela hiwrædene, *Mt.* 10, 6: *Ex.* 2, 1. Hiwrædene þinre fæder *familiæ tuæ pater, Gen.* 28, 2.

Hiwscipe, es; *m. A house, family;* familia:—*L. Ps.* 118, 17.—Hiwscipas *families, L. Ps.* 21, 28.—Hiwscipes fæder *master of a family, Bd.* 5, 12.

Hiwung, hiwing, hiwwing, gehiwung, gehywung, e; *f.* 1. *A forming, creation;* creatio, formatio. 2. *A pretence, counterfeiting, hypocrisy, scoff, irony, ambiguity;* simulatio, hypocrisis:—1. *C. Ps.* 102, 13. 2. Mid þære hiwunga *with the pretences;* cum speciebus, *Bt.* 20.

Hiwung, e; *f.* [hiwa *a family*] *A marriage;* matrimonium:—*Ors.* 2, 2.

Hlad *Load;* onus, *Som.*

HLA'DAN, þu hlætst, he hlæt; *p.* hlód, gehlód; *pp.* hlæden, gehladen; *v. a.* [*Plat. Dut. Ger. Tat. Ot.* laden: *Dan.* ladde: *Swed.* ladda: *Icel.* hlada: *Fin.* ladan: *Pol.* laduje. If the sense of heaviness be considered as the first, this word belongs to hlad *or* lad *a load*] 1. TO LOAD, *burthen, heap up;* onerare. 2. *To* LADE, *draw out, empty;* haurire:— 1. Ongan ad hladan *began a pile to load, Cd.* 140. Gehlodon him, *Cd.* 174. 2. Wæter to hladanne, *Ex.* 2, 16. Hlod wæter, *Ex.* 2, 19.

p Hladung LADING; haustus, *Som.*

Hlæd *A heap;* agger:—*Past.* 21, 5.

Hlædder, hlæder; *g.* hlædre, hlæddre; *d.* hlædre. [*Plat.* ledder *f: Dut.* ladder *f: Frs.* hladder *n: Ger.* leiter *f: Not.* leitero: *Schwa.* laiter *m: Ker.* hleitar] LADDER; scala:— On ufeweardre þære hlædre, *Gen.* 28, 13. Hlædræ rærdon *ladders reared, Cd.* 80.

Hlæddisc *satira, R.* 30.

Hlæden *A bucket;* hauritorium: —*R.* 25, v. hladan.

Hlædle [*Plat. Dut.* lepel *m: Ger.* löffel *m.* hlædle *from* hladan *to lade*] LADLE; spatha, cochleare, *Som.*

Hlæd-weogl, hlæd-wiogl. *An engine* or *wheel of a well to draw water;* antlia:—*Cot.* 9, 101.

Hlæfdie, hlæfdig, hlæfdige, an; *f.* [*Icel.* lavdi *f.*] *Lady, queen;* domina:—Agar forseah hire hlæfdian, *Gen.* 16, 4: *Ps.* 122, 3. Hlæfdigan hete *a lady's hate, Cd.* 103: *Ors.* 4, 3: *L. Ps.* 44, 11. Hiredes hlæfdig *a mistress, Elf. gl.* 5.

Hlæhter, hlæter *laughter,* v. hleahtor.

Hlæn *a loan,* v. læn.

Hlænan *to lend,* v. lænan.

Hlæne, &c. *lean, Gen.* 41, 3, v. læne, &c.

q HLÆST [*Plat. Dut. Ger. Dan. Swed.* last *f: Frs.* hlest *f: Icel.* hlass *n.*] *A burthen, loading, the loading of a ship, merchandise;* navis onus, merces:—Mid hlæste *with lading, Cd.* 71. Holmes hlæst *burthen of the sea, Cd.* 74.—Hence our LAST, *a quantity of corn,* and BALLAST, is from bat *a boat,* and hlæst.

Hlæstan; *pp.* gehlæsted. *To freight, load;* onerare:—Gehlæsted þat scip *loaded the ship, Bd.* 5, 9.

Hlæst-scip *a ship of burthen.*

Hlætst *ladest,* v. hladan.

Hlæw, hlaw, [*Moes.* hlaiw] 1. *A heap, barrow, a small hill;* agger. 2. *A tract of ground gently rising:* hence denominated A LOWE, LOE, frequently used in the names of places; tractus terræ paulatim ascendens:— 1. *Bt. R.* p. 162. On hlæwe

(1) v hyse

Hiwgende dissembl-
ing Son v hiwian

(3

Hiwisc family Th. la

(4. Grm I p ~~229~~ 235
* Hlafdige

Hiwes any shape, colour, hue etc

1 Ælc stæf hæfð preo
(2 þincg, nomen, figura,
potestas þ. is nama,
7 hiw 7 miht - Hiw,
hu he gesceapen bið . (2
each letter has 3 things a
name, form + power. #
Form (i.e) how it is formed
Ælf gr. 2 Som p2 |44

~~Hlænian to
make lean Som v
lænian~~

~~Hlænnes lean
nes Som v lænis~~

(2)

2+ Hwa
þæm hlæste on-fen
who received the freight Beow
104

(4)

~~T Hlæw, hlaw + es; m.
a heap ~~of pebbles~~ barrow
+ grave, etc
Ofer þone hlæw
ridon Grm. Myth. Spl
CXXVI~~

Hit icapan
214, 41 + Hiw
figura
manner
Grimm

Hirwnes *contempt, T. Ps.* 118, 141, v. hyrwnes.
His, hys, *his, of him;* illius; *g. s. m. of* he.
Hiscan *To reprove;* exprobrare: *L. Ps.* 32, 10.
Hise, hyse [*Plat.* he, heken: *Ger.* er: *Dan. Swed.* han: *Icel.* hann] *A male;* mas, masculus:—Hise-cild, hyse-cild, hyse-rinc *a male child, Ors.* 1, 10: *Gen.* 17, 10, 12.
Hispan *to deride, Ps.* 2, 4, v. hyspan.
Hispanie, Ispanie *Spain;* Hispania:—*Chr.* 1087.
Hissæpe *Cedria, Lye.*
Hit, hyt [*Plat.* het, idt, et: *Dut.* het: *Ger.* es: *Isl.* izs: *Moes.* ita: *Dan.* det, dette: *Swed.* thet, det: *Icel.* thad *or* that] *It;* id. *nom. ac. s. n. of* he:—Ic hit eom *it is I, Gen.* 27, 24.
Hitan *to eat, Lev.* 7, 25, v. ytan.
Hið *a haven, port,* v. hyð.
Hiðende *destroying, Cot.* 95, v. hyðian.
Hiðer *hither,* v. hider.
Hiðfull *Hateful;* odiosus:—*Scint.* 1.
Hiu, heo *she;* illa; *nom. s. f. of* he.
Hiu, *hah;* hei, *Lye.*
Hiu *hue, hew, Lk.* 3, 22, v. hiw.
Hiw, heaw, hiwe, hyew, es. [*Plat.* hau *m*: *Dut.* houw *m*: *Frs.* hei *f*: *Ger.* hie *m.*] 1. *A form, fashion, face, appearance;* species, forma. 2. Hue, *colour;* color:—1. On oðrum hiwe, *Mk.* 16, 12. Wlitig on hiwe, *Gen.* 12, 11. Heofones hiw, *Mt.* 16, 3. 2. Ælces hiwes *of every colour, Bd.* 1, 1. Anes hiwes *of one colour, Elf. gr.* 49.
Hiwa, an; *m.* [*Icel.* hión: *Swed.* hion] *A family,* in the *pl. persons of the same family, domestics, servants;* familia, domestici:—Heora hiwan eall *all their domestics, Cd.* 133, *Th.* p. 168, 10. To hire hiwun, *Gen.* 39, 14. Mid hira hiwun, *Ex.* 1, 1. To þinum hiwun, *Mk.* 5, 19, v. hiwen.—Hiw-gedal *a separation of a family, a divorce, Mt.* 5, 31.
Hiw-cuð *known to a family, familiar, R.* 115.
Hiw-cuðlice; *adv. Familiarly;* familiariter:—*Bd.* 5, 2.
Hiwcuðrædnes, se; *f. Acquaintance, intimacy;* familiaritas:—*R.* 116.
Hiwen *Servants;* domestici:—Hiwenu beþurfon *domestici indigent, Gen.* 42, 33, v. hiwa.
Hiwere, es; *m.* [hiw *a form*] *One who puts on a form, a hypocrite, a fabricator, an inventor, a fowler;* simulator, fabricator, auceps:—*Elf. gl.* 25, *Prov.* 6.
Hiw-gedal *a divorce,* v. hiwa.
Hiwian, hywan, gehiwan; *part.* hiwigende; *p.* ode; *pp.* od, gehiwod; *v. a.* 1. *To form, fashion, shape, hew, transform;* formare. 2. *To feign, pretend, counterfeit;* simulare:—1. Þe hiwode eage, *C. Ps.* 93, 9. Þu hiwodest me, *C. Ps.* 138, 4. Sio godcunde fore teohhung eall þing gehiwað *the divine Providence fashions every thing, Bt.* 39, 6. 2. Hiwigende lang gebed, *Lk.* 20, 47. Þeah hit gehywod wære *though it were pretended, Job.* p. 166.
Hiwing, hiwwing, gehiwung *a pretence, Num.* 12, 8, v. hiwung.
Hiwisce *A family;* familia:—Æt hiwisce *per familias, L. In.* 44.—Hiwisc-fæder *a master of a family, C. Lk.* 13, 25.
Hiwislice; *adv. Familiarly;* familiariter, *Som.*
Hiwleás; *adj. Without form, deformed;* deformis:—*Elf. gl.* 8.
Hiwleasnes, se; *f. Deformity, foulness;* deformitas, *Som.*
Hiwlic; *adj.* [hiw *a form*] *Assuming a form, beautiful, figurative;* formosus, figurativus:—*Somn.* 101, 244.
Hiwlic; *adj.* [hiwa *a family*] *Relating to a family;* matronalis:—*Cot.* 129.
Hiwræden, e; *f.* [hiwa *family,* ræden *state, condition*] *A house, family, tribe;* familia:—To þam sceapum Israela hiwrædene, *Mt.* 10, 6: *Ex.* 2, 1. Hiwrædene þinre fæder *familiæ tuæ pater, Gen.* 28, 2.
Hiwscipe, es; *m. A house, family;* familia:—*L. Ps.* 113, 17. Hiwscipas *families, L. Ps.* 21, 28.—Hiwscipes fæder *master of a family, Bd.* 5, 12.
Hiwung, hiwing, hiwwing, gehiwung, gehywung, e; *f.* 1. *A forming, creation;* creatio, formatio. 2. *A pretence, counterfeiting, hypocrisy, scoff, irony, ambiguity;* simulatio, hypocrisis:—1. *C. Ps.* 102, 13. 2. Mid þære hiwunga *with the pretences;* cum speciebus, *Bt.* 20.
Hiwung, e; *f.* [hiwa *a family*] *A marriage;* matrimonium:—*Ors.* 2, 2.
Hlad *Load;* onus, *Som.*
Hla'dan, þu hlætst, he hlæt; *p.* hlód, gehlód; *pp.* hlæden, gehladen; *v. a.* [*Plat. Dut. Ger. Tat. Ot.* laden: *Dan.* ladde: *Swed.* ladda: *Icel.* hlada: *Fin.* ladan: *Pol.* laduje. If the sense of heaviness be considered as the first, this word belongs to hlad *or* lad *a load*] 1. *To* LOAD, *burthen, heap up;* onerare. 2. *To* LADE, *draw out, empty;* haurire:—1. Ongan ad hladan *began a pile to load, Cd.* 140. Gehlodon him, *Cd.* 174. 2. Wæter to hladanne, *Ex.* 2, 16. Hlod wæter, *Ex.* 2, 19.
Hladung LADING; haustus, *Som.*
Hlæd *A heap;* agger:—*Past.* 21, 5.
Hlædder, hlæder; *g.* hlædre, hlæddre; *d.* hlædre, [*Plat.* ledder *f*: *Dut.* ladder *f*: *Frs.* hladder *n*: *Ger.* leiter *f*: *Not.* leitero: *Schwa.* laiter *m*: *Ker.* hleitar] LADDER; scala:—On ufeweardre þære hlædre, *Gen.* 28, 13. Hlædræ rærdon *ladders reared, Cd.* 80.
Hlæddisc *satira, R.* 30.
Hlæden *A bucket;* hauritorium:—*R.* 25, v. hladan.
Hlædle [*Plat. Dut.* lepel *m*: *Ger.* löffel *m.* hlædle *from* hladan *to lade*] LADLE; spatha, cochleare, *Som.*
Hlæd-weogl, hlæd-wiogl. *An engine* or *wheel of a well to draw water;* antlia:—*Cot.* 9, 101.
Hlæfdie, hlæfdig, hlæfdige, an; *f.* [*Icel.* lavdi *f.*] *Lady, queen;* domina:—Agar forseah hire hlæfdian, *Gen.* 16, 4: *Ps.* 122, 3. Hlæfdigan hete *a lady's hate, Cd.* 103: *Ors.* 4, 3: *L. Ps.* 44, 11. Hiredes hlæfdig *a mistress, Elf. gl.* 5.
Hlæhter, hlæter *laughter,* v. hleahtor.
Hlæn *a loan,* v. læn.
Hlænan *to lend,* v. lænan.
Hlæne, &c. *lean, Gen.* 41, 3, v. læne, &c.
HLÆST, [*Plat. Dut. Ger. Dan. Swed.* last *f*: *Frs.* hlest *f*: *Icel.* hlass *n.*] *A burthen, loading, the loading of a ship, merchandise;* navis onus, merces:—Mid hlæste *with lading, Cd.* 71. Holmes hlæst *burthen of the sea, Cd.* 74.—Hence our LAST, *a quantity of corn, and* BALLAST, is from bat *a boat,* and hlæst.
Hlæstan; *pp.* gehlæsted. *To freight, load;* onerare:—Gehlæsted þat scip *loaded the ship, Bd.* 5, 9.
Hlæst-scip *a ship of burthen.*
Hlætst *ladest,* v. hladan.
Hlæw, hlaw, [*Moes.* hlaiw] 1. *A heap, barrow, a small hill;* agger. 2. *A tract of ground gently rising:* hence denominated A LOWE, LOE, frequently used in the names of places; tractus terræ paulatim ascendens:—1. *Bt. R.* p. 162. On hlæwe

on a hill, Menol. 500. 2. Hundes-hlaw Hound's-low; canum tumulus. Leod, Lude-hlaw Ludlow; populi tumulus. Winnes-hlaw Winnes-low, Winslow; pugnæ tumulus, vel forsan Windes-hlaw ventosus tumulus. Mere-hlaw Mer-low; mariscis circumdatus tumulus; denique East-hlaw East-low; orientalis tumulus. West-hlaw West-low; occidentalis tumulus, &c.

HLA'F, es; m. [Ger. lab, laib, leib n. most commonly connected with brot bread, but also used alone to designate bread: Old Ger. hlaf: Moes. hlaifs, hlaibs: Lat. mid. leibo, libo] Bread, LOAF; panis:—Þinne hlaf etan to eat thy bread, Cd. 43.—Ic eom lifes hlaf, Jn. 6, 35, 48.—Hlafas wyrcan to make loaves, Cd. 228.—Cnapa hæfð fif berene hlafas, Jn. 6, 9.—Hlaf-æta a loaf-eater, domestic, menial servant, L. Ethelb. 25.—Hlaf-gang the procession of the host, L. Const. p. 112.—Hlaf gebrocht broken bread, Menol.—Hlaf-leaste want of bread, Nath. 7.—Hlaf-mæsse loaf-mass, v. in alphabetical order.—Hlaf-ofn loaf-oven, an oven.

Hlafdig, hlafdia a lady, C. Jn. 20, 16, v. hlæfdie.

Hlaf-mæsse [mæsse a mass] The loaf-mass or feast, the feast on the first of August, called Lammas-day, when the Saxons offered an oblation of loaves made from new corn. After rejecting h and f, we have lamæsse, hence LAMMAS; panis [sive frumenti primitiarum] festum, Ors. 6, 19.

Hlaford, es; m. [Icel. lávardr tutor collegii] A LORD; dominus:—Of his hlafordes godum, Gen. 24, 10: Mt. 21, 30. ¶ Cyne-hlaford, Gecynde-hlaford his lawful or liege lord.—Hlaford-hyld allegiance to a lord, Ors. 6, 37.—Hlaford-searwe, hlaford-swice disloyalty, infidelity; dominii proditio.—Hlaford-swica a traitor.

Hlafordleas LORDLESS; sine domino:—L. Ethel. 2.

Hlafordóm, es; m. Dominion, lordship; dominium:—Past. 28.

Hlafordscipe, es; m. Lordship; dominatio:—Ps. 144, 13: Bt. 7, 2.

Hlagole Ridiculous; promptus ad risum:—Off. Reg. 15.

Hlahende laughing, v. hlihan.

Hlammessa lammas, Chr. 1009, v. hlafmæsse.

Hlanca Lank; macilentus:—Jdth. 11.

Hland, hlond [Icel. hland n.—hence in Lanc. to this day they use, in the same sense, land or lant] Urine; lotium, urina:—Cot. 176.

Hlaw an elevation, a hill, v. hlæw.

Hleaf-gewrit [hleaf leave, gewrit written] A written license, a diploma; cautio, diploma.

Hleahtor, hleahter [Plat. Dut. lach m: Ger. gelächter n: Ker. hlatre, hlahtre: Dan. latter c: Swed. löje n: Icel. hláter m.] LAUGHTER; risus:—Bt. 16, 2. ¶ Hleahtor-bære a laugher, C. R. Ben. 4.—Hleahter-ful full of laughter, Guth. vit. pref.—Hleahter-lic laughable, Id.—Hleahtor-smith laughter-smith, laugher, Cd. 144.

Hleap a leap, v. hlyp.

Hleápan, he hlypð; p. hleop, we hleopon; pp. gehleápen [Plat. Dut. loopen: Frs. hlapa: Ger. laufen: Ot. laufan: Wil. lofen: Mons. louffan: Ker. hlauffan: Moes. hlaupan: Dan. löbe: Swed. löpa: Icel. hlaupa, hleypa: Heb. חלף hlp a passing] To LEAP, jump; saltare, salire:—Hleop on þæs cyninges stedan leaped on the king's steed, Bd. 2, 13.

Hleapende, Bd. 5, 2.

Hleápere, es; m. 1. A LEAPER, messenger, courier; saltator, cursor. 2. A leper; leprosus:—1. Butan twegen hleaperas but two couriers, Chr. 889. 2. Som.

Hleapestre A female dancer; saltatrix, Som.

Hleape-wince Lapwing; vanellus, Som.

Hleappettan To leap up; exsilire:—Bd. 5, 2.

Hleapung, e; f. LEAPING; saltatio, Som.

Hlear the cheek, jaw, face, R. 71, v. hleor.

Hleat bowed, v. hlutan, lutan.

Hlece Leaky; rimosus:—Hlece scip a leaky ship, Past. 57, 1.

Hleda, hlede A seat; sedile:—Elf. gr. 9, 2.

Hlega A traitor; proditor:—C. Lk. 6, 16.

Hleglende A humming; sonans:—Cot. 24.

Hlehter a laugher, Gen. 21, 6, v. hleahtor.

Hlehter-full full of laughter.

Hlem a sound, Past. 26, 5, v. hlyn.

Hlemman To make a noise, to crackle; crepitare ut flamma:—Cod. Exon. 97, b.

Hlence the proud, Cd. 151, v. wlænce.

Hlenortear hyssopus, L. Ps. 50, 8.

HLEO, hleow [Plat. löve f. a bower: Dut. luwte f. a shelter, calm place: Frs. hli f. a shed: Ger. laube f. a bower: Dun. Swed. loge m: Dan. læ: Icel. hlif f. hlie n.] 1. A shade, shelter, a basking in the sun while sheltered from the wind; umbraculum, apricitas. 2. An asylum, refuge; asylum, refugium:—1. On þisses holtes hleo in the shadow of this holt, Cd. 39. Under swegles hleo sub ætheris umbraculo, Cod. Exon. 16, b. 2. His recedes hleow his dwellings shelter, Cd. 112. Earmra hleo a refuge of the poor, Cd. 203, v. hlyðe.—Hleo-hræstnes a supplanter, L. Ps. 40, 10.

Hleohtor laughter, v. hleahtor.

Hleom a limb, Bd. 3, 9, v. lim.

Hleomæg, es; m. [hleo a house, mæg a relation] A kinsman, relation; consanguineus:—Ne can ic hleomæges sið I know not a kinsman's path, Cd. 48.

Hleomoc, hleomoce The herb pimpernel; anagallis:—L. M. 1, 2, 38.

Hleonade, hleonodon leaned, rested, inclined; p. of hlynian.

Hleonung Seat; discubitus:—C. Lk. 20, 46, v. hlining.

Hleop leaped, v. hleapan.

HLEOR, hlear [Plat. gluur] A face, countenance, cheek, jaw; vultus:—Tearig hleor tearful face, Cd. 104: 43.—Hleor-ban maxilla, L. Ps. 131, 5.

Hleor-lora A scholar; discipulus:—Cd. 92.

Hleótan, he hlyt; p. hleát, gehleat, we hluton; pp. hloten, gehloten [Plat. lotten: Dut. loten: Ger. losen: Icel. hlutaz, v. hlot a lot] To cast lots, to appoint or ordain by lot; sortiri:—Uton hleotan, Jn. 19, 24. Hi hluton they cast lots, Bd. 5, 11.

Hleoðo, hleoðu, hliðu Mountain tops; juga:—Cd. 72: 86, v. heoðo.

HLEOÐOR, 1. A sound; sonus, strepitus. 2. A revelation, an oracle; revelatio:—1. Þa cwom wuldres hleoðor then came a glorious sound, Cd. 162: 181. Hleoðrum gedælde in sounds divided, Cd. 81. 2. Æt hleoðre by revelation, Cd. 64.

Hleoðor-cwyd, es; m. [hleo a shady place, Þor Thor, cwyd a saying] The speech of Thor, an oracle, a revelation; oraculum, revelatio:—Abraham bewand þa hleoðor-cwidas on hige sinum Abraham turned these revelations in his mind, Cd. 107: 109.

2 3 Hlanc lank ~~Hlan~~ 10 flanca

Hleo, hleow, cs; m a shelter, etc. l 19 hlyewd
~~Hleo~~-burh a shelter city; an asylum Beo K 1817

b) c) l 10 Hleahtor-smid a laugher

1 b) gm I p 267, 11 ? hladan to lade haurire id. 10.

a Hlast, ~~cs m~~ a trace footstep Beo gl v last

d Hleapan, l 1 p. l 9 1/3 II 1 to leap jump 2 to run; currere etc

1 Hléápan leton fealwe mearas let fallow horses run Beo K 1722

7 ~~Hleo-burh asylum~~ Beo. 70 — ~~Hleo-mæg a kinsman~~ ~~cd 40 H 61, 34~~

Hleónian to lean Beo K 2830 v hlynian

II ~~Hleor~~ Beo v

3 Hleo-blæce paleness of the face Som

1 hleibort, leibort

3

a Hláf-ord nutritor, dominus gm I p 2293 Die volle form ins goth. Hlaifwards Hlaifondis. Valth.

Bes hlede see sedile Ps ~~gr~~ 9. 7 Som p 8. 14

d ~~Hleaford~~ socn ei ~~The Lord's protection to his man or Tenant~~ Som ~~Gavelkynd p 134~~ 21

e ~~Hleat~~ a lot from Aelfh p 642 v hlot

f Hleat lotted, allotted p of hleotan

g Hlehan to laugh ~~Som~~ Som v hlehan

h Hlem, es; m a sound, noise; prayor Beo gl

i 4 Hlemman ~~pp~~ hlam we hlummon to sound, resound ~~Th An~~

7)

a Hleodrymd Loud, shrill, making a great noise; So norus Som

a Hlim-bed for hlin-bed a death ~~back~~ bed Beo K 6063

b) b Hlimman to sound; sonare Cod Ex 81, b Leo gt v ~~hlynnan~~ 1pl hlemman

c Hlin-scua an; m incumbens umbra Cod Ex 73 b Beo gt in-scua

Hlom urine Ben v hlond

Hlond adl. c. f strangury

Hlotan to lot, Som Bendye v hleotan

Hlod-bót

c Hlid-geat a back door Som

a Hlist hearing Som v hlyst &c

e Hlid, hleod, es; n ~~a cover~~ opereulum, clivus Beo K 3781

a covering, refuge, declivity

Hleoðor-stede [stede *a place*] *A place of an oracle, a tabernacle;* oraculi locus :—*Cd.* 109.

Hleoðre *by revelation*, v. hleoðor.

Hleoðrian; *p.* ode; *pp.* od. 1. *To make a noise* or *tumult, to rebuke;* resonare. 2. *To sound, sing;* canere. 3. *To fall to, betake himself to;* incumbere:—1. Forþan efne find þine hleoðrodon, *Ps.* 82, 2: *Bd.* 3, 19. 2. Hleoðrade *sang, Cd.* 188: *C. Ps.* 57, 2. 3. Geornlice on gebede hleoðrede *obnixe in precibus voce sua incumbebat, Bd.* 4, 3.

Hleoðrung, e; *f. A noise, rebuking, chiding;* increpatio:—*Ps.* 37, 15.

Hleow *a shade, an asylum,* v. hleo.—Hleow-fæst *warm;* calidus, *R. Ben.* 55.—Hleow-feðeras *guardian wings, Cd.* 131.—Hleow-magas *relations.*—Hleow-stede *a sunny place, Elf. gr.* 27.—Hleow-stole *place of defence, an asylum, Cd.* 94.

Hleowan, hleowian [*Icel.* hlúa] 1. *To bubble, to make the noise of boiling;* ebullire. 2. *To nourish, cherish;* fovere:—1. Oð hit hleowe to wylme *till it bubbles with heat, L. In.* 78. 2. *Som.*

Hleowð, *A warmth, as of the sun while sheltered from the wind, a shade, an asylum;* apricitas, umbraculum:—*Elf. gr.* 27, v. hleo. — Hleowð-magas *relations,* v. hleomæg.

Hlet *a lot, Bd.* 2, 20, v. hlot.

Hlewan *to low as a cow, Elf. gr.* 26, v. hlowan.

Hliccetung, e; *f. Lightning;* coruscatio:—*V. Ps.* 143, 8.

Hlichan *to laugh, Elf. gr.* 26, v. hlihan.

Hlid, gehlid [*Plat. Dut.* lid *n*: *Frs.* hlid *n*: *Ger.* lied *n.* still used in the compound word augenlied *eye-lid*: *Ker.* lid: *Tat.* lido: *Moes.* lith: *Dan. Swed.* led *n*: *Icel.* hlid *a door*] A lid, *cover;* tegmen:—*Mt.* 27, 60.—Hlid-fæst *a fast lid.*—Hlid-gata *a back door, R.* 29.

Hlida-ford [*Flor.* Lideforda: *Brom. Hunt.* Lideford.—Lida *the name of a river,* ford *a ford*] Lidford, *Devonshire, Chr.* 997.

Hlidan; *p.* behlad, hi behlidon; *pp.* gehlidad, gehlyd; *v. a.* [hlid *a cover*] *To cover with a lid, to cover, close, shut;* tegere:—Hi þone pytt eft behlidon, *Gen.* 29, 3. Heo siððan togædere behlad *the* [eorðe *earth*] *then closed together, Ors.* 3, 3.

Hliet *a lot,* v. hlot.

Hlifendre *Red lead;* minium, *Som.*

Hlifian, hlifigan, hlifigean; *p.* ode; *pp.* od. 1. *To arise, raise up, tower, soar, to be conspicuous;* eminere. 2. *To smear, cover with vermilion;* linire:—1. Geseah þa gearo hlifigean *saw then arise complete, Cd.* 66. Gesawon salo hlifian *saw halls arise, Cd.* 109. Se wer geseah hlifigan hea dune *vir vidit eminere altum montem, Cd.* 139. Hlifigan, *Cd.* 205. 2. *Som.*

Hligað, *probably for* hnigað *incline;* inclinant:—*Cd.* 190, *Lye.*

Hlihan, hlihhan, ic hlihhe, hlihð, we hliað; *p.* hlóh, ahlóh, gehlóh, þu hloge we hlógon, gehlógon. [*Plat. Dut. Ger. Not.* lachen: *Frs.* hlaka: *Tat.* lahan: *Moes.* hlajan: *Dan.* lee: *Swed.* le: *Icel.* hlæa] *To laugh, deride;* ridere:—Ne hloh ic—ac þu hloge, *Gen.* 18, 15. Hlogon on bysmor, *L. Ps.* 21, 6. Hlihende *laughing, Cd.* 95.

Hlihtan *To* light, *alight;* descendere ab equo:—*Bd.* 3, 14.

Hlinc A linch, *balk, ridge of land left unploughed as a boundary;* agger limitaneus:—*Cod. Exon.* p. 56, a, *Heming.* p. 144.

Hlinian *to lean,* v. hlynian.

Hlining, hlinung, e; *f. A sitting down, a seat;* discubitus:—Þa forman hlininga, *Lk.* 20, 46.

Hlinode *leaned,* v. hlynian.

Hlionian *to lean,* v. hlynian.

Hliosa *fame, Bt.* 39, 11, v. hlisa.

Hlioðo *mountain-tops,* v. hleoðo.

Hlioðrian *to make a noise, to sing,* v. hleoðrian.

Hlip *a leap,* v. hlyp.

Hlisa, hlysa, hliosa, an; *m.* [*Dut.* leus, leuze *f. a sign*: *Icel.* lysa] *Fame, rumour, renown, glory, favour, esteem;* fama:—Þære brædinge his hlisan *of a spreading of his glory, Bt.* 19, *Card.* p. 106, 2: *Elf. T.* p. 13, 22: *Mt.* 24, 6. To habbenne þone idelan hlisan *to have vain fame, Bt.* 19, *Card.* p. 104, 24. — Hlis-bære *fame bearing, famous.*—Hlis-eadig *renowned, famous, Bt.* 13.—Hlis-eadignes *celebrity, Bt.* 33, 1.—Hlis-full *famous, Gen.* 6, 4.—Hlis-geadig *famous, Bt.* 33, 1.

Hlistnere *A listener, one who is obedient;* auscultator, *Som.*

Hlið, 1. *A declivity, slope, the side of a hill;* clivus. 2. *Lithe, gentle, quiet;* flexilis, mollis, v. lið:—1. Be hliðe heare dune *by a slope of a high hill, Cd.* 122. On hliðe nerede *preserved on a mountain's side, Cd.* 173. 2. *Som.*

Hliðu *heights, Cd.* 166, v. hleoðo.

Hliwð *warmth, L. Can. Edg. pn.* 16, v. hleowð.

Hlocan *To rush on;* irruere, *Lye.*

Hlód *loaded; p. of* hladan.

Hlodd *a portion, lot,* v. hlot.

Hlóge *laughedst.*—hlóh *laughed,* v. hlihan.

Hlond *urine.* — hlond-adl *the strangury,* v. hland.

Hlosan *to perish,* v. losian.

Hlosnan, hlosnian; *part.* hlosnende, hlosniende. *To expect with anxiety, to fear;* expectare suspense:—*C. R. Lk.* 19, 48.

Hlot, hlyt, gehlot [*Plat.* lott *n*: *Dut. Fr.* lot *n*: *Frs.* hlot *n*: *Ger.* los *n*: *Ot.* loz, loza: *Tat.* lozze: *Swed.* lott *m*: *Icel.* hluti *m. pars*] Lot; sors:—Wurpon hlot *miserunt sortem, Mt.* 27, 35. Wurpon hlotu *miserunt sortes, Lk.* 23, 34. On handum þinum hlyt min, *Ps.* 30, 18. On hlyte *by lot, Elf. gr.* 38. — Hlot-beod *a lot-bed, a balloting-box.*

Hloten *lotted,* v. hleotan.

HLOÐ. 1. *A band* or *company of robbers, from seven to thirty-five;* prædonum turma. 2. *What is taken by robbers, booty, spoil;* præda:—1. Þeofas we hatað oð seofon men, from seofon hloð oð fif and þrittig, and siððan bið here *thieves we call to seven men, from seven to thirty-five a band, and after that number an army, L. In.* 12, *W.* p. 17, 11: *Ors.* 3, 1. 2. *Bd.* 1, 34: 2, 20.—Hloðum *in crowds,* v. þeof, here.—Hloð-bot *compensation for robbery, L. Alf. pol.* 26, *W.* p. 40, 24, 26.

Hloða *a blanket, Cot.* 118, v. loða.

Hloðere *A robber;* prædator:—*Cot.* 170.

Hloðian *To rob, plunder;* prædas agere:—*Bd.* 1, 12, 14.

Hloðum *in crowds,* v. hloð.

Hlowan [*Plat.* lüen, luyen: *Dut.* loeyen: *Old Ger.* lutan: *Lips. gl.* ludon] *To* low, *bellow;* mugire, boare:—*Cot.* 188.

Hloweng *bombus, Cot.* 27, *Lye.*

Hlowung, e; *f.* A lowing; mugitus, *Som.*

Hlúd, lud [*Plat.* luud: *Dut.* luid: *Frs.* hlud: *Ger.* laut: *Isd.* hlud: *Ot.* lut: *Icel.* hlióð, ludr *m. a trumpet*] Loud, *talkative;* sonorus:—On stemne hludre *cum voce sonora, Ps.* 32, 3. — Hlud-clipol *calling aloud, R. Ben. interl.* 7.—Hluddra-sang *a chorus, R.* 34.

—Hlud-stefn, hlud-stemn *a loud voice, Cot.* 105. — Hlud-swege *a loud sound;* altisonus, *Elf. T.* p. 25.

Hlud-geat *a back door,* v. hlid, &c.

Hludnes, se; *f. Loudness;* sonoritas, *Som.*

Hludur *concisius; Cot.* 53.

Hluin *a sound, Jdth.* 11, v. hlyn.

Hluta *A fortune-teller,* v. hlyta.

Hlutan; *p.* hleat. *To bend, bow, C. Mk.* 5, 22, v. lutan.

HLUTER, hlutor, hluttor, hluðer; *g.* hluttres, hlutres; *m.* hluttre; *f. def.* se hlutra; seo, þæt hluttre [*Plat.* luter: *Dut.* louter: *Ger.* lauter: *Ot.* lutar: *Isd.* hlutro: *Dan. Swed.* lutter: *Wel.* llather *bright, shining*] *Pure, lucid, limpid, clear, simple, unmixed;* purus:— Gif þin eage byð hluttor, *Lk.* 11, 34. Mid hluttrum eagum his modes *with pure eyes of his mind, Bt.* 34, 8: *R.* p. 182. Hluttor wæter *pure water, Cd.* 191. Hluttre willan *pure wells, Bd.* 2, 16. Hluttres ealoð, þrittig ambra *of pure ale, thirty tubs, L. In.* 70. Twa tunnan fulle hlutres aloð *two barrels full of pure ale, Chr.* 852. Hluttor gebed *pura oratio, R. Ben.* 20.

* Hluton *cast lots; p. of* hleotan.

Hluttorlice; *adv. Purely, simply, merely;* luculenter:—*Greg.* 2, 20: *Bd.* 4, 22: 5, 13.

Hluttornes, se; *f. Purity, simplicity, sincerity;* puritas:—*Bd.* 2, 5, 15.

Hlyd *a noise, T. Ps.* 9, 7, v. gehlyd.

Hlydan; *p.* hlydde. *To make a noise, to be tumultuous, to vociferate, chatter;* tumultuari, clamare:—Þine fynd hlydað *inimici tui tumultuantur, Jud.* 5. Þa hlyddon hig, *Lk.* 23, 5. Hlydende, *Mt.* 9, 23.

Hlydanford *Lidford,* v. Hlidaford.

Hlydde *loud, loudly, Jdth.* 10, v. hlud.

Hlyd-monað [hlyd *loud, tumultuous;* monað *a month*] *March;* Mensis Martius:—*Menol.* 71, v. hreðe-monað.

Hlyhende *laughing,* v. hliban.

HLYN, hlynn, hlem [*Old Ger.* lamm, limme, laimb, lami *n*: *Icel.* hliómr *m.*] *A sound, noise, din;* sonus:— Hlyn awehte *sonum excitavit, Cd.* 52: 119: *Ors.* 1, 12. Hlynn wearð on ceastrum *a din was in cities, Cd.* 119.

Hlynan, hlynnan *To sound, make a noise, resound;* sonare:— Hlydde hlynede *tumultuose obstrepebat, Jdth.* 10.

HLYNIAN, hlinian, *part.* hlyniende, hlinigende; *p.* hlinode, hleonade, we hleonodon [*Plat. Dut.* leunen: *Ger.* lehnen: *Ker.* hlinen: *Wil.* leinen: *Dan.* læne: *Swed.* luta] *To* LEAN, *incline, rest on;* recumbere:—Hlinode on þæs Hælendes bearme, *Jn.* 13, 23. Hlyniende, *Bd.* 3, 17.

b Hlynna *A brook;* torrens:—*R. Jn.* 18, 1.

HLYP, hlip, hleap, es; *m.* A LEAP, *jump;* saltus:—Heorta hlypum *with harts' leaps, Cd.* 203.

Hlypa *A stirrup;* scansile:—*Ors.* 6, 24.

Hlyrian *To play, sound an instrument;* buccinare:—*L. Ps.* 80, 3.

Hlysan *To celebrate, illustrate;* celebrare, *Som.*

Hlyse, hlysa *fame,* v. hlisa.

Hlys-full *famous,* v. hlisa.

Hlysnend *attonitus, Cot.* 7, *Lye.*

Hlyst, gehlyst *The sense of hearing;* auditus:—On þæs folces hlyste, *Lk.* 7, 1: *Cd.* 181.

Hlystan, gehlystan; *v. a.* [*Plat.* lüstern, lustern: *Dut.* luisteren: *Ger.* lauschen: *Old Ger.* and in the dialect of the common people in *South. Ger.* laustern, losen, luzen: *Moes.* hlausjan: *Dan.* lure *to lurk, listen:* *Swed.* lura: *Icel.* hlusta] *To* LISTEN, *hear, attend to, obey;* audire:—Sunu min hlyste minre lare, *Gen.* 27, 8. Hig hliston him, *Lk.* 16, 29.

Hlyt *a lot,* v. hlot.

Hlyt *cast lots,* v. hleótan.

Hlyta, hlytta, an; *m. One who casts lots, a fortune-teller;* sortilegus:—*Ors.* 4, 7. Hlytan, hlyttan *fortune-tellers.*

Hlyðe *Slender, empty;* tenuis: Þa seofon hlyðran ear *septem tenues aristæ, Gen.* 41, 27.

Hlytte *A collector;* tributi exactor:—*Chr.* 911.

Hlyttrian *To melt, purify;* liquare:—*Elf. gr.* 37.

Hlyttrung, e; *f. A melting;* liquatio, *Lye.*

Hlywa *warm,* v. hleo.

c Hlywing *A refuge;* refugium:—*R. Conc.* 11.

Hlywð *A refuge, support, sustenance;* refugium:—*L. Eccl.* 32, v. hleowð.

Hnæcan [*Dut.* nekken *to slay, kill secretly:* *Plat.* nikken *to bend the neck,* from whence is called in *Plat.* nikker *m. an executioner, and the devil:* *Ger.* nicken: *Ker.* keneiken: *Not.* nichen: *Dan.* nikke: *Swed.* nicka. — *from Dan.* nokken, nökker: *Swed.* necken: *Icel.* nikr, nykr *m. a water spirit, the devil*] *To kill;* necare:—*Elf. gr.* 24.

Hnægan [*Plat.* neitern, nichen: *Dut.* grinniken: *Swed.* gnägga: *Icel.* hneggia] *To* NEIGH; hinnire:—*Elf. gr.* 22, 30.

Hnægung, e; *f.* NEIGHING; hinnitus:—*Elf. gr.* 1.

Hnæp, hnæpp, nappe [*Plat.* napp *n*: *Dut.* nap *m.* napje *n*: *Ger.* napf *m*: *Old Ger.* naff: *Mon.* napho: *Schw.* napfe: *Old Fr.* hanap, napf: *Swed.* napp *m*: *Icel.* hnappr *m.*] *A cup, goblet, bowl;* calix:—*Elf. gl.* 21.

Hnæppian, hnappian; *p.* ode; *pp.* od; *v. n. To* NAP, *take a nap, to sleep, rest, lie;* dormire:—Se þe hnæppað, *Ps.* 40, 9: *Bt.* 39, 7. Hnæppode, *Ps.* 3, 5. Hnappiende, *Ps.* 77, 71.

Hnæppung, hnappung, e; *f. Napping, sleeping;* dormitatio:—*Ps.* 131, 4.

Hnah *bowed,* v. hnigan.

Hneaw *Sparing, niggardly, covetous;* tenax:—*Cd.* 136.

Hneawlice; *adv. Sparingly, covetously:* tenaciter:—*Cd.* 86.

d Hneawnes, se; *f. Parsimony, niggardliness;* tenacitas, *Som.*

HNECCA, an; *m.* [*Plat.* nakken *m*: *Dut.* nek *m*: *Ger.* nacken *m*: *Dan.* nakke *c*: *Swed.* nacke *m*: *Icel.* hnacki *m. occiput:* *Fr.* nuque *f*: *It.* nuca: *Hung.* nyak: *Lap.* nikke] A NECK; cervix, occiput:—Fram þam fot-wolmum of þone hneccan, *Deut.* 28, 35.

Hnehsud *softened,* v. hnescian.

Hneomagas *relations,* v. cneomagas.

HNESC, hnysc, nesc; *adj. Tender, soft,* NESH; tener:— Þonne hys twig byð hnesce, *Mt.* 24, 32. Hnescum gyrlum gescrydne, *Mt.* 11, 8. Hwi ferde ge to gesonne þone man mid hnescum reafum gescrydne, *Lk.* 7, 25. Hnesce lufu *tender love, Past.* 17, 11. Þat ælc wuht bið innanweard hnescost *that every creature is inwardly softest, Bt.* 34, 10.

Hnescian, anescian, ahnescian; *p.* hi gehnesctun, hnescodon; *pp.* gehnescod. *To make nesh, to soften, mitigate, mollify, effeminate;* mollire:—Hi hnescodon spræca his, *Ps.* 54, 23, 24: *Ors.* 5, 3.

Hnesclic; *adj. Soft, effeminate;* mollis:—*Ors.* 1, 12.

Hnesclice; *adv. Gently, softly;* molliter:—*Past.* 21, 5.

Hnescnys, se; *f. Softness, tenderness, delicacy;* mollities:—*Scint.* 43.

Hnexian *to soften, Elf. gr.* 30, v. hnescian.

(2)

Hlūde loudly Th. an

Hlynsian, ode ϸpod To resound, strepere Beo K 1534

Hnægan i (from ϸ hnāh ϸ of hnigan) To subdue subigere Beo K 2637

Hnah adj Bowed, humble, weak; subactus, humilis, pravus Beo K 2637

(1) Hnigéan, rode to bond, submit Bos H 5028

a Hniglan parings, shala dan v hnyglā

(4)

(7)

(7)

2a)

b Hnit, e; f! a lentil ym: 267, 19

b)

(3)

(7)

c Hnol*es; m the top of the head Uhan

d)

e) Hnut, hnyt

e Hnyt* of a nut

(4)

a Ho, hoh i g. hos hough, heel.

Hoh. l 7

* Hoh- sinu

* Hohing, es; m anxiety suffering patibulum; rode Hofinge' rode

* the suffer of the cross

Hnifele, hnifol *The brow, forehead*; frons, *Som.* — Hnifol-crumb, hnifol-crump *wrinkled brows, Cot.* 45, 56.

Hnigan, hnigian, ic hníge, he hníhð; *p.* hnáh, we hnigon; *pp.* hnigen. [*Plat.* nigen: *Dut.* nygen: *Ger.* neigen: *Ot.* neigan: *Ker.* kehneigen: *Al.* hneigen: *Moes.* hneiwan: *Dan.* neje: *Swed.* niga: *Icel.* hnegia] *To bow, bow down, descend, sink;* caput inclinare:—Hnigan mid heafdum *to bow with (our) heads, Cd.* 35. Þa he to helle hnigan sceolde *when he to hell must descend, Id.* 221. He hnah to eorðan, *Num.* 22, 31.

Hnipan [*Icel.* hnippaz *concidere*] *To bend* or *cast down;* concidere: — Hnipað of dune *he bends downwards, Bt. R.* p. 197. Hnipod of dune *inclinavit deorsum, concidit vultus ejus, Past.* 34, 5.

Hnitan [*Plat.* niten: *Icel.* hnióta *labare*: *Icel.* hnibba *cornu petere*] *To butt, push, gore with the horns;* cornu petere:—Gif oxa hnite, *Ex.* 21, 28.

Hnit-cudu *mastic,* v. hwit-cudu.

Hnitel, hnitol; *adj. Butting, pushing, prone, bent down;* petulcus: — Gif se oxa hnitel wære *si bos petulcus esset, Ex.* 21, 29, 36.

Hnitu [*Plat.* nete *f*: *Dut.* neet *f*: *Ger.* nisse, nüsse *pl*: *Old Ger.* nizze: *Dan.* gnid *c*: *Swed.* gnet *f*: *Icel.* nyt *f.*] 1. A nit; lens,-dis. 2. *A lentil;* lens,-tis:—1. *R.* 23.—*Cot.* 16, 167. 2. Hnite, *Gen.* 43, 11.

Hnoc *A seal;* mutinus:—*R.* 22.

Hnol Knoll, *top, summit, crown, pate;* vertex:—*Ps.* 7, 17, v. cnoll.

Hnoppa [*Plat.* nobben, nubben *f*: *Dut.* nop *f.*] *Nap of cloth;* villus, *Som.*

Hnot *Shorn, cut, notted;* tonsus, mutilum:—*Elf. gr.* 9, 3.

Hnut, hnutu [*Plat.* nöt, nut *f*: *Dut.* noot *f*: *Frs.* noth *f.* nuwt *c*: *Ger.* nuss *f*: *Wil.* nuz: *Dan.* nöd *c*: *Swed.* nöt *f*: *Icel.* hnyt *f.* nyt *f.*] A nut, *wallnut;* nux, juglans: — *R.* 45.-Hnut-beam, hnutte-beam *a nut-tree, an almond-tree, Num.* 17, 8.—Hnute-hula *nut-hulls.*

Hnygela *Locks, cut wool, parings;* tomentum:—*R.* 64. Hnyglan *parings, shreds, Cot.* 152.

Hnylung Kneeling; accubitus: —*R.* 65.

Hnysc *soft, R.* 63, v. hnesc.

Hnyte *a nut, Somn.* 181, v. hnut.

Hó *I hang,* v. hón.

Ho; *g.* hoh *A heel;* calx, calcaneum:—Aheofð hys ho ongean me, *Jn.* 13, 18: *Gen.* 3, 15. Unrihtwysnys hos mine *iniquitas calcanei mei, Ps.* 48, 5: 55, 6.

Hobanca *A bedstead;* sponda:—*Cot.* 168.

Hoc, hoce, hooc, es; *m.* [*Dut.* haak: *Plat. Ger.* haken *m*: *Old Ger.* hahgen: *Dan.* hage *c*: *Swed.* hake *m*: *Icel.* haki: *Pol.* hak: *Heb.* חכה hce a *hook,* from חך hc *to scratch*] A hook, *a smith's instrument;* uncus, hamus:—*Cot.* 102: *R.* 18, 27. Hocas, *Bd.* 1, 12, *Som.*

Hoc *a hollyhoc,* v. holihoc.

Hocer, hooer, hocor-wyrd *A mocking, reproach;* irrisio:—*Lup. Serm.* 17.

Hoc-leaf *A mallow, hollyhoc;* malva:—*Elf. gl.* 14.

Hocnera-tun, es; *m.* [*Flor.* Hokenertune: *Hunt.* Hockeneretune: *Brom.* Hockemeretune] Hook-Norton, *Oxfordshire, and Hockerton, Notts., Chr.* 917.

Hód [for cognate words, v. hád] Hood, *a covering of the head;* cucullus, caputium:—*Cot.* 31.

Hoeg *hay, R. Mt.* 6, 30, v. heg.

Hoehtan *to persecute, R. Mt.* 5, 12, v. ehtan.

Hoehtnis *persecution, R. Mt.* 5, 10, v. ehtnes.

Hoelende *Calumniating;* calumnians:—*R. Mt.* 5, 44.

Hóf, hofe, [*Plat.* hoof *n. horse's hoof*: *Dut.* hoef *m*: *Ger.* huf *m*: *Dan.* hov *c*: *Swed.* hof *m*: *Icel.* hófr *m. horse's hoof*] Hoof; ungula:—*Elf. gl.* 3: *R.* 7.—Readhófe *redhoof, L. M.* 1, 2, *perhaps* hedera terrestris *alehoof.*

Hof; *pl.* hofu, *n.* [*Plat.* hof *m.* hove *f. a farm, and the house upon it,* also *the court of a prince*: *Dut.* hof *n. the court of a prince, and of justice*: *Frs.* hoaf *a garden, a court of a prince*: *Ger.* hof *m*: *Dan.* hof *n*: *Swed.* hof *n*: *Icel.* hof *n. the court of a prince*] *A house, dwelling, cave, den;* domus, spelunca: — Cynges hof *a king's dwelling, Prov.* 20. Ongan þat hof wyrcan *began the house to build, Cd.* 66. On þat hof *into that house, Cd.* 67. On hofun, *Ex.* 8. 24.—Lytel hof *a small house, R.* 107: *hence* hofel *a* hovel.—Hofweard *a house-steward, R.* 8.

Hóf, he hófe, we hófon hove, *lifted; p. of* hebban.

Hofer *A swelling on the back;* gibbus:—*Elf. gr.* 28, *Som.*

Hofered, gehoferod *Humpbacked;* gibbosus:—*Elf. gr.* 28.

Hoffingas *Spheres;* orbes, *Lye.*

Hof-rede *a bedridden person, R.* 77.

Hof-þela *rough places, woody, hard of access.*

Hófull *Careful;* sollicitus, *Som.*

Hoga, hogu, hige, hyge [*Icel.* hagr *dexter,* hagsynn *prudens*] *Prudent, careful, anxious;* prudens:—Hogo *prudentes, C. R. Mt.* 10, 16. Hoga wosan *sollicitus esse, C. R. Lk.* 12, 11.

Hoga, hoge *anxiety of mind, care, fear, R. Ben.* 53, v. hige, oga.

Hogan *to take heed,* v. hogian.

Hogascipe, hogescipe, es; *m. Prudence, wisdom;* prudentia: —*R. Lk.* 1, 17.

Hogfæst, hogofæst; *adj. Wise, prudent, skilful;* prudens:—*C. Mt.* 11, 25.

Hogfull *full of care,* v. hohfull.

Hogfullice; *adv. Anxiously;* sollicitè: *Fulg.* 32.

Hogian; *p.* hogode, gehogode, behogode, we hogodon; *pp.* gehogod [*Plat.* högen *to think*: *Dut.* heugen *to recollect*: *Icel.* huga *to have care.*—hogu, hige *the mind.*] 1. *To meditate, study, think, to be wise;* studere. 2. *To think too much, to be anxious, to lament, grieve;* sollicitus esse. 3. *To determine, condemn, despise;* spernere:—1. Ymb fleam hogodon *thought about flight, Bd.* 3, 18. 2. Ne beo ge na hogiende, *Mt.* 6, 34. 3. God hogode hig, *T. C. Ps.* 52, 7.

Hogofæst *wise, C. Mt.* 25, 2, v. hogfæst.

Hogoscipe *wisdom, C. Lk.* 2, 47, v. hogascipe.

Hogu *care, R. Ben.* 36, 53, v. hige.

Hogung, e; *f.* 1. *Care, effort, endeavour;* cura. 2. *Contempt;* contemptus:—1. *Hymn.* 2. *Som.*

Hoh *A heel,* hough, *ham;* calx, poples:—*Elf. gr.* 9, 72. ¶ On hoh *on the heels, behind, Cd.* 69, v. ho.—Hoh-fot *a heel, footstep;* calcaneum, *L. Ps.* 55, 6.—Hoh-scanc *the hough-shank;* crus.—Hoh-sin *hough-sinew;* poplitis nervus.—Hoh-spor *the heel;* calx, *R.* 75.

Hón *hang,* v. hón.

Hoh *high,* v. heah.

Hohfull, hogfull; *adj. Anxious, full of care;* sollicitus:—*R. Ben. interl.* 2: *Scint.* 9.

Hohfullnys, se; *f. Grief, vexation, anxiety;* dolor:—*Bd.* 3, 22.

Hohinge-rode *The yoke* or *suffering of the cross;* patibulum crucis:—*W. Cat.* p. 294.

Hohmod [mod *the mind*] *Anxiety,*

sorrow; sollicitus animo, mœstus:—*Off. Reg.* 15, *Lye.*

Hohmodnys, se; *f. Anxiety, grief, vexation;* sollicitudo, *Som.*

HOL, hal; *pl.* holu [*Plat.* holl, höl, höle *f: Dut.* hol *n: Ger.* höhle *f: Not. Wil.* hol *n: Moes.* holund: *Dan.* hule: *Swed.* håla *f: Lettish.* ula: *Icel.* hola *f.*] 1. A HOLE, *cavern, den;* caverna. 2. *A breathing hole;* spiraculum. 3. *A little hole, dot, point;* apex:—1. On þis dimme hol *in this dim hole, Bt.* 2. Foxas habbað holu, *Lk.* 9, 58. On holum, *Ps.* 16, 13. 2. *Som.* 3. Hol stæfes, *R. Mt.* 5, 18.

Hol *Detraction, slander;* calumnia:—*Off. Episc.* 8.

Hol; *adj.* HOLLOW; cavus:—Hol stan *a hollow* or *excavated stone, Cot.* 93. Hol-hlaf *cavus panis, collyra, Ex.* 29, 23. Hol-dene *cava vallis, Ps.* 59, 6.

Holan *To rush in;* irruere, *Som.*

Holc *a vein, L. M.* 1, 72, v. hylea.

HOLD, ahold [*Plat. Ger. Not.* hold: *Dut.* hulde *f.* holda houda *m: Moes.* hulths: *Dan.* huld: *Swed.* hylla: *Icel.* hollr] *Faithful, friendly, true;* fidus:—*Gen.* 39, 21. Hehþegen and hold *high minister and faithful, Cd.* 196.—Hold-að *oath of fidelity, Chr.* 1086.—Hold-mod *fidelity;* fidelis animo.—Hold-scipe *fidelity, Chr.* 1070.

Hold, es; *m. A nobleman who was higher than a thane, governor, captain;* præpositus, imperator:—Holdes and heh-gerefan wergyld is IIII þusend þrymsa, *L. Lund. W. p.* 71, 39. Agmund hold *Agmund governor, Chr.* 911. He gesohte þa holdas *he sought the captains, Chr.* 918.

HOLD [*Icel.* hold *n. flesh*] *A dead body, carcass;* cadaver:—Swa hwær swa hold byð, *Mt.* 24, 28: *Gen.* 15, 11.

Hold *Friendship, entertainment;* hospitium:—*Cot.* 85, 203.

Holdeoranes, se; *f.* [hol deora ness *cavæ Deiræ promontorium*] HOLDERNESS, *Yorkshire, Som.*

Holdlice; *adv. Friendly, kindly;* fideliter:—*Cd.* 220.

Hole-dene *a valley* or *dale.*

Holegn, holen *Holly* or HOLM-*tree;* aquifolium:—*Cot.* 6, 165.

Holen *hidden, C. Lk.* 8, 17.

Holenga, holinga, holonga, holunge; *adv. In vain, to no purpose, without cause;* nequicquam, frustra:—*Cot.* 193: *Bd.* 2, 20.

Holh *a ditch, cavern,* v. hol.

Holian *To* HOLLOW, *to make a hole, dig through;* excavare, *Som.*

Holiende *calumniating, L. Ps.* 118, 121, v. hoelende.

Holi-hoc HOLLYHOC; malva hortensis, *Som.*

Holinga *in vain, Bd.* 2, 15, v. holenga.

Holl *a cavern, R.* 110, v. hol.

HÓLM, es; *m.* [*Plat. Dan. Ger.* holm *a small island: Swed.* hólme *m: Icel.* holmi *m. an island*] 1. *Water, sea, ocean, abyss;* aqua, mare. 2. *A river island, a green plot of ground environed with water, and just rising above it;* hence, from being level and green, meadows, especially near rivers, are to this day called, HOLMES *or* HOMES. Hence, also, the names of places of a similar locality; insula, planities aquis circumfusa:—1. Holmas dælde waldend ure *our ruler parted the waters, Cd.* 8. Ofer holm boren *born over sea, Cd.* 6. Ofer holmes hrincg *over the orb of ocean, Cd.* 69. 2. Flat-holm *from its flatness.* Steep-holm *from being surrounded with high cliffs, two islands in the mouth of the Severn.* Æt þam Holme *at Holmwood, in Sussex, Chr.* 902.—Holm-ærn *an ocean-house, a ship, Cd.* 71.—Holm-weall *a sea-wall, Cd.* 166.

Holmeg *Wet, stormy;* pluviosus, procellosus:—*Cd.* 148.

Holoce *a vein,* v. holc.

Holonga *in vain, Bd.* 5, 1, v. holenga.

Holpen *helped; pp. of* helpan.

Holt *a handle, Cot.* 48, 147, v. hilt.

HOLT, es; *n.* [*Plat. Frs.* holt *n: Dut.* hout *n: Ger.* holz *n: Ot. Not. Wil.* holz] A HOLT, *grove;* lucus:—Plantode ænne holt, *Gen.* 21, 33. Innan on þisses holtes hleo *within a shadow of this grove, Cd.* 39.—Holt-hana *a woodcock.*

Hol-tihte *Slander;* calumnia:—*R.* 15.

Holunga, holunge *in vain, Cd.* 48, v. holenga.

Hom *a garment, jacket,* v. hama.

Hom *the ham, back part of the knee, Med. Quad.* 8, 13, v. ham.

Hóm. 1. *Bile;* cholera. 2. *Rust;* rubigo:—1. *L. M.* 1, 2. 2. *Prov.* 25, v. om.

Homa *The erysipelas;* ignis sacer:—*Med. ex Quadr.* 6, 1.

Homela, an *A fool, an idiot, discredit;* morio:—To homelan *with discredit, L. Alf. pol.* 31.

Homer *a hammer, Beo.* 39, 18, v. hamur.

HÓN, ahón, ic hó, ahó, anhó hóh, he héhð, we hóð; *p.* heng, ahencg, we hengon; *imp.* hóh, hóð ge; *pp.* hangen; *v. a.* [v. cognate words in hangian] *To hang, crucify;* suspendere:—He het hon on gealgan, *Gen.* 40, 22. Pharao hæt þe ahon on rode, *Gen.* 40, 19. Hine man heng *hunc ille suspendit, Gen.* 41, 13. Hoh hyne *crucifige illum, Mk.* 15, 13: *Jn.* 19, 6. Nime ge hyne and hoð, *id.* Sceal ic hon eowerne cyning, *Jn.* 19, 15.

Hona *a cock.*—hon-ered *cock-crowing, Bd.* 3, 19, v. hana.

Hond *a hand, Chr.* 853.—Hond-dyntas, hond-smællas *blows with the hands, cuffs, C. Jn.* 18, 22.—Hond-seten *a setting of the hand, a signature, Heming.* p. 164.—Hond-steore *limpus, Cot.* 125: for the other compounds of hond, v. hand, &c.

Honed *Calcaneus, R.* 77.

Hong *hung,* v. hón.

Hooc *a hook, R.* 3, v. hoc.

Hood *a hood,* v. hod.

Hóp HOOP, *circle;* circulus, *Som.*

HOPA [*Plat.* hop, häpje *f: Dut.* hoop, hope *f: Frs.* hoape *f: Swed.* hopp *n: Icel.* happ *n. bona sors*] HOPE; spes:—*Scint.* 2, 8.

Hop-gehnastes, hopa-gehnæstes *hope of victory, Cod. Ex.* 101, b.

Hopian; *p.* ode; *pp.* od. *To* HOPE, *trust;* sperare:—He hopode þæt he gesawe sum tacen, *Lk.* 23, 8. Þæt we hopien to Gode *that we should trust in God, Bt.* 42. Þa hopiendan on þe *sperantes in te, Ps.* 16, 8.

Hoppa *A stud, brooch;* bulla:—*Ors.* 4, 10.

Hoppada *A monk's garment;* ependyton:—*R.* 112.

Hoppan [*Plat.* hüppen, hüppern, hippen: *Dut.* huppelen: *Ger.* hüpfen, hupfen: *Dan.* hoppe: *Icel.* hoppa.—from the *Moes.* hup, or the *A.-S.* hype *the hip.* In Westphalia *the hip* is called hüppe] *To* HOP, *leap, dance;* salire, *Som.*

Hoppere A HOPPER, *dancer;* saltator, *Som.*

Hoppestre *A female dancer;* saltatrix, *Som.*

Hoppetende *leaping for joy, Past.* 2, 8, *from* hoppetan, hoppan.

Hopp-scytan *A sheet;* linteamentum:—*Wulfar. Test.*

Hopu *Privet;* ligustra:—*Cot.* 122.

Horas *Phlegm, filth, excrement;* pituita:—*R.* 78. ¶ Hora-seaðe *a sink, privy, Bt.* 37, 2.

Hol hollow. l 3

Hol-hlaf: l 5 Hol-...

Hond-sporu, a hand spur, referring to the claws of the monster Grendel Beo K 1965

Holdræden, e; f Fidelity, devotion Th an

Holdscipe Tes; m Fidelity Th an

Hond-ge-stealla an m a hand companion, a comrade Beo K 4333:

Hond-ge-slyht, e; f a hand blow Beo K 5854: 5940

Hond-locen hand locked Beo K 642: 1096

Hond-ge-mot, es, n a hand, or hostile meeting Beo K 3051

Hollenc holly hoc Som v hole-hoc

Holm-clif es; n a sea rock Beo K 458

Holm-wylm, es; m a sea wave Beo K 4818

3 Som. says steep, difficult, hard; diversus

Holt, es n a grove

Holt-wudu es; m grove wood, a wood Beo K 2738 — shield wood Beo K 4674

Hom, es m a covering Beo K 3007 v hama

Hom... an m ... Beo K 3007 ... v hama

Homor-secg sedge carices genus L M 1, 5, 6 Som

Hond-ge-sel, les; m a hand companion, a comrade Beo K 2961

Hond-lean es; n a hand reward, retribution reward Beo K 3082

(But hond-lean)

Hond-sciō, a hand shoe, a glove Beo K 4147

Hond-ræs, es; m hand ... close encounter

Hond-rond, es; m a hand shield, a shield Beo K 5215

... staff; twig, vimen;

Hop, es; m of hop, ... circulus ... a twig, not vimen

Hop ... circulus ... Lye Beo 5? ... also Fen-hop Grein II 452, 37

Hongiad hang ... Beo K 2725, 2785 Thk 104, 5

v hangian

Hop-scyte, an; f a sheet

3 V pl. of hop an olier be

...

Horn-geap a curved or pinnacled horn, Beo K 163

Hord-ærn, es; m a treasure - l 11 Hord-cleofa: l 13 Hord-fæt, es; n a treasure vessel, a treasury. Jos 7. 11

Hord-wela, an; m hoarded treasure, Beo K 4682

(1) Hord-weorðung, e; f treasure honour, a treasure Beo K 1897

Hord-wyn, e; f treasure pleasure, a treasure Beo K 4555

Horh, horig squalid Th Apb

Horn-geap a curved or pinnacled horn, Beo K 163

Horrung a whizzing sound v horn-ung

Hors ... l 9 Hors-steal: l 11 Hors-hnægung

Hors-bestridan to get on horse back Som

Hoðma, an; m perhaps a veil, a cloud; velamen, nubes Beo p 183 K 4911

(8)

(9) Hra, an; m A body, carcase cadaver Beo K 3176

(4)

Hrade readily Beo K v hrade

l 1641 Hræd-wæn, es; m

(6)

(9) Sea horse, morse trichichus rosmarus see Turner's Anglo-Saxon Hist. ... back A

Horsian to supply with horses Th An

Horn, es; m, n a horn

Þu eart se horn (m) minre hælo tu es cornu salutis meæ Ps Th 17.3

Horn-adl horned

Horu, wes, we; n filth, pollution; sordes, Th Apb Th Ap

Horwa-dl Horwian with impurities, filth Job p 167. 36

Hos, hosu, e; f [Moes. Goth. hansa a multitude crowd] An assembly troop crowd; coetus, turba Beo p 7 K 1842

Hræding, e; f hurry, haste Th An

Hor-cwen *a harlot, L. Cnut. pol.* 4.

Hórd, [*Ger.* hort *m*: *Isd. Ker. Tat. Moes.* haurd *or* haurda] Hoard, *treasure*; thesaurus:—*Elf. gl.* 27. Horde onfengon *a treasure received, Cd.* 71. ¶ Hence boc-hord *book-hoard, a library.*—Gold-hord *a gold-hoard, treasury.*—Hord-ærn *a storehouse, V. Ps.* 143, 16.—Hord-burh *a treasury, Cd.* 93. Hord-cleofa, hord-cofa *a cupboard, Ex.* 8, 3.—Hord-ern *a storehouse, Bd.* 3, 8.—Hord-fæte *a treasury, Jos.* 7, 11.—Hord-gestreon *gain, riches, Bt. R.* 170.—Hord-mægen *a treasure-house, Cd.* 209.—Hord-rædan *a keeping, R. Ben. interl.* 6.—Hord-weard *a treasurer, Cd.* 144.

Hordan *To* hoard, *store*; thesaurizare:—*Ass. S. Jn. Lye.*

Horder *A keeping*; custodia:—On æpla hordera *in pomorum custodiam, Ps.* 78, 1.

Hordere; *g.* horderes, hordres. A hoarder, *treasurer*; thesaurarius:—*L. Ethelst.* 3.

Hordres *of a treasurer,* v. hordere.

Horehte *Phlegmatic*; phlegmaticus, *Som.*

Horewen *Filth, excrement*; sordes, *Som.*

Horg, horh [*Plat.* hor, hoor: *Frs.* hor *f.*] *Phlegm, filth*; phlegma, sordes:—*Cot.* 86, v. horas.

Horig; *adj. Filthy, dirty*; sordidus:—*Scint.* 7, 21.

Horines, se; *f. Filthiness*; sordes, *Som.*

Horingas *Adulterers*; adulteri:—*Lup.* 1, 19, *Lye.*

Horiþi, horiti *The* Horiti; Harudes, populus:—Be eastan Dalamensam sindon Horiþi *east of the Dalmentians are the Horiti.* Be norðan Horiti is Mægþaland *to the north of the Horiti is Mazovia, Ors.* 1, 1.

Horlic *filthy,* v. horig.

Horn, hyrne [*Plat.* hoorn *n*: *Dut.* hoorn *m*: *Frs.* hoarn *n*: *Ger. Dan. Swed. Icel.* horn *n*: *Moes.* haurn. All these words signify *a horn,* and *a corner*; but the *Dan.* use hjörne, and the *Swed.* hörn, to denote *a corner.*—*Heb.* קרן qrn *a horn, what shoots forth* or *extends*] 1. A horn; cornu. 2. *A trumpet*; buccina:—1. And his upahafen swa anhyrnende horn, *Ps.* 91, 10: 17, 3: 74, 4. 2. Aoth bleow bealdlice his horn *Ehud inflavit fortiter ejus buccinam, Jud.* 3, 27: *Cd.* 151.—Horn-bær *horn-bearing*; corniger, *Elf. gr.* 8.—Horn-blawere *horn-blower, Elf. gl.* 6.—Horn-boga *corneus arcus, Jdth.* 11.—Horn-bora *a horn-blower, Cot.* 42.—Horn-pic *a pinnacle, C. R. Lk.* 4, 9.—Horn-sale *a pinnacled dwelling, a pinnacle, Cd.* 86.—Horn-sceaðe *a pinnacle, C. Mt.* 4, 5.

Hornleás; *adj.* Hornless; cornua non habens:—*Somn.* 410.

Hornung, e; *f. Whoring, adultery, fornication*; mœchatio, adulterium:—Hornung-sunu *a son of fornication, a bastard, Cot.* 142.

Horo-seaða *a sink, Bt.* 37, 2, *C.,* v. horas, &c.

Horr *a hinge, Elf. gr.* 9, 3, v. heor.

Hors, heors, es; *n.* [*Plat. Dut.* ros *n*: *Old Dut.* hors, ors: *Frs.* hors *m*: *Old Ger.* hors: *Dan.* hest: *Swed.* häst *m*: *Icel.* hross *n. a mare*: *Icel.* hestr *m. a horse*: *Old Icel.* hors *a mare*] A horse; equus:—Nyllege beon swa swa hors, *Ps.* 31, 11: *Bd.* 3, 5.—Hors-steall *horse-stall, a prison, R.* 61.—Hors-hnægung *horse neighing.*—Hors-bær *a horse-bier, hearse, Bd.* 4, 6.—Hors-camb *a horse-comb, Elf. gl.* 22.—Hors-cræt *a cart* or *chariot drawn by two horses.*—Hors-ele, hors-elene *horse-heal*; helenium, *Elf. gl.* 16.—Hors-ern *a stable.*—Hors-here *a horse-army, cavalry.*—Hors-hierde, hors-hyrde *a horse-keeper, hostler, Cot.* 172.—Hors-hwæl *a horse-whale, Ors.* 1, 1.—Hors-mint *horse-mint.*—Hors-syðða *a hearse, Bd.* 4, 6.—Hors-þegen *a horse-thane, an equery, Chr.* 897.—Hors-wain *a horse-wain, waggon, R.* 48.—Hors-wealh *an equery, L. In.* 33.—Hors-weard *horse-ward, hostler.*

Horsc; *adj. Sagacious*; prudens:—*Cd.* 191.

Horslice; *adv. Prudently, sagaciously, valiantly*; prudenter:—*Cot.* 138.

Horu, horuwe *filth,* v. horewen.

Horwa *Filth, dirt*; sordes:—*Job.* p. 161.

Hor-weg *Out of the way*; devius:—*Cot.* 61.

Hos *the heels, Ps.* 48, 5, v. ho.

Hos hosa [*Plat.* hase *f*: *Dut.* hoze, hoos *f*: *Dan.* hose *c*: *Icel.* hosa *f. a hose*] *Stockings,* hose, *hosen, a bramble*; caliga, ocrea, rhamnus:—*Elf. gl.* 19.—Hose-bendas *hose-bands, garters.*

Hosp *Reproach, scorn, mockery*; opprobrium:—*Ps.* 14, 4: 21, 5: *Lk.* 1, 25. Na ic do hosp *non faciam irritum, Ps.* 88, 34. To hospe gedon *contumelia afficere, Elf. T.* p. 12.

Hóð *hang*; *imp. of* hón.

Hou *A mountain*; mons, *Lye.*

Hr, the Anglo-Saxons frequently aspirated *r* by prefixing *h,* as in

Hraca, an; [*Plat. Ger.* rachen *m*: *Dut.* kaak *f*: *Rab. Maurus* hracho: *Icel.* hráki *m. spittle*] *A throat, the jaws, a cough, phlegm*; guttur, tussis:—On hracan heora *in gutture suo, Ps.* 113, 15.

Hraçca *The* rack, *neck, the hinder part of the head*; occiput, *Som.*

Hracod Raked, *ragged*; laceratus, *Som.*

Hrád *rode, Bd.* 3, 9; *p. of* ridan.

Hrad *ready, rash, Ps.* 13, 6, v. hræd.

Hradian; *p.* geradode; *pp.* geradod. *To hasten, to be ready, prosper*; properare:—*V. Ps.* 15, 3.

Hradung, e; *f. A hastening*; festinatio:—*R. Ben.*

Hræcan *To retch, hawk*; niti ad vomitum:—*Elf. gr.* 26.

Hræc-gebræc *The rheum*; branchus:—*R.* 10.

Hræctung, hræcung, e; *f. Retching, hawking*; screatio, saliva, pituita:—*R.* 78.

Hræd, hrad, ræd, geræd; *comp.* ra; *sup.* est; *adj.* [*Plat.* reed, rede: *Dut.* gereed: *Frs.* red: *Ger.* bereit: *Dan.* reede: *Swed.* reds: *Icel.* hradr *quick*] Ready, *swift, nimble, quick, rash*; celer:—On hrædum færelde *in a swift course, Bt.* 4. Se gast is hræd, *Mt.* 26, 41.—Hræde spræce, gerǽde spræce *prose*; prompta loquela, *Bd.* 5, 23, *S.* p. 648, 27.—Hræd-bita *a quick biter, a beetle.*—Hræde-monað *march,* v. hreðe-monað.—Hræd-fernes *a swift course, Bt.* 32, 2.—Hræd-hydignes *rashness, Past.* 49, 1.—Hræd-wæn *a ready waggon, a vehicle, Bt.* 36, 2.—Hræd-wilnes *vehement desire, rashness, Past.* 23, 2.

Hrædels *a riddle,* v. rædels.

Hrædinge; *adv. Shortly, quickly*; brevi:—*Lup.* 1, 20.

Hrædlic; *adj. Quick, speedy, sudden*; citus:—Hrædlice deað *sudden death, Bd.* 4, 23: *Ors.* 1, 10.

Hrædlice; *adv.* Readily, *shortly, quickly, immediately*; statim:—*Mt.* 3, 16: 13, 5, 20. Hrædlicor *more quickly, very soon, Bd.* 3, 14.

Hrædlicnys, se; *f. Readiness, haste, quickness*; celeritas:—*Guth. Vit.* 2.

Hrædnes, se; *f.* Readiness,

quickness, swiftness; agilitas:—*Greg.* 2, 9. On hrædnesse *quickly*; cito, *Bd.* 1, 14.
Hræfen *a raven, the Danish standard*, v. hrefen.—Hræfen-fot *raven-foot, horse-thyme, cinquefoil, Herb.*
Hræfnan *to support, C. R. Mt.* 6, 24, v. ræfnan.
Hræge *A doe, goat*; damula:—*R.* 19.
Hræge-heafd [heafod *a head*] GATESHEAD, *in Durham, Bd.* 3, 21.
HRÆGEL *Clothes, raiment, a garment*, RAIL; vestimentum:—Ge gemetaþ an cild hræglum bewunden, *Lk.* 2, 12. On hrægle *in raiment, Cd.* 195. *Spolium, Ps.* 67, 13. ¶ Nihtes-hrægl *night-rail or clothing.*—Hrægle-gewæd *clothes, Cot.* 118.—Hrægl-hus *a vestry, C. R. Ben.* 67.—Hrægl-þegn *a groom of the stole, C. R. Ben.* 55.—Hrægl-weard *a keeper of clothes, a vestry-keeper, Cot.* 175.
Hræglung, e; *f. Clothing*; vestitus:—*R.* 62.
Hræm *a raven, Elf. gr.* 6, v. hrem.
Hræm *a shout*, v. hream.
Hræman *to cry out*, v. hreman.
Hræmde *hindered, L. Ps.* 77, 37, v. hremman.
Hræmn *a raven, Elf. gr.* 8, v. hrem.
Hræn *A little goat, a kid*; capreolus, *Som.*
Hræron *should fall, Ps.* 117, 13, v. hreosan.
Hræs *A gushing*; impetus:—*C. Mt.* 8, 32.
Hræsto *Resting*; accubitus, *Som.*
Hræswan *To meditate*; meditari:—*Bt.* 22, 2, *C.*
Hræð *swift, Bd.* 4, 6, v. hræd.
Hræða *A garment of goat-skin*; melotes, *Som.*
Hræð-bita *a beetle*, v. hræd, &c.
Hræðe *quickly, R. Mt.* 4, 17; hræðor *sooner*, v. hraðe.
Hræð-fornes, se; *f. Quickness*; celeritas, *Som.*
Hræð-monað *March*, v. hreðe-monað.
Hræw *a corpse, Cd.* 144, v. hreaw.
Hrafyl *Rapine, ruin*; rapina:—*Beo.* 4, 40.
Hragra [*Plat.* reier *n*: *Dut. Ger.* reiger *m*: *Dan.* heire *m*: *Swed.* hägr *m.*] *A hern, heron*; ardea:—*Elf. gl.* 11: *Cot.* 12.
Hragyfra *Lamentable, mournful, cruel*; funestus:—*Cot.* 90.
Hralic *Belonging to a funeral, mournful*; funebris:—*Cot.* 88.
Hramma [*Plat.* ramm *m.*] 1. *A canker in the flesh*; cancer. 2. *A cramp*; spasmus:—1. *Cot.* 206. 2. *R.* 10.
Hramsa, hramse, an. *Henbane*; allium ursinum:—*Cot.* 7, 166. Hramsan crop *allii sylvestris cimæ.*
Hran *A whale*; cetus:—*Cot.* 23. Musculus, *R.* 102, v. hrón.
Hrán *touched*, v. hrinan.
Hranas [*Dan.* rensdyr: *Icel.* hreinn *m.* hrein dyr *n.*] *Reindeer*; cervi quidam cornua habentes ramosa:—Þa deor hi hataþ hranas *the deer they call reins, Ors.* 1, 1, *Ing. lect.* p. 62, 6.
Hraðe, hræðe; *comp.* rhaðor; *adv.* [hræd *ready*] *Of one's own accord, readily, quickly, soon, immediately*; hence our word RATHER; ultro:—Ga hraðe on þa stræta, *Lk.* 14, 21: 16, 6. To hraðe *too readily, too soon, Bt.* 3, 1: *Bd.* 4, 1.
Hraðre *to a mind, Bt. R.* p. 187, v. hreðer.
Hrawlic *mournful*, v. hralic.
Hreac, es; *m.* A RICK, *stack, heap*; strues:—Hreacas *ricks, Cot.* 18. Hræges-hreac *hayrick.*
Hread *a reed, R. Mt.* 12, 20, v. hreod.
Hreadydon *Hastened*; acceleraverunt, v. hradian.
Hreafian *to seize, L. Ps.* 49, 23, v. reafian.
Hream; *m.* [*Icel.* hreimr *m. a sound*: *Heb.* רוּם rum *elevated*, from רם rm *to lift*] *A din, clamour, a crying out, wailing*; clamor:—*Gen.* 18, 20.
Hreamig *exulting*, v. hremig.
Hrean *A consumption*; phthisis:—*L. M.* 2, 41.
Hreas *fell*; *p. of* hreosan.
Hreaþe-mus *a bat*, v. hreremus.
Hreaw, reaw; *adj.* [*Plat. Ger.* roh: *Dut.* raauw: *Dan.* raa: *Swed.* rå: *Icel.* hrái *m. rawness*] RAW; crudus:—*Herb.* 135, 2.
Hreaw, *repented*; *p. of* hreowan.
Hreaw, hræw, [*Dut.* rif *n*: *Frs.* hres *n*: *Isd.* hreve: *Ot.* reve: *Glos. Lips.* ref] 1. *A carcass*; cadaver. 2. *What relates to a dead body, funeral*; funus:—1. Heora fædera hreaw beon fornumene, *Num.* 14, 33. Hræwas *carcases, L. Ps.* 78, 2. 2. *Elf. gl.* 26.
Hrecca *a neck*, v. hracca.
Hrecg *a back*, v. hric.
Hreconlice; *adv. Quickly*; cito, *Som.*
HREDDAN; *v. a.* [*Plat. Dut.* redden: *Ger.* retten: *Dan.* redde: *Swed.* rädda: *Icel.* rétta *jus in aliquem exequi*] *To* RID, *seize, take*; rapere:—God wolde hreddan hea rice *God would take (his) proud kingdom, Cd.* 208.
Hredding A RIDDING, *delivering, redemption*; ereptio:—*W. Bd.* p. 310.
Hredlice *readily, L. Ps.* 6, 10, v. hrædlice.
Hred-mod *fierce, cruel*; ferus, *Som.*
Hred-monað *March*, v. hreðe-monað.
Href *A person diseased with leprosy*; leprosus:—*R. Mt.* 8, 2: *Lk.* 17, 2.
Hrefen *A crab*; cancer:—Hrefen, þe sume menn hataþ crabba, *W. Cat.* p. 168.
HREFEN, hræfen, ræfen; *g.* hrefnes; *m.* [*Plat.* rave *c*: *Dut.* raaf *m.* rave *c*: *Ger.* rabe *m*: *Wil.* raban: *Not.* rammo: *Dan.* ravn *m*: *Swed.* ramn *m*: *Icel.* hrafn *m.*] A RAVEN, *the Danish standard*; corvus:—Besceawiaþ þa hrefnas, *Lk.* 12, 24: *Chr.* 878. *Cant.*—Hrefn-cynn *raven-kind, Lev.* 11, 17.—Hrefnes-fot *raven's foot, Herb.* 28, *crow's foot.*—Hrefnes-leac *raven's leek*; satyrion, *Herb.* 16.
Hrefnan *to suffer, Cd.* 224, v. ræfnan.
Hrege *a she goat, Bd.* 3, 21, v. hræge.
Hregle *with a garment*, v. hrægel.
Hregnan *to rain, C. Mt.* 3, 45, v. rinan.
Hreh *A deluge*; inundatio, *Som.*
HREM, hræm, hræmn, hremm, hremn [hream *a noise, a shout*] *A raven*; corvus:—*Gen.* 8, 7.
Hremnes-fot *raven's foot, Elf. gl.* 14, v. hrefen.
Hreman *to cry, weep, cry out, boast, Mk.* 5, 7, v. hryman.
Hremig *Noisy, exulting, triumphant, querulous*; querulus, stridulus, *Conb.*; compos, *Lye*:—Since hremig *with wealth exulting, Beo.* 26, 132. Frætwum hremig *with ornaments exulting, Beo.* 28, 179.
Hremman; *p.* hræmde; *pp.* gehremmed. *To hinder, disquiet*; impedire:—*L. Ps.* 77, 37.
Hremming *A hinderance, disquieting*; impedimentum:—*Basil. R.* 2.
Hrendan *to rend, C. Lk.* 13, 17, v. rendan.
Hrenian. *To scent*; redolere:—*Scint.* 28, *Lye.*
Hreo *rough*, v. hreog.
Hreoce *A roach, rocket*; rubellio, *Som.*
HREÓD, hread, reod, es; *n.* [*Plat.* reet, riet, reit *n*: *Dut.* riet *n*: *Frs.* reid *n*: *Ger.* rieth, rohr *n*: *Moes.* raus: *Swed.* rör *n.*] 1. A REED, *sedge*; arundo. 2. *A path*; orbita:—1. Þu þrea wyldeor hreodes, *Ps.* 67, 33: *Mt.* 11, 7. Hwi ferde ge geseon þat hreod, *Lk.* 7, 24.

a)

Hran, es; m a whale or

Hran

b

Hrægel, hrægles, n

Hrægel a garment &

Hrægel.

Hræfn raven

3) Hræm, es; m a raven

Hc Ælfgr §6, 18 Som p5

c) Hræn, hran, es m a goat, etc.

d Hrærg. træf the tent of a heathen temple

Mone 15 1134

v hearg. træf

(3)

d / Hreaw [28 a 8]

Hrea-wic, es; n

[hreaw a carcass]

a corpse dwelling, a sepulchre Bes K 2428

c)

d Hrec moderamen

Ben

e)

Hreow, es; m
Pain, grief; mœror
dolor Beo K 4252

Hreof, hreofl a
mycel hreofla
Hreofl, es, m; hreofla
an; m. A leprous man
a leper
Hreoflic, hreflig
leprous

Bd 5. 2
Smith 614, 44

Hreop-sæt, es m
Hreop-sæta, an m
an inhabitant of Repton

Hreóh-mod
Hreoh mod sad-minded Beo K 4259

Rheornis a town
Rheornis a town
Ben v hreames

Hrepian, hreppan
To touch

Hreowian, hede
to lament Bd 1, 27 Resp
8 Smith 495, 40

Hred, es; m cruelty
ferocitas Beo K 5746

2. *Cot.* 145. — Hreod - bedd hreod-ihtig *a reed-bed, a place where sedge grows, Ex.* 2, 3.—Hreod-writ *a writing reed, a pen, C. Ps.* 44, 2.

Hreodea *Rough*; asper:—*Bd.* 4, 27.

Hreodford [hread *a reed*, ford *a ford*] *Redbridge, Hants, Bd.* 4, 16, *S.* p. 584, 29.

Hreof [*Plat.* rüdig: *Dut.* rappig: *Ger.* räudig: *Not.* rudig] Rough, *rugged, scabby;* callosus, scabiosus:—*Cot.* 47. Leprosus, *R. Mt.* 8, 2.

Hreof *A scab;* scabies:—*Past.* 11, 5.

Hreofl, hreoflic, hreoflig; *def.* se hreofla; *adj. Scabby, leprous;* scabiosus:—*Ex.* 4, 6.

Hreofla, an; *m. A leprous man, a leper, leprosy;* leprosus, elephantiasis: — On Simones huse anes hreoflan, *Mk.* 14, 3. Se hreofla hym fram ferde, *Lk.* 5, 13.

Hreofnys, se; *f. Roughness; scabbiness, leprosy;* callositas, *Mk.* 1, 42.

Hreog, hreoh [*Plat.* rau, rü: *Dut.* ruw: *Ger.* rauh, roh: *Old Ger.* rug: *Dan.* raa: *Swed.* râ] *Rough, fierce, stormy, cruel;* turbidus, ferus:—Hreoh weder, *Mt.* 16, 3.—Hreoh sæ, *Jn.* 6, 18. — Hreoh-mod *savage minded, Cd.* 186.

Hreohehe *Fannus, piscis, Cot.* 213.

Hreohfull; *adj. Rueful, stormy;* turbidus: — Hreohfull gear *turbidus annus, Cal. Jan.*

Hreohmodnes, se; *f. Cruelty;* ferocitas, *Som.*

Hreohnes, hreones, se; *f.* A roughness, *tempest, storm;* tempestas, scabrities:—*Ps.* 49, 4: *Bd.* 3, 15.

Hreol, reol [*Plat.* rull *f*: *Dut.* rol *f*: *Ger.* rolle *f*: *Dan.* rul, ruld: *Swed.* rulle *m*: *Icel.* hræll *m*: *Lat. mid.* rollus] A reel; girgillus:—*R.* 111.

Hreopan, we hreopon, hwreopon [*Plat.* ropen: *Dut.* roepen: *Frs.* hropa: *Ger.* rufen: *Isd.* hreofun: *Moes.* hropjan: *Dan.* raabe: *Swed.* ropa: *Icel.* hrópa] *To cry, scream;* clamare:—*Cd.* 150: 151.

Hreopan-dun, Hreope-dun, Hrypa-dun, e; *f.* [*Flor.* Hrepandun: *Malm.* Rependuna: *Hunt.* Rependun: *Dunel.* Repadun, Reopedun: *Hovd.* Repandun: *Brom.* Repandune.—*litoralis, collis, Som.*] Repton, *now only a village in Derbyshire, situate on an eminence near the river Trent.* It was anciently a large town, and had a monastery, where the Mercian kings were buried. The Danes, opposing Burhed, king of Mercia, wintered here in A. D. 874, and destroyed the monastery. *Ingulf* says, "Monasterium, quæ celeberrimum omnium regum Merciorum sacratissimum mausoleum funditus destruxissent," 26. It is remarkable, in the present day, for its well-endowed and celebrated grammar school. All the feelings, arising from gratitude and juvenile recollection, are associated with the name of Repton, for here the writer of this article was educated:—Æþelbald, Myrcna cyning lið on Hreopandune *Ethelbald, king of the Mercians, lieth at Repton, Chr.* 755. Her for se here from Lindesse to Hreopedune and þær winter-setl nam *here the army went from Lindsey to Repton, and there took winter-quarters, Chr.* 874. Her for se here from Hreopedune, *Chr.* 875.

Hreop-sæte, Hrypp-sæta *the people of Rippon,* v. Ripum.

Hreósan, behreosan, gehreosan, he hryst; *p.* ic, he hreás, hrysede, þu hrure, we hruron; *sub.* rhyre; *pp.* gehroren [*Plat.* risan: *Old South Ger.* and *Swiss dialects,* risan, zerisan, reysen, abreysen: *Ger.* rauschen *to rustle,* riseln *to fall drop by drop: Moes.* driusan: *Icel.* hrasa] *To* rush, *shake, waver, fall, fall* or *tumble down;* ruere:—Þe hreosað, *C. Ps.* 144, 15. He hreas and feoll on eorðan, *Bd.* 4, 31. Behreosað on helle *rush into hell, Lup.* 5, 8.

Hreose; *adj. Frail, ruinous, rushing on, violently approaching;* caducus, ruiturus:—*Bt.* 41, 3.

Hreosendlic; *adj. Frail, perishable;* caducus:—*Bt.* 14, 2.

Hreoða, an; *m.* [reow *raw*] *What is made of raw hides;* quidvis e crudis coriis confectum:—Bord-hreoða, scyld-hreoða *a buckler.*

Hreoðnys *a raging, C. Lk.* 8, 24, v. hreohnes.

Hreoðor, hreoðor-hyrde *an ox,* v. hryðer.

Hreoung *shortness of breath,* v. hristung.

Hreow, hrere *Raw,* rear, *cruel, fierce;* crudus:—Ne eton ge of þam nan þing hreowes, *Ex.* 12, 9: *Cd.* 220.

Hreowan, hreowsian, behreowsian, he hrywð; *p.* hreáw, gehreáw, we hruwon; *pp.* hrowen. *To* rue, *repent, to be sorry for, grieve, lament;* pœnitere:—Ne hit furðum him ne læt hreowan *nor indeed suffer himself to repent of it, Bt.* 39, 12. Mec hreoweð, *R. Mt.* 15, 32. Hreaw him, *Ps.* 105, 42.

Hreowe [*Plat.* rou, roue, rau *f.* beroue, berau *f*: *Dut.* rouw *m*: *Ger.* reue *f*: *Isd.* hreuu: *Ker.* hriuun: *Ot.* riu: *Moes.* reigo] *Repentance, penance;* pœnitentia: — Hreowe don *pœnitentiam agere, Bd.* 1, 27, *resp.* 8.

Hreowe; *adj. Repenting,* pœnitens:—Hreowum tearum *pœnitentibus lacrymis, Bd.* 4, 25.

Hreowig *Penitent;* pœnitens:—Hof hreowig mod *penitent minded wept, Cd.* 37: 38.

Hreowlic, hrywlic; *adj. Cruel, mournful;* crudelis:—*L. Lund.* 12.

Hreowlice; *adv. Cruelly, mournfully;* crudeliter:—*Bd.* 1, 15: *Ors.* 3, 7.

Hreownes, se; *f.* 1. *Repentance;* pœnitentia. 2. *Cruelty, roughness;* crudelitas:—1. *Mt.* 21, 29. 2. *Elf. T.* p. 35, 10.

Hreowsian *to repent, Mt.* 27, 3, v. hreowan.

Hreowsung, e; *f. Repentance;* pœnitentia:—*Bt.* 44, 3: *Lk.* 10, 13.

Hrepan, hreppan; *pp.* gehrepod, ahrepod; *v.a.* [*Plat. Old Dut.* reppen: *Swed.* repa *to catch, to take*] *To touch;* tangere:—God bebead us þat we ne æton, ne we þat treow ne hrepodon, *Gen.* 3, 3. Ic hrepe, *Ex.* 11, 1.

Hrepingas *Lipingale, Lincolnshire, Chr.* 675, *Ing.*

Hrepsung *The evening;* vesper, *Bridf. Rames.*

Hrepung, hreppung, e; *f. Feeling, touch;* tactus:—*Elf. gr.* 11, 43.

Hreran [*Plat.* rören: *Dut.* roeren: *Frs.* rieren: *Ger.* rühren: *Isd. Ot. Not.* ruoren: *Moes.* reiran: *Dan.* röre: *Swed.* röra: *Icel.* hræra] *To move, agitate, raise;* agitare:—Swa swa yða for winde þa sæ hrerað *as waves, through the wind, agitate the sea, Bt.* 39, 1: *Bt. R.* p. 191, v. ræran.

Hrere *rear, raw,* v. hreow.

Hrere-mus A reremouse, *bat;* vespertilio:—*Elf. gl.* 12.

Hrerenes *a tempest,* v. hreohnes.

Hresigende *Sick of a fever;* febricitans:—*H. Mk.* 1, 3.

Hrestan *to rest, stop, Bt. R.* p. 164, v. restan.

Hretan *To spread;* sternere:—*Prov.* 10.

Hreð, hreðe *savage, cruel, Cd.* 103, v. reð.

Hreða *a garment*, *Cod.* 133, v. hræða.

Hréðe-monað, hrede-monað, hræde-monað, hred-monað [Hreð *severe, rough*; Hræd, *Bd.* says, "from the goddess Rheda, to whom the A.-S. then sacrificed;" others say, from hræd *prepared*, because they then prepared for agriculture, navigation, and war; monað *a month*] *The month of March*; Martius:—Se Hreð-monað Martius, *W. Cat.* p. 106. On þæm þriddan monðe on geare bið an and þrittig daga, and se monað is nemned on læden Martius, and on ure geþeode hred-monað, *Menol. Sax. Hick. Thes.* I. p. 218, 70.

Hreðer; *d.* hreðre. *The breast, mind*; pectus, animus:—Hreðer-gleaw *prudent in mind*, *Cd.* 143. Hæfde on hreðre *had in mind*, *Cd.* 161, *Th.* p. 201, 2. Of þam hatan hreðre *of the hot mind*, *Cod. Exon.* 24, b.—Hreðer-cofa *the mind's cave, the breast*, *Cod. Exon.* p. 27, b.—Hreðer-loca *the mind's enclosure*, *Cod. Exon.* 23, b.

Hreðian; *p.* we hreðdon. *To rage, excite, cheer*; sævire:—*Cd.* 170.

Hreðig *severe, proud*, *Jdth.* 11, v. reðig.

Hreðleás; *adj.* WRATHLESS, *mild*; mitis:—*Cod. Exon.* 46, a.

HRIC, hricc, hricg, hrycce, hrycg; es [*Plat.* rugg, rugge *m*: *Dut.* rug *m*: *Frs.* hreg, reg *f*: *Ger.* rücken *m*: *Ker.* hrucki: *Isd.* hrucca: *Ot.* rugge: *Not.* rukke: *South Ger.* ruck, ruggen: *Dan.* ryg *c*: *Swed.* rygg *m*: *Icel.* hryggr *m.*] RIDGE, *back of a man* or *beast*; dorsum, fastigium:—Fynd mine þu sealdest me on hricc, *Ps.* 17, 42. On hrycce urum, *Ps.* 65, 10. Þa æftran hrices *posteriora dorsi*, *Ps.* 67, 14. Þonne bið tobrocen hrycg, *Ps.* 31, 4. Þæs temples hricg *templi fastigium*, *Lk.* 4, 9.—Hricg-ban *ridge-bone, back-bone*, *L. Ps.* 31, 4.—Hricg-hrægl *back-clothing, clothing*, *Wulfari. Test.*

Hriddel *A sieve*, RIDDLE; cribrum, *Som.*

Hridder, es; *m.* [*Plat.* ridder *m.*] *A fan to winnow corn*; capisterium:—*R.* 50: *Cot.* 170.

Hridrian; *p.* ode; *pp.* od, ud; *v. a. To sift, shake*; ventilare:—Satanas gyrnde þat he eow hridrude, *Lk.* 22, 31.

Hriefþo *Scabs, scurf, scales*; scabies:—Heafod hriefþo *scabs* or *scales on the head*, *L. M.* 2, 30. Hwite hriefþo *white scurf, the leprosy*, *id.*

Hries *A rushing*; impetus, *Som.*

HRIF, hrifé, hryfe, rif [*Plat.* rif, rift: *Dut.* rif *n, a carcass*: *Ger.* riff *n*: *Isd.* hrere *venter*] *The womb, bowels*; uterus, venter:—*C. Lk.* 11, 27: *Ors.* 1, 12. Uferre and niðerre hrife *superior et inferior venter*, *Som.*

Hrifteung, e; *f. A pain in the bowels*; iliaca passio:—*R.* 10.

Hrifþo *scabs*, v. hriefþo.

Hrifwerc *a pain in the bowels*, *R.* 10, v. hrifteung.

Hrig *a rick*, v. hreac.

Hrilæcung, e; *f. Reasoning*; ratiocinatio, *Ben.*

Hrim, hrime RHIME, *hoar frost*; pruina:—*T. Ps.* 118, 83.

Hriman *to cry out*, *Num.* 13, 31, v. hryman.

Hriman *to number*, *Past.* 57, 1, v. riman.

[b] Hrimig; *adj.* RHIMY; pruinosus:—*Menol.* 459.

HRIN *A touch*; tactus:—*Solil.* 2, v. hrinenes.

Hrinan, he hrinð; *p.* hrán; *pp.* hrinen. *To touch, strike, adorn, bewail*, v. gehrinan.

Hrinc, hrincg *a ring*, v. hring.

Hrind *rind*, *R.* 59, v. rind.

Hrinenes, gehrines, se; *f. The touch, a touching, contact*; tactus:—*Bd.* 4, 19, 31.

HRING, hrinc, hrincg, ring [*Plat.* ring, rink, krink *m*: *Dut.* ring, kring *m*: *Frs.* hring *m*: *Ger. Dan. Swed.* ring *m*: *Icel.* hringr *m.*] A RING, *orb, circle, circuit, garland, a girdle, what fastens a girdle, a buckle*; annulus, orbis, ambitus:—Syllað hym hring on his hand, *Lk.* 15, 22: *Bd.* 4, 18. Lytel hring *a little ring*, *R.* 65. Ofer holmes hringc *over ocean's circuit*; super maris ambitum, *Cd.* 69. Hrincg þæs hean landes *the circuit of the high land*, *Cd.* 137.—Hring-fag, hring-faag *a ringed* or *variegated garment*, *Gen.* 37, 3.—Hring-mæled *ring-hilted*, *Cd.* 93.—Hring-seta *a contender in a circus*, *Cot.* 43.—Hring-sete, hring-stede *a circus*, *Cot.* 183.—Hring-windle *a sphere*.

Hringan; *pp.* gehringed [*Ger.* ringen: *Dan.* ringe: *Swed.* ringa: *Icel.* hringia] *To* RING, *to sound a bell, to give alarm*; pulsare campanas:—Hringe tacn *sonet signum*, *R. Concord.* 47.

Hringed byrne *a shirt of mail*, *Cot.* 121, *Som.*

Hrínon *to touch*; tangere:—*Cd.* 69, *Th.* p. 84, 11, v. hrinan.

Hrinung, e; *f. A touch*; tactus:—*Solil.* 3.

Hriofol *Leprosy*; lepra:—*C. Mt.* 8, 3.

[c] Hrioh *rough*, *Bt. R.* p. 155, v. hreog.

Hriohnes *a tempest*, v. hreohnes.

Hriopan *to pluck*, *R. Mt.* 12, 1, v. ripan.

Hriord *a feast*, *C. Lk.* 14, 12, v. gereord.

Hriordian, riordian *To dine, feast, rejoice*; prandere:—*C. Jn.* 21, 12.

Hrioung *a shortness of breath*, v. hreoung.

Hrip *the womb*, v. hrif.

Hripe-man *a reaper*, *C. Mt.* 13, 39, v. ripere.

Hripphis, hrippe *a harvest*, *C. Mt.* 13, 39, v. rip.

Hris [*Ger.* reis *n*: *Dan.* ris *c*: *Icel.* hrís *a shrub*] *Tops of trees, small branches*, RICES; frondes:—*Cot.* 93.

Hriscian *To shake, vibrate, frizzle, to make a rustling noise*; vibrare:—Hriscende, *Cot.* 85, *Som.*

Hriseht *Bristly*; setosus:—*Cot.* 186.

Hrisel, hrisle *A weaver's shuttle*; radius textorius:—*R.* 110; ebredio, *Cot.* 71.

Hristenda *astridulus*, *Cot.* 5.

Hristlan [*Plat.* russeln: *Dut.* ritselen: *Ger.* rasseln: *Dan.* rasle: *Swed.* rasla: *Icel.* hrista] *To* RUSTLE; crepere, *Som.*

Hristlung, e; *f.* A RUSTLING; strepitus, *Som.*

Hristung, e; *f. A difficulty of breathing*; difficultas spirandi:—*L. M.* 2, 4.

Hrið-adl *A fever, an ague*; febris, *Som.*

Hriðer *an ox* or *cow*, v. hryðer.

Hriðian; *p.* ode; *pp.* od. *To be sick of a fever* or *ague*; febricitare:—*Mt.* 8, 14: *Mk.* 1, 30.

[d] Hriðing *Feverishness*; febricitatio, *Som.*

Hriung *an asthma*, v. hreoung.

HROC [*Plat.* rook, röke *f*: *Frs.* roek *c*: *Dut.* kaauw: *Ger.* kolkrabe *m*: *South Ger.* ruch *m.*, and, in some parts, rak] A ROOK, *crow*; cornix, graculus:—Se selð nytenum mete, and briddum hroca cigendum hine, *Ps.* 146, 10.

Hroden, gehroden *Adorned, arranged*; ornatus, instructus:—*Jdth.* 10, *Thw.* p. 21, 27.

Hroder *the sky*, *R.* 94, v. roder.

Hroeran *to move*, *C. R. Mt.* 27, 39, v. hreran.

Hroernes, se; *f. A moving*; motus, *Som.*

HRÓF, es; *m.* [*Dut.* roef *f. the cabin of a small vessel*: *Frs.* rof *n. a roof*] A ROOF, *top*; culmen:—Hi openodon þone hrof, *Mk.* 2, 4: *Lk.* 5, 19. Wið þæs hean hrofes *towards the high roof*, *Bt.* 41, 5. Under

a Hrēðe adv readily, soon quickly Beo K 1975 v hrade

b ✗ Hrēð-monað the month of March ✗ Hreð-monað, ba es; m

hryf, rif

a ✗ Hrif, e; f the wa

uterus, venter, L 6

✗ superioris et inferioris ventris

c)

b

c

ⓓ æt-hrin Gen II, 12, 28 XII 17, 25

✗ Hrive rein Som v hryre

✗

a

✗ Hreð-hyrde a

herds man Som v hryde.

hyrde

e Hrinde-bearwas circum rhymati ringed woods Beo K 2726

f

g Hring-boga an m

What is bowed as a ring, a serpent curved sicut annulus curvatus, serpens Beo K 5118

d)

j Hringian p ode th od i a To place in a ring Beo K 652 apx

n Hring-naca an m a ringed ship Beo K 3720

k Hring-iren, es n ringed iron, a coat of mail Beo K 642

o Hring-net, es; n a ring net, coat of mail Beo K 3773

l Hring-locas, an m ringed enclosure, a coat of mail th an

ringmael sword

6 Hring-sele a ring hall Beo K 4615

e

m Hring-mal, es m Beo K 3042 π

n Hringed ringed, annulis instructus Beo K 64

Hroden-hilt, es; n adorned hilt Beo K ...

1a

1 Hringed-byrne ar a coat of Mail Beo 2491

r ✗ hung about, ... surrounded with ornaments Beo ... in hreodan

p Hring-weorðung, e; f ring honouring, or dignity Beo K 6030

q ✗ Hring-windel a sphere

(2)

a Hróf-sele a roofed ~~house~~ hall Beo K 3029

b ~~Hromde hembane Son v hramse~~

~~Hrycg~~
~~2 Hrycg, es m the back; dorsum Beo K 937 v spl hric~~

~~c Hron-fisc, es; m a whale fish, a whale Beo K 1075~~

~~Hryf, e; f the breast, etc.~~

d 2 Hrór excited; excitatus Beo K 3257

~~e Hroder, dl- cattle v hryder~~

f es, m, n?
~~Hroder, an advantage, benefit, ~~comfort~~ comfort commodum, beneficium Beo K abv 4891: Ca. 48: Schleo and to hroter Cod Ex 25~~

30

(x)

hrofas *under roofs, Cd.* 170.—Hrof-gefor *a roofed vessel, Cd.* 67.—Hrof-tigel *roof-tile, R.* 58.—Hrof-wyrhta *a roof-worker, carpenter, R.* 9.

Hrofes-ceaster, Hrofe-ceaster, Hroue-ceaster [*Flor.* Rhovecestre: *Malm.* Rovecestria: *Hunt.* Rouecestre, Roueceastre: *Dunel.* Rovecester.—ceaster *the city: Bd.* says Hrofes *of Roffer: Som.* hrof *covered, because enclosed with hills,* or rof *eminent*] ROCHESTER, *Kent.* On Hrofes-ceastre, *Chr.* 644: 604: 986.

Hrohung, e; *f. Excreatio, Mod. confit.* 5.

Hromese *acitula, Cot.* 206.

Hrón, hran, es; *m. A whale;* grampus, balæna:—*Cot.* 161. Hronas *delphini, Bd.* 1, 1.—Hron-mere *a whale-pond, the sea, Bt. R.* p. 155.—Hron-rad *the whale's road, Cd.* 10.

Hrond-sparwa *A sort of sparrow;* passerum genus:—*C. Mt.* 10, 29.

Hrooc *a rook, cricket,* v. hroc.

Hrop *A distaff;* colus:—Hropwyrc *coli opus, R.* 11.

HROR; *adj. Prone, bent down;* pronus:—*Bt.* 41, 5.

Hroren *fallen, desolate,* v. gebroren.

Hrorenlic *Ready to fall* or *fail;* ruiturus, *Som.*

Hrost [*Plat.* rust, rast *f*: *Dut.* roest *m.*] A ROOST; petaurum. — Henna-hrost *a henroost.*

Hrot *Filth, scum;* sordes:—*L. M.* 2, 28.

Hroð *a commotion,* v. hruð.

Hroðer *cattle, Cd.* 48, v. hryðer.

Hroð-hund *A useless dog;* inutilis canis:—*Elf. gl. Som.* p. 59, v. riðða.

Hrowen *repented; pp. of* hreowan.

Hrug, hruh, hruhge *rough,* v. rug.

Hrum, hrym [*Icel.* hrím] *Soot;* fuligo:—*Martyr.* 25. *Aug. Cacobatus, Cot.* 42.

Hrumig; *adj. Sooty;* fuliginosus:—*Cot.* 31.

Hrure, hruron *fell, L. Ps.* 19, 9, v. reósan.

HRUSE, an; *f.* [*Plat. Dut.* rots *f.*] 1. *A rock, hill;* rupes. 2. *Earth, land, region;* terra, regio:—1. Hyllas and hrusan þec wurðiað *hills and rocks thee adore, Cd.* 192. 2. Hefig hrusan dæl *ponderosa terræ moles, Bt. R.* p. 195. Snaw hrusan leccað *snow moistens lands, Bt. R.* p. 196. Hungor ofer hrusan *fames per regionem, Chr.* 975.

Hrut *balidus, Cot.* 28.

Hrutan *To* ROUT *in sleeping, snore, snort;* stertere:—*Elf. gr.* 28.

Hruð *A commotion, raging;* æstus:—*L. M.* 2, 24.

Hruðer *cattle, Ex.* 34, 19, v. hryðer.

Hruwon *repented; p. of* hreowan.

Hruxle *A noise, rustling;* strepitus, *Som.*

Hry, es; *m. A thorn;* spina:—Hrygas *thorns, C. Mt.* 7, 16: 13, 7.

Hrycas, hrycg *a back, Ps.* 31, 4, v. hric.—Hryc-rib, hrycg-rib *a back rib, Cot.* 163.—Hrycryple, hrycg-riple *the vertebræ.*

Hryf *the bowels, Ps.* 21, 8, v. hrif.

Hryft *a cloak, R. Mt.* 5, 40, v. rift.

Hryg *a back,* v. hric.—Hrygilebuc *a wooden vessel, a pail, back bucket,* v. æscen.—Hrygmærh-lið *back-marrow-joint, the vertebræ.*

Hryman *To give way, depart;* discedere:—*Elf. gr. de 3 conjugat.*

Hryman, hreman, hriman; *p.* de [*Plat.* römen: *Dut.* roemen: *Ger.* rühmen: *Ot.* ruamen: *Ker.* ruomen: *Dan.* berömme: *Swed.* berömma *to boast: Swed.* råma *mugire: Icel.* hreima *resonare: Icel.* rymia.—hream *a cry*] *To cry out, vociferate:* clamare:—He hrymð *clamat, Mt.* 12, 19. Cnapan hrymað to hyra efengelicum, *Mt.* 11, 16. Ic hrimde *clamavi, Gen.* 39, 15. Hrymde *clamavit, Gen.* 39, 14. Hig hrymað to me, *Ex.* 22, 23.

Hryme *soot, Cot.* 82, v. hrum.

Hrympelle *A rumple, fold;* ruga:—*Cot.* 178.

Hrypa-dun *Repton, Guth. vit. C.* 2, v. Hreopandun.

Hrypan *to rip, break through, C. Mt.* 6, 19, v. rypan.

Hryp-sæta *the people of Rippon,* v. Hreop-sæta.

Hryre *Should fall;* caderem:—*C. T. Ps.* 117, 13, v. hreosan.

HRYRE, es; *m. A rushing, falling, violence, destruction, ruin;* prolapsio, ruina:—Hægles hryre *a falling of hail, Mk.* 5, 13. Gemænigfyld is on heom hryre, *Ps.* 105, 28. He gefylde hryras *implebit ruinas, Ps.* 109, 7: *Ors.* 4, 9.

Hryrednes, se; *f. Hastiness;* præcipitatio:—*L. Ps.* 51, 4.

Hryre-mus *a bat, Prov.* 30, v. hreremus.

Hryrenes, se; *f. A storm;* procella:—*L. Ps.* 106, 25.

Hrysc, hrysca *A bursting* or *rushing in;* irruptio, *Som.*

Hrysede, hrysedon *shook, rushed, Ps.* 21, 6; as if *from* hrysan; *p.* ede *for* hreósan.

Hrysel, hrysl *Fat of a hog* or *swine, lard;* adeps, abdomen:—*R.* 73.

Hrysiende *shaking, T. Ps.* 28, 7, v. hreósan.

Hryst *falls,* v. hreósan.

HRYÐER, hriðer, hruðer, hróðer [*Frs.* reder, rither *m*: *Icel.* hrútr *m. a ram*] *Neat, cattle, an ox, a cow, heifer;* quadrupes, bos:—Twentig hryðera *twenty of red cattle, Ors.* 1, 1, *Ing. Lect.* 62, 10. Of hriðerum *de bovibus, Lev.* 1, 2. Hryðeru *boves, L. In.* 70. Hryðera *of cattle, Deut.* 14, 26: *Jos.* 6, 21. Heo þe hroðra oftihð *she shall deny thee her cattle, Cd.* 48, *Th.* p. 62, 21. Iung hryðer *juvenculus, R.* 22. An þri wintre hryðer *a heifer of three years.* Hryðera heord *a herd of cattle, Cot.* 3: *Gen.* 45, 10.—Hryðer-heard, hryðer-hyrde *a herdsman.*—Hryðer-heawere *a cattle-hewer, a butcher.*

Hryðða *a mastiff,* v. riðða.

Hrywð *laments,* v. hreowan.

Hrywlic *cruel, Nathan.* 8, v. hreowlic.

Hrywsian; *p.* ode; *pp.* od. *To lament, be sorry for;* deflere:—Hi heora synna sceoldon hrywsian *they should lament their sins, Ors.* 6, 2. Hrywsode him *pœnituit eum, C. Ps.* 105, 42, v. hreowan.

Hú [*Plat.* wo: *Dut.* hoe: *Frs.* ho: *Ger.* wie: *Ot.* wio: *Tat.* so: *Wil.* suie: *Dan.* hvor: *Swed.* huru] How, *in what manner;* quam, quomodo:—Hu god *how good, Ps.* 72, 1. Hu mæg man, *Mt.* 12, 29. Hu magon ge *how can ye? Mt.* 12, 34. Hu fela *how many? Ps.* 77, 7: *Mt.* 27, 13: *Mk.* 5, 20. Hu lange, *Mt.* 17, 17. Hu micel *quam multus, quam magnus.* ¶ Hu ne *not, whether or not;* nonne, *Mt.* 6, 26.—Hu geares *however.*—Hu hugu, hu hwego *about, almost, Bd.* 4, 19.

Hua *who,* v. hwa.

Huæstrian *To murmur;* murmurare:—*C. Jn.* 7, 32.

Huæstrung, e; *f. A murmuring, muttering;* murmuratio, *Som.*

Hualf *a convexity,* v. hwealf.

Huars *Space, distance;* spatium:—*C. Lk.* 24, 13.

Hucs, husce, hucx [*Plat.* jux] HOAX, *irony, slight;* ironia:—Mid hucse *with slight, Cd.* 107. Þurh hucx *per ironiam, Cot.* 186.

Hudenian [hude, hyde *a hide*] *To unhide, examine;* excutere:

—Hudenige ærest hine selfne *excutiat prius seipsum, Past.* 64.

Hudig *heedful*, v. hydeg.

Hueol *a wheel*, v. hweohl.

Huer *an ewer*, v. hwer.

Huf *A round spungy substance covering the glottis, a disease;* uvula:—*R.* 71.

Húfe [*Plat.* huve *f*: *Dut.* huif *f*: *Frs.* huwe *f*: *Ger.* haube *f*: *Old Ger.* schaube *f*: *Dan.* hue *f*: *Swed.* hufwa *f*: *Icel.* húfa *f. a hat*: *Lat. mid.* cuphia, coiffa] *A round ornament for the head;* cidaris, tiara:—*R.* 64. Biscopes hufe *a bishop's mitre.* Hufan hættes *mitres.*

Hufian *To put on a head-dress;* tiaram sive mitram imponere:—Hufode *tiaram imposuit, Lev.* 8, 13.

Hugu, hugu-dæl; *adv. A little, but a little, at least;* parum:—Hwylce hugu tid *quantillum temporis, Bd.* 4, 22. Hu hugu *about, nearly, Bd.* 3, 27.

Hui, huig; *interj. Ho;* hui:—*Elf. gr.*

Huil *while, C. Mt.* 26, 40, v. hwil.

Hul, hula *a hill*, v. hill: *a hull, shell*, v. halstan.

Hulc, hulcl *A den, cabin, cottage;* cubile:—*Elf. gr.* 8: *gl.* 26.

Hulfestre *Rainy;* pluvialis:—*R.* 38.

Hulic *of what sort, Ors.* 4, 12, v. hwylc.

Hulme HULME, *Holm-castle, in Normandy, Chr.* 1094.

Hulpon *helped; p. of* helpan.

Hul-wyrt HILL-WORT, *wild thyme;* pulegium montanum, *Som.*

Humber HUMBER, *a river in Yorkshire.*—Be suðan Humbre *near south of Humber, Chr.* 827. Humbran muða *Humber's mouth;* Humbri ostium, *Chr.* 993.

Humeta *How, in what manner;* quomodo:—*Mt.* 22, 12.

Hun, hune *consumption;* tabes:—*Cot.* 192.

Hunas *The* HUNNS; Hunni:—Ætla Huna cyninge *Attila, king of the Hunns, Chr.* 443.

HUND, es; *n.* [*Plat. Ger.* hundert: *Dut.* honderd: *Frs.* huwndert, hondert: *Tat.* hund: *Moes.* hund, hunda: *Dan.* hundred: *Swed.* hundra, hundrade: *Icel.* hundrad: in the poem upon Saint Anno, hunterit: in older dialects the latter part of this word is not found; for instance, in the Salic laws, chunna: the *Moes.* and *A.-S.* hund: *Welsh,* and *Celt. Bret.* cant: *Albanish,* kinnt, to which corresponds the *Lat.* centum, derived by some from the *Grk.* κεντεω, *to prick;* it being a practice, in earlier times, to make a dot after each hundred. The terminating syllables ert, red *or* ret, which took their origin by transposition of red, rath, signified, according to *Wachter, a number;* but, according to *Ihre,* more justly, *a stroke;* it being the ancient custom to count or number by strokes or lines. The *Plat.* ret signifies *a rent* or *line,* which the ancients made on the wooden staff or stick, used to cast up their accounts. For this reason, the syllables red, ert, rad, have been added in the *Swed.* and other northern languages to the tens instead of the *Ger.* zig, as the *Swed.* attraed, *Ger.* achtzig, *eighty:* niraed, *Ger.* neunzig *ninety.* In ancient times hund only signified *ten: Moes.* taihun-taihund: *A.-S.* hund-teontig designates *ten times ten.* In the *A.-S.* hund-seofontig is *seventy.* In old *Ger.* MSS. they use, instead of hundret, zehenzig: *Isd.* zehanzo. Fragment on Charlemagne, zehenzig. For *two hundred, Wil.* uses zuirenzehenzog, and *Ot.* zuirozehanzug; and for a *thousand years* zenstunt zenzech iuro] A HUNDRED; centum. The *A.-S.* prefixed hund to numerals, from seventy to a hundred and twenty, but it was sometimes omitted, when hund preceded; as, scypa an hund and eahtatig *of ships one hundred and eighty.* When units are combined with tens, the units, as in *Dut.* and *Ger.,* are placed first with and; as, an and twentig *twenty-one;* but in *A.-S.* after the word hund *or* hundred, the smaller number is last, and the substantive repeated; for if the smaller number were set first, it would denote a multiplication; as, an hund wintra and þrittig wintra *a hundred and thirty years;* hund teontig wintra and seofon and XL wintra *a hundred and forty-seven years;* feower hund wintra and þrittig wintra *four hundred and thirty years;* þreo hund manna and eahtatyne men *three hundred and eighteen men.* Instead of twa hund, we find also tu hund. The others are simply thus; þreo hund, fif hund, &c. *Rask:*—Gyf hwylc mann hæfð hund sceapa, and him losað an of þam hu ne forlæt he þa nigon and hund nigontig *on* þam muntum, *Mt.* 18, 12.—Hund-eahtatig *eighty, Gen.* 16, 16.—Hund-enlufontig *a hundred and ten.*—Hund-feald *hundred-fold, Mt.* 13, 8.—Hund-nigontig *ninety, Gen.* 5, 9.—Hund-seofontig *seventy.*—Hund-teontig *a hundred.*—Hund-teontig-fealdlic *a hundred-fold, Bd.* 5, 19.—Hund-twelftig *a hundred and twenty.*

HUND, es; *m.* [*Dut.* hond *m*: *Plat. Ger. Dan. Swed.* hund *m*: *Icel.* hundr *m*: *Moes.* hunds] A HOUND, *dog;* canis:—Ymbsealdon me hundas manige *circumdederunt me canes multi, Ps.* 21, 15. Hundes beo *dog-bee, dog* or *horse-fly, Cot.* 54. Hundes fleoga, *Id. Ors.* 1, 7. Hundes lus, *Id. Elf. gl.* 12. Hundes berien *hound* or *dog-berry.*—Hundes tunge *hound's tongue;* cynoglossa, *Id. Elf. gl.* 42.—Hundes-wyrm *dog-worm;* ricinus, *R.* 24.—Hunda hus *dog's house, a kennel.*—Hund-wealh *canum servitor, R.* 8.

Hundhoge HUNCOT, *Lincolnshire, Chr.* 1124.

Hundrað *Hundredth;* centesimus:—*C. Mt.* 13, 8.

Hundred, hundryd, es; *n. pl. nom. ac.* hundredu. *A hundred, a division of a county;* centuria:—Innan his hundrede *within his hundred, L. Cnut. pol.* 16.—Hundred-man *a centurion;* centurio, *Mk.* 15, 44.—Hundredes man, *Id.*—Hundredes-ealdor, *Id. Mt.* 8, 5.

Hunduelle *A hundred-fold;* centuplus:—*C. Mt.* 13, 8.

Hu-ne, hu-la-ne *whether or not;* numquid:—*Mt.* 5, 46, 47, v. hu.

Hune *the Hunns, Bd.* 5, 9, v. Hunas.

Hune *Horehound;* marrubium, *Som.*

Hunel *Shameless, wanton;* procax, *Som.*

HUNGER, hungor, hungur; *g.* hungres; *d.* hungre. [*Dut. Frs.* honger *n*: *Plat. Ger. Dan. Swed.* hunger *m*: *Icel.* húngr *n*: *Ot.* hungar] HUNGER, *famine;* fames:—On hungre forwurðe, *Lk.* 15, 17.—Hungras; *pl. Mt.* 24, 7.—Hunger-biten *hunger-bitten, Chr.* 1096.—Hunger-læwa *one afflicted with hunger;* famelicus:—*Cantic Annæ.*

Hungreg, hungrig, hungri HUNGRY; famelicus, esuriens:—*Cot.* 191: *Cd.* 72.

Hungrian *to hunger*, v. hingrian.

Hungrie HUNGARY; Hungaria:—*Chr.* 1096.

a Hweol, rad a wheel
trisel Som v hweohl
b)
c)
Hu geare
Hu geares how
soever: qualiter-
cunque Som v hu
(a See Ref. Halbertsma
p. XIII & 18)
d Hygdig cauterius
Lye v. hydig
e)
f+ Humber, g. humbres m.
3+ Humbra, an; m the river
Humber

Huniflowende Huniflowende hone
flowing: melliflua
Mone B. 28

Grein II 277. 15

a) l 19 * Hunig-tear

a Hupan gretlum re-
vocare Bsw

† Ete man þ
hunig. Mone
p 509 b 45

01 [6ab]

Hunig awylled
honey boiled, mede
Som

* Hunta au m
a hunter, spider, etc

b Hus-bryne es; m
a house burning
Lye

c) † Husincle es; n
a small house
domuncula Gr. II 347, 18

huætn
ghwates

1) Hwæt m.f.p. hwæs, d
hwæm (hwam) ac
hwone (hwane) at
hwi

3) Hwæcce a chest Gr. I 264, 43
etc

d)

e)

HUNIG, huni [*Plat.* honnig *m*: *Frs.* huninge *f*: *Dut. Ger.* honig *m*: *Ker. Isd.* honec: *Not.* honanc: *South Ger.* hönig: *Dan.* honning *c*: *Swed.* honing, håning *m*: *Icel.* hunáng *n.*] HONEY; mel:—*Num.* 16, 14. Feld-beon hunig *field-bees' honey.* Wudu hunig *wood-honey;* sylvestre mel, *Mt.* 3, 4: *Mk.* 1, 6. Huniges dropa *drops of honey;* mel stillatitium, *L. M.* 2, 46.—Hunig-æppel *honey-apple;* pastillus, *Cot.* 155.—Hunig-camb *honey-comb, R. Conc.*—Hunig-sucle *honey-suckle.*—Hunig-swete *honey-sweating.*—Hunig-tear *honey-tears, drops of honey, Cot.* 43.—Hunig-tearlic *like nectar, Cot.* 138.—Huni-suge *privet;* ligustrum, *R.* 47.

Hunspera, hunspura *A staff* or *stick with a spear in it;* dolo:—*Cot.* 62.

HUNTA, an; *m.* A HUNTER; venator:—Preost ne beo hunta *a priest should not be a hunter, L. Can. Edg.* 64. Butan þær huntan gewicodon *except where hunters dwelt.*

Hunta, an; *m.* *A spider;* araneæ genus:—Huntan bite *a spider's bite, L. M.* 1, 68. Hunta, þæt swiðre oðre naman gangel-wefra, *L. M.* p. 1, c. 68.

Huntandun, Huntendun [*Hunt.* Huntendune: *Ric.* Huntadun: *Hovd.* Huntendun: *Brom.* Huntingdon:, *Kni.* Huntyngdon.—huntan *a hunter's,* dun *a hill*] HUNTINGDON; venantis dunum, oppidum Icenorum:—*Chr.* 656: 921: 963.—Huntandune-scyre, Huntadun-scire HUNTINGDONSHIRE, *Chr.* 1011.

Huntað, huntoð [huntað *from* huntian *to hunt*] *A hunting;* venatio:—*Ors.* 1, 1: *Gen.* 25, 28.

Huntian, ic huntige; *p.* ode; *pp.* od. *To* HUNT; venari:—*Coll. Monast. Elf. gr.* 24.

Huntigend, es; *m.* *A hunter;* venans:—Of grine huntigendra *e laqueo venantium, Ps.* 90, 3: 123, 6.

Huntigspere HUNTING-SPEAR; venabulum:—*R.* 51.

Huntnað, huntnoð *A hunting, chase;* venatio:—*L. Can. pol.* 77: *Bd.* 3, 14.

Huntung, e; *f.* A HUNTING; venatio:—*Bd.* 1, 1.

Hunu *How now;* nonne:—*Ps.* 38, 11.

Huoerf *exchange, C. Mk.* 8, 37, v. hwerf.

Huomm *a corner,* v. hwom.

Huon *a little, few,* v. hwon.

Huonlice *a little while,* v. hwonlice.

Hup-ban *a hip-bone, Cot.* 126, v. hipe.

Hup-seax *A dagger, short sword;* pugio, gladiolus:—*Jdth.* 12.

Hure [hyre *a reward,* hyrian *to hire*] WHORE; meretrix, *Som.*

Huredóm, es; *m.* WHOREDOM; meretricium, *Som.*

Huru, huru-þinga *At least, at all events, yet, only, indeed, especially;* saltem, tantum:—*Elf. T.* p. 36, 17: *Gen.* 16, 2: *Jos.* 1, 18.

HU'S, es; *n.* [*Plat. Dan.* huus *n*: *Dut.* huis *n*: *Ger.* haus *n*: *Frs. Isd. Ker. Ot.* and all the other old *South Ger.* writers, *Moes. Swed. Icel.* hus *n*: *Slavon.* and *Wendish.* hisha: *Wach.* derives this word, as well as the *Ger.* haut *skin,* and *Ger.* hütte *cottage,* from the *Old Ger.* hüten *to cover, protect, hide;* so that it would properly designate *a covered* or *protected place*] A HOUSE, *building, cottage;* domus, ædes:—*Mt.* 12, 25.—Hus be wege *a house by the way, a stable, Elf. gl.*—Hus of bredan *a tavern;* taberna, *R.* 55.—Hus-bonda, husbunda *husband;* domûs magister, *Ex.* 3, 22.—Hus-brec, hus-bryce *house-breaking, L. Cnut. pol.* 61.—Hus-bricel, hus-brycel *house-breaker, Cot.* 209.—Hus-carl, husceorl *a house-carl, house-churl, servant, Chr.* 1036.—Husehere *a dwelling, T. Ps.* 101, 7.—Hus-hefen *an arched roof, Cot.* 119.—Hus-hiwræden, hus-hywræden *a dwelling, Ps.* 117, 3.—Hus-hlaford *the house-lord, master, Lk.* 22, 11.—Hus-hleow *house protection, hospitality, L. Can. Edg.* 15.—Husincle, hus-incleof *a dwelling, Ps.* 101, 7.—Hus-ræden *a dwelling, L. Ps.* 47, 12.—Hus-scipe, hus-scype *houseship, domestic state, a family.* Hus-stede *the place* or *site of a house, Herb.* 52, 1.—Husweard *a house-ward, master.*—Hus-wist *a house, L. Ps.* 5, 8.

Husa *A domestic;* domesticus:—*C. Mt.* 10, 36.

Husc *slight, Cd.* 109, v. hucs.

HUSEL, husul; *g.* husles [*Ger.* hostie *f*: *Moes.* hunsl, hunsle: *Icel.* husl: *Lat. mid.* hostia *a sacrifice*] *The sacrament;* panis sacer, sive eucharisticus:—*Bd.* 2, 5: 4, 24. Husl syllan *to give the sacrament.* Husles wyrð *worthy of the sacrament.* ¶ Husel-box *the sacramental box, paten.*—Husel disc *the sacramental dish, paten.*—Husel-fatu *the sacramental vessels, Bd.* 1, 29.—Husel-gang *a going to the sacrament* or *partaking of it, L. Can. Eccl.* 19.—Husel-genga *a goer to the sacrament, a communicant, L. In.* 19.—Huselportic *a vestry, Bd.* 2, 1.

Husian; *pp.* gehused. *To* HOUSE, *entertain;* domo excipere:—*L. Can. Edg.* 14.

Husl *the sacrament,* v. husel, &c.

Huslian; *pp.* gehuslud. *To administer* or *celebrate the communion* or *sacrament;* eucharistiam celebrare:—*L. Can. Ælf.* 16, 31.

Husol *A subdeacon* or *an attendant on the priest at the sacrament;* acolythus, *Som.*

Husting [hus *a house,* þing *a thing, cause, council*] HUSTING, *a place of council;* conciliabulum, concilium:—Leadon hine to heora hustinga *led him to their place of council* [*hustings*], *Chr.* 1012.

Husul *the sacrament, C. Mt.* 12, 7, v. husel, &c.

Hu-swiðe *how great.*

Huð, huðe. 1. *Prey, booty, spoil;* præda. 2. *A port;* portus:—1. Mid micelre huðe, *Num.* 31, 12: *Jos.* 8, 2: *Cd.* 174. 2. *L. Ps.* 106, 30, v. hyð.

Huðe *permitted, for* uðe; *from* unnan.

Huxlic *Disgraceful, vile;* turpis:—*Elf. gr.* 9, 21.

Huxlice *Disgracefully, shamefully;* turpiter:—*Elf. T.* p. 16.

Hw, or the *w* aspirated. The modern English always places the *h* after the *w*; thus, hwa *who,* hwæðer *whether,* hwile *while, &c.*

Hwá *Who;* qui, quis:—*Mt.* 21, 23.

Hwæcca [*Chauc.* wiche] A HUTCH, *chest;* arca:—Cornhwæcca *a corn-chest, Som.*

HWÆDE, gehwæde; *adj.* *Small, little, mean, moderate;* exiguus:—Ge hwædes geleafan, *Lk.* 12, 28. Ge gehwædes geleafan, *Mt.* 6, 30.

Hwæder; *adv.* *Whither;* quò:—Hwæder ga ic *quonam abibo, Gen.* 37, 30: *Ex.* 21, 13. ¶ Elles-hwæder *else whither, Elf. gr.* Swa hwæder swa *whithersoever, Mt.* 8, 19.

HWÆG [*Plat.* waje, waddik, hei, heu *n*: *Dut.* wei, hui *f*: *Dan.* valde, valle *c*: *Swed.* wassla *f.*] WHEY; serum lactis:—*R.* 33.

HWÆL, hwal, es; *m.* [*Plat.* wal, walfisk *m*: *Dut.* walvisch *m*: *Ger.* wallfisch *m*: *Tat.* uual: *Dan.* hval, hvalfisk *m*: *Swed.* hwal, hwalfisk *m*: *Icel.* hvalr, hvalfiskr *m.* From the old word bal, wall *great*] WHALE; cetus:—On þæs hwæles innoðe, *Mt.* 12, 40. Hwalas þec herigað *whales praise thee, Cd.* 192. ¶ Hwæl-hunta *a whale-hunter, Ors.* 1, 1.—Hwæl-huntað *whale-hunting, Ors.* 1, 1.

Hwæl *slaughter, a carcass, Cd.* 151, v. wæl.

Hwæl *around, Cd.* 150, v. hweohl.

Hwæm *a corner, T. Ps.* 117, 21, v. hwom.

Hwæm, hwam *to whom; d. of* hwá.

Hwæne, hwone *Whom;* quem, quam; *ac. of* hwá.

Hwæne, hwene *Somewhat, almost, a little, scarcely;* aliquantum:—*Bd.* 1, 27, *resp.* 3. ¶ Hwæne ær *or* hwene ær *a little before, Bd.* 5, 19.—Hwæne læs *a little less, L. Ps.* 8, 6.

Hwænne, hwenne, hwonne, ahwænne *When;* quando:—*Mt.* 2, 7.

Hwær, hwar [*Plat.* waar, woor: *Dut.* waar: *Ger.* wo: *Ot.* waar: *Wil.* wa: *Moes.* hwar: *Dan.* hvor: *Swed.* hwar: *Icel.* hvar] WHERE; ubi:—*Mt.* 2, 2. ¶ Swa hwær swa *wheresoever, Mt.* 24, 28.

Hwær-boll, hwær-cytel *a frying-pan.*

Hwærf *departed; p. of* hweorfan.

Hwærflung, e; *f. Error;* aberratio:—*C. Mt.* 24, 24.

Hwæs; *adj. Bitter, sharp;* acerbus:—*Cod. Ex.* 29, a, 6.

Hwæs *Whose;* cujus; *g. of* hwá.

Hwæstran, hwæstrian *to murmur, C. Jn.* 6, 43, v. hwastran.

Hwæstrung *a murmur, C. Jn.* 7, v. hastrung.

Hwæt *quick, brisk, Ors.* 3, 7, v. hwat.

Hwæt; *pron. nom. n. of* hwá. 1. WHAT; quid. 2. Used for hwa *who;* quis:—1. Hwæt wenst þu *quid sentis tu? Mk.* 4, 41. 2. Hwæt wæs se þe *quis erat ille qui? Gen.* 27, 33. Hwæt is þes *quis est hic? Mk.* 4, 41. ¶ Hwæt elles *what else.*—Hwæt lytles *a little, somewhat.*—Hwæt þa *what then, but, Elf. T.* p. 2, 26.—Hwæt hugu *somewhat, a little, almost, nearly, Bd.* 2, 5, 6.—Hwæt-hwæga, hwæt-hweg, hwæt-hwega, hwæt-hwugu, hwæt-hwygu *about, a little, somewhat, Bt.* 39, 7.—Hwæt-hwara *somewhere.*

Hwæt; *adv. conj. Moreover, besides, but, wherefore, but yet, in short, indeed, because;* hinc, tandem:—*Gen.* 9, 23.

Hwæte, es; *m.* [*Plat.* weten *m*: *Dut.* weit *f*: *Ger.* weitzen *m*: *Moes.* wait, waitei: *Dan.* hvede *n*: *Swed.* hwete *n*: *Icel.* hveiti *n*: *Heb.* חִטָּה hthe *the wheat.* These words probably have their origin from the white colour of the wheat] WHEAT; triticum:—Fulne hwæte on þam eare, *Mk.* 4, 28.—Hwæte-god *wheat-goddess, Ceres.*—Hwæte-gryttan *wheat-grits, R.* 50.

Hwætene; *adj.* WHEATEN; triticeus:—Hwætene hlaf *wheaten loaf, R.* 66.—Hwætene corn *a wheat corn, Jn.* 12, 24.

Hwæðer; *pron.* WHETHER, *which of the two;* uter:—Hwæðer þara twegra, *Mt.* 21, 31. Hwæðer is mare, *Mt.* 23, 17, 19.

Hwæðre; *conj. adv. Whether, nevertheless, yet, if, but;* utrum, tamen, verum:—*Gen.* 18, 21: *Mt.* 26, 25. ¶ Hwæðer, þe- - - -þe *whether- - - -or.*

Hwætlice; *comp.* hwætlicor; *adv. Shortly, soon, diligently;* cito:—*Cot.* 138: *Coll. Monast.*

Hwætnes, se; *f. Quickness, velocity, vigour;* velocitas:—*Bt.* 24, 3.

Hwætscype, es; *m. Quickness, valour;* virtus:—*Ors.* 1, 10.

Hwæt-stan *a whetstone,* v. hwetstan.

Hwal, hwale *a whale, Gen.* 1, 21, v. hwæl.

Hwalf *a climate, Cot.* 50, v. hwealf.

Hwalfian *to arch,* v. hwealfian.

Hwall *Wanton;* procax:—*Cot.* 171.

Hwalwa *Declining;* devexus:—*Cot.* 67.

Hwám *To whom;* cui; *d. of* hwá.

Hwamm *a corner, V. Ps.* 117, 21, v. hwom.

Hwan, hwane, hwone *Whom;* quem:—*Mt.* 26, 8; *ac. s. of* hwá.

Hwan *Calamity;* calamitas, *Som.*

Hwanan, hwanon *Whence;* unde:—*Mt.* 13, 27, 54.

Hwanung, e; *f. A waning;* deficientia, *Som.*

Hwar *where, Mt.* 15, 33, v. hwær.

Hwarf *wharf, space,* v. hweorf.

Hwarne, ne hwarne long *Not far;* non procul:—*C. Mt.* 8, 30.

Hwastas *molles, Som.*

Hwastran, hwastrian, hwæstrian; *p.* we hwastredon. *To murmur, whisper, rumble;* susurrare:—*L. Ps.* 40, 8.

Hwastrung, hwæstrung, e; *f. A murmuring;* murmuratio:—*Confess. Peccat.*

HWAT, hwæt; *def.* se hwata; *adj. Quick, brisk, ready, strenuous;* acer:—Se hwata esne *fortis vir, Bt.* 40, 3.

Hwata [*Icel.* hvata *f. the goddess Hertha, Ertha, the earth,* mentioned by Tacitus. The Danish island, Sealand, contains still, at Hlethraburg, the remains of the temple *Hertha*] *Omens, divinations, soothsayings;* omina, auguria:—Ne gimon hwata, *Lev.* 19, 26: *Deut.* 18, 10.

Hwaðre *whether, Bt.* 40, 3, v. hwæðer.

Hwatung, e; *f. Soothsaying;* divinatio, *Som.*

Hweal *Urine;* lotium:—*R.* 78.

Hwealf; *adj. Convex, bending;* convexus:—Hwealfum lindum *convexis scutis, Jdth.* 11.

Hwealfa [*Plat.* welfte, wolfte, gewolfte *n*: *Dut.* verwelf, gewelf *n*: *Ger.* wölbung *f*: gewölbe *n*: *Dan.* hvælving *c*: *Swed.* hwälfning *f*: *Icel.* hvelfing *f.*] *A convexity, arch, expanse, climate;* convexitas:—Þæs heofones hwealfa *the heaven's expanse, Bt.* 19.

Hwealfian *To ceil, to vault;* camerare, *Som.*

Hweal-hafoc *Welsh-hawk, a stranger,* v. wealh.

Hweallæg [*Dunel.* Walalege] WHALEY, *Lancashire, Chr.* 798.

Hwear *where,* v. hwær.

Hwearf *A wharf, bank, shore;* crepido:—*Cd.* 169.

Hwearf *turned; p. of* hweorfan.

Hwearfian; *p.* ode; *pp.* od [*Plat.* werveln: *Ger.* wirbeln: *Old Ger.* werben, werweln: *Dan.* hvirvle: *Swed.* hwirfla: *Icel.* hverfa] *To fly, turn* or *wind round, to change, advance;* circumvolitare, circumvolvi:—*L. Can. eccl.* 4. Swá swá on wænes eaxe hwearfað þa hweol *as on a waggon's axle the wheels turn, Bt.* 39, 7: 25. Swa þu gesceope þa saule þat hio sceolde ealne weg hwearfian on hire selfne *so hast thou created the soul that she should always turn upon herself, Bt.* 33, 4. Guð hwearfode *war advanced;* prælium conversum est, *Cd.* 149, v. hweorfan.

Hwearftlian *to turn, Elf. gr.* v. hwearfian.

Hwearfum *by turns, Jdth.* 12, v. hwyrftum.

Hwearfung, gehwearf, e; *f. A turning, change, mutability;* versio:—Þe was þeos hwearfung sælða *to thee was this change better, Bt.* 7, 3.

Hweg *whey,* v. hwæg.

Hwega; *adv. At least, almost;* pene, *Som.*

Hwelan; *pp.* hweled. *To wither, pine away, putrify;* contabescere:—*Scint.* 15.

Hwelc *who, what,* v. hwylc.

q gedden. e f

1 + Hwæten wheaten Th. An

2 Hwætlic quick than

Hwealfa, an; m

1 + ~~Hwm~~ Grm II 58. 13.

+ Hwealfe a vault + Th. An

2 6 Hwealf, es m. A ~~turning~~ convexity, what is ~~ ~~ bent over, a canopy; convexum Beok 114.

b

1 Hwæt, m. n; f hwata g m n hwates; f hwætre adj: see Beo gl. in hwæt

3

Hwat-dl

c 2 + Hwæt, interj. What! lo! behold! ~~~~ Said Beok 1.

~~~~ Hwate Beo K 4170 Beo gl. has hwæte

+ Hwata def. m. hwates g. m n of hwæt
~~~~

a

Hwípan, p hweop
to weep; lugere Beo K 4531

b

b"

-wil
c Hwer. well; les
m Whirwell

Hwirfan to turn
& hweorfan

(x) (3)

(d) Hwi part of hwa
who LK. 3157

Hwirf-póle a
whirlpool Som
& hwyrfe-póle

Hwiccia an; m
The county bordering
on the Severn th An

(4)

f Hwel, e; f white
time Th An.
Beo gl

(3)

(7)

Hwile awhile
diu Beo K 210

Hwele *Putrefaction, rottenness;* putrefactio, *Som.*

HWELP, es; *m.* [*Plat.* wölp, wulp: *Dut.* welp *n*: *Old Ger.* welf *m*: *Dan.* hvalp *m*: *Swed.* hwalp *m*: *Icel.* hvelpr *m.*] WHELP; catulus:—Hwelp leona *catulus leonis, Ps.* 16, 13. Þa hwelpas etað of þam crumum, *Mt.* 15, 27: *Mk.* 7, 28.

Hwelung, e; *f. The sound of a trumpet;* clangor tubæ:—*Cot.* 109.

Hwem *a corner, quarter,* v. hwom.

Hwene *scarcely, a little, Bt.* 23, v. hwæne.

Hwenne *when, Gen.* 19, 35, v. hwænne.

Hweogl, hweogul *a wheel, Cot.* 145.

Hweohl, HWEOL, hweowol, es; *n.* [*Dut.* wiel *n*: *Dan. Swed.* hjul *n.*] A WHEEL, *circle, the world;* rota, orbis:—Þæt hweol hwerfð ymbutan *the wheel turns round, Bt.* 39, 7, *Card.* p. 338, 21. Þæs hweohles felga *fellies of the wheel, Id. Card.* p. 340, 21. Stefn þunurrada þinre on hweohle, *Ps.* 76, 17.

Hweolere, es; *m. A soothsayer, diviner;* augur:—*R.* 4.

Hweolp *a whelp, C. Mt.* 15, 27, v. hwelp.

Hweop A WHIP; flagellum, *Som.*

Hweóp WHOOPED, *called out, wailed, Cd.* 166: 125, v. wepan.

Hweóp *cry, Cd.* 148, v. wop.

Hweopan *To* WHIP, *scourge;* flagellare, *Som.*

Hweor-ban, hwyrf-ban WHIRLBONE; vertibulum, vertebra, *Som.*

Hweorf [*Plat. Frs.* warf *m*: *Dut.* werf *f*: *Ger.* werft *n*: *Dan.* verft *n*: *Swed.* hwarf *n*: *Icel.* hvarfi *n.*] WHARF, *distance;* spatium:—*R. Lk.* 24, 13.

Hweorfa *A whirl, what is hastily turned round, a spool;* verticillum:—*Cot.* 161: mola. 133.

Hweorfan, hwyrfan, gehweorfan, þu hweorfest, he hwyrfð; *p.* hwearf, gehwearf, hi hwurfon, gehwurfon; *pp.* hworfen, gehworfen, gehwyrfed, ahworfen, ahwerfed [*Dut. Kil.* wervelen] *To turn, turn* or *go away, depart, change, convert, wander, return;* vertere, discedere, convertere:—Gif seo wyrd swa hweorfan mot *if the fortune may so turn, Bt.* 4, *Card.* p. 12, 12. Þæt seo wyrd swa hwyrfan sceolde *that the fortune should so turn, Bt.* 4, *Card.* p. 12, 4. On wræc hweorfan *into exile, to depart, Cd.* 48. Lætað hine eft hweorfan to minum larum *let him again return to my precepts, Bt.* 3, 1, *Card.* p. 6, 19.

Hweorif *A beast of burden;* jumentum:—*R.* 20.

Hweosan *To* WHEEZE, *foam;* difficulter respirare.

Hweoð, hweoða *a gale, Ps.* 106, 29, v. hwið.

Hweoðerung *a murmuring,* v. hwastrung.

Hweowol *a wheel, Ps.* 82, 12, v. hweohl.

Hwer, huer *An ewer, a kettle;* cacabus, lebes:—*R.* 26: *Cot.* 120.

Hwerf, huoerf *An exchange, a loan;* commutatio:—*C. Mt.* 16, 26.

Hwerfa *vertigo, R.* 74.

Hwerfan, he hwerfð; *part.* hwerfende. *To turn, Bt.* 39, 7: 7, 2, v. hweorfan.

Hwerflic *Changeable;* mutabilis:—*Bt.* 11, 1.

Hwerfung, e; *f. A changing, change;* mutatio:—*Bt.* 7, 3.

Hwer-hwette, hwer-hwette *a wild cucumber, R.* 40.

Hwern *nowhere,* v. na-hwær.

Hwer-wille, Hwere-wille [*Flor. Malm.* Werewella: *Brom.* Werewell: *Kni.* Warewell] WHERWELL or WHORWELL, *Hants., Chr.* 1048.

Hwet *wet, Cot.* 120, v. wæt.

Hwetstan WHETSTONE; cos:—*Ors.* 4, 13.

Hwettan, ahwettan; we hwetton; *pp.* gehwetted [*Plat. Dut.* wetten: *Ger.* wetzen: *Ot.* wezzan: *Dan.* hvædse: *Icel.* hvessa] *To* WHET, *sharpen;* acuere:—Hi hwetton swa swa sweord tungan heora, *Ps.* 63, 3.

Hwi; *conj. adv.* [*Plat. Dut.* waarom: *Frs.* hwerom: *Ger.* warum: *Dan.* hvi: *Swed.* hwi: *Icel.* hví] WHY, *wherefore, for what, indeed;* cur, quamobrem:—Hwi didest þu þat, *Gen.* 3, 13. Hwi yt eower lareow, *Mt.* 9, 11. For hwi *for why, wherefore, Jn.* 7, 45.

Hwiccas [wic *a creek, from the winding of the Severn*] *People of Worcestershire;* Huiccii:—Hwicca mægð *Huicciorum provincia, Bd.* 4, 23. Hwicna bisceop *Huicciorum episcopus, Bd.* 5, 23: *Chr.* 800.

Hwider *whither, Gen.* 16, 8.—Hwider-wega *somewhere,* v. hwyder.

Hwidre *whether, Bt.* 22, 2, v. hwyder.

Hwig *why,* v. hwi.

HWIL, hwile, huil [*Plat.* wile *f*: *Dut.* wyl *f. time*: *Frs.* wile *f. rest*: *Ger.* weile *f*: *Ker.* wilu: *Ot.* wila: *Moes.* hweila. The latter three also under the signification of *an hour*: *Dan.* hvile *c. rest*: *Swed.* hwila *f. rest, leisure*: *Pol.* chwila: *Icel.* hvílld *f.*] A WHILE, *time, space, duration;* tempus:—On dæges hwile *in a day's space, Cd.* 191. On an byrhtm-hwile *in momento temporis, Lk.* 4, 5. Ic beo sume hwile mid eow, *Jn.* 7, 33. ¶ Þa hwile or þa hwile þe *the while, so long as, Mt.* 5, 25.—Hwil-fæc *a while, space, a pause.*—Hwil-sticce *a fragment of time, a short time, L. Alf. pol.* 39.—Hwil-tid *a while, time, a moment, C. Lk.* 4, 5.

Hwilc *what, which, who,* v. hwylc.

Hwilcnes, se; *f. A quality, manner, sort;* qualitas, *Som.*

Hwilendlic, hwilwendlic, hwilewendlic *For a time, temporary;* temporalis:—*Mt.* 13, 21.

Hwilon, hwilum, hwylum [*Dut.* wylen: *Ger.* weiland: *Ot.* wila: *Poem on St. Anno* wilen; hence *Spen. Old Eng.* whilom] *Sometime, awhile, for a time, once, now;* quondam, aliquando:—Hwilon ær *jam antea, Gen.* 43, 20. Hwilon an, hwilon twa *now one, now two.* Hi hwylum gelyfað, *Lk.* 8, 13.

Hwiolad WHEELED; rotas habens, *Lye.*

Hwiol-fag *A kind of woman's garment;* cyclas:—*Cot.* 49.

Hwioða *a gale, Cot.* 13, v. hwið.

Hwisprian [*Plat.* wispeln: *Ger.* wispern, wispeln: *Dan.* hviske: *Swed.* hviska: *Icel.* hvisla] *To* WHISPER, *murmur;* susurrare:—*R. Lk.* 19, 7.

Hwisprung, e; *f.* A WHISPERING, *murmuring;* susurratio:—*R. Jn.* 8, 12.

Hwistlan [*Swed.* hwissla: *Dan.* hvidsle, hvisle] *To* WHISTLE; fistulari, *Som.*

Hwistle A WHISTLE; fistula:—*Elf. gl.*

Hwistlere, es; *m.* A WHISTLER, *piper;* fistulator:—Geseah hwistleras and hlydende menigeo, *Mt.* 9, 23.

Hwistlung, e; *f.* A WHISTLING; sibilatio:—*R.* 49.

HWIT, hwita [*Plat. Dut.* wit: *Frs.* hwit: *Ger.* weiss: *Moes.* hueits: *Dan.* hvid: *Swed.* hwit: *Icel.* hvítr] WHITE; albus:—Swa hwite swa snaw, *Mt.* 17, 2: 28, 3: *Mk.* 9, 3. His reaf hwit scinende *ejus vestis candide splendens, Lk.* 9, 29. ¶ Gedon hwitne, *Mt.* 5, 36. Hwite gedon *to make white, Mk.* 9, 3.—Hwit-cudu, hwite-cweodu *mastic.*—Hwite-clæfr *white clover.*—Hwit-fot *white foot, Cot.* 12.—Hwit-leac *white leek, R.* 41.—Hwit-metas *white meats, what is made of milk, Mod. confit.* 7.—Hwit-papi, hywt-popig *white poppy, Herb.* 54.—Hwit-stan *white stone, a medical stone.*—Hwit-stow *a white place, mount Libanus, Ps.* 71, 16.—Hwit-man *a white man, a man clothed in white.*—Hwit-wingeard *a white vine, R.* 44.

Hwita *A worker;* faber:—Used in composition as sweord-hwita *a sword-maker, L. Alf. pol.* 19.

Hwit-circe [hwit *white,* circe *a church*] WHITCHURCH, *Hants. and the name of many other places, Chr.* 1001.

Hwitel; *d.* hwitle. 1. A WHITTLE, *a kind of cloak, mantle, a priest's cope;* pallium. 2. *A whittle, carving-knife;* cultellus:—1. Sem and Iafeth dydon anne hwitel on hira sculdra, *Gen.* 9, 23. Mid hire hwitle, *Jud.* 4, 18. 2. *Som.*

Hwitern [hwit *white,* ern *a place; Bd.* says, candida casa] WHITTERNE, *Whitehorne, in Galway:*—*Chr.* 560: 763: *Bd.* 5, 23, *S.* p. 646, 31.

Hwið, hwiða *A blast, a gentle wind;* aura lenis:—*L. Ps.* 106, 21.

Hwitian; *pp.* gehwitod. 1. *v. a.* To WHITEN; candefacere. 2. *v. n. To be* or *become white;* albescere, *Som.*

Hwiting-treow *Variculus arbor, Elf. gl.*

Hwitod *Whited;* dealbatus, *Lye.*

Hwit-sand[hwit *white,* sand *sand*] WHITSAN; nomen loci maritimi prope Calais:—*Chr.* 1095.

Hwolf *an expanse, a covering,* v. hwealf.

HWOM, hwem, hwæm, wæm, mes; *m. A corner, quarter, coast;* angulus:—Heafod hwommys *head of a corner, C. Ps.* 117, 21. Þa feower hwemmas ealles middan-eardes *the four corners of all the world, Som.* On stræta hwommum, *C. R. Mt.* 6, 5.—Hwom-stan *a corner-stone, C. Mt.* 21, 42.

Hwon; *adv. A little, little while, rarely;* paululum:—Þanon hwon agan, *Mk.* 1, 19. Us hwon restan, *Mk.* 6, 31. ¶On hwon, to hwon *how little.*—Be hwon *unde, Bd.* 2, 2.—For hwon *quare, Bd.* 4, 3.

Hwona, hwonan, behwon *Whence, where;* unde:—*C. R. Lk.* 1, 18. Na hwonan utane *nowhere without, Bt.* 34, 7.

Hwonlice; *comp.* hwonlicor; *sup.* hwonlicost; *adv. A little, a little while;* parumper:—*Æqu. Vern. R. Ben.* 30.

Hwonn *a little,* v. hwon.

Hwonne *when, Bd.* 3, 12. v. hwænne.

Hwonon *whence, Bt.* 5, 3, v. hwona.

Hworfen, hworfon *turned, wandered, Cd.* 214, v. hweorfan.

Hwosta *A cough;* tussis:—*Elf. gr.*

Hwostan [*Plat.* hosten: *Dut.* hoesten: *Ger.* husten: *Ot.* huasten: *Dan.* hoste: *Swed.* hosta: *Icel.* hósta] *To* WHOOST, HOST, *cough;* tussire, *Som.*

Hwoðeran [*Plat.* wooden: *Dut.* woeden: *Ger.* wüthen: *Old Ger.* wuthern: *Not.* wuoten] *To murmur, to make a rumbling noise;* murmurare:—Se brym hwoðerod *the sea murmured, Som.*

Hwrædel *A button, buckle;* fibula:—*R.* 65, *Lye.*

Hwreopon *screamed, Cd.* 151, v. hreopan.

Hwu *how,* v. hu.

Hwugu *at least.*—Hwugu fæc *a moment's space,* v. hugu.

Hwurf *An error, deceit;* illusio:—*C. Mt.* 27, 64.

Hwurf-fulnes, se; *f. Changeableness;* mutabilitas:—*Bt.* 20.

Hwurfon *turned; p. of* hweorfan.

Hwy *why,* v. hwi.

Hwyccas *people of Worcestershire, Bd.* 4, 13, v. hwiccas.

Hwyder, hwider. WHITHER; quo:—Hwyder he gæð *quò abit, Jn.* 3, 8: 12, 35. Hwyder gæst þu *quonam iturus es, Jn.* 13, 36.

Hwylc, hwilc, hwelc; *pron.*[*Plat. Dut.* welk: *Frs.* hwelk: *Ger.* welcher: *Ker. Isd.* huuelich, welicher: *Moes.* hweileiks: *Dan.* hvilken: *Swed.* hwilken: *Icel.* hvilikr.—hwa *who,* lic *like*] WHICH, *who, what, what sort, any;* quis, quænam, quidnam, qualis, ullus:—Hwylc man is of eow, *Mt.* 7, 9: 12, 11: *Lk.* 15, 4. Hwylc is min modor? *Mk.* 3, 33. Hwilc tacn sy? *Mt.* 24, 3. Hwylcum bigspelle? *Mk.* 4, 30. On hwylcum anwealde? *Mk.* 11, 28, 29. Hwylc is man! *Ps.* 24, 13. Gif hwylc cyning, *Lk.* 14, 31. ¶ Hwylce hugu *what little, somewhat, Bd.* 3, 10. Swa hwylc swa *whoever, Mt.* 10, 42. Swa hwylcere swa *of or to whomsoever;* cujuscunque, cuicunque.

Hwylca *varix, R.* 76.

Hwylum *awhile, for awhile, Lk.* 8, 13, v. hwilon.

Hwyrfan, he hwyrfð *to turn, change, vary,* v. hweorfan.

Hwyrfban *the whirlbone, R.* 11, v. hweorban.

Hwyrfe-pol *a whirlpool, Cot.* 59.

Hwyrfolung, e; *f. A changing;* mutatio, *Som.*

Hwyrft, *A circle, circuit, revolution, orbit;* orbis, circuitus:—Sume tunglu habbað scyrtran hwyrft þonne sume habban *some stars have a shorter revolution than others have, Bt.* 39, 3. Þu wille hwyrft don *tu vis circuitum facere, Cd.* 91, 190.

Hwyrfð *turns; from* hweorfan.

Hwyrftum, hwearfum *In turns, round;* alternatim:—*Cd.* 227.

Hwytel *a cloak, Elf. gl.: R. Ben.* 55, v. hwitel.

Hwyt-popig *white poppy,* v. hwit-papi.

Hycend *Accusing;* accusans, *Lye.*

Hycgan *to think, endeavour, Cd.* 22, v. hicgan.

Hyd *a hide,* v. hyde.

HYDAN, gehydan; *p.* gehyd, gehydde, behyd, hi ahyddon; *pp.* hidden, gehyded, gehyden, ahyded; *v. a.* [*Plat.* höden: *Dut.* hoeden: *Ger.* hüten: *Ker. Moes.* huotan: *Dan.* hytte, all in the sense *to take care of, to protect, to shelter*] *To* HIDE, *conceal;* abscondere:—He fande hidde *he found hid, Chr.* 963. Þat hi hyddon grynu, *Ps.* 63, 5.

Hydd-ern *a hiding-place, Elf. gl.*

HYDE; *g.* hyde; *f.* [*Plat.* huud, huut *f: Dut.* huid *f. Frs.* huwd *f: Ger.* haut *f: Ot.* hut: *Not.* hiute: *Dan.* hud, ham *f: Swed.* hud *f: Icel.* hydi *n.*] 1. A HIDE; corium, cutis. 2. *A hide of land, which was about one hundred and twenty acres,* (Gale *Script.* p. 472: 475, 481.) *Also as much land as could be tilled with one plough, or support one family, a family possession, families;* tanta fundi portio, quanta unico per annum coli poterat aratro vel ad alimoniam unius familiæ sufficeret. Beda vocat possessionem familiæ:—1. Binnan heora ægenre hyde *within their own skin, Bt.* 14, 2, *Card.* p. 68, 12. For his won hydum *pro squalida cute, Beo.* 6, 124. Þa hyde bringan *to bring the hide, Ors.* 4, 6, *Bar.* p. 147, 13. 2. Hyd landes *a hide of land;* hida terræ. Wæs þæs landes ealles hund-twelftig hida *duodecim possessiones decem erant familiarum,* i. e. *simul omnes centum viginti, scilicet familiæ, Bd.* 3, 24. Seofon and hund-eahtig hida landes *terram* LXXXVII *familiarum, Bd.* 4, 13. Is þæs ylcan ealondes gemet æfter Angelcynnes æhte, twelf hund hida *est autem ejusdem insulæ mensura, juxta Anglorum æstimationem*

(1)

a)

b Hwiterr. ss (a) Hwurfulee mod
~~m~~ whitehone suspectae mentes
c Past 35, 5 Lye
d

(1)

2 ~~Hygian~~ Be [?] i hyge

2) ~~Þa~~ Na þu minne
~~pearfe~~ ~~pearft~~ pearft
hafalan hydan thou
needest not my head of
mist (hide) Beo K 886

b
c Hwylp a whelp
Ben v. hwelp

d

* Hyd

Hynde

Hynden, e, f injury, affront, insult, th. an. Beo

(1) Hyder-cyme, es m. a hither coming, a coming i hider-cyme (2)

Hygd, es; m the mind animus v Beo gl in hygge

(3x) Hygeleast, e; f thoughtlessness, scurility

Hyge-mede mind weary Beo K 5879

Hyht, e; f hope or Beo K 356

Hyht-wyn, e; f joy of hope, pleasure, joy of hope; spei gaudium Beo K Th an

7 * Hylda, hyldu, e; f grace fidelity th. an

3. Hyge-bend, e; f a mind bond Beo K 3753

Hyge-geomor mind sad, or sorrowful Beo K 4881

Hyge-sorh; g. -sorge, f mind sorrow id. 4651 v hige

* Hyr wages hire wages v under hyre corrected

Hynden, ne; f a society. Hynden l 9 twy-hynden-men l 10 l 11

Hyder-cyme, es; m. a-hither coming, a coming v hidercyme

Hygd, es; m. the mind animus v Beo K in hyge

Hyge-least, e; f. thoughtless ness, scurrility

Hyge-mede mind weary Beo K 5879

Hyht, e; f. hope Beo K 356

Hyht-wyn, e; f. hope pleasure, joy of hope, spei gaudium Th An

Hylda, hyldu, e; f. grace fidelity Th An

Hyge-bend, e; f. a mind bend Beo K 2753

Hyge-geomor mind sad, or sorrow ful Beo K 4811

Hyge-sorh, g. -sorge, f mind sorrow id. 4651 v hige

Hynd

Hyndo

Hynde, e; f. injury, opprobrium, insult, loss Th An Beo K

Hyr wages hire wages v under hyre corrected

Hynden, ne; f. a society

Hynden l 9 twy-hynden-men l 10 l 11

seo heord todræfed, *Mt.* 26, 31. Ge synd hyrdas, *Gen.* 46, 32: *Ex.* 2, 17, 19: *Lk.* 2, 8, 15, 18, 20.—Scep-hyrde, sceapa-hyrde *a shepherd, Jn.* 10, 2.—Hyrde-man *a herdsman, Gen.* 13, 7.—Hyrde-wyrt *shepherd's plant, a pig-nut, L. M.* 1, 2.

Hyrdel, hyrdl [*Plat.* hordt *f*: *Dut.* horde *f*: *Ger.* hurde *f*: *Old Ger.* huirste.—*Old Ger.* hirten *to protect*] A HURDLE; crates:—*Ælf. gl.*: *R.* 29, 49.

Hyrdeleás; *adj. Without a shepherd;* pastore carens:—*Bd.* 2, 20.

Hyrdnes, gehyrdnes, se; *f. A keeping, custody, prison;* custodia, carcer:—Gif hwa befæst his feoh to hyrdnysse, *Ex.* 22, 7. Syllað eow on hyrdnyssa, *Lk.* 21. 12.

Hyrd-ræden, ne; *f. A keeping, guard;* custodia:—Þa gesette God æt þam infære engla hyrdrædene, *Gen.* 3, 24.

Hyrdung *instructio, R.* 62.

HYRE [*Plat.* hüür *f*: *Dut.* huur *f*: *Frs.* hira *f*: *Ger.* heuer *f*: *Dan.* hyre *c*: *Swed.* hyra *f*: *Arab.* أجر ajr *a recompence, hire*] HIRE, *usury, interest;* conductio, usura:—To hyre *ad usuram, Deut.* 23, 19: *Lk.* 10, 23.—Hyre-gildan *hired by money, mercenaries, R.* 8.

Hyre, hire *of* or *to him* or *her;* ejus, ei; *g. d. of* he.

Hyred *a family,* v. hired.

Hyrednes, se; *f. Hearsay, report;* fama, *Som.*

Hyr-efter *hereafter, L. With.*

Hyre-man *an auditor, a parishioner,* v. hyrman.

Hyrenes, se; *f. Obedience, imitation;* obedientia, *Som.*

Hyrian, ahyrian, ic hyrige; *p.* ode; *pp.* od; *v. a.* [hyre *a reward*] 1. *To* HIRE, *to procure assistance* or *obedience by a reward;* conducere. 2. *To follow, imitate, resemble;* imitari:—1. Us nan man ne hyrode, *Mt.* 20, 7. Þe uteode ahyrian, *Mt.* 20, 1. He bið ahyrod, *Jn.* 10, 13. 2. Hio hyrigað monnum *they imitate men, Bt.* 41, 5. Hyrigende *imitating,* v. hyran.

Hyrigman *a hearer, parishioner, L. Eccl.* 28.

Hyrling HIRELING, *servant;* mercenarius:—Hi heora fæder Zebedeo on scipe forleton mid hyrlingum, *Mk.* 1, 20.

Hyr-man *A hearer, one who is obedient, a servant;* auditor, subditus:—Cwist þu bist þu ure cyning, oððe beoð we þine hyrmen, *Gen.* 37, 8.

Hyrnde *Horned;* cornutus:—Hyrnde ciolas *rostratæ naves, Bt. R.* p. 188.

Hyrne, an; *f.* A HORN, *corner;* cornu, angulus:—On þæs weofodes hyrnan *on the horns of the altar, Ex.* 29, 12: *Lev.* 4, 18: 8, 15. On stræta hyrnum *in vicorum angulis, Mt.* 6, 5, v. horn.

Hyrned, hyrnen, hyrnend *Horned, horny;* corneus:—Hyrned-nebba *a horned nib* or *beak, Jdth.* 11.

Hyrnes, se; *f. What is subject* or *obedient, a province, parish;* subjectio, subjecta terra, parœcia:—*L. Eccl.* 4.

Hyrnet, hyrnete, hyrnyt [*Plat.* hornke *f*: *Dut.* horzel *m*: *Ger.* horniss *f*: *South Ger.* horneiss] A HORNET; crabro:—Ic asende hyrnytta, *Ex.* 23, 28.

Hyrn-stana *corner-stone,* v. hyrne.

Hyron *to obey, Bd.* 3, 21, v. hyran.

Hyrra *a hinge, Prov.* 26, v. heor.

Hyrra, hyrre *higher,* v. heah.

HYRST *An ornament, decoration;* ornamentum:—Hyrste gerim *tell (its) ornaments, Cd.* 100. Hyrsta *ornaments, Cot.* 88: *Jdth.* 12: *Bt. R.* p. 170.

Hyrst þu *hearest thou, hark you,* v. hyran.

Hyrstan; *pp.* hyrsted, gehyrsted, hyrst. *To adorn, dress, deck;* ornare:—Hyrsted gold *fretted gold, Cd.* 98.—Hyrstedne hrof *adorned roof, Cd.* 46.

Hyrstan, hierstan, gehyrstan *To murmur, to fry* or *make the noise of frying;* murmurare:—*C. R. Lk.* 15, 2; frigere, *Ælf. gr.*

Hyrsting, hiersting, hyrstincg, hyrstung, e; *f. A frying, hearth;* frixio, focus:—*L. Ps.* 101, 4.—Hyrsting-panne *a frying-pan.*

Hyrsudon *assembled;* concurrerunt, *Bd.* 3, 14, *b.*

Hyrsum, hirsum, gehyrsum; *adj. Hearing, obedient;* obediens:—*Bd.* 1, 25: 2, 12: *Ex.* 24, 7: *Mt.* 6, 24.

Hyrsumian, hersumian, gehyrsumian *To obey;* obedire:—Windas and sæ hym hyrsumiað, *Mt.* 8, 27: *Lk.* 8, 25.

Hyrsumnes, hersumnes, gehyrsumnes, se; *f. Obedience;* obedientia:—*Bd.* 5, 23.

Hyrt [*Ger.* hurt, hort *m.*] *Hurt, wounded;* læsus, *Som.*

Hyrtan, heertan; *pp.* gehyrted, gehyrt. *To* HEARTEN, *encourage, comfort;* animare:—*L. Can. Edg. pn.* 3: *Ex.* 23, 12.

Hyrðil *a hurdle,* v. hyrdel.

Hyrðling *an earthling, a farmer,* v. yrðling.

Hyrtling-beri [yrðling *a farmer,* burh *a town;* agricolarum burgus, sive vicus] IRLINGBOROUGH, ARTLEBOROUGH, *Northamptonshire, Chr.* 1137.

Hyrwe A HARROW; occa, *Lye.*

Hyrwend, es; *m. A blasphemer;* blasphemus:—Led ut þone hyrwend, *Lev.* 24, 14.

Hyrwian; *p.* ode, de; *pp.* gehyrwed. *To blaspheme, condemn,* HARROW, *vex, afflict;* blasphemare, condemnare, vexare:—Hyrwde Godes naman, *Lev.* 24, 11. Þa hyrwdon hig ealle hyne, *Mk.* 14, 64. Ne hyrwe ge utan-cymene man, *Lev.* 19, 33.

Hyrwnes, hirwnes, se; *f. Contempt, reproach, blasphemy;* contemptus, vexatio:—Gefylled we synd hyrwnessum, *T. Ps.* 122, 4: 118, 141.

Hys *of him, his;* ejus, illius; *g. of* he.

Hyse *a male,* v. hise.—Hyse-berðling, berðling *puerperium, R.* 5.

Hysian *To* HISS, *mock;* irridere:—Se þe eardað on heofonum hyseð hy, *T. Ps.* 2, 4.

Hysop HYSSOP; hysopum, *Som.*

HYSPAN, hispan; *p.* de, te; *v. a. To deride, slander, reproach, reprove;* irridere, exprobrare:—To geanes me hyspton, *Ps.* 40, 8. Hu lange, God, hyspeð feond, *Ps.* 73, 11. Þa ongan he hyspan þa burga, *Mt.* 11, 20: *Bt.* 18, 4. Hyne hyspdun *eum exprobrarunt, Mt.* 27, 44.

Hyspe *fornaculum, fornacale, Som.*

Hyspend, es; *m. A slanderer;* calumniator:—Fram stemne hyspendes, *Ps.* 43, 18.

Hysping, e; *f. Reproach, reviling;* exprobratio:—*Bt.* 18, 4.

Hyspnes, se; *f. A reproach, upbraiding;* exprobratio:—*T. Ps.* 43, 15.

Hyss, hysse, es; *m. A youth, stripling, one past fourteen years of age;* hirquitallus, juvenis:—Noldon þeah þa hyssas *yet the youths would not;* noluerunt autem juvenes, *Cd.* 183. Het scufan þa hyssas in bæl blyse *commanded to shove the youths to the pile blaze, Cd.* 184: 188: 195: 196.

Hyst *a whirlwind, storm,* v. yst.

Hyt *it;* id, illud, v. hit.

HYÐ [*Plat.* hode *f. a guard*: *Ger.* hut *f. protection*] HITHE, *port, haven;* portus:—Sio an hyð byð simle smyltu æfter ystum *this is the only haven ever calm after storms, Bt.* 34, 8.—Hyð-weard *a keeper of a port, Beo.* 27.

Hyð *a wave, flood,* v. yð.

Hyx- æcend
um

(2)

~~Hyxlice shamefu~~
~~th. An v hux~~
~~huxlice~~

:if

Iac, es, a cuckoo
Sm. v gæc

I Iandswæred
antwered v
andswarian

2 Ibrohte brought
p of bringan
th. An

I boren born
th. An. pp
of beran

I byldan to
imagine, draw
v gebyldan

Icoren chosen
th. An v gecoren

for. gifen
Iafen given Chr
1137

(2) Idel - hende
Beo gl in hand

Ief men; d. ac. me

Icend An increaser,
augmentator Som
Iege increased heaped up, in? ve,
getus. magnus. eximius Beo
K 2208

(5)

(3)

Iersian *to be angry*, *Cot.* 182, v. yrsian.
Ierð-land *the earth*, *Cot.* 15, v. yrð, &c.
Ierusalem *Jerusalem*, *Chr.* 448, v. Hierusalem.
Iesendas *Bowels*; exta:— *Cot.* 77: 177, *Som.*
Iest *east*, *C. R. Mt.* 24, 27, v. east.
Ietan *to confirm*, *Chr.* 675, v. geatan.
Ieteld *a tent*, *Cot.* 174, v. geteld.
Ieð *easy*, *Ors.* 2, 6, v. eað.
Ieðelic *easy*, v. eaðelic.
Ieðian *to flow*, v. yðian.
Ieðnes *easiness*; quies, v. eðnes.
Iette *yet*, v. get.
Iewian, eowian *to shew*, *Cd.* 30, v. ywan.
Ific [*Plat.* iloof, ewig *n.* ive: *Ger.* epheu, eppich *m*: *Old Ger.* ebeheue] Ivy; hedera:—Ifig þe on stane weax *ivy which grows on stone, rock-ivy*, *L. M.* 3, 3.—Ifig þe on eorðan wixð *ivy which grows on the earth, ground-ivy*, *L. M.* 3, 31: *Som.*—Ifig-crop *a bunch of ivy-berries*.—Ifig-tearo, ifig-taro *ivy-tears, ivy-gum*, *L. M.* 1, 58.
-ig [*Ger.* -ig: *Icel.* -igt, -ugt: *Eng.* -y.—Some think from ican *to eke, add*; thus, blodig *bloody*, i. e. *blood, add a noun*, as *sword*, &c.] In the present *Eng.* ig is changed into y; as, dreorig *dreary*; hefig *heavy*; sarig *sorry*; twentig *twenty*.
Ig *An island*; insula, v. ealand.
Igbernia Hibernia:—Igbernia, þat we Scotland hatað *Hibernia which we call Scotland*, *Ors.* 1, 1, v. Hibernia.
Igbuend *an islander*, v. icgbuend.
Igdæges *of the same day*, v. idæges.
Iggað, igeoð, iggeoð, igoð. *An island*; insula, *Chr.* 894, v. ealand.
Igil, igl *a hedgehog*, *R.* 24, v. il.
Igland *island*, *Ps.* 96, 1, v. ealand.
Iglea, Æglea [*Asser.* Æcglea: *Flor.* Ecglea.—ig *an island*, lea *plain*; campus insularis] *Iley Mead, near Meltsham, Chr.* 878, *Ing.* p. 105, 18.
Iglond *an island*, *Bt.* 38, 1, v. igland.
Igoð *an island*, *Elf. T.* p. 32, v. iggað.
Iht *increased*, v. ecan.
-iht [*Ger.* -icht: *Lat.* -osus: *Eng.* -ous] a termination of adjectives.
Ii, Hi, Hii. *The island Iona*, Hy Hu, now called *Ikolmkill* or *Colmkill*, contracted from Columbkill, that is, Columbæ cella *one of the Hebrides near Mull*:— Igland þe man Ii nemnað *an island which men call Ii*, *Chr.* 560: 728.
Iil *a hedgehog*, *Past.* 35, 5, v. il.
Iken-yld-stræt [*Icenorum antiqua via*, *Som.*] Ikenild-street, *a Roman road in England*, so called because it passed through the *Iceni*, or *Norfolk, Suffolk*, &c.
Il, iel, iil, igil, igl; *m.* [*Plat. Dut.* egel *m*: *Ger. Not.* igel *m*: *Swed.* igelkott *m*: *Icel.* igull *m*.] *A hedgehog*; erinaceus:—*Elf. gl.* 13: *L. Ps.* 103, 19. Se læssa il *a hedgehog*; erinaceus. Se mara il *a porcupine*; histrix, *Cot.* 116.
Il, es; *m. Hardness, hard skin, sole of the foot*; callus, plantæ pedum:— Fram his hnolle ufeweardan, oð his ilas neoðewerde *a vertice capitis ejus superne ad plantas pedis ejus deorsum*, *Job.* p. 166, *R.* 78.
Ilc *the same*, *Cot.* 113, v. ylc.
Ildan *to delay*, *Past.* 33, 4, v. yldan.
Ildenn, ilding *A delay, deceiving*; dilatio, *Lye.*
Il-fetu *A swan*; olor, *Som.*
Ilitend *infindens*, *Cot.* 111.
Ill *hardness*, v. il.
Ille-racu *A surfeit*; crapula, *Cot.* 52.
Imb *about*, v. ymb.
Imbefliten *Placito curiæ adjudicatus*, *Test. Elfred. D. Mann.*
Imb-erdling, imb-yrdling [ymb *about*, yrdling, yrðling *a farmer*] *A native*; domesticus colonus, *Gen.* 17, 27.
Imb-gæð *goes about*, *Gen.* 2, 13, v. ymb-gan.
Imbutan *about*, *Lev.* 3, 8, v. ymbeutan.
Imen *ambrosianum*, *C. R. Ben.* 25.
Immerca *A superscription*; inscriptio, *C. Mk.* 12, 16.
Imne *a hymn*, *C. T. Ps.* 64, 14, v. ymn.
Impan, impian; *pp.* impod, geimpod. [*Ger.* impfen: *Not.* impiton.—from the *Wel. Eng.* imp: *Swed.* ymp *m*: *Dan.* ympe *a cion*] To imp, *engraft, plant*; plantare, *Lye.*
In *in, into*, *Bd.* 2, 3.—In on *into*, *Mt.* 27, 5, v. on, innan.
In-adl *an inward disease*.
In-afaran *to go into*, *L. Ps.* 62, 9.
In-asendan *to let down*, *Mk.* 2, 4.
In-bærnis *incense*, v. anbærnys.
In-belædan; *p.* anbelæd. *To lead in, introduce.*
In-beornan *to light*, *R. Mt.* 5, 15.
In-beslean *to prick, stab.*
In-bewunden *wrapped up.*
In-birding *a native*, v. imb-erdling.
In-birig *A porch*; vestibulum, *Som.*
In-blawen *puffed up.*
In-borh Inborough, *bail, pledge*; pignus ad damnum resarciendum datum, *L. Edw.* 6.
In-bryrdnys *compunction*, *Bd.* 4, 24, v. onbryrdnys.
In-burh *A hall, house, dwelling*; atrium, *Elf. gl.*— Inburh-fæste *a steward, porter.*
In-byran *to bring in*, *L. In.* 78.
In-byrd, in-byrdling *a native*, *Gen.* 17, 12.
In-byrdnys, se; *f. Instruction*; instructio, *Bd.* 4, 17.
Inc, incg; *nom. d. ac. pron. You, ye, you two*; vos, vos duo:— Wariað inc (twegen) wið þone wæstm *beware you (two) of that fruit*, *Cd.* 13, *Th.* p. 15, 20. Inc (twegen) agen-yrnð sum man, *Mk.* 14, 13. Gelyfe gyt þat ic inc (twegen) mæg gehælan, *Mt.* 9, 28. Nys me inc (twegen) to syllenne *non est [apud] me vobis (duobus) concedere*, *Mt.* 20, 23: *Mk.* 10, 40. Inc (twam) sceal sealt wæter wunian *to you (two) shall (the) salt water abide*, *Cd.* 10, *Th.* p. 13, 6.
Inca, an; *m. A scruple, doubt, fault, offence*; scrupulus, querela:—Butan incan *without doubt*, *Bd.* 5, 6. Hi nænige incan to him wiston *illi nullam querelam contra eum norunt*, *Bd.* 4, 24.
Inca *of you, your*, *Cd.* 163, v. incer.
Ince *An* inch; uncia, *Som.*
Incer, incere, incre *your, of you*, *Ex.* 10, 17: *Cd.* 10; *g. d. of* inc.
Incit [inc gyt] *You, you two*; vos duo:—Restað incit her *rest you here*, *Cd.* 169.
In-cleofa, in-clyfa *a bed, nest, den*, *Ps.* 4, 5: 35, 4.
In-cnapa *a servant.*
In-cniht *a servant, client.*
In-cofa *a bed-chamber*, *L. Ps.* 4, 5; *the mind*, *Bt. R.* p. 183.
In-coða, in-coðe *Choler*; cholera, *Som.*
Incre *of* or *to your*, v. incer.
Incrum *to you, to you two*; vobis, vobis duobus, *Cd.* 43; *d. of* inc.
In-cuman *to come in, enter*, *Ex.* 21, 8.
In-cund; *adj. Internal, inward, intimate*; intime notus:—Incund freond *an intimate friend*, *Som.*
Incundnes, se; *f. An inward quality*; qualitas interna, *Som.*
Incuð *ignorant, unknown*, *C. Jn.* 3, 10.—Incuðlice *ignorantly, unconsciously*, *Elf. T.* p. 36, 1.
Indea India; India, *Chr.* 883.
Indeas Indians; Indi, *Ors.* 1, 2.

a Indepan to dip in c Lk 16, 24

b Indrencan to drink in, dye

c Indsa in ounce son v yndsa

e In-eardian to inhabit son

f) ed, in [illegible]

7 x In-fær, es m an infraire th an

Beo offering Bl Curt p 64, 19

2 In-frod [illegible] Beo 483 K 4893 (3744)

(1 x) ing was the ancient form, as ing is not found in Beowulf Grm II 354, 13 –

of those that [illegible] (or denoting [illegible]) action f. Grm II 354, 31 Rask § 30

of Personal nouns or nouns denoting substan[illegible] in Rask § 293 – Grm II 354, 8

Patronimics certainly ing – Grm II 351, 3 Rask § 293 v -ling

b Inflow flowed in Lk 6, 49 p of in-flowan v flowan

a In-gebyrdling es m [illegible] born in the same house, son

b 3 x Ingang, es; m in entrance Beo K 1098

c ingat, a; um

d 1 Ingebringan p ingebrohte to bring in th[illegible]

£ 3 x Ingehid, inge-hygd, es; m intention, knowledge concerning deep [illegible] than

2 In-genga m one who enters [illegible] Beo 34 K 3556 Grm II 760, 21

H In-ge-steald, es; m a family, household [illegible] Beo K 2303

In-gewadan to enter, penetrate, [illegible]

In-lædan to lead in, conduct th an Bd 4. 24

II Inge you son v inc

denotes people inhabitants v [illegible] ware, wara Grm II. 351, 3 Ontingas Cd 1052 Ing p 23[illegible] 15

In-lifan to live in, or for th. an

Inn, inne *into, within*, *Lk.* 11, 40, v. innan.
Inna *The womb*; uterus, *C. Lk.* 1, 15.
Innan; *adv.* [*Plat. Dut.* binnen: *Ger.* inn, inne, innen: *Ker.* inne: *Moes.* inn, inna: *Dan.* inden: *Swed. Icel.* innan, inni] *Within, inwardly*; intus, intra:—Ge synt innan fulle reaflaces, *Mt.* 23, 25, 27, 28: *Mk.* 7, 21.
Innan, innon; *prep. d. ac. In, into, within*; in:—Þa he sæt innan huse, *Mt.* 9, 10. Innan þa sæ, *Ex.* 14, 17: *Mt.* 21, 21. Ne ga ge innan Samaritana ceastre, *Mt.* 10, 5.
Innan *To go in, to enter*; ingredi:—He werodað syððan he innað *it grows sweet after it enters in*, *Bt.* 22, 1.
Innan-cund *inward*, v. in-cund.
Innane *within*, *Mt.* 7, 15, v. innan.
Innan-forhæfd *constipated bowels*, *L. M.* 2, 55.—Innan-fortogennes *a drawing together of the bowels, the cholic*, *L. M.* 2, 33.
Innan-teon *to draw within, to introduce*, *Ælfr. Vern.* 34.
Innan-weard *inward*, *Bt.* 34, 10.
Innað *the womb*, *Past.* 54, 1, v. innoð.
Inn-bewunden *wound round.*
Inne *within*, v. inn.
Inne *an inn*, v. inn.
Innelfe, innelue, innilue *the bowels*, v. inelf.
Innemest, innemyst Inmost; intimus, *Elf. gr.*: *Scint.* 4.
Innenddisc *Household-stuff*; supellex, *R.* 58.
Inner Inner; interior, *Bd.* 4, 13.
Inneðas *the bowels*, *Cot.* 183, v. innoð.
Innewærde, innewerde *the inwards, bowels*, *Ex.* 12, 9.
Inneward, inneweard, inweard; *adj.* Inward, *internal, entire*; internus, interior:—Mid inneweardum mode, mid inneweardan mode *with inward mind*; intima mente, *Bt.* 22, 1. He draf his heorde to inneweardum þam westene, *Ex.* 3, 1.
Inneweard; *adv. Inwardly*; intus:—Eall inneweard *all within*, *Cd.* 216.
Inn-faran *to go in, to enter*, *Deut.* 28, 63.
Inn-gehyd *Conscience*; conscientia, *Scint.* 60.
Inn-heard-men *soldiers*, *C. Mt.* 8, 9.
Inn-here *An army of natives, militia*; exercitus popularium, *Chr.* 1006.
Inn-hiwan *domestics*, *L. In.* 5.

Innian *To enter, to receive as a guest*; ingredi, hospitari, *Chr.* 1048.
Innierf *furniture*, *Bt.* 14, 2, *C*, v. in-erfe.
Inniht *Within*; intus, v. beboren.
Innilue *the bowels*, v. in-elf.
Inn-lændisc *indigenous*, *R. Conc.*, v. inlandisc.
Innon *within*, *Bt.* 35, 3, v. innan.
Innor *Inner*; interior, *Lye.*
Innorf *household-stuff*, v. in-erfe.
Innost *Inmost*; intimus, *Lye.*
INNOD, es; *m.* [*Ger.* innerste *n*: *Icel.* innisti] *The heart, stomach, bowels, womb*; interior pars corporis, cor, venter, uterus:—Ealle þas yfelu of þam innoðe cumað *omnia hæc scelera a corde proveniunt*, *Mk.* 7, 23. Ineode swa swa wæter on þa innoðas his *intravit sicut aqua in intestina ejus*, *Ps.* 108, 17. Bið swiðe liðe on þam innoðe *is very mild in the stomach*, *Bt.* 22, 1. Eadig is se innoð þe þe bær, *Lk.* 11, 27. Mæg he eftcuman on his modor innoð *potest ille revenire in ejus matris uterum*, *Jn.* 3, 4. ¶ Fæst innoð *costive bowels*, *Herb.* 12.—Fæstnes innoðes *costiveness of bowels*, *Herb.* 62.—Tobrocene innoð *ruptured bowels*, *L. M.* 2, 3.—Innoðes astyrung *a rumbling of the bowels.*—Innoðes flewsa *a flux.*—Innoðes forhæfdnes *costiveness of bowels.*—Innoðes meltung *digestion*, *L. M.* 2, 64.—Innoðes sar *pain in the bowels.*—Innoð-tidernes *tenderness of bowels, the flux*, *L. M.* 2, 33.
Innung [*Ger.* innung *f. a guild, society*: *Icel.* inni *n. a house*] *That which is included* or *contained, an* inning, *abode*; mansio, actus manendi, *Bt.* 32, 2.
Innweardlice; *adv. Diligently*; diligenter, *C. Mt.* 2, 7, 8.
Innyra, an; *m. The bowels*; interior, *C. Ps.* 108, 17.
In-orf *household-stuff*, *Gen.* 31, 36, v. in-erfe.
Inra *the bowels*, v. innyra.
Inræcan *To heap up*; ingerere, *Cot.* 105.
Inræsan *To rush on*; irrumpere, *Cot.* 106.
Inre *Inner*; interior, *R.* 74.
Insægl *a seal*, v. insegel.
Insæglian *to seal*, v. inseglian.
In-segel. 1. *A seal*; sigillum. 2. *A sealing, signing*; obsignatio. 3. *A jewel*; monile:—1. *Elf. gl.* 22. 2. *Som.* 3. *R.* 29.
Inseglian; *p.* geinseglode; *pp.* geinsegelod, geinsegluded. *To seal, to impress with a seal*; obsignare:—Inseglodun þone stan, *Mt.* 27, 66: *Deut.* 32, 34.
Insettan *To appoint*; instituere:—Insette *instituit*, *Bd.* 4, 23.
Insiht *A narration, history*; narratio, *Jn. pref. MS. C.*
Insiðian *to enter, enter in*, *Cd.* 76.
In-somnian *to assemble*, *Bd.* 4, 4.
In-spinn *Opificium netorium*, *R.* 110.
In-stæpe, in-stepe *Forthwith, quickly*; immediate, *Bd.* 2, 12.
In-steppan *to step in*, *L. Ps.* 25, 4.
In-sticce *in pieces.*
In-stice *a prick* or *stitch in the side*, *L. M.* 2, 54.
In-stondlic *substantialis.*
In-swane *the swine-herd of the lord's court* or *farm place.*
In-swapen *inwardly moved, provoked*, *Cot.* 105.
In-swogennis, se; *f. An invasion*; invasio, *Bd.* 2, 5.
In-þing *a cause*, *C. Mt.* 19, 3, v. intinga.
In-tihtan *to invite*, *Chr.* 957.
In-timbernes, se; *f. Instruction, provision*; instructio, *Som.*
Intimbred *Furnished, instructed*; instructus, *Bd.* 5, 8.
In-tinga, an; *m.* 1. *Cause, sake, reason*; causa rationabilis. 2. *Judicial cause, action, quarrel*; causa judicialis. 3. *A fault*; causa condemnationis, culpa. 4. *Business*; negotium:—1. Min sawul lybbe for þinum intingan, *Gen.* 12, 13. For hwilcum intingan sædest þu, *Gen.* 12, 19. Buton intingan *without cause, in vain*, *Ps.* 3, 7: *Mt.* 15, 9. 2. Tosceað intingan minne *discerne causam meam*, *Ps.* 42, 1: 73, 23. 3. Ne finde ic nanne intingan on þyssum men, *Lk.* 23, 4, 14. 4. *Bd.* 4, 5.
Into; *prep. d.* Into, *in*; in:—Into þam arce, *Gen.* 6, 18: 7, 7: *Mt.* 4, 24.
In-trahtnung *an interpretation.*
In-trifelung *a grinding*, *Cot.* 109.
In-trymedun *prevailed*, *Lk.* 23, 23, v. trymian.
In-undor *in, under, within*, *Cd.* 112.
In-weard *inward*, *Nic.* 31, v. inneward.
In-weardlice; *adv.* Inwardly, *thoroughly, entirely*; intime, penitus:—Þat ic mæge þe inweardlice lufian *that I may thoroughly love thee*, *Bt. R.* p. 149: *Bd.* 1, 26.
In-werdlic *internal*, *Med. ex. Quadr.* 3, 1, v. inneweard.
In-wid *deceit*, *T. Ps.* 14, 3, v. inwit.
Inwidd; *def.* se inwidda; *adj. Deceitful, bad, wicked*; dolo-

Iren-preat, es; m. iron crowd Beo K 658

d.

3 Inwit-feng, es; m. hostile grasp Beo K 2893

Inwit-gast, es; m. a deceitful guest Beo K 5396

Inwit-hrof, es; m. a treacherous roof tectum dolosum Beo 2311 K 6241

d. Inwit-net, es; n. an insidious net Beo K 4329

c. Inwit-scear, es; m. a deceitful shear Beo K 4337

Inwit-panc, es; m. a deceitful thought insidiosa cogitatio Beo K 491 Beo 192

Beo

Inwit-searo, es; n. hostile deceit Beo K 2195

h Inwit-sorh, ge; f. grievous sorrow Beo K 3470

Io-meowle, an; f. an old woman Beo K 5857

Inwit-wrasn, e; f. a treacherous deceitful band: insidiosa catena Cod Verc i 129: 1895 Beo 2 in wrasn

2 Isen-bend, es; m. an iron band, fetter; ferreum vinculum vel uncus Beo K 1542

Isen-byrne, an; f. an iron breast plate Beo 2217 K 5968 v isern-byrne

3 Isen-heard, iron hard, hard as iron Beo K 2217

Inwit-nið, es; m. deceitful malice Beo K 3712

Irlic angry Beo

Irringa adv. angrily, furiously; irate Beo K 3130: 5924

7

Isern-wyrhta, an; m. an iron worker, a smith R. 2

Is-gebind, es; n. an ice bond; glaciale vinculum Beo 2259

Is-gicel, es; m. an ice drop, an icicle v Ic.

Isælig happy v gesælig v Th.

Isæligelice happily v gesælig

Is-ceald ice cold Cod Ex 818

Isen iron Beo

Isen-graft a chariot, wagon; carpentum Som

Isen-wyrhta an iron worker a smith Elf gl R 2

Isern-byrne an iron breast plate; lorica ferrea Beo 52, K 1536

Isern-scur, es; m. an iron shower, a shower of darts imber ferreus Beo K 6227

Isund sound v gesund

Ithacige Ithaca

Ityng *a way*, v. yting.
Iu *you*, *R. Mt.* 5, 32, v. eow.
[k]Iu *formerly*, *Bd.* 1, 1, v. geo.
Iuc *a yoke*, *Cot.* 110, 164, v. geoc.
Iuc-boga *a sign of the zodiac, called Orion.*
Iuch *to you*; vobis, *C. Mt.*, v. eow.
Iucian; *pp.* geiuked. *To yoke, to join together*; jugare, *Som.*
Iudan-byrig *Jedburgh, Scotland*, *Chr.* 952.
Iudea, JUDEA; Judæa:—On Iudea, *Mt.* 2, 22: 4, 25: *Mk.* 3, 7. On þam westene Iudeæ *in deserto Judææ*, *Mt.* 3, 1. Iudea þeod, *Mt.* 3, 5.
Iudeas; *m.* JEWS; Judæi:—Þa Iudeas cwædon to hym, *Jn.* 2, 20. Iudea ealdras, *Lk.* 7, 3. Betwux þam Iudeum, *Jn.* 10, 19.
Iudeisc JEWISH; Judaicus:—Iudeisc rice, *Mk.* 1, 5. Eom ic Iudeisc *sum ego Judæus*, *Jn.* 18, 35: 4, 9. On Iudeisce endas *in Judaicos fines*, *Mt.* 19, 1.
Iueg, iuig *ivy*, v. ifig.
Iuer, iuerr *your*, *C. Mt.* 6, 14, v. eower.
Iugoð, iuguð *youth*, *Gen.* 8, 21, v. geoguð.
Iuh, iuih *you*, *C. Mt.* 10, 41, v. eow.
Iul *yule, Christmas*, v. geol.
Iuncglic, iunglic *young*, *Elf. T.* p. 33, v. geonglic.
Iung *young*, *Bd.* 5, 1, v. geong.
Iunga *a young man, a youth*, *Ps.* 67, 29, v. geong.
Iunglic *young*, v. iuncglic.
Iungling, iunglincg A YOUNGLING, *youth, young man*; adolescentulus:—Sum iungling him fyligde, *Mk.* 14, 51. Iunglincg, *Gen.* 4, 23: *Bd.* 5, 19, v. geongling.
Iur, iure *your*, *Chr.* 656, v. eower.
Iurþymyl *Rust*; rubigo, *Cot.* 218.
Iutas *the Jutes*, *Chr.* 449, v. Iotas.
Iw [*Plat.* ibe *f.* ive: *Ger.* eibe *f*: *Fr.* if *m*: *Lat. mid.* ivus, euves: *Swed.* id *f.*] YEW, taxus:—*Elf. gl. R.* 46: *Cot.* 165.
Iwh *you*, *C. Mt.* 26, 21, v. eow.
Iwian *To think*; putare, *Solil.* 2.

K

[m]Though the *A.-S.* generally used *c*, even before *e*, *i* and *y*, as *k* is sometimes found, the following words are given. Those words not found here, must be sought for under C.
Kadum *Caen in Normandy*; Cadomus, *Chr.* 1070.
Kalca-ceaster *Tadcaster, Yorkshire*, or *Newton-kyme*; Calcaria Antonini, *Bd.* 4, 23.
Kalend, kalendus *The first day of the month*; calendæ, *Menol.* 13, 59.
Kantwara-byrig *Canterbury*, *Chr.* 656, v. Cantwaraburhge.
Karleasnes, se; *f.* CARELESSNESS; incuria, *Lye.*
Kasere *an emperor*, *Bt.* 38, 1, v. casere.
Keld *A fountain*; fons, *S. Dunelm, an.* 1070.
Kene *keen*, *Past.* 33, 4, v. céne.
Kentingas *Kentish men*, *Som.*
Kersan *To grow*; crescere, *R.* 42.
Kertl *a kirtle, garment*, *H. Mt.* 7, 25, v. cyrtel.
Ketering KETTERING, *Northamptonshire*, *Chr.* 963.
[n]Kiæres-burh CHERBOURG, *in Normandy*, *Chr.* 1091.
Kicena *a kitchen*, *R. Ben.* 53, v. cycene.
Kine-cynn *royal race*, *Ors.* 1, 2, v. cyning.
Kinges-tun *Kingston*, *S. Dunel. an.* 924, v. cyngestune.
Kitelung, e; *f.* *A tickling*; titillatio, *Cot.* 174.
Kitte [*Dut.* kit *f. a tankard, pot*: hence, perhaps, KIT *a milk-pail*] *A vessel, bottle*; uter:—*T. Ps.* 118, 83.
Kok *a cock*, *Past.* 63, 64, v. cocc.
Kycgl, kygel *A dart*; jaculum, *Past.* 40, 5.
Kyf *a vat*, *Dial.* 1, 9, v. cyf.
Kyneg, kyng, *a king*, *Jos.* 10, 3: *Chr.* 963, v. cyning.
Kynren *a generation*, *Deut.* 32, 11, v. cynnryn.
Kyntlingtun [*Flor.* Kyrtlinege: *Hovd.* kirding: *Brom.* Kerling] KIRTLINGTON, *Oxfordshire*, *Chr.* 977.
Kyrriole [*Plat.* krijölen: *Dut.* krioelen *to cry out for joy*: hence our CAROL] *A chanting at the nativity.*
Kyð *a relation*, *T. Ps.* 73, 9, v. cuða.
Kyðan *to make known*, *Deut.* 32, 7, v. cyðan.

L

[o]The *A.-S.* sometimes aspirated the *l*; hence *h* is placed before *l*, as hlaf *a loaf*, hlid *a lid*, hlot *a lot*, hlud *loud*. Such words will be found in H.
L and *n* are often written double, or single, indiscriminately at the end of monosyllables, but the reduplication ceases when, in lengthening the word, a consonant follows: as, well *or* wel *well*; eall *all*; *ac.* ealne *all*; omnem: ic sylle *I give*; þu sylst *thou givest*; he sylð *he gives.*
La *O! Oh!* Lo! *Behold*:—La næddrena cyn *O viperarum generatio*, *Mt.* 3, 7: 12, 34.

C – [67a 1]

Lác, es; n.: m. a gift, present. [1] a b c
x th. an: Beo:
Lád hateful th. ag. v lád
Ládlic odious th. a. v ládlic
Ládu, e; f. a going, a journey; pro
cessio, conductus, iter
Beo K 1132: 209, 6: 101,
K 2640 Grein
502, 35

[Moes laikan salire:
Norse leika ludere: Old Ger leih ludus, saltus;
Moes laiks: Norse leikr] Beowulf in lác
to play, exult;
ludere, saltare Beo K 5660: 5692

b
2 Lácan Beowulf in
lác

Lácnend, lacnigend; es; m. A
physician; medicus
Som

1x Grein I, 642, 31

[For lade f. proof, evidence: Old
Ger leita]
Lade f. a defence,
[illegible] from
an accusation by
evidence or proof;
defensio, purgatio
Grm. Recht 855, 908
[1925]

(i)

1x Lædder, of lad-
dre f a ladder
th. a.

2)

Læg *lay*, Gen. 9, 21, v. licgan.
Læge *a law*, H. Mt. 5, 17, v. lagu.
Læge-ceaster, Lega-ceaster, Ligceaster. [*Brom.* Lega-cestre: *Wel.* Caër-legion, Caër-leon *castra legionis*] *West-Chester, Chester*, Bd. 2, 2: Chr. 894.
Læge-gleaw *a lawyer*, H. Lk. 11, 45.
Læget, læget *lightning*, Chr. 1086, v. liget.
Lægre-ceastre-scire *Leicestershire*, Chr. 1088, v. Legra-ceaster.
Læhte *seized, taken*, v. gelæccan, læccan.
Læi *law, for* læg, v. licgan.
Læl, læle, lela. *A mole, freckle, scar, mark from beating, a weal;* nævus, tumex:—L. Alf. eccl. 19: Ex. 21, 25.
Læland LAALAND, *an island in the Baltic belonging to Denmark*, Ors. 1, 1, v. Weonodland.
Lælian *To be black and blue;* livere, Cot. 119.
Læmen *Made of earth, earthen;* fictilis:—Læmen fæt *earthen vessel*, R. 26.
Læn, læne [*Plat. Dut.* leen *n*: *Dut.* leening *f*: *Ger.* lehen *n*: *Old Ger.* len: *Dan.* laan, len *n*: *Swed.* lån *n*: *Icel.* len, lien *n. feudum censuale*] A LOAN, *gift, reward;* mutuo datum, commodatum, præmium:—Se þe æt his nehstan hwæt to læne abit, *Ex.* 22, 14. Þe biddaŏ manega þeoda þines þinges to læne, *Deut.* 28, 12. Læne syllaŏ *make a loan;* mutuum date, *Lk.* 6, 35. Syle him to læne *da ei mutuum*, *Deut.* 15, 8. Laŏan læn *an enemy's gift*, *Cd.* 29. Læn Godes *a reward of God;* præmium Dei, *Cd.* 32. Of þyssum lænan *from these rewards*, *Cd.* 60, v. lean.
Lænan; *p.* gelænde; *pp.* gelæned, alæned; *v. a.* [læn *a loan*] *To* LEND; commodare:—Hig lænaŏ eow and ge ne lænaŏ him, *Deut.* 28, 44. Ealne dæg he miltsaŏ and lænŏ, *Ps.* 36, 27. Læn me þry hlafas, *Lk.* 11, 5. Alæned feoh *lent money, a pledge*, *R.* 4.
Læncten *the spring*, *Elf. gr.* v. lencten.
Lænctenlic *vernal*, v. lenctenlic.
Lændenu *the loins*, v. lenden.
Læne, hlæne; *adj.* [*Plat.* leen *lean*] *Fragile*, LEAN, *slender, frail, passing;* fragilis:—Læne dream *a slender joy*, *Cd.* 169. Lænes lifes *of fragile lives*, *Cd.* 156. On oŏrum lænum weorŏscipum *on other frail advantages*, *Bt.* 24, 3, *Card.* p. 128, 9. Hu lytel he biŏ and hu læne *how little he is and how transitory*, *Bt.* 18, 1. Æghwilc þing lænu sindon *omnes res fragiles sunt*, *Bt. R.* p. 182. Ofer lichoman lænne and sænne *super corpus fragile et segne*, *Bt. R.* p. 191.
Lænend, es; *m.* *A lender on usury;* fœnerator, *Som.*
Læng *long*, *Elf. gr.* v. leng.
Længian *to long for*, v. langian.
Længten *spring*, v. lencten.
Lænian, gehlænian; *pp.* ed. *To be lean, to make lean;* macrere, *Cot.* 183, 137.
Lænian *To restore, repay;* reddere, *Gen.* 50, 15.
Lænig *weak, lean*, v. læne.
Lænis, se; *f.* LEANNESS; tenuitas, *Lye.*
Lænlic; *adj.* *Fragile, temporary;* temporalis, *L. Eccl.* p. 173.
Lænten *the spring*, *Cal. Jan.* v. lencten.
Læp *a basket*, v. leap.
Læpeldre *level*, v. læfeldre.
Læpeo *a part*, *L. Edw. Guth.* 10, v. læppa.
Læppa, lappa, an; *m.* [*Plat. Frs.* lappe *f*: *Dut. Dan.* lap *m*: *Ger.* lappen *m*: *Mon.* lappa: *Swed.* lapp *m*: *Icel.* lappi *m.*] 1. A LAP, *border, hem;* fimbria. 2. *A piece, portion;* pars:—1. Þæt niŏer astygeŏ on læppan his hrægles, *C. Ps.* 132, 3. 2. Lifre læppan *jecoris portiones*, *R.* 76.
Læran, gelæran; *p.* lærde; *pp.* gelæred; *v. a.* [lar *lore, learning*] 1. *To teach, instruct, inform;* docere, erudire. 2. *To advise, suggest, persuade, exhort;* suadere:—1. Þu lærst us, *Jn.* 9, 34. Ic lære *I will teach*, *Ps.* 33, 11. Lær us, *Lk.* 11, 1. Læraŏ ealle þeoda *docete omnes gentes*, *Mt.* 28, 19. 2. We læraŏ hyne *nos suadebimus ei*, *Mt.* 28, 14. Lære Pharao, *Gen.* 40, 14: *Bd.* 4, 19, *S.* p. 587, 30.
Lære *doctrine;* ac. of lar.
Lærestre, *A female teacher, an instructress;* doctrix, *Scint.* 77.
Lærig *Teachable, a tyro;* docilis, tyro, *Mann.*—*Mr. Thorpe translates it a shield*, *Cd.* 154, *Th.* p. 192, 29.
Lærinc-man *a disciple*, *R. Ben.* 5.
Lær-læst *Unlearned;* indoctus, *Som.*
Lærnes, se; *f.* [*Dut. Kil.* laer *empty*] *Emptiness;* vacuitas, *Herb.* 1, 18.
Lær-wita *a teacher, doctor.*
Lærystre *a female teacher*, v. lærestre.
Læs; *adv.* LESS; minus:—*Bd.* 4, 25. An læs twentig *one less than twenty, nineteen.* Mid læs worda *with less words*, *Bt.* 35, 5. ¶ Læs hwon, þe læs, þe læs þe, þy læs, þy læs þe *lest, lest that;* ne, ne forte, ne quando:—Þe læs hig swelton *ne moriantur*, *Ex.* 19, 21, 24. Þe læs þe he cume *ne ille veniat*, *Gen.* 32, 11. Þy læs þe we swulton *ne moriamur*, *Gen.* 3, 3.—Læs-boren *less-born, inferior birth*, *L. Can. Edg.* 13, v. læss, leas.
Læs, læsew, læsuw, e; *f.* [*Ger.* lese *f.*—hence LESOWES *pastures*] *A pasture, a* LEESE *or common;* pastura, pascuum:—On læsum *in pascuis*, *Gen.* 37, 12. Sceap læswe þinre *oves pasturæ tuæ*, *Ps.* 73, 1: 78, 14. Fint læse *inveniet pasturam*, *Jn.* 10, 9. Gemæne læs *a common pasture*, *R.* 96.
Læse *false*, *Scint.* 33, v. leas.
Læsest *least*, v. lytel.
Læsew *a pasture*, v. læs.
Læsewian *to feed*, *Elf. gr.*, v. læsian.
Læs-hosum [læs *less, inferior;* hos *calcaneum*, i. e. *inferior incedens super calcanea sua*] *Cernuus, incurvatus*, *R.* 28.
Læsian, læswian; *p.* de; *pp.* od, gelæswod. *To pasture, feed;* pascere:—Hig man læswode on Morium lande, *Gen.* 41, 2. Læswiende, *Mt.* 8, 30. Læswigende, *Mk.* 5, 11.
Læss; *def.* se læssa; seo, þæt læsse; *adj.* [*comp. of* lytel] LESS; minor, inferior:—Þat læsse leoht *the less light*, *Gen.* 1, 16. Gaderodon sum mare sum læsse, *Ex.* 16, 17. Ic eom læssa þonne ealle þine miltsunga, *Gen.* 32, 10. Se þe læssa is *qui minimus est*, *Mt.* 11, 11: *Lk.* 7, 28.
Læst; *adj.* [*sup. of* lytel] LEAST; minimus:—An of þysum læstum bebodum, *Mt.* 5, 19. Þat læst fæc *the least space*, *Bd.* 2, 13.
Læstan, gelæstan; *v. a.* [*Plat.* leesten, lösten: *Dut.* lysten: *Frs.* lasta: *Ger. Ot. Not. Wil.* leisten] 1. *To observe, perform, fulfil, execute;* observare. 2. *To follow, pursue;* sequi. 3. *To* LAST, *endure, continue, adhere;* durare:—1. Heo Godes willan lengest læsten *they God's will long performed*, *Cd.* 13. Þu læstan scealt *thou shalt execute*, *Cd.* 25. Þu hit mæge gelæstan *thou canst perform it*, *Bd.* 36, 3, *Card.* p. 272, 9. 2. Gif hi læstan dorsten *if they durst follow*, *Bt. R.* p. 151. And symle him gelæste, *Ex.* 13, 22. 3. Eowre bleda gelæston, *Jn.* 15, 16. Hi him gelæstan woldon *they would adhere to him*, *Chr.* 920.

[illegible]de, for lede
led, pp. of lecgan

Læs, e; f. a pasture
Ju 10, 9 v Ælf læsu

Læsc-hiwung, e, f. a false appearance
hypocrisy Som Ben
Lye

Læsung, falsehood, etc.
leasing, v
leasung

Læsu, g. d. ac. læswe
læse, f. a pasture
etc

Læl, lel, e; f. a weal
or stroke (1)

(2)

(1) Som & Ben have
læppe q
+ pam læppan
illi parti to that
part or party.
Lye - therefore m
or n

(2)

d.
Læn-dæg, es; m.
a fragil day, life of
man Bes K 5178

Læringc-mæden a
female pupil Th. Apol

(e)

Læstend, es; m. one who does a thing; an executor Som.

Læswe, e; f. a pasture Th. An.

b) Læt m.; f. læte; gen m. lætes; f. lætre; comp. lætra; sup. lætost, latemest etc. v. Elements of A.S. gr. 28:25

d * Læt, adv. late, long diu Sk 1,21 v late

e * Læte, adv. late v late

Læð an injury, hate harm Th. An. v Lað

Lævend, es; m. a betrayer Som. part. of lævan

1+ Laf is often used in compound words & signifies the remainder, what is left, reliquiæ as Yrfe-laf Beo K 251

c Lafere, e; f. a lark, etc. v. Ml. lawerce

Laford a lord Th. An. v hlaford

Lág, e; f. law, obligation Th. An. v lagu, lah

Lagon pt. pl. of licgan

Lagu-sið

Lagu, e; f. water, sea, a lake Beo K 3260

Lagu-stræt, e; f. a lake path Beo K 476

Láh lent, pp. of lihan Beo K 291

Lah low, pl. lage Th. An

Lah-brecend, es; m. a law breaker, a transgressor Som. Ben

Lám, laam, etc. loam, etc. Gen I 380,24

Lambren lamb Gen I 644,28 pr. of lamb

CPSIA information can be obtained
at www.ICGtesting.com
Printed in the USA
BVHW040339140621
609171BV00012B/58